P9-CQG-207

HANDBOOK OF STRESS

HANDBOOK OF STRESS
Theoretical and Clinical Aspects

Edited by

Leo Goldberger and Shlomo Breznitz

THE FREE PRESS
A Division of Macmillan, Inc.
NEW YORK

Collier Macmillan Publishers
LONDON

Copyright © 1982 by The Free Press
A Division of Macmillan Publishing Co., Inc.

All rights reserved. No part of this book may be reproduced or transmitted in any form or by any means, electornic or mechanical, including photocopying, recording, or by any information storage and retrieval system, without permission in writing from the Publisher.

The Free Press
A Division of Macmillan, Inc.
866 Third Avenue, New York, N.Y. 10022

Collier Macmillan Canada, Inc.

First Free Press Paperback Edition 1986

Printed in the United States of America

printing number

1   2   3   4   5   6   7   8   9   10

Library of Congress Cataloging in Publication Data

Main entry under title:

Handbook of stress.

   Includes index.
   1. Stress (Psychology) 2. Stress (Physiology)
I. Goldberger, Leo. II. Breznitz, Shlomo [DNLM:
I. Stress, Psychological. WM 172 H239]
BF575.S75H35   1982   155.9   82-8448
ISBN 0-02-911950-2   AACR2

This book is dedicated to *Jessica, Dan, Ruth,* and *Nurit.*

Contents

Preface

The concept of stress and, indeed, research on stress have reached an all-time peak in popularity during the past few years. An ever increasing number of books and journals devoted exclusively to stress are being published, courses and seminars are being offered in this area, and references to stress in the mass media abound. With this heightened awareness of stress—meaning here essentially all that is unpleasant, noxious, or excessively demanding—a concomitant interest in stress reducing techniques, or stress management, has given birth to a new specialty in the health sciences.

The tremendous proliferation of stress literature has made a single, comprehensive text on the subject a forbidding undertaking. Instead, the time seems more than ripe for this handbook, the aims of which are to gather within one volume a wide array of authoritative articles on the many facets of stress; provide researchers and clinicians in the field with a forum for critical reflection on the perennial definitional and conceptual problems and methodological complexities peculiar to stress research and stress treatment; and, ideally, to provide readers with a state of the art overview of those areas in which a body of solid findings exists.

The stress field is a sprawling one, characterized by unevenness and lack of coordination (not unlike many other domains within the behavioral and mental health sciences), with pockets of substantial development separated by faddish, superficial, or one-time forays. We believe there is much to be gained by the student of stress in confronting a cross-section of current developments in the field as a whole.

This volume allows the reader to take stock of where we are and to discern links and overlaps among the several disciplinary lines; cross-fertilization of the multiple perspectives on stress is necessary if the field is to maintain its vitality. The idea for the *Handbook of Stress,* born in our recognition of timeliness of such a reference work, surely would have failed to materialize had it not resonated with our colleagues—the distinguished group of authors whom we invited to contribute chapters summarizing topics closest to their current concerns. Their enthusiasm and ready acceptance of the task testified to the shared purpose of our venture.

In choosing the topics included in the handbook, we faced the obvious constraint of space. We could neither cover all disciplinary perspectives and broad categories—biological, psychological, and sociological—nor be exhaustive within a given perspective or category. The reader will undoubtedly compose his/her own list of missing chapters. Clearly, we had to make choices and though these choices were inevitably biased by our professional training as psychologists, we tried to provide a balanced view at least within the field of psychological stress. In other words, we set out to achieve a balance among theoretical viewpoints, as well as a balance between theory and research. Although not all topics covered in the *Handbook of Stress* have reached the level of maturity that permits a state of the art overview, some were nonetheless included because they have significance for the field.

The volume begins with a brief outline of our own perspective on stress and suggestions for future directions of investigation. Dr. Hans Selye—the pioneer in the field of stress whose ideas and influence are discernible in many of these chapters—provides an appropriate historical introduction. The main body of the handbook consists of seven parts. The headings for each part are self-explanatory and reflect our concern for a balanced treatment of stress. The reader should note that quite a few chapters deal with several aspects of their particular topic—theory, research, and/or clinical issues—and some areas are addressed in more than one chapter, for example, the measurement of both stress and coping and the use of life events scales. Our purpose was to provide more intensive treatment of issues that have a singular, pragmatic value for the stress investigators who would, we thought, welcome ready access to this material.

The *Handbook of Stress* is intended for the professional and the student in the behavioral and mental health fields actively working or interested in the stress area. It should have considerable utility as a reference work—as an aid in locating significant bodies of research; as a guide to metrics, tests, scales, and questionnaires in the stress-coping field; and, for the practicing clinician, as a guide to some of the increasingly popular techniques for the prevention and treatment of stress related disorders. The volume also should be useful as a reference work for general readers who wish to gain familiarity with the current scientific yield in the field of stress.

Finally, it should be noted that the contributors were discouraged from being as expansive as they might have wished and from using an overabundance of tables, figures, and references—this decision reflected our concern with conserving space to allow a wide representation of topics. We are grateful for having had such in impressive group of colleagues cooperate with us and give of their time and expertise in preparing their chapters and we appreciate their forbearance in regard to space constraints and editorial cuts.

Our appreciation also goes to a number of other people whose help was invaluable. At New York University our thanks go to Roberta Gordon, Nancy Koch, Bettie Brewer, and William T. Francis for administrative and secretarial help; at Haifa University, our thanks to Ruth Maos and Dinah Katz. Kitty Moore, senior psychology editor at The Free Press, has our warm gratitude for her advice, support, and enthusiastic interest throughout this project.

Leo Goldberger
Shlomo Breznitz

About the Contributors

CATHY ANDERSON received her Ph.D. in experimental psychology from the University of Colorado. After completing her dissertation research, she was affiliated with the University of Colorado Health Sciences Center, where she engaged in psychophysiological research on stress-related disorders, and the University of Denver, where she was a research associate on the Mental Health Systems Evaluation Project. Currently, she supervises the test research and selection activities for the state of Colorado.

ALEXANDER R. ASKENASY is research scientist at the New York State Psychiatric Institute and assistant professor of clinical social sciences in psychiatry at Columbia University. He received his Ph.D. from Columbia University in 1962. He is the author of a book entitled *Attitudes toward Mental Patients: A Study Across Cultures,* and among his articles are "Some effects of social class and ethnic group membership on judgments of the magnitude of stressful life events" (with B. P. Dohrenwend and B. S. Dohrenwend).

J. BASTIAANS is professor and chairman of the Department of Psychiatry of the State University Leyden–Holland, where he has been since 1964. In the period of 1954–1963, he was director of the Psychoanalytic Institute in Amsterdam. He has been president of many societies in the area of psychiatry; at present, he is president of the International College of Psychosomatic Medicine. His main work deals with psychiatric and psychosomatic consequences of war stress. Since 1957 he has concentrated all his efforts on the treatment of survivors of man-made disasters. In later years, he and his co-workers published three books on the aftereffects of terrorists' acts in Holland.

DEBORAH BELLE is research associate and lecturer at the Harvard Graduate School of Education, where she is also director of the Stress and Families Project. She earned her Ed.D. in 1976 at the Laboratory of Human Development, Harvard Graduate School of Education. She is co-editor of *The Mental Health of Women* and editor of the forthcoming *Lives in Stress: A Context for Depression.*

ANDREW G. BILLINGS is a research associate in the Social Ecology Laboratory at the Veterans Administration and Stanford University Medical Centers.

ARTHUR S. BLANK, JR., M.D., was a psychiatrist in the Army in Viet Nam in 1965–1966 and has taught at Yale University and practiced in New Haven since then. He has been a principal consulting psychiatrist to the Veterans Administration nationwide system of 126 Viet Nam Vet Centers since 1979 and is currently engaged in the study of the continuing effects of the war experience on veterans. He was recently appointed national director of the country's counseling program for Viet Nam veterans.

JOSEPH V. BRADY is professor of behavioral biology at the Johns Hopkins University School of Medicine. He received his Ph.D. from the University of Chicago in 1951 and participated for the next two decades in the development and conduct of the interdisciplinary research program in Neuropsychiatry at the Walter Reed Army Institute of Research. His published reports have focused upon the experimental analysis of emotional behavior, behavioral physiology, and behavioral pharmacology, with a recent contribution on "Learning and Conditioning" (in *Behavioral Medicine: Theory and Practice,* O. F. Pomerleau and J. P. Brady, eds.).

SHLOMO BREZNITZ is professor of psychology and director of the Ray D. Wolfe Center for Study of Psychological Stress, Haifa University, Israel. He has written extensively in the area of anticipatory fear, false alarms, and health psychology. He is the editor of a book entitled *Denial Of Stress,* published in 1982.

ROY CAMERON is associate professor of psychology at the University of Saskatchewan, Saskatoon. He received his Ph.D. from the University of Waterloo, Ontario, in 1976. He has collaborated with Dr. Meichenbaum on a number of cognitive-behavioral projects and in the development of stress–inoculation training. Dr. Cameron has authored a number of chapters on such topics as cognitive-behavioral interventions, patient's resistance, and behavioral medicine.

MARGARET A. CHESNEY is the director of the Behavioral Medicine Program at SRI International (formerly Stanford Research Institute). She received her doctorate in counseling–clinical psychology from Colorado State University and was a postdoctoral fellow in the Behavior Therapy Unit at the Eastern Pennsylvania Psychiatric Institute in the School of Medicine. She is currently conducting a program of behavioral medicine research focused on identifying the coronary-prone features of the Type A behavior pattern, the etiologic mechanisms linking behaviors to disease, the predictors of adherence to health behaviors, and the development and evaluation of behavioral interventions in the occupational setting for such health problems as essential hypertension.

SIDNEY COBB, M.D., M.P.H., is professor emeritus of community health and psychiatry at Brown University. He has taught epidemiology and done research at the University of Pittsburgh, the University of Michigan, and Brown University. While at Michigan, he was a program director in the Survey Research Center and held a Career Scientist Award from the National Institute of Mental Health. He is a member of various professional organizations, including the American Psychosomatic Society, for which he served as president.

LEONARD R. DEROGATIS is currently director of the Division of Medical Psychology and associate professor of medical psychology and oncology at the Johns Hopkins University School of Medicine. His major areas of research include clinical measurement and psychopathology, with a particular focus on psychological assessment in the medical environment. In this area, he has been particularly interested in the psychological problems of the cancer patient. Dr. Derogatis also functions as the director of research for the Sexual Behaviors Consultation Unit at Hopkins and has done considerable research in the assessment of sexual disorders. He is the author of 10 distinct psychological tests and rating scales and has published over 60 scientific papers.

BARBARA SNELL DOHRENWEND is professor and head of the division of Sociomedical Sciences in the School of Public Health, Columbia University. She received her Ph.D. in psychology from Columbia University. She is the co-author (with Bruce P. Dohrenwend) of *Social Status and Psychological Disorder* and co-editor (with him) of *Stressful Life Events.* She is past president of the Division of Community Psychology of the American Psychological Association. She is corecipient with Bruce P. Dohrenwend of the 1980 Distinguished Contributions Award of the Division of Community Psychology, American Psychological Association.

BRUCE P. DOHRENWEND is Foundations' Fund for Research in Psychiatry professor in the College of Physicians and Surgeons of Columbia University. He received his Ph.D. in social psychology from Cornell University. Dr. Dohrenwend is director of Columbia's Research Training Program in Psychiatric Epidemiology supported by the National Institute of Mental Health and principal investigator on two NIMH research grants in the field of psychiatric epidemiology. He holds a Research Scientist Award from that institute and is corecipient with Barbara Snell Dohrenwend of the 1980 Distinguished Contributions Award of the Division of Community Psychology, American Psychological Association. He is the co-author (with Barbara Snell Dohrenwend) of *Social Status and Psychological Disorder* and co-editor (with her) of *Stressful Life Events: Their Nature and Effects.*

JEAN EDWARDS is currently a psychometrist at Toronto East General Hospital and a research associate in the Department of Psychology, York University. She received her M.A. degree from York University in 1973. Her publications include (with N. S. Endler), "Person by Treatment Interactions in Personality Research" (in *Perspectives in Interactional Psychology,* L. A. Pervin and M. Lewis, eds.).

NORMAN S. ENDLER is currently professor of psychology, York University. He received his Ph.D. from the University of Illinois in 1958. Dr. Endler is the co-editor (with D. Magnusson) of two books on interactional psychology: *Interactional Psychology and Personality* and *Personality at the Crossroads: Current Issues in Interactional Psychology.* He has also written numerous articles on personality, anxiety, and social influence. Dr. Endler is the former chairman of the Psychology Department, York University, and a recipient of the Canadian Silver Jubilee Medal (Queen Elizabeth II), 1978.

SEYMOUR EPSTEIN is professor of psychology and chairman of the Personality Program at the University of Massachusetts. He received his Ph.D. from the University of Wisconsin in 1953 and is a diplomate in clinical psychology and a fellow of the American Psychological Association. He has served on several editorial boards for professional journals, been an editorial consultant for many others, served on study sections for the National Institute of Mental Health, and done consulting work for many national and international organizations.

SUSAN L. FARBER is assistant professor of psychology in the Clinical Psychology Program at New York University. She received her Ph.D. from Teachers College, Columbia University, in 1973. In addition to *Identical Twins Reared Apart: A Reanalysis,* she has written in the areas of adoption, testing, and child development.

MARJORIE FISKE is professor of social psychology, and formerly director, in the Human Development and Aging research and doctoral program at the University of California, San Francisco. Among her publications are *Four Stages of Life, Middle Age,* and some 100 articles and chapters in professional books and journals. She holds or has held office in the American Sociological, Psychological, and Gerontological Societies and serves as advisor or board member to several journals and educational organizations. Professor Fiske's major research interests are personal/social change and stress/adaptation in adulthood.

CALVIN J. FREDERICK is chief, Psychology Service, Veterans Administration Medical Center in Los Angeles, California, and professor in residence, Department of Psychiatry, at the University of California, Los Angeles. He has served as advisor in Central and South America to the Pan American Health Organization on studies of violent deaths. His work has been widely published, and he has served on numerous government committees dealing with emergency mental health, including the Governor's Advisory Panel on health studies at Three Mile Island.

LEO GOLDBERGER is professor of psychology and director of the Research Center for Mental Health, New York University. He has published extensively in the area of sensory deprivation, personality, and cognitive style. He is currently editor-in-chief of *Psychoanalysis and Contemporary Thought,* a quarterly journal.

NORMA HAAN is research scientist at the Institute of Human Development, University of California, Berkeley. She is the author of *Coping and Defending: Processes of Self-Environment Organization* and of a number of papers concerned with the accommodation to life stress and the stress produced by moral conflict and political dissent. She is co-editor of the recently published *Past and Present in Middle Life.*

VERNON HAMILTON is senior lecturer and tutor in psychology, University of Reading, England. He received his Ph.D. in 1956 and his Diploma in Abnormal Psychology in 1956. He is co-editor of two volumes: *The Development of Cognitive Processes* (with M. D. Vernon) and *Human Stress and Cognition: An Information Processing Approach* (with D. M. Warburton).

ALAN H. HARRIS is associate professor of behavioral biology at the Johns Hopkins University School of Medicine. He received his Ph.D. in 1969 from Columbia University. His research interests are in the areas of conditioning and learning, particularly as these relate to the environmental–behavioral control of cardiovascular functioning.

KENNETH A. HOLROYD is associate professor of clinical psychology in the Department of Psychology and Division of Psychiatry and Behavioral Medicine at Ohio University. Dr. Holroyd is interested in the application of current theoretical models of stress phenomena to unresolved problems in the prevention and clinical management of stress-related disorders. His research has evaluated stress management interventions in the treatment of recurrent headache, the prevention of essential hypertension, and the identification of individuals at risk for these disorders.

ROBERT R. HOLT received his Ph.D. from Harvard in 1944. After two years in survey research, he was a clinical psychologist in the Veterans Administration (1946–1949); from 1948 to 1953 he worked at the Menninger Foundation, becoming its director of psychological staff. From 1953 through 1969, he was director of the Research Center for Mental Health at New York University, where is now professor of psychology. He holds a Research Career Award from the National Institute of Mental Health.

MARDI J. HOROWITZ, M.D., is professor of psychiatry at the University of California, School of Medicine, San Francisco, where he is director of the Center for the Study of Neuroses of the Langley Porter Psychiatric Institute. He received his medical training at the University of California, his psychiatric training at the Langley Porter Psychiatric Institute, his research training through an NIMH Research Career Program Award, and his psychoanalytic training at the San Francisco Psychoanalytic Institute. His books include *Image Formation and Cognition, Stress Response Syndromes, Hysterical Personality, States of Mind, Psychosocial Function in Epilepsy,* and the forthcoming *Personality and Brief Therapy.*

FREDERIC W. ILFELD, JR., M.D., is an associate clinical professor in the Department of Psychiatry and the University of California at Davis Medical School and is engaged in the private practice of psychiatry at the Alhambra Psychotherapy Center in Sacramento. His behavioral science background began in the undergraduate years at Yale University, where he majored in culture and behavior. He then obtained his M.D. from Harvard Medical School and his psychiatric residency and an M.A. in sociology from Stanford University. Dr. Ilfeld received the Pawlowski Peace Prize for his article ''Alternatives to Violence: Strategies for Coping with Social Conflict.''

IRVING L. JANIS is professor of psychology at Yale University. He has long been a leading contributor to research on psychological stress, attitude change, and decisionmaking. Janis is author of a well-known book on *Stress and Frustration* and co-author (with L. Mann) of the highly influential book *Decision Making,* which presents an analysis of decisional conflicts in terms of stress-coping patterns. In recognition of his many significant theoretical and empirical contributions to scientific psychology, the American Psychological Association presented its Distinguished Scientific Contributions Award to Professor Janis in August 1981. Among Janis's other special honors and awards are the Hofheimer Prize of the American Psychiatric Association (1958), the American Association for the Advancement of Science Socio-Psychological Prize (1967), and election to the American Academy of Arts and Sciences (1974).

ROBERT D. KAMINOFF is currently a Ph.D. candidate in environmental psychology at the City University of New York. He is a principal in CONTEXT, a consulting firm specializing in the behavioral analysis of architectural design, and also teaches human design factors at Pratt Institute.

STANISLAV V. KASL is currently professor of epidemiology in the Department of Epidemiology and Public Health at the Yale University School of Medicine. Before coming to Yale in 1969, he spent some ten years working at the University of Michigan's Institute for Social Research. His primary research interests center on social and psychological factors affecting health status, health effects of work environments, and "stress-and-disease" issues.

LAWRENCE KRASNOFF is a postdoctoral fellow in the Division of Biostatistics and Research Associate in the Division of Sociomedical Sciences, School of Public Health, Columbia University. He received his Ph.D. degree in clinical psychology from the City University of New York in 1979. He is a co-author (with B. S. Dohrenwend, B. P. Dohrenwend, and A. R. Askenasy) of "Exemplification of a Method for Scaling Life Events: The PERI Life Events Scale" and co-author (with I. Levav and B. S. Dohrenwend) of "Sources of Concern in an Israeli Community: The Israeli PERI Life Events Scale."

LOTHAR LAUX is presently a professor of psychology in the Department of Psychology at the University of Mainz. He received his doctoral degree (doctor rer. nat.) from the University of Mainz. He teaches experimental, general, and personality psychology. His main fields of interest are anxiety, stress, emotion, and personality. He contributed several chapters to *Stress and Anxiety* (C. D. Spielberger and I. G. Sarason, eds.) and is co-editor (with H. W. Krohne) of *Achievement, Stress and Anxiety*.

RICHARD S. LAZARUS has had 34 years of research experience on the dynamics of human adaptation since receiving his Ph.D. in 1948. Now a professor at the University of California at Berkeley, he has published extensively on the theory of stress and coping and on his empirical research. His current work has been extended to stress and coping in aging and has been supported by the National Institute on Aging and the MacArthur Foundation.

HOYLE LEIGH is professor of psychiatry at Yale University School of Medicine and assistant chief of psychiatry and director of the Division of Psychiatric Consultation-Liaison and Outpatient Services, as well as director of the Yale Behavioral Medicine Clinic at Yale–New Haven Hospital. He is a fellow of the American Psychiatric Association and the International College of Psychosomatic Medicine. His publications include two books: *The Patient: Biological, Psychological and Social Dimensions of Medical Practice* (with M. F. Reiser) and (as editor) *Psychiatry in the Practice of Medicine,* plus approximately 50 other publications in the area of psychosomatic medicine and consultation-liaison psychiatry.

MORTON A. LIEBERMAN received his Ph.D. in social psychology from the University of Chicago in 1958 and has been a faculty member there since 1957. He has had two enduring interests over the past twenty years. The first, "solving the puzzle of what conditions in the group setting lead to change in participants," he has pursued a variety of studies, emphasizing comparative analyses of various people-changing groups. His other interest has been in the latter half of the life span. He is the author of books in both areas: *Psychotherapy Through the Group Process* (with D. S. Whitaker), *Encounter Groups: First Facts* (with I. Yalom and M. Miles), *Last Home for the Aged* (with S. Tobin), *Self-Help Groups for Coping with Crises* (with L. Borman), and a forthcoming book entitled *Adaptation and Survival in Later Life* (with S. Tobin).

JAMES N. LOGUE is currently chief of the Epidemiology Section in the Epidemiologic Studies Branch, Bureau of Radiological Health of the U.S. Food and Drug Administration. He received his Dr.P.H. in epidemiology in 1978 from Columbia University. In addition to his interest and activities in disaster research, he has been involved in environmental and occupational epidemiologic research.

DAVID MAGNUSSON received his Ph.D. from the University of Stockholm, where he is presently chairman of the Department of Psychology. A former chairman of the Swedish Association of University Professors, Dr. Magnusson has published numerous books, including *Interactional Psychology and Personality* (co-editor with N. S. Endler) and *Toward a Psychology of Situations*.

GEORGE MANDLER is professor of psychology and director, Center for Human Information Processing, University of California, San Diego. He is a member of numerous professional societies and has published three books: *The Language of Psychology* (with W. Kessen), *Thinking: From Association to Gestalt,* and *Mind and Emotion.*

Don Meichenbaum is a professor of psychology at the University of Waterloo, Ontario. He received his Ph.D. from the University of Illinois in 1966. He has been a major contributor to the area of cognitive-behavior modification. His books on the subject include *Cognitive-Behavior Modification: An Integrative Approach, Stress Prevention and Management* (co-editor with M. Jaremko), *Pain and Behavioral Medicine* (co-author with D. Turk and M. Genest), and *Coping with Stress.*

Mary Evans Melick is senior research scientist for the New York Office of Mental Health and is an associate professor (part time) at the Albany College of Pharmacy of Union University, Albany, and at Union College, Schenectady. Her professional education began in nursing, where she was particularly interested in the care of patients with endocrine and metabolic problems. In her doctoral work in sociology, Dr. Melick became interested in the health outcomes associated with stressful events and wrote her dissertation on the health consequences of disaster.

Norman A. Milgram received his Ph.D. from Boston University in 1958 and taught at Nebraska College of Medicine, Catholic University of America, and Temple University. He has been at Tel-Aviv University since 1971. He is a diplomate of the American Board of Professional Psychology in Clinical Psychology and a fellow of two APA divisions. He organized two international conferences on war-related stress and recently edited Volume 8 of the Spielberger and Sarason series, *Stress and Anxiety,* which deals with war-related stress in Israel.

Rudolph H. Moos is a research career scientist and director of the Social Ecology Laboratory at the Veterans Administration and Stanford University Medical Centers. He is also a professor in the Department of Psychiatry and Behavioral Sciences at the Stanford University School of Medicine.

Leonard I. Pearlin is a research sociologist in the Laboratory of Socio-Environmental Studies of the National Institute of Mental Health. His interests have covered a variety of aspects of social structure and personality. For the past several years, he has been conducting a program of research in the social origins of stress and of coping.

David V. Perkins is assistant professor of psychology at the State University of New York at Buffalo. He received his Ph.D. in psychology from Indiana University in 1978. His published research is in the areas of stressful life events, environmental assessment, person–environment interaction, alcoholism, and program evaluation.

Anne C. Petersen is director, Laboratory for the Study of Adolescence, Michael Reese Hospital and Medical Center, and associate professor, Department of Psychiatry, at the University of Chicago. She received her Ph.D. from the University of Chicago in 1973. Her research interests include the biopsychosocial development at adolescence, sex differences, and methods for longitudinal research. She is the author of numerous books including *Adolescence and Youth,* 3rd ed. (with J. J. Conger, in press), co-editor of *Adolescent Health* (with T. Coates and C. Perry, in press), and *Girls at Puberty* (with J. Brooks-Gunn).

Herbert Peyser is assistant clinical professor of psychiatry and associate attending psychiatrist at Mt. Sinai Medical Center, New York City. He received his M.D. in 1948 from the Columbia University College of Physicians and Surgeons and is a diplomate of the American Board of Psychiatry and Neurology and a fellow of the American Psychiatric Association. He is a consultant to numerous county, state, and national committees on substance abuse. Among his numerous publications is a volume of which he was recently co-editor (with S. Gitlow): *Alcoholism: A Practical Treatment Guide.*

HAROLD M. PROSHANSKY is professor of environmental psychology and president of the Graduate School and University Center, City University of New York. His primary research interests lie in the study of privacy and the conceptualizations needed in defining place-identity and other environmental concepts.

JUDITH GODWIN RABKIN is research scientist, New York State Psychiatric Institute, and adjunct assistant professor of public health (epidemiology) in psychiatry, College of Physicians and Surgeons, Columbia University. She received her Ph.D. in clinical psychology from New York University in 1967 and her M.P.H. degree in epidemiology in 1978 from the Columbia University School of Public Health. In addition to publications in the area of stress research in *Science* and *Psychological Bulletin,* she has recently published a study of ethnic density and risk for psychiatric hospitalization in the *American Journal of Psychiatry* and is co-editor (with D. F. Klein) of a volume on research in anxiety.

RAY H. ROSENMAN, M.D., is a graduate of the University of Michigan. He is senior research physician in the Behavioral Medicine Program of SRI International (formerly Stanford Research Institute) and associate chief, Department of Medicine, Mount Zion Hospital and Medical Center, San Francisco. He has practiced clinical cardiology since 1950 while devoting half time to research in coronary heart disease and hypertension. He is co-author of the book, *Type A Behavior and Your Heart,* and author of about 240 scientific articles and 38 textbook chapters. He formerly was associate director of Mount Zion Hospital's Harold Brunn Institute.

HAROLD A. SACKEIM is currently an associate professor of psychology in the doctoral training program in clinical psychology at New York University and a research scientist and deputy chief of the Department of Biological Psychiatry, New York State Psychiatric Institute. He was educated at Columbia University, Magdalen College at Oxford University, and the University of Pennsylvania. His primary research focus is affective lateralization and the psychobiology of affective disorders.

JOSEPH D. SARGENT, M.D., F.A.C.P., graduated from the University of Michigan Medical School in 1958. He had a one-year psychosomatic residency at The Menninger Foundation and is presently chief of Internal Medicine and head of the Headache Research and Treatment Center at that same institution. He was elected to fellowship in the American College of Physicians in 1972 and is currently president of the Kansas Society for Internal Medicine. His numerous papers on headache include "Psychosomatic Self-Regulation of Migraine Headaches" in *Seminars of Psychiatry,* vol. 3, and "Use of Biofeedback in the Treatment of Headache Problems" in *International Review of Applied Psychology,* vol. 27.

HANS SELYE is emeritus professor at the University of Montreal and president of the International Institute of Stress and the Hans Selye Foundation, both recently established by him in Montreal. His famous and revolutionary concept of stress opened countless new avenues of treatment through the discovery that hormones participate in the development of many degenerative diseases. At present, most of his research is concerned with formulating a code of behavior based on the laws governing the body's stress resistance in dealing with personal, interpersonal, and group problems. He is the author of 38 books and more than 1,700 technical articles. In addition to his earned doctorates, he holds 20 honorary degrees from universities around the world. He counts among his medals the Starr Medal, the Prix de l'Oeuvre Scientifique, the Killam Scholarship, the International Kittay Award, and the American Academy of Achievement's Golden Plate Award.

JUDITH T. SHUVAL is professor of sociology at Hebrew University in Jerusalem.

ARON WOLFE SIEGMAN is professor of psychology, University of Maryland, and adjunct professor in the Department of Psychiatry at the University of Maryland Medical School. He received his Ph.D.

from Columbia University in 1957. He has published numerous articles in professional journals and four books.

Donald P. Spence is professor of psychiatry at the College of Medicine and Dentistry of New Jersey, Rutgers Medical School, Piscataway. He received his Ph.D. from Teachers College, Columbia University, trained at the New York Psychoanalytic Institute, and was formerly a professor of psychology at New York University. Spence is the editor of two books and the author of a forthcoming critical study of psychoanalytic theory entitled *Narrative Truth and Historical Truth*.

Ralph Spiga is assistant professor in the Department of Psychology at Auburn University, Montgomery. His research interests include stress and cardiovascular disease, the development of coronary-prone behavior, and the experimental analysis of behavior—specifically, schedule-induced behavior.

Johann Stoyva received his Ph.D. from the University of Chicago in 1961. Working first in the areas of sleep, dreaming, and hypnosis, he later shifted his research interests to biofeedback, psychosomatic disorders, and behavioral medicine. He is former president of the Biofeedback Society of America and was the founding editor of the journal *Biofeedback and Self-Regulation*. Since 1966, he has been in the department of psychiatry, University of Colorado School of Medicine, Denver.

Jaylan S. Turkkan is assistant professor in behavioral biology at the Johns Hopkins University School of Medicine. Her doctoral degree in experimental psychology under Dr. William N. Schoenfeld at the City University of New York (1977) focused on classically conditioned heart rate and blood pressure responses of the rhesus monkey. Recent work as a postdoctoral fellow with Dr. Alan H. Harris at Johns Hopkins has involved studies with baboons trained to raise their blood pressure with biofeedback and operant conditioning techniques. She is currently also involved in a project that will investigate the cardiovascular effects of noise.

Elizabeth Taylor Vance is associate professor at Cleveland State University in Ohio. She received her Ph.D. in psychology from Washington University and has taught at Case Western Reserve University. She is the author of several articles on psychopathology and competence.

Gerhard Vossel is assistant in the Department of Psychology at the University of Mainz. He received his doctoral degree (doctor rer. nat.) from the University of Mainz. He teaches both general and experimental psychology. Main fields of interest are attention, psychophysiology of individual differences, and stress. He published (with W. D. Froehlich) "Life Stress, Job Tension, and Subjective Reports of Task Performance Effectiveness" in *Stress and Anxiety*, vol. 6, and has written several articles for research journals.

Sara L. Weber is a Ph.D. candidate in clinical psychology at New York University, where she is doing research on the development of functional brain asymmetry in the regulation of emotion. Since completing her internship at Albert Einstein College of Medicine/Bronx Psychiatric Center, she has been a consultant to Head Start in Newark, New Jersey, and an adjunct instructor in the Masters in Dance Therapy Program at Hunter College. She received her undergraduate degree from Boston University.

Leonard S. Zegans, M.D., is currently director of education and professor of psychiatry at the University of California–San Francisco Department of Psychiatry. He is former director of graduate and postgraduate education at the Yale School of Medicine Department of Psychiatry. He is a graduate of Princeton University and of the New York University School of Medicine; he did his residency in psychiatry with the University of Michigan. He was awarded an NIMH special fellowship to the Tavistock Clinic and served in the public health service at St. Elizabeth's Hospital. Dr. Zegans's publications include articles in the area of human aggression, ethology, emotions and seizure disorders, adolescents, and stress and human physiology.

PHILIP G. ZIMBARDO is professor in the Department of Psychology at Stanford University. His research into the personal and social dynamics of shyness began with his classic prison simulation experiment in 1971. Observing how readily subjects surrendered their basic freedoms in the prisoner role, Zimbardo wondered about the pervasive power of psychological prisons in everyday life. The silent prison of shyness is generated by social constraints and self-imposed by fears of rejection. Unique in Zimbardo's systematic study of this widespread phenomenon is the combination of laboratory and field research with children and adults across cultures, with a theoretical focus guiding clinical applications.

PART I

INTRODUCTION

Stress Research at a Crossroads

Shlomo Breznitz   Leo Goldberger

ORIENTATION TO STRESS

The proliferation of research on stress over the past two decades makes it difficult to penetrate the universe of discourse in this area: Nonetheless, we shall try to identify the basic themes in the literature.

Stressors are external events or conditions that affect the organism. The description of stressors and their impact on behavior is an open-ended task, and current research considers an increasing number of events and conditions to be stressors. Most of this effort is still in the qualitative domain and parametric investigations are by and large rare.

The stressors themselves impinge on an organism that has specific characteristics of its own. Thus, another open-ended challenge is the systematic exposure of different species to a particular stressor. Such research can provide insight into phylogenetic and evolutionary processes, as well as into the general themes that cut across species boundaries. Within the same species it is, of course, possible to investigate the impact of a given stressor on different organisms, and the study of individual differences is a rapidly growing branch of stress research. The individual differences of most relevance in human research have to do with the *cognitive appraisal* of stressors. In line with Lazarus's (1966: Lazarus & Launier, 1978) formulation, cognitive appraisal plays a major role in the transaction between the person and the potentially stressful environment. Accordingly, researchers have sought to uncover the differential effects of a variety of cognitive styles upon the impact of stressors.

Another central element in the adaptational equation relates to *coping*. After appraising the stressor, the organism will use one or more coping strategies in an attempt to adjust to the situation. A relatively large body of stress research addresses various coping strategies. Here, again, the issue of individual differences and predispositions plays a key role.

Finally, investigators are interested in stress effects themselves. Ranging all the way from minor changes in behavior to dramatic clinical symptoms, such effects are often viewed as the raison d'être for stress research and stress management approaches.

Somewhere between the stressor and its effects lies the subjective, phenomenological experience of stress itself. Although from the individual's point of view experiencing stress is the most germane factor in confronting stressful conditions, such experience lies outside the realm of objective inquiry.

Accordingly, behaviors classified as stress effects can also be categorized as the effects of anxiety, the effects of conflict, etc. Insofar as expressions of emotion, performance deterioration, or symptom manifestations are concerned, stress is interchangeable with these other concepts. Its unique features thus have to be more specifically elaborated.

As this volume illustrates, there is substantial disagreement over the definition of *stress*. Different scholars have different definitions and oftentimes abide by those most suitable to the pursuit of their particular interests. Thus, for instance, Selye's (1956) focus on the nonspecific *general adaptation syndrome* forces an extreme response based definition, and the exact nature of the stressor becomes largely irrelevant. By contrast, Lazarus's (1966) focus on cognitive appraisal presumes that specific kinds of information are operative in appraising a particular stimulus as a stressor. Although this lack of agreement on the definition of stress is seen by some as indicative of a paradigm crisis, the absense of consensus more properly reflects the rapid expansion of stress research in many divergent directions and may be more conducive to future theorizing than a premature closure (see Kaplan, 1964, for a cogent argument on tolerance of ambiguity in the conduct of inquiry).

Whereas diversity in definition and emphasis may be helpful, such is not the case, however, with research tools. One of the main reasons that many basic questions relating to the effects of stress on adjustment remain unresolved is the lack of standardization in choosing the stressor, measuring its parameters and effects, and selecting the subjects for specific experiments. The absence of an adequate taxonomy of stressful situations and the paucity of parametric research in this area make it difficult to compare results from different studies. The systematic accumulation of knowledge cannot proceed without comprehensive, long-term research.

FUTURE DIRECTIONS

Reviewing the state of the art from the vantage point of the *Handbook of Stress,* we can trace some major ideas and biases in stress research. The following review points out broad themes and suggests possible directions for scientific inquirys in the future.

Repeated Exposure to Stressors

From Selye's initial formulation of the general adaptation syndrome to the diametrically opposite notion of *stress innoculation,* the analysis of the potential impact of repeated stressors is at the core of many theories (e.g., Breznitz, 1980; Frankenhaeuser, 1980). Investigators are interested in learning whether repeated exposure to the same stressors will result ultimately in immunization, habituation, or breakdown.

Duration of Exposure to Stressors

Our understanding of adaptation will be seriously deficient as long as we are unable properly to estimate the impact of duration of exposure to stressors on behavior. This need is particularly critical in the analysis of chronic versus acute stressors. In both epidemiological and clinical research on risk factors conducive to somatic as well as psychiatric problems, the relatively minor but everyday stressors seem to be emerging as the main culprit.

Pacing of Stressors

A question related to repetition and duration of exposure is the interstressor interval. What is the rate at which stressors follow one another? Is there a critical threshold in terms of pacing? The *recent life changes paradigm* is a case in point. Proponents of this view argue that different kinds of events produce a cumulative deleterious impact only if they follow one another at a rate above a certain critical level (Breznitz, 1972; Cleary, 1979; Holmes & Masuda, 1974; Lloyd, Alexander, Rice, & Greenfield, 1980).

Recovery from Stress

A crucial but neglected area in understanding stress concerns the temporal characteristics of recovery from stressful encounters. Repeated exposure, duration, and pacing are intimately associated with the recovery function. This problem is examined by Stoyva and Anderson in Chapter 45 and by Cameron and Meichenbaum in Chapter 42.

THE OPTIMISTIC BIAS

Although stress research is concerned mainly with maladjustment, interest in successful coping is increasingly apparent in the field. The major displacement of focus from the concept of *anxiety*, which relates primarily to an internal, personal problem, to the concept of *stress,* which is basically an external, environmental problem, deserves analysis. In our view, this shift indicates a tendency toward the denial of major and often unmanageable difficulties. Advocates of the new approach argue that since stress is caused by factors "out there," it is necessary only to devise ways to change the stressful features of the environment and all will be well. This view may to a certain extent account for the proliferation in Western societies of simplistic techniques of stress management. In any event, the domain of stress research now puts heavy emphasis on coping. Interest in coping strategies and predispositions, as well as in the teaching of coping skills, indicates an essentially optimistic bias. Whether pursued in the military or in the wide variety of stress inoculation programs, these practices rest on the assumption that given the right tools, one can cope effectively with most sources of stress.

Another sign of this optimistic outlook is the importance accorded the idea of control. Many workers in the field make the value judgment (implicitly or explicitly) that an internal locus of control is preferable to an external one; they argue that self-control can be used effectively to combat the potentially deleterious effects of stress. However, many critical stressors do not leave room for control, and passive acceptance may be the most appropriate coping strategy in such situations (e.g., Lazarus, 1982; Selye, 1956).

THE PSYCHOLOGY OF HEALTH

We suggest that stress research and theory are about to undergo a major change in emphasis—a change that may be yet another expression of the "optimistic bias" just noted. Concern with the negative, illness related impacts of stress will gave way to consideration of stress as a force conducive to health. Although health is still defined primarily as the lack of illness, the absence of symptoms is a very limited and unsatisfactory criterion of well-being. A concept denoting the *opposite* of stress would enrich our way of looking at person-environment interactions. In other words, can the active influence of positive factors in principle enhance health? Just as Lazarus and Launier (1978) posited daily uplifts as the opposite of daily hassles, some events may act as *antistressors*. Indeed, stress itself may produce positive effects. Selye (1974) saw the need to coin the concept of *eustress* essentially to account for certain seemingly harmless or even beneficial stressors. In Chapter 15, Haan, referring to her own research (1977), makes the point that stress can lead to gains as well as losses. (This issue has been examined by Breznitz and Eshel [1982] and by Yarom [1982].) Unless our sense of direction is off the mark, psychology and medicine will see an upsurge of interest along the above lines, and the field of stress will significantly increase its relevance.

REFERENCES

BREZNITZ, S. *The effect of frequency and pacing of warnings upon the fear reaction to a threatening event*. Jerusalem: Ford Foundation, 1972.

————. Stress in Israel. In H. Selye (ed.), *Selye's guide to stress research,* vol. 1. New York: Van Nostrand, 1980.

BREZNITZ, S., & ESHEL, J. Life events: Stressful ordeal or valuable experience? In S. Breznitz (ed.), *Stress in Israel.* New York: Van Nostrand, 1982.

CLEARY, P. J. *Life events and disease: A review of methodology and findings.* Stockholm: Laboratory for Clinical Stress Research, 1979.

FRANKENHAEUSER, M. Psychoneuroendocrine approaches to the study of stressful person-environment transactions. In H. Selye (ed.), *Selye's guide to stress research,* vol. 1. New York: Van Nostrand, 1980.

HAAN, N. *Coping and defending: Processes of self-environment organization.* New York: Academic, 1977.

HOLMES, T. H., & MASUDA, M. Life changes and illness susceptibility. In B. S. Dohrenwend & B. P. Dohrenwend (eds.), *Stressful life events: Their nature and effects.* New York: Wiley, 1974.

KAPLAN, A. *The conduct of inquiry: Methodology for behavioral science.* San Francisco: Chandler, 1964.

LAZARUS, R. S. *Psychological stress and the coping process.* New York: McGraw-Hill, 1966.

————. The costs and benefits of denial. In S. Breznitz (ed.), *The denial of stress.* New York: International Universities, 1982.

LAZARUS, R. S., & LAUNIER, R. Stress-related transactions between person and environment. In L. A. Pervin and M. Lewis (eds.), *Perspectives in interactional psychology.* New York: Plenum, 1978.

LLOYD, C., ALEXANDER, A. A., RICE, D. G., & GREEFIELD, N. S. Life change and academic performance. *Journal of Human Stress,* 1980, *6,* 15–25.

SELYE, H. *The stress of life.* New York: McGraw-Hill, 1956.

————. *Stress without distress.* Philadelphia: Lippincott, 1974.

YAROM, N. Facing death in war: An existential crisis. In S. Breznitz (ed.), *Stress in Israel.* New York: Van Nostrand, 1982.

2

History and Present Status
of the Stress Concept

Hans Selye

NOWADAYS, EVERYONE SEEMS TO BE TALKING about stress. You hear about this topic not only in daily conversation but also on television, via radio, in the newspapers, and in the ever increasing number of conferences, centers, and university courses devoted to stress. Yet remarkably few people define the concept in the same way or even bother to attempt a clear-cut definition. The businessperson thinks of stress as frustration or emotional tension; the air traffic controller, as a problem in concentration; the biochemist and endocrinologist, as a purely chemical event; and the athlete, as muscular tension. This list could be extended to almost every human experience or activity, and, somewhat surprisingly, most people—be they chartered accountants, short-order cooks, or surgeons—consider their own occupation the most stressful. Similarly, most commentators believe that ours is the "age of stress," forgetting that the caveman's fear of attack by wild animals or of death from hunger, cold, or exhaustion must have been just as stressful as our fear of a world war, the crash of the stock exchange, or overpopulation.

Ironically, there is a grain of truth in every formulation of stress because all demands upon our adaptability do evoke the stress phenomenon. But we tend to forget that there would be no reason to use the single word "stress" to describe such diverse circumstances as those mentioned above were there not something common to all of them, just as we could have no reason to use a single word in connection with the production of light, heat, cold, or sound if we had been unable to formulate the concept of energy, which is required to bring about any of these effects. My definition of *stress* is the *nonspecific* (that is, common) *result of any demand upon the body,* be the effect mental or somatic. The formulation of this definition, based on objective indicators such as bodily and chemical changes that appear after any demand, has brought the subject (so popular now that it is often referred to as "stressology") up from the level of cocktail party chitchat into the domain of science.

One of the first things to bear in mind about stress is that a variety of dissimilar situations—emotional arousal, effort, fatigue, pain, fear, concentration, humiliation, loss of blood, and even great and unexpected success—are capable of producing stress; hence, no single factor can, in itself, be pinpointed as the cause of the reaction as such. To understand this point, it is necessary to consider certain facts about human biology. Medical research has shown that while people may face quite different problems, in some respects their bodies

7

respond in a stereotyped pattern; identical biochemical changes enable us to cope with any type of increased demand on vital activity. This is also true of other animals and apparently even of plants. In all forms of life, it would seem that there are common pathways that must mediate any attempt to adapt to environmental conditions and sustain life.

HISTORICAL DEVELOPMENT

Even prehistoric man must have recognized a common element in the sense of exhaustion that overcame him in conjunction with hard labor, agonizing fear, lengthy exposure to cold or heat, starvation, loss of blood, or any kind of disease. Probably he soon discovered also that his response to prolonged and strenuous exertion passed through three stages: first the task was experienced as a hardship; then he grew used to it; and finally he could stand it no longer. The vague outlines of this intuitive scheme eventually were brought into sharper focus and translated into precise scientific terms that could be appraised by intellect and tested by reason. Before turning to contemporary science, it will be helpful to review some of the intervening developments that laid the foundation for the modern theory of stress.

In ancient Greece, Hippocrates, often considered the "father of medicine," clearly recognized the existence of a *vis medicatrix naturae,* or healing power of nature, made up of inherent bodily mechanisms for restoring health after exposure to pathogens. But early investigations were handicapped by the failure to distinguish between distress, always unpleasant, and the general concept of stress, which also encompasses experiences of intense joy and the pleasure of self-expression.

The nineteenth-century French physiologist Bernard (1879) enormously advanced the subject by pointing out that the internal environment of a living organism must remain fairly constant despite changes in the external environment: "It is the fixity of the *milieu intérieur* which is the condition of free and independent life" (p. 564). This comment had enormous impact; indeed, the Scottish physiologist Haldane (1922) was of the opinion that "no more pregnant sentence was ever framed by a physiologist" (p. 427). But this influence was due largely to various meanings that subsequently were read into Bernard's formulation. Actually, inanimate objects are more independent of their surroundings than are living beings. What distinguishes life is adaptability to change, not fixity. Bernard's more enduring legacy was the stimulation of later investigators to carry forward his pioneering studies on the particular adaptive changes by which the steady state is maintained.

The German physiologist Pflüger (1877) crystallized the relationship between active adaptation and the steady state when he noted that "the cause of every need of a living being is also the cause of the satisfaction of that need" (p. 57). The Belgian physiologist Fredericq (1885) expressed a similar view: "The living being is an agency of such sort that each disturbing influence induces by itself the calling forth of compensatory activity to neuralize or repair the disturbance" (p. 34).

In this century, the great American physiologist Cannon (1939) suggested the name "homeostasis," from the Greek *homoios,* meaning similar, and *stasis,* meaning position, for "the coordinated physiologic processes which maintain most of the steady states in the organism" (p. 333). Homeostasis might roughly be translated "staying power." Cannon's classic studies established the existence of many highly specific mechanisms for protection against hunger, thirst, hemorrhage, or agents tending to disturb normal body temperature, blood pH, or plasma levels of sugar, protein, fat, and calcium. He particularly emphasized the stimulation of the sympathetic nervous system, with the resulting hormonal discharge from the adrenal glands, which occurs during emergencies such as pain or rage. In turn, this autonomic process induces the cardiovascular changes that prepare the body for flight or fight.

It was against this cumulative background that, as a medical student, I eventually was drawn to the problem of a stereotyped response to any exacting task. The initial focus of my interest was what I thought of as the "syndrome of just being sick." In my second year of training I was struck by how patients suffering from the most diverse diseases exhibited strikingly similar signs and symptoms, such as loss of weight and appetite, diminished muscular strength, and absence of ambition. In 1936, the problem presented itself under conditions suited to analysis. While seeking a new ovarian hormone, co-workers and I at McGill University injected extracts of cattle ovaries into rats to see whether their organs would display unpredictable changes that could not be attributed to any known hormone. Three types of changes were produced: (1) the cortex, or outer layer, of the adrenal glands became enlarged and hyperactive; (2) the thymus, spleen, lymph nodes, and all other lymphatic structures shrank; and (3) deep, bleeding ulcers appeared in the stomach and upper intestines. Being closely interdependent, these changes formed a definite syndrome (see Figure 2-1).

FIGURE 2-1. Typical triad of alarm reaction: (A) adrenals; (B) thymus; (C) group of three lymph nodes; and (D) inner surface of stomach. The organs on the left are those of a normal rat; those on the right, of a rat exposed to the frustrating psychological stress of being immobilized. Note the marked enlargement and dark discoloration of the adrenals caused by congestion and the discharge of fatty secretion granules; the intense shrinkage of the thymus and the lymph nodes; and the numerous blood covered stomach ulcers in the alarmed rat (*from Selye, 1952:225*).

NORMAL   ALARMED

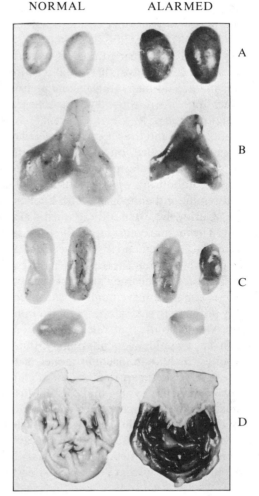

It was soon discovered that all toxic substances, irrespective of their source, produced the same pattern of responses. Moreover, identical organ changes were evoked by cold, heat, infection, trauma, hemorrhage, nervous irritation, and many other stimuli. Gradually, I realized that this was an experimental replica of the "syndrome of just being sick," which I had noted a decade earlier. Adrenal enlargement, gastrointestinal ulcers, and thymicolymphatic shrinkage were constant and invariable signs of damage to a body faced with the demand of meeting the attack of any disease. These changes became recognized as objective indices of stress and furnished a basis for developing the entire stress concept.

The reaction was first described in *Nature* as "a syndrome produced by diverse nocuous agents." Subsequently it became known as the *general adaptation syndrome* (GAS) or *biologic stress syndrome* (Selye, 1936). In the same report, I also suggested the name "alarm reaction" for the initial response, arguing that it probably represented the somatic expression of a generalized call to arms of the body's defensive forces.

THE GENERAL ADAPTATION SYNDROME

The alarm reaction, however, was evidently not the entire response. After continued exposure of the organism to any noxious agent capable of eliciting this reaction, a stage of adaptation or resistance ensues. In other words, a state of alarm cannot be maintained continuously. If the agent is so drastic that continued exposure becomes incompatible with life, the animal dies during the alarm reaction (that is, within the first hours or days). If the organism can survive, this initial reaction is necessarily followed by the *stage of resistance*. The manifestations of this second phase are quite different from, and in many instances the exact opposite of, those that characterize the alarm reaction. For example, during the alarm reaction, the cells of the adrenal cortex discharge their secretory granules into the bloodstream and thus become depleted of corticoid-containing lipid storage material; in the stage of resistance, on the other hand, the cortex becomes particularly rich in secretory granules. In the alarm reaction, there is hemoconcentration, hypochloremia, and general tissue catabolism, whereas during the stage of resistance there is hemodilution, hyperchloremia, and anabolism, with a return toward normal body weight.

Curiously, after still more exposure to the noxious agent, the acquired adaptation is lost. The animal enters into a third phase, the *stage of exhaustion,* which inexorably follows as long as the demand is severe enough and applied for a sufficient length of time. It should be pointed out that the triphasic nature of the general adaptation syndrome gave us the first indication that the body's adaptability, or *adaptation energy,* is finite, since, under constant stress, exhaustion eventually ensues. We still do not know precisely what is lost, except that it is not merely caloric energy: food intake is normal during the stage of resistance. Hence, one would think that once adaptation had occurred and ample energy was available, resistance would go on indefinitely. But just as any inanimate machine gradually wears out, so does the human machine sooner or later become the victim of constant wear and tear. These three stages are reminiscent of childhood, with its characteristic low resistance and excessive response to any kind of stimulus, adulthood, during which the body has adapted to most commonly encountered agents and resistance is increased, and senility, characterized by loss of adaptability and eventual exhaustion, ending with death.

Our reserves of adaptation energy might be compared to an inherited bank account from which we can make withdrawals but to which we apparently cannot make deposits. After exhaustion from excessively stressful activity, sleep and rest can restore resistance and adaptability very close to previous levels, but complete restoration is probably impossible. Every biologic activity causes wear and tear; it leaves some irreversible chemical scars, which accumulate to constitute the signs of aging. Thus, adaptability should be used wisely and sparingly rather than squandered.

Mechanisms of Stress

Discoveries since 1936 have linked nonspecific stress with numerous biochemical and structural changes of previously unknown origin. There has also been considerable progress in analyzing the mediation of stress reactions by hormones. However, the carriers of the alarm signals that first relay the call for adaptation have yet to be identified. Perhaps they are metabolic by-products released during activity or damage, or perhaps what is involved is the lack of some vital substance consumed whenever any demand is made upon an organ. Since the only two coordinating systems that connect all parts of the body with one another are the nervous and the vascular systems, we can assume that the alarm signals use one or both of these pathways. Yet, while nervous stimulation may cause a general stress response, deafferented rats still show the classic syndrome when exposed to demands; so the nervous system cannot be the only route. It is probable that often, if not always, the signals travel in the blood.

The facts that led us to postulate the existence of the alarm signals would be in agreement with the view that the various cells send out different messengers. In that case the messages must somehow be tallied by the organs of adaptation. Whatever the nature of the *first mediator,* however, its existence is assured by its effects, which have been observed and measured. The discharge of hormones, the involution of the lymphatic organs, the enlargement of the adrenals, the feeling of fatigue, and many other signs of stress can all be produced by injury or activity in any part of the body.

Through the first mediator, the agent or situation disruptive of homeostasis eventually excites the hypothalamus, a complex bundle of nerve cells and fibers that acts as a bridge between the brain and the endocrine system (see Figure 2–2). The resulting nervous signals reach certain neuroendocrine cells in the median eminence (ME) of the hypothalamus, where they are transformed into CRF (corticotrophic hormone releasing factor), a chemical messenger that has not yet been isolated in pure form but is probably a polypeptide. In this way, a message is relayed to the pituitary, causing a discharge into the general circulation of ACTH (adrenocorticotrophic hormone).

ACTH, reaching the adrenal cortex, triggers the secretion of corticoids, mainly glucocorticoids such as cortisol or corticosterone. Through gluconeogenesis these compounds supply a readily available source of energy for the adaptive reactions necessary to meet the demands made by the agent. The corticoids also facilitate various other enzyme responses and suppress immune reactions and inflammation, thereby helping the body to coexist with potential pathogens.

Usually secreted in lesser amounts are the pro-inflammatory corticoids, which stimulate the proliferative ability and reactivity of the connective tissue, enhancing the *inflammatory potential.* Thus, they help to build a strong barricade of connective tissue through which the body is protected against further invasion. Because of their prominent effect upon salt and water metabolism, these hormones have also been refered to as *mineralocorticoids* (e.g., desoxicorticosterone and aldosterone). The somatotrophic hormone (STH), or growth hormone, of the pituitary likewise stimulates defense reactions.

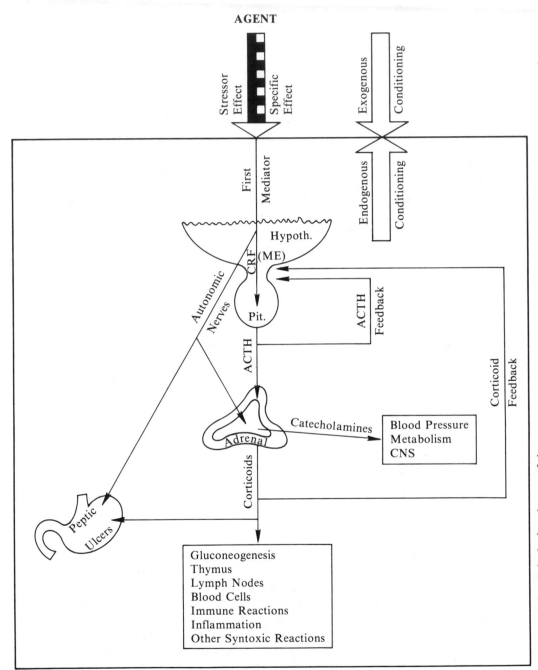

FIGURE 2-2. Principal pathways of the stress response.

This chain of events is cybernetically controlled by several feedback mechanisms. For instance, if there is a surplus of ACTH, a short-loop feedback returns some of it to the hypothalamus-pituitary axis and this shuts off further ACTH production. In addition, through a long-loop feedback, a high blood level of corticoids similarly inhibits too much ACTH secretion.

Simultaneously with all these processes, another important pathway is utilized to mediate the stress response. Hormones such as catecholamines are liberated to activate mechanisms of general usefulness for adaptation. Adrenaline, in particular, is secreted to make energy available, to accelerate the pulse rate, to elevate the blood pressure and the rate of blood circulation in the muscles, and to stimulate the central nervous system (CNS). The blood coagulation mechanism is also enhanced by adrenaline, as a protection against excessive bleeding if injuries are sustained in the state of affairs eliciting stress.

Countless other hormonal and chemical changes during stress check and balance the body's functioning and stability, constituting a virtual arsenal of weapons with which the organism defends itself. The facts known today may lead us to believe that the anterior pituitary and the adrenal cortex play the cardinal roles in stress, but this view probably reflects the active part endocrinologists have taken in elucidating the syndrome. Also, the techniques required to investigate the role of the nervous system are much more complex than those heretofore used. It is considerably easier, for example, to remove an endocrine gland and substitute injected extracts for its hormones than it is to destroy minute nervous centers selectively and then restore their function to determine the role they may play.

Syntoxic and Catatoxic Responses

In the course of human evolution, the body has developed two basic mechanisms for defense against potentially injurious aggressors, whether of external or internal origin. These two types of reactions, on which homeostasis mainly depends, are known as *syntoxic,* from *syn,* meaning together, and *catatoxic,* from *cata,* meaning against. The former help us put up with the aggressor while the latter destroy it. Syntoxic stimuli, acting as tissue tranquilizers, create a state of passive tolerance, which permits peaceful coexistence with aggressors. In the case of catatoxic agents, chemical changes, mainly the induction of destructive enzymes, generate an active attack on the pathogen, usually by accelerating its metabolic degradation.

Corticoids, substances produced by the adrenal cortex, are among the most effective syntoxic hormones. Of these, the best known are the anti-inflammatory group, including cortisone, and related substances that inhibit inflammation and many other defensive immune reactions such as the active rejection of grafted foreign tissues, that is, hearts or kidneys.

The main purpose of inflammation is to prevent the spread of irritants into the bloodstream by localizing them within a barricade. However, when the foreign agent is itself innocuous and causes disease only by inciting an exaggerated defense reaction, the suppression of inflammation is advantageous. Thus, anti-inflammatory corticoids have proved effective in treating diseases whose major complaint is inflammation of the joints, eyes, or respiratory passages.

On the other hand, when the aggressor is dangerous, the defensive reaction should be increased above the normal level. This is accomplished by catatoxic substances carrying a chemical message to the tissues to fight the invader even more actively than usual.

Stressors

The agents or demands that evoke the patterned response are referred to, quite naturally, as *stressors*. Something is thus a stressor to the same degree that it calls forth the syndrome. Stressors, it should be noted, are not exclusively physical in nature. Emotions—love, hate, joy, anger, challenge, and fear—as well as thoughts, also call forth the changes characteristic of the stress syndrome. In fact, psychological arousal is one of the most frequent activators. Yet it cannot be regarded as the only factor, since typical stress reactions can occur in patients exposed to trauma, hemorrhage, etc., while under deep anesthesia. Anesthetics themselves are commonly used in experimental medicine to produce stress, and stress of anesthesia is a serious problem in clinical surgery.

STRESS AND DISEASE

In general, the nervous and hormonal responses outlined above aid adaptation to environmental change or stimuli. Sometimes, however, they are the cause of disease, especially if the state of stress is prolonged or intense. In the latter case, the body passes through successive stages of the GAS, described earlier.

As we have seen, a fully developed GAS consists of the alarm reaction, the stage of resistance, and the stage of exhaustion. Yet it is not necessary for all three stages to develop before we can speak of a GAS; only the most severe stress leads rapidly to the stage of exhaustion and death. Most of the physical or mental exertions, infections, and other stressors that act upon us during a limited period produce changes corresponding only to the first and second stages. At first the stressors may upset and alarm us, but then we adapt to them.

Normally, in the course of our lives we go through these first two stages many, many times. Otherwise we could never become adapted to all the activities and demands that are man's lot. Even the stage of exhaustion does not always need to be irreversible and complete, as long as it affects only parts of the body. For instance, running produces a stress situation, mainly in our muscles and cardiovascular system. To cope with this, we first have to limber up and get these systems ready for the task at hand; then for a while we will be at the height of efficiency in running; eventually, however, exhaustion will set in. This sequence could be compared with an alarm reaction, a stage of resistance, and a stage of exhaustion, all limited primarily to the muscular and cardiovascular systems; yet such an exhaustion is reversible—after a good rest we will be back to normal.

It nevertheless remains true that the adaptive response can break down or go wrong because of innate defects, understress, overstress, or psychological mismanagement. The most common stress diseases—the so-called diseases of adaptation—are peptic ulcers in the stomach and upper intestine, high blood pressure, heart accidents, and nervous disturbances. This is a relative concept, however. No malady is just a disease of adaptation. Nor are there any disease producers that can be so perfectly handled by the organism that maladaptation plays no part in their effects upon the body. Such agents would not produce disease. This haziness in its delimitation does not interfere with the practical utility of our concept. We must put up with the same lack of precision whenever we have to classify a disease. There is no pure heart disease, in which all other organs remain perfectly undisturbed, nor can we ever speak of a pure kidney disease or a pure nervous disease in this sense.

The indirect production of disease by inappropriate or excessive adaptive reactions is well illustrated by the following example drawn from everyday life. If you meet a loudly insulting but obviously harmless drunk, nothing will happen if you take the syntoxic attitude of going past and ignoring him. But if you respond catatoxically, by fighting or even only preparing to fight, the outcome may be tragic. You will discharge adrenalinelike hormones that increase blood pressure and pulse rate, while your whole nervous system becomes alarmed and tense. If you happen to be a coronary candidate, you might end up with a fatal brain hemorrhage or cardiac arrest. In that case, your death will have been caused by your own biologically suicidal choice of the wrong reaction.

THE PRESENT STATUS OF RESEARCH

In this short chapter, it is impossible to give a meaningful sketch of all that has been learned about the structure of stress hormones, the nervous pathways involved, the medicines that have been developed to combat stress, and the diagnostic aids that this approach has offered. Nevertheless, the medical, chemical, and microscopic approaches to the problem have all been extremely fruitful. Since the very first description of the GAS, the most important single discovery was made only recently: the brain produces certain simple chemical substances closely related to ACTH. These substances have morphinelike, painkilling properties, and since they come from the inside (*endo*), they have been called *endorphins*. (I am especially proud that one of my former students, Dr. Roger Guillemin, was one of the three American scientists who shared the 1977 Nobel Prize for this remarkable discovery, although it was made at the Salk Institute quite independently of me.) The endorphins have opened up an entirely new field in medicine, particularly in stress research. Not only do they have antistress effects as painkillers, but also they probably play an important role in the transmission of the alarm signal from the brain to the pituitary, and their concentration is especially high in the pituitary itself. Thus, they may shed some light on the nature of the first mediator.

Significant breakthroughs have also been made with the discovery of tranquilizers and psychotherapeutic chemicals to combat mental disease. These have reduced the number of institutionalized mental patients to an unprecedented low. Also worth mentioning are the enormously potent anti-ulcer drugs that block the pathways through which stress ulcers are produced.

However, all these purely medical discoveries are applicable only by physicians, and the general public cannot use them in daily life without constant medical supervision. Futhermore, most of these agents are not actually directed against stress but rather against some of its morbid manifestations (ulcers, high blood pressure, or heart accidents). Therefore, increasing attention has been given to the development of psychological techniques and behavioral codes that anybody can use, after suitable instruction, to adjust to the particular demands made by his life.

Among these not strictly medical approaches are the relaxation techniques. We should spend a little time each day at complete rest, with our eyes closed and our muscles relaxed, breathing regularly and repeating words that are either meaningless or heard so often that they merely help us not think of anything in particular. This is the basis of Transcendental Meditation, Benson's relaxation technique, and an infinite variety of other procedures. These practices should not be underestimated merely because science cannot explain them; they have worked for so long and in so many forms that we must respect them.

More recently, biofeedback has added a great deal to the psychological approach. A number of highly sophisticated instruments have been developed that inform the user constantly about body changes characteristic of stress, for example, in blood pressure, pulse rate, body temperature, and even brain activity. We do not yet have a scientific explanation for biofeedback, but if people learn to identify, instinctively or through instrumentation, when they are under stress, they can automatically avoid, or at least reduce, their responses.

A SCIENTIFIC ETHICS

The drunk illustration I used earlier shows how certain well-known facts about the demands of everyday life can make clearer some of the principles involved in the unconscious, wired-in stress responses mediated by the neurohumoral system. Yet it is also true that the latter can refine our knowledge of the former. Laboratory observations on the body's methods for fighting distress have already helped us to lay the foundations for a biologically justifiable code of behavior, one designed to achieve the pleasant stress of fulfillment (known technically as *eustress*—from the Greek *eu* meaning good, as in euphemia and euphoria) without the harmful consequences of damaging stress, that is, *distress* (Selye, 1974).

At first it seems odd that the laws governing life's responses at such different levels as the cell, the whole person, and even the nation should be so essentially similar. Yet this type of uniformity is true of all great laws of nature. For example, in the inanimate world, arrangement of matter and energy in orbits circulating around a center is characteristic of the largest celestial bodies, as well as of individual atoms. Why is it that on these opposite levels, the smallest and the largest, the satellites circling a huge planet and the minute electrons around an atomic nucleus, should go around in orbits? We find comparable similarities in the laws governing living matter. Countless phenomena run in cycles, such as the periodically recurring needs for food, water, sleep, and sexual activity. Damage is unavoidable unless each cycle runs its full course.

In formulating a natural code of behavior, these thoughts have fundamental importance. We must not only understand the profound biological need for the completion and fulfillment of our aspirations but also know how to handle these in harmony with our particular inherited capacities. Not everybody is born with the same amount of adaptation energy.

Work: A Biological Necessity

Most people consider their work their primary function in life. For the man or woman of action, one of the most difficult things to bear is enforced inactivity during prolonged hospitalization or after retirement. Just as our muscles degenerate if not used, so our brain slips into chaos and confusion unless we constantly use it for work that seems worthwhile to us. The average person thinks he works for economic security or social status, but at the end of a most successful business career—when he finally has achieved this goal—there remains nothing to fight for. There is no hope for progress and only the boredom of assured monotony. The question is not whether we should or should not work, but what kind of work suits us best.

In my opinion, today's insatiable demand for less work and more pay does not depend so much on the number of working hours or dollars as on the degree of dissatisfaction with life. We could do much, and at little cost, by fighting this dissatisfaction. Many people suffer because they have no particular taste for anything, no hunger for achievement. These, and not those who earn little, are the true paupers of mankind. What they need more than money is guidance.

Without the incentive to work out his role as *homo faber,* a person is likely to seek destructive, revolutionary outlets to satisfy the basic human need for self-assertive activity. Man may be able to solve the age-old problem of having to live by the sweat of his brow, but the fatal enemy of all utopias is boredom. What we shall have to do after technology makes most "useful work" redundant is to invent new occupations. Even this will require a full-scale effort to teach "play professions," such as the arts, philosophy, crafts, and science, to the public at large; there is no limit to how much each man can work on perfecting himself and on giving pleasure to others.

"Earn Thy Neighbor's Love"

Each person must find a way to relieve his pent-up energy without creating conflicts with his fellow men. Such an approach not only insures peace of mind but also earns the goodwill, respect, and even love of our neighbors, the highest degree of security and the most noble status symbol to which the human being can aspire.

This philosophy of hoarding a wealth of respect and friendship is merely one reflection of the deep-rooted instinct of people and animals to collect—a tendency as characteristic of ants, bees, squirrels, and beavers as of the capitalist who collects money to put away in the bank. The same impulse drives entire human societies to build systems of roads, telephone networks, cities, and fortifications, which they view as necessary ingredients of their future security and comfort.

In man, this urge first manifests itself when children start to amass matchboxes, shells, or stickers; it continues when adults collect stamps or coins. This natural proclivity is not artificial. By collecting certain things, one acquires status and security in the community. The guideline of earning love merely attempts to direct the hoarding instinct toward what I consider the most permanent and valuable commodity that man can possess: a huge capital of goodwill that protects him against personal attacks by others.

To live literally by the biblical command to "love thy neighbor as thyself" leads only to guilt feelings because this teaching cannot be reconciled with the laws of objective science. Whether we like it or not, egoism is an inescapable characteristic of all living beings. But we can continue to benefit by the wisdom of this time-honored maxim if, in the light of modern biological research, we merely reword it. Let our guide for conduct be the motto "Earn thy neighbor's love."

REFERENCES

BERNARD, C. *Leçons sur les phénomènes de la vie commune aux animaux et aux végétaux,* vol. 2. Paris: Baillière, 1879.

CANNON, W. B. *The wisdom of the body.* New York: Norton, 1939.

FREDERICQ, L. Influence du milieu ambiant sur la composition du sang des animaux aquatiques. *Archives de Zoologie Experimental et Génerale,* 1885, *3,* 34.

HALDANE, J. S. *Respiration.* New Haven: Yale University Press, 1922.

PFLÜGER, E. Die teleologische mechanik der lebendigen *Natur. Pflüger's Archiv für die gesamte Physiologie des menschen umd der tiere,* 1877, *15,* 57.

SELYE, H. A syndrome produced by diverse nocuous agents. *Nature,* 1936, *138,* 32.

——————. *The story of the adaptation syndrome.* Montreal: Acta, 1952.

——————. *Stress without distress.* Philadephia: Lippincott, 1974.

——————. (ed.). *Selye's guide to stress research,* vol. 1. New York: Van Nostrand, 1980.

PART II

BASIC PSYCHOLOGICAL PROCESSES

3

Stress, Coping, and Somatic Adaptation

Kenneth A. Holroyd   Richard S. Lazarus

CONTEMPORARY RESEARCH ON PSYCHOLOGICAL STRESS emerged more than a quarter of a century ago, stimulated by the desire to understand breakdowns in adaptive behavior observed in extreme situations. Situations that were of immediate concern at that time included military combat (Grinker & Spiegel, 1945), the concentration camp (Bettelheim, 1943), bereavement (Lindemann, 1944), and traumatic injury (Hamburg, Hamburg, & deGoza, 1953). The disturbances in functioning that had been observed were often as dramatic as the extreme situations themselves and included psychotic behavior, severe anxiety, bleeding ulcers (Paster, 1948; Swank, 1949), and hypertension (Graham, 1945). By conceptualizing these phenomena as consequences of stress, investigators could formulate general principles that transcended the particular situation (e.g., battlefield or concentration camp) in which their observations had been made. Hypotheses about sources of stress, mechanisms of stress production, and factors that increase or decrease the psychological and somatic costs of stress could then be developed.

In subsequent decades the scope of stress research expanded from field studies of the casualties of extreme situations to laboratory analogue studies examining the conditions under which skilled performance deteriorates, as well as the impairment of morale, overall functioning, and somatic health in a wide variety of naturalistic settings (Lazarus, 1981; Lazarus & Folkman, 1982). Currently, popular and scientific interest in stress phenomena—and how they might be managed—is at an all-time high; at the same time, controversies about key concepts and research strategies in the field abound (cf. Mason, 1975b; McGrath, 1970; Rose & Levin, 1979).

Because obviously stressful events such as natural disasters and war so dramatically disrupt people's lives, it has been natural to search for the determinants of the stress experience in the characteristics of the stressful events themselves (e.g., Holmes & Masuda, 1974). For example, a great deal of effort has been expended to demonstrate that the adaptational consequences of stress can be predicted from life event scales that purport to measure the adjustment demands posed by stressful events (e.g., Dohrenwend & Dohrenwend, 1974; Gunderson & Rahe, 1974). Although research has failed to find the strong relationship between these two variables that was expected (cf. Rabkin & Struening, 1976), it tends to be

Preparation of this chapter was supported in part by grants from NIMH (1-F32-17H08327-01) to Kenneth A. Holroyd and from NIA (AG00799) to Richard S. Lazarus.

assumed that this will change with the methodological refinement of measurement instruments. Thus, Dohrenwend and Dohrenwend (1979) argued that if we could "measure the magnitude of life events with something approaching the incisiveness with which we measure the magnitude of electric shock or exposure to combat" (p. 119), the predicted relationships would emerge.

Others, including ourselves, would argue that even in extreme circumstances the consequences of stress cannot be understood merely in terms of the stressful event (Benner, Roskies, & Lazarus, 1980). Stressful circumstances do not take their toll from a passive individual, as is implicitly assumed by stimulus definitions of stress, but from an individual who is imbuing stressful circumstances with personal meaning and struggling to control and master these circumstances. Because these mediating psychological processes are important determinants of the stress experience, it is inevitable that situations will be encountered in which there is little or no relationship between the severity of the adjustment demands impinging on the individual and the adaptational consequences of these demands, or between the demands and complex qualitative patterns of reaction.

This is not to deny that environments such as prolonged combat (Kinston & Rosser, 1974) or the concentration camp (Eitinger & Strom, 1973) are sufficiently brutal to damage almost everyone exposed to them, although it is worth noting that a few individuals emerge even from such extreme circumstances apparently unscathed (Antonovsky, Maoz, Dowty, & Wijsenbeck, 1971). It is rather to assert that the success of our efforts to understand the impact of stress on human adaptation will be heavily dependent on the success with which we are able to conceptualize these mediating psychological processes. We now turn to this problem.

KEY CONCEPTS

Stress

We define *stress* relationally by reference to both the person and the environment (Coyne & Lazarus, 1980; Holroyd, 1979; Lazarus & Launier, 1978). This contrasts with definitions of stress phrased either solely in terms of the occurrence of events consensually regarded as stressful (Holmes & Masuda, 1974) or solely in terms of responses that are *sometimes* consequences of stress, such as physiological mobilization (Selye, 1976), cognitive disruption (Horowitz, 1976), or behavioral disorganization.

At the psychological level, which is our primary focus here, mediational processes involving evaluation and judgment are crucial to the stress reaction. Psychological stress requires a judgment that environmental and/or internal demands tax or exceed the individual's resources for managing them. This judgment and the individual's efforts to manage and shape the stress experience are conceptualized in terms of two interacting processes: appraisal and coping (Lazarus, 1966; Lazarus & Folkman, 1982).

Appraisal

Appraisal refers to the evaluative process that imbues a situational encounter with meaning for the person. The term refers to our sense that something of importance is jeopardized or at stake, as well as to our evaluation of the ways opposing demands and options, constraints and resources moderate this sense of jeopardy. Appraisals can be separated into those that are concerned with the recognition that the individual is in jeopardy (appraisal of what is at stake) and those that are concerned primarily with the evaluation of resources and options available for managing potential or actual harm (appraisal of coping). Although these two processes are highly interdependent and not separable in many contexts, this distinction is nevertheless of value in drawing attention to different sets of variables that interact in determining stress responses, coping patterns, and adaptational outcomes.

Appraisal of what is at stake refers to the sensed judgment that a transaction is either irrelevant to our well-being, benign or positive in its implication, or stressful. Stressful appraisals can be further placed in three categories. Appraisals of *threat* and *harm-loss* are distinguished primarily by their time perspective, with threat referring to the anticipation of imminent harm and harm-loss referring to the judgment that damage has already occurred. *Challenge* involves not only the judgment that a transaction contains the potential for harm *and* the potential for mastery or gain but also the judgment that this outcome can be influenced by the individual. Thus, in challenge, appraisals of stakes and a sense of positive control are fused.

If we consider the question implicit in the appraisal of stakes to be "Am I okay or in trouble?" then the question implicit in the appraisal of coping is "What can be done about the situation?" This evaluation of coping options and constraints is influenced by previous experiences in similar situations, generalized beliefs about the self and the environment, and the availability of personal (e.g., physical strength or problem-solving skills) and environmental (e.g., social support or money) resources (Wrubel, Benner, & Lazarus, 1981). It should not be assumed, however, that the appraisal process is necessarily rational; this assessment may not reflect extensive information processing of the sort that is assumed by computer models of human decision making (Folkman, Schaefer, & Lazarus, 1979). To the contrary, when threat is great or personal agendas and commitment are activated, coping may follow only the most minimal and biased processing of information and appear quite irrational to an outside observer (see also Janis & Mann, 1977).

Adaptational Consequences of Appraisal

One reason the concept of appraisal is central to stress theory is that appraisal serves as a final common pathway through which diverse personal and environmental variables influence the outcomes of stressful encounters. Today, with the advent of the "cognitive revolution" (Dember, 1974), it is readily conceded that the impact of environmental demands on the stress experience and on adaptational outcomes is mediated cognitively. It is less frequently acknowledged that demographic and personality variables can influence adaptational outcomes through the same mechanism (Bowers & Kelly, 1979; Depue, Monroe, & Shackman, 1979). Depue and co-workers (1979) offered a cogent analysis of the ways appraisal processes may mediate the impact of personality characteristics on health outcomes.

> At a specific level, certain psychological characteristics (e.g., dependency) may operate directly on the appraisal process and may predispose the individual to perceive a particular class of events (e.g., loss) as highly threatening to personal security. At a more general level, certain psychological characteristics may lead to the development of a more general "cognitive schema" predisposing the individual to appraise a wider range of events as threatening . . . .
>
> Whether one is considering more specific psychological characteristics (e.g., dependency) or

more general cognitive schemas (e.g., self-efficacy expectations) as psychological predisposing factors, viewing their influence as operating on the appraisal of life events places these factors in a central position with respect to moderating the impact of the environment on individuals. By increasing the potential threat of psychosocial stimuli, psychological predisposing variables may play a key role in exacerbating the emotional-biologic mediators that serve to "activate" biologic predisposing biases [leading to disease]. (Pp. 13–14)

Some of the most intriguing questions in stress research concern the possible adaptational consequences of different types of appraisals. Typically it is assumed that the individual who responds to the potential for gain in a stressful encounter and is challenged is likely to fare better than the person who responds primarily to the potential for harm or loss. To the extent this assumption proves correct, the distinction between challenge and threat would parallel the distinction emphasized by Selye (1976) between constructive and destructive stress (Lazarus, Cohen, Folkman, Kanner, & Schaefer, 1980).

Common sense suggests that the challenged individual may cope more persistently or effectively and thereby experience less stress than the threatened one. Psychological states such as challenge may also be associated with hormonal response patterns that are more adaptive or have fewer somatic costs than those associated with threat (Lazarus, 1977; Lazarus et al., 1980). Supporting this latter possibility, recent research suggests that threat is associated with elevations in both catecholamine and cortisol levels, whereas challenge is associated only with elevations in catecholamine levels, with cortisol levels remaining normal or even declining (Frankenhaeuser, 1980; Rose, 1980). However, the individual who is constantly challenged by even relatively innocuous occupational and social demands and who is, as a result, repeatedly mobilized for struggle may be particularly vulnerable to certain disorders (Glass, 1977). In any case, the consequences of appraisal can be expected to depend upon the context in which the appraisal occurs. Thus, it is an oversimplification to assume, as is often done in popular writing on holistic medicine, that particular attitudes can be adopted that will prove stress reducing in all contexts.

Coping

Early research from the Lazarus group was designed to demonstrate the value of the appraisal construct and, more generally, the advantages of cognitive-mediational accounts of human stress phenomena in a psychological climate dominated by S-R theory (Lazarus, 1966, 1968; Lazarus, Averill, & Opton, 1970). More recent research has focused on coping as a determinant of the stress experience and of adaptational outcomes, first with respect to well-defined and localized stressors such as surgery (Cohen & Lazarus, 1973) and later with respect to the stresses that occur in naturalistic settings such as the home and the workplace (Folkman & Lazarus, 1980).

The term "coping" refers broadly to efforts to manage environmental and internal demands and conflicts among demands (Lazarus, 1966, 1981). This definition focuses explicitly on *efforts to manage,* that is, on the dynamic constellation of thoughts and acts that constitute the coping process. The emphasis on what people are actually thinking and doing during a stressful encounter contrasts with the more dominant approach to understanding individual differences in response to stress, which focuses solely on relatively static *moderator variables*—for example, personality traits (Kobasa, Hilker, & Maddi, 1979), motive patterns (McClelland, 1979; McClelland, Floor, Davidson, & Saron, 1980), or historical events in the individual's life, say, the death of a parent during childhood (Brown & Harris, 1978).

We have two reservations about this moderator variable approach. First, because moderator variables tend to be related only weakly to actual coping activity, they are likely to be related only weakly to adaptational outcomes that are shaped by the coping process itself. Second, even if moderator variables successfully predicted individual differences in response to stress and in adaptational outcomes, we would remain ignorant of mediational processes, that is, what is being done in what types of situations that leads to observed differences in outcome.

Because of its breadth, our definition of coping risks overinclusiveness. However, we believe this problem is preferable to the difficulties that are created when attention is restricted to intrapsychic defensive processes (Haan, 1969, 1977) while more rational problem-solving efforts are ignored or, conversely, while attention is restricted to rational problem-solving efforts (Bedell, Archer & Marlowe, 1980; Spivack & Shure, 1974), with the adaptive function of defensive processes such as denial ignored (Lazarus & Golden, 1981). Because of our limited knowledge of coping, restrictive formulations of this sort invariably run the risk that the coping activities most strongly related to the outcomes of interest will be just those that are underemphasized or ignored.

When we attend to coping process we learn quickly that coping is multifaceted. Stresses that are encountered outside the well-controlled laboratory environment are seldom met with the restricted range of coping responses that are the focus of most laboratory research. Moreover, the difficulties posed by the environment and the coping strategies used by the individual evolve in meaningful ways during a stressful encounter. A recent examination of the coping strategies used by 100 middle-aged adults during more than 1300 stressful encounters indicated that stresses encountered in the naturalistic environment are met not with a single coping response but by a dynamic constellation of both problem-focused and emotion-focused coping activities (Folkman & Lazarus, 1980).

COPING AND ADAPTATION

The last decade has seen an important change in perspective in the health field. It has been increasingly acknowledged that health outcomes are a product of effective coping rather than simply a consequence of the presence or absence of stress (cf. Antonovsky, 1979; Henry & Stephens, 1977; Roskies & Lazarus, 1980). Within psychology this change in perspective is reflected in a renewed interest in the psychological determinants of health (cf. Cohen, 1979; Sexton, 1979; Ursin, 1980; Weiner, 1982) and in the emergence of health psychology and behavioral medicine as subdisciplines (cf. Davidson & Davidson, 1980; McNamara, 1979; Millon, Green, & Meagher, 1982; Stone, Cohen, & Adler, 1979); these trends have stimulated research on the role of coping in predisposing and initiating disease processes (Glass, 1977; Weiss, 1977) and in influencing the course of illness initiated by other factors (Cohen & Lazarus, 1979; Moos, 1982; Shontz, 1982). Disciplines that are concerned primarily with environmental sources of stress, such as epidemiology and sociology, have experienced a parallel growth in interest in environmental resources believed to moderate the health consequences of stress by facilitating effective coping (Cassel, 1976; Henry & Stephens, 1977; Jenkins, 1979; Kaplan, Cassel, & Gore, 1977; Rahe & Ranson, 1978).

In order to formulate hypotheses about the health consequences of different coping processes or to improve health outcomes through the enhancement of coping skills, it is not sufficient merely to acknowledge the importance of coping; we must move beyond this acknowledgment to an analysis of the mechanisms through which coping affects health. As an initial step in this direction we will outline four general pathways.

First, coping affects health outcomes by influencing the frequency, intensity, and patterning of neuroendocrine stress responses. This may occur in three ways. By preventing stressful events from occurring or by enabling the individual to avoid or resolve difficulties that do occur, *problem-focused coping* may eliminate environmental demands that otherwise could lead the individual to mobilize for action; however, if it is inept, problem-focused coping may aggravate stressful circumstances so that the individual is continually mobilized for struggle. *Emotion-focused coping* also can either moderate stress emotions and associated physiological mobilization or intensify and prolong the stress emotions that occur in response to even minor difficulties. Furthermore, particular coping styles or types of coping activity may affect health outcomes because they are associated with *patterns* of physiological mobilization that predispose to certain disorders but not to others.

The potential damaging effects of repeated or prolonged elicitation of neuroendocrine stress responses were recognized half a century ago (Cannon, 1932), and the concept that these responses play an important etiological role in a wide variety of disorders has been explored scientifically and popularized by Selye (1976). We now know that neuroendocrine stress responses can influence virtually every cellular and metabolic process in the body (Mason, 1968, 1975a). However, the somatic consequences of the mobilization are not always as straightforward as might be expected. For example, stress related fluctuations in neuroendocrine activity may alter kidney function, thereby biasing hemodynamic control systems in the early stages of essential hypertension (Kaplan, 1979), or they may reduce the effectiveness of the immune response, increasing the individual's vulnerability to whole classes of disorders (Bowers & Kelly, 1979; Morillo & Gardner, 1979; Rodgers, Dubey, & Reich, 1979). However, in other circumstances stress hormones may enhance the effectiveness of the immune response, acting protectively against disease processes (Amkraut & Solomon, 1974). Therefore, straightforward notions about the damaging consequences of mobilization (Stoyva, 1976) probably are, if not incorrect, at least incomplete and overstated.

Because laboratory paradigms in the biological sciences have tended to isolate stress responses from their psychological and social context, our knowledge of how coping shapes physiological stress responses is quite limited. Research typically employs either injurious agents such as bacteria or toxins or physical mutilation to mobilize physiological stress responses and severely restricts or entirely eliminates options for combating the stressor. This has enabled researchers reliably to elicit hormonal stress responses in order to document the important role of adrenal medulla and adrenal cortex secretions in mobilization. However, because it largely ignores factors that lead some individuals but not others to respond to a noxious stimulus with mobilization, and some individuals but not others to remain mobilized for prolonged periods, such laboratory research is unable to provide information about the determinants of these responses in individuals functioning in less restricted settings.

Fortunately, behavioral scientists have begun to examine biobehavioral responses to stress in a more integrated fashion. For example, Glass (1977; Glass, Krakoff, Contrada, Hilton, Kehoe, Manucci, Collins, Snow, & Elting, 1980) argued that fluctuations in catecholamines sufficiently dramatic to influence the pathogenesis of coronary heart disease are elicited by a coping style that alternates between intense efforts to control stressful transactions and helplessness when coping efforts fail. Similarly, Obrist (1981; Obrist, Light,

Langer, Grignolo, & McCubbin, 1978) contrasted cardiovascular responses associated with active and passive coping and presented evidence that only active coping is accompanied by sympathetic stimulation of the heart and is thus likely to generate the hemodynamic changes pathogenic for essential hypertension. This research, although confined to the laboratory setting, represents an important step toward understanding stress responses in their psychosocial context, something that must be done if we are to trace the genesis of stress related illness.

A second pathway through which coping can influence health outcomes comes into being when illness behavior (i.e., reporting symptoms and/or seeking treatment) or actual physiological symptoms serve coping functions. Illness behavior may serve stabilizing functions in conflicted families (Minuchin, Rosman, & Baker, 1978) or be maintained by secondary gains or reinforcements (Whitehead, Fedoravicius, Blackwell, & Wooley, 1979). Some physiological symptoms can probably also be acquired and maintained in a similar manner (Whitehead et al., 1979), although this pattern has been difficult to demonstrate. However, Miller (1980; Miller & Dworkin, 1977) speculated that essential hypertension may develop when elevations in blood pressure serve as coping responses. Drawing on research indicating that baroreceptor stimulation inhibits reticular formation activity and thereby produces sedativelike effects, Miller suggested that individuals who are unable to manage stress psychologically may learn to cope physiologically; that is, by elevating blood pressure so as to produce the sedativelike effects that accompany baroreceptor stimulation. These elevations in blood pressure would then continue to occur in stressful situations because they are reinforced by immediate reductions in stress emotions. However, over the long run they could be expected to contribute to the hemodynamic disregulation (Schwartz, 1977) that occurs in the early stages of essential hypertension.

Third, coping may contribute to disease because it involves changes in health behaviors that expose the individual to injurious agents such as alcohol, tobacco smoke, or allergens. When symptoms co-vary in a systematic manner with the occurrence of stressful events, the possibility that symptoms are triggered by changes in health behaviors and not by the mobilization of physiological stress responses is apt ro receive insufficient attention. For example, disease processes may be initiated or aggravated when men at risk for coronary heart disease increase their smoking in response to stress (Horowitz, Hulley, Alvarez, Reynolds, Benfari, Blair, Borhani, & Simon, 1979), or when peptic duodenal ulcer sufferers increase their consumption of alcohol in response to work stress (Weisman, 1956).

Finally, the way the individual copes with the threat of acute illness (Moos, 1982) or with the demands of chronic illness (Cohen & Lazarus, 1979; Shontz, 1982) can be an important determinant of the course of the illness and of the medical care received. Even in many chronic conditions the patient is likely to spend less than a total of one day per year in direct contact with doctors or nurses. As a result, patients' persistent efforts to regulate their disorders can often be a more important determinant of medical outcome than the medical care that is received. The asthmatic who responds to the intermittent threat of airway obstruction with high levels of fear or panic will typically be prescribed more steroid medication than the patient who is less fearful and more persistent in efforts to cope with threat, even when objective measures indicate similar levels of pulmonary function. Moreover, patterns of self-medication tend to be incorporated into these general styles of coping, with symptoms influencing the outcome of the disorder. For example, asthmatics who respond with high levels of fear frequently return to the hospital because they have overmedicated themselves, probably because they perceive few options other than the immediate use of medication, whereas asthmatics who cope with threat by persisting in their daily activities and ignoring the early warning signs of an attack return to the hospital because they fail to medicate themselves until it is too late to control an attack (Jones, Kinsman, Dirks, & Dahlem, 1979).

FACILITATING EFFECTIVE COPING

Currently there is considerable popular interest in psychological interventions that are designed to reduce the psychological and somatic costs of stress by facilitating effective coping (cf. Everly, Rosenfeld, Allen, Brown, Sobelman, & Wain, 1981; Meichenbaum & Jeremko, 1982). Such interventions necessarily make assumptions about the impact of particular coping processes on adaptational outcomes, and their success is likely to be dependent on the validity of the assumptions that are made. In this section we will contrast the views of coping that are implicit in the two most popular approaches to stress management: biofeedback and cognitive behavior therapy.

Biofeedback seeks to reduce the toll taken by stress by teaching people to control the physiological components of the stress response. The goal of treatment is typically to enable people to control the somatic consequences of stress either by controlling physiological responses that can lead to particular symptoms (Shapiro & Surwit, 1979) or by evoking a more generalized state of reduced arousal (Stoyva, 1976).

There is now a substantial body of research indicating that people can exert voluntary control over a wide variety of physiological responses when appropriate feedback is provided in a relaxed laboratory environment (cf. Miller, 1978; Shapiro & Surwit, 1979). However, the biofeedback approach to stress management further assumes that stress responses occurring in more naturalistic settings can be isolated from their psychological context and autonomously controlled by the individual in a similar manner. Unfortunately, the uncritical acceptance of this assumption has led investigators to minimize the importance of psychological processes in biofeedback (Holroyd, 1979; Lazarus, 1975) and in the transfer of training from the laboratory to stressful encounters in more naturalistic settings (Lynn & Freedman, 1979).

Our transactional perspective leads us to expect the management of physiological stress responses to require more extensive cognitive and behavioral changes than is assumed by biofeedback approaches to stress management. Because physiological stress responses result from appraisals of harm, threat, or challenge, they are expected to be firmly embedded in the individual's transactions with the environment and not readily modified without changing these transactions. It is therefore not surprising that the self-control of physiological responses painstakingly acquired during biofeedback training is readily disrupted by stresses encountered outside the laboratory, so that one seldom sees this learning transfer to other settings (Lynn & Freedman, 1979). People simply are unable to exert control over specific physiological responses while they are engaged in transactions with the environment that generate the very same responses. There is relatively good evidence in the case of tension and migraine headache that biofeedback does produce symptom improvements that extend beyond the therapeutic situation (Blanchard, Andrasik, Ahles, Teders, & O'Keefe, 1980). However, where biofeedback is effective, its effectiveness appears to have little to do with the ability to control symptom related physiological responses acquired during biofeedback. In fact, contingencies during biofeedback can be reversed—for example, tension headache sufferers can be taught to *increase* rather than *decrease* frontal muscle tension—without reducing the effectiveness of treatment (Andrasik & Holroyd, 1980; Holroyd & Andrasik,

1982; Kewman & Roberts, 1980). Following biofeedback, successfully treated headache patients also report dramatic changes in the ways they manage headache related stresses, such as more assertive behavior, rational evaluation of headache related stresses, and avoidance of situations that had previously elicited headache (Andrasik & Holroyd, 1980). The mechanisms whereby biofeedback and other psychological therapies produce change may thus be more similar than has previously been thought. In fact, biofeedback may be effective because it indirectly induces patients to alter the way they cope with headache related stresses, not because it enables patients more directly to control symptom related physiological responses.

Cognitive-behavioral interventions seek to reduce the somatic costs of stress by helping people psychologically to manage stress more effectively rather than by teaching people directly to regulate stress related physiological responses (Holroyd, 1979). When the patient has acquired more effective coping strategies, the somatic consequences of stress are reduced through pathways like those outlined above. Intervention focuses on (1) identifying patterns of thinking and behavior that aggravate and maintain stress responses, (2) practicing and evaluating potentially useful strategies for coping with stress, and (3) flexibly adapting these coping strategies to changing environmental demands and personal needs.

Initial applications of cognitive-behavioral interventions were restricted to anxieties commonly occurring in normal populations (Holroyd, 1976; Meichenbaum, 1972). More recently, however, these therapies have been applied to an increasingly wide range of problems, including the prevention of stress related illness in individuals who are in high-risk occupations (e.g., Novaco, 1977), who are undergoing difficult life transitions (e.g., Granvold & Welch, 1977), or who are at risk for disorders such as coronary heart disease or essential hypertension (e.g., Roskies, 1980); the treatment of psychological problems such as anxiety or depression (e.g., Rush, Beck, Kovacs, & Hollon, 1977) or of psychophysiological disorders such as recurrent (tension and migraine) headache and bronchial asthma (e.g., Holroyd, Appel, & Andrasik, 1982); and the management of stresses that are consequences of illness and medical care (e.g., Kendall, 1982a). The considerable research activity in this area is reported in three recent volumes (Emory, Hollon, & Bedrosian, 1981; Kendall, 1982b; Meichenbaum & Jeremko, 1982).

A growing body of research suggests that cognitive-behavioral interventions may be a promising method of preventing and treating some stress related disorders (Holroyd, 1979; Meichenbaum & Jeremko, 1982). However, we suspect that the continued advancement of this approach to stress management will depend more on the development of reliable methods of assessing coping processes than on the sort of clinical innovation that has characterized this work to date. Without the ability to assess coping processes we have no way of determining the impact our interventions are having on the coping activity of our clients. In the absence of empirical feedback, therapeutic innovation tends to be shaped by therapists' personal beliefs and conventional wisdom concerning what constitutes effective coping, and this approach to stress management will very likely prove another passing therapeutic fad. The successful development of a cognitive-behavioral approach to stress management is therefore likely to be highly dependent upon advances in basic research on stress and coping.

Research evaluating the effectiveness of stress management interventions also appears to provide an unusual opportunity to examine fundamental relationships between coping and adaptation. In contrast to research on the adaptational consequences of coping, which has been restricted to descriptive and correlational studies, research evaluating the effectiveness of stress management intervention provides a unique opportunity to examine the impact of *changes* in coping on adaptational outcomes. This is because cognitive-behavioral interventions are designed to produce dramatic changes in coping over the course of a few months.

CONCLUSION

Popular and scientific concern about the health consequences of stress has increased steadily during the past decade, as has interest in psychological interventions designed to reduce the toll taken by stresses encountered in modern industrial society. Further significant advances in stress research will require substantial change in the theory and research strategies that currently govern the field.

In this chapter we alluded to four fundamental changes in perspective and research strategy that will be required: (1) the discarding of stimulus and response conceptions of stress in favor of relational formulations that do not artificially isolate the personal and environmental determinants of the stress experience; (2) the deemphasis of trait and moderator variables in favor of process focused research methods that attempt to describe and assess coping processes as they evolve in the course of stressful transactions; (3) the deemphasis of exclusively normative research in favor of ipsative research that attempts to describe the social, psychological, and physiological mechanisms that operate as health outcomes improve, remain constant, or worsen in the face of stress; and (4) the deemphasis of laboratory research in favor of field research that examines stress phenomena in their psychosocial context, describing the sources of stress that operate in naturalistic settings and the full range of coping activities that people perform.

We outlined a theoretical approach to stress that conceptualizes the psychological determinants of the stress experience in terms of interacting processes of appraisal and coping and attempted to elucidate relationships between these two central constructs and adaptational outcomes in the area of somatic health. Because appraisals of harm-loss, threat, and challenge serve as a final common pathway through which personal and environmental variables influence the stress experience, we suggested that appraisal can serve as a valuable unifying concept in stress theory. We also attempted to move beyond the mere acknowledgment of the importance of coping as a determinant of health outcomes to an analysis of mechanisms, identifying four general pathways through which coping affects health.

Next, we discussed some of the implications of this theory for stress management, noting that intervention inevitably involves assumptions about the nature of coping and the coping activities most likely to moderate the negative consequences of stress. Biofeedback approaches to stress management are of interest not only because they are popular but also because they appear to many to have circumvented the theoretical and methodological difficulties that are involved in dealing with coping by focusing exclusively on readily quantifiable physiological stress responses. We argued that this appearance is largely illusory because without reference to the construct of coping, we cannot adequately explain the effectiveness of biofeedback in those instances where it is effective, nor are we likely to develop effective methods of transferring the learning that occurs during biofeedback training to stressful encounters occurring outside the laboratory.

Approaches to stress management that seek to reduce the toll taken by stress by facilitating effective coping avoid some of the limitations of purely physiologically focused stress management. The successful development of these psychological approaches to stress management, which are still in their infancy, depends heavily on basic research on stress and coping, in particular the construction of reliable methods of assessing coping processes. As a result, clinical research on stress management and basic research on stress and coping are likely to be increasingly interdependent in the coming years.

REFERENCES

AMKRAUT, A., & SOLOMON, G. F. From the symbolic stimulus to pathophysiologic response: Immune mechanisms. *International Journal of Psychiatry in Medicine,* 1974, *5,* 541–563.

ANDRASIK, F., & HOLROYD, K. A test of specific and non-specific effects in the biofeedback treatment of tension headache. *Journal of Consulting and Clinical Psychology,* 1980, *48,* 575–586.

ANTONOVSKY, A. *Health, stress, and coping.* San Francisco: Jossey-Bass, 1979.

ANTONOVSKY, A., MAOZ, B., DOWTY, N., & WIJESENBECK, H. Twenty-five years later. *Social Psychiatry,* 1971, *6,* 186–193.

BEDELL, J. R., ARCHER, R. P., & MARLOWE, H. A. A description and evaluation of a problem solving skills training program. In D. Upper & S. M. Ross (eds.), *Behavioral group therapy.* Champaign: Research, 1980.

BENNER, P., ROSKIES, E., & LAZARUS, R. S. Stress and coping under extreme conditions. In J. E. Dimsdale (ed.), *Survivors, victims, and perpetrators: Essays on the Nazi Holocaust.* Washington, D.C.: Hemisphere, 1980.

BETTELHEIM, B. *The informed heart: Autonomy in a mass age.* New York: Free Press, 1943.

BLANCHARD, E., ANDRASIK, F., AHLES, T. A., TEDERS, S. J., & O'KEEFE, D. Migraine and tension headache: A meta-analytic review. *Behavior Therapy,* 1980, *11,* 613–631.

BOWERS, K. S., & KELLY, P. Stress, disease, psychotherapy, and hypnosis. *Journal of Abnormal Psychology,* 1979, *88,* 490–505.

BROWN, G. W., & HARRIS, T. (eds.). *Social origins of depression: A study of psychiatric disorder in women.* New York: Free Press, 1978.

CANNON, W. B. *The wisdom of the body.* New York: Norton, 1932.

CASSEL, J. The contribution of the social environment to host resistance. *American Journal of Epidemiology,* 1976, *104,* 107–123.

COHEN, F. Personality, stress, and the development of physical illness. In G. C. Stone, F. Cohen, & N. E. Adler (eds.), *Health psychology: A handbook.* San Francisco: Jossey-Bass, 1979.

COHEN, F., & LAZARUS, R. S. Active coping processes, coping dispositions, and recovery from surgery. *Psychosomatic Medicine,* 1973, *35,* 375–389.

—————. Coping with the stresses of illness. In G. C. Stone, F. Cohen, & N. E. Adler (eds.), *Health psychology: A handbook.* San Francisco: Jossey-Bass, 1979.

COYNE, J. C., & LAZARUS, R. S. Cognitive style, stress perception, and coping. In I. L. Kutash & L. B. Schlesinger (eds.), *Handbook on stress and anxiety: Contemporary knowledge, theory, and treatment.* San Francisco: Jossey-Bass, 1980.

DAVIDSON, P. O., & DAVIDSON, S. M. *Behavioral medicine: Changing health life styles.* New York: Brunner/Mazel, 1980.

DEMBER, W. N. Motivation and the cognitive revolution. *American Psychologist,* 1974, *29,* 161–168.

DEPUE, R. A., MONROE, S. M., & SHACKMAN, S. L. The psychobiology of human disease: Implications for conceptualizing the depressive disorders. In R. A. Depue (eds.), *The psychobiology of the depressive disorders: Implications for the effects of stress.* New York: Academic, 1979.

DOHRENWEND, B. P. & DOHRENWEND, B. S. The conceptualization and measurement of stressful life events: An overview of the issues. In R. A. Depue (ed.), *The psychobiology of the depressive disorders: Implications for the effects of stress.* New York: Academic, 1979.

DOHRENWEND, B. S., & DOHRENWEND, B. P. (eds.). *Stressful life events: Their nature and effects.* New York: Wiley, 1974.

EITINGER, L. H., & STROM, A. *Mortality and morbidity after excessive stress.* New York: Humanities, 1973.

EMORY, G., HOLLON, S., & BEDROSIAN, R. *New directions in cognitive therapy: A casebook.* New York: Guilford, 1981.

EVERLY, G. S., ROSENFELD, R., ALLEN, R. J., BROWN, L. C., SOBELMAN, S., & WAIN, H. J. *The nature and treatment of the stress response: A practical guide for clinicians.* New York: Plenum, 1981.

FOLKMAN, S., & LAZARUS, R. S. An analysis of coping in a middle-aged community sample. *Journal of Health and Social Behavior,* 1980, *21,* 219–239.

FOLKMAN, S., SCHAEFER, C., & LAZARUS, R. S. Cognitive processes as mediators of stress and coping. In V. Hamilton & D. M. Warburton (eds.), *Human stress and cognition: An information-processing approach.* New York: Wiley, 1979.

FRANKENHAEUSER, M. Psychobiological aspects of life stress. In S. Levine & H. Ursin (eds.), *Coping and health.* New York: Plenum, 1980.

GLASS, D. C. *Behavior patterns, stress, and coronary disease.* Hillsdale: Erlbaum, 1977.

GLASS, D. C., KRAKOFF, L. R., CONTRADA, R., HILTON, W. F., KEHOE, K., MANUCCI, E. G., COLLINS, C., SNOW, B., & ELTING, E. Effect of harassment and competition upon cardiovascular and plasma catecholamine responses in type A and type B individuals. *Psychophysiology,* 1980, *17,* 453–463.

GRAHAM, J. D. P. High blood pressure after battle. *Lancet,* 1945, *1,* 239–246.

GRANDVOLD, D. K., & WELCH, G. Intervention for postdivorce adjustment problems: The treatment seminar. *Journal of Divorce,* 1977, *1,* 81–92.

GRINKER, R. R., & SPIEGEL, J. P. *Men under stress.* New York: McGraw-Hill, 1945.

GUNDERSON, E. K. E., & RAHE, R. H. *Life stress and illness.* Springfield: Thomas, 1974.

HAAN, N. A tripartite model of ego functioning: Values and clinical research applications. *Journal of Nervous and Mental Disease,* 1969, *148,* 14–30.

—————. *Coping and defending.* New York: Academic, 1977.

HAMBURG, D. A., HAMBURG, B., & deGOZA, S. Adaptive problems and mechanisms in severely burned patients. *Psychiatry,* 1953, *16,* 1–20.

HENRY, J., & STEPHENS, P. *Stress, health, and the social environment: A sociobiologic approach to medicine.* New York: Springer, 1977.

HOLMES, T. H., & MASUDA, M. Life change and illness susceptibility. In B. S. Dohrenwend & B. P. Dohrenwend (eds.), *Stressful life events: Their nature and effects.* New York: Wiley, 1974.

HOLROYD, K. Cognition and desensitization in the group treatment of test anxiety. *Journal of Consulting and Clinical Psychology,* 1976, *44,* 991–1001.

—————. Stress, coping, and the treatment of stress related illness. In J. R. McNamara (ed.), *Behavioral approaches in medicine: Application and analysis.* New York: Plenum, 1979.

HOLROYD, K., & ANDRASIK, F. A cognitive behavioral approach to the treatment of recurrent tension and migraine headache. In P. C. Kendall (ed.), *Advances in cognitive behavior therapy.* New York: Academic, 1982.

HOLROYD, K., APPEL, M., & ANDRASIK, F. A cognitive behavioral approach to the treatment of psychophysiological disorders. In D. Meichenbaum & M. Jeremko (eds.), *Stress prevention and management: A cognitive behavioral approach.* New York: Plenum, 1982.

HOROWITZ, M. *Stress response syndromes.* New York: Aronson, 1976.

HOROWITZ, M. J., HULLEY, S., ALVAREZ, W., REYNOLDS, A. M., BENFARI, R., BLAIR, S., BORHANI, N., & SIMON, N. Life events, risk factors, and coronary disease. *Psychosomatics,* 1979, *20,* 586–592.

JANIS, I. L., & MANN, L. *Decision making.* New York: Free Press, 1977.

JENKINS, C. D. Psychosocial modifiers of response to stress. *Journal of Human Stress,* 1979, *5,* 3–15.

JONES, N. F., KINSMAN, R. A., DIRKS, J. F., & DAHLEM, N. W. Psychological contributions to chronicity in asthma: Patient response styles influencing medical treatment and its outcome. *Medical Care,* 1979, *17,* 1103–1118.

KAPLAN, H. B., CASSEL, J. C., & GORE, S. Social support and health. *Medical Care,* 1977, *15*(5), 47–58.

KAPLAN, N. M. The Goldblatt Memorial Lecture. Part II: The role of the kidney in hypertension. *Hypertension,* 1979, *1,* 456–461.

KENDALL, P. C. Preparation for surgery. In D. Meichenbaum & M. Jeremko (eds.), *Stress prevention and management: A cognitive behavioral approach.* New York: Plenum, 1982. (a)

———— (ed.). *Advances in cognitive behavior therapy.* New York: Academic, 1982. (b)

KEWMAN, D., & ROBERTS, R. H. Skin temperature biofeedback and migraine headaches. *Biofeedback and Self-regulation,* 1980, *5,* 327–345.

KINSTON, W., & ROSSER, R. Disaster: Effects on mental and physical state. *Journal of Psychosomatic Research,* 1974, *18,* 437–456.

KOBASA, S. C., HILKER, R. R., & MADDI, S. R. Who stays healthy under stress? *Journal of Occupational Medicine,* 1979, *21,* 595–598.

LAZARUS, R. S. *Psychological stress and the coping process.* New York: McGraw-Hill, 1966.

————. Emotions and adaptation: Conceptual and empirical relations. In W. J. Arnold (ed.), *Nebraska Symposium on Motivation.* Lincoln: University of Nebraska Press, 1968.

————. A cognitively oriented psychologist looks at biofeedback. *American Psychologist,* 1975, *30,* 553–561.

————. Psychological stress and the coping process. In Z. S. Lipowski, D. R. Lipsitt, & P. C. Whybrow (eds.), *Psychosomatic medicine: Current trends and clinical applications.* New York: Oxford University Press, 1977.

————. The stress and coping paradigm. In C. Eisdorfer, D. Cohen, A. Kleinman, & P. Maxim (eds.), *Theoretical bases for psychopathology.* New York: Spectrum, 1981.

LAZARUS, R. S., AVERILL, J. R. & OPTON, E. M., JR. Toward a cognitive theory of emotions. In M. Arnold (ed.), *Feelings and emotions.* New York: Academic, 1970.

LAZARUS, R. S., COHEN, J. B., FOLKMAN, S., KANNER, A., & SCHAEFER, C. Psychological stress and adaptation: Some unresolved issues. In H. Selye (ed.), *Selye's guide to stress research,* vol. 1. New York: Van Nostrand, 1980.

LAZARUS, R. S. & FOLKMAN, S. Coping and adaptation. In W. D. Gentry (ed.), *The handbook of behavioral medicine.* New York: Guilford, 1982.

LAZARUS, R. S., & GOLDEN, G. The function of denial in stress, coping, and aging. In E. McGarraugh & S. Kiesler (eds.), *Biology, behavior, and aging.* New York: Academic, 1981.

LAZARUS, R. S., & LAUNIER, R. Stress-related transactions between person and environment. In L. A. Pervin & M. Lewis (eds.), *Perspectives in interactional psychology.* New York: Plenum, 1978.

LINDEMANN, E. Symptomatology and management of acute grief. *American Journal of Psychiatry,* 1944, *101,* 141–148.

LYNN, S. J., & FREEDMAN, R. R. Transfer and evaluation in biofeedback treatment. In A. P. Goldstein & F. Kanfer (eds.), *Maximizing treatment gains: Transfer enhancement in psychotherapy.* New York: Academic, 1979.

MASON, J. W. Organization of psychoendocrine mechanisms. *Psychosomatic Medicine,* 1968, *30,* 565–608.

————. Clinical psychophysiology. In M. F. Reiser (eds.), *American handbook of psychiatry,* vol. 4. New York: Basic Books, 1975. (a)

————. A historical view of the stress field (in two parts). *Journal of Human Stress,* 1975, *1,* 6–12; *1,* 22–37. (b)

MCCLELLAND, D. C. Inhibited power motivation and high blood pressure in men. *Journal of Abnormal Psychology,* 1979, *88,* 182–190.

MCCLELLAND, D. C., FLOOR, E., DAVIDSON, R. J., & SARON, C. Stressed power motivation, sympathetic activation, immune function, and illness. *Journal of Human Stress,* 1980, *6,* 11–19.

MCGRATH, J. E. *Social and psychological factors in stress.* New York: Holt, 1970.

MCNAMARA, J. R. *Behavioral approaches to medicine: Application and analysis.* New York: Plenum, 1979.

MEICHENBAUM, D. Cognitive modification of test anxious college students. *Journal of Consulting and Clinical Psychology,* 1972, *39,* 370–380.

MEICHENBAUM, D., & JEREMKO, M. (eds.). *Stress prevention and management: A cognitive behavioral approach.* New York: Plenum, 1982.

MILLER, N. E. Biofeedback and visceral learning. *Annual Review of Psychology,* 1978, *29,* 373–392.

————. Effects of learning on physical symptoms produced by psychological stress. In H. Selye (eds.), *Selye's guide to stress research,* vol. 1. New York: Van Nostrand, 1980.

MILLER, N. E., & DWORKIN, B. R. Critical issues in therapeutic applications of biofeedback. In G. E. Schwartz & J. Beatty (eds.), *Biofeedback.* New York: Academic, 1977.

MILLON, T., GREEN, C., & MEAGHER, R. (eds.), *Handbook of clinical health psychology.* New York: Plenum, 1981.

MINUCHIN, S., ROSMAN, B. L., & BAKER, L. *Psychosomatic families.* Cambridge: Harvard University Press, 1978.

MOOS, R. Coping with acute health crises. In T. Millon, C. Green, & R. Meagher (eds.), *Handbook of clinical health psychology.* New York: Plenum, 1982.

MORILLO, E., & GARDNER, L. Bereavement as an antecendent factor in thyrotoxicosis of childhood: Four case studies with survey of possible metabolic pathways. *Psychosomatic Medicine,* 1979, *41,* 545–555.

NOVACO, R. W. A stress inoculation approach to anger management in the training of law enforcement officers. *American Journal of Community Psychology,* 1977, *5,* 327–346.

OBRIST, P. *Cardiovascular psychophysiology: A perspective.* New York: Plenum, 1981.

OBRIST, P., LIGHT, K., LANGER, A., GRIGNOLO, A., & MCCUBBIN, J. Behavioral-cardiac interactions: The psychosomatic hypothesis. *Journal of Psychosomatic Research,* 1978, *22,* 301–325.

PASTER, S. Psychotic reactions among soldiers of World War II. *Journal of Nervous and Mental Disease,* 1948, *108,* 54–66.

RABKIN, J. G., & STRUENING, E. L. Life events, stress, and illness. *Science,* 1976, *194,* 1013–1020.

RAHE, R. H., & RANSON, R. J. Life change and illness studies: Past history and future directions. *Journal of Human Stress,* 1978, *4,* 3–15.

RODGERS, M., DUBEY, D., & REICH, P. The influence of the psyche and the brain on immunity and disease susceptibility: A critical review. *Psychosomatic Medicine,* 1979, *41,* 147–164.

ROSE, R. M. Endocrine responses to stressful psychological events. *Psychiatric Clinics of North America,* 1980, *3,* 251–276.

ROSE, R. M., & LEVIN, M. A. (eds.). The crisis in stress research: A critical reappraisal of the role of stress in hypertension, gastrointestinal illness, and female reproductive dysfunction. *Journal of Human Stress,* 1979, *5,* 2–48.

ROSKIES, E. Considerations in developing a treatment program for the coronary-prone (type A) behavior pattern. In P. O. Davidson & S. M. Davidson (eds.), *Behavioral medicine: Changing health life styles.* New York: Brunner/Mazel, 1980.

ROSKIES, E., & LAZARUS, R. S. Coping theory and the teaching of coping skills. In P. O. Davidson & S. M. Davidson (eds.), *Behavioral medicine: Changing health life styles.* New York: Brunner/Mazel, 1980.

RUSH, A. J., BECK, A. T., KOVACS, M., & HOLLON, S. Comparative efficacy of cognitive therapy and pharmacotherapy in the treatment of depressed outpatients. *Cognitive Therapy and Research,* 1977, *1,* 17–37.

SCHWARTZ, G. E. Psychosomatic disorders and biofeedback: A psychobiological model of disregulation. In J. D. Maser & M. E. P. Seligman (eds.), *Psychopathology: Experimental models.* San Francisco: Freeman, 1977.

SELYE, H. *The stress of life* (rev. ed.). New York: McGraw-Hill, 1976.

SEXTON, M. M. Behavioral epidemiology. In O. F. Pomerleau & J. P. Brady (eds.), *Behavioral medicine: Theory and practice.* Baltimore: Williams & Wilkins, 1979.

SHAPIRO, D., & SURWIT, R. S. Biofeedback. In O. F. Pomerleau & J. P. Brady (eds.), *Behavioral medicine: Theory and practice.* Baltimore: Williams & Wilkins, 1979.

SHONTZ, F. Adaptation to chronic illness and disability. In T. Millon, C. Green & R. Meagher (eds.), *Handbook of clinical health psychology.* New York: Plenum, 1982.

SPIVACK, G., & SHURE, M. B. *Social adjustment of young children: A cognitive approach to solving real-life problems.* San Francisco: Jossey-Bass, 1974.

STONE, G. C., COHEN, F., & ADLER, N. E. (eds.). *Health psychology: A handbook.* San Francisco: Jossey-Bass, 1979.

STOYVA, J. Self-regulation and the stress-related disorders: A perspective on biofeedback. In D. Mostofsky (ed.), *Behavior control and modification of physiological activity.* Englewood Cliffs: Prentice-Hall, 1976.

SWANK, R. L. Combat exhaustion. *Journal of Nervous and Mental Disease,* 1949, *109,* 475–508.

URSIN, H. Personality, activation, and somatic health: A new psychosomatic theory. In S. Levine & H. Ursin (eds.), *Coping and health.* New York: Plenum, 1980.

WEINER, H. Psychosomatogenesis. In T. Millon, C. Green, & R. Meagher (eds.), *Handbook of clinical health psychology.* New York: Plenum, 1982.

WEISMAN, A. A study of the psychodynamics of duodenal ulcer exacerbations with special reference to treatment and the problem of specificity. *Psychosomatic Medicine,* 1956, *18, 2–42.*

WEISS, J. M. Ulcers, In J. D. Maser & M. E. P. Seligman (eds.), *Psychopathology: Experimental models.* San Francisco: Freeman, 1977.

WHITEHEAD, W. E., FEDORAVICIUS, R. S., BLACKWELL, B., & WOOLEY, S. A behavioral conceptualization of psychosomatic illness: Psychosomatic symptoms as learned responses. In J. R. McNamara (ed.), *Behavioral approaches to medicine: Application and analysis.* New York: Plenum, 1979.

WRUBEL, J., BENNER, P., & LAZARUS, R. S. Social competence from the perspective of stress and coping. In J. Wine & M. Smye (eds.), *Social competence.* New York: Guilford, 1981.

4

Stress and Personality

Norman S. Endler   Jean Edwards

IN THE PAST DECADE there has been much empirical and theoretical interest in redefining the most appropriate paradigm for the study of personality. Historically, four models of personality have predominated: trait, psychodynamic, situationism, and interactionism (Endler & Magnusson, 1976c). A principal difference in the models is the assumed locus of the major determinants of behavior. Clinicians (Freud, 1959; Rapaport, Gill, & Schafer, 1945) and personality trait theorists (Allport, 1966; Cattell, 1946; Guilford, 1959) have emphasized traits and their dynamic sources within the individual; whereas social psychologists, sociologists, and social-learning theorists (Cooley, 1902; Dewey & Humber, 1951; Mead, 1934; Mischel, 1968; Rotter, 1954) have emphasized situations and their psychological meaning for individuals. The interactionist position recognizes the essential contributions of both person and situation factors.

The views of the proponents of any model are, of course, heterogeneous and models themselves change over time. Nonetheless, it is instructive to note that the core position of each model has had broad influence on its adherents regarding types of laws sought; determinants of behavior considered, units of analysis; the consistency versus specificity issue; developmental aspects probed; research strategies employed; and populations sampled. (See Endler and Magnusson [1976c] for contrasts and comparisons of these models.) The trait model dominated much of the work in personality until the mid-1960s (Endler & Magnusson, 1976c), when a reexamination of core issues was triggered by the mounting controversy surrounding the primary determinants of behavior. More recently the focus has shifted from the question of whether the person or situation is the primary factor to an exploration of theories and methodologies that can examine how persons and situations interact to determine outcome (Endler, 1973). Awareness of the interaction between persons and situations has affected the areas of stress and anxiety, influencing theories, measurement techniques, and research strategies.

INTERACTIONISM

The concept of *interactionism* is not new. It can be traced back to the time of Aristotle (Shute, 1973). Kantor (1924, 1926), one of the first to offer a psychological interpretation of interactionism, stated that "a personality conception must be predominantly functional and must place great emphasis upon the stimuli conditions and the interaction of the person with them" (1924: 91). Other examples of the early recognition of interactionism can be found in Koffka's (1935) discussion of perception and Lewin's (1935, 1936) emphasis on the interdependence of the various elements in the person-environment relationship. An important aspect of Murray's (1938) need-press theory of personality was the interaction between person factors and situation factors. More recently, Rotter's (1954) social-learning theory of personality proposed that the basic unit of analysis should be the interaction between the person and his/her meaningful environment.

Although there was early theoretical interest in an interactionist position (see Endler, 1982, for a more extensive review), empirical studies on interactionism did not begin until the late 1950s (Endler & Hunt, 1966; Endler, Hunt, & Rosenstein, 1962; Raush, Dittmann, & Taylor, 1959a) and were not integrated with the earlier theoretical writings. Only in the late 1960s and early 1970s did the theoretical discussion of interactionism again gain prominence (Endler, 1976; Endler & Hunt, 1969; Endler & Magnusson, 1976b; Hunt, 1965; Magnusson & Endler, 1977; Raush, 1965). Extensive reviews of studies relating to interactionism appear in Argyle and Little (1972), Bowers (1973), Ekehammar (1974), Endler (1976), Endler and Magnusson (1976b), Magnusson (1976), Magnusson and Endler (1977), Mischel (1973), and Pervin (1968).

In discussing current interactional psychology, it is useful to distinguish between dynamic and mechanistic concepts of interaction (Endler & Edwards, 1978; Endler & Magnusson, 1976c; Olwcus, 1977; Overton & Reese, 1973). *Mechanistic interaction* concerns the joint influence of two or more independent variables on the dependent variable. The basic analytic tool from this perspective is the analysis of variance. The concept of *dynamic interaction* relates to process. Here researchers examine the bidirectional interplay between independent and dependent variables. Although there has been some interesting work in the area (see Block, 1977, on longitudinal studies; Raush, 1977, on Markov chains; Pervin, 1977, on methods for having subjects generate their own situations; White, 1976, on intensive case studies; Argyle, 1977, on investigating rules for social interaction; Mischel, 1973, 1977, on encoding and decoding strategies), much innovative research is needed to establish techniques for investigating dynamic interaction. Most of the available research on the interaction of personality and situational factors is restricted to mechanistic interaction (Endler & Edwards, 1978).

According to Endler and Magnusson (1976c), there are four basic postulates to interactional psychology: (1) behavior is a function of a continuous and bidirectional process of person-situation interaction; (2) the individual is an intentional, active agent in this process; (3) motivational, emotional, and cognitive variables play important determining roles on the person side; and (4) the psychological meaning that the situation has for the person is an essential determining factor of behavior.

The development of theory and research on stress and anxiety in some respects parallels that in the broader field of personality. At various points in the study of stress and anxiety, emphasis has been placed on either the person or the situation. However, investigators have gradually shifted from viewing anxiety and stress as global constructs inherent in either the person or the situation toward viewing them as multidimensional constructs that are part of an ongoing process of person-situation interaction. The changing orientation has shaped the questions posed, the relationships sought, the approaches taken to the study of the development of anxiety, and the measurement instruments and research strategies used.

Several theorists have emphasized the need to examine the process of interaction in understanding stress and anxiety (Endler, 1975, 1980; Lazarus & Launier, 1978; Spielberger, 1975). The perception of the situation and the individual's active participation in the interaction are focal in these discussions. For instance, Lazarus and Launier (1978) stated that "threat cannot be described in terms of person or environment alone, but must be defined by both" (p. 288). They pointed out that the relationship between person and environment is one of "reciprocity of causation," as the person actively impinges on the environment, receives feedback from these efforts, and is confronted with a more or less potent environment. The interaction is a dynamic process that takes place over time. These points are similar to those set out by Endler and Magnusson (1976c).

Lazarus and Launier (1978) noted that "the meaning sphere encompassed by the term 'stress' is any event in which environmental or internal demands (or both) *tax or exceed the adaptive resources* of an individual, social system or tissue system" (p. 296). They elaborated the steps in the stress process. *Primary cognitive appraisal* is the mental process of evaluating an event in terms of its significance for one's well-being: is it irrelevant, benign-positive, or harmful? *Secondary appraisal* is the evaluation of one's coping options and resources in relation to the event. Secondary appraisal may influence primary appraisal, as well as the individual's coping activity. *Reappraisal* is reevaluation resulting from feedback, reflection, and/or defensiveness. Lazarus and Launier (1978) then dealt at some length with the coping process, noting that "there are intuitive and empirical grounds for believing that the ways people cope with stress are even more important to overall morale, social functioning, and health/illness than the frequency and severity of episodes of stress themselves" (p. 308). Throughout their discussion they emphasized "a transactional, mediational, time-oriented, and process-oriented perspective" (p. 321).

Recently, Endler (1975, 1980) proposed an *interactional model of anxiety*. The interaction model, with its emphasis on both person determinants and situational determinants and on the continuing process, appears to have promise in resolving some of the conceptual confusion that has arisen in the study of stress and anxiety. In the following sections we will review some of the prominent definitions of stress and anxiety, techniques for assessing anxiety, the interaction model, and the empirical support for this model.

ANXIETY AND STRESS

Anxiety and stress, ancient companions of man, have become in the last quarter century topics of intense interest among both laymen and psychologists. May (1977) characterized the mid-twentieth century as the "age of anxiety" and cited works from science, politics, the arts, religion, and philosophy that explore this phenomenon. His examples included W. H. Auden's poem "The Age of Anxiety" and Leonard Bernstein's symphony on the same theme. Camus also pondered the "century of fear" and Kafka presented powerful images of anxiety.

In the psychological literature anxiety has also gained prominence. May (1969) stated that although Freud considered the role of anxiety in neurosis, the concept of normal anxiety slowly gained acceptance in the 1950s. According to Lewis (1970), the number of articles on anxiety increased from 37 in 1950 to over 200 in 1966. From 1950 to 1970, approximately 5000 books and articles on anxiety were published (Spielberger, 1972) and during the 1970s approximately 3500 (Endler, 1980).

Anxiety has been variously defined as stimulus, response, drive, motive, and trait

(Endler, 1975). Lewis (1970) reviewed the historical and linguistic meaning of the "ambiguous word anxiety" and concluded by defining it as "an emotional state, with the subjectively experienced quality of fear or a closely related emotion (terror, horror, alarm, fright, panic, trepidation, dread, scare)" (p. 77). According to Lewis, the emotion is unpleasant, is directed toward the future, and is out of proportion to the threat; moreover, anxiety involves bodily disturbances. According to May (1977), "The special characteristics of anxiety are the feelings of *uncertainty* and *helplessness* in the face of danger" (p. 205).

Stress, too, has been of growing concern in the literature. The work of Hans Selye (1956, 1976), while concentrating on physiological responses in the *general adaption syndrome,* has acted as an impetus to the interest of many. As with anxiety, however, stress has been defined in diverse ways and, indeed, confusion between the two terms has occurred. Spielberger (1971, 1976) pointed out that the terms "anxiety" and "stress" have been used interchangeably in the literature.

Selye (1976) defined stress as the "nonspecific response of the body to any demand" (p. 472). Similarly, Lazarus (1976) noted that "stress occurs where there are demands on the person which tax or exceed his adjustive resources" (p. 47). Levitt (1980) found that "the word *stress* is used constantly in connection with emotional states; it appears almost as often in discussions of anxiety as does the word 'anxiety' itself" (p. 9). Lazarus (1966) construed stress as referring to "the whole area of problems that includes the stimuli producing stress reactions, the reactions themselves, and the various intervening processes" (p. 27). May (1977) defined the relationship between stress and anxiety thus: "Anxiety is how the individual relates to stress, accepts it, interprets it. Stress is a halfway station on the way to anxiety. Anxiety is how we handle stress" (p. 113; italics omitted). Stress, then, like anxiety has been defined as a stimulus, a response, and an intervening state of the individual. Furthermore, the relationship between the two concepts has not been clearly established.

In order to bring greater coherence to the field, Spielberger (1976) proposed that the term "stress" indicate the *objective* stimulus properties of a situation and that the term "threat" refer to the person's *perception* of a situation as being potentially dangerous for him/her. As pointed out by Spielberger (1976), "Typically, situations that are objectively stressful will be perceived as threatening; however a stressful situation may not be perceived as threatening by an individual who either does not recognize the inherent danger or has the necessary skills and experience to cope with it" (p. 5). Other researchers similarly have recognized that the perception of threat is central. May (1977), for example, stated that "psychologically speaking, how the person *interprets* the threat is crucial."

Both person factors and situation factors affect this perception-interpretation process. Lazarus (Coyne & Lazarus, 1980) emphasized the role of cognitive appraisal of threat and the transactional nature of the stress-anxiety process. He stated that "the important role of personality factors in producing stress reactions requires that we define stress in terms of transactions between individuals and situations rather than either one in isolation" (Lazarus, 1966:5). Spielberger (1979) concluded that "stress . . . can be defined by transactions between the person and the environment in which stressors are linked to anxiety reactions by the perception of threat" (p. 47).

The interaction model of anxiety (Endler, 1975, 1980) defines stress as a situational variable, the perception of which is influenced by the individual's predisposition to react to stress with increased anxiety. The perception of stress (threat) in turn mediates increases in the anxiety state. Let us now consider the development of the person-situation interaction model of anxiety.

THE INTERACTION MODEL OF ANXIETY

The interaction model of anxiety emphasizes the complex interplay between the person and the situation. Two conceptual distinctions have been of particular importance in developing the interactional model of anxiety: state anxiety (*A-state*) and trait anxiety (*A-trait*). Before the Christian era, Cicero made a basic distinction between *angor* and *anxietas:* "*Angor* is transitory, an outburst; *anxietas* is an abiding predisposition" (quoted in Lewis, 1970:62). Cattell and Scheir (1958, 1961) differentiated between trait, or chronic, anxiety—a relatively stable characteristic—and state, or acute, anxiety—a transitory condition. Spielberger (1972) suggested that some of the conceptual and empirical confusion in anxiety research has occurred because of the failure to differentiate between A-state and A-trait. Endler and Magnusson (1976a) concluded that the distinction between A-state, a transitory emotional condition, and A-trait, a relatively stable predisposition to respond to certain types of stress, is fundamental. Spielberger (1972) defined A-state as a reaction "consisting of unpleasant consciously-perceived feelings of tension and apprehension, with associated activation or arousal of the autonomic nervous system" (p. 29). Trait anxiety "refers to relatively stable individual differences in anxiety proneness, i.e. to differences among people in the disposition or tendency to perceive a wide range of situations as threatening and to respond to these situations with differential elevations in state anxiety" (Spielberger, 1975:137).

The state-trait distinction entails a consideration of both person factors and situation factors in predicting changes in state anxiety. In stressful situations persons high in A-trait would be expected to show higher levels of A-state than would persons low in A-trait. In neutral situations no differences in A-state would be anticipated. Although Spielberger (1972) proposed that research on anxiety investigate and specify the stress stimuli that elicit differential levels of state anxiety for those differing in trait anxiety, the measures of anxiety developed and the research produced by Spielberger and his colleagues have tended to emphasize ego threatening anxiety to the exclusion of other anxiety dimensions. In contrast, Endler's (1975, 1980) interaction model insists that anxiety is multidimensional. Endler, Hunt, and Rosenstein (1962) factor-analyzed data from the S-R Inventory of Anxiousness, a self report measure of anxiety, and found three situational factors: interpersonal (ego) threat, physical danger, and ambiguous threat. This finding suggests that the extent to which trait anxiety is expressed is dependent on the type of eliciting stimulus. That is, the interpersonal threat dimension would be expressed in a situation involving an ego or status threat. The physical danger dimension would be expressed in a situation involving potential physical hurt or pain. Endler and Magnusson (1976a) and Endler, Magnusson, Ekehammar, and Okada (1976) have found additional support for the multidimensionality of trait anxiety.

The interaction model of anxiety proposes that both the *type* of threat perceived in a stressful situation and the *dimension* of A-trait must be considered in predicting changes in A-state. A person-situation interaction producing changes in A-state would be expected to occur only when the dimension of A-trait and the type of stress in the situation were congruent. That is, an individual high in physical danger A-trait would be predicted to show increases in A-state in a physically dangerous situation; no such changes would be predicted for an individual low in physical danger A-trait. When the dimension of A-trait and the situational stress are not congruent, no interaction prompting changes in A-state would be anticipated. Thus, it is necessary for research on stress and anxiety to consider persons, situations, and the multidimensionality of the constructs. A schematic presentation of the interaction model of anxiety (Endler, 1975) may be useful in summary (see Figure 4–1).

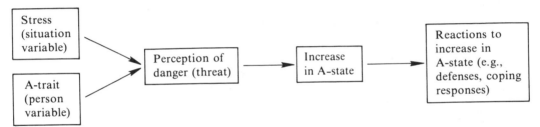

FIGURE 4-1. Stress and the anxiety process.

The remainder of this chapter will focus on the development of appropriate measures of individual proneness to respond to stress with anxiety and on research supporting the interactional model of anxiety.

MEASURES OF ANXIETY

Endler, Hunt, and Rosenstein (1962) pointed out that a trait such as anxiousness can be conceptualized in at least seven ways: (1) in the proportion of situations in which persons exhibit the class of anxiety responses, (2) in the kinds of situations in which persons exhibit the class of anxiety responses, (3) in the number of different responses, within the anxiety construct, that persons exhibit, (4) in the prevalence of the various subclasses of responses within the anxiety construct (e.g., overt versus physiological responses), (5) in the intensity of the responses observed, (6) in the duration of the responses observed, and (7) in the relative provocativeness of the situations that elicit the responses. Most of the techniques for measuring anxiety have concentrated on some combination of the proportion of situations in which the responses occurs, the number of different responses, and the intensity of the responses.

Levitt (1980) reviewed physiological, projective, and inventory techniques used to measure anxiety. Physiological measures focus on skin resistance and potential, heart rate, blood pressure, blood volume, respiratory rate, volume of saliva, gastric motility, pupillary diameter, muscular tension, brain waves, or adrenal hormones. Problems encountered in the interpretation of physiological measures and in relating them to each other and to reported levels of anxiety have limited their usefulness.

Projective techniques, principally the Rorschach test, also pose problems in interpretation, as well as in administration and quantification of results, which have limited their usefulness for research purposes.

Anxiety inventories (scales and questionnaires), while admittedly susceptible to bias introduced by notions of social desirability, have been the most frequently used measurement technique. Their ease of administration and scoring strongly recommend them. The development of the various inventories has closely followed theoretical advances—progressing from global measures to measures that take into account person-situation interactions—and has in turn strongly affected research. The increasing awareness of the role of situations in evoking anxiety in individuals with identified specific predispositions to respond is reflected in a number of specific anxiety scales.

The Taylor (1951, 1953) Manifest Anxiety Scale (MAS) had a striking impact on research. Studies on anxiety increased dramatically from 1952 to 1957, an increase in part attributable to the appearance of the MAS (Levitt, 1980). The MAS was developed within the Hull-Spence theory as a measure of drive. Items were selected from the Minnesota

Multiphasic Personality Inventory by clinicians as reflections of anxiety. The MAS is a global measure of anxiety reflecting primarily the ego involving dimension. In 1957 the Institute for Personality and Ability Testing (IPAT) developed the Anxiety Scale Questionnaire, a similar trait measure of anxiety.

As noted earlier, by the mid-1960s concern was growing over the inadequacies of traditional trait measures to take into account the influence of situations on the expression of personality. Accordingly, multidimensional measures of anxiety were developed, including the S–R Inventory of Anxiousness (Endler, Hunt, & Rosenstein, 1962) and the Inventory of Personal Reactions (Zuckerman, 1977). Also in the mid-sixties, Spielberger and his colleagues developed the State-Trait Anxiety Inventory (Spielberger, Gorsuch, & Lushene, 1970; Spielberger, Gorsuch, Lushene, & Vagg, 1977). The test includes separate but related forms to assess trait and state anxiety. Subjects are asked to respond by means of four-point intensity scales to 20 items assessing "How you *feel* right now, that is, *at this moment*" (A-state) and to respond by means of four–point frequency scales to 20 items assessing "How you *generally* feel" (A-trait). Zuckerman's (1960) Affect Adjective Checklist also can be used as a measure of either state or trait anxiety: the respondent can be instructed to rate how he/she feels "in general," a measure of A-trait, as opposed to how he/she feels "now-today," a measure of A-state.

In Endler's (1975, 1980) interaction model of anxiety, both trait and state anxiety are treated as multidimensional, and the measures developed by him and his colleagues incorporate this perspective. Endler, Hunt, and Rosenstein (1962) factor-analyzed the S–R Inventory of Anxiousness and found three factors: interpersonal (ego) threat, physical danger, and ambiguous threat. Endler and Okada (1974, 1975) constructed the S–R Inventory of General Trait Anxiousness (S–R GTA) to include these dimensions. The revised version of the S–R GTA presents four types of general situations to the respondent: (1) social evaluation, (2) physical danger, (3) ambiguous, and (4) daily routines. The respondent is asked separately to indicate his/her reaction to each of 15 responses to each situation by means of five–point intensity scales. The Present Affect Reaction Questionnaire (PARQ) is a 20–item measure of state anxiety that includes cognitive worry and emotional arousal subscales. The respondent is asked to indicate by means of five–point intensity scales how she/he feels in the present situation. A third questionnaire, the Perception of Situations Rating Form, is used to assess the respondent's perception of the type and degree of threat in given situations, (Endler, 1980).

In addition to the above inventories, a number of more specific anxiety measures have been developed, including state anxiety measures such as the Subjective Stress Scale (Kerle & Bialek, 1958), the Anxiety Differential (Alexander & Husek, 1962), the Clyde Mood Scale (Clyde, 1963), and the Mood Adjective Checklist (Nowlis, 1970). Other scales have been developed to assess test and achievement anxiety: the Test Anxiety Questionnaire (Mandler & Sarason, 1952), the Test Anxiety Scale (Sarason, 1978), the Test Anxiety Inventory (Spielberger, Gonzalez, Taylor, Anton, Algaze, Ross, & Westberry, 1980), and the Achievement Anxiety Test (Alpert & Haber, 1960). In addition, a number of scales for measuring anxiety in children are available: the Children's Manifest Anxiety Scale (Castaneda, McCandless, & Palermo, 1956), the State–Trait Anxiety Inventory for Children (STAIC) (Spielberger, Edwards, Lushene, Montour, & Platzek, 1973), the Test Anxiety Scale for Children, and the and General Anxiety Scale for Children (Sarason, Davidson, Lighthall, Waite, & Ruebush, 1960). For a more extensive review of anxiety measures currently available see Levitt (1980).

RESEARCH SUPPORTING THE STATE–TRAIT DISTINCTION AND THE INTERACTION MODEL

The usefulness of the state–trait distinction has been demonstrated by Spielberger and others. Auerbach (1973a), Hodges (1968), O'Neil, Spielberger, and Hansen (1969), and Rapaport and Katkin (1972) found that person (A-trait) by situation (stress) interactions affect state anxiety in ego threatening situations. However, in physical danger situations, similar results were not found (Auerbach, 1973b; Hodges, 1968; Hodges & Spielberger, 1966; Katkin, 1965; Spielberger, Gorsuch, & Lushene, 1970). It appears that while the Spielberger scales make an important contribution in the state–trait distinction and thus emphasize the interplay between situation stressors and individual predisposition, they focus on the ego threat dimension of anxiety and neglect dimensions such as physical danger and ambiguity.

Endler and his colleagues and students carried out a number of studies demonstrating the effectiveness of the multidimensional concept of trait anxiety in predicting increases in A-state. Endler and Okada (1974), in a laboratory experiment, found changes in A-state associated with an interaction between a physical threat situation (threat of shock) and the congruent physical danger A-trait dimension. The physical threat situation did not interact with the noncongruent dimensions of A-trait.

A series of field studies also have lent support to the interaction model. Endler and Magnusson (1977), in a study of Swedish university students, found an interaction between social evaluation (interpersonal) A-trait and a stressful classroom examination situation. Endler, King, Kuczynski, and Edwards (1980), studying Canadian high school students, and Phillips and Endler (1980), studying Canadian university students, found similar patterns of interaction. Endler, Edwards, and McGuire (1979) studied anxiety experienced by actors prior to both an important stage performance and rehearsal. Even though the sample was small, there was a trend toward an interaction between social evaluation A-trait and the congruent situational stress in affecting A-state. Diveky and Endler (1977), working with middle managers in business, asked each to specify a stressful social evaluation situation experienced on the job and a nonstressful off-the-job situation. They obtained the predicted social evaluation A-trait by stressful situation interaction. Flood and Endler (1980) found similar results when the field setting was a stressful social evaluation track and field meet; the subjects were young athletes competing in this event.

Kendall (1978) compared the Spielberger (1972) state–trait anxiety model with Endler's (1975, 1980) interaction model of anxiety. The results of Kendall's investigation supported the interaction model of anxiety: interactions appeared only when the dimensions of A-trait were *congruent* with the situational stressors.

SUMMARY AND CONCLUSIONS

This chapter discussed the recent evolution in personality theory from models that emphasize either the person or the situation as the prime determinant of behavior to an interactionist approach that emphasizes the complex interplay between person variables and situation variables. The history of interactionism was briefly described and the distinction between mechanistic and dynamic interaction presented. The basic postulates of modern interactionism were set out and the parallel between developments in personality and in stress and anxiety theory and research were noted. We also reviewed definitions frequently found in the literature on stress and anxiety. The interaction model of anxiety was discussed, and we described the distinction between state and trait anxiety, as well as the concept of anxiety as multidimensional. Finally, we reviewed current measures of anxiety and research supporting the interaction model.

An interactionist model that takes into account both person variables and situation varliables holds the most promise for research on stress and anxiety. Work by Spielberger and by Endler has demonstrated that consideration of both individual predisposition (A-trait) and the stressfulness of the situation is necessary to predict changes in A-state. Further work is needed to examine other steps in the stress process. There has been theoretical interest in the individual's perception and appraisal of the stressful situation; Lazarus and his colleagues have investigated this area. Here, too, much work remains to be done. Endler has emphasized the person's active role in selecting the situations he/she confronts. Examination of how this selection process affects the individual's encounters with stressful events would be useful. Finally, empirical exploration of the coping process is important in understanding the stress process.

Lazarus, Endler, Spielberger, and others have pointed out the need to work toward a process model of stress. Exploration of those factors that the individual brings into this process and how he/she changes and is changed by interaction with the situation should prove a challenging task for future researchers.

REFERENCES

Alexander, S., & Husek, T. The anxiety differential: Initial steps in the development of a measure of situational anxiety. *Educational and Psychological Measurement,* 1962, *12,* 325–348.

Allport, G. W. Traits revisited. *American Psychologist,* 1966, *21,* 1–10.

Alpert, R., & Haber, R. N. Anxiety in academic achievement situations. *Journal of Abnormal and Social Psychology,* 1960, *61,* 207–215.

Argyle, M. Predictive and generative rules models of P × S interaction. In D. Magnusson & N. S. Endler (eds.), *Personality at the crossroads: Current issues in interactional psychology.* Hillsdale: Erlbaum, 1977.

Argyle, M., & Little, B. R. Do personality traits apply to social behavior? *Journal for the Theory of Social Behavior,* 1972, *2,* 1–35.

Auerbach, S. M. Effects of orienting instructions, feedback information, and trait anxiety on state anxiety. *Psychological Reports,* 1973, *33,* 779–786. (a)

————. Trait-state anxiety and adjustment to dental surgery. *Journal of Consulting and Clinical Psychology,* 1973, *40,* 264–271. (b)

Block, J. Advancing the psychology of personality: Paradigmatic shift or improving the quality of research? In D. Magnusson & N. S. Endler (eds.), *Personality at the crossroads: Current issues in interactional psychology.* Hillsdale: Erlbaum, 1977.

Bowers, K. S. Situationism in psychology: An analysis and a critique. *Psychological Review,* 1973, *80,* 307–336.

Castaneda, A., McCandless, B. R., & Palermo, D. S. The children's form of the Manifest Anxiety Scale. *Child Development,* 1956, *27,* 317–326.

Cattell, R. B. *The description and measurement of personality.* New York: World, 1946.

CATTELL, R. B., & SCHEIER, I. H. The nature of anxiety: A review of 13 multivariate analyses comparing 814 variables. *Psychological Reports* (monograph supp.), 1958, *5*, 351–388.

————. *The meaning and measurement of neuroticism and anxiety.* New York: Ronald, 1961.

CLYDE, D. J. *Manual for the Clyde Mood Scale.* Coral Gables: Biometric Laboratories, 1963.

COOLEY, C. H. *Human nature and the social order.* New York: Scribner's, 1902.

COYNE, L. C., & LAZARUS, R. S. Cognitive style, stress perception, and coping. In I. L. Kutash & L. B. Schlesinger (eds.), *Handbook on stress and anxiety: Contemporary knowledge, theory, and treatment.* San Francisco: Jossey-Bass, 1980.

DEWEY, R., & HUMBER, W. J. *The development of human behavior.* New York: Macmillan, 1951.

DIVEKY, S., & ENDLER, N. S. The interaction model of anxiety: State and trait anxiety for banking executives in normal working environments. Manuscript, York University, Toronto, 1977.

EKEHAMMAR, B. Interactionism in personality from a historical perspective. *Psychological Bulletin,* 1974, *81,* 1026–1048.

ENDLER, N. S. The person versus the situation: A pseudo issue? A response to Alker. *Journal of Personality,* 1973, *41,* 287–303.

————. A person-situation interaction model of anxiety. In C. D. Spielberger & I. G. Sarason (eds.), *Stress and anxiety,* vol. 1. Washington, D.C.: Hemisphere, 1975.

————. Grand illusions: Traits or interactions? *Canadian Psychological Review,* 1976, *17,* 174–181.

————. Person-situation interaction and anxiety. In I. L. Kutash & L. B. Schlesinger (eds.), *Handbook on stress and anxiety: Contemporary knowledge, theory, and treatment.* San Francisco: Jossey-Bass, 1980.

————. Whence interactional psychology? In A. Furnham & M. Argyle (eds.), *Social behavior in context.* Boston: Allyn & Bacon, 1982.

ENDLER, N. S., & EDWARDS, J. Person by treatment interactions in personality research. In L. A. Pervin & M. Lewis (eds.), *Perspectives in interactional psychology.* New York: Plenum, 1978.

ENDLER, N. S., EDWARDS, J., & McGUIRE, A. The interaction model of anxiety: An empirical test in a theatrical performance situation. Manuscript, York University, Toronto, 1979.

ENDLER, N. S. & HUNT, J. McV. Sources of behavioral variance as measured by the S–R Inventory of Anxiousness. *Psychological Bulletin,* 1966, *65,* 336–346.

————. Generalizability of contributions from sources of variance in the S–R Inventories of Anxiousness. *Journal of Personality,* 1969, *37,* 1–24.

ENDLER, N. S., HUNT, J. McV., & ROSENSTEIN, A. J. An S–R inventory of anxiousness. *Psychological Monographs,* 1962, *76*(17), 1–33.

ENDLER, N. S., KING, P. R., KUCZYNSKI, M., & EDWARDS, J. *Examination induced anxiety: An empirical test of the interaction model.* York University, Department of Psychology report no. 97. Toronto, 1980.

ENDLER, N. S., & MAGNUSSON, D. Multidimensional aspects of state and trait anxiety: A cross-cultural study of Canadian and Swedish college students. In C. D. Spielberger & R. Diaz-Guerrero (eds.), *Cross-cultural anxiety.* Washington, D.C.: Hemisphere, 1976. (a)

————. Personality and person by situation interactions. In N. S. Endler & D. Magnusson (eds.), *Interactional psychology and personality.* Washington, D.C.: Hemisphere, 1976. (b)

————. Toward an interactional psychology of personality. *Psychological Bulletin,* 1976, *83,* 956–974. (c)

————. The interaction model for anxiety: An empirical test in an examination situation. *Canadian Journal of Behavioural Science,* 1977, *9,* 101–107.

ENDLER, N. S., MAGNUSSON, D., EKEHAMMAR, B., & OKADA, M. The multidimensionality of state and trait anxiety. *Scandinavian Journal of Psychology,* 1976, *17,* 81–93.

ENDLER, N. S., & OKADA, M. *An S–R inventory of general trait anxiousness.* York University, Department of Psychology report no. 1. Toronto, 1974.

————. A multidimensional measure of trait anxiety: The S–R Inventory of General Trait Anxiousness. *Journal of Consulting and Clinical Psychology,* 1975, *43,* 319–329.

FLOOD, M., & ENDLER, N. S. The interaction model of anxiety: An empirical test in an athletic competition situation. *Journal of Research in Personality,* 1980, *14,* 329–339.

FREUD, S. *Collected papers,* vols. 1–4 New York: Basic Books, 1959.

GUILDFORD, J. P. *Personality.* New York: McGraw-Hill, 1959.

HODGES, W. F. Effects of ego threat and threat of pain on state anxiety. *Journal of Personality and Social Psychology,* 1968, *8,* 364–372.

HODGES, W. F., & SPIELBERGER, C. D. The effects of threat of shock on heart rate for subjects who differ in manifest anxiety and fear of shock. *Psychophysiology,* 1966, *2,* 287–294.

HUNT, J. McV. Traditional personality theory in the light of recent evidence. American Scientist, 1965, *53,* 80–96.

KANTOR, J. R. *Principles of psychology,* vol. 1. Bloomington: Principia, 1924.

————. *Principles of psychology,* vol. 2. Bloomington: Principia, 1926.

KATKIN, E. S. The relationship between manifest anxiety and two indices of automatic response to stress. *Journal of Personality and Social Psychology,* 1965, *2,* 324–333.

KENDALL, P. C. Anxiety: States, traits—situations? *Journal of Consulting and Clinical Psychology,* 1978, *46,* 280–287.

KENRICK, D. T., & STRINGFIELD, D. O. Personality traits and the eye of the beholder: Crossing some traditional philosophical boundaries in the search for consistency in all of the people. *Psychological Review,* 1980, *87,* 88–104.

KERLE, R. H., & BIALEK, H. M. The construction, validation, and application of a subjective stress scale. Staff memorandum, U.S. Army Leadership, Human Research Unit, Monterey, 1958.

KOFFKA, K. *Principles of Gestalt psychology.* New York: Harcourt, 1935.

LAZARUS, R. S. *Psychological stress and the coping process.* New York: McGraw-Hill, 1966.

————. *Patterns of adjustment* (3d ed.). New York: McGraw-Hill, 1976.

LAZARUS, R. S., & LAUNIER, R. Stress-related transactions between person and environment. In L. A. Pervin & M. Lewis (eds.), *Perspectives in interactional psychology.* New York: Plenum, 1978.

LEVITT, E. E. *The psychology of anxiety* (2d ed.). Hillsdale: Erlbaum, 1980.

LEWIS, K. *A dynamic theory of personality: Selected papers.* New York: McGraw-Hill, 1935.

————. *Principles of topological psychology.* New York: McGraw-Hill, 1936.

LEWIS, A. The ambiguous word "anxiety." *International Journal of Psychiatry,* 1970, *9,* 62–79.

MAGNUSSON, D. The person and the situation in an interactional model of behavior. *Scandinavian Journal of Psychology,* 1976, *17,* 253–271.

MAGNUSSON, D., & ENDLER, N. S. Interactional psychology: Present status and future prospects. In D. Magnusson & N. S. Endler (eds.), *Personality at the crossroads: Current issues in interactional psychology.* Hillsdale: Erlbaum, 1977.

MANDLER, G., & SARASON, S. B. A study of anxiety and learning. *Journal of Abnormal and Social Psychology,* 1952, *47,* 166–173.

MAY, R. *Love and will.* New York: Norton, 1969.

————. *The meaning of anxiety.* New York: Norton, 1977.

MEAD, G. H. *Mind, self, and society.* Chicago: University of Chicago Press, 1934.

MISCHEL, W. *Personality and assessment.* New York: Wiley, 1968.

————. Toward a cognitive social learning reconceptualization of personality. *Psychological Review,* 1973, *80,* 252–283.

—————. The interaction of the person and situation. In D. Magnusson & N. S. Endler (eds.), *Personality at the crossroads: Current issues in interactional psychology.* Hillsdale: Erlbaum, 1977.

MURRAY, H. A. *Explorations in personality.* New York: Oxford University Press, 1938.

NOWLIS, V. Mood: Behavior and experience. In M. Arnold (ed.), *Feelings and emotions.* New York: Academic, 1970.

OLWEUS, D. A critical analysis of the modern interactionist position. In D. Magnusson & N. S. Endler (eds.), *Personality at the crossroads: Current issues in interactional psychology.* Hillsdale: Erlbaum, 1977.

O'NEIL, J. F., SPIELBERGER, C. D., & HANSEN, D. N. The effects of state anxiety and task difficulty on computer-assisted learning. *Journal of Educational Psychology,* 1969, *60,* 343–350.

OVERTON, W. F., & REESE, H. W. Models of development: Methodological implications. In J. R. Nesselroads & H. W. Reese (eds.), *Life span developmental psychology: Methodological issues.* New York: Academic, 1973.

PERVIN, L. A. Performance and satisfaction as a function of individual–environment fit. *Psychological Bulletin,* 1968, *69,* 56–68.

—————. The representative design of person-situation research. In D. Magnusson & N. S. Endler (eds.), *Personality at the crossroads: Current issues in interactional psychology.* Hillsdale: Erlbaum, 1977.

PHILLIPS, J. B., & ENDLER, N. S. *Academic examinations and anxiety: The interaction model empirically tested.* York University, Department of Psychology report no. 99. Toronto, 1980.

RAPAPORT, D., GILL, M., & SCHAFER, R. *Diagnostic psychological testing* (2 vols). Chicago: Year Book, 1945.

RAPAPORT, H., & KATKIN, E. S. Relationships among manifest anxiety, response to stress, and the perception of autonomic activity. *Journal of Consulting and Clinical Psychology,* 1972, *38,* 219–224.

RAUSH, H. L. Interaction sequences. *Journal of Personality and Social Psychology,* 1965, *2,* 487–499.

—————. Paradox, levels, and junctures in person-situation systems. In D. Magnusson & N. S. Endler (eds.), *Personality at the crossroads: Current issues in interactional psychology.* Hillsdale: Erlbaum, 1977.

RAUSH, H. L., DITTMANN, A. T., & TAYLOR, T. J. The interpersonal behavior of children in residential treatment. *Journal of Abnormal and Social Psychology,* 1959, *58,* 9–26. (a)

—————. Person, setting, and change in social interaction. *Human Relations,* 1959, *12,* 361–378. (b)

ROTTER, J. B. *Social learning and clinical psychology.* Englewood Cliffs: Prentice-Hall, 1954.

SARASON, I. G. The Test Anxiety Scale: Concept and research. In C. D. Spielberger & I. G. Sarason (eds.), *Stress and anxiety,* vol 5. New York: Wiley, 1978.

SARASON, S. B., DAVIDSON, K. S., LIGHTHALL, F. F., WAITE, R. R., & RUEBUSH, B. K. *Anxiety in elementary school children.* New York: Wiley, 1960.

SELYE, H. *The stress of life.* New York: McGraw-Hill, 1956.

—————. *The stress of life* (2d ed.). New York: McGraw-Hill, 1976.

SHUTE, C. Aristotle's interactionism and its transformations by some 20th century writers. *Psychological Record,* 1973, *23,* 283–293.

SPIELBERGER, C. D. Trait-state anxiety and motor behavior. *Journal of Motor Behavior,* 1971, *3,* 265–279.

—————. Anxiety as an emotional state. In C. D. Spielberger (eds.), *Anxiety: Current trends in theory and research,* vol. 1. New York: Academic, 1972.

—————. Anxiety: State-trait process. In C. D. Spielberger & I. G. Sarason (eds.), *Stress and anxiety,* vol. 1. New York: Wiley, 1975.

————. The nature and measurement of anxiety. In C. D. Spielberger & R. Diaz-Guerrero (eds.), *Cross-cultural anxiety*. Washington, D.C.: Hemisphere, 1976.

————. *Understanding stress and anxiety*. New York: Harper & Row, 1979.

Spielberger, C. D., Edwards, C. D., Lushene, R. E., Montuori, L., & Platzek, D. *Preliminary test manual for the State-Trait Anxiety Inventory for Children*. Palo Alto: Consulting Psychologist, 1973.

Spielberger, C. D., Gonzalez, H. P., Taylor, C. L., Anton, U. D., Algaze, B., Ross, G. R., & Westberry, L. G. *Preliminary professional manual for the Test Anxiety Inventory*. Palo Alto: Consulting Psychologists, 1980.

Spielberger, C. D., Gorsuch, R. L., & Lushene, R. E. *Manual for the State-Trait Anxiety Inventory*. Palo Alto: Consulting Psychologist, 1970.

Spielberger, C. D., Gorsuch, R. L., Lushene, R. E., & Vagg, P. R. *The State-Trait Anxiety Inventory: Form Y*. Tampa: University of South Florida, 1977.

Taylor, J. A. The relationship of anxiety to the conditioned eyelid response. *Journal of Experimental Psychology,* 1951, *41,* 81–89.

————. A personality scale of manifest anxiety. *Journal of Abnormal Psychology,* 1953, *49,* 285–290.

White, R. W. *The enterprise of living: A view of personal growth* (2d ed.). New York: Holt, 1976.

Zuckerman, M. Development of an affect adjective check list for measurement of anxiety. *Journal of Consulting Psychology,* 1960, *24,* 457–462.

————. Development of a situation-specific trait-state test for the prediction and measurement of affective responses. *Journal of Consulting and Clinical Psychology,* 1977, *45,* 513–523.

5

Conflict and Stress

Seymour Epstein

HISTORICAL BACKGROUND

Modern views of conflict have developed within several traditions, including the physiological, the psychodynamic, the behavioral, and the phenomenological tradition. However, the study of conflict is not new. Socrates, in Plato's *Republic* (cited in Smith, 1968), described a conflict between desire and reason. He noted that desire is linked with pleasure, and reason with forbearance. Desire bids a man to drink; reason forbids drinking. Socrates believed that peace of mind can be achieved only through the dominance of reason, which advocates temperance. Aristotle, in *de Anima* (cited in Smith, 1968), described a conflict between desire for immediate gratification and delay of gratification. He noted that an important way in which man differs from the other animals is that man has a sense of time, which allows him to consider objects not present and to delay gratification. In his *Nichomachean Ethics,* Aristotle (cited in Smith, 1968) discussed a conflict that arises from engaging out a sense of duty in acts that are not pleasurable. The conflict is between conscience and desire to avoid unpleasantness, as in the case of a person who engages in virtuous acts although he is no lover of virtue.

The Physiological Tradition

Homeostatic regulation of physiological functions has traditionally been accounted for by the interaction of opposing systems, as in the case of sympathetic and parasympathetic activity. The functioning of the nervous system itself is attributed to the interaction of excitatory and inhibitory neural impulses. Coordinated motor activity is explained by the firing of neurons that activate, and others that inhibit, response tendencies (Sherrington, 1906). Although Pavlov (1927) was a physiologist, he proposed a psychological theory of behavior based on the assumption that learning can be explained by the interaction of excitatory and inhibitory impulses. According to Pavlov, the nature and breadth of inhibition determine whether the behavior will be adaptive or maladaptive. Thus, from a variety of viewpoints, a common conclusion is that conflict between opposing forces can account for a wide range of physiological processes, adaptive and maladaptive.

The Psychodynamic Tradition

Freudian psychoanalytic theory is, at its core, a conflict theory. The energy to support psychological functions is assumed to be borrowed from inhibited biological drives, such as sex and aggression. Other conflicts exist between the individual and society; among the structures of the human mind—id, ego, and superego; between instincts, such as the life instinct and death instinct; and between motivational and inhibitory psychodynamic forces. Although other psychoanalytic schools have diverged from the Freudian school in many important respects, all have continued to accord a central role of conflict. Socially oriented psychoanalytic theories, such as those formulated by Adler (1954), Erikson (1963), Horney (1950), and Fromm (1955), have shifted the emphasis from biologically based to socially derived conflicts. Jung's theory emphasizes the bipolarity of human nature and attributes growth to the resolution of discrepancies. In his later years, Jung (1953) introduced the concept of *self,* which represents a high level of integration of differentiated personality structures. Interestingly, following a different path, Adler (1954) arrived at a similar conclusion.

In the psychoanalytic tradition, conflict can be either a destructive force or a source of growth. Resolution of conflict occurs either through the removal of restraining forces and the expression of inhibited impulses or through assimilation of repressed material into a conscious conceptual system.

The Behavioral Tradition

Within the behavioral tradition, four basic conflicts have generally been recognized, namely, approach-approach, approach-avoidance, avoidance-avoidance, and double approach-avoidance. Lewin (1931) is usually credited with having introduced the first three of these conflicts, which he referred to simply as type 1, type 2, and type 3. Smith and Guthrie (1921) and Kantor (1926) actually predated Lewin in recognizing the first three types of conflict (cf. Smith, 1968). Hovland and Sears (1938) introduced double approach-avoidance conflict and also introduced the approach-avoidance terminology. Hull (1938) translated Lewin's model into the language of stimulus-response theory. Miller (1944) later modified and extended Hull's model. It is Miller's *model of conflict* that is best known today and that we shall consider in greater detail later.

Until recently, it was widely accepted that there are only four basic types of conflict. The recognition by Miller and others that avoidance gradients need not always be steeper than approach gradients cleared a path for the discovery of a fifth conflict, avoidance-approach conflict. Avoidance-approach conflict was introduced by Kelman (1961) and, in different contexts, by others, often unaware of its previous introduction (Astin, 1962; Cutter, 1964; Epstein, 1978; Firestone, Kaplan, & Moore, 1974; Heilizer, 1964; Kaplan, Firestone, Degnore, & Moore, 1974). I shall have more to say about this interesting conflict later.

The Phenomenological Tradition

In a small, important book, Lecky (1945) introduced a phenomenological theory of personality. One of his key assumptions was that to understand an individual it is necessary to reconstruct that individual's world view. Lecky was the first of several self theorists who assumed that one of the most basic needs of all individuals is to maintain the unity of their conceptual systems. Lecky believed that two major sources of stress producing incompatibilities are inconsistencies within the self-system and inconsistencies between the self-system and reality. Shortly following the publication of Lecky's book, Snygg and Combs (1949) elaborated a similar theory from a Gestalt point of view. Soon thereafter, Rogers (1951, 1959, 1961) presented the first of a series of books and articles that together represented the most detailed development of the self theories. According to Rogers, three kinds of conceptual incompatibility that can produce high levels of stress are incompatibility between an individual's ideal and actual self, between conscious and subconscious perceptions, and between external reality and perception.

Cognitive personality theorists, such as Kelly (1955), Sarbin (1952), Hilgard (1949), and Epstein (1972, 1980), and social psychologists, such as Festinger (1957), Brehm and Cohen (1962), and Rokeach (1973), also have emphasized cognitive incongruity as a major source of stress.

CENTRAL CONCEPTS IN CONFLICT THEORY

Miller (1944) listed the basic incompatibilities as follows: chemical incompatibilities, neural incompatibilities, perceptual incompatibilities, mechanical or motor incompatibilities, and incompatibilities between acquired processes. *Chemical incompatibilities* refer to antagonistic biochemical or hormonal reactions, such as those that occur when a person eats while emotionally excited and as a result suffers from the simultaneous release of acetylcholine and epinephrine, which interferes with intestinal peristalsis. To illustrate an *antagonistic neural reaction,* Sherrington (1906) cited the case of a dog who, when simultaneously tickled on both sides, fails to exhibit the scratch reflex that tickling on only one side would produce. *Perceptual incompatibilities* refer to perceptions that interfere with or prevent other perceptions, as in the case of reversible illusions. *Motor incompatibilities* refer to antagonistic physical or mechanical responses. Finally, *incompatibilities between acquired processes* refer to conflicts that occur through learning antagonistic response tendencies, as in conflicts associated with toilet training and the inhibition of sexual impulses.

Brown (1957) suggested that conflicts be divided into temporal, spatial, and discrimination induced conflicts. He noted that most laboratory research on conflict has been concerned with *spatial conflict,* as in the case of a rat trained to approach and avoid the same goal at the end of a runway. Brown provided an extended discussion of *temporal conflict.* He noted that approach-avoidance gradients can be demonstrated as a function of nearness in time to an event that is both desired and feared and that both temporal and discrimination induced conflicts are similar in operation to spatial conflict. Epstein (1978) and others have argued that the basic consideration in all the above conflicts is *discrimination,* as the effects of time and space are dependent on the discrimination of cues.

Conflicts have also been divided according to whether they are conscious or unconscious. Other investigators have used content to classify conflicts, grouping together those that involve sexual impulses, for example.

The classification system that has evoked, by far, the most interest divides conflicts according to various combinations of approach and avoidance tendencies. As previously noted, there are five such conflicts: approach-approach, approach-avoidance, avoidance-avoidance, double approach-avoidance, and avoidance-approach. *Approach-approach conflict* is illustrated by the story of the ass who starved to death halfway between two bales of hay. Despite the ass's fate, the conflict generally is regarded as benign because a move in either direction resolves it. However, as Miller (1944) pointed out, what appears to be a simple approach-approach conflict may not be benign because in reality it is a double approach-avoidance conflict, in which the selection of either goal means the loss of the other. *Approach-avoidance conflict* has received the most attention because it, too, establishes a stable equilibrium in the absence of external force. In effect, the individual becomes imprisoned by his own drives, being able neither to achieve a desired goal nor to abandon it. How this occurs will be clarified in the next section. In *avoidance-avoidance conflict,* the individual is confronted with two unattractive alternatives. In the absence of restraint he would simply leave the field. *Double approach-avoidance conflict* is a complication of approach-avoidance conflict in which the individual is faced with a choice between two goal objects, each of which has both positive and negative features. *Avoidance-approach conflict* has been ignored until recently because a person in such a conflict would appear not to be in conflict at all, as he would simply stay away from the conflicting goal. However, should the person through either accident or coercion be placed in the vicinity of the goal, he would rapidly approach what he had previously avoided.

MILLER'S CONFLICT MODEL

Miller's (1944) model of conflict has stimulated a great deal of research and theorizing, which has both extended the model and identified some of its limitations. It is not possible to review all the relevant material here. Fortunately, thorough reviews are available in a series of articles by Heilizer (1977a, 1978).

Approach-Avoidance Conflict

Although Miller (1944, 1959; Dollard & Miller, 1950) recognized the four basic conflicts referred to by Hovland and Sears, he emphasized approach-avoidance conflict because of its implications for psychopathology. His core assumptions about approach-avoidance conflict follow: (1) There is a gradient of approach; i.e., the tendency to approach a goal is stronger the nearer the person is to the goal. (2) There is a gradient of avoidance; i.e., the tendency to avoid a goal is stronger the nearer the person is to the goal. (3) The gradient of avoidance is steeper than the gradient of approach; i.e., the strength of avoidance increases more rapidly with nearness to the goal than does the strength of approach. (4) The strength of approach and avoidance tendencies varies directly with the strength of the drives upon which they are based; an increase in drive raises the height of the entire gradient. (5) When there is a choice between two incompatible responses, the stronger one will be selected. The most critical assumption is the third, for it establishes that the gradients will intersect in a manner such that the approach gradient will be higher than the avoidance gradient at a distance from the goal and less high closer to the goal. As a result, an individual with an approach-avoidance conflict will approach the goal when at a distance but will avoid it when close. A stable equilibrium is thus established in which the individual vacillates around the point of intersection of the gradients (see Figure 5–1). The model not only predicts symptoms of conflict, such as vacillation and sustained high levels of fear and arousal in the absence of coercion, but also explains how conflicts can be maintained without reinforcement. According to the model, the individual, in effect, is imprisoned by his own desires, as he can neither relinquish nor obtain the goal object.

Other deductions of interest concern the effects of increases and decreases in the drives underlying the approach and avoidance tendencies. If both gradients are raised in a manner that keeps the distance from the point of intersection to the goal constant, there is no change in the individual's approach to the goal, but the individual will experience increased fear and arousal. If only the drive underlying the approach tendencies is increased (see Figure 5-2), the individual will move closer to the goal, but at the cost of experiencing increased fear, as he will be driven further up the avoidance gradient. Of course, should he repeatedly reach the goal by this procedure, the conflict would eventually be extinguished. However, give the sharp increase in fear and arousal that occurs before the goal is reached, it is more likely that

FIGURE 5-1. Theoretical gradients of approach and avoidance tendencies as a function of distance from a goal (*adapted from Dollard & Miller, 1950:356*).

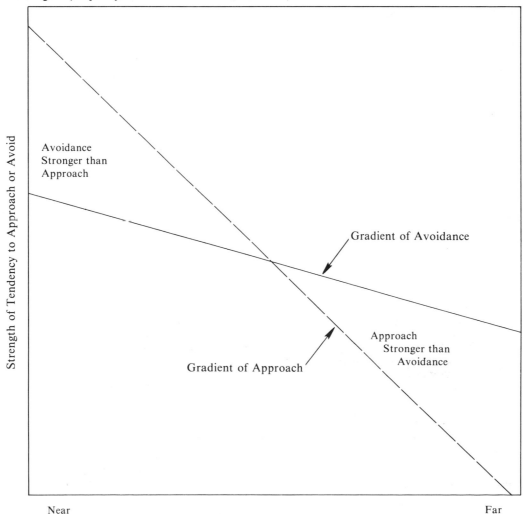

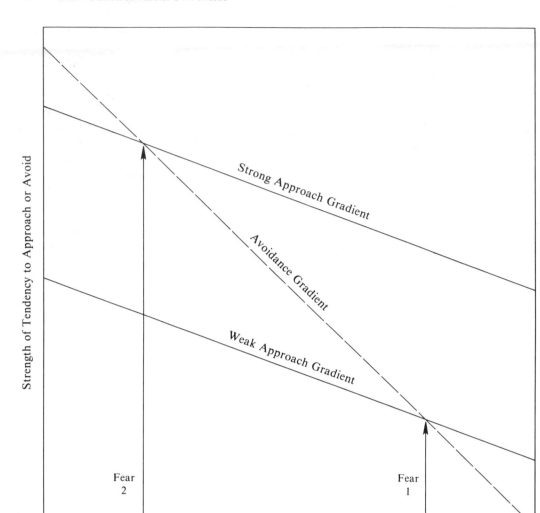

FIGURE 5-2. Conflicts produced by the intersection of stronger and weaker approach gradients with the same avoidance gradient. Fear 1 indicates the fear that would be experienced with the weaker approach gradient; Fear 2, the fear that would be experienced with the stronger approach gradient. It is apparent that an increase in approach markedly increases the fear that is experienced because it motivates the animal more closely to approach the feared goal (*adapted from Dollard & Miller, 1950:358*).

the individual would leave the field before reaching the goal. Thus, Miller (1944, 1959) considered raising the approach gradient in an approach-avoidance conflict to be a poor therapeutic strategy.

A preferable strategy, according to Miller, is to lower the avoidance gradient. When this is done, an interesting anomaly, the negative therapeutic effect, may occur. The *negative therapeutic effect* refers to an increase in overall anxiety that occurs in psychotherapy as fears are reduced. It can be seen in Figure 5-3 that the effect of lowering

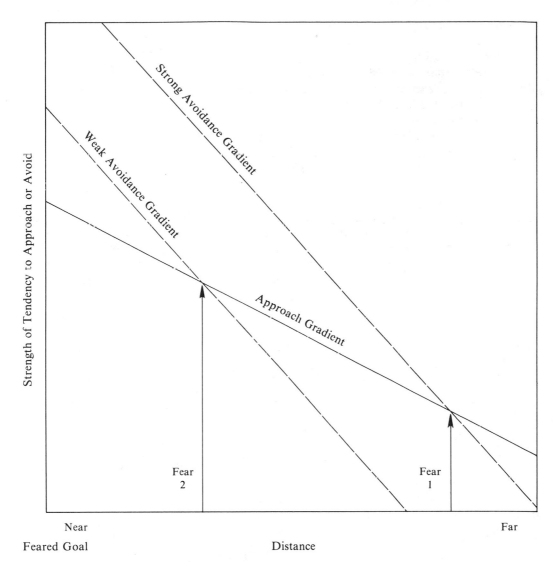

FIGURE 5–3. Conflicts produced by the intersection of stronger and weaker avoidance gradients with the same approach gradient. Fear 1 indicates the fear that would be experienced with the stronger avoidance gradient; Fear 2, the fear that would be experienced with the weaker avoidance gradient. It is apparent that a reduction in avoidance increases the fear that is experienced because it motivates the animal more closely to approach the feared goal (*adapted from Dollard & Miller, 1950:361*).

the avoidance gradient is to bring the individual closer to the conflicting goal, which produces a net increase in fear. Thus, there is a strange effect in an approach-avoidance conflict that lowering fear produces a net increase in fear. The increase in fear, however, is less than would occur if the approach gradient were raised.

The effect of raising the avoidance gradient is also of considerable interest. Raising the avoidance gradient drives the individual further from the goal. Thus, making the goal more fearful results in a net decrease in fear.

Miller's Displacement Model

According to Miller (1959), the spatial model of approach-avoidance conflict can be converted to a *displacement model* by substituting a dimension of stimulus dissimilarity for a dimension of physical distance. In the displacement model, the gradients are generalization gradients (see Figure 5–4), and the approach and avoidance tendencies refer to tendencies to produce or to avoid producing goal–relevant responses. Given the assumption that the generalization gradient of avoidance is steeper than that of approach, it follows that stimulus displacement will occur. An individual with an approach-avoidance conflict will, therefore, add an increment of goal relevance to his responses to stimuli at a distance from

FIGURE 5–4. Theoretical curves of expression and inhibition as a function of relevance of stimuli to an object about which there are conflicting tendencies. It is apparent that the maximum increase in goal relevance of the response as a result of the conflict occurs to stimuli at an intermediate point along the dimension (point B) of stimulus relevance (*adapted from Dollard & Miller, 1950:174*).

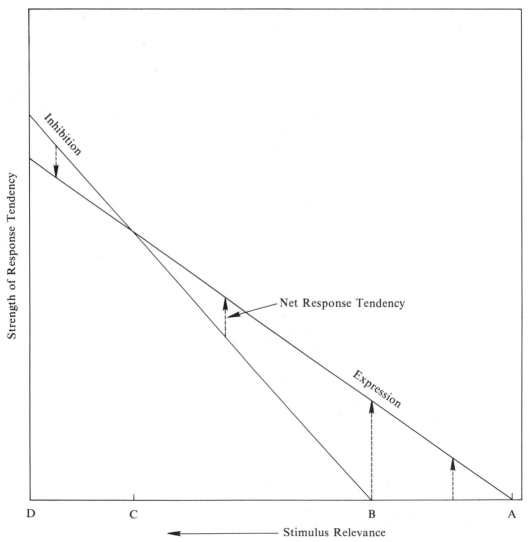

the goal and a decrement to stimuli more closely associated with the goal. This will occur because responses to stimuli that are highly similar to the goal object will be inhibited, while responses to more remote stimuli will be expressed, with maximum expression occurring at an intermediate level of dissimilarity from the goal (see Figure 5–4). As an example, consider an individual with an unresolved Oedipal complex. Sexual attraction to women viewed as highly similar to the mother will be inhibited, while women who are not at all similar will have no appeal. Women who are perceived as related to the mother to just the right degree will be maximally appealing.

Miller's model of stimulus displacement can be adapted to response displacement by substituting a dimension of response dissimilarity for one of stimulus dissimilarity. From the model of response displacement, it follows that a person with an approach-avoidance conflict will tend to produce displaced responses that are related only indirectly to the object of the conflict. Stimulus displacement and response displacement will tend to occur together; these patterns can be represented by a three-dimensional model (e.g., Epstein, 1962; Murray & Burken, 1955). The double displacement model has interesting implications for the interpretation of dreams, responses to projective tests, and intrusive thoughts.

Critique of Miller's Conflict and Displacement Models

According to Heilizer (1977a, 1978), there is support for many of the deductions from Miller's model. It has been found that there are conditions corresponding to approach-avoidance conflict in which an animal approaches when at a distance from a goal and avoids when closer to the goal (Brown, 1957). There is also evidence that vacillation occurs around an intermediate point along a spatial dimension and that changes in the strengths of the drives that underlie the approach and avoidance tendencies shift the point of greatest aproach in the directions predicted. There is support for both stimulus and response displacement. With respect to the most fundamental assumption on which the model is based, however, the avoidance gradient has not been found to be always steeper than the approach gradient, nor can such an assumption be logically defended (cf. Epstein, 1978; Maher, 1966). Miller (1959) has conceded that avoidance gradients were found to be steeper than approach gradients in the early studies because the approach gradients were based on the hunger drive, an internal state, and the avoidance gradients were based on shock received in the goal box, an external condition. As a result, the avoidance gradient varied more as a function of external cues than did the approach gradient.

A second difficulty with the Miller model is its treatment of drive (Champion, 1961). Miller (1944) endorsed Hull's theory of learning. According to Hull (1938), a multiplicative interaction between nonspecific drive and "habit strength" determines the directional tendencies of reactions. An increase in drive, according to Hull, will increase the slope, as well as the height, of a gradient of reaction tendency. Yet, Miller (1944), in his graphic representation of the effect of an increase in drive, raised the entire gradient without increasing its slope, thereby assuming an additive combination of drive and cues. Miller provided no explanation for the additive assumption, which is very likely untenable, considering that it indicates there could be a strong motive state in the absence of either drive or goal-relevant cues so long as one or the other is present. If Hull's assumption of a multiplicative relationship is substituted for Miller's assumption of an additive relationship, Miller's model loses much of its elegance, as approach gradients can then be steeper or less steep than avoidance gradients, depending on the drive strengths on which they are based.

It should be noted that neither of the above limitations is critical with respect to Miller's model. These features nevertheless suggest modifications that would make the model less simple and not quite as elegant as it initially appeared. However, the model remains an impressive tool that not only has enhanced our understanding of an important conflict but also has stimulated a great deal of research and has received a fair degree of confirmation.

MODIFICATIONS AND EXTENSIONS OF MILLER'S MODELS

Reconceptualization of the Gradients

Sometimes Miller's gradients represent response tendencies and sometimes actual responses. He did not spell out what the gradients represent in broader theoretical terms, such as how they relate to Hull's or other theories of learning or motivation. Nor is it clear in what sense Miller used the term "drive" in discussing his gradients. As noted above, if Miller conceived of drive in the Hullian sense of an intervening variable that intensifies responses, it is difficult to understand why he did not assume a multiplicative relationship between drive and habit strength. It is also not clear what the term "response tendency" means in Miller's model. Is it a hypothetical construct equivalent to Hull's (1943) *reaction potential,* or is it something more tangible that has directly measurable attributes apart from its effect on approach and avoidance behavior? How, if at all, is either concept related to measures of physiological arousal?

Much of the confusion about gradients can be removed by redefining them as motives that have directional and arousal properties subject to independent measurement. In Epstein's (1962) variation of Miller's model, it is assumed that motives are a multiplicative function of an inner state, such as that produced by food deprivation, and goal-relevant cues, such as the sight or odor of food. It follows from this assumption that when either the drive or the cue function is zero, the strength of the motive is zero and that, given a dimension of goal-relevant cues and a receptive inner state, the stronger the cues, the greater the strength of the motive. The directional component of the motive can be measured in animal studies by traditional measures such as running speed and strength of pull. With humans, measures of approach and avoidance can consist of ratings of enthusiasm and fear (Epstein, 1962, 1967; Epstein & Fenz, 1965) and of goal-relevant responses to stimulus dimensions in projective tests with specially built-in dimensions (Epstein, 1966; Fenz & Epstein, 1962). The arousal component can be assessed by physiological measures (Epstein, 1967; Fenz & Epstein, 1967).

The revised model was tested in a series of studies on different kinds of conflict, including conflicts over hostile impulses, sexual impulses, and parachute jumping (Epstein, 1962, 1967; Fenz & Epstein, 1967). Independent variables including temporal dimensions and stimulus dimensions. Dependent variables included autonomic measures, ratings of approach tendencies and fear, and goal-relevant responses to specially constructed projective tests. The results provided strong support for the model with respect to the arousal component of conflict and mixed support for the directional component, the measurement of which was found to be more complicated than anticipated. Gradients of autonomic arousal were obtained that distinguished conflict groups from control groups at extremely high levels of reliability, often with no overlap between groups.

The Modulation of Anxiety and Arousal

In Millers' (1959) displacement model, the fear gradient is a source of inhibition of unacceptable impulses. In the studies of sport parachuting, (Epstein, 1962, 1967; Epstein & Fenz, 1965; Fenz & Epstein, 1962) a conflict was observed in which fear itself was inhibited. That is, a conflict was observed between a tendency to express fear and a tendency to inhibit fear. Of particular interest, as mastery progressed, monotonic gradients of autonomic reactivity and ratings of fear along time and cue dimensions changed to inverted V-shaped curves, the peaks of which became increasingly displaced (see Figures 5–5 and 5–6). The data

FIGURE 5–5. Tonic skin conductance of novice and experienced parachutists as a function of the sequence of events leading up to and following a parachute jump (*from Fenz & Epstein, 1967:37*).

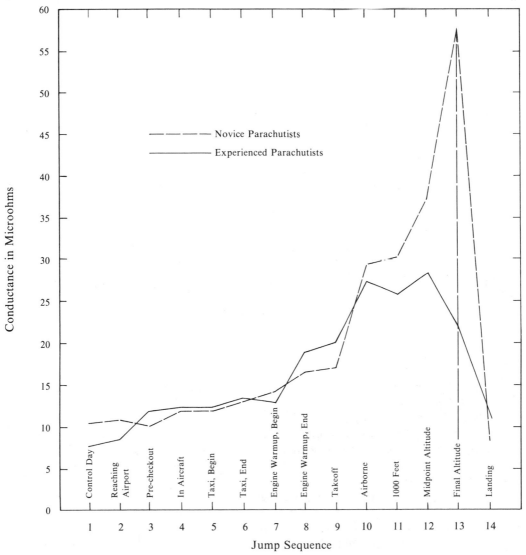

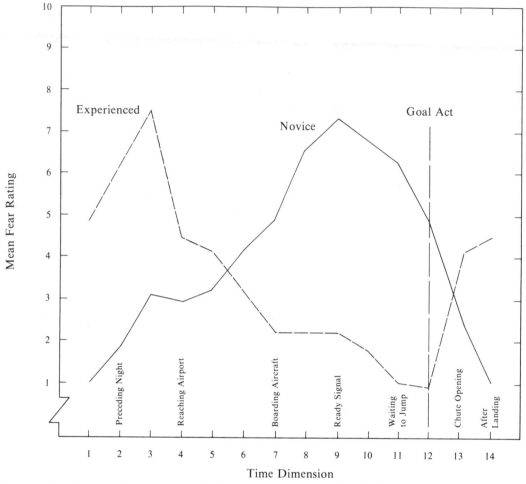

FIGURE 5-6. Mean ratings of relative fear at different points in time before and after a jump for novice and experienced parachutists. For experienced parachutists, the point of greatest fear occurs on the morning of the jump; for novices it occurs at the ready signal, shortly before the jump (*from Fenz & Epstein, 1967:34*).

could be accounted for by assuming that in the subject with successful experience, fear does not simply dissipate but is inhibited, and the gradient of inhibition becomes increasingly steeper and higher than the gradient of fear (see Figure 5-7). The mastery of anxiety as it develops by the above process has two distinct advantages over the mastery of anxiety that would occur if gradients simply declined in steepness over time. First, it provides an increasingly early warning signal of anxiety while, at the same time, reducing anxiety at the moment of critical action. Second, it forces attention to be shifted, as mastery progresses, over the full range of threat-relevant cues.

The above model for the mastery of anxiety has been extended to the modulation of all arousal by the proposal of a general *law of excitatory modulation* (LEM) (Epstein, 1967). According to the LEM, as arousal mounts, it triggers an inhibitory reaction that mounts more rapidly, thereby reducing high levels of arousal more than low levels. Space does not permit further discussion of the LEM here. The interested reader can find an extended treat-

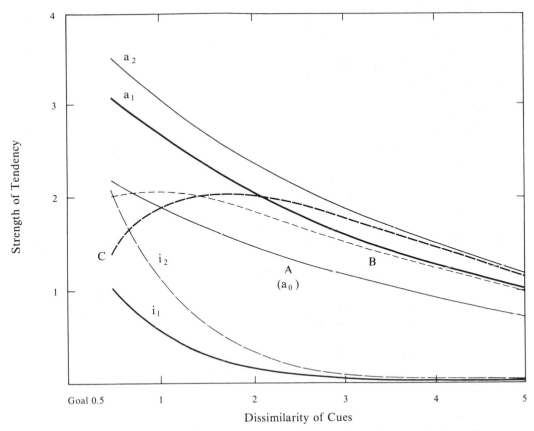

FIGURE 5-7. The production of curves of anxiety that peak increasingly early along time or cue dimensions (curves A, B, and C) as a result of the interaction of theoretical curves of conditioned anxiety (a_1 and a_2) and inhibition (i_1 and i_2), the latter with gradients that become increasingly steeper than those of the former (*from Epstein, 1967:17*).

ment in Epstein (1967). Suffice it to note that the theory can account for a variety of phenomena that are not easily explained otherwise, such as the sequence of paradoxical responses observed by Pavlov in traumatized dogs and the afterdischarge of anxiety that sometimes occurs after a crisis (Epstein, 1967).

Avoidance-Approach, the Fifth Basic Conflict

Once it is recognized that approach gradients can be steeper than avoidance gradients, the possibility of a conflict in which a steeper gradient of approach intersects a gradient of avoidance is suggested. In such a situation, which has been referred to as avoidance-approach conflict, avoidance prevails at a distance from the goal and approach close to the goal. As a result, an individual with such a conflict usually appears not to be in conflict at all, but simply remains outside the conflict zone. However, should accidental circumstances or coercion place him on the goal side of the intersection of the gradients, he would exhibit behavior dramatically out of character, for he would rapidly approach a goal he had previously avoided.

Avoidance-approach conflict was introduced by Kelman (1961) to explain how forced actions can result in attitude change. If avoidance tendencies happened to be more internalized than approach tendencies, he argued that the gradient of avoidance would be less steep than the gradient of approach. As a result, an individual with such approach and avoidance tendencies would exhibit a dramatic change in attitude if circumstances forced him into the vicinity of a goal that he had previously avoided. To illustrate, Kelman described a person who is forced by circumstances into close association with a minority group he had previously disowned. Rather than finding the relationship distasteful, the person finds, to his surprise, that he relates positively to the group and maintains the relationship voluntarily thereafter.

Avoidance-approach conflict has been used to account for both antisocial behavior (Astin, 1962) and ego-alien behavior (Epstein, 1978), such as when a model boy commits a violent crime of passion. This concept has also been used to account for drug abuse, including alcoholism (Heilizer, 1964), and the influence of formal versus informal communications on attitude formation (Firestone, Kaplan & Moore, 1974; Kaplan, Firestone, Degnore, & Moore, 1974).

The most efficient therapeutic procedure for resolving avoidance-approach conflict is to raise the approach gradient by coercion, temptation, or persuasion. For approach-avoidance conflict, it will be recalled, raising the approach gradient is contraindicated. Thus, it is important to distinguish between the two conflicts, as the preferred method of treatment is opposite. Of course, if the approach tendency in either an avoidance-approach or an approach-avoidance conflict consists of antisocial impulses, then resolution of the conflict by facilitating goal attainment through any means is contraindicated. For a more detailed discussion of resolution of these two conflicts, see Epstein (1978).

CONCEPTUAL CONFLICT

Up to now, I have emphasized conflicts involving behavioral impulses. Yet, the most prevalent kind of conflict in humans is, undoubtedly, conceptual conflict. *Conceptual conflict* refers to incompatibilities between beliefs or values. Conceptual conflict is the source of most impulse conflict as impulses would not give rise to conflict if events were construed differently. Expressed otherwise, a major way of resolving impulse conflicts is cognitively to reconstrue events. Conceptual conflict not only consists of incompatibilities between single thoughts or values but also includes incompatibilities between entire organizational systems, as in the case of multiple personalities and clashes between isolated belief systems and an individual's overall conceptual system (Epstein, 1980).

Maintaining coherence in an individual's conceptual system is of critical significance because without a unified system events cannot be adequately anticipated and coped with (Epstein, 1980; Kelly, 1955; Lecky, 1945). Emotionally significant experiences that cannot be assimilated into a coherent system have been shown to generate high levels of anxiety even in nonhuman animals. In a classic experiment in Pavlov's (1927) laboratory, a dog was fed when a circle appeared but not when an ellipse appeared. No punishment was employed. After the dog learned to distinguish the circle from the ellipse, the ellipse was made gradually to approach the circle in appearance. Finally, the dog could no longer discriminate. A remarkable transformation then took place. The dog exhibited what Pavlov described as an animal neurosis. It struggled and howled, tore at the apparatus, and lost its ability to make previous discriminations. The dog became chronically fearful and was particularly disturbed whenever cues reminiscent of the laboratory appeared. The experiment has since been replicated with other animals and stimuli (cf. Gantt, 1944). If maintaining a coherent conceptual system is critically significant for a dog, how much more important must it be for a human being? Some psychologists, such as Lecky (1945), believe it is the single most important motive in human behavior.

There are at least five basic sources of conceptual incompatibility: (1) incompatibilities between an individual's beliefs and the occurrence of events inconsistent with those beliefs, (2) incompatibilities between an individual's ideal self and actual self, (3) incompatibilities between different beliefs or values of which the individual is aware, (4) incompatibilities between beliefs in what is and what should be or should have been, and (5) incompatibilities between beliefs at different levels of awareness.

With respect to *incompatibilities between beliefs and events,* Rogers (1951) noted that there are three main methods of coping. The individual can ignore the experience, distort or deny it, or accept and assimilate it. In the third pattern, anxiety will occur, but assimilation and growth also will take place.

The importance of *incompatibilities between an individual's perception of his actual and his ideal self* has been emphasized by James (1907), Rogers (1951), and Horney (1950), among others. Rogers's theory has stimulated considerable research. The research has often relied on Q-sorts in which statements referring to the actual and the ideal self are rated according to how accurately they describe the individual. The two Q-sorts are then correlated, and the magnitude of the correlation is taken as an index of correspondence between actual and ideal selves. The procedure has produced mixed results (Wylie, 1974). A major complicating factor is the influence of defensiveness on the correspondence between the two selves. Friedman (1955) found that psychotics obtained self-ideal discrepancies that were closer to those obtained with normals than to those obtained with neurotics; he attributed the low discrepancies in psychotics to defensiveness. By denying reality, a person obviously can perceive himself to be as he ideally would like to be. An important challenge for future research is to develop measures of self-evaluation that are not easily distorted by defensiveness.

Incompatabilities between what is and what should be or should have been fall in a broad category that includes self-ideal discrepancies. Horney (1950) introduced the phrase the "tyranny of the should" to describe a common problem observed in her patients. Cognitive therapists, such as Ellis (1962) and Beck (1976), have accorded a central place in therapy to teaching their clients to accept reality for what it is and not to dwell on what it should be. Buddah (cited in Hall & Lindsey, 1978) expressed a similar view several millennia earlier and suggested "insight meditation" as a means of conflict resolution through developing nonattachment.

Incompatibilities also can occur *between beliefs of which the individual is aware, between beliefs of which the individual is unaware,* and *between beliefs existing at different levels of awareness.* When at least one component of a conflict is unconscious (i.e., is not accessible to awareness), it is apt to have uniquely destructive effects, as the individual is unable to confront the conflict with his most powerful resource, his verbally mediated conceptual system (Dollard & Miller, 1950).

Psychoanalysts have particularly emphasized the importance of unconscious conflict. They view such conflict as a clash between two forces, one striving for expression and the other exercising an inhibitory influence. Symptoms are assumed to arise from the tension associated with the two forces and from the indirect expression of blocked impulses. An alternative explanation that does not make the dubious assumption of psychic energy that is continuously striving for discharge assumes, instead, that the conflict is between incompatible cognitions (Epstein, 1980). According to this view, the mind continuously strives to assimilate cognitions into a coherent conceptual system. When assimilation fails, stress occurs in the conceptual system, which is subjectively experienced as anxiety. The impression of an impulse striving for discharge is created by the mind continuously striving to assimilate the unassimilable. As a result, thoughts and images related to the unassimilated material repeatedly appear in dreams or intrude into consciousness.

CONFLICT IN ONE INDIVIDUAL AS A SOURCE OF CONFLICT AND STRESS IN OTHERS

An approach-avoidance conflict in one person can become a source of conflict and stress in associates of that person. A person with an approach-avoidance conflict over intimacy will seek relationships when they are unavailable and reject them when they are available. This behavior pattern will create a most confusing situation for the person who is the target of the reaction. If that person responds to the overtures of the conflicted person by exhibiting affection beyond a certain degree (corresponding to the intersection of the approach and avoidance gradients of the first person), the conflicted person will withdraw. If the target person responds, in turn, by withdrawing, the conflicted person will attempt to pursue the relationship. As a result, both individuals may be trapped in an unsatisfactory relationship. If either severs the relationship, the conflicted person will tend to establish a similar relationship with another person.

In the above example, the individual who was the object of the conflicted person's attention was an adult who could abandon the relationship if he so wished. The consequences would be far more serious if the conflict involved a child who was dependent on the conflicted individual for the child's very existence. Bateson (1972) proposed that schizophrenia has its roots in "double-bind" communications, in which the parent gives mixed messages to the child. The result is that no matter what the child does, his or her behavior is considered unsatisfactory. According to Bateson, the double-bind occurs because the parent is both hostile to the child and guilty about the hostility. Consequently, the parent denies the hostility and requires the child to do the same. It is noteworthy that the problem corresponds to an approach-avoidance conflict in which the approach tendency consists of hostile feelings and the avoidance tendency of the inhibition of expression of hostile feelings. Epstein (1967) described a somewhat different approach-avoidance conflict. According to Epstein, some mothers of schizophrenic and autistic children have an approach-avoidance conflict regarding their children that is similar to the one described above for adults. That is, the mother approaches the child, but when the child reciprocates, the mother withdraws. When the child responds by withdrawing, the mother approaches the child, and the cycle repeats itself. The relationship is sufficiently enticing to keep the child in a high state of arousal and tension. Ultimately this sequence results in the child exhibiting a broad disengagement from reality, which no longer can be endured. At this point, the mother's unconscious conflict subsides, and she becomes concerned about the disturbed child. It should be noted that the view that some cases of autism and childhood schizophrenia are produced by such a mechanism does not deny that other cases may have a biological etiology.

CONFLICT RESOLUTION

To do justice to the topic of conflict resolution would require a review of the major schools of psychotherapy, which is well beyond the scope of this chapter. Space will permit but a few brief comments on five broad principles of resolution of approach-avoidance conflict.

One source of resolution lies in goal attainment through either reducing avoidance or increasing approach. As previously noted, both procedures result in a net increase in fear, but the former is preferable as it increases fear to a lesser extent. Of course, if approach tendencies involve antisocial behavior, then goal attainment is not a reasonable solution.

A second approach, one that is suitable for conflicts in which approach tendencies are destructive, is to raise the avoidance gradient. This reduces conflict as the individual is kept so far from the goal that the conflict, in effect, does not exist. The disadvantage with the approach is that it requires the individual to avoid a range of situations. How serious the disadvantage is depends on the nature of the situations that must be avoided. Many experiences can be avoided without any serious loss. The avoidance of others, however, such as intimate relationships, is another matter.

A third approach involves discrimination training. Conflicts can often be resolved by determining under what circumstances and in what form approach tendencies can appropriately be expressed. Of course, the development of fine distinctions is easier said than done and is far more difficult than learning broad prohibitions, which corresponds to raising the entire avoidance gradient.

The fourth way to resolve conflict is a nonspecific procedure that reduces all strong drives. Many problems in living arise from desires and fears that are excessive. By changing the belief that certain outcomes are necessary and that it would be catastrophic if they did not occur to one in which certain outcomes are recognized as desirable, but not essential, the intensity of all drives and conflicts can be reduced (cf. Ellis, 1962). As a result, conflict will be diminished.

The fifth principle is, in a way, opposite to the fourth as it is based on increasing the intensity of motivation. To the extent that a particular motive becomes dominant, other motives will become relatively unimportant. It is commonly observed, for example, that engaging in highly dangerous and absorbing tasks, such as hunting lions, climbing mountains, or sky diving, can be therapeutic by diverting attention from inner problems and conflicts. A related and safer approach is the development of lifelong goals that give meaning to existence (Frankl, 1960).

RECOMMENDATIONS FOR RESEARCH

Most research on conflict has been done with nonhuman animals. As a result, conflict between impulses has been stressed to a far greater extent than conceptual conflict. It would be desirable to redress this imbalance. This is not to deny the need for research on conflicts between opposing response tendencies. Further research is required on determining the factors that influence the relative steepness of approach and avoidance gradients and on establishing whether a mutiplicative or an additive model better represents the interactive effect of inner states and cues on motive strength. Research can profitably be done in which behavioral impulses are measured by physiological correlates in situations in which a goal is made to approach a stationary human or animal as well as the reverse. There is also a need for studies on avoidance-approach conflict in both humans and animals.

With respect to conceptual conflict, many questions beg for answers. What is the role of conceptual conflict in psychosomatic illness? Is stress that is produced by conceptual incompatibilities different from other kinds of stress, such as physical stress and fear of specific events? What is the relative incidence of disturbances produced by different kinds of conceptual discrepancies, such as discrepancies between actual and ideal selves, between experiences and beliefs, between perceptions of how things are and ought to be, and between cognitions at different levels of awareness? It is important to examine in real life, as well as in the laboratory, how people deal with such discrepancies in both constructive and destructive ways. Of particular importance is the examination of experiences that conflict with the basic assumptions in an individual's implicit theory of reality (cf. Epstein, 1980). What is the relationship between stress and repression? Does repression, when it is sufficiently deep, produce no stress, but simply exist as a potential source of disturbance that can be activated by circumstances, or is repression always a source of stress?

The application of the displacement model to the content of dreams, to responses in projective techniques, and to spontaneous thought is a rich area for further research. For example, content in dreams might be explored in relationship to a dimension of time elapsed since the occurrence of a threatening event. If the expression-inhibition model for the modulation of anxiety is correct, direct threat-relevant content should not be expressed directly, if at all until several days after the event.

Physiological reactions along cue and time dimensions concerns another promising area for further research. Physiological measures can also be used to examine reactions to stimulation at subthreshold levels of awareness. Interest in perceptual defense has faded although the fundamental problems have not been resolved. It would be worthwhile to resume such research, with an emphasis on the stress producing effects of unconscious conflict.

Finally, a promising area for research is the modulation of arousal according to the conflict model presented earlier.

REFERENCES

Adler, A. *Understanding human nature.* New York: Fawcett, 1954.

Astin, A. W. "Bad habits" and social deviation: A proposed revision in conflict theory. *Journal of Clinical Psychology,* 1962, *18,* 227–231.

Bateson, S. *Steps to an ecology of mind.* New York: Chandler, 1972.

Beck, A. T. *Cognitive therapy and the emotional disorders.* New York: International Universities, 1976.

Brehm, J. W., & Cohen, A. R. *Explorations in cognitive dissonance.* New York: Wiley, 1962.

Brown, J. S. Principles of intrapersonal conflict. *Conflict Resolution,* 1957, *1,* 135–154.

Champion, R. A. Motivational effects in approach-avoidance conflict. *Psychological Review,* 1961, *68,* 354–358.

Cutter, H. S. G. Conflict models, games, and drinking patterns. *Journal of Psychology,* 1964, *58,* 361–367.

Dollard, J., & Miller, N. E. *Personality and psychotherapy.* New York: McGraw-Hill, 1950.

Ellis, A. *Reason and emotion in psychotherapy.* New York: Lyle Stuart, 1962.

Epstein, S. The measurement of drive and conflict in humans: Theory and experiment. In M. R. Jones (ed.), *Nebraska Symposium on Motivation.* Lincoln: University of Nebraska Press, 1962.

————. Toward a unified theory of anxiety. In B. A. Maher (ed.), *Progress in experimental personality research,* vol. 4. New York: Academic, 1967.

————. The nature of anxiety with emphasis upon its relationship to expectancy. In C. D. Spielberger (ed.), *Anxiety: Current trends in theory and research,* vol 2. New York: Academic, 1972.

————. Avoidance-approach: The fifth basic conflict. *Journal of Consulting and Clinical Psychology,* 1978, *46,* 1016–1022.

————. The self-concept: A review and the proposal of an integrated theory of personality. In E. Staub (ed.), *Personality: Basic issues and current research.* Englewood Cliffs: Prentice-Hall, 1980.

EPSTEIN, S., & FENZ, W. D. Steepness of approach and avoidance gradients in humans as a function of experience: Theory and experiment. *Journal of Experimental Psychology,* 1965, *70,* 1–12.

ERIKSON, E. H. *Childhood and society* (2d ed.). New York: Norton, 1963.

FENZ, W. D., & EPSTEIN, S. Theory and experiment on the measurement of approach-avoidance conflict. *Journal of Abnormal and Social Psychology,* 1962, *64,* 97–112.

————. Gradients of psychological arousal of experienced and novice parachutists as a function of an approaching jump. *Psychosomatic Medicine,* 1967, *29,* 33–51.

FESTINGER, L. *A theory of cognitive dissonance.* Evanston: Row, Peterson, 1957.

FIRESTONE, I. J., KAPLAN, K. J., & MOORE, M. The attitude-gradient model. In A. A. Harrison (ed.), *Explorations in psychology.* Monterey: Brooks/Cole, 1974.

FRANKL, V. E. *The doctor and the soul.* New York: Knopf, 1960.

FRIEDMAN, I. Phenomenal, ideal, and projected conceptions of self. *Journal of Abnormal and Social Psychology,* 1955, *51,* 611–615.

FROMM, E. *The sane society.* New York: Holt, 1955.

GANTT, W. H. *Experimental basis for neurotic behavior.* New York: Hoober, 1944.

HALL, C. S., & LINDZEY, G. *Theories of personality* (3d ed.). New York: Wiley, 1978.

HEILIZER, F. Conflict models, alcohol, and drinking patterns. *Journal of Psychology,* 1964, *57,* 457–473.

————. A review of theory and research on the assumptions of Miller's response competition (conflict) models: Response gradients. *Journal of General Psychology,* 1977, *97,* 17–71. (a)

————. A review of theory and research on Miller's response competition (conflict) models. *Journal of General Psychology,* 1977, *97,* 227–280. (b)

————. Approach-withdrawal response competition (AW-RC), displacement, and behavior modification. *Journal of General Psychology,* 1978, *99,* 181–204.

HILGARD, E. R. Human motives and the concept of the self. *American Psychologist,* 1949, *4,* 374–382.

HORNEY, K. *Neurosis and human growth.* New York: Norton, 1950.

HOVLAND, C. I., & SEARS, R. R. Experiments on motor conflict. Part I: Types of conflict and their modes of resolution. *Journal of Experimental Psychology,* 1938, *23,* 447–493.

HULL, C. L. Principles of behavior. New York: Appleton-Century-Crofts, 1943.

HULL, S. L. The goal-gradient hypothesis applied to some "field force" problems in the behavior of young children. *Psychological Review,* 1938, *45,* 271–299.

JAMES, W. *Psychology: The briefer course.* New York: Holt, 1907.

JUNG, C. G. Psychology and alchemy. In *Collected works,* vol. 13. Princeton: Princeton University Press, 1953.

KANTOR, J. R. *Principles of psychology,* vol. 2. Bloomington: Principia, 1926.

KAPLAN, K. J., FIRESTONE, I. J., DEGNORE, R., & MOORE, M. Gradients of attraction as a function of disclosure probe intimacy and setting formality: On distinguishing attitude oscillation from attitude change. *Journal of Personality and Social Psychology,* 1974, *30,* 638–646.

Kelly, G. *The psychology of personal constructs* (2 vols.). New York: Norton, 1955.

Kelman, H. C. The induction of action and attitude change. In G. Nielsen (ed.), *Proceedings of the XIV International Congress of Applied Psychology.* Copenhagen: Munksgaard, 1961.

Lecky, P. *Self-consistency: A theory of personality.* Long Island City: Island Press, 1945.

Lewin, K. Environmental forces in child behavior and development. In C. Murchison (ed.), A handbook of child psychology. Worcester: Clark University Press, 1931.

Maher, B. A. *Principles of psychopathology: An experimental approach.* New York: McGraw-Hill, 1966.

Miller, N. E. Experimental studies of conflict. In J. McV. Hunt (ed.), *Personality and the behavior disorders,* vol. 1. New York: Ronald, 1944.

————. Liberalization of basic S–R concepts: Extensions to conflict behavior, motivation, and social learning. In S. Koch (ed.), *Psychology: A study of a science.* Vol. 2: General systematic formulations, learning, and special processes. New York: McGraw-Hill, 1959.

Murray, E. J., & Berkun, M. M. Displacement as a function of conflict. *Journal of Abnormal and Social Psychology,* 1955, *51,* 47–56.

Pavlov, I. P. *Conditioned reflexes,* trans. G. V. Anrep. New York: Oxford University Press, 1927.

Rogers, C. *Client-centered therapy: Its current practice, implications, and theory.* Boston: Houghton Mifflin, 1951.

————. A theory of therapy, personality, and interpersonal relationships as developed in the client-centered framework. In S. Koch (ed.), *Psychology: A study of a science.* Vol. 3: *Formulations of the person in the social context.* New York: McGraw-Hill, 1959.

————. *On becoming a person.* Boston: Houghton Mifflin, 1961.

Rokeach, M. *The nature of human values.* New York: Free Press, 1973.

Sarbin, T. R. A preface to a psychological analysis of the self. *Psychological Review,* 1952, *59,* 11–22.

Sherrington, C. S. *The integrative action of the nervous system.* New Haven: Yale University Press, 1906.

Smith, N. W. On the origin of conflict types. *Psychological Record,* 1968, *18,* 229–232.

Smith, S., & Guthrie, E. R. *General psychology in terms of behavior.* New York: Appleton, 1921.

Snygg, D., & Combs, A. W. *Individual behavior.* New York: Harper, 1949.

Wylie, R. *The self-concept* (rev. ed.), vol. 1. Lincoln: University of Nebraska Press, 1974.

6

Decisionmaking under Stress

Irving L. Janis

DURING THE PAST THREE DECADES, *rational-choice models,* based on *game theory* and *subjective-expected utility theory,* have been dominant in the psychological research literature on decisionmaking. These models assume that decisionmakers deliberately choose their courses of action on a rational basis by taking account of the values and the probabilities of the consequences that would follow from selecting each of the available alternatives (e.g., Edwards, 1954; Miller & Star, 1967; Raiffa, 1968). Models of rational choice have led to the development of formal methods for decision analysis, which provide useful normative rules that specify how people should make sound decisions when they have to take risky actions (Wheeler & Janis, 1980). One central idea is that it is essential to make the best estimates of the probability that each of the expected consequences will occur; another is that the relative importance of each of the anticipated favorable and unfavorable consequences should be taken into account—their expected utility value from the decisionmaker's own standpoint.

Although valuable for prescriptive purposes, rational models run into considerable difficulty when they are proposed as *descriptive* theories that explain how people actually do make decisions (Broadhurst, 1976; Kahneman & Tversky, 1979; Lee, 1971; Rapoport & Wallsten, 1972; Simon, 1976; Slovic, Fishhoff, & Lichtenstein, 1977). One major reason that people deviate from a rational model pertains to the cognitive limitations of the human mind (Simon, 1976). People simply cannot understand and keep in mind all the relevant information needed for an optimal solution to the decisionmaking problems they face. Nor do they have at their command all the necessary knowledge about cause and effect relationships and all the baseline data essential for making accurate probability estimates of alternative outcomes. Another major reason that people do not consistently follow rational procedures has to do with the effects of emotions on the cognitive processes involved in decisionmaking. This is where stress enters the picture.

DETRIMENTAL EFFECTS OF STRESS

One source of stress arises from the decisionmakers' awareness of their own limited knowledge and problem-solving capabilities. This type of *cognitive stress,* as George (1974)

This chapter is based on more extensive discussions of the same topic in Janis (1983) and in Janis and Mann (1977).

labeled it, is well illustrated by something President Warren Harding told a friend when he was struggling with a major domestic problem.

> John, I can't make a damn thing out of this tax problem. I listen to one side and they seem right, and then God! I talk to the other side and they seem just as right, and there I am where I started. I know somewhere there is a book that would give me the truth, but hell, I couldn't read the book. I know somewhere there is an economist who knows the truth, but I don't know where to find him and haven't the sense to know him and trust him when I did find him. God, what a job! (George, 1974:187, quoted from Fenno, 1959:36)

Other sources of stress include fear of suffering from various losses that would occur no matter which alternative were chosen, worry about unknown things that could go wrong when vital consequences are at stake, concern about making a fool of oneself in the eyes of others, and losing self-esteem if the decision works out badly. Vital decisions often involve conflicting values, which convinces the decisionmaker that any choice he or she makes will require the sacrifice of ideals. As a result, the decisionmaker's anticipatory anxiety, shame, or guilt is increased, which adds to the level of stress (Janis & Mann, 1977).

When the level of stress is very high, the decisionmaker is likely to display *premature closure*—terminating the decisional dilemma without generating all the alternatives and without seeking or appraising the available information about the outcomes to be expected for the limited set of alternatives under consideration. A high level of stress reduces the decisionmaker's problem-solving capabilities, especially when dealing with the complicated cognitive tasks posed by decisions rendered difficult by numerous competing values. The person's attention and perceptions are somewhat impaired and there are various manifestations of cognitive rigidity. These cognitive deficiencies result in narrowing the range of perceived alternatives, overlooking long-term consequences, inefficient searching for information, erroneous assessing of expected outcomes, and using oversimplified decision rules that fail to take account of the full range of values implicated by the choice. George (1980) listed various cognitive crutches that policymakers are especially likely to rely on when they are beset by uncertainties and threats that generate stress: (1) using a minimally satisfactory criterion of choice—what Simon (1976) called "satisficing"—rather than using optimizing criteria; (2) confining the alternative choices to small incremental changes when gross alterations may be required; (3) deciding on the basis of what people in the organization seem to want without considering the main outcomes to be expected; (4) giving undue weight to historical analogies, and (5) relying on either a general formula based on ideological principles or an operational code as a guide to action without carrying out detailed analyses of the specific policy issues at hand.

Stress encroaches most profoundly on decisionmaking processes when the decisionmaker is in a dilemma about what to do about imminent threats of physical suffering, bodily injury, or death. Elstein and Bordage (1979) pointed out that at times of acute distress, one of the main assumptions of theories of rational choice is violated, namely, that preferences will remain sufficiently stable so that the person will regard any given outcome as having essentially the same utility shortly after making a decision as he or she did at the time the decision was made: "A patient in severe pain or grave distress may evaluate a variety of outcomes quite differently than when pain and distress are absent. Consequently, a set of utility estimates obtained under one condition may not apply when conditions are altered" (p. 363).

These and other changes arising from stress account for gross deviations from the decisionmaking behavior predicted by descriptive rational models for many vital decisions, such as those made by patients who need medical treatment or surgery. For example, the vast majority of patients with acute myocardial infarctions, according to Hackett and Cassem (1975), realize that they may be having a heart attack but delay calling a physician for four or five hours. "The decision making process," the authors asserted, "gets jammed by the patient's inability to admit that he is mortally sick" (p. 27). Similar maladaptive delay, which significantly increases a patient's chances of dying, has been observed among people suffering from symptoms of cancer (Blackwell, 1963; Kasl & Cobb, 1966). Few patients who postpone a medical examination are unaware of the danger. The majority have been found to be familiar with the warning signs of cancer, more so than patients who promptly seek medical aid (Goldsen, Gerhardt, & Handy, 1957; Kutner, Makover, & Oppenheim, 1958). The most plausible explanation for the delay seems to be that the patients fail to make a decision on a rational basis because they are trying to ward off anxiety by avoiding exposure to threat cues, such as distressing information from a physician.

The same criticisms also apply to the *health-belief model* developed by Hochbaum (1958), which incorporates essentially the same assumptions about rational choices as the subjective–expected utility model. Nevertheless, it is quite possible that for certain types of decisions pertaining to preventive measures, such as cutting down on smoking, made at a time when people are not emotionally aroused, a rational model may predict fairly well (Becker & Maiman, 1975; Kirscht & Rosenstock, 1979; Mausner & Platt, 1971). Ultimately, a comprehensive theory needs to be developed to predict and explain when choices will be made on a rational basis and when not.

A CONFLICT–THEORY ANALYSIS

Stress does not always have detrimental or maladaptive effects. On the contrary, anticipatory fear of excessive losses sometimes prevents premature closure. Such concerns can serve as incentives to carry out the adaptive "work of worrying," which leads to careful information search and appraisal (Janis, 1958, 1971; Janis & Mann, 1977). This brings us to another major problem that requires theoretical analysis and empirical research: under what conditions does stress have favorable versus unfavorable effects on the quality of decisionmaking? In other words, when is stress healthy and when not?

The *conflict-theory analysis* formulated by Janis and Mann (1977) attempted to answer this question, as well as the broader question posed earlier concerning the conditions under which people will use sound decisionmaking procedures to arrive at a rational choice. This analysis focused on different ways people deal with stress when they are making vital decisions, contrasting coping patterns that result in defective forms of problem–solving with a vigilant coping pattern, which generally meets the standards of rational decisionmaking. Janis and Mann began their analysis by specifying the main criteria that can be used to judge whether or not a person's decision is of high quality with regard to the problem-solving procedures that lead up to the act of commitment. The following seven criteria were extracted from the extensive literature on effective decisionmaking. The decisionmaker (1) thoroughly canvasses a wide range of alternative courses of action; (2) takes account of the full range of objectives to be fulfilled and the values implicated by the choice; (3) carefully weighs whatever he or she knows about the costs or drawbacks and the uncertain risks of negative consequences, as well as the positive consequences, that could flow from each alternative; (4) intensively searches for new information relevant for further evaluation of the alternatives; (5) conscientiously takes account of any new information or expert judgment to which he or she is exposed, even when the information or judgment does not support the course of action he or she initially preferred; (6) reexamines the positive and negative consequences of all known alternatives, including those originally regarded as unacceptable, before making a final choice; and (7) makes detailed provisions for implementing the chosen course of action, with special attention to contingency plans that might be required if various known risks were to materialize.

Failure to meet any of these seven criteria is assumed to be a defect in the decision-making process. The more such defects are present before the decisionmaker becomes committed, the greater the chance that he or she will undergo unanticipated setbacks and postdecisional regret, which favor reversal of the decision. Although systematic data are not yet available on this point, it seems plausible to assume that *high-quality decisions*—in the sense of satisfying these procedural criteria—have a better chance than others of attaining the decisionmaker's objectives and of being adhered to in the long run.

Janis and Mann (1977) postulated that stress engendered by decisional conflict frequently is a major determinant of failure to meet the criteria for high-quality decisionmaking. *Decisional conflict* refers to simultaneous tendencies within the individual to accept and to reject a given course of action. The most prominent symptoms of such conflicts are hesitation, vacillation, feelings of uncertainty, and signs of acute psychological stress (anxiety, shame, guilt, or other unpleasant affect) whenever the decision comes to the focus of attention. Such conflicts arise whenever the decisionmaker is concerned about the material and social losses he or she might suffer from whichever course of action is choosen—including the costs of failing to live up to prior commitments. The more severe the anticipated losses, the higher the level of stress. Stress is augmented when the person recognizes that his or her reputation and self-esteem as a competent decisionmaker are also at stake.

In assuming that the stress itself is frequently a major cause of errors in decisionmaking, Janis and Mann (1977) did not deny the influence of other common causes, such as ignorance, prejudice, and bureaucratic politics. They maintained, however, that many ill-conceived and poorly implemented decisions reflect the motivational consequences of decisional conflict, particularly attempts to ward off the stresses generated by agonizingly difficult choices.

In line with their initial assumptions, Janis and Mann (1977) postulated that there are five basic patterns of coping with the stresses generated when people have to make a vital choice. Each pattern is associated with a specific set of antecedent conditions and a characteristic level of stress. These patterns, listed below, were derived from an analysis of the research literature on psychological stress bearing on how people react to warnings that urge protective action to avert disasters, health hazards, or other serious threats.

1. *Unconflicted inertia.* The decisionmaker complacently decides to continue whatever he or she has been doing, ignoring information about associated risks.

2. *Unconflicted change.* The decisionmaker uncritically adopts whichever new course of action is most salient or most strongly recommended, without making contingency plans and without psychologically preparing for setbacks.

3. *Defensive avoidance.* The decisionmaker evades the conflict by procrastinating, by shifting responsibility to someone else, or by constructing wishful rationalizations that bolster the least objectionable alternative, minimizing the expected unfavorable consequences and remaining selectively inattentive to corrective information.

4. *Hypervigilance.* The decisionmaker, in a paniclike state, searches frantically for a way out of the dilemma, rapidly shifts back and forth between alternatives, and impulsively seizes upon a hastily contrived solution that seems to promise immediate relief. He or she

overlooks the full range of consequences of his or her choice because of emotional excitement, repetitive thinking, and cognitive constriction (manifested by reduction in immediate memory span and by simplistic ideas).

5. *Vigilance.* The decisionmaker searches painstakingly for relevant information, assimilates information in an unbiased manner, and appraises alternatives carefully before making a choice.

While the first two patterns occasionally are adaptive in saving time, effort, and emotional wear and tear, especially for routine or minor decisions, they often lead to defective decisions when the individual must make a choice that has serious personal or family consequences or profound implications for the organization he or she represents. Similarly, defensive avoidance and hypervigilance may be adaptive in certain extreme situations but generally reduce the decisionmaker's chances of averting serious losses. Consequently, all four are regarded as defective patterns of decisionmaking. The fifth pattern, vigilance, although occasionally maladaptive if danger is imminent and a split-second response is required, generally leads to decisions that meet the main criteria for rational or sound decisionmaking.

Janis and Mann (1977) postulated that people will weigh the benefits of a recommended course of action against the perceived costs of, or barriers to, taking that action, as is assumed by rational-choice models, *only when their coping pattern is vigilance.* When any of the four defective coping patterns is dominant, the decisionmaker will *fail* to carry out adequately the cognitive tasks that are essential for arriving at stable decisions. Then when they experience undesirable consequences, such as the usual unpleasant side effects of a standard medical treatment or unexpected demands for overtime work shortly after starting on a new job, they are likely to overreact. They suffer not just from the distressing setback but also from strong feelings of postdecisional regret, which may interfere with their ability to curtail the losses or to make a sound new decision that will enable them to recover rapidly from the setback. Postdecisional regret entails intense emotional arousal, such as anxiety and rage, which creates a high level of stress and could give rise to psychosomatic disorders (Janis, Defares, & Grossman, 1982).

What are the conditions that foster vigilance and how do they differ from those that underlie each of the four defective coping patterns? The answer to this question is presented in Figure 6–1, which is a schematic summary of the Janis and Mann (1977) conflict model of decisionmaking. This model specifies the psychological conditions responsible for the five coping patterns and the level of stress that accompanies them. The coping patterns are determined by the presence or absence of three conditions: (1) awareness of serious risks associated with whichever alternative is chosen (i.e., arousal of conflict), (2) hope of finding a better alternative, and (3) belief that there is adequate time in which to seek information and to deliberate before a decision is required. Although there may be marked individual differences in preference for one or another of the coping patterns, all five patterns are assumed to be in the repertoire of every person when he or she functions as a decisionmaker. In different circumstances the same person will use different coping patterns depending on which of the three crucial conditions are present or absent.

Janis and Mann (1977) did not claim that the five patterns occur *only* as a result of specified conditions. Rather, they argued that the patterns are linked dependably with the mediating psychological conditions specified in Figure 6–1—a claim that has numerous implications, including descriptive hypotheses about environmental circumstances that generate vigilance and prescriptive hypotheses about deliberate interventions that could be used to counteract the beliefs and perceptions responsible for defective coping patterns.

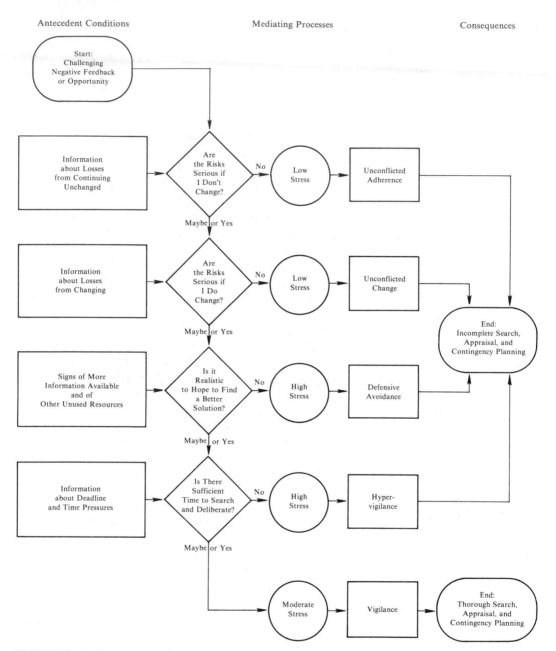

FIGURE 6–1. The conflict-theory model of decisionmaking *(after Janis & Mann, 1977:70).*

In their review of social–psychological studies bearing on premature closure, postdecisional regret, and a number of other aspects of decisional behavior, Janis and Mann (1977) called attention to scattered findings consistent with predictions about the behavioral consequences of vigilant versus nonvigilant coping patterns, from which they concluded that their theoretical analysis is plausible. They also described a few of their own experiments that were designed to test hypotheses derived from their conflict model. One such experiment by

Mann, Janis, and Chaplin (1969), for example, dealt with threats of the type encountered by many people who have to make decisions about taking medications or undergoing medical treatments that create nausea and other temporary side effects that are harmless but unpleasant. As predicted by the conflict-theory model, subjects who were led to believe that no additional information could be expected (which reduced their hope of finding a more adequate solution) tended to bolster the alternative they had originally preferred, which is a manifestation of defensive avoidance. Bolstering was evidenced by a spread in the relative attractiveness of the alternatives. In contrast, among subjects who were led to expect more information, there was virtually no tendency to bolster—another finding consistent with the conflict model, which specifies that vigilance will be the dominant coping pattern under such circumstances. The results indicated that bolstering occurs before overt commitment if the conditions that foster defensive avoidance are present.

None of the studies carried out so far can be regarded as crucial experiments that definitively test the conflict-theory model or enable one to decide that this model is better in general than other psychological theories of decisionmaking. In the present early stage of research on decisionmaking under stress, the conflict-theory model appears to have heuristic value in that it calls attention to neglected variables that affect decisionmaking behavior.

Effects of Warnings

Any theory of decisionmaking under stress should have something important to say about the effects of warnings about impending dangers. Throughout their lives, people are exposed to an unending stream of challenging warnings that call attention to the risks of suffering serious losses unless they decide to adopt a new course of protective action. The challenging information is sometimes conveyed by disturbing events, as when a heavy smoker develops a chronic cough. Fairly often, however, the challenging information that initiates the decisionmaking process is contained in impressive communications, such as a weather bureau's warning of an oncoming tornado or a physician's warning to stop smoking after a physical checkup has revealed precancerous cells in a patient's lungs. Just as with scare propaganda, authentic warnings that arouse intense emotional reactions can lead to resistance to change, misattributions, erroneous judgments, and defective decisions, sometimes as a result of panic or extreme reactions of defensive avoidance. What can be done to prevent such adverse reactions? Under what conditions are fear arousing warnings most likely to be effective in evoking decisions to take adaptive action?

Some tentative answers have come from social–psychological studies of the effects of warnings and emotional appeals (Janis, 1967, 1971; Leventhal, 1973; McGuire, 1969; Rogers & Mewborn, 1976). Dozens of controlled attitude change experiments have been carried out to determine whether acceptance of precautionary recommendations increases or decreases when strong fear appeals, as compared with milder ones, are used. One set of such experiments dealing with real-life threats of illness or other adverse consequences, indicated that there can be diminishing returns as the level of fear arousal is increased (Janis & Feshbach, 1953; Janis & Terwilliger, 1962; Rogers & Thistlethwaite, 1970). These experiments support the following conclusion, which is consistent with the Janis and Mann (1977) conflict model: when fear is strongly aroused by a communication but is not fully relieved by reassurances that build up hope of averting the danger, the recipients will display a pattern of defensive avoidance as manifested by tendencies to ignore, minimize, or deny the importance of the threat. On the other hand, another set of experiments dealing with similar threats showed that strong threat appeals can be more effective than milder ones. These experiments pointed to the facilitating effects of fear arousal (Insko, Arkoff, & Insko, 1965; Leventhal, Singer, & Jones, 1965).

Taken together, the two sets of results suggest that changes in feelings of vulnerability to a threat and subsequent adoption of a recommended course of action depend upon the relative strength of facilitating and interfering reactions, both of which are likely to be evoked whenever a warning by an authority arouses fear. If so, we cannot expect to discover any simple generalization applicable to warnings given by authoritative sources that will tell us whether strong fear arousing presentations that vividly depict the expected dangers or milder versions that merely allude to the threats will be more effective. Rather, we must expect the optimal level of fear arousal to vary for different types of threat, for different types of recommended action, and for different personalities.

Social–psychological investigators generally agree that the effectiveness of any fear arousing communication urging people to take protective action depends partly upon three content variables that interact in complex ways (Hovland, Janis, & Kelley, 1953; McGuire, 1969; Rogers & Mewborn, 1976):

1. magnitude of the threat (if it were to materialize)
2. probability of the threat's materializing (if no protective action is taken)
3. probable effectiveness of the recommended protective action (if that action is taken)

These three components are among the key components of the subjective–expected utility model and the health-belief model, discussed earlier. According to these rational-choice models, people suffering from an illness can be expected to accept their physicians' recommendations if they believe that the probable consequences of doing what is recommended—despite all the costs in terms of money, time, effort, and discomfort—are preferable to the consequences of the untreated illness. But, as I have already stated, this model is expected to hold only in the presence of the conditions necessary for a vigilant pattern of coping. Some of the findings cited earlier on delay of treatment and other maladaptive responses among patients suffering from heart disease or cancer appear to bear out this assumption.

The crucial role of the third component—perceived effficacy of the recommended means for averting or minimizing the threat—is repeatedly borne out by social-psychological research on the effects of public health messages that contain fear arousing warnings (Chu, 1966; Leventhal, 1973; Leventhal, Singer, & Jones, 1965; Rogers & Deckner, 1975; Rogers & Thistlethwaite, 1970). Rogers and Mewborn (1976), for example, found that assertions about the efficacy of recommended protective actions had a significant effect on college students' intentions to adopt the practices recommended in three different public health communications dealing with well-known hazards that produce preventable human suffering—lung cancer, automobile accident injuries, and venereal disease.

The findings just cited appear to be consistent with the following hypothesis derived from the conflict-theory model: when a warning message presents realistic information about the unfavorable consequences of alternative courses of action—such as consent forms that describe the risks and suffering that could arise from undergoing surgery or painful medical treatments—it is most likely to induce vigilance and to instigate sound decisionmaking procedures if it is accompanied by impressive information about the expected efficacy of the recommended course of action, which instills hope about dealing effectively with anticipated threats. Vigilance is likely to be replaced by unconflicted inertia, however, once people have been given warnings that turn out to be false alarms. Breznitz's (1967, 1976) laboratory experiments using the threat of electric shock indicated that when people are warned about an impending threat and then told that the danger has been postponed or canceled, they show a characteristic false-alarm reaction in response to subsequent warnings about the same danger; they tend to display much less fear and to ignore the new warnings.

Hypervigilance

The grossest errors in decisionmaking are to be expected whenever hypervigilance is the dominant stress reaction. The emotional state of panic or near panic that is at the core of the hypervigilant pattern might involve what Selye (1956) called the initial *alarm reaction* of the *general adaptation syndrome* evoked by powerful stressors. According to Selye, this stage, which is distinguised by a marked increase in sympathetic-adrenal activity, is followed by a *stage of physiological resistance* and then a final *stage of exhaustion or collapse.*

Fortunately, the paniclike state that characterizes hypervigilance seldom occurs in everyday life or even in extreme emergencies (Schultz, 1964). On those rare occasions when hypervigilance is elicited by warnings of, or actual confrontations with, danger, cognitive functioning is seriously impaired.

Many controlled psychological experiments have tested cognitive performance after exposure to threats, such as telling subjects that they are going to be given painful electric shocks. In general, it appears that minor threats have little or no effect but serious threats can evoke temporary impairment in cognitive functioning (Hamilton, 1975; Janis, 1971; Janis & Leventhal, 1968).

Excessive alertness to all signs of potential threat results in diffusion of attention. This is one of the main sources of cognitive inefficiency whenever someone becomes hypervigilant, and it probably accounts for some of the failures to meet the criteria for effective decisionmaking. Persons in a hypervigilant state are strongly motivated to engage in thorough search and appraisal. But as they try to carry out essential cognitive tasks, such as searching for reliable information about what seems to be a promising course of action (by consulting an expert) or trying to remember what happened when they tried to deal with similar threats in the past, they are constantly distracted and their train of thought gets derailed. Their attention shifts rapidly to all sorts of other threat cues, many of which are inauthentic or unimportant but nevertheless alarming. They are also likely to be distracted from essential cognitive tasks by obsessional ideas about all the things that could go wrong or about the worst possible outcomes. Because of their indiscriminate attentiveness to all sorts of threats, relevant and irrelevant, much of the time and energy available for working out a satisfactory decision about the best available course of protective action is wasted. Then when a deadline is at hand, they are likely to seize upon an ill-conceived solution that is useful mainly for mitigating whichever source of danger happens to be most salient at the moment but that may be a poor solution because it overlooks other threats that need to be taken into account. For example, in a state of near panic after hearing a horror story from an ill-informed and thoughtless visitor, a cancer patient in dire need of extensive surgery may suddenly decide not to have a recommended operation and leave the hospital.

An experiment by Sigall and Helmreich (1969) provided impressive evidence of the tendency for people in a state of high fear to fail to discriminate between credible and non-credible sources of a persuasive communication, which results in indiscriminate acceptance of the message. The failure to make such discriminatory evaluations and also the failure to adopt a critical stance in evaluating the authenticity, plausibility, and personal applicability of warning messages may be caused partly by the diffusion of attention and partly by the lowering of mental efficiency that occurs whenever a person is in a state of high emotional arousal.

Along with cognitive constriction there is a marked tendency toward stereotyped thinking in terms of oversimplified categories and reliance on simpleminded decision rules. In fire emergencies that occur in crowded theaters or restaurants, for example, where fear is very high and decision time is very short, people tend to follow the simple decision rule that the best way to escape is to do what everyone else is doing, i.e., to run to whichever exit the crowd is heading for. Other available escape routes are overlooked as everyone converges on the same exit, which soon becomes blocked; as a result, many people unnecessarily lose their lives (Schultz, 1964). But if someone who is perceived as a leader is present in panic inducing situations, mass convergence into a bottleneck can be prevented by authoritative directives. In such instances, the simple decision rule to do whatever others are doing appears to be replaced by the equally simple rule to do whatever an authority figure tells one to do. Both decision rules may reflect a general increase in social dependence that occurs under conditions of high fear, which is manifested by overt efforts to avoid being separated from companions, strong preference for contact with authority figures who are capable of giving reassurances, and increased compliance (Janis, 1958, 1971; Schachter, 1959).

Other behavioral consequences of strong fear arousal have been investigated in field studies of natural disasters and in laboratory experiments. Closely related to the temporary loss of cognitive efficiency is the temporary loss of perceptual acuity, perceptual-motor coordination, and motor skills (Duffy, 1962). Clumsiness on manual tasks results partly from the muscular tenseness that occurs in states of fear arousal, which is manifested by the stiffening of muscles all over the body and by muscular tremors. Facial expressions also tend to become rigid, partly because of taut facial muscles (Ekman, Freisen, & Ellsworth, 1972; Izard, 1971).

Lazarus (1966, 1976) pointed out that coping with stress is essentially a matter of problem-solving under conditions wherein it is not clear what to do. Because problem-solving activities become grossly inefficient when people are in a state of hypervigilance, they are likely to fail to choose an adaptive course of action that will reduce the risks posed by the anticipated danger. Efforts to escape or to aggress against the perceived source of threat are likely to be misdirected and ineffectual.

When people suddenly realize that they may be entrapped in a danger situation, such as a rapidly approaching tornado, they tend to become so agitated that they fail to use whatever time is available to find the best available escape route and fail to notice obvious defects in the one they impulsively choose (see Fritz & Marks, 1954). Similar failures to make full use of their cognitive capabilities have been observed in the emergency decisionmaking of jittery people who display less extreme forms of hypervigilance, when confronted with community warnings about potential radiation hazards in a nearby atomic energy plant or with personal warnings from a physician about the possibility that a skin growth might be malignant. Many such people become obsessed with images of horrifying things that may happen to them and fall prey to informational overload as they indiscriminately pat attention to all sorts of warnings, advice, and rumors about the threat (Horowitz, 1976; Janis, 1971). Sometimes a person's impulsive action takes the form of unwarranted fight rather than flight.

> The disruptive effects of a high level of stress in circumstances requiring immediate protective activity are illustrated by the thoughtless action taken by a law enforcement agent during the race riot in Detroit in 1967, as described in the Report of the National Advisory Commission on Civil

Disorders (1968, p. 98). A white National Guardsman believed that his own life was in immediate danger from snipers when he heard shots nearby after having been summoned by a nightwatchman to investigate looting. Instead of taking cover and watching to see what was going on, he promptly decided to shoot to kill when he caught sight of a black man holding a pistol. The victim turned out to be the nightwatchman, who had shot his pistol into the air to scare off the looters. (Janis & Mann, 1977:61)

During and immediately after tornadoes, earthquakes, explosions, conflagrations, air raids, or other major disasters, large numbers of survivors admit that they feel terrified and at the same time, they display marked signs of high physiological arousal (Janis, 1951, 1971; Rachman, 1978). Most disaster survivors recover rapidly, within a half hour after the danger has subsided, but in a minority of cases symptoms of jitteriness persist for days and sometimes weeks, along with excessive physiological arousal in response to noises and minor threats, which appear to be reactivations of the alarm reaction. When this occurs, the person repeatedly displays the characteristic symptoms of psychological trauma—trembling of the hands, preoccupation with possible recurrences of danger, and terrifying nightmares and intrusive daytime visions in which traumatic events are reexperienced (Horowitz, 1976; Janis, 1951). This persisting state of hypervigilance, which continues to interfere with effective decisionmaking, may alternate with feelings of numbness, denial of loss, efforts to ward off exposure to reminders of the disaster, and other manifestations of extreme defensive avoidance tendencies (Horowitz, 1976).

The readiness to become jittery, agitated, and preoccupied with frightening images in response to any threat of physical danger is thought to be related to a number of personality variables. Among the predisposing attributes frequently mentioned in the literature on personality research are chronic anxiety neurosis, low ego strength, low self-confidence, low problem-solving ability, and low capacity for developing or using a network of social supports (e.g., Jenkins, 1979). Empirical findings bearing on such variables, however, are not clear-cut and sometimes are mutually contradictory. Obviously, methodological refinements are needed in personality research in order to pin down the predisposing variables related to different ways of coping with threat (Cohen & Lazarus, 1979).

Somewhat more dependable evidence is available on situational variables that are thought to be determinants of ineffective coping. The evidence points to a number of primary and secondary causal factors that contribute to hypervigilant reactions.

Near-miss Experiences, Time Pressures, and Other Causal Factors

Considerable evidence of the traumatizing effects of exposure to danger stimuli has accumulated from case studies and surveys of people who have been injured or have undergone narrow escapes in accidents or disasters (Janis, 1971). Even among the most stable personalities, hypervigilance apparently occurs at least temporarily following direct involvement in a disaster. Why do some survivors fail to recover rapidly from emotional shock and display hypervigilant reactions for many weeks each time they are exposed to reminders of how close they came to being either badly hurt or killed? One of the critical determinants of sustained hypervigilance seems to be what MacCurdy (1943) labeled a *near-miss experience*. Studies of wartime and peacetime disasters have indicated that the most intense and prolonged symptoms of hypervigilance tend to develop among survivors who were in close proximity to actual danger and experienced a near miss, such as narrowly escaping serious injury when their home was destroyed, being pinned down by fallen debris, losing relatives or friends, and seeing maimed bodies (Janis, 1951; Rachman, 1978; Wolfenstein, 1957). Survivors who had *remote-miss experiences*, on the other hand, showed a marked tendency toward increased tolerance of stress, manifested by decreased fear with successive exposure to the same type of danger, presumably as result of habituation or emotional adaptation.

Survey data on 544 combat flying officers (Grinker, Willerman, Bradley, & Fastarsky, 1946) indicated that fliers who had developed extreme fear and symptoms of traumatic neurosis during combat duty were much less likely to give affirmative answers to questions about feelings of personal invulnerability ("While others might be hurt or killed, it couldn't happen to me") than were fliers who had undergone similar tours of duty without developing severe fear or anxiety symptoms. Although such correlational findings cannot establish a causal sequence, they are consistent with the hypothesis that when people develop the characteristic pattern of hypervigilance following exposure to danger, the mediating psychological process is a change in attitude concerning personal vulnerability. This hypothesis appears to be plausible in light of impressionistic observations in peacetime disasters (Janis, 1962; Wolfenstein, 1957), but has not yet been tested systematically.

In the extensive research literature on human fear reactions, a number of other factors in addition to near-miss exposures have been described that apparently augment fear during disasters and that may hamper decisionmaking after frightening encounters with extreme danger. Among the factors most frequently implicated as antecedents of hypervigilant reactions are lack of contact with family members or other supportive persons, restrictions of activity, lack of perceived control over dangerous events, and lack of preparatory information about the stressful events to be expected and about what to do to build up one's coping skills (Cox, 1978; Epstein, 1973; Janis, 1971; Janis & Rodin, 1979; Monat & Lazarus, 1977; Rachman, 1978). Both field studies and laboratory experiments have indicated that these factors can increase the probability of sustained hypervigilance, although not in all circumstances. Considerable research is required to determine the conditions under which each of these factors has the expected detrimental effect as against a favorable effect or no effect at all.

Janis and Mann's (1977) analysis of emergency decisionmaking emphasized *time pressure* as one of the major determinants of hypervigilance when people are exposed to serious threats of physical injury or death. Disaster studies indicate that panic, the most extreme form of hypervigilance, tends to occur when people perceive that danger is imminent and that escape routes are rapidly closing off. That is to say, people facing danger are likely to become hypervigilant if they expect to be helpless to avoid being victimized unless they act very quickly. Under these conditions, the most extreme instances of cognitive impairment, poor judgment, and maladaptive impulsive decisions are likely to occur. There is even some evidence suggesting that when people are told that a disaster is expected to strike within a few minutes, their frantic escape attempts are so unrealistic that they increase rather than decrease the danger and that most poeple would be better off with no warning at all (Fritz & Marks, 1954).

In a series of laboratory experiments that confronted subjects with the threat of painful electric shocks, Kelley and his co-workers (1965) found that paniclike reactions resulting in entrapment were likely when subjects were under extreme time pressure. The findings indicated that when fear is aroused in a threat situation that allows only a short time for escape, people frantically take action without regard for the available opportunities that would enable them to escape successfully.

Janis and Mann (1977) postulated that the hypervigilant pattern is fostered by deadline pressures whenever people must take action to avert a threatened loss, whether it concerns their personal safety, career goals, social or financial status; or other important values. At a time when decisionmakers are in a state of acute decisional conflict because of the perceived risks entailed by whichever available course of action is chosen, the likelihood that they will become excessively preoccupied with the threatened losses and will display the other symptoms of hypervigilance increases if they receive information about an impending deadline that leads them to believe that they have insufficient time to search for a good solution. Under these pressing conditions, people become indiscriminately receptive to rumors about terrible things that might happen. They fail to take account of evidence indicating the improbability of exaggerated dangers, vacillate as they try to avoid each of the risky alternatives that could lead to catastrophe, and finally choose hastily whichever course of action appears at the moment to be least dangerous.

Some persons may be under constant time pressure as a result of either situational demands that create an overloaded daily schedule of urgent obligations or personality predispositions or both. Whatever the cause may be, such persons can be expected to become hypervigilant much more readily than others in response to warnings and approaching deadlines, which leads to ill-considered decisions that are frequently followed by postdecisional conflict and frustration. It is noteworthy that a chronic sense of time urgency has been found to be a major component of *type A personalities,* who are at high risk with regard to coronary heart disease (see Glass, 1977).

The combination of sudden, unexpected threat, with extreme time pressure to avert the danger, appears to be one of the conditions that most consistently fosters a state of hypervigilance, in which people are likely to commit themselves impulsively to courses of action that they soon will have cause to regret. This treacherous combination is most likely to occur, according to Janis and Mann (1977), when decisionmakers have failed to react vigilantly to earlier warnings about the threat. When reactions to initial warnings take the form of defensive avoidance rather than vigilance, people ignore the warnings, fail to search for relevant information, and do not adequately appraise the risks entailed by the alternative courses of action. They evade decisional conflict by shifting responsibility for the decision to someone else, by procrastinating, and/or by constructing wishful rationalizations that bolster the least objectionable alternative, which results in their minimizing the losses to be expected. As Figure 6-1 indicated, this defective coping pattern is most likely to occur when people in a state of high decisional conflict about the risks entailed by choosing any of the available alternatives have little hope of finding a satisfactory solution.

When defensive avoidance is the dominant pattern, decisionmakers remain inattentive to corrective information until they are confronted by a dramatic threat that catches them by surprise, which sets the stage for a hypervigilant reaction. The same thing is likely to happen if decisionmakers misunderstand or fail to grasp the significance of earlier warnings and, as a result, feel genuinely unconcerned about the risks or dangers that might lie ahead. This pattern of unconflicted inertia leaves decisionmakers just as unprepared for sudden bad news about threats of serious losses as does defensive avoidance. Unconflicted inertia and defensive avoidance in response to early warnings about a given threat can be regarded as psychological reactions that increase the probability of hypervigilance in response to a subsequent confrontation with the danger.

PREVENTION OF DEFECTIVE COPING PATTERNS

In recent years a variety of psychological techniques have been designed to prevent the onset of defective coping patterns in threatening situations or to minimize such reactions if they already exist. These include benign preexposure to the threatening situation, stress inoculation via preparatory communications, and controlled breathing and relaxation procedures designed to moderate physiological responses to emotion arousing situations. Studies of these techniques, although seldom sufficiently well controlled to provide definitive results, have suggested that each of them is at least partially successful for some people in some circumstances (Janis, Defares, & Grossman, 1982).

The conflict-theory analysis of decisionmaking (Fig. 6–1) leads us to expect that counseling can be an effective aid to making decisions under stressful conditions insofar as it counteracts the conditions underlying defective coping patterns and promotes the psychological conditions conducive to vigilance. A number of interventions have been developed for this purpose, including an awareness-of-rationalizations procedure, new forms of role-playing in structured psychodramas, and a balance-sheet procedure to induce awareness of the full range of consequences (Janis & Mann, 1977).

Perhaps the most promising type of intervention for fostering a vigilant approach to recurrent threats that are likely to be disruptive and demoralizing is *stress inoculation*. This technique is usually applied shortly after a decision has been made but before it is implemented. Inoculation for emotional stress involves exposing the decisionmaker to preparatory information that vividly describes what it will be like to experience the expected negative consequences of the chosen course of action. Preparatory information functions as a form of inoculation if it enables the person to increase his or her tolerance for postdecisional stress by developing effective reassurances and coping mechanisms (Janis, 1958, 1971; Meichenbaum, 1977; Meichenbaum & Turk, 1976). This type of intervention is called inoculation because it may be analogous to the process whereby antibodies are induced in response to injections of mildly virulent toxins.

The underlying principle is that accurate preparatory information about an impending crisis gives people the opportunity to anticipate the loss, to start working through their anxiety or grief, and to make plans that will enable them to cope more adequately. The psychological processes stimulated by preparatory information include correcting faulty beliefs, reconceptualizing the threat, and engaging in realistic self-persuasion about the value of protective action, as well as developing concepts and self–instructions that enable the person to deal more effectively with setbacks (Janis, 1971, 1982).

We would expect stress inoculation procedures to be effective for any decision that entails severe short-term losses before substantial long-term gains are attained. Most decisions concerning personal health problems belong in this category because they usually require the person to undergo painful treatments and deprivations before his or her physical well-being improves. Much of the evidence concerning the effectiveness of stress inoculation procedures has come from studies of such decisions—voluntary submission to abdominal surgery, painful medical treatments, and the like. Correlational results from Janis's (1958) studies of surgical patients indicated that those who received information about the unpleasant consequences beforehand were less likely to overreact emotionally to setbacks and adverse events during the postdecisional period. Supporting evidence has come from a number of controlled field experiments with people who decided to accept their physicians' recommendations to undergo surgery (Egbert, Battit, Welch, & Bartlett, 1964; Johnson, 1966; Schmidt, 1966; Schmitt & Wooldridge, 1973; Vernon & Bigelow, 1974). These studies indicated that when physicians or nurses gave preoperative information about the stresses of surgery and ways of coping with those stresses, adult patients showed less postoperative distress and sometimes better recovery. Positive results on the value of stress inoculation also were found in studies of childbirth (Breen, 1975; Levy & McGee, 1975) and of noxious medical examinations requiring patients to swallow tubes (Johnson & Leventhal, 1974). Field experiments by Moran (1963) and by Wolfer and Visintainer (1975) with children on pediatric surgery wards yielded similar results.

A completely different area, that of work decisions, also has produced evidence that stress inoculation can dampen postdecisional conflict and minimize the tendency to reverse the decision when setbacks are encountered. New employees who are given realistic preparatory information at the time they are offered the job, or immediately after they accept the job, are more likely to stay with the organization (Gomersall & Myers, 1966; Macedonia, 1969; Wanous, 1973; Youngberg, 1963).

All these findings support the conclusion that many people will display higher stress tolerance in response to undesirable consequences if they have been given advance warnings about what to expect, together with sufficient reassurance, so that fear does not mount to an intolerably high level. There are exceptions, of course, such as neurotic personalities who are hypersensitive to any threat cues. But such considerations do not preclude the possibility that techniques of stress inoculation might be developed and used by decision counselors to help mitigate the impact of a wide variety of anticipated postdecisional setbacks, especially when the chosen course of action requires undergoing temporary losses in order to achieve long-term goals.

Meichenbaum's (1977) stress inoculation training program involves three main steps: (1) discussing the nature of stress reactions to provide clients with a conceptual framework and to motivate them to acquire new coping skills; (2) teaching and inducing rehearsal of coping skills—such as collecting information about what is likely to happen and arranging for ways to deal effectively with anxiety engendering events; and (3) encouraging the client to practice and apply the newly acquired coping skills to stressful conditions, by means of either role-playing in imagined stress situations or actual exposure to real-life stresses. This type of training has been found to be at least partially successful in increasing adherence to a number of stressful choices, including decisions to reenter phobic situations (Meichenbaum & Cameron, 1973) and to undergo pain (Turk, 1975). Some negative results, however, were reported by Girodo and Roehl (1976) for the decision to travel by plane by college women who were afraid of flying. After reviewing the positive and negative outcomes of studies employing stress inoculation training, Girodo (1977) suggested that the successful components are those that induce the person to reconceptualize the threat into nonthreatening terms and that all other self-statements serve merely as attention diversion mechanisms. Any such generalization, however, gives undue weight to a limited set of findings and is premature until we have well-replicated results from a variety of investigations that carefully test the effectiveness of each component of stress inoculation. It remains for the next phase of research to determine which components are the necessary and sufficient ingredients for promoting effective coping in stressful situations.

Related types of psychological intervention also need to be investigated, especially those that may help people to reconceptualize the stresses engendered by a stressful course of action, such as going through with a divorce, a drastic career change, or a surgical operation. For example, an effective coping device developed for use by counselors in hospitals and other medical settings by Langer, Janis, and Wolfer (1975) involves encouraging an optimistic reappraisal of anxiety provoking events to build up the clients' realistic hopes of dealing effectively with whatever suffering or setbacks might be encountered.

By inducing people to arrive at an accurate blueprint of the consequences that might be in store for them and of the coping resources at their disposal, decision counselors should be able to help clients build a basic attitude of self-confidence, maintain a vigilant approach throughout all the stages of decisionmaking, and develop realistic reassurances. This type of reassurance can have a dampening effect whenever a postdecisional setback occurs that otherwise might evoke a high degree of stress, resulting in defective coping reactions.

REFERENCES

Becker, M. H., & Maiman, L. A. Sociobehavioral determinants of compliance with health and medical care recommendations. *Medical Care,* 1975, *13,* 10–24.

Blackwell, B. The literature of delay in seeking medical care for chronic illnesses. *Health Education Monographs,* 1963, *3*(16), 3–31.

Breen, D. *The birth of a first child: Towards an understanding of femininity.* London: Tavistock, 1975.

Breznitz, S. Incubation of threat, duration of anticipation, and false alarm as determinants of fear reaction to an unavoidable frightening event. *Journal of Experimental Research in Personality,* 1967, *2,* 173–180.

————. False alarms: Their effects on fear and adjustment. In I. G. Sarason & C. D. Speilberger (eds.), *Stress and anxiety,* vol 3. New York: Wiley, 1976.

Broadhurst, A. Applications of the psychology of decisions. In M. P. Feldman & A. Broadhurst (eds.), *Theoretical and experimental bases of the behavior therapies.* New York: Wiley, 1976.

Chu, C. C. Fear arousal, efficacy, and imminency. *Journal of Personality and Social Psychology,* 1966, *4,* 517–524.

Cohen, F., & Lazarus, R. S. Coping with the stresses of illness. In G. C. Stone, F. Cohen & N. E. Adler (eds.), *Health psychology.* San Francisco: Jossey-Bass, 1979.

Cox, T. *Stress.* New York: Macmillan, 1978.

Duffy, E. *Activation and behavior.* New York: McGraw-Hill, 1962.

Edwards, W. The theory of decision making. *Psychological Bulletin,* 1954, *51,* 380–417.

Egbert, L., Battit, G., Welch, C., & Bartlett, M. Reduction of post-operative pain by encouragement and instruction. *New England Journal of Medicine,* 1964, *270,* 825–827.

Ekman, P., Freisen, W., & Ellsworth, P. *Emotion in the human face.* Oxford: Pergamon, 1972.

Elstein, A. A., & Bordage, G. Psychology of clinical reasoning. In G. C. Stone, F. Cohen, & N. E. Adler (eds.), *Health psychology.* San Francisco: Jossey-Bass, 1979.

Epstein, S. Expectancy and magnitude of reaction to a noxious UCS. *Psychophysiology,* 1973, *10,* 100–107.

Fenno, R. F. *The president's cabinet.* Cambridge: Harvard University Press, 1959.

Fritz, C., & Marks, E. The NORC studies of human behavior in disaster. *Journal of Social Issues,* 1954, *10,* 26–41.

George, A. Adaptation to stress in political decision making: The individual, small group, and organizational contexts. In G. V. Coelho, D. A. Hamburg, & J. E. Adams (eds.), *Coping and adaptation.* New York: Basic Books, 1974.

————. *Presidential decision making in foreign policy: The effective use of information and advice.* Boulder: Westview, 1980.

Girodo, M. Self-talk: Mechanisms in anxiety and stress management. In C. D. Spielberger & I. G. Sarason (eds.), *Stress and anxiety,* vol. 4. New York: Wiley, 1977.

Glass, D. *Behavioral antecedents of coronary heart disease.* Hillsdale: Erlbaum, 1977.

Goldsen, R. K., Gerhardt, P. T., & Handy, V. H. Some factors related to patient delay in seeking diagnosis for cancer symptoms. *Cancer,* 1957, *10,* 1–7.

GOMERSALL, E. R., & MYERS, M. S. Breakthrough in on-the-job training. *Harvard Business Review,* 1966, *44,* 62–72.

GRINKER, R. R., WILLERMAN, B., BRADLEY, A. D., & FASTARSKY, A. A study of psychological predisposition to the development of operational fatigue. *American Journal of Orthopsychiatry,* 1946, *16,* 191–214.

HACKETT, T. P., & CASSEM, N. H. Psychological management of the myocardial infarction patient. *Journal of Human Stress,* 1975, *1,* 25–38.

HAMILTON, V. Socialization, anxiety, and information processing: A capacity model of anxiety-induced performance. In I. G. Sarason & C. D. Spielberger (eds.), *Stress and anxiety,* vol. 2. New York: Wiley, 1975.

HOCHBAUM, G. *Public participation in medical screening programs: A sociopsychological study.* PHS publication no. 572. Bethesda: U.S. Public Health Service, 1958.

HOROWITZ, M. J. *Stress response syndromes.* New York: Aronson, 1976.

HOVLAND, C. I., JANIS, I. L., & KELLEY, H. H. *Communication and persuasion.* New Haven: Yale University Press, 1953.

INSKO, C. A., ARKOFF, A., & INSKO, U. M. Effects of high and low fear arousing communications upon opinions toward smoking. *Journal of Experimental Social Psychology,* 1965, *1,* 256–266.

IZARD, C. *The face of emotion.* New York: Appleton, 1971.

JANIS, I. L. *Air war and emotional stress.* New York: McGraw-Hill, 1951.

————. *Psychological stress,* New York: Wiley, 1958.

————. Psychological effects of warnings. In D. Chapman & G. Baker (eds.), *Man and society in disaster.* New York: Basic Books, 1962.

————. Effects of fear-arousal on attitude change. In L. Berkowitz (ed.), *Advances in experimental social psychology,* Vol. 3. New York: Academic, 1967.

————. *Stress and frustration.* New York: Harcourt, 1971.

————. The patient as decision maker. In D. Gentry (ed.), *Handbook of behavioral medicine.* New York: Guilford, 1983.

JANIS, I. L., DEFARES, P. B., & GROSSMAN, P. Hypervigilant reactions to threat. In H. Selye (ed.), *Selye's guide to stress research,* vol. 3. New York: Van Nostrand, 1982.

JANIS, I. L., & FESHBACH, S. Effects of fear-arousing communications. *Journal of Abnormal and Social Psychology,* 1953, *48,* 78–92.

JANIS, I. L., & LEVENTHAL, H. Human reactions to stress. In E. Borgatta & W. Lambert (eds.), *Handbook of personality theory and research.* Chicago: Rand McNally, 1968.

JANIS, I. L., & MANN, L. *Decision making: A psychological analysis of conflict, choice, and commitment.* New York: Free Press, 1977.

JANIS, I. L., & TERWILLIGER, R. An experimental study of psychological resistance to fear-arousing communications. *Journal of Abnormal and Social Psychology,* 1962, *65,* 403–410.

JENKINS, C. D. Psychosocial modifiers of response to stress. *Journal of Human Stress,* 1979, *5,* 3–15.

JOHNSON, J. E. *The influence of purposeful nurse-patient interaction on the patient's postoperative course.* ANA monograph series no. 2: Exploring medical-surgical nursing practice. New York: American Nurses' Association, 1966.

JOHNSON, J. E., & LEVENTHAL, H. Effects of accurate expectations and behavioral instructions on reactions during a noxious medical examination. *Journal of Personality and Social Psychology,* 1974, *29,* 710–718.

KAHNEMAN, D., & TVERSKY, A. Prospect theory: An analysis of decision under risk. *Econometrica,* 1979, *47,* 263–292.

KASL, S. V., & COBB, S. Health behavior, illness behavior, and sick role behavior. *Archives of Environmental Health,* 1966, *12,* 246–541.

Kelley, H. H., Condry, J. C., Jr., Dahlke, A. E., & Hill, A. H. Collective behavior in a simulated panic situation. *Journal of Experimental Social Psychology,* 1965, *1,* 20–54.

Kirscht, J. P., & Rosenstock, I. M. Patients' problems in following recommendations of health experts. In G. C. Stone, F. Cohen, & N. E. Adler (eds.), *Health psychology.* San Francisco: Jossey-Bass, 1979.

Kutner, B., Makover, H. B., & Oppenheim, A. Delay in the diagnosis and treatment of cancer: A critical analysis of the literature. *Journal of Chronic Diseases,* 1958, *7,* 95–120.

Langer, E. J., Janis, I., & Wolfer, J. Reduction of psychological stress in surgical patients. *Journal of Experimental Social Psychology,* 1975, *1,* 155–166.

Lazarus, R. S. *Psychological stress and the coping process.* New York: McGraw-Hill, 1966.

————. *Patterns of adjustment.* New York: McGraw-Hill, 1976.

Lee, W. *Decision theory and human behavior.* New York: Wiley, 1971.

Leventhal, H. Changing attitudes and habits to reduce risk factors in chronic disease. *American Journal of Cardiology,* 1973, *31,* 571–580.

Leventhal, H., Singer, R. E., & Jones, S. Effects of fear and specificity of recommendations. *Journal of Personality and Social Psychology,* 1965, *2,* 20–29.

Levy, J. M., & McGee, R. K. Childbirth as crisis: A test of Janis' theory of communication and stress resolution. *Journal of Personality and Social Psychology,* 1975, *31,* 171–179.

MacCurdy, J. *The structure of morale.* New York: Macmillan, 1943.

Macedonia, R. M. Expectations-press and survival. Doctoral dissertation, New York University, 1969.

Mann, L., Janis, I. L., & Chaplin, R. The effects of anticipation of forthcoming information on predecisional processes. *Journal of Personality and Social Psychology,* 1969, *11,* 10–16.

Mausner, B., & Platt, E. S. *Smoking: A behavioral analysis.* Oxford: Pergamon, 1971.

McGuire, W. J. The nature of attitudes and attitude change. In G. Lindzey & E. Aronson (eds.), *The handbook of social psychology,* vol. 3. Reading: Addison-Wesley, 1969.

Meichenbaum, D. *Cognitive-behavior modification: An integrative approach.* New York: Plenum, 1977.

Meichenbaum, D., & Cameron, R. An examination of cognitive and contingency variables in anxiety relief procedures. Manuscript, University of Waterloo, Waterloo, Ontario, 1973.

Meichenbaum, D., & Turk, D. C. The cognitive-behavioral management of anxiety, anger, and pain. In P. O. Davidson (ed.), *The behavioral management of anxiety, depression, and pain.* New York: Brunner/Mazel, 1976.

Miller, D. W., & Star, M. K. *The structure of human decisions.* Englewood Cliffs: Prentice-Hall, 1967.

Monat, A., & Lazarus, R. S. (eds.). *Stress and coping: an anthology.* New York: Columbia University Press, 1977.

Moran, P. A. An experimental study of pediatric admission. Master's thesis, Yale University School of Nursing, 1963.

Rachman, S. J. *Fear and courage.* San Francisco: Freeman, 1978.

Raiffa, H. *Decision analysis.* Reading: Addison-Wesley, 1968.

Rapoport, A., & Wallsten, T. S. Individual decision behavior. In P. H. Mussen & M. R. Rosenzweig (eds.), *Annual review of psychology,* vol. 23. Palo Alto: Annual Reviews, 1972.

Rogers, R. W., & Deckner, W. C. Effects of fear appeals and physiological arousal upon emotion, attitudes, and cigarette smoking. *Journal of Personality and Social Psychology,* 1975, *32,* 220–230.

Rogers, R. W., & Mewborn, C. R. Fear appeals and attitude change: Effects of a threat's noxiousness, probability of occurrence, and the efficacy of coping responses. *Journal of Personality and Social Psychology,* 1976, *34,* 54–61.

ROGERS, R. W., & THISTLETHWAITE, D. L. Effects of fear arousal and reassurance upon attitude change. *Journal of Personality and Social Psychology,* 1970, *15,* 227–233.

SCHACHTER, S. *The psychology of affiliation.* Stanford: Stanford University Press, 1959.

SCHMIDT, R. L. An exploratory study of nursing and patient readiness for surgery. Master's thesis, Yale University School of Nursing, 1966.

SCHMITT, F. E., & WOOLDRIDGE, P. J. Psychological preparation of surgical patients. *Nursing Research,* 1973, *22,* 108–116.

SCHULTZ, D. P. (ed.). *Panic and behavior: Discussion and readings.* New York: Random House, 1964.

SELYE, H. *The stress of life.* New York: McGraw-Hill, 1956.

SIGALL, H., & HELMREICH, R. Opinion change as a function of stress and communicator credibility. *Journal of Experimental Social Psychology,* 1969, *5,* 70–78.

SIMON, H. A. *Administrative behavior: A study of decision-making processes in administrative organization* (3d ed.). New York: Free Press, 1976.

SLOVIC, P., FISHHOFF, B., & LICHTENSTEIN, S. Behavioral decision theory. *Annual Review of Psychology,* 1977, *28,* 1–38.

TURK, D. T. Cognitive control of pain: A skills-training approach. Master's thesis, University of Waterloo, Waterloo, Ontario, 1975.

VERNON, D. T. A., & BIGELOW, D. A. The effect of information about a potentially stressful situation on responses to stress impact. *Journal of Personality and Social Psychology,* 1974, *29,* 50–59.

WANOUS, J. P. Effects of a realistic job preview on job acceptance, job attitudes, and job survival. *Journal of Applied Psychology,* 1973, *58,* 321–332.

WHEELER, D., & JANIS, I. L. *A practical guide for making decisions.* New York: Free Press, 1980.

WOLFENSTEIN, M. *Disaster: A psychological essay.* New York: Free Press, 1957.

WOLFER, J. A., & VISINTAINER, M. A. Pediatric surgical patients' and parents' stress responses and adjustment as a function of psychologic preparation and stress-point nursing care. *Nursing Research,* 1975, *24,* 244–255.

YOUNGBERG, C. F. An experimental study of job satisfaction and turnover in relation to job expectations and self-expectations. Doctoral dissertation, New York University, 1963.

7

Stress and Thought Processes

George Mandler

THOUGHT AND COGNITION

Any discussion of thought and stress must take into account the new approaches to cognition that have come to dominate psychology over the past two decades. Cognitive psychology—the new mentalism—does not restrict its domain to the contents of consciousness, much less to the aspects of those contents that can be verbalized. This discipline considers as mental events all those complex processes and mechanisms that need to be ascribed to the organism in order to make its thoughts and actions comprehensible. We have also learned to speak about consciousness, both as a personal datum and as an inferred mechanism the detailed functions of which still need to be explored (Mandler, 1975a).

Traditionally, and certainly earlier in this century, there was a significant tie between cognitive and phenomenological concerns. Cognitive psychologists often used as primitive terms those terms of the common language that referred to cognitive processes; frequently, these terms were coextensive with phenomenological usage. Thus, intuitively "obvious" judgmental words such as "good" and "bad," comparative terms such as "better" and "similar," and processes such as "conscious" and "self" formed the basic vocabulary of cognitive theories. The cognitive, human information processing approach searches instead for the processes and mechanisms that generate not only these terms and usages but in fact language as such. This approach to problems of thought and stress informs the following pages.

A Point of View and Some Definitions

We need to specify the kinds of events that are to be included under the term "thought processes." In the first instance we must distinguish between thought considered traditionally (and usually philosophically) and thought recast in the modern mold. Traditionally, thought processes were seen as coextensive with the contents of consciousness. Both thought

This chapter is a revised version of "Thought Processes, Consciousness and Stress," published in V. Hamilton and D. W. Warburton (eds.), *Human Stress and Cognition: An Information Processing Approach* (New York: Wiley, 1979). Copyright © 1978, 1982 by George Mandler.

and mental life frequently were considered to be characterized by consciousness, although the notion of unconscious thought has been popular at least since Freud. In the sense to be used here, *thought processes* refer to all complex transformations performed on environmental inputs, as well as intermediate products of the information processing chain. In this sense, the unconscious use of proper syntactic rules is as much a thought process as is the conscious interpretation of a passage of poetry. In considering all such processes as thoughts there is a danger of including all the organism's inferred activities as relevant to thought processes. However, I shall confine myself to those thought processes that are involved in complex activities, particularly problem-solving, and I shall frequently use measures of cognitive efficiency as the observable evidence for the operation of internal thought processes.

I have emphasized that thought processes can be found in both the conscious and the nonconscious mode. When I discuss stress and thought I shall be concerned to a large extent with an interaction between stress and conscious thought. My usual reference to *conscious states* and *events* will be to the limited-capacity system that has variously been identified with consciousness or focal attention. My own preference has been to view that capacity as being limited in the number of organized chunks of information it can simultaneously keep in the conscious state, i.e., that can be apprehended or kept in a working memory. Typically about five such chunks can be accommodated. However, my position in no sense excludes interpretations that ascribe the limitation to effort or some other variable. Agreement as to some limitation is now well established, regardless of niceties of theoretical interpretation of what it is that is limited or why it is so limited.

The notion that human information processing capacity is limited has been current in one form or another for at least a couple of centuries (Mandler, 1975c). However, the use of such a view for the explanation of interfering and capacity limiting events (such as stress) is relatively recent. One influential model relevant to the present discussion is Kahneman's (1973). He suggested that the capacity available varies with arousal (theoretically rather than autonomically defined); he defined "spare capacity" as the amount of capacity that remains after most of the available capacity has been appropriated for the primary task at hand. I shall argue that the definition of a "primary task" is at least difficult and that the amount of capacity available for any task facing the individual is a function of other tasks and other capacity demanding inputs with which some fixed limit of capacity must be shared.

What is it that becomes conscious? I cannot examine this question in detail here, but a more extended discussion is available elsewhere (Mandler, 1975a,c; Marcel, in preparation). I shall summarize some of the major charcteristics of conscious states, with particular reference to how and why they function in problem-solving and memory tasks. The first set of characteristics deals with consciousness during problem-solving in the broad sense. I shall discuss when and why particular structures are in the conscious state and when it is that conscious processes are both useful and necessary.

Consciousness and Problem-solving

I assume that the limited capacity characteristic of consciousness serves to reduce further the "blooming confusion" that the physical world potentially presents to the organism. Just as sensory end organs and central sensory transducers radically reduce and categorize the world of physical stimuli to the functional and manageable world that is in fact registered, the conscious process further radically reduces the available information to a small and manageable subset. Similarly, Marcel (in preparation) proposed that conscious states are constructed so that they are functionally useful and make optimal sense of all the available data. I assume, somewhat circularly, that the limitation of conscious capacity defines what is in fact cognitively manageable. While we do not know why the reduction is of the magnitude that we observe, it is reasonable to assume that some reduction is necessary. Consider a need for pairwise comparisons (in a choice situation) among *n* chunks in consciousness; clearly, that number must be limited if the organism is to make a choice within some reasonable time span.

I shall also emphasize that the human organism is preprogrammed to represent certain events consciously; among these are intense stimuli and, most important for the present discussion, internal physiological events such as autonomic nervous system activity. Whenever such events claim and preoccupy some part of the limited-capacity system, other cognitive functions will suffer, i.e., they will be displaced from conscious processing and problem-solving will be impaired. Particularly in the case of the interruption or failure of ongoing conscious and unconscious interactions with the world, signals from both the external and the internal world will demand conscious representation.

When are conscious processes most obvious? First of all, they are evident in the *construction and integration of mental and action structures.* Essentially, this use of consciousness applies to the learning process. Thoughts and actions typically are conscious before they become well integrated and subsequently automatic. Thus, for example, learning to drive a car is a conscious process, but the skilled driver acts automatically and unconsciously. Second, conscious processes are active during the *exercise of choices and judgments,* particularly with respect to the action requirements of the environment. These choices, often novel ones, require the consideration of possible outcomes and consequences and frequently involve *covert trial and error.* Third, conscious processes exercise an important function during *troubleshooting.* Thus, many automatic structures become conscious when they somehow fail in their functions—when a particular habitual way of acting fails or when a thought process cannot be brought to an appropriate conclusion. The experienced driver becomes aware of where she is and what she is doing when something new and different happens; for instance, when a near miss, a police car, or a traffic light suddenly registers. The troubleshooting function of consciousness permits repair of unconscious and automatic structures and subsequent choice from among other alternatives.

These arguments stress in particular the role of consciousness in action, in contrast to a contemplative, reflective view of conscious states. The specific role of consciousness in the execution and the voluntary initiation of actions has been explored by Norman and Shallice (1980).

Consciousness and Memory

Conscious processes also enter into the storage and retrieval mechanisms of memory. While it is commonplace to note that what is not attended to cannot be remembered, it is less clear how consciousness and memorial processes interact. Is consciousness both necessary and sufficient at the time of storage and retrieval? Despite recent arguments that attention to encoding cues is essential for later retrieval, there is increasing evidence that retrieval is possible through cues that may not have been encoded or attended to at the time of storage (cf. Anderson & Pichert, 1978). Fortunately, we need not solve these problems here. All that needs to be noted for present purposes are the conditions in which conscious processes obviously interact with memory, so that we can examine later how stress interacts with these conditions.

Storage mechanisms involve consciousness when attention is clearly paid to ongoing contexts within which some to-be-remembered events take place. In a sense, all conscious commentary on ongoing environmental events and activities produces some storable structures that may later be retrieved and that, conversely, may be interfered with under conditions of stress. We often construct some retrieval structures specifically for subsequent use, as, for example, when we note, "I must remember that John passed his examination and congratulate him the next time I see him." Both deliberate and incidental mnemonic devices fall under this rubric.

At the *retrieval* end, many memory search processes, particularly those involving complex searches, require conscious processing. Among these are the search processes that involve the generation of possible retrieval candidates ("His name started with an F; what was it?") and those that are usually preceded by wh——— questions like "Where did I leave my watch?" "What is his name?" or "When am I supposed to be in his office?"

I shall argue that the most important effect of stressors on thought processes is that they interfere specifically with the smooth operation of these conscious cogitations and cognitions.

A Cognitive Definition of Stress

Let me start with a psychological, rather than a physiological, definition of stress. External *stressors* are effective to the extent that they are perceived as dangerous or threatening, that is, to the extent that they are cognitively interpreted as inimical. One of the difficulties with so-called objective definitions of stressors has been their neglect of these cognitive mediators. Mason (1975), in a critique of Selye's stress concept, noted that emotional arousal is one of the most ubiquitous reactions in situations that are considered stressful. However, these emotional responses depend on psychological interpretive mechanisms. What determines the emotional quality of an event, such as its noxiousness or attractiveness, is not a question I can deal with in detail here. I shall assume, however, that the major consequence of such an interpretation or appraisal is the activation of a stress reaction that is psychologically functional. In other words, the consequence must be perceptible. I refer here primarily to the perception of autonomic nervous system (ANS) activity, particularly sympathetic activation. Thus, a situation is defined as *stressful* if and when the interpretive cognitive activities of the organism transform the input in such a way that a perceptible internal change results. I shall confine myself to the interaction between autonomic activity and stress. However, it is possible to entertain other reactions, such as hormonal release, that would have perceptible effects, as well as conditions under which some physiological activity occurs without direct cognitive interpretation. Thus, Selye (1975), in his reply to Mason, insisted that stress responses (physiologically defined) do and can occur even when no emotional arousal (or appraisal) is observed. If they do, and if they are perceived by the organism, then they properly belong under the rubric of thought and stress.

I shall neither consider problems of the milder stresses in this chapter nor undertake any fine-grained analysis of the limited-capacity system. Both tasks were performed admirably by Broadbent (1971). His major concern was not, as he himself noted, to generalize to and from real-life stresses but, rather, to refine the information model itself, particularly with respect to the decision processes that must be produced within such a system.

A THEORETICAL APPROACH TO STRESS AND THOUGHT

From a theoretical point of view, and following the general position outlined previously, the following processes and mechanisms need to be explored. What are the conditions and events that lead to autonomic activity; specifically, how is psychological stress initiated? What is the function of autonomic activity; how does it affect cognitive functioning? Finally, how does autonomic arousal affect conscious thought processes?

The Conditions of Stress

Questions about the conditions that produce psychological stress have bedeviled most theories of stress and emotion. Most frequently, answers have taken the form of lists of such conditions. These lists enumerate what might be evaluated as dangerous or noxious but rarely provide a categorical principle that unites the instances. Psychoanalytic theory has taken a step in this direction by speaking about the threat or danger (perceived by the individual) of excess stimulation or unmanageable impulses. However, stress theory in general has defined stressors as that class of events that produce stress reactions in the organism. I shall use an approach that I (Mandler, 1964, 1975c), previously advanced, namely, *interruption theory*. This position has cognate but discontinuous predecessors in the so-called conflict theories of emotion dating back at least to Herbart in the early nineteenth century (cf. Mandler, 1979a).

The basic premise of interruption theory is that automatic activity results whenever some organized action or thought process is interrupted. The term "interruption" is used in as neutral a sense as possible. That is, any event, external or internal to the individual, that prevents completion of some action, thought sequences, plan, or processing structure is considered to be interrupting. Such interruption might consist of either active or passive blocking by environmental events; it might be an internal thought process that prevents or blocks the completion of another process; or it may occur when one or another plan or processing strategy cannot be brought to completion because it is inconsistent or discrepant with some other currently active processing activity. Interruption can occur in the perceptual, cognitive, behavioral, or problem-solving domains—the consequence will always be the same, namely, autonomic activity. It is important to note that interruption should not be imbued with negative characteristics; this process simply and neutrally involves the disconfirmation of an expectancy or the noncompletion of some initiated action. Interruption is not synonymous with frustration or other related terms. Interruption may be interpreted emotionally in any number of ways, ranging from the most joyful to the most noxious.

The degree of autonomic activity depends primarily on two factors: the degree of organization of the interrupted process and the severity of the interruption. *Degree of organization* refers to the stereotypy and habitual character of the act or thought process. An action or thought sequence that is in the process of organization still has much variance associated with it. As a result, much irrelevant thought and behavior occurs within the sequence; there is no well-organized structure to be interrupted. However, when the sequence has become invariant and its parts occur with a high degree of expectancy or even with certainty, then the interruptive process will run its course. *Severity of interruption* presumably has its main source in an iterative process. If the environment, for example, not only supports but actually demands the execution of a particular action or cognitive process that is interrupted, then there will be repeated attempts to take up the sequence again, which action, when repeatedly interrupted, will potentiate the arousal. In other words, interruption is severe when the process is continuously reinitiated and reinterrupted. In addition, some cognitive structures are more salient than others to the current plans and goals of the individual; the more salient, the more severe the autonomic reaction to interruption. However, we know relatively little about the psychological structure of salience.

In short, I assume that most (but not necessarily all) psychologically stressful situations are the result of interruption. Stressors are interruptors, but not all interruptors are stressors.

The Functions of Autonomic Nervous System Arousal

If interruption produces autonomic activity and if that activity produces the major intrapsychic consequence of stress, how does peripheral autonomic activity interact with the information processing apparatus? I shall not discuss here the function of autonomic arousal in potentiating, coloring, and distinguishing the experiences usually called emotional. I (Mandler, 1975c) have extensively addressed these issues elsewhere, noting that *autonomic activity* is more than a homeostatic mechanism, related to the internal economy of the organism; it has other important adaptive functions in selecting and coding important events and in providing a secondary alert system.

The autonomic nervous system functions as a secondary support system in response to events that require extensive cognitive interpretation. Thus, with the individual focused and attending to some set of events, another occurrence in the environment might signal an interruption—an unexpected and unprepared for set of circumstances. This interruption automatically triggers the autonomic nervous system, and feedback from autonomic events tells the organism that some event is occurring in the environment that requires immediate attention. The system has the paradoxical advantage of being slow; thus, it acts as a backup. During the one to two seconds of its initiation, other cognitive sensory events may take place that handle the situation. If they do not, then the autonomic reaction is available as the second signal (assuming that the first sensory-perceptual one has been ignored). If no appropriate action has been taken to adapt to the new environmental events, then the secondary signal will draw the attention of the organism to some initially cognitively unspecified emergency. The attention to, and cognitive evaluation of, that new state of affairs follow the action of the autonomic signal.

The evidence for an attentional effect of autonomic arousal is threefold. The Laceys (1974) showed that attentional activity is accompanied by cardiac deceleration. Such deceleration would attenuate the internal, attention demanding, "noisy" aspect of cardiac activity (acceleration). Thus, the primitive response of the organism is a parasympathetic one that not only conserves energy but also prepares the organism for more adequate coping with the environmental situation. Second, there is an independent response of cardiac deceleration in response to acceleration. Here again, though with a longer latency (1.0–1.5 seconds), a noise reducing response occurs automatically in response to sympathetic activation. First, then, attention reduces internal noise; subsequently, internal noise produces its own negative feedback. The third line of evidence comes primarily from Frankenhaeuser (e.g., 1975, 1976), who suggested that autonomic activity and the accompanying catecholamine release are not obsolete, primitive responses. Rather, she argued that such activity facilitates adjustment to cognitive and emotional pressure. In brief, there is some evidence that the autonomic nervous system may be involved in environmental scanning and attention to important events.

Attentional Effects of Stress and Autonomic Arousal

Stress—defined as an emergency signaling interruption—can have the effect of increasing attention to crucial events in the environment. Under these circumstances, the stressful situation produces highly adaptive reactions and improves the coping response. On the other hand, autonomic activity may act as noise in the cognitive system. I am referring here to the organism's conscious perception of autonomic activity, which automatically demands attentional capacity. If the individual attends to these internal events, then less focal attention is available for other task-directed and coping activities. Therefore, to the extent that autonomic activity is past the point of alerting the individual, continuing autonomic arousal will be registered within consciousness and will interfere with ongoing cognitive efficiency. In that sense, then, autonomic activity becomes noise.

There is another aspect of the stress situation that requires attentional or conscious capacity, namely, the conditions that themselves produce the stress. These conditions—whether external or internal—are the primary causes of autonomic noise. As such they may be considered noxious (e.g., interpreted negatively) by the individual and therefore subject to some effort toward their removal. For example, during the performance of some skill or task, continuous comments from a co-worker or loud noises may be interpreted as stressful. As a result, some effort, involving conscious capacity, might be made to remove these noxious conditions. Hamilton (1975), following Kahneman's (1973) analysis, looked at these capacity demanding efforts. In a discussion of anxiety, he referred to attempts at avoiding the stressful conditions as a secondary task that interferes with the primary task facing the individual.

In short, the problem of stress is twofold: both the internal autonomic signals and the conditions that generate these signals require some conscious capacity and thereby interfere with the performance of targeted tasks.

I now turn to a specific application of these general theoretical considerations. I shall start with a rather antiquated but still serviceable notion embodied in the *Yerkes-Dodson law,* (1908) which describes the relation between efficiency and stress (or stimulation). I will then bring that view into contact with modern concepts and consider some current evidence on the effect of stress and autonomic activity on attention and consciousness. From that vantage point I shall then consider the more general relation among thought, consciousness, and stress.

THE YERKES–DODSON LAW, THEN AND NOW

I have assumed that the effect of physically or environmentally defined stressors depends on their analysis as threats and stresses. There are, of course, stressors that demand a stressful interpretation or that automatically produce stress reactions (particularly, autonomic nervous system reactions). When such a demand or effect is obvious, we need not speak complexly about cognitive interpretations but can talk directly of stressor effects. Among these are inescapably painful (because extremely intense) stimuli, such as electric shock. Talking about stressors rather than about interpreted stresses and threats enables us to make contact with an older (frequently behaviorist) literature that defined stresses exclusively in terms of environmental, physical variables. Perhaps the oldest and single most important finding in that tradition is enshrined in the Yerkes-Dodson law. Yerkes and Dodson (1908) discovered that while performance on an easy discrimination task improves with increasing shock intensity, performance on a difficult task is worse with weak and strong shocks and optimal with intermediate-level shocks. This curvilinear relationship constitutes the Yerkes-Dodson law.

In 1940, Freeman confirmed an inverted U-shaped relationship between arousal and cognitive efficiency. This statement was important because it set the stage for several decades of preoccupation with the rather vague concept of arousal, specifically, arousal as a theoretical entity rather than as a measurable and observable set of events that occupy attentional capacity. Indexes of arousal have varied widely, from general muscular activity, to sympathetic nervous system activity, to activity of the reticular activating system. In the process it has been pointed out that there is no single unitary and useful concept of arousal (cf. Lacey, 1967). I shall avoid the vagueness of the arousal concept by restricting myself to the stress or threat induced effects of peripheral autonomic nervous system activity. Consequently, I shall use the terms "autonomic activity" and "autonomic arousal" interchangeably.

The next step in the evolving understanding of the inverted U–shaped function that relates performance, efficiency, and cognitive competence to arousal was Easterbrook's (1959) *cue utilization hypothesis*. Easterbrook suggested that "the number of cues utilized in any situation tends to become smaller with increase in emotion" (p. 197). Since he equated emotion with emotional drive, the extension to arousal has frequently been made in the past. Furthermore, Easterbrook related the restricted utilization of cues to changes in attention, without, however, providing mechanisms for the restriction in attention associated with emotion or arousal.

I can now return to my initial discussion of the effects of autonomic arousal on the limited-capacity system. Given the presence of attention demanding occurrences, it is to be expected that with increasing autonomic activity the number of events (cues) that can share conscious attention will be limited. Easterbrook (1959) noted that in some cases restrictions in attention (and effective cues) may improve cognitive efficiency. Clearly, when the excluded cues are irrelevant to the thought processes at hand, efficiency will be improved, but when a task requires attention to a wide range of cues, then narrowing of attention will have deleterious effects.

A position that cannot be maintained is that there exists some specific law relating efficiency to arousal. Understanding the relation between efficiency and stress requires an analysis of specific stressors, an approach to arousal that assigns it definable properties rather than global, unspecified effects, and knowledge about the requirements of the task and, finally, the individual's perception of the task and the ensuing stress. Hockey and MacLean (1981) developed an approach to stress that involves such an analysis, focusing on the interaction between different stressors and the component requirements of a task.

COGNITIVE EFFICIENCY AND EXTREME STRESS

Stress may be experienced in the most innocuous situations. Whether trying to open a door that is stuck, to fill out a complicated bureaucratic form, or to assemble a child's toy, most of us have experienced states of high stress. Repeated attempts to open the door, to follow the instructions, or to fit part A between parts B and C may fail; autonomic arousal then increases; and irrelevant ideation ("Those idiots, incompetents, and fools!!!") and paniclike behavior may ensue. Each failure is an interrupted sequence, and each interruption further potentiates autonomic arousal.

The notion that such sequences have attention narrowing consequences is not new.

Callaway and Dembo (1958) concluded that "emotional states, such as anxiety, panic, and orgasm . . . produce a . . . narrowing of attention. . . . a correlation between narrowed attention and central sympathomimetic activity is demonstrated" (p. 88). Similarly, the tendency to engage in task-irrelevant behavior is well known. Bachrach (1970) described the psychological problem of panic in deep-sea diving as "a strong, fearful perception by an individual that he is out of control, that he is not capable of coping with the situation in which he finds himself, leading to behaviors that not only do not solve the problem posed by the danger but actually may work directly against such solution" (p, 125).

Baddeley (1972) published the best analysis and summary of the available evidence on cognitive efficiency in dangerous environments. His conclusion is worth citing in full:

> [It] appears that one way in which danger affects performance is through its influence on the subject's breadth of attention. A dangerous situation will tend to increase the level of arousal which in turn will focus the subject's attention more narrowly on those aspects of the situation he considers most important. If the task he is performing is regarded by him as most important, then performance will tend to improve; if on the other hand it is regarded as peripheral to some other activity, such as avoiding danger, then performance will deteriorate. With experience, subjects appear to inhibit anxiety in the danger situation and hence reduce the degree of impairment. We still do not know what mechanisms mediate the effect of arousal on the distribution of attention, or what is involved in the process of adaptation to fear. (Pp. 545)

The evidence for Baddeley's conclusion comes from a variety of sources, which I shall review briefly, together with more recent evidence. First, Baddeley (1971) and others found that equal degrees of nitrogen narcosis (when air is breathed at its highest pressure) diminished efficiency to different degrees when the test was conducted in the open sea or in a pressure-chamber situation. The greater impairment in the more realistic situation could be ascribed only to the greater degree of danger perceived by the subjects. In addition, more anxious subjects were more easily influenced, (i.e., their functioning impaired) by the increased "danger" of the more realistic situation.

Given these observations, does the perception of danger behave like arousal; can it be subsumed under the cue utilization hypothesis of Easterbrook? Hockey (1970) showed that an increase in noise improved performance on centrally attended stimuli at the expense of peripheral ones. While Poulton (1976a) questioned some of Hockey's results on procedural grounds, another study by Bacon (1974) made the same point more persuasively. Bacon found not only that arousal impaired attention to peripheral cues but also that it narrowed the range of cues processed by systematically "reducing responsiveness to those aspects of the situation which initially attract a lesser degree of attentional focus" (p. 81). Bacon attributed this loss to a diminution in subjects' sensitivity and argued that arousal affects the capacity limitation directly.

The bridge to the danger situation was provided by Weltman, Smith & Egstrom (1971), who demonstrated the same diminution of attention to peripheral stimuli in a task simulating danger. Experimental subjects showed both increased autonomic activity and decrease in attention to peripheral stimuli, but no decrement in performance of a central task.

Thus, the conclusion holds that stress, like noise, reduces attentional capacity and narrows it to central tasks. Recurring to Bacon's (1974) results, we can assume that what is perceived as psychologically central will be determined by the initial attention assigned to it. What is originally maximally attended to is central; whatever receives less attention is perceived as peripheral and will suffer the greater loss of attention under stress. Whenever the target task is central, increased autonomic arousal may well improve performance. This point was made clearly by Baddeley (1972) and subsequently adumbrated by Poulton (1976b) in an attack on the notion that noise necessarily interferes with efficiency.

Whereas most of the early research on the effect of noise on human performance used relatively high levels of noise (95dB or greater), recent studies have indicated that these effects can also be found with moderate levels. Broadbent (1981) reviewed these studies and he concluded that levels of noise found in home or office (70–90dB) affect efficiency, that such effects are especially likely to be found when the allocation of effort between two or more activities is measured and that the nature of these effects seems to be related to a general state of reactivity or arousal.

Finally, we must deal with the observation that experienced subjects show few or none of the deleterious effects of stress (environmentally defined). First, I note again that stress must be subjectively defined. For the experienced subject the perception of subjectively or objectively defined stress must necessarily be different from that shown by the naive observer. Apart from what is perceived or judged to be stressful, the effect of the stressor differs radically for experienced and inexperienced subjects. Hammerton and Tickner (1967) showed increased efficiency prior to a parachute jump as a function of previous jumping experience. Similarly, Epstein and Fenz (1965) found that novice jumpers had a high pulse rate before a jump, which dropped to a normal level upon landing, while experienced jumpers showed the reverse effect. The same lack of stress responses has been found in highly trained astronauts and has been explained in identical fashion (Mandler, 1967).

The effect of experience must be related to the proposition that autonomic arousal is, to a very large degree, a function of the interruption of ongoing behavior, plans, and expectations. Stress, under this explanation, occurs when no actions or though structures are available to handle the situation the individual faces. Astronauts, as an example, are trained to have available response sequences, plans, and problem-solving strategies for all imaginable emergencies. Emergencies are thus transformed into routine situations and by definition are not stressful. Conversely, the novice parachutist ruminates on possible outcomes, none of which he is able to handle—emergencies that he either imagines or remembers and for which no action structures are available. At the end of the jump, this interruptive effect, interrupting thoughts about successful completion of the jump, is eliminated: the original plan (to complete the jump successfully) has been achieved. At the more speculative level, one might assume that for the experienced parachutist who enjoys the jump (both emotionally and cognitively), landing interrupts that enjoyment or even elation; more concretely, landing terminates a complete and competent action structure. Confirming reports are available anecdotally from sky divers who cannot wait to go up again for the next jump.

As far as Baddeley's (1972) final question about the mechanisms that mediate the effect of arousal on attention are concerned, I have provided such a mechanism in the introductory theoretical passages. Autonomic arousal narrows attention in two ways: first, automatically by the direct action of the autonomic nervous system and, second, indirectly by occupying some of the limited capacity of attention/consciousness and thereby reducing the attentional capacity available for those events or stimuli originally perceived as central (cf. Bacon, 1974).

STRESS, COPING, AND MASTERY

Stress may result in cognitive processes that draw attention to centrally important aspects of the environment. Such efforts are often described as relevant to the *mastery of stress,* to our ability to control a particular situation. Mastery refers to the perception that the events in our personal world may be brought under our control. This sense of mastery may be important not so much because it has direct effects on our actions but because a sense of control, or mastery, colors the cognitive interpretation of our world. It is generally seen as good to be in control of our world, and as the world is appraised as good the emotional tone will be positive. Things that frighten us may become amusing when we have a sense of mastery, even though our actual control of the situation has not changed. What has changed is the relevance of the event to our ongoing plans. If events or conditions are seen as relevant and as impeding (interrupting) ongoing action, they may become frightening; however, if they are seen as irrelevant, or impeding only in the short term, they may become amusing and tolerable. When a friendly colleague criticizes our work, the remark is often seen as constructive and conducive to mastery, while the identical remark from a supervisor may easily appear threatening. The objective absence of control is not necessarily seen as negative; consider the enjoyment some people experience on a rollercoaster, while others in the identical situation are frightened. It is the subjective sense of control that is important rather than the objective control of the environment.

Without doubt, the sense of mastery in many cases reduces the deleterious effects of stress and alleviates the subjective sense of emotional disturbance. I assume that this effect may occur under two conditions:

1. Any action related directly to the threatening, interrupting situation or event may change that event and reduce its threatening aspect, i.e., interrupting effect. In that case an action by the individual has changed the situation from one that is arousing (and interpreted as threatening) to one that is nonarousing and thereby has removed its threatening aspects.

2. Without any changes in its objective aspects, a situation may be reinterpreted in such a way that it is no longer perceived as interrupting. The overall structure or plan under which the situation or event is perceived has changed significantly to remove its interrupting aspect or to reinterpret the interruptive event as beneficial. In the latter case, the autonomic arousal will persist but will be positively interpreted. The rollercoaster ride seen as a joyful situation that will terminate when planned thus becomes nonfrightening. The cognitive removal of interruptive aspects occurs less frequently. Consider the case of a student who received a grade of 66 on an examination. She had hoped for at least a 75 in order to pass the course. With her plans disrupted, the student is in a state of autonomic arousal. Then she notices a slip of paper appended to the examination that says that the test was unusually difficult and that 66 will be recorded as a passing grade. The same event is now reinterpreted; its interruptive, as well as negative, aspect has been removed.

This discussion leads into the general topic of coping, appraisal, and reappraisal. The most important contribution to this problem has been made by Lazarus and his colleagues (e.g., Folkman, Schaefer, & Lazarus, 1979; Lazarus, 1975). Gal and Lazarus (1975) examined the question of why activity as such apparently has the capacity to lower stress reactions. They distinguished between threat related and non-threat related activities. The former lower stress reactions because they provide a feeling of control or mastery. Non-threat related activities, however, distract or divert attention from threat. This latter explanation should be added to the account I have given here. It is certainly likely that in some cases of threat a restriction of attention may reduce the perception of both the threatening event, as well as the internal autonomic activity. However, activity as such is not stress reducing in all cases. In panic situations, for example, continuing interrupted activity not only fails to reduce the experience of stress but usually increases it. In general, the question of mastery and control, as well as of the effects of activity as such, requires detailed analysis of the task, the perceived situation, and the general structures that guide thought and action at each point in time.

STRESS AND INTELLECTUAL EFFICIENCY

An area in which questions about the mastery of threat and the effect of interpreted threat on efficiency have been of continuing interest is the performance of complex intellectual tasks. This area of research permits us to come relatively close to observing the outcomes of complex thought processes, while at the same time addressing a topic of practical importance. Specifically, investigators are concerned with the effect of perceived threat on the performance of testlike tasks.

The general conclusions accepted today derive from a few studies published some decades ago. The major strategy is to select individuals who report (on paper and pencil tests) high and low degrees of anxiety or concern about test situations (e.g., Mandler & Sarason, 1952). These test anxiety scales have been variously interpreted as measuring anxiety drive, traits, or attitudes. My own preference (Mandler, 1972) has been to assume that the "high anxious subject tells himself that . . . appropriate (not necessarily useful or adaptive) behavior in a test situation consists of observing his own behavior, of examining his failures, of ruminating about . . . his emotional reactions" (p. 407). The low anxious individual, on the other hand, "orients his behavior and cognitions towards the specific requirements of the task, excluding extraneous ideations" (p. 407). This line of thought is an elaboration of a distinction between task-relevant and task-irrelevant responses originally proposed by Seymour Sarason and me.

In our original study (Mandler & Sarason, 1952), we noted that high anxious individuals performed worse on intelligence tasks and that the absence of any further instructions was most beneficial for this group; on the other hand, information that they had failed was most helpful for low anxious individuals. In a subsequent study, I. G. Sarason (1961) found that high anxious subjects solved anagrams more efficiently than did low anxious individuals when the situation was nonthreatening, that is, when subjects were instructed that they were not expected to finish all the anagrams because they were very difficult and harder than usual. When subjects were told that the task was related directly to intelligence level and that they should finish easily if of average intelligence, low anxious individuals performed significantly better than did high anxious ones.

These and other studies confirm that many people bring stress into a situation, just as situations bring out the individual's stress potential. Both a potentially threatened individual and a properly interpretable situation are needed to produce the stress reaction. In turn, this reaction presumably takes two forms; first, the individual ruminates about the irrelevant aspects of the task, including his own state, performance, and reactions; second, the threat interpretation produces autonomic activity, which itself demands attention. Both sets of internal events vie for the individual's limited cognitive capacity and thereby reduce the attentional, conscious capacity available for thought processes required by the task itself.

THE STRANGE AND THE UNUSUAL: SOME CONDITIONS OF STRESS

In this section I want to explore some further aspects of events that are usually called stressful and to consider how they come to be stressful.

It is generally assumed that the strange, the unusual, and the unexpected are stressful. Clearly, this everyday language usage refers exactly to the kinds of events that are interruptive in the sense used here. Two major positions in the psychology of stress and emotion have emphasized the importance of the strange and the unusual. In the framework of his attachment theory, Bowlby (e.g., 1969) sensitively described the general problem of fear and its ontogeny. Similarly, Hebb (e.g., 1946) discussed the occurrence of fear in response to perceptual discrepancies. It is clear from both expositions that fear of the strange does not occur until familiarity and expectations have been developed. Stranger anxiety in infants does not occur until schemata for faces have developed. Chimpanzees are terrorized by detached parts of chimp bodies only after having experienced intact bodies. Thus, the strange is interruptive because the structures that are evoked in and by a particular situation are violated; the strange is unassimilable. However, apart from the violation of specific expectations by the strange and the unusual, another characteristic of human cognition produces fright. In the presence of events and perceptions that are new, i.e., for which no current schemata or structures are appropriate, the human individual will search for an appropriate way to interpret the surround—an automatic process that I previously called *meaning analysis* (1975c). In a novel situation, no such appropriate structure will be found, but in the search process each attempted structure will fail of environmental support and thus be interrupted. I consider this unavailability of appropriate response or action alternatives, this helplessness in the face of the environment, to be the essential psychological basis of the set of subjective reactions subsumed under the label "anxiety."

Shifting to intrapsychic stressful events, consider first the condition under which ongoing cognitive structures are interrupted by their own consequences. Consider some plan that is not executed but is examined within the conscious system. If a consequence of this plan is discovered to be incompatible with some other, maybe hierarchically higher, plan, or with some expected environmental condition, then we are once again confronted with an interruption, an intrapsychic cognitive one. These thought processes will lead to arousal just as an external event will. For example, planning to attend the theater and then remembering a previous engagement for the same evening would lead to stress and coping activities.

Plans and cognitive structures are hierarchically arranged (cf. Miller, Galanter, & Pribram, 1960), and the stress produced by the interruption of a particular plan will vary with the number of plans subordinate and superordinate to the interrupted one that are disrupted at the same time. For example, the interruption of a low-level plan ("I want to have eggs for breakfast, but there aren't any in the house") may not be too arousing and stressful because a higher priority is not affected ("I want to have breakfast and might as well eat some cereal"). The important point is that any interruptive event must be analyzed in terms of the level of plan and the hierarchy involved. Thus, when all levels of plans are threatened (cannot be completed) by some event, the degree of autonomic arousal will be intense and the stress most severe.

Both action structures and intrapsychic cognitive structures may be interrupted either when an expected event or sequence fails to occur or when something unexpected happens. Both cases involve interruption and autonomic arousal and usually, in the kind of situation considered in this chapter, are interpreted as negative and unpleasant. In either case, the interruption of a current cognitive structure automatically focuses consciousness on that structure and the interruptive event or thought. I noted earlier that one of the functions of consciousness is that it becomes the arena for troubleshooting when conscious or unconscious structures fail. This phenomenon was labeled the *law of awareness* by Claparède (1934): people become aware of automatic actions when these are disrupted or fail. It is reasonable to assume that one of the adaptive functions of interruption is to bring some problem into consciousness, where repair and coping activities can take place. If such "snapping into consciousness" takes place, we expect the field of focal attention to be narrowed and, under many circumstances, other ongoing activity to be impaired because of the restricted amount of focal capacity that remains available. However, much troubleshooting will occur without any stressing sequelae. When working on a complex problem, we often expect to find one or more structures to be inadequate for the solution of the problem at hand. In that case, the operative executive plan expects interruptions and the expected does not lead to autonomic arousal. Expected interruptions of this kind will be innocuous only if they are not perceived as destructive of the executive plan. The anxious individual, in contrast, who expects to fail, will perceive these interruptions as fatal or at least deleterious to the goal at hand. Previously I noted that well-trained individuals (e.g., astronauts) have exactly the useful kinds of expectations that include troubleshooting; consequently, interruption may not produce a stress response.

PROBLEM-SOLVING, MEMORY, AND STRESS

How is stress likely to affect the efficiency of memory and its component mechanisms? It is generally agreed that the degree of elaboration of an event will determine how efficiently its details are recorded and how easily the memory can be retrieved. The position was introduced under the rubric "depth of processing" but has recently been discussed more frequently in terms of elaboration (Craik & Lockhart, 1972; Craik & Tulving, 1975) I (Mandler, 1979b) have suggested that elaboration describes the complexity of interstructural links that are developed in the process of encoding and that these links provide better access at the time of retrieval. Both integrative (intrastructural) and elaborative (interstructural) requirements make demands on conscious capacity and thereby limit the amount of storage activities possible under various circumstances (see the discussion of isocapacity functions in Mandler, 1979b).

These assumptions about memory and storage retrieval suggest that the restriction of conscious capacity that occurs as a function of stress should have obvious effects on memory functions. Not only will events be less elaborately coded under conditions of stress (we remember fewer things that occur under stress and these less well), but also—with central focusing during stress—we should remember a few salient events that occurred under stress extremely well. Anecdotal evidence, at least, bears out this hypothesis. One would also expect retrieval under stress to show similar characteristics, with the stressful occurrence itself possibly providing additional retrieval cues.

Unfortunately, there is little experimental evidence on the effects of stress on complex storage and retrieval processes. The available data tend to be rather dated and limited to supporting the point that stress (frequently defined as failure) impairs memory. Much of this evidence was collected under behaviorist paradigms and therefore tends to emphasize drive-performance interactions and pays little heed to underlying cognitive processes. The only extensive set of data concerns the effect of stress on short-term memory and shows that practically any kind of stress, failure experience, or uncontrollable noise will impair short-term memory retrieval. Since short-term memory, as used in the experimental literature, is to some extent coextensive with span of attention or consciousness, such a finding is not suprising and adds little to our understanding of more complex processes. To the extent that short-term memory experiments require the holding in consciousness (or working memory) of the to-be-remembered material, we would naturally expect that any set of events that makes demands on limited processing capacity at the same time will interfere with these short-term storage processes.

If the experimental literature on stress and memory has failed to elucidate underlying cognitive processes, experimental work on stress and problem-solving has failed equally. Both lay people and psychologists recognize that under stress the thought processes involved in problem-solving demonstrate the kind of narrowing and stereotyping that we would expect on the basis of the present analysis. If much of problem-solving involves the manipulation in consciousness of alternatives, choices, probable and possible outcomes and consequences, and alternative goals, then the internal noise of stress and autonomic arousal should and does interfere with problem-solving. Thought processes become narrowed in the sense that only obvious alternatives are considered and no conscious capacity is available to assess new alternatives. In the same sense, thought becomes stereotyped and habitual. Conversely, the possibility of bringing in new strategies and weighing their possible effect is reduced; thought becomes repetitive and unelaborated. In a sense, the restriction on memorial elaboration refers to the very same elaboration that is restricted during problem-solving under stress. We have seen examples of these consequences in the discussion of the available data on the problem of central and peripheral processing under stress.

What is needed are some fine-grained experimental analyses of these processes during problem-solving. How and when does the introduction of stress (however produced or defined) restrict the available alternatives in the conscious state? Which processes are suppressed or removed from consciousness and in what order? Does the stress induced inability to solve a problem potentiate further stress reactions because of the interruptive process of the failure to solve the problem? How is hypothesis sampling affected by stress conditions? Under what circumstances can the focusing that occurs under stress be beneficial? How does attention to centrally relevant problems under stress promote more efficient problem-solving? The research potential is indeed great, but our preoccupation with the unstressed mind has restricted experimental work on these problems.

I hope that the present analysis will stimulate such explorations. More important, however, is the demonstration that modern cognitive and information processing analyses are not confined to purely cognitive problems but can be fruitfully extended to problems that have previously been segregated under discussions of emotions, motivations, and drives.

REFERENCES

ANDERSON, R. C., & PICHERT, J. W. Recall of previously unrecallable information following a shift in perspective. *Journal of Verbal Learning and Verbal Behavior,* 1978, *17,* 1–12.

BACHRACH, A. J. Diving behavior. In *Human performance and scuba diving.* Chicago: Athletic Institute, 1970.

BACON, S. J. Arousal and the range of cue utilization. *Journal of Experimental Psychology,* 1974, *102,* 81–87.

BADDELEY, A. D. Diver performance. In J. D. Woods & J. N. Lythgoe (eds.), *Underwater science.* New York: Oxford University Press, 1971.

————. Selective attention and performance in dangerous environments. *British Journal of Psychology,* 1972, *63,* 537–546.

BOWLBY, J. *Attachment and loss,* vol. 1. London: Hogarth & Institute of Psychoanalysis, 1969.

BROADBENT, D. E. *Decision and stress.* New York: Academic, 1971.

————. The effects of moderate levels of noise on human performance. In J. V. Tobias & E. D. Schubert (eds.), *Hearing research and theory.* New York: Academic, 1981.

CALLAWAY, E., III, & DEMBO, D. Narrowed attention: A psychological phenomenon that accompanies a certain physiological change. *AMA Archives of Neurology and Psychiatry,* 1958, *79,* 74–90.

CLAPARÈDE, E. *La genèse de l'hypothese.* Geneva: Kundig, 1934.

CRAIK, F. I. M., & LOCKHART, R. S. Levels of processing: A framework for memory research. *Journal of Verbal Learning and Verbal Behavior,* 1972, *11,* 671–684.

CRAIK, F. I. M. & TULVING, E. Depth of processing and the retention of words in episodic memory. *Journal of Experimental Psychology,* 1975, *104,* 268–294.

EASTERBROOK, J. A. The effect of emotion on cue utilization and the organization of behavior. *Psychological Review,* 1959, *66,* 183–201.

EPSTEIN, S., & FENZ, W. D. Steepness of approach and avoidance gradients in humans as a function of experience: Theory and experiment. *Journal of Experimental Psychology,* 1965, *70,* 1–13.

FOLKMAN, S., SCHAEFER, C., & LAZARUS, R. S. Cognitive processes as mediators of stress and coping. In V. Hamilton & D. M. Warburton (eds.) *Human stress and cognition: An information processing approach.* London: Wiley, 1979.

FRANKENHAEUSER, M. Experimental approaches to the study of catecholamines and emotion. In L. Levi (ed.), *Emotions: Their parameters and measurement.* New York: Raven, 1975.

————. The role of peripheral catecholamines in adaptation to understimulation and overstimulation. In G. Serban (eds.), *Psychopathology of human adaptation.* New York: Plenum, 1976.

FREEMAN, G. L. The relationship between performance level and bodily activity level. *Journal of Experimental Psychology,* 1940, *26,* 602–608.

GAL, R., & LAZARUS, R. S. The role of activity in anticipating and confronting stressful situations. *Journal of Human Stress,* 1975, *1,* 4–20.

HAMILTON, V. Socialization anxiety and information processing: A capacity model of anxiety-induced performance deficits. In I. G. Sarason & C. D. Spielberger (eds.), *Stress and anxiety,* vol. 2. Washington, D.C.: Hemisphere, 1975.

HAMMERTON, M., & TICKNER, A. H. Tracking under stress. *Medical Research Council Report,* 1967, no. APRC 67/CS 10(A).

HEBB, D. O. On the nature of fear. *Psychological Review,* 1946, *53,* 259–276.

HOCKEY, G. R. J. Effect of loud noise on attentional selectivity. *Quarterly Journal of Experimental Psychology,* 1970, *22,* 28–36.

HOCKEY, R., & MACLEAN, A. State changes and the temporal patterning of component resources. In A. D. Baddeley & J. Long (eds.), *Attention and performance,* vol. 9. Hillsdale: Erlbaum, 1981.

KAHNEMANN, D. *Attention and effort.* Englewood Cliffs: Prentice-Hall, 1973.

LACEY, B. C., & LACEY, J. I. Studies of heart rate and other bodily processes in sensorimotor behavior. In P. A. Obrist, A. Black, J. Brener, & L. DiCara (eds.), *Cardiovascular psychophysiology: Current mechanisms, biofeedback, and methodology.* Chicago: Aldine-Atherton, 1974.

LAZARUS, R. S. The self-regulation of emotion. In L. Levi (ed.), *Emotions: Their parameters and measurement.* New York: Raven, 1975.

MANDLER, G. The interruption of behavior. In D. Levine (ed.), *Nebraska Symposium on Motivation: 1964.* Lincoln: University of Nebraska Press, 1964.

————. Invited commentary. In M. H. Appley & R. Trumbull (eds.), *Psychological stress: Issues in research.* New York: Appleton Century Crofts, 1967.

————. Comments. In C. D. Spielberger (ed.), *Anxiety: Current trends in theory and research.* New York: Academic, 1972.

————. Consciousness: Respectable, useful, and probably necessary. In R. Solso (ed.), *Information processing and cognition: The Loyola Symposium.* Hillsdale: Erlbaum, 1975. (a)

————. Memory storage and retrieval: Some limits on the reach of attention and consciousness. In

P. M. A. Rabbitt & S. Dornic (eds.), *Attention and performance,* vol. 5. New York: Academic, 1975. (b)

————. *Mind and emotion.* New York: Wiley, 1975. (c)

————. Emotion. In E. Hearst (ed.), *The first century of experimental psychology.* Hillsdale: Erlbaum, 1979. (a)

————. Organization and repetition: Organizational principles with special reference to rote learning. In L. G. Nilsson (ed.), *Perspectives on memory research.* Hillsdale: Erlbaum, 1979. (b)

MANDLER, G., & SARASON, S. B. A study of anxiety and learning. *Journal of Abnormal and Social Psychology,* 1952, *47,* 166–173.

MARCEL, A. J. Conscious and unconscious perception: Visual masking, word recognition, and an approach to consciousness. *Cognitive Psychology,* in press.

MASON, J. W. A historical view of the stress field. *Journal of Human Stress,* 1975, *1,* 6–12, 22–36.

MILLER, G. A., GALANTER, E. H., & PRIBRAM, K. *Plans and the structure of behavior.* New York: Holt, 1960.

NORMAN, D. A., & SHALLICE, T. *Attention to action: Willed and automatic control of behavior.* CHIP technical report no. 99. San Diego: University of California Center for Human Information Processing, 1980.

POULTON, E. C. Arousing environmental stresses can improve performance, whatever people say. *Aviation, Space, and Environmental Medicine,* 1976, *47,* 1193–1204. (a)

————. Continuous noise interferes with work by masking auditory feedback and inner speech. *Applied Ergonomics,* 1976, *7,* 79–84. (b)

SARASON, I. G. The effects of anxiety and threat on the solution of a difficult task. *Journal of Abnormal and Social Psychology,* 1961, *62,* 165–168.

SELYE, H. Confusion and controversy in the stress field. *Journal of Human Stress,* 1975, *1,* 37–44.

WELTMAN, G., SMITH, J. E., & EGSTROM, G. H. Perceptual narrowing during simulated pressure-chamber exposure. *Human Factors,* 1971, *13,* 99–107.

YERKES, R. M., & DODSON, J. D. The relation of strength of stimulus to rapidity of habit-formation. *Journal of Comparative and Neurological Psychology,* 1908, *18,* 459–482.

8

Cognition and Stress:
An Information Processing Model

Vernon Hamilton

ALL OF US KNOW WHAT WE MEAN BY STRESS, yet few are able to define this term completely to our own satisfaction or to that of others. We talk about the noticeable effects of stress, using as cues signs of tension or irritability, poorly coordinated motor movements, and inability to concentrate or to execute tasks efficiently.

Following Selye (1956), we have sophisticated models of the stress response at the physiological and biochemical levels. Furthermore, we have been exposed for a number of years to a variety of nonphysiological approaches to the study of so-called intrapsychic or behavioral stress. Such research has looked primarily at the interaction between stress vulnerability and environmental stressors, taking cognisance of the development and capacity of individually tailored coping behavior. The general conclusion of many researchers seems to be that although the term "stress" may be used colloquially, precision of argument and reductively oriented research require distinction among types of stress, particularly between *stress as an effect* and *stress as an agent.* These issues will be elaborated a little further along.

Having recently co-edited a comprehensive text in the general area of cognition and stress (Hamilton & Warburton, 1979), I do not propose to trespass on either that volume or the fields of expertise of other contributors to the *Handbook of Stress,* except where necessary. To anticipate the subsequent discussion, however, I will argue in support of an information processing concept of stress as an agent, where stress as an effect is seen as the consequence of the type and amount of information processing mediated by *stressors,* which contain and generate stressful information.

Cognition, broadly interpreted here as the behavior involved in knowing, occurs as the result of acquiring a store of information of the self, of the external environment, and of their interaction in the pursuit of behavioral goals. These goals range from the infant's capacity to recognize significant caretakers and to solicit their support, to spatial, temporal, and logical problem-solving, and to the development and application of social skills in complex community settings. These examples of behavior, and all others requiring cognition, depend on organized information-carrying structures in the cell systems of the cortex, which

This Chapter was written while holding a Visiting Professorship at Emory University, Atlanta, Georgia, January–March, 1981. I am grateful for the facilities provided by the Psychology Department.

are capable of activation at any time. These structures constitute the information storage and integrating system, and we refer to them as *long-term memory* (LTM), or *permanent memory*. Memory structures contain the results of all the individual's exprience: those transmitted by sensory external signals or events, as well as those that have been internally generated as the result of autonomous activities (e.g., fantasy or daydreaming). To utilize the information encoded in LTM structures, the response organizing system requires cognitive processes or operations. Whereas the structures represent the content of knowledge domains, the processes utilize selected items of content to meet situational demands. The most important processes are various types of attention; *short-term memory* (STM), or *working memory,* as it is frequently termed; encoding and retrieval of information; response integration; rehearsal of subsidiary processing steps; and preresponse testing that response selection matches situational constraints and facilitations (i.e., the T of the TOTE process).

Following Broadbent (1958, 1971), many psychological experiments have shown that human cognitive processing capacity is finite at any given point in time. Limited processing can be regarded as a function of neurological and electrophysiological constraints and of differential allocation both of reserves of processing capacity and of energy resources (Kahneman, 1973). If we now regard stressors as stimulus events presenting information of a particular and usually aversive kind to the cognitive processing system while this system is engaged in another task, then in this situation the information processing capacity of the system is pushed to or beyond its limits. Thus, an informational reanalysis of psychogenic or situational stressors permits a quantitative approach to the well-documented unfavorable effect of what is loosely called stress on even well-practiced skills and capacities. The cognitive load on the information processing system will be increased even further if the system has at its disposal only inadequate so-called coping strategies. I will argue, however, that the very need to employ additional stressor reducing or defending strategies requires additional cognitive work because at least two, if not three, masters have to be served: a socially required task, stressor analyzing operations, and stressor reduction or denial.

These considerations are not intended to supersede or controvert models of stress that lay emphasis on the role of biochemical processes in the emergence paticularly of psychosomatic illness (Mason, 1968; Selye, 1956). Nor is it desirable to ignore the role of corticosteroids in either the stress response or its control (see Warburton, 1979, for a recent review). Two related arguments will be pursued, however, for which evidence appears to be accumulating: first, the excitatory, activating, and arousing characteristics of a person under stressor strain are not reliably related to performance decrements: second, these biological events are consequences, rather than precursors, of stressor related suboptimal behavior whatever their subsequent role in the development of psychosomatic symptoms or other impairments of adaptation. From this point of view, two conclusions follow naturally: physiological events constitute a necessary but not a sufficient explanation of behavioral decrements in a person under stress, and cognitive restructuring intervention by self or others is the more fundamental approach to raising the threshold for vulnerability to stressors. In the context of this chapter, therefore, the emphasis will be on *stress as information* or *cognitive data* and ona cognitive–information processing approach to the detrimental interaction between stimulation interpreted as aversive for and by the person and an optimally efficient and satisfying lifestyle. Here *lifestyle* applies to capacity exhibited at any point of the life cycle, from infancy to old age, in situations ranging from academically oriented problem-solving to the recognition and solution of social and personal dilemmas.

STRESSORS AS COGNITIVE DATA

Although I regard stress as an effect primarily from the point of view of its influence on skilled performance through its influence on optimal cognitive processes and operations, *limited processing* is a biological concept that is amenable to extension beyond the area of cognition. It seems appropriate to suggest, for example, that the whole human adaptive system draws its energy for repairing, developing, or elaborating its many functions from a unitary source that, like cognitive capacity, is limited at any given point in time. For this reason, it is plausible to argue in favor of physiological, biochemical, and pharmacological sources of strain and load. These need to be distinguished both from cognitive and psychogenic stressors and from those sources of strain that are self-induced as a result of the individual's evaluating his biological impairments as threatening important short- or long-term life plans.

Physiological Stressors

Among the *physiological stressors* are body injury, pain, fever, fatigue or exhaustion, extreme temperatures, intense and intermittent noise, and sleep loss. To this list must be added the biological aspects of affective and mood states and of emotionality, to the extent that parts of the organic system *interpret* these states as stressing. With this elaboration, however, we establish a possible conceptual hiatus since the word "interpret," as well as the activity it describes, indicates a primary cognitive component in the physiological stress response. What, for example, is actually implied by a study such as that done by Mason, Sachar, Fishman, Hamburg, & Handlon (1965), in which volunteer subjects produced a large secretion of corticosteroids in the first 24 hours of a 14-day period of corticosteroid response examination, which response subsequently declined over the next 13 days? As Warburton (1979) put it, the adrenocortical response occurred as a result of subjects' *interpreting* their participation in the study with apprenhension and uncertainty and their environment as having novel, ambiguous, and uncertain implications for them.

Warburton's (1979) approach to the physiological stress response indicates that this response is initated by cognitive events in the system, events that by the identification of externally and internally generated stimuli trigger the adrenocorticotrophic system to supply energy, and stress steroids. In this conceptualization, psychogenic or cognitive stressors precede physiological and psychopharmacological stressors. Once the system is working under the influence of stress hormones, the resulting changes in brain chemistry assume a more dominant role by facilitating cognitive processes that may either reduce—through conditioned feedback pathways—or increase the flow of corticosteroids. Corticosteroid activity will diminish if the cognitive system has coped with stimulus inputs that it initially interpreted as stressful, but such activity will increase while the response generating apparatus searches for an adaptive response strategy with some element of efficiency, method, and control. The strategy may deteriorate if subunits of cognitive control "perceive" a severe and unmanageable response demand, and behavior deficits at various levels may then occur. The level, severity, and persistence of deficits will then depend on the system's vulnerability to cognitively identified stressors and its capacity for generating stressor reducing response decisions. The term "response" is used here in a somewhat idiosyncratic way that will be elaborated subsequently.

In the rest of this chapter, the participation of the physiological and psychopharmacological stress responses in psychogenic, cognitive, and behavioral strain is taken for granted; elucidation of their precise role is left to those more competent in these areas. The role that my own theoretical approach assigns to the biophysiological and cognitive systems in responses to stressor strain is sketched in Figure 8–1. This figure attempts not only to show, in oversimplified form, the many interactions among the principal subsystems but also to indicate at this early stage that I regard psychogenic, cognitive, and biophysiological stressors as *information* that the different subsystems need to identify, process, and act upon in order to maintain or reestablish an optimum internal and external environment for the whole person. Figure 8–1 also proposes that it may be appropriate to regard the sum of stressors and the strain that they induce as a *load factor* on the total organismic system.

Techniques are now available to attach some quantitative index to task performance by which behavioral deficit attributed to stressors may be more objectively demonstrated than in earlier work. Inferences of the extent of psychogenic stressors have been and are still being made either on the basis of systematic observation and interviewing or on the basis of responses to questionnaires and projective techniques in appropriate areas of personality or motivation. Although a body of opinion now regards these efforts only as the beginning of a more rigorous approach to the assessment of people's dominant goal seeking characteristics (Hamilton, 1983), inferences of this sort serve well as an approximation of psychogenic needs, their frustrating effects, and the type and load of anxiety they may generate. A quan-

FIGURE 8–1. Information processing model of load, stressors, and strain *(from Hamilton, 1979, p. 73, with permission).*

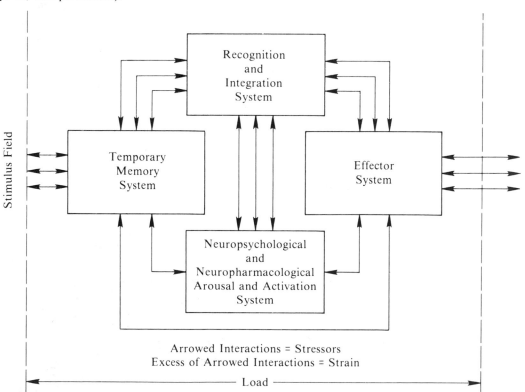

titative index of psychogenic stressors of adequate validity is thereby available to pursue the testing of a quantitative interaction between cognitive and motivational stressor variables. The quantification of biophysiological stressors seems to be very much a question of the development of sophisticated techniques to supersede the existing, quite useful analyses of urine excretion by which Frankenhaeuser (1971) and Frankenhaeuser and Johansson (1976), for example, demonstrated the effect of task stressors on neuroendocrine activity (see also Mason, Sachar, Fishman, Hamburg, & Harlon, 1965).

Cognitive Stressors

By definition, *cognitive stressors* are those cognitive events, processes, or operations that exceed a subjective and individualized level of average processing capacity. This statement assumes that the human brain is constantly at work processing information—a condition tacitly assumed but rarely spelled out—otherwise the EEG patterns during sleep, even dreamless sleep, would be slower and flatter than they are. While a great deal of evidence indicates that sleep accompanied by rapid eye movements (REM sleep) reflects the cognitive events leading to and represented in dream content (e.g., Dement, 1974), there is as yet no evidence that slow-wave, non-REM sleep is necessarily associated with cognitive work. The very conception of a cognitive processing system of limited capacity leads to the plausible inference, however, that the conceptual, experience integrating work of the long-term memory stores is optimally carried out when these data stores are not simultaneously supporting and facilitating ongoing response selection for immediate adaptive use. This does not mean that what Bartlett (1932) long ago called the organization of schemata of knowledge and experience needs to be carried out during sleep. Such organizational activity may make only limited demands on the information processing system in a modality other than that which becomes the focus of current stimulus and response integration. Cognitive organizing and restructuring certainly accompanies both daydreaming and conceptually and functionally related activities.

Two related approaches are open to us in deciding which stressors to call cognitive stressors. By categorizing stressors as either biophysiological, or cognitive, or psychogenic, I have already indicated that it may be useful to differentiate between the content, or material, operated upon by cognitive processes *and* the degree to which the subunits of the processing system and its operations are being utilized, extended, or overloaded. This section presents a utilization and loading interpretation of cognitive stressors.

Partly by convention and partly for explanatory convenience, cognitive psychologists have divided the cognitive processing system into a set of interrelated and interacting components and functions. In doing so everyone is aware that this reifying approach may be conceptually retarding, but because of the close relationship between physiological and cognitive psychology and the more recent specialization of neuropsychology, extreme and misleading concretization has been avoided successfully so far. The need for a caveat in this situation is particularly clear when considering the processes termed short-term, or working, memory and selective attention. Caution is even more relevant perhaps when attempting to concretize that which is called variously response control, executive function, processor, or process integrator. The generally accepted components of the cognitive or information processing apparatus are shown schematically in Figure 8–2, together with the most commonly agreed directions of interaction between them. The specialization of LTM indexed here refers to the more fundamental and analytic information that needs to be accessed by stimuli

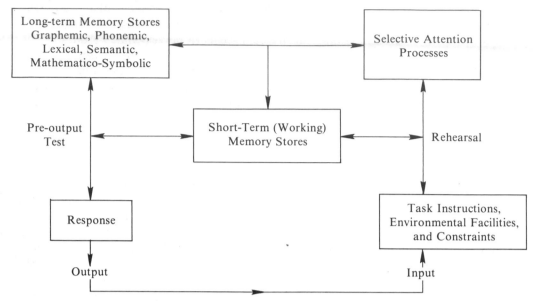

FIGURE 8–2. Model of integrated cognitive processing system.

that contain written or spoken symbols. For example, before the possibly ego threatening content of the word "failure" can be conveyed, the word must be read or heard. In the process of hearing or reading, the visual or auditory configurations or features need to be identified and the separate items combined to make a word. For the practiced adult exposed to clear print or good enunciation, without loss of information due to tachistoscopic exposure or voice distortion, this is a fast process; the graphemic and phonemic identifications and combinations have become habitual, especially if the verbal stimulus is a common one. The next stage is the meaning of the word, which is obtained from the lexical store of memory. Only then are we able to respond on request with the dictionary definition.

The different stages of word identification just described cannot be carried out entirely by the LTM system. Let us assume, by reference to Figure 8–2, that the person has been instructed to say what the word "failure" means. The word and the instructions have to be held in the short-term, working memory component of the system while the identification and labeling process is under way. Although this process may be virtually instantaneous in this example, it nevertheless requires a number of checking and rehearsal operations so that the word "failure," rather than "feature," is perceived. In these operations, data from the LTM are matched with data in the STM prior to the response.

Let us now suppose that a person is presented with a short list of words with the instruction to say what they have in common or in which way they are similar. Take knife, screwdriver, hammer, spanner, and spoon. An oral presentation makes the task more difficult than a visual presentation without inspection-time limit; in the former case, the complete list requires periodic rehearsal to keep each item in the working memory. In addition to the analytic procedures already described for single-word recognition, the new task requires operations in and on semantic LTM—initially to retrieve the known characteristics and uses of each word. This may be a prolonged search process during which some of the data retrieved need to be temporally held and rehearsed while others are discarded. It should be clear by now that the logical and conceptual process of induction required here before the response "tools" can be made depends on selective attention. Moreover, the task just described could be made considerably more difficult by increasing the length of the word series, by offering less frequently used words, by accelerating the presentation, by distorting any one or all of the words, or by employing combinations of these tactics. Common sense, personal experience, and extensive experimental verification lead to the conclusion that in the presence of a limited-capacity processing system, the whole system, as well as its individual components, will be overloaded by the most extreme combination of performance conditions.

Although it is possible to carry out more than one verbal-symbolic task at the same time, provided that somewhat different skills are required (e.g., Allport et al. (1972)), even this ability is impaired when one or both of the tasks are either unpractised or difficult within the usual meaning of the term. We may conclude, therefore, that heavy cognitive work loads are synonymous with cognitive stress. And this must be the case even before an individual's dominant personality and motivational characteristics start interpreting *failure under work load* as a threat to self-esteem or a signal for the emergence of social anxieties.

A great deal of effort has been expended on the study of attention (e.g., Broadbent, 1971; Moray, 1969; Treisman, 1969), and especially on its selective function and capacity. This is not the occasion for a detailed review of this area. However, one or two points should be made at this stage relating to our cognitive stressor discussion. The first of these concerns ambiguities, which appear to attach to attentional function itself. In behaviorally oriented psychology, attention is regarded as a process dealing selectively with signals arising *external* to the person. There is a great deal of justification, however, for pointing to a dominant role for selective attention in relation to *internal* information. This role entails sequential or other strategic search programs directed toward data in the LTM until a suitable item has been retrieved as, for example, in the tasks described above. Of even greater interest in the present context is the role of selective attention vis-a-vis internal, self-generated stimulation, whose information content may be regarded as the prime source of psychogenic stressors.

Subtle distinctions are also required, but are not always spelled out, concerning the characteristics of the attentional process. In a lucid and provocative paper, Wachtel (1967) drew attention to a number of parameters that are optimal for describing the process. The following dimensions seem to be required: degrees of arc of an attentional beam, degrees of movement of the beam, number of stops of a sweeping beam at focal points, and regularities or irregularities of the sweeping operation. This type of analysis seems to be of primary relevance to an individual difference dimension. It has implications, however, for the *amount of information* gathered by attentional effort; it refers to the checking or testing function of focal attention and thereby says something about the close relationship that must exist between short-term, working memory and selective attention. Since the working task is held in the STM system, which is the only system that knows which kind of response is required, there are grounds for suggesting that the selective functions of the attentional process are in fact determined by the working memory and that attention is merely an energized information seeking and focusing beam without independent executive function.

Although this argument throws the weight of information processing load on the short-term, working memory system, it does not diminish the amount of work to be done by attention during a difficult task or in multiple tasks. Simultaneous or fast-paced demands for information from the working memory system may quickly exhaust its capacity to perform.

Previously I referred to the convention, derived from computer science, that one of the cognitive processing subsystems is concerned with the integration of stimulus demands and the information made available by long- and short-term memory operations, with the assistance of attentional processes to meet those demands. There is probably no single identifiable subsystem that facilitates tasks required of a central and general processor. It is much more likely that the final decision of what is or is not an appropriate response is made by the working memory system, to which all relevant information, including the task demands, are channeled. Therefore, if we wished to identify the most sensitive component of the human information processing system, that which is most vulnerable to processing overload, we would have to select the short-term, working memory component. The STM is the only system that has all the required information, including the adequacy of the selected response. Furthermore, and somewhat parenthetically in the present context, if one were to inquire as to the location and identity of states of awareness, or consciousness, or knowledge of one's own organized behavior as it emerges, it seems plausible again to refer to the short-term memory system of the cognitive apparatus. To know that I know, and even not wanting to know what I know I know, requires juxtapositions and integration of information that can be held only by this working component. In a cognitively oriented approach to the relationship between stress and behavior, therefore, it is most relevant to consider the role played by short-term, temporary memory events in the generally accepted unfavorable relationship between performance and personally stressful experience.

Psychogenic Stressors

I have made the distinction between cognitive and psychogenic stressors to indicate that the human adaptively responding system may be under stressor strain even without intrapsychic aversive stimulation. I will eventually argue that this distinction is not fundamental. It was necessary to show, however, that the amount of speech or written instruction that is placed before us, the speed with which a response is required, the difficulty level of the words used, or the number of tasks that may have to be done virtually simultaneously, irrespective of their semantic interpretation or motivational implication, may contribute to an information processing load. Because biochemical, neurological, or physiological processing is itself limited at any given moment, information processing capacity is limited. In the absence of processing space and time, the system will be under strain and be unable to perform satisfactorily. The strain is the result of the stressors imposed on the components of the processing system, which together define the load. As a consequence, we fail to perform adequately and report feeling tired or exhausted.

Our discussion has focused so far on external sources of information and on external stimuli presented to our sensory surfaces. I will now define *psychogenic stressors* as internal stimuli deriving from internal sources of information that present the internal analyzing system with information that is unpleasant, aversive, threatening, or dangerous for the person. Many chapters in this volume are concerned with the sources of this type of information and I do not propose to present a detailed analysis. Instead, I will briefly discuss the nature of the information, how it becomes a source of internal stimulation, and how I conceive of the interaction between psychogenic, cognitive, and physiological stressors.

Psychogenic stressors are events (or the anticipation of events) that have unfavorable implications and/or potentially unfavorable outcomes for the person. I (Hamilton, 1979, 1980) have argued elsewhere in some detail that the largest number of aversive expectancies belongs to events, persons, objects, or situations that at their most fundamental level threaten social isolation and rejection. Expectancies are foreknowledge of the consequences of a stimulus whose meaning has been interpreted on the basis of already existing data in long-term, permanent memory. Also encoded in memory are alternatives of a particular set of outcome expectancies and, frequently also, objective or imagined estimates of the probability with which outcomes O_1, O_2, or O_3 may occur. Expectancies depend, therefore, on earlier, actual, or imagined stimulation or behavior. The more important the experience area for the individual, and the more frequent the involvement of the appropriate memory data, the more highly elaborated we would expect the cognitive structures to be that have encoded earlier events. In Bartlett's terms (1932), the size, elaboration, and complexity of a memory schema and its patterned relationship to other schemata depend upon and reflect the subjective importance of any particular behavior area under discussion. For example, a high-scoring introvert is characterized as such by the number of times and situations in which he demonstrates a preference for seclusion, daydreaming, quiet occupations, minimal social interaction, avoiding noise, or avoiding anxiety provoking situations or tasks. Questionnaire measures and clinical ratings of anxiety inquire into the number of situations in which and the frequency and intensity with which anxiety has been experienced. The occurrences, as well as the capacity to report them, reflect the schematic organization of the anxiety stressor.

Similar analyses can be presented for every human motive, every personality trait, and every emotion or mood, whether within normal range or not. This somewhat strong statement can be made for several reasons. First, motives and traits are defined not only by knowledge of the *goals of behavior* but also by a decisionmaking process that selects *methods of goal approach* for which an optimal outcome is anticipated. Second, emotions and moods are primarily neither feeling tones nor clearly differentiated patterns of peripheral and/or electrocortical arousal but *distinctive thought processes* about the self in relation to the actions of others or the constraints or temptations of objects, events, and situations in the person's life space (Hamilton, 1983).

This deliberate emphasis on the cognitive components of what historically have been termed *noncognitive parameters* has received considerable empirical and theoretical support from many quarters (e.g., Hamilton & Warburton, 1979; Sarason, 1975; Schachter & Singer, 1962; Weiner, 1974). This perspective does not deny the importance of the occurrence, or question the relevance, of experienced feeling tones but emphasizes cognitive events that have interpreted incoming or self-generated stimuli along the particular lines encoded in permanent memory schemata. Therefore, the person with widely elaborated, fine-grained schemata encoding anxiety will be sensitive to anticipated attacks on or injury to self-esteem, to threats of social rejection, to nonachievement of goals, to situations in which performance may be adversely evaluated, or to any situations that are ambiguous with respect to meaning or personal implications and that therefore signal unstable or uncertain events.

This analysis represents a cognitive approach to anxiety that has led me to propose a model of the interaction between the anxiety stressor and performance in which cognitive and psychogenic stressors may be considered as summating amounts of information, which in the most unfavorable circumstances will predictably and systematically reduce the power of the cognitive processing apparatus.

A COGNITIVE STRESSOR MODEL OF ANXIETY

I have no dispute with the common proposition that anxiety is stressful and that excessive anxiety will impair a wide variety of behaviors. The reasons advanced in support of this view are founded on overwhelming experimental evidence (Liebert & Morris, 1967; Mednick, 1958; Sarason, 1975; Spence, 1964; Spielberger, 1966, 1972; Wine, 1971). Explanations have ranged from the adverse effect of high arousal or drive, to "worry," "preoccupation," "lack of concentration," "negative self-evaluations," and "anticipated threats or dangers." I have suggested on a number of occasions that these so-called causes of the effect of anxiety are insufficiently explanatory because they offer no systematic account of *what* anxiety actually *is*, nor do they provide a sufficiently fundamental conceptualization of *why* anxiety interferes with externally prescribed tasks. Instead, I would argue that *anxiety* should be considered a particular set or network of connotative data that, on the basis of past experience and autonomous elaboration of their cognitive structures, provides a store of long-term memories. These are available for retrieval when stimulated, just like other long-term memory data (Hamilton, 1975, 1976, 1979, 1980). In the context of the preceding discussion, it follows that if anxiety is high it may be regarded as a psychogenic stressor, which adds an information processing load to the cognitive processing system.

This interpretation obtains support from various sources. Anticipation of any form of danger, expectancies of threats, the probability that any one of a number of painful, unpleasant, or aversive outcomes may be contingent, say, on what a person does at any given moment or on how well he thinks he is doing it—all these must depend on having available knowledge of potential outcomes. This, however, requires a store of information, reality based or fantasied, by which to anticipate and calculate the probability of an event that will be aversive and threatening for the person. My emphasis at this point is not only on the organization or consistency of structures but also on the amount of aversive information, on its generalization to objects, events, or persons that characterize the high anxious person, and on the method of encoding the information. Usually this information is unrelated to and irrelevant for the task the person is asked to carry out, which task will contain its own quantum of information processing demands. However, the greater the predispositon to generate aversive expectancies or behavior outcomes, the greater the appropriate memory store, the lower the retrieval threshold for this type of information, and the greater the response bias toward primary processes of identifying and avoiding real or potential aversiveness. If this analysis is correct, then it follows that the high anxious person when performing any task is, in fact, in a two-task situation, which requires multiple channels and parallel cognitive processes.

Only one additional factor is required to provide a parasimonious explanation of why high anxiety impairs performance. This factor is to be found in the generally accepted propositions of data and resource limitations in human information processing capacity (e.g., Broadbent, 1971; Kahneman, 1973; Norman & Bobrow, 1975). An early, neat illustration of these limits was provided by Conrad (1951), who was investigating limitations of human vigilance. As with performance by high anxious subjects, two sources of information were observed in this experiment: signal rate and number of dials. Predictably, the number of responses possible was a decreasing function of the total information processing load.

If for high anxious individuals anxiety is cognitive information with low retrieval thresholds and high priorities for selective attention to stimuli that have no specific relationship to the task, and if the processing resources of the person are limited at any given time, then two general predictions can be made. First, high anxious subjects should perform worse than low anxious subjects when a task becomes more difficult, that is, when there is a substantial increase in its information processing demands. ("Worse" here is defined by either increased slowness or increased errors—to avoid the awkward trade-off effect.) Second, these performance deficits should not co–vary necessarily with levels or changes in levels of skin conductance or heart rate, i.e., the most favored explanation for the unfavorable interaction.

This analysis converts psychogenic stressors into cognitive stressors. This would be true even if, as is obvious, we could not ignore the physiological and electrocortical arousal parameters: the function of these processes *is* to arouse, with the direction of arousal governed by the ongoing cognitive processes. In other words, in the presence of anxiety stressors, arousal will be used by the information processing system to generate associated long-term memory data. Their function, in the service of adaptive, anxiety avoidance responses, is to retrieve previously employed response strategies that led to anxiety reduction. In the high anxious person, however, avoidance and reduction are likely to be preceded by the retrieval of a large amount of aversive long-term memory data—mainly those data that define what we mean by high anxiety. However, any adaptive system also has produced defensive cognitive strategies. As a result, the retrieval of ego threatening cognitive data is accompanied by other cognitive data that encode—also in long-term memory—defensive-denial-restructuring information and strategies. From this it will need to be argued, as I shall do below, that psychogenic defense operations and mechanisms required for coping may increase rather than reduce the cognitive load on the information processing system.

To permit more precise predictions of the adverse effect of the anxiety stressor on task performance and to provide a more reductionist and rational explanation of this interaction, a quasi-mathematical model of maximum adaptive capacity is offered:

$$APC + SPC > I_{eps} + I_{i(eps)} + I_{i(A)} + I_{i(D)} + I_{i(RSO)}$$

APC is average cognitive processing capacity; SPC is spare processing capacity; I_{eps} is externally presented information that is primary as well as secondary for the purpose of stimulus evaluation and interpretation; $I_{i(eps)}$ is internally generated information that the processing system regards as relevant for the selection of an appropriate response eps; $I_{i(A)}$ is internally generated information relevant to anxiety; $I_{i(D)}$ is the defensive information generated by anxiety; and $I_{i(RSO)}$ is the information generated by the involvement of cognitive restructuring strategies and operations that are initiated by anxiety data and the defenses against them.

Several terms of the formalized statement are already quantifiable, such as task difficulty (e.g., Hamilton, 1982; Hamilton & Moss, 1974); levels of anxiety and defensiveness by questionnaire or clinical rating scores; and even the number of competing responses triggered by the external stimulus, which are most probably a function of intelligence and experience with the stimulus. For the purpose of testing the cognitive stressor model of anxiety, my students and I initially concentrated on devising a problem task that varied systematically in difficulty. It consisted of mathematical equations in which various terms were progressively reexpressed in different form; subjects had to verify whether or not a final mathematical equation expressed equality. We developed a problem series in which sets of items required 10, 20, 25, or 30 analyzing steps, respectively, to solve the task (Hamilton, 1980; Hamilton & Moss, 1974). Eight experiments have been carried out so far on high and low test anxious subjects. The general prediction was that high anxious subjects would be slower, as well as make more errors, than low anxious subjects. More specific predictions said that time pressure, self-esteem sensitizing instructions, and ego threatening *false* feedback of poor performance would enhance the differences predicted generally. Apart from the problem-solving series just described, the tasks included very short-term memory tests and the ability to deal with dual tasks. Figure 8–3 shows in summary the results obtained with the problem-solving task. I have indicated (in the publications previously cited) that these results were not systematically related to peripheral arousal measures that is, to physiological stressors.

Since the most pronounced differences between the experimental groups were defined

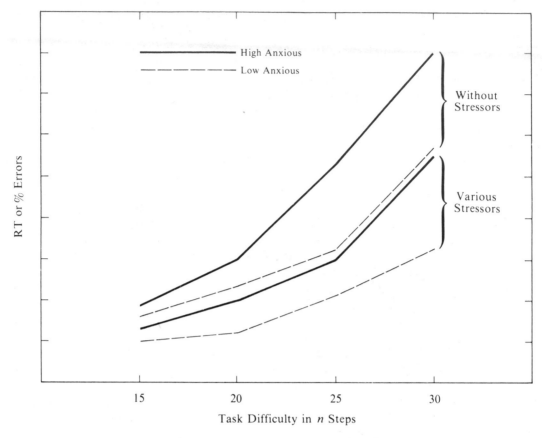

FIGURE 8–3. Summary relationship between test anxiety and problem-solving performance.

by their responses to anxiety questionnaires, the most plausible explanation of these and similar studies on the effects of anxiety needs to be sought in those organized cognitive structures from which subjects deduce or induce their responses to questionnaire items. In other words, the type and intensity of self-generated cognitive interference appears to be a function of the content and elaboration of long-term memory schemata that encode the subjective experience, knowledge, anticipation, and response requirements of potential threats and dangers. Thus, the interaction of one particular personality and motivational potential stressor system—anxiety—with external situations is governed by cognitive processes that integrate external-temporary and internal-more durable goal-directed processes. In this way, anxiety increases the total information processing load on the cognitive system.

COPING AND THE LANGUAGE OF COGNITION— STRESS INTERACTION

In this final section I will attempt to deal with two issues that present themselves for reanalysis following the preceding reinterpretation of stress as a primarily cognitive event. The first issue is how to conceptualize the process of coping with stressors in the light of a cognitive model of anxiety; the second and probably more interesting issue concerns the *nature of the data* on which the components of the cognitive processing system work.

When a person who is exposed to a frightening or depressing experience engages in behavior that indicates that he can tolerate and overcome his anxiety or grief without damage to himself, others, or the environment, we say that he is *coping with stress.* This definition is not peculiar to psychologists since the layperson would offer a similar one. The psychological contribution has been twofold: coping is the outcome of intervening stress reducing processes that lead to the avoidance of unpleasant emotions, and coping is effected by cognitive processes of primary and secondary appraisal and by reappraisal Lazarus (1966, 1974). If this is a valid summary of the theoretical position, and if we relate it to the title of a recent essay by Folkman, Schaefer, and Lazarus (1979), "Cognitive Processes as Mediators of Stress and Coping," then the situation seems very similar to that presented by the undifferentiated use of the term "stress." That is, coping is both an agent *and* an outcome, a conceptual position that has been rejected in relation to stress.

In relation to stress I have suggested that we should refer to stressors as agents and to strain and load as outcomes. An event does not become a stressor until a cognitive processing system has identified it as such on the basis of existing long-term memory data. Stressors are minimized, or an adaptation to them is effected, by searching memory data for a previous stressor reducing response, by reanalyzing the original stimulus to verify its stressing implications, and by utilizing a previously employed *strategy* available in long-term memory, possibly in association with stimulus input of a particular kind, by which the stressing stimulus meaning or content is prevented from reaching perceptual threshold. In other words, coping is not merely the consequence of cognitive processes mediating between the individual and the environment, as in the imprecise sense; rather, *coping is a cognitive process.* And *appraisal* is the process of matching, testing, comparing, and decisionmaking in short-term, working memory.

My cognitive analysis of stressors depends critically on conventional notions about the organized conceptual-schematic structures of permanent memory. The retrieval of stored information enables us to identify internal and external stimuli and to select a stimulus-appropriate response. *How do we know how to respond or what to respond to?* An empiricist answer is still valid: we know what things are because we know either what they do or what they do to us. And we employ classification systems of things, people, and events to simplify the process of responding. Our classifications are categories of referents in our experience field, each of which has accrued through interaction with sets of attributes. A *cognitive schema,* therefore, is an organization of attributes around referents. In order to distinguish between different referents and attributes, the cognitive system requires a coding, or labeling, convention. In neurophysiological terms this is likely to be provided by patterns of neurophysiological activity, with each pattern differing in some detail from another. Present theorizing, while maintaining the distinctive functional properties of cortical specialization, argues in favor of cross-referenced, cross-modality connection forming as the basis of stimulus-appropriate behavior (Hebb, 1949; Pribram, 1971).

A system of neurophysiological codes cannot be sufficient, however, for an adapting organism, which must be responsive to fine-grained social cues in the environment and to the equally fine-grained distinctions between two or three variants of the same stimulus. In order to *know* that a response is going to be adequately adaptive, the *meaning of the stimulus,* as well as the *meaning of the response and its outcome,* has to be available to the response organizing and integrating system. Whereas animals and human infants appear to possess an inherited capacity to interpret the primary *sign releasers* of facial expression, posture, gesture, type of touch, or tone of voice, which must be regarded, therefore, as a primitive symbolic language, more mature humans have a complex and highly efficient code of verbal language. A gradually amassed lexicon enables us to distinguish clearly most of the time between one referent or attribute and another. Each lexical term, however, is not just an isolated symbolic representation of an object, person, event, or situation, since each of these simultaneously conveys the general as well as the idiosyncratic and subjective meanings and implications of the so labeled stimulus. Psycholinguists and cognitive psychologists refer here to the superordinate system of semantics, which by definition must reside in long-term memory. Moreover, because semantics develop as the result of verbal learning, the physiological structures of semantic language are located predominantly in the left hemisphere (Hamilton, 1983).

Let us now consider the nature of the data by which conditions, events, etc., are identified as stressors. Why do we respond with anxiety if we think that are we being followed while walking through a dark and empty park? Clearly, we *interpret,* rightly and wrongly, the situation as being favorable to a mugging. We impose a *meaning* on a stimulus field on the basis of what we mean—as a result of learning—by being alone in the dark and being followed. The meaning is established vocally, subvocally, or without vocalization by retrieving the implications of "walking behind," "dark," "lonely," and "mugging." These lexical units form a so-called semantic network. Should it transpire that the stranger following is the park keeper, the whole interpretation and its lexicon is revised. The identification of this official person changes the semantic network and, therefore, the conceptual structure of the previous anxiety response to one of support and relief.

This type of analysis makes it plausible to propose not only that the cognitive structures of anxiety and other stressors depend on a previous history of experience but also that this history is semantically encoded. A new consensus appears to be developing among cognitive psychologists and even among artificial intelligence theorists that concept formation, the utilization of concepts in problem-solving, and even so-called perceptual processes require semantic, as well as lexical, codes and structures (e.g., Bobrow & Norman 1978; Findler, 1979; Hayes-Roth & Hayes-Roth, 1977; Norman & Bobrow, 1975).

There are obviously substantial gaps in the derivation of my propositions, but ongoing work at Reading University is attempting to fill these in. Some studies, for example, have already produced support for the hypothesis that high anxious subjects will take longer and make more errors, compared with low anxious subjects, on a relatively simple verbal task with words of low imageability directed to the left hemisphere (Hamilton, 1983). In more general terms, it now seems possible to attempt a cognitive reappraisal of theories of personality and motivation, so that the many confirmed instances of interaction between cognitive and so-called noncognitive variables can be given a rational basis and so that individually characteristic goal seeking may be seen for what it is: a problem-solving task requiring complex cognitive decisionmaking on strategies with differential outcomes for the person.

REFERENCES

Allport, D. A., Antonis, B., & Reynolds, P. On the division of attention: A disproof of the single channel hypothesis. *Quarterly Journal of Experimental Psychology,* 1972, *24,* 225–235.

Bartlett, F. C. *Remembering.* Cambridge: Cambridge University Press, 1932.

Bobrow, D. G., & Norman, D. A. Some principles of memory schemata. In D. G. Bobrow & A. M. Collins (eds.), *Representation and understanding: Studies in cognitive science.* New York: Academic, 1978.

Broadbent, D. E. *Perception and communication.* New York: Pergamon, 1958.

—————. *Decision and stress.* New York: Academic, 1971.

CONRAD, R. Speed and load stress in a sensorimotor skill. *British Journal of Industrial Medicine,* 1951, *8,* 1–7.

DEMENT, W. C. *Some must watch while some must sleep.* San Francisco: Freeman, 1974.

FINDLER, N. V. (ed.). *Associative networks: Representation and use of knowledge by computers.* New York: Academic, 1979.

FOLKMAN, S., SCHAEFER, C., & LAZARUS, R. S. Cognitive processes as mediators of stress and coping. In V. Hamilton & D. M. Warburton (eds.), *Human stress and cognition: An information processing approach.* Chichester: Wiley, 1979.

FRANKENHAEUSER, M. Experimental approaches to the study of human behavior as related to neuro-endocrine functions. In L. Levy (ed.), *Society, stress, and disease.* Vol. 1: *The psychosocial environment and psychosomatic diseases.* New York: Oxford University Press, 1971.

FRANKENHAEUSER, M., & JOHANSSON, G. Task demands as reflected in catecholamine excretion and heart rate. *Journal of Human Stress,* 1976, *2,* 15–23.

HAMILTON, V. Socialization and information processing: A capacity model of anxiety-induced performance deficits. In I. G. Sarason & C. D. Spielberger (eds.), *Stress and anxiety,* vol. 2. Washington, D.C.: Hemisphere, 1975.

—————. Cognitive development in the neuroses and schizophrenias. In V. Hamilton & M. D. Vernon (eds.), *The development of cognitive processes.* New York: Academic, 1976.

—————. Personality and stress. In V. Hamilton & D. M. Warburton (eds.), *Human stress and cognition: An information processing approach.* New York: Wiley, 1979.

—————. A information processing analysis of environmental stress and life crises. In I. G. Sarason & C. D. Spielberger (eds.), *Stress and anxiety,* vol. 7. Washington, D.C.: Hemisphere, 1980.

—————. A cognitive model of anxiety: Implications for theories of personality and motivation. In C. D. Spielberger & I. G. Sarason (eds.), *Stress and anxiety,* vol. 10. Washington, D.C.: Hemisphere, 1982.

—————. *The cognitive structures and processes of human personality and motivation.* New York: Wiley, 1983.

HAMILTON, V., & Moss, M. A method of scaling conservation of quantity problems by information content. *Child Development,* 1974, *45,* 737–745.

HAMILTON, V., & WARBURTON, D. M. (eds.). *Human stress and cognition: An information processing approach.* New York: Wiley, 1979.

HAYES-ROTH, B., & HAYES-ROTH, F. Concept learning and the recognition and classification of exemplars. *Journal of Verbal Learning and Verbal Behavior,* 1977, *16,* 321–338.

HEBB, D. O. *The organization of behavior.* New York: Wiley, 1949.

KAHNEMAN, D. *Attention and effort.* Englewood Cliff: Prentice-Hall, 1973.

LAZARUS, R. S. *Psychological stress and the coping process.* New York: McGraw-Hill, 1966.

—————. Cognitive and coping processes in emotion. In B. Weiner (ed.), *Cognitive views of human motivation.* New York: Academic, 1974.

LIEBERT, R. M., & MORRIS, L. W. Cognitive and emotional components of test anxiety: A distinction and some initial data. *Psychological Reports,* 1967, *20,* 975–978.

MASON, J. W. A review of psychoendocrine research on pituitary-adrenal cortical system. *Psychosomatic Medicine,* 1968, *30,* 576–607.

MASON, J. W., SACHAR, E. J., FISHMAN, L. A., HAMBURG, P. S., & HANDLON, J. H. Corticosteroid responses to hospital admission. *Archives of General Psychiatry,* 1965, *13,* 1–8.

MEDNICK, S. A. A learning theory approach to research in schizophrenia. *Psychological Bulletin,* 1958, *55,* 316–327.

MORAY, N. *Attention: Selective processes in vision and hearing.* London: Hutchinson, 1969.

Norman, D. A., & Bobrow, D. G. On data-limited and resource-limited processes. *Cognitive Psychology,* 1975, *1,* 44–64.

Pribram, K. *Languages of the brain.* Englewood Cliff: Prentice-Hall, 1971.

Sarason, I. G. Anxiety and self-preoccupation. In I. G. Sarason & C. D. Spielberger (eds.), *Stress and anxiety,* vol. 2. Washington, D.C.: Hemisphere, 1975.

Schachter, S., & Singer, J. E. Cognitive, social, and physiological determinants of emotional state. *Psychological Review,* 1962, *69,* 379–399.

Selye, H. *The stress of life.* New York: McGraw-Hill, 1956.

Spence, K. W. Anxiety (drive) level and performance in eyelid conditioning. *Psychological Bulletin,* 1964, *61,* 129–139.

Spielberger, C. D. (ed.). *Anxiety and behavior.* New York: Academic, 1966.

————. *Anxiety: Current trends in theory and research.* New York: Academic, 1972.

Treisman, A. M. Strategies and models of selective attention. *Psychological Review,* 1969, *76,* 282–299.

Wachtel, P. L. Conceptions of broad and narrow attention. *Psychological Bulletin,* 1967, *68,* 417–429.

Warburton, D. M. Physiological aspects of information processing and stress. In V. Hamilton & D. M. Warburton (eds.), *Human stress and cognition: An information processing approach.* New York: Wiley, 1979.

Weiner, B. (ed.). *Cognitive views of human motivation.* New York: Academic, 1974.

Wine, J. Test anxiety and direction of attention. *Psychological Bulletin,* 1971, *75,* 92–104.

PART III

BASIC BIOLOGICAL PROCESSES

9

Genetic Diversity and Differing Reactions to Stress

Susan L. Farber

THIS CHAPTER OFFERS A BRIEF INTRODUCTION to the hypothesis that people may be more or less susceptible to stressors because of individual differences in endogenous factors. One of these factors is genotype.

A number of recent articles have argued that racial, ethnic, and/or sexual groups differ in various abilities because of hypothetical genetic differences. The word "differ" frequently is interpreted to indicate inherent superiority or inferiority. Some have gone so far as to try to rank-order racial groupings on IQ (Eysenck & Kamin, 1981) or to argue that females are inferior to males in certain cognitive abilities (e.g., Benbow & Stanley, 1980). Such conclusions can be demonstrated to be implausible on numerous grounds (e.g., Block & Dworkin, 1976; Eysenck & Kamin, 1981; Jencks, 1972; Kamin, 1974; MacKenzie, 1980; Taylor, 1980; Tomizuka and others, 1981). However, the public frequently is unaware of more judicious opinions in this area and the exploration of innate differences is therefore suspect. To rectify the imbalance, I first briefly comment on aspects of methods and terminology. Subsequently, I discuss research findings in an illustrative, not exhaustive, review designed for heuristic purposes.

HERITABILITY

Heritability, perhaps the most widely used and misused term in the field of behavior genetics, refers to the proportion of variance in a group that can be associated with genetic variance. Thus, if the heritability of milk production in a given population of dairy cows is 80%, it is assumed that 80% of the variance in milk production is associated with genetic variation in the herd, leaving 20% of variance associated with environmental factors. Similarly, if the heritability of disorder X in a sample is estimated at 80%, one would link approximately 20% of the variance in the sample with environmental factors.

Note that heritability is a population statistic and predicts nothing about individuals. A person with disorder X does not fall ill 80% because of his genes and 20% because of his environment. The figures refer, instead, to the population to which he belongs. Furthermore, such statistics can be computed by various methods, none of them satisfactory and each offering somewhat different results (Plomin, DeFries & McClearm, 1979). Moreover, heritability statistics apply only to the population being studied and are *not* informative about differences between groups. Similarly, they would be expected to change for the same population if the environment(s) of that population changed. Finally, and perhaps most important, heritability statistics are based on a cross-sectional, nondevelopmental approach and frequently are interpreted as though the actions of genes (or environment) were static and indeed immutable from the moment of conception. The notion of immutability—whether implicit or explicit—is incorrect and may lead to serious errors in understanding and intervention.

DEVELOPMENTAL PROPOSITIONS

Genes switch on and off in the course of development. Baldness, for example, rarely occurs in middle childhood, usually emerging in mid-adulthood. Just as embryonic and fetal development is determined, in part, by the actions of genes (Schaie, Anderson, McClearn & Money, 1975), so also is postnatal development probably influenced by endogenous factors. Key issues that influence research strategies, as well as interpretation of results, are whether it is more appropriate to focus attention on specific traits (such as height, phobias, or IQ) or on the overall pattern of development (growth spurts, onset of landmarks, or emergence of discrete cognitive skills). While either approach in an extreme form is unlikely to be satisfactory, there is ample evidence in the literature that heritabilities for the same trait in the same population shift over time. The implication is that interaction exists not only between heredity and environment but also among heredity, environment, and the organism's developmental stage.

In other words, genetic action may, in the long run, be best understood when viewed as a developmental process involving differentiation and reorganization. For the moment, note is made only of the fact that heritability or concordance-discordance rates estimate endpoints alone and offer no information on the multileveled, shifting, and reshifting interactions between genes and environment that lead to outcome. Such concepts are useful for flagging traits worthy of investigation but do not necessarily indicate that a given trait is significantly influenced in a direct fashion by the actions of genes. Environmental factors (such as a virus or psychological interaction system common to many or all members of a group) may remain explanatory, as do congenital but nongenetic influences (common birth trauma or cerebral lateralization, for example). Another possibility is that the genetic blueprint influences the individual's developmental sequencing, which in turn may influence the timing and form of a trait emergence. This latter view may be most important when examining complex traits such as those involved in personality or cognition.

INFECTIOUS DISEASES: A MODEL
OF DIFFERENTIAL SUSCEPTIBILITY

Communicable diseases such as polio, tuberculosis, or leprosy fall toward the environmental end of the spectrum since all are determined by the interaction between virus or bacillus and host. However, although almost everyone falls ill in epidemics of certain diseases (such as measles), the more typical pattern when a large population is exposed to an infectious organism is for most people to remain asymptomatic, a smaller group to have mild, sometimes unidentifiable symptoms, and the smallest group to show the classic form of the disease (Ashley, 1973). "The organism," as Ashley noted, "is relatively constant, the variable factor is the reaction of the host" (p. 550).

Variable reaction of the host is one way of describing differential susceptibility in a population. Twin studies suggest that a degree of differential susceptibility is associated with genetic factors. For example, identical twins are more frequently concordant than are fraternal twins with respect to leprosy, tuberculosis, or poliomyelitis (Chakravartti & Vogel, 1973; Gedda, 1961; Propping & Vogel, 1976; Stern, 1973). Concordance extends beyond tallies of whether both twins have fallen ill to similarities in form, severity, and localization of the disease. For example, concordance tends to occur for the tuberculoid versus lepromatous form of leprosy. The hypothesis of genetic susceptibility is further strengthened by cases of fraternal twins in which only one twin has fallen ill; the ill twin, nonetheless, having the form of leprosy found recurrently in the family line. Concordance for tuberculosis also is sometimes highly specific in identical twins. Documented cases, for example, testify to similar, or identical localization, say, in a specific area of the lung, or, interestingly, to mirror-image localizations in identical twins who are mirror-images of each other (Gedda, 1961; Stern, 1973).

Heritabilities have been offered of .53–.65 for tuberculosis, compared to only − .06 for death from acute infection (Cavalli-Sforza & Bodmer, 1978). Stern (1973) listed identical versus fraternal twin concordance at 95% versus 87% for measles, 36% versus 6% for poliomyelitis, and 64% versus 47% for scarlet fever.

Concordance rates have been used to estimate the form of inheritance involved. For example, it has been postulated that a simple Mendelian mode may lead to a specific defect in the immune system (as in the T-cell system), which in turn makes some individuals more susceptible to lepromatous leprosy. However, identical twins are not concordant for type of leprosy in 100% of cases, hinting at a more complex mode of transmission (Propping & Vogel, 1976).

Thus, investigation of infectious diseases indicates that some individuals may be particularly susceptible to the effects of external stressors. However, even when susceptibility can be postulated, the interaction between genotype and environment in the most straightforward cases is complex.

CORONARY HEART DISEASE

Heart disease is one of the leading causes of death in many industrialized nations and, as such, has been the focus of extensive research. It is known that coronary disease tends to run in families. Likewise, blood pressure, including hypertension, is estimated at 62–63% heritability (Cavalli-Sforza, 1978; Farber, 1981; Harvald & Hauge, 1965; Rose, Fulker, Miller, Grim & Christian, 1980). However, epidemiologic studies of coronary heart disease (CHD) have focused the public's attention on stressors such as diet, inactivity, type A and B personalities, high cholesterol, high blood pressure, smoking, and drinking. Twin studies uniformly find identical twins more concordant than fraternals but, as yet, have been unable to explain either concordance or discordance on the basis of the most frequently mentioned environmental stressors (Cederlof, Friberg, Jonsson & Kaij, 1966; de Faire, 1974, 1976; Harvald & Hauge, 1970; Liljefors, 1970, 1976). All such reasearch suggests a noteworthy genetic contribution to susceptibility and many studies underscore the genetic hypothesis with the finding that concordance rises the more broadly one scores for presence of heart disease. For example, twin sets discordant for death from CHD frequently are concordant for elevated blood pressure, serum cholesterol, and the like, and concordance tends to rise the longer sets are followed through the ages of highest risk. The few cases of identical twins reared apart also support the patterns cited in the larger literature (Farber, 1981).

However, not all individuals at risk develop CHD and not all identical twins are concordant, whether scored by narrow or broad criteria. The public emphasis on the role of stressors such as drinking, smoking, and overeating might suggest that identical twins discordant for CHD also are discordant for some or all of these types of factor. As yet, no clear-cut pattern has emerged in the literature. For example, Liljefors (1970, 1976) found no association between blood pressure, serum cholesterol, or smoking habits and the presence or absence of overt symptoms of CHD. Similarly, no direct association could be demonstrated between heavy drinking and manifest or subclinical coronary disease (Myrhed & Floderus, 1976), although slightly higher values for certain pathological trends were found in the heavier drinking group. Although Kringlen (1980) suggested an association between hospitalization and the twin with the more stressful work environment, Koskenvuo and co-workers (1980) found no significant association between type A personality and CHD. However, they left open the possibility that the association may emerge in prospective studies, since type A individuals, by raw score, had more history of CHD.

Overall, the literature strongly suggests a noteworthy genetic element in susceptibility to CHD. Although all studies surveyed acknowledged the probable influence of known stressors—well documented in the epidemiologic literature—none found a straightforward association between the known stressors taken either singly or in combination that could fully explain why one or both partners in genetically identical pairs were concordant or discordant for illness or death. As Liljefors (1976) noted, genetic predisposition is so strongly implicated in CHD that it might be most efficient to shift a portion of attention away from epidemiologic studies and to look instead for environmental variance in genetically homogeneous populations such as identical twin pairs.

ALCOHOL CONSUMPTION

Animal studies support the hypothesis that endogenous factors contribute to individual differences in alcohol consumption. Selective breeding produces lines that differ both in preference for alcohol and in the effects following ingestion. Some strains can be induced in early development to consume ethanol in large quantities but revert to nondrinking status when later offered free choice, while other nondrinking strains continue to show a preference for alcohol in maturity after exposure as juveniles (Fuller & Thompson, 1978).

Several twin studies reported higher concordance among identicals than fraternals for drinking patterns (Kaij, 1960; Partanen, Bruun, & Markkanen, 1966), but one recent investigation found virtually identical correlations for identicals and fraternals (Clifford, Fulker, Gurling, & Murray, 1980). While earlier studies also found increasing concordance with increasing levels of drinking, more recent research suggests a complex interaction of influences of varying degrees of heritability. Sex differences in drinking frequently are noted in the literature. Highly limited data from studies on twins reared apart support high concordance—irrespective of degree of contact—with no sets discordant in the heavy drinking group (Farber, 1981). However, when twins reared together are discordant for alcoholism, morphological and psychological deterioration is associated with the alcohol use and is not a pattern exhibited by both twins (Gurling, Murray, & Clifford, 1980).

One particularly interesting study of reared together twins indicated that ethanol metabolism is almost entirely gene determined, with heritability estimated at .98 (Vesell, Page, & Pasanti, 1971). Seven identical and seven fraternal twin pairs were followed every half hour after ingesting 1ml/kg of 95% ethanol diluted with ice water. Metabolic rates of the fraternals sometimes differed markedly. In contrast, identicals were highly alike, with most showing zero difference.

Cultural, family environment, and sex differences are all implicated as significant variables in the literature on alcoholism. However, twin, family, and adoption studies have indicated that some degree of genetic susceptibility to alcoholism is likely (Goodwin, 1976; Goodwin, Schulsinger, Hermansen, Guze & Winokur, 1973; Goodwin, Schulsinger, Knop, Mednick & Guze, 1977a, b; Roe, 1944; Schuckit, Goodwin, & Winokur, 1972; Conterio & Chiarelli, 1962).

ASTHMA

Harvald and Hauge (1965) found identical twins significantly more concordant than fraternal twins for asthma. Cavalli-Sforza and Bodmer (1978) gave heritability estimates of .58–.71 and McKusick (1978) noted the possible association between HLA–W6 and intrinsic asthma. Two cases of identical twins reared apart both were concordant (Farber, 1981).

ULCERS

Literature on genetic susceptibility to ulcers is equivocal (Levitan, 1977), although the hypothesis of some degree of *polygenic inheritance* (the interaction of many genes) is widely entertained (Cavalli-Sforza & Bodmer, 1978; Fraser Roberts & Pembry, 1978). The finding that families of gastric ulcer patients have a higher incidence of gastric ulcers than does the normal population, whereas relatives of duodenal ulcer probands have about three times the average rate of duodenal ulcers (Beeson & McDermott, 1975), suggests some degree of family transmission and also suggests that predisposition to gastric versus duodenal ulcer may be independently transmitted.

Harvald and Hauge (1965) found no appreciable difference in rates of peptic ulcer for identical and fraternal twins, which led them to speculate that environment may be more important than heredity in this condition. In six cases of twins reared apart, only one set (possibly two) was concordant (Farber, 1981). However, the literature on twins reared together and those reared apart indicates that when clinical evaluation is done with every subject—regardless of symptom report—concordance goes up (Farber, 1981; Harvald & Hauge, 1965). X ray, for example, may show gastric ulcers in both partners, although only one reports symptoms. Similarly, in three out of four discordant cases of identicals reared apart, both partners were troubled with high acidity.

Thus, although environmental factors are known to be salient, the underlying patterns, plus the discussion in the literature on a possible relationship among duodenal ulcers, blood group O, and secretor-nonsecretors (Cavalli-Sforza & Bodmer, 1978; Fraser Roberts & Pembry, 1978; Levitan, 1977), suggest some degree of genetically based susceptibility to this condition.

MIGRAINE

Most evidence points to a high degree of heritability for migraine. McKusick (1978), for example, suggested that only the pattern of inheritance is unclear. When two people affected with migraine mate, estimates of incidence in their children range from 69% to 83%. When only one parent is affected, incidence drops to 44–61 percent. Finally, when neither parent is affected, incidence is estimated at 3–29%.

Twins reared apart are highly concordant for migraine. In the international literature, four out of five reporting cases were concordant (Farber, 1981), with even the age of onset and the pattern of headache greatly alike (Juel-Nielsen, 1980). Preliminary results from the Minnesota study of identicals reared apart (Chen, 1979; Holden, 1980) also indicate striking concordance in the migraine pattern.

COLITIS

Literature on the heritability of ulcerative colitis is limited. However, the disease is known to run in families, and associations are suggested between ulcerative colitis and ankylosing spondylitis, which now is linked to a specific immune-system defect (HLA-B27) (Fraser Roberts & Pembry, 1978; Janowitz, 1975; McKusick, 1978; Riccardi, 1977). Two twin studies reported extremely high concordance for colitis—63% and 100%, respectively—although their sample sizes and selection methods leave them open to question (Janowitz, 1975; Lynch, 1976).

Two sets of identical female twins reared apart and discordant for colitis were reported by Shields (1962). Environmental factors were suggested by the discordance and by the fact that in both instances the affected twin had had an extremely late and presumably traumatic separation from her rearing environment (4 and 12 years of age, respectively). Furthermore, in both sets, the affected twin had had more illnesses throughout the life span. However, association with an immune-system defect was suggested by the case of an affected twin who also reported "osteoarthritis" (recall the link with ankylosing spondylitis).

"PSYCHOSOMATIC" SYMPTOMS
AND HABIT DISTURBANCES

Menstrual complaints traditionally have been regarded as psychosomatic and it is known that both the cycle and the degree of symptom reporting are influenced by environmental factors (Frieze, Parson, Johnson, Ruble & Zellman, 1978). The interaction between genes and environment can be seen in the fact that identicals reared apart fall between identicals and fraternals reared in the same home in the number of months' difference in onset of menstruation (Farber, 1981). However, the presumably innate physiological basis of menstrual functioning is supported by Rybo and Hallberg's (1966) finding that degree of blood loss during menstruation is significantly more similar for identicals than for fraternals (intraclass correlations of .64 and .07, respectively) and by the serendipitous finding that identical twins reared apart—irrespective of degree of possible mutual influence—tend to report the same menstrual symptoms, often in highly similar terms, and frequently to report them as occurring during the same periods of life (Farber, 1981). Further research on identicals reared apart, on cultural factors and on prostoglandin metabolism in women of varying degrees of consanguinity should illuminate this area.

Enuresis is another symptom often attributed to emotional stress. Whether stress is necessary or whether enuresis is simply an expression of disturbance in stage IV (non-REM) sleep is moot. However, twin studies imply that an underlying genetic susceptibility is necessary before the symptom is expressed, whatever the stressor. Enuretic children tend to come from families with histories of enuresis, and identicals are consistently more concordant than fraternals (Badalyan and others, 1971; Bakwin, 1971).

According to limited data on twins reared apart, globulus hystericus symptoms were 100% concordant, nail biting was highly concordant, and nervous mannerisms were similar often enough to indicate the need for further investigation. One of the most striking findings with twins reared apart is that even highly separated identicals frequently describe the experience of anxiety in a highly similar manner (Farber, 1981; Juel-Nielsen, 1980). This information is reminiscent of Lacey's (1962) findings on arousal patterns and dovetails with hypotheses of underlying arousal patterns and phenotypic personality patterns from workers as divergent as the experimentalist Claridge (1967) and the psychoanalysts Korner (1964), Fries (1977; Fries & Wolff, 1953), Escalona (1963, 1968), and Thomas, Chess, and Birch (1968). The data are provocative enough to lead to speculation that each individual is born with the potential for a discrete cluster of symptoms, the expression of which will depend on the interaction among congenital and genetic factors and environmental stressors (Farber, 1981).

PSYCHOSIS

Twin, adoption, and fostering studies generally support the hypothesis that a genetic predisposition is a necessary precondition for the development of schizophrenia or severe affective disorder (e.g., Bertelsen, Harvald & Hauge, 1977; Depue, 1979; Gottesman, 1976; Gottesman & Shields, 1972; Tsuang & Vandermey, 1980). Twin concordance often is found to increase with increasing severity of disturbance, a pattern noted previously in CHD and alcoholism, suggesting that some individuals may be more susceptible because of a greater *genetic load*. This formulation frequently is described as a *diathesis-stressor model:* the greater the innate susceptibility (diathesis), the lower the degree of external stressors needed to bring the individual over the threshold into symptom expression. There also are suggestions in the literature that, to some degree, disorders breed true and may be somewhat independent of each other. However, the current transitional period in psychiatric diagnosis may lead to the reevaluation of patients reported in early studies, with some affective disorders reinterpreted as schizophrenia and vice versa.

Current work often takes the genetic hypothesis as given and seeks either to estimate the form of transmission or to develop methods of predicting which individuals are at highest risk. For example, the rate of mood disorder among relatives of bipolar patients is 10–20 times the general population rate (Tsuang & Vandermey, 1980). Put another way, roughly 30% of the children of bipolar parents can be expected to exhibit affective disorder at some point in life. Scattered case reports suggest that some offspring of bipolar parents exhibit a distinctive group of symptoms, including hyperactivity, short attention span, poor frustration tolerance, explosiveness, and school performance below expectations (Dyson & Barcai, 1970). Kestenbaum (1979) found a similar constellation of symptoms, plus a verbal IQ significantly greater than performance IQ on cognitive tests. A recent trial study (Decina, Kestenbaum, Farber, Kron, Gargan, & Fieve, 1981) compared 31 offspring of bipolar lithium responding parents with a control group of children from families with no history of either schizophrenia or affective disorder. Approximately one-third of the bipolar offspring exhibited the constellation of symptoms reported in the literature, more, when subclinical manifestations were counted. The verbal-performance discrepancy was found in 39% of the BP offspring. Blind evaluations of test protocols also produced 16 Rorschachs with color greater than form percentages, 15 of which were in the bipolar group (Kestenbaum, Decina, Farber, Kron, Sackeim, Gargan & Fieve, 1982). However, the relationship among these variables was unclear, no single variable or group of variables being significantly associated with diagnosis.

Future studies on larger groups of children and on offspring reared away from bipolar parents may prove illuminating. As with research on children of schizophrenic parents, it is likely that the patterns of those genuinely at high risk will be less simple than now postulated at the early stages of investigation. Nonetheless, the possibility remains that an approach assuming genetic transmission may lead to earlier intervention and new insights into the nature of the disorder itself.

FUTURE DIRECTIONS

The discipline of behavior genetics is still in its infancy. While rooted in work done before the turn of the century, it has emerged as a discipline in its own right only within the past decade or so. As in many emergent disciplines, the claims and counterclaims are sometimes strident and almost certainly overstated. The advocates of a strongly hereditarian or a strongly environmentalist position probably will have to alter formulations as better and richer data emerge and as the complexity of human gene–environment interactions becomes clearer.

For those curious enough and patient enough to wait until science gains precedence over politics in the field—as inevitably will happen over time—the area offers a wealth of new viewpoints with which to approach old dilemmas. For example, more accurate identification of populations at risk for particular disorders should lead to earlier and better interventions. For those interested in examining specific traits or disorders with an eye toward etiology, the refinement in selecting target populations should, in the long run, lead to a more thorough understanding of precursors and of the disorders themselves. For those, like myself, interested in the process of development, the field may prove revolutionary. At the moment, there is a split in the types of investigations being done. Many researchers are following the established route of studying discrete traits at specific moments in time. Others, however, are beginning to look at longitudinal data with an eye toward process rather than endpoints. Soon, the issues in this area will no longer hinge on heritabilities but on how the genetic blueprint predetermines developmental sequences and how, in turn, environment activates or inhibits the blueprint and transforms into new levels of organization.

REFERENCES

ASHLEY, D. J. B. Infectious diseases. In A. Sorsby (ed.), *Clinical genetics* (2d ed.). London: Butterworths, 1973.

BADALYAN, L. O., ORADOVSKAIA, I. V., & LOPOVETSKAIA, N. G. Nocturnal enuresis in twins (clinico-genetic analysis). *Urololgy Nefrology (Moscow)*, 1971, *36*(2), 44–48 (in Russian with English summary).

BAKWIN, H. Enuresis in twins. *American Journal of Diseases of Children,* 1971, *121*(3). 222–225.

BEESON, P. D., & McDERMOTT, W. (eds.). *Textbook of medicine* (14th ed.). Philadelphia: Saunders, 1975.

BENBOW, C. P., & STANLEY, J. C. Sex differences in mathematical ability: Fact or artifact? *Science,* 1980, *210* 1262–1264.

BERTELSEN, B., HARVALD, B., & HAUGE, M. A Danish study of manic-depressive disorders. *British Journal of Psychiatry,* 1977, *130,* 330–351.

BLOCK, N. J., & DWORKIN, G. *The IQ controversy.* New York: Pantheon, 1976.

CAVALLI-SFORZA, L. L., & BODMER, W. T. *The genetics of human populations.* San Francisco: Freeman, 1978.

CEDERLOF, R., FRIBERG, L., JONSSON, E., & KAIJ, L. Respiratory symptoms and angina pectoris in twins with reference to smoking habits. *Archives Environmental Health,* 1966, *13,* 726–737.

CHAKRAVARTTI, M. R., & BOGEL, F. *A twin study on leprosy.* Stuttgart: Thieme, 1973.

CHEN, E. Twins reared apart: A living lab. *New York Times Magazine,* 9 December 1979, pp. 112-126.

CLARIDGE, G. S. *Personality and arousal.* New York: Pergamon, 1967.

CLIFFORD, C. A., FULKER, D. W., GURLING, H. M. D., & MURRAY, R. M. A twin study of alcohol use: Workshop on twin research in smoking, drinking, and substance exposure. *Acta Geneticae Medicae et Gemellologiae.* (Rome), 1980, *29,* 64.

CONTERIO, F., & CHIARELLI, B. Study of the inheritance of some daily life habit. *Heredity,* 1962, *17,* 347–359.

DECINA, P., KESTENBAUM, C. J., FARBER, S., KRON, L., GARGAN, M., & FIEVE, R. R. Children of bipolar patients. Paper presented to the annual meeting of the American Psychiatric Association, New Orleans, 1981.

DE FAIRE, U. Ischemic heart disease in death-discordant twins. *Acta Medicae Scandinavica* (supp.), 1974, 568.

————. Ischemic heart disease in death-discordant twins. *Acta Geneticae Medicae et Gemellologiae.* (Rome), 1976, *25,* 271–275.

DYSON, W. L., & BARCAI, A. Treatment of children of lithium-responding parents. *Current Therapeutic Research,* 1970, *12*(5), 286–290.

ESCALONA, S. Patterns of experience and the developmental process. *Psychoanalytic study of the child,* 1963, *8,* 197–244.

————. *The roots of individuality.* Chicago: Aldine, 1968.

EYSENCK, H. J., & KAMIN, L. J. *The intelligence controversy.* New York: Wiley, 1981.

FARBER, S. L. *Identical twins reared apart: A reanalysis.* New York: Basic Books, 1981.

FRASER ROBERTS, J., & PEMBRY, M. E. *An introduction to medical genetics.* New York: Oxford University Press, 1978.

FRIES, M., & WOLFF, P. Some hypotheses on the role of the congenital activity type in personality development. *Psychoanalytic Study of the Child,* 1953, *8,* 48–64.

————. Longitudinal study: Prenatal period to parenthood. *Journal of the American Psychoanalytic Association,* 1977, *25*(1), 115–140.

FRIEZE, I. J., PARSON, J. E., JOHNSON, P. B., RUBLE, D. N., & ZELLMAN, G. L. *Women and sex roles: A social psychological perspective.* New York: Norton, 1978.

FULLER, J. L., & THOMPSON, W. R. *Foundations of behavior genetics.* St. Louis: Mosby, 1978.

GEDDA, L. *Twins in history and science.* Springfield: Thomas, 1961.

GOODWIN, D. W. *Is alcoholism hereditary?* New York: Oxford University Press, 1976.

GOODWIN, D. W., SCHULSINGER, F., HERMANSEN, L., GUZE, S. B., & WINOKUR, G. Alcohol problems in adoptees raised apart from alcoholic biological parents. *Archives of General Psychiatry,* 1973, *28,* 238–243.

Goodwin, D. W., Schulsinger, F., Knop, J., Mednick, S., & Guze, S. B. Alcoholism and depression in adopted-out daughters of alcoholics. *Archives of General Psychiatry,* 1977, *34,* 751–755. (a)

————. Psychopathology in adopted and nonadopted daughters of alcoholics. *Archives of General Psychiatry,* 1977, *34,* 1005–1009. (b)

Gottesman, I. I. A critical review of recent adoption, twin, and family studies of schizophrenia: Behavioral genetic perspectives. *Schizophrenia Bulletin,* 1976, *2,* 360–453.

Gottesman, I. I., & Shields, J. *Schizophrenia and genetics: A twin study vantage point.* New York: Academic, 1972.

Gurling, H. M. D., Murray, R. M., & Clifford, C. A. Psychological deficit, brain damage, and the genetic predisposition to alcoholism: A twin study (workshop on twin research in smoking, drinking, and substance exposure). *Acta Geneticae Medicae et Gemellologiae* (Rome), 1980, *29,* 64.

Harvald, B, & Hauge, M. Hereditary factors elucidated by twin studies. In J. V. Neel, M. W. Shaw, & W. J. Schull (eds.), *Genetics and the epidemiology of chronic diseases.* PHS publication no. 1163. Washington, D.C.: U.S. Public Health Service, 1965.

Holden, C. Twins reunited. *Science 80, 1,* 7, 1980, 55–59.

Janowitz, H. D. Chronic inflammatory diseases of the intestine. In P. B. Beeson & W. McDermott (eds.), *Textbook of medicine* (14th ed.). Philadelphia: Saunders, 1975.

Jencks, C. *Inequality: A reassessment of the effect of family and schooling in America.* New York: Basic Books, 1972.

Juel–Nielsen, N. *Individual and environment: A psychiatric-psychological investigation of MZ twins reared apart* (rev. ed.). New York: International Universities, 1980.

Kaij, L. *Alcoholism in twins.* Stockholm: Almquist & Wiksell, 1960.

Kamin, L. J. *The science and politics of IQ.* New York: Wiley, 1974.

Kestenbaum, C. J. Adolescents at risk for manic-depressive illness: Possible predictors. *American Journal of Psychiatry,* 1979, *139,* 9.

Kestenbaum, C. J., Decina, P., Farber, S., Kron, L., Sackeim, H., Gargan, M., & Fieve, R. R. Offspring of bipolar parents. 1982. Unpublished Ms. Available from Kestenbaum, C. J.

Korner, A. Some hypotheses regarding the significance of individual differences at birth for later development. *Psychoanalytic Study of the Child,* 1964, *19,* 58–72.

Koskenvuo, M., Kaprio, J., Langinvainio, H., Romo, M., & Sarna, S. Coronary-prone behavior in adult like-sexed twins: An epidemiological study (workshop on psychosocial factors in cardiovascular disease). *Acta Geneticae Medicae et Gemellologiae* (Rome), 1980, *29,* 70.

Kringlen, E. Stress and coronary heart disease (workshop on psychosocial factors in cardiovascular disease). *Acta Geneticae Medicae et Gemellologiae* (Rome), 1980, *29,* 70.

Lacey, J. I., & Lacey, B. C. The law of initial value in the longitudinal study of autonomic constitution: Reproducibility of autonomic response and response patterns over a four-year interval. *Annuals of the New York Academy of Science,* 1962, *98,* 1257–1290.

Levitan, M. *Textbook of human genetics* (2d ed.). New York: Oxford University Press, 1977.

Liljefors, I. Coronary heart disease in male twins. *Acta Medicae Scandinavica* (supp.)., 1970, 511.

————. Coronary heart disease in male twins: Seven-year follow-up of discordant pairs. *Acta Geneticae Medicae et Gemellologiae* (Rome), 1976, *25,* 276–280.

Lynch, H. T. *Cancer genetics.* Springfield: Thomas, 1976.

Mackenzie, B. Hypothesized genetic racial differences in IQ: A criticism of three proposed lines of evidence. *Behavior Genetics,* 1980, *10*(2), 225–234.

McKusick, V. A. *Mendelian inheritance in man* (5th ed.). Baltimore: Johns Hopkins Press, 1978.

Myrhed, M., & Floderus, B. Alcohol consumption in relation to factors associated with ischemic heart disease: A co-twin control study. *Acta Geneticae Medicae et Gemellologiae* (Rome), 1976, *25,* 129–132.

PARTANEN, J. K., BRUUN, K., & MARKKANEN, T. Inheritance of drinking behavior: A study on intelligence, personality, and the use of alcohol of adult twins. *Finnish Foundation of Alcohol Studies,* 1966, *14,* 1–159.

PLOMIN, R., DeFRIES, J. C., & McCLEARN, G. E. *Behavioral genetics: A primer.* San Francisco: Freeman, 1980.

PROPPING, P., & VOGEL, F. Twin studies in medical genetics. *Acta Geneticae Medicae et Gemellologiae* (Rome), 1976, *25,* 249–258.

ROE, A. The adult adjustment of children of alcoholic parents raised in foster-homes. *Quarterly Journal of Studies on Alcohol,* 1944, *5,* 378–393.

ROSE, R. J., FULKER, D. N., MILLER, J. Z., GRIM, C. E., & CHISTIAN, J. C. Heritability of systolic blood pressure. *Actae Geneticae Medicae et Gemellologiae,* 1980, *29,* 143–149.

RYBO, G., & HALLBERG, L. Influence of heredity and environment on normal menstrual blood loss: A study of twins. *Acta Obstetrica Gynecologica Scandinavica* 1966, *45*(4), 389–410.

SCHAIE, K. W., ANDERSON, V. E., McCLEARN, G. E., & MONEY, J. (eds.). *Developmental human behavior genetics.* Lexington: Heath, 1975.

SCHUCKIT, M. A., GOODWIN, D. W., & WINOKUR, G. A study of alcoholism in half siblings. *American Journal of Psychiatry,* 1972, *128,* 122–126.

SHIELDS, J. *Monozygotic twins brought up apart and brought up together.* New York: Oxford University Press, 1962.

STERN, C. *Principles of human genetics.* San Francisco: Freeman, 1973.

TAYLOR, H. F. *The IQ game.* New Brunswick: Rutgers University Press, 1980.

THOMAS, A., CHESS, S., & BIRCH, H. G. *Temperament and behavior disorders in children.* New York: New York University Press, 1968.

TOMIZUKA, C., TOBIAS, S., STAGE, E. K., KARPLUS, R., CHIPMAN, S., EGELMAN, E., ALPER, J., LEIBONITZ, L., BECKWITH, J., LEVINE, R., LEEDS, A., MORAN, D. J., LUCHINS, E. H., & LUCHINS, A. S. Letters. *Science,* 1981, *212,* 114–121.

VESELL, E. S., PAGE, J. G., & PASSANTI, G. T. Genetic and environmental factors affecting ethanol metabolism in man. *Clinica Pharmacologia Therapeutica,* 1971, *12,* 192–201.

10

Stress and the Development of Somatic Disorders

Leonard S. Zegans

THE RELATIONSHIP BETWEEN MIND AND BODY has fascinated philosophers and scientists throughout history. In Greece an ancient Orphic tradition regarded the body as corrupt, imprisoning man's pure and immortal soul. Hebraic thought, like earlier primitive attitudes, was monistic, believing that a person's mental states and physical activities were part of an indivisible whole. The Elizabethans revered the body as a microcosmic representation of the divine universe, a belief given expression by many Renaissance poets and artists. According to the spirit of the times, then, we have reviled our bodies, objectified them, and revered them.

The prevailing cultural model defining the relationship of body to consciousness tends to be reflected in disease models. Ever since the Enlightenment we have viewed the body from a scientific-materialist perspective, comparing it to a machine, an assemblage of inter-working parts—each capable of autonomous breakdown or repair. Consciousness, feelings, and thoughts have been conceived of as epiphenomena of physical processes. This perspective was summed up by Cabanis in the eighteenth century: "Les nerfs—violà tout l'homme" (quoted in Shaeffer, 1967:343). To that savant, the brain secreted thoughts just as the liver produced bile.

Today we are beginning to develop a different perspective about mind-body issues. Exciting research in psychoimmunology, neuroendocrinology, and neurophysiology is encouraging us to take another look at the mind-body question and particularly at the issue of how psychosocial stress can effect pathological changes in body function. This chapter reviews current concepts about stress and discusses the new data that help us understand how tensions, conflicts, and losses contribute to the onset and progress of organic illness.

There has always been puzzlement about the fact that thoughts and feelings, which are immaterial, can produce alterations in body structure and function. For a thinker like Freud, who grew up in the scientific-materialist tradition, the clinical evidence that mental processes could bring about physical changes was remarkable; he called this transformation the "mysterious leap from mind to body" (Deutsch, 1959: 5). Freud was always uncomfortable that he could not root his theories of mental illness in some physicalistic soil.

Like others of his era, Freud was an heir of Descartes, who had taught that in the human being mind and body were separated into the realism of *res cogitans* and *res extensa*. (Descartes, 1952). Unlike mind, body was held to be divisible. By separating out the "thinking substance'' from corporality, Descartes in effect despiritualized the body, making it acceptable as an object of scientific inquiry. This model, dubbed with some irony by Ryle (1949) the doctrine of the "ghost in the machine," helped spur research into the structure and functions of the body. The anatomy and physiology of each organ could now be studied by careful techniques that illuminated the workings of every separate part. This led to the classical medical model, which emphasized the search for specific physiochemical agents that through their invasive, toxic, or degenerative properties caused disease. Illnesses were characterized by discrete morphological changes in tissues and organs.

As medical science came to understand the plumbing and wiring of the body better, it began to see all organismic phenomena strictly in physicalistic terms. The mind-body dilemma was resolved by denying mind any separate reality apart from physicochemical events. Thoughts came to be seen as effects only, never the cause of brain alterations. The modern epiphenomenalist position was put succinctly by Gerard (1959), who stated that "no twisted thought without a twisted molecule" (p. 1620).

The confidence of many biomedical scientists in this model stems from the stunning accomplishments of modern medicine using a materialist approach. This strategy has been particularly successful in the understanding and treatment of infectious disease.

With a shift of contemporary medical concern away from acute infections and toward chronic illness, awareness of multiple factors in pathogenesis has grown. There is a current trend to identify all those elements—invasive, genetic, and psychosocial—that can alter the internal milieu and create conditions favorable to pathological alterations. We are encountering in medicine today a greater acknowledgment of the importance of psychosocial factors such as bereavement, loss of social network, and change of social status in contributing to the onset and course of disease.

Medicine is gradually coming to regard thoughts, emotions, and environmental inputs as salient *biological* factors in disease and health processes. There is accumulating evidence that the brain and peripheral organs are linked in complex, mutually adjusting relationships tuned to *social,* as well as *physical,* alterations of the environment. We are returning to a viewpoint fostered by ancient Hellenic physicians, who understood that in treating an illness more than the diseased part and the proximate cause of the malady must be considered. The true physician is the person who "never thinks of the part without thinking of the whole, who always sees it as it affects and is affected by everything else" (Jaeger, 1944:26).

It has been difficult, however, for science to admit that quantitatively soft factors have the same weight as more clearly physical features. Biological thinking has for many years been dominated by the models and methods of classical physics and chemistry, with their emphasis on mathematics and quantitative measurement. Since the time of Galileo, scientists have held to the view that qualitative difference in perception (colors, tones, smells, tastes, sensations) are distinguished solely by quantitative differences in reality. Accordingly, scientific research has ransacked the subjective modes of our mental representations to find the real essence of bodies (and their relations).

Descartes designated the qualities that belong to bodies in themselves as *primary* and called those *secondary* that belong to a body by virtue of its action upon our senses. He allowed as primary qualities only shape, size, position, and motion. For him the physical body's reality coincided with its mathematical description. What was real and worthy of study was that which could be described and quantified by the prevailing mathematics of the day. The mathematics of the past 400 years has dealt largely with the size, shape, or movement of spacially discrete bodies; therefore, problems involving changes in patterns of behavior of objects rather than in their mass or velocity have escaped scientific inquiry and interest. When one attempts to understand the functioning of a human being as a symbol producing, communicating organism, the mathematics of primary qualities is inadequate. A more explicit mathematics of human biology would generate a formal system that gave *patterned* and not simply quantitative meaning to life events.

For years medicine ignored certain questions simply because phenomena involving symbolic meaning, rules of interaction, etc., are not reducible to classical mathematical equations. We are just beginning to address problems of human biology without denigrating meaning and feeling. In order to understand the impact of stress on physiological processes, we must first recognize meaning itself as a biological principle. As Laszlo commented, "Specialized science is simply irrelevant to the question of meaning in life. But the latter cannot be dismissed with a wave of the hand as specialists tend to do; there are good indications that there is such a thing as 'will to meaning' in man as one of his most basic motivational forces" (Laszlo, 1973:67). Harré and Secord (1973) also observed that "actions are mediated by *meanings,* that is considerations that arise from an understanding of the connection that actions have with one another, and with their consequences in complex patterns of social life" (p. 37).

The pioneering work of ethologists like Lorenz, Tinbergen, and Hinde forcefully argued that *styles of social behavior* are an essential part of an organism's inherited endowment, necessary for both individual and species survival. (Lorenz, 1965; Hinde, 1966) In lower animals, elaborate programs have been developed to subserve the functions of mating, predation, aggression, social bonding, infant care, and territorial defense. Social stimuli related to these functions not only produce perceptual alterations but also have critical impact on the autonomic, endocrine, and immune systems of the organism. Excess or deficit of relevant social stimulation has *stress* implications for the animal just as profound as deprivation of food, extreme thermal change, or parasitic injury.

Patterned social communication and ritualized symbolic exchange have their substrate in the genetic coding of all animal species. Social behavior may involve changes in skin color and body temperature and a host of other physiological alterations. The sight or sound of a predator, the absence of a nestling, and the display of a mate all mobilize and alter a variety of body processes. Social stimuli have significant implications for the health and diesease of an organism. A stimulus noxious to an animal is just as likely to involve some change in social functioning as it is to be concerned with invasion of a foreign body.

In humans and other higher primates, learning takes a role played in lower species by instinctive mechanisms. Yet *Homo sapiens* has behavioral needs whose cogency and thrust give them an instinctual character. Identification of these fundamental needs in humans varies widely. My own list would include six essential needs:

1. Physical security
2. Attachment to specific others who are concerned with the individual's growth, development, and survival
3. Affiliation with a larger social group, which provides clear definition of norms, rules, reinforcements, and status
4. Opportunities for intimate sexual experiences with another
5. Opportunities for experiencing mastery in an environment of moderate complexity and novelty
6. Exposure to coherent meaning structures, which relate the developing self, the social group, and the physical environment

What the literature refers to as *psychosocial stress* occurs in response to those conditions that threaten the human mechanisms for achieving security, bonding, status, meaning, intimacy, and optimal arousal. Anticipation of the loss of these basic needs produces not only compensatory behaviors but emotional and physiological reactions as well. Stress, therefore, is an organismic state that can contribute (under the proper circumstances) to changes in body function, which if intense or chronic may lead to disease. Yet it is important to heed Engels (1977) warning that we should not use the concept of stress as "some kind of 'bad' force to which the person falls helpless victim" (p. 187). He rightly cautioned against regarding stress in terms of evil psychological or social influences that *alone* cause the person to break down and become mentally or physically ill. To do so would be to view stress as the psychosocial equivalent of germs—that is, as a single causative agent that must be attacked, treated, or exorcised. It is important, instead, to see stress as a factor that can trigger a multiplicity of organismic reactions, some of which may contribute to illness, while others may produce healthy adaptive response and personal growth. We must avoid reducing the rich concept of stress to the older, single-entity, mechanistic model of disease.

If indeed we are more accepting today of a medical paradigm that is moving away from a reductionistic, physicalistic, single-cause model to include host adaptive capacities and psychosocial factors as contributing to the onset and maintenance of illness, what role does the concept of stress play in this approach? What do we really mean by stress? Does the concept have a clarity that makes it especially useful in thinking about illness and health in new ways, and how can stress of a psychosocial nature alter body processes?

WHAT IS STRESS?

Occasionally a word or phrase takes hold that appears to promise much in the way of explaining some difficult phenomenon or sharpening our ideas about a problem. The concept of stress seems to have had a special place in the minds of laymen and scientists ever since Seyle (1966) popularized the term in his writings on the *general adaptation syndrome.* However, one senses that as more theorists attempt to examine and define stress, this concept becomes more diffuse and complex. Lazarus (1966) abandoned the task of trying operationally to define stress and instead use the word as "a generic term for the whole area of problems that includes the stimuli producing stress reactions, the reactions themselves and the various intervening processes" (p. 27). He suggested considering the *field* of stress, which would include physiological, sociological, and psychological phenomena and related concepts. In his opinion, stress is not a stimulus, a response, or an intervening variable but a collective term for an area of study.

Lazarus also noted that there have been three main variations of the meaning of the term. The most common approach has been to regard stress as a *stimulus,* a condition that produces turbulence or some sort of reactive change. Other writers (Appley & Trumbull, 1977) have emphasized the *response* side, the nature of the turbulence itself. Lazarus himself favors the view that stress is a relational or transactional concept describing certain kinds of adaptive commerce between any organism and its environment.

Stress from the Perspective of the Stimulus: Life Events Research

Stress conceived as a stimulus has been used to describe situations characterized as new, intense, rapidly changing, sudden, or unexpected. Stressful stimuli can also include stimulus deficit, absence of expected stimulation, highly persistent stimulation, fatigue, and boredom. Lazarus (1966) also included as stress stimuli such events as failure or the threat of failure, noxious or unpleasant agents in the environment, isolation, bereavement, and rapid social change. Other stimulus situations mentioned in the literature as stressful are a. loss of personal, physical, cognitive, or affective functions; b. frustration of anticipated rewards or goal attainment; c. failure of or change in social feedback mechanisms; d. impulse flooding; and e. approach–avoidance conflict situations.

When one regards stress only from the vantage point of the stimulus there is a tendency to disregard the function of the interpretive *meaning* of the event. As Hinkle (1973) put it, "In view of the fact that people react to their life situations or social conditions in terms of the meaning of those situations to them, it is difficult to accept the hypothesis that certain kinds of situations or relationships are inherently stressful and certain others are not" (p. 46).

The stress as stimulus concept has triggered very active research on possible connections between stress and bodily illness. Many years ago, Meyer (1958) argued that certain alterations of life circumstances, such as changes of habitat, births, deaths, and new jobs, have a potent influence on the balance between health and illness. Holmes (1974), Rahe (1968), and their collaborators examined this perception in a series of studies geared to determine whether changes in a person's life could be statistically correlated with onset of illness. The *psychosomatic medicine movement* had long before associated certain internal psychological conflicts with predispositions to particular diseases (e.g. asthma, ulcers, ulcerative colitis). The *life events research model* hypothesized that it is possible to make predictions about stress and susceptibility to a much wider array of diseases (infectious, neoplastic, autoimmune) by determining the magnitude of critical life changes taking place within a limited span of time.

> These psychophysiological studies indicate that naturally occurring and experimentally induced life situations, which threaten the security of the individual and evoke attempts at adaptive behavior, also evoke significant alterations in the function of most bodily tissues, organs and systems. These physiological changes in their turn will lead to a lowering of the body's resistance to disease. The greater the magnitude of such life changes, the greater the risk of acquiring an illness of a serious nature. (Rahe, 1964:42)

Empirical studies by Holmes and Rahe (1967) generated a hierarchical list of life event changes likely to require significant alteration in the ongoing adaptive patterns of the individual. The events themselves need not be of a traumatic or negative character to provoke disease. The essential factor is the new demand on the usual adaptive patterns of the person. This line of research has not considered the psychological meaning or social desirability of life events but only their disruptive impact. Underlying this approach is the assumption that certain events require more intense and prolonged coping efforts than do others. The greater the strain on the coping mechanisms, the more likely that an inadequate or inappropriate response will be utilized, thus eliciting idiosyncratic or pathological physiological reactions. A Social Readjustment Rating Scale (SRRS) developed that rank-orders events judged to require the greatest adaptational effort and presumably to generate the greatest stress. Items such as death of a spouse, divorce, marital separation, jail term, and death of a close family member are thought to require the most adaptive change.

This work permitted Holmes and Rahe (1967) to determine the temporal relationship between a clustering of life changes and the onset and severity of illness. They discovered a strong relationship between major health changes and *life crisis,* the latter defined as an accumulation of at least 150 *life change units* (LCUs) during a period of one year. Each life change (as a stimulus) has a fixed numerical value; thus, the more life events that presumably require a shift in the usual mode of living, the greater the risk of illness. This research has been concerned more with establishing statistical correlations between observable events than with studying the process by which such pathological changes occur. Were the subjects who developed illness indeed more stressed than those who remained healthy? Did they share certain personality or physiological traits? Holmes and Masuda (1974) speculated that "life change events, by evoking adaptive efforts by the human organism that are faulty in kind and duration, lower 'bodily resistance' and enhance the probability of disease occurrence" (p. 67). This presumes that demanding life events must necessarily evoke faulty adaptive efforts, which will lead to pathogenic physiological change. Naturally, such a bold hypothesis has attracted its share of supporters and detractors (Cleary, 1974; Rabkin & Struening, 1976).

Many critics argue that life events theory ignores all intervening reactive variables, including coping responses, anticipatory reactions, and longitudinal difficulties of the individual. They suggest that an understanding of a life event's impact must take into account the physical susceptibility of the individual, the meaning of the social changes, the person's ability to cope with a variety of stresses, and the individual's social network, ethnic and class background, and cultural assumptions.

Serious alterations in a person's environment and capacities do create challenges for new accommodations in the psychological and biological spheres. Such new adaptations, however, need not be inadequate. The maturational process from infancy to adulthood constantly places novel demands on our self-image, social expectations, and sense of body organization. Sometimes the strains of these developmental epochs indeed trigger functional mental illness or organic disease. They can also foster a sense of dynamic growth, or even joy, and promote health. A life event change as a stimulus may be the occasion for precipitating a stress, but it is not a stress in itself.

Stress appears to be an altered state of the individual that arises as a consequence of adaptive failure and not adaptive challenge. Illness is the outcome of multiple characteristics of the organism, which interact with a variety of interdependent factors, including social context and disease agents. As Cleary (1974) and Rabkin and Struening (1976) have pointed out, the life events research while calling attention to an important source of stress has focused only on linear relationships between independent and dependent variables. The task of new investigation and theory is to go beyond the linkage of stimulus and probability of illness to illuminate those internal mechanisms through which life events are believed to have their pathological impact. In the face of these criticisms, many authors have observed that although certain events or situations are potential stress provokers, the stress itself lies on the response side of the equation.

Stress from the Perspective of the Response

We all know, as Gilbert and Sullivan put it, that "things are seldom what they seem." Much depends upon context, mood, and experience when we come to interpret the meaning of an event. The death of a partner can be a catastrophic blow to one child and a liberation for another. With the exception of extreme and sudden life threatening situations, no raw stimulus is a universal stressor. The stimulus itself may cause some impact damage, but the true consequences of stress arise from the manner in which the organism responds to the presumed danger. In an anaphylactic reaction, the direct tissue damage by the invading foreign agent may be slight, but the inflammation and edema of the allergic response can be life threatening. Thus, in this perspective it is the way in which the organism handles perceived stressors—the defenses it mobilizes and the alarm reactions ignited—that constitutes the true nature of the stress.

There may be something excessive or unusual about a reaction that produces psychological or physiological consequences detrimental to the organism. The presence of emotional activity has been used as a post facto index to determine the existence of stress. Some alteration of body function that exceeds or departs from the norm—increased heart rate, adrenocorticotrophic hormone (ACTH) excretion, galvanic skin response change, etc.—has been seen as a marker of stress. A linkage is made among a noxious stimulus, an emotional response, and some alteration of physiological function. From this perspective, stress would be regarded as the demands placed upon the organism to respond adaptively to a stimulus appraised as noxious. The emphasis in this model is upon the meaning of the stimulus, rather than the objective nature of the stimulus itself.

The work of Selye (1966) first set the mold for response theories of stress. In a later article (1978), Tache and Selye state that "stress is the nonspecific *'response* of the body to any demand made upon it,' that is, the rate at which we live at any one moment" (p. 5). He went on to describe the *triphasic response,* which he labeled an inevitable "call to arms" of the body's defenses. This response includes the *alarm reaction,* the *state of resistance* (during which the initial symptoms diminish or vanish), and, after prolonged exposure to a noxious stimulus, the *stage of exhaustion.* Selye called the physiological aspects of these states (thymolympathic involution, adrenal enlargement, and gastric ulcers) the *nonspecific* response of the body to any demand which is mediated through the hypothalamus by its production of corticotrophic releasing factor (CRF). He insisted that no matter how systemic damage is produced, it is always accompanied or followed by manifestations of the systemic defense, or *countershock.* In this theory, the hypothalamic-pituitary-adrenal axis organizes and expresses the defensive reactions and the physiological responses that may precipitate organic disease.

Selye's elucidation of the body's response to stress has led to a better grasp of the biochemical, anatomic, and neurohormonal changes that accompany adaptation to stress. However, as Froehlich (1978) pointed out, Selye did not explicitly include cognitive or emotional factors and their impact on the adaptive processes. Mason's (1975) pioneering work indicated that the psychological meaning of a stimulus, and not nonspecific stressful factors, activates the hypothalamic-pituitary-adrenal system. It has been suggested that when a set of predictable events is altered so that expectancies are not met, hypothalamic-pituitary-adrenal activity is increased. Levine and associates (1978) stated this point emphatically when discussing the role of the organism's evaluation of a threatening stimulus.

> Thus, if the organism evaluates the situation as threatening and uncertain, there will be a continuing high level of activation. However, if the organism evaluates the situation as being safe and one in which he can master the probable events, the resulting physiological response will be diminished, if not absent, even though the situation itself had been extremely threatening. (p. 6)

Theorists who define stress from a response perspective see it as an *imbalance* between the *requirements* to make an adaptive response and the *repertoire* of the individual. The greater the fracture of expectancies in a situation and the greater the perceived discrepancy between demand and response capacity and the higher the appraised cost of making such a reaction, the more stress there will be acting on the individual. A noxious stimulus perceived as a threat that can be handled by an available and inexpensive coping strategy would not create the same stress for the individual as would a similar stimulus for which the person had no adequate coping response. In short, stress involves a transaction in which resources must be mobilized, imposing a burden on the individual when automatic and sufficient resources and coping responses are not available to meet the demand.

COPING

Theorists have pointed to both intrapsychic and social factors in trying to determine why different individuals respond with different degrees of competence to similar threats and demands. Pearlin and Schooler (1978) defined coping as "the concept used to refer to any response to external life-strains that serves to prevent, avoid or control emotional distress" (p. 3). Interestingly, they emphasized external events, but obviously a maturational change (menopause or senility) also inflicts life strains that require elaborate coping strategies. However, these authors made a valuable distinction between social and psychological resources and specific coping responses. In their view, resources refer not to what people do but to what is available to them in developing their coping repertoires. Social resources would include crucial environmental supports, family, friends, and neighbors; psychological resources refer to personality characteristics that are drawn upon to help withstand threats. This framework would include both classical defense mechanisms (displacement, projection, denial, etc.) and characterological variables (self-esteem, anxiety threshold, problem-solving abilities). *Coping,* in contrast to resources, refers to that variety of behaviors, physiological reactions, cognitions, perceptions, and motor acts that control either the demand placed upon the organism directly or the interpretation placed on its anticipated consequences. Pearlin and Schooler distinguished three major types of coping responses: responses that change the situation out of which the strainful experience arises; responses that control the meaning of the strainful experience after it occurs but before the emergence of stress; and responses that function more for the control of stress itself after it has emerged.

Menninger (1954) elaborated a series of stages for coping with stress that proceeds from exaggeration of normal functions, to partial detachment from reality, through hypertrophy and solidification of emergency measures (making for pathology), and finally to disorientation, disorganization, and complete collapse of ego control. Each stage has unique psychological and, in many instances, physiological characteristics. Clearly, the stress response is far more complex than Selye originally envisioned, involving perceptual, interpretive, behavioral, and physiological adjustments. The physiology of one stress stage may differ dramatically from that of another further down the chain and involve entirely different demands upon the organism. The following section is a hypothetical sketch of the sequence of stages comprising the stress response.

STAGES OF THE STRESS RESPONSE

Stage of Alarm. A noxious stimulus is identified, leading to increased arousal, orientation toward the stimulus, and cessation of ongoing activities.

Stage of Appraisal. An assessment is made about the nature of the stressful provocation—including a scanning of past occurrences and the current meaning of the stimulus. Does the stimulus mean physical threat, loss, frustration, etc.? The appraisal function includes not only what the stimulus is but also what it has meant in the past, how it was met, and what current significance it has for the individual. A stimulus can be accurately appraised, but the consequences for the individual can be denied, distorted, minimized, or exaggerated. Appraisal must entail both identification of the stressor and clarification of its meaning for the person. An appraisal must determine whether the stimulus should be ignored, investigated further, or acted on immediately. There is no simple relationship between the initial recognition of the stressor and a corresponding emotion.

The appraisal thus combines a raw identification of the stimulus; a review of previous encounters; a tabulation of current meanings and possible consequences of the impact of the stimulus; and a rough assessment of coping possibilities. An array of emotions may be provoked until some final appraising judgment is made about what the stimulus is and what its consequences for the individual are likely to be. Characterological traits are important at this stage; they influence the identification of the stimulus, its meaning, and its salience with regard to coping.

Stage of Searching for a Coping Strategy. Dysphoric emotional arousal provoked by a stressor is decreased when there is anticipation of control or mastery through the implementation of a successful coping strategy (Levine, Weinberg, & Ursin, 1978). For any given stressor there are several possibilities for anticipating adequacy or inadequacy of response:

The stressor may be familiar because it was actively encountered in the past. In this case, either an adequate coping strategy was previously used or the coping approach was unsuccessful. A coping strategy can be unsuccessful because it is either inappropriate or inadequately applied. Memories of failed coping strategies provoke anxiety and encourage the search for new, more successful strategies.

The stressor may be familiar but only in a passive fashion. The individual has had no direct encounter with the stimulus situation but has experienced it vicariously. Coping responses are only secondhand or inferential in this instance. A soldier entering combat for the first time has only boot camp experience and the recounted coping strategies of veterans to rely upon. Often, analogous situations are drawn upon to provide a template for new coping responses. When the stressor has not been actively encountered but is familiar through the experience of others, the relationship with these sources may determine the level of emotional (and physiological) arousal.

The stressor may be totally unfamiliar and therefore no coping strategy exists in the individual's repertoire. Clearly, the affective accompaniment of the third stage will depend upon whether the individual believes that an adequate coping strategy is available. Coping strategies may be divided into those that deal either directly with the stimulus or indirectly with the ontological consequences of the stimulus. Control in the latter case is gained by dealing with the meaning of the stressor and not its direct noxious impact.[1] That is, when coping does not succeed in altering the situation and eliminating the problem, the impact of the stimulus may be buffered by responses that control the meaning of the situation. The cognitive neutralization of threats that are experienced makes it possible to avoid or minimize stresses that might otherwise evoke the responses associated with the next stage.

Stage of the Stress Response. This stage involves acutely dysphoric affect states (grief, anxiety, anger, panic), inadequate ego defenses, poor cognitive organization, and activation of altered autonomic and neuroendocrine patterns. This response comes from inadequate, inappropriate deactivated, or excessively prolonged coping reactions. The final outcome may be a state of either disorganization or exhaustion, affecting both mental and physiological processes.

Relation of Stages of the Stress Response to Alterations in Body Processes. Each of the above stages is accompanied by physiological reactions. Physical problems can occur with prolonged alarm, inadequate appraisal, inadequate coping, and prolonged coping. These reactions form the basis for stress related disease. Psychosocial stress can lead to either decreased resistance to disease processes or increased susceptibility to disease agents. Different disease vulnerabilities are related to changes in the host-pathogen interaction, which is mediated by neuroendocrine and immune functions. Alterations in the neuroendocrine, autonomic, and immune balance, which is related (hypothetically) to dysphoric affect states and regressive ego patterns, increase susceptibility to disease agents or processes. A question that has haunted research on stress related diseases has been whether the disturbed physiological functions are related in any specific way to either the nature of the stimulus or the personality of the individual undergoing the stress. Are pathophysiologically significant alterations of neuroendocrine-autonomic responses related to any or all of the following factors?

the nature of the stressor
the nature of the appraisal
the particular coping mechanism employed
the affects provoked by a failure of coping responses
constitutional factors interacting with general physiological arousal
developmentally learned physiological reactions

THE PSYCHOSOMATIC PERSPECTIVE

Whereas the life events approach focuses on stress as a stimulus that triggers a generalized vulnerability to illness, the psychosomatic movement began with an interest in identifying those personal response mechanisms that place some individuals by virtue of their personality and life history at selective risk for certain diseases. Research in this area takes as its starting point the patient's psyche, which through its conflicts, character patterns, and ego defenses intervenes between life event and illness (Pancheri, 1978; Kubie, 1953; Lidz, 1959).

The earliest psychoanalytic studies of illness by authors such as Ferenczi and Jellife regarded physiological disturbances as displaced, unconscious, symbolic expressions of repressed instinctual drives. Freud's theory of the origin of the conversion phenomena served as the template for these explanations of disturbed physiological function. The symptom was a form of symbolic communication that expressed some wish or impulse in disguised form because its normal path of expression was blocked. Ferenczi, for example, considered diarrhea to be an aggressive form of giving to others, which substituted for real performance (see Reiser, 1975, on the history of the psychosomatic movement).

Later writers such as Dunbar (1954) abandoned the concept of symbolic communication in favor of the idea that certain personality types were more vulnerable to certain illnesses. She described the ambitious, hard-driving executive, who was likely to develop cardiovascular disease, a profile that fits the type A personality. Dunbar was looking for *specific* personality or emotional factors that could be linked with specific diseases.

Alexander (1950) had a different idea. First, he attempted to relate specific unresolved unconscious conflicts with certain illnesses. He believed that these conflicts could occur in people with a variety of characterological traits. He emphasized that current stresses reactivated unresolved childhood conflicts. Real or anticipated life crises stirred up these fixated, unconscious conflicts, setting in motion both the person's immature psychological defenses and activation the specific physiological responses that had been associated with these conflicts in childhood. Alexander also postulated a particular constitutional vulnerability of a tissue, organ, or system that influenced the somatic localization of the physiological dysfunction brought on by the conflict. In this model, a critical life event by itself would not trigger the disease process without a reactivated conflict and a sensitized organ system.

Other writers such as Grinker (1950) and Schur (1955) were concerned not only with the reactivation of old conflicts but also with the primitivization of ego function that accompanied them. They regarded the pathophysiology of the psychosomatic disorder as stemming from a reactivation of the body response patterns of infancy and early childhood. Discomfort or stress in early childhood is accompanied by rather global, intense, and undifferentiated activation of the cardiovascular, visceral, and respiratory systems. With maturity, these diffuse reactions become modified and differentiated as we improve our coping abilities in handling stress. In some individuals, primitive body reactions may manifest themselves when normal psychological and behavioral adaptive patterns no longer work.

Thus, the psychosomatic school looked within the individual to examine his symbolic modes of communication, early conflicts, personality organization, and defensive operations to explain why the body was sometimes involved in stress situations. As Reiser (1975) commented, the early work in this field paid little attention either to broader genetic, interpersonal, or socioecological factors or to the mediating role of the central nervous system (CNS). There was no theory to account for how cognitive, affective, and perceptual mechanisms are ultimately linked to peripheral neurovegetative and immune patterns. Of course, these investigators lacked the rich information we have today about the brain and its multiple neuronal and hormonal connections with the rest of the body.

TOWARD A THEORY OF STRESS AND ILLNESS

Certain environmental, maturational, and intrapsychic events can initiate the stress response. Each stage of this response has associated cognitive, affective, and physiological components. Failure adequately to perceive, interpret, or cope with stress provoking stimuli may have serious pathophysiological consequences. Different physiological responses are possible during each of the intermediate stages of the stress response. The final outcome of the stress response is mastery, exhaustion, or disorganization. *Mastery* occurs when the coping strategies of the individual are appropriate and adequate to resolve the stressful situation. *Exhaustion* indicates that the coping reaction was appropriate in kind but not in degree to handle the threat. This leads either to a search for a new strategy or to a continuation of the old approach. Because of prolongation of the coping phase, fatigue occurs. This may result in feelings of depression or hopelessness, low arousal, inability to concentrate, physical inertia, and irregularities of autonomic and endocrine function. *Disorganization* occurs when either a deficient strategic repertoire or anxiety prevents an adequate integration and execution of coping responses. Feelings of panic and disintegration ensue, with a primitivization of both ego defenses and physiological responses. Exaggerated fight-flight mechanisms occur, eliciting peripheral organ emergency response. Obviously, different physiological patterns are activated when central coping mechanisms result in either exhaustion or disorganization. The physiological patterns that occur in these situations are specific to the state of the *central adaptational system* of the organism and not to the provoking stimulus. When a given stimulus is appraised as a threat to one of the basic needs outlined earlier, there is both a cognitive-affective and a physiological component to the reaction.

The distinction between abnormal physiological processes provoked by generalized failure of coping abilities and those triggered by appraisals of specific threats may reconcile the differences in approach to stress taken by the life events and psychosomatic schools. The former is concerned with the general failure of coping mechanisms as a result of mass demand on system capacity. The more numerous and difficult the life changes that are encountered, the greater the likelihood of adaptive failure, leading to disorganization or exhaustion. The collapse of the central adaptational system (mediating cognitive, affective, and physiological responses) represents a nonspecific strain on the entire psychobiological axis. This activates abnormal neuroendocrine and autonomic responses; diurnal rhythms are disrupted; balance between excitatory and inhibitory pathways is interrupted; and emergency hypothalamic-pituitary-adrenal responses are evoked. This state resembles Selye's general adaptation syndrome in the variety of tissues and systems involved. Any constitutional or acquired tissue weakness may be irritated by such an intense generalized reaction. When the threshold of tolerance of a given organ is breached, then the stage is set for pathology.

However, physiological events also occur throughout all stages of the stress response that do not involve such generalized consequences. When the individual appraises a given stimulus as a threat to a basic need (which may be involved in a neurotic conflict), then a very specific cognitive-affective-physiological complex is activated. There is no overall collapse of coping mechanisms, with an attendant disorganized physiological response. Instead, a more specific reaction occurs, linking appraisal, emotion, and target organ system. It is this process that interested the psychosomatic theorists. Clearly, a focal problem left unresolved may lead to a generalized adaptive collapse and each person uses his adaptive resources and coping skills to forestall that possibility. On the other side, loss of social supports, new job challenges, and change of status not only create new adaptive demands but also may unravel a coping strategy mediating a chronic neurotic problem centering on insecurity about a basic need.

The organ system can be activated, therefore, at any of the way stations of the stress response. This process can occur

1. as a concomitant physiological response to a failure of coping (exhaustion, disorganization)
2. as a concomitant physiological response to an appraisal of a threat to basic needs
3. as a nonspecific activation pattern during the state of orientation-alarm
4. as a physiological response when the stimulus has been correctly appraised but no adequate coping mechanism is either available or used (the individual is then vulnerable to the direct noxious impact of the stimulus)

Though the body does react during the different phases of the stress response, overt disease is not necessarily inevitable. The critical issue is what causes these transient events to become transformed into processes involving pathology of tissues and organs. A number of hypotheses exist:

1. The acute body response itself may cause damage, particularly if an already compromised organ is involved.
2. The acute response may cause transient insult to a tissue, but repeated occurrence of the stress may cause permanent tissue damage.

3. The acute physiological reaction can become chronic if it becomes conditioned to a benign stimulus resembling the stressor. Such a benign stimulus may be a more regular part of the individual's environment and provoke an unnecessary coping response.

4. A coping strategy may be used successfully but the physiological component is not terminated when the challenge is mastered. A *reverberating circuit* is established, which puts unusual strain on the body.

5. A minor stress provocation releases an inappropriately severe physiological response. Modulation is lacking that grades the body's reaction according to the nature of the threat. When all stresses are responded to as major assaults, abnormal physiological reactions are possible.

6. A physiological response appropriate and adequate to cope with a given threat may result in damage to some other aspect of the body through inhibiting a benign but vital body process or stimulating an irritating one.

7. Coping strategies can misfire when the behavioral component is inhibited but the physiological aspect is expressed (fight behavior inhibited but not its physiological component). The physiological aspects of a blocked action can be continuously repeated since no appropriate cutoff signal is received.

Our knowledge of how these interfaces between cognitive-affective components of the stress response and their physiological correlates produce serious tissue damage is limited. Different animal species have developed specific hormonal and autonomic responses to mediate important psychosocial stimuli. These responses occur in concrete situations that are vital to the survival needs of the organism. They occur in order to achieve some genetically programmed consummatory goal, reduce threats, or maintain group cohesion and social order. The endocrine-autonomic responses to biosocially significant stimuli are mediated by specific CNS circuits. Whenever a vital biological need of a lower animal is threatened, a stress response will occur. In man, whenever a stimulus is perceived to threaten or block a fundamental need, the stress response also will be initiated. Imagination can produce its own stressors and prompt a neuroendocrine-autonomic response that itself poses a real threat to the organism. Man, with his vast learning potential and vulnerability to neurotic conflicts, has an infinitely broad scope of concrete or fantasy stimuli that can provoke the stress response.

Although the brain itself ultimately identifies threats, activates alerting, appraising, and coping processes, and integrates body reactions with thoughts and feelings, all parts of the body can experience a major stress response when coping breaks down. Some regions are particularly vulnerable:

hypothalamic-pituitary-endocrine axis
autonomic nervous system–adrenal medulla
immune system
reticular activating system
involuntary and striated muscle systems
cognitive-affective integrating centers of the brain

By engaging these important integrative systems, stress can cause disease by

lowering or exaggerating the immune response (Stein, Keller, & Schleifer, 1981)
creating endocrine problems through either hypoactivity or hyperactivity (Lipton, 1976)

altering the balance of autonomic control, resulting in changes in the cardiovascular, respiratory, secretory, and visceral system (Lisander, 1979)

altering sleep patterns, with attendant impact on protein metabolism, hormone secretion, and other vegetative functions (Weitzman, Boyar, Kapen, & Hellman, 1975)

changes in peptide release in extra-CNS sites (Marx, 1979)

affecting the neurotransmitter, neuromodulator, and neuroendocrine functions of the brain itself, which can have profound impact on health through a variety of mechanisms, including changes in eating and health habits (exercise, drug or alcohol consumption, and accident-prone behavior) (Antelman & Caggivla, 1977).

The brain is organized to treat provocative stimuli and foreign symbols as basic threats to its organizational integrity. It mobilizes cognitive, affective, motor, and humoral defenses to operate synergistically with one another. We are rapidly learning how the cerebro-cortical-limbic-hypothalamic-pituitary axis translates symbolic messages into neurochemical impulses, which can alter any system in the body, including the immune system.

Critical to any theory that claims that stress of a psychosocial nature can alter body function is the demonstration that brain structures exist that can mediate between cognitive-affective representations in higher cortical centers and those lower nuclei systems that regulate hormonal and autonomic activity. Can grief, panic, or hope alter the great neuronal and endocrine pathways that lead from the hypothalamus and pituitary to every gland, artery, and viscus in the body? Modern neuroanatomical and neuropsychological studies suggest that such linkages do exist, which make possible the alteration of organ function through the influence of stress. Brodal (1981) pointed out that the prefrontal cortex has two-way connections with structures involved in "emotional and behavioral changes and in the regulation of the internal milieu of the organism." Lesions, particularly in the orbitofrontal region of the cortex, tend to create profound disturbances in emotional reactivity and to interfere with appropriate social behavior. Lesions of the dorsomedial thalamic nucleus produce essentially the same alterations as do ablations in the orbitofrontal zone. This suggests a linkage between the highest centers of the cortex and the diencephalic region that may relate emotional responses to messages to peripheral body organs.

Listing the structures that mediate between higher and lower centers of the brain, Brodal (1981) mentioned the amygdala, the hippocampus, the septum, and the cingulate gyrus. These structures, with their connections to the hypothalamus and the neocortex, comprise the so-called limbic system. Brodal reported that the amygdala influences the secretion of hormones through its action on the hypothalamus. Recent studies have identified the role of this structure in modulating the secretion of gonadotrophic hormone, adrenocorticotrophic hormone, thyrotrophin, and vasopressin. Isaacson (1974), in his review of limbic function, suggested that each structure within this system may be highly specialized and tuned to specific changes in the internal or the external environment. Henry and Meehan (1981) speculated that the hippocampus is linked to the pituitary-adrenal cortical system, which in turn is closely linked to depression and the perception of loss of control, while the amygdala is associated with the fight-flight aspects of the sympathetic adrenal medullary response. *Surveying extrahypothalamic centers in neuroendocrine integration,* Ellendorf and Parvizi (1980) stated that the limbic system–midbrain circuit possibly represents the largest input to the hypothalamus and "encompasses components involved in neuroendocrine integrative mechanisms" (p. 297). The function of the limbic system may be to coordinate the cognitive aspects of stimulus appraisal with their affective components and integrate both with the appropriate bodily expression of emotion. Since lesions in the rostrohypothalamic area result in degenerative patterns in the amygdala, amygdala-hypothalamic relations are considered to be reciprocal. Similar findings have been made with regard to the hippocampus. Schur (1955) estimated that 65% of the median eminence neurons alter their firing pattern in response to dorsal hippocampus stimulation. This effect is critical since the median eminence plays a major role in the transport of neuroendocrine releasing factors from the hypothalamus to the anterior pituitary. According to Ellendorf and Parvizi, it is well established that the amygdala participates in the mechanisms that control gonadotrophin secretion. In addition, the amygdala appears to be one of the most important extrahypothalamic structures involved in the regulation of growth hormone (GH), while the hippocampus also appears to have a stimulatory effect on GH release.

Perhaps of greatest interest with regard to stress and illness (particularly with reference to alterations in immunological competence) is the relationship between limbic structures and pituitary release of ACTH. Numerous studies have found that the pituitary-adrenal axis may be activated or inhibited by fear, anger, rage, pain, or adverse environmental conditions. With regard to ACTH regulation it was long believed that its release was dependent on circulating epinephrine levels, circulating adrenal cortical hormone levels, or hypothalamic action effected through the hypophysial portal vessels. It now appears that hypothalamic control may be dependent upon extrahypothalamic integrative mechanisms. There is suggestive evidence that the amygdala may be largely facilitory of ACTH release while the hippocampus is inhibitory to corticotrophin releasing factor and ACTH release. Reichlin (1979), in his review of the anatomical and physiologic basis of anterior pituitary regulation, observed that "the functions of the central biogenic systems are under the domination of inputs from various parts of the 'visceral brain' and are thereby responsive to stress and emotional disturbance" (p. 9). He reported that drugs that act as dopamine agonists stimulate the release of growth hormone and inhibit the release of prolactin. Noradrenergic agonists also stimulate GH release and the release of gonadotrophins and thyroid stimulating hormone (TSH). On the other hand, serotonin agonists suppress TSH release.

Bioaminergic systems that influence pituitary hormone release are, as Reichlin (1979) pointed out, also involved in the determination of affective states, sleep and wakefulness, appetite, and drinking behavior. Neuroleptic agents, widely used in psychiatry to modify mood or cognition, act in part by stimulating or suppressing central bioaminergic pathways and thus may interfere with or modify anterior pituitary function. A common example is the administration of chlorpromazine, which inhibits GH secretion and stimulates prolactin release. Thus, stress may operate through an alteration of bioaminergic transmitters, not only influencing thought processes and affect but also changing pituitary secretion, with far-reaching consequences for health. Does stress effect neurochemical changes in the brain, which then influence vital neurotransmitter systems that may operate among the limbic system, hypothalamus, and pituitary? In a massive review of this literature, Anisman (1978) observed that there is good evidence for this sequence. For example:

1. Moderate levels of stress tend not to affect the endogenous level of norepinephrine (NE) and serotonin (5-HT). It is probable that stress increases both synthesis and release of NE and 5-HT.
2. With intense stress, a decline in endogenous levels of NE and 5-HT is seen. Presumably, synthesis does not keep up with utilization. The effectiveness of NE released apparently is also reduced by increased reuptake of NE.
3. With mild stress, dopamine (DA) and acetyl choline (ACh) are unaffected. As stress

severity increases, ACh levels rise. DA may decrease, but the effect of stress on DA is less prounounced than that on NE neurons.

4. Under conditions of stress, activity of the anterior pituitary hormones increases, as do levels of plasma corticosterone.
5. Under conditions in which control over stress is possible, *NE levels do not decline.* Reports also indicate that with controllable stress neither ACh nor corticosterone levels are affected.
6. After repeated exposure to stress, neurochemical adaptation may occur.
7. Stimuli associated with stress may come to elicit the same neurochemical changes as does the provocative stimulus itself.

Anisman's conclusions are worth quoting:

> It seems evident that although stress of a physical nature may affect neurochemical activity, such factors as control (coping) over stress may be influential in determining neurochemical activity. As such it needs to be considered that the physical stimulus per se does not influence neurochemical activity, but we are left with two alternatives that are not necessarily mutually exclusive. First, cognitive factors act as a modulator of the physiological response to stress; second, under conditions in which the organism is unable to deal effectively with stress, subsidiary mechanisms (in terms of neurochemical activity) are called upon. (p. 160)

STRESS AND IMMUNOLOGY

One of the most exciting fields in medicine today is immunology. New findings are revolutionizing our ideas about how the body protects itself from outside invasive forces and monitors itself for signs of malignant cytological change. There has also been ferment in the field of psychoimmunology, as researchers attempt to understand the relationship between the immune system and events that occur in the central nervous system. There is increasingly solid experimental evidence that the brain plays an important role in modulating and responding to changes in immune status. These changes seem to be mediated by the hypothalamus and by pituitary hormones. Many of the hormones produced by the pituitary or by the brain itself appear to have some impact on immunological competence. Many factors can alter the body's immune responses: time of day, age of the individual, pregnancy, and, of course, stress. High doses of exogenous steroids are known to have immunosuppressive effects on both humoral and cellular immune responses. Physiological levels of corticosteroids have been found to be required for normal functioning of immunity. Other hormones—including the thyroid hormone, growth hormone, sex hormones, and insulin—are also necessary for the development and functioning of the immune system. Any stressful process that alters the normal physiology of these hormones will naturally have an impact on immunological behavior. As Solomon and Amkraut hypothesized, if the central nervous system does influence immunological function, then we should expect emotional distress to alter the incidence or severity of those diseases for which immunological resistance or deficiency states are found. We should also hope to find that hormones regulated by the CNS influence immune mechanisms; that experimental manipulation of parts of the CNS affects immunological processes; that experimental manipulations of behavior have immunological consequences; and that cells involved in the immunological processes have receptor sites for neuroendocrines, neurotransmitters that would be the instruments of brain influence. A growing literature indicates that many of these hypotheses have solid experimental evidence to support them. The interested reader is referred to Solomon and Amkraut (1981) and to Stein, Keller, and Schleifer (1976) and Rogers, Dubey, and Reich (1979).

CONCLUDING THOUGHTS

There appears to be anatomical, physiological, and neurochemical evidence that cognitive-affective responses to stress can alter the functioning of those vital hypothalamic-pituitary pathways that modulate endocrine, autonomic, and immune processes. Alteration of these systems and of the brain sets the stage for the onset of disease. The fact that the brain itself can be a target organ for hormones produced both by its own neurosecretory cells and by the pituitary (ACTH, vasopressin) suggests that brain functioning can be altered by stress. Increasing knowledge about the production of peptides in the brain and other body organs and the relation of this process to stress will add new dimensions to our understanding. The full picture is undoubtedly far more complex than this short overview can suggest. If Freud's leap from mind to body occurs, it is probable that its mysteries are to be found at the point at which emotional factors alter those neurotransmitters that mediate between the limbic system and the hypothalamus.

As we move away from the traditional mechanistic model of medicine, we are redefining the way in which we think about disease so that the interplay of behavioral, social, and physical factors can be understood as contributing to the onset, prevention, diagnosis, treatment, and reversal of disease. To explain any disease process, both researcher and clinician must take into account psychological factors, including response to environmental stress, changes in developmental functioning, intrapsychic conflict, learning deficits, and inadequate coping mechanisms.

NOTES

1. Pearlin and Schooler (1978) reported that although responses that modify the situation directly represent the most decisive way of dealing with a stressor, they are not the ones most commonly employed.

REFERENCES

ALEXANDER, F. *Psychosomatic medicine*. New York: Norton, 1950

ANISMAN, H. Neurochemical changes elicited by stress. In H. Anisman & G. Bignami (eds.), *Psychopharmacology of adversely motivated behavior*. New York: Plenum, 1978

ANTELMAN, S. M. & CAGGIULA, A. R. Norephinephrine-dopamine interations and behavior. *Science,* 1977, *195:* 646–653.

APPLEY, J. J. & TRUMBULL, R. The concept of psychological stress. In A. Monat & M. Lazerus (eds.), *Stress and coping*. New York: Columbia University Press, 1977.

BRODAL, A. *Neurological anatomy* (3rd edition), New York: Oxford University Press, 1981

CLEARY, P. J. Life events and disease: A review of methodology and findings. In *Reports from the laboratory for clinical stress research* (Stockholm), 1974, *3:* 1–50.

DESCARTES, R. Meditations on the first philosophy. In B. Rand (ed.), *Modern Classical philosophers*. Boston, Mass: Houghton Mifflin, 1952.

DEUTSCH, F. *On the mysterious leap from the mind to the body,* New York: International University, 1959.

DUNBAR, H. F. *Psychosomatic diagnosis.* New York: Hoeber, 1943

ELLENDORF, F. & PARVIZI, N. Role of extrahypothalamic centers in neuroendocrine integration. In M. Motta (eds.), *The endocrine functions of the brain.* New York: Raven Press, 1980

ENGELS, G. L. A unified concept of health and disease. In T. Millon (ed.), *Medical behavior science.* Philadelphia: Saunders, 1975.

FROEHLICH, W. D. Stress, anxiety and the control of attention: A psychophysiological approach. In C. D. Spielberger (ed.), *Stress and anxiety,* vol. 5. Washington, D.C.: Hemisphere, 1978.

GERARD, R. Neurophysiology: brain and behavior. In S. Arieti (ed.), *American handbook of psychiatry,* Vol. 1. New York: Basic Books, 1959.

GRINKER, R., SR. *Psychosomatic research,* New York: Norton, 1950.

HARRÉ, H. & SECORD, P. F. *The explanation of social behavior.* Totawa: Littlefied, Adams, 1973.

HENRY, J. P. & MEEHAN, J. P. Psychosocial stimuli, physiological specificity and cardiovascular disease. In H. Weiner, M. A. Hofer, & A. J. Stunkard (eds.), *Brain, behavior and bodily disease.* New York: Raven, 1981

HINDE, R. *Animal behavior.* New York: McGraw-Hill, 1966.

HINKLE, L. E. The concept of stress in the biological and social sciences. In *Sciences, medicine and man,* Vol. I. New York: Pergamon, 1973.

HOLMES, T. H. & MASUDA, M. Life change and illness susceptibility. In B. S. Dohrenwend & B. P. Dohrenwend (eds.), *Stressful life events.* New York: Wiley, 1974.

HOLMES, T. H. & RAHE, R. H. The social readjustment rating scale. *Journal of Psychosomatic Research,* 1967, *II:* 213–218.

ISAACSON, R. L. *The limbic system.* New York: Plenum, 1974

JAEGER, W. *Paidea: The ideals of Greek culture.* New York: Oxford University Press, Vol. 3, 1944

KUBIE, L. S. The central representation of the symbolic process in psychosomatic disorders. *Psychosomatic Medicine,* 1953, *15:* 1–7.

LAZARUS, R. *Psychological stress and the coping process.* New York: McGraw Hill, 1966.

LASZLO, E. *Introduction to systems philosophy.* New York: Harper Torchbook, 1973.

LEVINE, S., WEINBERG, J., & URSIN, H. Definition of the coping process and statement of the problem. In H. Ursin (ed.), *Psychobiology of Stress.* New York: Academic, 1978.

LIDZ, T. General concept of psychosomatic medicine. In S. Arieti (ed.), *American handbook of psychiatry,* Vol. I. New York: Basic Books, 1959.

LIPTON, M. A. Behavioral effects of hypothalamic polypeptide hormones in animals and man. In E. J. Sachar (ed.), *Hormones, behavior and psychopathology.* New York: Raven, 1976.

LISANDER, B. Somato-autonomic reactions and their higher control. In C. Brooks, K. Koizumi, & A. Sato (eds.) *Integrative functions of the autonomic nervous system.* New York: Elsevier, 1979.

LORENZ, K. *Evolution and modification of behavior.* Chicago: University of Chicago Press, 1965.

MARX, J. L. Brain peptides. *Science,* 1979, *205:* 886–889.

MASON, J. W. Emotions as reflected in patterns of endocrine integration. In L. Levi (ed.), *Emotions: The parameters and measurement.* New York: Raven, 1975.

MENNINGER, K. Regulatory devices of the ego under major stress. *International Journal of Psychoanalysis,* 1954, *35:* 412–20..

MEYER, A. *Psychobiology: A science of man,* translated by E. F. Winters and A. M. Bower. Springfield, Ill: Charles Thomas, 1958.

PANCHERI, P. & BENAISSA, C. Stress and psychosomatic illness. In C. D. Spielberger (ed.), *Stress and anxiety,* vol. 5. Washington, D.C.: Hemisphere, 1978.

PEARLIN, L. I. & SCHOOLER, C. The structure of coping. *Journal of Health and Social Behavior,* 1978, *19:* 2–21.

RABKIN, J. G. & STRUENING, E. L. Life events, stress and illness. *Science,* 1976, *194:* 1013–1020.

RAHE, R. H. Life-change measurement as a predictor of illness. In *Proceedings of the Royal Society of Medicine,* 1968, *61:* 1124–1126.

RAHE, R. H., MEYER, M., SMITH, M., KJAERG, G., & HOLMES, T. H. Social stress and illness onset. *Journal of Psychosomatic Research,* 1964, *8:* 35–44.

REICHLIN, S. An overview of the anatomical and physiological basis of anterior-pituitary regulation. In G. Tolis, F. Labire, J. Martin, & N. Naftolin (eds.), *Clinical Neuroendocrinology.* New York: Raven, 1979.

REISER, M. Changing theoretical concepts of psychosomatic medicine. In S. Arieti (ed.), *American handbook of psychiatry,* Vol. 4. New York: Basic Books, 1975.

ROGERS, M. P., DUBEY, D., & REICH, P. The influence of the psyche and the brain on immunity and disease susceptibility: A critical review. *Psychosomatic Medicine,* 1979, *41:* 147–164.

RYLE, G. *Concept of the mind.* London: Hutchinson, 1949.

SCHUR, M. Comments on the metapsychology of somatization. In *Psychoanalytic Study of the Child,* 1955, *10:* 119–164.

SELYE, H. *The stress of life.* New York: McGraw Hill, 1966.

SHAEFFER, J. Mind-body problems. In P. Edwards (ed.), *The encyclopedia of philosophy.* New York: Macmillan, 1967.

SOLOMON, G. E. & AMKRAUT, A. A. Psychoneuroendocrinological effects of the immune response. *Annual Review Microbiology,* 1981, *35:* 155–184.

STEIN, M., KELLER, S., & SCHLEIFER, S. The hypothalamus and the immune response. In H. Weiner, M. Hofer, & A. Stunkard (eds.), *Brain, behavior and bodily disease.* New York: Raven, 1981.

STEIN, M., SCHIAVI, R., & CAMERINO, M. Influence of brain and behavior on the immune system, *Science,* 1976, *191:* 435–440.

TACHE, J. & SELYE, H. On stress and coping mechanisms. In C. D. Spielberger & I. G. Sarason (eds.), *Stress and anxiety,* Vol. 5. Washington, D.C.: Hemisphere, 1978.

WEITZMAN, E. D., BOYAR, R. M., KAPEN, S., & HELLMAN, L. The relationship of sleep and sleep stages to neuroendocrine secretion and biological rhythms in man. *Recent Progress Hormone Research,* 1975, *31:* 399–446.

11

Animal Studies of Stressful Interactions: A Behavioral-Physiological Overview

Jaylan S. Turkkan   Joseph V. Brady

Alan H. Harris

THE TOPIC OF STRESS has traditionally presented methodological and conceptual challenges to scientists and professionals of every persuasion. In recent decades, the field has been cultivated assiduously, and current lively interest in the problem is amply reflected in the comprehensive coverage provided by this book. But dedication and industry do not always guarantee achievement. In both scientific and professional endeavors, wide gaps frequently separate experimental observations and interpretive formulations.

The quasi-technical use of the word "stress" as a referent for a bewildering range of phenomena continues to produce semantic, linguistic, and taxonomic confusion. Of course, the observations to which the term refers cannot be easily denied. But persistent reification of stress as a substantive thing that affects and is, in turn, affected by other things obscures the legitimate conceptual status of stress as a construct emerging from the empirical relationship between environmental circumstances and behavioral-physiological activities. To the extent that such interactions involve significant departures from accepted norms of stimulus and/or response function (e.g., in frequency or intensity), their metaphorical characterization as stressful has served generally descriptive purposes for popular discourse on this ubiquitous topic. From a scientific perspective, however, more precise definition of terms and functional relationships is required.

The animal studies to be reviewed represent an experimental approach to stress within just such an operational framework. Careful specification of methods and procedures, including measurement techniques, in the laboratory provides for essential definitional clarity and functional analysis. The obvious advantages of such controlled investigative conditions have enriched an extensive literature in this important problem area, and the necessarily selective overview that is to follow has been based for the most part, upon studies that meet the following criteria:

1. controlled experimental methodology
2. characteristically extreme environmental, behavioral, and/or physiological conditions
3. relevance to human clinical circumstances

The authors would like to thank Kathryn Arvin for typing the manuscript through numerous stages.

BEHAVIORAL METHODS AND STRESSFUL INTERACTIONS

Two methodologically distinguishable approaches to the experimental analysis of stressful interactions can be identified in an animal laboratory literature that goes back almost a century to Pavlov. Early contributions focused upon *response-independent* circumstances, characterized by the occurrence of environmental events (e.g., food, electric shock) that preceded behavioral-physiological changes (e.g., increased motor activity, heart rate). More recently, observations in the animal laboratory have called attention to a second *response-dependent* group of stressful interaction procedures, which focus upon the relationship between a performance (e.g., limb movement) and its effect upon the environment (e.g., food presentation, shock termination). While this distinction between response-independent and response-dependent procedures, based upon the temporal ordering of stimulus and response events, ignores obvious overlaps in methodology and empirical findings, some heuristic value may attach to thus organizing the extensive literature on animal studies of stressful interactions.

Response-independent Models

Perhaps the prototypical animal studies of response-independent stressful interactions are to be found in Pavlov's early reports of experimental neurosis in laboratory dogs. The basic procedure involved presentation of a circle as the *conditional stimulus,* which was always followed by food (CS +), and an ellipse, which was never followed by food (CS −) (Gantt, 1953; Pavlov, 1928). After repeated exposure of the animal to this discrimination procedure, salivation, the measured *conditional response* (CR), occured reliably following presentation of the circle but not of the ellipse. The form of the circle was then progressively changed so that it more and more resembled an ellipse. Not only did the salivation discrimination break down, but changes occurred in other behavior: "The dog which formerly stood quietly on his bench now was constantly struggling and howling" (Pavlov, 1928:342). Later, Miminishvili (1960), in a study with rhesus monkeys in which a CS that had been reliably terminated with shock was next presented immediately following a food CS, reported similar neurotic behavioral changes, consisting of excitability and cessation of eating, followed by torpor, drowsiness, and loss of both weight and fur. After the monkeys had been 18 months in the experiment, temporary termination of the procedure resulted in both weight gain and fur improvement, but resumption of the experiment reversed these gains.

Lapin and Cherkovich (1971), extending Miminishvili's (1960) investigation of experimental neurosis, described procedures with a colony of laboratory baboons. The dominant male was placed in a cage separate from the females and the lower hierarchy males. In one situation, the females were fed first, before the dominant male (normally the dominant male eats first in baboon society); in another arrangement, a lower status male was placed in the adjoining cage with the females. Both procedures produced radical changes in behavior:

> This situation led to the most violent excitation, expressed in rushing about the cage, furious cries and attacks on the wirenetting separating the rival. In one of the experiments, the monkey attacked the netting so furiously that he broke his tooth. Four or five months of life under such conditions lead to considerable stable changes in the higher nervous activity which we regard as neurosis. (p. 268)

The cardiovascular changes that developed are detailed in a later section of this review.

Aversive control procedures involving response-independent electric shock presentations have been studied under somewhat more circumscribed laboratory conditions of obvious relevance to the experimental analysis of stressful interactions. The pairing of a *neutral stimulus* (e.g., tone, light) with delivery of electric shocks to the feet or tail of an experimental animal has been shown to produce marked behavioral changes as conditional responses to subsequent presentations of the same light or tone as a conditional stimulus. In rats, for example, suppression of motor activity and consummatory behaviors is extreme and is reported to be accompanied in many instances by defecation, urination, and piloerection (Brady & Hunt, 1951; Hunt & Otis, 1953; Garcia & Koelling, 1966). In rhesus monkeys, the behavioral effects of such response-independent aversive conditioning procedures have included agitated vocalization, piloerection, and striking increases in motor activity (Brady, 1970), accompanied by a range of endocrinological and autonomic changes detailed in subsequent sections of this chapter. Ulrich (1967) described significant increases in aggressive attack behaviors with animals in response to presentation of a CS previously associated with electric shock.

Within the extended framework of this response-independent model, such aggressively stressful interactions have been experimentally analyzed in considerable detail. The early observations of Ulrich and Azrin (1962) of rearing, striking, and biting in pairs of chamber-confined rats following foot shock, for example, have been extended in a number of studies exploring the conditions under which these behaviors occur. Subsequent research has confirmed that shock intensities in the 2mA range represent optimal levels for eliciting these aggressive behavior changes (higher intensities produce grid-floor biting, running, and/or jumping) and that chamber size must be considered an important variable (the effects are not observed in large chambers). The probability of fighting also increases if the rats are facing each other when the shocks are presented. Finally, the methodological overlap between response-independent and response-dependent procedures for the experimental analysis of aggressively stressful interactions is clearly reflected in the studies of Azrin, Hutchinson, and McLaughlin (1965), who found that squirrel monkeys learn chain-pulling to produce a ball, upon which they then launch a biting attack following shock.

Response-dependent Models

Performances that operate upon the environment (*operant behavior*) are maintained by schedule arrangements between those performances (e.g., lever-presses) and their environmental consequences (e.g., food presentations). The properties of such *schedules of reinforcement* (Ferster & Skinner, 1957) have been shown, in at least some instances, to generate interaction patterns with evident stressful concomitants. Pigeons, for example, have been shown to attack restrained target birds when food delivery no longer follows every lever-press (*extinction*), after extended training on a *continuous reinforcement schedule,* which provides food after every lever-press (Azrin, Hutchinson, & Hake, 1966). *Intermittent reinforcement schedules* like high-value *fixed-ratio schedules* for food (piecework arrangements that require relatively large numbers of response units, like lever-presses, for each food pellet delivered) also have been shown to result in aggressive behaviors (Gentry, 1968). The magnitude of the aggressive response has been directly related to the size of the ratio (Hutchinson, Azrin, & Hunt, 1968) and the degree of food deprivation (Azrin and others, 1966). Similarly, *fixed-interval schedules* for food (delivery of food pellets for responses occurring only after a specified time interval has elapsed since delivery of the previous food pellet) have been reported to produce aggressively stressful interactions (Richards & Rilling, 1972). In both the fixed-interval and the fixed-ratio case, attack incidents occur most frequently during the pause that characteristically follows food delivery under such schedule arrangements (Ator, 1980; Hutchinson, Azrin & Hunt, 1968; Richards & Rilling, 1972). Both these food schedules also generate escape behaviors when responses on a second manipulandum produce periods of *time-out* from the schedule of reinforcement (Azrin, 1961; Brown & Flory, 1972; Thompson, 1964, 1965). Schedule induced escape tends to occur in the pause following pellet delivery as well; this response varies as a bitonic function of the interreinforcement interval (Ator, 1980; Brown & Flory, 1972; Thomas & Sherman, 1965).

Intermittent schedules of food delivery have produced such aberrant performances as *pica* (inappropriate feeding) in rhesus monkeys (Villarreal, 1967) and *polydipsia* (excessive water drinking) in several species of animals (for reviews see Falk, 1971; Staddon, 1977). Schedule induced polydipsia, for example, has been reported to involve the ingestion within a single experimental session of water quantities that can approximate one-half the animal's body weight and does not appear to be a function of either dry mouth (Falk, 1967) or adventitious schedule-behavior interactions (Falk, 1971). Rather, two of the critical variables seem to be meal size and length of the interval imposed between occurrences of individual eating episodes by the schedule of reinforcement in effect during the experimental session (Falk, 1971). Moreover, when alcohol solutions are made available in place of water under such conditions, similarly excessive fluid intake occurs, with repeated exposure resulting in addictive levels of alcohol preference (Falk, Samson, & Winger, 1972).

In general, these *adjunctive behaviors* (attack, escape, pica, polydipsia, etc.), which have been shown to occur in close association with performances under reinforcement schedule control, all appear to be functionally related to the same variables. The following four characteristics, for example, are commonly observed under such apparently stressful interaction conditions:

1. generated by intermittent events (e.g., food, electric shock)
2. observed in the immediate postreinforcement period (Falk, 1961)
3. correlated stimuli (i.e., with each type of adjunctive behavior) sufficient to sustain schedule behavior (Falk, 1971; Thompson, 1964)
4. related to reinforcement frequency by a bitonic function

In addition to such schedule induced effects, aversive control procedures involving escape and avoidance of electric shocks have been extensively investigated in the animal laboratory under conditions of obvious relevance to the experimental analysis of response-dependent stressful interactions. For the most part, attention has focused upon the visceral and autonomic changes that accompany such performances; subsequent sections of this chapter review key findings. Some directly observable behavioral effects have been described in relationship to such shock delivery schedules in primates, however, including hyperactivity and aggression (Forsyth & Harris, 1970) and increased alcohol drinking in preference to water consumption (Clark & Polish, 1960). Kinney and Schmidt (1979) confirmed the preference for an ethanol-sucrose solution over a pure sucrose solution in rats during cued inescapable shock periods. They also noted that the ethanol drinking appeared to occur in bursts after shock delivery, indicating that it may be related to the previously described adjunctive behaviors.

Indeed, it has been suggested that the development of adjunctive behaviors under certain response-dependent arrangements of stimulus delivery may constitute evidence of "schedule aversiveness" (Richards & Rilling, 1972). The generality of this interpretive formulation would appear questionable, however, in light of the finding that response-independent delivery of stimuli (e.g., food, shock) can also generate such adjunctive performances (Flory, 1969; Ulrich & Azrin, 1962). Although a unifying conceptual framework has yet to be developed for encompassing these somewhat counterintuitive adjunctive behaviors, the extreme, intense, and frequently maladaptive effects observed under such conditions more than justify their inclusion within the stressful interaction context of this behavioral-physiological overview.

CARDIOVASCULAR ADAPTATIONS AND STRESSFUL INTERACTIONS

The observation that environmental circumstances and behavioral activities can have profound and enduring effects upon cardiovascular functions has been repeatedly confirmed in both the laboratory and the clinc (for recent reviews see Brady & Harris, 1977; Cohen & Obrist, 1975; Galosy & Gaebelein, 1977; Harris & Brady, 1974; Schneiderman, 1978). Both the basic functional relationships characterizing environmental-behavioral-cardiovascular interactions, on the one hand, and the pathological consequences of such cardiovascular adaptations to more stressful circumstances, on the other, have been extensively investigated, although the time frames of experimental analysis have varied widely. For the most part, studies that focus upon functional relations and general laws attend to relatively brief intervals (seconds to minutes) preceding and following the onset of specifically programmed experimental events (e.g., stimuli, responses). A somewhat longer view is generally taken by those investigators interested in cardiovascular pathology, with physiological processes studied over periods of months and even years. Both long- and short-term approaches have generated a robust and productive investigative analysis of the cardiovascular adaptations and adjustments to stressful interactions.

Acute responses of the cardiovascular system to physically salient environmental stimulus events (*unconditional stimuli,* or USs) and to neutral stimuli that have been temporally (i.e., conditionally) associated with such USs have been explored for just about every imaginable permutation of CS and US modality, intensity, temporal pattern, and duration. For the most part, heart rate changes provided the dominant focus for these studies until the 1960s because of the presumed relevance of such autonomic indexes to emotional states and the relative ease of measurement of heart rate compared to other hemodynamic variables like blood pressure and blood flow. Heart rate changes (CR) at the onset of CS have assumed many forms as a function of the particular trial of a session (Black & Black, 1967; Jaworska & Soltysik, 1962); the particular subject in an experiment (Cohen & Durkovic, 1966; Newton & Perez-Cruet, 1967); or the duration of an experiment (Lynch, 1973; McDonald, Stern, & Hahn, 1963). Moreover, several independent variables have been shown to affect CR form such as the conditioning paradigm—e.g., trace or delay (where CS terminates prior to, or coincident with US) (Black, Carlson, & Solomon, 1962; Fitzgerald & Martin, 1971; Turkkan, 1979) or backward conditioning (where US precedes CS) (Fitzgerald & Walloch, 1966); the mode or intensity of CS and US (Gantt, 1960; Lynch & McCarthy, 1969); the species of subject (Cohen & Obrist, 1975); the performance of a subsequent instrumental response by the subject (Schoenfeld, Matos, & Snapper, 1967); the pre–CS baseline heart rate (Ramsay, 1970); and the CS–US interval (Dronsejko, 1972; Hastings & Obrist, 1967). Thus, in accordance with the results of individual experiments, the cardiac CR form has been described as a montonic acceleration of heart rate from CS onset to the end of the CS–US interval (Cohen & Pitts, 1968; Obrist & Webb, 1967); a monotonic deceleration over the course of the CS–US interval (Hein, 1969; McAllister, Farber, & Taylor, 1954; VanDercar & Schneiderman, 1967); or a phasic response with distinguishable acceleratory and deceleratory components (Geer, 1964; Wilson, 1969). Most frequently, an acceleratory phase has been observed to precede a deceleratory phase in the CS-US interval, although, occasionally, the deceleratory phase occurs first (Fitzgerald & Martin, 1971; Newton & Perez-Cruet, 1967). Finally, polyphasic responses (multiple cycles of acceleration and deceleration) have been reported (Bowers, 1971; Gatchel & Lang, 1974; Turkkan, 1979).

At least some of the variability in cardiac conditional response form can be explained by species differences. In primates, for example, the cardiac rate CR has almost always been reported as biphasic: acceleration followed by deceleration in the CS–US interval (for the rhesus, Nathan & Smith, 1968; Ramsay, 1970; Snapper, Pomerleau, & Schoenfeld, 1969; for humans, Geer, 1964; Wilson, 1969; Zeaman, Deane, & Wegner, 1954). Moreover, other species that have demonstrated monotonic acceleration or deceleration at CS–US intervals under four seconds sometimes have revealed a biphasic CR form in studies examining longer intervals (in dogs, Brown & Peters, 1967; in rabbits, Deane, 1965, Kosupkin & Olmsted, 1943; in rats, Schoenfeld, Matos, & Snapper, 1967). Movement artifacts have also been shown to affect CR form. Black, Carlson, and Solomon (1962), for example, found relatively stable CR forms in curarized dogs compared with undrugged dogs. Also in this regard, Randall and Smith (1974) noted that in trials involving motor activity, monotonic heart rate accelerations were observed during the CS; in trials with such activity absent, the CRs were biphasic.

Numerous studies have attempted to identify the neural processes that participate in classically conditioned heart rate responses (see Cohen, 1974, for a review). Overall, those studies examining CRs with an acceleratory component, whether the entire response form is monotonic or biphasic, find contributions from both sympathetic and parasympathetic branches of the autonomic nervous system, although it seems probable that an increase in sympathetic activity is the larger contributor (Bond, 1943; Kadden, Schoenfeld, & Bindler, 1975; Klose, Augenstein, Schneiderman, Manas, Abrams, & Bloom, 1975). Those studies examining CRs with a deceleratory component, whether the deceleration is part of a monotonic or a biphasic response, seem to point mostly to an increase in vagal restraint on the heart as the primary source of heart rate deceleration (Sampson, Francis, & Schneiderman, 1974; Turkkan & Kadden, 1979). Again, however, both components of the autonomic nervous system can be seen to contribute since neither vagal nor sympathetic blockade alone abolishes the heart rate CR, although combined blockade does (Cohen & Pitts, 1968; Kadden, Schoenfeld, & Bindler, 1975; Kazis, Milligan, & Powell, 1973; Klose et al., 1975). Finally, there is some evidence that sympathetic influences predominate early in training, whereas vagal influences predominate as training progresses (Cohen & Pitts, 1968; Turkkan & Kadden, 1979).

In addition to heart rate, other hemodynamic measures have been obtained during classical conditioning. Systolic and diastolic blood pressure, aortic blood flow, coronary blood flow, left and right ventricular pressure, cardiac output, and rate of change measures (i.e., indexes of the contractile state of the heart) have all been described under such conditions. Blood pressure changes during the CS periods preceding shock, for example, appear to consist of an initial increase in pressure, a subsequent decrease, and a final increase (Kadden, Schoenfeld, McCullough, Steele, & Tremont, 1980; Randall, Brady, & Martin, 1975; Randall, Kaye, Randall, Brady, & Martin, 1976; Turkkan & Schoenfeld, 1979). Myocardial contractility (Randall & Smith, 1974) and aortic blood flow (Smith & Stebbins, 1965) also increase in the CS– US interval. Coronary blood flow and coronary vascular resistance vary inversely after CS onset, with initial decreases in flow accompanied by alpha-adrenergically mediated increases in coronary vascular resistance (Billman & Randall, 1980, 1981).

Disturbances in cardiac rhythm and EKG form have also been examined during and after shock associated events. Animals with an occluded coronary artery showed various EKG abnormalities and arrythmias during presentations of conditioned stimuli that had been previously paired with electric shock, such as elevations of the of the ST segment of the EKG complex in the monkey (Randall & Hasson, 1977) and R on T phenomena in dogs (Corbalan, Verrier, & Lown, 1974). Shock delivery was also shown to decrease the threshold at which electrical pacemaker pulses would produce ventricular arrythmias and fibrillation in dogs (Lown, Verrier, & Corbalan, 1973). When animals had been previously habituated to the experimental environment, however, increases occurred in the latency to ventricular fibrillation after coronary artery occlusion (Skinner, Lie, & Entman, 1975).

Additional complexities in the stress related development of cardiac rhythm and rate disturbances were described by Randall and Hasson (1981). This experiment extended the coronary artery occlusion–CS presentation paradigm to situations involving not only shock but also food delivery as unconditioned stimuli. Food US trials were as likely (in some cases, more likely) to produce ventricular arrythmias after coronary artery occlusion in rhesus monkeys as were shock US trials. The variable that appeared to determine arrythmic occurrence was a critical range of heart rates during trials, leading the authors cautiously to suggest that the most stressful situations may not be the most arrythmogenic and that a critical range of such conditions may be important in producing electrical disturbances of the heart.

When Pavlovian conditioning trials are superimposed upon ongoing operant behavior, a paradigm results that has been termed *conditioned emotional response* (CER), or, less subjectively, *conditioned suppression*. Estes and Skinner (1941) found that when a tone shortly followed by shock was presented during ongoing lever-press behavior maintained by an operant food schedule, lever-press responding decreased during the tone-shock (CS–US) interval. This reduction in lever-pressing rate (accompanied by such autonomic signs as defecation and piloerection) during CS after shock pairings (Brady, 1975) prompted an extensive experimental literature describing the cardiovascular consequences of such conditioned emotional response interactions (Brady, Kelly, & Plumlee, 1969; Marshall, Zeiner, & Smith, 1978; Nathan & Smith, 1968; Parrish, 1967; Smith, Astley, DeVito, Stein, & Walsh, 1980; Snapper, Pomerleau, & Schoenfeld, 1969). The form and magnitude of the cardiovascular changes during the CER appear to depend upon some of the same parameters that determine form and magnitude of CRs during classical conditioning; for instance, stage of training (Brady, Kelly, & Plumlee, 1969), presence or absence of bodily movement during CS presentation (Marshall, Zeiner, & Smith, 1978), individual differences (Kelly, 1980), and, uniquely for the CER paradigm, free-feeding versus response-contingent food delivery (Kelly, 1980). Smith and collaborators (1980) examined a number of hemodynamic variables during CER trials in the baboon. At the onset of a one-minute CS preceding an electric shock US, heart rate, mean blood pressure, mean renal resistance, and mean terminal aortic flow all increased, whereas mean renal flow, mean terminal aortic resistance, and lever-pressing (on a *variable-interval food schedule,* where the duration of required time between reinforced responses varies from trial to trial) decreased. Although acute reversals in the functions were apparent, these trends generally continued until the onset of the shock.

The CER paradigm extends information from classical conditioning experiments by affording opportunities to examine cardiovascular and behavioral interactions. When systolic and diastolic pressures, heart rate, and lever-press rate were examined in rhesus monkeys under such CER conditions, cardiovascular and behavioral responses were dissociated during both acquisition and extinction (Brady, Kelly, & Plumlee, 1969). Moreover, in a recent study with baboons, hypothalamic lesions after CER training eliminated cardiovascular changes in the CS–US interval, whereas lever-press suppression was unaltered (as were the cardiovascular accompaniments to exercise and free-feeding) (Smith et al., 1980). It thus appears that cardiovascular and schedule controlled behavior components of the CER are "separable but interacting" (Brady, 1975).

Under such circumstances, a priori assignment of emotional or stressful properties to stimulus and response events must be undertaken only with great caution. It has been shown, for example, that both presentation of various positive unconditioned stimuli such as food or water to deprived organisms and intracranial stimulation (in the so-called reward centers of the brain) generate lever-press suppression in the CS–US interval when superimposed on responding maintained by different positive reinforcers (Azrin & Hake, 1969). Other investigators have noted that suppression or facilitation of lever-press responding depends importantly upon the CS–US interval duration (Meltzer & Brahlek, 1968; Pomerleau, 1970).

The fact that cardiovascular changes of substantial magnitude and duration can be shown to occur in the presence of previously neutral stimuli that regularly precede salient environmental events like electric shock has been interpreted as indicating that the conditional cardiovascular changes (i.e., CR) that occur under such circumstances are metabolically appropriate to the behavioral and physiological adjustments required by the US (e.g., electric shock) onset (Cohen & Obrist, 1975; Ellison & Zanchetti, 1971; Schneiderman, 1972). Experimental support for this formulation is provided by the finding that the magnitude of a limb blood flow CR during CSs paired with graded treadmill exercise (US) varied systematically with the degree of exercise (Bolme & Novotny, 1969). Ebel and Prokasy (1963) also showed that the temporal overlap between CR and US that develops in the classical eyeblink conditioning to an air puff may function to attenuate the unconditioned effects of the air puff stimulus.

To some extent at least, the expanding literature (e.g., Miller, Grossman, Richardson, Wistow, & Thomas, 1978; Weiss, 1971a, b, c, 1972) on such presumably protective, or immunizing, effects of adaptively functioning CSs that precede noxious and/or deleterious environmental events is at variance with the observation that CSs can acquire the physiologically detrimental properties characterizing the US events with which they have been associated (Corbalan, Verrier, & Lown, 1974; Randall & Hasson, 1977). With respect to the cardiovascular consequences of such conditional arrangements, however, it may be that the deleterious effects of the CS become evident only in myocardial electrical instability—and then only in those circumstances that involve coronary artery occlusion. There is also to be considered in the resolution of these apparent inconsistencies the experimental literature on the differential effects of signaled and unsignaled environmental events (Weiss, 1971a, b, c,), which will be detailed subsequently.

For the most part, investigations of the cardiovascular concomitants of classical Pavlovian conditioning procedures have focused upon acute phasic changes occurring during the CS–US interval, and little is known about the chronic effects of such stimulus arrangements on tonic (resting) levels of heart rate and blood pressure. Dykman and Gantt (1960) reported no chronic changes in overall blood pressure levels following 13 months of such conditioning, although their studies did show that cardiac CRs can persist for such extended intervals. In this regard, for example, Newton and Gantt (1966) demonstrated in dogs that a single conditioning trial pairing a bell with a strong electric shock led to a persistance of the heart rate CR to the bell for over a month. Long-term effects of selected experimental procedures have also been examined by Miminishvili, Magakian, and Kokaia (1960) under conditions that exposed rhesus monkeys to a combination of Pavlovian and operant procedures involving inconsistent and conflicting CS functions (e.g., CSs that had preceded food stimuli became paired with shock, or CSs that had been paired with shock were presented in conjunction with food CSs). After 12 months of continuous exposure to these procedures, some subjects developed hypertension, and others showed coronary insufficiency of the left ventricle, as indicated in EKG tracings.

Experimental attention to the more chronic cardiovascular consequences of behaviorally stressful interactions has also been increasingly evident in studies conducted within the framework of response-dependent models. Procedures providing for postponement of electric shock contingent upon an appropriate response (Sidman, 1953), for example, have been extensively investigated in relationship to cardiovascular adaptations (for a review see Galosy & Gaebelein, 1977).

In the most commonly used *Sidman avoidance paradigm* (Sidman, 1953) for examining the cardiovascular concomitants of such response-contingent aversive control procedures, shocks are delivered at regular intervals (e.g., every 30 seconds) unless a response (e.g., lever-press) occurs within that interval to postpone the shock another 30 seconds. Under such conditions, the animal can avoid virtually all shocks by pressing the lever at least once every 30 seconds. Several recent studies examined the cardiovascular changes occurring during intervals that precede regularly scheduled exposures to such shock avoidance procedures (Anderson & Brady, 1971; Anderson & Tosheff, 1973; Galosy, Clarke, & Mitchell, 1979; Lawler, Obrist, & Lawler, 1975). In contrast to the actual shock postponement performance, which is characterized by evident elevations in heart rate, cardiac output, and blood pressure during lever-pressing, the preavoidance period is generally marked by decreased levels of heart rate and cardiac output, accompanied by increased levels of blood pressure and total peripheral resistance. Stroke volume remains unchanged during the avoidance period, according to some investigators (Anderson & Tosheff, 1973), while others have demonstrated increases (Lawler, Obrist, & Lawler, 1975).

Increased cardiac performance during avoidance sessions has also been reflected in elevations both in maximal rate of left ventricular pressure development and in left ventricular systolic pressure (Galosy, Clarke, & Mitchell, 1979). These findings, combined with assessments made on the basis of pharmacological blockade studies, suggest that sympathetic control of the heart predominates during such avoidance periods (Anderson & Brady, 1976; Anderson, Yingling, & Brady, 1976; Galosy, Clarke, & Mitchell, 1979). The hemodynamic mechanisms involved in the preavoidance blood pressure elevations (accompanied by heart rate decreases) are less well understood (Galosy & Gaebelein, 1977). The fact that neither beta- nor alpha-adrenergic blockade appears to affect this preavoidance pattern would seem to implicate cholinergic mechanisms (Anderson & Brady, 1976; Anderson, Yingling, & Brady, 1976). Galosy and associates (1979), however, reportedly found high heart rates during preavoidance periods, which they attributed, along with evidence of decreased maximal rate of left ventricular pressure development, to a withdrawal of vagal tone during preavoidance. Some of these discrepant findings may be the result of procedural differences and we must await their clarification by further experimental study.

Tonic changes in blood pressure levels over a two-week period were reported in dogs performing an avoidance task (Galosy, Clarke, & Mitchell, 1979). Monkeys have also shown increases in heart rate and blood pressure during avoidance training, which effect then declined over subsequent weeks (Forsyth, 1968). When even longer durations (months) of avoidance training are involved, most monkeys show progressive elevations in pressure (Forsyth, 1969; Forsyth & Harris, 1970), with variable times on onset.

In general, monkeys working on avoidance schedules with shorter intervals (e.g., 5–7 seconds) between programmed shocks (thus requiring higher lever-pressing rates to postpone shock) have been reported to maintain higher blood pressure levels than animals required to avoid shocks programmed at longer intervals (e.g., every 20–30 seconds). Moreover, elevations approximating 30mmHg above baseline in systolic pressure observed after seven months' exposure to such shock avoidance requirements were not restricted to the avoidance periods but were maintained throughout the nonavoidance periods of the day as well (Forsyth, 1969; Forsyth & Harris, 1970).

Systemic and regional blood flow measurements were obtained from monkeys working for 72 continuous hours on Sidman avoidance schedules (Forsyth, 1971). The approximately 18–27mmHg increases in blood pressure were observed to be accompanied initially by increases in both cardiac output and heart rate (with little or no change in stroke volume) and by relatively high regional blood flow to skeletal muscle, heart, and liver. As the 72-hour avoidance session progressed, however, the elevated blood pressures were maintained by increases in peripheral resistance, and the maintained high level of regional blood flow to the heart and the liver was augmented by an increased flow to the spleen and the pancreas. It is of some interest that the temporal course of these hemodynamic changes in laboratory primates exposed to performance requirements involving shock postponement is at least somewhat similar to the temporal sequence of hemodynamic events frequently observed in human hypertensive disorders (Lund-Johansen, 1967).

Cardiovascular changes have also been examined in relationship to response-dependent procedures involving other shock delivery arrangements (Findley, Brady, Robinson, & Gilliam, 1971; Herd, Morse, Kelleher, & Jones, 1969). In these studies, the schedule either required the animal to press a lever a fixed number of times for postponement or termination of shock delivery (FR escape-avoidance) or required a single response after a prespecified time interval had elapsed in order to prevent shock delivery (FI escape-avoidance). In both cases, successful completion of the lever-press requirement produced a short time-out. In a study with squirrel monkeys, mean arterial pressures were observed to increase progressively over successive months of such escape-avoidance conditioning (Herd, Morse, Kelleher, & Jones, 1969). Although only one of three monkeys developed chronic hypertension (mean arterial pressure above 139mmHg) with prolonged exposure to the FR escape-avoidance procedure, all three animals maintained on the FI escape-avoidance procedure showed hypertensive pressure levels. A subsequent report by Findley and associates (1971) described a similar long-term study with baboons exposed to an FR escape-avoidance requirement for periods up to and exceeding a year. Although transient elevations in blood pressure and heart rate were observed throughout the extended course of the study, chronic hypertension failed to develop in any of the three animals involved in the experiment.

These experiments suggest that long-term elevations in blood pressure may or may not occur depending upon the temporal parameters of the reinforcement schedule. Sidman avoidance schedules using shorter intervals between shocks have been reported to produce higher blood pressure levels (Forsyth & Harris, 1970), although neither the rate of shocks delivered nor the response rate was consistently related to blood pressure level (cf. Herd and others, 1969). In both Sidman and fixed-interval schedules of shock avoidance, responding (in the absence of a specifically programmed warning signal of impending shock delivery) tends to occur throughout the intershock interval (i.e., is not localized to the period just prior to shock). Though not causally related to such avoidance response rates, blood pressure elevations may also, through extended exposure, persist throughout the intershock interval (as well as throughout the day), as reported by Herd and associates (1969) for prolonged training under fixed-interval avoidance requirements. Alternatively, interval avoidance schedules and ratio avoidance schedules may provide different opportunities for adventitious reinforcement of blood pressure level (Findley, Brady, Robinson, & Gilliam, 1971).

Indeed, blood pressure and heart rate modifications by direct reinforcement have now been reliably demonstrated in nonhuman primates (Benson, Herd, Morse, & Kelleher, 1969; Engel & Gottlieb, 1970; Harris, Gilliam, Findley, & Brady, 1973; Plumlee, 1969; Turkkan & Harris, 1981), in rats (DiCara & Miller, 1968), and, less reliably, in humans (see Goldstein, 1979, for a review). In a format combining food reward, shock avoidance, and visual biofeedback, all contingent upon diastolic blood pressure, for example, baboons were conditioned, in three to four months, both to raise their blood pressure 30–50% (25–40mmHg) above preconditioning baseline levels and to maintain the increased pressures during daily 12-hour training sessions (Harris, Gilliam, Findley, & Brady, 1973; Harris & Turkkan, 1981a, b). Over the course of several months of conditioning, the criterion diastolic level was made progressively higher for food procurement and shock cancelation, typically beginning with a requirement of 65mmHg diastolic and ending with 90mmHg diastolic (maintained for 12 hours daily). Diastolic pressure levels during the sessions pregressively shifted upward with increases in the criterion level to such an extent that diastolic pressures frequently occurred at levels that had never appeared in the preconditioning phase (Turkkan & Harris, 1981). Although neither alpha- nor beta-adrenergic blockade above eliminated the conditioned blood pressure elevations, combined alpha- *and* beta-adrenergic blockade did significantly attenuate the increase in diastolic blood pressure (Goldstein, Harris, & Brady, 1977). These findings, along with data that show increases in plasma epinephrine and norepinephrine during conditioning sessions (Goldstein, Harris, Izzo, Turkkan, & Keiser, 1981), indicate that sympathetic adrenergic activity participates to some extent in conditioned hypertension.

Several reports describing irreversible cardiovascular pathology have focused upon necrotic changes in the myocardium of animals exposed to avoidance conditioning procedures for extended periods (Corley, Mauck, & Shiel, 1975; Corley, Mauck, Shiel, Barber, Clark, & Blocher, 1979; Corley, Shiel, Mauck, & Greenhoot, 1973). Chair-restrained squirrel monkeys yoked to avoidance subjects received shocks whenever the avoidance monkey did but had no control over shock occurrence. Myocardial pathology (fuchsinophilia, necrosis, and fibrosis) appeared to occur more frequently in the avoidance subjects, while physical debilitation, bradycardia, and ventricular arrest occurred in yoked animals. When the animals on a shock avoidance schedule either were vagotomized or received beta-blockade (propranolol), the results suggested that the myocardial pathology resulted from increased sympathetic activity. Cardiac arrest, however, occurred in both vagotomized and beta-blockaded animals, leading the authors to conclude that an imbalance of either sympathetic or parasympathetic input can produce this effect (cf. also Randall & Hasson, 1981). Other studies have also found myocardial electrical instability during performance on shock avoidance schedules (Lang, 1967; Lawler, Botticelli, & Lown, 1976).

Conflict schedules in rats genetically compromised by selective breeding for susceptibility to hypertension have also been observed to result in cardiovascular disorders (Friedman & Dahl, 1977; Lawler, Barker, Hubbard, & Allen, 1980). The rats were first trained on a baseline schedule of either food procurement (Friedman & Dahl, 1977) or shock avoidance

(Lawler, Barker, Hubbard, & Allen, 1980). The conflict aspect of the procedure consisted of explicitly punishing with electric shock the occurrence of responses emitted to meet the requirement of the baseline schedule. Elevated blood pressures (systolic pressures at 150–190mmHg) consistently occurred in the genetically susceptible rats under the conflict condition as compared to various control conditions (random shocks, food deprivation, maturation level, genetically resistant and normotensive strains), which failed to produce such pressure elevations. With the food procurement baseline at least, the blood pressures returned to normotensive levels when the experiment was discontinued, suggesting that duration of exposure to the schedule was an important determinant of chronic blood pressure elevation, as others have reported (Forsyth, 1969; Herd, Morse, Kelleher, & Jones, 1969; Miminishvili, Magakian, & Kokaia, 1960). While these findings provide general support for the interaction between hereditary and environmental factors in the etiology of hypertension (Guttman & Benson, 1971), it has recently been reported (McMurty, Wright, & Wexler, 1981) that genetically normotensive rat pups (Sprague-Dawley but not Wistar-Kyoto) will develop hypertension if suckled by a rat dam of the spontaneously hypertensive strain (Okamoto & Aoki, 1963). It has not yet been determined whether a "hypertensinogenic factor" was transmitted through the mother's milk, or whether the spontaneously hypertensive rat dam's hyperkinetic behavior was responsible for the effect.

The cardiovascular effects of so-called combination stress have been described by several investigators with procedures that exposed laboratory rats to high-intensity flashing lights, loud noise, and cage oscillation (Hudak & Buckley, 1961; Perhach, Ferguson, & McKinney, 1975; Rosecrans, Watzman, & Buckley, 1966; Smookler & Buckley, 1969; Smookler, Goebel, Siegel, & Clarke, 1973; Yamori, Matsumoto, Yamabe, & Okamoto, 1969). Blood pressures reliably increased soon after onset under such conditions, although some habituation has been reported to occur with prolonged exposure (Hudak & Buckley, 1961). When the spontaneously hypertensive rat strain was used, the combination procedure (which also added immobilization) augmented the progressive blood pressure elevation typical in this strain (Yamori, Matsumoto, Yamabe, & Okamoto, 1969).

A contrasting procedural approach has been described for rats housed in pairs in soundproof rooms (Marwood & Lockett, 1977). No external sounds penetrated the chamber, and self-generated sounds such as breathing and eating were not over 45dB. The "sound withdrawal hypertension" reported to develop under such conditions over a 4-week period was characterized by an elevation in mean systolic blood pressure to 192mmHg followed by stabilization at a lower level still markedly elevated over that of controls housed in nonsoundproofed rooms. If sounds from the control rat chamber were relayed to the soundproofed chamber, the pressure elevations did not develop. In this study, the increased pressure levels appeared to be irreversible since transferring sound-withdrawn rats to the normal rat chamber did not result in lower pressures. Additionally, after the rats had spent 12 weeks in the soundproofed chamber, pathological changes were evident in the arterioles, characterized by reduced lumen diameters.

These findings, along with the observation that high-intensity sound alone can produce hypertension (Andriukin, 1961; Farris, Yeakel, & Medoff, 1945; Medoff & Bongiovanni, 1945), suggest that, for rats at least, too little sound or too much sound can adversely affect blood pressure regulation. Primate data on the cardiovascular effects of noise are more equivocal and much less plentiful. High-intensity sound exposure for nine months has recently been reported to produce significant blood pressure elevations in rhesus monkeys (Peterson, Augenstein, Tanis, & Augenstein, 1981), although no such chronic effects were observed with African green monkeys under similar exposure conditions for periods up to six months (Schreyer, 1979).

ENDOCRINE REGULATION AND
STRESSFUL INTERACTIONS

The extensive research literature on general relationships between hormonal response patterns and behavioral interactions has been comprehensively described by Mason (1968a) and by Stone (1975). Historically, attention has focused upon procedures involving aversive environmental circumstances and responses of the pituitary-adreno-cortical system—mostly adrenocorticotrophic hormone (ACTH), growth hormone, and corticosteroids—circumstances that make appropriate contact with the present behavioral-physiological overview of stressful interactions. Traditionally, the activity of the sympatho-adreno-medullary system—the catecholamines, epinephrine (E), norepinephrine (NE), and dopamine—has been more difficult to assay under such conditions. However, sensitive radio-enzymatic techniques have now been developed to detect small amounts of catecholamines in the peripheral circulation (Peuler & Johnson, 1977). Additionally, investigators have sought more sensitive indexes of noradrenergic activity in measurements of rates of turnover of norepinephrine or dopamine. If both synthesis and utilization of norepinephrine increase, for example, norepinephrine turnover is increased considerably, although total levels may not be changed (Stone, 1975).

A range of environmental and behavioral factors have been reported to influence the hormonal response pattern to both response-dependent and response-independent procedures involving aversive stimulus presentation. In the first instance, *prior experience* (Pavlovian conditioning) may determine either the basal levels of hormones or the acute response of hormones even when basal levels are unchanged (McCarty & Kopin, 1978; Sackett, 1973). McCarty and Kopin (1978), for example, showed that when previously shocked rats were placed in the shock chamber, they had more acute elevations in plasma catecholamines relative to those seen in rats that were also placed in the chamber but had never been shocked. However, basal catecholamine levels of these two groups did not differ.

A second parameter influencing hormone response patterns is the *duration of exposure* to aversively stressful procedures. Rhesus monkeys, for example, required to engage in weekly 72-hour continuous shock avoidance sessions initially showed elevated corticosteroid levels (urinary 17-hydroxycorticosteroids, or 17-OHCS) during avoidance as compared to levels during the rest period each week (Brady, 1965). As exposure to the procedure continued, however, 17-OHCS levels in response to avoidance decreased and then increased over the 65-week experiment independently of any changes in response rate or shock frequency, which remained low and stable throughout. Similarly, variable changes have been described by Stone (1975) in an extensive review of the effects on catecholamine tissue levels depending upon the chronicity of exposure to aversive environments (e.g., immobilization, noise, conditioned avoidance, unavoidable foot shock, treadmill exercise, cold swim, burns, hemorrhage). In general, acutely stressful circumstances were found to reduce brain NE levels and to increase NE turnover in the brain and periphery. Increased concentrations of NE in plasma and urine have also been typically described under such conditions (Mason, 1968b). More chronic preparations, however, have been reported to show either progressive returns to baseline after depressed levels or gradual increases in brain NE level, a maintenance of increased turnover, and a reduction in reuptake of NE.

The *presence or absence of warning signals* under circumstances requiring response-dependent shock avoidance (e.g., Sidman avoidance) has also been shown differentially to affect hormonal levels. The addition of a 5-second warning signal after 15 seconds of the programmed 20-second response-shock interval have elapsed in a Sidman avoidance procedure has been shown markedly to reduce the plasma 17-OHCS response as compared to responses in experimental sessions without the warning signal (Mason, Brady, & Tolson, 1966; Sidman, Mason, Brady, & Thach, 1962). When, on the other hand, warning signals are superimposed on an operant food baseline, steroid elevations are observed (Mason, Mangan, Brady, Conrad, & Rioch, 1961).

Finally, the *availability of an aversive stimulus delay or escape contingency* appears to exert a significant influence on hormone responses under stressful conditions (Anisman, Pizzino, & Sklar, 1980; Hanson, Larson, & Snowdon, 1976; Mason, Brady, & Tolson, 1966; Weiss, Stone, & Harrel, 1970). When the plasma cortisol response of rhesus monkeys was compared under conditions of escapable and inescapable high-intensity noise, for example, significantly higher cortisol levels were observed in monkeys who could not escape the noise. Large-magnitude, acute elevations in steroids have also been observed when procedural changes prevent the animal's well-practiced performances from postponing or escaping all or even some of the programmed aversive stimuli (Hanson, Larson, & Snowdon, 1976; Levine, Gordon, Peterson, & Rose, 1970; Mason, Brady, & Tolson, 1966; Sidman, Mason, Brady, & Thach, 1962).

Although hormone levels appear in some studies to be related to response and/or shock rates (Anisman, Pizzino, & Sklar, 1980; Brown, Schalch, & Reichlin, 1971; Sidman, Mason, Brady, & Thatch, 1962), other experiments, sometimes using the same subjects (Sidman et al., 1962), have shown that hormonal reactions may vary independently of such response and shock rates (Brady, 1965; Mason, Brady, & Tolliver, 1968). Dissociations between overt bodily activity and hormone levels have been reported (DiCara & Stone, 1970; McCarty & Kopin, 1978; Welch & Welch, 1968), and individual differences in the responsiveness of hormones have been observed, for example, during paradigms involving electric shock (Levine, Gordon, & Rose, 1968; Mason, Brady, & Tolliver, 1968). In this regard, as well, rated behavioral aggressiveness in rhesus monkeys has been reported reliably to differentiate hormonal levels, with aggressive animals showing higher urinary 17-OHCS (Levine, Gordon, Peterson, & Rose, 1970). And in experiments with rats subjected to inescapable foot shock, only those rats that died had elevated plasma catecholamines throughout the course of exposure to these stressful conditions (Weick, Ritter, & Ritter, 1980). Mason, Wool, Wherry, Pennington, Brady, and Beer (1968) showed that growth hormone in rhesus monkeys may increase or decrease during experimental sessions depending upon presession baseline hormone levels.

Mason and colleagues (1968a, b), in an extensive series of investigations relating hormonal response patterns to long shock avoidance sessions in rhesus monkeys, demonstrated a separation between two subgroups of hormones in terms of their direction of change and time course. In the initial hours of a 72-hour avoidance session, for example, 17-OHCS, catecholamines, thyroxin, and growth hormone were all observed to increase, while sex hormones and insulin initially decreased. The hormone elevations that occurred during avoidance were followed by decreases in the postavoidance period. The hormones that decreased during avoidance, on the other hand, showed later elevations during a 72-hour postavoidance period. This hormonal response pattern to "emotional" stimuli was interpretively related to energy mobilization requirements, as in the classical fight or flight account provided by Cannon (1923). Such adaptational accounts of endocrine regulation in response to behaviorally stressful interactions are of course similar to interpretations offered in the extensive literature on cardiovascular response patterns under such circumstances (Schneiderman, 1972, 1978), reviewed above.

It is of some interest in this regard that research on endocrine regulation and stressful interactions has relied heavily upon procedures involving aversive stimulation. While this focus is understandable in view of the robust effects that have been demonstrated under such conditions, the neglect of procedures based upon more appetitive environmental events may obscure endocrinological-behavioral relationships of at least as great interest and importance. In a few instances (e.g., Mason, Brady, & Sidman, 1957), hormonal accompaniments of food maintained schedules of reinforcement were investigated, and similar increases in brain norepinephrine turnover with rats were reported during performance on a variable-interval schedule of water reinforcement (Lewy & Seiden, 1972) as during conditional shock avoidance performance (Weiss, Stone, & Harrel, 1970). The finding that plasma corticosterone activity was significantly reduced in rats during exposure to a food delivery schedule that concurrently generated polydipsic drinking (Brett & Levine, 1979) suggests a range of interesting investigative possibilities with regard to an extended analysis of such schedule induced adjunctive phenomena (excessive water drinking, aggression, escape, inappropriate feeding). The bitonic function relating the incidence and duration of adjunctive behaviors to schedule parameters (the ratio in FR or the interval in FI schedules of food reinforcement) may reflect a temporal patterning of hormone changes detectable in assays (e.g., catecholamines) based upon plasma samples withdrawn continuously from indwelling catheters, for example, during the interreinforcement intervals typically identified with the occurrence of such adjunctive performances.

GASTROINTESTINAL REACTIVITY TO STRESSFUL INTERACTIONS

In 1956, Sawrey and Weisz first reported the production of gastric ulcers in rats exposed to an instrumental conflict procedure, although later studies clearly suggested that the effects of multiple interacting factors, including food deprivation, shock, weight loss, and even social experience, could not be readily teased apart in such conflict produced alterations (Conger, Sawrey, & Turrell, 1958; Sawrey, Conger, & Turrell, 1956; Weisz, 1957). A subsequent series of studies at the Walter Reed Medical Center focused upon the production of peptic ulcers in rhesus monkeys exposed to recurrent instrumental avoidance performance requirements; this investigation further confirmed the complexity of such effects (Brady, 1958, 1963; Brady & Polish, 1960; Brady, Porter, Conrad, & Mason, 1958; Polish, Brady, Mason, Thach, & Neimeck, 1962; Porter, Brady, Conrad, Mason, Galambos, & Rioch, 1958). Two additional studies, however, were able to provide support for the relationship between instrumental avoidance performances and gastrointestinal reactivity (Davis & Berry, 1963; Rice, 1963).

Some further support for the role of conflict and related procedures in the production of gastric lesions in laboratory rats has been provided by studies focusing upon approach-avoidance methods and comparisons involving individual and group stress exposure (Lower, 1967; Sawrey, 1961; Sawrey & Long, 1962; J. Sawrey & W. Sawrey, 1964, 1966; W. Sawrey & J. Sawrey, 1963, 1964), but replication and confirmation of the reported relationships continue to present problems (Ader, Beels, & Tatum, 1960; Ader, Tatum, & Beels, 1960; Pare, 1964). Similarly, recent descriptions of avoidance performance effects upon the gastrointestinal system have presented something less than a constant picture with regard to the conditions under which ulcers are most likely to occur. The reported incidence of peptic ulcers in rhesus monkeys intermittently exposed to free-operant shock avoidance requirements (Brady, Conrad, Porter, Conrad, & Mason, 1958) has proven difficult to repeat under some laboratory conditions (Folz & Miller, 1964), including those under which the study originated (Brady, 1964). Additionally, several investigations with laboratory rats in escape-avoidance situations have failed to find a greater incidence of gastric lesions in experimental animals than in controls; in some instances, yoked animals receiving unavoidable shocks showed a greater degree of ulceration than did their avoiding partners (Moot, Cebulla, & Crabtree, 1970; Paré, 1971; Weiss, 1971a). In his 1971 review of the research in this area Ader was nonetheless able to document the general observation that with laboratory animals at least, gastrointestinal changes of pathological proportions can be related to environmental-behavioral interactions; he noted that such observations had long served as a basis for considering peptic ulcer (which accounts for more than 10,000 deaths each year) a model for so-called psychosomatic disease and the behavioral-physiological consequences of stressful interactions.

To some extent, a clarification and at least partial reconciliation of the apparently conflicting developments emerging from the animal laboratory in this area was suggested by Weiss (1970, 1971a, b, c) on the basis of a systematic series of experiments with rats. These studies started with the observation that animals who received intermittent tail shock following presentation of a 10-second beep developed significantly less gastric ulceration than did animals receiving the same shock without the warning. Weiss then added an operant escape-avoidance panel-press to the procedure. Under these conditions, markedly fewer gastric lesions were found in the escape-avoidance animals when compared with yoked controls similarly exposed to warning signals and shocks but noncontingently. The interactions between warning signals and escape-avoidance responses were tested in a subsequent experiment in which rats received electric shock preceded by either a warning signal, a series of signals providing an external clock, or no signal at all. Under all three conditions, animals who could avoid and/or escape shock developed less ulceration than did yoked animals. In addition, there was a clear difference in favor of the warning signal condition in reducing ulcerations as compared to the no-signal condition, regardless of whether the animals could or could not escape or avoid the shock.

Relying on these experiments, Weiss theorized that the incidence of peptic ulcers may be a function of the interaction between the strength of the escape-avoidance performance (response rate) and the probability of discriminable response-contingent signals associated with the absence of aversive stimuli (i.e., feedback about shock-free conditions). In these terms, the occurrence of peptic ulcers in monkeys performing on free-operant avoidance can be explained by their high rate of response in the absence of warning stimuli. The yoked monkeys, by contrast, emit few responses, receive only a few shocks well distributed in time (because of the high performance rate of the experimental animals), and have been found to be free of gastrointestinal pathology. Some further confirmation of this hypothesis was provided by Weiss (1971c) in a subsequent series of experiments: the frequency of ulcers was increased in "avoidance" rats, which were punished with shock for responding (creating a situation in which a high rate of response was associated with low feedback about shock-free conditions), and decreased in animals receiving a brief tone with each occurrence of avoidance responses (i.e., strong feedback about shock-free conditions).

A recent experiment with rhesus monkeys involving performance on various shock schedules (avoidance, escape, punishing escape responses, and punishing avoidance responses) found lesions in the mucosa of the stomach and duodenum in seven out of eight subjects (Natelson, Dubois, & Sodetz, 1977). The lesions appeared to be most severe in the avoidance conflict procedure, in which up to 20% of avoidance responses were followed immediately by shock (200msec at 5 mA) (cf. Weiss's, 1971c, findings with rats). Periodic examination of the lesions by fiberoptic endoscopy revealed that the lesions were extremely transient (they healed within a week). All monkeys in this study experienced the same order of experimental conditions, with the highest lesion producing procedure (avoidance conflict) introduced last (5.5–8 weeks after the onset of the shock schedules). Moreover, because the avoidance conflict procedure was the longest studied (a median 2.5 weeks), a durational effect cannot be discounted.

IMMUNOLOGICAL RESPONSES
TO STRESSFUL INTERACTIONS

Increased susceptibility to infectious agents has been demonstrated in studies involving electric shock delivery. Both Coxsackie B2 virus (Friedman, Ader, & Glasgow, 1965; Johnsson, Lavender, Hultin, & Rasmussen, 1963) and poliomyelitis virus (Johnson & Rasmussen, 1965), for example, have been shown to be enhanced in virulence under conditions that involve exposure of mice to a shock avoidance procedure. Exposure for 56 days to a procedure involving inescapable shock (1mA for 15 seconds duration, repeated daily for 15 minutes) has also been shown to result in an increased incidence of dental caries in rats fed a cariogenic diet and inoculated with cariogenic bacteria (Borysenko, Turesky, Borysenko, Quimby, & Benson, 1980).

Response contingency likewise has been shown to exert an important influence upon the immunological response to stressful interactions (Sklar & Anisman, 1979). In this study it was shown that in mice injected with tumor cells, those animals able to escape from shock in a shuttle-box avoidance task lived longer than did mice exposed to the same shock but lacking an escape contingency. Duration of exposure also appeared to be an important variable determining survival in this study: mice that received inescapable shocks over 10 daily sessions had smaller tumor areas and longer survival times than did mice that received 1 or 5 daily sessions of inescapable shock. The mechanisms that account for this somewhat counterintuitive finding have not yet been determined, although the possible relationship of these observations to previously reviewed evidence for cardiovascular and endocrine habituation with prolonged exposure to shock schedules would seem to suggest a fruitful direction for more detailed experimental analysis.

Recent studies described by Riley (1981) examined rotation stress in rodents and found that rotation induced increases in adrenal corticoids and other hormones resulted in injury to elements of the immunological apparatus (e.g., the thymus and thymus dependent T-cells), often leaving the subjects vulnerable to pathological processes that are normally held in check. Recent reviews that documented these and similar findings may be found in Rogers, Dubey, and Reich (1979) and in Monjan (1981).

A BEHAVIORAL–PHYSIOLOGICAL OVERVIEW

Despite the broad range of response-independent and response-dependent behavioral procedures and the widely varying physiological participants encompassed by this review, some general relationships can be identified among the variables that appear critically to determine the characteristically extreme conditions defining stressful interactions. The parameters of interest, not necessarily in order of importance, are outlined in this concluding section.

Intermittency of Events

The modality of event can vary widely, such as food, shock, noise, or performance on various reinforcement schedules. An important modulating variable would seem to be the interval between events, as in optimal interfood intervals for producing adjunctive behavior (Staddon, 1977). Additionally, the length of the intershock interval in Sidman avoidance has been shown to be correlated with the degree of elevation in hormone (Sidman, Mason, Brady, & Thatch, 1962) and blood pressure levels (Forsyth & Harris, 1970). Significantly, inter-event intervals of two to five seconds (e.g., for FI food and Sidman shock avoidance schedules) have been found to generate the greatest blood pressure elevations (Forsyth & Harris, 1970), the highest plasma 17-OHCS levels (Sidman, Mason, Brady, & Thatch, 1962), and the most extreme amounts of polydipsic drinking (Falk, 1971). A similarly critical temporal dimension, though of a different order of magnitude, is suggested by the finding that a six-hour on, six-hour off Sidman avoidance schedule compared to either longer or shorter on-off formats maximizes the degree of ulceration observed in laboratory animals (Brady, 1958; Rice, 1963).

Availability of a Warning Signal

It has been generally observed that pairing a warning signal with otherwise unsignaled aversive events may reduce the magnitude and/or the duration of behavioral and/or physiological departures from response norms (Mason, Brady, & Tolson, 1966; Miller et al., 1978; Sidman, Mason, Brady, & Thatch, 1962; Weiss, 1972).

Availability of Escape or Avoidance Contingencies

Ameliorating effects, similar to those observed in the case of warning signal availability, have been described that suggest that response-dependent escape or avoidance contingencies can attenuate the behavioral and physiological consequences of exposure to aversive environmental events (Anisman, Pizzino, & Sklar, 1980; Sklar & Anisman, 1979; Weiss, 1971a, b, c; Weiss, Stone, & Harrel, 1970).

Duration of Exposure

Short durations of exposure to stressful interactions may not have chronic consequences since recuperative processes can operate to reverse deleterious effects (Friedman & Dahl, 1977). In general, medium-range durations of exposure may be most effective in producing pathological changes (Forsyth, 1969; Forsyth & Harris, 1970; Herd, Morse, Kelleher, & Jones, 1969) since longer exposure may result in habituation (Desiderato & Testa, 1976; Hudak & Buckley, 1961; Natelson, Krasnegor, & Holaday, 1976; Schreyer, 1979; Sklar & Anisman, 1979). From a physiological perspective, the various bodily systems may have their own short, medium, and long time frame; in some instances, the time course appears triphasic rather than biphasic, i.e., initial large-scale changes followed by adaptation and then further chronic changes (Brady, 1965; Forsyth, 1969; Rosecrans, Watzman, & Buckley, 1966). While this latter sequence may appear to be consistent with the hypothesized alarm, resistance, and exhaustion stages of the *general adaptation syndrome* (Selye, 1946), the more frequent case would seem to be repetitive or cyclic patterning of responses specific to the tonic (Mason, Brady, & Sidman, 1957) or acute (Turkkan, 1979) properties of the stressful interaction.

Changes in Established Procedure

Situations introducing conflict arrangements in which aversive events (e.g., shock) are made contingent upon performances maintained by appetitive consequences (e.g., food) appear to produce pathological effects in both genetically compromised subjects (Friedman & Dahl, 1977; Lawler and others, 1980) and nongenetically selected subjects (Natelson and others, 1977). Significantly, such changes in established procedure have been shown to produce deleterious effects under response-independent Pavlovian arrangements in which either CSs paired with shock were presented with CSs paired with food or the CS–shock US interval was lengthened unpredictably (Miminishvili, Magakiau, & Kokaia, 1960), as well as under response-dependent conditions. In the latter case, for example, presentation of non-contingent shocks during ongoing operant performances maintained by either shock avoidance or food delivery has been shown to produce extensive endocrine changes (Brady, 1975; Levine, Gordon, Peterson, & Rose, 1970; Sidman, Mason, Brady, & Thatch, 1962), as has the complete removal of escape or avoidance response contingencies previously in effect (Hanson, Larson, & Snowdon, 1976; Mason, Brady, & Tolson, 1966).

Event Intensity

Extreme values of certain variables in either direction appear to produce pathological changes as in the hypertensive effects of both combination stress (Smookler & Buckley, 1969; Smookler et al., 1973) and sound withdrawal (Marwood & Lockett, 1977). Similarly, the development of behavioral derangements has been observed under conditions of both crowding (Henry, Meehan, & Stephens, 1967) and social isolation (Sackett, 1973). On the other hand, shock elicited aggression occurs only within a certain range of shock intensities (Ulrich & Azrin, 1962), and schedule induced polydipsic drinking varies as a function of meal size (Falk, 1967).

Historical and Constitutional Factors

Animals selectively bred, for example, have been shown to be more susceptible to blood pressure elevations and to the development of related cardiovascular pathologies (Friedman & Dahl, 1977; Lawler, Barker, Hubbard, & Allen, 1980; Yamori, Matsumoto, Yamabe, & Okamoto, 1969). The influence of prior experience has been convincingly demonstrated in the extensive literature on Pavlovian conditioning, as well as by more recent experimental initiatives (McCarty & Kopin, 1978; Sackett, 1973). Additionally, differences in both overt behavior (Levine, Gordon, Petterson, & Rose, 1970; Weiss, 1972) and physiological levels (Randall & Hasson, 1981) have been shown to influence the gastrointestinal and cardiovascular consequences of exposure to stressful interactions.

A final comment on the state of the art as it relates to this overview of animal studies on stressful interactions would seem to be in order. While the literature to date reveals an appropriate emphasis upon the production of more or less specific and clinically relevant pathologies under stressful interaction conditions, a more detailed analysis of the functional relationships between systematically varied environmental-behavioral parameters and operationally defined biochemical-physiological processes now seems to be required. In this regard, for example, a more comprehensive coverage of critical interaction effects is likely to be provided by attending not only to the periods in which experimental variables are being actively manipulated but also to the intervals that separate programmed sessions in the laboratory and to more extended durations of exposure appropriate to the behavioral and physiological processes of interest. Under such circumstances, important aspects of reversibility and recovery within individual animals can be carefully examined. Most important, technological advances now make possible concurrent measurements in multiple response systems, so that interaction effects can be explored and delineated by surgical, physiological, pharmacological, and behavioral interventions. Within the context of these emerging approaches, animal laboratory studies promise to provide important insights into the behavioral-physiological processes that determine and define stressful interactions.

REFERENCES

ADER, R. Experimentally induced gastric lesions. In *Advances in Psychosomatic Medicine,* vol. 6. Basel: Karger, 1971.

ADER, R., BEELS, C. C., & TATUM, R. Social factors affecting emotionality and resistance to disease in animals. Part II: Susceptibility to gastric ulceration as a function of interruptions in social interactions and the time at which they occur. *Journal of Comparative and Physiological Psychology,* 1960, *53,* 455–458.

ADER, R., TATUM, R., & BEELS, C. C. Social factors affecting emotionality and resistance to disease in animals. Part I: Age of separation from the mother and susceptibility to gastric ulcers in the rat. *Journal of Comparative and Physiological Psychology,* 1960, *53,* 446–454.

ANDERSON, D. E., & BRADY, J. V. Pre-avoidance blood pressure elevations by heart rate decreases in the dog. *Science,* 1971, *172,* 595–597.

————. Prolonged pre-avoidance effects upon blood pressure and heart rate in the dog. *Psychosomatic Medicine,* 1976, *38,* 181.

ANDERSON, D. E., & TOSHEFF, J. Cardiac output and total peripheral resistance changes during pre-avoidance periods in the dog. *Journal of Applied Physiology,* 1973, *34,* 650–654.

ANDERSON, D. E., YINGLING, J., & BRADY, J. V. Cardiovascular responses to avoidance conditioning in the dog: Effects of alpha adrenergic blockade. *Pavlovian Journal of Biological Sciences,* 1976, *11,* 150.

ANDRIUKIN, A. A. Influence of sound stimulation on the development of hypertension. *Cor et Vasa,* 1961, *3,* 285–293.

ANISMAN, H., PIZZION, A., & SKLAR, L. S. Coping with stress, norepinephrine depletion, and escape performance. *Brain Research,* 1980, *191,* 583–588.

ATOR, N. A. Mirror pecking and timeout under a multiple fixed-ratio schedule of food delivery. *Journal of the Experimental Analysis of Behavior,* 1980, *34,* 319–328.

AZRIN, N. H. Time-out from positive reinforcement. *Science,* 1961, *133,* 382–383.

AZRIN, N. H., & HAKE, D. F. Positive conditioned suppression: Conditioned suppression using positive reinforcers as the unconditioned stimuli. *Journal of the Experimental Analysis of Behavior,* 1969, *12,* 167–173.

AZRIN, N. H., HUTCHINSON, R. R., & HAKE, D. F. Extinction-induced aggression. *Journal of the Experimental Analysis of Behavior,* 1966, *9,* 191–204.

AZRIN, N. H., HUTCHINSON, R. R., & McLAUGHLIN, R. The opportunity for aggression as an operant reinforcer during aversive stimulation. *Journal of the Experimental Analysis of Behavior,* 1965, *8,* 171–180.

BENSON, H., HERD, J. A., MORSE, W. H., & KELLEHER, R. T. Behavioral induction of arterial hypertension and its reversal. *American Journal of Physiology,* 1969, *217,* 30–34.

BILLMAN, G. E., & RANDALL, D. C. Classic aversive conditioning of coronary blood flow in mongrel dogs. *Pavlovian Journal of Biological Science,* 1980, *15,* 93–101.

—————. Mechanisms mediating the coronary vascular response to behavioral stress in the dog. *Circulation Research,* 1981, *48,* 214–223.

BLACK, A. H. CARLSON, N. J., & SOLOMON, R. L. Exploratory studies of the conditioning of autonomic responses in curarized dogs. *Psychological Monographs* whole no. 548), 1962, *76,* 1–31.

BLACK, R. W., & BLACK, P. E. Heart rate conditioning as a function of interstimulus interval in rats. *Psychonomic Science,* 1967, *8,* 219–220.

BOLME, P., & NOVOTNY, J. Conditional reflex activation of the sympathetic cholinergic vasodilator nerves in the dog. *Acta Physiologica Scandinavica,* 1969, *77,* 58–67.

BOND, D. D. Sympathetic and vagal interaction in emotional responses of the heart rate. *American Journal of Physiology,* 1943, *138,* 468–478.

BORYSENKO, M., TURESKY, S., BORYSENKO, J. Z., QUIMBY, F., & BENSON, H. Stress and dental caries in the rat. *Journal of Behavioral Medicine,* 1980, *3,* 233–243.

BOWERS, K. S. The effects of UCS temporal uncertainty on heart rate and pain. *Psychophysiology,* 1971, *8,* 382–389.

BRADY, J. V. Ulcers in "executive" monkeys. *Scientific American,* 1958, *199,* 95–100.

—————. Further comments on the gastrointestinal system and avoidance behavior. *Psychological Reports,* 1963, *12,* 742.

—————. Behavioral stress and physiological change: A comparative approach to the experimental analysis of some psychosomatic problems. *Transactions of the New York Academy of Sciences,* 1964, *26,* 483–496.

—————. Experimental studies of psychophysiological responses to stressful situations. *Symposium on medical aspects of stress in the military climate.* Washington, D.C.: U.S. Government Printing Office, 1965.

—————. Endocrine and autonomic correlates of emotional behavior. In P. Black (ed.), *Physiological correlates of emotion.* New York: Academic, 1970.

—————. Toward a behavioral biology of emotion. In L. Levi (ed.), *Emotion: Their parameters and measurement.* New York: Raven, 1975.

BRADY, J. V., & HARRIS, A. H. The experimental production of altered physiological states. In W. K. Honig & J. E. R. Staddon (eds.), *Handbook of operant behavior.* Englewood Cliffs: Prentice-Hall, 1977.

BRADY, J. V., & HUNT, H. F. A further demonstration of the effects of electro-convulsive shock on a conditioned emotional response. *Journal of Comparative and Physiological Psychology,* 1951, *44,* 204–209.

BRADY, J. V., KELLY, D., & PLUMLEE, L. Autonomic and behavioral responses of the rhesus monkey to emotional conditioning. *Annals of the New York Academy of Sciences,* 1969, *159,* 959–975.

Brady, J. V., & Polish, E. Performance changes during prolonged avoidance. *Psychological Reports,* 1960, *7,* 554.

Brady, J. V., Porter, R., Conrad, D., & Mason, J. Avoidance behavior and the development of gastroduodenal ulcers. *Journal of the Experimental Analysis of Behavior,* 1958, *1,* 69–72.

Brett, L. P., & Levine, S. Schedule-induced polydipsia suppresses pituitary-adrenal activity in rats. *Journal of Comparative and Physiological Psychology,* 1979, *93,* 946–956.

Brown, C. C., & Peters, J. E. The effects of different durations of conditional stimulus on the magnitude of conditional cardiac acceleration. *Conditional Reflex,* 1967, *2,* 159.

Brown, G. M., Schalch, D. S., & Reichlin, S. Patterns of growth hormone and cortisol responses to psychological stress in the squirrel monkey. *Endocrinology,* 1971, *88,* 956–963.

Brown, T. G., & Flory, R. K. Schedule-induced escape from fixed-interval reinforcement. *Journal of the Experimental Analysis of Behavior,* 1972, *17,* 395–403.

Cannon, W. B. *Bodily changes in pain, hunger, fear, and rage.* New York: Appleton, 1923.

Clark, R., & Polish, E. Avoidance conditioning and alcohol consumption in rhesus monkeys. *Science,* 1960, *132,* 223–224.

Cohen, D. H. Analysis of the final common path for heart rate conditioning. In P. Obrist, A. Black, J. Brener, & L. DiCara (eds.), *Cardiovascular psychophysiology.* Chicago: Aldine, 1974.

Cohen, D. H., & Durkovic, R. G. Cardiac and respiratory conditioning, differentiation, and extinction in the pigeon. *Journal of the Experimental Analysis of Behavior,* 1966, *9,* 681–688.

Cohen, D. H., & Obrist, P. A. Interactions between behavior and the cardiovascular system. *Circulatory Research,* 1975, *37,* 693–706.

Cohen, D. H., & Pitts, L. H. Vagal and sympathetic components of conditioned cardio-acceleration in the pigeon. *Brain Research,* 1968, *9,* 15–31.

Conger, J. J., Sawrey, W. L., & Turrell, E. S. The role of social experience in the production of gastric ulcers in hooded rats placed in a conflict situation. *Journal of Comparative Physiological Psychology,* 1958, *51,* 214–220.

Corbalan, R., Verrier, R., & Lown, B. Psychological stress and ventricular arrhythmias during myocardial infarction in the conscious dog. *American Journal of Cardiology,* 1974, *34,* 692–696.

Corley, K. C., Mauck, H. P., & Shiel, F. O'M. Cardiac-responses associated with "yoked-chair" shock avoidance in squirrel monkeys. *Psychophysiology,* 1975, *12,* 439–444.

Corley, K. C., Mauck, H. P., Shiel, F. O'M, Barber, J. H., Clark, T. S. & Blocher, C. R. Myocardial dysfunction and pathology associated with environmental stress in squirrel monkey: Effect of vagotomy and propranolol. *Psychophysiology,* 1979, *16,* 554–560.

Corley, K. C., Shiel, F. O'M, Mauck, H. P., & Greenhoot, J. Electrocardiographic and cardiac morphological changes associated with environmental stress in squirrel monkeys. *Psychosomatic Medicine,* 1973, *35,* 361–364.

Davis R. C., & Berry, F. Gastrointestinal reactions during a noise avoidance task. *Psychological Reports,* 1963, *12,* 135–137.

Deane, G. E. Cardiac conditioning in the albino rabbit using 3 CS–US intervals. *Psychosomatic Science,* 1965, *3,* 119–120.

Desiderato, O., & Testa, M. Shock-stress, gastric secretion, and habituation in the chronic gastric fistula rat. *Physiology and Behavior,* 1976, *16,* 67–73.

DiCara, L. V., & Miller, N. E. Instrumental learning of systolic blood pressure responses in curarized rats: Dissociation of cardiac and vascular changes. *Psychosomatic Medicine,* 1968, *5,* 489–494.

DiCara, L. V., & Stone, E. A. Effect of instrumental heart-rate training on rat cardiac and brain catecholamines. *Psychosomatic Medicine,* 1970, *32,* 359–368.

DRONSEJKO, K. Effects of CS duration and instructional set on cardiac anticipatory responses to stress in field dependent and independent subjects. *Psychophysiology,* 1972, *9,* 1–13.

DYKMAN, R. A., & GANTT, W. H. Experimental psychogenic hypertension: Blood pressure changes conditioned to painful stimuli (schizokinesis). *Bulletin of the Johns Hopkins Hospital,* 1960, *107,* 72–89.

EBEL, H. C., & PROKASY, W. F. Classical eyelid conditioning as a function of sustained and shifted interstimulus intervals. *Journal of Experimental Psychology,* 1963, *65,* 52–58.

ELLISON, G. D., & ZANCHETTI, A. Sympathetic cholinergic vasodilation in muscles: Specific appearance during conditioned movement. *Nature,* 1971, *232,* 124–125.

ENGEL, B. T., & GOTTLIEB, S. H. Differential operant conditioning of heart rate in the restrained monkey. *Journal of Comparative and Physiological Psychology,* 1970, *73,* 217–225.

ESTES, W. K., & SKINNER, B. F. Some quantitative properties of anxiety. *Journal of Experimental Psychology,* 1941, *29,* 390–400.

FALK, J. L. Production of polydipsia in normal rats by an intermittent food schedule. *Science,* 1961, *133,* 195–196.

————. Control of schedule-induced polydipsia: Type, size, and spacing of meals. *Journal of the Experimental Analysis of Behavior,* 1967, *10,* 199–206.

————. The nature and determinants of adjunctive behavior. *Physiology and Behavior,* 1971, *6,* 577–588.

FALK, J. L., SAMSON, H. H., & WINGER, G. Behavioral maintenance of high concentrations of blood ethanol and physical dependence in the rat. *Science,* 1972, *177,* 811–813.

FARRIS, E. J., YEAKEL, E. H., & MEDOFF, H. Development of hypertension in emotional gray Norway rats after air blasting. *American Journal of Physiology,* 1945, *144,* 331.

FERSTER, C. B., & SKINNER, B. F. *Schedules of reinforcement.* New York: Appleton, 1957.

FINDLEY, J. D., BRADY, J. V., ROBINSON, W. W., & GILLIAM, W. J. Continuous cardiovascular monitoring in the baboon during long-term behavioral performances. *Communications in Behavioral Biology,* 1971, *6,* 49–58.

FITZGERALD, R. D., & MARTIN, G. K. Heart rate conditioning in rats as a function of interstimulus interval. *Psychological Reports,* 1971, *29,* 1103–1110.

FITZGERALD, R. D., & WALLOCH R. A. Changes in respiration and the form of the heart rate CR in dogs. *Psychosomatic Science,* 1966, *5,* 425–426.

FLORY, R. Attack behavior as a function of minimum inter-food interval. *Journal of the Experimental Analysis of Behavior,* 1969, *12,* 825–828.

FOLZ, E. L., & MILLER, F. E., JR. Experimental psychosomatic disease states in monkeys. Part I: Peptic ulcer "executive monkeys." *Journal of Surgical Research,* 1964, *4,* 445–453.

FORSYTH, R. P. Blood pressure and avoidance conditioning. *Psychosomatic Medicine,* 1968, *30,* 125–135.

————. Blood pressure responses to long-term avoidance schedules in the restrained rhesus monkey. *Psychosomatic Medicine,* 1969, *31,* 300–309.

————. Regional blood-flow changes during 72-hour avoidance schedules in the monkey. *Science,* 1971, *173,* 546–548.

FORSYTH, R. P., & HARRIS, R. E. Circulatory changes during stressful stimuli in rhesus monkeys. *Circulation Research* (supp. 1), 1970, *26–27,* I-B-I-20.

FRIEDMAN, R., & DAHL, L. K. Psychic and genetic factors in the etiology of hypertension. In D. Wheatley (ed.), *Stress and the heart.* New York: Raven, 1977.

FRIEDMAN, S. B., ADER, R., & GLASGOW, L. A. Effects of psychological stress in adult mice inoculated with coxsackie B viruses. *Psychosomatic Medicine,* 1965, *27,* 361–368.

GALOSY, R. A., CLARKE, L. K., & MITCHELL, J. H. Cardiac changes during behavioral stress in dogs. *American Journal of Physiology,* 1979, *236,* H750–H758.

GALOSY, R. A., & GAEBELEIN, C. J. Cardiovascular adaptation to environmental stress: Its role in the development of hypertension, responsible mechanisms, and hypotheses. *Biobehavioral Reviews,* 1977, *1,* 165–175.

GANTT, W. H. Principles of nervous breakdown-schizokinesis and autokinesis. *Annals of the New York Academy of Sciences,* 1953, *56,* 143–163.

————. Cardiovascular component of the conditional reflex to pain, food, and other stimuli. *Physiological Review,* 1960, *40,* 266–291.

GARCIA, J., & KOELLING, R. A. Relation of cue to consequence in avoidance learning. *Psychonomic Science,* 1966, *4,* 123–124.

GATCHEL, R. J., & LANG, P. J. Effects of interstimulus interval length and variability on habituation of autonomic components of the orienting response. *Journal of Experimental Psychology,* 1974, *103,* 802–804.

GEER, J. H. Measurement of the conditioned cardiac response. *Journal of Comparative and Physiological Psychology,* 1964, *57,* 426–433.

GENTRY, W. D. Fixed-ratio schedule-induced aggression. *Journal of the Experimental Analysis of Behavior,* 1968, *11,* 813–817.

GOLDSTEIN, D. S. Instrumental cardiovascular conditioning: A review. *Pavlovian Journal of Biological Science,* 1979, *14,* 108–127.

GOLDSTEIN, D. S., HARRIS, A. H., & BRADY, J. V. Sympathetic adrenergic blockade effects upon operantly conditioned blood pressure elevations in baboons. *Biofeedback and Self-regulation,* 1977, *2,* 93–105.

GOLDSTEIN, D. S., HARRIS, A. H., IZZO, J., TURKKAN, J. S., & KEISER, H. Plasma catecholamines and renin during operant blood pressure conditioning in baboons. *Physiology and Behavior,* 1981, *26,* 33–37.

GUTTMAN, M. C., & BENSON, H. Interaction of environmental factors and systemic arterial blood pressure: A review. *Medicine,* 1971, *50,* 543–553.

HANSON, J. D., LARSON, M. E., & SNOWDON, C. T. The effects of control over high intensity noise on plasma cortisol levels in rhesus monkeys. *Behavioral Biology,* 1976, *16,* 333–340.

HARRIS, A. H., & BRADY, J. V. Animal learning: Visceral and autonomic conditioning. *Annual Review of Psychology,* 1974, *25,* 107–133.

HARRIS, A. H., GILLIAM, W. J., FINDLEY, J. D., & BRADY, J. V. Instrumental conditioning of large-magnitude, daily, 12-hour blood pressure elevations in the baboon. *Science,* 1973, *182,* 175–177.

HARRIS, A. H., & TURKKAN, J. S. Generalization of conditioned blood pressure elevations: Schedule and stimulus control effects. *Physiology and Behavior,* 1981, *26,* 935–940. (a)

————. Performance characteristics of conditioned blood pressure elevation in the baboon. *Biofeedback and Self-regulation,* 1981, *6,* 11–24. (b)

HASTINGS, S. E., & OBRIST, P. A. Heart rate during conditioning in humans: Effect of varying the interstimulus (CS-UCS) interval. *Journal of Experimental Psychology,* 1967, *74,* 431–442.

HEIN, P. L. Heart rate conditioning in the cat and its relationship to other physiological responses. *Psychophysiology,* 1969, *5,* 455–464.

HENRY, J. P., MEEHAN, J. P., & STEPHENS, P. M. The use of psychosocial stimuli to induce prolonged systolic hypertension in mice. *Psychosomatic Medicine,* 1967, *29,* 408–432.

HERD, A. J., MORSE, W. H., KELLEHER, R. T., & JONES, L. G. Arterial hypertension in the squirrel monkey during behavioral experiments. *American Journal of Physiology,* 1969, *217,* 24–29.

HUDAK, W. J., & BUCKLEY, J. P. Production of hypertensive rats by experimental stress. *Journal of Pharmaceutical Sciences,* 1961, *50,* 263–264.

HUNT, H. F., & OTIS, L. S. Conditioned and unconditioned emotional defecation in the rat. *Journal of Comparative and Physiological Psychology,* 1953, *46,* 378–382.

HUTCHINSON, R. R., AZRIN, N. H., & HUNT, G. M. Attack produced by intermittent reinforcement of a concurrent operant response. *Journal of the Experimental Analysis of Behavior,* 1968, *11,* 489–495.

JAWORSKA, K., & SOLTYSIK, S. Studies on the aversive classical conditioning. Part III: Cardiac responses to conditioned and unconditioned defensive (aversive) stimuli. *Acta Biologiae Experimentalis,* 1962, *22,* 193–214.

JOHNSSON, T., LAVENDER, J. F., HULTIN, F., & RASMUSSEN, A. F., JR. The influence of avoidance-learning stress on resistance to coxsackie B virus in mice. *Journal of Immunology.* 1963, *91,* 569–575.

JOHNSSON, T., & RASMUSSEN, A. F., JR. Emotional stress and susceptibility to poliomyelitis virus infection in mice. *Archiv fur die Gesamte Virusforschung,* 1965, *18,* 393–396.

KADDEN, R. M., SCHOEFELD, W. N., McCULLOUGH, M. R., STEELE, W. A., & TREMONT, P. J. Classical conditioning of heart rate and blood pressure in *Macaca mulatta. Journal of the Autonomic Nervous System,* 1980, *2,* 131–142.

KAZIS, E., MILLIGAN, W., & POWELL, D. Autonomic-somatic relationships: Blockade of heart rate and corneo-retinal potential responses. *Journal of Comparative and Physiological Psychology,* 1973, *84,* 98–110.

KELLY, D. D. Enhancement of conditioned autonomic responses in monkeys when preshock signals occasion operant suppression. *Journal of the Experimental Analysis of Behavior,* 1980, *33,* 275–284.

KINNEY, L., & SCHMIDT, H., JR. Effect of cued and uncued inescapable shock on voluntary alcohol consumption in rats. *Pharmacology, Biochemistry, and Behavior,* 1979, *11,* 601–604.

KLOSE, K. J., AUGENSTEIN, J. S., SCHNEIDERMAN, N., MANAS, K., ABRAMS, B., & BLOOM, L. J. Selective autonomic blockade of conditioned and unconditioned cardiovascular changes in rhesus monkeys *(Macaca mulatta). Journal of Comparative and Physiological Psychology,* 1975, *89,* 810–818.

KOSUPKIN, J. M., & OLMSTED, J. M. Slowing of the heart as a conditioned reflex in the rabbit. *American Journal of Physiology,* 1943, *139,* 550–552.

LANG, C. M. Effects of psychic stress on atherosclerosis in the squirrel monkey. *Proceedings of the Society for Experimental Biology and Medicine,* 1967, *126,* 30–34.

LAPIN, B. A., & CHERKOVICH, G. M. Environmental changes causing the development of neuroses and corticovisceral pathology in monkeys. In L. Levi (ed.), *Society, stress, and disease,* vol. 1. New York: Oxford University Press, 1971.

LAWLER, J. E., BARKER, G. F., HUBBARD, J. W., & ALLEN, M. T. The effects of conflict on tonic levels of blood pressure in the genetically borderline hypertensive rat. *Psychophysiology,* 1980, *17,* 363–370.

LAWLER, J. E., BOTTICELLI, L. J., & LOWN, B. Changes in cardiac refractory period during signalled shock avoidance in dogs. *Psychophysiology,* 1976, *13,* 373–377.

LAWLER, J. E., OBRIST, P. A., & LAWLER, K. A. Cardiovascular function during pre-avoidance, avoidance, and post-avoidance in dogs. *Psychophysiology,* 1975, *12,* 4–11.

LEVINE, M. D., GORDON, T. P., PETERSON, R. H., & ROSE, R. M. Urinary 17–OHCS response of high- and low-aggressive rhesus monkeys to shock avoidance. *Physiology and Behavior,* 1970, *5,* 919–924.

LEVINE, M. D., GORDON, T. P., & ROSE, R. M. Individual differences in urinary 17–OHCS levels during chronic free operant avoidance. *Proceedings of the American Psychological Association,* 1968, *3,* 265–266.

LEWEY, A. J., & SEIDEN, L. S. Operant behavior changes norepinephrine metabolism in rat brain. *Science,* 1972, *175,* 454–456.

LOWER, J. S. Approach-avoidance conflict as a determinant of peptic ulceration in the rat. Doctoral dissertation, Case Western Reserve University, 1967.

LOWN, B., VERRIER, R., & CORBALAN, R. Psychologic stress and threshold for repetitive ventricular response. *Science,* 1973, *182,* 834–836.

LUND-JOHANSEN, P. Hemodynamics in early essential hypertension. *Acta Medica Scandinavica* (supp. 482), 1967, *00,* 1–101.

LYNCH, J. J. Pavlovian inhibition of delay in cardiac somatic responses in dogs: Schizokinesis. *Psychological Reports,* 1973, *32,* 1339–1346.

LYNCH, J. J., & MCCARTHY, J. F. Social responding in dogs: Heart rate changes to a person. *Psychophysiology,* 1969, *5,* 389–393.

MARSHALL, L. B., ZEINER, A. R., & SMITH, O. A. Development of conditioned suppression and associated cardiovascular responses in the monkey. *Physiology and Behavior,* 1978, *20,* 441–446.

MARWOOD, J. F., & LOCKETT, M. F. Stress-induced hypertension in rats. In D. Wheatley (ed.), *Stress and the heart.* New York: Raven, 1977.

MASON, J. W. Organization of the multiple endocrine responses to avoidance in the monkey. *Psychosomatic Medicine,* 1968, *30,* 744. (a)

————. A review of psychoendocrine research on the sympathetic-adrenal medullary system. *Psychosomatic Medicine,* 1968, *30,* 631. (b)

MASON, J. W., BRADY, J. V., & SIDMAN, M. Plasma 17-hydroxycorticosteroid levels and conditioned behavior in the rhesus monkey. *Endocrinology,* 1957, *60,* 741–752.

MASON, J. W., BRADY, J. V., & TOLLIVER, G. A. Plasma and urinary 17-hydroxycorticosteroid responses to 72-hour avoidance sessions in the monkey. *Psychosomatic Medicine,* 1968, *30,* 608–630.

MASON, J. W., BRADY, J. V., & TOLSON, W. W. Behavioral adaptations and endocrine activity. In R. Levine (ed.), *Proceedings of the Association for Research in Nervous and Mental Diseases.* Baltimore: Williams & Wilkins, 1966.

MASON, J. W., MANGAN, G., BRADY, J. V., CONRAD, D., & RIOCH, D. Concurrent plasma epinephrine, norepinephrine, and 17-hydroxycorticosteroid levels during conditioned emotional disturbances in monkeys. *Psychosomatic Medicine,* 1961, *23,* 334–353.

MASON, J. W., WOOL, M. S., WHERRY, F. E., PENNINGTON, L. L., BRADY, J. V., & BEER, B. Plasma growth hormone response to avoidance sessions in the monkey. *Psychosomatic Medicine,* 1968, *30,* 760–773.

MCALLISTER, W. R., FARBER, I. E., & TAYLOR, J. E. *Conditioned heart rate as a function of anxiety and CS–UCS interval.* Iowa State University, Department of Psychology technical report no. 1. 1954.

MCCARTY, R., & KOPIN, I. J. Changes in plasma catecholamines and behavior of rats during the anticipation of foot shock. *Hormones and Behavior,* 1978, *11,* 248–257.

MCDONALD, D. G., STERN, J. A., & HAHN, W. W. Classical heart rate conditioning in the rat. *Journal of Psychosomatic Research,* 1963, *7,* 97–106.

MCMURTY, J. P., WRIGHT, G. L., & WEXLER, B. C. Spontaneous hypertension in cross-suckled rats. *Science,* 1981, *211,* 1173–1175.

MEDOFF, H. S., & BONGIOVANNI, A. M. Blood pressure in rats subjected to audiogenic stimulation. *American Journal of Physiology,* 1945, *143,* 300–304.

MELTZER, D., & BRAHLEK, J. Quantity of reinforcement and fixed-interval performance. *Psychosomatic Science,* 1968, *12,* 207–208.

MILLER, D. G., GROSSMAN, Z. D., RICHARDSON, R. L., WISTOW, B. W., & THOMAS, F. D. Effect of signalled versus unsignalled stress on rat myocardium. *Psychosomatic Medicine,* 1978, *40,* 432–434.

MIMINISHVILI, D. I. Experimental neurosis in monkeys. In I. A. Utkin (ed.), *Problems of medicine and biology in experiments on monkeys.* New York: Pergamon, 1960.

MIMINISHVILI, D. I., MAGAKIAN, G. O., & KOKAIA, G. I. Attempts to obtain a model of hypertension and coronary insufficiency in monkeys. In I. A. Utkin (ed.), *Problems of medicine and biology in experiments on monkeys.* New York: Pergamon, 1960.

MONJAN, A. A. Stress and immunologic competence: Studies in animals. In R. Ader (ed.), *Psychoneuroimmunology.* Academic, 1981.

MOOT, S. A., CEBULLA, R. P., & CRABTREE, J. M. Instrumental control and ulceration in rats. *Journal of Comparative and Physiological Psychology,* 1970, *71,* 405–410.

NATELSON, B. H., DUBOIS, A., & SODETZ, F. J. Effect of multiple-stress procedures on monkey gastroduodenal mucosa, serum gastrin, and hydrogen ion kinetics. *Digestive Diseases,* 1977, *22,* 888–897.

NATELSON, B. H., KRASNEGOR, N., & HOLADAY, J. W. Relationship between behavioral arousal and plasma cortisol levels in monkeys performing repeated free-operant avoidance sessions. *Journal of Comparative and Physiological Psychology,* 1976, *90,* 958–969.

NATHAN, M. S., & SMITH, O. A., JR. Differential conditional emotional and cardiovascular responses: A training technique for monkeys. *Journal of the Experimental Analysis of Behavior,* 1968, *11,* 77–82.

NEWTON, J. O., & GANTT, W. H. One trial cardiac conditioning in dogs. *Conditional Reflex,* 1966, *1,* 251–265.

NEWTON, J. E., & PEREZ-CRUET, J. Successive-beat analysis of cardiovascular orienting and conditional responses. *Conditional Reflex,* 1967, *2,* 37–55.

OBRIST, P. A., & WEBB, R. A. Heart rate during conditioning in dogs: Relationship to somatic-motor activity. *Psychophysiology,* 1967, *4,* 7–34.

OKAMOTO, K., & AOKI, K. Development of a strain of spontaneously hypertensive rats. *Japanese Circulation Journal,* 1963, *27,* 282–293.

PARÉ, W. P. The effect of chronic environmental stress on stomach ulceration, adrenal function, and consummatory behavior in the rat. *Journal of Psychology,* 1964, *57,* 143–151.

————. Six-hour escape-avoidance work shift and production of stomach ulcers. *Journal of Comparative and Physiological Psychology,* 1971, *77,* 459–466.

PARRISH, J. Classical discrimination conditioning of heart rate and bar-press suppression in the rat. *Psychonomic Science,* 1967, *9,* 267–268.

PAVLOV, I. P. *Lectures on conditioned reflexes,* trans. W. H. Gantt. New York: International, 1928.

PERHACH, J. L., JR., FERGUSON, H. C., & MCKINNEY, G. R. Evaluation of antihypertensive agents in the stress-induced hypertensive rat. *Life Sciences,* 1975, *16,* 1731–1736.

PETERSON, E. A., AUGENSTEIN, J. S., TANIS, D. C., & AUGENSTEIN, D. G. Noise raises blood pressure without impairing auditory sensitivity. *Science,* 1981, *211,* 1450–1452.

PEULER, J. D., & JOHNSON G. A. Simultaneous single isotope radioenzymatic assay of plasma norepinephrine, epinephrine, and dopamine. *Life Sciences,* 1977, *21,* 625–636.

PLUMLEE, L. A. Operant conditioning of increases in blood pressure. *Psychophysiology,* 1969, *6,* 283–290.

POLISH, E., BRADY, J. V., MASON, J. W., THACH, J. S., & NIEMECK, W. Gastric contents and the occurrence of duodenal lesions in the rhesus monkey during avoidance behavior. *Gastroenterology,* 1962, *43,* 193–201.

POMERLEAU, O. F. The effects of stimuli followed by response-independent shock on shock-avoidance behavior. *Journal of the Experimental Analysis of Behavior,* 1970, *14,* 11–21.

PORTER, R. W., BRADY, J. V., CONRAD, D., MASON, J. W., GALAMBOS, R., & RIOCH, D. McK. Some experimental observations on gastrointestinal lesions in behaviorally conditioned monkeys. *Psychosomatic Medicine,* 1958, *20,* 379–394.

RAMSAY, D. A. Form and characteristics of the cardiovascular conditional response in rhesus monkeys. *Conditional Reflex,* 1970, *5,* 36–51.

RANDALL, D. C., BRADY, J. V., & MARTIN, K. H. Cardiovascular dynamics during classical appetitive and aversive conditioning in laboratory primates. *Pavlovian Journal of Biological Science,* 1975, *19,* 66–75.

RANDALL, D. C., & HASSON, D. M. A note of ECG changes observed during Pavlovian conditioning in a rhesus monkey following coronary arterial occlusion. *Pavlovian Journal of Biological Science,* 1977, *12,* 229–231.

————. Cardiac arrhythmias in monkey during classically conditioned fear and excitement. *Pavlovian Journal of Biological Science,* 1981, *16,* 97–107.

RANDALL, D. C., KAYE, M. P., RANDALL, W. C., BRADY, J. V., & MARTIN, K. H. Response of primate heart to emotional stress before and after cardiac denervation. *American Journal of Physiology,* 1976, *230,* 988–995.

RANDALL, D. C., & SMITH, O. A. Ventricular contractility during controlled exercise and emotion in the primate. *American Journal of Physiology,* 1974, *226,* 1051–1059.

RICE, H. K. The responding-rest ratio in the production of gastric ulcers in the rat. *Psychological Reports,* 1963, *13,* 11–14.

RICHARDS, R. W., & RILLING, M. Aversive aspects of a fixed-interval schedule of food reinforcement. *Journal of the Experimental Analysis of Behavior,* 1972, *17,* 405–411.

RILEY, V. Psychoneuroendocrine influences on immunocompetence and neoplasia. *Science,* 1981, *212,* 1100–1109.

ROGERS, M. P., DUBEY, D., & REICH, P. The influence of the psyche and the brain on immunity and disease susceptibility: A critical review. *Psychosomatic Medicine,* 1979, *41,* 147–164.

ROSECRANS, J. A., WATZMAN, N., & BUCKLEY, J. P. The production of hypertension in male albino rats subjected to experimental stress. *Biochemical Pharmacology,* 1966, *15,* 1707–1718.

SACKETT, G. P., BOWMAN, R. E., MEYER, J. S., TRIPP, R. L., & GRADY, S. S. Adrenocortical and behavioral reactions by differentially raised rhesus monkeys. *Physiological Psychology,* 1973, *1,* 209–212.

SAMPSON, L. D., FRANCIS, F., & SCHNEIDERMAN, N. Selective autonomic blockades: Effects upon classical conditioning of heart rate and lever-lift suppression in rabbits. *Journal of Comparative and Physiological Psychology,* 1974, *87,* 953–962.

SAWREY, J. M., & SAWREY, W. L. Ulcer production with reserpine and conflict. *Journal of Comparative and Physiological Psychology,* 1964, *57,* 307–309.

————. Age, weight, and social effects on ulceration rate in rats. *Journal of Comparative and Physiological Psychology,* 1966, *61,* 464–466.

SAWREY, W. L. Conditioned responses of fear in relationship to ulceraton. *Journal of Comparative and Physiological Psychology,* 1961, *54,* 347–348.

SAWREY, W. L., CONGER, J. J., & TURRELL, E. S. An experimental investigation of the role of psychological factors in the production of gastric ulcers in rats. *Journal of Comparative and Physiological Psychology,* 1956, *49,* 457–461.

SAWREY, W. L., & LONG, D. H. Strain and sex differences in ulceration in the rat. *Journal of Comparative and Physiological Psychology,* 1962, *55,* 603–605.

SAWREY, W. L., & SAWREY, J. M. Fear conditioning and resistance to ulceration. *Journal of Comparative and Physiological Psychology,* 1963, *56,* 821–823.

————. Conditioned fear and restraint in ulceration. *Journal of Comparative and Physiological Psychology,* 1964, *57,* 150–151.

SAWREY, W. L., & WEISZ, J. D. An experimental method of producing gastric ulcers. *Journal of Comparative and Physiological Psychology,* 1956, *49,* 269–270.

SCHNEIDERMAN, N. Response system divergencies in aversive classical conditioning. In A. H. Black & W. F. Prokasy (ed.), *Classical conditioning: Current theory and research.* New York: Appleton, 1972.

————. Animal models relating behavioral stress and cardiovascular pathology. In T. Dembroski (ed.), *Proceedings of the forum on coronary-prone behavior.* DHEW publication no. (NIH) 78-1451. Washington, D.C.: U.S. Government Printing Office, 1978.

SCHOENFELD, W., KADDEN, R., & BINDLER, P. Autonomic nervous system control of the cardiac conditional rate response in the rhesus monkey. Paper presented to the annual meeting of the Society for Neuroscience, New York City, 1975.

SCHOENFELD, W. N., MATOS, M. A., & SNAPPER, A. C. Cardiac conditioning in the white rat with food presentation as unconditional stimulus. *Conditional Reflex,* 1967, *2,* 56–67.

SCHREYER, N. K. The effects of sound stress on blood pressure and norepinephrine responsiveness. Doctoral dissertation, Hahnemann Medical College and Hospital of Philadelphia, 1979.

SELYE, H. The general adaptation syndrome and the diseases of adaptation. *Journal of Clinical Endocrinology,* 1964, *4,* 117.

SIDMAN, M. Avoidance conditioning with brief shock and no exteroceptive warning siganl. *Science,* 1953, *118,* 157–158.

SIDMAN, M., MASON, J. W., BRADY, J. V., & THACH, J. Quantitative relations between avoidance behavior and pituitary-adrenal cortical activity. *Journal of the Experimental Analysis of Behavior,* 1962, *5,* 353–362.

SKINNER, J. E., LIE, J. T., & ENTMAN, M. L. Modification of ventricular fibrillation latency following coronary artery occlusion in the conscious pig. *Circulation,* 1975, *51,* 656–667.

SKLAR, L. S., & ANISMAN, H. Stress and coping factors influence tumor growth. *Science,* 1979, *205,* 513–515.

SMITH, O. A., ASTLEY, C. A., DEVITO, J. L., STEIN, J. M., & WALSH, K. E. Functional analysis of hypothalamic control of the cardiovascular responses accompanying emotional behavior. *Federation Proceedings,* 1980, *39,* 2487–2494.

SMITH, O. A., & STEBBINS, W. C. Conditioned blood flow and heart rate in monkeys. *Journal of Comparative Physiological Psychology,* 1965, *59,* 432–436.

SMOOKLER, H. H., & BUCKLEY, J. P. Relationships between brain catecholamine synthesis, pituitary adrenal function, and the production of hypertension during prolonged exposure to environmental stress. *International Journal of Neuropharmacology,* 1969, *8,* 33–41.

SMOOKLER, H. H., GOEBEL, K. H., SIEGEL, M. I., & CLARKE, D. E. Hypertensive effects of prolonged auditory, visual, and motion stimulation. *Federation Proceedings,* 1973, *32,* 2105–2110.

SNAPPER, A. G., POMERLEAU, O. F., & SCHOENFELD, W. N. Similarity of cardiac CR forms in the rhesus monkey during several experimental procedures. *Conditional Reflex,* 1969, *4,* 212–220.

STADDON, J. E. R. Schedule-induced behavior. In W. K. Honig & J. E. R. Staddon (eds.), *Handbook of operant behavior.* Englewood Cliffs: Prentice-Hall, 1977.

STONE, E. A. Stress and catecholamines. In A. Friedhoff (ed.), *Catecholamines and behavior,* vol. 2. New York: Plenum, 1975.

THOMAS, J. R., & SHERMAN, J. A. Time out from a fixed-ratio schedule. *Psychonomic Science,* 1965, *3,* 489–490.

THOMPSON, D. M. Escape from S^D associated with fixed-ratio reinforcement. *Journal of the Experimental Analysis of Behavior,* 1964, *7,* 1–8.

————. Punishment by S^D associated with fixed-ratio reinforcement. *Journal of the Experimental Analysis of Behavior,* 1965, *8,* 189–194.

Turkkan, J. S. Varying temporal location of a conditioned stimulus in heart rate conditioning of *Macaca mulatta. Pavlovian Journal of Biological Science,* 1979, *14,* 31–43.

Turkkan, J. S., & Harris, A. H. Shaping blood pressure elevations: An examination of acquisition. *Behavior Analysis Letters,* 1981, *1,* 97–106.

Turkkan, J. S., & Kadden, R. M. Classically conditioned heart rate responses in *Macaca mulatta* after beta-adrenergic, vagal, and ganglionic blockade. *Journal of the Autonomic Nervous System,* 1979, *1,* 211–227.

Turkkan, J. S., & Schoenfeld, W. N. Classical conditioning of blood pressure in *Macaca mulatta* with cardiac rate controlled. *Pavlovian Journal of Biological Science,* 1979, *14,* 10–19.

Ulrich, R. E. Pain-aggresion. In G. A. Kimble (ed.), *Foundations of conditioning and learning.* New York: Appleton, 1967.

Ulrich, R. E., & Azrin, N. H. Reflexive fighting in response to aversive stimulation. *Journal of the Experimental Analysis of Behavior,* 1962, *5,* 511–520.

VanDercar, D. H., & Schneiderman, N. Interstimulus interval functions in different response systems during classical discrimination conditioning of rabbits. *Psychonomic Science,* 1967, *9,* 9–10.

Villarreal, J. Schedule-induced pica. Paper presented to the annual meeting of Eastern Psychological Association, Boston, 1967.

Weick, B. G., Ritter, S., & Ritter, R. C. Plasma catecholamines: Exaggerated elevation is associated with stress susceptibility. *Physiology and Behavior,* 1980, *24,* 869–874.

Weiss, J. M. Somatic effects of predictable and unpredictable shock. *Psychomatic Medicine,* 1970, *32,* 397–408.

————. Effects of coping behavior in different warning signal conditions on stress pathology in rats. *Journal of Comparative and Physiological Psychology,* 1971, *77,* 1–13. (a)

————. Effects of coping behavior with and without a feedback signal on stress pathology in rats. *Journal of Comparative and Physiological Psychology,* 1971, *77,* 22–30. (b)

————. Effects of punishing the coping response (conflict) on stress pathology in rats. *Journal of Comparative and Physiological Psychology,* 1971, *77,* 14–21. (c)

————. Psychological factors in stress and disease. *Scientific American,* 1972, *226,* 104–113.

Weiss, J. M., Stone, E. A., & Harrel, N. Coping behavior and brain norepinephrine level in rats. *Journal of Comparative and Physiological Psychology,* 1970, *72,* 153–160.

Weisz, J. D. The etiology of experimental gastric ulceration. *Psychosomatic Medicine,* 1957, *19,* 61–73.

Welch, A. S., Welch, B. L. Reduction of norepinephrine in the lower brainstem by psychological stimulus. *Proceedings of the National Academy of Sciences,* 1968, *60,* 478–481.

Wilson, R. S. Cardiac response: Determinants of conditioning. *Journal of Comparative and Physiological Psychology Monograph,* 1969, *68*(1, Pt. 2), 1–23.

Yamori, Y., Matsumoto, M., Yamabe, H., & Okamoto, K. Augmentation of spontaneous hypertension by chronic stress in rats. *Japanese Circulation Journal,* 1969, *33,* 399–409.

Zeaman, D., Deane, G., & Wegner, N. Amplitude and latency characteristics of the conditioned heart response. *Journal of Psychology,* 1954, *38,* 235–250.

Zeaman, D., & Smith, R. W. Review and analysis of some recent findings in human cardiac conditioning. In W. F. Prokasy (ed.), *Classical conditioning: A symposium.* New York: Appleton, 1965.

12

Functional Brain Asymmetry in the Regulation of Emotion: Implications for Bodily Manifestations of Stress

Harold A. Sackeim   Sara L. Weber

OVER THE PAST CENTURY, considerable attention has been devoted to the functional differences between the sides of the brain in subserving cognition. This work derived originally from observations in neurological populations of associations between particular sensorimotor and cognitive deficits and side of unilateral brain damage (Broca, 1861; Werneicke, 1874). Subsequent neuropsychological research with normal samples (Harnad, Doty, Goldstein, Jaynes, & Krauthamer, 1977) and with patients who had undergone corpus callosotomy for the control of intractable epilepsy further specified the nature of cognitive lateralization (Gazzaniga, 1970; Sperry, 1968).

Despite long-standing indications from observations of unilaterally brain-damaged patients that the sides of the brain are also functionally asymmetric in subserving affect (Alford, 1933; Babinski, 1914), until recently this issue was not systematically investigated. Initial studies of functional brain asymmetry in the regulation of mood and emotional expression suggested that in most individuals affective states were subserved more by the right side of the brain than by the left side (Mills, 1912; Sackeim, Gur, & Saucy, 1978; Schwartz, Davidson, & Maer, 1975). There is substantial evidence now, however, that the direction of functional brain asymmetry in the regulation of emotion is not uniform across affective states. Rather, it appears that in most individuals the right side of the brain subserves negative affective states to a greater extent than does the left side, whereas the reverse holds for positive affective states (Ahern & Schwartz, 1979; Sackeim, 1982a; Sackeim, Greenberg, Weiman, Gur, Hungerbuhler, & Geschwind, 1982; cf. Tucker, 1981).

As negative affective states, particularly depression and anxiety, are common concomitants and/or consequences of stress, the role of functional brain asymmetry in subserving affect is of particular interest here. We begin our discussion with a brief review of the sources of evidence that indicate how the sides of the brain differ in regulating emotion. Following this description, we examine bodily asymmetries in the manifestation of

We thank Paolo Decina, Dennis M. Grega, Sidney Malitz, and Donna M. Zucchi for their comments. Preparation of this chapter and some of the research reported herein were supported in part by NIMH grants MH34494 and MH35636, as well as by a Research Challenge Award from New York University.

psychiatric and physical illness. The occurrence of at least some of these illnesses is thought to be related to stress. We propose that consistent bodily asymmetry in their manifestation may reflect the role of functional brain asymmetry in mediating the effects of stress.

FUNCTIONAL BRAIN ASYMMETRY IN THE EXPERIENCE OF EMOTION

Diverse lines of investigation with brain-damaged, psychiatric, and normal population have indicated that there is a significant degree of functional brain asymmetry in the regulation of emotion. Studies with each type of sample have suggested that there is a degree of specificity to the type of emotion most subseved by each side of the brain.

Brain Damage and Mood

Patients with unilateral lesions on opposite sides of the brain are likely to display contrasting changes in mood and personality. An indifferent-euphoric reaction has been associated with right-side damage, whereas a dysphoric reaction is associated with left-side damage (Cutting, 1978; Gainotti, 1972; Hécaen, 1972; Hommes, 1965). Patients manifesting the *indifferent-euphoric reaction* may be unusally placid or carefree in mood, may engage in inappropriate humor and punning, and/or may be socially disinhibited. The *dysphoric reaction* is accompanied by anxiety and/or depression, self-reproach, tearing, and social withdrawal.

Similar mood changes have been observed acutely using the Wada procedure to barbiturate temporarily one side of the brain. In preneurosurgery candidates, it is often critical to determine the nature of deficits that might be produced by surgery. This can be accomplished by infusing one side of the brain with a short-acting barbiturate (Branch, Milner, & Rasmussen, 1964). A group of investigators have reported that barbituration of the left side is associated with a marked dysphoric response, while right-side sedation produces euphoric behavior (Rossi & Rosadini, 1967; Terzian, 1964; cf. Milner in Rossi & Rosadini, 1967; Tsunoda & Oka, 1976). In a small group of patients who were administered barbiturates on one and then the other side of the brain, we also observed side-specific mood changes.[1]

The mood changes observed acutely after unilateral brain damage and unilateral barbituration may share features with, but are not necessarily identical to, classic psychiatric affective disorders. Clinically, it would appear that the incidence of affective disorders is relatively high among brain-injured populations (Geschwind, 1975). There have been few attempts to relate systematically type of affective disorder to predominant side of destructive lesion (Lishman, 1968). Review of case reports and clinical studies (Busch 1940; Hillbom, 1960; Keschner, Bender, & Strauss, 1936; Serafetinides & Falconer, 1962) indicates that where inappropriate positive changes in emotion (e.g., manic symptoms) were noted, damage was most often primarily right-sided. With one exception (Lishman, 1968), inappropriate negative changes in emotion (e.g., depressive symptoms) were more likely following left-side damage. In studies using the Minnesota Multiphasic Personality Inventory (MMPI) to contrast groups with left- and right-side lesions, when differences were found, elevated depression scores were associated with left-side damage and increased tendencies toward extroversion or hypomania were linked to right-side damage (Black, 1975; Gasparrini, Satz, Heilman, & Coolidge, 1978).

These findings from studies of brain-damaged patients raise the possibility that the sides of the brain differ in their roles in the regulation of emotion. However, there are two central interpretive problems in this research. First, it is conceivable that in many, if not all, cases, affective changes subsequent to brain damage are secondary or psychological reactions to deficits in other domains. It would not be surprising, for instance, to observe depression in a patient with left-side damage who is paralyzed and aphasic. Second, even if mood change in many of these cases is produced directly by changes in brain functioning, linking side of damage to type of mood change does not explicate the role of each side of the brain in subserving the altered emotional state. Unilateral destructive lesions may disinhibit emotional behavior subserved by the same or opposite side of the brain.

Recently, Sackeim, Greenberg, Weiman, Gur, Hungerbuhler, and Geschwind (1982) examined both these issues. In their first study, they collected reports of patients with destructive lesions presenting the disorder of pathological laughing and/or crying. Patients with this disorder have uncontrollable outbursts of laughing and/or crying that are unrelated to environmental events or subjective mood. The outbursts cannot be initiated or stopped voluntarily. Their onset may precede other signs of brain damage. In this respect, pathological laughing and crying is a disorder of emotional expression that is believed to be a direct result of changes in brain functioning produced by damage. Sackeim and associates found that in patients with laughing outbursts damage most often was predominantly right-sided; crying outbursts were associated with predominant left-side damage. Therefore, these investigators concluded that dysphoric reactions and uncontrollable crying are consequences of left-side damage, whereas indifferent-euphoric reactions and uncontrollable laughing are consequences of right-side damage. Since the pathologic outbursts are thought to be primary effects of brain damage, it is likely that in many cases mood changes subsequent to lesions are a direct result of alteration in brain functioning.

In another study, Sackeim and colleagues (1982) collected reports of uncontrollable laughing and/or crying as components of epileptic seizures. Seizures are a result of hyperexcitability in neuronal aggregates that comprise foci. Integrated behavioral acts or sensory alterations during seizures are thought to be caused by release of function in such regions (Mauguiere & Courjon, 1978; Penfield & Jasper, 1954). Few cases of crying during seizures have been reported, while ictal laughing outbursts (gelastic epilepsy) are relatively common. Sackeim and associates observed that epileptic foci in gelastic epilepsy were predominantly left-sided. This suggested that hyperexcitability and release in the left side of the brain are associated with ictal laughing outbursts. They argued that mood change and uncontrollable emotional outbursts following destructive (nonepileptogenic lesions) result from disinhibition of the contralateral (opposite) side of the brain. In short, they claimed that in most cases the left side of the brain subserves certain positive emotional states to a greater extent than does the right side, while the reverse obtains for some negative emotional states.

Psychiatric Affective Disorders

Differences observed in the types of mood change associated with side of unilateral brain insult suggested that there are asymmetries in resting levels of hemispheric activation among psychiatric samples that differ in affective symptomatology (d'Elia & Perris, 1973). Most research in this area has concentrated on depressed patients, examining electroencephalographic (EEG) measures of asymmetry in hemispheric activation during the resting state. With the exception of work by Flor-Henry (1976; Flor-Henry, Kiles, Howarth, & Burton, 1979), the effects of cognitive processing on the indices studied in affective patients are undetermined. There has also been initial investigation of asymmetries in event related potentials (Perris, 1974; Roemer, Shagass, Straumanis, & Amadeo, 1978).

Despite a range of methodological problems, the research on lateral asymmetries in the psychophysiological behavior of depressives has produced a relatively consistent set of findings. In virtually every study that compared depressives with schizophrenics, lateral asymmetries in the two groups were opposite in direction. Investigators frequently interpreted their findings as suggesting either greater right-side activation or greater left-side suppression in depressives. Flor-Henry and associates (1979) reported data suggestive of left-side hyperactivation in both schizophrenic and manic disorders. Four studies that compared depressives to normals suggested greater right than left hemisphere involvement in clinical depression (Flor-Henry, 1976; Flor-Henry & Koles, 1980; Myslobodsky & Hoesh, 1978; Roemer et al., 1978). The available evidence from this research appears to favor the view that depressive states are characterized by greater right- than left-side activation. Preliminary evidence indicates that manic states are characterized by greater left-side activation, with some evidence of right-side dysfunction.

Electroconvulsive therapy (ECT) is a common and efficacious form of treatment for major depressive disorders (Fink, 1979). ECT may be administered bilaterally, to both sides of the brain, or stimulating electrodes may be applied to one side, in unilateral administrations. While both types of treatment evoke generalized seizures, the effects on cognitive functioning and physiological activity are specific to the side or sides of the brain stimulated. In line with cognitive lateralization, transient verbal amnesic disturbance is more severe following ECT administered to the left side. Greater disturbance in memory for nonverbal, visuoperceptual material is associated with right ECT (d'Elia, Lorentzson, Raotma, & Widepalm, 1976; Squire & Slater, 1978). Most investigators have found that unilateral ECT results in a greater amount of EEG slowing on the same side of the brain, that is, *ipsilateral* to the stimulation (e.g., Small, 1974; Stromgren & Jensen, 1975). Likewise, Risberg and colleagues (Silfverskiöld, Gustafson, Johanson, & Risberg, 1979) reported that right ECT resulted in decreased right hemisphere *regional cerebral blood flow* (rCBF), with no change in left hemisphere rCBF. Therefore, it appears that ECT produces suppression of activity most on the side of the brain ipsilateral to electrode placement.

There seems to be a difference between left and right ECT in therapeutic efficacy. When differences between these two modes of treatment have been noted, clinical effects with right ECT have been more pronounced (Cohen, Penick, & Tarter, 1974; Deglin, 1973; Halliday, Davison, Browne, & Kreeger, 1978). In line with this finding, it has been hypothesized that suppression of activity on the right side is tied to clinical improvement in patients with major depressive disorders (Malitz, Sackeim, & Decina, in press).

Normal Populations and Mood

The mood states observed in brain-damaged and psychiatric populations are often intense and pathological. Investigation of brain lateralization in the emotional experience of normal groups (neurologically intact, nonpsychiatric populations) should serve to determine whether there is consistency in the functional differences between the two sides of the brain in subserving mild to severe positive and negative emotional states. To date there has been relatively little investigation of these issues with normal samples. Initial findings have been reported in four areas: electrocortical asymmetries during induced mood states, lateral eye movements and head turns as a function of mood, asymmetry in facial electromyography (EMG) in response to affective questioning, and emotional response to material presented to the left and right visual fields.

Two studies examined asymmetry in EEG alpha indices during experimentally induced positive and negative mood states (Davidson, Schwartz, Saron, Bennet, & Goleman, 1979; Tucker, Stenslie, Roth, & Shearer, 1981). In both studies, subjects were asked to reflect on mood-relevant personal material. The findings in both studies suggest greater relative right-side frontal activation during dysphoric states and greater relative left-side frontal activation during euphoric states.

A number of investigators have used direction of conjugate lateral eye movements (CLEMs) following questioning as an index of contralateral hemispheric activation (Kinsbourne, 1972; Schwartz, Davidson, & Maer, 1975; see Erlichman & Weinberger, 1978, for a review). Tucker, Roth, Arneson, and Buckingham (1977) examined CLEMs in subjects under stress and nonstress conditions. A greater percentage of left CLEMs was obtained in the stress condition, suggesting greater relative right hemisphere activation. Ahern and Schwartz (1979) presented subjects with questions about affectively loaded topics that were either positive or negative in nature. They obtained more left CLEMs following negative emotional questions and more right CLEMs following positive emotional questions.

The study of differences between left and right sides of the face in voluntary emotional expression has provided inroads for investigation of the functional brain asymmetry in the expression of emotion (Sackeim, Gur, & Saucy, 1978). To date there has been little methodologically sound research on facial asymmetry in spontaneous emotional expression (see Sackeim & Gur, 1982, for a review). Asking subjects to respond to emotionally laden questions, Schwartz, Ahern, and Brown (1979) compared facial EMG on the two sides of the face. They found that negative emotional questions resulted in greater relative activity (muscle tension) on the left side of the face; there was a trend for greater relative activity on the right side following positive emotional questions.

Dimond and Farrington (1977) compared heart rate response of subjects viewing films in either the left or the right visual field. Subjects were fitted with specially constructed contact lenses so that vision could be restricted to one visual field for long durations. Subjects viewing films in the left visual field showed a greater increase in heart rate when watching an unsettling surgical operation than did right-field viewing subjects. The opposite pattern was obtained for a humorous cartoon. Left-field viewing subjects rated films overall as more horrific and unpleasant than did right-field viewing subjects (Dimond, Farrington, & Johnson, 1976).

Rather few studies to date have examined the role of functional brain asymmetry in regulating positive and negative emotional states in normal populations. The available evidence supports the notion that this dimension of hemispheric specialization extends to normal variation in mood. Research with neurologic, psychiatric, and normal groups lends credence to the view that in most individuals the right side of the brain subserves negative affective states to a greater extent than does the left side, whereas the reverse hold for positive affective states. Negative affective states are likely to augment stress or to be experienced as a consequence of stress. In this respect, there may be greater right hemisphere involvement in stress related disorders. This hypothesis can be evaluated, in part, by examining bodily asymmetries in the manifestation of disease.

BODILY ASYMMETRIES IN MANIFESTATIONS OF DISEASE

Stress has been linked to a number of psychiatric and organic conditions that manifest in bodily asymmetries. Since sensorimotor functioning in each half of the body is represented primarily in the contralateral side of the brain, asymmetry in bodily manifestation of disease may be an outcome of functional brain asymmetry. We have reviewed evidence that indicates that in most individuals the right side of the brain subserves negative affective states to a greater extent than does the left side. To the degree that negative affective states contribute to manifestation of disease and to the degree that there is contralateral neurological control over the bodily manifestations, one might expect an overrepresentation of left-sided symptoms in stress related disorders. However, consistent asymmetry in bodily manifestation for any particular disorder is not necessarily an outcome of lateralization in the regulation of emotion. Alternative explanations could point either to peripheral asymmetries in structure or use of body parts or to central brain asymmetries for functions other than affect. Consistent left-sided overrepresentation observed across various types of disease states would increase the possibility that central brain asymmetry in the regulation of affect contributes to these manifestations.

The following sections summarize the available evidence on lateral distribution of symptoms for various psychiatric and organic conditions. We also indicate some areas that are likely to have strong psychosomatic components but that have not been investigated in regard to this issue. The conditions are presented in an order that corresponds roughly to the degree to which stress is believed to contribute to their manifestation.

Hysterical Conversion Reactions

The psychiatric literature has long suggested that unilateral hysterical conversion reactions are most likely to be manifested on the left side of the body (Briquet, 1850, cited in Gainotti, 1979; Ferenczi, 1926; Pitres, 1891; Purves-Stewart, 1931). Recent retrospective studies in the main have supported this suggestion (Bishop, Mobley, & Farr, 1978; Fallik & Sigal, 1971; Fleminger, McClure, & Dalton, 1980; Galin, Diamond, & Braff, 1977; Magee, 1962; Stern, 1977). Magee (1962) reported on 50 cases of hysterical hemiplegia and hemianesthesia (paralysis and loss of sensation on one half of the body): only 3 patients exhibited right-sided symptoms. Galin and associates (1977) reviewed the records of 52 patients (42 female, 10 males) with unilateral sensory and/or motor conversion symptoms. In 63% of cases, symptoms were left-sided and this effect held particularly for females. Stern (1977) reviewed the records of 191 patients (140 female, 51 male) and also found left-side overrepresentation of sensory and motor conversion symptoms. This effect was obtained in both right-handed and left-handed subsamples and there were no gender differences. Fleminger and associates (1980) interviewed 106 psychiatric patients, taking histories of presumed psychogenic sensory and motor symptoms. They also reported a left-side overrepresentation in the 24 patients with clearly lateralized symptoms.

In contrast, Fallik and Sigal (1971) reported a preponderance of right-sided symptoms in 40 cases of conversion reactions. The sample was highly unusual. Ninety percent were male; 85% were under the age of 30 years; and 65% of the sample had had previous lesions on the side of the presumed conversion reaction. Bishop and co-workers (1978) reported on 22 cases. Males and females were equally represented, although the sample was drawn from a larger group of cases in which females outnumbered males three to one. No effect of body side was observed in this study, and the investigators suggested that the left-sided over-representation of conversion symptoms may be particular to females.

Overall it does appear that hysterical conversion reactions are manifested more frequently on the left side of the body. Whether this effect is moderated by individual differences such as sex or handedness is not established. Various factors might account for the left-sided overrepresentation in this disorder. In particular, the literature has focused on whether similar processes underlie symptom manifestation in conversion reactions and sensorimotor changes produced by suggestion and/or hypnosis (see Sackeim, Nordlie, & Gur, 1979, for a review). There is some evidence that among right-handers hypnosis results in greater right than left hemisphere activation (Frumkin, Ripley, & Cox, 1978; Gur & Gur, 1974; McKeever, Larrabee, Sullivan, Johnson, Ferguson, & Rayport, 1981; Morgan, MacDonald, & Hilgard, 1974). Fleminger and co-workers (1980) administered a suggestion test outside the context of hypnosis to a patient sample and a sample of nurses. The suggestion concerned a tingling feeling that could be experienced in either hand. In the total sample, more subjects reported experiencing the sensation in the left hand. Among the patient group, those who had reported unilateral psychogenic symptoms also responded on the same side of the body to the suggestion test. Of note, however, in a previous study Fleminger, Dalton, and Hsu (1978) did not observe a consistent direction of response when this suggestion test was administered to a mixed sample of 100 psychiatric patients. Recently, Sackeim (1982b) administered nine hypnotic suggestions in individual sessions with 80 right-handers. Overall, there was greater responsiveness to the suggestions on the left side of the body. Therefore, it is possible that the overrepresentation of left-sided symptoms in hysterical conversion reactions reflects the same underlying processes that determine asymmetry of bodily response to hypnotic suggestion. Alternatively, it is conceivable that the greater role of the right side of the brain in negative affective states is implicated in the bodily asymmetry in conversion reactions.

Psychogenic Pain

The hysterical symptoms examined in the studies reviewed above involved principally loss of motor and/or sensory functioning, as in disorders of paralysis, weakness, anesthesia, blindness, etc. Psychiatric patients frequently present with complaints of pain for which there is no evident organic basis. For some time it has been debated whether psychogenic pain should be classified among the conversion reactions and/or distinguished from hypochondrical pain (Whitlock, 1967). In this and the three subsequent sections we review the evidence concerning bodily asymmetries in manifestations of various types of pain. Our classification of this research into studies of psychogenic pain, hypochondriasis, rheumatic pain, and chronic pain is admittedly arbitrary.

At the outset we should consider the possibility that asymmetries in bodily manifestations of pain may be related to bodily asymmetry in pain perception and tolerance thresholds. A number of studies have found that among right-handers the left side of the body has a lower threshold for the perception and tolerance of pain (Haslam, 1970; Weinstein & Sersen, 1961; Wolff & Jarvik, 1964). Weinstein and Sersen (1961) tested pressure sensitivity in the palm, forearm, and sole on each side and found that across these bodily regions right-handers evidenced lower thresholds on the left side. The consistency across regions, the absence of significant asymmetry in left-handers, and findings from previous work with brain-damaged populations led Weinstein and Sersen to suggest that bodily asymmetry in pressure sensitivity is an outcome of brain lateralization of function. It would appear that thresholds for the perception and tolerance of pain are lower in the right hemispheres of most right-handers. Given the strong affective components in pain perception and tolerance (Melzack, 1973), this dimension of functional asymmetry may be related to lateralization in the regulation of emotion.

Walters (1961) reported on 430 cases of regional pain for which no peripheral cause could be found, in which the location did not conform either to sites of pain with local physical lesions or to sites of referred pain, and that appeared to be psychogenic in character. In the total sample, lateralization of sites of pain was not described. However, 9 (5 male, 4 female) case reports were presented. In 6 of these 9 patients, symptoms were exclusively left-sided; in 1 case symptoms appeared to be left-sided; 1 patient experienced bilateral pain; and only 1 case of right-sided pain was reported.

Hypochondriasis

Kenyon (1964) reviewed the records of 512 patients who had received diagnoses of either primary hypochondriasis ($n = 301$) or hypochondriasis secondary to another psychiatric diagnosis ($n = 211$). Of patients with secondary hypochondriasis, 82.4% had a primary diagnosis of affective disorder. Furthermore, 30.5% of patients with primary hypochondriasis had psychiatric histories of affective disorder. The symptoms most associated with hypochondriasis were depression and anxiety. Unilateral symptoms were present in 18.9% and 12.3% of patients with primary and secondary hypochondriasis, respectively. Of the unilateral groups, 65.0% and 80.7%, respectively, of primary and secondary hypochondriacs had left-sided symptoms. Therefore, hypochondriasis was most frequently accompanied by affective disorder and when unilaterally manifested was significantly more frequent on the left than on the right side.

Rheumatic Pain

Two studies examined lateral distributions of rheumatic pain and related conditions (Edmonds, 1947; Halliday, 1937). A number of investigators have suggested that emotional factors may elicit rheumatic symptomatology and/or that complaints of rheumatism may often be psychogenically based (see Edmonds, 1947, for a review). Halliday (1937) presented 21 cases of rheumatism. As he noted:

> The sites of the pain, etc., may be grouped as follows: neck only, four patients; neck and left arm, seven patients; left arm only, six patients; right arm only, one patient. The predominance of pain in the left arm compared with the right is remarkable—namely, 13 patients to one. Another point to be noted is that the pain was usually felt on the extreme left aspect of the body—namely, the top of the shoulder and outer side of the left arm. (P. 265)

Edmonds (1947) reported on 87 patients who presented both neuroses and muscular pain or nonarticular rheumatism. In all cases, the manifestation of pain was thought clinically to be related to emotional factors. Pain was predominantly unilateral in 51 cases. Of these, 44 patients presented left-sided pain, and only 7 had right-sided symptoms.

A related type of muscular pain, *pectoral fibrositis,* is seen frequently in so-called soldier's or effort syndrome (Wood, 1941). Pain in the left thoracic region is reported and patients may believe that they are having a heart attack. Pain on the right side of the chest has been found to be less frequently reported even on inquiry (Wood, 1941). Of course, the association of cardiac functioning with the left side of the body may play a role in the left-sided predominance of presumably psychogenically based pectoral fibrositis.

Chronic Pain

Agnew and Merskey (1976) reported on 128 patients who were seen in clinical practice and presented chronic pain. To be included in the sample, patients had to have experienced pain for at least three months; typically duration exceeded six months. A large subgroup ($n = 63$) of the patients had psychiatric diagnoses, and among these patients headache was the most common pain reported. Depressive disorders constituted the largest group of psychiatric diagnoses, followed by anxiety and hysteria. A variety of pain symptoms were reported within the group that received diagnoses of either organic disorder ($n = 46$) or both organic and psychiatric disorders ($n = 19$). In the combined sample of patients with psychiatric or organic diagnoses and unilateral pain symptoms, pain was experienced more often on the left side of the body. This effect was clearly significant in the psychiatric group and manifested as a trend within the group with organic diagnoses. Furthermore, although not noted by Agnew and Merskey, the combined sample showed a significant sex difference in side of reported pain. Among males, 73.68% had unilateral left-sided pain, whereas only 52.22% of females had pain on this side alone. An overrepresentation of left-sided chronic pain in psychiatric patients without evidence of organic lesion was reported also by Merskey and Boyd (1978) and by Spear (1965).

Breast Disease

Haagensen (1971) examined 2017 women with gross cysts in the breasts. Initial development of cysts was bilateral in 10.41% of cases. Of cases of unilateral cysts, 55.78% were left-sided, a highly significant effect. Haagensen also reported that carcinoma was more frequent in the left breast: he stated, "I have no explanation for this phenomenon" (p. 158). Johnsén (1975) similarly reported that breast disease was more common on the left side.

The factors contributing to the greater frequency of left-sided breast disease are unknown. Several possibilities should be considered. Johnsén (1975) suggested that there is consistent asymmetry in breast size, with the left breast larger. This issue has not been examined systematically. Johnsén suggested that the larger left breast may contain more parenchyma, tissue particularly susceptible to breast disease. If this explanation is valid, the cause of the consistent size asymmetry would still be at issue. Another possibility is that physiological processes within the breast or central representations of the breast area are consistently asymmetric in response to internal or external stimulation. Weinstein (1963) found that among right-handed women the left breast displayed a lower threshold for pressure sensitivity than did the right breast.

Johansson (1976) performed breast thermography on 1456 women. The sample included 155 women with breast carcinoma, 1070 women with benign cysts, and 231 women free from breast disease. Positive thermograms, indicating hot spots, were obtained more frequently in the left breast for all three groups. Of those with positive thermograms, 69.0%

of the cancer group, 85.9% of the benign lesion group, and 87.5% of the disease-free group had hot spots in the left breast. Therefore, even in women without breast disease hot spots showed a marked tendency to be left-sided. Overall, thermography was moderately sensitive in discriminating between groups with and without cancer. In the cancer group, 81.3% of cases had positive thermograms, while 47.0% of the benign cyst cases and 38.1% of the disease-free cases had positive thermograms. Furthermore, within the cancer group, side of hot spots and side of lesion were significantly related. Replicating Haagensen's (1971) finding, 55.48% of the carcinomas were left-sided. Of these 86 women, 76 had positive thermograms, of which 74 were left-sided. Size of breasts was estimated clinically in disease-free and cancer groups. Size was found to be unrelated to the frequency of positive thermograms.

It would appear, therefore, that the left breast of disease-free women displays a greater frequency of hot spots than does the right breast and that the presence of cancer is associated with greater frequency and side of hot spots. The greater frequency of left-sided than right-sided gross cysts and carcinomas may be related to the process that determines asymmetry in thermal characteristics of the breasts. This asymmetry may be the result of peripheral anatomic features of the breasts and/or of central processes that may be stress related. Another possibility is that the observed asymmetry in incidence of breast disease was an artifact of patient self-selection. Since most individuals are right-handed, a spouse is more likely to palpate the left breast and women may find it easier more thoroughly to examine the left breast. The data indicating that left-sided hot spots are more common in disease-free women would not be subject to this possible artifact.

DISCUSSION

A variety of psychiatric and organic conditions that are believed to be stress related—hysterical conversion reactions, psychogenic pain, hypochondriasis, rheumatic pain, chronic pain, and breast disease—are manifested more frequently on the left than on the right side of the body. In some cases the evidence for this claim is only suggestive and in some cases conradictory findings exist. Nonetheless, the overrepresentation of left-sided symptoms in this diverse collection of disease states warrants scrutiny.

There have not been systematic epidemiological studies of side of symptom manifestation in a number of disorders either known or suspected to be stress related. If a preponderance of left-sided symptoms is found in an additional set of disease states, involving different peripheral physiological systems, the possibility will loom larger that the overrepresentation of left-sided symptoms is caused by a factor related to lateralization of brain function.

We suggest that migraine headache and idiopathic dental erosion are two disorders that should be examined in this light. Emotional factors, and stress in particular, have long been considered to play an important role in a large proportion of manifestations of migraine headache (Gittleson, 1961; Merskey, 1965; Wolff, 1948). Care must be taken in assessing side of disturbance in migraine. Not infrequently, patients may experience head pain on the same side or on the side contralateral to neurologic motor and sensory signs. For instance, hemiplegia associated with migraine may occur either on the same or the opposite side of the body as the hemicranial pain. When pain and neurologic symptoms are lateralized on opposite sides, it may be that the head pain reflects cerebrovascular disturbance of a peripheral nature. Headache on the same side as neurological signs may reflect a more central etiology. In either case, determining side of brain involvement on the basis of motor and sensory neurological signs is likely to be more valid than relying only on side of head pain. We informally collected cases diagnosed as migraine headache from the literature (Adie, 1930; Basser, 1969; Bradshaw & Parsons, 1965; Engel, Ferris, & Romano, 1945; Kennard, Gawel, Rudolph, & Rose, 1978; Marshall, 1978; Slatter, 1968; Whitty, 1953). Cases were excluded in which clear-cut neurophathology (e.g., meningioma) had been found. Of 76 case reports, 38 presented unilateral neurological signs (e.g., hemiplegia, hemianopia, hemianesthesia) at the onset of or during migraine. Twenty-four of the 38 cases, or 63%, had neurological signs on the left side ($p = .07$). These data tentatively suggest a greater frequency of right than left hemisphere involvement in migraine and contrast with Bradshaw and Parsons's (1965) findings. In an informal survey of cases of hemiplegic migraine, they noted a greater frequency of right-sided hemiplegia. The possible role of affective lateralization in migraine headache is of further interest since this condition is often associated with depression or anxiety and is frequently treated effectively with antidepressants.

Idiopathic dental erosion is a disorder marked by erosion-abrasion lesions of dental surfaces of unknown etiology. Looking at a random sample of 10,000 extracted teeth, Sognaaes, Wolcott, and Xhonga (1972) found that 19% had erosionlike lesions. Since dental erosion has been shown in acrylic and vulcanite dentures that are chemically inert, some cases of erosion are attributable to frictional forces and possibly to hyperactivity of oral soft tissue (Brodie & Sognaaes, 1974). On the other hand, the mouth region contains several hundred glands, and stress can lead to hypersecretion of erosion producing substances.

Frequently, patterns of idiopathic dental erosion are asymmetric. When observed on the buccal surfaces of the left-side teeth, the erosion is often attributed to intense brushing with the right hand. An alternative, however, is that stress induced hyperactivation of the right hemisphere may lead either to hyperactivity of left-side facial muscles (Sackeim & Gur, 1978, Sackeim & Gur, 1982) or to hypersecretion of left-side glands, thereby producing erosion by frictional and/or chemical processes. There has been no investigation to date of lateral distributions of idiopathic dental erosion.

The disorders discussed in this chapter are believed to be stress related to varying extents. A number of organic conditions that are not linked to stress also result in consistent asymmetries in symptom manifestation. For instance, congenital hypoplasia of the depressor anguli oris muscle, or congenital unilateral lower-lip palsy, is one of the most common congenital facial disturbances (Kobayashi, 1979). Patients manifest unilateral paralysis caused by weakness of the lower-lip depressor muscles, a pattern especially evident on emotional expression. The disorder is also referred to as *asymmetric crying facies* (Perlman & Reisner, 1973). Four studies had independent samples of patients with this disorder as a congenital manifestation (Kobayashi, 1979; McHugh, Sowden, & Levitt, 1969; Papadatos, Alexiou, Nicolopoulos, Mikropoulos, & Hadzigeorgiou, 1974; Pape & Pickering, 1972). In each sample there was a greater incidence of left-side weakness, and in most cases the left-side overrepresentation was significant. However, when this disorder is observed with congenital heart disease, the right side is more frequently affected. Cayler (1969) found right-side weakness in 12 of 14 newborns; all had heart disease, with 12 showing ventricular septal defect.

Trigeminal neuralgia, or *tic douloureux,* is a disorder associated with short bursts of pain along the distribution of the trigeminal, or fifth cranial, nerve. Its etiology is unknown. The disorder is more frequent among females and is more commonly right-sided than left-sided when unilateral. Voorhies and Patterson (1981) estimated that the overrepresentation of right-sided disturbance is 1.7 to 1.0, which agrees with White and Sweet's (1969) retrospective study of over 7000 cases.

Consistent asymmetry in bodily location of disorders that are believed to be unrelated to stress is important on two grounds. First, this pattern suggests caution in attributing necessarily consistent asymmetries in specific stress related disorders to affective lateralization even if location is predominantly left-sided. As in congenital unilateral lip palsy, some disease states apparently affect the body in a consistent asymmetric fashion. Even in cases of stress related disorders, it is possible that asymmetries in location result from either peripheral neuropathology or central factors that are independent of functional brain asymmetry. Indeed, we raised a number of alternative explanations for the asymmetries noted in the various stress related disorders. Second, both congenital heart disease associated with unilateral lower-lip palsy and trigeminal neuralgia demonstrate that some disease states characteristically affect the right side of the body with greater frequency than they do the left side. This indicates that the left side of the human body is not typically subject to malfunction or disease to a greater extent than is the right side, regardless of disease pathogenesis or type. This fact, coupled with the seeming consistency in left-sided overrepresentation among stress related disorders, strengthens the possibility that the observed consistency across such disorders indeed reflects the role of functional brain asymmetry in the regulation of emotion. It may be that disorders unrelated to stress may manifest predominantly on either the left or the right side of the body, while stress related disorders are consistently left-sided in their manifestation. At present there is considerable evidence that in most individuals the right hemisphere subserves negative affective states to a greater extent than does the left side of the brain. That a variety of stress related disturbances are all manifested more frequently on the left side of the body suggests that this asymmetry in central brain function plays a role in bodily manifestations of stress.

NOTES

1. Observations of intracarotid injections of sodium amytal in preneurosurgery patients were made in collaboration with Raquel E. Gur, Ruben C. Gur, and Neil Sussman at Graduate Hospital, Philadelphia.

REFERENCES

ADIE, W. J. Permanent hemianopia in migraine and subarachnoid haemorrhage. *Lancet,* 1930, *2,* 237–238.

AGNEW, D. L., & MERSKEY, H. Words of chronic pain. *Pain,* 1976, *2,* 73–81.

AHERN, G. L., & SCHWARTZ, G. E. Differential lateralization for positive versus negative emotion. *Neuropsychologia,* 1979, *12,* 693–698.

ALFORD, L. B. Localization of consciousness and emotion. *American Journal of Psychiatry,* 1933, *12,* 789–799.

BABINSKI, J. Contribution à/'étude des troubles mentaux dans l'hemiplegie organique cerebral (anosognosie). *Revue neurologique,* 1914, *27,* 845–848.

BASSER, L. S. Relation of migraine and epilepsy. *Brain,* 1969, *92,* 285–300.

BISHOP, E. R., MOBLEY, M. C., & FARR, W. F. Lateralization of conversion symptoms. *Comprehensive Psychiatry,* 1978, *19,* 393–396.

BLACK, F. W. Unilateral brain lesions and MMPI performance: A preliminary study. *Perceptual and Motor Skills,* 1975, *40,* 87–93.

BRADSHAW, P., & PARSONS, M. Hemiplegic migraine: A clinical study. *Quarterly Journal of Medicine,* 1965, *34,* 65.

BRANCH, C., MILNER, B., & RASMUSSEN, T. Intracarotid sodium amytal for the lateralization of cerebral speech dominance. *Journal of Neurosurgery,* 1964, *21,* 399–405.

BROCA, P. Remarques sure l siège de la faculté du langage articulé, suivies d'une observation d'aphemie (perte de la parole). *Bulletin de la Société anatomique de Paris* (2d ser.), 1861, *6,* 330–357.

BRODIE, A. G., & SOGNAAES, R. F. Erosionlike denture markings possibly related to hyperactivity of oral soft tissues. *Journal of the American Dental Association,* 1973, *88,* 1012–1017.

BUSCH, E. Psychical symptoms in neurosurgical disease. *Acta Psychiatrica et Neurologica Scandinavica,* 1940, *15,* 257–290.

CAYLER, G. C. Cardiofacial syndrome: Congenital heart disease and facial weakness, a hitherto unrecognized association. *Diseases of Childhood,* 1969, *44,* 69–75.

COHEN, B. D., PENICK, S. B., & TARTER, R. E. Antidepressant effects of unilateral electric convulsive shock therapy. *Archives of General Psychiatry,* 1974, *31,* 673–675.

DAVIDSON, R. J., SCHWARTZ, G. E., SARON, C., BENNETT, J., & GOLEMAN, D. Frontal versus parietal EEG asymmetry during positive and negative affect. *Psychophysiology,* 1979, *16,* 202–203.

DEGLIN, V. L. A clinical study of unilateral electroconvulsive surgery. *Zhurnal nevropatologii i psikhiatrii* (Moscow), 1973, *73,* 1609–1621.

D'ELIA, G., LORENTZSON, S., RAOTMA, H., & WIDEPALM, K. Comparison of unilateral dominant and non-dominant ECT on verbal and non-verbal memory. *Acta Psychiatrica Scandinavica,* 1976, *53,* 85–94.

D'ELIA, G., & PERRIS, C. Cerebral functional dominance and depression. *Acta Psychiatrica Scandinavica,* 1973, *49,* 191–197.

DIMOND, S. J., & FARRINGTON, L. Emotional response to films shown to the right or left hemisphere of of the brain measured by heart rate. *Acta Psychologia,* 1977, *41,* 255–260.

DIMOND, S. J., FARRINGTON, L., & JOHNSON, P. Differing emotional response from right and left hemispheres. *Nature,* 1976, *261,* 690–692.

EDMONDS, E. P. Psychosomatic non-articular rheumatism. *Annals of Rheumatic Disease,* 1947, *6,* 36–49.

ENGEL, G. L., FERRIS, E. B., & ROMANO, J. Focal encephalographic changes during scotomas of migraine. *American Journal of Medical Science,* 1945, *209,* 650.

ERLICHMAN, H., & WEINBERGER, A. Lateral eye movements and hemispheric asymmetry: A critical review. *Psychological Bulletin,* 1978, *85,* 1080–1101.

FALLIK, A., & SIGAL, M. Hysteria: The choice of symptom site. *Psychotherapy and Psychosomatics* (Basel), 1971, *19,* 310–318.

FERENCZI, S. An attempted explanation of some hysterical stigmata. In S. Ferenczi (ed.), *Further contributions to the theory and technique of psychoanalysis.* London: Hogarth, 1926.

FINK, M. *Convulsive therapy: Theory and practice.* New York: Raven, 1979.

FLEMINGER, J. J., DALTON, R., & HSU, G. Lateral response to suggestion in relation to handedness. *Perceptual and Motor Skills,* 1978, *46,* 1344–1346.

FLEMINGER, J. J., McCLURE, G. M., & DALTON, R. Lateral response to suggestion in relation to handedness and the side of psychogenic symptoms. *British Journal of Psychiatry,* 1980, *136,* 562–566.

FLOR-HENRY, P. Lateralized temporal-limbic dysfunction and psychopathology. *Annals of the New York Academy of Science,* 1976, *280,* 777–795.

FLOR-HENRY, P., & KOLES, Z. J. EEG studies in depression, mania, and normals: Evidence for partial shifts of laterality in the affective psychoses. *Advances in Biological Psychiatry,* 1980, *4,* 21–43.

FLOR-HENRY, P., KOLES, Z. J., HOWARTH, B. G., & BURTON, L. Neurophysiology studies of schizophrenia, mania, and depression. In J. Gruzelier & P. Flor-Henry (eds.), *Hemisphere asymmetries of function in psychopathology.* New York: Elsevier, 1979.

Frumkin, L. R., Ripley, H. S., & Cox, G. B. Changes in cerebral hemispheric lateralization with hypnosis. *Biological Psychiatry,* 1978, *3,* 741–750.

Gainotti, G. Emotional behavior and hemisphere side of the lesion. *Cortex,* 1972, *8,* 41–55.

————. The relationships between emotions and cerebral dominance: A review of clinical and experimental evidence. In J. Gruzelier & P. Flor-Henry (eds.), *Hemisphere asymmetries of function in psychopathology.* New York: Elsevier, 1979.

Galin, D., Diamond, R., & Braff, D. Lateralization of conversion symptoms: More frequent on the left. *American Journal of Psychiatry,* 1977, *134,* 578–580.

Gasparrini, W., Satz, P., Heilman, K. M., & Coolidge, F. L. Hemispheric asymmetries of affective processing as determined by the Minnesota Multiphasic Personality Inventory. *Journal of Neurology, Neurosurgery, and Psychiatry,* 1978, *41,* 470–473.

Gazzaniga, M. S. *The bisected brain.* New York: Appleton, 1970.

Geschwind, N. The borderland of neurology and psychiatry: Some common misconceptions. In D. E. Benson & D. Blumer (eds.), *Psychiatric aspects of neurologic disease.* New York: Grune & Stratton, 1975.

Gittleson, N. L. Psychi.... headache: A clinical study. *Journal of Mental Science,* 1961, *107,* 403.

Gur, R. C., & Gur, R. E. Handedness, sex, and eyedness as moderating variables in the relation between hypnotic susceptibility and functional brain asymmetry. *Journal of Abnormal Psychology,* 1974, *83,* 635.

Haagensen, C. D. *Diseases of the breast* (2d ed.). Philadelphia: Saunders, 1971.

Halliday, A. M., Davison, D., Browne, M. W., & Kreeger, L. C. A comparison of the effects of depression and memory of bilateral ECT and unilateral ECT to the dominant and nondominant hemispheres. *British Journal of Psychiatry,* 1979, *135,* 77–78.

Halliday, J. L. Psychological factors in rheumatism: A preliminary study. *British Medical Journal,* 1937, *1,* 264–269.

Harnad, S., Doty, R. W., Goldstein, L., Jaynes, J., & Krauthamer, G. (eds.). *Lateralization in the nervous system.* New York: Academic, 1977.

Haslam, D. R. Lateral dominance in the perception of size and of pain. *Quarterly Journal of Experimental Psychology,* 1970, *22,* 503–507.

Hécaen, H. Clinical symptomatology in right and left hemispheric lesions. In V. B. Mountcastle (ed.), *Interhemispheric relations and cerebral dominance.* Baltimore: Johns Hopkins Press, 1962.

Hillbom, E. After-effects of brain injuries. *Acta Psychiatrica et Neurologica Scandinavica* (supp. 142), 1960, *35.*

Hommes, O. R. Stemmingsanomalien als neurologisch symptoom. *Nederlands Tijdschrift voor Geneeskunde,* 1965, *109,* 588–589.

Johansson, N. T. Thermography of the breast: A clinical study with special reference to breast cancer detection. *Acta Chirurgica Scandinavica* (supp. 460), 1976,

Johnsén, C. Breast disease: A clinical study with special reference to diagnostic procedures. *Acta Chirurgica Scandinavica* (supp. 454), 1975,

Kennard, C., Gawel, M., Rudolph, N. deM., & Rose, F. C. Visual evoked potentials in migraine subjects. *Research in the Clinical Study of Headache,* 1978, *6,* 73–80.

Kenyon, F. E. Hypochondriasis: A clinical study. *British Journal of Psychiatry,* 1964, *110,* 478–488.

Keschner, M., Bender, M. B., & Strauss, I. Mental symptoms in cases of tumor of the temporal lobe. *Archives of Neurology and Psychiatry,* 1936, *35,* 572–596.

Kobayashi, T. Congenital unilateral lower lip palsy. *Acta Otolaryngol* (Stockholm), 1979, *88,* 303–309.

Lishman, W. A. Brain damage in relation to psychiatric disability after head injury. *British Journal of Psychiatry,* 1968, *114,* 373–410.

Magee, K. Hysterical hemiplegia and hemianaesthesia. *Postgraduate Medicine,* 1962, *31,* 339–345.

MALITZ, S., SACKEIM, H. A., & DECINA, P. ECT in the treatment of major affective disorders: Clinical and basic research issues. *Psychiatry Journal of the University of Ottawa,* in press.

MARSHALL, J. Cerebral blood flow in migraine without headache. *Research in the Clinical Study of Headache,* 1978, *6,* 1–5.

MAUGUIERE, F., & COURJON, J. Somatosensory epilepsy. *Brain,* 1978, *101,* 307–332.

MCHUGE, H. E., SOWDEN, K. A., & LEVITT, M. N. Facial paralysis and muscle agenesis in the newborn. *Archives of Otolaryngology,* 1969, *89,* 131–143.

MCKEEVER, W. F., LARRABEE, G. J., SULLIVAN, K. F., JOHNSON, H. J., FURGUSON, S., & RAYPORT, M. Unimanual tactile anomia consequent to corpus callosotomy: Reduction of anomic deficit under hypnosis. *Neuropsychologia,* 1981, *19,* 171–178.

MELZACK, R. *The puzzle of pain.* Baltimore: Penguin, 1973.

MERSKEY, H. The characteristics of persistent pain in psychological illness. *Journal of Psychosomatic Research,* 1965, *9,* 291–298.

MERSKEY, H., & BOYD, D. B. Emotional adjustment and chronic pain. *Pain,* 1978, *5,* 173–178.

MORGAN, A. H., MACDONALD, H., & HILGARD, E. R. EEG alpha: Lateral asymmetry related to task task and hypnotizability. *Psychophysiology,* 1974, *11,* 275–282.

MYSLOBODSKY, M. S., & HORESH, N. Bilateral electrodermal activity in depressive patients. *Biological Psychology,* 1978, *6,* 111–120.

PAPADATOS, D., ALEXIOU, D., DICOLOPOULOS, D., MIKROPOULOS, H., & HADZIGEORGIOU, E. Congenital hypoplasia of depressor anguli oris muscle: A genetically determined condition? *Archives of Disease in Childhood,* 1974, *49,* 927–931.

PAPE, K. E., & PICKERING, D. Asymmetric crying facies: An index of other congenital anomalies. *Journal of Pediatrics,* 1972, *81,* 21–30.

PENFIELD, W., & JASPER, H. *Epilepsy and the functional anatomy of the human brain.* Boston: Little, Brown, 1954.

PERLMAN, M., & REISNER, S. H. Asymmetric crying facies and congenital anomalies. *Archives of Disease in Childhood,* 1973, *48,* 627–629.

PERRIS, C. Average evoked responses (AER) in patients with affective disorders. *Acta Psychiatrica Scandinavica* (supp. 255), 1974, 89–98.

PITRÈS, A. *Leçons cliniques sur l'hystérie et l'hypnotisme.* Paris: Dolin, 1891.

PURVES-STEWART, J. *The diagnosis of nervous diseases* (7th ed.). London: Arnold, 1931.

ROEMER, R. A., SHAGASS, C., STRAUMANIS, J. J., & AMADEO, M. Pattern evoked potential measurements suggesting lateralized hemispheric dysfunction in chronic schizophrenics. *Biological Psychiatry,* 1978, *13,* 185–202.

ROSSI, G. F., & ROSADINI, G. Experimental analysis of cerebral dominance in man. In C. H. Millikan & F. L. Darley (eds.), *Brain mechanisms underlying speech and language.* New York: Grune & Stratton, 1967.

SACKEIM, H. A. Self-deception, depression, and self-esteem: The adaptive value of lying to oneself. In J. Masling (ed.), *Empirical studies of psychoanalytic theory,* vol. 1. Hillsdale: Erlbaum, 1982a.

SACKEIM, H. A. Lateral asymmetry in bodily response to hypnotic suggestions. *Biological Psychiatry,* 1982b, *17,* 437–447.

SACKEIM, H. A., GREENBERG, M. S., WEIMAN, A. L., GUR, R. C., HUNGERBUHLER, J. P., & GESCHWIND, N. Hemispheric asymmetry in the expression of positive and negative emotions: Neurological evidence. *Archives of Neurology,* 1982, *39,* 210–218.

SACKEIM, H. A., & GUR, R. C. Lateral asymmetry in intensity of emotional expression. *Neuropsychologia,* 1978, *16,* 473–481.

―――――. Facial asymmetry and the communication of emotion. In J. T. Cacioppo and R. E. Petty (eds.), *Social psychophysiology.* New York: Guilford, 1982.

SACKEIM, H. A., GUR, R. C., & SAUCY, M. C. Emotions are expressed more intensely on the left side of the face. *Science,* 1978, *202,* 434–436.

SACKEIM, H. A., NORDLIE, J. W., & GUR, R. C. A model of hysterical and hypnotic blindness: Cognition, motivation, and awareness. *Journal of Abnormal Psychology,* 1979, *88,* 474–489.

SCHWARTZ, G. E., AHERN, G. L., & BROWN, S. L. Lateralized facial muscle response to positive and negative emotional stimuli. *Psychophysiology,* 1979, *16,* 561–571.

SCHWARTZ, G. E., DAVIDSON, R. J., & MAER, F. Right hemisphere lateralization for emotion in the human brain: Interactions with cognition. *Science,* 1975, *190,* 286–288.

SERAFETINIDES, E. A., & FALCONER, M. A. The effect of temporal lobectomy in epileptic patients with psychosis. *Journal of Mental Science,* 1962, *109,* 584–593.

SILFERSKIÖLD, P., GUSTAFSON, L., JOHANSON, N., & RISBERG, J. Regional cerebral blood flow related to the effect of electroconvulsive therapy in depression. In J. Obiols, C. Gallus, E. Gonzalez, N. Onclus, & J. Pujol (eds.), *Biological psychiatry today.* New York: Elsevier, 1979.

SLATTER, K. H. Some clinical EEG findings in patients with migraine. *Brain,* 1968, *91,* 85.

SMALL, J. G. EEG and neurophysiological studies of convulsive therapies. In M. Fink, S. Kety, J. McGaugh, & T. A. Williams (eds.), *Psychobiology of convulsive therapy.* Washington, D.C.: Winston, 1974.

SOGNAAES, R. F., WOLCOTT, R. B., & XHONGA, F. A. Dental erosion. Part I: Erosion-like patterns occurring in association with other dental conditions. *Journal of the American Dental Association,* 1972, *84,* 571–576.

SPEAR, F. G. A study of pain as a symptom in chronic psychiatric illness. M.D. thesis, University of Bristol, 1965.

SPERRY, R. W. Hemisphere deconnection and unity in conscious awareness. *American Psychologist,* 1968, *23,* 723–733.

SQUIRE, L. R., & SLATER, P. C. Bilateral and unilateral ECT: Effects on verbal and nonverbal memory. *American Journal of Psychiatry,* 1978, *135,* 1316–1320.

STERN, D. B. Handedness and the lateral distribution of conversion symptoms. *Journal of Nervous and Mental Disease,* 1977, *164,* 122–128.

STROMGREN, L. S., & JENSEN, P. J. EEG in unilateral and bilateral electroconvulsive therapy. *Acta Psychiatrica Scandinavica,* 1975, *51,* 340–360.

TERZIAN, H. Behavioural and EEG effects of intracarotid sodium amytal injection. *Acta Neurochirurgica,* 1964, *12,* 230–239.

TSUNODA, T., & OKA, M. Lateralization for emotion in the human brain and auditory cerebral dominance. *Proceedings of the Japan Academy,* 1976, *52,* 528–531.

TUCKER, D. M. Lateral brain function, emotion, and conceptualization. *Psychological Bulletin,* 1981, *89,* 19–46.

TUCKER, D. M., ROTH, R. S., ARNESON, B. A., & BUCKINGHAM, V. Right hemisphere activation during stress. *Neuropsychologia,* 1977, *15,* 697–700.

TUCKER, D. M., STENSLIE, C. E., ROTH, R. S., & SHEARER, S. L. Right frontal lobe activation and right hemisphere performance decrement during a depressed mood. *Archives of General Psychiatry,* 1981, *38,* 169–197.

VOORHIES, R., & PATTERSON, R. H. Management of trigeminal neuralgia (tic douloureux). *Journal of the American Medical Association,* 1981, *245,* 2521–2523.

WALTERS, A. Psychogenic regional pain alias hysterical pain. *Brain,* 1961, *84,* 1–19.

WEINSTEIN, S. The relationship of laterality and cutaneous area to breast sensitivity in sinistrals and dextrals. *American Journal of Psychology,* 1963, *76,* 475–479.

WEINSTEIN, S., & SERSEN, S. A. Tactual sensitivity as a function of handedness and laterality. *Journal of Comparative and Physiological Psychology,* 1961, *54,* 665–669.

WERNICKE, C. Der Aphusische Symptomencomplex. Breslau: MaxCohen & Weigert, 1874.

WHITE, J. C., & SWEET, W. H. *Pain and the neurosurgeon* (2d ed.). Springfield: Thomas, 1969.

WHITLOCK, F. A. The aetiology of hysteria. *Acta Psychiatrica Scandinavica,* 1967, *43,* 144–162.

WHITTY, C. W. M. Familial hemiplegic migraine. *Journal of Neurology, Neurosurgery, and Psychiatry,* 1953, *16,* 172–177.

WOLFF, B. B., & JARVIK, M. E. Relationship between superficial and deep somatic thresholds of pain with a note on handedness. *American Journal of Psychology,* 1964, *77,* 589–599.

WOLFF, H. G. *Headache and other head pain.* New York: Oxford University Press, 1948.

WOOD, P. Da Costa's syndrome (or effort syndrome). *British Medical Journal,* 1941, *1,* 767–851.

PART IV

RESEARCH PARADIGMS AND MEASUREMENT

13

Paradigms in Stress Research: Laboratory versus Field and Traits versus Processes

Lothar Laux   Gerhard Vossel

THERE IS NO SINGLE PARADIGM IN STRESS AND COPING RESEARCH and certainly no one on which all authors in the field agree. Indeed, the recent contributions of Lazarus and his colleagues suggest a paradigmatic crisis. After calling into question the paradigms traditionally employed in stress research Lazarus and Launier (1978) concluded: "We are certain that only a radical change in outlook, research paradigm, and conceptual language, will allow us to escape the doldrums into which research and theory on psychodynamics and adaptation have lapsed using the research models and language of the recent past" (p. 321). One essential criticism concerns the limitations of the laboratory paradigm, and Lazarus and Launier (1978) would like to see complete reliance on field studies. Another controversy surrounds the assumption that traits are stable dispositions that importantly govern behavior. This "very paradigm personologists have been employing" (Block, 1977:38) has come under serious attack especially from stress and anxiety researchers who suggest replacing the dominant emphasis on structural factors or traits (e.g., habitual coping styles) with a transactional process orientation (Lazarus & Launier, 1978).

This chapter describes the current paradigmatic shifts in stress research. Our discussion centers around two pairs of polar themes: *laboratory* versus *field* and *traits* versus *processes*. Limitations of space prevent us from looking at psychologists' understanding of the term "paradigm" (cf. Kuhn, 1970). Likewise, we shall not pursue the question of whether psychology should adopt a preparadigmatic, an apardigmatic, or a metaparadigmatic position (Marceil, 1977).

LABORATORY VERSUS FIELD

Evaluation of Laboratory and Field Research

Laboratory experiments have been repeatedly criticized as an inadequate strategy in stress research. It has been argued, for example, that practical and ethical reasons make it impossible to subject humans to the kinds and degrees of stress that are typical of everyday life. Furthermore, the laboratory experiment has been criticized on the ground that it studies behavior under artificial conditions; by the very nature of the setting, the subject knows he or she is in an experiment. Consequently, findings in laboratory experiments are said to have limited generalizability. Several authors have even advocated abandoning laboratory research and studying stress and its consequences solely in real-life settings (e.g., Lazarus, 1980; Lazarus & Launier, 1978).

It should be noted that the conclusions about the advantages and disadvantages of field and laboratory research are frequently biased in favor of field research (cf. Laux & Vossel, 1982). As the thorough review of research strategies and discussion of their characteristic strengths and weaknesses by Runkel and McGrath (1972) showed, the most desirable features of any empirical study—realism, precision, and generality—cannot be maximized at the same time. And each available strategy—laboratory experiment, field experiment, field study—can serve only *some* aims of research well. Therefore, one should not search for the single right strategy but choose that strategy that is best for one's own purposes and try to minimize its inherent weaknesses.

In a reply to the frequently raised objections against the laboratory experiment, we offer some examples of psychological stress research in which this strategy has been successfully used. The work of Lazarus and colleagues (Lazarus, 1968; Lazarus, Averill, & Opton, 1970) with motion picture films comes first to mind. This research clearly demonstrated the important mediating role of *cognitive appraisal* which can be understood as evaluative judgments related to person's well-being or to available coping resources in stress-related transactions. Without this program of laboratory research, the formulation of a psychological stress theory from a cognitive point of view (Lazarus, 1966) would scarcely have been possible. A second example of the usefulness of the laboratory experiment in stress research is provided by a series of studies performed within the context of *test anxiety theory* (Sarason, 1978) and of *trait-state anxiety theory* (Spielberger, 1972, 1975). These studies demonstrated that ego involving laboratory situations that do not differ from naturalistic situations with regard to the intensity of state anxiety reactions elicited are possible and that the results of such laboratory experiments can be generalized to real-life situations with some justification (cf. Epstein, 1981). Further examples of promising laboratory paradigms and standardized laboratory techniques may be found in Weick (1970), who concluded from his discussion of methodological problems that there is reason for optimism about the future of laboratory studies, since this approach is sufficiently flexible to handle most of the crucial problems in stress research.

In general, discussions on strategies in stress research have been overly concerned with the question of choosing adequate settings (laboratory versus field), contrasting the advantages and disadvantages of the laboratory experiment with the field study (cf. McGrath, 1970). Other possibilities of field research, especially true field experiments and quasi-experiments (cf. Cook & Campbell, 1976), have only rarely been considered. These methods, however, would permit us to overcome some of the weaknesses of typical field studies—especially their high vulnerability to threats to internal validity—at the same time providing for a higher degree of realism than do laboratory experiments.

Combinations of Research Strategies

Previous discussions on strategies in stress research also have underestimated the possibility of combining laboratory and field investigations. Two kinds of combinations may be distinguished: in the first, predictions derived from laboratory research are tested in a field setting; in the second, hypotheses are formulated on the basis of field observations and are subsequently examined in controlled laboratory experiments. The work of Glass and Singer (1972, 1975) provides a good example of such a research strategy. In order to investigate the behavioral aftereffects of stress, they ran a series of laboratory experiments that demonstrated that exposure to a variety of stressors (e.g., noise, electric shock, social stressors) had deleterious effects on performance in the poststressor condition. As a check of the external validity of these results, several field studies were performed. One of these studies, for example, investigated the effects of traffic noise on reading ability and auditory discrimination in children (Cohen, Glass, & Singer, 1973). An inverse relationship between the children's verbal skills and the noisiness of their apartments was found that could be interpreted as a negative aftereffect of prolonged exposure to noise. The advantages of such a mixed strategy are also manifest in the work of Houston (1982) on the relationships between trait anxiety and cognitive behavior in coping with stress.

The main characteristic of the second kind of combined laboratory-field research is the systematic alternation between settings. Elsewhere (Laux & Vossel, 1982) we referred to this strategy as an *interplay* between laboratory and field research. Such an approach starts with a set of concepts and hypotheses that are examined with regard to completeness and adequacy in a field setting. The next step is the construction of a laboratory situation that permits the investigator to evaluate the hypotheses by experimental methods and, if necessary, to reformulate them. Then the investigator returns to the field and reexamines his or her concepts and hypotheses. An excellent example of such a research cycle is provided by the work of Schönpflug and colleagues (Schönpflug, 1979; Schulz & Schönpflug, 1982) on regulator activity during states of stress. In order to investigate the effects of various stressors typical of clerical jobs in industry, the authors first conducted individual interviews in the industrial setting. They then used these interviews to make a detailed analysis of working conditions and to create experimental tasks intended to simulate the most important features of the field setting. The tasks, for example, were decision problems consisting of four alternatives of a decision and five additional pieces of information. Subjects were asked to select the optimal solution. In a series of laboratory experiments, the effects of personality variables (e.g., introversion), task variables (e.g., difficulty), and stressor conditions (e.g., noise, uncertainty, evaluative feedback) on task performance, casual attributions, and physiological measures were studied. On the basis of the results obtained in the laboratory, futher studies in the industrial setting were performed, which, in turn, led to a modified experimental approach. This alternation between field investigation and laboratory experiment can be continued until convergence of results permits the formulation of a theory, say, a theory of stress, fatigue, and economics of behavior (Schönpflug, 1981), that adequately describes similar paradigms in very different settings.

In conclusion, we agree with McGrath (1982) that research in both settings—laboratory and field—has inevitable costs and potential benefits. The proposed abandonment of the laboratory experiment as a strategy in stress research therefore is not justified, especially since this approach can be fruitfully combined with real-life research.

TRAITS VERSUS PROCESSES

The Consistency Issue

An enduring controversy in research on stress and coping concerns the importance of traits. This debate recently has been given new impetus by some active stress researchers who have attacked the dominant trait orientation in the study of stress and coping (e.g., Lazarus & Cohen, 1978; Lazarus & Launier, 1978).

The controversy centers around *consistency*. In brief, to what extent is behavior consistent (stable) across situations? In most trait models an individual's specified behavior is assumed to be stable across situations not in an *absolute* sense but *relative* to the behavior of others (Magnusson & Endler, 1977). That is, individuals should retain their relative positions on a response variable across situations. It is essential to distinguish between relative consistency across situations that are *similar* and relative consistency across situations that are *dissimilar* (Magnusson & Endler, 1977). In a large number of test-retest reliability studies, behavior was observed in situations that differed in time but otherwise were similar. In general, these studies indicated an impressive degree of relative consistency of reactions *(temporal stability)*.

The debate on behavioral consistency, however, focuses on consistency across dissimilar situations. Long before the current controversy stimulated by modern interactionists, stress researchers had turned their attention to the issue of *consistency-specificity*. Stopol (1954), for example, examined the hypothesis that individuals who show a loss of efficiency in one kind of stress situation will also show a loss of efficiency in other types of stress situations. Stopol examined performance impairment on a digit-symbol test under failure (deprecatory statements) and distraction (presentation of extraneous stimuli) conditions. The insignificant correlations between scores from both situations led him to adopt a situation-specific point of view:

> The data bearing upon the major problem posed by this study, that of consistency of behavior from one type of stress situation to another, indicate that stress tolerance is not a unitary characteristic. The ability to withstand failure stress and the ability to withstand distraction stress are essentially independent of each other. (P. 25)

Alfert (1966) compared responses to a vicarious stress situation (accident film) with responses to a direct stress situation (threat of shock). *Change scores* (the difference between rest and experimental periods) derived from adjective checklists and physiological variables were used. To examine the consistency of behavior under stress, Alfert correlated responses for each variable across stress situations. She concluded from the high correlations obtained for autonomic and mood variables that there is striking agreement between the stress reactions to vicarious and direct threats.

The contradictory results reported by Alfert (1966) and by Stopol (1954) and the empirical evidence reported by Magnusson and Endler (1977) indicate that consistency versus specificity of behavior under different kinds of stressors should be evaluated with reference to the method chosen for measuring stress. For example, there might be more consistency for subjective and physiological variables than for performance. Moreover, even high correlations cannot be straightforwardly interpreted as indicative of consistency. Ratings obtained in different situations might correlate appreciably merely because the same method of measurement has been used. An appropriate way to tackle this problem of method variance appears to be a *multitrait-multimethod analysis*. Such an analysis uses at least two different stress situations and at least two different measures of stress. Comparison of various groups of correlation coefficients can distinguish method variance from variance caused by consistency of reactions (see Laux, 1976, for a fuller discussion of the multitrait-multimethod strategy in stress research).

Research over the years has revealed little empirical evidence of consistency of reactions across dissimilar situations. The specificity of most reaction variables has led stress researchers to question the belief in broad traits presumed to determine a person's reaction in various stress situations. In short, behavior appears to lack the generality supposed in the trait measurement model, which underlies personality tests (Magnusson & Endler, 1977).

Reformulation of Trait Conceptions

To overcome the deficiencies and inadequacies of the traditional trait orientation, at least three theoretical positions and related research strategies have been proposed by stress researchers.

Situation-specific Traits. The critique of the traditional trait model has led to the conception of narrowly defined traits closely tied to situations. Tests developed to measure these traits are called *narrow,* or *situation-specific,* since they specify the situation in the test item (Spielberger, 1980; Zuckerman, 1979). In the area of anxiety, for example, such tests focus on individuals' dispositions to be anxious in selected classes of stressful situations (e.g., taking examinations or making speeches). According to Mellstrom, Zuckerman, and Cicala (1978), the idea of situation-specific traits can be conceived as a redefinition of the trait concept that takes into consideration the situation and the person by situation interaction.

In contrast to situation-specific tests, *general tests of trait anxiety,* such as the State-Trait Anxiety Inventory (STAI), developed by Spielberger, Gorsuch, and Lushene (1970), do not specify situations in the items of the tests. A number of studies compared the predictive validity of situation-specific trait anxiety scales to that of general tests of trait anxiety (Laux, Glanzmann, & Schaffner, 1982; Mellstrom and others, 1978). The typical procedure is to pretest subjects on general and situation-specific trait anxiety measures (e.g., speech anxiety) and later to expose them to the actual criterion situation (e.g., speech situation). On the whole, results indicated that situation-specific trait anxiety tests are more predictive of behavioral and subjective anxiety in the corresponding criterion situation than are general trait anxiety measures.

Traits as a Summary of States. Situation-specific trait measures based on self-report questionnaires have undoubtedly exceeded the low order of prediction found for general trait measures. An even better prediction of behavior may be achieved by measuring a sample of a person's *states* in certain classes of similar situations. The theoretical basis for such a procedure was provided by Zuckerman (1976), who suggested that "personality might be better assessed as a summary of responses over time rather than in terms of hypothetical traits that are supposed to predict these responses" (p. 169). From Zuckerman's empirical investigations, based on self-report scales, the hypothesis may be derived that a limited number of state measurements (e.g., two or three self-reports on anxiety) in a certain stress situation would predict the future state level in this particular situation better than would any general or situation-specific trait test. In addition, it can be assumed that a better prediction of performance and physiological responses could be made from self-report state scales given in situ. This research strategy is not limited to self-report state measures but can also be used with performance and physiological measures as predictors.

Coherent Patterns of Behavior. The frequent finding that behavior across different situations shows a rather low degree of consistency does not necessarily imply that situations are the prime deteminants of behavior. Magnusson and Endler (1977) cogently argued that behavior can be lawful and thus predictable without being stable in either an absolute or a relative sense. An individual's behavior across situations of different character may form a unique pattern of reactions and this pattern is characteristic of him or her. Magnusson and

Endler (1977) referred to this lawful and predictable variation of behavior as *coherence,* a phenomenon that may be studied by observing a sample of individuals in certain kinds of stress situations. The individual process of person by situation interaction may be described as a number of *cross-situational profiles,* yielding one profile for each variable of the stress reaction. The idiographic pattern of changing and stable reactions across situations for an individual would be reflected in the total pattern of such profiles (see Magnusson, Duner, & Zetterblom, 1975, for an empirical study).

Some researchers argue that the coherence of behavior is dependent upon continuous mediating processes (described in terms of hypothetical variables) responsible for the selection and interpretation of situational information. Such a model of personality, linking the unique cross-situational pattern of actual behavior to a consistent functioning of the mediating system, corresponds, for example, to Allport's (1966) trait model.

Transaction and Process

In psychological stress theory, Lazarus and colleagues (Lazarus, 1980; Lazarus & Launier, 1978) suggested that stress can be most adequately described in terms of a transaction between person and environment. According to Pervin (1968), who proposed the distinction between transaction and interaction, *transaction* focuses on *reciprocal causation,* while *interaction* denotes *unidirectional causality.* That is, interaction—following the logic of the analysis of variance model—refers only to the causal interplay between two variables (person and environment) that influence behavior. Transaction, on the other hand, means not only that the environment influences the person but also that the person is an active agent in influencing the environment. This distinction corresponds to the one proposed by Overton and Reese (1973) between the *reactive organism* (mechanistic) and the *active organism* (organismic) model of man and to Magnusson and Endler's (1977) distinction between *mechanistic* and *dynamic interactions.* Reciprocity of causation is especially evident in the study of bereavement, which involves a complex sequence of different coping processes on the part of the bereaved person over time: "As the initial shock and numbness wear off, depression, anger, guilt, anxiety, and other affects come in their place. The coping task is now to accept the loss, and ultimately to reinvest in new love objects, commitments, and activities" (Lazarus & Launier, 1978:291). These coping processes change the psychological environment, while at the same time information about these changes is fed back to the person, influencing his or her future behavior.

According to Lazarus (1980) and Pervin and Lewis (1978), a transaction, which is brought about by the interaction between personal and environment variables, should be considered a new entity with unique characteristics. The term "threat," for example, expresses a new unit of psychological analysis. There is no person or environment but only a person-environment relationship described by the word "threat." Lazarus distinguished three kinds of stressful appraisals of person-environment transactions: harm-loss, threat, and challenge. All three involve a more or less negative evaluation of a person's present or future state of well-being. *Harm-loss* refers to damage that has already occurred; *threat,* to harm or loss that is anticipated; and *challenge,* to the possibly risky and difficult to attain but probable mastery of an imbalance between environmental demands and reponse capabilities (cf. Lazarus & Launier, 1978).

In Lazarus's view (1980), one of the main characteristics of a transactional perspective is its *process orientation.* The traditional interactive perspective is criticized because it is usually deterministic. That is, it focuses on static or structural variables of persons (traits) and environments. When statistical interactions are found, they tend to be interpreted in terms of actual interactive processes. It is assumed, for example, that in persons under threat of surgery differences in the coping process account for different reaction patterns. Most heavily researched are the so-called *vigilant* and *avoidant* modes of coping. Patients using a vigilant mode of coping are overly alert to the threatening aspects of the medical experience while patients using an avoidant mode of coping deal with the threat by not admitting it. Normally only trait measures of avoidance and vigilance are applied, while no attempt is made to examine which coping processes are actually used. Some research data, however, show that a trait measure of coping is, at least in certain instances, not predictive of actual coping processes and their consequences during threat of surgery (Cohen & Lazarus, 1973). Instead of emphasizing relatively stable structure or trait determinants and their role in mediating the stress response, a transactional view, therefore, concentrates on the description of actual behavior in a stressful situation and its consequences. Such a process orientation focuses on real-life interchanges between person and environment and investigates such interchanges over time and across situations.

Our discussion of reciprocal action does not mean to diminish the important influence of person-situation (mechanistic) interactions on behavior. We still have not fully explored the nature of mechanistic interactions in many areas of stress research. Endler and Edwards (1978) even suggested that in the first instance investigators should focus on mechanistic interaction "in order to further our understanding of the effective and predictive variables and the functional relationships between antecedent conditions and the behavior they influence" (p. 160). Once we have established such a frame of reference, the ultimate goal of understanding personality in terms of dynamic and process views of interaction should be approached. Such a position does not completely contradict the transactional perspective proposed by Lazarus (1980), who did not intend to abandon traditional research guided by a mechanistic model but only to redress the balance in favor of a dynamic model.

One might further wonder whether most relevant interactions in stress research (except for interactions between persons) are best conceived as reciprocal. Ideally, research should be guided by a model that allows for the investigation of reciprocal action but includes the possibility that interactions do not involve such exchanges (for a fuller discussion see Howard, 1979; Pervin & Lewis, 1978).

CONCLUSION

This chapter indicated that there is a strong need for stress researchers to abandon older paradigms and seek innovative approaches. Though we recognized the limitations of traditional conceptualizations and research strategies, we argued that a radical paradigm shift is not necessary.

We showed, for example, that an emphasis on naturalistic observation does not prevent laboratory research provided that the phenomenon studied in the laboratory is relevant to behavior in the natural environment and that the results of laboratory experimentation are checked against information based on real-world events.

With regard to the trait versus process issue, we demonstrated that there is good reason to adopt the concepts and research strategies of refined trait models, as well as the assumptions and methodology of process oriented approaches. In future research and theorizing, special interest should be devoted to a joint consideration of trait and process oriented point of views. The concept of coherence and the definition of reciprocal interaction as an extension rather than a contradiction of mechanistic interaction could serve as examples.

REFERENCES

Alfert, E. Comparison of responses to a vicarious and a direct threat. *Journal of Experimental Research in Personality,* 1966, *1,* 179–186.

Allport, G. W. Traits revisited. *American Psychologist,* 1966, *21,* 1–10.

Block, J. Advancing the psychology of personality: Paradigmatic shift or improving the quality of research? In D. Magnusson & N. S. Endler (eds.), *Personality at the crossroads: Current issues in interactional psychology.* Hillsdale: Erlbaum, 1977.

Cohen, S., Glass, D. C., & Singer, J. E. Apartment noise, auditory discrimination, and reading ability in children. *Journal of Experimental Social Psychology,* 1973, *9,* 407–422.

Cohen, F., & Lazarus, R. S. Active coping processes, coping dispositions, and recovery from surgery. *Psychosomatic Medicine,* 1973, *35,* 375–389.

Cook, T. D., & Campbell, D. T. The design and conduct of quasi-experiments and true experiments in field settings. In M. D. Dunnette (ed.), *Handbook of industrial and organizational psychology.* Chicago: Rand McNally, 1976.

Endler, N. S., & Edwards, J. Person by treatment interactions in personality research. In L. A. Pervin & M. Lewis (eds.), *Perspectives in interactional psychology.* New York: Plenum, 1978.

Epstein, S. The stability of behavior. Part II: Implications for psychological research. *American Psychologist,* 1980, *35,* 790–806.

Glass, D. C., & Singer, J. E. *Urban stress: Experiments on noise and social stressors.* New York: Academic, 1972.

————. Effects of noise on human performance. In A. Damon (ed.), *Physiological anthropology.* New York: Oxford University Press, 1975.

Houston, B. K. Trait anxiety and cognitive coping behavior. In H. W. Krohne & L. Laux (eds.), *Achievement, stress, and anxiety.* Washington, D.C.: Hemisphere, 1982.

Howard, J. A. Person-situation interaction models. *Personality and Social Psychology Bulletin,* 1979, *5,* 191–195.

Kuhn, T. S. *The structure of scientific revolutions.* Chicago: University of Chicago Press, 1970.

Laux, L. The multitrait-multimethod rationale in stress research. In I. G. Sarason & C. D. Spielberger (eds.), *Stress and anxiety,* vol. 3. Washington, D. C.: Hemisphere, 1976.

Laux, L., Glanzmann, P., & Schaffner, P. General versus situation-specific traits as related to anxiety in ego-threatening situations. In C. D. Spielberger, I. G. Sarason, & P. B. Defares (eds.), *Stress and anxiety,* vol. 9. Washington, D.C.: Hemisphere, 1982.

Laux, L., & Vossel, G. Theoretical and methodological issues in achievement-related stress and anxiety research. In H. W. Krohne & L. Laux (eds.), *Achievement, stress, and anxiety.* Washington, D.C.: Hemisphere, 1982.

Lazarus, R. S. *Psychological stress and the coping process.* New York: McGraw-Hill, 1966.

————. Emotions and adaptation: Conceptual and empirical relations. In W. J. Arnold (ed.), *Nebraska Symposium on Motivation.* Lincoln: University of Nebraska Press, 1968.

————. The stress and coping paradigm. In C. Eisdorfer, D. Cohen, & A. Kleinman (eds.), *Theoretical bases for psychopathology.* New York: Spectrum, 1980.

Lazarus, R. S., Averill, J. R., & Opton, E. M., Jr. Toward a cognitive theory of emotion. In M. Arnold (ed.), *Feelings and emotions.* New York: Academic, 1970.

Lazarus, R. S., & Cohen, J. B. Environmental stress. In J. Altman & J. F. Wohlwill (eds.), *Human behavior and the environment.* New York: Plenum, 1978.

Lazarus, R. S., & Launier, R. Stress-related transactions between person and environment. In L. A. Pervin & M. Lewis (eds.), *Perspectives in interactional psychology.* New York: Plenum, 1978.

MAGNUSSON, D., DUNER, A., & ZETTERBLOM, G. *Adjustment: A longitudinal study.* New York: Wiley, 1975.

MAGNUSSON, D., & ENDLER, N. S. Interactional psychology: Present status and future prospects. In D. Magnusson & N. S. Endler (eds.), *Personality at the crossroads: Current issues in interactional psychology.* Hillsdale: Erlbaum, 1977.

MARCEIL, J. C. Implicit dimensions of idiography and nomothesis: A reformulation. *American Psychologist,* 1977, *32,* 1046–1055.

McGRATH, J. E. Major methodological issues. In J. E. McGrath (ed.), *Social and psychological factors in stress.* New York: Holt, 1970.

————. Methodological problems in research on stress. In H. W. Krohne & L. Laux (eds.), *Achievement, stress, and anxiety.* Washington, D.C.: Hemisphere, 1982.

MELLSTROM, M., ZUCKERMAN, M., & CICALA, G. A. General versus specific tests in the assessment of anxiety. *Journal of Consulting and Clinical Psychology,* 1978, *46,* 423–431.

OVERTON, W. F., & REESE, H. W. Models of development: Methodological implications. In J. R. Nesselroade & H. W. Reese (eds.), *Life span developmental psychology.* New York: Academic, 1973.

PERVIN, L. A. Performance and satisfaction as a function of individual-environment fit. *Psychological Bulletin,* 1968, *69,* 56–68.

PERVIN, L. A., & LEWIS, M. Overview of the internal-external issue. In L. A. Pervin & M. Lewis (eds.), *Perspectives in interactional psychology.* New York: Plenum, 1978.

RUNKEL, P. J., & McGRATH, J. E. *Research on human behavior: A systematic guide to method.* New York: Holt, 1972.

SARASON, I. G. The Test Anxiety Scale: Concept and research. In C. D. Spielberger & I. G. Sarason (eds.), *Stress and anxiety,* vol. 5. Washington, D.C.: Hemisphere, 1978.

SCHÖNPFLUG, W. Regulation und Fehlregulation im Verhalten. Part I: Verhaltensstruktur, Effizienz und Belastung—theoretische Grundlagen eines Untersuchungsprogramms. *Psychologische Beiträge,* 1979, *21,* 174–203.

————. Stress, fatigue, and the economics of behavior. In R. B. Hockey (ed.), *Stress and fatigue.* New York: Wiley, 1981.

SCHULZ, P., & SCHÖNPFLUG, W. Regulatory activity during states of stress. In H. W. Krohne & L. Laux (eds.), *Achievement, stress, and anxiety.* Washington, D.C.: Hemisphere, 1982.

SPIELBERGER, C. D. Anxiety as an emotional state. In C. D. Spielberger (ed.), *Anxiety: Current trends in theory and research,* vol. 1. New York: Academic, 1972.

————. Anxiety: State-trait process. In C. D. Spielberger & I. G. Sarason (eds.), *Stress and anxiety,* vol. 1. Washington, D.C.: Hemisphere, 1975.

————. *Test Anxiety Inventory ("Test Attitude Inventory").* Palo Alto: Consulting Psychologists, 1980.

SPIELBERGER, C. D., GORSUCH, R. L., & LUSHENE, R. E. *Manual for the State-Trait Anxiety Inventory.* Palo Alto: Consulting Psychologists, 1970.

STOPOL, M. S. The consistency of stress tolerance. *Journal of Personality,* 1954, *23,* 13–29.

WEICK, K. E. The "ess" in stress: Some conceptual and methodological problems. In J. E. McGrath (ed.), *Social and psychological factors in stress.* New York: Holt, 1970.

ZUCKERMAN, M. General and situation-specific traits and states: New approaches to assessment of anxiety and other constructs. In M. Zuckerman & C. D. Spielberger (eds.), *Emotions and anxiety: New concepts, methods, and applications.* Hillsdale: Erlbaum, 1976.

————. Traits, states, situations, and uncertainty. *Journal of Behavioral Assessment,* 1979, *1,* 43–54.

14

Conceptualizing and Measuring Coping Resources and Processes

Rudolph H. Moos   Andrew G. Billings

ALTHOUGH COPING RESOURCES PLAY A CENTRAL ROLE in contemporary theories of stress, we still know relatively little about the specific coping processes people use in adapting to stressful life circumstances. How have different theoretical perspectives contributed to current conceptualizations and measures of coping resources? What are the most important coping resources and how are they related to the responses selected in actual stressful encounters? What are the major domains of appraisal and coping responses and how can these domains be measured? Do people typically vary their coping styles depending on the type of stressor they experience, or do they tend to use one coping style irrespective of the situation? We shall address these questions first by describing four lines of theory and research that have shaped current concepts and measures of coping. We shall then use ideas derived from this literature to formulate a conceptual framework to focus on the coping factors involved in mediating the connection between stress and functioning. Finally, we shall review selected methods by which coping resources and processes have been assessed and discuss some relevant conceptual and methodological issues.

THEORETICAL ANTECEDENTS OF COPING CONCEPTS

Four related perspectives have enlightened the search for formulations and measures of coping resources and processes: psychoanalytic theory, life cycle theory, evolutionary theory and behavior modification, and cultural and social-ecological approaches. These perspectives have pointed to the major domains that need to be included in a conceptual framework of coping processes and their determinants and effects.

Psychoanalytic Theory and Ego Psychology

Freud believed that ego processes serve to resolve conflicts between an individual's impulses and the constraints of external reality. Their function is to reduce tension by enabling

Preparation of the chapter was supported by NIAAA grant AA02863 and Veterans Administration Medical Research funds. We wish to thank Ruth Lederman and Deborah Shields for bibliographic assistance and Ruth Cronkite, John Finney and Roger Mitchell for valuable comments on an earlier draft of the manuscript.

the individual to express sexual and aggressive impulses indirectly, without recognizing their "true" intent. These ego processes are cognitive mechanisms (although they may have behavioral expression) whose main functions are defensive (reality distorting) and emotion focused (oriented toward tension reduction). Subsequently, ego psychologists emphasized reality oriented processes of the "conflict-free" ego sphere such as attention, perception, and memory. The concepts and measures that have emerged from these ideas include Witkin's (Witkin & Goodenough, 1977) work on field orientation and Haan's tripartite theory of ego processes.

Life Cycle Perspectives

In addition to emphasizing the processes of defense and coping, psychoanalysis and ego psychology provided the basis for formulating developmental perspectives that focused on the gradual accumulation of personal coping resources over an individual's life span. For instance, Erikson (1963) described eight life stages, each of which represents a new challenge, or crisis, that must be negotiated successfully in order for the individual to cope adequately with the next stage. Personal coping resources (such as the development of trust and autonomy) accrued during the adolescent and young adult years are integrated into the self-concept and influence the process of coping in adulthood and old age. This perspective assumes that adequate resolution of the transitions and crises that occur at each point in the life cycle leads to coping resources that can help resolve subsequent crises. Successful encounters with environmental stressors build a sense of efficacy and ego integrity.

These formulations spawned a set of procedures to measure such general coping resources as self-esteem, ego identity, competence motivation, novelty needs, and stimulus seeking behavior (Moos, 1974). These resources can affect the appraisal of potentially stressful situations, as well as the selection of coping responses to handle such situations. For instance, a sense of competence may lead a person to perceive a potential stressor as less threatening and to choose a reality oriented coping response that fosters a successful outcome. Coping resources can also help people anticipate and take action to avoid expected social stressors. Although many characteristics of an individual can be seen as coping resources, such constructs as self-efficacy, internal control, sense of mastery, and ego maturity have received the most attention.

Evolutionary Theory and Behavior Modification

Darwin's evolutionary perspective on adaptation provided the basis for a behaviorally oriented counterpoint to the psychoanalytic concern with intrapsychic and cognitive factors. This orientation led to an emphasis on behavioral problem-solving activities that contribute to individual and species survival. Initial applications of the behaviorist tradition emphasized the functional aspects of problem-solving behavior, although more recent clinical treatment procedures have included cognitively oriented components.

Cognitive behaviorism is concerned both with problem-solving skills and with an individual's cognitive appraisal of the meaning of an event. Recent investigations in this area have focused on the importance of a sense of self-efficacy as a coping resource. Bandura (1977) noted that individuals must believe that they can successfully accomplish a task in order for them to engage in active efforts to master that task. Successful coping increases future expectations of self-efficacy, which, in turn, lead to more vigorous and persistent efforts to master threatening tasks and situations. The measurement procedures that have emerged from this orientation typically assess coping strategies involved in handling specific situations, although a few techniques pertain to more general coping styles (Platt & Spivack, 1975; Tyler, 1978).

Cultural and Social-Ecological Perspectives

Aside from emphasizing the adaptive qualities of behaviorally oriented problem-solving, the evolutionary approach focused on the relationship between organisms or groups of organisms and the environment. Adaptation to the conditions of the physical and cultural environment is facilitated by the cooperative efforts of the human community, which are essential in adapting to the environment. The concept of enviromental coping resources emerged from this perspective. One important domain of such resources is the provision of culturally mandated coping resolutions and methods of teaching the skills necessary to attain such resolutions. Another domain is composed of social networks, which can provide such interpersonal resources as emotional understanding, cognitive guidance, and tangible support. These environmental resources can affect the appraisal of the threat implied by an event, as well as the choice, sequence, and relative effectiveness of coping responses.

An Integrative Conceptual Framework

The elements identified by the four perspectives we have reviewed are integrated in a framework that conceptualizes the link between life stress and functioning as mediated both by personal and environmental coping resources and by cognitive appraisal and coping processes, as well as their interrelationships. This framework views life events as typically developing from a combination of personal and environmental factors. *Life events* are relatively discrete, short-term stressors (such as an argument with one's boss), as well as longer-term, sequential stressors (separation, divorce, school problems with one's child) and chronic life strains (a monotonous job or a stultifying marriage). With respect to personal factors, impulse control can help an individual avoid stressors, whereas an impulsive lifestyle often precipitates stressful events. An impulsive person is more likely to make major life changes (moving, switching jobs) and may take risks that increase the probability of experiencing events such as accidents or legal difficulties. In terms of environmental factors, living in an inner-city area increases the risk of being the victim of a crime while having a large social network makes experiencing the death of a relative or friend more likely.

The conceptual model illustrates that life events, and the personal and environmental coping resources related to such events, can affect the appraisal-reappraisal process, as well as the selection of coping responses and their effectiveness. Although this process is transactional and reciprocal feedback occurs at each stage, research has typically focused on either descriptions of one or two of the sets of factors or cross-sectional analyses of the relationships among several factors. However, a considerable amount of work has addressed the problem of developing measures of coping resources and responses. An overview of recent work on some aspects of environmental coping resources is presented elsewhere (Moos and Mitchell, 1982); we shall focus here on selected measures of both personal coping resources and appraisal and coping processes.

ASSESSING PERSONAL COPING RESOURCES

As previously described certain person centered factors mediate the perception of stressful events and the selection of specific coping responses. *Coping resources* are a complex set of personality, attitudinal, and cognitive factors that provide the psychological context for coping. Such resources are relatively stable dispositional characteristics that affect the coping process and are themselves affected by the cumulative outcome of that process. Selecting from numerous variables in this domain, we shall briefly review some measures of ego development; self-efficacy and related factors, such as sense of mastery and internal control; cognitive styles; and general problem-solving abilities.

Ego Development

Loevinger (1976) conceptualized *ego development* as the "master trait," encompassing an individual's frame of reference and the processes through which psychological and environmental experiences are integrated into a coherent whole. The ego progressively unfolds to achieve a more differentiated perception of the self and the social world. Each step represents a qualitatively different stage of structural organization. Although the sequence of developmental stages is invariant, individuals differ in the final stage they attain. Loevinger assumed that the measurement of ego development requires a projective technique that permits a person to reveal her own "unbiased" frame of experience.

Loevinger's Sentence Completion Test of Ego Development (SCT) measures a respondent's impulse controls, interpersonal style, conscious preoccupations, and cognitive style by responses to 36 sentence stems (such as "Raising a family_____" and "When they avoided me_____"). Each response is matched to one of nine stages of ego development, varying from impulsive and self-protective to individualist, autonomous, and integrated. Experienced judges can achieve relatively high interrater reliability. Holt (1980) recently published national norms for a 12-item version of the SCT based on the responses of approximately 3500 college and age matched noncollege youth.

Since ego development is a theoretically broad concept, no single behavioral criterion can be used to validate the SCT. Existing results are generally supportive of the theory and measure (for a review see Hauser, 1976), and research has shown that the SCT is not simply a reflection of intelligence or verbal fluency. Ego development has been related to complex patterns of behavior such as help giving, empathy, and independence, as well as to global measures of maturity and moral development (Loevinger, 1979; McCrae & Costa, 1980). In addition, the general relationships between the SCT and Haan's (1977) measures of ego processes indicate that higher levels of ego development are moderately associated with a greater variety and effectiveness of coping strategies.

Self-efficacy, Social Competence, and Related Beliefs

Personality researchers have sought to measure those aspects of the self-concept that provide general personal resources in handling adverse environmental events (Wylie, 1979). Persons with higher levels of *self-efficacy* are thought to be more active and persistent in their efforts to handle threatening situations, while those with lower levels are less active or tend to avoid such situations. A large body of work has attempted to differentiate between persons who actively manipulate and seek to control their environment and those who are less likely to engage in such behaviors. Following the initial contributions of Rotter (1966), a number of measures of internal-external control orientation have been developed (Lefcourt, 1976). Utilizing this construct in life events research, Johnson and Sarason (1978) found that the relationship between recent stressful life changes and anxiety and depression was stronger among persons with an *external* as compared to an *internal locus of control.*

Pearlin and Schooler (1978) considered a related construct, *sense of mastery,* which they described as a core resource, along with high self-esteem and freedom from self-denigration. They measured mastery using a seven-item composite (items such as "I have little control over the things that happen to me"). In their study, these personal resources attenuated the impact of life strain on perceived marital, parental, financial, and occupational stress. In comparison to women, men reported higher psychological resources, which provided them with greater resistance to the effects of life strains.

Several theorists have definded the *competent self* as involving a set of favorable self-attitudes (such as high self-esteem); a sense of personal efficacy and interpersonal trust; and realistic goal setting and an active approach to coping with the environment. To measure this last component, Tyler (1978) developed the Behavioral Attributes of Psychosocial Competence Test (BAPC). The revised BAPC is a 45-item, forced-choice questionnaire that probes the respondent's usual reactions to a variety of situations and problems. The BAPC has differentiated exemplary from marginal high school students and is basically free of academic aptitude and social desirability bias. The Exploration Preference Scale is a related measure that assesses students' use of social exploration as a style of coping with the high school environment (Edwards & Kelly, 1980). In general, students with a high preference for exploration have higher levels of self-esteem, are more involved in classroom and extracurricular activities, and experience less depression and fewer social problems.

Cognitive Styles

Our "cognitive glasses"—habitual patterns of perception and information processing—have formative effects on learning and adaptive processes. A considerable amount of early research was conducted on the construct of repression-sensitization (Chabot, 1973), but field orientation is currently the most extensively studied cognitive style. A *field-dependent* individual's perceptions of a figure are strongly influenced by the surrounding perceptual context, while those who experience figures as separate and unaffected by the perceptual context are designated *field-independent.* Although initially measured with the Rod and Frame Test, field dependence is now more widely assessed with the Embedded Figures Test, (Witkin, Oltman, Raskin, & Karp, 1971) which can be administered individually or in groups. People are highly consistent in field orientation, and women tend to be somewhat more field dependent than men.

Field-dependent persons are more attuned to their social environments and hence are perceived as warmer and friendlier. They are attracted to social situations, have better social skills, and tend to be more emotionally expressive. In contrast, field-independent persons have a more well-defined identity and are more autonomous and sensitive to their internal needs. The adaptive value of each cognitive orientation depends upon the nature of the situation. Field-independent persons tend to be more analytic and structured in their thinking and are likely to be more successful in dealing with situations that require logical analysis and self-reliance. Those who are field-dependent may utilize their social skills to solve interpersonal problems more effectively. However, highly field-dependent persons may look to their environment for readily available solutions to life problems, as suggested by the finding that alcoholics are more field-dependent than are nonalcoholics (for reviews of this work see Witkin & Goodenough, 1977; Witkin, Moore, Goodenough, & Cox, 1977).

Field orientation may be related to affect regulation. Although field-dependent and field-independent persons experience comparable arousal levels under stress, studies with the Defense Mechanisms Inventory (DMI) have shown that persons who are field independent are likely to express anger and hostility directly against others, while those who are field dependent express such feelings indirectly (Gleser & Ihilevich, 1969). Field-dependent persons tend to use global defenses such as turning against the self and reversal, while field-independent persons prefer differentiated defenses such as turning against the object and projection (Gleser & Ihilevich, 1969; Rohsenow, Erickson, & O'Leary, 1978).

Problem-solving Abilities

Social-learning approaches have emphasized the importance of *effective problem-solving behaviors* for successful adaptation (Kendall & Hollon, 1980). To quantify such behaviors, several studies have used Platt and Spivack's (1975) Means-Ends Problem-solving Procedure (MEPS), a series of 10 written scenarios with only a beginning and an end. A need, goal, or problem is aroused in the protagonist at the beginning of each scenario, while at the end of the scenario the situation is successfully resolved. The individual responds by indicating the means by which the protagonist resolved the situation. The responses are coded as to the number and relevance of means, the amount of elaboration given for each mean, and the number of obstacles mentioned that might obstruct successful resolution. The MEPS originally covered only social interaction; Platt and Spivack (1977) later developed the Emotional Means-Ends Problem-solving Procedure to assess problem-solving relating to strong emotional states. Similar in format to the initial MEPS, this procedure includes scenarios dealing with emotional states such as anxiety and depression.

The MEPS has been used to differentiate patient from nonpatient groups and to assess the effectiveness of clinical and educational interventions aimed at ameliorating problem-solving deficits. Spivack, Platt, and Shure (1976) identified four key elements of problem-solving: recognizing the existence of a problem, defining the problem, generating possible solutions, and selecting the best solution after evaluating consequences of all alternatives. A training program organized around these elements was shown to improve the problem-solving skills of primary grade children and to lead to improved sociability with peers and more initiative and autonomy in the classroom, as measured by the MEPS (Spivack, Platt, & Shure, 1976). Intagliata (1978) found that the use of this program significantly improved the problem-solving of hospitalized alcoholics, as well as the specificity of their posthospitalization planning as assessed during a discharge interview.

Self-control interventions have also been aimed at managing disruptive emotional states such as extreme anger and anxiety and at teaching people to cope with specific stressful situations. For example, Chaney, O'Leary & Marlatt (1978) developed the Situational Competency Test to assess the effectiveness of a skills training program designed to improve alcoholics' coping responses in situations that might be relapse inducing. The respondent role-plays responses to temptation situations involving frustration and anger, other negative emotional states such as depression, and social pressure to drink. Responses are scored for latency, duration, efforts to change the outcome of the situation, and specification of nondrinking alternatives. Such procedures can help in the design of relevant skills training programs and can serve as one measure of their effectiveness.

CLASSIFYING AND MEASURING APPRAISAL AND COPING PROCESSES

Although several attempts have been made to classify appraisal and coping responses (Haan, 1977; Lazarus & Launier, 1978; Moos, 1976, 1977; Pearlin & Schooler, 1978), no accepted method has yet emerged. We have organized the dimensions of appraisal and coping included in selected measurement procedures into three domains according to their primary focus on appraising and reappraising a situation, dealing with the reality of the situation, and handling the emotions aroused by the situation. *Appraisal-focused coping* involves attempts to define the meaning of a situation and includes such strategies as logical analysis and cognitive redefinition. *Problem-focused coping* seeks to modify or eliminate the source of stress (destroying an alcoholic husband's liquor supply), to deal with the tangible consequences of a problem (taking over family responsibilities when the head of household is ill), or actively to change the self and develop a more satisfying situation (learning new skills and enhancing independence). *Emotion-focused coping* includes responses whose primary function is to manage the emotions aroused by stressors and thereby maintain affective equilibrium.

These categories are not mutually exclusive. Appraisal-focused coping can be directed at either the instrumental or the affective aspects of a situation (or both). Furthermore, problem-focused coping can help the person deal with the emotions aroused by a situation (studying for an exam may reduce anxiety; seeking advice may generate emotional support), while emotion-focused coping can provide the resources necessary to handle a problem (meditating to reduce anxiety may help one in studying for an exam; expressing tension by crying or shouting may elicit advice about alternative ways of handling a problem). We shall use this preliminary classification scheme to categorize coping responses into nine types.

Appraisal-focused Coping

Logical Analysis. Strategies in this category include trying to identify the cause of the problem, paying attention to one aspect of the situation at a time, drawing on relevant past experiences, and mentally rehearsing possible actions and their consequences.

Cognitive Redefinition. This category includes cognitive strategies by which an individual accepts the reality of the situation but restructures it to find something favorable. Such strategies involve reminding oneself that things could be worse, thinking of oneself as well off with respect to other people, concentrating on something good that might develop from the situation, and altering values and priorities in line with changing reality.

Cognitive Avoidance. Included here are such strategies as denying fear or anxiety under stress, trying to forget the whole situation, refusing to believe the problem really exists, and engaging in wishful fantasies instead of thinking realistically about the problem.

Problem-focused Coping

Seek Information or Advice. Responses in this category involve seeking more information about the situation; obtaining direction and guidance from an authority; talking with one's spouse, other relatives, or friends about the problem; and asking someone to provide a specific kind of help, such as lending money.

Take Problem-solving Action.   These strategies include making alternative plans, taking specific action to deal directly with the situation, learning new skills directed at the problem, and negotiating and compromising to try to resolve the issue.

Develop Alternative Rewards.   This strategy involves attempts to deal with the problematic situation by changing one's activities and creating new sources of satisfaction. Examples are building alternative social relationships, developing greater autonomy and independence, and engaging in substitute pursuits such as doing volunteer work or studying philosophy or religion.

Emotion-focused Coping

Affective Regulation.   These strategies involve direct efforts to control the emotion aroused by the problem by consciously postponing paying attention to an impulse (suppression), experiencing and working through one's feelings, trying not to be bothered by conflicting feelings, maintaining a sense of pride and keeping a stiff upper lip, and tolerating ambiguity by withholding immediate action.

Resigned Acceptance.   This category includes such responses as waiting for time to remedy the problem, expecting the worst, accepting the situation as it is, deciding that nothing can be done to change things, and submitting to fate.

Emotional Discharge.   Included here are verbal expressions to let off steam, crying, smoking, overeating, and engaging in impulsive acting out. These responses may involve a failure of affective regulation, but we categorize them separately in order to distinguish persons who alternate between emotional control and emotional discharge.

In using these nine domains to characterize existing measures of appraisal and coping processes, we have taken some liberties with the descriptions provided by the original authors. We believe that our reformulations are justified by the need to develop common conceptual domains of coping responses to guide the organization of measurement procedures. The following discussion distinguishes between measures of coping processes obtained when respondents focus on a specific life stressor or strain and those obtained from life history interviews or experimenter derived situations, which attempt to tap a typical process or hierarchy of coping preferences that characterizes an individual during at least one life transition or life stage.

Situation-specific Measures of Coping Processes

Most measures of coping processes contain items that focus on one type of stressful situation. In this section, we shall consider measures of coping with ongoing marital and occupational strains, family separations, a spouse's alcoholism, and acute physical health crises (see also Moos, 1981). The nine categories of appraisal and coping responses are used to provide some conceptual comparability among assessment procedures.

Onging Family and Work Strains.   How do individuals cope with the persistent life strains they encounter in their enduring family and work roles? Pearlin and Schooler (1978) focused on this question by identifying several constellations of coping responses individuals use to handle marital, parental, financial, and occupational strains. Some of the strategies were identified in only one or two role areas, but all appear to be relevant to each type of strain. In Table 14–1 we classify these strategies as follows: *making positive comparisons*

TABLE 14-1
Selected Examples of Dimensions of Coping Processes

	Family and Work Strains	Family Separations	Alcoholism	Cancer	Haan's Tripartite Model
Appraisal-focused Coping					
Logical analysis	Make positive comparisons				Objectivity Intellectuality Logical analysis Concentration Ego regression
Cognitive redefinition				Accept but redefine	
Cognitive avoidance	Selective ignoring		Cognitive avoidance	Try to forget Think about other things Project blame	Denial-repression Projection Isolation
Problem-focused Coping					
Seek information or advice	Seek help or advice	Seek information	Seek help	Seek information Seek advice Talk with others	
Take problem-solving action	Negotiate in marriage Parental discipline Direct action	Maintain family integrity Establish independence Live up to role expectations	Active confrontation Safeguard family interests Establish independence	Take firm action Negotiate alternatives	
Develop alternative rewards	Substitution of rewards	Build new interpersonal relationships Strengthen religious involvement			
Emotion-focused Coping					
Affective regulation	Controlled reflectiveness				Sublimation Suppression Tolerance of ambiguity
Resigned acceptance	Passive forbearance Helpless resignation		Behavioral withdrawal	Withdraw socially Accept the inevitable	Regression Doubt
Emotional discharge		Reduce tension	Acting out	Reduce tension Act out	Displacement

220

(appreciating one's own marriage after seeing what other marriages are like) and *selective ignoring* are examples of controlling the meaning of a stressful situation by cognitive redefinition; problem-focused coping includes *seeking help or advice, negotiation in marriage,* relying on *discipline* to cope with *parental strain,* taking *direct action* to handle occupational problems, and *substitution of rewards* (adapting to problems on the job as long as the pay is good); *controlled reflectiveness, passive forbearance,* and *helpless resignation* are forms of emotion-focused coping.

In general, Pearlin and Schooler (1978) found that the use of coping responses reduced the effect of role strains in the marriage, parental, and financial areas, though not in the occupational area. Self-reliance (not seeking help) and controlled reflectiveness were most efficacious in coping with marital strains, while self-reliance and making positive comparisons were most useful in coping with parental strains. Cognitive redefinition (devaluation of money and selective ignoring) was most helpful in coping with financial strains. In comparing the stress buffering effects of personal resources and specific coping responses, Pearlin and Schooler found the former to be more important in regard to financial and job problems, in which persons often have little direct control. They also noted that a varied repertoire of coping responses was helpful in fending off distress, and that men and the more educated and affluent respondents tended to use the most effective modes of coping.

Coping with Family Separation.   McCubbin and his colleagues (McCubbin, 1979; Boss, McCubbin, & Lester, 1979) examined the coping strategies used by women to manage three types of family separation: short (one week), repeated separations caused by a husband's business travel; separations of longer duration (eight months) caused by a husband's deployment aboard a navy carrier; and prolonged separations (average of six years) caused by a husband's being missing in action in Vietnam. They described the development and common dimensions of each of their measures; related coping repertoires to sociodemographic, attitudinal, and environmental factors; and conceptualized the use of coping patterns in relation to family role patterns and family stress.

Some of the coping styles identified by McCubbin and associates' (McCubbin, 1979; Boss, McCubbin, & Lester, 1979) measurement procedures were primarily problem focused (seek information, maintain family integrity, establish independence, live up to role expectations, build new interpersonal relationships, maintain and strengthen an involvement in religion), while one was primarily emotion focused (reducing tension by crying, smoking, or drinking alcohol). Most of the active behavioral responses involved in coping with family separations (such as establishing independence and autonomy) were not directed at changing the initial problem. We would classify such responses as problem oriented because they involve changing the self or the environment to meet the new demands engendered by the situation. This research also indicated the importance of distinguishing between a *coping resource* (e.g., a strong religious belief) and a *coping response* in a specific situation (e.g., strengthening religious involvement as a way of developing alternative rewards).

Adapting to a Spouse's Alcoholism.   Several recent studies examined the coping efforts of women married to men with a serious drinking problem (e.g., Wiseman, 1980). Attempts have been made to measure the relevant strategies by asking women to describe specific responses they have used to cope with a husband's alcohol abuse. Although analyses conducted on alternative versions of a questionnaire on coping with drinking have identified somewhat different factor structures (Orford, Guthrie, Nicholls, Oppenheimer, Egert, & Hensman, 1975), the factors can be grouped into five of our nine categories (see Table 14–1): cognitive avoidance, or trying not to think about the problem; active confrontation of the husband (pleading with him to stop drinking) or with the alcohol itself (destroying or hiding the liquor supply); safeguarding family interests (hiding money from the husband, paying the bills); establishing independence (finding a job); help seeking (asking an employer to intervene, contacting Al-Anon); behavioral withdrawal (avoiding the husband, keeping the children out of his way), and acting out or tension reduction (trying to make him feel jealous, trying to stop his drinking by getting drunk).

When wives of alcoholic men are asked about their use of such coping styles, the results show that almost all women tend to employ more than one style, that the severity of the husband's drinking problem is positively related to the number of different coping responses used, that behavioral withdrawal is the single most prevalent style, and that membership in Al-Anon is related to changes in preferred types of coping responses (from direct confrontation to establishing independence). There is some evidence that actively confronting the alcohol itself is positively related to the husband's treatment outcome, whereas emotional discharge strategies directed against the husband are related to poor treatment outcome (Gorman & Rooney, 1979; Orford et al., 1975).

Experiencing a Heart Attack. In an attempt to predict the course of recovery following myocardial infarction (MI), Hackett and Cassem (1974) constructed an interview based denial scale to explore an individual's response to having a heart attack. Although denial is a cognitive process, the authors developed items with specific behavioral or verbal referents. For instance, the items tap the delay in seeking medical care for symptoms, the extent to which the patient minimizes symptoms, the verbal denial of fear, the use of humorous clichés when speaking about death, and verbal complaints or criticisms about "unnecessary" restrictions in the coronary care unit (CCU). Hackett and Cassem suggested that denial (cognitive avoidance in our framework) is the most common ego defense used by MI patients while they are in the CCU and that it is positively related to the liklihood of survival in the immediate post-MI period. Other studies have shown that denying patients report less mood disturbance during the rehabilitation process and that blue-collar patients are more likely than white-collar patients to use denial in responding to a heart attack (Hackett & Cassem, 1976).

Living with Cancer. Interested in the unique problems cancer patients experience, Weisman (1979) described four psychosocial phases related to the stage, treatment, and progression of cancer: existential plight, accommodation and mitigation, recurrence and relapse, and deterioration and decline. Weisman and Worden (e.g., Weisman & Worden, 1976–77) developed an interview rating procedure to obtain information about the coping strategies used by cancer patients throughout the four stages. This procedure was used to identify appraisal-focused (accept the situation but redefine it by finding something favorable, try to forget, attempt to distract oneself), problem-focused (seek more information, confront the problem by taking firm action, negotiate feasible alternatives), and emotion-focused (withdraw socially, submit to the situation and accept the inevitable, reduce tension by drinking and overeating, engage in impulsive acting out) coping strategies (see Table 14–1).

In studying the existential phase, Weisman and Worden found that less disturbed patients were likely to confront the problem by taking firm action, accept but redefine the situation, and seek medical direction and comply with treatment. More disturbed patients tended to use withdrawal and disengagement from others, externalization or projection of blame (cognitive avoidance), tension reduction through excessive use of alcohol or drugs, and passive acceptance or submission. Seeking information, talking with others, and thinking about other things (distraction) had equivocal relationships with problem resolution and emotional functioning. Weisman and Worden explained the findings by noting that these strategies can be used either for coping (that is, directed toward the problem) or for defense (that is, directed toward emotional concomitants of the problem). For instance, information seeking may be employed either to assist in decisionmaking and problem resolution or to continue to question the facts, to search interminably for treatment alternatives, and to postpone selecting an acceptable course of action.

Process Oriented Measures of Coping Strategies

Some investigators have assumed that individuals have relatively stable preferences for particular coping strategies to handle different life situations (Menninger, 1963; Vaillant, 1977). We shall consider two examples of relevant measures here.

Gleser and Ihilevich (1969) constructed the Defense Mechanism Inventory (DMI) to tap the relative intensity of usage of five groups of defenses. The DMI consists of 10 brief stories, 2 in each of five conflict areas (such as authority, independence, and competition), followed by questions about the respondent's actual behavior, fantasy behavior, thoughts, and feelings in the situations described. Each question provides five responses typifying the defenses of projection, intellectualization, reversal (responding positively or neutrally to an object that would be expected to evoke a negative reaction), turning against object (hostility-out), and turning against self (hostility-in). We would classify the first three categories as primarily appraisal focused; turning against object, as mainly problem focused; and turning against self, as mainly emotion focused.

The DMI subscales are predictably related to standard personality scales such as the Minnesota Multiphasic Personality Inventory (MMPI) and the Sixteen Personality Factors Questionnaire (16PF.) Persons who turn their hostility inward are likely to be higher on anxiety, guilt, and feminine sexual identity, to show greater decreases in estimates of their own ability after a failure experience, and to fail to take appropriate precautions against unwanted pregnancies (Cramer & Carter, 1978; Gleser & Sacks, 1973; Kendall, Finch, & Montgomery, 1978; Rader, Bekker, Brown, & Richart, 1978). The defense mechanisms of intellectualization and reversal are associated with less anxiety, depression, and psychopathology among alcohol abusers. In addition, alcoholic patients who prefer reversal defenses have been shown to be more likely to complete a long-term treatment program and less likely to be rehospitalized after treatment (Rohsenow, Erickson, & O'Leary, 1978). There is some evidence that individuals who are more consistent across the 10 DMI situations show more predictable behavior in an experimental setting (Gleser & Sacks, 1973).

Haan (1977) formulated a more general taxonomy of 10 generic ego processes that may be expressed in three modes: coping, defense, or fragmentation. According to Haan, coping is the reality oriented, normative mode. *Coping* involves purpose, choice, flexibility, and adherence to consensual reality and logic; whereas *defensiveness* is compelled, negating, and rigid and distorts logic and reality. Defense is emotion focused in that it allows covert impulse expression and focuses on the relief of anxiety without directly addressing the problem. *Fragmentation* is automated, ritualistic, affectively directed, and irrational.

Haan's (1977) 10 ego processes are divided according to four functions. (1) Cognitive functions underlie the active, outward directed, instrumental aspects of problem-solving efforts and include the coping processes of objectivity, intellectuality, and logical analysis. (2) The attention focusing function of selective awareness includes the coping process of concentration. (We group these four processes under *logical analysis* (in Table 14-1.) (3) The affective impulse regulation functions use such coping processes as sublimation and suppression to attempt to accommodate feelings and emotions that are not expressed directly. (4) The reflexive-intraceptive functions reflect the person's engagement with her own thoughts, feelings, and intuitions and include the coping processes of tolerance of ambiguity (which we would classify as affective regulation) and regression in the service of the ego (we would classify this as logical analysis). Each of the coping processes has a defensive counterpart. We would categorize these ego defenses as appraisal- and emotion-focused response (see Table 14-1 for examples).

Three data collection procedures have been used with this model of ego processes: normative ratings, Q-sorts, and empirically derived questionnaires. In the rating procedure, judges use five-point scales to rate an individual's use of each ego process and then develop an ego map of the person. The Q-sort technique includes items representing various facets of each of the coping and defensive processes (fragmentations are not included because of their infrequency). The ego process scales, composed of items drawn from the California Psychological Inventory (CPI) and the MMPI, assume that the way individuals use their ego processes in responding to a test taking situation is representative of the way that they use them in other situations. Findings on the reliability and internal validity of these measures are encouraging, although there is some evidence that the rating and questionnaire procedures may tap different sets of ego processes or at least different aspects of such processes (Haan, 1977).

It is difficult to summarize the results of the more than 40 studies that have been conducted using Haan's (1977) perspective. In general, coping processes are positively associated with intellectual functioning and development, adult socioeconomic status and social mobility, intellectual and affective enjoyment of test situations, perceived internal control, and moral development. Coping processes also tend to be negatively related to obesity, problem drinking, and acute adverse drug reactions. The direction of these relationships is typically reversed for defensive processes.

In research focused on how alterations in family living situations affect ego processes, Haan (1977) found that women who had experienced family changes during adolescence were more empathetic as adults. Men who had experienced changes in the early adult years were more tolerant of ambiguity and showed more isolation and empathy during middle age. Haan concluded that effective coping is facilitated by accommodation and instrumental attacks at the problem, as well as by periods of assimilation, which are fostered by such ego processes as tolerance of ambiguity and regression in the service of the ego. Furthermore, there is evidence that the development of these two ego processes in adulthood is enhanced by family conflict during adolescence and that moral development in the preadult period is fostered by ego processes that permit stress to be experienced and resolved rather than simply negated. These findings illustrate the potential growth enhancing effect of encountering stressful life events. Although there are some problems in measurement, Haan's tripartite model is a well-developed conceptualization of ego processes that differentiate among individuals and may act as "resistance resources" in stressful circumstances.

CONCEPTUAL AND METHODOLOGICAL ISSUES

We have identified some common domains of coping resources and processes and suggested a framework to stimulate future research. We now shall use the foregoing material to focus on three issues: identifying domains of coping processes, evaluating the cross-situational consistency of coping, and specifying the connection between coping processes and adaptational outcomes. Other issues involved in the assessment of coping and its effectiveness are discussed elsewhere (Cohen & Lazarus, 1979; Moos, 1974).

Identifying Domains of Coping Processes

Efforts to subdivide coping responses into smaller classes, or domains, are at an early stage. We have described nine types of appraisal and coping responses based on a rational categorization of current measures into three underlying domains. Although this classification system is preliminary, it encompasses the major types of responses identified by existing measurement devices and can be used as a guide in constructing new procedures.

The way in which stressors are cognitively appraised is a central factor in the selection and utilization of coping responses. Cognitive appraisal and the generation of problem-focused and emotion-focused coping responses are closely allied processes, both of which are influenced by personal and environmental resources. Subsequent (or perhaps simultaneously) to the use of other coping responses, the residual level of threat or challenge and the remaining task components are reevaluated, thus either resolving the situation or reinitiating the coping process.

With respect to the other two domains, problem-focused coping is defined here somewhat more broadly than usual by including responses that attempt to develop alternative sources of gratification when the focal problem (such as having a husband who is missing in action) cannot be addressed directly. Other theorists believe that many (if not all) types of coping responses can be directed either at the problem or at the emotion. For instance, Roskies and Lazarus (1981) noted that type A individuals may engage in problem-solving action in order to reduce their anxiety, while Weisman (1979) pointed out that information seeking can be used for either instrumental or palliative ends. The fact that the problem often *is* an emotion (such as loneliness after a recent separation) exemplifies the complexity of the issues involved in classification. A possible alternative to a classification system is a procedure to rate coping responses on a continuum of common dimensions (such as the degree to which they are problem or emotion focused).

In studies employing this logic, the appraisal of life conditions has been measured along many dimensions, among the most important of which are the stressor's relative desirability or undesirability, its magnitude or severity, and the extent to which the stressor is expected and the individual feels that he or she has some control over it and its consequences. Fontana and his colleagues (Fontana, Hughes, Marcus, & Dowds, 1979) found some overlap between the appraisal of events on the dimensions of desirability, adjustment, anticipation, and control. Undesirable events that required considerable adjustment tended to be those whose occurrence could not be anticipated; however, the dimension of controllability was relatively separate from the other three aspects of cognitive appraisal. These findings highlight the need for clarification of both the dimensions of appraisal and coping processes and their interrelations.

In pursuing this endeavor, researchers should recognize that psychometric procedures such as internal consistency and factor-analytic techniques may have only limited usefulness in evaluating the adequacy of measures of coping. These techniques assume positive inter-item co-variation on similar coping responses, even though the successful use of one response in a domain may effectively reduce stress and thus lessen the utilization of other responses in that domain. With respect to help seeking, for instance, eliciting a particular type of assistance from one member of a social network may satisfy a "coping need" and reduce or eliminate other "networking responses". We believe that a combination of conceptual and empirical approaches will eventually prove most fruitful in formulating conceptualizations of coping dimensions, much as has occurred in constructing measures of social environments (Moos, 1979).

Evaluating the Cross-situational Consistency of Coping

Do persons who use logical analysis or seek information or advice in one problematic situation also use these coping responses in other situations? Although there is evidence of considerable long-term stability in preferred ego processes and cognitive styles (Haan, 1977; Witkin & Goodenough, 1977), the degree of cross-situational consistency in the use of specific domains of coping responses remains to be determined. Some investigators have tried to address this issue by assessing the same coping responses in different situations. For instance, Sidle, Moos, Adams, and Cady (1969) examined individual and situational consistency in coping strategies by obtaining information about the use of 10 coping responses in each of three problem-story situations. They found some individual consistency (respondents tended to use preferred coping responses irrespective of the problem situation), as well as some situational variability (the three stories elicited different coping responses). The finding that person-situation interactions accounted for as much of the variance in two of the DMI measures (turning against object and reversal) as did stable individual differences led Richert and Kettering (1978) to conclude that coping styles such as defensiveness should not necessarily be conceptualized as global traits.

Folkman and Lazarus (1980) developed an inventory, Ways of Coping, composed of items that can be classified into problem-focused and emotion-focused categories. One hundred respondents were interviewed several times over a nine-month period and asked to respond to the inventory in terms of how they had coped with intervening life stressors. Both problem-focused and emotion-focused responses were used in nearly every coping episode. There was some stability in the use of specific coping responses for a person across episodes, but in general individuals were characterized more by variability than by stability in coping patterns. With respect to the context of the event, work situations were associated with more problem-focused coping and health situations with more emotion-focused coping.

In examining the consistency of individual appraisal across stressors, Dohrenwend and Martin (1979) found only minor variability in the degree to which different individuals anticipated and felt they controlled life events. Their conclusion that appraisal is more situationally than personally determined (at least it was among their normal community respondents) has been further supported by evidence that appraised desirability is influenced primarily by the situation; that is, most persons agree on which events are positive and which are negative (Fontana et al. 1979). In line with our conceptual framework, this body of research suggests that persons are likely to vary across situations in their appraisal and coping processes and that both personal and environmental factors need to be considered in examining the selection and use of specific coping responses.

Coping Processes and Adaptational Outcomes

Although the connections between coping responses and individual functioning are complex, there is growing evidence that the use of such strategies as logical analysis, cognitive redefinition, information seeking, problem-solving action, and affective regulation is positively related to some indexes of adaptation (Haan, 1977; Vaillant, 1977; Weisman, 1979). As noted previously, Pearlin and Schooler (1978) found that self-reliance, controlled reflectiveness, and selective ignoring reduced the statistical effect of life strains on distress and that a varied repertoire of coping responses was more effective then reliance on a single response.

Billings and Moos (1981) constructed measures of active cognitive coping (logical analysis and cognitive redefinition), active behavioral coping (information seeking and taking positive action), and avoidance or tension reduction coping (cognitive avoidance, resigned acceptance, and emotional discharge). In exploring the nature of the coping process among a representative group of adult community members, we found some evidence that these coping responses moderated the relationship between stressful events and indexes of negative mood and physical symptoms. Specifically, persons who were more likely to use active cognitive strategies and less likely to use avoidance strategies showed better adaptational outcomes.

Some recent studies have examined the connections between the appraisal of life events and indexes of functioning. McFarlane and his colleagues (McFarlane, Norman, Streiner, Roy, & Scott, 1980) found that undesirable events over which the respondent had control were not related to strain, whereas events perceived as uncontrollable had an adverse effect on functioning irrespective of whether or not they were anticipated. Persons who perceived an event as controllable should be able to mobilize more effective problem-focused coping responses and consequently may experience less emotional arousal and distress. Folkman and Lazarus (1980) in fact noted that individuals were more likely to employ defensive or emotion-focused coping in response to stressors that they appraised as having little potential for amelioration (uncontrollable).

We believe that the relationship between coping processes and functioning will vary in relation to a number of factors: the temporal stage of the coping episode, the intensity and flexibility of specific types of responses, the nature of the stressor and the outcome criterion, and the personal and environmental context of coping. For instance, initially responding to a physical sign or symptom (a breast lump or severe chest pain) by cognitive avoidance may neutralize anxiety but can delay medical attention and result in a less favorable eventual outcome. Although the presence of social resources (such as a concerned spouse) can effectively counter the avoidance process and lead to earlier medical care, it may also encourage reality oriented information seeking that shatters hope by resolving ambiguity. Furthermore, behavioral withdrawal can be an effective way to cope with the overarousal that may occur when interacting with an involved but critical family member (Vaughn & Leff, 1976), while giving up in response to one stressor may enable an individual to conserve energy and handle another stressor more successfully.

Future research needs to address certain high-priority problems in addition to developing better conceptual formulations and more refined measures of appraisal and coping. One issue involves the long-term adaptive consequences of experiencing and coping successfully with earlier stressors and the identification of the personal and environmental resources that facilitate such successful experiences. In this connection, Ruch and her colleagues (Ruch, Chandler, & Harter 1980) found that women who had experienced more stressful events in the preceding year were better able to cope with the emotional aftermath of rape. Personal resources such as internal control may also enable individuals to remain healthy in the face of high levels of life stress and to reappraise potentially disabling traumatic events as opportunities for personal growth. Coping resources and processes can affect the degree to which events are anticipated and thus avoided or overcome. For instance, we found some stability in the rate at which persons encountered stressful events; individuals who used problem-focused coping responses tended to experience fewer life stressors (Billings & Moos, 1982).

A second issue concerns the biopsychological mechanisms by which coping resources affect functioning criteria. In focusing on this area with respect to physical illness, Cohen and Lazarus (1979) pointed out that coping responses may affect physiological reactivity and thereby influence bodily resistance to illness. Coping styles may also involve habits that are directly injurious to health, such as excessive smoking or drinking in response to the death of a significant other or maintaining a high level of physical activity after experiencing a myocardial infarction. On the other hand, persons with high self-esteem and an internal control orientation may be attuned to small bodily changes and seek medical help without undue delay, while those who are field dependent may use their personal skills to establish closer relationships with health care staff and thereby obtain better treatment.

We believe that the conceptual framework presented in this chapter can contribute to a more systematic understanding of the conditions under which these and other mechanisms influence the coping-adaptation system, as well as foster the development of more effective clinical interventions. Even though coping processes insure behavioral variability by constructing unique resolutions to problematic situations, such understanding may further the search for predictable relationships between coping responses and adaptational outcomes.

REFERENCES

BANDURA, A. Self-efficacy: Toward a unifying theory of behavioral change. *Psychological Review,* 1977, *84,* 191–215.

BILLINGS, A. G., & MOOS, R. H. Stressful life events and symptoms: A longitudinal model. *Health Psychology,* 1982, *1,* 99–117.

————. The role of coping responses in attenuating the impact of stressful life events. *Journal of Behavioral Medicine,* 1981, *4,* 139–157.

BOSS, P. G., MCCUBBIN, H. I., & LESTER, G. The corporate executive wife's coping patterns in response to routine husband-father absence. *Family Process,* 1979, *18,* 79–86.

CHABOT, J. A. Repression-sensitization: A critique of some neglected variables in the literature. *Psychological Bulletin,* 1973, *80,* 122–129.

CHANEY, E., O'LEARY, M., & MARLATT, G. A. Skill training with alcoholics. *Journal of Consulting and Clinical Psychology,* 1978, *46,* 1092–1104.

COHEN, F., & LAZARUS, R. S. Coping with the stresses of illness. In G. C. Stone, F. Cohen, & N. E. Adler (eds.), *Health psychology.* San Francisco: Jossey-Bass, 1979.

CRAMER, P., & CARTER, T. The relationship between sexual identification and the use of defense mechanisms. *Journal of Personality Assessment,* 1978, *42,* 63–73.

DOHRENWEND, B. S., & MARTIN, J. Personal versus situational determination of anticipation and control of the occurrence of stressful life events. *American Journal of Community Psychology,* 1979, *7,* 453–468.

EDWARDS, D. W., & KELLY, J. G. Coping and adaptation: A longitudinal study. *American Journal of Community Psychology,* 1980, *8,* 203–215.

ERIKSON, E. H. *Childhood and society* (2d ed.). New York: Norton, 1963.

FOLKMAN, S., & LAZARUS, R. S. An analysis of coping in a middle-aged community sample. *Journal of Health and Social Behavior,* 1980, *21,* 219–239.

FONTANA, A., HUGHES, L., MARCUS, J., & DOWDS, B. Subjective evaluation of life events. *Journal of Consulting and Clinical Psychology,* 1979, *47,* 906–911.

GLESER, G. C., & IHILEVICH, D. An objective instrument for measuring defense mechanisms. *Journal of Consulting and Clinical Psychology,* 1969, *33,* 51–60.

GLESER, G. C., & SACKS, M. Ego defenses and reaction to stress: A validation study of the Defense Mechanisms Inventory. *Journal of Consulting and Clinical Psychology,* 1973, *40,* 181–187.

GORMAN, J. M., & ROONEY, J. F. The influence of Al-Anon on the coping behavior of wives of alcoholics. *Journal of Studies on Alcohol,* 1979, *40,* 1030–1038.

HAAN, N. *Coping and defending: Processes of self-environment organization.* New York: Academic, 1977.

HACKETT, T., & CASSEM, N. Development of a quantitative rating scale to assess denial. *Journal of Psychosomatic Research,* 1974, *18,* 93–100.

————. White collar and blue collar responses to heart attack. *Journal of Psychosomatic Research,* 1976, *20,* 85–95.

HAUSER, S. T. Loevinger's model and measure of ego development: A critical review. *Psychological Bulletin,* 1976, *83,* 928–955.

HOLT, R. Loevinger's measure of ego development: Reliability and national norms for male and female short forms. *Journal of Personality and Social Psychology,* 1980, *39,* 909–920.

INTAGLIATA, J. Increasing the interpersonal problem-solving skills of an alcoholic population. *Journal of Consulting and Clinical Psychology,* 1978, *46,* 489–498.

JOHNSON, J. H., & SARASON, I. G. Life stress, depression, and anxiety: Internal-external control as a moderator variable. *Journal of Psychosomatic Research,* 1978, *22,* 205–208.

KENDALL, P. C., FINCH, A. J., JR., & MONTGOMERY, L. E. Vicarious anxiety: A systematic evaluation of a vicarious threat to self-esteem. *Journal of Consulting and Clinical Psychology,* 1978, *46,* 997–1008.

KENDALL, P. C., & HOLLON, S. D. (eds.), *Assessment strategies for cognitive-behavioral interventions.* New York: Academic, 1980.

LAZARUS, R. S., & LAUNIER, R. Stress-related transactions between person and environment. In L. A. Pervin & M. Lewis (eds.), *Perspectives in interactional psychology.* New York: Plenum, 1978.

LEFCOURT, H. M. *Locus of control: Current trends in theory and research.* Hillsdale: Erlbaum, 1976.

LOEVINGER, J. *Ego development: Conceptions and theories.* San Francisco: Jossey-Bass, 1976.

————. Construct validity of the Sentence Completion Test of Ego Development. *Applied Psychological Measurement,* 1979, *3,* 281–311.

MCCRAE, R. R., & COSTA, P. T. Openness to experience and ego level in Loevinger's Sentence Completion Test: Dispositional contributions to developmental models of personality. *Journal of Personality and Social Psychology,* 1980, *39,* 1179–1190.

MCCUBBIN, H. I. Integrating coping behavior in family stress theory. *Journal of Marriage and the Family,* 1979, *41,* 237–244.

MCFARLANE, A., NORMAN, G., STREINER, D., ROY, R., & SCOTT, D. A longitudinal study of the influence of the psychosocial environment of health status: A preliminary report. *Journal of Health and Social Behavior,* 1980, *21,* 124–133.

MENNINGER, K. *The vital balance.* New York: Viking, 1963.

MOOS, R. H. Psychological techniques in the assessment of adaptive behavior. In G. V. Coelho, D. A. Hamburg, & J. E. Adams (eds.), *Coping and adaptation.* New York: Basic Books, 1974.

————. Improving social settings by social climate measurement and feedback. In R. Munoz, L. Snowden, & J. Kelly (eds.), *Social and psychological research in community settings.* San Francisco: Jossey-Bass, 1979.

————. Coping with acute health crises. In T. Million, C. Green, & R. Meagher (eds.), *Handbook of clinical health psychology.* New York: Plenum, 1981.

————. (ed.), *Coping with physical illness.* New York: Plenum, 1977.

————. (ed.), *Human adaptation: Coping with life crises.* Lexington, Heath, 1976.

MOOS, R. H., & MITCHELL, R. E. Conceptualizing and measuring social network resources. In T. A. Wills (ed.), *Basic processes in helping relationships.* New York: Academic, 1982.

ORFORD, J., GUTHRIE, S., NICHOLLS, P., OPPENHEIMER, E., EGERT, S., & HENSMAN, C. Self-reported coping behavior of wives of alcoholics and its association with drinking outcome. *Journal of Studies on Alcohol,* 1975, *36,* 1254–1267.

PEARLIN, L. I., & SCHOOLER, C. The structure of coping. *Journal of Health and Social Behavior,* 1978, *19,* 2–21.

PLATT, J. J., & SPIVACK, G. *Manual for the Means-Ends Problem-Solving Procedure (MEPS): A measure of interpersonal cognitive problem-solving skill.* Philadelphia: Hahnemann Medical College and Hospital, Hahnemann Community Mental Health/Mental Retardation Center, 1975.

―――――. *Measures of interpersonal problem-solving for adults and adolescents.* Philadelphia: Hahnemann Medical College and Hospital, Hahnemann Community Mental Health/Mental Retardation Center, 1977.

RADER, G. E., BEKKER, L. D., BROWN, L., & RICHART, C. Psychological correlates of unwanted pregnancy. *Journal of Abnormal Psychology,* 1978, *87,* 373–376.

RICHERT, A. J., & KETTERING, R. Psychological defense as a moderator variable. *Psychological Reports,* 1978, *42,* 291–294.

ROHSENOW, D. J., ERICKSON, R. C., & O'LEARY, M. R. The Defense Mechanism Inventory and alcoholics. *International Journal of the Addictions,* 1978, *13,* 403–414.

ROSKIES, E., & LAZARUS, R. S. Coping theory and the teaching of coping skills. In P. Davidson (ed.), *Behavioral Medicine: Changing health life styles.* New York: Brunner/Mazel, 1981.

ROTTER, J. B. Generalized expectancies for internal versus external control of reinforcement. *Psychological Monographs* (whole no. 609), 1966, *80.*

RUCH, L. O., CHANDLER, S. M., & HARTER, R. A. Life change and rape impact. *Journal of Health and Social Behavior,* 1980, *21,* 248–260.

SIDLE, A., MOOS, R. H., ADAMS, J., & CADY, P. Development of a coping scale: A preliminary study. *Archives of General Psychiatry,* 1969, *20,* 226–232.

SPIVACK, G., PLATT, J. J., & SHURE, M. B. *The problem-solving approach to adjustment.* San Francisco: Jossey-Bass, 1976.

TYLER, F. B. Individual psychological competence: A personality configuration. *Educational and Psychological Measurement,* 1978, *38,* 309–323.

VAILLANT, G. E. *Adaptation to life.* Boston: Little, Brown, 1977.

VAUGHN, C., & LEFF, J. The influence of family and social factors on the course of psychiatric illness: A comparison of schizophrenic and depressed neurotic patients. *British Journal of Psychiatry,* 1976, *129,* 125–137.

WEISMAN, A. *Coping with cancer.* New York: McGraw-Hill, 1979.

WEISMAN, A., & WORDEN, J. The existential plight in cancer: Significance of the first 100 days. *International Journal of Psychiatry in Medicine,* 1976–77, *7,* 1–15.

WISEMAN, J. The "home treatment": The first steps in trying to cope with an alcoholic husband. *Family Relations,* 1980, *29,* 541–549.

WITKIN, H. A., & GOODENOUGH, D. R. Field dependence and interpersonal behavior. *Psychological Bulletin,* 1977, *84,* 661–689.

WITKIN, H. A., MOORE, C. A., GOODENOUGH, D. R., & COX, P. W. Field-dependent and field-independent cognitive styles and their educational implications. *Review of Educational Research,* 1977, *47,* 1–64.

WITKIN, H. A., OLTMAN, P. K., RASKIN, E., & CARP, S. A. *A Manual for the Embedded Figures Test.* Palo Alto, Ca: Consulting Psychologists, 1971.

WYLIE, R. C. (ed.). *The self-concept: Theory and research on selected topics,* vol. 2. Lincoln: University of Nebraska Press, 1979.

15

Situational Determinants of Stress: An Interactional Perspective

David Magnusson

A DISCUSSION OF THE ROLE OF SITUATIONAL EFFECTS in the area of stress presupposes a conceptualization of situation. Since the concept of situation is subsumed in the more general concept of environment, it is necessary first to clarify the meaning and use of the term "environment" in the social sciences. The environment can be viewed and analyzed in two ways: as it actually is before it has been interpreted by an individual, here designated the *actual environment,* and as it is perceived, interpreted, and cognitively represented in the minds of individuals, here designated the *perceived environment.* In the first approach, the environment is described and analyzed in terms of its physical and sociocultural properties. In the second approach, it is described and analyzed in terms of individuals' perceptions, cognitions, emotions, reactions, and actions.

THE ACTUAL ENVIRONMENT APPROACH

The actual environment approach has a long history in social science. Geographers, architects, cultural anthropologists, economists, and others have explained individual behavior in terms of an environment that is objectively describable by its physical and sociocultural properties. The environment can be conceptualized in terms of ecological structure (spatial, geographical, architectural, and organizational dimensions) and assessed independently of the interpretations made by individuals acting in the environment.

The actual environment approach has been particularly dominant in the stimulus-response (S-R) tradition of experimental psychology, strongly influenced by psychophysics and classical behaviorism. This tradition of psychological research has directed attention to studying behavior in relation to objectively defined physical and social stimuli. It is assumed that the individual reacts to quantitative variations in stimuli that are presented by the experimenter but lacks the freedom to reconstruct the situation as defined by the experimenter. Watson (1924) defined a situation as being "resolvable into a complex group of stimuli" (p. 20). This view of the environment has changed in many respects since the 1920s, but the conceptualization and description of the environment in physical and social terms have been

Comments from Vernon Allen, Irwin Sarason, and Bertil Törestad are highly appreciated.

advocated by researchers in different fields (see, e.g., Barker, 1965; Chein, 1954; Krause, 1970; Sells, 1963; Sherif & Sherif, 1956). In the rapidly growing field of environmental psychology (see, e.g., Proshansky, Ittelson, & Rivlin, 1970), much interest is devoted to the physical properties of the environment and its effect on individuals' well-being. The implications and limitations of this approach have been discussed by Orne (1962) and Rosenthal (1966) (see also Harré & Secord, 1972; Lazarus & Launier, 1978).

Early stress related research began with the actual environment approach. Research on fear is a good example. The fear survey schedules that have been presented in a number of versions primarily measure individuals' reactions to objectively defined objects of fear (Braun & Reynolds, 1969; Geer, 1965; Lang & Lazovick, 1963; Scherer & Nakamura, 1968; Wilson, 1968; Wolpe & Lang, 1964). In the early stages of research on the effects of crowding, the concept was defined and measured in objective, physical terms (Stokols, 1972). The research on life events (death of a close friend, divorce, personal illness, change in residence, etc.) as important stress factors in individuals' lives has related stress symptoms to quantitative measures of life events, most often in terms of frequency of such events. Research on the relation between the frequency of stressful events per se and the strength of stress symptoms has implicitly assumed that life events have a general and nonspecific impact on somatic and psychic illness (e.g., Holmes & Rahe, 1967; Lundberg & Theorell, 1976; Theorell & Rahe, 1971, 1975). The effect on behavior of objectively described aspects of stressful situations has been discussed, among others, by Holmes and Rahe (1967), Kagan and Levi (1974), Lazarus (1966), Levi and Andersson (1975), Levine and Scotch (1970), McGrath (1970), Mechanic (1975), and Paykel, Dienelt, Klerman, Lindenthal, Myers, and Pepper (1969).

THE PERCEIVED ENVIRONMENT APPROACH

The importance of considering the meaning of the environment, i.e., how it is perceived, interpreted, and cognitively represented in the minds of individuals, has been emphasized for decades not only by psychologists advocating different theoretical approaches (see, e.g., Angyal, 1941; Bowers, 1973; Endler, 1975; Jessor, 1956; Kelly, 1955; Koffka, 1935; Lewin, 1935; Magnusson, 1971, 1978; Rogers, 1959; Rotter, 1954; Schneider, 1973; Stagner, 1976) but also by sociologists and anthropologists (e.g., Berger & Luckman, 1967; Goffman, 1964; Mead, 1934; Thomas, 1927, 1928). Obviously, the "real world" in which we experience, feel, think, and act is the world as we perceive it and to which we give meaning. Or, as formulated by Thomas (1928) in what Merton (1957) called the Thomas theorem: "If men define situations as real, they are real in their consequences."

The perceived environment approach has important consequences for personality theories that attempt to explain social behavior. This approach has been particularly important in interactional personality theory (a perspective discussed later). And this view has greatly influenced research on stress and anxiety. It has changed the focus from an interest in how external stimulation per se provokes emotional, physiological, and behavioral anxiety reactions to an interest in how stress and anxiety reactions are elicited by expectations about the consequences of stressful conditions (Magnusson & Stattin, 1981a). Lazarus (1966, 1976) emphasized in his research the cognitive appraisal of a stressful situation as the important factor underlying stress and anxiety reactions. In Endler's (1975) model of anxiety, the perception of situational interpersonal threat, physical danger threat, or inanimate threat determines the extent to which individuals experience state anxiety in a given situation. In research on crowding, the effects of perceived density of people rather than density per se has become a central issue. Research on life events and their stressful effects has been strongly affected by theories dealing with the moderating effects of perceived social support, perceived predictive and behavioral control, etc. (Sarason & Sarason, 1981).

For theory and research on stress, the essential aspect of this change of focus from the actual to the perceived environment is the growing awareness that it is the perceived qualities of stressful environmental conditions that are the important determinants of stress.

The rapidly growing interest in the perceived environment is only natural, given the nature of the phenomena that are important in psychology. Of course, this does not mean that the actual environment should be neglected. Analyses of actual environments are of interest in themselves. For effective theories and models for behavior in relation to the environment in general (and in relation to stressful situations), we obviously need both the actual and the perceived environment approach (e.g., Lantermann, 1978; Pugh, 1977). Two of the most important issues in psychology are the way an individual's conceptions of the external world are formed on the basis of information about the environment "as it is" (obtained in a continuous interplay with the environment) and the way these conceptions function in relation to the actual, objective conditions at a specific time and place.

THE SITUATION

The environment can be conceptualized and analyzed along a dimension from the microlevel to the macrolevel. Both for theorizing and for empirical research on environmental influences on human behavior we need to identify appropriate units of analysis along the micro-macro continuum. The concept of situation, as a part of the total environment, has been used in personality theories and in research on stress and anxiety in a wide variety of senses. Definitions have ranged from single stimuli that affect behavior at a certain occasion to lifelong influences. The vagueness of the concept of situations requires a more precise definition of its use here.

Two distinct definitions of the term "situation" can be offered: the *actual situation*, or that part of the environment that is accessible in relatively stable fashion to sensory perception, and the *perceived situation*, or the perception, interpretation, and cognitive representation of an actual situation. These definitions exclude more general stressful aspects of the environment, which are sometimes discussed under the heading of life events or life situations (see, e.g., Magnusson & Stattin, 1981a; Sarason & Sarason, 1980).

In a discussion of situational determinants of stress, there are two main reasons for directing interest to situations as defined here. One reason is *developmental:* it is in actual situations that we encounter the world, form our conceptions about it, and develop specific kinds of behaviors for coping. In that process, situations present the information that we deal with and provide the necessary feedback for constructing valid conceptions of the outer world; these conceptions, in turn, form the basis for valid predictions about what will happen (including the outcomes of our actions). The other reason for being interested in situations is *environmental:* behavior takes places in actual situations. Behavior does not exist except in relation to certain situational conditions, and it cannot be understood and explained in isolation from them. Stress and anxiety reactions are elicited by actual situational conditions both directly and indirectly (i.e., as they are perceived and interpreted). Thus, the situation must play a decisive role in any adequate model of behavior, including models of stress and anxiety.

STRESS AND STRESSORS:
AN INTERACTIONAL PERSPECTIVE

It should be noted that *stress* is a concept that is bound to persons. In its most general form, stress is defined as an individual's psychic and somatic reactions to demands that approach or exceed the limits of his coping resources. For discussions of the concept of stress, see Appley and Trumball (1967), Glass (1977), Lazarus (1976), and Sarason and Sarason (1980).

The physical and psychosocial elements of a situation that impose demands on individuals and that lead to stress reactions are usually discussed in terms of *stressors*. Any aspect of an actual situation can serve as a stressor. Some physical stressors, such as cold, heat, viruses, and pollution, impose demands on the individual's resources directly, without any intervening cognitive appraisal. Other physical and psychosocial conditions become stressors via cognitive appraisal and interpretation of threat.

These formulations imply, among other things, that what becomes a stressor is not determined solely by the nature of the situation or by the individual and his dispositions. A stress reaction in an individual is the joint effect of his psychic and somatic dispositions *and* the stress provoking quality of situational conditions, the stressors, as illustrated in Figure 15-1. This figure of course, is drawn arbitrarily to demonstrate the general principle. The relation is assumed to be, at least partly, specific for individuals, variables, and types of stressor. Some situations—for example, extreme cold or extreme heat but also certain psychological situations—are so stress provoking that all or most individuals will show stress

FIGURE 15-1. Stress reactions as a product of the vulnerability of the individual and the stress provocation of the situation.

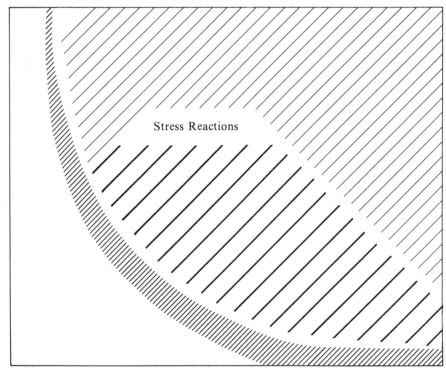

Vulnerability

Stress Reactions

Stress Provocation

reactions. On the person side, the occurrence of stress is determined by the individual's *vulnerability,* defined in terms of physiological predispositions, perceptual-cognitive appraisals, and coping competence. (Zubin and Spring [1977] introduced the concept of vulnerability to explain individual differences in reactions to schizophrenic episodes.) An individual's current vulnerability is the result of a process of maturation and learning within the limits of inherited potentialities. Vulnerability may be specific, i.e., restricted to certain kinds of stressful conditions (e.g., phobic situations), or general, i.e., referring to most environmental stressors.

In the continuous person-situation interaction process, an important aspect of an individual's proneness to react with stress is the functioning of his perceptual-cognitive system in selecting and appraising environmental information (the role of cognitive appraisal in the situational determination of stress reactions is addressed in a later section).

For purposes of subsequent discussion it should be noted that *stress* and *anxiety* are not synonymous. Anxiety always entails stress, but the reverse does not necessarily hold. Cold, heat, and illness may lead to stress but not necessarily to anxiety. Which stressors lead to stress depends upon the individual's appraisal of them as threatening in some sense. Though it may seem reasonable to separate the physiological (Selye, 1976) and the psychological aspects of stress, they are, in fact, strongly related. Mason (1975) even asserted that psychological process, in the form of attribution of expected harm to a situation, precedes most physiological stress reactions.

TWO BEHAVIORAL MODELS—
TWO TYPES OF SITUATIONAL EFFECT

Basic to the discussion of situational determinants of individual behavior (and fundamental for the purpose of this chapter) is the distinction between *general* and *differential* situational effects on behavior.

In conceptualizing the relation between situational conditions and emotional, physiological, and behavioral reactions, two main models can be distinguished (see Figure 15-2). They are connected with two models of behavior that have been designated the

FIGURE 15-2. Cross-situational profiles of individuals A, B, and C for a certain behavior, according to a traditional measurement model (left) and an interactional model (right).

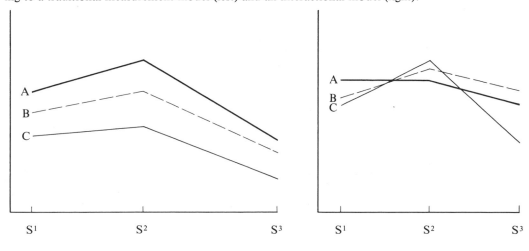

relative consistency model and the *coherence model* (Magnusson, 1976). The relative consistency model is closely bound to a *trait measurement model,* which guided most empirical research in the field of personality for decades and is still influential, especially by its effect on the methods used for collecting and treating data that are closely bound to the model. The second approach, an *interactional model* of behavior, gained acceptance over the seventies following a long period of theoretical discussion. The two models differ with respect to the situational effects that are considered: the relative consistency model assumes and considers only general situational effects, but the coherence model assumes both general *and* differential effects.

In the relative consistency model, the rank-order of individuals for a certain reaction is the same across situations, independent of the nature of the situations (see Figure 15-2). If only general situational effects exist, the true variance of a person by situation matrix of data for a certain reaction can be explained totally by main effects for person and situation factors, without interaction. According to this model, individuals differ in terms of their emotional, physiological, and behavioral reactions to stressful situations only with respect to the level of cross-situational profiles. Means of reactions across situations are sufficient to account for differences among individuals.

An implication of the assumption about differential situational effects in the coherence model of behavior is that the rank-order of individuals for a certain behavior will vary across situations (Figure 15-2). In terms of data, individuals differ not only on the level of their cross-situational profiles for a certain kind of behavior but also on the pattern of the profiles. The existence of differential situational effects is revealed in the interaction variance of a person by situation data matrix. True interaction variance then reflects the existence of partially unique individual profiles across situations for the behavior under consideration. That such partially unique profiles contribute to the total person by situation matrix has been shown in a number of studies, including ones concerned with reactions to stressful situations (for summaries, see Bowers, 1973; Endler & Magnusson, 1976; Magnusson, 1976; Sarason, Smith, & Diener, 1975). That such profiles show stability over time has been empirically demonstrated (Magnusson & Stattin, 1981b). Thus, according to an interactional coherence model, individuals differ behaviorally with respect to two main paramenters: the mean level of intensity of reactions across situations *and* partially unique cross-situational profiles.

COGNITIVE APPRAISAL

I noted earlier that most physical and psychosocial stressors do not elicit stress reactions directly but rather by way of cognitive appraisal of demand and threat. Thus, a central and decisive role is given to the individual's cognitive system of conceptions and abstractions about the external world. This cognitive system determines (as far as there are alternatives) which situations to seek or avoid, which elements in a situation to attend to, the appraisal of these elements, and the strategies used to cope with demands and threats (cf. Averill, 1979; Lazarus, 1976; Lazarus & Launier, 1978).

An individual's system of cognitive abstractions and conceptions about the world (including self-conceptions) is formed by, and gradually changes in continuous interaction with, environments that are encountered. By assimilating new knowledge and new experiences into existing categories and by accommodating old categories and forming new ones, each individual develops an integrated system of mental structures and contents. Within the limits of inherited dispositions, affective tones become bound to the interpretation of environmental elements, and cognitive strategies develop for dealing with various kinds of environments and situations in an ongoing learning process. In this way, physical, biological, social, and cultural aspects of the environment that an individual encounters are of decisive importance for the development of his more permanent ways of conceptualizing and dealing with the actual world (Hebb, 1958; Lewis, 1978; Matheney & Doland, 1975; Runyan, 1978; Wohlwill & Kohn, 1976). During this process and particularly at early stages of development, generalizations and discriminations in the perception and appraisal of situations and events develop. The experience of threat in an achievement demanding situation, for example, may generalize to a wide range of similar situations, resulting in, say, avoidance behavior. According to the traditional stimulus-response theory of learning, behavior (including anxiety and stress reactions) is acquired by association with stimuli or the events that precede them in the learning situation, and these and similar stimuli will elicit the same behavior in subsequent settings. In contrast to this view, cognitive learning theorists argue that people learn two kinds of expectancies: *situation outcome contingencies* (i.e., that certain situational conditions are followed by certain outcomes) and *behavior outcome contingencies* (i.e., that certain behaviors lead to certain consequences). Expectations and anticipations play a central role in such theories of behavior, as well as in theories of anxiety (e.g., Bandura, 1977; Cattell, 1966; Epstein, 1967, 1972; Mandler & Watson, 1966; Rotter, 1954, 1955; Seligman, 1975). The basis of an individual's anxiety or stress reactions in psychosocial situations is, then, his anticipation of future harm. The anxiety and stress are not in the situation per se but in the appraised anticipation of harmful outcomes. Forming situation outcome and behavior outcome contingencies has adaptive value for the person in that it enables him to control and influence the environment to some extent. The information provided by the situation forms the basis for his predictions about the outcomes of alternative behaviors and makes it possible for him to prepare himself and to act appropriately (at least within his own framework of action).

Thus, in the process of learning and maturation, individuals develop total cognitive systems that are partly unique with respect to the affective tones bound to specific situations and with respect to the expectations, coping skills, and strategies they use for dealing with situational and stored information. An individual's interpretation of a certain situation has a history, as well as a current frame of reference, and is influenced by plans and expectations. Among other things this implies that individuals differ to some extent with respect to how they select, perceive, interpret and use information from a certain situation, and, therefore, act in the situation and react to it emotionally and physiologically. Averill (1979) emphasized the importance for psychological stress of the individual's appraisal of potential harm in the stressor and pointed to individual differences in this respect: "To become a source of threat, an event must be appraised as potentially harmful . . . what may be appraised as harmful by one person may be appraised as benign by another, or by the same individual at some later time" (p. 367). Selye's (1976) conclusion that "once again we meet the basic principle that what matters is not really what happens to you but the way you take it" (p. 394) is an endorsement of the importance of individuals' partly unique appraisals of surrounding stressful circumstances. In this way, differences in people's cognitive systems of abstractions and conceptions about the environment account for individual differences in cross-situational profiles for stress reactions, which were discussed earlier in connection with an interactional model of behavior.

EMPIRICAL ILLUSTRATIONS

In order to demonstrate the systematic and lawful nature of the relation between situational conditions and an individual's perceptions of and reactions to stressful situations, I shall discuss five empirical studies performed at the University of Stockholm. Although these studies were directed to the more general area of anxiety and stress, the results are equally valid as a basis for drawing conclusions about situational determinants of stress.

Individual Differences in Reactions to Stressful Situations

As described previously, in an interactional model of behavior individuals are characterized, on the data level, by partly unique cross-situational profiles of stable and changing behaviors. Individuals differ not only with respect to levels but also with respect to patterns of such profiles. This implies an approach to understanding and explaining individual reactions and actions more in terms of the total patterns of cross-situational profiles for a relevant set of variables than in terms of profiles across a number of basic personality factors, disregarding situational effects, as has been the main approach in traditional empirical personality research for decades.

The importance of considering both general and differential situational effects on individual reactions in the field of stress and anxiety—as they are reflected in partly unique cross-situational profiles—can be illustrated by results from a study reported by Magnusson and Ekehammar (1975).

Teenage boys and girls (15–17 years of age) answered an S-R inventory, employing 17 situations and 18 modes of response. For each situation the subject had to report the degree of experienced intensity of each mode of response. The inventory included three main types of situation: threat of punishment, anticipation fear, and inanimate threat. The 18 modes of response represented two types of anxiety reaction: somatic and psychic anxiety.

Two main types of analysis were made. First, individuals were classified, for each sex separately, into homogeneous groups on the basis of cross-situational profile similarity by *latent profile analysis* (LPA). Three groups of individuals were obtained for both girls and boys. Second, a five-way analysis of variance with partially nested sets, comprising the following factors, was performed: sex profiles (LPA) nested within sex, individuals nested within profiles and sex, responses, and situations. Figure 15-3 shows the results of the analysis of data for the girls, and in Table 15-1 results concerning transsituational response consistency are presented. For girls, profile I (59% of the girls) was characterized by low anxiety level, high transsituational consistency, and high response consistency; profile II (17%) was characterized by high anxiety level, comparatively high transsituational consistency, and low response consistency; and profile III (24%) was characterized by moderate anxiety level, low transsituational consistency, and low response consistency. Low response consistency means that the difference between psychic and somatic reactions was large. For boys, profile I (53%) was characterized by a low anxiety level, high transsituational consistency, and high response consistency; profile II (36%), by moderate anxiety level, comparatively high transsituational consistency, and low response consistency; and profile III (11%), by high anxiety level, low transsituational consistency, and moderate response consistency.

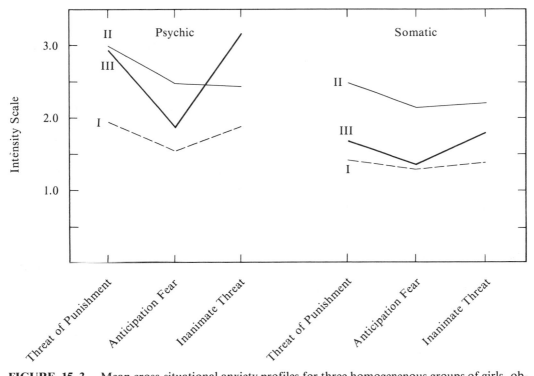

FIGURE 15–3. Mean cross-situational anxiety profiles for three homogenenous groups of girls, obtained by latent profile analysis *(from Magnusson & Ekehammar, 1975:36).*

The results support a conclusion that is basic for our purpose here: what is stressful to some individuals is not especially so for others. Person-situation interactions are important in the field of research on stress and anxiety and in application of the results of such research to the development of more effective prevention in the physical and social environment. Among other things, this implies that fruitful research on stress and anxiety cannot be done without considering the specific situational conditions under which individuals are observed.

TABLE 15–1
Profile Characteristics of Each Latent Profile Analysis (LPA) Group by Sex

Profile characteristic	Girls			Boys		
	Profile I	Profile II	Profile III	Profile I	Profile II	Profile III
Transsituational inconsistency *(MS_S)*	.05	.10	.44	.03	.05	.39
Response inconsistency *(MS_R)*	.27	.32	1.76	.13	.58	.33
Mean overall anxiety	1.56	2.50	2.12	1.29	1.68	2.01

Source: Magnusson & Ekehammar (1975:40).

Age Differences in the Perception of Stressful Situations

In a recent study, boys and girls aged 12–18 were asked to report the three most anxiety provoking situations that came to mind and to describe why each situation made them anxious. In the analysis of the youngsters' motives for anxiety, a rather obvious age difference appeared. The preadolescents often referred to the physical properties of situations, external bodily consequences, and possible external sanctions; by contrast, older teenagers referred to psychological consequences such as anticipated shame, guilt, separation, or lack of personal integrity. Whereas the younger subjects spoke about spatially and temporally close sanctions, older ones referred to anticipated consequences in the future (in professional life, in marriage, etc.). The preadolescent boys and girls even had difficulty conceptualizing the consequences for themselves. A preadolescent explanation in response to the described situation "I am afraid when I ski down a steep hill" was "Because the hill is so steep" and did not refer to the possibility of physical injury, a common explanation among older subjects.

Based on our observations and Piaget's (1951, 1952) theory of cognitive development, a study was performed to investigate age variations in perceptions and interpretations of anxiety provoking situations, from preadolescence to postadolescence (Stattin, 1980). The basic assumption was that preadolescents would see relations between situations in terms of manifest physical characteristics, while older subjects would conceptualize resemblances between situations more in terms of latent psychological, anticipated consequences.

Data were obtained for three age groups (11–12, 14–15, and 17–18). From a sample of nearly 1000 descriptions of anxiety provoking situations given by youngsters in the same age groups, 11 were selected for the present study. The hypothesis was tested by the use of similarity ratings. All possible combinations of the 11 situations were rated with respect to perceived similarity on a four-point scale.

Ratings of similarity between two situations were possible on two different grounds. According to the first principle, situations could be judged as similar with reference to a common central object or person that was clearly visible and salient in the situations. In this respect, situations could have one of the following four elements in common: classmate, brother, relative, or dog. These were designated *manifest characteristics*. According to the second principle, similarity could be judged on the basis of common anticipated consequences. Four types of consequences were used: physical injury, separation, guilt, and shame. These were designated *latent characteristics*. An example will illustrate the way this procedure works. Two situations were described as follows: "An angry dog nips at you when you are out walking" and "Your dog is sick and has to be taken to the veterinarian." According to the main hypothesis, these two situations will be judged similar by preadolescents because of the common element dog but different by postadolescents since the anticipated consequences are different (physical injury and separation). Mean ratings of similarity for situations *without* common manifest and latent characteristics were used in testing the significance of similarity ratings based on manifest and latent characteristics, respectively.

The overall result is presented in Figure 15-4. As the hypothesis suggested, for both boys and girls there was a gradual decrease with increasing age in similarity ratings based on manifest characteristics and a corresponding increase in similarity ratings based on latent characteristics. The study thus supported the assumption that the perception and interpretation of environmental threats change in nature from preadolescence to postadolescence.

This result is of interest in different perspectives (for a discussion see Stattin, 1980). One

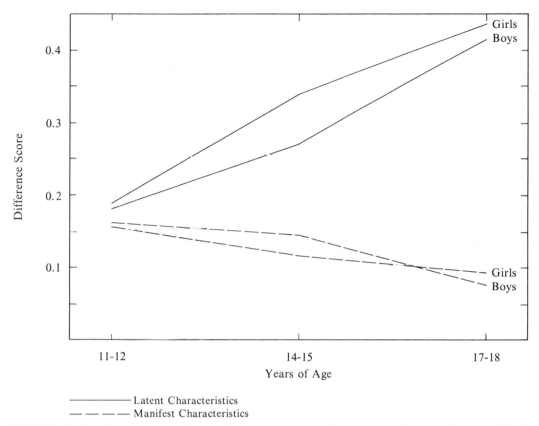

FIGURE 15-4. Development change in situation perception for boys and girls *(from Stattin, 1980:6).*

implication that is important for further theorizing and research on stress and anxiety can be emphasized. During the 1970s, the problem of personality consistency—both in a cross-situational and in a longitudinal perspective—was a central and controversial theme. The result presented here indicates a clear change in the perception and interpretation of anxiety provoking situations from preadolescence to postadolescence. To the extent that behavior is a function of how we perceive and construe the outer world as we encounter it in actual situations, the environmental conditions that determine cross-situational stability in actual behavior vary with age; i.e., what constitutes a stable environment as a prerequisite for behavioral consistency varies with age. For preadolescents a stable environment is characterized strongly by similarity in physical, external properties; postadolescents, on the other hand, interpret situations predominantly with respect to psychological, latent qualities. Age differences in the perception and interpretation of threatening, stressful situations can be assumed to imply age differences in coping with such situations. These speculations suggest a series of important and fruitful problems for systematic research on stress and anxiety with respect to age differences.

Sex Differences in Reactions to Stressful Situations

A review of the literature shows that the size and direction of sex differences in stress reactions observed in empirical research vary according to the type of variable that is under consideration (e.g., emotions, cognitive worries, or physiological reactions), the type of data used for analysis (e.g., self-reports or objective measures of physiological reactions), and the way situations are presented to subjects (e.g., whether responses refer to real-life situations or to hypothetical cases presented verbally or visually). A fourth important factor influencing the size and direction of sex differences, and one that is germane here, is the character of the situations in which behavior occurs.

The existence of important sex by stressful situation interactions has been demonstrated in empirical research. Bergman and Magnusson (1978), Frankenhaeuser (1980), and Lundberg (1980) studied sex differences in physiological reactions in stressful psychosocial situations. In a series of studies, Frankenhaeuser (1980) and her associates consistently found stronger adrenaline reactions in males than in females in situations involving stress, while such differences were not observed in neutral everyday situations. A result in the same direction was presented by Bergman and Magnusson (1978). They found no significant correlation between relative achievement as a rather stable person characteristic and adrenaline excretion in a neutral school situation, but a strong significant correlation for boys in a school situation involving demands for intellectual achievement.

In all these studies, males consistently showed higher adrenaline excretion than did females in stressful situations. However, it should be noted that all the situations demanded some sort of achievement. Of particular interest, then, is a recent study reported by Lundberg (1980) in which fathers' and mothers' physiological reactions to a situation involving a threat to their children were measured. In this case, the expected sex difference was not found; rather, a tendency in the reverse direction was observed.

Magnusson and Törestad (1980) undertook to investigate sex by situation interactions by systematically manipulating the character of the situation. They used data on anxiety reactions in 15-year-old boys and girls toward various anxiety provoking situations.

The situations were chosen to represent four categories of anxiety provoking situations found to form distinct categories in earlier empirical research. In addition, neutral situations were included. Thus, five a priori groupings of situations were used:

1. innocuous, nonprovocative situations
2. achievement demanding situations
3. physical threat situations
4. threat of punishment situations
5. inanimate situations

Data were obtained from 15-year-old boys and girls randomly drawn from a school within Sweden's undifferentiated, compulsory school system.

Figure 15–5 gives a summary of the results. The figure indicates mean reactions of boys and girls for the different types of situation; the situation categories are ordered on the basis of their anxiety provocation, expressed in total means of reactions. Figure 15–5 shows, first, a significant sex by situation interaction in anxiety reactions ($p < .01$); second, there was an increasing sex difference as the mean anxiety reaction increased. Figure 15–5 also reveals another interesting feature. For boys, mean reactions varied insignificantly and unsystematically across anxiety provoking situation types. For girls, in contrast, a one-way analysis of variance for the differences in mean reaction in the five types of situation gave a significant result ($p < .02$).

The exact form of the curve in Figure 15–1, representing intensity of anxiety reactions

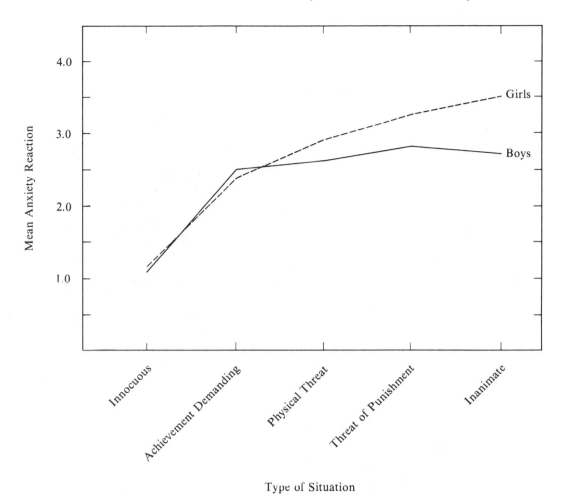

FIGURE 15-5. Sex differences in reactions to different types of anxiety provoking situations *(from Magnusson & Törestad, 1980:6).*

as a function of type of situation, should be viewed with caution: all inanimate situations do not provoke higher anxiety reactions than do all other situations and so on. The form of the curve will depend to some extent upon the sampling of situations that represent each category. It should also be emphasized that the form of the sex by situation interaction found in this study cannot be generalized to all types of stressful situation. As indicated by the results presented by Lundberg (1980), in some instances the sex difference is reversed. Further research on sex differences in reactions to stressful situations must study sex by situation interactions in a more varied set of stressful situations.

The main conclusion that can be drawn from the Magnusson and Törestad (1980) study is that meaningful investigations of sex differences in reactions to stressful situations cannot be accomplished without controlling the situational conditions under which observations are made. And for understanding and explaining observed sex differences, the properties of the situational conditions under which the observations are made are of crucial importance.

Sex and Age Differences in Activating Conditions and Expected Consequences in Stressful Situations

For systematic research on person-situation relations in the field of stress and anxiety the following questions are fundamental. Which situations are actually stressful? What is the population of stressful situations? What is the structure of that population? Are there age differences in these respects? Do the populations of stressful situations differ among situations for a given age group?

Researchers in the field of stress and anxiety have presented different lists of categories of stressful situations. For example, Spielberger (1972) restricted his theory of trait and state anxiety and the construction of STAI-S and STAI-T to ego threatening situations; Endler (1975), in his trait anxiety scale (GTA), distinguished three types of threatening situation (interpersonal, physical danger, and inanimate); and Schalling (1975) identified seven categories (criticism, anticipation, aggression, pain–medical, pain, thrill, and boredom). Common to these and other lists is that the categorizations are not based on data that meet the requirement of representative sampling of persons and situations. The categories may have been obtained by an empirical procedure, but the representativeness of the results is often unknown because of lack of adequate sampling of situations for a known representative group of individuals. The following procedure was used to meet the requirement of sampling anxiety provoking situations for studying sex and age differences (Magnusson & Stattin, 1981b). Boys and girls aged 12, 15, and 18 were asked to report the three most anxiety provoking situations that came to mind. For each situation they described *what* in the situation was connected with the experience of anxiety and *why* it was so. For categorizing the situations a classification scheme was worked out, based on an informal content analysis. The scheme consisted of two subparts, one classifying the situations in terms of *activating conditions* (the description of *what* is connected with the experience of anxiety, i.e., the stressor) and one classifying situations in terms of *expected consequences* (*why* a certain situational condition arouses anxiety). The categories of the two subschemes are presented in Tables 15–2 and 15–3. A study with teenagers in Hungary (Magnusson & Olah, 1981) and one with Swedish youngsters (Stattin & Magnusson, 1981) were conducted using this procedure.

Figure 15–6 shows the percentage of boys and girls at each age level in the Swedish study who reported the various categories of activating conditions as the most threatening (Stattin & Magnusson, 1981). Situations exceeding 10% at any age level were included. Figure 15–7 shows the corresponding age curves for expected consequences. The two subschemes can be used separately, as demonstrated in Figures 15–6 and 15–7; however, their combination permits a more subtle analysis of situation outcome contingencies for threatening experiences. The two subschemes can be matched in a contingency table with m rows (the number of categories for activating conditions) and n columns (the number of categories for expected consequences).

Stattin and Magnusson's (1981) results illustrate the need for adequate sampling of situations, among well-defined samples of individuals, in order to arrive at meaningful classifications of situations as a basis for studying the role of situational conditions. For example, in research on anxiety one of the important situation categories that has been frequently used is anticipation of pain. According to the present study, such situations are reported as especially threatening by a rather small number of individuals.

TABLE 15-2
Activating Conditions

Person
1. Self
2. Parents
3. Other closely related adults
4. Siblings
5. Authorities
6. Equals
7. "Dangerous" people
8. People in general
9. Achievement situations
10. Medical situations
11. Accidents
12. Common phobias
13. Animals
14. Archaic situations*
15. Supernatural-horror
16. Macrosocial

* Often referred to as inanimate situations.
Source: Magnusson & Stattin (1981b:70).

TABLE 15-3
Expected Consequences

Physical-Bodily
1. Physical pain
2. Physical injury
3. Uneasiness
4. Unrealistic
Personal-Interpersonal
5. Personal inadequacy
6. Loss of self-control
7. Death
8. Punishment
9. Guilt
10. Shame
11. Rejection
12. Separation
Global
13. Societal

Source: Magnusson & Stattin (1981b:77).

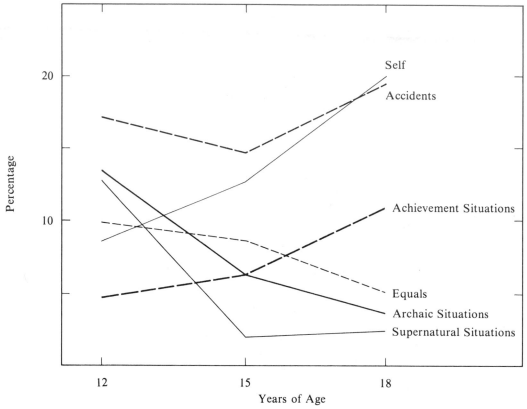

FIGURE 15-6. Activating situational conditions at different ages *(from Stattin & Magnusson, 1981:5).*

Cultural Differences in Reactions to Stressful Situations

To some extent, physical-geographical conditions and sociocultural patterns govern the conditions that will be perceived as particularly threatening for a population. Through common laws, norms, rules, and attitudes, cultural and social factors regulate individuals' perception and interpretation of the situational circumstances they encounter. Through its institutions, society also governs to a degree the kinds of factual situations that people encounter. In one sense, general physical-geographical and sociocultural factors homogenize peoples' experiences, making some situations more likely than others to be appraised as threatening. Although the environment at the macrolevel standardizes experiences to a certain extent, on lower levels it leaves considerable room for variation. Subcultural factors will make different groups of individuals sensitive to different threatening conditions. Therefore, one can assume that different situational conditions will be perceived as threatening by subjects from different geographical locations (for example, rural and urban districts), different ethnic groups, different socioeconomic levels, etc. Furthermore, at the microlevel there will be considerable individual variation in the perception and interpretation of the environment that reflects upbringing and unique experiences in the course of development.

In a crosscultural study of reactions to anxiety provoking situations, youngsters in

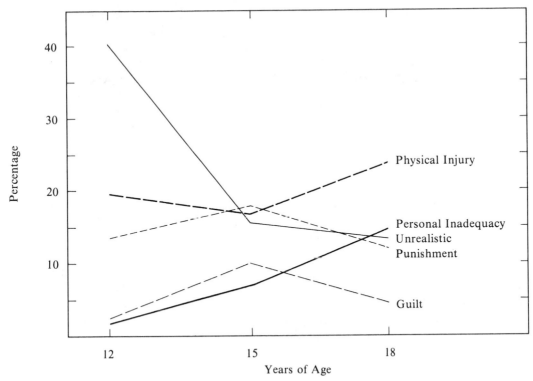

FIGURE 15-7. Expected consequences of anxiety provoking situations at different ages *(from Stattin & Magnusson, 1981:6).*

Hungary, Japan, and Sweden rated their own reactions to a number of hypothetical situations (Magnusson & Stattin, 1978). Figure 15-8 shows reaction profiles across three situations for youngsters in the three countries. The situations belonged to the same category of anxiety provoking situation, according to data from Swedish youngsters.

Figure 15-8 clearly reveals that youngsters in the three countries differed not only on the mean level of anxiety reaction across situations but also (and of no less interest) on their characteristic profiles of reaction across situations. The results underline a point emphasized

FIGURE 15-8. Cross-situational anxiety reaction profiles for youngsters in Hungary, Japan, and Sweden *(from Magnusson & Stattin, 1978:330).*

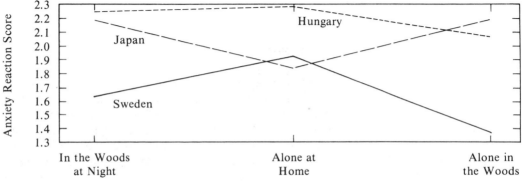

earlier: what is stressful depends upon the physical, social, and cultural environment in which individuals are reared and live. What is anxiety provoking in one culture—with its specific physical, geographical, and social characteristics—is not necessarily disturbing in a culture with other characteristics. With few exceptions (e.g., Lazarus, Opton, Tomita, & Kodama, 1966), most research on cross-cultural differences has been performed without reference to specific situations. The results presented by Magnusson and Stattin (1978) clearly illustrate the importance of using situation-specific data in cross-cultural research on stress and anxiety.

CONCLUSION

The studies presented in the preceding section documented a systematic interaction between person characteristics and type of situation. The studies were directed toward the investigation of anxiety reactions, but the consequences that can be drawn for theorizing and research on anxiety are equally valid for theorizing and research on stress. It should be underlined again that the studies were not presented in order to show final, decisive results for the form of person-situation interaction in the field of stress and anxiety; however, they are suggestive and indicate fruitful directions for further research on stress and anxiety. A challenging task would be to investigate person-situation interactions for different situation types and for different person characteristics, using different types of data.

Empirical Research

The main conclusion that can be drawn for the field of stress and anxiety is that individual differences, age differences, sex differences, cultural differences, etc., cannot be meaningfully and productively investigated and understood without reference to the specific characteristics of the situation in which the behavior is observed. This implies, for empirical research, a need to use situation-specific data, rather than traditional trait-bound inventory data and ratings. It leads to a demand for the development and use of appropriate methods and strategies of data collection. For example, the prediction of state anxiety in a certain situation from trait anxiety data will be dependent on the extent to which the trait measure refers to the same type of stressful situation as the one for which the prediction is being made (cf. Endler's interactional model of anxiety, 1975; Magnusson, 1980a). The conclusion also implies a need for considering situational features in planning and conducting empirical research on stress and anxiety.

Systematic Description and Classification of Situations

The conclusions noted here for theorizing and research on stress and anxiety imply that we need to know the characteristics of the situation under which behavior is being investigated. However, psychological theorizing and research has focused almost entirely on the person side of the person-situation interaction. That there is a great need for systematic research that can yield descriptions and classifications of situations in relevant terms has been increasingly emphasized during the past decade. Research leading to useful knowledge implies a series of conceptual, theoretical, and methodological problems. See, for example,

Magnusson (1978, 1981a) and Pervin (1978) for analyses of these problems in general and Magnusson and Stattin (1981a) for a discussion of problems in the analysis of stressful situations. These problems must be attacked so that we can obtain the knowledge about situations that is necessary to enable us both to consider situational conditions in a systematic way when planning and conducting empirical research on stress and anxiety and to incorporate situational conditions in more appropriate models of the way individuals cope with stressful situations.

Theories of Stress and Anxiety

To understand why an individual feels, thinks, and acts as he does in a certain situation we need knowledge about the operating person factors and their functional interplay; knowledge about the operating situation factors and their functional interplay; and a theory (model) linking these two networks in the continuous process of bidirectional person-situation interaction. In an interactional model of personality, a crucial role in this process is played by the perceptual-cognitive system (with its affective tones and coping strategies and its connections and interplay with physiological processes). On the person side it is also important to consider physiological factors, which contribute to the vulnerability of individuals to stress provocation. For more effective theorizing and empirical research in psychology we need a functional theory of personality that incorporates and integrates situational conditions, cognitive and physiological processes, and behavior (Magnusson, 1980b, 1981b). Such a theory will help us understand why individuals feel, think, and act as they do not only in situations that imply stress and anxiety but also in situations in general.

REFERENCES

ANGYAL, A. *Foundations of a science of personality.* Cambridge: Harvard University Press, 1941.

APPLEY, M. S., & TRUMBALL, R. *Psychological stress.* New York: Appleton, 1967.

AVERILL, J. R. A selective review of cognitive and behavioral factors involved in the regulation of stress. In R. S. Depue (ed.), *The psychobiology of the depressive disorders: Implications for the effects of stress.* New York: Academic, 1979.

BANDURA, A. *Social learning theory.* Englewood Cliffs: Prentice-Hall, 1977.

BARKER, R. G. Explorations in ecological psychology. *American Psychologist,* 1965, *20,* 1–14.

BERGER, P., & LUCKMAN, T. *The social construction of reality.* New York: Doubleday, 1967.

BERGMAN, L. R., & MAGNUSSON, D. Overachievement and catecholamine excretion in an achievement-demanding situation. *Psychosomatic Medicine,* 1979, *41,* 181–188.

BOWERS, K. S. Situationism in psychology: An analysis and a critique. *Psychological Review,* 1973, *80,* 307–336.

BRAUN, P., & REYNOLDS, D. J. A factor analysis of a 100-item fear survey scale. *Behavior Research and Therapy,* 1969, *7,* 399–402.

BRONFENBRENNER, U. Toward an experimental ecology of human development. *American Psychologist,* 1977, *32,* 513–531.

———. *The ecology of human development.* Cambridge: Harvard University Press, 1979.

CATTELL, R. B. Anxiety and motivation: Theory and crucial experiments. In C. D. Spielberger (ed.), *Anxiety and behavior.* New York: Academic, 1966.

CHEIN, I. The environment as a determinant of behavior. *Journal of Social Psychology,* 1954, *39,* 115–127.

ENDLER, N. S. The case for person-situation interactions. *Canadian Psychological Review,* 1975, *16,* 12–21.

ENDLER, N. S., & MAGNUSSON, D. Toward an interactional psychology of personality. *Psychological Bulletin,* 1976, *83,* 956–974.

EPSTEIN, S. Toward a unified theory of anxiety. In B. A. Maher (ed.), *Progress in experimental personality research,* vol. 4. New York: Academic, 1967.

————. The nature of anxiety with emphasis upon its relationship to expectancy. In C. D. Spielberger (ed.), *Anxiety: Current trends in theory and research,* vol. 2. New York: Academic, 1972.

FRANKENHAEUSER, M. Psychoneuroendocrine approaches to the study of stressful person-environment transactions. In H. Selye (ed.), *Selye's guide to stress research,* vol. 1. New York: Van Nostrand, 1980.

GEER, J. H. The development of a scale to measure fear. *Behavior Research and Therapy,* 1965, *3,* 45–53.

GLASS, D. C. *Behavior patterns, stress, and coronary disease.* Hillsdale: Erlbaum, 1977.

GOFFMAN, E. The neglected situation. *American Anthropologist,* 1964, *66,* 133–136.

HARRÉ, R., & SECORD, P. F. *The explanation of social behavior.* Oxford: Blackwell, 1972.

HEBB, D. O. The mammal and his environment. In E. E. Maccoby, T. M. Newcomb, & E. L. Hartley (eds.), *Readings in social psychology* (3d ed.). New York: Holt, 1958.

HOLMES, T. H., & RAHE, R. E. The Social Readjustment Rating Scale. *Journal of Psychosomatic Research,* 1967, *11,* 213–218.

JESSOR, R. Phenomenological personality theories and the data language of psychology. *Psychological Review,* 1956, *63,* 173–180.

JESSOR, R., & JESSOR, S. L. The perceived environment in behavioral science. *American Behavioral Scientist,* 1973, *16,* 801–828.

KAGAN, R. R., & LEVI, L. Health and environmental-psychological stimuli: A review. *Social Science and Medicine,* 1974, *8,* 225–241.

KELLY, G. A. *The psychology of personal constructs.* New York: Norton, 1955.

KOFFKA, K. *Principles of Gestalt psychology.* New York: Harcourt, 1935.

KRAUSE, M. S. Use of social situations for research purposes. *American Psychologist,* 1970, *25,* 847–753.

LANG, P. J., & LAZOVIK, A. S. Experimental desensitization of a phobia. *Journal of Abnormal Social Psychology,* 1963, *66,* 519–525.

LANTERMANN, E.-D. Situation und Person: Inter-individuelle Differenzen des Verhaltens als Folge und Ursache Idiosynkratischer Konstruktion von Situationen. In C. F. Grauman (ed.), *Ökologische Perspektiven in de Psychologie.* Bern: Huber, 1978.

LAZARUS, R. S. *Psychological stress and the coping process.* New York: McGraw-Hill, 1966.

————. *Patterns of adjustment.* New York: McGraw-Hill, 1976.

LAZARUS, R. S., & LAUNIER, R. Stress-related transactions between person and environment. In L. A. Pervin & M. Lewis (eds.), *Perspectives in interactional psychology.* New York: Plenum, 1978.

LAZARUS, R. S., OPTON, E., JR., TOMITA, M., & KODAMA, M. A crosscultural study of stress reaction patterns in Japan. *Journal of Personality and Social Psychology,* 1966, *4,* 622–633.

LEVI, L., & ANDERSSON, L. *Psychosocial stress: Population, environment, and quality of life.* New York: Halsted, 1975.

LEVINE, S., & SCOTCH, N. A. *Social stress.* Chicago: Aldine, 1970.

LEWIN, K. A. *A dynamic theory of personality.* New York: McGraw-Hill, 1935.

LEWIS, M. Situational analysis and the study of behavioral development. In L. A. Pervin & M. Lewis (eds.), *Perspectives in interactional psychology.* New York: Plenum, 1978.

LUNDBERG, U. Catecholamine and cortisol excretion patterns in three-year-old children and their parents. Manuscript, University of Stockholm, 1980.

LUNDBERG, U., & THEORELL, T. Scaling of life changes: Differences between three diagnostic groups and between recently experienced and non-experienced events. *Journal of Human Stress,* 1976, *2,* 7-17.

MAGNUSSON, D. An analysis of situational dimensions. *Perceptual and Motor Skills,* 1971, *32,* 851-867.

—————. The person and the situation in an interactional model of behavior. *Scandinavian Journal of Psychology,* 1976, *17,* 253-271.

—————. Personality in an interactional paradigm of research. *Zeitschrift für Differentielle und Diagnostische Psychologie,* 1980, *1,* 17-34. (a)

—————. Trait-state anxiety: A note on conceptual and empirical relationships. *Personality and Individual Differences,* 1980, *1,* 215-217. (b)

—————. Interaktionales Modell des Verhaltens. In H.-N. Hoefert (ed.), *Person und Situation* interaktionspsychologische Untersuchungen. Göttingen: Verlag für Psychologie Hogrefe, 1981. (a)

—————. Wanted: A psychology of situations. In D. Magnusson (ed.), *Toward a psychology of situations: An interactional perspective.* Hillsdale: Erlbaum, 1981. (b)

MAGNUSSON, D., DUNÉR, A., & ZETTERBLOM, G. *Adjustment: A longitudinal study.* New York: Wiley, 1975.

MAGNUSSON, D., & EKEHAMMAR, B. Anxiety profiles based on both situational and response factors. *Multivariate Behavioral Research,* 1975, *10,* 27-44.

MAGNUSSON, D., & ENDLER, N. S. Interactional psychology: Present status and future prospects. In D. Magnusson & N. S. Endler (ed.), *Personality at the crossroads: Current issues in interactional psychology.* Hillsdale: Erlbaum, 1977.

MAGNUSSON, D., & OLAH, A. Anxiety provoking situations: Sex and age differences in activating factors and expected consequences. Manuscript, University of Stockholm, 1981.

MAGNUSSON, D., & STATTIN, H. A cross-cultural comparison of anxiety responses in an interactional frame of reference. *International Journal of Psychology,* 1978, *13,* 317-332.

—————. *Methods for studying stressful situations.* In H. W. Krohne & L. Laux (eds.), Washington, D.C.: Hemisphere, 1981. (a)

—————. *Situation-outcome contingencies: A conceptual and methodological analysis of threatening situations.* University of Stockholm, Department of Psychology report no. 571. 1981. (b)

MAGNUSSON, D., & TÖRESTAD, B. *Situational influences on sex differences in anxiety reaction.* University of Stockholm, report no. 559. 1980.

MANDLER, G., & WATSON, D. L. Anxiety and the interruption of behavior. In C. D. Spielberger (ed.), *Anxiety and behavior.* New York: Academic, 1966.

MASON, J. W. A historical view of the stress field (in two parts). *Journal of Human Stress,* 1975, *1,* 6-36.

MATHENY, A. P., JR., & DOLAN, A. B. Persons, situations, and time: A genetic view of behavioral change in children. *Journal of Personality and Social Psychology,* 1975, *32,* 1106-1110.

McGRATH, J. E. (ED.), *Social and psychological factors in stress.* New York: Holt, 1970.

MEAD, G. H. *Mind, self, and society.* Chicago: University of Chicago Press, 1934.

MECHANIC, D. Some problems in the measurement of stress and social readjustment. *Journal of Human Stress,* 1975, *1,* 43-48.

MERTON, R. K. *Social theory and social structure.* New York: Free Press, 1957.

ORNE, M. T. On the social psychology of the psychological experiment: With particular reference to demand characteristics and their implications. *American Psychologist,* 1962, *17,* 776–783.

PAYKEL, E. S., MYERS, J. K., DIENELT, M. N., KLERMAN, G. L., LINDENTHAL, J. J., & PEPPER, M. P. Life events and depression: A controlled study. *Archives of General Psychiatry,* 1969, *21,* 753–760.

PERVIN, L. A. Definitions, measurements, and classifications of stimuli, situations, and environments. *Human Ecology,* 1978, *6,* 71–105.

PIAGET, J. The child's conception of physical causality. London: Routledge & Kegan Paul, 1951.

————. The origins of intelligence in children. New York: International Universities Press, 1952.

PROSHANSKY, H. M., ITTELSON, W. H. & RIVLIN, L. S. (EDS.), *Environmental psychology: Man and his physical setting.* New York: Holt, 1970.

PUGH, W. M. Assessment of environmental effects: Method and model. *Organizational Behavior and Human Performance,* 1977, *18,* 175–187.

ROGERS, C. A. Theory of therapy, personality, and interpersonal relationships as developed in the client-centered framework. In S. Koch (ed.), *Psychology: A study of a science,* vol. 3. New York: McGraw-Hill, 1959.

ROSENTHAL, R. *Experimental effects in behavioral research.* New York: Appleton, 1966.

ROTTER, J. B. *Social learning: A clinical psychology.* Englewood Cliffs: Prentice-Hall, 1954.

————. The role of the psychological situation in determining the direction of human behavior. In M. R. Jones (ed.), *Nebraska Symposium on Motivation.* Lincoln: University of Nebraska Press, 1955.

RUNYAN, W. M. The life course as a theoretical orientation: Sequences of person-situation interaction. *Journal of Personality,* 1978, *46,* 569–593.

SARASON, I. G., & SARASON, B. R. *Abnormal psychology.* Englewood Cliffs: Prentice-Hall, 1980.

————. The importance of cognition and moderator variables in stress. In D. Magnusson (ed.), *Toward a psychology of situations: An interactional perspective.* Hillsdale: Erlbaum, 1981.

SARASON, I. G., SMITH, R. E., & DIENER, E. Personality research: Components of variance attributable to the person and the situation. *Journal of Personality and Social Psychology,* 1975, *32,* 199–204.

SCHALLING, D. Types of anxiety and types of stressors as related to personality. In I. G. Sarason & C. D. Spielberger (eds.), *Stress and anxiety,* vol. 1. Washington, D.C.: Hemisphere, 1975.

SCHERER, M. W., & NAKAMURA, C. Y. A fear survey schedule (Fss-Fc): A factor analytic comparison with manifest anxiety (CMAS). *Behavior Research and Therapy,* 1968, *6,* 173–182.

SCHNEIDER, D. J. Implicit personality theory: A review. *Psychological Bulletin,* 1973, *79,* 294–309.

SELIGMAN, M. E. P. *Helplessness.* San Francisco: Freeman, 1975.

SELLS, S. B. An interactionist looks at the environment. *American Psychologist,* 1963, *18,* 696–702.

SELYE, H. *The stress of life.* New York: McGraw-Hill, 1976.

SHERIF, M., & SHERIF, C. W. *An outline of social psychology.* New York: Harper, 1956.

————. Varieties of social stimulus situations. In S. B. Sells (ed.), *Stimulus determinants of behavior.* New York: Ronald, 1963.

————. Crowding, perceived control, and behavioral after effects. *Journal of Applied Social Psychology,* 1974, *4,* 171–186.

SPIELBERGER, C. D. Anxiety as an emotional state. In C. D. Spielberger (ed.), *Anxiety: Current trends in theory and research,* vol. 1. New York: Academic, 1972.

STAGNER, R. Traits are relevant: Theoretical analysis and empirical evidence. In N. S. Endler & D. Magnusson (eds.), *Interactional psychology and personality.* Washington, D.C.: Hemisphere, 1976.

STATTIN, H. *The appraisal of relations between emotionally threatening events: A developmental study*. University of Stockholm, Department of Psychology report no. 563. 1980.

STATTIN, H. & MAGNUSSON, D. Situation-outcome contingencies of threatening experiences: age and sex differences. Department of Psychology, University of Stockholm, Report No. 580, 1981.

STOKOLS, D. On the distinction between density and crowding: Some implications for future research. *Psychological Review,* 1972, *79,* 275–277.

THEORELL, T., & RAHE, R. H. Psychosocial factors and myocardial infarction: An inpatient study in Sweden. *Journal of Psychology Research,* 1971, *15,* 25–31.

————. Life change event, ballistocardiography, and coronary death. *Journal of Human Stress,* 1975, *1,* 18–24.

THOMAS, W. I. The behavior and the situation. *American Sociological Society: Papers and Proceedings,* 1927, *22,* 1–13.

————. *The child in America.* New York: Knopf, 1928.

WATSON, J. B. *Behaviorism.* New York: Norton, 1924.

WILSON, G. D. The principal components of phobic stimuli. *Journal of Clinical Psychology,* 1968, *24,* 191.

WOHLWILL, J. F., & KOHN, I. Dimensionalizing the environmental manifold. In S. Wapner, S. B. Cohen, & B. Kaplan (eds.), *Experiencing the environment.* New York: Plenum, 1976.

WOLPE, J., & LANG, P. J. A fear survey schedule for use in behavior therapy. *Behavior Research and Therapy,* 1964, *2,* 27–30.

ZUBIN, J., & SPRING, B. Vulnerability: A new view of schizophrenia. *Journal of Abnormal Psychology,* 1977, *86,* 103–126.

16

The Assessment of Coping, Defense, and Stress

Norma Haan

BEFORE ASSESSING, INVESTIGATORS NEED DEFINITIONS of what they want to assess. Investigators of coping, defense, and stress are handicapped by a lack of consensus on the meaning of these terms. The concept of stress is used and understood by laypersons, but its scientific study has proven difficult. Plainly, *stress* is whatever stresses people, but its essential properties are not clear. Is stress whatever upsets people (Paykel, Prusoff, & Uhlenhuth, 1971) or is it whatever requires them to adjust (Holmes & Rahe, 1967)? To discuss assessment of the concepts of coping, defense, and stress, then, I shall first indicate how I understand these words. My definitions draw on common sense, hoping that its modest consensual definitions will make it possible to discuss, without too much equivocation, the issues and means of assessing coping, defending, and stress. I shall agrue, that we must start with common sense to resolve the "crisis in stress research" (Rose & Levin, 1979).

PRELIMINARY DEFINITIONS

Stress

We commonly understand that stress ensues when situations are "bad" from a personal point of view, for example, the cancelation of an eagerly anticipated "good" event. Despite our seemingly contradictory recognition that stress is in the eye of the beholder, we well understand the commonsense meaning of stress in our everyday lives. We know when we and others are stressed. Of course, we may have special, deeper understandings of another person's plight if we have experienced the same stress. Acknowledgment that stress has common, shared human meanings is the underlying justification for the methodology used in life events research. As Holmes and Rahe (1967) showed, when people make impersonal social judgments about the stressfulness of events—all other matters of living being held equal—their agreements are rather good, whatever the criticisms about the items in different lists or the psychometric errors committed.

No one disagrees that traumatic events like losing a loved one, experiencing the Holocaust, being a POW, or serving as one of Milgram's subjects are stressful, but mild or moderate stresses occasion argument. Many are probably stressful in the eye of the beholder, constructed for reasons of personal history or cultural background. For example,

254

women admit more readily than men to being stressed, and Hinkle's (1974) studies suggest that Hungarian refugees were more stressed than Chinese refugees by the necessity of immigration, apparently for reasons of cultural facilitation and vulnerability. Socioeconomic disadvantage is a well-understood stress. Common sense suggests other sources of individual differences: if persons have experienced numerous, intense, or prolonged episodes of stress, their resistance will be reduced. But as yet we have little researched based understanding of personal vulnerabilities.

The experience of stress, moreover, does not inevitably lead, in commonsense terms, to personal deterioration. Although we expect deterioraton, we contrarily expect that stress benefits people, making them more tender, humble, and hardy. Both gains and losses have been identified in longitudinal studies (Haan, 1977). When subgroups divided on the basis of incidence of hospitalizations and illnesses were compared, the more frequently ill were seen at later dates as typically more empathic and tolerant of ambiguity, although less able smoothly to regulate their affect. Moreover, people like stress in some ways. Stimulation by some difficulty keeps us interacting, and to experience stress and survive gives us knowledge of ourselves. To rust out is seen, at least in this culture, as even less desirable than to burn out. Once the stress has passed, we relish telling our stories of war, surgery, and divorce. We imply that we have proven ourselves and are better and wiser for our experience. Many research designs do not include provisions for assessing personal gains and thus the unstated supposition that stress is invariably decremental in effect is reified. Common sense is far wiser about the wear and tear of life; the ubiquitous hope is to manage stress and survive.

Our culture's idolization of success seems to evoke the idea—particularly in researchers of the behaviorist persuasion—that the strong person is invulnerable to stress. In this perspective, he or she simply does not become aroused. In fact, an assumption of research using scales like Holmes-Rahe's (1967) is that it is better not to have anything happen to one, not even marriage or pregnancy. Dubos (1959) has countered this position. Being human, he wrote, means having the capacity to experience stress. Invulnerability to stress may be a massive defensive maneuver. At root, these are contrasting value judgments about the best way to live.

In sum, stress is either a bad event or a good event that did not come about; its meanings are commonly understood even though some people's histories may be especially vulnerable to certain kinds of stress. Contrasting values about the best way to live—invulnerability or reactivity—permeate stress research. Finally, stress does not invariably lead to deterioration. It may facilitate growth by tempering arrogance and by enhancing our tenderness toward ourselves and others.

Coping and Defending

Coping and defense are no less controversial concepts than is stress. *Coping* is described as either a subcategory of defense (Cohen & Lazarus 1979) or a reaction that appears only in extremis (White, 1974). More often, its meanings are concretized as particular strategies appropriate for the special situation under study, like adjusting to college life (Coelho, Hamburg, & Murphey, 1963). Alternatively, I (Haan, 1977) have argued that coping is commonly understood to be a good way to handle problems; moreover, coping can be distinguished from defense. In *Webster's Third Unabridged Dictionary* coping means "to maintain a contest or combat, usually on equal terms or even with success . . . or to face, encounter . . . or overcome problems and difficulties." Concurring with clinical usage, *Webster's* supplies the following ideas about defense: "defendents' denial, answer, or plea opposing the truth of prosecutor's claims . . . fortification, justification . . . manner of self-protection." Thus, in common parlance, coping is not an action evoked solely by trauma, nor is coping a defense. Instead, it is an attempt to overcome difficulties on equal terms; it is an encounter wherein people reach out and within themselves for resources to come to terms with difficulties. *Defense* is unyielding fortification. Notice that a self-protective maneuver, undertaken with awareness, could be a sensible coping response in a situation of dangerous oppressiveness. Whether an action is coping or not can be decided only within context. Thus, coping does not insure a successful outcome because not all situations permit just or reasonable solutions.

The features that set coping and defense apart from one another are plain, so a question arises as to why some researchers shy away from explicit recognizing their differences, particularly when the differentiation clarifies conceptualizations and differentiates research designs. The positivists' mandate that social scientists be value-neutral probably accounts for this reluctance because coping does represent the value based conclusion of common sense that there are good and better, and bad and worse ways of handling stress.

The definitive and essentially epistemological argument that social science has only pretensions of being value-neutral cannot be taken up here. The basic point is that social-psychological knowledge is a human construction and it does not have the same objective reality that physical constructs do. Bernstein (1976), for instance, analyzed social science's confusion in this regard and suggested that our pretensions to value neutrality lie at the root of our frequent crises, which are then set aside by the claim that social science is still in its infancy. The solution most observers propose is that social science should admit its value basis and then proceed with analyses relying on the common value (Haan, 1977; Haan, Bellah, Rabinow, & Sullivan, 1981; Habermas, 1971, 1981).

Our lack of objective targets can be seen in stress research. We "know" what kind of experiences are stressful because we are in commonsense agreement that people are stressed when they have stress experiences. If we were to admit openly that our knowledge of stress arises from common, shared understandings and not from objective reality, the insight would be liberating. We could then use what we already know in our everyday lives: stress is handled in "richer and poorer, effective and less effective ways" (Frenkel-Brunswik, 1954).

In any event, we are not more value-neutral for focusing exclusively on the defensive, destructive ways in which stress is handled and its detrimental results of personal decrement. In fact, the concept of defense is also value-based; it rests on the assumption that negating, distorting, and obscuring both self-knowledge and contextual knowledge is not as good as knowing the "truth." Furthermore, we are not entitled as scientists to obscure or circumvent certain classes of human actions (Frenkel-Brunswick, 1954), nor do we have license to revise the common meanings of words. The conceptual position of attempting to achieve in the social sciences the value-neutral stance of physical science turns us away from life and distorts our use of garden-variety values.

ACHIEVING GENERALITY IN STRESS REASEARCH

For stress researchers to obtain a general understanding of the conditions and effects of stress, identification of stressors, coping, and defensive reactions that transcend situationally specific stresses and personal processes is needed. Otherwise research will generate small facts but no insights. No listing of so-called objective, situationally specific stress stimuli is likely to be satisfactory because stress is the result of a situation's having a certain meaning.

Fortunately, such meanings may have some common properties that could help us construct a taxonomy of stress situations.

Both common sense and research (McGrath, 1970) suggest that people's *assimilation* of undesirable circumstances is more difficult (1) when they have not anticipated a bad event or their hopes for good news have been dashed, (2) when the onset is out of their control, (3) when the conditions of their situation are ambiguous, (4) when they think that they will be stressed, (5) when the situation resembles other poorly resolved events, (6) when they are already stressed by other matters, and (7) when their efforts to secure pertinent information are defeated. *Accommodations* to stress are more difficult (1) when one has little or no possibility of diminishing the stress—its outcome is beyond one's control (Seligmann, 1975), (2) when the stress is intense, (3) when stressful experiences closely follow one on another, and (4) when one has had no previous experience with the particular kind of stress. Moreover, researchers have recently recognized what common sense already taught: lack of social or institutional supports exacerbates stress reactions, whereas such support facilitates effective reactions.

If this taxonomy of properties has face validity, then it might be useful for researchers to begin classifying stress situations not only according to their content—like bereavement—but also according to their stress properties. For instance, controversy has centered on the positive events included in the original Holmes-Rahe (1967) list, which could be differentiated by such a taxonomy. By and large, their life course events, like the birth of a baby, are to be expected; however, when a life event occurs off schedule, such as having a baby at age 15 or age 45 (Neugarten, 1979), its meaning changes. It is not expected and it becomes an adventitious stressful event.

A concomitant of the growing awareness that stress can be defined only in a circular fashion is the theme that stress involves interaction between events and people. Thus, *interaction*—not only personal responses to stress stimuli—must be assessed if we are to understand stress and stressed people. Temporal sequences need to be measured by assessing and reassessing *both* situations and people. The relevant personal aspects in this context are the processes people use to interact. Therefore, most stress researchers, unlike traditional personologists, have turned to the study of person's processes. Traits will not do because they denote the perseveration of the same response over time.

Surely in interacting, people would prefer to cope if they could. However, most often in stress situations we not only cope but also defend and frequently *fragment,* however briefly, in a sequence or in some desperate, random combination of all three modes. Following methodological convention, we tend to type people, in the manner of early personality theorists, as all or forever good or bad, as either copers or defenders. But in their attempts to unravel a stressful event, the same people—even psychotics—cope, defend, and fragment, so measures of all three reaction modes are needed.

Coping, defending, and fragmenting are general approaches, not specific processes. People have more specific ways of dealng with stress that are represented in their hierarchies of preferred ego processes. For instance, a professor faced with an emotional interpersonal problem may rely first on logical analysis, not on empathy, or he or she may intellectualize in an attempt to resolve the difficulty. But again, preferred, specific processes are readily abandoned in a situation if they do not work. People's intelligence in reacting appropriately to the features of different situations and their virtuosity in inventing new ways of interacting have been the bane of traditional personologists. These capabilities generated the controversy over cross-situational consistency in personality. In sum, then, coping and defense cannot be understood outside the context of the situational stress, and stress is not known apart from the ways people interact with it. To elucidate the interaction between people and stress, research designs need to include the features reviewed in the next section.

ASSESSMENT PROVISIONS IN RESEARCH DESIGN

Time Frame

Assimilating and accommodating to stress necessarily take place over time. Thus, designs need a time frame of a length appropriate to the problem under investigation. Hosack's (1968) study should alert us to the possibility of reaching erroneous conclusions when data are collected at a single point in time. She found that mothers whose first child was malformed and who later coped with the baby's condition by health professionals' standards of appropriate care were intelligently upset at the baby's birth, in contrast to defensive mothers, who were seemingly more tranquil both early and later. If Hosack's model of successfully handling stress had been the characterologically nonaroused person, she might have been content with a single data collection immediately following the baby's birth. But then she would have concluded that the defensive mothers had handled the stress of the baby's condition in the most effective way. To cope with stress, it must be admitted, but to admit stress has to be upsetting, at least in the beginning.

Transcending Specific Situations

In order for social scientists to achieve general understanding of the meanings that stress has for people (so useful recommendations about public policy can eventually be made), coping, defense, and stress need to be operationalized in general, not situationally bound terms. In other words, the variables need to be sufficiently abstract to transcend specific contexts and particular kinds of maneuvers. As suggested earlier, stressful situations could be classified according to commonly understood properties, like anticipated or not, controlled or not. Likewise, the person's processes of handling stress need to be generalized, as many investigators already recognize.

Capturing a Wide Array of Processes

Because attempts to resolve stressful events involve sequences of interactions as persons make more or less apt responses in an attempt to preserve their own integrity, an array of processes usually appears. Consequently, the net for assessing process variables needs to be thrown wide. Moreover, as Bem and Funder (1978) observed, not all people use all processes. If for reasons of methodological simplicity and rigor, the design permits only one or two processes to be assessed or collapses discrete processes into global notions like overall coping, the analysis of some person-stress interactions will be incomplete or wrong.

Repeated Assessments

Focus on interactions means not only that the person's processes need to be assessed at different points during the process of resolution but also that stressful situations need to be assessed and reassessed at different points.

Effective and Ineffective Ways of Handling Stress and Its Outcomes

Provisions need to be made for evaluating effective processes and personal gains, as well as ineffective processes and personal losses, in relation to the stress experience. Thus, both coping, as a value based representation of the more effective and richer ways of processing stress, and defensiveness, as the less effective and narrower way, must be assessed. We need to know what kinds of stress, handled with what kinds of processes in the context of what kinds of exogenous support, eventually have humanizing and actualizing, as well as detrimental, effects.

Supports of All Kinds

The effects of stress can be exacerbated or tempered by varying the person's social supports (Brown, 1978; Cobb, 1976), or, more comprehensively, "resistance resources" (Antonovsky, 1979). However, social support is only one environmental resource for alleviating stress; economic, financial, or political power also expands response options (Pearlin & Schooler, 1978). Moreover, social support must go beyond tender care to include help in sorting out the implications of one's experience, discarding one's exaggerations and distortions, and consensually validating the reality of one's reactions and the situation. Crisis intervention clinics and self-help groups now formally provide such support for the process of working through stress. Crisis clinics base their operation on the accumulated wisdom that stressed people adopt, usually by six weeks, truly equilibrated or false, rigid solutions because prolonged and unremitting stress is intolerable.

Studies of social support have tended to be only correlative in design. Research distinguishing the mechanisms and effects of the different kinds of support—social, material, and cognitive-clarifying—is much needed.

Naturalistic Study

Although psychologists earlier studied artificially aroused stress in laboratories, many workers now prefer naturalistic study. The meanings of stress experienced in the laboratory turned out to be unpredictably constructed by subjects (Haan, 1969; Lazarus, Opton, Tomita, & Kodama, 1966; Maguire, Maclean, & Aitken, 1973). However, the study of naturalistic events is not an easy road to truth. First, the variety of stress events is enormous. Second, investigators must know the subjects' status prior to the stress in order to isolate the effects of stress. Third, all manner of events other than the target stress may be experienced by subjects during the investigation. Still, the advantages of studying real-life interactions undoubtedly outweigh the disadvantages. Researchers who conduct naturalistic investigations will have to tolerate error variance and prediction failure (Bem & Funder, 1978).

MEASUREMENT OF COPING AND DEFENDING

In this section, measurement of stress is not directly taken up because other chapters in this volume cover the topic well. However, the reverberations between people and events means that the measurement of people cannot be divorced from the evaluation of situations.

The two main ways of measuring coping and defending are (1) observations by professionals or intimates of stressed persons and (2) self-reports of behaviors or responses to test items. The distinction between observations and self-reports may not be as important in advancing stress research as is the scheduling of measurements; assessments need to be made within the situation of stress or outside it, the latter to include ratings done before, after, or during but still removed from the target event.

An ideal design would include measurements of coping and defending made before stress—to evaluate input status; within the situation—to assess actual reactions; and afterward—to assess enduring effects. Naturalistic situations almost never permit premeasurements because the investigator usually comes upon the scene when the stress is under way. Moreover, premeasurements of large samples at risk for experiencing a particular stress—like a coronary attack—are prohibitively expensive.

An alternative is to attempt to trigger a stressful experience in a naturalistic way. However, these designs also have difficulties. Paramount is the ethical hazard of investigators' deliberately invoking stress. If they first give fully informed consent, subjects will react to the stressful situation in unnatural ways. Plainly, Milgram's (1974) subjects would not have been troubled had they known that the electric shock they were asked to administer was bogus. In an ongoing project, my colleagues and I inform subjects (at first adolescent but subsequently young adult friendship groups) that we are studying morality. We tell subjects that they will be given moral problems to solve as groups and that, as a result, they are likely to become angry with their friends and argue. Our forewarning probably accounts for one general result, although our subjects do become angry and stressed: stressful problems result in significantly lower levels of coping than do nonstressful problems, but not in markedly higher levels of defensiveness, as we unthinkingly hypothesized. Thus, informed consent may allow subjects to cope instead of defend.

Despite the difficulties, within-situation measurement of coping and defending may have the greatest payoff for stress research for several reasons. First, the controversy over cross-situational consistency of personality is evidence in itself that theories of personality based solely on persons' predispositions do not tell us enough about how people act in stressful circumstances. Second, the lengthy inferential reach required to connect actions taken in stress situations with predispositions is obviated by within-situation measurement; instead, the actual reaction needs to be measured. Finally, studies including within-situation measurement are rare so that we know little about how people actually interact with stress. Of course, within-situation measurement is not an end in itself: societies need to predict in order to construct policies that might prevent breakdowns and decompensations.

Measures Taken outside the Stress Situation

I have limited the subsequent presentation to measurements of processes and I evaluate them substantively and conceptually instead of psychometrically. Readers will want firsthand information about the psychometric status of measures. How much unreliability an investigator will tolerate with complex variables is a personal decision that may put validity at risk whenever reliability is too high or too low.

Human virtuosity in selecting and sequencing processes in accordance with specific situations means that an array of measures, not just one or two, should be used; otherwise, the reactive processes of some persons will slip through the assessment net. Paper and pencil measures do not directly represent the objective reality of persons' processes, or even their traits, but instead their processes of test taking—that is, only what they are willing to have the investigator know. I suggest, however, that interactions with investigators are not markedly different from interactions with others in the person's life.

An early study by Miller and Swanson (1960) illustrates the need for flexibility in measurement. Their observational assessment included only defense mechanisms, which they aroused by various stimuli. However, a number of subjects did not become defensive. Because these investigators had no conceptual provisions for handling nondefensive behavior—which may have been coping behavior—they eliminated these subjects from their analyses. They may have thereby excluded from scrutiny an important segment of the range of human reaction.

The use of paper and pencil measures brings up the issue of social desirability, which in the process oriented view becomes a defense in itself, not an extraneous intrusion that can be corrected with the expectancy that the "real truth" about the individual's personality will be revealed. For example, I (Haan, 1977) found that defensive denial scores were positively associated with the Minnesota Multiphasic Personality Inventory (MMPI's) lie, K, and social desirability scales at the .001 level (correlations ranged from .44 to .52) and with the California Psychological Inventory (CPI's) good impression and commonality scores at the .001 and the .05 level, respectively (correlations were .34 and .21) in samples of 85 men and 90 women. The MMPI F-scale was positively associated with defensive doubt and defensive regression at the .001 level (r's of .41 and .39, respectively). According to this view, stress researchers should not want to correct scores for test taking attitudes.

Locus of Control. Although the Locus of Control instrument was not constructed to represent a process, it seems to do so. *Internal control* attributes agency to oneself, a coping procedure, whereas *external control* gives agency to others or to fate (presumably a defensive expectation that leads to helplessness) (Seligmann, 1975). Both aspects of control are likely to occur in situations of stress.

To discuss this instrument at length is not possible here. However, investigators using the Locus of Control in stress research need to take its several substantive limitations into account. First, people cannot realistically attribute responsibility to themselves for many stressful events, although they may habitually think that they determine their own fate. In fact, an almost invariant property of a stressful situation is that people are not able to control its onset or outcome. Dohrenwend (1973) illustrated this point well when she showed that women and blacks experience more stressful life events than do white males, an understandable finding in view of their lower status. Women and blacks are also known to have lower internal control scores than do white males. This limitation may not always be an important drawback if assessment is done before or after stress or even during mild stress that does not color all the interpretations that persons make of themselves and their lives. Thus, the problem is to separate specific reactions to stress from habitual expectations but, of course, this problem accompanies any measure made outside the stress situation.

Second, internal locus of control is a global measurement of general coping and investigators may want greater differentiation among coping processes. Furthermore, external control seems to include several ways of defending, e.g., displacement and projection. Kuypers (1972) found, as evidence, that persons higher on internal locus of control were also higher than externals on all 10 of Haan's coping processes, significantly higher on 6 of these, and lower on 9 of the 10 defensive processes but significantly lower on only 1. In sum, differentiation of the coping behaviors used by internals cannot be attained with this measure and some kinds of defensive behavior may not be assessed for externals.

Cognitive Controls. During the late 1950s and early 1960s, a series of publications described certain cognitive styles as typical of persons who preferred certain defenses, and it was reasonably shown that these cognitive styles, regarded as ways of organizing information, accounted for individual variations in adaptive behavior (see Gardner, Holzman, Klein, Linton, & Spence, 1959). For example, Gardner, Holtzman, Klein, Linlon, & Spence, (1959) showed that *cognitive leveling* was associated with repressive tendencies and that *cognitive scanning* was related to isolating tendencies. Leveling (or sharpening) referred to persons' tendency to mute (or maximize) differences in their experience, whereas scanning refers to their tendency to cast about for different solutions. Witkin and his associates (Witkin, Dyk, Faterson, Goodenough, & Karp, 1962) took part in this early work and developed the concept of field independence-dependence, which seems near in meaning to locus of control. *Field independents* have agency; *field dependents* allow the field to organize them. Moos (1974) reviewed recent research on cognitive styles and general adaptation, not stress and coping per se, but investigators who consider using cognitive controls and styles would be rewarded by reading his account. In the original work by the Gardner and Witkin teams, a variety of interesting quasi-experimental measures were developed to measure the cognitive controls of leveling, sharpening, tolerance for unrealistic experiences, focusing, constricted-flexible, and field independence-dependence. Additional measures indexed the styles persons use in reacting to Rorschach blots. Sharpening of differences, as opposed to leveling, and field independence, as opposed to field dependence, were regarded as good styles— coping styles I would say—, although the investigators did not admit the value bias underlying their procedures.

MMPI Scales. Scanning the appendix of the *MMPI Handbook,* volume 2, (Dahlstrom, Welsh, & Dahlstrom, 1960), which lists specially developed scales, indicates that measurement of processes in stress research need not start from scratch. The titles of the following special scales suggest that they measure the kinds of processes likely to occur with some frequency in stress situations (I do not credit their authors; I am merely mentioning possibilities): facilitation-inhibition, conflict resolution, sensitivity, perceptual distortion, rigidity, use of the will to set and hold goals, blaming self, feeling sorry for self, punishing self, self-rejection distress, concern for health, acting out, ego control, neurotic overcontrol, neurotic undercontrol, acting out hostility, resisting being told what to do, blaming others, criticism of others, demandingness, and possibly Barron's (1953) ego strength, which may measure character more than it does processes.

In 1965, I published a study that I had done on developing preliminary coping and defensive scales based on MMPI items. The scales included intellectualizing, doubt, denial, projection, regression, displacement, repression, and primitive defense, Joffe and Naditch (1977) subsequently used larger samples and more sophisticated statistical techniques, primarily on CPI items but also on MMPI items, to develop coping and defensive scales based on my ego model (Haan, 1977). Their scales are discussed in the next section. In reviewing the validity of my original scales, Morrissey (1977) suggested that their usefulness was uneven, but investigators will find his careful review helpful.

CPI Scales. Most of the standard CPI scales developed by Gough (1957) do not appear on their face to measure processes. Gough had wanted to measure folk concepts about personalities, but the line of demarcation between process and personality is sometimes thin. Several of his scales do seem to measure coping processes, namely, tolerance, good impression, achievement conformance, achievement independence, intellectual efficiency, psychological mindedness, and flexibility. In addition, Gough (1976, 1977) developed a modernity scale that measures the extent to which people favor social change and experimentation and indicates whether they are optimistic about the future and their capacity to cope with new experiences. Persons with high and low scores on modernity should handle stress differently.

Joffe and Naditch (1977) constructed a set of CPI and MMPI based coping and defending scales. As mentioned earlier, their scales undoubtedly are an excellent replacement for my preliminary coping and defending scales (Hahn, 1965). Scales that Joffe and Naditch regarded as "probably acceptable by existing standards," which were replicated for both sexes, were the coping scales of intellectuality, logical analysis, tolerance of ambiguity, regression in the service of the ego, and total coping, along with the defense scales of intellectualizing, doubt, and regression. "Less acceptable" scales for both sexes, which did not meet all criteria of validation, reliability, or discriminant validity, were sublimation and substitution (coping) and rationalization (defending). Another set of scales met either the strict or the relaxed criteria for one or the other of the sexes: for men, expressiveness (coping) and projection, isolation, primitive defense, and total defense (defending); for women, denial, displacement, projection, structured defense, and primitive defense (defending). Joffe and Naditch (1977) also developed several MMPI based ego scales for projection and regression (defense) and concentration and suppression (coping). (The recency of these scales' development means that only two published studies so far have tested their validity in separate samples of stressed persons, blind males and Marine recruits being discharged for nonperformance [Joffe & Bast, 1978; Vickers, & Hervig, 1981].)

Coping as Measured by Shanan. Shanan (1973) developed an articulated and dynamic definition of coping and proposed methods of its assessment by means of a sentence completion test and the Thematic Apperception Test (TAT). The distinctive features of this definition of coping are (1) the availability of free cathetic energy for directing attention to difficulty and identifying complexity, (2) the articulation of transactions between field and self, (3) the tendency to confront or avoid complexity and conflict, and (4) the optimal balance between demands of reality and self. Measurements are accomplished as follows: *energy:* the number of stems completed on a sentence completion test and the total number of all words and verbs indicating activity used in TAT stories; *transaction between field and self:* the number of sentence completion responses that refer to other persons and objects, as opposed to the self and the number of complex situations describing conflict in TAT stories, along with the number of time dimensions and ambiguous endings; *dealing with complexity and conflict:* the number of sentence completions that indicate tendencies to give up as opposed to persevere and, within the TAT stories, the same tendencies in the actions of characters. Shanan did not state how optimal balances between the demands of reality and self are to be measured. His conceptualization and convincing operationalizations of coping are interesting and relevant to stress research and he did report several validating studies. However, his methods may be too time-consuming for many investigators.

The Defense Mechanism Inventory. Gleser and Ihilevich (1969) developed an objective instrument for the measurement of five clusters of defenses: turning against the object, projection, principalization (splitting affect from content and repressing content), turning against the self, and reversal (responding positively or neutrally to a frustrating object). They defined these mechanisms in the classical way as processes whereby the "ego attacks, distorts, or become selectively unaware of certain aspects of the internal or external world" (p. 52). The instrument includes 10 stories; after reading each story, the person responds to questons that refer to actual behavior, impulsive behavior, thoughts, or feelings. Five alternative answers for each question correspond to each of the five defense clusters. The respondent indicates the alternatives that are most and least representative of what he or she would be likely to do. Gleser and Sacks (1973) used this inventory, with results that confirmed hypotheses, to assess defense reactions in undergraduates prior to their being told that their performance was deficient on a test of scholastic ability. Vickers, and Hervig (1981) investigated the relationship of the inventory's scores with clinical ratings of defense in a group of men who were presumably stressed because they were being discharged from the Marine Corps prior to completing their basic training. Here the results were disappointing as compared to those with the Joffe-Naditch (1977) scales. Nevertheless, the original validation studies and the conceptual framework for this instrument suggest that it may be useful in stressful research.

Persons' Self-Described Coping and Defending. Another recently developed method of assessing coping by self-report is illustrated by the work of Pearlin and Schooler (1978), Folkman and Lazarus (1980), and Billings and Moos (1981). All these studies used nonsymptomatic community samples. Subjects were asked to report how they usually coped with noxious events or with specific experiences. At the same time, subjects also reported their stresses, strains, and negative life events. The investigators developed these instruments by surveying the literature, testing pilot samples, and/or relying on their own theories or common sense. This method differs from those discussed previously because it is based on the presumption that people *can* directly describe their coping strategies with the aid of a checklist or questionnaire. This assumption needs to be supported by comparisons of such self-reports with clinical observations.

Folkman and Lazarus included only coping items in their inventory, whereas the other two investigations had mixtures of coping and defense. From the standpoint of the present distinction between coping and defending, a question must be raised as to whether people can describe their defenses inasmuch as these are customarily thought to operate at the preconscious level. People should be able to describe their coping efforts because a hallmark of coping is conscious choice. Our accrued understanding from psychotherapeutic situations, which is the context par excellence for observing processes in action, is that people do not ordinarily recognize their defenses. In fact, the purpose of psychotherapy is to facilitate clients' recognition of their defenses so that they can choose how to act—in other words, how to cope. If this reasoning is correct, this self-report method should elicit more coping than defense responses.

Folkman and Lazarus (1980) and Billings and Moos (1981) used a rather similar classification of coping, the division between *problem-focused* and *emotion-focused coping.* However, this separation does not seem to be conceptually clear. Stress situations that can be resolved by problem-focused coping must also involve emotions and vice versa. As it turns out, in 98% of the stress incidents reported by Folkman and Lazarus, both kinds of coping were used despite modest correlations of about .45 between the two measures. But differences were still discernible: people used more problem-focused coping in situations in which they thought "something could be done" and more emotion-focused coping when they thought they could only accept the situation. This result seems to tell us exactly what we would expect.

The Folkman-Lazarus (1980) checklist, called Ways of Coping, contains 64 items—24 for problem-focused coping and 40 for emotion-focused coping. Examination of these items indicates that almost all could represent coping as it is defined in this chapter. In fact, Folkman and Lazarus came close to endorsing such a definition: "Coping is defined as the cognitive and behavioral efforts made to master, tolerate, or reduce external and internal demands and conflicts among them" (p. 223). However, whether or not items are coping or defending depends on the situation and the respondent's level of awareness. Endorsing the idea of coping is a clear loss if the price is to discard defense, a time-honored and well-understood means of handling stress. To its credit, the Billings-Moos (1981) instrument of 19 items includes both coping and defense items (e.g., "Sometimes took it out on other people when I felt angry or depressed," "Tried to step back from the situation and be more objective").

A final problem of conceptual clarity needs to be mentioned. These instruments include a conglomeration of coping (or defense) processes, a characteristic that reduces differentiation; at the same time, the processes included may be insufficiently abstract to permit the eventual generalizations that stress research needs. In fact, Folkman and Lazarus (1980) expressed concerned that "it may be that to identify coping styles that transcend situational contexts, we must look at another level of abstraction" (p. 229).

The Pearlin-Schooler (1978) study of 2300 persons took a sociological approach and thus used variables like household economics and "limited societal opportunity structures." Psychologists tend to overlook their subjects' objective resources, which generate response options, and then implicitly assign the better coping of their objectively advantaged subjects to intrinsically better character. However, all data in this study came from self-reports and the distinction between coping and defense is not made. Subjects were asked to make fine distinctions among stresses, strains, coping resources, and coping responses. For example, in the content area of spouse, strain was operationalized as nonacceptance by spouse; stress, as being unhappy, bothered, frustrated, tense, bored, discontented, and so forth with the spouse; coping resources, as self-denigration, mastery, and self-esteem; and coping responses, as self-reliance versus advice seeking, controlled reflective versus emotional discharge, selective ignoring versus paying attention.

Measurements Made inside the Stress Situation

To show how people interact with stressful experiences, measurements made within the stress situation are needed. However premeasurements are also required if effects of the stress itself are to be separated from effects related to prior status. Within-measurements of naturalistic situations will almost always be based on observations because there are ethical questions involved in asking stressed persons to make self-reports like answering yes or no to items on a personality inventory for the purpose of psychologists' research. A different interpersonal exchange obtains when professionals extract measures of coping and defending from interviews that have the purpose of helping persons with their feelings and problems. For this reason, transcribed interviews conducted in crisis intervention clinics seem an excellent data base for obtaining measurements of stress.

The full force of the conceptual difficulties in systematizing the ways people cope and defend is felt when the multifaceted, real-life reactions of stressed persons are confronted. Here the means of assessment must almost always be ratings in some form. A common approach is to take the content of a specific stress situation and deduce the likely dimensions. For example, Silber and his associates (Silber, Coelho, Murphey, Hamburg, Pearlin, & Rosenberg, 1961), in their study of competent adolescents coping with the problem of college entrance, organized their observations according to such headings as the use of environmental resources in learning about colleges, application strategies, assessment of the potential self-college fit, and parents' roles in students' choice of college.

In order to generalize the most common processes people use in dealing with all kinds of stress, various schemes of either coping or coping and defending have been offered. Cohen and Lazarus (1979) suggested that the four main modes of coping are information seeking, which has a self-evident meaning; direct actions, for which the authors gave the examples of running away, arguing, or "in short, doing something about the problem"; inhibition of action, which they briefly stated is "a mode of coping"; and intrapsychic processes, for which the examples of the defenses of denial, avoidance, and the like were given. This scheme well illustrates the conceptual problems that develop when coping is regarded as defense. Not only are all intrapsychic coping processes classified as defenses, but also intrapsychic processes are apparently thought to be conceptually different from cognitive processes and unrelated to action. Taking action and inhibiting action probably are the two extremes of the same dimension. Too much information seeking may be an obsession and the prudence of acting or not acting depends on the nature of the situation. However, Cohen and Lazarus remained true to their own position; they did not posit a good way to handle stress.

Moos and Tsu (1977) offered an integrated and comprehensive scheme specifically to describe coping within the context of physical illness; however, most of their dimensions have generality. They identified six separate processes: denying or minimizing the seriousness of the crisis; seeking relevant information; requesting reassurance; learning specific illness related procedures; setting concrete, limited goals; rehearsing alternative outcomes; and finding a general purpose or meaning in the event.

Finally, the multidimensional scheme of coping, defending, and fragmentation that I (Haan, 1977) proposed is most easily understood by recounting its development. Each of the 10 coping and 10 fragmenting processes was constructed to represent the same general processes involved in 10 classical defense mechanisms; however, the coping and fragmenting items have different properties from those of their defense counterparts. For example, within the same generic ego process of interpersonal sensitivity, projection is the defense, empathy is the coping counterpart, and delusions are the fragmented manifestation.

In this model (Haan, 1977), five properties identify coping: open consideration of options; orientation to the realities and future implications of the situation and to the implications of one's possible reactions; differentiated thinking that integrates rational, conscious considerations and preconscious elements; flexible and inventive creation of response options; and governance of disturbing affects and tempered affective expression. In a few words, coping rests on the value of accuracy in assimilating the critical elements of one's situation and one's reactions and accuracy in acting and accommodating, after consideration of the various possible transactions that might be undertaken and their future consequences.

In contrast, the common and classical meanings of defense involve negation of choice; slanting the present situation in terms of the past; disregarding future implications and the consequences of one's action; distorted and undifferentiated cognitive considerations; separation of thought from concomitant feelings; expectancies that disturbing feelings can be magically removed; and impulse gratification by subterfuge. Intersubjective and intrasubjective inaccuracies typify defensive strategies.

Still another set of properties describes the fragmented processes of persons we ordinarily think of as psychotic (or those of normal people for brief moments). Here the processes are repetitive, ritualistic, and automated; assumptions about reality and the future are privatistically based and nonresponsive to the requirements of the present situation; affect determines reactions; and unmodulated gratification of impulse occurs.

My colleague (Kroeber, 1963) and I hoped that the resulting trios of coping, defensive, fragmenting process was near to being a comprehensive map of the main ego processes that encompassed cognitive, affective, intraceptive, and attention focusing functions. Moreover, we reasoned that the values underlying coping—and defense, too, for that matter—might be at some distance from our personal values. A main difficulty of the model seems to be that it is too abstract from a nonclinical investigator's point of view.

Assessment of the relevant variables in most of these schemes to represent coping and for defense usually must be done by ratings; sometimes, unobtrusive measures can be used. For instance, information seeking (coping) by a physically ill patient could be evaluated by nurses on the ward. Although some investigators are discomfited by so-called soft measures, like ratings, others take the position that human reactions and interactions are so complex that they can be captured only by equally flexible and complex human minds. Until we have a consensual taxonomy of human processing of stress, most researchers will undoubtedly develop rating systems of within-situation stress reactions that express their own theoretical preferences. For instance, my 60-item Q-Sort of Ego Processes (Haan, 1977) includes three items for the 10 coping and 10 defensive processes; I did not include fragmenting processes because I work mostly with normal subjects, who do not fragment frequently.

CONCLUSION

A rosy picture of the art of assessing coping, defending, and stress could not be painted in this chapter. We lack consensus about the meanings of these terms and about the likely connections among them. Undoubtedly, if we had consensus, measures would be quickly developed. I suggested that our difficulties emanate from our continued pretension that stress research is a science that concerns objective realities. Not only is stress the construction of the stressed, but also we know by common sense that there are both good (accurate, logical, socially sensitive, and informed) and bad (distorted, decompensated, and socially destructive) ways of handling stress. But this admission would invalidate the social scientist's claims of value neutrality.

The parent of stress research is the long worked but chaotic field of personology, which aims to conceptualize and understand the whole person. The basic parameters of stress research are much clearer: we are interested in the effects of environments that lead people to feel trapped, helpless, and oppressed and we seek to understand how people handle these experiences. The long-term goal is plainly a humane one—knowledge of how societies might organize themselves to avoid the unnecessary stresses that people experience and to buffer the inevitable stresses that citizens must suffer. In a way, interest in psychometric assessment at this time is premature because our debates have not yet resolved the basic questions of definition: what is stress, coping, and defending? But then social science never proceeds in an orderly way.

REFERENCES

ANTONOVSKY, A. *Health, stress, and coping.* San Francisco: Jossey-Bass, 1979.

BARRON, F. An ego-strength scale which predicts response to psychotherapy. *Journal of Consulting Psychology,* 1953, *17,* 327–333.

BEM, D., & FUNDER, D. Predicting more of the people more of the time: Assessing the personality of situations. *Psychological Review,* 1978, *85,* 485–501.

BERNSTEIN, R. *The restructuring of social and political theory.* New York: Harcourt, 1976.

BILLINGS, A., & MOOS, R. The role of coping responses and social resources in attenuating the stress of life events. *Journal of Behavioral Medicine,* 1981.

BROWN, G., & HARRIS, T. *The social origins of depression.* New York: Free Press, 1978.

COBB, S. Social support as a moderator of life stress. *Psychosomatic Medicine,* 1976, *38,* 300–314.

COELHO, G. V., HAMBURG, D. A., & MURPHEY, E. B. Coping strategies in a new learning environment. *Archives of General Psychiatry,* 1963, *9,* 433–443.

COHEN, F., & LAZARUS, R. S. Coping with the stresses of illnesses. In G. C. Stone, F. Cohen, & N. E. Adler (eds.), *Health psychology.* San Francisco: Jossey-Bass, 1979.

DAHLSTROM, W., WELSH, G., & DAHLSTROM, L. *An MMPI handbook* (rev. ed.), vol. 2. Minneapolis: University of Minnesota Press, 1975.

DOHRENWEND, B. S. Social status and stressful life events. *Journal of Personality and Social Psychology,* 1973, *28,* 225–235.

DUBOS, R. *Mirage of health.* New York: Harper, 1959.

FOLKMAN, S., & LAZARUS, R. An analysis of coping in a middle-aged community sample. *Journal of Health and Social Behavior,* 1980, *21,* 219–239.

FRENKEL-BRUNSWIK, E. Social research and the problem of values. *Journal of Abnormal and Social Psychology,* 1954, *49,* 466–471.

GARDNER, R. W., HOLZMAN, P. S., KLEIN, G. S., LINTON, H. P., & SPENCE, D. P. Cognitive control: A study of individual consistencies in cognitive behavior. *Psychological Issues,* 1959, *1,* 1–186, whole issue.

GLESER, G., & IHILEVICH, D. An objective instrument for measuring defense mechanisms. *Journal of Consulting and Clinical Psychology,* 1969, *33,* 51–60.

GLESER, G., & SACKS, M. Ego defenses and reaction to stress: A validation study of the Defense Mechanism Inventory. *Journal of Consulting and Clinical Psychology,* 1973, *40,* 181–187.

GOUGH, H. *Manual for the California Psychological Inventory.* Palo Alto: Consulting Psychologists, 1957.

————. A measure of individual modernity. *Journal of Personality Assessment,* 1976, *40,* 3–9.

————. Further validation of a measure of individual modernity. *Journal of Personality Assessment,* 1977, *41,* 49–57.

HAAN, N. Coping and defense mechanisms related to personality inventories. *Journal of Consulting Psychology,* 1965, *29,* 373–378.

————. A tripartite model of ego functioning, values, and clinical and research applications. *Journal of Nervous and Mental Disease,* 1969, *148,* 14–30.

————. Two moralities in action contexts. *Journal of Personality and Social Psychology,* 1978, *36,* 286–305.

————(ed.). *Coping and defending: Processes of self-environment organization.* New York: Academic, 1977.

HABERMAS, J. *Knowledge and human interests,* trans. J. J. Shapiro. Boston: Beacon, 1971.

HINKLE, L. E. The effect of exposure to cultural change, social change, and changes in interpersonal relationships on health. In B. S. Dohrenwend & B. P. Dohrenwend (eds.), *Stressful life events.* New York: Wiley, 1974.

HOLMES, T. H. & RAHE, R. H. The social adjustment rating scale. *Journal of Psychosomatic Research,* 1967, *11,* 213–218.

HOSACK, A. A comparison of crises: Mother's early experiences with normal and abnormal first-born infants. Doctoral dissertation, Harvard University School of Public Health, 1968.

JOFFE, P. E., & BAST, B. E. Coping and defense in relation to accommodation among a sample of blind men. *Journal of Nervous and Mental Disease,* 1978, *166,* 537–552.

JOFFE, P. E., & NADITCH, M. Paper and pencil measures of coping and defense processes. In N. Haan (eds.), *Coping and defending: Processes of self-environment organization.* New York: Academic, 1977.

KROEBER, T. C. The coping functions of the ego mechanisms. In R. White (ed.), *The study of lives.* New York: Atherton, 1963.

KUYPERS, J. A. Internal-external locus of control, ego functioning, and personality characteristics in old age. *Gerontologist,* 1972, *12,* 168–173.

LAZARUS, R. S., OPTON, E., TOMITA, M., & KODAMA, M. A cross-cultural study of stress-reaction patterns in Japan. *Journal of Personality and Social Psychology,* 1966, *4,* 622–633.

MAGUIRE, G., MACLEAN, A., & AITKEN, R. Adaptation on repeated exposure to film-induced stress. *Biological Psychology,* 1973, *1,* 43–51.

McGRATH, J. *Social and psychological factors in stress.* New York: Holt, 1970.

MILGRAM, S. *Obedience to authority.* New York: Harper & Row, 1974.

MILLER, D., & SWANSON, G. E. *Inner conflict and defense.* New York: Holt, 1960.

MISCHEL, W. *Personality and assessment.* New York: Wiley, 1968.

MOOS, R. Psychological techniques in the assessment of adaptive behavior. In G. Coelho, D. Hamburg, & J. Adams (eds.), *Coping and adaptation.* New York: Basic Books, 1974.

MOOS, R., & TSU, V. The crisis of physical illness: An overview. In R. H. Moos (ed.), *Coping with physical illness.* New York: Plenum, 1977.

MORRISSEY, R. The Haan model of ego functioning: An assessment of empirical research. In N. Haan (ed.), *Coping and defending: Processes of self-environment organization.* New York: Academic, 1977.

NEUGARTEN, B. L. Time, age, and the life cycle. *American Journal of Psychiatry,* 1979, *136,* 887–894.

PAYKEL, E. S., PRUSOFF, B. A., & UHLENHUTH, E. H. Scaling of life events. *Archives of General Psychiatry,* 1971, *25,* 340–347.

PEARLIN, L., & SCHOOLER, C. The structure of coping. *Journal of Health and Social Behavior,* 1978, *19,* 2–21.

ROSE, R., & LEVIN, M. The crisis in stress research. *Journal of Human Stress,* 1979, *5,* whole issue.

SELIGMAN, M. E. P. *Helplessness.* San Francisco: Freeman, 1975.

SHANAN, J. Coping behavior in assessment for complex tasks. *Proceedings of the 17th International Congress of Applied Psychology,* 1973, *1,* 313–321.

SILBER, E., COELHO, G., MURPHEY, D., HAMBURG, D., PEARLIN, L., & ROSENBERG, M. Competent adolescents coping with college decisions. *Archives of General Psychiatry,* 1961, *5,* 517–527.

VICKERS, R., & HERVIG, L. Comparison of three psychological defense questionnaires as predictors of clinical ratings of defense. *Journal of Personality Assessment,* 1981, 45, *6,* 630–638.

WHITE, R. Strategies of adaptation: An attempt at systematic decription. In G. Coelho, D. Hamburg, & J. Adams (eds.), *Coping and adaptation.* New York: Basic Books, 1974.

WITKIN, H. H., DYK, R. B., FATERSON, H. F., GOODENOUGH, D. R., & KARP, S. H. *Psychological differentiation: Studies of development.* New York: Wiley, 1962.

17

Self-report Measures of Stress

Leonard R. Derogatis

ALTHOUGH THE DEVELOPMENT of the first psychological questionnaire is usually attributed to Galton (1883), credit for the application of the method of self-report to the study of emotional integration belongs to Woodworth (1918). His Personal Data Sheet, designed as a screening test for emotionally unstable recruits in World War I, is the prototype for all self-report tests of psychological status that were developed subsequently. It is interesting to note that although we have become much more sophisticated psychometrically since that time, several of the tests covered in the current review, such as the Minnesota Multiphasic Personality Inventory (MMPI) (Hathaway & McKinley, 1940) and the SCL-90-R (Derogatis, 1975), reflect items and principles derived directly from Woodworth's pioneering effort.

In reviewing self-report measures of stress understanding will probably be facilitated by first discussing the fundamental characteristics of the self-report modality, then moving on to the structures and limitations placed on measurement by stress theory, and finally constructing a rough taxonomic framework within which to discuss individual measures. Emphatically, the present review is not intended to be comprehensive, given the hundreds of psychological test instruments that have been applied or constructed to provide one or another operational definition of stress over the years. Instead, my plan here is to be selective—to focus on those tests and inventories that possess a productive history in stress research and to include reviews of recent instruments that show promise based on their underlying construct theory (Messick, 1981) and/or early validation data.

CHARACTERISTICS OF THE SELF-REPORT MODALITY

A review of the attributes of self-report measurement suggests that this modality of assessment has many desirable characteristics to recommend it. A very important property of self-report inventories concerns their *economy of professional effort:* most self-report scales can be administered and scored by nonprofessional personnel, who, with a bit of additional training, can also deliver basic interpretive information. Through this mechanism the professional is freed from personal involvement in appropriating fundamental assessment data, information that may in fact be utilized in a screening or triage model to determine which individuals require professional time.

A second attractive feature of self-report measurement is that such instruments are highly amenable to *actuarial methods of scoring* (Meehl & Dahlstrom, 1960). Through this and other characteristics, they also lend themselves to smooth integration into computer based clinical decision systems (Fowler, 1969; Glueck & Stroebel, 1969), a property that is becoming increasingly important with expanded utilization of patient-interactive computer testing.

Self-report inventories also tend to be *cost-efficient, brief* (with some exceptions), and, by virtue of these two properties, highly *cost-beneficial* if they are well designed; self-report measures are also *highly transportable* in the sense that the low levels of technology and professional training required for their administration and scoring enable them to be utilized in a broad spectrum of evaluation environments. This latter feature has led to their use and demonstrated *sensitivity in an extremely broad range of measurement contexts,* so that in all probability self-report measures have been addressed to more psychological attributes than has any other form of psychological assessment.

Probably the most compelling feature of the self-report modality has to do with the fact that data derived from self-report arise from the individual experiencing the phenomena in question—*the test respondent himself.* All other observers are limited to reporting apparent versions of the individual's experiences based upon the interpretation of manifest behavior or its absence. Even though the individual is clearly subject to need induced distortions in his representations, he is obviously much closer to the phenomena than any external observer can be.

Although self-report measurement may claim many positive attributes, it also possesses a number of potential liabilities. Wilde (1972) cautioned that adoption of the self-report modality tacitly assumes that validity of the "inventory premise": that is to say, the respondent *can* and *will* accurately describe his relevant experiences and behaviors. We know from experience that this is not always the case, with particular difficulties arising from identified response biases (e.g., social desirability, acquiescence) and certain defensive maneuvers on the part of the respondent.

To help place these problems in perspective, however, it should be noted that a number of critical investigations have tended to minimize the impact of response biases in clinical assessment, with the exception of social desirability (Rorer, 1965). However, the latter appears to function in a selective and complex manner (Fiske, 1971; Norman, 1967), and a number of investigators have cast serious doubt on social desirability as a unitary measurement construct (e.g., Wiggins, 1964). Individual defense mechanisms like denial or rationalization do have the capacity to distort self-report, but these mechanisms also tend to operate in other measurement modalities. The trained clinical observer may be able accurately to document the presence of such mechanisms, but he is often no more previleged to the undistorted underlying material than is the interpreter of self-report.

It would appear, then, that self-report psychological assessment is an extremely useful and flexible measurement modality with a rich past and a promising future. Like all other scientific approaches to measurement, it possesses strengths as well as weaknesses; however, the former seem to outweigh the latter, particularly when consideration is given to methods of reducing or eliminating sources of motivational distortion within respondents.

THEORIES OF STRESS AND THE STRUCTURE OF MEASUREMENT

In most areas of science the nature of the theories proposed frequently dictates operational definitions and through these definitions specifies, or at least imposes a structure upon, the nature of measurement. The area of stress research is no exception in this regard and because of the variation in theories has produced a complicated and sometimes confusing array of psychological and physical stress measures. Our task here is to deal only with the former class and, within that category, only with self-report instruments.

As Lazarus (1966) and others have noted, models or theories of stress may be partitioned into three types: stimulus oriented theories, response oriented theories, and organism oriented, or interactional, theories. Although few instruments currently used to measure stress can boast a stress construct determined strategy of development, many had been adopted or utilized as a direct result of the fit between the construct(s) they measure and investigators' beliefs that such constructs are exemplars of stress defined in either stimulus or response terms.

Stimulus oriented theories view stress as a potential residing within the stimulus properties of the organism's environment; according to this approach, those aspects of the environment that are demanding or disorganizing for the individual impose stress upon him. Cox (1978) pointed out that stimulus theorists frequently use an engineering analogy that possesses surface appeal although it often is too simplistic a model for human stress phenomena. The engineering model essentially states that each individual has an innate capacity to withstand environmental stressors (something akin to coefficient of tolerance); when the cumulative stress experienced is greater than that value, the individual begins to undergo a deterioration in function—the reaction to stress. Models based on this reasoning focus measurement efforts on the characteristics of the individual's environment (e.g., life events, time demands, external and internal noxious conditions) and attempt to utilize instruments that will accurately reflect cumulative environmental stress.

Response oriented theory defines stress in a different light. It is the response of the individual to the events of the environment that is treated as defining the presence of stress. In particular, the pattern and amplitude of emotional responses (at least at the psychological level) are used to evaluate presumptive levels of stress. Response oriented theorists owe much in their position to the work of Selye (1970) and his elucidation of the *general adaptation syndrome*. More recent theories arising from this position tend to be more interactional in nature (e.g., Kagen & Levi, 1974); however, they continue to define stress in terms of response variables and hold that this response pattern is a precursor to, or instrumental in, the development of functional derangement and diseases (of adaptation). Response oriented models tend to direct psychological assessment toward measures of disorganized functioning; psychological symptom inventories, scales measuring negative affect and mood, and instruments reflecting general psychological adjustment have explicitly or implicitly been used as stress measures by these theorists.

The third major group of theorists—those holding with an *interactional point of view*—emphasizes the characteristics of the organism as major mediating mechanisms between stimulus characteristics of the environment and the response they invoke. Interactionist theorists are critical of the unelaborated stimulus and response theories in that both these theories dismiss the important variable of person in the stress equation and, with it, the large number of important mediating characteristics that form the basis for individual differences. Most theorists in this group insist that theirs is actually a *transactional* approach: not only does the individual mediate the impact of environmental stimulus events upon responses in a linear fashion but also the perceptual, cognitive, and physiological characteristics of the individual can affect and become a significant part of the environment (e.g., Cox & Mackay, 1976; Lazarus, 1976, 1981). These theorists describe a dynamic cybernetic system in which reciprocal interactions occur between the individual's cognitive, perceptual, and emotional functions, on the one hand, and the characteristics of the external environment, on the other. Feedback loops allow for constant interplay among the components of the system to provide for a dynamic equilibrium.

Transactional theorists have so far not provided a strong impetus for new developments in stress measurement, in part because the transactional position is rather new in stress research. A second reason has to do with the fact that measurement of a system in dynamic equilibrium poses certain psychometric difficulties. The transactional position holds that perceptual, cognitive, and emotional mediating processes of the individual actively affect the *demand characteristics* of the environment so that the status of the system is constantly changing. For these investigators, the ongoing *relationship* between the person's adaptive mechanisms and the stimulus properties of the environment is central to the definition of stress. Such a definition carries the implication that accurate measurement of the stimulus field, the response spectrum, or stable mediating traits of the individual would be insufficient to capture the essence of the phenomenon since the dynamic reciprocal relationship among them would constantly alter component values. The conundrum may be more apparent than real, however, in that all measurement, even of dynamic systems, must have a stable time referent; what may emerge from the transactional position may be an innovative sequential measurement approach, which is what Lazarus (1980) appears to be striving for with his "ipsative-normative research designs."

Stimulus Oriented Measures

As mentioned previously, stimulus oriented stress research focuses on the intrinsic potential for stress residing in the environment. Logically then, measurement arising from such an orientation would address the significant characteristics of the environment that impinge upon the individual and would include scaling methods that assign weights or otherwise quantify the stress value of environmental stimuli. Although numerous aspects of the environment can be demonstrated to be stress inducing (see Weitz, 1970), few have given rise to a consistent psychological measurement approach. An exception in this regard is *life events research,* and this tradition will be the primary focus of my review of stimulus oriented measures.

It is important to note at the beginning that research on the impact of life events is not a new area of investigation even though most people tend to date it to the past decade or two. As Rahe (1978) correctly pointed out, Adolph Meyer, the first Henry Phipps Professor of Psychiatry at Johns Hopkins, made life events a central part of his theoretical model and attempted to relate such events to the medical status of individuals through his "life chart" method (Meyer, 1951).

Modern research on life events can be dated to the publication of the first version of the Schedule of Recent Experience (SRE) (Hawkins & Holmes, 1957), or more precisely to its revision, accomplished in 1964 (Rahe, Meyer, Smith, Kjaer, & Holmes, 1964). The original SRE contained 42 items and was conceptualized as a life events incidence measure. Although many minor alterations have occurred through the years (Rahe, 1978), the 42 original items have remained by and large intact. Rahe (1974) more recently integrated 13 "productive new life change questions" with the original set and added instructions for subjective life change scaling. According to Rahe, the resulting instrument, the Recent Life Changes Questionnaire (RLCQ), was designed for prospective research on life change and illness.

A source of confusion for many people attempting to appreciate this area of investigation stems from the fact that a parallel program of research has been conducted by these same investigators on *life change scaling*. The first of these studies was designed to measure the magnitude of adjustment associated with each of the 42 events (Holmes & Rahe, 1967). The investigators used direct magnitude estimation, a psychophysical scaling technique, to arrive at mean life change scores for the 42 events. The instrument involved was termed the Social Readjustment Rating Questionnaire (SRRQ), and the mean values derived from this scaling exercise became labeled *life change units* (LCUS) (Rahe, McKean, & Arthur, 1967). When the life events included in these studies are rank-ordered by mean LCU score, the resulting scale is termed the Social Readjustment Rating Scale (SRRS) (Holmes, 1979).

Despite the constraints inherent in a stimulus oriented definition of stress, life events scales nonetheless hold out great promise as sensitive predictive measures of the construct. They tend to be less affected by response biases and memory distortions than are many other measures and through the acceptance of stress as a cumulative phenomenon facilitate the summation of differential event weights (including unit weights) to achieve a total stress score. These scores may then be used in nomothetic or ipsative (i.e., studies which constrast the subject's status with his own previous status rather than normative values derived from a group) designs to evaluate the relationships of stress to disease, job performance, psychiatric symptoms, or numerous other variables.

A large number of empirical studies have demonstrated correlations between life events and health status. Rahe (1968) showed an affiliation between life stress and deterioration of health and subsequently Rahe and Lind (1971) revealed a connection between life events and sudden cardiac death, the mechanisms for which were thoughtfully reviewed by Engel (1971). Edwards (1971) observed a link between life events and subsequent myocardial infarction, as did Theorell and Rahe (1971). Gorsuch and Key (1974) demonstrated a relationship between life stress and complications with birth and pregnancy. Both Cline and Chosey (1972) and Marx, Garrity, and Bowers (1975) confirmed a bearing of life events upon health. The general conclusion of these studies seems to be that life events reduce resistance to disease in a nonspecific fashion, so that the individual's general susceptibility to illness is increased by the cumulative effects of life stress.

Consistent linkages have also been reported between life events and psychiatric symptomatology. Paykel and his colleagues (1969) observed a significant relationship between life stress and depressive disorder, a connection confirmed by Markush and Favero (1974), Ilfeld (1977), and Warheit (1979). Meyers and his associates (Meyers, Lindenthal, & Pepper, 1971, 1972) and Dekker and Webb (1973) also demonstrated a clear affiliation between life events and psychiatric disorder in general, as did Uhlenhuth and Paykel (1973) with psychiatric intensity. Barrett (1979) published a comprehensive review of the relationship between psychiatric disorder and life stress. Other thorough reviews of life events research in general were made by Dohrenwend and Dohrenwend (1974) and by Rabkin and Struening (1976).

Although the first blush appraisal of life events instruments as presumptive measures of stress is quite favorable, conceptual and methodological critiques of the approach have raised serious questions about it. To begin with, the original postulations concerning life events stress held that desirability of the events was irrelevant to their potential to produce stress; the cumulative impact of life change associated with the events was identified as the etiologic agent (Homes & Rahe, 1967). Subsequent research has argued strongly against this position. Brown (1974) seriously challenged the idea that profoundly negative events are no more stressful than positive events, and Vinokur and Selzer (1975) demonstrated convincingly that stress related measures of affect and symptoms correlated selectively with negative, as opposed to positive, life events. Subsequently, Zeiss (1980) demonstrated a high correlation between LCU scores and aversiveness of events, and Byrne and White (1980) showed that life events as discriminators of patients with myocardial infarction have little power unless the patients' subjective interpretation of the events is taken into account. To increase the predictive power of life change assessment, Horowitz and his colleagues (Horowitz, Wilner, & Alvarez, 1979) developed a life events scale that measures the subjective impact of the events.

A second problem with life stress measures concerns the differential weighting schemes for events. The LCU scores computed from the differential weights of the SRRS are widely used in life stress studies, as are other differential weighting systems. Evidence is increasingly accumulating that differential weighting of life events may be predictively irrelevant. Grant, Sweetwood, Gerst, and Yager (1978) contrasted four different weighting schemes (including SRE unit weights) and found no appreciable enhancement of event-symptom correlations associated with the differential weighting. Similarly, predicting the outcome from psychometric theory, Lei and Skinner (1980) demonstrated a correlation of .97 between SRE unit weights and differential weights developed from the SRRS. They further showed that the SRRS approach results in a reduction of internal consistency reliability. These same investigators also produced very high SRE-SRRS correlations (.93–.98) when life event scores were dimensionalized into six subdomains via factor analysis.

In addition to these problems, the issue of dimensionality has been raised regarding life stress instruments (Miller, Bentz, Aponte, & Brogan, 1974; Rahe, Pugh, & Erickson, 1971). Typically, life events instruments have represented life stress as unidimensional, with events contributing to an overall stress score. If, in fact, there are distinct dimensions or domains to life events stress, then a single overall score can easily obscure significant relationships between such specific dimensions and important variables like disease, psychiatric disorder, or job performance. Following a similar logic, Skinner and Lei (1980) determined six life event dimensions factor-analytically in a sample of 353 alcohol and drug abuse patients. They demonstrated, as one would expect, that internal consistency reliability estimates for these scales, equal in length to the SRE, were significantly higher than that for the unidimensional SRE. More important, they were able to demonstrate in many cases somewhat higher correlations for the specific dimensions with important health and demographic variables.

More general critiques of life events research have also been forthcoming. Cleary (1980) cited 10 methodological problems that have plagued this area of research and called for more rigorous designs. Goldberg and Comstock (1976) reviewed prospective studies of the relationship between life events and subsequent illness and cautioned that there is little evidence for predictive power in these prospective investigations. Minter and Kimball also raised serious questions about this connection and concluded that only with more reliable definitions and measures of health status will the question of relationship be resolved. Andrews and Tennant (1978) somewhat ominously noted that when initial hopes concerning an agent's etiological significance are not fulfilled in the psychological and medical sciences we frequently see a period of preoccupation with methodology; this reaction sometimes results in an attempt to solve with enhanced precision what is basically a problem of irrelevance.

Before closing on life events measurement, it is only accurate to point out that there are numerous other scales beyond the SRE and the SRRS that measure life stress. For example, Sarason, Johnson, and Siegel (1979) recently published data on their scale, the Life Experiences Survey (LES), and Horowitz, Schaefer, Hiroto, Wilner, and Levin (1977) proposed a number of new life stress measures.

In the final analysis, the conclusions one reaches concerning the adequacy of this approach to stress measurement are determined in large part by one's measurement requirements. If the goal is to achieve group measurement of the stress potential inherent in the environment, then with some increases in methodological rigor and some psychometric fine-tuning, these scales appear capable of accomplishing the task handily. If, on the other hand, one's purpose is to achieve precise individual measurement and prediction, then these measures do not appear to hold much promise in and of themselves. Reliabilities are compromised for a variety of reasons, and the issue of person oriented mediating variables (Johnson & Sarason, 1979) so alters the ultimate effects of environmental stressors from one individual to the next that life events scores appear to share insufficient unique variance with the criterion variables to allow effective prediction.

Response Oriented Measures

Unlike stimulus oriented life events measurement, which arose more or less from a theoretical basis in stress research, response oriented measurement has its theoretical underpinnings in pscyhopathology. Cognitive aberrations, altered affect states, and disorganized interpersonal and social relationships—long-standing hallmarks of psychiatric disorders—have come to be adopted by investigators in this area as prima facie evidence of the presence of stress.

There are literally hundreds of self-report measures that have been developed in the various areas of psychopathology, mood, psychological adjustment, personality, social competence, etc., that in one sense or another could fit the definition of a response oriented stress measure. I will not attempt to provide a comprehensive review or evaluation of this very broad area but rather focus upon a few measures that I consider to be exemplary of these various classes. For more thorough reviews the reader may consult Buros (1978), Comrey, Backer, and Glaser (1973), Hargreaves, Attkisson, Siegel, and McIntyre (1975), and Waskow and Parloff (1975).

The classes of self-report instruments that have figured most prominently as presumptive measures of stress are *psychological symptom inventories* and *scales that measure negative affect*. Most of these instruments have been multidimensional, reflecting the multiple syndromes and dysphoric emotions that exist; however, specific syndromes (e.g., anxiety) that figure prominently in psychological disorder have fostered dedicated unidimensional instruments.

Multidimensional Psychological Symptom Inventories

The MMPI The Minnesota Multiphasic Personality Inventory is one of the best-known psychological tests in existence (Hathaway & McKinley, 1940). An enormous amount of rescarch has been done using the instrument in an extremely diverse range of clinical situations and with a broad spectrum of samples. The MMPI has been pivotal in the development of personality research over a 25-year period and has provided enormous heuristic as well as scientific value (Dahlstrom & Welsh, 1960, 1972). In spite of its broad appeal, the MMPI is not without problems (Butcher, 1972). The 566 items of the scale make it extremely lengthy, and since it possesses both state and trait measurement characteristics, it is somewhat difficult for stress researchers to separate emotional responses (to stress) from some of the cognitive characteristics that mediate them. In a recent collection evaluating psychotherapy change measures (Waskow & Parloff, 1975), of the four authors assigned to evaluate self-report instruments, Dahlstrom (1975) recommended the MMPI highly, Gleser (1975) was consistently critical of the instrument, and Imber (1975) and Cartwright (1975) did not mention it at all.

In spite of ambivalent reviews, the MMPI continues to be used as a general outcome measure by stress researchers, in all probability motivated primarily by the large research literature on the scale. Examples of recent studies are a report by Miyabo, Asato, and Mizushima (1979), showing a relationship between cortisol and growth hormone levels and MMPI scores in neurotic patients, as well as a study by Bieliauskas (1980), which failed to find a relationship between 17-hydroxycorticosteroid (17-OHCS) levels and K-scale scores on a shortened version of the MMPI. Keegan, Sinha, Merriman, and Shipley (1979) observed only marginal differences between type A and type B cardiac patients on the MMPI, in spite of significant differences between the two groups in terms of medical conditions and interpersonal and social measures. Pancheri and associates (1978) found the MMPI to discriminate clearly between improved an nonimproved patients who had suffered a severe myocardial infarction, and Davis and Widseth (1978) observed the scale to be sensitive to stress among male college students.

The SCL-90-R

The SCL-90-R is a multidimensional self-report symptom inventory designed to measure symptomatic psychological distress. A prototypical version of the scale was developed in 1973 (Derogatis, Lipman, & Covi, 1973); the final version of the instrument was published two years later (Derogatis, 1975). An introductory paper by Derogatis, Rickels, and Rock (1976) was followed by the publication of the administration and scoring manual (Derogatis, 1977). The SCL-90-R is related most closely to the Hopkins Symptom Checklist (HSCL) (Derogatis, Lipman, Rickels, Uhlenhuth, and Covi, 1974 a, b); however, some items may be traced back to the original self-report inventory—Woodworth's (1918) Personal Data Sheet.

The SCL-90-R has demonstrated high levels of both test-retest and internal consistency reliability (Derogatis, 1977; Edwards, Yarvis, Mueller, Zingale, & Wagman, 1978), and validation has been approached in a programmatic manner. Derogatis, Rickels, and Rock (1976) demonstrated very high convergent and discriminant validity for the SCL-90-R in comparison with the MMPI in a sample of symptomatic volunteers, while Boleoucky and Horvath (1974) provided a similar demonstration using the Middlesex Hospital Questionnaire (MHQ) (Crown and Crisp, 1966) in a sample of nonpatient normals. In a large factor-analytic study, Derogatis and Cleary (1977a) confirmed the clinical-rational structure of the instrument, contributing to its construct validity, and in a subsequent report Derogatis and Cleary (1977b) revealed factorial invariance of the primary symptom dimensions across sex.

The SCL-90-R has proven very sensitive to change in a broad variety of clinical and medical contexts. Research on depression has shown the "90" to be particularly discriminating regarding the presence and alteration of depressive conditions. In a study focused on the distinctions between primary and secondary depression, the "90" proved to be particularly effective in demonstrating differential severity of symptoms between the groups (Weissman, Pottenger, Kleber, Rubin, Williams, & Thompson, 1977), while in a second investigation by this research team, the SCL-90-R was demonstrated capable of accurately appraising depression occurring in five psychiatric populations and a community sample (Weissman, Sholomskas, Pottenger, Prusoff, & Locke, 1977).

The SCL-90-R reflects psychological distress in terms of nine primary symptom dimensions and three global indexes of distress. Somatization (SOM), obsessive-compulsive (OBS), interpersonal sensitivity (INT), depression (DEP), anxiety (ANX), hostility (HOS), phobic anxiety (PHOB), paranoid ideation (PAR), and psychoticism (PSY) are the primary symptom constructs. The three global indexes represent summary measures of psychological disorder that, although correlated, have been shown to display distinct aspects of psychopathology (Derogatis, Yevzeroff, & Wittelsberger, 1975). The general severity index (GSI) combines information on numbers of symptoms and intensity of distress; the positive symptom total (PST) reflects only numbers of symptoms; the positive symptom distress index (PSDI) is a pure intensity measure, adjusted for numbers of symptoms present.

Currently, there are three formal published norms associated with the SCL-90-R; these were developed with psychiatric outpatients, psychiatric inpatients, and nonpatient normals. In each case, separate norms are available for men and women. Each norm represents the raw score distributions of the nine symptom dimensions and three globals in terms of *area* T-scores. Two new norms, one for adolescents and one based upon industrial executives, will be introduced during 1982, and the first of a series of change norms will soon be completed for psychiatric outpatients. Beyond formal norms, profile data are available for numerous specific clinical groups on the SCL-90-R.

The SCL-90-R has also proven sensitive to psychological distress arising from sexual disorders (Derogatis, Meyer, & Gallant, 1977; Derogatis, Meyer, & King, 1981); from conditions associated with sleep disturbance (Kales, Kales, Soldatos, Caldwell, Charney, & Martin, 1980); from chronic pain (Hendler, Derogatis, Avella, & Long, 1977); from headache (Harper & Stegler, 1978); and from cancer (Craig & Abeloff, 1974; Derogatis, Abeloff, & McBeth, 1976).

Use of the SCL-90-R specifically in stress research has been reported by Carrington and her associates (Carrington, Collings, Benson, Robinson, Wood, Lehrer, Wolfolk, & Cole, 1980), who showed the instrument to be highly sensitive to differences in various meditation interventions in stress, and by Horowitz and his group (Horowitz, Wilner, Kaltreider, & Alvarez, 1980), who carefully profiled the *DSM-III* post–traumatic stress disorders in terms of the SCL-90-R. Horowitz, Krupnick, Kaltreider, Wilner, Leong, and Marmar (1981) also demonstrated high discriminative sensitivity for the instrument concerning the stress inherent in parental death, helping people who require therapeutic help in dealing with this event. Derogatis, Abeloff, and Melisaratos (1979) revealed the SCL-90-R to be capable of discriminating long- from short-term survivors of metastic breast cancer on the basis of their affective coping pattern, a finding that was concurrently confirmed by Rogentine and his associates (Rogentine, VanKammen, Fox, Docherty, Rosenblatt, Boyd, & Bunney, 1979) with patients suffering from melanoma.

An important additional characteristic of the instrument is that the SCL-90-R does not exist solely as a distinct psychological test but rather is one component in a matched series of test instruments. A brief form of the scale, the Brief Symptom Inventory (BSI), measures the same nine symptom dimensions and three globals as the "90" and correlated very highly with it in a psychiatric population (Derogatis, 1977). In addition, two matched clinical observer's scales—have been developed to measure the same nine symptom constructs (Derogatis, 1977). The two observer's scales differ primarily in the level of sophistication in psychopathology required to use them. These instruments greatly expand the nature of the research that may be done with the SCL-90-R and enormously facilitate doctor-patient comparisons (Abramowitz & Herrera, 1981; Derogatis, Abeloff, & McBeth, 1976; Derogatis, Freeland, & Abeloff, 1979).

Unidimensional Psychological Symptom Measures

Even a cursory review of the domain of unidimensional symptom scales indicates that it is vast indeed. Limiting her focus to anxiety measures, deBonis (1974) documented 27 distinct inventories in use. Today, there are probably many more, and the same can be said for constructs other than anxiety. My selection of instruments from this large array to serve as examples of the class was dictated by two principles: first, since anxiety and depression are the emotional symptom complexes most often identified with stress, these constructs should be the primary measurement target; second, the instrument must possess an established track record of predictive validity across a range of clinical research contexts. With these two notions in mind, I selected four instruments to discuss; obviously, many more can be found that fit these criteria.

The BDI The Beck Depression Inventory is a unidimensional instrument focused upon the measurement of depression. In his introductory paper, Beck (Beck, Ward, Mendelson, Mock, & Erbaugh, 1961) described the BDI as "an instrument designed to measure the behavioral manifestations of depression" (p. 53). More recently, he (Beck & Beamesderfer, 1974) described the BDI as "an inventory for measuring the depth of depression" (p. 154). The BDI arose in part from a dissatisfaction with the vagaries of clinical judgment, reflecting both the idiosyncracies of individual practitioners and the inherent weaknesses in the nosological system. The use of a self-report inventory was perceived as a more objective approach and one that enabled the power of psychometrics to be brought to bear on the problem of measuring depression.

The BDI rests upon 21 "symptom-attitude categories," which were clinically derived by Beck and his colleagues and judged to be characteristic of their patients and specific for depression. Each category represents a characteristic manifestation of depression. (e.g., pessimism, self-dislike, fatigability), which the patient rates himself on using a series of four-point ordinal scales. Individual category scores are summed to produce a total BDI score. Beck (Beck & Beamsderfer, 1974) indicated that the particular form of the BDI was dictated by his observations that (1) severity of depression and numbers of symptoms are correlated, (2) intensity of distress and severity of depression are correlated, and (3) frequency of depressive symptoms has a stepwise distribution through the continuum from nondepressed to severely depressed.

Beck and Beamesderfer (1974) reported internal consistency reliability for the scale of .86 but for some reason skirted the issue of test-retest reliability, arguing in a less than compelling fashion that memory could bias findings over the short term and that natural fluctuations in the condition would reduce coefficients over any appreciable duration. Concurrent validity studies, with clinician ratings and other self-report measures, are numerous for the BDI, and a series of studies related to construct validation are well documented (Beck Beamesderfer, 1974).

In 1972, a 13-item short form of the BDI was introduced (Beck & Beck, 1972); however, little information on reliability was provided. This shortcoming was recently resolved through a study by Reynolds and Gould (1981), who demonstrated internal consistency coefficients of .83 for the short form, .85 for the long form, and a correlation of .93 between the two.

Although the BDI is unidimensional in the sense that it measures a single construct, a number of factor-analytic studies have isolated several distinct factors consistently from patient cohorts. These factors appear to represent the physiological-vegetative aspects of depression, hopelessness-despair, guilt–self-abasement, and fatigue-inhibition. In spite of these findings there has been no real attempt to accomplish multidimensional scoring or interpretation of the BDI.

In an insightful response to the question of cutoff scores to determine "caseness" with the BDI, Beck and Beamesderfer (1974) pointed out that it is not possible to identify a single score whereby to make assignments. The relevance of any score depends upon the cohort being predicted from, the selectivity and specificity associated with various cutoffs in that sample, and the utility functions involved in determining the "cost" of false negatives and false positives in the particular context in question. It is important to note, however, as Reynolds and Gould (1981) observed, that there are significant sex differences on the BDI (particularly the short form) and this fact should be taken into account when using cutoff scores.

The BDI is broadly used to measure stress and distress associated with psychological disorders (Beck & Beamesderfer, 1974) and has been shown also to be sensitive to the stress associated with inpatient (Schwab, Bialon, Brown, & Holzer, 1967) and outpatient (Nielsen & Williams, 1980) medical disorders. The scale is often used as a measure of depression in life events studies (e.g., Johnson & Sarason, 1978) and recently has been shown to be applicable to disordered adolescents (Strober, Green, & Carlson, 1981).

The STAI   The State-Trait Anxiety Inventory is a self-report symptom-mood inventory designed to provide an operational distinction between anxiety as an enduring personality characteristic—*trait anxiety*—and anxiety as a transient emotional experience—*state anxiety*. Spielberger and his colleagues (Spielberger, Gorsuch, & Lushene, 1970) developed the STAI with the notion of creating two distinct scales with high internal consistency that would provide valid measurement of these separate but related components of anxiety as postulated by state-trait anxiety theroists (Cattell, 1960, 1966; Spielberger, 1966, 1972).

The STAI is comprised of two sets of 20 statements concerning how an individual feels. The respondent endorses one set with instructions to do so regarding how he feels *at a particular moment (A-state);* while the second set of items is responded to in terms of how the individual *generally* feels (*A-trait*). There is a children's version of the instrument, the STAIC (Spielberger, 1973), and a Spanish edition of the adult scale (Spielberger, Gonzalez-Reigoza, & Martinez-Urrutia, 1971).

Smith and Lay (1974) compiled an annotated bibliography of research done with the STAI through 1972 and documented sensitivity for the instrument in a wide variety of stress contexts. Stress conditions ranged from surgery (Delong, 1971; Florell, 1971), through dental treatment (Lamb & Plant, 1972), to public speaking (Lamb, 1970). Kendal and his associates (Kendall, Finch, Auerbach, Hook, & Mikulka, 1976) did a tripartite study of the STAI investigating the factor structure of the instrument. They discovered a unitary trait anxiety factor but observed two distinct dimensions of state anxiety. Relationships between high and low trait anxiety and levels of the two state anxiety measures under self-esteem and physical threat conditions were evaluated; mixed support was observed for the relationship predicted from theory.

Several recent examples of the use of the STAI in stress research may be found in Johnson and Sarason (1978), who utilized the instrument in life events research, and in Sarason, Johnson, and Siegle (1979), who demonstrated that negative life change scores had a significant correlation with the measures of the STAI, while positive life change scores correlated approximately zero with this feeling based measure of stress. Because of its brevity and ease of use, as well as the distinction between current emotional reaction versus what may very well turn out to be a mediating variable in stress experiences, the STAI continues to be an attractive instrument in stress research.

The SDS and the SAS   The Self-rating Depression Scale and the Self-rating Anxiety Scale were published by Zung in 1965 and 1971, repectively. Each scale was devised to provide an operational definition of the relevant symptom construct as a *clinical disorder*. The instruments were generated from a systematic program of research designed to provide objective operational definitions of these important clinical entities.

The Self-rating Depression Scale was developed in an effort, according to Zung (1974), "to define depressive disorders by an operational definition qualitatively, and construct a rating scale which would quantify the symptomatology" (p. 171). Review of a great deal of prior and contemporary clinical and multivariate research on depression led Zung to conclude that four characteristics of clinical depression are commonly observed: pervasive affect disturbances, physiological disturbances, psychomotor disturbances, and psychological disturbances. Twenty items were then developed from these four primary areas. Each item is provided on a four-point ordinal scale of proportional applicability to the respondent, who is asked to indicate how applicable the item is to him at the time of testing. A numerical index is developed for the SDS by dividing the sum of scores on the 20 items by 80 and converting the resulting decimal to a whole number distribution that ranges from 25 to 100. This is not a standardized distribution, however, but something akin to a percentage distribution that has been arbitrarily truncated at the lower end.

In discussing reliability and validity, Zung (1974) argued strongly that *content* validity is important for such a scale and observed that the operations that had generated the scale adequately fulfilled this criterion. He also cited a number of studies demonstrating predictive validity in terms of the criterion of psychiatric diagnosis, along with a number of convergent validity studies with instruments such as the BDI, the MMPI D-scale, and the Hamilton Depression Rating Scale. The level of discriminative validity shown by the SDS was less clear from these reports.

Zung (1972) reported on a broad range of studies measuring depression in clinical populations, as well as on a number of cross-cultural studies and studies in normal populations. It is important to note that the SDS has a matching clinical observer's scale, the Depression Status Inventory (DSI) (Zung, 1972), a 20-item semistructured interview that correlates .87 with the SDS.

Although published a number of years later, the Self-rating Anxiety Scale was developed to rectify a similar lack. Zung (1974) pointed out that "the need for a standardized method of evaluating and recording the presence of anxiety as a clinical disorder has not been met by most scales today" (p. 180).

The SAS consists of 20 items designed to reflect the major characteristics of clinical anxiety disorders. The SAS also has a matching clinical observer's scale termed the Anxiety Status Inventory (ASI) (Zung, 1974, 1975). Scoring of both scales follows Zung's unique procedure of dividing the sum of item scores by the maximum of 80 and multiplying by 100. Since items are scored from 1 through 4, this procedure results in a truncated distribution ranging from 25 to 100.

Reliability on validity data are less available on the SAS than on the SDS. Zung (1974, 1979) heavily stressed the importance of content validity for both scales and provided data on convergent validity using the Taylor Manifest Anxiety Scale and the Hamilton Anxiety Scale. He also reported predictive validity using the presence of psychiatric anxiety disorders as a criterion, and demonstrated correlations between the SAS and ASI of .66 in a heterogeneous group of psychiatric patients and .74 for a sample limited to anxiety disorders (Zung, 1979, 1979). I could find no data on reliability for either the SAS or the ASI.

Although not widely used in stress research, both the SDS and the SAS have a number of characteristics to recommend them. They arose from systematic, ongoing programs of clinical measurement, and they are brief and simple to administer. Although psychometric studies remain to be done with the scales, matching observer's forms are a measurement bonus; moreover, the sensitivity of the measures is now well documented and they will probably see more utilization in future stress research.

Affect and Mood Scales

In addition to response oriented measures based upon psychiatric symptoms, affect and mood scales constitute a second significant class of measures. By their nature, moods and affects tend to be more transient than other signs of stress, such as psychological symptoms; therefore, consistency reliability for these measures is by definition somewhat lower. In my experience, however, simple mood measures repeatedly have shown themselves to be the first instruments to reveal impending therapeutic change; futhermore, they are extremely cost-efficient and cost-beneficial. Typically, such instruments are collections of adjectives that depict various mood states, often selected on the basis of factor-analytic studies. Although a large number of adjective mood scales exist, only two will be discussed here: one because of its proven sensitivity in many clinical research contexts and the second because of its unusual approach to the measurement of affect.

The POMS The Profile of Mood States is a 65-item adjective checklist that reflects measurement in terms of six primary mood states derived through repeated factor analyses (McNair, Lorr, & Droppleman, 1971). The mood dimensions are labeled tension-anxiety, depression-dejection, confusion, anger-hostility, vigor, and fatigue.

Each item of the POMS is scaled on a five-point scale from not at all to extremely; the measurement context is "the past week including today." The scale takes approximately 10–15 minutes to complete, and language levels have been assessed to keep word difficulty at a minimum.

Reported internal consistency coefficients for the POMS range from .74 to .92, with test-retest coefficients of .61–.69 based on a one-month interval (McNair & Lorr, 1964). Repeated factor analyses of the instrument have confirmed its basic factor structure (Lorr, McNair, & Weinstein, 1963; McNair & Lorr, 1964), and separate male and female norms are available for the instrument based upon a large sample seen at a university health center.

The POMS has shown predictive validity in a broad spectrum of clinical change studies involving both psychotherapy (Imber, 1975) and psychopharmacology (McNair, 1974). In a fascinating study, Haskell, Pugatch, and McNair (1969) demonstrated independent predictive variance associated with symptoms, as measured by the Hopkins Symptom Checklist, and affective status, as measured by the POMS. The instrument is well conceived and developed and should prove to be a sensitive response oriented measure of stress.

The ABS A review of the majority of adjective mood scales reveals that most dimensions of these scales focus upon negative affect states. When used as measures of current status or treatment induced change, these instruments are limited to operational definitions totally dependent upon the status of dysphoric affects.

Many of us have made the clinical observation, however, that current assessment or prognosis is equally dependent upon the status of positive affects in the individual. Much as the ultimate response to stress depends not only upon levels of stressors but also upon coping resources, so the most accurate assessment of an individual's emotional status must examine both positive and negative affects. Consistent with this appreciation, I (Derogatis, 1975) developed an adjective mood scale, the Affect Balance Scale, that includes positive affect dimensions (joy, contentment, vigor, and affection), as well as four negative dimensions (anxiety, depression, guilt, and hostility).

The ABS is a 40-item adjective instrument that scales mood adjectives on a five-point scale from not at all (0) to extremely (4). Summations across the eight affect dimensions lead to positive and negative affect totals; an overall difference score between these two (the affect balance index) provides the summary score for the instrument.

Currently there are published norms available for the ABS on psychiatric inpatients, sexually dysfunctional patients, and nonpatient normals (Derogatis, 1975). Norms for psychiatric outpatients are currently being developed, as are change norms based upon this group. The ABS takes three to five minutes to complete.

Although formal reliability studies are in progress, five studies have reported on the predictive validity of the scale. Derogatis, Meyer, and Vasquez (1978) showed the ABS to be highly sensitive to the dysphoric affect status of male gender dysphorics; this affect posture was distinct from that of female gender dysphorics (Derogatis, Meyer, & Boland, 1981). Negative affect states associated with both male and female sexual dysfunction have also been clearly documented with the ABS (Derogatis & Meyer, 1979), and Derogatis, Abeloff, and Melisaratos (1979) demonstrated that mechanisms associated with affect status significantly discriminated long-term from short-term survivors with metastic breast cancer. Most recently, Hoen-Saric (1981) was able to show the ABS to be highly sensitive to distinctions among anxiety states.

I (Derogatis, 1982) recently completed a structure confirming factor analysis of the ABS based upon 417 psychiatric outpatients. All four negative affect dimensions were confirmed, along with vigor and affection in the positive domain. The joy and contentment dimensions blended together to form a single dimension. A higher order analysis of the correlations among the primary factors resulted in two distinct dimensions, one reflecting positive, the other negative, affect items.

Although his work arose from a different research perspective (community samples), Bradburn (1969; Bradburn & Caplovitz, 1965) convincingly argued for the notion of independence of positive and negative affects, asserting that mental health status is most accurately related to the balance between them. Although his scale is quite different in structure from the ABS, Bradburn also developed a 10-item instrument termed the Affect Balance Scale. This work is central to the emerging theoretical position that *psychological health* is independently important to psychological well-being and that the conceptualization health is an essential counterpart to disorder or disease (see Fontana, Marcus, Dowds, & Hughes, 1980). The separation of positive and negative affect states is an important component in this theoretical approach and may prove highly relevant in research on resisitance to stress. For this reason, the ABS developed in our laboratory may be a useful measure in future stress research.

INTERACTION ORIENTED MEASURES

As I pointed out earlier, interactional theorists are particularly interested in the cognitive, perceptual, and other characteristics of the individual that serve to mediate responses to stress. Personality traits, coping styles, psychodynamic mechanisms of defense, as well as many other person variables, enter into interactional postulations concerning stress.

The interactional position is somewhat newer than the stimulus and response orientations to stress and partly for this reason has not yet given rise to a variety of psychological measures in the stress field. However, this situation is rapidly changing. This section first examines the instrument that is probably the most familiar of all stress measures and then reviews a number of promising new interactional measures.

The JAS

The Jenkins Activity Survey is a self-report screening instrument developed by Jenkins and his colleagues (Jenkins, Rosenman, & Friedman, 1967; Jenkins, Zyzanski, & Rosenman, 1975, 1976) to measure a specific pattern of behavior thought to have high a association with proneness to coronary disease: this behavioral complex has come to be known as the *type A behavior pattern*. The scale actually represents a more rigorous and objective operational definition of a pattern of behavior originally described via interview methods (Friedman & Rosenman, 1959).

The JAS has been repeatedly demonstrated to have convergent validity (70–73% agreement) with structured interviews designed to measure the same behavior complex (Jenkins & Zyzanski, 1980) and has shown substantial predictive validity concerning the prevalence of coronary heart disease (Jenkins, 1971, 1976; Jenkins, Rosenman, & Zyzanski, 1974). Also, in a fascinating and systematic series of laboratory and field experiments, Glass has (Glass, 1977) made a significant contribution to the construct validity of the type A behavior pattern.

The JAS consists of 52 items scaled in terms of multiple-point descriptors. Jenkins and Zyzanski (1980) indicated that the instrument is comprised of four scales, only one of which is the type A scale: the latter was derived through discriminant function analysis. The remaining three scales were derived through a factor analysis of the items that discriminated type A behavior from other patterns (i.e., type B). These are described as "three independent dimensions, which are uncorrelated with each other but each is correlated with Type A" (p. 159). The corresponding factors have been labeled speed and impatience, job involvement, and hard-driving–competitive. Obviously, the item loadings of the scales are not univocal, and, as we know from previous experience with the MMPI (Norman, 1972), the artifactual correlations resulting from joint keying of items can often obscure predictive relationships.

Nonetheless, the JAS has been used almost universally in stress research (at least that aspect related to coronary heart disease); the instrument has been translated into numerous languages, including Dutch, Polish, Russian, and Swedish (Jenkins & Zyzanski, 1980). Space limitations prevent my reviewing the enormous literature involving the JAS; excellent reviews have been provided by Glass (1977), Goldband, Katkin, and Morell (1979), Jenkins (1971, 1976), and Jenkins and Zyzanski (1980), and an interesting editorial on the topic was published by Marmot (1980). I shall present a few examples.

Recent research with the JAS indicated increased risk of coronary artery disease when both type A behavior and social insecurity were present (Jenkins, Zyzanski, Ryan, Flessas, & Tannenbaum, 1977); however, a therapeutic exercise program disproportionately reduced physiologic coronary risk factors in type A subjects (Blumenthal, Williams, Williams, & Wallace, 1980). Another report demonstrated that hostility and the type A behavior pattern are independently predictive of atherosclerosis (Williams, Haney, Lee, Kong, Blumenthal, & Whalen, 1980), and Nielson and Dobson (1980) found that the type A behavior pattern was virtually uncorrelated with a series of measures of trait anxiety among college students.

As with all instruments, one could wish for certain improvements in the JAS. Although convergent validity studies are plentiful, with the exception of the few reports mentioned previously, we have not seen sufficient evidence of discriminative validity for the scale. Scoring of the JAS is unnecessarily complicated, and the psychometric relationships between type A and the other dimensions of the instrument remain obscure. They are obviously not independent; however, there is insufficient information on the degree of correlation of the factored scales with type A to determine whether the latter is simply a linear combination of the other three.

In spite of these objections, the JAS has proven to be an extremely productive research instrument that has facilitated an enormous amount of research on the important topic of the relationship between physical disease and psychological-behavioral mediators. Although limited to a specific area of stress research, the JAS represents a measurement benchmark that has proven most useful.

The DSP

The Derogatis Stress Profile is a new stress instrument, with introductory psychometric analyses being completed at the time of this writing. The DSP is mentioned here first because it is one of the very few measures whose constructs came directly from stress theory and second because it explicitly incorporates stimulus, response, and interactional elements. Also, preliminary validation data suggest that the instrument is sensitivite to stress phenomena across a broad spectrum.

The DSP is a 77-item test with 11 underlying dimensions and two global scores. One global represents a summation of scores over the 11 primary dimensions, while the second is an analogue measure of the individual's subjectively perceived current level of stress. The test takes 10–15 minutes to complete and is easily hand scored.

Three of the 11 DSP scales measure stimulus elements arising from the job environment, the home environment, and the health environment. These scales are termed vocational satisfaction, domestic satisfaction, and health posture. Five dimensions measure characteristic attributes and coping mechanisms that have been shown to have significant mediating effects regarding stress. These are termed time pressure, which is self-defining; driven behavior, which reflects the compulsive need to be constantly involved in behavior deemed constructive; attitude posture, which reflects the achievement ethic; relaxation potential, which measures the potential for healthy diversions; and role definition, which is designed to measure the role determined expectancy of bearing sole responsibility for life demands. The three remaining dimensions reflect the primary response oriented measures of stress via the emotion-symptom constructs of aggression-hostility, tension-anxiety, and depression. The two former measures gain fundamental support as valid measures of stress through Cannon's (1929) original postulation of the neuroendocrine mechanisms of the fight-flight response. Depression finds support as a valid measure of stress via Selye's (1970) work with the general adaptation syndrome and subsequent explication by a number of theorists (Horowitz, 1979; McLean, 1976).

The DSP was conceived to be a truly interactional measure of stress. The three stimulus scales provide an indication of the level of environmental stress the individual is subjected to; the five mediating behavior scales may be thought of as a lens system capable of magnifying or reducing the impact of stressors; finally, the three response measures indicate the level of conscious emotional distress the individual is experiencing as a result of stressor-mediator interaction. Each scale has an equal opportunity to contribute to the overall interactional stress score.

Norms (area T-scores) are now being developed on a number of populations (executives, students, psychiatric patients) and fundamental reliability and confirmatory factorial studies are in progress.

The RSL

The Rating of Statements List is a Dutch instrument designed to measure a fundamental dimension of what is termed the "infarction personality" (van Dije & Nagelkerke, 1980). This construct is quite similar to the type A behavior pattern, measured by the JAS, and test development also paralleled Jenkins's methods in that the original pool of 69 items was first subjected to discriminant function analysis to identify those items that distinguished between MI patients and healthy males; these 27 items were subsequently factor-analyzed. This analysis identified four factors that accounted for 90% of the variance in the matrix, namely depressiveness, hostility, work involvement and job involvement, and job responsibility.

The scale has shown predictive validity of the retrospective type in discriminating established MI patients from healthy controls (van Dijl & Negelkerke, 1980), and an earlier version of the scale also demonstrated predictive validity prospectively by discriminating MI patients and high-risk (for MI) controls from low-risk controls (van Dooren, 1980).

The instrument is brief and appears to possess substantive predictive value. The item content of the RSL should be stabilized and its formal psychometric properties further developed.

The MQ

The Maastricht Questionnaire is another recently developed Dutch scale (Appels, 1979, 1980). The MQ has a particular focus upon detecting the prodromata of MI and sudden death. Sixty-three items, plus 14 "fillers," comprise the instrument, and Appels (1980) recently showed that a subset of 40 items successfully discriminated between a group with cardiovascular disease and healthy controls. Hierarchical cluster analysis demonstrated that discriminating items appeared to measure such things as tiredness, loss of vitality, depression, helplessness-hopelessness, and sleep disturbance. Appels suggested that the construct measured by the test is "a syndrome of vital exhaustion and depression" (p. 193) and that such a behavioral complex is a prodromal developmental phase moving from the type A behavior pattern to coronary disease.

A convergent and predictive validity study reported that the MQ correlated well with the JAS in discriminating MI patients from healthy controls (Verhagen, Nass, Appels, vanBastelaer, & Winnubisi, 1980). These same authors reported Cronbach α's for the scale of over .80.

The idea of a devolpmental path for the individual with coronary-prone behavior that ultimately passes through an identifiable prodromal stage of "vital exhaustion and depression" is intriguing and not without support. It is hoped that Appels will formalize this instrument in the near future and provide appropriate psychometric analyses.

CONCLUSION

Upon completion of this chapter, it occurs to me that reviewing self-report measures of stress at the end of the twentieth century may not be unlike the task that faced European cartographers and navigators of the fifteenth century in charting a direct westward route to India. Although there are some promising reports, the goal in question may ultimately be unattainable as originally stated.

It is possible, as Hinkle (1979) argued, that the construct of stress has become adorned with too much excess meaning to serve any longer as a useful scientific construct relative to the pathogenesis of disease. He suggested that stress is a construct devoid of precise explanatory value and that we should redirect our attention to specific psychologically mediated events at physiological levels (e.g., catecholamine discharge, sympathetic arousal) that have demonstrated relationships to health status. It is also possible that Hinkle's critique is premature or incorrect (or both) regarding the scientific value of the construct, particularly if it lends itself to reliable measurement.

One of the most demanding requirements that can be placed upon any construct is that it serve as the basis for effective operational measurement. That is to say, the construct theory must delineate the boundaries, dimensions, and relationships of the domain in question and insure, in Messick's (1981) words, that "a miniature test of the construct theory is afforded at the item level" (p. 575). Hallmarks of constuct validation are convergent and discriminant studies that confirm the meaning of test scores as operational definitions of the construct and integrate observed relationships with other variables and construct measures. Although we have seen numerous convergent studies in the stress literature, the same cannot be said of discriminant validity reports, and these are much needed to provide precise delineations of our constructs.

As stress theory has moved toward a more interactional, and subsequently transactional, posture, a more realistic appreciation of the phenomenon appears to have emerged. I believe this transition will have an important effect upon those involved in attempting to measure stress: they will become less like the three blind men trying to describe an elephant. At this point, it is too early to tell whether the stress concept will survive the ensuring decades; however, if it does, such a result can be realized only through sound operational measurement.

REFERENCES

ABRAMOWITZ, S. I., & HERRERA, H. R. On controlling for patient psychopathology in naturalistic studies of sex bias: A methodological demonstration. *Journal of Consulting and Clinical Psychology,* 1981, *49,* 597–603.

ANDREWS, G., & TENNANT, C. Life event stress and psychiatric illness. *Psychological Medicine,* 1978, *8,* 545–549.

APPELS, A. Psychological prodromata of myocardial infarction and sudden death. *Psychotherapy and Psychosomatics,* 1980, *34,* 187–195.

APPELS, A., POOLS, J., & LUBSEN, T. Psychische prodromen van het hartinfaret. *Nederlands Tijdschrift Psychologie,* 1979, *34,* 213–223.

BARRETT, J. E. (ed.). *Stress and mental disorder.* New York: Raven, 1979.

BECK, A. T., & BEAMESDERFER, A. Assessment of depression: The depression inventory. In P. Pichot (ed.), *Modern problems in pharmacopsychiatry,* vol 7. Basel: Karger, 1974.

BECK, A. T., & BECK, R. W. Screening depressed patients in family practice: A rapid technic. *Postgraduate Medicine,* 1972, *52* (6), 81–85.

BECK, A., WARD, C., MENDELSON, M., MOCK, J., & ERBAUGH, J. An inventory for measuring depression. *Archives of General Psychiatry,* 1961, *4,* 53–63.

BIELIAUSKAS, L. Life events, 17-OHCS measures, and psychological defensiveness in relation to aid-seeking. *Journal of Human Stress,* 1980, *6,* 28–36.

BLUMENTHAL, J. A., WILLIAMS, R. S., WILLIAMS, R. B., & WALLACE, A. G. Effects of exercise on the type A (coronary prone) behavior pattern. *Psychosomatic Medicine,* 1980. *42,* 289–296.

BOLEOUCKY, Z., & HORVATH, M. SCL-90 rating scale: First experience with the Czech version in healthy male scientific workers. *Activitas Nervosa Superior,* (Praha), 1972, *16,* 115–116.

BRADBURN, N. M. *The structure of psychological well-being.* Chicago: Aldine, 1969.

BUROS, O. K. *The eighth mental measurement yearbook.* Highland Park: Gryphon, 1978.

BUTCHER, J. N. (ed.). *Objective personality assessment: Changing perspectives.* New York: Academic, 1972.

BYRNE, D. G., & WHYTE, H. M. Life events and myocardial infarction revisited: The role of measures of individual impact. *Psychosomatic Medicine,* 1980, *42,* 1–10.

CANNON, W. B. *Bodily changes in fear, hunger, pain, and rage: An account of recent researches into the function of emotional excitement* (2d ed.). New York: Appleton, 1929.

CARRINGTON, P., COLLINS, G. H., BENSON, H., ROBISON, H., WOOD, L. W., LEHRER, P. M., WOOLFOLK, R. L., & COLE, J. The use of meditation-relaxation techniques for the management of stress in a working population. *Journal of Occupational Medicine,* 1980, *22,* 221–231.

CARTWRIGHT, D. S. Patient self-report measures. In I. E. Waskow & M. B. Parloff (eds.), *Psychotherapy change measures.* Rockville: National Institute of Mental Health, 1975.

CATTELL, R. B. The dimensional (unitary-component) measurement of anxiety, excitement, effort stress, and other mood reaction patterns. In L. Uhr & J. G. Miller (eds.), *Drugs and behavior.* New York: Wiley, 1960.

—————. Anxiety and motivation: Theory and crucial experiments. In C. D. Spielberger (ed.), *Anxiety and behavior.* New York: Academic, 1966.

CLEARY, P. J. A checklist for life event research. *Journal of Psychosomatic Research,* 1980, *24,* 199–207.

CLIVE, D., & CHOSY, J. A prospective study of life changes and subsequent health changes. *Archives of General Psychiatry,* 1972, *27,* 51–53.

COMREY, A. L., BACKER, T. E., & GLASER, E. M. *A sourcebook for mental health measures.* Los Angeles: Human Interaction Research Institute, 1973.

COX, T. *Stress.* Baltimore: University Park Press, 1978.

COX, T., & MACKAY, C. J. A psychological model of occupational stress. Paper presented to the Medical Research Council meeting on mental health in industry, London, 1976.

CRAIG, T. J., & ABELOFF, M. D. Psychiatric symptomatology among hospitalized cancer patients. *American Journal of Psychiatry,* 1974, *131,* 1323–1327.

DAHLSTROM, W. G. Recommendations for patient measures in evaluating psychotherapy: Test batteries and inventories. In I. E. Waskow & M. B. Parloff (eds.), *Psychotherapy change measures.* Rockville: National Institute of Mental Health, 1975.

DAHLSTROM, W. G., WELSH, G. S., & DAHLSTROM, L. E. *An MMPI handbook. Vol. 1: Clinical interpretation* Minneapolis: University of Minnesota Press, 1972.

DAVIS, D. A., & WEDSETH, J. C. A Minnesota Multiphasic Personality Inventory indicator of psychological distress in male students. *Journal of Counseling Psychology,* 1978, *25,* 469–472.

DEBONIS, M. Content analysis of 27 anxiety inventories and rating scales. In P. Pichot (ed.), *Modern problems in pharmacopsychiatry,* vol. 7. Basel: Karger, 1974.

CROWN, S. & CRISP, A. H. A short clinical diagnostic self-rating scale for psychoneurotic patients: The Middlesex Hospital Questionnaire (MHQ). *British Journal of Psychiatry,* 1966, *112,* 917–923.

DEKKER, D. J., & WEBB, J. T. Relationships of the social readjustment rating scale to psychiatric patient status, anxiety, and social desirability. *Journal of Psychosomatic Research,* 1974, *18,* 125–130.

DELONG, R. D. Individual differences in patterns of anxiety arousal, stress-relevant information, and recovery from surgery. *Dissertation Abstracts International,* 1971, *32*(B), 554.

DEROGATIS, L. R. *The Affects Balance Scale.* Baltimore: Clinical Psychometric Research, 1975. (a)

————. *The SCL-90-R.* Baltimore: Clinical Psychometric Research, 1975. (b)

————. *SCL-90-R administration, scoring, and procedures manual,* vol. 1. Baltimore: Clinical Psychometric Research, 1977.

————. *The Derogatis Stress Profile (DSP).* Baltimore: Clinical Psychometric Research, 1980.

DEROGATIS, L. R., ABELOFF, M. D., & FREELAND, C. Doctor versus patient perception of psychological distress among cancer patients. Paper presented to the annual meeting of the American Society of Clinical Oncology, New Orleans, 1979.

DEROGATIS, L. R., ABELOFF, M. D., & MCBETH, C. D. Cancer patients and their physicians in the perception of psychological symptoms. *Psychosomatics* 1976, *17,* 197–201.

DEROGATIS, L. R., ABELOFF, M. D., & MELISARATOS, N. Psychological coping mechanisms and survival time in metastic breast cancer. *JAMA,* 1979, *242,* 1504–1508.

DEROGATIS, L. R., & CLEARY, P. Confirmation of the dimensional structure of the SCL-90: A study in construct validation. *Journal of Clinical Psychology,* 1977, *33,* 981–989. (a)

————. Factorial invariance across gender for the primary symptom dimensions of the SCL-90. *British Journal of Social and Clinical Psychology,* 1977, *16,* 347–356. (b)

DEROGATIS, L. R., LIPMAN, R. S., & COVI, L. SCL-90: An outpatient psychiatric rating scale: Preliminary report. *Psychopharmacology Bulletin,* 1973, *9,* 13–27.

DEROGATIS, L. R., LIPMAN, R. S., RICKELS, K., UHLENHUTH, E. H. & COU, L. The Hopkins Symptom Checklist (HSCL): A self-report symptom inventory. *Behavioral Science* 1974a, *19,* 1–15.

DEROGATIS, L. R., LIPMAN, R. S., RICKLES, K., UHLENHUTH, E. H. & COVI, L. The Hopkins Symptom Checklist (HSCL): A measure of primary symptom dimensions. In P. Pichot (ed.), *Psychological Measurements in Psychopharmacology.* Basel: Karger, 1974b.

DEROGATIS, L. R., & MEYER, J. K. A psychological profile of the sexual dysfunctions. *Archives of Sexual Behavior,* 1979, *8,* 201–223.

DEROGATIS, L. R., MEYER, J. K., & BOLAND, P. A psychological profile of the transsexual. Part II: The female. *Journal of Nervous and Mental Disease,* 1981, *169,* 157–168.

DEROGATIS, L. R., MEYER, J. K., & GALLANT, B. W. Distinctions between male and female invested partners in sexual disorders. *American Journal of Psychiatry,* 1977, *134,* 385–390.

DEROGATIS, L. R., MEYER, J. K., & KING, K. M. Psychopathology in individuals with sexual dysfunction. *American Journal of Psychiatry,* 1981, *138,* 757–763.

DEROGATIS, L. R., MEYER, J. K., & VASQUEZ, N. A psychological profile of the transsexual. Part I: The male. *Journal of Nervous and Mental Disease,* 1978, *166,* 234–254.

DEROGATIS, L. R., RICKELS, K., & ROCK, A. The SCL-90 and the MMPI: A step in the validation of a new self-report scale. *British Journal of Psychiatry,* 1976, *128,* 280–289.

DEROGATIS, L. R., YEVZEROFF, H., & WITTELSBERGER, B. Social class, psychological disorder, and the nature of the psychopathologic indicator. *Journal of Consulting and Clinical Psychology,* 1975, *43,* 183–191.

DOHRENWEND, B. S., & DOHRENWEND, B. P. (eds.). *Stressful life events: Their nature and effects.* New York: Wiley, 1974.

EDWARDS, D. W., YARVIS, R. M., MUELLER, D. P., ZINGALE, H. C., & WAGMAN, W. J. Test-taking and the stability of adjustment scales. *Evaluation Quarterly,* 1978, *2,* 275–291.

EDWARDS, M. K. Life crises and myocardical infarction. Master's thesis, University of Washington, 1971.

ENGEL, G. L. Sudden and rapid death during psychological stress: Folklore or folk wisdom? *Annals of Internal Medicine,* 1971, *74,* 771–782.

FISKE, D. W. *Measuring the concepts of personality.* Chicago: Aldine, 1971.

FLORELL, J. L. Crisis intervention in orthopedic surgery. *Dissertation Abstracts International,* 1971, *32*(B), 633.

FONTANA, A. F., MARCUS, J. L., DAWDS, B. N., & HUGHES, L. A. Psychological impairment and psychological health in the psychological well-being of the physically ill. *Psychosomatic Medicine,* 1980, *42,* 279–288.

FOWLER, R. D. Automation and the computer. In J. N. Butcher (ed.), *MMPI: Research developments and clinical applications.* New York: McGraw-Hill, 1969.

FRIEDMAN, M., & ROSENMAN, R. H. Association of specific overt behavior pattern with blood and cardiovascular findings. *Journal of the American Medical Association,* 1959, *169,* 1286–1296.

GALTON, F. *Inquiries into human faculty and its development.* New York: Macmillan, 1883.

GLASS, D. C. Stress, behavior patterns, and coronary disease. *American Scientist,* 1977, *65,* 177–187.

GLESER, G. C. Evaluation of psycohotherapy outcome by psychological tests. In I. E. Waskok & M. B. Parloff (eds.), *Psychotherapy change measures.* Rockville: National Institute of Mental Health, 1975.

GLUECK, B. C., & STROEBEL, C. F. The computer and the clinical decision process. *American Journal of Psychiatry (supp.),* 1969, *125,* 2–7.

GOLDBAND, S., KATKIN, E. S., & MORELL, M. A. Personality and cardiovascular disorder: Steps toward demystification. In I. G. Sarason & C. D. Spielberger (eds.), *Stress and anxiety,* vol. 6. New York: Wiley, 1979.

GOLDBERG, E. L., & COMSTOCK, G. W. Life events and subsequent illness. *American Journal of Epidemiology,* 1976, *104,* 146–158.

GORSUCH, R. L., & KEY, M. K. Abnormalities of pregnancy as a function of anxiety and life stress. *Psychosomatic Medicine,* 1974, *36,* 352.

GRANT, I., SWEETWOOD, H., GERST, M. S., & YAGER, J. Scaling procedures in life events research. *Journal of Psychosomatic Research,* 1978, *22,* 525–530.

HARGREAVES, W. A., ATTKISSON, C. C., SIEGAL, L. M., & MCINTYRE, M. H. *Resource material for community mental health program evaluation,* part 4. Rockville: National Institute of Mental Health, 1975.

HARPER, R. G., & STEGER, J. C. Psychological correlates of frontalis EMG and pain in tension headache. *Headache Journal,* 1978, *18,* 215–218.

HASKELL, D., PUGATCH, D., & MCNAIR, D. M. Time-limited psychotherapy for whom? *Archives of General Psychiatry,* 1969, *21,* 546–552.

HATHAWAY, S. R., & MCKINLEY, J. C. A multiphasic personality schedule (Minnesota). Part I: Construction of the schedule. *Journal of Psychology,* 1940, *10,* 249–254.

HAWKINS, N. C., DAVIES, R., & HOLMES, T. H. Evidence of psychosocial factors in the development of pulmonary tuberculosis. *American Review of Tuberculosis and Pulmonary Disorders,* 1957, *75,* 768–780.

HENDLER, N., DEROGATIS, L. R., AVELLA, J., & LONG, D. EMG biofeedback in patients with chronic pain. *Diseases of the Nervous System,* 1977, *38,* 505–509.

HINKLE, L. E. Commentary: "On stress and cardiovascular disease." *Cardiovascular Medicine,* 1979, *26,* 192–202.

HOEHN-SARIC, R. Characteristics of chronic anxiety patients. In D. F. Klein & J. Rabkin (eds.), *Anxiety: New research and changing concepts*. New York: Raven, 1981.

HOLMES, T. H. Development and application of a quantitative measure of life change magnitude. In J. E. Barrett *Stress and mental disorder*. New York: Raven, 1979.

HOLMES, T. H., & RAHE, R. H. The Social Readjustment Rating Scale. *Journal of Psychosomatic Research*, 1967, *11*, 213–218.

HOROWITZ, M. J. Depressive disorders in response to loss. In I. G. Sarason & C. D. Spielberger (eds.), *Stress and anxiety*, vol. 6. New York: Wiley, 1979.

HOROWITZ, M. J., KRUPNICK, J., KALTREIDER, N., WILNER, N., LEONG, A., & MARMER, C. Initial psychological response to parental death. *Archives of General Psychiatry*, 1981, *38*, 316–323.

HOROWITZ, M., SCHAEFER, C., HIROTO, D., WILNER, N., & LEVIN, B. Life event questionnaires for measuring presumptive stress. *Psychosomatic Medicine*, 1977, *39*, 413–431.

HOROWITZ, M., WILNER, N., & ALVAREZ, W. Impact of event scale: A measure of subjective stress. *Psychosomatic Medicine*, 1979, *41*, 209–218.

HOROWITZ, M., WILNER, N., KALTREIDER, N., & ALVAREZ, W. Signs and symptoms of posttraumatic stress disorder. *Archives of General Psychiatry*, 1980, *37*, 85–92.

ILFELD, F. W., JR. Current social stressors and symptoms of depression. *American Journal of Psychiatry*, 1977, *134*, 161–166.

IMBER, S. D. Patient direct self-report techniques. In I. E. Waskow & M. B. Parloff (eds.), *Psychotherapy change measures*. Rockville: National Institute of Mental Health, 1975.

JENKINS, C. D. Psychologic and social precursors of coronary disease. *New England Journal of Medicine*, 1971, *284*, 244–317.

————. Recent evidence supporting psychologic and social risk factors for coronary disease (in two parts). *New England Journal of Medicine*, 1976, *294*, 987–994, 1033–1038.

JENKINS, C. D., ROSENMAN, R. H., & FRIEDMAN, M. Development of an objective psychological test for the determination of the coronary-prone behavior pattern in employed men. *Journal of Chronic Diseases*, 1967, *20*, 371–379.

JENKINS, C. D., ROSENMAN, R. H., & ZYZANSKI S. J. Prediction of clinical coronary-prone behavior pattern. *New England Journal of Medicine*, 1974, *290*, 1271–1275.

JENKINS, C. D., & ZYZANSKI, S. J. Behavioral risk factors and coronary heart disease. *Psychotherapy and Psychosomatics*, 1980, *34*, 149–177.

JENKINS, C. D., ZYZANSKI, S. J., & ROSENMAN, R. H. Risk of new myocardial infarction in middle-aged men with manifest coronary heart disease. *Circulation*, 1976, *53*, 342–347.

JENKINS, C. D., ZYZANSKI, S. J., RYAN, T. J., FLESSAS, A., & TANNENBAUM, S. I. Social insecurity and coronary-prone type A responses as identifiers of severe atherosclerosis. *Journal of Consulting and Clinical Psychology*, 1977, *45*, 1060–1067.

JOHNSON, J. H., & SARSON, I. G. Life stress, depression, and anxiety: Internal-external control as a moderator variable. *Journal of Psychosomatic Research*, 1978, *22*, 205–208.

————. Moderator variables in life stress research. In I. G. Sarason & C. D. Spielberger (eds.), *Stress and anxiety*, vol. 6. New York: Wiley, 1979.

KALES, J. D., KALES, A., SOLDATOS, C. R., CALDWELL, A. B., CHARNEY, D. S., & MARTIN, E. Night terrors: Clinical characteristics and personality patterns. *Archives of General Psychiatry*, 1980, *37*, 1406–1410.

KEEGAN, D. L., SINHA, B. N., MERRIMAN, J. E., & SHIPLEY, C. Type A behavior pattern. *Canadian Journal of Psychiatry*, 1979, *24*, 724–730.

KENDALL, P. C., FINCH, A. J., JR., AUERBACH, S. M., HOOKE, J. F., & MILKULKA, P. J. The state-trait anxiety inventory: A systematic evaluation. *Journal of Consulting and Clinical Psychology*, 1976, *44*, 406–412.

LAMB, D. H. The effects of public speaking on self-report physiological and behavioral measures of anxiety. *Dissertation Abstracts International,* 1970, *31*(4B), 2284.

LAMB, D. H., & PLANT, R. Patient anxiety in the dentist's office. *Journal of Dental Research,* 1972, *51,* 986–989.

LAZARUS, R. S. *Psychological stress and the coping process.* New York: McGraw-Hill, 1966.

————. *Patterns of Adjustment.* New York: McGraw-Hill, 1976.

————. The stress and coping paradigm. In C. Eisdorfer, D, Cohen, A. Kleinman, & P. Maxim (eds.), *Models for clinical psychopathology.* New York: Spectrum, 1981.

LEI, H., & SKINNER, H. A. A psychometric study of life events and social readjustment. *Journal of Psychosomatic Research,* 1980, *24,* 57–66.

LORR, M., McNAIR, D. M., & WEINSTEIN, G. J. Early effects of chlordiazepoxide (Librium) used with psychotherapy. *Journal of Psychiatric Research,* 1963, *1,* 257–270.

MARKUSH, R. E., & FAYERO, R. V. Epidemiologic assessment of stressful life-events, depressed mood, and psychophysiological symptoms: A preliminary report. In B. S. Dohrenwend & B. P. Dohrenwend (eds.), *Stressful life events: Their nature and effects.* New York: Wiley, 1974.

MARMOT, M. Type A behavior and ischaemic heart disease. *Psychological Medicine,* 1980, *10,* 603–606.

MARX, M. B., GARRITY, T. F., & BOWERS, F. R. The influence of recent life experience on the health of college freshman. *Journal of Psychosomatic Research,* 1975, *19,* 87.

McLEAN, P. D. Depression as a specific response to stress. In I. G. Sarason & C. D. Spielberger (eds.), *Stress and anxiety,* vol. 3. New York: Wiley, 1976.

McNAIR, D. M. Self-evaluations of antidepressants. *Psychopharmacologia,* 1974, *37,* 281–302.

McNAIR, D. M., & LORR, M. An analysis of mood in neurotics. *Journal of Abnormal and Social Psychology,* 1964, *69,* 620–627.

McNAIR, D. M., LORR, M., & DROPPLEMAN, L. F. *Profile of mood states.* San Diego: Educational and Industrial Testing Service, 1971.

MEEHL, P. E., & DALHSTRON, W. C. Objective configural rules for discriminating psychotic from neurotic MMPI profiles. *Journal of Clinical and Consulting Psychology,* 1960, *21,* 375–387.

MESSICK, S. Constructs and their vicissitudes in educational and psychological measurement. *Psychological Bulletin,* 1981, *89,* 575–588.

MEYER, A. The life chart and the obligation of specifying positive data in psychopathological diagnosis. In E. Winters (ed.), *The collected papers of Adolph Meyer,* vol. 3. Baltimore: Johns Hopkins Press, 1951.

MILLER, F. T., BENTZ, W. K., APONTE, J. R., & BROGAN, D. R. Perception of life crisis events. In B. S. Dohrenwend & B. P. Dohrenwend (eds.), *Stressful life events: Their nature and effects.* New York: Wiley, 1974.

MIYABO, S., ASATO, T., & MIZUSHIMA, N. Psychological correlates of stress-induced cortisol and growth hormone releases in neurotic patients. *Psychosomatic Medicine,* 1979, *41,* 515–523.

MYERS, J. K., LINDENTHAL, J. J., & PEPPER, M. P. Life events and psychiatric impairment. *Journal of Nervous and Mental Disorders,* 1971, *152,* 149–157.

————. Life events and mental status: A longitudinal study. *Journal of Health and Social Behavior,* 1972, *13,* 398–406.

NIELSEN, A. C., III, & WILLIAMS, T. A. Depression in ambulatory medical patients. *Archives of General Psychiatry,* 1980, *37,* 999–1004.

NIELSON, W. R., & DOBSON, K. S. The coronary-prone behavior pattern and trait anxiety: Evidence for discriminant validity. *Journal of Consulting and Clinical Psychology,* 1980, *48,* 546–547.

NORMAN, W. T. On estimating psychological relationships: Social desirability and self report. *Psychological Bulletin,* 1967, *67,* 273–293.

—————. Psychometric considerations for a revision of the MMPI. In J. N. Butcher (ed.), *Objective personality assessment: Changing perspectives.* New York: Academic, 1972.

PANCHERI, P., BELLATERRA, M., MATTEOLI, S., CRISTOFARI, M., POLIZZI, C., & PULETTI, M. Infarct as a stress agent: Life history and personality characteristics in improved versus non-improved patients after severe heart attack. *Journal of Human Stress,* 1978, *5,* 16–22.

PAYKEL, E. S., MYERS, J. K., DIENETT, M. N., KLERMAN, G. L., LINDENTHAL, J. J., & PEPPER, M. P. Life events and depression: A controlled study. *Archives of General Psychiatry,* 1969, *21,* 753–760.

RABKIN, J. G., & STRUENING, E. L. Life events, stress, and illness. *Science,* 1976, *194,* 1013.

RAHE, R. H. Life change measurement as a predictor of illness. *Proceedings of the Royal Society of Medicine,* 1968, *61,* 1124–1126.

—————. The pathway between subjects' recent life changes and their near future illness reports: Representative results and methodological issues. In B. S. Dohrenwend & B. P. Dohrenwend (eds.), *Stressful life events: Their nature and effects.* New York: Wiley, 1974.

—————. Life change measurement clarification. *Psychosomatic Medicine,* 1978, *40,* 95–98.

RAHE, R. H., & LIND, E. Psychosocial factors and sudden cardiac death: A pilot study. *Journal of Psychosomatic Research,* 1971, *15,* 19.

RAHE, R. H., McKEEN, J. D., & ARTHUR, R. J. A longitudinal study of life change and illness patterns. *Journal of Psychosomatic Research,* 1967, *10,* 355.

RAHE, R. H., MEYER, M., SMITH, M., KJAER, G., & HOLMES, T. H. Social stress and illness onset. *Journal of Psychosomatic Reseach,* 1964, *8,* 35–44.

RAHE, R. H., PUGH, W. M., ERICKSON, J., GUNDERSON, E. K. E., & RUBIN, R. T. Cluster analyses of life changes. Part I: Consistency of clusters across large navy samples. *Archives of General Psychiatry,* 1971, *25,* 330.

REYNOLDS, W. M., & GOULD, J. W. A psychometric investigation of the standard and short form Beck Depression Inventory. *Journal of Consulting and Clinical Psychology,* 1981, *49,* 306–307.

ROGENTINE, D. S., VanKAMMEN, D. P., FOX, B. H., DOCHERTY, J. P., ROSENBLATT, J. E., BOYD, S. L., & BUNNEY, W. E. Psychological factors in the prognosis of malignant melanoma: A prospective study. *Psychosomatic Medicine,* 1979, *41,* 647–655.

RORER, L. G. The great response-style myth. *Psychological Bulletin,* 1965, *63,* 129–156.

SARASON, I. G., JOHNSON, J. H., & SIEGAL, J. M. Assessing the impact of life changes. In I. G. Sarason & C. D. Spielberger (eds.), *Stress and anxiety,* vol. 6. New York: Wiley, 1979.

SCHWAB, J. J., BIALOW, M., BROWN, J. M., & HOLZER, C. E. Diagnosing depression in medical inpatients. *Annals of Internal Medicine,* 1967, *67,* 695–707.

SELYE, H. The evolution of the stress concept. *American Journal of Cardiology,* 1970, *26,* 289–299.

SKINNER, H. A., & LEI, H. Differential weights in life change research: Useful or irrelevant? *Psychosomatic Medicine,* 1980, *42,* 367–370.

SMITH, R. C., & LAY, C. D. State and trait anxiety: An annotated bibliography. *Psychological Reports,* 1974, *34,* 519–594.

SPIELBERGER, C. D. Theory and research on anxiety. In C. D. Spielberger (ed.), *Anxiety and behavior.* New York: Academic, 1966.

—————. Anxiety as an emotional state. In C. D. Spielberger (ed.), *Anxiety: Current trends in theory and research,* vol. 1. New York: Academic, 1972.

—————. *Preliminary test manual for the State-Trait Anxiety Inventory for Children ("How I feel Questionnaire").* Palo Alto: Consulting Psychologists, 1973.

SPIELBERGER, C. D., GONZALEZ-REIGOSA, F., & MARTINEZ-URRUTIA, A. Development of the Spanish edition of the State-Trait Anxiety Inventory. *Interamerican Journal of Psychology,* 1971, *5,* 3–4.

SPIELBERGER, C. D., GORSUCH, R. C., & LUSHENE, R. E. *Manual for the State-Trait Anxiety Inventory.* Palo Alto: Consulting Psychologists, 1970.

STROBER, M., GREEN, J., & CARLSON, G. Utility of the Beck Depression Inventory with psychiatrically hospitalized adolescents. *Journal of Consulting and Clinical Psychology,* 1981, *49,* 482–483.

THEORELL, T., & RAHE, R. H. Psychosocial factors and myocardial infarction. Part I: An inpatient study in Sweden. *Journal of Psychosomatic Research,* 1971, *15,* 25–31.

UHLENHUTH, E. H., & PAYKEL, E. S. Symptom intensity and life events. *Archives of General Psychiatry,* 1973, *28,* 473–477.

VAN DIJL, H., & NAGELKERKE, N. Statistical discrimination of male myocardial infarction patients and healthy males by means of a psychological test and a tracing of basic dimensions of the infarction personality. *Psychotherapy and Psychosomatics,* 1980, *34,* 196–203.

VAN DOORNEN, L. J. P. The coronary risk personality: Psychological and physiological aspects. *Psychotherapy and Psychosomatics,* 1980, *34,* 204–215.

VERHAGEN, F., NASS, C., APPELS, A., VAN BASTELIER, A., & WINNUBST, J. Cross-validation of the A/B typology in the Netherlands. *Psychotherapy and Psychosomatics,* 1980, *34,* 178–186.

VINOKUR, A., & SELZER, M. L. Desirable versus undesirable life events: Their relationship to stress and mental distress. *Journal of Personality and Social Psychology,* 1975, *32,* 329.

WARHEIT, G. J. Life events, coping stress, and depressive symptomatology. *American Journal of Psychiatry,* 1979, *136,* 502–507.

WASKOW, I. E., & PARLOFF, M. B. (eds.). *Psychotherapy change measures.* Rockville: National Institute of Mental Health, 1975.

WEISSMAN, M. M., POTTENGER, M., KLEBER, H., RUBEN, H. L., WILLIAMS, D., & THOMPSON, W. D. Symptom patterns in primary and secondary depression: A comparison of primary depressives with depressed opiate addicts, alcoholics, and schizophrenics. *Archives of General Psychiatry,* 1977, *34,* 854–862.

WEISSMAN, M. M., SHOLOMSKAS, D., POTTENGER, M., PRUSOFF, B. A., & LOCKE, B. Z. Assessing depressive symptoms in five psychiatric populations: A validation study. *American Journal of Epidemiology,* 1977, *106,* 203–214.

WEITZ, J. Psychological research needs on the problems of human stress. In J. E. McGarth (ed.), *Social and psychological factors in stress.* New York: Holt, 1970.

WIGGINS, J. S. Convergences among stylistic response measures from objective personality tests. *Education Psychological Measurement,* 1964, *24,* 551–562.

WILDE, G. J. S. Trait description and measurement by personality questionnaires. In R. B. Cattell (ed.), *Handbook of modern personality theory.* Chicago: Aldine, 1972.

WILLIAMS, R. B., HANEY, T. L., LEE, K. L., KANG, Y., BLUMENTHAL, J. A., & WHALEN, R. E. Type A behavior, hostility, and coronary atherosclerosis. *Psychosomatic Medicine,* 1980, *42,* 539–549.

WOODWORTH, R. S. *Personal data sheet.* Chicago: Stoelting, 1918.

ZEISS, A. M. Aversiveness versus change in the assessment of life stress. *Journal of Psychosomatic Research,* 1980, *24,* 15–19.

ZUNG, W. W. K. A self-rating depression scale. *Archives of General Psychiatry,* 1965, *12,* 63–70.

————. A rating instrument for anxiety disorders. *Psychosomatics,* 1971, *12,* 371–379.

————. The depression status inventory: An adjunct to the Self-Rating Depression Scale. *Journal of Clinical Psychology,* 1972, *28,* 539–543.

————. The measurement of affects: Depression and anxiety. In P. Pichot (ed.), *Modern problems in pharmacopsychiatry,* vol. 7. Basel: Karger, 1974.

————. Assessment of anxiety disorder: Qualitative and quantitative approaches. In W. E. Fann (ed.), *Phenomenology and treatment of anxiety.* New York: Spectrum, 1979.

18

Verbal Indicators of Stress

Donald P. Spence

THE SEARCH FOR VERBAL INDICATORS of stress has had a long history and a mixed press. Results are inconsistent; positive findings frequently go unreplicated; and response measures tend to outrun clear rationales. Recently, interest has seemed to shift from verbal to nonverbal markers. In the first six months of 1971, the *Journal of Personality and Social Psychology* published one paper bearing on speech related indicators of stress and one on nonverbal measures; in the corresponding period of 1980, the same journal published six papers from the second category and only one from the first. In this chapter, I review the more significant work on verbal markers of stress and suggest some fruitful options for future work.

What is speech and why should it be vulnerable to stress? The function of speaking would seem to vary enormously according to the circumstances surrounding the speaker, but these are rarely, if ever, taken into account by investigators. In the case of the released Iranian hostages, to take a recent example, speaking to one another assumed critical significance after a long period of isolation and deprivation, and even though these persons were under considerable stress, it can be argued that the very act of speaking became a cathartic release, which may well have served to reduce anxiety. A search for *speech markers of stress* (e.g., stuttering, repetition, tongue-slip) under these circumstances might have been self-defeating because the longer the subject talked, the less stress there would be to measure and the less chance one would have to detect signs of *leakage*—to use a term introduced by Ekman (Ekman & Friesen, 1969) in relation to nonverbal behavior—because speaking by itself was sufficient to dissipate the residual tension.

Consider now the anxious patient in psychotherapy. Here speech takes on a somewhat different function because the patient may use words to avoid painful thoughts. Under these conditions, it seems more reasonable to look for signs of leakage: the act of speaking is probably not sufficient to discharge the underlying tension. The leakage may be related directly to the content of the patient's anxiety (i.e., *lexical leakage*), or it may take the form of a disturbance in the speech process, such as an increase in stuttering or hesitation.

This distinction between form and content has an important bearing on the extent to which speech, as a particular form of complex motor behavior, can be considered vulnerable to stress. It could be argued (Mahl, 1956) that because speech is a complex and highly organized piece of behavior, it is particularly vulnerable to the intrusive interference of stress. Yet, because we rely heavily on feedback to monitor speech (the speech of deaf people, deprived of auditory feedback, is significantly distorted with respect to rhythm and pitch), the speech function may be unusually well protected and therefore not a good measure of the effects of stress. At this point, form and content make a difference. Although speech is carefully monitored, our attention is usually focused more on *what* we are saying than on *how* we are saying it. From this it follows that disturbances in the form of an utterance—e.g., hesitations, stutters, incompletions, and the use of noncontent fillers—should be relatively more indicative of stress than disturbances in content would be. Under certain circumstances, however, leakage might spread to content, as long as the superficial meaning of the utterance conformed to the speaker's intended message; examples of this phenomenon will be considered later in the chapter.

If we assume that the content of speech is more important to preserve than the form, it would follow that the speaker will protect the former with much more effort than he will protect the latter. One way in which he protects content is through the careful management of the unfilled pause. In a series of studies, Goldman-Eisler (1968) explored the relation between the length of the pause and the complexity of the subsequent utterance. In general, she found that the *unfilled pause* (i.e., silence) seems to operate as a buffer period during which the speaker can organize his thoughts. Long pauses are followed by more sophisticated and more concise linguistic formulations, whereas short pauses and filled pauses are followed by less sophisticated linguistic achievements. Her studies suggest that the *filled pause*—the use of "ah" during sentence construction—can be understood as a partial attempt to plan the next verbal sequence. Because planning is at issue, the filled pause would seem to represent an effort to exert control over the utterance and should be considered separately from speech faults that represent *lack* of control. We can think of the unfilled pause as representing the greatest control; followed by the filled pause (the "ah"), a sign of partial control; followed by speech faults that are probably outside the speaker's awareness. I discuss support for this distinction when I review specific studies.

At this juncture, I would like to suggest a tentative rationale of speech markers. First, I will arrange the dependent measures along a *continuum of speaker control*. The least controlled indicators of stress are changes in quantity and rate of speaking. Next come the noncontent disturbances such as stutters, hesitations, sentence corrections, and repetitions. Then come filled and unfilled pauses: the former represent unsuccessful planning and, therefore, partial loss of control; whereas the latter, often followed by well-turned phrases, represent more successful control. Finally, signs of stress may be detected in word choice although the outward form of the sentence does not show any obvious disruption. Because they conform to all outward criteria of careful speech, examples of lexical leakage are usually the hardest to detect and represent the best control.

This arrangement of response measures also conforms to a *continuum of visibility*. Changes in amount and rate of speaking and speech faults are among the more obvious signs of distress; they are clear manifestations of underlying anxiety. On the other hand, unfilled pauses, as long as they do not go on for too long, are rather easily overlooked, particularly if they are followed by examples of good speech. Examples of lexical leakage usually go unnoticed. It could be argued that speech markers at the more visible (and less controlled) end of the continuum constitute greater evidence of stress because they represent a more profound invasion of the speech function; we might also expect them to occur somewhat earlier in the speech sample because the emotional discharge function of speech has not yet been brought into play. Speech markers at the more controlled end of the spectrum seem to represent more muted expressions of stress and might be expected to appear somewhat later in the speech sample.

There is an important paradox here that deserves emphasis. The less controlled measures, precisely because they are more visible, are more likely to attract the speaker's attention and be brought under some kind of management. As a result, we might expect their frequency to decline as the speech sample continues. The more controlled responses, on the other hand, can be understood as compromise formations that probably lie on the fringe of the speaker's awareness and are therefore more apt to be continued throughout the protocol; although harder to score, they may represent a more frequent and therefore a more reliable and robust sign of stress. It follows from these distinctions that the different kinds of speech measures may not be highly intercorrelated and should always be scored separately.

Consider now the function of each type of marker in the psychic economy of the speaker. If we are analyzing the utterances of recently released hostages, we might expect more response measures from the visible end of the continuum, and we might restrict our analysis to the more visible signs of loss of control. Signs of this kind might be particularly frequent at the beginning of the speech sample because of the cathartic function of speaking, which I discussed earlier. If we analyzed a psychotherapy protocol, on the other hand, and had reason to think that the patient was using a good deal of denial, isolation, and other modes of overcontrol, we might look for markers at the less visible end of the spectrum. As therapy progressed and overcontrol gave way to more expressive behavior, other measures might be used. Thus, the choice of markers would seem to depend on the function of the speech sample for the speaker, the temporal progression of the sample, and the confluence of external and internal events during the speaker's performance. I now turn to some of the more important studies.

VISIBLE MARKERS: QUANTITY AND RATE

Murray (1971) offered the most comprehensive account of research on quantity and rate of speech as a function of stress. Reviewing 26 studies, he found that *verbal quantity*—how much the person talks—is increased by what Murray termed *concurrent* and *dispositional anxiety* but decreased by *situational anxiety*. Subjects seem to speak less when under environmental stress (state anxiety), but they speak more if they are characterologically anxious (trait anxiety). This last finding gives us an example of how speech may operate as cathartic release; the innately anxious subject seems motivated simply to speak more. Murray's findings suggest that verbal output cannot be interpreted unless we know the diagnostic makeup of the subject in question; clearly, speech productions cannot be used as a general measure of stress under all circumstances. This inconsistency may be related to the fact that quantity is a highly visible measure, rather easily brought into the speaker's awareness and therefore open to many forms of control. The high visibility of this marker may also explain many of the inconsistent findings in the literature.

According to Murray (1971), *rate of speaking* is not related to any of the three kinds of anxiety. This negative finding has an important implicaton for the common convention of converting speech output into words per minute in order to equalize for differences in fluency among speakers. If Murray's findings are supported by future studies and it turns out that the absolute amount of speech is a more sensitive indicator than rate of speaking, it may be a mistake automatically to express absolute data in relative terms. This rule may be extended to other kinds of measures; it may be more revealing, for example, to count the absolute number of speech faults in a corpus rather than express this figure as a function of faults per 1000 words because such a conversion may eliminate the very detail we want to study. We may want to look at all speech markers in more absolute terms and find other statistical ways of adjusting for individual differences (co-variance and autoregression are two possible approaches to the problem).

NEAR–VISIBLE MARKERS: SPEECH FAULTS

Under this heading I include the markers that traditionally have been used to indicate disturbance in the *motor function* of speech. The list has proved remarkably stable; first defined by Mahl (1956), the same indicators were used two decades later in a study by Horowitz, Sampson, Siegelman, Wolfson and Weiss (1975). Here is the original list, with a brief example of each speech fault, reproduced from a study by Kasl and Mahl (1965:426):

1. Sentence change   Well she's . . . already she's lonesome.
2. Repetition   Cause they . . . they get along pretty well together.
3. Stutter   It sort of well l . . . l . . . leaves a memory.
4. Omission   She mour . . . was in mourning for about two years.
5. Sentence incompletion   Well I'm sorry I couldn't get here last week so I could . . . ah . . . I was getting a child ready for camp and finishing up swimming lessons.
6. Tongue-slip   We spleat the bitches (for "split the beaches").
7. Intruding incoherent sound   I see a girl now I'd like to take out . . . I just . . . dh . . . ask her.

In a typical study (Kasl & Mahl, 1965), one group of subjects was given a control interview followed by a stress interview; a second group was given two control interviews. Information gathered in the first interview, together with information obtained from the Minnesota Multiphasic Personality Inventory (MMPI), was used to generate the stressful areas of the experimental interview. Twenty-four of the 25 subjects in the experimental group showed an increase in speech faults during the second interview; only 12 of the 20 control subjects showed a similar change. All seven categories of markers showed an increase during the stress interview, but not all subjects were affected in the same way. No information was given as to the relative contribution of each type of marker to the overall variance.

These seven types of speech faults would seem to be reasonable candidates for the measurement of stress, but there may well be other measures that are just as sensitive and perhaps more reliable. The literature fails to provide us with a comprehensive rationale for the response measures; they seem to be sanctioned more by tradition than by theory. In the absence of a correlation matrix, furthermore, it is not clear to what extent the different measures are substitutes for one another or to what extent they represent different aspects of speech behavior. A comprehensive theory of speech as an expression of complex motor behavior might direct us to measures that have not yet been used. Some of these measures may be less under the speaker's control and therefore more sensitive to underlying variations in stress; because they are less intuitively obvious, however, they will never be discovered by inspection alone.

Little is known, furthermore, about the extent to which each of these speech faults can be sensed by the speaker and thus brought under some kind of voluntary control. Changes in the form of the sentence and perhaps other kinds of syntactical mistakes are close to the awareness of most speakers; the best evidence on this point came from Deese (1978), who reported that only 2% of all sentences in a corpus of 20,000, taken from a variety of samples of natural language, were grammatically incorrect. This statistic suggests that as we speak we pay continual attention to the form of the utterance. From Deese's data we might conclude that sentence change, repetition, omission, and sentence incompletion would be relatively insensitive to moderate stress; that they would tend to appear early in the speech sample but might be rather quickly brought under control; and that when they *did* appear, they would probably indicate a high level of underlying stress.

Less obvious, in part because they loom somewhat smaller in the utterance, are the tongue-slip and the intruding incoherent sound. We might assume that both are more likely to occupy only the fringe of the speaker's awareness and thus to be less susceptible to corrective feedback. On the other hand, Deese (1978) reported a rate of no more than one tongue-slip per 100 sentences, and in almost all cases the error was detected and corrected by the speaker.

As we reduce the search space to microseconds of utterance, we increase our chances of picking up indicators that lie completely outside the speaker's awareness. But they may also lie outside the experimenter's awareness, and here we are brought up against another kind of problem. Only highly trained transcribers have the ability to detect the more subtle speech faults; as the size of the fault becomes smaller and smaller, more and more training is needed to achieve suitable levels of reliability. At some point, the sensitivity of a particular measure to underlying stress may be more than offset by its cost of detection, and further research is needed to tell us where the two lines cross.

Future research might consider the use of new kinds of hardware. The voice print, for example, can detect changes in the stress and contour of an utterance that are inaudible to the naked ear. Certain kinds of detectors might be developed that could pick up changes in accent or rhythm. In general, it seems that we should place less and less reliance on the naive transcriber because in our everyday role of listening to impure speech, we have trained ourselves to overlook the very measures we are trying to record. Thus, a certain amount of untraining is necessary before we can produce a reasonably reliable transcriber, and even these professionals make a certain number of mistakes. The more we can take this activity out of human ears, the more reliable our data and the broader their scope.

Despite their somewhat heterogeneous nature, Mahl's (1956) original markers continue to be used and continue to be used and continue to be sensitive to underlying stress. Siegman and Pope (1965) compared the effects of low and high anxiety arousing topics on the speaker's verbal behavior and found that the latter produced a significantly higher number of speech faults; once again, we have no information about the relative contribution of each type of speech fault. Pope, Blass, Siegman and Raher (1970) studied the daily speech samples of six inpatients over a three-month period. From daily ratings of depression and anxiety, these investigators picked eight high and eight low samples on each scale. Anxiety produced a significant increase in the seven Mahl indicators, but no additional information was provided as to the relative sensitivity of each measure. In a related study, Krause and Pilisuk (1961) examined the influence of stress on break, correction, speech fragment, distortion, repetition, procrastination, and intrusion (the last being defined as any nonverbal sound, such as a sign, laugh, cough, throat clear, or deep breath, that might intrude on the flow of speech). Only the intrusion measure discriminated significantly between stress and control stimuli. Although some of the other Mahl indicators might have been affected, they were not scored. This study extended slightly the scope of available response measures and stressed once again the need for a comprehensive rationale that would help us decide which measures could be usefully pursued and which measures could be dropped. A comprehensive set of measures, to be used in *all* studies, would contribute substantially to the impact of any one experiment.

LESS VISIBLE MARKERS:
FILLED AND UNFILLED PAUSES

Ah-filled speech is perhaps one of the more distressing mannerisms of the nonfluent speaker; although painfully noticeable to the listener, however, this device often appears to be outside the speaker's awareness. But even though it seems relatively difficult to control, the filled pause has not proved a good measure of underlying anxiety. One reason for this insensitivity may stem from the fact that ah-usage is partly a stylistic indicator: some speakers say "ah" all the time, under all conditions; other speakers do so relatively rarely. According to Deese (1978), "A small minority of speakers—four or five out of the nearly fifty speakers we have listened to thus far—show no filled pauses at all. These persons pause, often for very long times, but they do not, like the rest of us, 'um' and 'uh.' They simply stop for a while and plan ahead" (p. 318). Second, as already noted, the filled pause is used partly for planning purposes and therefore seems to tell us more about what is coming than about the speaker's current state of stress.

Originally included in Mahl's list of speech faults, the filled pause was soon found to behave quite differently from the other measures, and by now the "ah" is scored separately. Kasl and Mahl (1965) found that the ah-ratio was not affected by anxiety; Siegman and Pope (1965) noted a similar lack of effect; and Pope and associates (1970) found that while the ah-ratio was significantly lower in speech samples from depressed patients, it did not change as a function of anxiety. Despite its rather poor history, the filled pause continues to be counted; I suspect that its popularity has to do more with its visibility (this fault is easier to score than many others) than with any other attribute.

The unfilled pause, or silence, has a different history. Although not part of Mahl's (1956) original scoring scheme, it has become increasingly popular as a measure that can be scored quite easily and that seems moderately sensitive to underlying stress. Unfortunately, the sensitivity of this marker is somewhat hard to replicate. In his comprehensive review, Murray (1971) reported that silence was *positively* correlated with situational and concurrent anxiety and *negatively* correlated with dispositional anxiety. Siegman and Pope (1965) found no correlation. Pope and associates (1970) found that the "silence quotient"—the total pause duration divided by the total length of the speech sample—was *decreased* by what could be called concurrent anxiety (a finding opposite to Murray's) and increased with depression. Measures of articulation rate showed that anxious patients spoke significantly faster, and it would thus follow that the silence quotient might decrease. But it should also be clear that the kind of stress measured in daily ratings by nursing staff (Pope et al., 1970) is quite different from the underlying stress of a well-controlled psychotherapy patient, and this point brings us back to our earlier concern about the different uses of speech.

When talking has a cathartic function, silence is likely to be used in planning the next utterance, as Goldman-Eisler (1968) reported, and might therefore correlate *positively* with underlying stress. Of critical importance are the boundaries of the silence—what might be called its semantic and syntactic surround. A pause followed by a flawless phrase or a highly unusual word is likely to be a sign of planning, control, and perhaps evasion; Goldman-Eisler found a high negative correlation between the length of the pause and the likelihood of the next word. A pause followed by a garbled sentence, on the other hand, or a word salad, is probably an index of some less voluntary interruption. It should be clear that a simple counting of pauses will not lead to a meaningful score; if silence is used as a measure of stress, its linguistic function must be evaluated as well as its length. Here is another case in which ease of scoring may have unnecessarily increased the popularity of a measure.

INVISIBLE MARKERS: LEXICAL LEAKAGE

Consider the following classified advertisement:

Radiation Oncology
Growth Position
Edward W. Sparrow Hospital

A close reading suggests a semantic overlap between the word "growth" and the background context of cancer; it might be argued that the use of "growth" is determined partly by these background concerns. When a farmer applying for drought relief complains, "We're drowning in red tape," one is tempted to reach the same conclusion; the word "drowning" is inspired partly by the need for water. Lexical leakage can be defined as a choice of words that is influenced by unconscious and preconscious background factors but that conforms to all local semantic and syntactic requirements. Leakages are to be contrasted with slips of the tongue or other speech faults that by definition violate one or more rules of speech. Lexical leakages, as we have seen, tend to occupy only the fringes of our awareness and for this reason may be thought to be particularly good choices for the measurement of stress.

How can such phenomena be identified? Elsewhere I (Spence, 1980) specified three steps. First, we may sense a "semantic overlap between the choice of word in the target sentence and the surrounding context" (p. 146). Second,

> we can detect leakage by statistical means. . . . if certain words are overdetermined by background factors, they will appear with a greater frequency in all contexts. Thus a simple word count of specific markers will prove the hypothesis. Third, we can look for subtle errors in usage. If certain words are being forced into the [syntactical] frame, they will probably displace other, more appropriate choices; a careful reading of the passage, asking at every point is this the one and only word to be used, might uncover subtle mistakes. Pp. 146–147.

Lexical leakage may be particularly responsive to stress for three additional reasons; they are all related to the fact that we are studying spoken, as opposed to written, language.

> Because of the looseness of expressive syntax in natural language, the choice of specific words is much less constrained than is the case with prose or poetry. This syntactical freedom allows other factors to play a much larger role than would be the case in the more restricted genres. There is the second point that size of vocabulary is much less important as a constraint on word choice. This idea follows from the fact that natural language shows a strong preference for the most frequent words; thus, only a small proportion of the speaker's vocabulary is ever being used, and therefore differences in vocabulary size introduce relatively little variation. Third, since the rate of language production (an average of five words per second) is considerably higher in spoken language than in written language, it becomes impossible for a speaker to monitor each and every word. (Spence, 1980:148)

In a study of 62 women who were at risk for cervical cancer, Spence and associates (1978) determined the frequency of two clusters of marker words (hope and hopeless) in the interview transcript of each patient. The interview was conducted after the patient had been admitted to the hospital for cone biopsy but before the results of the biopsy had been told to the patient; both patient and interviewer were unaware of the diagnosis. Two clusters of words were created to measure the two themes of hope and hopelessness: the hopeless cluster was derived from an interview by Kübler-Ross (1969) with an overtly depressed patient in the terminal stages of cancer; the hope cluster was derived from three content-analysis dictionaries. Frequencies of each cluster were counted by computer, and separate scores were determined for utterances by patient and utterances by interviewer. To control for attitudes toward cancer that might influence the findings, we rated all patients on a scale that ranged from complete denial of danger (1 = "There's nothing wrong with me") to open worry and concern (7 = "I'm sure I have cancer"). Two judges rated each interview after it had been stripped of all information about biopsy outcome and age; reliability between judges was .94.

In the patients' speech, the hope cluster was used significantly more often by patients with negative biopsy ($n = 35$) than by patients with positive biopsy ($n = 27$) (Spence, Scarborough, & Ginsberg, 1978). Rates of the hopeless cluster were about the same in the two groups. When we controlled for patients' attitudes toward cancer, the findings became more significant. In the concerned half of the sample (ratings above the median) both the hope and the hopeless cluster significantly discriminated the 17 cases of ongoing cancer (positive biopsy) from the 15 false-alarm cases (negative biopsy). However, in patients in the defended half of the sample (ratings below the median), neither cluster discriminated between positive and negative biopsy.

In the interviewer's speech (the same person conducted all interviews), significantly more hopeless words were used when he was talking with a patient with positive biopsy. The difference was even greater for the concerned patients. The hope cluster did not discriminate between the two groups.

We can assume that long before the patient arrived at the hospital, she had accumulated a certain amount of information about her probably status. Some of this information could have been transmitted by her personal physician in the process of collecting and evaluating the initial Pap smears; other information could have been transmitted during the cone biopsy at the hospital. It can be argued that this reservoir of conscious and preconscious information about her condition played a significant role in the patient's choice of words during the interview. The influence of this information appears to have been modulated by the patient's attitude about illness; if she was openly concerned about the risk of cancer, she was apparently more expressive of her inner feelings and allowed more of the hopeless marker words to appear in her speech. More defended patients, on the other hand, apparently were able to mute the influence of this background information and speak in more neutral language.

If we think of the risk of cervical cancer as a gradually accumulating stress of which the patient is particularly aware and which she attempts to control by her preferred defensive style, these data would suggest that lexical leakage may be one way of measuring the impact of stress on natural language. It would seem that the more concerned patients, perhaps because they are more expressive in their speech, give us more opportunities to measure the effect. It could be argued that the interview assumed more of a discharge function for concerned patients (Spence, Scarborough, & Ginsberg, 1978). Defended patients, on the other hand, may be more selective in their vocabulary and significantly reduce the opportunities for leakage. Thus, the earlier distinction between expressive and controlling aspects of speech may well have played a significant part in the present study. Future studies are needed to bring these variables under stricter control, as well as to correlate signs of lexical leakage with the other measures of stress described previously in the chapter.

Turning to the evidence for leakage in the interviewer's speech, Spence and associates (1978) found that he used significantly more hopeless words when he was speaking to positive biopsy patients. These data suggest not only that he was picking up information of which he was only partly aware but also that he was introducing cues into the conversation that might have been sensed by the patient, affecting the subsequent course of the interview. Sequential analysis might reveal an interaction between interviewer and patient, and we might expect that the more defended patients were the most sensitive to disturbing cues. Just as certain kinds of speech faults may be more apparent early in the speech sample, before stress has been released by the act of speaking, so we may find that certain kinds of leakages tended to appear early in the interview, before the patient had been alerted to the possibility that she was saying more than she intended. The time course of the various marker words may be even more revealing than the overall total. Sequential analysis might indicate which of the marker words emitted by the interviewer were detected by the patient, producing either an increase or a decrease in similar indicators.

IMPLICATONS FOR FUTURE RESEARCH

This review of selected studies has suggested that verbal markers of stress have yet to live up to their original promise. Speech faults and other kinds of verbal indicators may indeed reflect the presence of background tension under certain conditions, but because many of these markers are continuously monitored by the speaker, their usefulness may be less than expected. We have yet to establish which markers show the best promise of indicating stress while also evading voluntary control. It seems fairly clear that the more visible markers are probably poor candidates for the very reason that they are easy to count; if they can be reliably detected by the experimenter, they can also be accurately monitored by the speaker. Refined hardware may lead us to a new set of "microfaults" that can be reliably measured and that fall outside the speaker's control; new research along these lines is urgently needed.

More attention must also be paid to the time course of the interview or speech sample. Some way must be found to chart the changing pattern of speech over time and to document shifts in response to variations in the speaker's level of stress and to changes in the other voice or voices in the conversation. Allowance must be made for the fact that we are always responding to signals from the other speaker, and if these signals are stressful, as seemed to be the case in the cervical cancer study (Spence, Scarborough, & Ginsberg, 1978), then the speech of the target subject is apt to change accordingly. Some method must be found to show how each speaker's stress markers are triggered by, and in turn act as the trigger for, the markers of the other speaker; contingency analysis of this kind will yield significant information about speech as a dynamic process, exquisitely sensitive to external influence. As we have seen, some indicators of stress may abound in the earlier portions of the speech sample, and we may find that our choice of markers is significantly reduced as the speech sample continues—as the subject becomes more aware of both what he is saying and how he is saying it and more aware of what the interviewer may be listening for. We can assume that the amount of information being leaked to the outside world is always under fairly tight control; to the degree that this information represents anxiety, stress, or other ego-dystonic variables, the need to conceal these sources increases accordingly.

This line of argument brings us to the function of the speech sample in the speaker's view of the world. If, as in some studies, he is answering stressful questions and trying to defend himself against a stressful interviewer, we are likely to find many fewer markers. On the other hand, if the circumstances are more relaxed and the speech sample more spontaneous, we can assume that less self-monitoring is taking place and that more verbal markers may emerge. But a speech situation, even under these conditions, is potentially unstable; any sign of interest in a particular response measure is likely to make it disappear. The ideal interviewer should probably be unaware of what markers are being measured and perhaps even unaware of the presumed relation between stress and speech faults.

A review of selected studies makes it clear that we are still without a comprehensive theory of speech and its psychological function. In the absence of theory, the number of response measures has tended to increase with each new study, and many of the more popular measures, because they represent the more visible aspects of the speech process, are probably doomed to extinction. We have no data, furthermore, on the relative research effectiveness of any of the more traditional speech faults or any way of evaluating the extent to which each of these can be brought under voluntary control. In addition, ways are needed for determining which speakers do and do not depend on filled pauses; for measuring the extent to which speech faults are within a speaker's awareness; and for understanding the function of speech itself in the particular context being studied. Just as spoken language has certain characteristics that make it distinct from written language, so spoken language takes unique forms: conversational speech in a social setting differs considerably from the speech of an employment interview or a psychotherapy session. Better knowledge of background conditions would alert us to the more promising stress markers in each situation. In similar fashion, general knowledge of certain kinds of speech faults, such as filled and unfilled pauses, would make us better able to separate signal from noise; to tell when a long pause, for example, is used for emphasis as opposed to delay or evasion.

In the final analysis, the search for discrete markers may give way to the discovery of specific patterns. Stress, after all, is not an intermittent event but something much more like muscle tension or hormonal discharge, which has a measurable time course with a beginning, a middle, and an end. By evaluating a broad range of stress markers, we should be able to identify the point in the interview at which the stress first appeared; to see how fast it developed and along how broad a channel; to trace its effects on the visible and less visible markers, the form and content of the speech process; and, finally, to determine the conditions under which it disappeared. We would be able, for example, to discover the conditions under which a formal speech fault, such as a stutter, gives way to a change in content and the occasions on which a burst of the less visible markers signals the emergence of a more visible response measure. Pattern analysis of this kind has much greater face validity than a simple counting of discrete markers. Concentration on broad-gauged patterns would also make it easier to look at interactions between speakers and better to approximate the moment at which the target speaker first becomes aware that he is "saying too much." If we can detect changes in strategy and shifts to another response measure, we can significantly improve the sensitivity of our techniques and come closer to finding reliable indicators of underlying stress.

REFERENCES

Deese, J. Thought into speech. *American Scientist,* 1978, *66,* 314–321.

Ekman, P. & Friesen, W. V. Nonverbal leakage and clues to deception. *Psychiatry,* 1969, *32,* 88–105.

Goldman-Eisler, F. *Psycholinguistics.* New York: Academic, 1968.

Horowitz, L., Sampson, H., Siegelman, A., Wolfson, A., & Weiss, J. On the identification of warded off mental contents. *Journal of Abnormal Psychology,* 1975, *84,* 545–558.

Kasl, S. V. & Mahl, G. F. Disturbance and hesitation in speech. *Journal of Personality and Social Psychology,* 1965, *1,* 425–433

KRAUSE, M. S. & PILISUK, M. Anxiety in verbal behavior: A validation study. *Journal of Consulting Psychology,* 1961, *25,* 414–419.

KUBLER-ROSS, E. *On death and dying.* New York: Macmillan, 1969.

MAHL, G. F. Disturbances and silences in the patient's speech in psychotherapy. *Journal of Abnormal and Social Psychology,* 1956, *53,* 1–15.

MURRAY, D. C. Talk, silence, and anxiety. *Psychological Bulletin,* 1971, *75,* 244–260.

POPE, B., BLASS, T., SIEGMAN, A. W., & RAHER, J. Anxiety and depression in speech. *Journal of Consulting and Clinical Psychology,* 1970, *35,* 128–133.

SIEGMAN, A. W., & POPE, B. Effects of question specificity and anxiety-producing messages on verbal fluency in the initial interview. *Journal of Personality and Social Psychology,* 1965, *2,* 522–530.

SPENCE, D. P. Lexical leakage. In R. W. Rieber (ed.), *Applied psycholinguistics and mental health.* New York: Plenum, 1980.

SPENCE, D. P., SCARBOROUGH, H. S., & GINSBERG, E. Lexical correlates of cervical cancer. *Social Science and Medicine,* 1978, *12,* 141–145.

19

Nonverbal Correlates of Anxiety and Stress

Aron Wolfe Siegman

THE RESEARCH DISCUSSED in this chapter is part of a long-standing attempt on the part of psychologists to find objective, quantifiable correlates of stress induced and other types of anxiety arousal. In the past, this search focused primarily on physiological measures, but more recently it has come to encompass a wide variety of behavioral measures, especially nonverbal behaviors. The interest in the latter is motivated by the expectation that nonverbal, unlike physiological, manifestations can provide nonobtrusive indexes of anxiety arousal and stress. From a practical point of view, such nonobtrusive indexes are critical in situations that preclude the cooperation necessary for physiological measurements, as in the case, for example, of negotiating with terrorists. However, even when the necessary cooperation can be obtained, the obtrusiveness, if not the outright intrusiveness, of physiological measures can be a source of serious confounding. The very presence of monitoring devices can be anxiety arousing. Furthermore, they inevitably betray the investigator's purpose, which may give rise to various countermeasures on the part of the subject. For example, in criminal investigations, the subject may make himself deliberately anxious throughout the investigation, so as to minimize the differences between control and critical questions. This is not to say that similar maneuvers cannot be attempted even in the absence of obtrusive instruments, but this is more difficult to accomplish when one does not know what aspect of one's behavior is being monitored and when. Therefore, the search for nonobtrusive, nonverbal correlates of stress and anxiety is a matter of practical importance.[1]

ANXIETY AROUSAL AND SPEECH

Siegman and Pope (1965a, 1972; Pope et al., 1970) investigated the effects of anxiety arousal on speech within the context of the clinical interviews. Differential anxiety levels were aroused in interviewees by means of topical manipulation. Specifically, interviewees were selected so that questions focusing on their family relations would be more anxiety arousing than questions focusing on their school experiences. A postinterview questionnaire revealed that this manipulation was effective, although even the family questions proved to be only mildly anxiety arousing. Siegman and Pope looked at the effects of anxiety arousal on disruptions, in the interviewee's speech, at the effects of anxiety arousal on interviewees's productivity levels, and at the effects of anxiety arousal on the temporal racing of speed.

Speech disruption was measured by Mahl's (1956) Speech Disturbance Ratio (SDR), which includes categories such as incomplete sentences, sentence corrections, repetitions, stutters, and tongue-slips. The interviewer's anxiety arousing questions were found to be associated with higher SDR scores than were the neutral questions. With a notable early exception (Boomer & Goodrich, 1961), this association between anxiety arousal and speech disruption has been documented by many investigators (e.g., Cook, 1969; Feldstein, Brenner, & Jaffe, 1963; for a comprehensive review see Rochester, 1973). Interviewees' responses to the anxiety arousing questions, in contrast to their responses to the neutral ones, were also associated with a faster *speech rate,* a faster *articulation rate,* and fewer long *silent pauses*—that is, with a more accelerated pacing of speech (including fewer *filled pauses,* i.e., use of "ah" and "ehm"). *Speech rate* was obtained by dividing number of words by response time, which included silent pauses. *Articulation rate* was obtained by dividing number of words by response time minus the duration of the silent pauses. Speech rate, then, was a function of a speaker's articulation rate and the duration of his silent pauses. Finally, interviewees gave more productive, or longer responses to the anxiety arousing than to the neutral questions. Siegman and Pope (1972) suggested that these findings can be readily explained in terms of a drive conceptualization of anxiety arousal (see Taylor, 1951; Taylor & Spence, 1952).

One methodological problem with the Siegman and Pope (1965, 1972) study, and with other investigations in which anxiety arousal is achieved via topical manipulation, is that different topics have been shown to be associated with different productivity levels and speech rates (Siegman & Reynolds, 1981a, c). Also, the finding that anxiety arousal is associated with relatively short silent pauses is contradicted by an earlier finding (Mahl, 1956). In that study, one of the earliest on the effects of anxiety arousal on temporal features of speech, it was noted that interviewee responses that were characterized by high conflict induced anxiety arousal were also associated with *longer* silent pauses than were interviewee responses characterized by low conflict induced anxiety arousal. Other studies, however, have found that experimentally produced anxiety is indeed associated with an accelerated speech rate, independent of topical focus. For example, in a series of word association studies by Kanfer (1958a, b), subjects were administered intermittent shocks, which were preceded by an auditory warning signal. Subjects showed an increase in posttone speech rate (in anticipation of the shock) and a decrease in postshock speech rate, suggesting that anxiety arousal had an accelerating effect on speech rate. Sauer and Marcuse (1958) similarly reported that anxiety over the presence of a tape recorder had an accelerating effect on subjects' responses to Thematic Apperception Test (TAT) cards.

Recent findings on the temporal speech patterns of coronary-prone, type A personalities also support the hypothesis that stress induced anxiety arousal may be associated with an accelerated speech rate. For the past two decades, evidence has been accumulating that certain behavior patterns or personality traits are significant risk factors in coronary heart disease (CHD) (Friedman & Rosenman, 1959; Rosenman, 1978). These traits, which include ambitious, hard-driving, competitive, hostile, impatient, and time-pressured behavior patterns, are characteristic of *type A individuals.* The relative absence of these traits or, more positively stated, a relaxed lifestyle is characteristic of *type B individuals* and is associated with a low risk for CHD. Behavior typing is achieved either by means of objective paper and pencil questionnaires or by means of a specially structured interview. Recent evidence suggests that the interview based behavior typing is more effective than the questionnaires in predicting clinical CHD and severity of atherosclerosis (Blumenthal et al, 1978). The interview is designed to be a moderately stressful experience. This condition is achieved by asking some of the questions in a rapid-fire style, by dragging out others, and by interrupting the interviewee in the midst of giving responses. Recent studies have indicated that the responses of type A and type B individuals to this kind of stressful interview can be distinguished on the basis of their vocal and temporal characteristics: in such interviews, type A's, in contrast to type B's, have shorter response latencies, faster articulation rates, and louder voices (Howland & Siegman, in press; Scherwitz, Berton, & Leveuthal, 1977; Schucker & Jacobs, 1977). In fact, a regression equation consisting of response latency and voice volume was able correctly to identify the A and B behavior ratings of 89% of a group of 66 patients (Howland & Siegman, *in press*). These findings suggest that stress tends to elicit a *time-pressured speech pattern,* characterized by a fast reaction time and a fast speech rate, but they also suggest that this pattern may be true for only some individuals (i.e., type A's) and not for others (i.e., type B's)

THE MODERATING EFFECT OF ANXIETY LEVEL AND OF TASK COMPLEXITY

In discussing the energizing-facilitating effect of arousal on behavior, a number of authors have argued that this effect is likely to reach an asymptote with increasing levels of arousal and eventually will reverse itself (Duffy, 1962; Fiske & Maddi, 1961; Hebb, 1955). If so, then even if mild and moderate levels of anxiety arousal tend to accelerate speech, very high levels of anxiety arousal should be associated with a slower speech rate and longer silent pauses. Although this hypothesis, usually referred to as the *inverted U-curve hypothesis,* seems reasonable enough both from a theoretical and a commonsense point of view, it is difficult to test empirically. It is difficult to calibrate levels of anxiety arousal and to identify in advance precisely which anxiety levels will produce a facilitating effect and which will produce the reverse. Failures to obtain the hypothesized asymptote or reversal can always be attributed, post hoc, to insufficient arousal.

Perhaps the most clear-cut evidence in favor of the inverted U-curve hypothesis came from a study by Fenz and Epstein (1962), which, incidentally, is one of the few studies on the effects of naturalistically occurring anxiety, rather than experimentally manipulated anxiety, on speech. Fenz and Epstein obtained stories in response to TAT-like cards from a group of novice parachutists on their day of jumping and from a control group of nonparachutists. In addition, the parachutists served as their own controls by responding to the cards on a nonjumping day. Subjects always responded to three kinds of cards: neutral (no relevance to parachute jumping), low relevance, and high relevance. The reaction-time (RT) data clearly suggest that anxiety arousal has an activating effect on response latency. Conditions that can be assumed to have aroused mild to moderate anxiety were associated with a decrease in RT. On the other hand, the one condition that probably aroused very high anxiety levels, namely, the high relevance cards on the day of jumping, was associated with a steep increase in RT. Pauses in the parachutists' stories on the day of jumping also showed an activation effect, with lower pause ratios in the low relevance than in the neutral cards and higher pause ratios in the high relevance than in the low relevance cards. There were no significant differences in the control group. Subjects' verbal rate data also followed a similar pattern, but these differences were not significant. By and large, the results of the Fenz and Epstein study provide fairly strong support for the inverted U-curve hypothesis, as far as anxiety and temporal indexes of speech are concerned.

The results of another study, however, appear to be inconsistent with the inverted U-curve hypothesis (Pope, Blass, Siegman, & Raher, 1970). In this study, six hospitalized psychiatric patients spoke into a tape recorder each morning for their entire hospitalization, describing for about 10 minutes any of their experiences from the preceding day. The patients were also rated each day by a team of trained nurses on a number of manifest anxiety scales. Speech samples recorded during each patient's eight most anxious and eight least anxious days were compared. It should be noted that all patients had psychosomatic diagnoses and that they all occasionally manifested extreme anxiety, as well as stretches of calm and relaxed behavior. The results were based on a within-subjects comparison (high anxiety versus low anxiety days) and were not confounded by subjects' psychiatric diagnoses. Speech samples recorded during high anxious days, in contrast to speech samples recorded during low anxious days, were associated with faster speech rates, lower pause ratios, and faster articulation rates, but only the differences for speech rate and pause ratio were significant (this study did not yield RT scores). These findings, then, suggest that even high anxiety arousal—it seems reasonable indeed—is associated with a higher speech rate, due to a reduction in silent pauses.

Perhaps the conflicting findings can be reconciled if we consider the different tasks that were involved in the two studies. From a drive theory point of view, the effect of arousal on behavior is in part a function of the nature of the task. For example, it has been shown that the same level of anxiety arousal that facilitates simple learning tasks (tasks in which the predominant response tendency is the correct one) will interfere with complex learning tasks (tasks that elicit competing response tendencies) (Siegman, 1957; Taylor & Spence, 1952). By the same token, the effects of anxiety arousal and stress on the temporal pacing of speech should also be a function of the nature of the speaking task. The same arousal level that accelerates highly habituated speech sequences, or automatic speech, such as is involved in discussing a familar topic, it likely to slow down speech that requires planning and decision-making, such as is involved in making up stories in response to TAT cards. This could account for the fact that even fairly high anxiety levels accelerated patients' speech when they were asked to talk about anything that occurred to them (Pope, Blass, Siegman, & Raher, 1970) but had the opposite effect on subjects in the Fenz and Epstein (1962) study, who were asked to make up creative stories about ambiguous TAT-like cards.

Direct empirical support for the hypothesized mediating role of task complexity came from a recent study in which subjects were asked to give truthful responses to a series of routine questions and to make up imaginative responses to a set of similar questions (Siegman & Reynolds, 1981b). In postexperimental ratings, subjects indicated that the make-believe task was considerably more difficult than the control condition. As hypothesized, subjects' anxiety scores, obtained on Eysenck's (1959) neuroticism scale, correlated negatively with their RT scores in the control condition and positively in the make-believe condition.

Thus, there is considerable evidence that anxiety arousal is associated with an accelerated speech style—specifically, with short reaction times, relatively fast articulation rates, and few and/or short silent pauses—and with a relatively high level of speech disruptions, provided the speech task does not involve complex decisionmaking. However, at least two research areas suggest that under certain circumstances, stress induced anxiety arousal can be associated with generally decelerated rather than accelerated, speech, i.e., with long response latencies, slow articulation rates, and long silent pauses. Moreover, under such circumstances the stress induced anxiety arousal may not be associated with an increase in speech disruptions. These two research areas involve the effects of stage fright and deception on speech. We will now take a closer look at this research and its implications for understanding the effects of anxiety arousal on speech.

AUDIENCE ANXIETY AND SPEECH

Public speaking is a stressful situation for many people. Considering the effects of situational anxiety on speech, summarized earlier in this chapter, one would expect public speaking, in contrast to dyadic conversation, to have several distinguishing extralinguistic features. First and foremost, one would expect public speaking, to the extent that it is in fact anxiety arousing, to be associated with speech disruptions as measured by Mahl's (1956) SDR. Second, public speaking should be associated with an accelerated speech tempo if the speaking task is a simple one and with a reduced speech tempo if the speaking task is complex. Findings will be reviewed separately for each of the speech variables.

Speech Disturbances

A number of investigators have looked at the effect of public speaking anxiety, or *audience anxiety,* as it is referred to in the literature, on speech disturbances. Some studies combined the speech disturbance categories with silent pauses and filled pauses into a single *dysfluency index* (e.g., Levin, Baldwin, Gallwey, & Paivio, 1960), which makes evaluation of results difficult. Of several investigators who looked specifically at the impact of audience anxiety on either the SDR or its separate major categories, none obtained the expected disruptive effect (Geer, 1966; Levin & Silverman, 1965; Paivio, 1965; Reynolds & Paivio, 1968). Considering the consistency with which situational anxiety has been found to be associated with an increase in the SDR, this is a puzzling finding. Before attempting to provide an explanation for this finding, I will first present some other data.

Temporal Measures

A number of investigators have looked at the effects of audience anxiety on the temporal patterning of speech. By and large, the evidence suggests that audience anxiety slows down the speaker's pace. However, as has been pointed out elsewhere (Siegman, 1978), most studies of this relationship involved complex tasks, such as making up stories in response to TAT cards and interpreting cartoons, rather than the highly habituated speech that is found in most dyadic conversation. However, even the few studies that used relatively simple speaking tasks found a slowing effect on speech. For example, Reynolds and Paivio (1968) looked at the effects of audience anxiety on speech in a group of college students whose task was to define a series of abstract and concrete nouns, the latter certainly being a simple task. The experimental manipulation had no significant independent effect on either of the two temporal indexes: response latency and pause ratio. However, as far as the silent pauses were concerned, there was a significant interaction between subjects' scores on an inventory designed to measure audience sensitivity (ASI) and the experimental manipulation. While high ASI scorers showed an increase in silent pauses from the control to the public speaking condition, low ASI scorers showed a decrease. Moreover, in the control condition, the high scorers had lower pause rates than did the low scorers. A similar interaction between subjects' ASI scores and public versus private speaking was reported by Paivio (1965) in relation to speech rate. If one makes the assumption that the public speaking situation produced mild anxiety arousal in the low ASI scorers and fairly high anxiety in the high ASI scorers, then the results of these two studies are consistent with the inverted U-curve hypothesis; namely, mild anxiety arousal accelerates speech, whereas strong arousal has the reverse effect.

The Reynolds and Paivio (1968) study also clearly indicated that a high level of audience anxiety can be associated with a decelerated speech pattern even if the speech task is relatively simple. This finding, of course, is contrary to that obtained by Pope and associates (1970) with psychiatric patients, whose speech was accelerated on the days when they were very anxious. The difference may lie in the circumstances surrounding the anxiety arousing conditions of the two studies. It is not at all obvious that the patients in the study by Pope and associates were aware of their anxiety arousal; moreover, if they were, there is no particular reason why they should have been motivated to conceal it. By way of contrast, people with high audience anxiety are likely to be aware that they become very anxious when having to address an audience. Moreover, when placed in such a situation, they probably do not want the audience to be aware of their discomfort, and they are likely to engage in measures designed to cover up their anxiety arousal. Knowing that when they become anxious they tend to speak much more quickly, they are likely to make an effort to speak slowly. However, as is frequently the case with such attempts, they may overshoot their mark, resulting in a slower pace than normal. Alternatively, people high on audience anxiety may deliberately adopt a markedly slow pace, knowing from experience that in so doing they can avoid the speech disruptions that are normally associated with anxiety arousal. Whatever the explanation, the puzzling absence of speech disruptions in speakers with high audience anxiety may very well be related to the relatively slow pace of their speech.[2]

In other words, the effects of anxiety arousal on the temporal pacing of speech is a function not only of task complexity but also of the speaker's motivation to conceal his or her anxiety arousal. Should the speaker be so motivated, then anxiety arousal may not have the expected accelerating effect on speech, even if the task involves simple speech sequences. In fact, when the speaker is so motivated, anxiety arousal may be associated with deliberate and slow speech. Of course, this can be no less a telltale sign of anxiety arousal than is a fast speech rate. Implicit in what has been said thus far is the assumption that should they so desire, speakers can regulate the pacing of their speech at will, or at least they can slow down the rate. Results obtained by Sloan (1976) clearly support this assumption. Moreover, this assumption is not necessarily at variance with yet another assumption that the vocal channel is a relatively "leaky" channel, i.e., it is likely to betray a speaker's true feelings which he or she is trying to conceal. Leakage is a function not only of controllability but also of awareness. Speakers may be relatively unaware of naturally occurring changes in their speech rate yet may be able to regulate their speech rate when instructed to do so by others or by themselves. More important, the so-called leakiness of the vocal channel may be a function of factors other than speech rate and silent pauses.

TELLING LIES

Recently there has been a surge of research activity on the nonverbal correlates of deceptive communications, with some studies focusing on the veridical nonverbal correlates of deceptive messages and other studies focusing on the nonverbal cues that listeners use in detecting lies. Viewed against the assumption that for most people lying is a stressful experience, causing the liar to feel guilty and/or anxious about being caught, this research should have obvious implications for the central concern of this chapter: the effects of stress and anxiety arousal on nonverbal behavior. In a review of the literature, Zuckerman, DePaulo, and Rosenthal (1981) found that deceptive communications were associated with relatively high levels of speech disruption, which, of course, is what one would expect if lying is indeed a stressful, anxiety arousing experience. One the other hand, they found no evidence that speakers accelerated their speaking pace when engaged in deceptive communications. In fact, there was a nonsignificant trend in the opposite direction. How are we to reconcile this finding with the previous conclusion that anxiety arousal is associated with accelerated speech rate? At the outset, it should be pointed out that, on first glance, subjects in the typical laboratory study on deception should have very little reason, if any, to be anxious about their lying; usually they are instructed to lie by the experimenter. In justifying the relevance of such laboratory studies to lying in the real world, investigators argue that if lying has been conditioned to anxiety in the past, deception in the lab is likely to elicit some anxiety in spite of the experimenter's sanction. Moreover, in order to make the deception task anxiety arousing, the experimenter may tell subjects that if they are detected, it will reflect negatively on their professional potential or entail some other negative consequence. It is not at all clear, however, that this instruction will evoke anything comparable to the anxiety involved in real-life lying. There is yet another problem. In many laboratory studies, the lying task requires that the subject concoct a fictitious response, which may be cognitively demanding, thereby confounding the deception manipulation with task complexity. In such studies the deceptive response may or may not be anxiety arousing, but it clearly involves more complex processes than telling the truth. There is considerable evidence that difficult and complex tasks are associated with more hesitant speech, with slower articulation rates, and longer silent pauses than are simple tasks (Siegman, 1978, 1979). Thus, the task complexity associated with the deceptive communications in such studies may mask or reverse the otherwise accelerating effect of anxiety arousal on speech. Of course, in the real world, too, lying can be cognitively demanding, although it is by no means clear that this is always or even typically the case. In short, the implications of deception studies for the effects of anxiety arousal on speech are compromised to the extent that the lying manipulation is confounded with task complexity.

A recently completed study was free from the above two strictures (Reynolds, 1981). The lying was neither feigned nor especially difficult to achieve. Subjects were enticed by the experimenter's confederate into cheating and deviating from the prescribed experimental procedure. Subsequently, they, as well as control subjects who had had no opportunity to cheat, were asked in a postexperimental interview to describe the procedures that they had followed during the experiment. This made it possible to compare unfeigned deceitful and truthful responses. Although confounding with task complexity was not an issue, the deceptive responses were clearly associated with longer reaction times, longer silent pauses, and slower speech rates than were the truthful responses. I would suggest that although anxiety arousal has an accelerating effect on speech, this is true only if the subject is motivated to speak, but not if the speech act per se arouses an approach-avoidance conflict. This conflict is likely to occur when someone is questioned about his or her transgressions. On the one hand, there is the normal motivation to respond; on the other, however, there is the motivation not to respond lest one reveal one's transgression. Such conflict is bound to slow down speech. This explanation can also account for Mahl's (1956) finding, cited earlier, that interviewee responses indicating conflict induced anxiety arousal were associated with relatively long silent pauses.

In their review of the deception literature, Zuckerman, DePaulo, and Rosenthal (1981) divided the studies into those in which subjects were strongly motivated (by means of appropriate positive or negative contingencies) not to be detected in their deceptions and those in which there was little, if any, such motivation. One might assume that subjects in the former group of studies were probably more anxious about lying and, therefore, more likely when lying to manifest the nonverbal correlates of anxiety arousal than subjects in the latter group. In fact, the opposite was the case. For example, the positive association between lying and speech disruptions reported earlier was significant only in the low motivation studies. The same was true of other known correlates of anxiety arousal. For example, in the low motivation studies, there was a significant positive correlation between deception and rate of eye blinking, which, of course, is to be expected if deception is anxiety arousing. Yet in the high motivation studies, in which subjects presumably were more anxious about their deceptions than in the low motivation studies, there was a significant negative correlation between the two.

How are we to account for these paradoxical findings? The point made at the conclusion of the preceding section on audience anxiety probably applies here as well. The nonverbal correlates of anxiety arousal are a function of the subject's willingness to evidence his or her anxiety. The nonverbal correlates the deception in the low motivation studies apparently represented a direct manifestation of subjects' anxiety arousal, even though they probably were only minimally aroused. On the other hand, the nonverbal correlates of deception in the high motivation studies probably represented subjects' attempt to hide and counteract their anxiety arousal; hence the absence of speech disruptions and the reduced incidence of eye blinks. The very motivation not to be detected, which caused subjects in the high motivation studies to be more anxious than subjects in the low motivation studies, may also make them want to cover up all telltale signs of anxiety arousal. It is of interest to note that subjects in the high-motivation studies were less productive when lying than when telling the truth. This finding, too, is consistent with the suggestion that these subjects were motivated to conceal, as much as possible, any signs of being anxious. By way of summary, then, I would suggest that the effects of anxiety arousal on speech disruptions and speech rate also depend, in addition to the factors identified earlier, on the speaker's willingness to manifest anxious behavior. Anxiety arousal per se is associated with an accelerated speech rate and with a relatively high level of speech disruptions. However, if subjects are strongly motivated to hide their anxiety, then they may manifest the very opposite behavior: a slow pacing of speech and no increase in speech disruptions. In fact, the very intensity of a subject's anxiety arousal may motivate the subject to hide his or her anxiety.

PERSONALITY AS A MEDIATING VARIABLE

A distinction has been made between *state* anxiety and *trait* anxiety (Spellberger, 1966). State anxiety refers to a person's momentary or situational anxiety, and it varies over time and across settings. Trait anxiety, on the other hand, refers to a person's more stable, characteristic overall anxiety level. The discussion thus far has dealt with the effects of state anxiety on speech, but what about the effects of trait anxiety? One might reasonably expect that the effects of *trait anxiety,* on speech would correspond to the effects of *state anxiety,* as described earlier. The available empirical evidence, however, provides only partial support for this expectation. Contrary to expectation, there is no evidence for a positive correlation between measures of trait anxiety, such as the Taylor's (1953) Manifest Anxiety Scale (MAS), and Mahl's SDR (Siegman, 1978). On the other hand, trait anxiety apparently has an accelerating effect on speech. In a review article, Murray (1971) cited six studies that correlated measures of trait anxiety with response latency. All six correlations were negative; three, significantly so. Similarly, Siegman and Pope (1965b) obtained a significant positive correlation between the Taylor MAS and articulation rate. Other investigators, however, reported significant positive correlations between trait anxiety and indexes of silent pausing (Helfrich & Dahme, 1974). It is possible, of course, that trait anxiety is associated with short response latencies, and even with a fast articulation rate, and at the same time with intermittent, long silent pauses.

In an attempt to reconcile these apparently paradoxical findings, I (1978) suggested elsewhere that chronically anxious individuals may compensate for their quick response times and their fast articulation rates by resorting to more frequent long silent pauses in order to insure fluent speech, free from speech disruptions. Scherer (1979), on the other hand, suggested a social-psychological explanation for the positive correlation between the Taylor MAS and articulation rate. There is considerable evidence that listeners are attracted, and attribute positive personality traits to, individuals who speak with a relatively fast articulation rate and without unduly long silent pauses (Brown, 1980; Feldstein & Crown, 1979; Siegman & Reynolds, 1982a). High MAS scorers tend to be socially insecure and anxious individuals, with a heightened sensitivity to social evaluation. Scherer suggested that such individuals are likely to accelerate their speech rate so as to make a positive impression on listeners. Of course, by the same token, they should also want to avoid long silent pauses. Scherer explained the evidence to the contrary in two ways. First, speaking more quickly, such individuals need longer within-response silent pauses for their planning and information processing. Alternatively, he suggested that their concerns about self-presentation have sensitized them to signals of listener reaction, which they monitor closely. Unexpected listener signals such as a frown of doubt or disapproval should severely interfere with their ongoing thought and speech processes, requiring long silent pauses to reorient and restructure the content and manner of their responses. Recent findings confirm Scherer's assumption that socially insecure individuals will evidence relatively long within-response silent pauses in dyadic interactions (Siegman & Reynolds, 1982b).

Perhaps the paradoxical findings on the relationship between the Taylor MAS and various temporal indexes are related to that scale's multifactorial composition. Some of the items seem to involve an other-directedness, which is rooted in a sense of social inadequacy and insecurity, but others seem to index autonomic nervous system arousal. While the latter is likely to have an accelerating effect on speech, the former may have a slowing effect. Researchers interested in the relationship between trait anxiety, as assessed by the MAS, and the temporal patterning of speech may be well advised to look at the effects of each of these dimensions on a broad variety of temporal indexes. As pointed out earlier, yet another source of individual differences in response to stress induced anxiety is the type A–type B behavior pattern. Finally, recent research indicates that extroversion and acting skills are two potent sources of variance in people's ability to regulate their expressive vocal behavior (Siegman & Reynolds, 1981b, 1982b).

OTHER NONVERBAL CORRELATES OF STRESS AND ANXIETY AROUSAL

Thus far, this discussion on the effects of anxiety arousal on nonverbal behavior has focused primarily on speech disruptions and the temporal pacing of speech, primarily because these variables have been looked at in a variety of anxiety arousing situations (e.g., topical anxiety, fear of electric shock, anxiety associated with being tape-recorded, public speaking anxiety, anxiety linked to lying and parachutists' fear of falling), so that the results, to the extent to which they show consistent trends, possess a measure of ecological and construct validity. However, investigators have looked at a number of other nonverbal indexes, some of which are strong candidates for the role of nonverbal indicators of anxiety arousal.

Vocal Correlates

The increase in muscle tone under stress and the deepening of respiration and dilation of the bronchi under stress (Gray, 1971) would lead one to expect higher intensity and higher fundamental frequency in the speech signal, caused by increased subglottal pressure and higher medial compression and tension of the vocal folds, as well as a shift of the energy concentration in the spectrum to higher frequencies. Some of the most realistic studies on the effects of stress on the speech signal have involved air-to-ground communications in flights made under dangerous conditions. Most studies have reported an increase in fundamental frequency (F_0) with increasing danger (for a recent review of the literature see Scherer, 1981). In their review of the deception literature, Zuckerman, DePaulo, and Rosenthal (1981) also found lying to be associated with an increase in pitch. However, in a laboratory study on the effects of task induced stress on the acoustic signal, Hecker, Stevens, von Bismarck and Stevens (1968) reported that while some subjects always produced a higher fundamental frequency when under stress, others always produced a lower fundamental frequency. Similar individual differences were reported by Friedhoff, Alpert, and Kurtzberg (1964), who studied the effect of stress (in a lying situation) on loudness.

In part, such differences may reflect different emotional responses to the identical stress producing stimulus: some individuals may respond with anger, others with anxiety, and yet others with shame or various combinations thereof. Furthermore, facing the same emotional reaction, different individuals resort to different coping strategies. For example, consider two individuals who respond to the same stressful situation with anxiety; one may openly express such symptoms, while the other, as pointed out earlier, may supress all such symptoms or overcompensate for them. Whatever the explanation, individual variations in response to stress complicate matters enormously for anyone trying to develop a theoretical model of the effects of stress behavior. However, from a practical point of view, as long as we know an individual's baseline response, significant deviations therefrom, whether above or below baseline, can be viewed as indications of stress.

Recently there has been considerable interest in a stress measuring device, the Psychological Stress Evaluator (PSE), which according to its developers measures the absence of microtremors in the voice (Holden, 1975). Microtremors are supposed to be present under normal conditions but ostensibly disappear under stress. The PSE has been used most extensively as a lie detection instrument. In reviewing this literature, Scherer (1981) concluded that the PSE's accuracy does not exceed chance. The PSE has also been used to assess the vocal effects of stress associated with upcoming hospitalization, final exams, and emotional disturbance. While some success in stress detection with the PSE has been claimed in these studies, Scherer (1981) concluded that "the justification for these claims cannot be properly established, since important methodological details are either not reported or remain unclear" (p. 175). Furthermore, even if it were possible to detect stress with the PSE, it is not at all clear what is actually being measured (Podlesny & Raskin, 1977); indeed, the very existence of voice tremors is considered problematic (Shipp & McGlone, 1973).

Hand Movements

It is frequently assumed that anxiety is associated with fidgeting; that is, individuals engage in more frequent postural shifts and body movements of various sorts when anxious than when relaxed. Until recently, there have been few careful empirical studies involving stress and body movement, probably because body movement does not readily lend itself to quantification. The absence of a generally accepted classification system contributes to the problem. Nevertheless, many of the deception studies did look at the effect of lying on various body and hand movements.

A classification system suggested by Ekman and Friesen (1972) divides hand movements into *emblems* (iconic signs, such as the V-sign), *illustrators* (acts that are intimately related either to what is being said or to the speech rhythm), and *adaptors* (rubbing, squeezing, or scratching various parts of one's body; playing with one's jewelry, pencil, cigarette, or other such objects). Adaptor type movements apparently are related to anxiety. A factor analysis of Overall and Gorham's (1962) Brief Psychiatric Rating Scale yielded three factors, one of which was labeled upsetness, or anxiety. In a group of psychiatric patients, subjects' upsetness, or anxiety, scores correlated significantly with their rate of adaptor type hand movements (Ekman & Friesen, 1972). Moreover, in their review of 12 deception studies, Zuckerman, DePaulo, and Rosenthal (1981) found lying to be significantly associated with adaptor type hand movements. Of 10 nonvocal cues usually associated with lying, this category of hand movements emerged as the second most reliable discriminator of deceptive communications. (Although pupil dilation was by far the best discriminator in the deception studies, this response is probably a concomitant of general arousal, rather than a specific marker of anxiety.)

CONCLUSION

This chapter reviewed the nonverbal communication research literature with the objective of finding reliable correlates of stress induced anxiety arousal. While a number of speech indexes (speech disruptions, temporal pacing of speech—e.g., speech rate and silent pauses—and pitch) and one movement variable (adaptor type hand movements) emerged as potential candidates, it is apparent that the relationships are complex and moderated by several factors. For example, while anxiety arousal up to a certain point has the effect of accelerating speech, this is true only if the information processing required by the speaking task is not too complex. Anxiety can have a slowing effect on speech if the arousal level is very high or if the task is cognitively demanding. Complicating prediction even further is the important fact that a speaker can, given sufficient warning, try deliberately to mask his or her anxiety symptoms, occasionally overshooting the mark. This frequently happens in stage fright and in some deception situations. In such cases, anxiety arousal is likely to manifest itself in a deliberate and slow speech style. Of course, this pattern, too, can be an indication of anxiety arousal. The problem of individual differences, which has plagued research on the physiological correlates of stress induced anxiety arousal, is no less troublesome in the nonverbal domain. Finally, the problem of distinguishing indicators of anxiety from indictors of emotionality and general arousal, which has long confounded physiological research, arises in the nonverbal domain as well. Nevertheless, the absence of a single, simple telltale sign of anxiety need not discourage us from continuing the search for patterns of nonverbal correlates of stress induced anxiety arousal.

NOTES

1. I have avoided defining stress and anxiety and discussing the distinctions between them. This has been done by others in the past (e.g., Appley & Trumbull, 1967; Lazarus, 1966), and these issues are examined elsewhere in this volume. In the absence of new insights, a discussion of these constructs here is bound to be redundant.
2. Other methodological problems concern the proper control condition for evaluating the effects of audience anxiety. For example, in studies by Levin and Silverman (1965) and by Reynolds and Paivio (1968), the control condition required that subjects speak into a tape recorder, with no other person present. Two problems arise here. First, speaking into a tape recorder, and certainly for the first time, can be stressful (Sauer & Marcuse, 1957). Second, the mere presence of another person or persons produces pressure on a speaker that he does not have to contend with when he is alone. It can be argued, therefore, that the proper control condition for audience anxiety is one in which the speaker addresses one other person. Finally, some studies have confounded audience size and status. In a study by Levin and Silverman (1965), in which the speakers were children, the audience consisted of higher status adults; in an investigation by Reynolds and Paivio (1968), in which the audience consisted of peers, the control condition involved the presence of a high-status experimenter. The evidence that listener status influences a speaker's paralinguistic behavior (Siegman, 1978) points to the seriousness of confounding audience size and status.

REFERENCES

APPLEY, M. H., & TRUMBULL, R. *Psychological stress.* New York: Appleton, 1967.

BLUMENTHAL, J. A., WILLIAMS, R., KONG, Y., SCHANBERG, S. M., & THOMSON, L. W. Type A behavior pattern and angiographically documented coronary disease. *Circulation,* 1978, *58,* 634–635.

BOOMER, D. S., & GOODRICH, D. W. Speech disturbance and judged anxiety. *Journal of Consulting Psychology,* 1961, *25,* 160–164.

BROWN, B. L. Effects of speech rate on personality attributions and competency evaluations. In H. Giles, W. P. Robinson, & P. M. Smith (eds.), *Language: Social psychological perspectives.* New York: Pergamon, 1980.

COOK, M. Anxiety, speech disturbances, and speech rate. *British Journal of Social and Clinical Psychology,* 1969, *8,* 13–21.

DUFFY E. *Activation and behavior.* New York: Wiley, 1962.

EKMAN, P., & FRIESEN, W. V. Nonverbal behavior and psychopathology. In R. J. Friedman & M. M. Katz (eds.), *The psychology of depression: Contemporary theory and research.* Washington, D.C.: U. S. Government Printing Office, 1972.

EYSENCK, H. J. *Manual of the Maudsley Personality Inventory,* London: London Press, 1959.

FELDSTEIN, S., BRENNER, M. S., & JAFFE, J. The effect of subject sex, verbal interaction, and topical focus on speech disruption. *Language and Speech,* 1963, *6,* 505–509.

FELDSTEIN, S., & CROWN, C. L. Interpersonal perception in dyads as a function of race, gender, and conversational time patterns. Paper presented to the annual meeting of the Eastern Psychological Association, Philadelphia, 1979.

FENZ, W. D. J., & EPSTEIN, S. Measurement of approach-avoidance conflict along a stimulus dimension by a thematic apperception test. *Journal of Personality,* 1962, *30,* 613–632.

FISKE, D. W., & MADDI, S. R. (eds.). *Functions of varied experience.* Homewood: Dorsey, 1961.

FRIEDHOFF, A. J., ALPERT, M., & KURTZBERG, R. L. An electro-acoustic analysis of the effects of stress on voice. *Journal of Neuropsychiatry,* 1964, *5,* 266–272.

FRIEDMAN, M., & ROSENMAN, R. H. Association of specified overt behavior pattern with blood and cardiovascular findings. *Journal of the American Medical Association,* 1959, *169,* 1286–1296.

GEER, J. H. Effects of fear arousal upon task performance and verbal behavior. *Journal of Abnormal Psychology,* 1966, *71,* 119–123.

GRAY, J. A. *The psychology of fear and stress.* New York: McGraw-Hill, 1971.

HEBB, D. O. Drives and the C.N.S. (conceptual nervous system). *Psychological Review,* 1955, *62,* 243–254.

HECKER, M. H. L., STEVENS, K. N., VON BISMARCK, G., & WILLIAMS, C. E. Manifestations of task-induced stress in the acoustical speech signal. *Journal of the Acoustical Society of America,* 1968, *44,* 993–1001.

HELFRICH, H., & DAHME, G. Sind Verzogerungsphanomene bein spontanen Sprechen Indikatoren personlichkeitsspezifischer Angstverarbeitung. *Zeitschrift fur Sozialpsychologie,* 1974, *5,* 55–65.

HOLDEN, C. Lie detectors; PSE gains audience despite critics' doubt. *Science,* 1975, *190,* 359–362.

HOWLAND, E. W., & SIEGMAN, A. W. Toward the automated measurement of the type-A behavior pattern. *Journal of Behavioral Medicine,* in press.

KANFER, F. H. Effect of a warning signal preceding a noxious stimulus on verbal rate and heart rate. *Journal of Experimental Psychology,* 1958, *55,* 78–80.

————. Supplementary report: Stability of a verbal rate change in experimental anxiety. *Journal of Experimental Psychology,* 1958, *56,* 182.(b)

LAZARUS, R. S. *Psychological stress and the coping process.* New York: McGraw-Hill, 1968.

LEVIN, H., BALDWIN, A. L., GALLWEY, M., & PAIVIO, A. Audience stress, personality, and speech. *Journal of Abnormal and Social Psychology,* 1960, *61,* 469–473.

LEVIN, H., & SILVERMAN, I. Hesitation phenomena in children's speech. *Language and Speech,* 1965, *8,* 67–85.

MAHL, G. F. Disturbances and silences in the patient's speech in psychotherapy. *Journal of Verbal Learning and Verbal Behavior,* 1956, *53,* 1–15.

MURRAY, D. C. Talk, silence, and anxiety. *Psychological Bulletin,* 1971, *75,* 244–260.

OVERALL, J. E., & GORHAM, E. R. The Brief Psychiatric Rating Scale. *Psychological Reports,* 1962, *10,* 799–812.

PAIVIO, A. Personality and audience influence. In B. A. Mahr (ed.), *Progress in experimental personality research,* vol. 2. New York: Academic, 1965.

PODLESNY, J. A., & RASKIN, D. C. Physiological measures and the detection of deception. *Psychological Bulletin,* 1977, *84,* 782–799.

POPE, B., BLASS, T., SIEGMAN, A. W., & RAHER, J. Anxiety and depression in speech. *Journal of Consulting and Clinical Psychology,* 1970, *35,* 128–133.

REYNOLDS, A., & PAIVIO, A. Cognitive and emotional determinants of speech. *Canadian Journal of Psychology,* 1968, *22,* 164–175.

REYNOLDS, M. Vocal correlates of unfeigned deceit. Master's thesis, University of Maryland Baltimore County, 1981.

ROCHESTER, S. R. The significance of pauses in spontaneous speech. *Journal of Psycholinguistic Research,* 1973, *2,* 51–81.

ROSENMAN, R. H. The interview method of assessment of the coronary-prone behavior pattern. In T. Dembroski, S. Weiss, J. Shields, S. Haynes, & M. Feinleib (eds.), *Coronary-prone behavior.* New York: Springer, 1978.

SAUER, R. E., & MARCUSE, F. L. Overt and covert recording. *Journal of Projective Techniques,* 1957, *21,* 391–395.

SCHERER, K. Personality markers in speech. In K. R. Scherer & H. Giles (eds.), *Social markers in speech.* New York: Cambridge University Press, 1979.

SCHERER, K. R. Vocal indicators of stress. In J. K. Darby (ed.), *Speech evaluation in psychiatry.* New York: Grune & Stratton, 1981.

SCHERWITZ, L., BERTON, B. S., & LEVENTHAL, H. Type A assessment and interaction in the behavior pattern interview. *Psychosomatic Medicine,* 1977, *39,* 299–240.

SCHUCKER, B., & JACOBS, D. R. Assessment of behavioral risk for coronary disease by voice characteristics. *Psychosomatic Medicine,* 1977, *39,* 219–228.

SHIPP, T., & MCGLONE, R. E. Physiologic correlates of acoustic correlates of psychological stress. *Journal of the Acoustical Society of America,* 1973, *53,* 63.

————. The telltale voice: Nonverbal messages of verbal communication. In A. W. Siegman & S. Feldstein (eds.), *Nonverbal behavior and communication.* Hillsdale: Erlbaum, 1978.

————. Cognition and hesitation in speech. In A. W. Siegman & S. Feldstein (eds.), *Of time and speech: Temporal speech patterns in interpersonal contexts.* Hillsdale: Erlbaum, 1979.

SIEGMAN, A. W., & POPE, B. Effects of question specificity and anxiety producing messages on verbal fluency in the initial interview. *Journal of Personality and Social Psychology,* 1965, *4,* 188–192. (a)

————. Personality variables associated with productivity and verbal fluency in the initial interview. *Proceedings of the American Psychological Association,* 1965, pp. 273–274. (b)

————. The effects of ambiguity and anxiety on interviewee verbal behavior. In A. W. Siegman & B. Pope (eds.), *Studies in dyadic communication.* New York: Pergamon, 1972.

SIEGMAN, A. W., & REYNOLDS, M. The effects of rapport and topical intimacy on interviewee productivity and verbal fluency. Manuscript, University of Maryland Baltimore County, 1981. (a)

————. Self-monitoring and speech style. Paper presented to the annual meeting of the Eastern Psylogical Association, New York City, 1981. (b)

————. Speaking without seeing: Intimacy and verbal behavior in the initial interview. Manuscript, University of Maryland Baltimore County, 1981. (c)

————. Interviewer-interviewee nonverbal communications: An interactional approach. In C. Arensberg & M. Davis (eds.), *Interaction rhythms.* New York: Human Services, 1982. (a)

————. The validity of Snyder's self-monitoring scale as a measure of expressive self-control. Paper presented to the annual meeting of the Eastern Psychological Association, Baltimore, 1982. (b).

SLOAN, B. Nonverbal patterns of speech as a function of introversion and extraversion. Master's thesis, University of Maryland Baltimore County, 1976.

SPIELBERGER, C. D. The effects of anxiety on complex learning and academic achievement. In C. D. Spielberger (ed.), *Anxiety and behavior.* New York: Academic, 1966.

TAYLOR, J. A. The relationship of anxiety to the conditioned eyelid response. *Journal of Experimental Psychology,* 1951, *41,* 81–92.

TAYLOR, J. A., & SPENCE, K. W. The relationship of anxiety level to performance in serial learning. *Journal of Experimental Psychology,* 1952, *44,* 61–64.

TAYLOR, Y. A. A personality scale of manifest anxiety. *Journal of Abnormal and Social Psychology,* 1953, *48,* 285–290.

ZUCKERMAN, M., DEPAULO, B. M., & ROSENTHAL, R. Verbal and nonverbal communication in deception. In L. Berkowitz (ed.), *Advances in experimental social psychology,* 1981.

20

The Assessment of Stress
Using Life Events Scales

David V. Perkins

LIFE EVENTS RESEARCH and the assessment of stress can be traced back to diverse sources from the first half of the twentieth century (for reviews see Holmes, 1979; Rahe, 1978), including Cannon's (1929) concept of emotional antecedents to physical change, Meyer's (1951) use of the "life chart" procedure in medical diagnosis, and numerous studies on the reactions of victims of natural or man-made disasters (e.g., Lindemann, 1944). Selye's (1956) subsequent elucidation of the *general adaptation syndrome* suggested that even when relatively mild stressful events occur in close succession, their effects on bodily resistance and disease can be cumulative and thus serious.

More recent investigators have systematically pursued the idea that discrete, time-limited events requiring change or adaptation are associated with, and may cause, a wide range of human disorders. The best-known researchers have been Holmes and Rahe and their colleagues (Holmes, 1979; Holmes & Rahe, 1967; Rahe, 1978). Their initial measure, called the Schedule of Recent Experience (SRE), contained 43 common human events (e.g., marriage, change in residence, major personal injury or illness), and a subject's life stress score was simply the number of events he or she reported experiencing during a recent interval of time (usually 6–24 months). Holmes and Rahe soon recognized that some of the 43 SRE items (e.g., death of spouse) required considerably more change and adaptation than did others (e.g., Christmas); accordingly, a subsequent instrument, the Social Readjustment Rating Scale (SRRS) (Holmes & Rahe, 1967), *weighted* each event using a ratio scale to estimate the amount of change or readjustment required on the part of the individual experiencing the event. The specific weights were derived from Stevens's (1966) psychophysical estimation procedures to obtain ratings from a large sample of predominantly white, middle-class adults. The estimate of total life stress experienced by a subject thus became the sum of the weights, or *life change units* (LCUs), for the events reported. Note that from this viewpoint both events that represent positive experiences (e.g., vacation) and those clearly negative in valence (e.g., fired from job) are seen to make adaptive demands on the individual and thus to produce stress. This particular conception of

Preparation of this chapter was greatly facilitated by many comments, criticisms, and suggestions from my colleague Murray Levine and by unpublished reviews of the life events literature prepared by Scott M. Monroe and Sharon Kraus.

stress, called the *change construct* (Dohrenwend, 1973), will be examined in some detail in this chapter.

Numerous other instruments, along with adaptations of the Holmes and Rahe approach, were developed in the 1970s, and during that decade the empirical literature on stressful life events grew at such a remarkable rate that Holmes (1979) estimated that over 1000 publications appeared based on the SRRS alone. The life events method has now been used with a wide variety of populations, different from the original samples in age (e.g., Coddington, 1972; Ruch & Holmes, 1971); racial and ethnic composition (Hough, Fairbank, & Garcia, 1976); and nationality (Cochrane & Robertson, 1973; Masuda & Holmes, 1967; Rahe & Theorell, 1971). Examination of this massive literature leaves little doubt that a significant relationship exists between the experience of stress, as assessed by life events scales, and a host of adverse physical and psychological conditions, including (but not limited to) tuberculosis, diabetes, arthritis, and cancer (for reviews see Holmes & Masuda, 1974; Rahe & Arthur, 1978); heart disease (Rahe & Lind, 1971); depression (Paykel, 1979); schizophrenia (Brown, Sklair, Harris, & Birlens, 1973); neurosis (Tennant & Andrews, 1978); accidents (Selzer & Vinokur, 1974); athletic injuries (Bramwell, Masuda, Wagner, & Holmes, 1975); and poor academic performance (Lloyd, Alexander, Rice, & Greenfield, 1980). For more complete reviews of the empirical literature, see Dohrenwend and Dohrenwend (1974) and Barrett, Rose, and Klerman (1979). The wide range of phenomena correlated with life stress measures is as puzzling as it is impressive. On the one hand, such diversity lends encouragement to researchers, but on the other it raises questions about artifacts of measurement and about confounding of criterion and predictor.

Recent years have seen some revision in thinking about, and tempering of enthusiasm toward, the life events method of assessing stress. Occasional negative results have been reported all along (e.g., Gersten, Langner, Eisenberg, & Simcha-Fagin, 1977; Goldberg & Comstock, 1976; Hudgens, Robins, & Delong, 1970; Wershow & Reinhart, 1974), and critical reviews (e.g., Rabkin & Struening, 1976; Sarason, de Monchaux, & Hunt, 1975) have pointed to the very modest size of stress-disorder correlations identified in this fashion (typically .30 or less, accounting for under 10% of variance). Some have questioned the extent to which the literature has actually established any causal connection between common life events and disorder (Rabkin, 1980; Rahe, 1979). The degree of risk (for virtually all outcomes studied) entailed by the kinds of life events found on the typical scale, no matter how many of them one reports experiencing, clearly seems to fall short of the expectation created by the early studies of major disasters (Dohrenwend & Dohrenwend, 1979). Several conceptual and methodological issues require discussion here, including the psychometric generalizability of stress assessments based on life events measures, the theoretical constructs used in conceptualizing stress, the content validity of many scales for the populations on which they are used, and the specific role of individual and social factors in mediating the stress-disorder relationship. Each of these issues will be discussed in the following sections.

GENERALIZABILITY

One cause of the low stress-criterion correlations obtained to date may be the poor generalizability of estimates of life event stress across important dimensions of measurement (Sarason, de Monchaux, & Hunt, 1975). For example, test-retest reliability coefficients have ranged from .26 to .90, with higher values associated with shorter intertest intervals (Rahe, 1974). Furthermore, the higher the test-retest reliability desired for recall of an event, the *longer* should be the interval of time over which recall is directed (Hurst, 1979), although recall of any given event may also depend to some extent on the degree of stress engendered by the event (Dohrenwend & Dohrenwend, 1979). Brown and associates (1973) recommended three to six months as the optimal time interval, although any cutoff up to the individual's entire lifetime seems arbitrary given that we know so little about the temporal effects of life event stress. For example, Grant, Sweetwood, Yager, and Gerst (1978) found no consistent time interval that seemed to separate life event occurrence and symptom change.

Interview procedures can improve recall reliability (Brown et al., 1973), but the lack of anonymity and full disclosure may be a trade-off here (Sarason, de Monchaux, & Hunt, 1975). One illustration of the potential threat to external validity is Caplan's (1975) report that some events of an innocuous nature tend to be overreported, while socially undesirable events often go underreported. Caplan went so far as to suggest that correction factors be empirically developed for use in adjusting a sample's raw responses to life events questionnaires. In addition to test-retest scheduling and various procedural formats, another important dimension of assessment involves the specific form taken by the life events scale. For example, Hough and associates (1976) pointed out that the order in which events are listed in a measure may introduce unwanted effects; they suggested that events be presented to subjects in randomized, counterbalanced orders.

Generalizability problems reflect methodological and conceptual issues. With respect to methodology, investigators should carefully evaluate instruments as to the generalizability of life stress estimates across occasions of measurement, alternate forms and procedural formats, and/or other dimensions within a multidimensional framework such as that offered by Cronbach's (Cronbach, Gleser, Nanda, & Rajaratnam, 1972) *theory of generalizability,* in which the systematic variance associated with each of one or more measurement dimensions is assessed using the analysis of variance procedure. On a theoretical level, problems are apparent in the specific constructs used to conceptualize stress. For example, one probable factor in poor test-retest reliability is that the criterion of self-reported stress may itself vary over time with respect to any given event (Horowitz, Schaefer, & Cooney, 1974), casting doubt on any approach that assumes that the stress experienced by an individual over many months could ever be assessed accurately at a single point in time. Moreover, there are probably individual differences in this respect, confounding the measurement of stress with the subject's cognitive style in remembering or reporting such experiences.

CONSTRUCT VALIDITY

The methodological breakthrough provided by the life events method was its quantification of what had been largely a qualitative area of study. That is, life events can provide a simple index of life stress. Several different life stress constructs or dimensions have been quantified to date, and the empirical limits to stress-disorder prediction noted previously may to some extent reflect construct validity problems in the life events scales. Holmes and Rahe (1967) adopted Selye's (1956) notion that life stress is the physical or psychological change elicited in response to an event, independent of the desirability of the event, and is eminently quantifiable in terms of either the number of events experienced (the SRE) or the additive total of changes required by all events (the SRRS).

The appealing parsimony of the stress equals change conception fades somewhat upon close examination of the quantitative assumptions it makes. For example, one implicit assumption is that the stress-disorder relationship is *linear;* that is, while catastrophic events elicit stress and high risk for disorder, everyday events also entail some stress and some risk, and some stress is always riskier than no stress. This assumption conflicts with intuitive notions that an *absence* of life events may entail just as much disequilibrium (and hence stress) as is created by some events. On the other hand, perhaps the absence of an event (e.g., a desired raise or promotion is denied) is simply another event itself. If so, then most event lists are deficient in failing to include these other sources of life stress.

The change construct also assumes that individual events are independent and additive and that the same event always elicits the same amount of stress. Evidence against this notion came from Horowitz, Schaefer, & Cooney (1974), who showed that the reported change elicited by some events (e.g., marital separation) consistently *increased* with each successive experience of the event, while that associated with other events (e.g., threats to self-esteem) decreased with repeated experiences. Even the practice of simply totaling the stress associated with different events has been criticized. For example, Wainer, Fairbank, and Hough (1978) presented evidence, based on a "latent trait" analysis, that the total stress associated with life events occurring in close temporal proximity may be a multiplicative rather than additive function of their individual unscaled magnitudes. The finding that some degrees of stress are growth promoting and positive is by now becoming widely accepted (Chiriboga & Dean, 1978; Finkel, 1975), yet advocates of a change conception of stress are hard put to integrate this finding into a simple linear model. Furthermore, thresholds for the effects of stress may exist; in other words, the individual must experience a minimum number of events or a minimum amount of change before any risk of disorder arises (Crandall & Lehman, 1977; Lloyd and associates, 1980). Other evidence suggests that an asymptote may also exist, i.e., a high level of life stress above which further events do not increase the risk appreciably (Hough, Fairbank, & Garcia, 1976). Thus, a power function may describe the stress-disorder relationship better than the simple additive model does.

Some nonquantitative problems plague the change construct of stress as well. As used in the life events literature, this construct entails a black box view of human experience in assuming that nothing of significance intervenes between the objectively quantifiable stimulus (the life event) and the individual's adaptive response, save for the perception that an event has occurred. Events are thus seen as *nonspecific stimuli* that impact on different people from different situations to approximately the same degree (i.e., no significant role is played by other factors such as the individual's cognitive appraisal of the event or the degree of social support available to him or her). One problem with implying that life events are nonspecific in their impact on people is that the precise nature of the changes elicited has never been clearly spelled out (Monroe, 1981). For example, it seems intuitively obvious that such changes could be physiological (pregnancy), behavioral (changing to a different line of work), and/or social (major change in social activities), *depending* on the particular event and on the person who experiences it (Mechanic, 1975). The conception of life stress as *nonspecific change* thus seems limited and oversimplified. Furthermore, on an empirical level, a study by Ruch (1977) used multidimensional scaling to show that subjects' ratings of the degree of change required by different life events in fact reflected at least two other dimensions: the desirability of the change and the life area in which the change had occurred.

An alternative construct for life events stress emphasizes not change but rather the psychological and emotional aspects of the response to events and differentiates events in terms of the degree of undesirability (Paykel, 1979) or threat (Brown and associates, 1973) they entail, and in some cases the individual's degree of anticipation or control over them as well (Dohrenwend, 1977). Advocates of the *undesirability construct* usually view events as *specific elicitors* of psychological and emotional responses and thus as encompassing many more dimensions than just the amount of change required. Furthermore, these characteristics of events *interact* with characteristics of the individual and the situation (e.g., cognitive appraisal, social support) in producing stress. However, the undesirability construct also needs further conceptual refinement (Monroe, 1981). For example, what specific response does the perception of an undesirable event elicit (e.g., depressive affect, anxiety, anger) and under what conditions?

The constructs of change, undesirability, anticipation, and control are not mutually exclusive, of course, and when used together to assess life stress may be much more powerful than any would be alone. Comparative evaluations of these constructs generally have produced two findings. First, the degree of undesirability of life events accounts for more variance in the criterion than do the other dimensions (Chiriboga, 1977; Crandall & Lehman, 1977; Gersten, Langner, Eisenberg, & Orzeck, 1974; Hough, Fairbank, & Garcia, 1976; Tennant & Andrews, 1978; Vinokur & Selzer, 1975; Zeiss, 1980). Second, although change, undesirability, anticipation, and control are conceptually distinct and independent constructs, subjects who rate events on two or more of these dimensions tend to correlate them highly (Hurst, Jenkins, & Rose, 1978; Ruch, 1977; Tennant & Andrews, 1978; Zeiss, 1980). Thus, until the stress construct is defined with more clarity (e.g., in behavioral and social, as well as physiological, terms), little progress will be made in understanding the specific risks entailed by the experience of life events (Monroe, 1981).

Differential weights for life events, regardless of the particular conceptual dimension adopted, present another set of issues worth considering: are the sums of weights superior to simple frequency counts of reported events as estimates of stress and, if they are, should standardized or individual weights be used? Evidence is available in support of both positions on the first issue, i.e., that differential weighting does provide superior prediction to that of nonweighting (e.g., Chiriboga, 1977; Myers, Lindenthal, & Pepper, 1974; Theorell, 1974) and that it does not (e.g., Gersten, Langner, Eisenberg, & Orzeck, 1974; Rahe, 1974). Most investigators seem now to agree that differential weighting is useful, and so the debate has centered on whether the weights should be standardized or left for individual subjects themselves to supply.

The use of standard weights is consistent with the nonspecific change conception of stress (i.e., the view that the important effects of life events are independent of individual and situational variables). However, although the generalizability of ratings across different subject populations was initially reported to be high (Holmes & Rahe, 1967; Masuda & Holmes, 1967; Rahe, 1969), more recent studies have identified many significant differences in estimating the weights of life events among samples differing in demographic background (Chiriboga, 1977; Hough, Fairbank, & Garcia, 1976; Miller, Bentz, Aponte, & Brogan, 1974). Standard weights, if used, probably should be derived from the specific population on which they will be applied (Caplan, 1975; Dohrenwend, Krasnoff, Askenasy, & Dohrenwend, 1978). However, some degree of caution is still in order here. Different methods of generating weights can produce different results (Hough, Fairbank, & Garcia, 1976), and formal training in psychophysical estimation apparently does not improve interrater reliability (Stone & Neale, 1978). Both Hurst and associates (1978) and Wershow and Reinhart (1974) noted that the 95% confidence interval for the true mean rating of an event typically spans the entire scale, a finding that adds little luster to the argument for standardized weighting. Also, subjects who have experienced an event tend to assign different weights from those supplied by naive subjects (Horowitz, Schaefer, & Cooney, 1974; Hurst, 1979).

A sizable group of life event researchers has argued that the additional variance introduced by using each subject's individual weights represents important systematic variance in the subject's experience of stress (Caplan, 1975; Chiriboga, 1977; Hurst, Jenkins, & Rose, 1978; Sarason, de Monchaux, & Hunt, 1975; Vinokur & Selzer, 1975). However, Dohrenwend (1979) argued that this variance actually reflects not stress but rather a subject's sense of "personal vulnerability" to each event; it may also reflect response style. Clearly, the issue of standardized versus individualized weights reflects disagreement over the nature of stress: is it a purely environmental phenomenon or is it inextricably bound up in dimensions of persons and situations? Dohrenwend and Dohrenwend (1978) insisted that standard ratings remain useful and urged the continued development of norms under increasingly more specific conditions, while Rahe and Arthur (1978) expressed little confidence in any approach beyond the mere counting of reported events. The measurement choice in any given situation may turn on whether the primary focus is *events* as they are exprienced by a broad range of individuals or a *specific target sample* of individuals themselves and the *meaning* to them of the life events they have experienced.

CONTENT VALIDITY

In recent years, most life events studies have used either the original 43-item SRE developed by Holmes and Rahe (1967) or a slightly revised SRE. Another explanation for the low stress-disorder relationships cited by critics is that any single events list presents items that may or may not be relevant to a specific target population (e.g., Dohrenwend, 1974; Hurst, 1979; Rabkin, 1980; Rabkin & Streuning, 1976). For example, many of the SRE items (e.g., retirement from work, foreclosure on a mortgage or loan, son or daughter left home) would have little direct relevance for a high-risk population like college students, for whom the experience of many events *not* on the SRE (e.g., involving academic difficulties or relationships with parents) would more closely reflect their exposure to stress. The basic argument is that the "events listed in a life events inventory must be ones for which the individuals in a study population would be at risk in the time span over which the study respondents would be required to report" (Hurst, 1979:18). More attention has recently been paid to tailoring events lists for specific populations (Hurst, 1979). Representatives of the target group itself nominate events based on what has happened to them or to people like them (Dohrenwend and associates, 1978).

Beyond the issue of *population-specific content, comprehensiveness* poses another problem in life events research. While any list presumably represents only a sample of the possible life experiences and sources of adversity confronted by subjects, its degree of comprehensiveness is important in providing an accurate and reliable estimate of stress. Two basic approaches here are either to keep the list succinct and to sample 40–60 items from the relevant corpus of events (as was done for the SRE) or to strive for completeness by attempting an exhaustive listing of events that may impact on the target population.

There are several problems with the *sampling approach*. First, how does the investigator justify the basis on which events are sampled? By definition, for example, a random sample means that every element in a set has an equal chance of being selected, yet few investigators would claim to have a clear idea of the exact size and content of the set of life events from which they sampled. A second problem with using relatively few events is that low event totals for subjects responding to shorter (or irrelevant) lists tend to skew the distribution of scores toward zero, attenuating any stress-criterion relationship that may be present (Hurst, 1979). Finally, since most of the life events experienced by people are relatively mild in severity (e.g., change in residence, vacation), the etiological significance with respect to disorder must come largely from a confluence of events occurring within a limited interval of time, and lists that include all these events will provide more powerful assessments of life stress.

The *comprehensive approach* may thus be more useful in general. This technique probably provides a more accurate and reliable estimate of life stress since it is based on a broader sample of relevant events. Such lists can be expanded and updated periodically by asking subjects to write in events not included on the current list (Dohrenwend and associates, 1978). As the number of new events identified in this way approaches zero, the list can be considered relatively complete. Moreover, the comprehensive list would be close enough to a 100% sample that any events not included presumably would be so rare as to detract negligibly from the list's validity for the population as a whole.

On the other hand, the comprehensive approach may exacerbate another problem with event lists: *item wording*. Events are often worded ambiguously: "change in sleeping habits" could represent either a change for the better or a change for the worse. Depending on the conception of stress used, these two experiences may or may not be equally stressful. Fuzzy wording of items—e.g., "sexual difficulties"—also can blur the distinction between discrete events and what might better be thought of as chronic stressors (cf. Ilfeld, 1976).

Another widely recognized content problem is the possible *confounding* of events (e.g., major illness) with the outcome states they are supposed to predict independently (e.g., admission to a hospital) (Brown, 1974; Dohrenwend, 1974; Fairbank & Hough, 1979; Hudgens, Robins, & Delong, 1970; Mechanic, 1975). In lieu of any guaranteed way to eliminate the possibility of confounding, Dohrenwend and Dohrenwend (1978) recommended sampling both events that clearly are confounded with outcome and events that clearly are not and analyzing data from the two kinds of events separately. Fairbank and Hough (1979) proposed even more stringent guidelines, arguing that any events even remotely under the subject's control should also be eliminated from analysis to avoid contaminating the stress-disorder relationship with individual differences. Needless to say, while Fairbank and Hough's suggestion may produce purer estimates of environmental stress, their method would also eliminate a great deal of interesting variance associated with person × event × outcome interactions.

MEDIATING FACTORS

The importance of assessing factors that may interact with characteristics of life events to influence outcome depends on the underlying stress construct. While nonspecific change advocates argue that life events research should seek increasingly "purer" estimates of environmental impact, specificity theorists hold that it is precisely those person and situation dimensions that "contaminate" the "clean" assessment of life stress that need to be examined further (cf. Mechanic, 1975; Nelson, 1974). Thus, once a theoretical position is taken, the approach to assessing life events and stress will be reasonably well laid out. Nonspecific change investigators will focus on more and more limited sources of variance in life stress, while specificity theorists, believing that life events by their very nature occur in important personal, social, and cultural contexts, will systematically introduce one or more variables from these domains into their assessments.

A few examples can illustrate the importance of *mediating factors*. For convenience, one may distinguish between dimensions of persons and dimensions of the environment other that life events. For example, one class of person factors with which the occurrence and the meaning of stress have been extensively associated is demographic background (Dohrenwend, Krasnoff, Askenasy, & Dohrenwend, 1978; Horowitz, Schaefer, & Cooney, 1974; Miller, Bentz, Aponte, & Brogan, 1974). Characteristics of demography and lifestyle, whether adopted by choice or by default, serve to place people at increased or decreased risk for stressful events and can thus influence even simple frequency counts of events reported, as well as subjective ratings.

Of greater interest to many psychologists is the evidence linking dimensions of personality with life events. In this vein, Rahe and Arthur (1978) identified processes of individual perception, ego defense, psychophysical responsiveness, and coping ability as mediating the effects of stressful events. Providing an empirical example, Smith, Johnson, and Sarason (1978) found in a study of college students that undesirable life change was significantly associated with psychological distress only among students who were low in "sensation seeking"; high sensation seeking students apparently were much more tolerant of undesirable life change. No direction of causality was established here, of course, and in many cases life events and disorder may both be caused by a personal incompetence factor (Fairbank & Hough, 1979).

Among the possible environmental mediators of life stress, social support has probably received the most attention (cf. Gore, 1974; Kaplan, Cassel, & Gore, 1977). Some debate exists over whether social support interacts with stress to predict outcome (Nuckolls, Cassel, & Kaplan, 1972) or is simply an independent predictor (Andrews, Tennant, Hewson, & Vaillant, 1978). In any event, investigators would do well to assess social support when estimating subjects' life stress (Rabkin & Streuning, 1976), and several useful measures of social support are now available (e.g., Hirsch, 1979).

CONCLUSION

Stress researchers have long debated the issues of subjective versus objective qualities of stress and the individual's role as a mediator in the stress response (Sarason, de Monchaux, & Hunt, 1975). I agree with a host of other investigators (Dohrenwend & Dohrenwend, 1978; Nelson, 1974; Rahe & Arthur, 1978) that the assessment of life stress using simple life events scales alone is destined to be replaced by multifactorial models encompassing individual differences and situational contexts as well. Life events interact with these mediators to predict outcome, so two or more components will have to be assessed in some way for most applications. Some stressors are probably so severe that almost anyone would be at risk for disorder, and some people may be so hardy that no set of events would induce stress in them, but the vast majority of situations lie somewhere in between these extremes (Dohrenwend & Dohrenwend, 1979). Progress in the near term may also require a leveling off of trends toward the complete quantification of phenomena and a measured return to interest in the qualitative aspects of life stress. Investigators will need to move closer to the phenomena of life stress and focus more explicitly on the individual, situational, and life event correlates of specific outcomes.

Initial conceptions of the life changes and illness work were necessarily simple and straightforward, but as the evidence for the validity of the general concept has mounted, it has also become necessary to think in terms of the complexity of the social, psychological, and physiological variables involved .... The enormously difficult task awaits us of filling in the crucial steps in an all-encompassing model which takes into account not only environmental variables but the social, psychological, and physiological characteristics of the individual. (Rahe & Arthur, 1978:13)

REFERENCES

ANDREWS, G., TENNANT, C., HEWSON, D. M., & VAILLANT, G. E. Life stress, social support, coping style, and risk of psychological impairment. *Journal of Nervous and Mental Disease,* 1978, *168,* 307–316.

BARRETT, J. E., ROSE, R. M., & KLERMAN, G. L. (eds.). *Stress and mental disorder.* New York: Raven, 1979.

BRAMWELL, S. T., MASUDA, M., WAGNER, N. N., & HOLMES, T. H. Psychosocial factors in athletic injuries. *Journal of Human Stress,* 1975, *1,* 6–20.

BROWN, G. W. Meaning, measurement, and stress of life events. In B. S. Dohrenwend & B. P. Dohrenwend (eds.), *Stressful life events: Their nature and effects.* New York: Wiley, 1974.

BROWN, G. W., SKLAIR, F., HARRIS, T. O., & BIRLEY, J. L. T. Life events and psychiatric disorders. Part I: Some methodological issues. *Psychological Medicine,* 1973, *3,* 74–87.

CANNON, W. B. *Bodily changes in pain, hunger, fear, and rage.* New York: Appleton, 1929.

CAPLAN, R. D. A less heretical view of life change and hospitalization. *Journal of Psychosomatic Research,* 1975, *19,* 247–250.

CHIRIBOGA, D. A. Life event weighting systems: A comparative analysis. *Journal of Psychosomatic Research,* 1977, *21,* 415–422.

CHIRIBOGA, D. A., & DEAN, H. Dimensions of stress: Perspectives from a longitudinal study. *Journal of Psychosomatic Research,* 1978, *22,* 47–55.

COCHRANE, R., & ROBERTSON, A. The Life Events Inventory: A measure of the relative severity of psycho-social stressors. *Journal of Psychosomatic Research,* 1973, *17,* 135–139.

CODDINGTON, R. D. The significance of life events as etiologic factors in the diseases of children. Part II: A study of a normal population. *Journal of Psychosomatic Research,* 1972, *16,* 205–213.

CRANDALL, J. E., & LEHMAN, R. E. Relationship of stressful life events to social interest, locus of control, and psychological adjustment. *Journal of Consulting and Clinical Psychology,* 1977, *45,* 1208.

CRONBACH, L. J., GLESER, G. C., NANDA, H., & RAJARATNAM, N. *The dependability of behavioral measurements: Theory of generalizability for scores and profiles.* New York: Wiley, 1972.

DOHRENWEND, B. P. Problems in defining and sampling the relevant population of stressful life events. In B. S. Dohrenwend & B. P. Dohrenwend (eds.), *Stressful life events: Their nature and effects.* New York: Wiley, 1974.

————. Stressful life events and psychopathology: Some issues of theory and method. In J. Barrett, R. Rose, & G. Klerman (eds.), *Stress and mental disorder.* New York: Raven, 1979.

DOHRENWEND, B. P., & DOHRENWEND, B. S. The conceptualization and measurement of stressful life events: An overview of the issues. In R. Depue (ed.), *The psychobiology of the depressive disorders: Implications for the effects of stress.* New York: Academic, 1979.

DOHRENWEND, B. S. Life events as stressors: A methodological inquiry. *Journal of Health and Social Behavior,* 1973, *14,* 167–175.

————. Anticipation and control of stressful life events: An exploratory analysis. In J. Strauss, H. Babigian, & M. Roff (eds.), *Origins and course of psychopathology.* New York: Plenum, 1977.

DOHRENWEND, B. S., & DOHRENWEND, B. P. (eds.). *Stressful life events: Their nature and effects.* New York: Wiley, 1974.

DOHRENWEND, B. S., & DOHRENWEND, B. P. Some issues in research on stressful life events. *Journal on Nervous and Mental Disease,* 1978, *166,* 7-15.

DOHRENWEND, B. S., KRASNOFF, L., ASKENASY, A. R., & DOHRENWEND, B. P. Exemplification of a method for scaling life events: The PERI life events scale. *Journal of Health and Social Behavior,* 1978, *19,* 205-229.

FAIRBANK, D. T., & HOUGH, R. L. Life event classifications and the event-illness relationship. *Journal of Human Stress,* 1979, *5,* 41-47.

FINKEL, N. J. Stress, trauma, and trauma resolution. *American Journal of Community Psychology,* 1975, *3,* 173-178.

GERSTEN, J. C., LANGNER, T. S., EISENBERG, J. G., & ORZECK, L. Child behavior and life events: Undesirable change or change per se? In B. S. Dohrenwend & B. P. Dohrenwend (eds.), *Stressful life events: Their nature and effects.* New York: Wiley, 1974.

GERSTEN, J. C., LANGNER, T. S., EISENBERG, J. G., & SIMCHA-FAGAN, O. An evaluation of the etiologic role of stressful life-change events in psychological disorders. *Journal of Health and Social Behavior,* 1977, *18,* 228-244.

GOLDBERG, E. L., & COMSTOCK, G. W. Life events and subsequent illness. *American Journal of Epidemiology,* 1976, *104,* 146-158.

GRANT, I., SWEETWOOD, H. L., YAGER, J., & GERST, M. S. Patterns in the relationship of life events and psychiatric symptoms over time. *Journal of Psychosomatic Research,* 1978, *22,* 183-191.

HIRSCH, B. J. Psychological dimensions of social networks: A multimethod analysis. *American Journal of Community Psychology,* 1979, *7,* 263-277.

HOLMES, T. H. Development and application of a quantitative measure of life change magnitude. In J. E. Barrett, R. M. Rose, & G. L. Klerman (eds.), *Stress and mental disorder.* New York: Raven, 1979.

HOLMES, T. H., & MASUDA, M. Life change and illness susceptibility. In B. S. Dohrenwend & B. P. Dohrenwend (eds.), *Stressful life events: Their nature and effects.* New York: Wiley, 1974.

HOMES, T. H., & RAHE, R. H. The Social Readjustment Rating Scale. *Journal of Psychosomatic Research,* 1967, *11,* 213-218.

HOROWITZ, M. J., SCHAEFER, C., & COONEY, P. Life event scaling for recency of experience. In E. K. E. Gunderson & R. H. Rahe (eds.), *Life stress and illness.* Springfield: Thomas, 1974.

HOUGH, R. L., FAIRBANK, D. T., & GARCIA, A. M. Problems in the ratio measurement of life stress. *Journal of Health and Social Behavior,* 1976, *17,* 70-82.

HUDGENS, R. W., ROBINS, E., & DELONG, W. B. The reporting of recent stress in the lives of psychiatric patients. *British Journal of Psychiatry,* 1970, *117,* 635-643.

HURST, M. W. Life changes and psychiatric symptom development: Issues of content, scoring, and clustering. In J. E. Barrett, R. M. Rose, & G. L. Klerman (eds.), *Stress and mental disorder.* New York: Raven, 1979.

HURST, M. W., JENKINS, C. D., & ROSE, R. M. The assessment of life change stress: A comparative and methodological inquiry. *Psychosomatic Medicine,* 1978, *40,* 126-141.

ILFELD, F. W. Characteristics of current social stressors. *Psychological Reports,* 1976, *39,* 1231-1247.

KAPLAN, B., CASSEL, J., & GORE, S. Social support and health. *Medical Care,* 1977, *15,* 47-58.

LINDEMANN, E. Symptomatology and management of acute grief. *American Journal of Psychiatry,* 1944, *101,* 141-148.

LLOYD, C., ALEXANDER, A. A., RICE, D. G., & GREENFIELD, N. S. Life events as predictors of academic performance. *Journal of Human Stress,* 1980, *6,* 15-25.

MASUDA, M., & HOLMES, T. H. The Social Readjustment Rating Scale: A cross-cultural study of Japanese and Americans. *Journal of Psychosomatic Research,* 1967, *11,* 227–237.

MECHANIC, D. Some problems in the measurement of stress and social readjustment. *Journal of Human Stress,* 1975, *1,* 43–48.

MEYER, A. The life chart and the obligation of specifying positive data in psychopathological diagnosis. In E. E. Winters (ed.), *The collected papers of Meyer.* Vol. 3: *Medical teaching.* Baltimore: Johns Hopkins Press, 1951.

MILLER, F. T., BENTZ, W. K., APONTE, J. F., & BROGAN, D. R. Perception of life crisis events: A comparative study of rural and urban samples. In B. S. Dohrenwend & B. P. Dohrenwend (eds.), *Stressful life events: Their nature and effects.* New York: Wiley, 1974.

MONROE, S. M. Life events and disease: The desirability-change debate and beyond. Manuscript, University of Pittsburgh, 1981.

MYERS, J. K., LINDENTHAL, J. J., & PEPPER, M. P. Social class, life events, and psychiatric symptoms: A longitudinal study. In B. S. Dohrenwend & B. P. Dohrenwend (eds.), *Stressful life events: Their nature and effects.* New York: Wiley, 1974.

NELSON, P. D. Comment. In E. K. E. Gunderson & R. H. Rahe (eds.), *Life stress and illness.* Springfield: Thomas, 1974.

NUCKOLLS, C., CASSEL, J., & KAPLAN, B. H. Psycho-social assets, life crises, and the prognosis of pregnancy. *American Journal of Epidemiology,* 1972, *95,* 431–441.

PAYKEL, E. S. Causal relationships between clinical depression and life events. In J. E. Barrett, R. M. Rose, & G. L. Klerman (eds.), *Stress and mental disorder.* New York: Raven, 1979.

RABKIN, J. G. Stressful life events and schizophrenia: A review of the research literature. *Psychological Bulletin,* 1980, *87,* 408–425.

RABKIN, J. G., & STREUNING, E. L. Life events, stress, and illness. *Science,* 1976, *194,* 1013–1020.

RAHE, R. H. Multi-cultural correlations of life change scaling: America, Japan, Denmark, and Sweden. *Journal of Psychosomatic Research,* 1969, *13,* 191–195.

————. The pathway between subjects' recent life changes and their near future illness reports: Representative results and methodological issues. In B. S. Dohrenwend & B. P. Dohrenwend (eds.), *Stressful life events: Their nature and effects.* New York: Wiley, 1974.

————. Life change measurement clarification. *Psychosomatic Medicine,* 1978, *40,* 95–98.

————. Life change events and mental illness: An overview. *Journal of Human Stress,* 1969, *5,* 2–10.

RAHE, R. H., & ARTHUR, R. J. Life change and illness studies: Past history and future directions. *Journal of Human Stress,* 1978, *4,* 3–15.

RAHE, R. H., & LIND, E. Psychosocial factors and sudden cardiac death: A pilot study. *Journal of Psychosomatic Research,* 1971, *15,* 19–24.

RUCH, L. O. A multidimensional analysis of the concept of life change. *Journal of Health and Social Behavior,* 1977, *18,* 71–83.

RUCH, L. O., & HOLMES, T. H. Scaling of life change: Comparison of direct and indirect methods. *Journal of Psychosomatic Research,* 1971, *15,* 221–227.

SARASON, I. G., DE MONCHAUX, C., & HUNT, T. Methodological issues in the assessment of life stress. In L. Levi (ed.), *Emotions: Their parameters and measurement.* New York: Raven, 1975.

SELYE, H. *The stress of life.* New York: McGraw-Hill, 1956.

SELZER, M. L., & VINOKUR, A. Life events, subjective stress, and traffic accidents. *American Journal of Psychiatry,* 1974, *131,* 903–906.

SMITH, R. E., JOHNSON, J. H., & SARASON, I. G. Life change, the sensation seeking motive, and psychological distress. *Journal of Consulting and Clinical Psychology,* 1978, *46,* 348–349.

STEVENS, S. S. A metric for the social consensus. *Science,* 1966, *151,* 530–541.

STONE, A. A., & NEALE, J. M. Life event scales: Psychophysical training and rating dimension effects on event-weighting coefficients. *Journal of Consulting and Clinical Psychology,* 1978, *46,* 849–853.

TENNANT, C., & ANDREWS, G. The pathogenic quality of life event stress in neurotic impairment. *Archives of General Psychiatry,* 1978, *35,* 859–863.

THEORELL, T. Life events before and after the onset of a premature myocardial infarction. In B. S. Dohrenwend & B. P. Dohrenwend (eds.), *Stressful life events: Their nature and effects.* New York: Wiley, 1974.

VINOKUR, A., & SELZER, M. L. Desirable versus undesirable life events: Their relationship to stress and mental distress. *Journal of Personality and Social Psychology,* 1975, *32,* 329–337.

WAINER, H., FAIRBANK, D. T., & HOUGH, R. L. Predicting the impact of simple and compound life change events. *Applied Psychological Measurement,* 1978, *2,* 311–320.

WERSHOW, H. J., & REINHART, G. Life change and hospitalization: A heretical view. *Journal of Psychosomatic Research,* 1974, *18,* 393–401.

ZEISS, A. M. Aversiveness versus change in the assessment of life stress. *Journal of Psychosomatic Research,* 1980, *24,* 15–19.

21

The Psychiatric Epidemiology Research Interview Life Events Scale

Barbara Snell Dohrenwend   **Lawrence Krasnoff**

Alexander R. Askenasy   **Bruce P. Dohrenwend**

CLINICAL INTEREST IN STRESSFUL LIFE EVENTS can be traced back to the 1930s, when Meyer advocated the use of the life chart in medical diagnosis (Dohrenwend & Dohrenwend 1974b). The *life chart* is a complete medical history from birth, together with "the changes of habitat, of school entrance, graduations or changes, or failures; the various 'jobs'; the dates of possible important births and deaths in the family, and other fundamentally important environmental incidents" (Meyer, 1951: 53). Meyer's influence was evident in the 1949 conference of the Association for Research in Nervous and Mental Disease, which was devoted to life stress and bodily disease. Papers were presented on the effects of life stress on disorders of growth, development, metabolism, the eye, the airways, stomach, colon, muscles, joints, and periarticular structures, as well as on headache and cadiovascular disease (Wolff, Wolf, & Hare, 1950).

Influenced by the work of Meyer, Wolff, and other participants of the 1949 conference, Holmes and Rahe (1967) developed the Social Readjustment Rating Scale (SRRS), the stressful life events scale most widely used in the 1970s (Gunderson & Rahe, 1974; Dohrenwend & Dohrenwend, 1974a). The list of events in the SRRS was generated by systematic study of life charts, initiated in 1949, of over 5000 patients (Holmes & Rahe, 1967). The SRRS brought together long-standing clinical interests with a powerful psychometric technique. The instrument represented a methodological advance over previous work primarily because Holmes and Rahe incorporated a scaling technique (Hough, Fairbank, & Garcia, 1976).

Since its publication in 1967, the SRRS has generated an extensive body of research, as well as a considerable amount of criticism (e.g., Brown, 1974; Hinkle, 1974; Hudgens, 1974). The research on this instrument has been generalized by its proponents to conclude

This chapter is an expansion of "Exemplification of a Method for Scaling Life Events: The PERI Life Events Scale," *Journal of Health and Social Behavior,* 1978, *19,* 205–229. The research was supported in part by a research grant (MH 10328) and a research scientist award (K5 MH 14663) from the National Institute of Mental Health to B. P. Dohrenwend. We would like to thank Maxine Lubner for her help in classifying events in our hypothesized pathogenic triad. We would also like to express our appreciation for the statistical advice and criticism we received from Alan Gross, Joseph L. Fleiss, and Patrick E. Shrout; however, responsibility for the analysis is solely our own.

that "the greater the magnitude of life change (or life crisis), the greater the probability that the life change would be associated with disease onset, and the greater the probability that the population at risk would experience disease" (Holmes & Masuda, 1974:68). Its critics have taken positions ranging from rejection of the premises underlying the SRRS to detailing of specific methodological failings in the procedures used by Holmes and Rahe to construct this scale. In this chapter we will first challenge the bases for rejecting the rationale of the SRRS and then propose procedural improvements for three aspects of scale construction.

ARE GENERALIZED RATINGS OF THE MAGNITUDE OF LIFE EVENTS USEFUL?

Critics have raised two questions about the usefulness of the SRRS and, by implication, any other life event scale in which weights, based on consensual judgments, are attached to individual events. The first question is whether the use of event-specific different weights offers any advantage over simply counting life events, that is, giving each event a weight of one. Empirical justification for raising this question comes from demonstrations by psychometricians that measures based on differentially weighted items do not yield better predictions than measures constructed simply by giving each item a weight of one (e.g., Wainer, 1976). However, this finding is based on research with scales constructed from test responses or other characteristics of individual subjects and is not necessarily applicable to life events. Moreover, research on stressful life events generally suggests that magnitude weights do provide useful information. The only empirically based suggestion that weights not be used of which we are aware was made by Rahe (1974) for a particular population. He pointed out that for young, single, navy men, whose life events tend to be those with low weights, the correlation between weighted and unweighted life event scores has been found to be as high as .89, indicating that results based on unweighted scores would differ little from those based on weighted scores. He suggested, therefore, that unweighted life event scores could be used for this population. At the same time, he recommended against using unweighted scores for middle-aged subjects, whose life events more often include those with large weights. Furthermore, as Rahe pointed out, direct evidence of the usefulness of weighted scores is provided by Theorell's (1974) finding that cardiac patients and their nonpatient controls did not differ in number of recent life events but did differ when the events were given magnitude weights. Another kind of evidence of the difference in results obtained with weighted and unweighted scores is the finding reported by Myers and his colleagues (Myers, Lindenthal, & Pepper, 1974) that social class was not related to the number of events reported but was related to a weighted score. In sum, the balance of evidence suggests that useful information is gained when life events are assigned different weights.

Despite the empirical evidence, critics continue to argue that high correlations between weighted and unweighted totals imply that one might as well simply count events (Lorimor, Justice, McBee, & Weinman, 1979). The implicit assumption in this argument is that if two variables have a correlation coefficient of .95, they may be used interchangeably as indicators of the construct to which they are both related. Goldstein, Fleiss, Goldstein, and Landovitz (1979) examined the problem of using *proxy variables*, variables that are more easily or economically obtained than the variables directly of interest, as substitutes for the true variables in regression analysis. They showed that even when proxy variables were highly correlated (e.g., .65 and .78) with the true variable of interest, they could give extremely misleading results when used to estimate the influence of the true variable on some other variable.[1]

One might assume that although problems exist for variables correlated about .70, they would not exist for variables correlated .95, which is so close to 1.0 that the variables are virtually identical. An examination of the mathematics of correlations reveals the error in this intuition. For example, we found a correlation of .95 between weighted and unweighted totals for the PERI list (Dohrenwend, Krasnoff, Askenasy, & Dohrenwend, 1979) but a correlation between the weighted total and various health indicators on the order of .316 (i.e., the square root of .10) (Krasnoff, 1979). Thus, the correlation between unweighted totals and such health indicators could range from .0042 to .5962.[2]

In addition, there are conditions under which correlations between weighted and unweighted totals are likely to be low. For example, if an investigation concerns subsets of events, rather than only the aggregate of all kinds of life events, the observed correlations in some subsets between weighted and unweighted scores may not be anywhere near 1.0. For example, we found that the correlation between weighted and unweighted scores for the subset of events on our list concerning childbearing and childrearing was .36 in a sample of residents of New York City. This low correlation is not predicted by Ghiselli's (1964) formula; if r is assumed to be .001, the hypothetical correlation between unweighted and weighted scores for this subset of events is .93.

Another problem with unweighted life events scores is their implicit assumption that meaningful group differences in perceptions of the stressfulness of specific life events do not exist. Yet Krasnoff (1979) found, first, that predictions of whether psychiatrists would judge an individual to be a case were consistently more accurate when the prediction equation included group-specific weighted life events scores than when it included life events scores based on weights that were not group-specific and, second, that group-specific weighted life events scores yielded consistently higher correlations with symptom measures than did non-group-specific scores. These findings argue against adopting a procedure that precludes measuring group differences in evaluations of the stressfulness of life events.

Another assumption implicit in the suggestion that unweighted scores are as efficient as weighted scores is that only one form of life event measure, the additive score, will prove useful. Yet in a study of age differences in recent life event experience, Mulvey (1979) found that the number of events experienced in one year did not vary with age. Nor, as Lorimor and his associates (1979) would predict from this finding, did weighted event totals differ. However, the average weight of events reported by individuals did vary as the investigator had predicted, increasing significantly with age (Mulvey, 1979).

In general, we suggest that life events weights are a useful research tool. We agree with Lorimor and his colleagues (1979) that when events are simply aggregated over an entire list, in the same way for all individuals, both unweighted and weighted scores should be tested and the former, simpler score adopted if the two approaches yield equivalent results. We also suggest, however, that the implication of their analysis should not be overgeneralized to the point that valuable information concerning subsets of stressful life events and group differences in perceptions and experiences of these events is lost to studies of the complex life stress process.

Critics have also debated whether generalized weights should be used or whether it would not be better to weight each individual's life events according to his own perception of their magnitudes. The empirical basis for this question is that a measure of an individual's perception of an event that he has experienced, ordinarily taken after the outcome of the event is known to the individual, yields closer relations to outcome measures than does an index based on generalized ratings of change (e.g., Hinkle, 1974; Theorell, 1974; Vinokur & Selzer, 1975). It would be surprising if the results were otherwise. The problem is that an individualized, ordinarily post hoc measure of change, while it may be useful for understanding and treating individual cases, is not a clean measure of environmental input in a stress process. Instead, this measure is some resultant of environmental input, the affected individual's predisposition, and his assessment of the outcome. If we are concerned with answering etiological questions about the impact of stressors in the environment on individuals' health we must obtain a measure of social environmental stressors that is not confounded with individual predispositions and vulnerabilities, let alone with outcomes.

Given this conclusion, we turn to three methodological problems in the procedures used to construct scales intended to represent general judgments: construction of the list of life events, selection of judges, and tests of whether judges agree on their ratings. Under each of these three topics we will present, first, exisiting problems; second, the method we propose for solving these problems; third, the specific procedures we used in applying this method to construction of the Psychiatric Epidemiology Research Interview (PERI) Life Events Scale; and fourth, the results obtained in this step of construction of the PERI Life Events Scale.

CONSTRUCTION OF A LIFE EVENTS LIST

Problems

Holmes and Rahe's (1967) list of 43 life events, which has influenced the contents of almost all other lists, was constructed by culling events "observed to cluster at the time of disease onset" from the life charts of patients (Holmes & Masuda, 1974:46). The most obvious problem with this procedure derives from the fact that the appearance of disease is often a subtle and gradual affair, so that identification of time of onset is difficult. As a result, one would expect that a list of life events that "cluster at the time of disease onset" would include some that are concomitants or effects rather than agents that may be responsible for producing a disorder, and Holmes and Rahe's list has been criticized on just this point. Hudgens (1974), for one, suggested that the problem is pervasive, estimating that 29 of the 43 events on Holmes and Rahe's list and 32 of the 61 events on the expanded list constructed by Paykel Prusoff, and Uhlenhuth (1971) are "often the symptoms or consequences of illness" (p. 131).

The events on Holmes and Rahe's (1967) list have also been criticized for the ambiguity of their descriptions. The particular type of ambiguity that has attracted most criticism concerns the desirability of the event, as in event descriptions such as "Change in responsibilities at work" or "Change in living conditions" (e.g., Miller, Bentz, Aponte, & Brogan (1974). This criticism has been generated, in part, by findings that the effects of losses differ from the effects of gains in kind and degree (e.g., Gersten et al., 1974; Paykel, 1974; Vinokur & Selzer, 1975), a finding that could be obscured by event descriptions that are ambiguous with respect to desirability.

Proposed Method

Neither Holmes and Rahe's (1967) list of 43 life events nor the expanded list of 61 events created by Paykel and his colleagues (1971) nor, for that matter, the list of 102 events that we will present can be said to exhaust the full range of possible life events. Any list of life events is, we assume, a sample representing a larger population. Accordingly, two major questions must be answered in order to construct a life events list: how do we define the events to be sampled and what is the population of events from which the sample is to be drawn? Although neither of these questions can be answered with the precision that is possible in solving more conventional sampling problems, they serve the important function of directing our attention to the fact that decisions we make in the construction of the list will determine the kinds of inferences and generalizations that we can make.

Investigators who have offered definitions of life events have either implicitly or explicitly been guided by the qualification "stressful"; that is, they have indicated what they considered could reasonably be meant by stressful life events (e.g., Antonovsky & Kats, 1967; Brown & Birley, 1968; Holmes & Rahe, 1967; Myers et al., 1972). The common denominator in these definitions is objective occurrences of sufficient magnitude to bring about change in the usual activities of most individuals who experience them. This common denominator seems to us to be as close as we can come to a workable definition of what is to be sampled in creating a list of life events in the context of studies of life stress.

We turn, then, to the second sampling question: from what population of events is the sample of events to be drawn? This general question generates several more specific questions related to various dimensions of the population of life events. As the first of these let us consider what breadth of human experience we want the listed events to represent. Ideally, we might try to represent the life experience of all humankind but, given the variety of social and cultural settings in which humans live, this aim seems unrealistic. Instead, life events lists have, in practice, been constructed from two subpopulations of events that are distinguished in terms of the generality of the settings in which they occur. The first of these subpopulations consists of events that represent the universals of human experience. These include marriages, births, illnesses, injuries, and deaths and constitute a core that will be included in any list no matter what the setting in which it is to be used.

The second subpopulation of events varies with social and cultural settings. Thus, for example, when Holmes and Rahe's (1967) list of 43 events, which was originally drawn from the experience of patients in an urban setting in the northwestern United States, was used by Miller and his colleagues (1974) in rural North Carolina, the latter group of researchers noted that "taking out a mortgage of greater than $10,000 is almost antithetical for the rural North Carolinian, whereas such a loan might be assumed with relative ease by the city dweller. In the rural South, a general pay-as-you-go philosophy still prevails" (p. 271).

A question related to what is to be sampled concerns how the sample is to be drawn. For the first subpopulation, researchers can probably rely safely on a few informants and may hope to draw up an exhaustive list. Furthermore, there is no reason to start anew in constructing lists of events in this subpopulation. In contrast, one probably cannot count on drawing a representative sample from the second subpopulation of events either by consulting only one's own and one's colleagues' experience or by relying on lists constructed in other settings. Instead, the most likely guarantee against sociocultural parochialism seems to be a query a sample of persons, preferably systematically drawn, from the setting in which the life events list will be used.

The last recommendation raises a specific issue related to the procedure used by Holmes and Rahe (1967) for constructing the list of events and their numerical ratings in the SRRS. They drew on the experience of approximately 5000 patients, most of whom were presumably residents of the northwestern United States. More specifically, they drew on this experience within a limited time period, near the onset of the patient's illness. We question whether this is the appropriate population of events from which to draw in constructing a list of events to be used in etiological research, since it severely limits the inferences that can be made. That is, one cannot draw conclusions from this list about the extent to which life events experienced by people living in that particular setting were associated with the onset of illness, but only about the extent to which life events previously associated with the onset of illness continued to be associated with the onset of illness. For this reason, we suggest that in order to permit more general and more interesting conclusions about the relation between life events and illness, a sample of life events that may be specific to a particular sociocultural setting should be drawn from the experience of the general population of persons living in the appropriate communities, as well as from other groups of special interest to the investigator.

There are two further questions concerning the population from which a list of life events is to be drawn. In discussing the first of these we will indulge in an analogy. In a study designed to predict the outcome of an election, the investigator could draw a sample of voters, paying no attention to their other characteristics, or he might decide, for example, to stratify the population on race and draw subsamples of black voters and white voters, particularly if he had an interest in predicting the votes of those two groups separately. As we mentioned earlier, one of the criticisms of Holmes and Rahe's (1967) list is that many of the events are described as changes without indicating whether the change is positive or negative. A related criticism of this and other lists is that they undersample positive changes (e.g., Rahe, 1974). This criticism suggests that life events should be stratified on desirability for the purpose of sampling in order to draw a more representative sample from each stratum and thereby achieve better tests of their separate effects on illness or other outcomes.

There are many other dimensions, such as novel versus previously experienced, on which events could also be stratified. However, since it is impractical to stratify on all dimensions that might conceivably be of interest, it is necessary to decide when constructing a list what dimensions have the greatest theoretical importance or predictive power and to stratify life events on these selected dimensions for purposes of sampling. This decision is of particular importance in the case of a sample of life events, for unlike the situation with voters, whose race will probably be recorded whether the sample is stratified on race or not, the characteristics of life events that were ignored when a list was drawn up are usually not ascertained in further uses of the list.

The final and very important question concerning the population of events to be sampled concerns the possibility of screening events in terms of their relation to the illness outcome to be predicted. It has been argued that many of the items on current lists of life events are either indicators or possible effects of illness rather than independent events that may contribute to the onset of the illness and should therefore, be screened out of the population of events before it is sampled (cf. Brown, 1974; Hudgens, 1974). To get a clear picture of this issue, let us consider concrete examples. Two of the events on Holmes and Rahe's (1967) list have been cited as particularly likely to be indicators rather than antecedents of a wide range of illness: change in eating habits and change in sleeping habits. Furthermore, items like illness and injury, unless carefully specified in terms of content in each case, present the same problem. By contrast, events such as deaths and others' illnesses are clearly neither indicators nor consequences of a subject's illness. It is obvious, then, that the first class of events should be considered for exclusion from the population to be sampled and that the second should not.

In addition to these relatively clear cases, there is a large class of events whose relation to illness is often ambiguous. These events are particularly numerous when the outcome to be predicted is psychological disorder rather than physical illness. Thus, being fired or being divorced, along with many other troubles, as well as achievements such as promotions, may be either effects or antecedents of the subject's psychological condition (cf. Dohrenwend, 1974). The question is whether events in this category should be excluded from the population to be sampled. On the one hand, Hudgens (1974) has taken the position that they should be included. On the other hand, Dohrenwend (1974) suggested that these events be considered as a separate stratum for puposes of sampling. More generally, he identified three strata that have different etiological implications for physical illness and for psychological disorder: events that are confounded with the psychological condition of the subject; events that consist of or indicate physical illness and injury; and events whose occurrences are independent of either the subject's physical health or his psychological condition.

In order to construct a comprehensive event list, we suggest that stratified sampling of the three classes of events identified by Dohrenwend (1974) is to be preferred over exclusion of the first two categories. Exclusion of the first category would preclude investigation of the role of events, such as divorce, that may be either independent of or confounded with psychological disorder or distress, depending on the circumstances. Progress in studying the effects of these events will depend on the development of appropriate probes to determine the circumstances and timing of the events. Exclusion of the second category would, likewise, preclude the investigation of important problems, those concerning relations between physical illness and psychological disorder or distress.

A further argument for comprehensiveness follows from an examination of extreme situations such as combat, concentration camps, and man-made and natural disasters. Analysis of such extreme situations suggests that they have in common a *pathogenic triad* of concomitant events and conditions, including *physical exhaustion, loss of social support,* and *fateful negative events* other than physical illness or injury whose occurrence is beyond the individual's control. In normal civilian life, stressful circumstances characteristic of such extreme situations may be approximated if, within a relatively brief period of time, an individual experiences, for example, physical exhaustion from illness or injury, loss of social support from geographical relocation, and a fateful negative event such as death of a loved one (Dohrenwend, 1979; Dohrenwend & Dohrenwend, 1978). It is particularly important, therefore, to make sure the events from all three elements of this hypothesized pathogenic triad of events are adequately represented.

In general, then, we propose that the construction of an event list be cast as a sampling problem and that attention be given to several crosscutting strata in carrying out this sampling.

Procedures Used to Construct the PERI Life Events List

The PERI Life Events Scale was constructed as part of a study in New York City designed to develop methods for psychiatric epidemiological research in community populations. A sample of life events that might be particularly characteristic of New York City was drawn from the experience of the local population. This sampling was done as part of two earlier studies in the Washington Heights section of the city (Dohrenwend, 1974; Dohrenwend, 1970–71).

The main question that we asked of the subjects in these studies to elicit their nominations of stressful life events was "What was the last major event in your life that, for better or for worse, interrupted or changed your usual activities?" If no response was forthcoming, the interviewer used the following standard probe: "For example, events affecting your occupation, your physical health, your living arrangements, your relations with other family members, your friends, or your personal values or beliefs." If a major event was recalled, the respondent was asked: "When did this occur?" "What happened?" Several other questions were asked about additional events "almost as important" since then.

The list of 102 events was constructed by drawing on previous lists, on the researchers' own experiences, and on the events reported in the two Washington Heights studies cited earlier. We excluded from the list events that are subjective rather than objective, in the sense that they are both theoretically and practically difficult or impossible to verify independently of subjects' reports of their occurrence. Because previous research suggested the importance of the desirability of events in predicting illness outcomes, we attempted to specify this characteristic in the descriptions of events included in the list, with the intention both of reducing their ambiguity and of increasing the representation of positive events.

Results

Table 21-1 shows the PERI list in the order and wording in which items are presented to respondents. Each event is classified first as to whether it probably occurs independently of any particular setting or is likely to be limited to some types of sociocultural settings and, second, as to whether it is a gain, a loss, or ambiguous in this respect. These classifications were based on consensus among four judges. Each event is also classified according to whether it is a possible consequence of the psychological condition of the subject who reports it, an indicator of physical illness or injury, or an occurrence independent of the subject's physical or psychological condition. This classification depends in part on whether the respondent was the central figure in the event. Note, however, that the central figure in an event is not specified in the event description but must be determined as an additional piece of information in queries about events that people have experienced. One consequence of this ambiguity in the event descriptions will be discussed when we consider the interpretation of magnitude ratings.

In the fifth column of Table 21-1, we indicate whether an event occurring to the respondent or, in a few cases, to someone close to the respondent (e.g., spouse or child) is a member of our hypothesized pathogenic triad; that is, a fateful negative event, an event likely to exhaust the individual physically, or an event (other than fateful negative events) likely to involve loss of social support. In some cases, an event, such as changed schools or training programs, could involve both loss of social support (from the old school) and gain of social support (from the new one), with no clear way from the event itself to tell whether losses outstripped gains. Such events are qualified by a question mark, meaning that more information is likely to be required to make the determination. Note also that the classification of events like physical illness or injury depends on whether they have occurred to the respondent or to someone close to the respondent.

The last column in Table 21-1 contains magnitude ratings of the events. How they developed is our next topic.

TABLE 21-1
Classifications and Total Sample Ratings of PERI Life Events

Topic area and event	Breadth of setting[a]	Desirability[b]	Relation to etiology when central figure is:[c] Respondent	Relation to etiology when central figure is:[c] Other	Elements of pathogenic triad[d]	Rating classification with elevation:[e] Uncontrolled	Rating classification with elevation:[e] Controlled	Arithmetic mean of subgroup ratings[f]	Rank of mean[g]
School									
1. Started school or a training program after not going to school for a long time	L	+	P	P		C (.7)	C (.6)	340	59.5
2. Changed schools or training programs	L	?	P	P	LSS	C (.8)	C (.7)	257	88
3. Graduated from school or training program	L	+	P	P		C (.7)	C (.6)	323	68
4. Had problems in school or in training program	L	−	P	P		C (.7)	C (.6)	268	86
5. Failed school, training program	L	−	P	P		I	I	302	69.5
6. Did not graduate from school or training program	L	−	P	P		C (.7)	C (.5)	300	71.5
Work									
7. Started work for the first time	L	+	P	P		C (.7)	S	386	44
8. Returned to work after not working for a long time	L	?	P	P		N	C (.7)	348	54
9. Changed jobs for a better one	L	+	P	P	LSS?	C (.7)	C (.6)	472	46
10. Changed jobs for a worse one	L	−	P	P	LSS?	C (.8)	C (.7)	359	69.5
11. Changed jobs for one that was no better and no worse than the last one	L	?	P	P		I	I	251	85
12. Had trouble with a boss	L	−	P	I		N	N	322	75
13. Demoted at work	L	−	P	I		C (.7)	C (.5)	379	53
14. Found out that was *not* going to be promoted at work	L	−	P	I		C (.7)	C (.6)	345	78

340

	Event									
15.	Conditions at work got worse, other than demotion or trouble with the boss	L	—	P	P		C(.7)	C(.5)	316	57
16.	Promoted	L	+	P	P		C(.7)	C(.5)	374	50
17.	Had significant success at work		+				C(.6)	C(.5)	350	56
18.	Conditions at work improved, *not* counting promotion or other personal successes	L	+	P	P		C(.7)	C(.6)	318	63.5
19.	Laid off	L	+	P	P	FN	C(.8)	C(.6)	325	59.5
20.	Fired	L	—	I	I	LSS	I	C(.6)	407	40
21.	Started a business or profession	L	+	P	P		C(.5)	C(.5)	471	33
22.	Expanded business or professional practice	L	+	P	P		N	S	478	35
23.	Took on a greatly increased work load	L	?	P	P		C(.6)	C(.5)	289	74
24.	Suffered a business loss or failure	L	—	P	I		C(.7)	C(.5)	510	30
25.	Sharply reduced work load	L	?	P	P		C(.8)	S	245	89.5
26.	Retired	L	?	P	P	LSS	C(.6)	C(.5)	461	31
27.	Stopped working, *not* retirement, for an extended period	L	?	P	P		C(.7)	C(.6)	456	48.5
	Love and Marriage									
28.	Became engaged	L	+	P	P	LSS	C(.6)	C(.5)	409	57
29.	Engagement was broken	L	—	P	P		S	S	309	81
30.	Married	L	—	P	P		modulus			22
31.	Started a love affair	U	+	P	P		N	C(.8)	381	65.5
32.	Relations with spouse changed for the worse, without separation or divorce	U	+	P	P		C(.6)	C(.5)	526	9.5
33.	Married couple separated	U	—	P	P	LSS	C(.7)	I	515	16
34.	Divorce	U	—	P	P	LSS	S	S	633	5
35.	Relations with spouse changed for the better	U	+	P	P		C(.7)	C(.5)	520	18
36.	Married couple got together again after separation	U	+	P	P		C(.7)	C(.7)	558	14
37.	Marital infidelity	U	+	P	P	LSS	C(.7)	S	558	17
38.	Trouble with in-laws	L	—	P	P		N	C(.7)	310	80
39.	Spouse died	U	—	I	I	FN	S	I	821	2

TABLE 21-1
Classifications and Total Sample Ratings of PERI Life Events (*cont.*)

Topic area and event	Breadth of setting[a]	Desirability[b]	Relation to etiology when central figure is:[c] Respondent	Other	Elements of pathogenic triad[d]	Rating classification with elevation:[e] Uncontrolled	Controlled	Arithmetic mean of subgroup ratings[f]	Rank of mean[g]
Having Children									
40. Became pregnant	U	?	P	P		C (.6)	C (.5)	419	32
41. Birth of a first child	U	+	P	P		C (.5)	C (.5)	577	6
42. Birth of a second or later child	U	?	P	P		C (.6)	S	448	26
43. Abortion	U	—	P	P		C (.6)	S	370	42.5
44. Miscarriage or still-birth	U	—	I	I	FN	S	N	457	19
45. Found out that cannot have children	U	—	I	I	FN	I	I	518	9.5
46. Child died	U	—	I	I	FN	S	S	1036	1
47. Adopted a child	U	+	P	I		C (.7)	C (.5)	458	27
48. Started menopause	U	?	I	I		N	N	336	48.5
Family									
49. New person moved into the household	U	?	P	P		N	C (.7)	297	71.5
50. Person moved out of the household	U	?	P	P	LSS	C (.7)	C (.6)	333	79
51. Someone stayed on in the household after he was expected to leave	U	—	P	P		N	C (.7)	285	76
52. Serious family argument other than with spouse	U	—	P	P		C (.8)	C (.7)	262	92.5
53. A change in the frequency of family get-togethers	U	—	P	P		C (.8)	C (.7)	262	92.5
54. Family member other than spouse or child dies	U	—	I	I	FN	S	I	463	25
Residence									
55. Moved to a better residence or neighborhood	L	+	P	P	LSS?	I	I	437	47

Item									
56. Moved to a worse residence or neighborhood	L	—	P	I	LSS?	C (.3)	C (.6)	463	39
57. Moved to a residence or neighborhood no better or no worse than the last one	L	?	P	P		N	C (.8)	241	89.5
58. Unable to move after expecting to be able to move	L	—	P	P		C (.8)	C (.7)	308	73
59. Built a home or had one built	L	+	P	P		C (.6)	S	548	29
60. Remodeled a home	L	+	P	P		C (.8)	C (.6)	314	65.5
61. Lost a home through fire, flood, or other disaster	L	—	P	I	FN	C (.6)	S	580	12.5
Crime and Legal Matters									
62. Assaulted	U	—	I	I	FN	S	S	383	52
63. Robbed	U	—	I	I	FN	N	C (.7)	314	63.5
64. Accident in which there were no injuries	U	—	I	I		N	N	254	45
65. Involved in a lawsuit	L	—	P	P	FN	N	C (.7)	408	37
66. Accused of something for which a person could be sent to jail	L	—	P	I		C (.6)	C (.5)	489	15
67. Lost driver's license	L	—	P	I		N	N	254	96
68. Arrested	L	—	P	I		C (.7)	C (.5)	475	21
69. Went to jail	L	—	P	I	LSS	C (.6)	S	566	4
70. Got involved in a court case	L	—	P	P		N	S	304	67
71. Convicted of a crime	L	—	P	I		C (.8)	C (.5)	539	8
72. Acquitted of a crime	L	+	P	P		C (.6)	C (.5)	468	24
73. Released from jail	L	+	P	P		C (.8)	C (.7)	497	11
74. Didn't get out of jail when expected	L	—	P	I		S	S	469	20
Finances									
75. Took out a mortgage	L	?	P	P		C (.7)	C (.6)	320	77
76. Started buying a car, furniture, or other large purchase on the installment plan	L	+	P	P		C (.8)	C (.7)	264	91
77. Foreclosure of a mortgage or loan	L	—	P	I		C (.7)		460	41
78. Repossession of a car, furniture, or other items bought on the installment plan	L	—	P	P		S	S	287	87

TABLE 21-1
Classifications and Total Sample Ratings of PERI Life Events (cont.)

Topic area and event	Breadth of setting[a]	Desira-bility[b]	Relation to etiology when central figure is:[c] Respondent	Other	Elements of pathogenic triad[d]	Rating classification with elevation:[e] Uncontrolled	Controlled	Arithmetic mean of subgroup ratings[f]	Rank of mean[g]
79. Took a cut in wage or salary without a demotion	L	—	I	I	FN	S	S	396	45
80. Suffered a financial loss or loss of property not related to work						S	C (.6)	446	51
81. Went on welfare	U	—	P	P		C (.8)	I	422	34
82. Went off welfare	L	?	P	I		C (.8)	C (.7)	352	61
83. Got a substantial increase in wage or salary without a promotion	L	+	P	P		C (.7)	C (.5)	352	61
84. Did not get an *expected* wage or salary increase	L	—	I	I	FN	N	N	343	62
85. Had financial improvement not related to work	U	+	P	P		C (.6)	C (.5)	517	36
Social Activities									
86. Increased church or synagogue, club, neighborhood, or other organizational activities	L	+	P	P		C (.8)	C (.7)	274	84
87. Took a vacation	L	++	P	P		C (.8)	C (.7)	273	82
88. Was not able to take a *planned* vacation	L	—	I	P	FN	N	S	221	98

344

No.	Life event	Breadth of setting[a]	Desirability[b]	Relation to etiology[c]		Elements of pathogenic triad[d]	Rating classification[e]	Rating classification[e]	Arithmetic mean[f]	Rank[g]
89.	Took up a new hobby, sport, craft, or recreational activity	L	+	P	P		I	I	281	99
90.	Dropped a hobby, sport, craft, or recreational activity	L	—	P	P		C(.8)	N	182	101
91.	Acquired a pet	U	+	P	P		N	S	163	102
92.	Pet died	U	—	I	I		N	S	196	100
93.	Made new friends	U	+	P	I		C(.8)	N	247	94
94.	Broke up with a friend	U	—	P	P	LSS	S	S	328	83
95.	Close friend died	U	—	I	I	FN	S	S	457	23
	Miscellaneous									
96.	Entered the armed services	L	?	P	P	LSS?	C(.6)	C(.7)	406	55
97.	Left the armed services	L	?	P	P	LSS?	C(.6)	S	360	42.5
98.	Took a trip other than a vacation	L	?	P	P		I	N	249	92.5
	Health									
99.	Physical health improved	U	+	H	P		C(.6)	C(.7)	562	28
100.	Physical illness	U	—	H	I	PE	S	C(.6)	668	3
101.	Injury	U	—	H	I	PE	C(.7)	N	560	12.5
102.	Unable to get treatment for an illness or injury	U	—	H	I	PE	S	S	611	7

[a] Breadth of setting: U = universal; L = limited.

[b] Desirability: + = gain; ? = ambiguous; — = loss.

[c] Relation to etiology: H = events concerning respondent's physical health and psychological condition; P = possibly confounded with respondent's psychological condition; I = certainly independent of respondent's physical health and psychological condition.

[d] Elements of pathogenic triad: FN = fateful negative event; LSS = loss of social support event or possible physical exhaustion event other than by fateful negative event; PE = possible physical exhaustion event; ? = depends on context.

[e] Rating classification: C = consensual; N = noisy due to CV greater than .8; I = noisy due to uninterpretable interaction effect. S = status dependent.

[f] The arithmetic mean was calculated as the mean of the actual sample means, as opposed to the arithmetic means of subgroup ratings, presented in the preceding column. In the actual sample means each person was weighted equally; therefore, subgroups of unequal size were weighted unequally, according to their size. These ranks therefore are not redundant with those in the previous column.

[g] These ranks were based on the actual sample means, as opposed to subgroups that happened to be overrepresented in the sample, presented in the preceding column, in order to avoid undue weight to subgroups that happened to be overrepresented in the sample.

SELECTION OF JUDGES

Problems

With the exception of a study in rural North Carolina (Miller et al., 1974), all of the ratings that have been reported for Holmes and Rahe's (1967) list of events were obtained from *samples of convenience* (i.e., selected because they are readily available rather than to represent a known population) of judges. Similarly, ratings of the event list constructed by Paykel and his colleagues (1971) were obtained from persons who were readily available, specifically psychiatric patients and their relatives, and ratings of an instrument based on a combination of these two lists were done by "medical personnel and . . . non-medical members of the local community . . . weighted toward the upper socioeconomic groups" (Tennant & Andrews, 1976:29). In the North Carolina study, a representative sample was selected from a rural county, but evaluation of the final sample of judges is difficult because no information is available concerning the numbers of persons in the original sample who did not complete the rating task.

It is apparent from descriptions of the results obtained from these samples of judges that they were intended to represent a larger population, sometimes a particular ethnic group (Komaroff et al., 1968), sometimes a geographical region (Miller, Bentz, Aponte, & Brogan, 1974), and sometimes a nation (Masuda & Holmes, 1967b). If the burden of proof rests on these investigators that their samples of judges actually represented the specified populations, it is clear that, possibly with the exception of Miller and his colleagues, they do not have the evidence to support this argument. However, if we shift the burden of proof to the critic, is there any reason to think that a sample of convenience would not represent the population from which it was drawn? There is indeed evidence from studies of social circles that a group of people recruited by dint of one set of common activities or associations is likely to be more homogeneous in other respects than a representative sample of the population (cf. Askenasy, Dohrenwend & Dohrenwend, 1977).

Proposed Method

Ratings of the magnitudes of life events can be generalized with confidence only if a probability sample of judges is selected from the appropriate population. This population is the one in which the magnitude judgments are to be used as measures of the stressfulness of particular events in studies of the effects of life events. If this population is heterogeneous with respect to characteristics such as ethnicity, which might be associated with differences in judgments of the stressfulness of some events, a stratified sample including equal numbers of judges from different groups rather than a representative sample might be chosen. This stratification would provide a more efficient basis for testing group differences in judgments, particularly if the groups to be compared were grossly unequal in the population to be sampled.

Sampling of Judges for PERI Life Events Ratings

The history of the sample of judges who rated the PERI life events list involves what one might call three sampling generations. The first sampling generation consisted of 2627 adults aged 21–64 drawn from all five boroughs of New York City on a strict probability basis. They had been interviewed approximately four years earlier about their physical health and health care by the Center for Social Research at the Graduate Center of the City University of New York. The completion rate in this study was an excellent 84%.

The second sampling generation aimed at a stratified subsample of 250 male and female heads of households, married or single, aged 21–64, for the purpose of studying the relation between life events and psychiatric symptomatology (Dohrenwend, 1976). For married couples, a procedure similar to a coin flip determined whether the male or female would be interviewed. In order to facilitate statistical comparisons, the sample drawn was 30% black, 30% Puerto Rican, and 40% non–Puerto Rican white. Within each of the three ethnic groups, similar proportions of each of three class levels were sought. These class levels, specified in terms of the number of years of education of the head of the household (the male head in the case of married couples), ranged from less than high school graduate; to high school graduate but less than college graduate; to college graduate or better. This time, however, the completion rate for the first round of interviews was only 60.4% of the 331 located subjects we set out to interview. This was lower than the 75.0% completion rate we had expected and left us with 200, rather than 250, interviews.

The PERI life event rating study used the third sampling generation, which involved visiting the 200 households in which interviews had been completed about two weeks earlier. This generation consisted originally of the spouses of the respondents interviewed for the second study (Dohrenwend, 1976). About 10% of these refused. Because 56 of the respondents selected for the second study had no spouses, the sample of judges was supplemented by 30 persons drawn from the original New York City sample. Rating interviews were ultimately obtained from 124 subjects. Obviously, we paid a considerable price in nonresponse for the advantage of being able to stratify as we wished on the basis of data from previous research. These 124 subjects represented only the residentially most stable and cooperative members of the original four-year-old citywide sample.

The Rating Task

The events to be rated were the 101 shown in Table 21–2, excluding married, which was used as the modulus against which the others were judged. The order of events was radomized. The events were then listed on four pages, which were rotated across judges to control possible order effects on the ratings.

The instructions used were those for rating change devised by Komaroff and associates (1968) for lower-class, less educated judges. These instructions are simpler in wording than the original readjustment instructions used by Holmes and Rahe (1967) but are otherwise equivalent. We used the simpler instructions because we included poorly educated, as well as highly educated, judges in our sample.

Results

There is no indication in previously published studies, all but one of which used samples of convenience, that any of the subjects had difficulty with the rating task. In retrospect we find this surprising, for we have strong indications that many of our judges had serious problems in making these judgments. When the completed interviews were examined, we had to discard 32 sets of ratings, disproportionately from lower-class judges, because the judges had not followed the rating instructions. The 32 judges were eliminated on the

TABLE 21-2

Ethnicity and Education of Household Head; Sex of 92 Judges Who Completed the Rating Task Satisfactorily and of 32 Judges Who Failed to Follow Instructions[a]

Years education of head of household	Ethnicity					
	Black		Puerto Rican		Non–Puerto Rican white	
	Male	*Female*	*Male*	*Female*	*Male*	*Female*
0–11	1 / / 4	4 / / 3	6 / / 4	10 / / 4	7 / / 1	8 / / 3
12–15	4 / / 5	4 / / 1	6 / / 1	10 / / 1	3 / / 1	6 / / 1
16+	3 / / 1	1 / / 1	0 / / 0	1 / / 0	12 / / 1	6 / / 0

[a] In each cell the number above the diagonal refers to judges who completed the task satisfactorily and the number below the diagonal to judges who did not do so.

following evidence. Fourteen were dropped because their ratings either were highly incomplete or appeared to at least two researchers to be arbitrary or grossly at odds with the instructions. Some of these 14 respondents gave seemingly rigid responses, like many 0's and 1000's; others wrote "less than 500" and "more than 500"; still others refused to accept the modulus married as 500 points, that is, they changed it to 1000 points, to 20 points, or to 0 points. One respondent claimed the modulus did not apply to him since he was single. Some respondents reported that the task was too difficult. Eighteen of the 32 judges were dropped on the basis of the previous finding that desirable events receive average change ratings well below the average for undesirable events (Dohrenwend, 1973; Vinokur & Selzer, 1975). Therefore, judges whose average change rating for desirable events was higher than their average for undesirable events were eliminated on the assumption that they had not followed the instruction to rate the events in terms of the amount of change they entail but had instead rated them on desirability. This problem may have been particularly prevalent among these judges because, before rating the life events, they had had the task of rating symptoms of psychological disorder in terms of social desirability. Some judges apparently carried this set over to the life events rating task.

Table 21-2 describes the 92 judges who completed the rating task successfully and the 32 who apparently did not follow instructions in making their ratings. It is possible that in previous studies subjects who would have experienced difficulty with the task simply did not volunteer to do it. If this is the case, the present group of 92 judges must be considered similar to a sample of convenience rather than to a representative sample of the general population in this respect. On the other hand, the sample of 92 judges contrasts with samples of convenience in that it clearly was not drawn from one or more social circles whose members, even if not formally organized, could be expected to share certain values, interests, and behavior patterns (Askenasy, Dohrenwend, & Dohrenwend, 1977).

AN EMERGENT PROBLEM: OCCASIONAL NON–TASK ORIENTED RATINGS

Among the ratings made by the 92 judges were some that could more readily be interpreted as expressions of feelings about particular events than as ratings of the amount of change that they entail. For example, one judge assigned 1 million points both to death of a child and to death of spouse. By contrast, he assigned only 900 points to birth of first child. Another respondent assigned 1 million points to death of spouse and 10 million points to death of a child but only 500 points to birth of first child. Viewed against the definition of the raters' task, ratings such as these, which seemed to express a judge's sense of outrage about an event rather than his assessment of the amount of change involved, were clearly errors. The presence of errors in the ratings was also suggested by an analysis of correlations between the mean ratings across the 101 events by judges who differed in social class (Askenasy, Dohrenwend, & Dohrenwend, 1977).

These apparently expressive ratings could not be ignored since they might produce misleading results in either of two ways in tests to determine whether judges from different status groups were in agreement in rating particular events. Depending on the distribution of the extreme ratings in the status groups being tested, expressive ratings could lead either to type 1 or to type 2 errors of statistical inference. If the extremely high ratings were concentrated in one group, they might, by elevating the mean of that group, erroneously produce a statistically significant group difference. On the other hand, if they did not have this effect, they might, by inflating within-group variance, lead to erroneous acceptance of the null hypothesis of no difference between groups. Thus, these apparently expressive and thereby erroneous judgments had to be dealt with before analyzing the ratings for group differences.

When there is reason to believe that some outlying scores in a distribution were sampled from a different population from the one that yielded the remainder of the distribution, a data trimming technique called *Winsorization* may be used (Winer, 1971). This procedure is appropriate, for example, when, as in our case, raters apparently do not follow instructions. This technique involves substituting the next highest score in the distribution of ratings for an event for one or more of the highest values and the next lowest score for an equal number of the lowest values in the distribution of ratings of that event. The adjustment of scores at the nonsuspect end of the distribution is designed to balance the effect on the mean of adjusting the suspect scores. In this respect, Winsorization is similar to simple trimming, in which equal numbers of scores are dropped completely at both ends of the distribution. In contrast to simple trimming, however, Winsorization does not reduce the number of scores on which the estimate of the mean of the distribution is based.

The major problem in implementing this technique is to decide how far to Winsorize. To make this decision, we examined the distributions of the ratings for each event. We noted that where high ratings occurred, their frequency declined with some regularity up to about 2000; higher ratings were generally isolated occurrences, although ratings of 5000 tended to pile up. Across all events, of the 43 ratings of 5000 or more, 19 were exactly 5000. Reasoning that these disproportionately frequent, round number ratings of 5000 might represent the point at which serious attempts to assess the amount of change entailed by an event left off and expressive responses began, we first Winsorized all ratings of 5000 or more, along with an equal number of low ratings for the same events. If an event had one rating of 5000 or more and more than one rating tied for lowest value, a die or coin was used to select the low rating to be changed to the next lowest value. In this way, 43 pairs of high and low ratings distributed among 26 events were changed to the next most extreme rating.

The decision to Winsorize ratings of 5000 or more did not eliminate all the high ratings that seemed to be isolated from the distributions in which they appeared. To test the effect of altering most of these relatively isolated ratings, we performed a further Winsorization of all ratings of 3000 or greater. This Winsorization involved 55 high-low rating pairs distributed among 33 events. Comparison of the results of the first Winsorization with those of this second, more radical Winsorization indicated that the more radical procedure reduced the

TABLE 21–3
Distribution of Pairs of Winsorized Scores According to
Status Characteristics of Judges

Status characteristics	Number of pairs
Years of education of household head	
0–11	22[a]
12–15	17
16 +	4
Ethnicity of household head	
Black	11[a]
Puerto Rican	2
Non–Puerto Rican white	30
Sex	
Male	20[a]
Female	23

[a] One judge accounted for nine of these high ratings.

variability of some of the less variable events. In contrast, the Winsorization limited to scores of 5000 or more reduced only the variability of highly variable events. Winsorization was, therefore, limited to high ratings of 5000 or more and paired low ratings of the same events. The distribution of Winsorized ratings among the judges according to social class, ethnicity, and sex is shown in Table 21–3. The distribution of these 43 pairs of ratings across events is reported elsewhere (Dohrenwend, Krasnoff, Askenasy, & Dohrenwend, 1978).

TESTS OF WHETHER JUDGES AGREE ON THEIR RATINGS

Problems

Holmes and his colleagues (Holmes & Rahe, 1967; Holmes & Masuda, 1974) argued on the basis of two findings that the ratings of life events on their list are universally agreed upon. The first finding is that correlations between mean ratings across all events were generally above .90 for judges grouped according to sex, ethnicity, age, or other characteristics (Holmes & Rahe, 1967). However, high correlations among the mean ratings of groups of judges across the entire list do not preclude differences among these groups in the magnitude of their ratings of particular events, and such differences have in fact been found (e.g., Miller, Bentz, Aponte, & Brogan, 1974).

The second finding on which Holmes and his colleagues based their argument for accepting the ratings of their list as universal concerns the nature of the variability among individual judges. Masuda and Holmes (1967a) showed that the standard error of the geometric means of the ratings increased as a linear function of the size of the geometric mean, thus conforming to Ekman's law which states that the variability of sets of scores increases as the means of the sets increase. However, even if some of the variability in a set of ratings can be explained by Ekman's law, the variability of the ratings of particular events may still be judged unacceptably large when tested against other explicit criteria.

Proposed Method: A General Decision Model

Judges' ratings of the amount of change entailed by a particular life event may reflect any of three mutually exclusive states: universal agreement, differences among persons as a function fo their social class or other identified characteristics, or differences among persons unrelated to any identified characteristic. We label the first state *consensus;* the second, *status-dependent differences;* and the third, *noise.* A decision model designed to classify event ratings into these three categories is shown in Figure 21-1.

The decision process starts with a conventional analysis of variance, asking first whether there are any significant interactions among the social status variables according to which the judges were classified. If a significant interaction effect is found, the next question is whether it relates meaningfully to the content of the event. If so, the event ratings are classified as reflecting status-dependent differences, indicated by the notation S. If not, they are classified as noisy, using the notation N_I to indicate a significant interaction. If no significant interactions are found among status variables, the next question, as in the usual analysis of variance, is whether there are any significant main effects. If so, the event ratings are, by a second route, classified as reflecting status-dependent differences (indicated by S). At this point, as well as where status-dependent differences are found through a significant interaction effect, it is also necessary for future reference to record the particular difference that has been identified.

At the point where no significant main effects are found, we have determined that the event ratings do not reflect differences related to any of the statuses identified in the data being analyzed. The remaining question is whether the ratings should be classified as consensual (C) or noisy (N). The answer to this question requires that we decide how much unexplained variance we will accept in ratings classified as consensual. Ideally, there should be no

FIGURE 21-1. Decision model for classifying the ratings of events as status dependent (S), noisy (N or N_I), or consensual (C). I = interaction; S = status main effect—sex, ethnicity, or social class; $SD/\overline{X}$ = coefficient of variation; V = cutting point for value of $SD/\overline{X}$ to be decided.

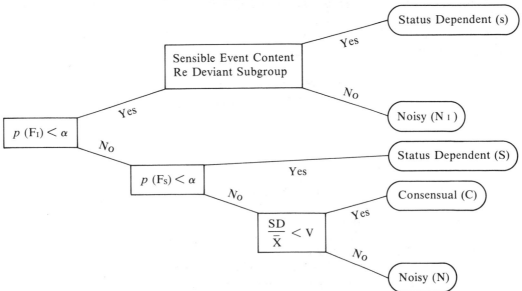

variability in these ratings. In practice, however, even in ratings of unambiguous physical stimuli, experience with magnitude estimation indicates that

> the judgment of subjective magnitude is inherently a "noisy" phenomenon. When people try to describe a sensation in quantitative terms they face a difficult task, and the factors that affect the outcome are numerous and subtle. Patience and experimental skill can probably clean up part of the variance, but there will always remain irreducible dispersions to set a level below which we sink into uncertainty. (Stevens, 1957:167)

The statistic on which we base the decision as to whether ratings of an event are consensual or noisy is the *coefficient of variation* (CV), which is the standard deviation of the ratings divided by their mean. This statistic is more appropriate than the standard deviation alone since it controls for the operation of Ekman's law, whereby variability increases as the mean increases. As we noted earlier, this relationship has been shown to hold in magnitude estimations of life events (Holmes & Masuda, 1974).

In the general decision model shown in Figure 21-1 no specific rule is set as to what CV separates consensual from noisy sets of event ratings. Instead, in the absence of any prior information about the amount of dispersion to be expected in ratings of life events, we have indicated that the user chooses a *value* (V) when he applies the decision model. Similarly, for earlier steps of the decision model concerning interaction and main effect of status variables, a particular value of alpha has not been set but must be chosen by the user.

When we applied the decision model to the PERI life events ratings we had to deal with other problems that arose from the attrition of our sample linked to refusals and to loss of judges who did not follow the instructions for the rating task. These problems concerned the distribution of judges in status subgroups and the number of judges relative to the number of events judged.

A Problem Concerning the Distribution of Judges in Status Subgroups in the PERI Life Events Rating Study

Before choosing values of alpha and V and applying the decision model to the PERI life event ratings, we had to deal with a problem that appeared when we examined the distribution of judges in the subgroups that would be formed in testing for interaction effects. As Table 21-3 shows, three of these subgroups were represented by only one judge each. In order to avoid the possibility of having to base interpretations of significant interaction effects on ratings by single judges, we eliminated these three from the analysis. Thus, our results for the PERI Life Events Scale came from the ratings of 89 judges.

Choice of Alpha and V for Application of the Decision Model to the PERI Life Events Ratings

In choosing alpha we had to consider type 1 and type 2 errors in relation to the F tests that comprise the first two stages of the decision model schematized in Figure 21-1. However, we should note at this point that these errors have different implications in the context of the decision model and in traditional experimental hypothesis testing. In the latter situation, the alternative to an experimental hypothesis is the null hypothesis. In the context of the decision model, the alternative to the hypothesis of group differences is not simply a null hypothesis of no differences between groups because of nonsignificant F ratio leads to implementation of a further stage in the decision model, where the ratings may be classified as consensual. Thus, a type 2 error in tests of group differences may lead to misclassification of the ratings as consensual. Because of the possibility of this erroneous classification, in choosing alpha we were concerned with the rate of type 2 errors as much as we were with the rate of type 1 errors. That is, the choice of alpha was designed to balance the different types of error that might be produced by the decision model.

In choosing alpha we were not able to solve the problem of predicting error rates for multiple F tests, in part because of the small number of judges relative to the number of tests we planned to perform. Given this limitation in our data, we chose an alpha level on the basis of the implications of a particular level for a single statistical test rather than for the 707 nonindependent tests involved in our design.

To choose an alpha level we considered its implications for type 2 errors by examining power curves appropriate to our sample size for the tests of group differences (Cohen, 1969). These curves will differ with the number of groups involved in a test. In our case, the tests for sex differences involved two group comparisons, while the tests for social class and ethnic main effects and for all interaction effects involved three group comparisons. The fact that the differences in power between two- and three-group comparisons were rather large when alpha equaled .01 and were considerably smaller for alphas of .05 and .10 argued for choosing an alpha greater than .01 in order to make tests for the various status effects as comparable as possible.

At the same time, the greater power provided by tests with alpha set at .10 rather than .05 seemed undesirable because most of the additional power would have involved increasing the probability of detecting between group differences that accounted for less than 6% of the variance in ratings and, therefore, perhaps had no practical import. Given these two considerations, we chose alpha of .05 for the application of the decision model to the PERI life events ratings.

In the absence of any general guiding principles or prior information about coefficients of variation of life event ratings, the choice of values of V was based on examination of the distribution of coefficients of variations for the PERI ratings. This distribution is shown in part A of Figure 21-2. We see that a V of less than .6 would largely preclude the finding of consensual events. On the other hand, a V on the order of 1.0 would make it difficult, on the face of it, to argue that an event was consensual. Within these limits, however, there seemed no obvious basis for choosing a particular figure. Our initial choice, therefore, was to report which events were classified as noisy and which as consensual at three levels of V: .6, .7, and .8.

Controls of Possible Rating Bias

Across all events, ratings by women were on the average 56 points higher than ratings by men. Ratings also differed according to the social class of the judge, with a spread of 94 points between the middle-class mean, which was highest, and the upper-class mean, which was lowest. The spread among ethnic groups was much less. The high and low mean, for blacks and non–Puerto Rican whites, respectively, differed by only 19 points.

These differences in group means possibly reflected true differences between groups in the way that they experienced life events. However, for the moment let us consider the alternate possibility that the differences arose from the rating process itself and therefore represented error or bias in the ratings.

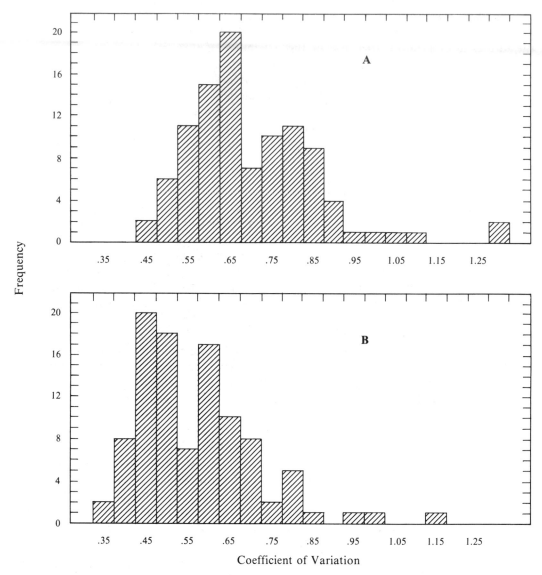

FIGURE 21-2. Distributions of coefficients of variation based on Winsorized ratings of 89 judges before controlling for elevation (A) and after controlling for elevation (B) in ratings.

Results from previous studies illustrate two possible sources of group differences that arise from the rating process. The first involves the modulus event. When Miller and his colleagues (1974) compared ratings by a rural sample of judges with the original ratings collected by Holmes and Rahe (1967) from an urban sample, they found that the modulus event, marriage, ranked fourth when rated by the urban judges and twenty-first when rated by the rural judges; furthermore, the rural judges gave higher ratings than did the urban judges to every event on the list. The most parsimonious explanation of this overall difference is that, as a consequence of the label "marriage," the value of the modulus, 500, represented less change to the rural judges than to the urban judges. Second, when Paykel and colleagues (1976), in England, compared ratings by American and English samples on a 21-point scale, with no modulus, they obtained significantly higher ratings from the English sample on 19 out of 61 events and a statistically significant overall mean difference between the two samples of judges. Before interpreting differences in the ratings obtained from the two samples, Paykel and his co-workers subtracted half the difference between the group means from the English ratings and added half to the American ratings, thus treating the difference between the groups as misleading error or bias in the ratings.

Although we were concerned, as were these investigators, that group differences in ratings might be misleading if not corrected for possible differences in rating bias, the procedure of correcting the judges' ratings directly in terms of a group difference, as Paykel and his colleagues (1976) did, seemed unsatisfactory on two counts: it does not correct for, and may distort, other group differences and it does not allow for individual differences in possible rating bias. For these reasons we took the mean of each judge's ratings of all events as a measure of his possible rating bias and made the correction at the individual level.

This individual mean score may represent the effect on a judge's ratings both of his perception of the modulus event and of his expressivity across all events. Since we could not determine the influence of each of these processes, we called this score, descriptively, *elevation,* so as not to prejudge its source. This descriptive title allows also for the possibility that these scores, rather than measuring a rating bias, may represent true differences between individuals and groups in the way that they experience life events. Given this uncertainty about interpretation, we will report the results of analyzing the ratings with the decision model both before and after we controlled for elevation.

When variability due to elevation was removed from the rating, it did not change the overall mean but it did reduce the variance and thus the size of the coefficient of variation for an event. This effect is shown in part B of Figure 21-2. As we noted earlier, V of less than .6 would create a nearly empty category of consensual events at the low end of the first distribution in Figure 21-2. However, when elevation is controlled, it becomes reasonable to introduce a category of consensual events having coefficients of variation lower than .5. Therefore, in reporting the results of application of the decision model to the ratings, we will indicate which are noisy and which consensual at four levels of V: .5, .6, .7, and .8.

Results

Table 21-1 shows the classification of events by application of the decision model to the ratings, with alpha set at .05 and the levels of V described above. Before elevation was controlled, ratings of the majority of events, 56 out of 101, were classified as consensual at V of .8 or better, 17 as status dependent, and 28 as noisy—8 of the 28 because of uninterpretable interaction effects and 20 because their CV was .8 or greater. After elevation was controlled, the ratings of 60 events were classified as consensual at V of .8 or better, 22 as status dependent, and 19 as noisy—11 because of uninterpretable interaction effects and 8 because their CV was .8 or greater.

These changes in the distribution of events among the three categories were based on 34 events that shifted among the three categories when elevation was controlled. The modal shift, 38% of the 34 events, was from noisy to consensual at V of .8 or less, reflecting the decrease in coefficients of variation after the variation due to elevation was removed from the ratings. The second most common shift, 26% was from consensual at .8 or less to status dependent. In contrast, only 6% of the events that shifted after controlling for elevation moved from status dependent to consensual at V of .8 or less. This pattern of shifts reflected the distribution of elevation scores within and between status groups. That is, none of the apparently large mean differences in elevation scores between groups was statistically significant because the variation in elevation scores within groups was very large. This fact, together with the pattern of shifts observed when elevation was controlled, indicates that the predominant effect of elevation was not to produce but to obscure group differences in event ratings.

This conclusion about the effect of elevation on group differences is strengthened by the results of a multivariate analysis of variance that we carried out on a subset of events. For this analysis we selected 14 events, a number small enough to permit us to do a multivariate analysis with data from 89 judges. These 14 events were selected (without regard to results of the univariate analysis) as ones that four judges readily agreed belonged among those that are universal with respect to the settings in which they occur. The events in this set of 14 are indicated in Table 21-1 by an asterisk next to U under the setting heading. The multivariate analysis was carried out both before and after elevation was controlled. When elevation was not controlled, the multivariate statistics for status group differences were not significant at the .05 level, raising questions about the interpretability of the group differences found with univariate tests for the 14 events in the analysis. In contrast, when elevation was controlled, some multivariate statistics were significant at the .05 level, suggesting that significant differences emerged in the ratings of these 14 events as a consequence of controlling elevation.

Turning again to the univariate analysis of the ratings of the total set of 101 events, the means of events classified as having status-dependent ratings either before or after control of elevation are shown in Table 21-4. Although the changes in the content of events whose ratings were classified as status dependent before and after control of elevation were fairly complex and not always meaningful, some of these changes argue for the appropriateness of this control. Thus, for example, only after elevation was controlled did we find that men and women differed in their rating of marital infidelity, with men rating it higher; similarly, only

TABLE 21-4
Group Means for Life Events that Have Status-dependent Ratings[a]

Topic area and event	Rank of total sample mean	Status Class: Ethnicity: Sex:	Level Low Black Male	Middle Puerto Rican Female	High Non-Puerto Rican white
Work					
7. Started work	44	Ethnicity:	*495*	*428*	*337*
22. Expanded business	35	Class:	*528*	*360*	*405*
25. Reduced work load	25	Ethnicity:	*251*	*332*	*213*
Love and Marriage					
29. Engagement broken	81	Sex:	234	344	
			248	333	
34. Divorce	5	Class:	506	748	555
			518	707	601
37. Marital infidelity	17	Sex:	*586*	*449*	
39. Spouse died	2	Ethnicity:	699	621	1022

(cont.)

TABLE 21–4
Group Means for Life Events that Have Status-dependent Ratings[a] (cont.)

Topic area and event	Rank of total sample mean	Status — Class Ethnicity: / Sex:	Level — Low Black / Male	Level — Middle Puerto Rican / Female	Level — High Non-Puerto Rican white
Having Children					
42. Birth of later child	26	Ethnicity:	*397*	*507*	*456*
44. Miscarriage	19	Sex:	374	619	
46. Child died	1	Class:	873	1158	610
		Ethnicity:	753	684	681
			754	*709*	*1132*
Family					
54. Other family member died	25	Sex:	415	551	
Residence					
59. Built a home	29	Class:	*542*	*447*	*386*
		Ethnicity:	*522*	*531*	*406*
61. Lost a home through disaster	12.5	Ethnicity:	*688*	*538*	*526*
Crime and Legal Matters					
62. Assaulted	52	Ethnicity:	*439*	*262*	*448*
			440	*278*	*436*
		Sex:	276	472	
			302	450	
69. Went to jail	4	Ethnicity:	*726*	*502*	*654*
70. Involved in court case	67	Ethnicity:	*366*	*405*	*256*
74. Didn't get out of jail	20	Class:	450	654	350
		Ethnicity:	*511*	*377*	*597*
			485	*406*	*582*
Finances					
77. Foreclosure of loan	41	Ethnicity:	*520*	*402*	*360*
78. Repossession	87	Class:	199	344	276
		Ethnicity:	*348*	*313*	*213*
79. Cut in wage	45	Ethnicity:	*453*	*470*	*315*
			445	*486*	*301*
		Sex:	334	443	
80. Financial loss	51	Class:	347	495	266
Social Activities					
88. Not able to take vacation	98	Ethnicity:	*218*	*301*	*177*
91. Acquired a pet	102	Class:	134	210	116
92. Pet died	100	Sex:	153	267	
94. Broke up with a friend	83	Class:	226	371	260
			237	*345*	*286*
95. Close friend died	23	Ethnicity:	526	260	666
			514	285	651
Miscellaneous					
97. Left armed services	42.5	Sex:	328	464	
Health					
100. Physical illness	3	Ethnicity:	696	*512*	685
102. Unable to get treatment	7	Ethnicity:	808	400	725
			699	*431*	*705*

[a] Means with elevation controlled appear in italics.

after this control was introduced did we find an inverse relation between social class and mean ratings of expanded business or professional practice.

SOME METHODOLOGICAL ISSUES RAISED BY THE PERI LIFE EVENTS SCALE

To What Extent Can a List Be Generalized?

The PERI list of life events was designed broadly to represent the experience, both positive and negative, of an urban population. Although the list was constructed from the experience of New Yorkers, limiting its use to this particular urban setting seems unnecessarily restrictive. On the other hand, this list of events surely does not represent well the experience of a rural population, and it almost certainly deviates in some respects from the experience of urban populations in other countries. It is, moreover, a sample of events taken at a particular time and may become less representative as time passes. Already two items—entered the armed services and left the armed services—are less prominent in the experience of the population whose life events were sampled than they were in 1974, when the United States was drafting men into the services. In sum, like any other list, this list should serve for a while to represent the life events of residents of a particular type of setting but should, we suggest, be reviewed critically as time passes and before being used in other sociocultural settings.

Can a Representative Sample of a Heterogeneous Community Population Rate the Magnitudes of Life Events?

The answer to this question seems to be in doubt because of two problems that arose in collecting ratings of the PERI life events list. The first problem was the high proportion of the originally designated sample who either were not contacted or refused to cooperate. As we noted earlier, this sample loss probably was caused at least in part by problems peculiar to the PERI sample design, which was based on a larger sample that was four years old and required the cooperation of both members of married couples.

In addition, however, the results of the PERI study raise the issue of whether, even if they were willing, all members of a representative community sample would be able to complete the rating task. In particular, the disproportionate failure among lower-class judges raises the question of whether it is feasible to get such ratings from a representative sample of this group.

Our experience with the PERI study does not provide a definitive answer to this question, in large part because of the apparently uneven performance of the interviewers. Although the numbers of rating interviews completed by individual interviewers were too few and too unequally distributed to permit a statistical test of interviewer differences, their supervisors developed the impression that some interviewers were more conscientious or better able than others to handle the task of instructing judges about how to carry out the event ratings. These impressions suggest that the interviewers were at least in part responsible for some of the failure. With sufficient interviewer training and supervision it may be possible, therefore, to increase the proportion of judges in a general community sample who can perform the rating task adequately and particularly, perhaps with extra care, the proportion of lower-class judges who can do so.

How Many Judges Are Needed?

The sample of judges who rated the 101 PERI life events was, unfortunately, too small to provide assurance that the status group differences that were found were reliable. A reasonable estimate is that if each combination of status levels were represented by 20 judges, the standard deviation of the group means would be low enough to give reliable estimates. By this criterion, for our design—which classified judges into three social classes and three ethnic groups and divided them by sex—we should have had 360 judges.

This number would also have provided a larger number of judges than events, thus enabling us to use multivariate analysis of variance to analyze the ratings of the 101 events. Another criterion, however, is that for multivariate analysis the number of judges should be several times the number of statistical tests to be made, say, about 2000 if 100 events are judged and therefore 700 tests are to be performed. However, since the purpose of the study was not, in a strict sense, to test experimental against null hypotheses but rather to increase the probability of correct classification of event ratings, it is not certain that this criterion should have been applied rigidly to decide exactly how many judges would have been sufficient. There is no question, however, that the number of judges should be larger than the number of events to be rated.

The number of judges required to classify event ratings reliably, as well as to get reliable estimates of group differences, raises for the future the problem of the cost of a sufficiently large probability sample. The decision will have to be made as to whether reliable estimates of the magnitudes of life events are worth the cost.

A Qualitative Limitation on the Generality of the Ratings

Recall that in sampling the PERI life events we did not specify whether the central figure in an event was the person who reported it or someone else, for example, a spouse or child. Therefore, when judges rated the events they were free to make whatever assumptions they chose to about this aspect of an event. However, we have some information about the likely choice from a pilot study in which judges were asked, after completing their ratings, what assumptions they had made. The pilot study judges reported that they generally had assumed themselves to be both the person reporting the event and the central figure. Exceptions were a few events such as pregnancy for male raters and entered armed services for female raters, in which they either could not have been or would not have been likely to be the central figure and therefore assumed that someone close to them was the central figure. Relying on their reports, which accord with common sense, we should probably assume that ratings based on the event descriptions on the PERI list provide a measure of magnitude only for events in which the central figure is the respondent and, in general, in the absence of a specification to judges on this point that ratings of events apply to those in which the respondent was the central figure.

How Should We Decide Which Ratings to Use in Studies of the Effect of Life Events?

In presenting the PERI life events ratings we left open at a number of points the question of which means to use in weighting events when studying their effects on illness or other outcomes. Specifically, the user would have to choose: (1) whether to use group-specific weights for events whose means varied across status groups; (2) which value of V to adopt to identify events with consensual as against noisy ratings; and (3) whether to use ratings before or after they were controlled for elevation (this decision would determine which group-specific weights might be used and which events would be classified as consensual at a given V).

Although the group differences found in the PERI life event ratings may not have been reliable, let us assume that they were for the sake of discussion the first of the three problems of choice just described. We can ask, then, whether the PERI results indicate that the use of group-specific ratings would have a nontrivial impact on life event change scores in a study of the effects of these events. In general, we would expect the effect on subjects' life change scores to be trivial if events with group-specific ratings were rare or if the sizes of the weights with group-specific ratings were small relative to the ratings of other events.

Although we have no reliable data on the frequency of occurrence of individual life events, the number of events on which group differences in ratings occurred is suggestive. In particular, when elevation was controlled, the ratings for 17 events varied as a function of the ethnicity of the raters. This number seems too large to permit us to assume with any certainty that the effect of ethnic group-specific weights would be trivial. However, the ratings of only 4 events differed with class and 3 with sex when elevation was controlled, or 7 with class and 7 with sex when elevation was not controlled, suggesting that group-specific weights for these two statuses might have little effect on subjects' total life change scores.

Concerning the size of possible group-specific weights relative to weights for other events, analysis of the results in Table 21-2 shows that only 5 of the 17 events whose ratings varied with ethnicity when elevation was controlled had an overall mean rating below the median for all events or, when elevation was not controlled, only 1 of 7 events whose ratings varied with ethnicity had an overall rating below this median. These results suggest that ethnic group-specific weights might have a nontrivial impact on subjects' life change scores. Apparently, then, we cannot dismiss the problem of deciding whether or not to use group-specific weights on the basis of results from the PERI rating study.

Nor can we decide which V to choose on the basis of information from the ratings themselves. In particular, there is no regularity in the relations between the size of mean ratings and the size of the coefficients of variation such that we could set a dividing point selectively to identify a group of noisy events with mean ratings low enough to add insignificantly to an individual subject's total life change score. The mean rating of events with a CV of less than .5, with elevation controlled, was 427 and the mean of events with a CV equal to or greater than .8 was 364, with intermediate groups of events having means of 243, 362, and 290.

As we noted earlier, there is no inherent basis in the elevation score for designating it as a measure of a particular kind of rating bias, or even as a measure of rating bias rather than of true differences between individuals and groups in the way that they experience life events. What this score actually represents can be determined only by means of studies of the effects of life events in which the events are weighted according to magnitude ratings. To the extent that group differences in elevation represent rating bias, life event weights in which the effect of elevation has been controlled should provide better predictions than uncontrolled weights of the effects of events on the relevant groups. On the other hand, to the extent that group differences in elevation represent true differences in experience, ratings that include the effect of elevation should provide better predictions.

In general, then, it does not seem that rules for making the decisions that were left open in presenting results can be developed from the ratings themselves. Instead, these decisions will have to be made either in terms of the design and purpose of a particular study of effects of events or on the basis of information about alternate sets of weights generated by further research.

CONCLUSION

Our purpose in this chapter was to present a procedure for scaling life events and a particular scale constructed with that procedure. Although the latter, the PERI Life Events Scale, has technical weaknesses, these are probably not unique to this scale but, instead, are more clearly visible than in scales constructed with less methodological rigor. We suggest, therefore, that despite its technical weaknesses, the PERI scale provides an improved measure of stressful life events. At the same time, we want to emphasize that, like any other scale, it is neither universal nor timeless. In contrast, we hope that the procedure we propose will lead to a general and permanent methodological gain in studies of stressful life events.

NOTES

1. They presented the general mathematical development and examples using real data on two aspects of air pollution and two health indicators. Given proxy variables that correlated .78 or .65 with the corresponding true measure of pollution and given that the true measure only accounts for a variation of 1% more in the health indicator than the proxy, the range of uncertainty for the estimated effect on health indicators was 2 to 16 times greater than the estimate of the effect. The range of uncertainty was even greater when the true variable accounted for more variance that was unexplained by the proxy.
2. These limits are based on the fact that a correlation matrix is symmetrical and composed of real numbers; therefore, the determinant of the matrix is greater than or equal to zero. Substituting the given correlations into the equation for the determinant, we get a quadratic equation in the unknown correlation that is greater than or equal to zero. The two limiting values are the roots of the quadratic equation. These limits show that, despite the high correlation with weighted totals, unweighted counts of events may be virtually uncorrelated with the consequences of stress previously related to weighted totals. Although these results are counterintuitive, they are mathematically dictated (Duncan, 1975).

REFERENCES

ANTONOVSKY, A., & KATS, R. The life crisis history as a tool in epidemiological research. *Journal of Health and Social Behavior,* 1967, *8,* 15–20.

ASKENASY, A. R., DOHRENWEND, B. P., & DOHRENWEND, B. S. Some effects of social class and ethnic group membership on judgments of the magnitude of stressful life events: A research note. *Journal of Health and Social Behavior,* 1977, *18,* 432–439.

BROWN, G. W. Meaning, measurement and stress of life events. In B. S. Dohrenwend & B. P. Dohrenwend (eds.), *Stressful life events: Their nature and effects.* New York: Wiley, 1974.

BROWN, G. W., & BIRLEY, J. L. Crises and life changes and the onset of schizophrenia. *Journal of Health and Social Behavior,* 1968, *9,* 203–214.

COHEN, J. *Statistical power analysis for the behavioral sciences.* New York: Academic, 1969.

DOHRENWEND, B. P. Problems in defining and sampling the relevant population of stressful life events.

In B. S. Dohrenwend & B. P. Dohrenwend (eds.), *Stressful life events: Their nature and effects.* New York: Wiley, 1974.

————. Background and description of program of methodological research. Paper presented to the annual meeting of the American Psychological Association, Washington, D.C., 1976.

————. Stressful life events and psychopathology: Some issues of theory and method. In J.F. Barrett, R. M. Rose, & G. L. Klerman (eds.), *Stress and mental disorder.* New York: Raven, 1979.

Dohrenwend, B. S. An experimental study of the effect of payment as respondent cooperation. *Public Opinion Quarterly,* 1970–71, *34,* 621–624.

————. Social status and stressful life events. *Journal of Personality and Social Psychology,* 1973, *28,* 225–235.

Dohrenwend, B. S., & Dohrenwend, B. P. (eds.). *Stressful life events: Their nature and effects.* New York: Wiley, 1974. (a)

Dohrenwend, B. S., & Dohrenwend, B. P. A brief historical introduction to research on stressful life events. In B. S. Dohrenwend & B. P. Dohrenwend (eds.), *Stressful life events: Their nature and effects.* New York: Wiley, 1974. (b)

————. Some issues in research on stressful life events. *Journal of Nervous and Mental Disease,* 1978, *166,* 7–15.

Dohrenwend, B. S. Krasnoff, L., Askenasy, A. R., & Dohrenwend, B. P. Exemplification of a method for scaling life events: The PERI Life Events Scale. *Journal of Health and Social Behavior,* 1978, *19,* 205–229.

————. Reply to comment by Lorimor et al. *Journal of Health and Social Behavior,* 1979, *20,* 306–308.

Duncan, O. D. *Structural equation models.* New York Academic, 1975.

Gersten, J. C., Langner, T. S., Eisenberg, J. G., & Orzek, L. Child behavior and life events: Undesirable change or change per se? In B. S. Dohrenwend & B. P. Dohrenwend (eds.), *Stressful life events: Their nature and effects.* New York: Wiley, 1974.

Ghiselli, E. E. *Theory of psychological measurement.* New York: McGraw-Hill, 1964.

Goldstein, I., Fleiss, J. L., Goldstein, M., & Landovitz, L. Methodological problems arising from the choice of an independent variable in linear regression, with application to an air pollution epidemiological study. *Environmental Health Perspectives,* 1979, *32,* 311–315.

Gunderson, E. K. E., & Rahe, R. H. (eds.). *Life stress and illness.* Springfield: Thomas, 1974.

Hinkle, L. E., Jr. The effect of exposure to culture change, social change, and changes in interpersonal relationships on health. In B. S. Dohrenwend & B. P. Dohrenwend (eds.), *Stressful life events: Their nature and effects.* New York: Wiley, 1974.

Holmes, T. H., & Masuda, M. Life change and illness susceptibility. In B. S. Dohrenwend & B. P. Dohrenwend (eds.), *Stressful life events: Their nature and effects.* New York: Wiley, 1974.

Holmes, T. H., & Rahe, R. H. The social readjustment rating scale. *Journal of Psychosomatic Research,* 1967, *11,* 213–218.

Hough, R. L., Fairbank, D. T., & Garcia, A. M. Problems in the ratio measurement of life stress. *Journal of Health and Social Behavior,* 1976, *17,* 70–82.

Hudgens, R. W. Personal catastrophe and depression: A consideration of the subject with respect to medically ill adolescents, and a requiem for retrospective life-event studies. In B. S. Dohrenwend & B. P. Dohrenwend (eds.), *Stressful life events: Their nature and effects.* New York: Wiley, 1974.

Komaroff, A. L., Masuda, M., & Holmes, T. H. The social readjustment rating scale: A comparative study of Negro, Mexican and White Americans. *Journal of Psychosomatic Research,* 1968, *12,* 121–128.

Krasnoff, L. The use of symptom and life event stress information in psychiatric judgment and case identification. Doctoral dissertation, City University of New York, 1979.

LORIMOR, R. J., JUSTICE, B., MCBEE, G. W., & WEINMAN, M. Weighting events in life-events research. *Journal of Health and Social Behavior,* 1979, *20,* 306–308.

MASUDA, M., & HOLMES, T. H. Magnitude estimations of social readjustments. *Journal of Psychosomatic Research,* 1967, *11,* 219–225. (a)

————. The social readjustment rating scale: A cross-cultural study of Japanese and Americans. *Journal of Psychosomatic Research,* 1967, *11,* 227–237. (b)

MEYER, A. The life chart and the obligation of specifying positive data in psychopathological diagnosis. In E. E. Winters (ed.), *The collected papers of Adolf Meyer,* Vol. 3: *Medical teaching.* Baltimore: Johns Hopkins, 1951.

MILLER, F. T., BENTZ, W. K., APONTE, J. F., & BROGAN, D. R. Perception of life crisis events. In B. S. Dohrenwend & B. P. Dohrenwend (eds.), *Stressful life events: Their nature and effects.* New York: Wiley, 1974.

MULVEY, M. A. The relationship of life events, gender and age: A community study of adulthood. Doctoral dissertation, City University of New York, 1979.

MYERS, J. K., LINDENTHAL, J. J., & PEPPER, M. P. Social class, life events, and psychiatric symptoms: A longitudinal study. In B. S. Dohrenwend & B. P. Dohrenwend (eds.), *Stressful life events: Their nature and effects.* New York: Wilcy, 1974.

MYERS, J. K., LINDENTHAL, J. J., PEPPER, M. P., & OSTRANDER, D. R. Life events and mental status: A longitudinal study. *Journal of Health and Social Behavior,* 1972, *13,* 398–406.

PAYKEL, E. S. Life stress and psychiatric disorder: Applications of the clinical approach. In B. S. Dohrenwend & B. P. Dohrenwend (eds.), *Stressful life events: Their nature and effects.* New York: Wiley, 1974.

PAYKEL, E. S., MCGUINESS, B., & GOMEZ, J. An Anglo-American comparison of the scaling of life events. *British Journal of Medical Psychology,* 1976, *49,* 237–247.

PAYKEL, E. S., PRUSOFF, B. A., & UHLENHUTH, E. H. Scaling of life events. *Archives of General Psychiatry,* 1971, *25,* 340–347.

PAYKEL, E. S., & UHLENHUTH, E. H. Rating the magnitude of life stress. *Canadian Psychiatric Association Journal,* 1972, *17,* SS93–SS100.

RAHE, R. H. The pathway between subjects' recent life changes and their near-future illness reports: Representative results and methodological issues. In B. S. Dohrenwend & B. P. Dohrenwend (eds.), *Stressful life events: Their nature and effects.* New York: Wiley, 1974.

STEVENS, S. S. On the psychophysical law. *Psychological Review,* 1957, *64,* 153–181.

TENNANT, C., & ANDREWS, G. A single scale to measure the stress of life events. *Australian and New Zealand Journal of Psychiatry,* 1976, *10,* 27–32.

THEORELL, T. Life events before and after the onset of a premature myocardial infarction. In B. S. Dohrenwend & B. P. Dohrenwend (eds.), *Stressful life events: Their nature and effects.* New York: Wiley, 1974.

VINOKUR, A., & SELZER, M. L. Desirable versus undesirable life events: Their relationship to stress and mental distress. *Journal of Personality and Social Psychology,* 1975, *32,* 329–337.

WAINER, J. Estimating coefficients in linear models: It don't make no nevermind. *Psychological Bulletin,* 1976, *83,* 213–217.

WINER, B. J. *Statistical principles in experimental design* (2d ed.). New York: McGraw-Hill, 1971.

WOLFF, H. G., WOLF, S. G., JR., & HARE, C. C. (eds.). *Life stress and bodily disease.* Baltimore: Williams & Wilkins, 1950.

PART V

COMMON STRESSORS

A. Environmental and Social Sources

22

The Social Contexts of Stress

Leonard I. Pearlin

THIS CHAPTER IS CONCERNED PRIMARILY with identifying social conditions that stand as sources of stress. In surveying the literature, one discovers rather quickly that an appreciable part of what we know about the social origins of stress has not come necessarily from work focused on stress. Indeed, prior to the 1960s there was relatively little research directed to any of the naturalistic cause of stress, social or other. There are probably many reasons for this lack. One is certainly that interest in how stress is aroused has been distinctly subordinate to interest in the consequences of stress for organismic functioning. To this day, most stress research is concerned with the response of the various organs and systems of the body to stress, not with the antecedents of the stress.

Researchers who are interested mainly in the effects of stress clearly do not have to depend on its spontaneous or naturalistic occurrence in order to carry out their studies. On the contrary, research into the biological and biochemical functioning of the organism can be conducted much more effectively when the stress is experimentally aroused and controlled in the laboratory. Moreover, the laboratory researcher often decides that animals are better suited than human subjects to his research purposes. The importance of laboratory based work to our understanding of the organismic manifestations of stress hardly needs acknowledgment. But as important as this kind of research is, we are not likely to acquire knowledge about social sources of stress from it.

While the tilt of current research is still prominently in the direction of the consequences of stress, a growing concern with its naturalistic origins can be discerned. In part, this development is linked to the emergence of questions and issues that cannot be dealt with by laboratory based research. In particular, there is a growing interest in the epidemiology of diseases thought to result from stress. The incidence of hypertension, cardiovascular ailments, and depression, to take but a few examples, varies with such factors as race, sex, marital status, and income. This kind of socioeconomic variation of disease indicates that the stresses that presumably dispose people toward these ailments are somehow anchored to the conditions that people confront as they occupy their various positions and statuses in the society. From a public health perspective, it becomes mandatory to identify these conditions, for the eventual control of diseases caused by stress depends on understanding the social etiology of the stress. And, of course, these goals can be accomplished only by moving research out of the laboratory.

The naturalistic sources of stress also have received some attention in several other fields. One is the study of rather cataclysmic events that occasionally befall large collectivities. Studies of disasters and of their effects on populations (e.g., Erikson, 1976) are but one step away, theoretically, from studies of other, less eruptive, naturalistic sources. Another area of research that has stimulated interest in the social origins of stress. Students struggling to satisfy the requirements for the Ph.D. (Mechanic, 1972) and air traffic controllers (Rose, Hurst, & Kreger, 1978), who labor with the constant awareness of the grim consequences of error, are examples of such groups. Next, large-scale studies of the well-being of people living in the community and engaged in ordinary life pursuits have contributed importantly to the interest in stressful conditions of social life (Gurin, Veroff & Feld, 1960; Srole, Langer, Michael, Opler, & Rennie, 1962). Later I shall discuss some of this research in greater detail.

It should be noted, finally, that current social perspectives of the stress process have been reinforced by a sensitivity to the fact that different people experiencing similar life conditions are not necessarily affected in the same manner; i.e., some may be stressed by these conditions and others not. In attempting to account for these differences, researchers have been intensively examining people's access to and use of support systems, along with their coping repertoires. The nature of supports and their distribution along lines of social demarcation have been widely documented (e.g., Brown, 1978). What may be less readily recognized, however, is that individuals' coping repertoires are also appreciably social. That is, the manner in which people attempt to avoid or remedy painful situations, the perceptual and cognitive behaviors they use to reduce threat, and their techniques for managing tensions are largely learned from the groups to which they belong. Although constellations of coping responses may be distinctive for individuals, coping dispositions to a considerable extent are acquired from the social milieu (Pearlin, 1980b; Pearlin & Schooler, 1978).

The history of research into stress, then, is characterized by preoccupation with bodily functioning, a concern that is not dependent on knowledge of the naturalistic sources of stress. This orientation has begun to change as a result of several conditions: greater awareness of the social epidemiology of ailments having a stress etiology; efforts to understand the consequences of disasters; concern with at-risk groups in the society; studies of people in their community settings; and greater attention to the soical influences underlying the mediators of stress, coping, and supports. These developments portend a rapid and rich growth in the future. At present, however, the boundaries of our knowledge about the social causes of stress are somewhat narrow and not always clearly discernible. In describing what is currently known—or assumed—about the social underpinnings of stress, I shall not attempt a detailed canvassing of the diffuse and uneven literature. Instead, I shall seek to convey an understanding of the scope and diversity of the origins of stress. This is a strategy that depends more on the selective presentation of work that will help to exemplify major lines of inquiry than on an exhaustive cataloguing of the literature. The first step toward this task is a brief specification of the concept of stress itself.

STRESS: A CONCEPTUAL GLIMPSE

Almost all stress researchers experience some confusion and despair about the field. Indeed, there is some doubt that the concept of stress is worth preserving. Pearlin, Lieberman, Menaghan & Mullan (1981) suggested that it is not the core meaning of the concept that is confusing, for there is general agreement that *stress* refers to a *response of the organism to a noxious or threatening condition.* The doubt and disagreement arise with regard to where and how to identify this response. Is stress, for example, to be recognized by the functioning of an organ or a system of organs, by biochemical or physiological alterations, by changes in emotional states, or by the presence of disease entities? Is it manifested in short-run reactions of the organism or in long-run dysfunctions? Are people aware of the stress they harbor to the extent that they can report it, or must its presence be determined by independent assays? Is stress a global, encompassing state, or is it confined to situations in which it is aroused? The real problem in understanding stress is not that there are no answers to these questions, but that the answer to each of them is yes. That is, manifestations of stress are found at every level of organismic functioning, from the microbiological to the emotional; stress can be both a short-run response and a pattern that emerges slowly over time; individuals may be keenly aware that they are host to stress, although stress may also be present at a level below consciousness; finally, stress responses can be highly contained and situationally bounded, but they also can develop into a prevailing state that persists through time and extends through space.

It is in the very nature of stress that it can be so many things, and we should not try to reduce the multidimensionality of this phenomenon by arbitrarily declaring that stress is only one thing or another. It is much more productive, I believe, to recognize the diffuse character of the stress phenomenon and to bend our efforts to understanding how its multiple manifestations are interconnected. But it is not likely that this shift will occur quickly, for research into the various ways in which stress can be manifested is closely organized around disciplines, and disciplinary lines are not easily breached. The social scientist is not likely to study the production of steroids, and the endocrinologist is equally unlikely to study the production of depression. Firmly and actively engaged in his chosen research, each investigator is convinced that the manifestations of stress that he is examining represent "real" stress.

My own conviction is that it is prudent to retain the concept of stress despite its problems and shortcomings. It is not unusual in science for the same concept to acquire diverse meaning and to recruit the interest of many disciplines. The confusion that inevitably results is forgivable and should not inhibit continued work at multiple levels.

I turn now to a consideration of what is central to this chapter: social contributions to the arousal of stress.

SOCIAL CONTRIBUTIONS TO PERSONAL STRESS

It is not an easy matter to assemble what is known about stressful social conditions. One major reason for this difficulty is that the sources of stress extend from the most immediate contexts of people's lives to the outermost boundaries of societies and cultures. A detailed treatment of social stressors touches, at one end, on the microenvironments of individuals and, at the other, on large-scale social organization. A second difficulty stems from a somewhat paradoxical source to which I have already alluded: some of the early writing that is highly relevant to social stress paid little attention to social stress. Scholarly work of this type was aimed more often at such matters as social disorganization, deviance, conflict, and racism than at stress per se. Thus, important intellectual roots of the field are planted quite outside the edges of the field.

The vastness and uneven quality of the literature, coupled with the theoretical range of relevant work, require that I be highly selective (and somewhat arbitrary) in the research that I bring into discussion and that I impose some sort of schema to find order in an unruly field. The schema is a simple one. It begins with the broadest sources of stress, those that are thought to reside in the very nature of societies and their cultures; it then narrows to an examination of those stressful conditions that reside within institutional contexts, such as stratification systems, work roles, and family; and, finally, it funnels in still further to examine sources of stress from the perspective of individual experience. Needless to say, the conditions that exist at these different levels are not insulated from one another. Nevertheless, each level can be treated as a separate context out of which stress may grow.

Society as Stressor

The social science literature reveals an established interest in certain overarching features of society that have the potential to arouse stress. Two general themes run through this literature. One calls attention to the faulty integration among systems of cultural values, beliefs, precepts, goals, and aspirations. The second theme also deals with cultural and structural malintegration but emphasizes rapid social change as the inevitable forerunner of such malintegration. I shall first illustrate these themes and then examine the assumptions on which they rest.

Several classical studies viewed society and culture as a reservoir of personal stress and maladjustment. Anthropologists, in particular, have been very sensitive to discrepancies between the real and the ideal, the differences between the principles and beliefs to which a society claims adherence and those that are reflected in the actions of members of the society. To the extent that individuals internalize both the idealized values and the discrepant norms regulating actions, they would presumably be host to inner conflict detrimental to their well-being. Perhaps the most comprehensive study reflecting this perspective was done not by an anthropologist but by a Swedish economist and observer of the United States (Myrdal, Steiner, & Rose, 1944). Myrdal and his collaborators argued that the deep commitment of the nation to an egalitarian ethos contrasted sharply with discriminatory practices directed against blacks. The resulting dilemma, they observed, was deeply imprinted on the character of Americans, residing there as an impediment to be struggled with.

Other scholars have pointed to conflicts that do not involve the uncongeniality of the real and the ideal but result, instead, from discrepancies between the behaviors to which people are socialized as children and those to which they are expected to conform as adults. The well-known work of Benedict (1938) is an outstanding case in point. She observed that boys are taught to be obedient and responsive to the will and directions of their elders and to be sexually neutral. By contrast, adult males are expected to be independent, autonomous, and sexually aggressive. To the extent that these incompatible elements have been incorporated into a man's personality, his inner conflicts presumably will reflect those existing in the society at large.

A third perspective on society as a stressor has influenced sociological orientations to stress more than any other approach has done. This view, embodied in Merton's important essay on "Social Structure and Anomie" (1957), is similar to those outlined above in that Merton, too, was concerned with cultural values, particularly those that emphasize achievement and success. But unlike the others, he was interested less in how continuous or discontinuous these values are with other values than in how the valuation of success fits with the structure of opportunities. Briefly, Merton suggested that the system of values stimulates motivations toward the attainment of monetary and honorific success among more people than could possibly be accommodated by the opportunity structure. Consequently, many of us who internalize the culturally prized success goals are doomed to failure. Failure, in turn, leads on to a variety of possible adaptive and maladaptive modes. For Merton, society stands as a stressor not by presenting uncongenial values but by stimulating values that conflict with the structures in which they are to be acted upon. This is a landmark theory of how people participating in the mainstream systems of social life can be caught between the goals and values to which they have been socialized and the constraints of the structures in which they must act.

The various types of societal conflict and stress that I have sketched may exist during periods of relative stability. It is a fairly common view, however, that stressful conditions are especially likely to arise out of rapid social change. That is, under conditions of profound change the kinds of social conditions I described above are apt to surface at an accelerated pace. When social institutions and the norms and belief systems that support them go through rapid alterations, it grows increasingly likely that people will come to hold mutually antagonistic values, that their early socialization will not be appropriate to the demands of current realities, or that there will be no opportunity structures or institutional contexts that can accommodate the goals and aspirations that have been internalized. In addition, of course, large-scale change can carry with it other problems; people may be physically uprooted, experience a weakening or destruction or social ties, or have an alien culture imposed on or incorporated into their native culture. And, when the social change entails increased industrialization and urbanization, people must obviously shift away from earlier economic activities; established kinship arrangements are often disrupted; and, usually, informal perparation for occupational life gives way to formal and specialized training. It is understandable that profound social change has been of interest to students of stress.

But what are the mechanisms by which social change undermines the will-being of people? Whether one looks at the intensification of value conflicts or at the erosion of established forms of social organization, one assumes a direct, causal tie between upheavals in our external world and those in our inner world. However, the stress that people experience may not be a simple and direct consequence of culture conflict and social disorganization. In this vein, Marris (1974) elucidated a number of indirect pathways through which the deleterious effects of change come about. He pointed out that change can leave people with a sense of loss of control over their own destinies; it can undermine people's ability to predict their futures; it can erode the precepts by which people interpret and derive meaning from experience; and it may engender a profound feeling of loss of the past, leaving people in a bereavementlike state. The adverse effects of change, therefore, do not stem from an inherent proclivity for stability. Such effects may result, instead, from a host of losses produced by the change.

I have suggested that the uncertainties and contradictions that arise in societies, especially during periods of extensive change, can act as precursors of stress. This emphasis, however, should not be interpreted to mean that societal disorganization and change inevitably translate into personal stress. Some conditions can neutralize the effects of the kinds of broad social forces that I have been discussing. And, although relatively little research has been directed at these conditions, it is possible to suggest a few of them. One such condition involves the separation of roles in time and space. Although we are many things—workers, parents, children, religious followers, political participants, and so on—fortunately, we are not all of them simultaneously. To the extent that internalized values are organized around the roles that people play, the spatial and temporal segregation of roles may enable people to avoid direct confrontations among incompatible values. A man can be both a shady businessman and a pious worshiper. And as long as he does not conduct his business in church, he is likely to escape the severe personal dilemma that would otherwise result from his conflicting commitments.

With regard to elements of childhood socialization that are not appropriate to current realities—the kind of discontinuity of which Benedict wrote—there again may be less personal conflict than might be assumed on logical grounds. When we recognize that socialization is a continuous process, occurring not only in childhood but extending over the life span, then we can understand that many of the things we learn early in life go through gradual transformations. Learning to be obedient as young children, for example, does not preclude learning to be assertive as adults; the socialization that occurs later can preempt that which occurred earlier. Consequently, if we compare only early training with later requirements, many discontinuities will appear, but if we take into account all the intervening training that takes place, the process of preparing people for adult roles will appear more continuous. Finally, and more generally, we need to understand how the violation of cherished norms may be supported by other, equally cherished, norms. As Williams (1970) noted, every society provides institutionalized evasions of institutionalized norms. To the extent that our evasions are as acceptable as the norms from which we are departing, whatever conflicts result are probably neither severe nor durable. Clearly, we must be very cautious in judging the stressfulness of societal forces solely on the basis of what appears to be logically reasonable. Societies are both sources of stress and sources of mechanisms by which people avoid stress.

Social Organizations as Stressors

Any society, if it is to survive, must organize its activities and structure the relationships among its collectivities. Social organization varies considerably in scope: it is very extensive, encompassing entire populations, and it is also more limited, involving, for example, elites or members of special communities. In this section I shall be concerned with the more overarching forms of social organization, attempting to convey how formal properties themselves may come to constitute sources of stress. For this purpose I shall first discuss selected aspects of systems of stratification and then turn to a consideration of a few institutionalized features of occupation and family.

In recent years there has been some rather tantalizing research into the stressful consequences of people's locations in stratified economies. Enough evidence has been accumulated to assure us that psychological distress increases linearly with a decrease in income level (e.g., Pearlin & Radabaugh, 1976). Furthermore, a variety of indicators of stress show that economic fluctuations have powerful aftereffects on the psychological functioning of populations (Brenner 1973; Catalano & Dooley, 1977). The struggles and uncertainties of people in lower economic echelons of the society are sources of stress whose importance has not been appreciated fully. If one attempts to trace personal stress back to its societal roots, one it likely to be led eventually to the economic organization of societies.

Societies are stratified along status and power dimensions, as well as along economic lines. The very multidimensional nature of stratification has itself been recognized as a social source of stress. The central point of the substantial literature concerned with this issue is that the consistency of one's standing in the various stratification orders may be as important to stress as is one's position within any one of them. To use an example with which young academics will be familiar, one may enjoy a relatively high occupational status along with an incommensurately low income. This kind of discrepency produces stress presumably because inconsistent statuses produce inconsistent elements of identity. At any rate, a number of studies have found a disproportionate concentration of stress symptoms among people whose standing on one dimension of stratification is higher than their standing on others (e.g., Hornung, 1977; Jackson, 1967). Such symptoms are especially likely to appear, according to Hornung (1978), when the inconsistency is accompanied by aspirations for social advancement. Thus, a woman who has a high income from a low-status occupation may be indifferent to the inconsistency if she is indifferent to status; the same inconsistent circumstances are likely to be more stressful if the person is a status striver.

Occupational settings and their organization represent more closely delineated contexts for stress than do extensive systems of social and economic stratification. This does not mean that their relationships to stress are more simple. On the contrary, overviews of work in this area have revealed that the formal features of occupational settings and their relationships to stress are highly complex (e.g., Gross, 1970). In identifying some of these features, I shall report primarily from the work of Katz and Kahn (1978).

As these workers noted, there are many approaches to identifying those formal aspects of occupational settings that have stressful consequences for their members. One such approach focuses on the various subsystems of occupations. Production is an example of a basic subsystem. The inherent task of production, Katz and Kahn (1978) pointed out, is the enhancement of proficiency, a goal that triggers a number of interlocking conditions leading to stress. Briefly, the achievement of proficiency often depends on increased specialization of work. This aspect of work, in turn, is conducive to overload, monotony, and the absence of variety, all of them seedbeds of stress. There are four additional subsystems: the production supportive, which regulates transactions between the organization and its environment; the maintenance subsystem, which regulates and manages the reward structure; an adaptive structure, which guides changes within the organization in response to changing external conditions; and, finally, the managerial system, which monitors and directs activities. Each subsystem can be viewed as operating in response to its own unique set of imperatives and as being capable of generating its own set of stressful conditions.

Katz and Kahn's (1978) perspectives are interesting and informative in their own right but they are notable also in that they attempt to account for stress strictly in terms of the organizational features of occupational contexts. That is, they identify the sources of occupational stress as inherent in the universal properties of formal organization. Within this conceptual framework, occupational stress can be considered not as something that now and then besets unfortunate workers but as a normal consequence of laboring in organized work settings. From this prespective, the absence, not the presence, of occupational stress is anomalous.

Inevitably, this scanning of institutional sources of stress must come to rest on the family. As in the case of occupation, I wish to identify a few institutionalized aspects of family life that potentially result in stress, a focus that is quite different from that which centers on the individual experiences of family members. Once more, I find it necessary to add the caveat that within these pages it is possible at best to skim a few of the more salient issues. For inclusive reviews, the reader needs to consult other sources (Croog, 1970; Mc-Cubbin, Joy, Canble, Comeau, Patterson, & Needle, 1980).

The family has multiple functions in the stress process. First, within the constellation of social institutions, the family can be seen as the one in which life strains that are engendered elsewhere can be expressed and acted upon most easily. For example, the distress that the alienated worker feels after an unpleasant encounter with his boss may be displaced in an overly punitive reaction to his child's transgressions; one may lose a job, but not family membership, by displaying outrage. Similarly, a child who suffers humiliation on the playground may engage in some puzzling rebelliousness at the dinner table. More than a target for displaced stress, the family is also a source of solace and sympathy when people suffer defeat in the outside world. The family stands in most contemporary societies as the welcoming haven where we can be refreshed and reassured. For many people, home may not be simply the preferred place to turn in times of distress but the only place in which one has access to acceptance and support.

However, even while it soothes and supports, the family also may inflict emotional pain and punishment. Several institutional and structural features of the contemporary family help make it a potential source of stress, as well as a source of succor. First, such factors as urbanization, geographic movement, and class mobility increase the likelihood that marital partners will come from significantly different social and economic backgrounds. An appreciable proportion of marriages, for example, involve partners whose fathers' occupational statuses are unequal. Status inequality by itself seems to be unrelated to marital stress (Pearlin, 1975); however, when the partner who "marries down" also holds values that bespeak a desire for status aggrandizement, marriages of unequal partners then become fertile ground for stress. Whether or not marriage is a source of stress, therefore, depends in part on both the background characteristics that spouses bring to the marriage and the manner in which these characteristics combine with values and aspirations.

One should not infer from this description that the course of marriage is dictated only by what is brought to the marriage at its inception. We know that socialization takes place across the entire life span; consequently, marriage itself is a context for learning and socialization. The relevance of this point for stress is that socialization will not be identical for the marital partners; they probably will change at different rates and in different directions. The inevitable strains produced by these differences can challenge severely the adaptational capacities of the partners. In addition to marital changes that inexorably stem from adult socialization, other equally inexorable changes come with adult role transitions. I refer, of course, to the family cycle and all of the role losses and role gains that it entails—from marrying, through childrearing, and ultimately ending in the death of a spouse. At this time there is an incomplete understanding of the conditions under which life cycle transitions are apt to lead to individual and marital stress. In general, however, it appears that the movement into and out of roles and statuses may result in less marital stress than has been assumed (Menaghan, 1980; Pearlin, 1980a).

The stresses generated within the family context involve parent-child relations, as well as marital relations. Problems with children spring out of a variety of social conditions. For example, one may point to the prolonged period of training required by industrialized societies, to the concomitant extended dependence, and to the parent-child conflict that can be fed by these conditions. Social change also may play a part in this conflict. The ultimate functions of the socialization of children are found not in childhood, but in adulthood. That is, training and rearing practices are directed toward the social roles that children will assume when they are adults, not toward the perfection of childhood behaviors. Parents typically evaluate the current behavior of their children in terms of its consistency with that they perceive as the requirements of their children's future roles. However, parental conceptions of what is good and worth striving after often are different from their children's conceptions. During periods of widespread change and upheaval, these intergenerational differences probably become intensified. Parents are then apt to arrive at the alarming conclusion that their children's course of development diverges from cherished goals. A distressing state, indeed.

Among the rich array of family based stresses are those that exist between adult children and their aged parents. The very people who are contending with the needs of their minor children may be contending at the be same time with the needs of their parents. As longevity is increased, this becomes a fairly common circumstance, one that is winning growing attention from researchers (Lieberman, 1978; Troll, 1971). Some of the strains and problems that can arise from the relations between aged parents and their adult children are self-evident. When there is debilitating illness or a decline in physical self-sufficiency, or when parents' economic resources are not adequate to their needs, a turnabout in the parent-child relationship may occur. Adult children at first may assume more of a peer relationship with their parents but, as problems continue, go on to assume a larger degree of responsibility for the latter's material, legal, and emotional well-being. The turnabout clearly has the potential for arousing stress; the adult child may find it a drain on energy, on emotions, and on resources; the aged parent, on the other hand, may find that this new dependence violates his desire for autonomy and self-direction. The internal conflicts of each party easily can develop into a conflict between the parties.

In sum, I have dealt in this section with ways in which people's actions and relationships are organized, looking specifically at the hierarchical ordering of people in stratification systems; the structuring of work and work tasks; and the network of family relations and their changes across the life course. I have sought to call attention to an important issue: people who are engaged in the mainstream institutional life of the society can be stressed as a sheer result of the organizational arrangements of these institutions and the changes that normally occur within them. From a social perspective, stress is not the consequence of bad luck, unfortunate encounters, or unique circumstances. It is, instead, the consequence of engagement in social institutions whose very structures and functioning can engender and sustain patterns of conflict, confusion, and distress.

STRESSFUL EXPERIENCES

Thus far, I have tried to indicate how the properties of societies and their institutions can evoke stress. Eventually, however, the researcher needs to ask how institutional conditions are incorporated into individual experience. Individual experience, of course, is ultimately inseparable from the larger social circumstances that I have been discussing. Nevertheless, in order to understand how these circumstances penetrate the lives of people, we must shift our focus from a societal and institutional to an individual level.

My own research into stress and coping is pitched largely at this level, and I shall be drawing on this research for much of the discussion here. Essentially, I distinguish two broad classes of experience, that which is eventful and that which is repeated or continuous. Both types of experience are likely to arise within the institutional settings of the society. That is, to a large extent, experience is organized around the roles and statuses we have as workers, spouses, parents, children, friends, and neighbors. This is not to say that people are never overtaken by events or confronted by continuing problems outside these roles. Anyone who has been the victim of a mugger or who daily sits in slow moving commuter traffic can attest to the ubiquitous nature of stressful experience. Nevertheless, because so much behavior is organized around major social roles, it is here that one is able to discover patterns of stressful experience.

Eventful experiences and their consequences for stress have been the focus of considerable research, much of it stimulated by the development of the Social Readjustment Rating Scale (Holmes & Rahe, 1967). This research has been subjected to a good deal critical scrutiny (e.g., Dohrenwend & Pearlin, 1981), which need not be recapitulated here. What I would like to emphasize about life events studies is that they increasingly regard the stressful impact of events as depending more on the quality of the events than solely on the magnitude of the changes they entail. The voluntary or involuntary character of events is one quality that has been addressed. Another quality, perhaps the most commonly considered, concerns the desirability of events. A third distinction, one that we have found useful (Pearlin & Lieberman, 1979), is between scheduled and unscheduled events. I shall explicate briefly the nature of this distinction.

Scheduled events are those that have, in advance, a high probability of occurrence. We may not know precisely when they will emerge, but we have a fair degree of certainty that they will emerge. Events of this type derive their scheduled character from being an inherent part of the life cycle; that is, they are found in those family and career transitions that represent the junctures between life stages (Lowenthal, Thurnher, Chiriboga, & Associates, 1975). Transitions typically involve the separation from one role or status and/or entrance into another. Marriage, having children, the movement of children toward their own eventual launching from the parental home, grandparenthood, retirement, and death of a spouse are scheduled transitional events.

On the face of the far-reaching life changes that are involved in many scheduled events, one could reasonably expect them to be stressful. Certainly, some transitional events entail a rather profound reorganization of life. Yet, our own work generally has indicated that there is no notable association between experiencing this kind of life event and manifesting symptoms of stress (Pearlin & Lieberman, 1979). It would be premature to discount scheduled events as antecedents of stress, but it is tempting to speculate that the very forecastable nature of scheduled events helps to minimize what would otherwise be their considerable stressful impact. Because these events can be foreseen long before their occurrence, they may be preceded by a great deal of anticipatory coping. By the time we actually assume a new role, we may already have considerable understanding of its demands. If transitional events are not clearly related to stress, therefore, it may be because of the coping that was initiated years before the person actually confronted the transition.

It is a different story with *unscheduled events*. Although events of this type do not always descend upon us without prior warning, they are not built into our set of expectations, as in the case of scheduled events. Divorce, injury and illness, job disruption, premature death, and ruptured friendships are examples of unscheduled events. In contrast to those that are scheduled, these events are notably associated with stress (Pearlin & Lieberman, 1979). One may wonder, too, whether they also differ from scheduled events in their sensitivity to different kinds of coping and social support interventions. I suspect that unscheduled crises, more than events having a long and explicit prelude, are likely to mobilize social supports and short-run coping responses. Obviously, these are questions that at this point in time are easier to raise than to answer.

Despite the unanswered questions, it is possible to underscore some promising gains being made by current research into the effects of eventful experience. First, it is obvious from my discussion of life events that there is a movement away from a concern with eventful change per se and a commensurately greater concern with identifying the quality of those events that are likely to exert a stressful impact. As far as emotional stress is concerned, eventful experiences are not equally provocative. Those that are voluntary, desired, or scheduled have no apparent emotional consequences; involuntary, undesired, and unscheduled events do.

Another area in which there are hints of progress involves the possibility that different kinds of eventful experience may call out different adaptive modes. As I noted previously, successful adjustment to scheduled or transitional experiences may rely on anticipatory coping and preparation to a considerable extent, while successful adjustment to eruptive events may depend more on the ability of people both to mobilize quickly an array of coping responses and to utilize various support measures. Future research into stress and coping can be expected to look more closely for a fit between types of eventful experience and types of mediators people can invoke to meet such contingencies.

Finally, research probably will be increasingly sensitive to the links between the emergence of particular events in the lives of people and life course processes. Life events are amenable to a number of conceptual classifications, but one of the particularly useful features of the scheduled-unscheduled distinction is that it helps to clarify how many events are systematically distributed along the life span. In general, research into eventful experiences as antecedents of stress will benefit by viewing the events within the organization of people's lives through time, not by treating them as temporally happenstance occurrences. We need to know how the stressful events one experiences as a young person become the contingencies for the events one will experience as an older person.

The second major type of stressful experience, it will be recalled, is that which is *repeated* or *chronic*. Efforts to identify the persistent experiences that are built into the fabric of daily life have been overshadowed somewhat in recent years by the burgeoning interest in life events. This disparity cannot be explained by the relative stressfulness of events and chronic strains. On the contrary, it appears that the latter exert a more powerful stressful impact than the former. Thus, we have been able to identify persistent elements of marital relations, of parent-child relations, and of occupational experience that bear a close association with various indicators of stress (Pearlin & Lieberman, 1979). If one were interested only in the more potent sources of stress, one would devote more attention to chronic stress and far less to life events.

However, we have learned that the parts played by life events and by chronic strains as sources of stress are understood most clearly by observing them together rather than by regarding them as separate and unrelated antecedents (Pearlin, Lieberman, Menaghan, & Mullan, 1981). Concretely, events—especially undesired, unscheduled events—arouse stress indirectly by changing adversely the conditions of life with which people must live. Let us take as an example the involuntary disruption of work. This is an event that has a moderately strong statistical relationship to symptoms of stress, but the relationship is explained largely by the effect of the event on the economic resources of people. That is, the life event contributes to stress through its negative effect on economic circumstances, an ongoing feature of one's world. If these two causes of stress were looked at separately, we would fail to see how they come together in a unitary process. Indeed, the challenge of future research is to understand how the antecedents of stress, its mediators, and its symptoms converge to constitute the stress process.

CONCLUSION

Perhaps the most salient message to be taken from this chapter is that the array of social sources of personal stress is highly diverse and ranges from the very distal to the very proximal. These sources may be seen as including some of the central features of society itself: its value systems, the stratified ordering of its populations, the organization of its institutions, and the rapidity and extent of changes in these elements.

Sources of stress also can be identified in the direct experiences of individuals. Both eventful experience, involving undesirable, unscheduled or involuntary change, and continuing experience, involving persistent problems within social roles, can be powerful conditions for stress. Although the empirical demonstration of the stressful consequences of some of these sources is far from convincing, overall we can be quite certain that stress is indeed often rooted in the social contexts in which individuals are engaged.

There is little reason to rest with the present state of our knowledge about the social origins of stress. First, as I noted, some of this knowledge is more putative than convincingly documented. But beyond the obvious need to be less assertive and more empirical in drawing out the connections between social life and stress, there is other work to be done. I would emphasize in particular the need to move away from attempts to identify separate sources of stress to the specification of the process leading to stress. Some start has been made in this direction in our own research, which shows the confluence of life events, chronic strains, and self-concept in producing stress. What is not sufficiently known is how life events and role strains themselves stem from broad-scale social and institutional organization and their changes. Not all personal stress can be traced to social contexts, of course, and not all problems in these contexts necessarily result in stress. However, if we are to understand personal problems as an expression of social problems, then we also must understand the processes by which features of our social system become transformed into features of the emotional interiors of individuals.

REFERENCES

BENEDICT, R. Continuities and incontinuities in cultural conditioning. *Psychiatry,* 1938, *2,* 161–170.

BRENNER, M. H. *Mental illness and the economy.* Cambridge: Harvard University Press, 1973.

BROWN, B. Social and psychological correlates of help-seeking behavior among urban adults. *American Journal of Community Psychology,* 1978, *6,* 425–439.

CATALANO, R., & DOOLEY, D. Economic predictors of depressed mood and stressful life events in a metropolitan community. *Journal of Health and Social Behavior,* 1977, *18,* 292–307.

CROOG, S. H. The family as a source of stress. In S. Levine & N. A. Scotch (eds.), *Social stress.* Chicago: Aldine, 1970.

DOHRENWEND, B., & PEARLIN, L. I. *Report of the panel on life events.* Washington, D.C.: Institute of Medicine, 1981.

ERIKSON, K. T. *Everything in its path: Destruction of community in the Buffalo Creek flood.* New York: Simon & Schuster, 1976.

GROSS, E. Work, organization, and stress. In S. Levine & N. A. Scotch (eds.), *Social stress*. Chicago: Aldine, 1970.

GURIN, G., VEROFF, J., & FELD, S. *Americans view their mental Health*. New York: Basic Books, 1960.

HOLMES, T. H., & RAHE, R. H. The Social Readjustment Rating Scale. *Journal of Psychosomatic Research*, 1967, *11*, 213–218.

HORNUNG, C. A. Social status, status inconsistency, and psychological stress. *American Sociological Review*, 1977, *42*, 623–628.

————. Status inconsistency, importance of getting ahead, and psychological stress. In A. Rappaport (ed.), *Avoiding social catastrophes and maximizing social opportunities*. Washington, D.C.: Society for General Systems Research, 1978.

JACKSON, E. H. Status consistency and symptoms of stress. *American Sociological Review*, 1967, *27*, 469–480.

KATZ, D., & KAHN, R. *The social psychology of organizations* (2d ed.). New York: Wiley, 1978.

LIEBERMAN, G. Children of the elderly as natural helpers: Some demographic differences. *American Journal of Community Psychology*, 1978, *6*, 489–498.

LOWENTHAL, F. F., THURNHER, M., CHIRIBOGA, D., & ASSOCIATES. *Four stages of life: A comparative study of women and men facing transitions*. San Francisco: Jossey-Bass, 1975.

MARRIS, P. *Loss and change*. London: Routledge & Kegan Paul, 1974.

McCUBBIN, H. I., JOY, C. B., CANBLE, A. E., COMEAU, J. K., PATTERSON, J. M., & NEEDLE, R. H. Family stress and coping: A decade review. *Journal of Marriage and the Family*, 1980, *42*, 855–871.

MECHANIC, D. *Students under stress*. New York: Free Press, 1972.

MENAGHAN, E. Assessing the impact of family transitions on marital experience: Problems and prospects. Doctoral dissertation, University of Chicago, 1980.

MERTON, R. K. Social structure and anomie. In R. K. Merton (ed.), *Social theory and social structure* (2d ed.). New York: Free Press, 1957.

MYRDAL, G., STEINER, R., & ROSE A. *An American dilemma*, vol 1. New York: Harper, 1944.

PEARLIN, L. I. Status inequality and stress in marriage. *American Sociological Review*, 1975, *40*, 344–357.

————. The life cycle and life strains. In H. M. Blalock, Jr. (ed.), *Sociological theory and research: A critical approach*. New York: Free Press, 1980.

————. Life-strains and psychological distress among adults. In N. J. Smelser & E. H. Erikson (eds.), *Themes of love and work in adulthood*. Cambridge: Harvard University Press, 1980.

PEARLIN, L. I., & LIEBERMAN, M. A. Social sources of emotional distress. In R. Simmons (ed.), *Research in community and mental health*, vol. 1. Greenwich: JAI, 1979.

PEARLIN, L. I., LIEBERMAN, M. A., MENAGHAN, E. G., & MULLAN, J. T. The stress process. *Journal of Health and Social Behavior*, 1981, *22*, 337–356.

PEARLIN, L. I., & RADABAUGH, C. Economic strains and the coping functions of alcohol. *American Journal of Sociology*, 1976, *82*, 652–663.

PEARLIN, L. I., & SCHOOLER, C. The structure of coping. *Journal of Health and Social Behavior*, 1978, *19*, 2–21.

ROSE, R. M., HURST, M. W., & KREGER, B. E. Predictors of hypertension in air traffic controllers: A prospective study. *Psychosomatic Medicine*, 1978, *40*, 86.

SROLE, L., LANGNER, T. S., MICHAEL, S. T., OPLER, M. K., & RENNIE, T. A. C. *Mental health in the metropolis*. New York: McGraw-Hill, 1962.

TROLL, L. The family in later life: A decade review. *Journal of Marriage and Family Living*, 1971, *33*, 263–290.

WILLIAMS, R. M., JR. *American Society* (3d ed.). New York: Knopf, 1970.

23

Stress as a Consequence of the Urban Physical Environment

Robert D. Kaminoff   Harold M. Proshansky

IN THIS CHAPTER OUR PRIMARY CONCERN is with stress that is experienced by individuals as a consequence of their urban physical environments, or what is sometimes referred to as the *built environment*. Our approach to these problems is rooted in the thinking and orientation of the environmental psychologist. This approach is not only problem focused and inter-disciplinary in its conceptual orientation but is real world oriented as well (cf Proshansky, 1976). To meet such requirements, environmental psychology is rooted in a methodology that embraces the physical environment of this world in all its complexity. In effect, the integrity of that experience we call human stress, as well as the physical and social environmental events that produce it, must be zealously guarded and maintained. Thus, laboratory research on human stress can never become a substitute for holistic longitudinal or cross-sectional methods in the field. It can, however, serve as a vehicle for testing out relationships between particular variables that allow themselves to be measured in the laboratory setting with a minimum of distortion.

The question of definition now arises: how is stress to be defined? By *stress* we mean that pattern of psychological, behavioral, and physiological responses of the individual to demands of the physical and social environment that exceed his capacity to cope effectively, that is, to carry out activities, realize goals, and experience satisfactions. Human stress can never be conceptualized meaningfully, however, by references to objective environmental conditions or measurable behavioral outcomes alone. Stress can and does occur without awareness of discomfort, as well as with such awareness. Similarly, the individual may or may not be conscious of precipitating environmental conditions or long-term personal consequences. Stress can sometimes be described in precise physical and phenomenological terms, but sometimes it cannot. Sometimes it is evident in the behavior of the individual, while at other times there is no direct, overt manifestation. Finally, the extent to which physiological, psychological, and behavioral factors are involved in stress may themselves vary.

THEORETICAL FRAMEWORK

Sources of human stress directly related to properties of urban settings are almost self-evident: intense noise, overcrowded spaces and places, air pollution, physical setting monotony and/or ambiguity and complexity, travel and distance obstacles, light and temperature extremes, fire, crime and safety problems, as well as many others. Yet to understand how, when, and why these environmental events induce stress in an individual, it is necessary that we establish the importance of several environmental needs and coping strategies that are central to the day-to-day functioning of the individual. What is critical in this regard is the extent to which the environment is either congruent or incongruent with what a person or group needs at a particular time and place to pursue immediate and long-term goals in the setting. The more that environment deviates from such personal or collective requirements, the more demanding it becomes and the greater the potential for stress to be experienced (Proshansky, Nelson-Shulman, & Kaminoff, 1979; Stokols, 1979; Zimring, 1981). From such an analysis of person-environment relationships, we should be better able to understand not only how and when individuals experience their physical settings as stressful but also how and to what extent they are capable of either adjusting to or exerting control over their environments in order to reduce the discrepancy between environmental conditions and personal requirements; that is, the degree to which they can mitigate both the experience and the consequences of stress.

Environmental Needs

We begin with the simple and safe assumption that no two individuals can occupy the same space at one point in time. Each of us must have a *personal space*—that "bubble" of least space that the individual requires in and around himself to maintain his physical and psychological integrity, thereby providing a physical boundary between the self and others (Hall, 1966; Sommer, 1969). As each individual stands, sits, or walks in a given path, he establishes—for longer or shorter periods of time—his personal space. The violation of an individual's personal space may directly produce pain for that individual and/or it may interfere with his ability to satisfy other social and physical needs. These kinds of effects of personal space invasion may be responsible for some *crowding* experiences, a critical and prevalent source of stress in most urban settings (Worchel, 1978).

That the individual has spatially related needs that go well beyond maintaining and protecting the relatively small bubble of personal space is evidenced by the human need for *privacy,* the ability to control unwanted stimuli. The individual may seek to achieve and maintain privacy for a number of reasons (Altman, 1975; Jourard, 1966; Laufer, Proshansky, & Wolfe, 1974; Westin, 1967). Most individuals need privacy to reflect upon past experiences, as well as to plan and rehearse future actions. It is also a requirement for the development of intimate relationships. Finally, privacy is needed to maintain distinctions among various role requirements, to engage in rational thought and creative fantasy, and to develop and maintain one's identity.

Privacy can involve either control over stimulation emanating from the environment (e.g., presence of other people, noise) or control over the disclosure of information about oneself (e.g., one's facial expressions, views, past history) and one's physical setting (e.g., messy room), or both. A number of critical issues are involved in the individual's experience of privacy. First, whether privacy is achieved by physically separating oneself from unwanted stimulation (e.g., closing a door) or through psychological means (e.g., withdrawing into oneself while stimuli are present), questions concerning the nature of the physical environment are always relevant. Second, desired levels of privacy and how they are achieved are determined both by social norms and by the individual's personal needs, goals, activities, abilities, and expectations. Thus, different people—as members of different cultures and as unique individuals—not only require varying amounts and types of privacy but are also socialized to achieve privacy in very different ways (cf. Rapoport, 1975).

Conceptually, the relationship between personal space and human privacy expresses the person's need to control his physical environment as a means of maintaining and protecting the identity of self through the satisfaction of a host of physical and social needs. If this assumption is correct, then a more spatially focused and encompassing environmental need or disposition is required, and, indeed, the concept of territoriality expresses this broader conceptual linkage. By *territoriality* we mean people's need to define, defend, or preserve places and spaces for themselves and the exercise of control over such space. Territories may be held on a very temporary basis (e.g., a spot on a movie line), on an intermittent basis (e.g., the space around one's desk at work) or on a relatively permanent basis (e.g., one's home). They may be held by individuals (e.g., a room) or by groups (e.g., a neighborhood). However large or small the territory or the time duration for which it is held, it is crucial that the individual or group occupying the territory can exert enough control over it to realize ongoing purposes, ranging from work and social interactions, to the need for privacy, sleep, and safety.

Whether to establish a territory, preserve personal space, or seek and maintain privacy, the person as a cognizant, feeling, goal-directed individual must successfully transact with the physical world. To achieve such success the person must obtain appropriate environmental skills. Thus, before we can orient ourselves in spaces, find our way through places, and use settings effectively, we must first understand them. *Environmental understanding* represents the sum of the individual's cognition about how a setting works. Knowing, of course, is not enough. We must also have *environmental competence,* the ability to move through, use, and indeed exert control over the physical environment in order to accomplish our goals. However, to understand and to be competent in his physical setting, the person must not only feel secure about himself but also about the environment. *Environmental security* refers to the extent to which the individual feels safe in his physical setting, free of anxiety and fear of events, people, or changes that might harm him. It is evident that understanding one's physical setting, feeling secure in it, and being competent in using it are three interrelated psychological processes. However much we understand and are competent in a physical setting, if it becomes threatening, that understanding and competence will be reduced because of anxieties and fears that tend to decrease what we know about and are able to do in the environment. Similarly, achieving competence in and understanding of a physical setting contributes to developing environmental security in that setting.

The fact that the real attributes and symbolic meanings provided by the physical environment may have a significance that reaches the very core of personality is reflected in the concept of place-identity (Proshansky & Kaminoff, 1981). *Place-identity* is that particular structure of the self-identity of the individual that consists of ideas, memories, beliefs, feelings, and attitudes about spaces, places, and their objects that define from moment to moment and over time who and what the person is. Places and spaces and their attributes—as well as social groups, roles, and relationships—serve to establish the self-identity of each person. In effect, the subjective sense of self is defined and expressed not simply by our identification with particular social roles and groups but also by the various physical settings that frame our daily lives.

The concepts we have discussed up to this point are essentially person-environment analytical tools that focus on the psychological properties of the *person* that relate particularly to his physical world. Clearly, to understand stress induced by this world it is necessary to expand our framework to include relational concepts that focus on the properties of physical settings. Thus, the satisfaction of privacy, personal space, or other environmental needs will depend both on the environmental skills of the person and on the details of the physical setting and what is going on it it. This brings us to the broad conception of person-environment fit.

Person-Environment Fit

The concept of *person-environment fit,* or *congruence,* is not new to discusions relating people to their physical settings. However, only recently has it been explicitly applied to analyses of human stress (Stokols, 1979; Zimring, 1981). This concept is generally used to describe the extent to which an environment accommodates, facilitates, or supports the needs and relevant behaviors of the individuals and groups who occupy and use it. We would define *maximal fit* as a person-environment relationship in which individuals and groups can pursue their goals with maximal support and minimal interference from the physical environment; conversely, with *minimal fit* people receive least support and maximum interference from the environment.

Lack of fit between the properties of the physical environment and the requirements of the person may induce stress in that person by creating demands that exceed his ability to cope and still pursue other goals in the setting. The extent to which there is a lack of fit between people and their environment, the degree to which this disparity induces stress in a given individual, and the way people attempt to reduce discrepancies between personal needs and environmental features all appear to be influenced by the complex interaction of three broad classes of determinants: (1) properties of the physical environment; (2) characteristics of the social system; and (3) attributes of the individual. Of course, none of these classes of determinants influences the person in isolation from the others. On the contrary, it is the compatibility of a particular physical environment with the individual's personal requirements and goals, given the norms operating in the particular social system, that ultimately determines the degree of fit or misfit.

A number of physical setting properties have clear implications for person-environment fit. In the context of an urban existence, or a built environment, the nature and intensity of *environmental stimulation,* including the extent to which it can be predicted and controlled, assumes considerable importance. Whether we think of light, sound, smell, heat, or cold, their particular nature and intensity has consequences for the person's goal achievement in a given physical setting. Spaces also vary in their *boundedness;* that is, the extent to which architectural barriers restrict and direct stimulation and movement. The *scale,* or relative size, of places and spaces also influences the behavior and experience of the individual and therefore the fit between his properties and those of the physical setting. Two other physical setting characteristics should be specified: first, the degree of *flexibility* of the setting—a factor that may increase the possibilities of fit—and second, the *clarity and appropriateness of meanings* provided by the physical environment.

Physical settings are, of course, also social settings; thus, such factors as *social-cultural norms* underlying the use and allocation of space influence person-environment fit. A group's *size, composition,* and *orientation* also may have such influence.

Finally, person-environment fit is related to *characteristics of the individual:* personality attributes, past experience, status, sex, stage in life cycle, as well as the environmental skills and needs we cited earlier. Individual factors have implications for person-environment fit largely through their influence upon environmental preferences and requirements, as well as through the potential they represent for environmental control.

The various levels of concepts that organize our theoretical framework for understanding the development of stress in relation to the physical environment are inextricably related, and it is not difficult to demonstrate these relationships. For example, environmental stimulation may be perceived as more or less intense depending on both cultural norms for noise and the personality of the individual. In the event that highly intense stimulation is perceived as such by the person, the individual may be motivated to obtain privacy or otherwise exert control over this stimulation. But such responses in turn depend on his environmental skills, e.g., competence and security, and no less so on the other properties of the physical setting in which the noise occurs. The flexibility of this setting, its boundedness, its size, and its differentiation, as well as the norms that pertain to its organization and use, may all contribute to the extent to which the person can escape from or even control the intense stimulation so that whatever stress is involved can be reduced or diminished.

Environmentally Induced Stress, Adaptation, and Control

Lack of fit between attributes of the physical environment and the individual's personal requirements may create demands that exceed the individual's capacity to cope and still realize goals in the setting and thereby induce stress in the individual. To the extent that stress is experienced, the individual is motivated to reduce the discrepancy between negatively perceived aspects of the environment and his own personal requirements. This can be accomplished by either adapting himself to the environment or exerting control over it. Both forms of discrepancy reduction entail change, but whereas *adaptation* refers to a change in either the individual's own perception or behavior, *control* entails bringing about a change either in the physical environment or in the behavior of others. Thus, faced with excessive amounts of noise while trying to concentrate on a task, the office worker may try to reduce this lack of fit in four basic ways. He might close his door (exerting physical control) or get others to be quiet (exerting social control). Alternatively, if features of the environment and/or social system preclude these changes, the individual may try to try to modify his own perception by tuning out the noise or by abandoning the task at hand in favor of one that requires less concentration. If these adaptations are not possible, he may simply leave the setting as a way of eliminating the stress involved. Frequently, people compromise their own behavior or experience, even of some degree of control is exerted over the environment; for instance, closing the door may alleviate noise distractions but also make the office hot and stuffy for the occupant or restrict a desirable view.

Whether control or adaptation occurs depends both upon the *change potential* of the physical and social environment and upon the individual's own *perceived control* over environmental events. Environments that are comprehensible, flexible, and predictable are generally more subject to change or control than those that are confusing, rigid, or random. The individual's own perception of environmental control is related to his self-perceptions involving environmental competence, environmental security, and environmental understanding. Through past experience with trying to reduce the discrepancy between desired and actual environmental features (environmentally induced stress), we may increase our understanding of features of the physical environment that render it controllable (e.g., doors, dimmer switches, furniture arrangements). We may also learn about features of the social system that may permit or prohibit our exerting control (e.g., norms, rules, status hierarchies), as well as about our own ability to change either the environment or the behavior of others. Much of this depends upon our evaluations and attributions of past successes and failures in trying to reduce discrepancies between desired and actual attributes of the environment, as well as upon the evaluations and attributions that are made by others in the social system.

ENVIRONMENTAL STIMULATION

The modern city dweller is bombarded with an inordinate array of physical, social, and information bearing stimuli. It is small wonder, then, that the concept of environmental stimulation has dominated the literature concerning environmentally induced stress. Linkages between various levels of environmental stimulation—what we would define as the spatial and temporal density of physical, informational, and social stimuli—and measures of physiological, psychological, and social pathology have been investigated by biologists, ecologists, ethologists, psychologists, physicians, sociologists, geographers, anthropologists, politicians, and still others. By now it is clear that stress can result either from too *little* stimulation, as documented by studies of sensory deprivation (Goldberger, this volume; Lilly, 1977; Riesen, 1975; Suedfeld, 1981; Zubek, 1969) and social isolation (Haggard, 1973; Suedfeld, 1974), or from too *much* stimulation, such as that produced by noise (Broadbent, 1978; Cohen & Weinstein, 1981; Jones, Chapman, & Auburn, 1981; Kryter, 1970), crowding (D'Atri, 1975; Epstein, 1981; Evans, 1979; Sundstrom, 1978), high temperatures (Bell, 1981; Griffitt & Veitch, 1971; Wilkinson et al, 1964), and air pollution (Evans & Jacobs, 1981; Lave & Seskin, 1970).

Such findings have led some theorists to suggest that for each individual there is an optimal level of stimulation, lying between the two extremes, that maximizes human task performance, cognitive functioning, developmental growth, physiological health, and aesthetic pleasure (Berlyne, 1960; Fiske & Maddi, 1961; Wohlwill, 1974). Since the urban environment is generally characterized by high, rather than low, levels of environmental stimulation, we will focus on *overstimulation* in this section. Moreover, we will give emphasis in our review to the two problems that have received the greatest amount of theoretical and empirical attention: noise and crowding.

Level of Stimulation

A review of the literature quickly reveals that knowing the level of a particular form of stimulation is not enough to predict whether or not that stimulation will produce stress for any given individual. Thus, whereas high noise levels have frequently been associated with lowered task performance (Boggs & Simon, 1968; Bronzcraft & McCarthy, 1975; Cohen, Glass, & Singer, 1973; Hockey, 1970), reduced helping behavior (Mathews & Cannon, 1975; Page, 1977), as well as various health problems ranging from nervousness, sleep difficulties, and headaches (Kokokusha, 1973) to increased blood pressure (Parvizpoor, 1976), elevated cholesterol levels (Khomulo, Rodinova, & Rusinova, 1967), and cardiac arrest (Capellini & Moroni, 1974), others have not found significant correlations (Gattoni & Tarnopolsky, 1973; Stevens, 1972).

Similarly, although the majority of studies investigating the effects of high concentrations of people have found crowding to be associated with one or more measures of physiological arousal (Aiello, Epstein, & Karlin, 1975; D'Atri, 1975; Saegert, 1975), social withdrawal (Bickman and associates 1973; Hutt & Vaizey, 1966; Valins & Baum, 1973), and various physical, psychological, and social pathologies (Dean, Pugh, & Gunderson, 1975; Levy & Herzog, 1975; McCain, Cox, & Paulus, 1976; Schmitt, 1966), others have found no such density effects (Freedman, Klevansky, & Ehrlich, 1971; Schmitt, 1963; Stokols, Rall, Pinner, & Schopler, 1973; Winsborough, 1965).

These contradictory findings have led many to suggest that it is not environmental stimulation per se that induces human stress (except extreme levels that inflict physiological damage) but the interaction of various physical, social, and individual factors. For each form of potential stressor it is thus necessary to distinguish between the objective level of physical stimulation that is impinging upon the individual and the individual's subjective psychological experience of that stimulation (Cohen & Weinstein, 1981; Kryter, 1970; Rapoport, 1975; Saegert, 1978; Stokols, 1972). Thus, whereas the terms "sound" and "density" refer to objective, physically defined levels of environmental stimulation, "noise" and "crowding" are psychological concepts that refer to the human perception and experience of such stimulation. Whether or not a given level of sound is experienced as noise or a particular density level is perceived as crowding depends upon other characteristics of the stimulus situation, as well as upon characteristics of the individual, the social system, and the setting (Lazarus, 1966; Rapoport, 1975; Stokols, Rall, Pinner, & Schopler, 1973). It is evident in this respect that the development of place-identity in the person, based on his continuing physical socialization from birth onward, must necessarily include his sound versus noise and density versus crowding conceptions.

Before reviewing the extensive empirical literature on the role the factors noted above, e.g., social system and setting, may play in moderating the individual's experience of stressful stimulation, it is necessary briefly to note the diversity of theoretical positions concerning how and why high levels of stimulation may lead to stress. Theories of noise vary in the extent to which they attribute decrements in task performance and negative affective states to heightened arousal (Broadbent, 1971), cognitive overload (Cohen, 1978), or distraction and interference (Poulton, 1979). Each of these theorists also attempted to explain the decrements in task performance that may *follow* exposure to noise (Glass & Singer, 1972). Whereas Broadbent (1971) talked about "learned helplessness" and Cohen (1978) about "cognitive fatigue," Poulton (1979) attributed such aftereffects to decreases in arousal that may follow the termination of noise.

With regard to theories of crowding, a distinction can be made between social overload models and behavioral constraint models (cf. Stokols, 1976). *Social overload models,* such as those proposed by Altman (1975), Valins and Baum (1973), Desor (1972), Milgram (1970), and Saegert (1973), suggest that crowding is stressful to the extent that it creates excessive or unwanted levels of social stimulation. *Behavioral constraint models*—such as those proposed by Freedman (1975), Proshansky, Ittelson, and Rivlin (1970), Stokols (1972), and Worchel (1978)—emphasize the restrictions that high concentrations of people impose upon the individual's behavioral freedom. In an effort to reconcile these contrasting theoretical perspectives, Saegert (1973) argued that the two sets of theories address two distinct components of density: high levels of *social density,* defined as the total number of people present in a setting, are more likely to induce a state of social overload than one of behavioral constraint; conversely, high levels of *spatial density,* the amount of space available per person, are more likely to result in behavioral constraint than in social overload. Now that we have at least mentioned the diversity of theoretical points of view, it is time to specify the conditions under which exposures to high levels of environmental stimulations leads to stress. In the remainder of this chapter, we will examine how various physical, social, and individual factors may moderate the experience and consequences of environmentally induced stress.

Stimulus Characteristics

Predictability and Controllability. The degree to which environmental stimulation is perceived to be predictable and controllable influences the extent to which it induces stress in the individual (Averill, 1973; Cohen, Glass, & Phillips, 1979). Noise that is unpredictable and uncontrollable has been found to produce poorer task performance and lower tolerance to frustration (Glass & Singer, 1972), as well as less helping behavior (Sherrod & Downs, 1974) and more aggression (Donnerstein & Wilson, 1976) than noise that is predictable and controllable. Cohen (1978) suggested that unpredictable stimuli are especially stress inducing because of their informational properties; that is, they place greater attentional demands on the individual's information processing capacities than do predictable stimuli, which lend themselves more easily to habituation.

It should be evident that the past place-identity experiences and current environmental skills of the person may also play a role in determining the extent to which a particular stimulus configuration is experienced as predictable or controllable. Whereas the ability to predict stimulus events requires environmental understanding, the ability to exert contol over such events depends on the person's environmental competence. Moreover, if unwanted stimuli are neither predictable nor controllable by the person, then clearly a decrease in environmental security may be the first consequence leading to stress. Sherrod (1974) suggested that the perception of stimulus control may be especially important: when subjects in this laboratory study had the option to leave a crowded room, they suffered less crowding stress than those who were not given this option. Individual factors related to perceived and actual control over the environment—such as personality dispositions, past experience, and life cycle stage—will be explored later in the chapter.

Meaning. The meanings communicated by a potential stressor have implications for whether or not an event or condition is indeed deemed stressful (Cohen, 1978; Lazarus, 1966). For example, the sounds of police and fire sirens, which signal dangers or emergencies, are considered more distressing than the sounds of church bells, which communicate peace and serenity (Southworth, 1969). The extent to which *social* meanings are communicated appears to be particularly important. Office workers consistently report being bothered more by noise generated by people conversing with one another than by noise emanating from office equipment (Brookes & Kaplan, 1972; Harris, 1978; Kaminoff and associates, 1980; Nemecek & Grandjean, 1973). Ostensibly, employees habitually tune out the more predictable and less informative machine noise, whereas their ability to understand what is being said in conversations leads them to direct their attention to speech sounds and they are therefore more apt to be distracted from their work.

Saegert (1978) noted that high population densities are particularly taxing to the individual's information processing system because of the social nature of the information provided by the people involved. The behavior of other people is generally less predictable and more socially meaningful than the patterns generated by strictly physical sources of stimulation. Moreover, the individual who is in a socially stimulating situation, in addition to choosing and carrying out his own course of action, must coordinate his behavior with that of others. This is why the composition and normative structure of the group may mediate the perception and the effects of crowding in high-density situations (Epstein, 1981).

Characteristics of the Social System

Group Composition and Orientation. Being with familiar and/or similar others renders people's behavior and physical characteristics more predictable (Rapoport, 1975). Fisher (1974) found individuals to feel less crowded when approached by an attitudinally similar confederate than when approached by a confederate who was considered dissimilar. In his study of extremely high household densities in Hong Kong, Mitchell (1971) found few adverse effects when only kin shared an apartment but many such effects when unrelated people shared the same dwelling unit. Saegert (1978) reasoned that being with people whom one trusts reduces the need to be constantly vigilant. This not only directly obviates stress in the situation, by reducing the threat of undesirable social encounters, but also helps to mitigate the experience and consequences of cognitive overload associated with vigilance. In a sense, one can assume that the demands on the environmental skills of the person (understanding, competence, etc.) are far less with familiar others than with a crowd of strangers. Certainly, problems of personal space, privacy, or territoriality can be more quickly resolved with known and trusted others than with strangers.

Being with familiar others not only renders the situation more predictable and less threatening and demanding but also is more likely to lead to coordinated behavior than is being in an unfamiliar and heterogeneous group. Groups that adopt a cooperative orientation have been found to experience less crowding stress than those that adopt a competitive one, because they are better able to pool their resources and coordinate their behaviors to try to achieve the greatest good for the greatest number (Baum, Harpin, & Valins, 1975; Epstein, 1981; Stokols et al., 1973). Not only is stress affected by the orientation of the group, but stress may itself influence the orientation adopted by the group. Thus, Valins and Baum (1973) found students living in a crowded dormitory to act more competitively on an interactive laboratory task than did students who experienced less crowding in their dorms. In a follow-up to this study, floor mates who were able to develop cooperative strategies experienced less crowding stress than did those who did not, despite comparable social and spatial densities (Baum, Harpin, & Valins, 1975).

Sociocultural Norms. Hall's (1966) contention that members of different cultures have varying personal space habits and requirements suggests cultural differences in response to crowding and other environmental stressors. In a comprehensive review of this literature, Altman and Vinsel (1977) found support for the view that persons from Arabic, Latin American, and Mediterranean societies are more tolerant of close spatial distancing than are other groups.

Not only do members of different cultures show a range of sensitivities to environmental stimulation, such as desired and required levels of privacy, but also they vary in the mechanisms employed for controlling such stimulation; that is, they differ in their ways of achieving privacy (Altman, 1975; Hall, 1966; Rapoport, 1975). To control unwanted stimulation or interaction can rely on a number of devices, ranging from physical distancing and the use of physical barriers, through reliance upon social rules that establish manners, status hierarchies, avoidance behavior, and/or time-space scheduling, to the extreme of psychological withdrawal when the physical presence of others is unavoidable (Rapoport, 1975).

Anderson (1972) reported a number of norms that emerged in Chinese culture to help mitigate the experience and consequences of crowding stress. Privacy for the family as a group is considered more important than that for the single individual, and it is considered desirable for large numbers of people to share housing units. There are also strict rules governing the timing, location, and nature of social interactions. Such norms have allowed the Chinese to develop a fair degree of both tolerance to and control over environmental stimulation, despite extremely high household densities (Anderson, 1972; Mitchell, 1971).

Within a given society or culture, moreover, the norms of particular social systems govern the degree of control members of that social system may exert over environmental stimulation. For example, in the office setting, different management styles allow employees varying degrees of privacy (Steele, 1973). Even within a single organization, management may permit privacy in certain situations while prohibiting it in others. Thus, Justa and Golan (1977) found norms operating in one corporation that allowed employees to close their doors when having confidential meetings but not when working alone on a task. Similarly, families allow varying amounts of privacy to their members, and for different purposes, that depend upon their concept of what it means to be a family (Kantor & Lehr, 1975).

Characteristics of the Individual

Although properties of the stimulus configuration and of the social system do determine, in part, the extent to which environmental stimulation has stressful implications, perhaps the greatest amount of variability occurs at the individual level. Here, the person's goals in the setting interact with personality dispositions, past experiences, sex, life cycle, and status characteristics to influence the degree of fit between desired and actual levels of privacy, territoriality, and personal space. And, of course, emerging from these differences in past experiences, personality dispositions, and the like are differences in both needs and abilities for environmental understanding, competence, and control. These needs and abilities, in turn, represent the goal directed individual's striving to provide a better match between the settings frequented on a daily basis and the individual's place-identity experiences and expectations in order to preserve, protect, and enhance self-identity.

Tasks, Purposes, and Goals. Perhaps the single factor that most determines the extent to which environmental stimulation evokes stress in the individual concerns the degree to which the former interferes with what the individual is trying to accomplish in the setting. Noise, for instance, produces greater decrements in task performance and greater physiological arousal when the individual is involved in complex tasks, rather than simple tasks, although whether this effect should be attributed to heightened arousal (Broadbent, 1971) or to cognitive overload (Cohen, 1978) is still open to debate. Similarly, sounds that mask important conversations are most apt to be labeled noise and are likely to pose stressful consequences for those involved (Kryter, 1970), a finding that may account for the reduced social interaction and helping behavior that is often associated with noise (Mathews & Cannon, 1975; Page, 1977).

Tasks that demand a great deal of scanning of, or interaction with, the environment are more likely to lead to performance decrements and other negative responses to crowding than are tasks that do not require such scanning and interaction (Baum & Davis, 1976; Saegert, Mackintosh, & West, 1975). This may account for the lack of density effects reported in laboratory studies utilizing paper and pencil tests (e.g., Freedman, Klevansky, & Ehrlich, 1971), which serve to divert the subject's attention away from the crowded environment. Whereas tasks requiring environmental scanning challenge the information processing capacities of the individual, those that require interaction pose the additional demand of coordinating one's movements with those of others, producing heightened levels of both social overload and behavioral constraint (Saegert, 1978).

Personality and Past Experience. We might expect individuals to differ in both the amount of environmental stimulation they seek and the amount they can tolerate. That people do vary along such dimensions has been documented by Mehrabian and Russell (1973) and by Zuckerman (1971). Evidence suggests that extroverts both seek (Hockey, 1972) and tolerate (Elliott, 1971) higher noise levels than do introverts. These results are consistent with findings that extroverts, compared to introverts, have higher sensory thresholds (Smith, 1968) and less tolerance for sensory deprivation (Petrie, Collins, & Solomon, 1960).

Individual differences also appear relevant to varying sensitivities to crowding stress. Both Cozby (1973) and Dooley (1974) found individuals who preferred greater amounts of personal space to have lower thresholds to crowding stress than did those requiring less personal space. Schopler and Walton (1974) found that individuals high in the trait of *external locus of control* (i.e., those who believe they have little control over environmental events) experienced a greater degree of crowding stress, underscoring the importance of the person's perceived control of the physical settings in mediating the effects of environmental stimulation. The more the individual perceives that he has such control, the less the crowding stress. Not only does perceived control influence the crowding experience, but also the reverse may be true. Rodin (1976) reported that children from high-density households exerted less control in an experimental setting that did children from lower density households. She attributed this finding to *learned helplessness,* whereby the child tends to perceive situations as uncontrollable, even when they are not, because of prior experience in crowded, uncontrollable environments.

Whether past experiences of the individual influence personality tendencies or directly impact upon one's sensitivity to stress, it is important to consider how prior exposure to stressful situations may influence the effects of later exposure to these situations. First, although people quickly adapt or habituate to noise experienced in the laboratory (Glass & Singer, 1972), this finding has not been demonstrated in longitudinal studies conducted in residential settings (Cohen & Weinstein, 1981). On the contrary, many of these studies have found increases in measures of annoyance over time (Jonnson & Sorensen, 1973; Weinstein, 1978). Similarly, crowding studies using repeated measures over time frequently have showed the opposite of adaptation to occur. A laboratory study reported by Aiello, Epstein, and Karlin (1975) found measures of physiological arousal to increase over time. In a study of people's responses to prolonged high-density conditions aboard ship, Smith and Haythorn (1972) reported that greater stress was experienced during the last half of a 21-day period.

On the other hand, studies investigating the influence of previous living experiences on current thresholds to crowding frequently have lent support to the notion of adaptation (Sundstrom, 1978). That is, people who have a history a high levels of social stimulation have been shown to have a higher tolerance to crowding stress (e.g., Wohlwill & Kohn, 1973). However, Paulus, Cox, McCain, and Chandler (1975) reported lower tolerances to crowding for inmates who had a longer history of imprisonment in high-density cells.

Saegert and Kaminoff (1982) attempted to sort through the various linkages among past density experiences, personality factors, and current responses to highly dense settings. Although their data are not yet fully analyzed, and space prohibits a full description of this study, a few interesting trends are worth noting. First, growing up in large cities, as opposed to smaller cities and suburban and rural areas, was found to be associated with the development of a *field-dependent* rather than a *field-independent cognitive style,* as revealed by an embedded figure task. That is, experience in large urban settings predisposes individuals to rely on environmental stimuli and events, rather than their own cognitive structures, to understand and act in the world. It is possible to interpret this finding as a learned helplessness effect: individuals growing up in cities, which present confusing arrays of environmental stimulation, may quickly give up trying to discriminate a figure when it is embedded within a complex background. However, when we look at the relationship between another measure of background density, the *density of the household(s)* lived in before the age of 12, and another personality measure, *stimulus screening,* a very different picture emerges. People growing up with high household densities show a greater tendency to screen stimulation that is impinging upon them than do those who experienced low household densities during their formative years. Whether past experience in overly stimulating environments leads to easier coping with such environments (i.e., less stress)—as *adaptation-level theory* (in which people adapt to the levels and types of stimulation that they are used to experiencing) would have it (Helson, 1964; Wohlwill, 1974)—or whether it leads to greater coping difficulties (i.e., more stress)—as learned helplessness theory might predict (Rodin & Baum, 1978; Seligman, 1975)—would seem to depend on the outcomes of past coping attempts and especially on the implications they hold for the individual's sense of environmental competence, security, and control.

Saegert and Kaminoff (1982) also investigated the role that these personality measures may play in mediating the individual's current susceptibility to highly dense settings by taking subjects into a supermarket under varying density conditions and having them perform a task requiring a great deal of scanning and interaction with the environment (cf. Langer & Saegert, 1977). Of the two personality measures, stimulus screening appeared to have the greater adaptive significance. Subjects scoring high on this measure performed better on the task than did low scorers. Screeners also reported feeling less edgy and more satisfied in the setting than did nonscreeners. Although field independents performed marginally better than did field dependents, there appears to be a cost associated with this superiority as far as affectively experienced stress is concerned. Individuals possessing a field-independent cognitive style felt less satisfied, less comfortable, and less friendly than did their field-dependent counterparts. This affective cost for better task performance experienced by field independents probably reflected their "fighting" the field in order to focus on the task at hand. Field dependents, on the other hand, probably made less of an effort to focus on task-relevant cues, choosing instead to "go with the flow" of the field, upon which they were more dependent.

Status. A concept that links the individual to the social system is the individual's status within that system. It is frequently observed that individuals occupying low-status roles are permitted less privacy than are higher status members of a given social system. This has been observed for clerical workers in office settings (Steele, 1973), inmates of residential psychiatric facilities (Wolfensberger, 1977), and children in household settings (Baldassare, 1977). That lack of control over environmental stimulation and interaction translates into greater stress for low-status members of a social system is evidenced by studies comparing the responses of children from high-density households with those of their parents (Stokols, 1978). Children are more apt to experience increased nervousness (Gasparini, 1973), to suffer greater decrements in intellectual development (Booth & Johnson, 1975), to have their social interactions curtailed, and to be blamed for household problems (Clausen & Clausen, 1973) than are parents in high-density residences.

By way of summary, the extent to which the individual experiences stress in response to high levels of stimulation depends upon a plethora of physical, social, and individual characteristics. Questions of who the individual is and what he or she is trying to accomplish within the setting—given the social norms, group composition, and orientation of a particular social system—are always relevant. Architectural features such as scale, boundedness, and clarity of environmental meanings are also important, as we shall see in the following sections.

BOUNDEDNESS OF SPACE

As we noted earlier, boundedness of space means the structural definitions of spaces and places that serve to distinguish and separate physical areas from each other in terms of sound, light, and other physical stimulation, including a person's access to and egress from one spatial area to another. It is evident that spatial boundaries can and do determine the control that individuals and groups have over environmental stimulation and social interaction. Boundaries between territories can be too permeable, causing privacy invasions and incompatible activities to conflict, or not permeable enough, creating problems of access and contact among isolated individuals and groups who require greater degrees of communication. Following Crowhurst (1974), we will define *territory* as a volume of space—such as a room, a house, a block, or a neighborhood—the outer limits of which are marked by a boundary. Territories may be under the exclusive control of specific individuals and groups, or their control may be ambiguous and/or open to competition among different persons or groups. A *boundary* defines the outer limit of a territory, often separating one territory from another.

Boundedness and Crowding

Various crowding studies have demonstrated that boundaries that clearly demarcate territories can help to mitigate the perception and effects of high social densities. In a doll-placement simulation experiment, Desor (1972) found that subjects placed more human figures in a partitioned room before it was perceived as crowded than they did in an open (not partitioned) space. In a real-world analogue to this study, Blake, Rhead, Wedge, and Mouton (1956) compared the social interaction levels of army personnel housed in barracks of either an open or a partitioned design. Although each of the barracks housed 60 recruits, one used partitions to create 10 fairly separate groups of 6 men each, while the other was left completely open. The partitioned barrack had doorways connecting the spaces, but no doors were provided. Although (and perhaps *because*) there was a greater number of potential interactions in the open barrack, more social interaction was reported to occur in the partitioned barrack. There were no measures of crowding in the Blake (1956) study, but the Desor (1972) experiment may be drawn on to help interpret these findings. Recruits living in the open barrack were more likely to perceive the setting as crowded given the undifferentiated social stimulation caused by the absence of boundaries, which serve to separate and distinguish groups of individuals from each other. Those living in the partitioned barrack, on the other hand, had a great deal of this stimulation screened out, allowing them to focus on interactions in their immediate area, which were at a more predictable, controllable, and manageable level.

Studies conducted in other residential settings have pointed more directly to the role of boundaries in influencing the ability to predict and control social interactions. Baum and Valins (1977) compared the behavior and experience of freshmen assigned to dormitories of either a double-loaded corridor design—dorm rooms on each side of a corridor—or a suite design. Although each dormitory had comparable spatial densities (floor area per resident), the arrangement of space created different levels of social density. In the double-loaded corridor design, 2 students shared each room but lounge and bathroom facilities were used by 36 students. Students assigned to suites also shared a room with another student, but shared a lounge and bathroom with only 5 others. Residents of the corridor design dormitories experienced more crowding stress and exhibited less social interaction and more competitive behavior than did their counterparts living in suites. Students living in the corridor designed dorms complained about their inability to predict and control undesired social interactions experienced on a daily basis. Suite residents, on the other hand, were subject to more manageable levels of social interaction and were able to devise cooperative strategies (such as time-place scheduling) that permitted suite mates to secure needed levels of privacy (Baum & Valins, 1977).

Studies conducted in institutional settings have underscored the importance of boundaries in offering the freedom to choose when and where social interactions will take place. Ittelson, Proshansky, and Rivlin (1970) found the behavior of residents of a psychiatric ward to be a function of the number of patients per room. As this number increased, the amount of both isolated active behaviors and social interactions decreased dramatically. Patients assigned to private rooms not only were more active and socially interactive than patients sharing bedrooms but also exhibited the widest *range* of activities. Taken together, these and other studies (e.g., Holahan & Saegert, 1973; Knight, Weitzer, & Zimring, 1978; Paulus, McCain, & Cox, 1978) suggest that the provision of clearly bounded private spaces affords people greater freedom of choice to pursue desired activities, as well as greater control over the physical and social environment. That a lack of boundedness has stressful implications is well documented (Paulus, McCain, & Cox, 1978). Comparing prisoners living in single cells, double cells, and dormitories, Paulus and associates reviewed prison records and found that inmates living in double cells and dormitories exhibited greater levels of stress than those living in single cells, as measured by the incidence of disciplinary problems and illness complaints and by death rate.

Boundaries in Family Settings

In household settings the boundedness of space has profound implications for intrafamily interactions, as well as for relationships between the family and immediate neighbors and the surrounding community. Within the household the degree of boundedness influences the degree to which the various activities of family members may conflict, how much time the family spends together as a unit, and how much privacy is allowed different family members for different purposes (Crowhurst, 1974).

In a study of apartment living, Becker (1974) reported conflicts over internal space use as a particularly salient issue when children were involved, especially when the conflicts concerned television viewing. Residents reported three major ways of dealing with such conflicts. Whereas *time territory* strategies entail different family members' utilizing the same space at different times, *space territory* strategies rely on the spatial distribution of simultaneously occuring activities. In a final arrangement, *cooperation-capitulation,* all family members engage in one activity that is determined by the dominant individual or subgroup (Becker, 1974).

Studies of household density frequently have uncovered boundedness problems since density is usually measured as persons per room (telling us little about the independent effects of family size and room size). Booth and Edwards (1976; Edwards & Booth, 1977) found high household densities to increase both the extent to which parents hit their children and the number of verbal quarrels, as well as negatively to affect the perceived quality of relationships with spouses. Lack of perceived privacy was reported to interfere particularly with sexual relationships.

Cultural appears to be an important mediator of the degree of boundedness required to minimize stress in family functioning. Despite extremely high household densities and few, if any, territorial markers and boundaries to separate activities, families living in Hong Kong (at least those who did not share a household with strangers or live on the upper floors of a high-rise) exhibited minimal levels of stress (Mitchell, 1971). Others have also commented upon the apparent lack of stress reactions among members of Eastern cultures in response to high population densities (Canter & Canter, 1971; Schmitt, 1963). These findings not only reflect differences in the amount of personal space or privacy required by members of different cultures but also can be attributed to cross-cultural variations in the mechanisms used to obtain privacy when it is required (Altman, 1975; Hall, 1966; Rapoport, 1969). Thus, Americans frequently require closed doors to achieve privacy, whereas members of other cultures often rely on more subtle strategies such as speaking in a polite, reserved manner and posturing themselves in a way that signals the desire to be alone (Hall, 1966). The fact that Americans often need boundaries that enable them to withdraw physically from social interactions may help us understand why American families make every attempt to provide separate rooms for each family member.

Children have very different boundary requirements at different stages of development. In infancy, boundaries that separate parent and child can evoke anxiety and stress in both (Pollowy, 1977). In the early stages of infancy, visual contact with the parent seems necessary since the child cannot perceive the existence of an apparently absent object or person (Piaget, 1951); by the end of the second year, however, the sound of mother may suffice if the infant is in familiar surroundings (Pollowy, 1977).

As the child progresses from one developmental stage to the next, his or her requirements for privacy become more pronounced (Wolfe, 1978). These privacy requirements reach their pinnacle in adolescence, when increased autonomy, surges in physical maturation, and concentrated intellectual activity, as well as experimentation with social and sexual intimacy, combine to create privacy needs that previously existed only in a more primitive, less distinctive form (Savin, Parke, & Dimicelli, 1975).

Boundaries are used not only to allow for the physical separation of individual family members but also to separate whole families from their neighbors. Kuper (1953) reported poor soundproofing between semidetached units, as well as the poor planning of adjacencies, to be a major complaint of residents. Because adjacent housing units had common living room walls, noise was easily transmitted from one family to the next. Such infringements upon a family's privacy occurred at an even more personal level since these units also shared bedroom walls. Residents expressed a great deal of embarrassment at being able to overhear the private conversations and activities of their neighbors and felt inhibited about their own activities and those of their children. Moreover, lack of boundedness between homes, apartment buildings, and the surrounding neighborhood poses obvious threats to people's environmental security, as far as fear of crime is concerned (Newman, 1972).

Boundaries in Other Settings

There is evidence that many everyday settings are becoming more open, or less bounded, in plan, such as homes (Cooper-Marcus & Hogue, 1976), offices (Brookes & Kaplan, 1972), and schools (Rivlin & Rothenberg, 1976). Open-plan offices, for instance, are said to result in greater communication among employees, increased cohesion within work groups, greater flexibility in the use of space, as well as financial savings (cf. Brookes & Kaplan, 1972). Yet there is a great deal of evidence that employees suffer from visual and auditory distractions, as well as from a lack of conversational privacy (Brookes & Kaplan, 1972; Nemecek & Grandjean, 1973). Of course, the degree of satisfaction with open-plan offices depends upon a host of physical, social, and individual factors. For example, managers, because of their past experience and current expectations and requirements regarding privacy, generally are more dissatisfied with the open plan than are other kinds of employees (Duffy, 1969; Harris, 1978; Nemecek & Grandjean, 1973).

Similarly, some teachers and students have complained about noise, increased disruptions, lack of display and storage space, and lack of territoriality in open-plan classrooms (Kyzar, 1971). Kyzar (1971) pointed out, however, that although the design of these rooms was open, the educational program was essentially conventional, underscoring the importance of fit between the physical setting and the curriculum approach. There is much evidence to suggest that teachers whose educational philosophies conflict with the physical configuration of their classrooms experience more difficulty than those whose orientations match such arrangements (Durlak, Beardsley & Murray, 1972; Rivlin & Rothenberg, 1976). Burnetti (1972) suggested that for teachers committed to an open style of teaching, large, unbounded spaces actually allowed for *more* privacy and *less* noise than did more conventional classrooms, containing four solid walls and row seating. If children wanted to work in small groups, they were able to go off to a remote corner to do so without distracting others with their activity. Similarly, if children desired privacy, they could easily remove themselves from the immediate presence of others.

SCALE

The scale of environments may be either too small comfortably to accommodate the people and the activities they contain, or too large, posing problems of distance, orientation, and complexity. Because of rising land and construction costs as well as soaring interest rates, the scale of the average home is becoming smaller; of course, the average family size also has become smaller (Cooper-Marcus & Hogue, 1976). When households are too small, the activities of their members tend to spill out into communal areas (Perin, 1972), often causing a great deal of tension and conflict among family members (Jephcott, 1971). The size of individual rooms can also make a difference. The kitchen, to take but one example, may be too small to contain both parent and child activities simultaneously, making it impossible for a mother to involve herself in meal preparation or cleanup activities while she supervises her child's play.

Dramatic increases in population levels generally, and in urban settings in particular, have led to the construction of large-scale buildings to contain these large numbers of people, as well as the machinery and equipment needed to support the living styles of the members of a complex industrial society. Presumably there is an economy offered by centrally located and massively scaled environments. However, both anecdotal and systematic evidence suggests that large-scale settings may have negative impacts on the human populations that inhabit or use them, ranging from disorientation in airports (Kilday, 1979), government buildings (Berkeley, 1973), and health care facilities (Izumi, 1970; Spivak, 1967); to alienation, social withdrawal, and fear of crime in high-rise apartment complexes (Newman, 1972; McCarthy & Saegert, 1978; Yancey, 1971); and finally to poorer quality of care in day care facilities (Prescott, 1970) and psychiatric institutions (Ullman, 1967).

In cities, shortages of space and large numbers of people combine to create a demand for increasingly tall buildings. In a study investigating people's general reactions to such tall structures, Haber (1977) found their most consistently disliked attributes to be waiting long periods of time for elevators, lack of greenery, fear of fire, impersonality, monotony, difficulty getting to the outside, fear of being trapped in elevators, general lack of environmental control, noise, and feelings of isolation. Positive responses to tall buildings included the views they offered from higher floors and their economical use of space.

High-rise apartment complexes represent the most controversial, as well as the most heavily studied, type of tall building (Cooper-Marcus & Hogue, 1975). Many studies comparing the behavior and satisfaction of residents living in single-family low-rise and in high-rise structures have found the latter to be associated with a number of potentially stressful events: crime in semipublic areas (Becker, 1974; Newman, 1972; Yancey, 1971), difficulties in raising children (Becker, 1974; British Department of the Environment, 1972; Jephcott, 1971; Maizels, 1961; Morville, 1969), social isolation and loneliness (Adams & Conway, 1974; Becker, 1974; British Department of the Environment, 1972), as well as less perceived privacy, friendliness, and helping behavior (McCarthy & Saegert, 1978). Such findings have led many to suggest that high-rise structures are inherently a poor form of housing and have resulted in a ban on their construction in Denmark and Toronto.

Many housing studies have been criticized on either methodological or substantive grounds. Cooperman (1977), for example, suggested that building height is often confounded with such variables as social class, physical mobility, residential choice, financial cost, and household, as well as neighborhood, density. Others have pointed out that high-rise housing may be satisfactory and even desirable for some groups, while it is inappropriate for others (Adams & Conway, 1972; British Department of the Environment, 1972; Homenuck, 1973; Michelson, 1973; Wekerle, 1974).

Childrearing Problems in High-rise Housing

Studies investigating the role of a family's stage in the lifecycle in determining housing satisfaction and preferences have consistently found families with young children to be the least satisfied with high-rise housing. This general finding was reported by Adams and Conway (1972), who also reported that parents of young children frequently complain that it is difficult, if not impossible, to supervise children's outdoor play activities while they themselves remain in the apartment (British Department of the Environment, 1972). The anxieties of parents seem to increase with floor height and center around fear for the safety of children on balconies, as well as in elevators, on staircases, and in ground-level play areas. It is particularly stressful for parents to be able to *see* their child in danger from a window yet be too far away to *do* anything about it. Consequently, many studies report that young children (those under five) living in high-rises play outdoors less frequently than do their counterparts living in low-rise buildings (British Department of the Environment, 1972; Maizels, 1961; Morville, 1969).

Preschoolers need to play close to parents or other supervising adults and yet have contact with peers. Perhaps no less important is their need to be able to explore and manipulate their environment—to run, make noise, stretch their muscles, and so on. In low-rise housing, children are frequently involved in flexible indoor-outdoor play while parents perform household chores and hobbies, e.g., gardening. Although a high-rise parent can take his or her child to a ground-level playground or park, he or she cannot be simultaneously involved in household activities. Therefore, such visits occur less frequently and are often much shorter than the more casual and flexible play opportunities offered to children in low-rise dwellings (Morville, 1969). High-rise children's play is often restricted to the apartment interior, creating tension and conflict among family members (Becker, 1974). Parents frequently report restraining their children's indoor play activities, especially those that would generate noise, in order to minimize both their own stress and complaints from neighbors (British Department of the Environment, 1972; Jephcott, 1971). Thus, for families with young children, high-rise living may not only inhibit play activities associated with the child's normal development but also contribute to conflicts and tensions among family members and among neighbors (Cooper-Marcus & Hogue, 1976).

Crime and Interaction Problems in High-rise Housing

Another problem associated with high-rise living is the lack of perceived control over the environment, especially control over the entry of nonresidents and social interactions with friends and neighbors (Becker, 1974; McCarthy & Saegert, 1976; Newman, 1972; Yancey, 1971). High-rise developments frequently have multiple entry points, as well as numerous stairwells, elevators, lengthy corridors, and other semipublic spaces. McCarthy and Saegert (1978) found the building densities of high-rises (number of apartments per building) to be too great to enable residents to recognize one another, making it virtually impossible for them to make distinctions with any degree of accuracy between those who belonged in the semipublic areas and those who did not. Newman (1972) characterized these semipublic spaces of many high-rises as not "defensible" because their boundaries are not clearly delineated and they cannot be watched by tenants from their apartments. All these factors contribute to findings of higher crime rates in the semipublic areas of high-rises located in moderate- or high-crime neighborhoods than in low-rise apartment buildings located in the same or similar neighborhoods (Becker, 1974; Newman, 1972; Yancey, 1971). Clearly, these same factors have implications for an evolving place-identity, in this instance one that is predicated on low environmental security, which may in turn undermine the person's feelings of environmental competence and understanding.

Fear of crime, as well as the general lack of control residents feel they have over social interactions, frequently induces residents to spend as little time as possible in semipublic areas. This not only exacerbates the crime problem (by resulting in less tenant surveillance of these areas) but also inhibits the development of social networks (Yancey, 1971). Bombarded with excessive amounts of unpredictable social interactions with unfamiliar others, tenants frequently withdraw into their own apartments (McCarthy & Saegert, 1978). Groups that lack the mobility to form friendships elsewhere in the city, such as the poor, the elderly, women, and young children, are particularly susceptible to the sense of alienation and isolation experienced in high-rises (Adams & Conway, 1974; Michelson, 1973; Yancey, 1971). Moreover, the finding that well-developed social networks help to mitigate the experience and consequences of stress in general is certainly important in the context of this volume.

Thus, high-rise residents who are unable to develop appropriate social supports are more apt to experience stress than are their counterparts who are better able to do so (Baldassare, 1977).

This discussion should not lead us to the conclusion that high-rises are inherently stress provoking to residents. On the contrary, many studies have found them to be a desirable form of housing for some groups under appropriate conditions (Adams & Conway, 1974; Cooper-Marcus & Hogue, 1976; Homenuck, 1973; Michelson, 1973; Wekerle, 1974). For instance, middle- and upper-class residents frequently prefer to live in high-rises rather than in other forms of housing (Michelson, 1973).

CLARITY OF ENVIRONMENTAL MEANING

The physical environment is filled with both empirical and symbolic meanings that communicate how we are expected to behave in any given setting (Hall, 1966; Hershberger, 1974; Spivak, 1976). These meanings tell us how to orient ourselves in, and navigate passages through, the spaces we need to frequent on either an occasional or a daily basis (Lynch, 1960; Moore, 1979; Weisman, 1979). Once we have arrived at our destination, the arrangement of spaces and objects tell us how they may or may not be used (Ruesch & Kees, 1970). They communicate personal information about the owners, designers, and users of the setting (Cooper, 1974). Finally, these meanings tell us where we fit within a given social system and how we are expected to relate to others in that setting (Steele, 1973; Wolfensberger, 1977).

Orientation and Wayfinding

Following Zimring (1981), we will define *orientation* as the individual's ability to relate his or her location to known features of the environment and *wayfinding* as the actual behaviors employed by the individual to find desired locations within the environment. Both anecdotal and systematic evidence suggests that orientation and wayfinding problems may induce stress in people (see Zimring, 1981, for a review). Kilday (1979) reported numerous incidents of emotional disturbance associated with the disorientation caused by the massive scale and confusing layout of the Dallas–Fort Worth Airport. Berkeley (1973) suggested that disorientation problems experienced in Boston City Hall may contribute to the anger and hostility people feel toward government. Disorientation problems encountered in a university art and architectural building led to feelings of "indignation" among users of the facility, who took great pride in their highly developed spatial ability, suggesting that one's perceived environmental competence and environmental security enter into such assessments (Dixon, 1968).

We might expect disorientation to pose a more serious threat to particular segments of society. Pastalan (1972) reported that when elderly groups are moved to new housing, mortality rates soar temporarily, a finding attributed in part to disorientation. When an orientation program was introduced that allowed residents to visit the new housing and get accustomed to it before moving in, residents were more likely to survive the trauma of relocation (Pastalan, 1972). Similarly, we might expect orientation and wayfinding to be especially difficult and stressful for visually impaired persons. Peake and Leonard (1971) found the heart rates of blind pedestrians to be significantly elevated when they were negotiating complex routes in shopping areas. Although Zimring (1979) was not able to replicate this physiological effect among his sample of blind travelers, he attributed this to the possibility that the route used was less complex than that employed in the Peake and Leonard (1971) study. Zimring (1979), however, did find more self-reported anxiety on complex than on simple routes.

Disorienting features of hospital and psychiatric facilities pose special difficulties for populations who may already be experiencing perceptual distortions (Izumi, 1970; Spivak, 1967). Spivak (1967) described the seemingly endless corridors in psychiatric facilities, which distort one's perceptions of both visual and aural stimuli. The walls, floors, and ceilings of these corridors have hard, shiny finishes that permit easy maintenance but produce inordinate amounts of glare and echo.

Researchers have suggested several ways to facilitate orientation and wayfinding within buildings. Weinstein (1979) rephrased a Gestalt principle of perception by calling for overall regularity of architectural form within a particular building, although he qualified this by suggesting that well-differentiated subareas also aid orientation and wayfinding. Sivadon (1970) emphasized the importance of perpendicular axes to provide a frame of reference and cautioned against the use of curved corridors because they do not provide adequate views. Evans and associates (1982, in press) found that color coding of an academic building facilitated both image formation and actual wayfinding. Zimring (1979) suggested that the redundant use of cues is helpful, particularly for visually impaired persons.

A study of museum orientation by Winkel and associates (1975) stressed the importance not only of signs and floor plans but also of a logical layout that conformed to the associations visitors made between exhibits. These researchers performed factor analyses on visitors' interest ratings of various museum exhibits of determine the cognitive connectedness of the different exhibits and recommended a physical layout that would parallel more closely visitors' perceptions of similarity.

Wener and Kaminoff (1979) found that the introduction of signs in a crowded visitor waiting area of a prison not only aided wayfinding but also significantly reduced self-reported levels of stress. In addition to making fewer navigational errors and taking less time to complete the visitor registration process, visitors experiencing the signs reported feeling less crowded, less confused, less angry, and more comfortable than counterparts who did not have directional signs available. The signs not only directly added cognitive clarity to the environment but also diverted visitors' information seeking behavior away from social cues; that is, instead of finding out where to go by watching others, visitors were able to attend to more directly relevant, nonsocial cues in order to get needed information. There is evidence that effective orientation and wayfinding reduces stress and that stress, in turn, may impair orientation and wayfinding (Langer & Saegert, 1977; Saegert, Mackintosh, & West, 1975). This research program, conducted in large urban stores, found the stress of crowding to impair people's ability to form accurate cognitive representations of the environment. Taken together, these studies suggest that complex urban settings provide a surfeit of information; cues utilized for orientation and wayfinding purposes must compete with physical and social stimulation that is irrelevant to the task at hand (in this case, getting from one place to another) but is still attention demanding. To aid wayfinding and mitigate stress, cues used for orientation must be easily discernible despite the presence of massive amounts of competing information.

Understanding Use and Symbolism

Once the individual arrives at his or her destination, the physical environment communicates empirical and symbolic meanings that prescribe *how* it may be used, as well as *who* may use it in particular ways and for particular purposes. The setting provides information about the tasks and personalities of its occupants and either reinforces or subverts existing social role relationships. Space may be clearly delineated and differentiated to tell us precisely what is permitted, expected, or possible in different areas, or such delineations may be unclear, creating uncertainty and anxiety as to use and allowing conflicting activities to take place in the same space. Thus, the extent to which environmental meanings are clear and comprehensible to the occupant of a setting and the degree to which they support individual needs, social relationships, organizational procedures, and collective needs and styles have clear consequences for the amount of stress that is experienced in a given setting by the individual.

Let us begin with a simple example. Before a door can be used, we must first recognize it as a door (Hershberger, 1974). Izumi (1970) described numerous contemporary designs that may make such recognition difficult. Assuming for the moment that the individual recognizes a wood panel as a door, symbolic features may render it either an invitation to enter or a formidable barrier to avoid. Similarly, design features may or may not communicate what the individual can expect to find on the other side of the door. The decision (or even the opportunity) to use the door in a particular way is further complicated when we consider relevant social norms that may be operating in the setting. For instance, Justa and Golan (1977) explored how social norms influenced the use of doors to achieve different types of privacy in an office setting. As we noted earlier, although it was considered acceptable to close one's door to insure privacy when meeting with others for confidential conversation, it was not considered appropriate to close one's door when working alone because being accessible to co-workers was a higher corporate priority than individual privacy. Thus, when confronted with one-person tasks requiring a great deal of concentration, some employees came to the office early, worked through lunch, or stayed late to do the job. Others brought such work home with them, even though this set the stage for possible family conflicts. When confronted with work of an individual nature that had to be done during regular office hours, employees either worked under distracting conditions with their doors open or closed their doors and experienced discomfort at having violated social norms. The important point is that the meaning and use of doors change from one situation to another. In this case, social norms operating in the setting prohibited some uses while sanctioning others. Although employees made various adaptations in order to execute tasks requiring concentration, each of these implied potentially stressful costs. (Of course, as the individual moves from one culture to another, environmental meanings change more dramatically. Difficulty in understanding the physical cues of alien cultures accounts, in part, for the stress that often accompanies foreign travel [Hall, 1966]).

The meanings provided by the physical environment communicate important information about oneself and others (Cooper, 1974; Proshansky & Kaminoff, 1982). After reviewing the relationship between housing quality and mental health, Schorr (1966) concluded that the occupants' self-image frequently mediated this relationship in important ways. Dilapidated housing was found adversely to affect psychological and social adjustment of the person largely because of the negative information it communicated about the self. An analysis of the meanings provided by the housing environment helps us understand why some urban renewal and relocation projects succeed in improving residents' self-concepts and mental health (MacKintosh, 1952; Wilner, Walkey, Pinkerton, & Tayback, 1962) while others fail to do so (Fried & Gleicher, 1961; Yancey, 1971). Improving the actual conditions of peoples' daily lives may enable them to embrace new feelings of pride and optimism, which may result in increased residential satisfaction, which in turn may result in an improved self-concept or improved mental health (MacKintosh, 1952; Schorr, 1966; Wilner and associates 1962). Yet the design of many housing projects suggests an insensitivity to particular meanings residents attach to their homes. Residents of urban slums, for example, attach a great deal of importance to the rich social life experienced on the stoops and streets in front of their low-rise tenements. This form of socializing is not possible in massively scaled high-rise projects. Thus, after being relocated from their old homes to new high-rise structures, many residents report feeling alienated, threatened, isolated, and grief stricken (Fried & Gleicher, 1961; Yancey, 1971).

The design of psychiatric and other institutions may communicate a range of negative meanings to both inmates and outsiders. The location of such facilities in remote, rural areas or their separation from the community by barriers like highways or railroad yards not only keeps residents apart from friends, relatives, and community services but also reinforces notions that inmates *must* be separated from the mainstream of society. As Wolfensberger (1977) noted, the degree to which the facade of the building fits into the surrounding neighborhood may influence the degree to which its residents are perceived (by themselves and others) to be deviant. Thus, both the dilapidated group home in the middle-class community and the modern chrome and glass facility located in a slum are lacking in neighborhood building congruity and may reinforce notions of deviance and/or arouse neighborhood hostility toward the facility. Even the names of many psychiatric facilities suggest to both residents and outsiders that they house a specific group. As Wolfensbeger noted, names communicate an image of separateness (Outwood, The Retreat), dependence (Carefree Lodge, Rest Haven) or, finally hopelessness (HELP School, SOS Workshop, Last Chance House). Moreover, many interior features of psychiatric facilities—such as hard, indestructible materials, inaccessible controls for lighting and temperature regulations, and doors that can be locked or unlocked only from the outside—communicate to residents that they are expected to, or probably will, behave in a wild, irresponsible manner, that they are incapable of making meaningful choices, and, therefore, that their movements must be restricted (Wolfensberger, 1977).

The physical environment not only communicates information about oneself and others but also provides messages about our relationship to others. In the corporate setting, the clerical worker who occupies a desk in an impersonal open area is always aware of the status differential between himself and the occupant of a large and private corner office. Characteristics of the executive office such as its size, the texture of the carpet, the number of windows, the proportions of the desk, the way it is decorated, and the placement of chairs communicate to subordinates the nature of the superior-subordinate relationship obtaining, and thereby indicate how they are to act in that room (Steele, 1973).

Social interaction difficulties occur both when social role definitions concerning this relationship are not clear and when place-identity expectations are not met; that is, when spaces and places are inappropriate for the individuals who occupy them. Thus, in addition to considering the clarity of environmental meaning, we must consider the *compatibility* of these meanings with respect to the social system governing any given setting. An open-plan office, in which executives, middle managers, and clerks share workspace in open areas, may be appropriate for corporations having a "flat" organizational structure, in which employees at all levels need direct access to one another to make decisions in a participatory fashion. However, such an office may create stress in a conventional company, wherein members have expectations regarding status and privacy that require that spaces by assigned on a more hierarchical basis (Duffy, 1969).

CONCLUSION

The foregoing review of the literature suggested a paucity of one-to-one relationships between physical features of the built environment and stressful outcomes for inhabitants. We indicated the importance of several person-environment concepts that mediate such relationships and thus enable us better to predict the circumstances under which stress is likely to result from particular environmental conditions. At root in this approach is the requirement to assess the degree to which physical characteristics of a setting—including the level of stimulation that is present, the clarity of meanings communicated, and the scale and boundedness of spaces that comprise it—are appropriate to both the social context and the goals and opportunities of individual occupants—including the person's needs for privacy, territoriality, and personal space, and his abilities to achieve environmental understanding, competence, and security given his unique constellation of place-identity experiences.

REFERENCES

ADAMS, B., & CONWAY, J. The social effects of living off the ground. *Proceedings of IABSE Tall buildings and people conference,* Oxford University, 1974, 150–157.

AIELLO, J. R., EPSTEIN, Y. M., & KARLIN, R. A. Effects of crowding on electrodermal activity. *Sociological Symposium,* 1975, *14,* 43–57.

ALTMAN, I. *The environment and social behavior: Privacy, territoriality, personal space, and crowding.* Monterey: Brooks/Cole, 1975.

ALTMAN, I., & VINSEL, A. M. Personal space: An analysis of E. T. Hall's proxemics framework. In I. Altman & J. F. Wohlwill (eds.), *Human behavior and environment,* vol. 2. New York: Plenum, 1977.

ANDERSON, E. N., JR. Some Chinese methods of dealing with crowding. *Urban Anthropology,* 1972, *1,* 141–150.

AVERILL, J. Personal control over aversive stimuli and its relation to stress. *Psychological Bulletin,* 1973, *80,* 226–303.

BALDASSARE, M. Residential density, household crowding, and social networks. In C. Fischer (ed.), *Networks and places.* New York: Free Press, 1977.

BAUM, A., & DAVIS, G. E. Spatial and social aspects of crowding perception. *Environment and Behavior,* 1976, *8,* 527–544.

BAUM, A., HARPIN, R. E., & VALINS, S. The role of group phenomena in the experience of crowding. *Environment and Behavior,* 1975, *7,* 185–198.

BAUM, A., & VALINS, S. *Architecture and social behavior.* Hillsdale: Erlbaum, 1977.

BECKER, F. D. *Design for living: The residents' view of multifamily housing.* Ithaca: Center for Urban Development Research, 1974.

BELL, P. A. Physiological comfort, performance, and social effects of heat stress. *Journal of Social Issues,* 1981, *37,* 71–94.

BERKELEY, E. P. More than what you want to know about Boston City Hall. *Architecture Plus,* February 1973, pp. 72–77.

BERLYNE, D. E. *Conflict, arousal, and curiosity.* New York: McGraw-Hill, 1960.

BICKMAN, L., TEGER, A., GABRIELE, T., MCLAUGHLIN, C., BERGER, M., & SUNADAY, E. Dormitory density and helping behavior. *Environment and Behavior,* 1973, *5,* 465–490.

BLAKE, R. R., RHEAD, C. C., WEDGE, B., & MOUTON, J. S. Housing and social interaction. *Sociometry,* 1956, *19,* 133–139.

BOGGS, D. H., & SIMON, J. R. Differential effects of noise on tasks of varying complexity. *Journal of Applied Psychology,* 1968, *52,* 148–153.

BOOTH, A., & EDWARDS, J. Crowding and family relations. *American Sociological Review,* 1976, *41,* 308–321.

BOOTH, A., & JOHNSON, D. The effect of crowding on child health and development. *American Behavioral Scientist,* 1975, *18,* 736–749.

British Department of the Environment. *The estate outside the dwelling.* London: HMSO, 1972.

BROADBENT, D. E. *Decision and stress.* New York: Academic, 1971.

—————. The current state of noise research: Reply to Poulton. *Psychological Bulletin,* 1978, *85,* 1052–1067.

BROOKES, M. J., & KAPLAN, A. The office environment: Space planning and affective behavior. *Human Factors,* 1972, *14,* 373–391.

BRONZCRAFT, A. L., & MCCARTHY, D. P. The effect of elevated train noise on reading ability. *Environment and Behavior,* 1975, *7,* 517–528.

BRUNETTI, F. Noise, distraction, and privacy in conventional and open school environments. In W. J. Mitchell (ed.), *Environmental design: Research and practice* vol. 1. Proceedings of the Environmental Design Research Association. Los Angeles: University of California, 1972.

CANTER, D., & CANTER, S. Close together in Tokyo. *Design and Environment,* 1971, *2,* 60–63.

CAPELLINI, A., & MORONI, M. Clinical survey on hypertension and coronary disease and their possible relations with the environment in workers of a chemical plant. *Medicina del lavoro* (Rome), 1974, *65,* 297–305.

CLAUSEN, J., & CLAUSEN, S. The effects of family size on parents and children. In J. Fawcett (ed.), *Psychological perspectives on population.* New York: Basic Books, 1973.

COHEN, S. Environmental load and the allocation of attention. In A. Baum, J. E. Singer, & S. Valins (eds.), *Advances in environmental psychology,* (vol. 1). Hillsdale: Erlbaum, 1978.

COHEN, S., GLASS, D. C., & PHILLIPS, S. Environment and health. In H. E. Freeman, S. Levine, & L. G. Reeder (eds.), *Handbook of medical sociology.* Englewood Cliffs: Prentice-Hall, 1979.

COHEN, S., GLASS, D. C., & SINGER, J. E. Apartment noise, auditory discrimination, and reading ability in children. *Journal of Experimental Social Psychology,* 1973, *9,* 407–422.

COHEN, S., & WEINSTEIN, N. Nonauditory effects of noise on behavior and health. *Journal of Social Issues,* 1981, *37,* 36–70.

COOPER, C. The house as symbol of the self. In J. Lang, C. Burnette, W. Moleski, & D. Vachon (eds.), *Designing for human behavior: Architecture and the behavioral sciences.* Stroudsburg: Dowden, Hutchinson & Ross, 1974.

COOPER-MARCUS, C., & HOGUE, L. Design guidelines for high-rise housing. *Journal of Architectural Research,* 1976, *5,* 34–39.

COOPERMAN, D. Social research on tall habitats: A critique and proposal for network analysis. In D. J. Conway (ed.), *Human response to tall buildings.* Stroudsburg: Dowden, Hutchinson & Ross, 1977.

COZBY, P. C. Effects of density, activity, and personality on environmental preferences. *Journal of Research in Personality,* 1973, *7,* 45–60.

CROWHURST, S. H. A house is a metaphor. *Journal of Architectural Education,* 1974, *27,* 35–41.

D'ATRI, D. A. Psychophysiological responses to crowding. *Environment and Behavior,* 1975, *7,* 237–250.

DEAN, L. M., PUGH, W. M., & GUNDERSON, E. K. E. Spatial and perceptual components of crowding: Effects on health and satisfaction. *Environment and Behavior,* 1975, *7,* 225–236.

DESOR, J. A. Toward a psychological theory of crowding. *Journal of Personality and Social Psychology,* 1972, *21,* 79–83.

DIXON, J. M. Campus city revisited. *Architectural Forum,* 1968, *129,* 28–43.

DONNERSTEIN, E., & WILSON, D. W. Effects of noise and perceived control on ongoing and subsequent aggressive behavior. *Journal of Personality and Social Psychology,* 1976, *34,* 774–781.

DOOLEY, B. B. Crowding stress: The effects of social density on men with "close" or "far" personal space. Doctoral dissertation, University of California, 1974.

DUFFY, F. Role and status in the office. *Architectural Association Quarterly,* 1969, *1,* 4–14.

DURLAK, J. T., BEARDSLEY, B. E., & MURRAY, J. S. Observation of user activity patterns in open and traditional plan school environments. In W. J. Mitchell (ed.), *Environmental design: Research and practice.* Vol. 1 Proceedings of the EDRA 3/AR 8 Conference. Los Angeles: University of California, 1972.

EDWARDS, J., & BOOTH, A. Crowding and human sexual behavior. *Social Forces,* 1977, *55,* 791–808.

ELLIOTT, C. D. Noise tolerance and extraversion in children. *British Journal of Psychology,* 1971, *62,* 375–380.

EPSTEIN, Y. M. Crowding stress and human behavior. *Journal of Social Issues,* 1981, *37,* 126–144.

EVANS, G. W. Behavioral and physiological consequences of crowding in humans. *Journal of Applied Social Psychology,* 1979, *9,* 27–46.

EVANS, G. W., FELLOWS, J., ZORN, M., & DOTY, K. Cognitive mapping and architecture. *Journal of Applied Psychology,* 1982 (in press).

EVANS, G. W., & JACOBS, S. V. Air pollution and human behavior. *Journal of Social Issues,* 1981, *37,* 95–125.

FISHER, J. Situation-specific variables as determinants of perceived environmental aesthetic quality and perceived crowdedness. *Journal of Research in Personality,* 1974, *8,* 177–188.

FISKE, D. W., & MADDI, S. *Functions of varied experience.* Homewood: Dorsey, 1961.

FREEDMAN, J. L. *Crowding and behavior.* San Francisco: Freeman, 1975.

FREEDMAN, J. L., KLEVANSKY, S., & EHRLICH, P. R. The effects of crowding on human task performance. *Journal of Applied Social Psychology,* 1971, *1,* 7–25.

FRIED, M., & GLEICHER, P. Some sources of residential satisfaction in an urban slum. *Journal of the American Institute of Planners,* 1961, *27,* 305–315.

GASPARINI, A. Influence of the dwelling on family. *Ekistics,* 1973, *216,* 344–348.

GATTONI, F., & TARNOPOLSKY, A. Aircraft noise and psychiatric morbidity. *Psychological Medicine,* 1973, *3,* 628–634.

GLASS, D. C., & SINGER, J. E. *Urban stress.* New York: Academic, 1972.

GRIFFITT, W., & VEITCH. Hot and crowded: Influences of population density and temperature on interpersonal affective behavior. *Journal of Personality and Social Psychology,* 1971, *17,* 92–98.

HABER, G. M. The impact of tall buildings on users and neighbors. In D. Conway (ed.), *Human response to tall buildings.* Stroudsburg: Dowden, Hutchinson & Ross, 1977.

HAGGARD, E. A. Some effects of geographic and social isolation in natural settings. In J. Rasmussen (ed.), *Man in isolation and confinement.* Chicago: Aldine, 1973.

HALL, E. T. *The hidden dimension.* New York: Doubleday, 1966.

HARRIS, L. AND ASSOCIATES, INC. *The Steelcase National Study of Office Environments: Do they work?* Grand Rapids: Steelcase, 1978.

HELSON, H. *Adaptation-level theory*. New York: Harper, 1964.

HERSHBERGER, R. G. Predicting the meaning of architecture. In J. Lang, C. Burnette, W. Moleski, & D. Vachon (eds.), *Designing for human behavior: Architecture and the behavioral sciences*. Stroudsburg: Dowden, Hutchinson & Ross, 1974.

HOCKEY, G. R. Effect of loud noise on attentional selectivity. *Quarterly Journal of Experimental Psychology,* 1970, *22,* 28–36.

————. Effects of noise on human efficiency and some individual differences. *Journal of Sound and Vibration,* 1972, *20,* 299–304.

HOLAHAN, C. J., & SAEGERT, S. Behavioral and attitudinal effects of large-scale variation in the physical environment of psychiatric wards. *Journal of Abnormal Psychology,* 1973, *82,* 459–462.

HOMENUCK, P. *A study of high-rise: Effect, preferences, and perceptions*. Toronto: Institute of Environmental Research, 1973.

HUTT, C., & VAIZEY, M. J. Differential effects of group density on social behavior. *Nature,* 1966, *209,* 1371–1372.

ITTELSON, W. H., PROSHANSKY, H. M., & RIVLIN, L. G. Bedroom size and social interaction on the psychiatric ward. *Environment and Behavior,* 1970, *2,* 255–270.

IZUMI, K. Psychosocial phenomena and building design. In H. M. Proshansky, W. H. Ittelson, & L. G. Rivlin (eds.), *Environmental psychology: Man and his physical environment*. New York: Holt, 1970.

JEPHCOTT, P. *Homes in high flats*. Edinburgh: Oliver & Boyd, 1971.

JONES, D. M., CHAPMAN, A. J., & AUBURN, T. C. Noise in the environment: A social perspective. *Journal of Environmental Psychology,* 1981, *1,* 43–59.

JONNSON, E., & SORENSEN, S. Adaptation to community noise: A case study. *Journal of Sound and Vibration,* 1973, *26,* 571–575.

JOURARD, S. M. Some psychological aspects of privacy. *Law and Contemporary Problems,* 1966, *31,* 307–318.

JUSTA, F. C. & GOLAN, M. B. Office design: Is privacy still a problem? *Journal of Architectural Research,* 1977, *6,* 5–12.

KAMINOFF, R., MALTZ, J., PAXSON, L., TROVATI, J., & NOBILE, V. *Environmental evaluation and design recommendations for the advertising department*. New York: Center for Human Environments, 1980.

KANTOR, D., & LEHR, W. *Inside the family*. San Francisco: Jossey-Bass, 1975.

KHOMULO, L. P., RODINOVA, L. P., & RUSINOVA, A. P. Changes in the blood lipid metabolism of man owing to the prolonged effects of industrial noise on the central nervous system. *Kardologia,* 1967, *7,* 35–38.

KILDAY, P. Travellers go crazy in big Dallas–Fort Worth Airport. *Associated Press News Service,* 8 July 1979.

KNIGHT, R. C., WEITZER, W. H., & ZIMRING, C. M. *Opportunity for control and the built environment: The ELEMR project*. Amherst: University of Massachusetts, Environmental Institute, 1973.

KOKOKUSHA, D. *Report on investigation of living environment around Osaka International Airport*. Osaka: Association for the Prevention of Aircraft Nuisance, 1973.

KRYTER, K. D. *The effects of noise on man*. New York: Academic, 1970.

KUPER, L. *Living in towns*. London: Cressett, 1953.

KYZAR, B. L. *Comparison of instructional practices in classrooms of different design*. Alua, Oklahoma: Northwestern State College, School Planning Laboratory, 1971.

LANGER, E., & SAEGERT, S. Crowding and cognitive control. *Journal of Personality and Social Psychology,* 1977, *35,* 175–182.

LAUFER, R. S., PROSHANSKY, H. M., & WOLFE, M. Some analytic dimensions of privacy. In R. Kuller (ed.), *Architectural psychology*. Stroudsburg: Dowden, Hutchinson & Ross, 1974.

LAVE, L., & SESKIN, E. Air pollution and human health. *Science, 1970, 169, 723–733.*

LAZARUS, R. S. *Psychological stress and the coping process*. New York: McGraw-Hill, 1966.

LEVY, L., & HERZOG, A. N. Effects of population density and crowding on health and social adaptation in the Netherlands. *Journal of Health and Social Behavior, 1974, 15, 228–240.*

LILLY, J. *The deep self*. New York: Simon & Schuster, 1977.

LYNCH, K. *The image of the city*. Cambridge: MIT Press, 1960.

MacKINTOSH, J. M. *Housing and family life*. London: Cassell, 1952.

MAIZELS, J. *Two to five in high flats*. London: Housing Center, 1961.

MATHEWS, K. E. JR., & CANNON, L. K. Environmental noise level as a determinant of helping behavior. *Journal of Personality and Social Pychology, 1975, 32, 571–577.*

McCAIN, G., COX, V., & PAULUS, P. The relationship between illness complaints and degree of crowding in a prison environment. *Environment and Behavior, 1976, 8, 289–291.*

McCARTHY, D., & SAEGERT, S. Residential density, social overload, and social withdrawal. *Human Ecology, 1978, 6, 253–271.*

MEHRABIAN, A., & RUSSELL, J. A. A measure of arousal seeking tendency. *Environment and Behavior, 1973, 5, 315–334.*

MICHELSON, W. *Environmental change*. University of Toronto, Center for Urban and Community Studies research paper no. 60. 1973.

MILGRAM, S. The experience of living in cities. *Science, 1970, 167, 1461–1468.*

MITCHELL, R. Some social implications of high density housing. *American Sociological Review, 1971, 36, 18–29.*

MOORE, G. T. Knowing about environmental knowing: The current state of theory and research on environmental cognition. *Environment and Behavior, 1979, 11, 33–70.*

MORVILLE, J. *Children's play on flatted estates* (English summary). Copenhagen: Statens Byggeforsknings Institut, 1969.

NEMECEK, J., & GRANDJEAN, E. Results of an ergonomic investigation of large-space offices. *Human Factors, 1973, 15, 111–124.*

NEWMAN, O. *Defensible space*. New York: Macmillan, 1972.

PAGE, R. A. Noise and helping behavior. *Environment and Behavior, 1977, 9, 311–334.*

PARVIZPOOR, D. Noise exposure and prevalence of high blood pressure among weavers in Iran. *Journal of Occupational Medicine, 1976, 18, 730–731.*

PASTALAN, L. Involuntary environmental relocation: Death and survival. In W. F. E. Prelser (ed.), *Environmental design research*, vol. 2. Stroudsburg, Pennsylvania: Dowden, Hutchinson & Ross, 1973.

PAULUS, P. B., COX, V. C., McCAIN, G., & CHANDLER, J. Some effects of crowding in a prison environment. *Journal of Applied Social Psychology, 1975, 5, 86–91.*

PAULUS, P. B., McCAIN, G., & COX, V. C. Death rates, psychiatric commitments, blood pressure, and perceived crowding as a function of institutional crowding. *Environmental Psychology and Nonverbal Behavior, 1978, 3, 107–116.*

PEAKE, P. & LEONARD, J. A. The use of heart rate as an index of stress in blind pedestrians. *Ergonomics, 1971, 14, 189–204.*

PERIN, C. Concepts and methods for studying environments in use. In W. J. Mitchell (ed.), *Environmental design: Research and practice*. Proceedings of the EDRA 3/AR 8 Conference. Los Angeles: University of California, 1972.

PETRIE, A., COLLINS, W., & SOLOMON, P. The tolerance for pain and sensory deprivation. *American Journal of Psychology, 1960, 123, 80–90.*

PIAGET, J. *Play, dreams, and imitation in childhood.* New York: Norton, 1951.

POLLOWY, A. *The urban nest.* Stroudsburg, Pennsylvania: Dowden, Hutchinson & Ross, 1977.

POULTON, E. C. Composite model for human performance in continuous noise. *Psychological Review,* 1979, *86,* 361–375.

PRESCOTT, E. The large day care center as a child-rearing environment. *Voice for Children,* 1970, *2,* (4).

PROSHANSKY, H. M. Environmental psychology and the real world. *American Psychologist, 1976, 4,* 303–310.

PROSHANSKY, H. M., ITTELSON, W. H., & RIVLIN, L. G. Freedom of choice and behavior in a physical setting. In H. M. Proshansky, W. H. Ittelson, & L. G. Rivlin (eds.), *Environmental psychology: Man and his physical setting.* New York: Holt, 1970.

PROSHANSKY, H. M., & KAMINOFF, R. D. Place-identity: The physical socialization of the self. Manuscript. New York: City University Graduate Center 1982.

PROSHANSKY, H. M., NELSON-SHULMAN, Y., & KAMINOFF, R. D. The role of physical settings in life-crisis experiences. In I. G. Sarason & C. R. Spielberger (eds.), *Stress and anxiety,* vol. 6. Washington, D.C.: Hemisphere, 1979.

RAPOPORT, A. *House form and culture.* Englewood Cliffs, New Jersey: Prentice-Hall, 1969.

—————. Toward a redefinition of density. *Environment and Behavior,* 1975, *7,* 131–158.

RIESEN, A. H. (ed.). *The developmental neuropsychology of sensory deprivation.* New York: Academic, 1975.

RIVLIN, L. G., & ROTHENBERG, M. The use of space in open classrooms. In H. M. Proshansky, W. H. Ittelson, & L. G. Rivlin (eds.), *Environmental psychology: People and their physical settings* (2d ed.). New York: Holt, 1976.

RODIN, J. Density, perceived choice, and responses to controllable and uncontrollable outcomes. *Journal of Experimental Social Psychology,* 1976, *12,* 564–578.

RODIN, J., & BAUM, A. Crowding and helplessness: Potential consequences of density and loss of control. In A. Baum & Y. M. Epstein (eds.), *Human response to crowding.* Hillsdale, New Jersey: Erlbaum, 1978.

RUESCH, J., & KEES, W. Function and meaning in the physical environment. In H. M. Proshansky, W. II. Ittelson, & L. G. Rivlin (eds.), *Environmental psychology: Man and his physical setting.* New York: Holt, 1970.

SAEGERT, S. Crowding: Cognitive overload and behavioral constraint. In W. Preiser (ed.), *Environmental design research,* vol. 2. Stroudsburg: Dowden, Hutchinson & Ross, 1973.

—————. The effects of spatial and social density on arousal, mood, and social orientation. *Dissertation Abstracts International,* 1975, *35,* 3649.

—————. High-density environments: Their personal and social consequences. In A. Baum & Y. M. Epstein (eds.), *Human response to crowding.* Hillsdale: Erlbaum, 1978.

SAEGERT, S., & KAMINOFF, R. D. Background density, personality, and current susceptibility to crowding phenomena. Manuscript. New York: Center for Human Environments, 1982.

SAEGERT, S., MACKINTOSH, E., & WEST, S. Two studies of crowding in urban public spaces. *Environment and Behavior,* 1975, *7,* 159–184.

SAWIN, D. B., PARKE, R. D., & DIMICELI, S. Privacy in the home: A developmental and situational analysis. Paper presented to the biennial meeting of the Society for Research in Child Development, 1975.

SCHMITT, R. C. Implications of density of Hong Kong. *Journal of the American Institute of Planners,* 1963, *24,* 210–217.

—————. Density, health, and social disorganization. *Journal of the American Institute of Planners,* 1966, *32,* 38–40.

Schopler, J., & Walton, M. The effects of structure, expected enjoyment, and participants' internality-externality upon feelings of being crowded. Manuscript, University of North Carolina, 1974.

Schorr, A. L. *Slums and social insecurity*. Washington, D.C.: U.S. Government Printing Office, 1966.

Seligman, M. *Helplessness*. San Francisco: Freeman, 1975.

Sherrod, D. R. Crowding, perceived control, and behavioral after effects. *Journal of Applied Social Psychology*, 1974, *4*, 171–186.

Sherrod, D. R. & Downs, R. Environmental determinants of altruism: the effects of stimulus overload and perceived control on helping. *Journal of Experimental Social Psychology*, 1974, *10*, 468–479.

Sivadon, P. Space as experienced: Therapeutic implications. In H. M. Proshansky, W. H. Ittelson, & L. G. Rivlin (eds.), *Environmental psychology: Man and his physical setting*. New York: Holt, 1970.

Sommer, R. *Personal space: The behavioral basis of design*. Englewood Cliffs: Prentice-Hall, 1969.

Smith, S. L. Extraversion and sensory thresholds. *Psychophysiology*, 1968, *5*, 293–299.

Smith, S. L., & Haythorn, W. W. Effects of compatability, crowding, group size, and leadership seniority on stress, anxiety, hostility, and annoyance in isolated groups. *Journal of Personality and Psychology*, 1972, *22*, 67–79.

Southworth, M. The sonic environment of cities. *Environment and Behavior*, 1969, *1*, 49–70.

Spivak, M Sensory distortions in tunnels and corridors. *Hospital and Community Psychiatry*, 1967, *18*, 24–30.

Steele, F. *Physical settings and organization development*. Reading: Addison-Wesley, 1973.

Stevens, S. S. Stability of human performance under intense noise. *Journal of Sound and Vibration*, 1972, *21*, 35–36.

Stokols, D. On the distinction between density and crowding: Some implications for future research. *Psychological Review*, 1972, *79*, 275–277.

————. The experience of crowding in primary and secondary environments. *Environment and Behavior*, 1976, *8*, 49–86.

————. A typology of crowding experiences. In A. Baum & Y. M. Epstein (eds.), *Human response to crowding*. Hillsdale: 1978.

————. A congruence analysis of human stress. In I. G. Sarason & C. D. Spielberger (eds.), *Stress and anxiety*, vol. 6. Washington, D.C.: Hemisphere, 1979.

Stokols, D., Rall, M., Pinner, B., & Schopler, J. Physical, social, and personal determinants of the perception of crowding. *Environment and Behavior*, 1973, *5*, 87–115.

Suedfeld, P. Social isolation: A case for interdisciplinary research. *Canadian Psychologist*, 1974, *15*, 1–15.

————. *Restricted environmental stimulation*. New York: Wiley, 1981.

Sundstrom, E. Crowding as a sequential process: Review of research on the effects of population density on humans. In A. Baum & Y. M. Epstein (eds.), *Human response to crowding*. Hillsdale: Erlbaum, 1978.

Ullman, L. *Institution and outcome: A comparative study of psychiatric hospitals*. New York: Pergamon, 1967.

Valins, S., & Baum, A. Residential group size, social interaction, and crowding. *Environment and Behavior*, 1973, *5*, 421–439.

Weinstein, N. D. Individual differences in reactions to noise: A longitudinal study in a college dormitory. *Journal of Applied Psychology*, 1978, *63*, 458–466.

Weisman, G. A study in architectural legibility. Doctoral dissertation, University of Michigan, 1979.

WEKERLE, G. R. Vertical village: The social world of a highrise complex. Doctoral dissertation, Northwestern University, 1974.

WENER, R. E., & KAMINOFF, R. D. Environmental clarity and perceived crowding. In A. D. Seidel & S. Danford (eds.), *Environmental design: Research, theory, and application.* Washington, D.C.: Environmental Design Research Association, 1979.

WESTIN, A. *Privacy and freedom.* New York: Atheneum, 1967.

WILKINSON, R. T., FOX, R. H., GOLDSMITH, R., HAMPTON, I. F. G., & LEWIS, H. E. Psychological and physiological responses to raised body temperature. *Journal of Applied Physiology,* 1964, *19,* 287–291.

WILNER, D. M., WALKEY, R. P., PINKERTON, T. C., & TAYBACK, M. *The housing environment and family life.* Baltimore: John Hopkins Press, 1962.

WINKEL, G. H., OLSEN, R., WHEELER, F., & COHEN, M. *The museum visitor and orientational media.* New York: Center for Human Environments, 1975.

WINSBOROUGH, H. The social consequences of high population density. *Law and Contemporary Problems,* 1965, *30,* 120–126.

WOHLWILL, J. Human response to levels of stimulation. *Human Ecology,* 1974, *2,* 127–247.

WOHLWILL, J., & KOHN, I. The environment as experienced by the migrant: An adaptation-level view. *Representative Research in Social Psychology,* 1973, *4,* 135–64.

WOLFE, M. Childhood and privacy. In I. Altman & J. Wohlwill (eds.), *Human behavior and the environment: Children and the environment,* vol. 3. New York: Plenum, 1978.

WOLFENSBERGER, W. The normalization principle and some major implications to architectural-environment design. In M. J. Bednar (ed.), *Barrier-free environments.* Stroudsburg: Dowden, Hutchinson & Ross, 1977.

WORCHEL, S. The experience of crowding: An attributional analysis. In A. Baum & Y. M. Epstein (eds.), *Human response to crowding.* Hillsdale: Erlbaum, 1978.

YANCEY, W. L. Architecture, interaction, and social control: The case of a large-scale public housing project. *Environment and Behavior,* 1971, *3,* 3–18.

ZIMRING, C. M. Cognitive mapping and the blind. Paper presented at the annual meeting of the Environmental Design Research Association, Buffalo, 1979.

————. Stress and the designed environment. *Journal of Social Issues,* 1981, *37,* 145–171.

ZUBEK, J. P. (ed.). *Sensory deprivation.* Englewood Cliffs: Prentice-Hall, 1969.

ZUCKERMAN, M. Dimensions of sensation seeking. *Journal of Consulting and Clinical Psychology,* 1971, *36,* 45–52.

24

Sensory Deprivation and Overload

Leo Goldberger

SENSORY DEPRIVATION and sensory overload are topics that appear to have found a permanent place in the literature as environmental sources of stress, that is, as external, physical stressors. This chapter presents a succinct and largely retrospective overview of sensory deprivation and, to a lesser extent, sensory overload research and highlights the substantive yield of knowledge in an area that has been characterized by a morass of misinformation, exaggeration, and confounding of variables. It should be noted at the outset that my focus will be the identification of effects, whether stressful or not, attributable primarily to either sensory restriction or excessive stimulation. Such obviously stressful situations as imprisonment, solitary confinement, being cast adrift, or experiencing urban noise and overcrowding—in which sensory deprivation or sensory overload per se are aspects or components but certainly not the most salient determinants—will be ignored in this overview. Experimentally induced sensory deprivation and sensory overload may indeed be experienced by many subjects as stressful, but these laboratory situations may also be experienced as tolerable and even pleasurable. The wide range of responses largely reflects mediation by cultural and individual differences (see Suedfeld, 1980, for a discussion of nonstressful response to sensory deprivation).

SENSORY DEPRIVATION

Even before the publication of the first findings on the "effects of decreased variation in the sensory environment" (Bexton, Heron, & Scott, 1954), word had spread about experiments at McGill University (conceived of by Hebb and his students) in which college student subjects, kept isolated and deprived of perceptual experiences, experienced vivid hallucinations, body image disturbances, and thought disorders. The first published report captured the imagination of psychiatric and psychological researchers, who quickly put together their own experimental setups (soundproofed rooms, respirators, or water tanks) to probe this area themselves. These early investigators—Lilly, Vernon, Solomon, Azima, Goldberger and Holt, Silverman, Cohen, Ruff, Freedman, and a handful of others—were essentially exploring the range and limits of this new experimental technique. Soon both the specialized journals and the popular press were filled with discussions of perceptual isolation and sensory or stimulus deprivation; reviews of anecdotal data appeared (C. Brownfield, 1965); and in 1958 the first symposium was organized bringing together the initial group of investigators (Solomon, Kubzansky, Leiderman, Mendelson, & Wexler, 1961). A new field had been born.

The widespread fascination with sensory deprivation in part reflected to the original tie-in with "brainwashing"—a timely subject in the early 1950s. This interest also had relevance to another popular concern, the Mercury space program, which included sensory deprivation among the stress procedures used to screen potential astronauts. But perhaps even more fundamental was the fact that on the face of it, here was a manipulation that made a *real difference*. To be able to induce major behavioral and physiological changes by psychological means was indeed worthy of attention. To induce a phenomenon experimentally is to get close to understanding its cause. Such was the promise held out by early research on sensory deprivation.

The field reached its peak in the 1960s, during which period increasingly more sophisticated and ingeniously controlled studies were being conducted, notably by Zubek, Zuckerman, Suedfeld, and Myers—all among the contributors to perhaps the most authoritative volume in the area, edited by Zubek (1969), which critically reviewed and summed up the field and included a bibliography of some 1300 items.

Methods

Sensory deprivation is the generic term for a variety of complex experimental conditions (frequently quite stressful) aimed at drastically reducing the level and variability of a person's normal stimulation from, and commerce with, his environment for a relatively prolonged period of time.

The original aim of sensory deprivation research was to determine the effects on human functioning of a drastic curtailment of sensory stimulation. The approach paralleled that used in animal experiments: human beings were placed in laboratory settings of three basic types: bed confinement in a sound attenuated or soundproofed room, confinement in a tank type respirator, or suspension in a water tank. The salient experimental variable was presumed to be a reduction of environmental stimulation—in either the variety or the amount of sensory input (as it turns out, the oft made conceptual distinction between perceptual isolation and sensory deprivation proper has only little empirical significance).

Typically, subjects were used either in short-term studies, as in the water immersion studies (up to 8 hours), or in long-term experiments, in which a 72-hour stretch was fairly characteristic, though in some cases as much as a week was used. The basic experimental paradigm called for baseline testing on a variety of psychological and physiological measures, with periodic testing during the study (usually via intercommunication arrangements) and a posttesting session. Subjects in the long-term studies generally were able to go to the toilet and to feed themselves, thus making any social contact unnecessary, except via the intercommunication system for emergency purposes, for periodic, self-regulated, subjective reports on thoughts and feelings, and for testing. The standardized, 242-item Isolation Symptom Questionnaire (Myers & Zubek, 1969) was increasingly used.

The original research aim met with obstacles from a variety of methodological sources, so that interpretation of findings was difficult. It was nearly impossible to control for each of the many potentially relevant parameters inherent in the complex of conditions. Among the variables found to affect and confound the interpretation of experimental results were type of confinement, instructions, duration, restriction of movement, expectations, and the everpresent variable of personality. And because each laboratory used its own experimental setup and its own procedures for assessing effects, comparability of data suffered. Effects originally ascribed to sensory reduction might in fact have been caused by any number of other variables, singly or in combination. Moreover, experience taught most investigators that another very troublesome obstacle to unambiguous findings lay in the fact that a subject undergoing sensory deprivation is in a totally altered life situation, which affects his defenses, fantasies, motivations, and cognitive and interpersonal stratagems.

Findings

In view of both the inherent methodological problems and the procedural differences marking the sensory deprivation field, it is surprising that any enduring, replicable, and meaningful findings emerged. But the bulk of the evidence gathered since the McGill report (Bexton, Heron, & Scott, 1954) does support the original claims, albeit with some qualifications necessitated by the additional specification of the variables responsible for the effects. To summarize briefly, it is still valid to assert that sensory deprivation induces an altered state of consciousness that is characterized

1. *neurologically* by a progressive slowing in mean alpha frequency and by the appearance of marked delta—and, in long-term studies, also of excessive theta—wave activity, especially in the temporal lobes;
2. *autonomically* by a decrease in skin resistance (i.e., increased arousal), though by no other consistent autonomic differences (e.g., in heart rate, respiration, temperature, blood pressure, metabolic rate);
3. *biochemically* by no consistent findings in urinary levels of oxycorticoids and catecholamines (except for subjects in the respirator setup), but by certain individual differences between "stayers" and "quitters" in pre-isolation levels of adrenaline and serum uric acid, as well as in urine excreted during deprivation. The evidence suggests, however, that the *major sources of stress* inhere in the *confinement, social isolation,* and *physical immobility* aspects of the total experimental situation rather than in sensory restriction per se;
4. *psychologically* by boredom, apathy, and a state of motivational loss, which in the realm of thought processes takes the form of mind wandering, reverie, and fantasy activity interspersed with periods of sleep and attendant hypnogogic and hypnopomic phenomena. Subjective reports of attention and concentration deficits and of impairment in the maintenance of logical, directed thinking receive support from objective cognitive test findings, with deficits revealed only on tasks requiring complex, self-directed efforts. Rote learning, simple digit-span performance, and memory for meaningful material, however, tend to be facilitated!

Most investigators have strongly cautioned against linking the phenomena subsumed under the generic label "hallucinatory activity"—vividly projected images, varying in content, complexity, and origin, rendered primarily in the visual mode and occurring most frequently during high to medium arousal—to hallucinations observed in the psychoses. Rather, these phenomena appear more akin to those found in certain drug induced hallucinatory states, albeit not as vivid, colorful, or persistent (Goldberger & Holt, 1958; Zubek, 1969).

Certain sensory effects, such as lowered thresholds and increased acuity, are a consistent concomitant of sensory deprivation, which is in keeping with the general sensitivity to minimal and residual stimulation and the stimulus hunger that subjects characteristically show.

Another consistent finding in relation to stress has been that about one-third of all subjects in sensory deprivation experiments quit before the official termination of the experimental run—no matter how long the scheduled duration. Individual differences have loomed large in regard not only to endurance to sensory deprivation but also to most other effect measures, but they have not been readily reducible to personality variables. In large part, this reflects the multidimensional nature of the total experimental situation. With systematic fractionation, each situational parameter or dimension would be found to have a special linkage to a set of personality characteristics. Effects such as anxiety and anger, for example, are clearly attributable to the extraneous and most stressful aspects of the situation, such as confinement, enforced passivity, and social isolation, and could be expected to relate to personality variables quite different from those linked to tolerance for the curtailment of external stimulation. Nevertheless, such personal characteristics as overall ego strength, tolerance for primary-process ideation, field dependence-independence, and sensation seeking needs have been consistently identified as meaningful individual difference correlates (Goldberger, 1961; Goldberger & Holt, 1961; Zuckerman, 1974).

Theoretical Formulations

The theoretical context of sensory deprivation studies has naturally varied in accordance with the special interest and focus of the investigator. Though the various theoretical constructs employed are by no means incompatible with one another, they derive from three different levels of behavior analysis: neurophysiological, psychoanalytic, and psychological.

The neurophysiological perspective was introduced by Hebb (1955), who saw in these experiments a way of clarifying sensory-cortical interaction. Within this formulation, repetitive, homogeneous, or drastically reduced stimulation is seen as causing the diffuse projection system of the *reticular formation*—the neurological system deemed essential for arousal and organized cortical activity—to become habituated. When this occurs, cortical functioning becomes disorganized and synchronous firing of cells takes place. The sensory deprivation effects are thus interpreted as a reflection of a general *habituation syndrome*.

From the psychoanalytic viewpoint, an intimate relationship between mode of thought and the presence or absence of reality contact is postulated (Rapaport, 1958). With diminished reality contact (as in sensory deprivation or sleep), a shift from the *secondary-process* (logical, realistic) to the *primary-process* (drive organized, developmentally primitive) mode takes place.

In the main, the psychological theories have involved a broad cognitive perspective in which constructs derived from information processing theory play a central role, along with a general social-psychological approach in which the key concepts revolve around the role of the subject's expectations and the demand characteristics of the situation. A narrower and more specialized conception posits a specific drive for sensory variation, termed *sensoristatis* (Schultz, 1965), and suggests that each person has an optimal level of arousal that is determined by a number of confluent factors, including constitution, age, learning, recent level of stimulation, task demands, and diurnal cycling.

Applications

One cannot help but be impressed by the many-sidedness of the sensory deprivation field. The range of topics, ideas, and foci in the literature is staggering. Though it is easy to criticize so-called method oriented research, it must be remembered that methods do legitimately open doors to the investigation of a variety of problems other than the ones to which they are first applied. Sensory deprivation is a powerful technique—a life-sized, temporally extended, projective test that calls for a real adaptive response rather than simply a test response. For many researchers this avenue of study has led not only to stress (i.e., Zuckerman, 1964) but also to personality, ego autonomy, response to unstructured situations (Goldberger, 1961), suggestibility, sensitivity to internal cues, stimulus seeking behavior, temporal orientation (see Zubek, 1965), clinical problems (e.g., the effects of post–eye surgery patching (Ziskind, 1965), and therapeutic application (Cooper, Adams, & Cohen, 1964). It has permitted exploration of the social psychology of the psychological experiment (Orne & Scheibe, 1964). It has brought within the sphere of the laboratory analogues of a number of real-life problems—space flight, work under arctic weather conditions, small-group confinement, monotony in assembly line jobs, long-distance truck driving, and geographic or social isolation in natural settings (Rasmussen, 1973). And it has required behavioral researchers at least to acknowledge such cognitive or phenomenological notions as purpose, meaning, doing, structure, and states of consciousness, along with such poorly understood phenomena as boredom, encapsulation, and sense of isolation.

SENSORY OVERLOAD

The concept of *sensory overload* (sensory overstimulation) designates a situation in which the organism is bombarded by higher than normal levels of sensory stimulation, usually in more than one sensory modality. It is the obverse of sensory deprivation (sensory underload) and is similarly classed as a potential stressor.

Considering the implications of sensory overload research for the comon experience of overstimulation in today's technologically advanced society, it is surprising that there has been only a handful of experimental studies on the effects of overload, in contrast to the large number of sensory deprivation studies (Zubek, 1969). Would-be investigators may be discouraged by the operational specification of stimulation as excessive and the frequently added definitional requirement that the stimulation be sudden and unpredictable, not to mention the methodological problems inherent in separating the attributes of diversity, instability, novelty, complexity, and meaningfulness of stimulation.

Despite the meager data base, references abound to the maladaptive effects of sensory overload, running the gamut of psychopathology from schizophrenic and organiclike symptoms to phenomena associated with so-called psychedelic states. Perhaps the most dramatic view of the consequences now broadly attributed to overstimulation is afforded by Toffler's (1970) *Future Shock,* in which the additional notions of *information overload* and *decision stress* are treated as sharing essential characteristics with sensory overload. Information overload, a concept introduced in 1959 by Miller (1964), is intimately connected with sensory overload: sensory input is usually also the conveyor of symbolic meaning (i.e., information). Nonetheless, the two concepts may be conceptually and operationally distinguished. Lipowsky (1975) placed still other areas within the orbit of sensory overload, such as field studies of urban life and experimental studies on the effects of crowding, population density, and noise. Lipowsky argued that sensory and informational overloads are vitally important concepts that have far-reaching implications for the psychological and physical well-being of man. A number of authors, among them McReynolds (1960) and Silverman (1972), have also seen sensory overload as a relevant construct for the understanding of schizophrenia. Finally, Spitz (1964), in discussing experiments by Calhoun (1962) that showed the deleterious effects of crowding and overstimulation on rats, extrapolated to clinical observations on infants who suffered emotional overload associated with the "wrong kind of mothering," "undisciplined parental behavior," and other excessive stimulation; he suggested the relevance of sensory overload to developmental disorders.

Theoretical Formulations

The scientific interest in sensory overload may be traced to Lindsley's (1961) proposal that the conditions of sensory overload, sensory underload, and sensory distortion have a common neurophysiological mechanism, namely, the ascending reticular formation. Lindsley viewed the ascending reticular formation as a barometer for both sensory input and sensory output; a homeostatic regulator of input-output relations that is subject to an adaptation level. Any deviation from the established level upsets the balance of the regulating system, resulting in a variety of disturbances. Specifically addressing the condition of overstimulation of two or more sense modalities (especially if there is a sudden and intense input from afferent and corticofugal sources), Lindsley noted that "blocking of the reticular formation may occur and behavioral immobilization and general confusion may result" (p. 176).

A number of related conceptions and theoretical elaborations have been introduced that have a bearing on sensory overload. Hebb (1955) proposed a homeostatic theory that views the organism as acting so as to produce an optimal level of excitation. Berlyne (1960) ascribed drive inducing properties to deviations from an optimum influx of arousal potential. Malmo (1959) and many others have written extensively about the notion of a general activation level, which in turn has been related to external sensory input and the inverted U-curve formulation: under conditions of excessive sensory input, a correspondingly high activation level will ensue, resulting in impaired performance across a variety of tasks. Mention should also be made of concepts that emphasize the organism's limited capacity to deal with a massive sensory influx: Freud's "protective barrier against stimulation" (Freud, 1922) (frequently viewed as a developmental precursor of the classic defense mechanisms); Pavlov's (1955) "protective inhibition" concept; and the "filter theory of attention," associated with Broadbent's (1958, 1971) work. Aside from speculating about defective filter mechanisms, or a "thin stimulus barrier" (Bergman & Escalona, 1969), some investigators have invoked various conceptions of cognitive control and stylistic or protective strategies as heuristic explanations for observed individual differences in habitual sensitivity and response to extreme stimulation (see for example, Silverman's [1964] work on scanning; Haer's [1971] on field dependence; and Petrie's [1967] on the augmenting-reducing dimension).

Experimental Studies

The experimental studies that have been conducted on sensory overload (Gottschalk, Haer, & Bates, 1972; Haer, 1970, 1971; Ludwig, 1971, 1972, 1973), including a series of experiments at Tohuku University in Japan and a few other investigations (see Lipowsky, 1975), have all been of short duration, averaging some 2.5 hours, in contrast to the fairly long runs characteristic of deprivation studies. This fact may in itself be a reflection of the greater aversiveness of the sensory overload condition. Most of the studies have aimed quite specifically at inducing an altered state of consciousness (or psychedelic state) by whatever psychological means seemed most promising and potent. This aim is apparent in the techniques used and, because of the obvious demand characteristics in Orne's (1962) sense, may have exerted a strong influence on subjects' responses.

Essentially, the procedure involves confining a subject in a so-called sensory overload chamber—a total sensory environment like a geodesic dome (10 feet in diameter)—in which the subject is surrounded by and immersed in visual and auditory input. Typically, the subject reclines comfortably on a carpeted floor; a 16mm movie projector displays films of various kinds (abstract, colored designs); electronic music or cacophonous sounds blare from all directions; and intense and changing colored illumination is provided. The experimental paradigm usually calls for the stimulation to be varied and random in presentation and maintained at high levels of intensity (experimental situations that are close analogues to 1960s discotheques featuring rock music and psychedelic light shows). In the studies by Ludwig (1971, 1973), which, within certain limits, allowed the subject to regulate the level and type of input by employing a fixed-ratio button-pressing method, the stimulation was totally devoid of symbolic meaning. By contrast, in the studies by Haer (1970, 1971) and by Gottschalk, Haer, and Bates (1972), emotionally arousing thematic contents were injected into the visual stimulation, although the themes appeared in quick succession and in random order.

Findings have varied somewhat from study to study as a function of the stimuli and the mode of presentation; nevertheless, the evidence suggests that overstimulation tends to be more aversive than understimulation. Subjects in the former condition show heightened arousal: they report vivid imagery (and occasionally also hallucinatory and delusional processes), body image distortion, temporal disorientation, and intellectual-cognitive impairment. Significant individual differences have also been noted. The findings are no more than preliminary and suggestive, however, subject to qualification as more systematic work is performed on the much needed specification of the separate variables and their effects. What, for example, are the effects attributable solely to the factors of confinement, enforced passivity and the demand characteristics? What are the specific contributions to the overall stress of such *cognitive* variables as predictability of and perceived control over stimulation? Taking a clue from Glass and Singer's (1972) research on noise, it may well be these cognitive mediators, along with such factors as the meaning of the stimulation—excessive or not—for the person and his ongoing activity, that determine stress response to sensory overload. (See also Kaminoff and Proshansky, Chapter 23, this volume).

REFERENCES

Bergman, P., & Escalona, S. K. Unusual sensitivities in very young children. *Psychoanalytic Study of the Child,* 1949, *4,* 333-352

Bexton, W. H., Heron, B., & Scott, T. H. Effects of decreased variation in the sensory environment. *Canadian Journal of Psychology,* 1954, *8,* 70-76.

Broadbent, D. E. *Decision and stress.* New York: Academic, 1971.

BROWNFIELD, C. A. *Isolation: Clinical and experimental approaches.* New York: Random House, 1965.

CALHOUN, J. Population density and social pathology. *Scientific American,* 1962, *206,* 139–148.

COOPER, G. D., ADAMS, H. B., & COHEN, L. D. Personality changes after sensory deprivation. *Journal of Nervous and Mental Disease,* 1965, *140,* 103–118.

FREUD, S. *Beyond the pleasure principle.* London. Hogarth, 1922.

GLASS, D. C., & SINGER, J. E. *Urban stress.* New York: Academic, 1972.

GOLDBERGER, L. Reactions to perceptual isolation and Rorschach manifestations of the primary process. *Journal of Projective Techniques,* 1961, *25,* 287–302.

GOLDBERGER. L., & HOLT, R. R. Experimental interference with reality contact (perceptual isolation): Method and group results. *Journal of Nervous and Mental Disease.* 1958, *127,* 99–112.

GOLDBERGER, L., & HOLT, R. R. *A comparison of isolation effects and their personality correlates in two divergent samples.* WADC technical report no. 61–417, contract AF33(616)–6103. Wright-Patterson Air Force Base, 1961.

GOTTSCHALK, L. A., HAER, J. L., & BATES, D. E. Effects of sensory overload on psychological state. *Archives of General Psychiatry,* 1972, *27,* 451–456.

HAER, J. L. Field dependency in relation to altered states of consciousness produced by sensory overload. *Perceptual and Motor Skills,* 1971, *33,* 192–194.

HEBB, D. O. Drives and the CNS (central nervous system). *Psychological Review,* 1955, *62,* 243–254.

LINDSLEY, D. Common factors in sensory deprivation, sensory distortion, and sensory overload. In P. Solomon, P. E. Kubzansky, P. H. Leiderman, J. H. Mendelson, & D. Wexler, (eds.), *Sensory deprivation.* Cambridge: Harvard University Press, 1961.

LIPOWSKY, Z. J. Sensory and information inputs overload: Behavioral effects. *Comprehensive Psychiatry,* 1975, *16,* 199–221.

LUDWIG, A. M., & STARK, L. H. Schizophrenia, sensory deprivation, and sensory overload. *Journal of Nervous and Mental Disease,* 1973, *157,* 210–216.

McREYNOLDS, P. Anxiety, perception, and schizophrenia. In D. Jackson (ed.), *The etiology of schizophrenia.* New York: Basic Books, 1960.

MILLER, J. G. Psychological aspects of communication overloads. In R. W. Waggoner & D. J. Carek (eds.), *International psychiatry clinics: Communication in clinical practice.* Boston: Little, Brown, 1964.

ORNE, M. On the social psychology of the psychological experiment: With particular reference to the demand characteristics and their implications. *American Psychologist,* 1962, *17,* 776–783.

ORME, M. T., & SCHEIBE, K. E. The contribution of non-deprivation factors in the production of sensory deprivation effects: The psychology of the panic button. *Journal of Abnormal and Social Psychology,* 1964, *68,* 3–12.

PAVLOV, I. P. *Selected Works.* Moscow: Foreign Languages Publishing House, 1955.

RAPAPORT, D. The theory of ego-autonomy: A generalization. *Bulletin of the Menninger Clinic,* 1958, *22,* 13–35.

RASMUSSEN, J. (ed.). *Man in isolation and confinement.* Chicago: Aldine, 1973.

SCHULTZ, D. P. *Sensory restriction: Effects on behavior.* New York: Academic, 1965.

SILVERMAN, J. Scanning-control mechanism and "cognitive filtering" in paranoid and nonparanoid schizophrenia. *Journal of Consulting Psychology,* 1964, *28,* 385–393.

SOLOMON, P., KUBZANSKY, P. E., LEIDERMAN, P. H., MENDELSON, J., & WEXLER, D. (eds.). *Sensory deprivation.* Cambridge: Harvard University Press, 1961.

SPITZ, R. The derailment of dialogue: Stimulus overload, action cycles, and the completion gradient. *Journal of the American Psychoanalytic Association,* 1964, *12,* 752–775.

Suedfeld, P. *Restricted environmental stimulation: Research and clinical application.* New York: Wiley Interscience, 1980.

Toffler, A. *Future shock.* New York: Random House, 1970.

Zubek, J. P. (ed.). *Sensory deprivation: Fifteen years of research.* New York: Appleton, 1969.

Zuckerman, M. The sensation-seeking motive. In B. Maher (ed.), *Progress in experimental personality research,* vol. 7. New York: Academic, 1974.

Zuckerman, M. Perceptual isolation as a stress situation. A review. *Archive General Psychiatry,* 1964, *11,* 225–276.

Ziskind, E. An explanation of mental symptoms found in acute sensory deprivation experiments: Researches 1958–1963. *American Journal of Psychiatry,* 1965, *121,* 939–946.

25

Occupational Stress

Robert R. Holt

WORK HAS ALWAYS BEEN considered at best a mixed blessing, if not an absolute curse. The lack of any need to work was the chief attraction of the Garden of Eden, and when Adam was expelled God proclaimed: "In the sweat of thy face shalt thou eat bread." For centuries, it was taken for granted that work is hard, that it is only rarely its own reward, or gratifying in itself, but that it is undertaken in the first instance for extrinsic benefits—those of survival first, then comforts, pleasures, luxuries, and higher cultural rewards. Among the latter was the moral benefit of keeping out of mischief: Satan finds work for idle hands. Or, as Voltaire put it in *Candide,* perhaps reversing historical order, "Work keeps at bay three great evils: boredom, vice, and need."

The industrial revolution, which so transformed Western civilization in a few decades around the turn of the nineteenth century, profoundly changed the nature and organization of work. The factory was a new social invention, a special workplace for large numbers of people away from their homes, in which power machinery greatly multiplied workers' productivity and also exposed them to both obvious and subtle dangers. The new industrial processes made possible a great and widespread increase in the standard of living, but subjected factory workers to amputations, burns, and other accidental traumas. Both travelers and workers on the newly invented forms of mechanical transportation (railways, automobiles, airplanes) now risked accidents more severe and frequent than the era of the stagecoach ever knew, and the condition of traumatic neurosis had to be named and treated. More recently, whole populations are being exposed to pathogenic chemicals and ionizing radiation by industry.

A less obvious consequence of the new organization of work was that the producer of goods lost the autonomy he had had under the guild system and became a part of a hierarchical organization in which he was expected to do what he was told, often without understanding the function or value of the task assigned because of the great growth in the division of labor. The machine had its own pace; man was expected to keep up with it. The clock came to dominate most aspects of the worker's life, adding a new kind of pressure, time urgency. Perhaps we shall one day look on much of the stress of modern life as a previously unrecognized externality of our mechanized means of production (Mumford, 1967, 1970).

Preparation of this chapter was supported by a U.S. Public Health Service research career award (5-K06-MH-12455) from the National Institute of Mental Health.

These properties of industrial work created not only danger and stress but also a great imbalance of power between the entrepreneur, who had the capital to start an enterprise, and the people he hired. The trade union was invented as an attempt to regain some of the workers' lost power. From the beginning, the union movement sought to gain control over the unwanted and threatening side effects of work, diminishing if not abolishing these dangers. Pressure on employers from unions and later from government reinforced the weaker influence of enlightened humanitarianism and has made work safer in many respects than it was a few generations ago, although new dangers are constantly being discovered and the need for vigilance is eternal.

Though the fact is seldom mentioned, it should be apparent that the field of occupational stress (OS) easily becomes embroiled in social controversy, labor-management struggles, and even politics (witness the attacks of the 1980 political campaigns on the Occupational Safety and Health Administration). A psychologist may naively believe that proposed research on OS is just a disinterested search for truth but soon find himself under pressure to produce results that will support one or the other side in a union organizing drive centered on job hazards or in a management campaign against federal regulation. Therefore, research funded by either management or unions falls under inevitable suspicion.

Marx introduced one of the first general critiques of work that went beyond the traditional recognition that labor is fatiguing and dirtying, with sometimes unpleasant physiological side effects. Work for the vast majority under capitalism, said Marx, is alienated, deprived of its true meaning and significance and thus of its proper intrinsic value. Only since the rise of the mental health movement, however, has society become generally aware of a new class of deleterious aspects of work, defined by their largely psychological effects or, in some cases, by their psychological and sociological repercussions. Just as publicity about physical dangers brought abrupt reforms in the organization and conduct of various kinds of work that have made it possible to accomplish the same useful purposes without the harmful impacts, so now we are seeing an era of change or proposed change in the social and psychological circumstances of work to accomplish the same benefit.

Thus, OS is not a new phenomenon, but it is a relatively new concept and field of study. Perhaps the two essential ingredients necessary for OS to come into being as a subdiscipline were the founding of the field of psychosomatic medicine by Dunbar and others and the pioneering work of Selye on stress and the *general adaptation syndrome* as a fresh conceptualization of the nature of much illness. New hypotheses appeared about diseases of previously puzzling or unknown etiology, like peptic ulcer and essential hypertension, and perhaps not coincidentally these conditions began greatly increasing in observed numbers. Surveys by the Life Extension Institute (of New York City), covering 40,000 health examinations annually, indicated that between 1958 and 1972 stress diseases seemed to become "epidemic" (Chase, 1972).

Another important historical event, helping to crystallize OS as a new field of research, was the passage of the Occupational Safety and Health Act of 1970, creating the Occupational Safety and Health Administration (OSHA), in the Department of Labor, and the National Institute of Occupational Safety and Health (NIOSH), in the Department of Health, Education, and Welfare the following year. The former was charged with setting and enforcing standards of industrial health and safety, the latter with conducting and funding the research necessary to undergird these standards. From its beginning, NIOSH was directed to include psychological, behavioral, and motivational factors in the investigations it sponsored and carried out (Cohen & Margolis, 1973).

Papers on OS often begin with the remark that the concept of stress is unclear and variously defined. The chief source of confusion is whether to conceive of stress as a situational factor (the distressing circumstances external to the person) or a reaction (the disturbance of a person's normal state, viewed either physiologically or psychologically). Selye (1956) preferred the second definition, calling the external initiators of an organismic stress reaction *stressors*. Ironically, hardly anyone follows this usage. Indeed, stress is almost never used as a technical concept but just as a general term of negative evaluation for a state of upset or its precipitant. McGrath (1976) and some other writers try to use the word "stress" nonevaluatively, as more or less equivalent to activation, but that convention makes cross-study comparisons difficult. I shall follow the general practice of not trying to define stress more precisely than as a pointer to the dark side of work.

Put in commonsense terms, the basic proposition of the whole field of OS might be expressed thus: some aspects of many kinds of work have bad effects on most people under certain circumstances. The expansion and specification of that simple statement have already busied a few generations of good minds, and plenty of work remains to be done. By a process sometimes called a response definition of the stimulus, the field of occupational stress then becomes the study of those aspects of work that either have or threaten to have bad effects. The prevalent research paradigm is *stress* (independent variable) → *undesirable consequences* (dependent variable) under certain *parametric conditions* (moderator variable), which are not always included. This chapter investigates each domain in turn.

TYPES OF OCCUPATIONAL STRESS

As an initial orientation to OS, let us look at Table 25–1, which displays the main independent variables of OS research. The table has two principal parts, depending on whether stress is defined objectively or subjectively. This is not the same distinction as Selye's (1956) differentiation of stressor from stress; operationally, it is a matter of whether the researcher (or another outsider) defines what is stressful or the person being stressed does so.

Objectively Defined Stress

The objective stress of noise occupies a special place among occupational hazards. Though very high levels directly cause damage to the middle and the inner ear, with consequent impairment of hearing, less severe noise is treated as a psychological stress because, though distressing, it does not cause physical damage. A good many studies have focused directly on the irritation, tension, fatigue, and impaired efficiency of workers exposed to annoying noise (e.g., Cohen, 1980; Glass & Singer, 1972), but perhaps because it does not seem psychological enough noise is often neglected as a complicating factor in studies of other kinds of OS. Ferguson (1973), however, found that telegraphers showing signs of neurosis differentially complained of noise in the workplace and held negative attitudes toward the job and supervision.

In general, noise resembles many other physical stressors in that normal environments, which most people find comfortable and conducive to work, contain moderate levels. Outside a range of stimuli to which people adapt without effort or attention, either too little or too much light, temperature, humidity, barometric pressure, etc., is obtrusive and involves some adaptive strain, while extreme values damage tissues. Certain other aspects of the physical environment (e.g., exposure to electromagnetic fields, microwaves, or ionizing radiation) seem to have no optima above zero, but since they are difficult or impossible to

TABLE 25-1
Types of Stress Measured in OS Research (Independent Variables)

Objectively defined
  Physical properties of the working environment
    Physical hazards, chronic dangers (Althouse & Hurrell, 1977)[a]
    Pollution, less immediate dangers (House, 1972)
    Extremes of heat, cold, humidity, pressure, etc. (Biersner and associates, 1971)
    Noise (Glass & Singer, 1972)
    Bad man-machine design (Swain & Guttmann, 1980)

  Time variables
    Change in time zone or length of workday (McFarland, 1974)
    Nonstandard working hours (shift work) (Rentos & Shepard, 1976)
    Deadlines (Pearse, 1977)
    Time pressure (Schmidt, 1978)

  Social and organizational properties of work and its setting[b]
    Machine pacing (Murphy & Hurrell, 1980)
    Organizational or administrative irrationality, red tape (Cummings & De Cotiis, 1973)
    Work load, overload (Caplan, 1972)
    Responsibility load (Cobb, 1973)
    Monotony (Quinn, 1975)
    Participation
    Availability of intrinsic rewards (House, 1972)
    Availability of extrinsic rewards (pay scale, prestige) (House, 1972)
    Piecework versus hourly pay
    Poor labor-management relations (Colligan & Murphy, 1979)
  Changes in job
    Loss of job (unemployment) (Cobb & Kasl, 1977; Jahoda, 1979)
    Demotion (Kasl & French, 1962)
    Qualitative changes in job (Lederer, 1973)
    Overpromotion (Brook, 1973)
    Transfer of job locus (Renshaw, 1976)
    Change in shift pattern (Theorell, 1974)
    Null changes (nonevents) (Jolly, 1979)

Subjectively defined
  Role related
    Role ambiguity versus clarity (Kahn, 1973)
    Role conflict (Kahn, 1973)
    Role strain (MacKinnon, 1978)
    Degree of control over work processes (Frankenhaeuser & Gardell, 1976)
    Responsibility for people (Caplan and associates, 1975)
    Responsibility for things (Cobb, 1973)
    Participation (Caplan and associates, 1975)
    Feedback and communication problems (Moch, Bartunek, & Brass, 1979)
  Miscellaneous
    Job complexity, qualitative load (Caplan et al., 1975)
    Quantitative overload or underload (Kahn, 1973)
    Relationship to supervisor (Theorell, 1974)
    Inadequate support from, or performance by, supervisors (Pearse, 1977)
    Relationship to, or isolation from, co-workers (Theorell, 1974)
    Conflict with, or inadequate performance by, subordinates (Pearse, 1977)
    Conflict with, or pressure from, customers and/or community (Kroes and associates, 1974)
    Ambiguity about future, job insecurity (Caplan et al., 1975)
    Monotony (Quinn, 1975)
    Inequality of pay (Caplan et al., 1975)
    Underutilization of abilities (Caplan et al., 1975)
    Quantity-quality conflict (Kahn, 1973)

Subjectively defined (cont.)
  Person-environment (job) fit
    Role ambiguity (Caplan et al., 1975)
    Responsibility for people (Caplan et al., 1975)
    Responsibility for things (French, 1973)
    Quantitative work load (Caplan et al., 1975)
    Job complexity (Caplan et al., 1975), qualitative work load (French, 1973)
    Degree of control over work processes (Harrison, 1976)
    Participation (French, 1973; Singer, 1975)
    Opportunity for advancement (French, 1973)
  Off-job stress
    Disturbed life pattern of miscellaneous stresses (Neves, 1969)
    Stressful life events (Dohrenwend & Dohrenwend, 1974)
    Demands of husband and children on working women (Waldron, 1978)

[a] References in this table and in Tables 24–2 and 24–3 are purely illustrative. They cite sources in which the variables listed are described and defined and are not intended in any way to be comprehensive.
[b] These items are inferred, for the most part, not measured.

sense directly their potential as psychological stressors is largely unknown. In general, people are so adaptable that they can learn to work for long periods, even all their lives, under conditions most of us would find intolerable—e.g., in arctic cold, aboard submarines, or in humid jungles.

Among other physical properties of the working environment, its dangerousness—the exposure of workers to possible loss of life or limb—would seem to be an important source of psychological stress. Quite aside from the physiological impact of bruises or broken bones, chronic exposure to such dangers (even when they are successfully avoided) should tend to arouse the general adaptation syndrome (Selye, 1956), with detectable results on mental or physical health. A study of 486 coal miners found, however, that they did not *report* more stress than did 452 workers in jobs of similar status level, although they did experience significantly more "affective strains"—anxiety, depression, irritation, and somatic complaints (Althouse & Hurrell, 1977). Here is a first indication that subjective and objective measures of stress may give different results, and it is not always evident which will have the greater effect on health.

Several types of OS are hardly definable in any other than an objective way. One such stressor is nonstandard hours of work, or shift work. The phenomenon is widespread in the United States, with about one in every four workers having something other than usual daytime hours (Smith, Colligan, & Hurrell, 1980); the proportion of manufacturing workers on evening shifts is as high as 43% in Detroit (Owen, 1976). For various reasons, notably the reduced cost of off-peak energy, the numbers of workers affected will probably continue to rise rapidly, so this may be expected to become a more prominent source of OS.[1]

The basic research findings to date may be summarized in the following scheme: evening or night work causes disturbed circadian rhythms (of sleep, body temperature, gastrointestinal function, etc.) (A) and disturbed rhythms of social living (B); A in turn causes bad moods, poor sleep, and digestive compalints (C), while B causes malfunctioning in social roles and disruption of the family (D); C and D interact to bring about individual and social pathology. The problems are a good deal more complex than this scheme suggests. There are diverse shift schedules; and there are great differences in stability, with scheduled rotations effected daily, weekly, less frequently, or not at all. Consequently, it is difficult to compare research findings.

Another complicating aspect of research on the health effects of shift work is that people who cannot tolerate it drop out. It has been estimated that as many as 20% of workers cannot adapt to shift work (Bruusgard, 1975). Hence, the statistics that are gathered, being limited to those who can adapt, tell us little about the intrinsic relation between this particular kind of stress and illnesses or other strains. There should be little surprise, therefore, that many surveys of studies that simply compared morbidity rates in shift and nonshift workers (e.g., Taylor, 1973) found little evidence of deleterious effects except for complaints most obviously related to disturbed circadian rhythms—difficulties in sleeping and complaints about digestive and eliminative functions (Axelsson & Lundberg, 1975; Levine, 1976; Tasto & Colligan, 1978). In one study, however, which compared workers who stayed with shift work for three years and those who dropped out after six months, those who stayed showed *more* of the same troubles all had initially reported—disturbed sleep and GI functioning, anxiety, etc. (Meers, Maasen, & Verhaegen, 1978). In a large and more sophisticated study conducted under NIOSH auspices, Tasto and Colligan (1978) studied 1200 nurses and 1200 food processors. In both occupations, those who were on rotating shifts had more serious illnesses and more accidents than did those on steady shifts. Shift work (especially evening and rotating shifts) seems to have a negative impact on the domestic lives of workers, especially their sexual activity and parental responsibilities (Mott, Mann, McLoughlin, & Warwick, 1965; Tasto & Colligan, 1978).

Machine pacing has been much studied ever since Kornhauser's (1965) classic study of assembly line workers in the automobile industry. As Murphy and Hurrell (1980) pointed out, machine pacing is much more complex than one might at first think; the degree of the worker's control, the rigidity of pacing, the amount of rest time, etc., vary widely. These are easily manipulated variables, however, so the problem lends itself to experimental study. The only well-established finding from such research so far is that as the pressure of externally imposed work demand increases, heart rate goes up (Amaria, 1974; Ettema & Zielhuis, 1971; Johansson & Lindstrom, 1975). Though these experiments generally lacked ecological validity, the finding was supported by a field study of Swedish sawmill workers, which documented a higher incidence of caridovascular and other psychosomatic disorders among machine-paced than among nonpaced workers (Frankenhaueser & Gardell, 1976). Machine pacing produced elevated levels of excreted adrenaline and noradrenaline, often cited as cardiac risk factors (see also Froberg, Karlsson, Levi, Lidberg, & Seeman, 1970). As Kornhauser (1965) reported, machine-paced workers also complain more of monotony and general mental strain (Frankenhaueser & Gardell, 1976). Caplan and associates (Caplan, Cobb, French, Harrison, & Pinneau, 1975) found that of the 23 occupations they studied, assemblers and relief men on a machine-paced assembly line reported the most boredom and dissatisfaction wih their work; machine tenders also were very high on these measures. These three kinds of workers rated themselves most anxious, depressed, and irritated as well, and somatic complaints were most frequent among assemblers and relief men; assemblers made most visits to dispensaries. All in all, these two groups of machine-paced workers had the highest stress and strain of the workers studied (over 2000 subjects). Using the same measures of strain, Wilkes, Slammerjohn, and Lalich (n.d.) reported that machine-paced poultry inspectors scored only slightly lower on dissatisfaction with job and workload, boredom, and somatic complaints. None of these studies was either prospective or longitudinal, but several studies along such lines are under way (under NIOSH auspices).

Most social and organizational properties of work listed in Table 25-1, when not measured by workers' reports, are inferred or generally observed properties of jobs, cited in interpretations of findings. For example, seeking to explain the well-replicated findings that general practitioners have significantly more coronary heart disease than do other physicians (Morris, Heady, & Barley, 1952; Russek, 1960), and that foremen have peptic ulcers much more often than do the men they supervise (Doll & Jones, 1951; Vertin, 1954), Cobb (1973) hypothesized that the additional responsibility for persons is pivotal.

It is no historical accident that unemployment, the focus of pioneering psychological studies during the Great Depression, was relatively neglected as a source of OS until the end of the 1970s. One important study followed 162 blue-collar workers from the initial announcement that two plants were closing through the period of unemployment until they were relocated, repeatedly collecting physiological and psychological data (Cobb & Kasl, 1977; Kasl, Gore, & Cobb, 1975). As compared both to control workers and to themselves upon reemployment, the unemployed men had higher blood pressure (especially diastolic) during the periods of anticipation and joblessness. Results with other blood consituents (e.g., uric acid, cholesterol) were less clear-cut. Other recent research concentrated on mental health outcomcs (Dooley & Catalano, 1980; Theorell, Lind, & Floderus, 1975). As Jahoda (1979) commented, the recent work found the same types of impact as did studies 40–50 years earlier: deterioration of family relationships, more depression and irrational self-doubt, lower self-esteem (also reported by Cobb & Kasl, 1972), and higher incidence of psychiatric disorders.

Subjectively Defined Aspects of Stress

With thc cmergence of internally consistent measures, workers' own reports about many aspects of OS have proven highly useful (the Institute of Social Research, at the University of Michigan, played a major part in developing such measures). It has long been known that little participation in decisionmaking, ambiguity about job security, and poor use of skills and abilities are correlated with such strains as job related tension and job dissatisfaction (Argyris, 1964; Likert, 1961; Quinn, Seashore, Kahn, Mangione, Campbell, Slaines & McCullough, 1971). Nonparticipation was correlated especially strongly with eight strain measures, including depressed mood, escapist drinking, and overall physical health, reported by 1500 workers in 12 occupations (Quinn & Shepard, 1974). Hamner and Tosi (1974) and Caplan and associates (1975) reported significant associations between job conflict and anxiety. Similarly, Hite (1976) found job challenge (a mixture of utilization of abilities, degree of control over work processes, etc.) to be positively related to job self-esteem and negatively to the Zung (1965) measure of depression. Singer (1975) reported that among 1148 male governmental employees, underutilization of abilities and insufficient participation on the job accounted for more variance in psychological and somatic symptoms than did nonoccupational life stresses. These two variables were among the most strongly correlated with job dissatisfaction (r's of .42 and .36, respectively) and boredom (r's .59 and .31) in a sample of 310 men in 23 occupations (Caplan et al., 1975), along with ambiguity about job future ($r = .39$ with job dissatisfaction, .36 with boredom, and .24 with depression). Compare the findings of Margolis, Kroes, and Quinn (1974) from another large national sample of U.S. workers: nonparticipation was correlated .34 with job dissatisfaction and .21 with depressed mood.

One of the oldest subjectively defined OS variables is *role ambiguity,* the opposite of clarity about what one is supposed to do on a job, its purpose, responsibilities, etc. Kahn, Wolfe, Quinn, Snoek, and Rosenthal (1964) reported substantial correlations of ambiguity with strain variables (measured by self-report in a national survey of 1500 respondents), some of which have been replicated: job satisfaction ($r = -.32$), job related tension (.51), and self-confidence ($-.27$). Among 205 NASA engineers, scientists, and administrators, French and Caplan (1970) found that role ambiguity was correlated with job satisfaction ($r = -.42$) and with feelings of job related threat to well-being (.40). Kahn (1973), studying 150 aerospace engineers and administrators, found role ambiguity to be associated with job satisfaction ($r = -.4$), job related threat (.5), self-esteem (.2), and a four-item measure of somatic symptoms of depression (.5). In a national sample of 1496 workers, Margolis, Kroes, and Quinn (1974) found significant but much lower correlations: job satisfaction ($-.13$) and self-esteem ($-.16$). Here, incidentally, is an example of a frequently noticeable trend: correlations that are strong in one occupation (or a cluster of closely related jobs) may become attenuated when sought in a vocationally heterogeneous sample.

The next step in the development of subjective measures was taken by French (1973) and his co-workers at the Institute of Social Research (ISR) (French, Rodgers, & Cobb 1974).[2] It became increasingly evident that psychological stress variables are like their physical counterparts in that the optimum is usually a middle, not an extreme, value. Hence, to find what is least stressful for any one person, one should ask him what level of, say, quantitative or qualitative work load he prefers and relate the response to the demand made upon him by his workrole, by supervisors, or by other apsects of the work environment. The resulting relational scores measure *person-environment (P-E) fit*.

Harrison (1976), using a representative subsample of 318 men from the Caplan et al. (1975) survey, demonstrated that while neither the worker's report of the actual complexity of his job nor the level he wanted was significantly related to depression, the P-E fit measure had a highly reliable curvilinear relation: when the fit was exact, depression was minimal. In a Canadian study, Coburn (1975) similarly reported a curvilinear effect on mental health of P-E fit with respect to job complexity. Harrison (1976) also was able to show that the absolute amount of misfit significantly improved the multiple correlations of the component P and E scores on job complexity with each of the six strains (job dissatisfaction, boredom, somatic complaints, anxiety, depression, and irritation). Further multiple regression analyses were carried out in which all 34 of the study's measures of stress were entered as predictors of the various strains; the great majority of the consistent independent predictors of overall job dissatisfaction and boredom were fit measures. Another important finding from this survey was that in every occupation studied, approximately equal numbers of men were dissatisfied because of either too much or too little job complexity or work load (see also London & Klimoski, 1975). Harrison (1976) noted the implication that proposals for job enrichment will improve fit for many workers but make it *worse* for others.

Although I found no clearly replicated results on the effects of off-the-job stress, a good theoretical case can be made that stressful events in the nonoccupational part of a worker's life can lower his threshold of resistance to OS or cause sensitization to certain classes of OS, thus contributing to an eventual pathological outcome (e.g., Cooper & Marshall, 1976).

The relative utility of objectively and subjectively defined stress measures is a more complex issue than might at first be supposed and surely is not a question to be decided in terms of ideological preference for one or the other type across the board. Some subjective indicators of stress take the form of direct questions (e.g., "Is your job stressful? Does anything about your work upset you, make you tense, or cause you any other difficulty?"). Such an approach runs up against the need of many persons (perhaps men in particular, and especially those in lower status, blue-collar jobs) to maintain a public posture of toughness or machismo. Such a hypothesis would help account for the anomalous fact that men in more objectively rigorous, physically demanding, and dangerous jobs often deny any stress yet exhibit the highest rates of stress diseases. Compare, for example, Cherry's (1978) report that in a representative sample of 1415 workers, the following proportions reported "nervous debility and strain": professionals, 54%; intermediate nonmanual (white-collar) workers, 57%; skilled nonmanuals, 44%; semiskilled nonmanuals, 50%; skilled manual (blue-collar) workers, 31%; semiskilled manuals, 15%; and unskilled manual laborers, 10%. Yet Smith, Colligan, and Hurrell (1980) found that unskilled laborers had by far the highest rates of stress diseases, both physical and mental, and that the top 12 occupations in terms of combined indexes included no professionals but did include mine operatives; college professors appeared among the 13 occupations with the fewest stress diseases.

The remarkable adaptability of human beings sometimes works to their detriment. Faced with the choice between a boring, dangerous, or otherwise stressful job and unemployment, most people will choose to work and will find a way to reduce the dissonance.[3] Some people are characterological complainers, while others take pride in never complaining, and there is no reason to suppose that these types are randomly distributed across occupations.

DEPENDENT VARIABLES IN OS RESEARCH

Table 25-2 lists the most important recurrent variables treated as effects or products of OS. With some misgivings, I have followed the prevalent practice of classifying these variables as strains or illnesses, but the distinction is arbitrary. What one author treats as a strain (a relatively minor side effect of working at an occupation), another takes as evidence of impaired health. To a degree, this lack of agreement represents the confused state of symptomatology and the controversial status of the concept of disease, especially outside the realm of physical and physiological medicine. Even more, however, it points to a necessary clash between methodological approaches. The traditional atomistic-analytic conception of scientific research makes investigators look for linear effects between stress and strain—causal variables and effect variables, each conceived of as continuously distributed and treatable in isolation even though the scientist recognizes that reality is more complex and that it will be necessary to put the pieces back together. By contrast, the clinical disciplines have been forced to recognize the intrinsically patterned and discontinuous nature of the troubles for which people consult practitioners.

Consider, for example, blood pressure, serum cholesterol, and serum uric acid, elevated levels of which are associated with coronary heart disease. Neither these nor any of the other physiological variables Caplan and associates (1975) managed with great difficulty and expense to measure on 390 men in eight occupations was related to any of their questionnaire measures of stress or strain. In an ongoing study of coronary heart disease among 400 managers and supervisors in an aerospace corporation, such so-called risk factors as uric acid, blood glucose, dopamine-beta-hydroxylase, and cholesterol were found to be related to one another and to cardiovascular status (pulse rate, blood pressure, etc.) but *not* to coronary heart disease (Chadwick, 1980). They were also unrelated to the only good predictor of heart attacks, *personality types A and B* (see below, p. 431 and Chapter 33). Chadwick (1980) therefore rejected the simple formula that stress causes strain causes heart disease and called for a consideration of "second order things: the person-environment fit and nonlinear interactions" (p. 28).

On the other hand, a researcher may accept as a fact of life the self-defined nature of illness and take as his dependent variable either the frequency of visits to dispensaries, physi-

TABLE 25-2
Types of Effects Measured in OS Research (Dependent Variables)

Strains
  Physiological
    Pulse rate, blood pressure (Caplan et al., 1975)
    Erythrocyte sedimentation rate, protein-bound iodine, serum iron (Froberg et al., 1970)
    Serum cholesterol, high- and low-density lipoproteins (Chadwick, 1980)
    Serum cortisol, thyroid hormones, serum glucose, serum uric acid (Caplan et al., 1975)
    Catecholamine excretion (Frankenhaeuser & Gardell, 1976)
    Electrocardiogram (Shirom et al., 1973)
    Lung function tests (House et al., 1979)
    Disrupted sleep, bowel function, or eating habits (Mott, 1976)
    Somatic complaints (Caplan et al., 1975)
  Psychological
    Job dissatisfaction (Caplan et al., 1975)
    Boredom, anxiety, depression, irritation (Caplan et al., 1975)
    Self-esteem: occupational (House, 1972) or general (Beehr, 1976)
    Alienation from, or confidence in, organization (Kahn, 1973)
    Tension, experienced conflict (Kahn, 1973)
    Fatigue (Beehr et al., 1976)
    Satisfaction with life (Iris & Barrett, 1972)
    Sexual maladjustment (Mott, 1976)
  Behavioral and social
    Authoritarian punitiveness (Fodor, 1976)
    Strikes (Belbin & Stammers, 1972)
    Early retirement, changing jobs (Jacobson, 1972; Powell, 1973)
    Burnout (Daley, 1979)
    Rate of smoking, caffeine intake (Caplan et al., 1975)
    Use of drugs or alcohol on the job (Mangione & Quinn, 1975)
    Counterproductive behaviors (spreading rumors; doing inferior work on purpose; stealing from employer; damaging property, equipment, or product on purpose; damaging property accidentally but not reporting) (Mangione & Quinn, 1975)
    Absenteeism (Akerstedt, 1976)
    Disrupted performance of social role as spouse and parent (Mott, 1976)
    Disrupted performance of social role as citizen (Gardell, 1976)
    Interference with friendships, socializing, dating (Mott, 1976)
Illnesses and mortality
  Somatic-physiological (including psychosomatic)
    Heart disease (Glass, 1977)
    Hypertension (Cobb & Rose, 1973)
    Cerebral accident (stroke) (*Work in America,* 1973)
    Peptic ulcer (Cobb & Rose, 1973; House et al., 1979)
    Arthritis (Cobb, 1971)
    Headache (Kimball, 1979)
    Respiratory illness (bronchitis, asthma, cough, phlegm) (Caplan et al., 1975)
    Dermatitis, other skin afflictions (House et al., 1979)
    Diabetes melitus (Cobb & Rose, 1973)
    General, diffuse sickness (Mechanic, 1974)
    Total rate of illness (Hinkle, 1974; Rahe et al., 1972)
    Frequency of visits to doctor or dispensary (Caplan et al., 1975)
    Mortality rates (Colligan et al., 1977)
  Psychological
    Mental health versus mental illness (Gavin, 1975)
    Visits to community mental health center (Colligan et al., 1977)
    Depression (Ilfeld, 1977)
    Alcoholism, drug abuse (Lederer, 1973)

Illnesses and mortality (cont.)
    Neurotic symptoms reported on questionnaire (House et al., 1979)
    Neurosis, character disorder, etc., diagnosed clinically (Ferguson, 1973)
    Mass psychogenic illness (Colligan & Murphy, 1979)
  Behavioral and social
    Violence (*Work in America,* 1973)
    Other antisocial acting out (e.g., white-collar crime) (*Work in America,* 1973)
    Delinquency of worker's children (*Work in America,* 1973)
    Impaired interpersonal relations (*Work in America,* 1973)
    Accidents and errors, with harm to self (Theorell, 1974)
    Accidents and errors, with harm to others (Colquhoun, 1976)
    Suicide (Karcher, 1978)

cians, or other medical facilities or the record of days lost on account of illness as the bottom line with which employers have to cope. Yet good data on these patterns are hard to get: even though a company has a dispensary, some employees may prefer to seek medical help elsewhere, and taking time off for illness is notoriously easy to abuse in some settings. Some people continue to work with clinically detectable, fully developed illnesses, while others stay home at every sniffle. This very difference may be related to stress, however. In one study of angina, when subjects were equated for the amount of reported chest pain and the condition of their coronary arteries was directly checked, those who had higher independently measured levels of stressful life events had more nearly *normal* arterial status than those who registered lower levels of stress (Chadwick, 1980). Apparently, feeling under pressure made the former group experience a milder degree of coronary pathology as acutely painful. Even when an illness can be objectively diagnosed with ease, to find all cases in a given population may require subjecting all members to a medical examination—an expensive and difficult undertaking.[4]

Let us consider next the evidence that the psychological strains listed in Table 25–2 are relevant to health and disease. A classical 15-year study of aging examined genetic inheritance, medical status, and use of tobacco in 268 volunteers and found that the best predictor of longevity was work satisfaction ($r = .26$) (Palmore, 1969). Among males who were most likely to be working full-time, the correlation was highest (.38). In three separate samples of 12, 16, and 36 occupational groups, Sales and House (1971) found negative relationships between average level of job satisfaction and mortality rates for heart disease, but not for any other morbidity measure. Those correlations existed across groups, not individuals. In a representative sample of 228 men from one community, House (1972) found no correlation between job satisfaction and several cardiac risk factors such as cholesterol and blood pressure; but when he analyzed the data by occupations, a negative correlation appeared in several white-collar groups. Occupational self-esteem has been found to be negatively related to cardiac risk factors (House, 1972; Kasl & Cobb, 1970) and to dispensary visits (Kasl & French, 1962). These results should be viewed with caution not only because of the negative findings on self-esteem and cardiac risk reported by Caplan (1972) and by French, Tupper, and Mueller (1965), and the lack of a clear association between job satisfaction and cardiac risk (Caplan and associates, 1975), but also because the alleged risk factors are often unrelated to morbidity in prospective research (Chadwick, 1980).

The central finding of Kornhauser's (1965) justly celebrated study of Detroit automobile workers was a positive relationship (not expressed as a correlation coefficient) between job satisfaction and mental health. Gechman and Wiener (1975) reported a similar finding, but Ronan, Cobb, Garrett, Lazarri, Mosser, and Racine (1974) found no correlation after having attempted to replicate Kornhauser's study, using his measures, over a fairly wide occupational distribution. Once again, because relationships may not generalize beyond the specific occupational groups in which they were originally found does not mean that they are of no interest. On the whole, job satisfaction is evidently highly relevant to OS and its pathogenic effects. For reviews of the extensive literature on the measurement and correlates of job satisfaction, see Katzell, Yankelovich, Fein, Oornati, and Nash (1975) and Locke (1976).

Fatigue has long been studied by industrial psychologists and is occasionally mentioned in OS research (e.g., Cameron, 1971), but I found no direct evidence linking it to illness. In a comprehensive review of research on OS in secretaries, Dainoff (1979) reported that the best-established findings were that sustained work with cathode-ray tube displays led to ocular fatigue and related complaints, and that keyboard operators complained of muscular distress. In both instances, correctable flaws in design and operator training apparently played large roles and the effects seemed to be reversible.

A few observers have noted the neglect of what are classified in Table 25-2 as behavioral strains—notably the "counterproductive behaviors" studied by Mangione and Quinn (1975) in a national sample of 1327 wage and salary workers: deliberately trying to make trouble or to harm the employer by spreading rumors; doing work badly or incorrectly; deliberately damaging property, equipment, or products; failing to report accidental damage; and stealing from the employer (Spector, 1975; *Work in America,* 1973). Especially in men over 30, counterproductive acts were related to job dissatisfaction.[5] These touchy topics *can* be investigated, but white-collar crime of all kinds, including bribery, cheating, and the interface between legitimate business and organized crime, remains as little touched by scientific study as by the criminal justice system.

Psychiatrists classify alcoholism and drug abuse among the character disorders, hence as diseases rather than strains. In a large survey, Margolis, Kroes, and Quinn (1974) found "escapist drinking" to be significantly associated with job stress. It is, of course, extremely difficult to prove cause. Persons like long-distance truckers, who must remain alert on a dangerous but soporific, monotonous job, are at risk of taking amphetamines (Harris & Mackie, 1972) and at times abuse such a seemingly innocuous drug as caffeine with serious (albeit usually reversible) effects on their health.

We come now to diseases in the narrower sense as dependent variables. A considerable variety of pathologies have been said to be caused or exacerbated by OS: cardiovascular diseases, mental illnesses of several kinds (including suicide), asthma and other respiratory illnesses such as bronchitis, thyroid disorders, skin diseases, arthritis of various types, obesity (also considered a strain), tuberculosis, migraine, peptic ulcers, ulcerative colitis, and diabetes (Cooper & Marshall, 1978; Kroes, 1976; Selye, 1976). Backing up such medical opinions or beliefs by hard evidence is a difficult matter. The simplest type of research, comparing morbidity rates across occupational groups or social statuses, leaves a great deal to be desired: the criterion groups differ in many respects other than inferred (or measured average) levels of stress, and the direction of casual influence is ambiguous. It could easily be that people who have a disease or a predisposition to it seek out certain kinds of jobs or are selected into them. Schizophrenics are found in disproportionately large numbers in the least skilled jobs with lowest status, for example, partly because many of them are unable to work at more demanding tasks.

A great deal of attention has focused on cardiovascular diseases, especially coronary heart disease (CHD), which has become in modern times the principal cause of death in the

United States. The origins of CHD are unclear and multiple, and OS has been clearly implicated (for earlier reviews see Cooper & Marshall, 1976; House, 1974; Jenkins, 1976). Evidence continues to accumulate of a significant positive association between various aspects of OS and heart disease—House, McMichael, Wells, Kaplan, and Landerman (1979) found links between eight measures of perceived stress and angina, hypertension, and other risk factors and Falger (1979) noted associations between work overload and myocardial infarction—but negative findings also have been reported (Haynes and associates, 1978).[6] The one well-established, frequently replicated finding links cardiovascular disease and the Type A behavior pattern: "excessive drive, aggressiveness, ambition, involvement in competitive activities, frequent vocational deadlines, and enhanced sense of time urgency" (Jenkins, Rosenman, & Friedman, 1968). (For a detailed review of Types A and B, see Chapter 33.)

If heart disease of several kinds is so closely related to OS, what about other cardiovascular disorders? The two principal possibilities are hypertension (high blood pressure) and cerebral vascular accident (stroke). Hardly any research has been done on the latter, perhaps because even though stroke is a frequent cause of death, it tends to occur at a late age, often after retirement. Here is one of the most difficult problems in occupational medicine: the pathogenesis of a number of major killers, notably including cancer, is a long, slow process. It not only complicates the legal process of demonstrating responsibility—for example, of an employer for subjecting workers to low levels of such radioactive carcinogens as radon, or such chemical carcinogens as benzene, or byssinosis-producing cotton dust—when years elapse between the exposure and the insidious onset of the disease; it also impedes research. Quite possibly, OS will someday be shown to have a presently undetected pathogenic influence on various diseases of delayed onset. As to hypertension, however, there has been a fair amount of research, but the only well-established finding links it to the Type A personality. Investigative designs tend to be more naive in blood pressure studies than they are in cardiac research. The state of knowledge about both hypertension and CHD will doubtless advance considerably a few years hence, when some large, sophisticated prospective studies have been completed and reported (Chadwick, 1980; Haynes and associates, 1980; Rose, Jenkins, & Hurst, 1978). At the benign end of the dependent variable, however, there is one well-established finding: scientists have significantly lower systolic blood pressure than do other occupational groups tested, e.g., administrators and air traffic controllers (Caplan, 1972; Caplan and associates, 1975).

Though in the popular conception peptic ulcer has long been the prototypical OS disease, medical opinion about the evidence has been divided: Susser (1967) concluded from a survey of research that there is a definite link; Weiner (1977), that none had been proved. It is to be expected, therefore, that more recent results should be fragmentary. In a group of blue-collar workers in a rubber factory, House and colleagues (1979) found a significant association between reported OS—particularly stressful relations with others—and ulcer, despite controls for seven possibly confounding variables. Air traffic controllers were found to have unusually high rates of peptic ulcer (Cobb & Rose, 1973), but in another study using self-report only they did not differ from other occupational groups (Caplan and associates, 1975). Doubtless, stable results must wait on more complex approaches. For example, Mendeloff and Dunn (1971) reported that young women who work and have family responsibilities have more ulcers than those with only one type of responsibility; Kahn and French (1970) found that rates of peptic ulcer rise as self-esteem declines.

Many of the people who show up in doctors' offices or clinics refuse to settle into diagnostic pigeonholes, "being bothered by all sorts of ailments, feeling weak all over, having undefined pains, lacking energy, feeling tense and nervous, feeling depressed, drowsiness, nervous stomach, having personal worries, being nervous, feeling blue, and having headaches" (Mechanic, 1974:90). A high proportion of the people who seek medical help do so for what seems to be poor general organismic functioning, not for specific organic diseases, yet most research has concentrated on the latter. Patients of the former kind are looked on as a nuisance, almost as an embarrassment; they are suspected of hypochondria or malingering, as if these patterns were not themselves forms of pathology worthy of study and correction. Though there is a dearth of information on days lost from work because of unclassifiable illness, Hinkle (1974) suggested that the number may be high and that the phenomenon is suitable for, and fully deserving of, much more intensive investigation.

One approach that has the merit of not excluding unclassifiable illnesses is having the worker rate his own general state of health or well-being. A few studies reported relations between OS variables and such measures, usually in specific occupations (Coburn, 1978; Rahe, Ganderson, Pugh, Rubin, & Arthur, 1972; Tung & Koch, 1980).

Faced with the choice between being considered a "mental patient" or being regarded as someone with a somatic illness, most people consciously or unconsciously choose the latter, socially more acceptable patient role. Small wonder, therefore, that there is a great deal of OS literature in which the dependent variables are bodily diseases or their precursors and very little in which specific neuroses, psychoses, or other established psychodiagnostic categories play that role. The only replicated result I found concerns depression: a couple of large epidemiological studies found that while life events as a whole seemed to play a small role in this etiology, OS was significantly associated with depression for married men (Holzer, Warheit, & Kuldau, 1978; Ilfeld, 1977).

A survey by occupation of all first admissions to 22 of the 27 community mental health centers in the state of Tennessee from January 1972 through June 1974 bypassed the diagnostic issues and showed striking differences among occupations (Colligan, Smith, & Hurrell, 1977). Occupations were ranked in terms of admission rate per 1000 employees, thus holding constant differences in the numbers of persons employed in different vocations, and these rates were compared with expected frequencies based on population norms. The group with by far the highest rate was health technology technicians, and five others of the top 20 in the list are relatively low-status health care occupations. Doubtless, these workers experience much pressure and authoritarian treatment to which they cannot respond directly, but they also should be better informed about mental health facilities and more inclined to seek help than are many other persons. The same artifactual influence may apply to registered nurses and social workers, also in the top 27. (After reviewing the literature on psychiatric illness in physicians, Murray [1974] found that they, their wives, and paramedics stand out in being prone to drug addiction and suicide. Since these persons have easy access to drugs, it is uncertain whether OS plays a role in the high morbidity rates.)

Waiters and waitresses had the second highest rate in the Tennessee study (Colligan, Smith, & Hurrell, 1977), and a fair number of other personal service occupations had high ranks, suggesting that the interpersonal strains in serving the public in subordinate, nonprofessional capacities may have an etiological role in stress related disorders. Telephone operators ranked seventeenth on clinic admission rates; a Russian study likewise found that 280 female intercity operators had a higher frequency of "nervous disorders and neurotic reactions" than did control workers (Ryzhkova, Lanskiy, Nevskaya, & Simonova, 1978).

Men in high-status, more intrinsically interesting occupations yield paradoxical findings: more job satisfaction but also more depression (Quinn & Shepard, 1974) or more "nervous strain" (Cherry, 1978). It is difficult to tell whether holders of high-level jobs report more "mental symptoms" because of OS, or because they are sophisticated enough to be more introspective and more willing to admit, or seek help for, conditions like depressed mood; or some interaction of the foregoing.

Incidentally, much of the OS literature deals with the special problems of specific occupations. Space does not permit a summary of findings. For specific reviews see Cooper (1980) on dentists, Davidson and Veno (1980) on policemen, and Marshall (1980) on nurses. A good deal of work recently has concentrated on human service occupations under the catchphrase "staff burnout" (e.g., Cherniss, 1980).

Outbreaks of mass psychogenic illness in work settings apparently have become more frequent in recent years. Colligan and Murphy (1979) concluded from a review of 16 published and unpublished studies that groups of workers reported physical symptoms (usually including headache, dizziness, and/or nausea) without ascertainable physical basis, often after experiencing an unusual odor. Affected workers were predominantly women who had been subject to considerable OS: boredom, production pressure, poor labor-management relations and communications, and a noisy, unpleasant working environment.

Accidents on the job have long been a subject of research, much of it an inconclusive attempt to identify accident proneness. There are no definitive demonstrations that industrial accidents are caused by OS, but enough positive indications from adequately complex research to warrant further careful study of accidents as the resultant of stressful conditions impinging on dissatisfied persons (perhaps with some degree of internally distracting anxiety or depression, or other nonspecific predisposition). Such research is urgently needed because, as Colquhoun (1976) pointed out, "even though an actual accident may be a rare event in any particular factory or plant, in more and more cases nowadays, such an accident could be disastrous"—not only to workers but to large sectors of the public. Since the accident at Three Mile Island, attention is beginning to be focused on human factors in workers at nuclear reactors (e.g., Swain & Guttmann, 1980), but it is distressing to report that to date there has been no published research on OS in control room operators and the Nuclear Regulatory Commission knows of no such work in progress in the United States. Compare, by contrast, the dozens of OS studies on air traffic controllers (reviewed by Crump, 1979).

It has long been known that mortality rates differ strikingly across occupations (e.g., Cobb & Rose, 1973; Sales & House, 1971), reminding us of the vital significance of OS. Research using death in general or a special form, such as suicide, as the dependent variable is usually of a large-scale, statistical kind. Studies of suicide rates by occupation and other demographic classifications, in the sociological tradition of Durkheim (Bsuglass & Duffy, 1978; Karcher, 1978; Reinhart, 1978), have found that such stresslike or strainlike inferred variables of the work setting as weakness of social organization and anomie are significantly associated with self-destructive acts or attempts.

MODERATOR VARIABLES AND INTERACTION EFFECTS

An important and fairly recent development in OS, toward more sophisticated and adequate research designs, is the explicit introduction of moderating (sometimes called *conditioning*) variables. Instead of merely attempting to connect stress with strain, investigators pursue the hypothesis that a given stress has deleterious effects on health only under specified parametric conditions. Table 25-3 lists some moderator variables that have been investigated in OS research.

So far, there seem to be very few replicated findings of this kind. Quinn (1972) and

TABLE 25-3
Moderating Variables Used in OS Research

Physiological
    Use of alcohol, drugs, caffeine (Cobb, 1974)
    Disruption of diet (Halberg & Nelson, 1976), low fat diet (Russek, 1973)
    Exposure to dust and chemical pollution (House et al., 1979)
    Exposure to microwave radiation (Becker, 1979)

Characteristics of individuals
    Age (House, 1972; Mangione & Quinn, 1975)
    Sex (Ramos, 1975)
    Ethnicity (Ramos, 1975)
    Nationality (Orth-Gomer, 1979)
    Stage of life (Kellam, 1974)
    Number of life changes (Cobb, 1974)
    Lark versus owl (capacity for wakefulness) (Ostberg, 1973)
    Work addiction (Theorell, 1974)
    Work values (Crain, 1974)
    Attachment to organization (Porter & Dubin, 1975)
    Neurotic anxiety (Kahn, 1973)
    Depressive tendencies (Mott, 1976)
    Schizoid or introvert lack of sociability (Mott, 1976)
    Neuroticism (Gulian, 1974)
    Self-esteem (London & Klimoski, 1975)
    Strength of higher order needs (Beehr et al., 1976)
    Flexibility-rigidity (Kahn, 1973)
    Effectiveness of defenses (Cobb, 1974)
    Resistance resources (Antonovsky, 1974)
    Type A (versus Type B) behavior pattern (Caplan, 1972)
    Machiavellianism (Gemmill & Heisler, 1972)
    Need for clarity at work (Miles & Petty, 1975)

Situational
    Size of work unit (Schriesheim & Murphy, 1976)
    Group cohesiveness (Beehr, 1976)
    Autonomy on job (Beehr, 1976), opportunity for formal control (Gemmill & Heisler, 1972)
    Social support from co-workers (Caplan et al., 1975)
    Social support from supervisors (Caplan et al., 1975)
    Job enrichment (Abdel-Halim, 1978)

Organizational
    Tall versus flat organizational structure (Ivancevich & Donnelly, 1975)
    Model I versus Model II (Argyris, 1973)
    Organizational climate (James & Jones, 1974)
    Structural dimensions of organization (James & Jones, 1976)

Sociological
    Social support from home (spouse, relatives, friends) (Caplan et al., 1975)
    Other interpersonal ties and involvements (Antonovsky, 1974)
    Community involvement (Antonovsky, 1974)

Cohen (1976) found symptoms of poorer mental health in stressed and dissatisfied workers who felt locked into jobs. Results of great plausibility and convincingness have been reported: House and colleagues (1979) found that perceived stress was positively related to the incidence of respiratory and dermatological symptoms only in rubber workers who had been exposed to possibly noxious fumes, and may yet be replicated.

    Social support as a moderator, or buffer, of stress effects has received a good deal of attention during recent years, especially by the investigative team at ISR (e.g., Caplan and associates, 1975; Cobb, 1976). According to Pinneau (1976): "Men with high support from either supervisor or co-workers generally reported low role conflict, low role ambiguity, and low future ambiguity, high participation, and good utilization of their skills" (p. 35). Interestingly, in light of the psychoanalytic expectation, depression was the strain measure most frequently correlated with support. Depression, anxiety, and irritation were affected by support both at home and on the job; most other strains were related only to support in the occupational setting—effects that remained significant across 16 occupational groups when the simultaneous and complicating effects of other stresses were controlled by multiple regression analyses (Pinneau, 1976). There was, however, no clear evidence of any buffering effect, no diminution of the pathological effect of a stress, when support was present, and Pinneau added that his scrutiny of previous research failed to find any either. The buffering hypothesis remains attractive, however, and deserves to be examined further, using the person-environment fit approach, especially in experimental attempts to modify strains. Social support should be most ameliorative when the amount available fits the amount wanted.

TRENDS IN OS THEORIES AND RESEARCH

The field of OS seems to have gone through four phases of development.

The first phase was marked by efforts to find simple cause and effect relationships, largely of this type: stress → illness or death. Both cause and effect tended to be objectively defined (that is, in terms of the researcher's judgment, not that of the affected persons). The few such correlations found were usually low; understanding of the mediating process was meager or wholly lacking. The work was methodologically naive, and the variables used were defined traditionally, uncritically accepted from sources outside the research field. I include here, also, clinical reports based on unsystematic and usually small samples.

The second phase was marked by increasing differentiation of independent and dependent variables and of the cause-effect chain. The latter often was expressed in terms of explicit theories; for example, environmental stressors → perceived stress → strain → illness. Interactions were not sought and only occasionally found. Investigators were more willing to make deliberate use of subjectively defined variables, or at least were clear which variables were objectively and which were subjectively defined. With better defined and psychometrically developed measures and with the strategy of looking for effects in subsamples (e.g., by sex, by age group, or by general classes of occupations like white- versus blue-collar), investigators sometimes reported larger effect sizes.

The third phase was signaled by the emergence of theories and designs in which interactions and moderator variables played an explicit role. Investigators recognized that low or negligible zero-order correlations between a kind of stress and an effect variable often meant that there were dissimilar or even opposite relationships in different parts of the original sample, which canceled each other out. This phase saw an increase in the sophistication of measurement, research designs, and statistical analyses necessary to detect such interactions and not just linear but curvilinear relationships.

Finally, in the currently emerging phase, prospective (longitudinal) designs have become more prominent; there is a new emphasis on amelioration in controlled studies of therapeutic programs derived from and testing theories of pathogenesis; awareness of the complexity of the phenomena has resulted in multidisciplinary research and movement away from linear conceptions of cause and effect toward explanatory models influenced by systems theories, incorporating various feedback loops.

Many of the problems of OS research are not unique to this field but are local manifestations of endemic defects in research in the human sciences. For obvious reasons, simple research designs are easier to carry out than more complex ones and are tried first. Unhappily, when we are dealing with such important human concerns as work and health, which are interrelated as parts of highly intricate, nested, and overlapping systems, we can expect a kind of Gresham's law to prevail: since oversimplified approaches are cheaper, quicker, and easier to explore than adequate ones, the products of inadequate investigations naturally tend to dominate the literature.

Apparently, certain basic truths need to be emphasized over and over again: people's feelings about their work are highly overdetermined and almost always mixed (ambivalent), hence not easily ascertained by a few blunt, direct questions with precoded answers; work takes place in a multilayered social and cultural context in which many important and often conflicting values intersect; workers are also members of families, and of social, religious, recreational, political, educational, and other institutions, from which they derive a mixture of costs and benefits, of stress and support, interacting with their work lives in highly variable ways depending on the person, the occupation, and other factors; health and illness are extraordinarily complex states that resist reduction to sociological, psychological, or biological terms alone. Nevertheless, a shrewd or lucky investigator can still uncover important links with relatively simple and manageable designs and samples of practicable size. Despite the complexities of occupational stress, some effects are big enough to be detectable with crude instruments and are nearly enough universal so that sophisticated sampling is not always necessary.

NOTES

1. *Ergonomics,* 1978, *21* (10), was devoted entirely to shift work.
2. A similar conception was set forth by Argyris (1957, 1964) in his "personality and organization theory."
3. Sheppard and Herrick (1972) found that workers on a dull, routine job reported the largest amount of dissatisfaction when they started working at it; after three to five years, they began to say that they were satisfied. Note, however, Korman's (1971) finding that people doing repetitive work were satisfied with it when they had poor self-acceptance, but those who did accept themselves expressed dissatisfaction with the same job.
4. Omitting from a study people who actually have an illness but do not define themselves as sick distorts findings, for true positives may get incorrectly classified as false negatives.
5. Ominously, a number of instances of sabotage at nuclear electrical facilities have occurred (Mullen, Davidson, & Jones, 1980), and such acts by disgruntled workers may be on the rise (Emshwiller, 1980).
6. One reason for failure to replicate is suggested by Byrne and White's (1980) finding that 120 myocardial infarct patients did not report more life events of a stressful kind than did 40 less severely ill heart patients but did rate the same events as more emotionally distressing.

REFERENCES

Abel-Halim, A. Employee affective responses to organizational stress: Moderating effects of job characteristics. *Personnel Psychology,* 1978, *31,* 561–579.

Akerstedt, T. Shift work and health: Interdisciplinary aspects. In P. G. Rentos & R. D. Shepard (eds.) *Shift work and health.* Washington, D.C.: U.S. Government Printing Office, 1976.

ALTHOUSE, R., & HURRELL, J. *An analysis of job stress in coal mining.* DHEW (NIOSH) publication no. 77–217. Washington, D.C.: U.S. Government Printing Office, 1977.

AMARIA, P. J. Effects of paced and unpaced work situations. In C. H. Gudnason & E. N. Corlett (eds.), *Development of production systems.* London: Taylor & Francis, 1974.

ANTONOVSKY, A. Conceptual and methodological problems in the study of resistance resources and stressful life events. In B. S. Dohrenwend & B. P. Dohrenwend (eds.), *Stressful life events: Their nature and effects.* New York: Wiley, 1974.

ARGYRIS, C. *Personality and organization.* New York: Harper, 1957.

—————. *Integrating the individual and the organization.* New York: Wiley, 1964.

—————. Personality and organization theory revisited. *Administrative Science Quarterly,* 1973, *18,* 141–167.

AXELSSON, R., & LUNDBERG, U. *Working environment of operating personnel in a nuclear power plant: A pilot study.* Report No. TA 875-R1, Bromma, Sweden, 1975.

BECKER, R. O. Brain pollution. *Psychology Today,* 1979, *9*(12), 124.

BEEHR, T. A. Perceived situational moderators of the relationship between subjective role ambiguity and role strain. *Journal of Applied Psychology,* 1976, *61,* 35–40.

BEEHR, T. A., WALSH, J. T., & TABER, T. D. Relationship of stress to individually and organizationally valued states: Higher order needs as a moderator. *Journal of Applied Psychology,* 1976, *61,* 41–47.

BELBIN, R. M., & STAMMERS, D. Pacing stress, human adaptation, and training in car production. *Applied Erogonomics,* 1972, *3,* 142–146.

BIERSNER, R. J., GUNDERSON, E. K., RYMAN, D. H., & RAHE, R. H. *Correlations of physical fitness, perceived health status, and dispensary visits with performance in stressful training.* USN Medical Neuropsychiatric Research Unit technical report no. 71-30. U.S. Navy, 1971.

BROOK, A. Mental stress at work. *Practitioner,* 1973, *210,* 500–506.

BRUUSGARD, A. Shift work as an occupational health problem. *Studia Laboris et Salutis* (Stockholm), 1975, *4,* 9–14.

BSUGLASS, D., & DUFFY, J. C. The ecological pattern of suicide and parasuicide in Edinburgh. *Social Science and Medicine,* 1978, *12,* 241–253.

BYRNE, D. G., & WHITE, H. M. Life events and myocardial infarction revisited: the role of measures of individual impact. *Psychosomatic Medicine,* 1980, *42,* 1–10.

CAMERON, C. Fatigue problems in modern industry. *Ergonomics,* 1971, *14,* 713–720.

CAPLAN, R. D. Organizational stress and individual strain: A social psychological study of risk factors in coronary heart disease among administrators, engineers, and scientists. *Dissertation Abstracts International,* 1972, *32*(11B), 6706B.

CAPLAN, R. D., COBB, S., FRENCH, J. R. P., JR., HARRISON, R. V., & PINNEAU, S. R., JR. *Job demands and worker health: Main effects and occupational differences.* DHEW (NIOSH) publication no. 75-160. Washington, D.C.: U.S. Government Printing Office, 1975.

CHADWICK, J. F. Psychological job stress and coronary heart disease: A current NIOSH project. In R. M. Schwartz (ed.), *New developments in occupational stress.* Cincinnati: National Institute for Occupational Safety and Health, 1980.

CHASE, D. J. Sources of mental stress and how to avoid them. *Supervisory Management,* 1972, *17,* 33–36.

CHERNISS, C. *Staff burnout: Job stress in the human services.* Beverly Hills: Sage, 1980.

CHERRY, N. Stress, anxiety, and work: A longitudinal study. *Journal of Occupational Psychology,* 1978, *51,* 259–270.

COBB, S. *The frequency of the rheumatic diseases.* Cambridge: Harvard University Press, 1971.

————. Role responsibility: The differentiation of a concept. *Occupational Mental Health,* 1973, *3,* 10–14.

————. A model for life events and their consequences. In B. S. Dohrenwend & B. P. Dohrenwend (eds.) *Stressful life events: Their nature and effects.* New York: Wiley, 1974.

————. Social support as a moderator of life stress. *Psychosomatic Medicine,* 1976, *38,* 300–314.

Cobb, S., & Kasl, S. V. Some medical aspects of unemployment. In G. M. Shatto (ed.), *Employment of the middle-aged: Papers from industrial gerontology seminars.* Springfield: Thomas, 1972.

————.*Termination: The consequences of job loss.* Cincinnati: National Institute for Occupational Safety and Health, 1977.

Cobb, S., & Rose, R. M. Psychosomatic disease in air traffic controllers: Hypertension, diabetes, and peptic ulcer. *Journal of the American Medical Association,* 1973, *224,* 489–492.

Coburn, D. Job-worker incongruence: Consequences for health. *Journal of Health and Social Behavior,* 1975, *16,* 198–212.

————. Work and general psychological and physical well-being. *International Journal of Health Services,* 1978, *8,* 415–435.

Cohen, A., & Margolis, B. Initial psychological research related to the Occupational Safety and Health Act of 1970. *American Psychologist,* 1973, *28,* 600–606.

Cohen, J. German and American workers: A comparative view of worker distress. *International Journal of Mental Health,* 1976, *5,* 138–147.

Cohen, S. Aftereffects of stress on human performance and social behavior: A review of research and theory. *Psychological Bulletin,* 1980, *88,* 82–108.

Colligan, M. J., & Murphy, L. R. Mass psychogenic illness in organizations: An overview. *Journal of Occupational Psychology,* 1979, *52,* 77–90.

Colligan, M. J., Smith, M. J., & Hurrell, J. J. Occupational incidence rates of mental health disorders. *Journal of Human Stress,* 1977, *3,* 34–39.

Colquhoun, W. P. Accidents, injuries, and shift work. In P. G. Rentos & R. D. Shepard (eds.), *Shift work and health.* Washington, D.C.: U.S. Government Printing Office, 1976.

Cooper, C. L. Dentists under pressure: A social psychological study. In C. L. Cooper & J. Marshall (eds.), *White collar and professional stress.* New York: Wiley, 1980.

Cooper, C. L., & Marshall, J. Occupational sources of stress: A review of the literature relating to coronary heart disease and mental ill health. *Journal of Occupational Psychology,* 1976, *49,* 11–28.

————. Sources of managerial and white collar stress. In C. L. Cooper & R. Payne (eds.), *Stress at work.* New York: Wiley, 1978.

————. (eds.). *White collar and professional stress.* New York: Wiley, 1980.

Crain, R. D. The effect of work values on the relationship between job characteristics and job satisfaction. *Dissertation Abstracts International,* 1974, *34*(11B), 5729B.

Crump, J. H. Review of stress in air traffic control: Its measurement and effects. *Aviation, Space, and Environmental Medicine,* 1979, *50,* 243–248.

Cummings, L. L., & DeCotiis, T. A. Organizational correlates of perceived stress in a professional organization. *Public Personnel Management,* 1973, *2,* 275–282.

Dainoff, M. J. *Occupational stress factors in secretarial/clerical workers: Annotated research bibliography and analytic review.* Cincinnati: National Institute for Occupational Safety and Health, 1979.

Daley, M. R. Burnout: Smoldering problem in protective services. *Social Work,* 1979, *24,* 375–379.

Davidson, M. J., & Veno, A. Stress and the policeman. In C. L. Cooper & J. Marshall (eds.), *White collar and professional stress.* New York: Wiley, 1980.

DOHRENWEND, B. S., & DOHRENWEND, B. P. (eds.). *Stressful life events: Their nature and effects.* New York: Wiley, 1974.

DOLL, R., & JONES, A. F. *Occupational factors in the aetiology of gastric and duodenal ulcers.* Medical Research Council special report no. 276. London: HMSO, 1951.

DOOLEY, D., & CATALANO, R. Economic change as a cause of behavioral disorder. *Psychological Bulletin,* 1980, *87,* 450–468.

EMSHWILLER, J. R. Sabotage by insiders: How serious is the threat to atomic facilities? *Wall Street Journal,* 3 September 1980, pp. 1,20.

ETTEMA, J. H., & ZIELHUIS, R. L. Psychological parameters of mental load. *Ergonomics,* 1971, *14,* 137–144.

FALGER, P. R. Changes in work load as a potential risk constellation for myocardial infarction: A concise review. *Gedrag: Tijdschrift voor Psychologie* (Tilburg, Netherlands), 1979, *7,* 96–114.

FERGUSON, D. A study of occupational stress and health. *Ergonomics,* 1973, *16,* 649–664.

FODOR, E. M. Group stress, authoritarian style of control, and use of power. *Journal of Applied Psychology,* 1976, *61,* 313–318.

FRANKENHAEUSER, M., & GARDELL, B. Underload and overload in working life: Outline of a multidisciplinary approach. *Journal of Human Stress,* 1976, *2,* 35–46.

FRENCH, J. R. P., JR. Person-role fit. *Occupational Mental Health,* 1973, *3,* 15–20; also in A. McLean (ed.), *Occupational stress.* Springfield: Thomas, 1974.

FRENCH, J. R. P., JR., & CAPLAN, R. D. Psychosocial factors in coronary heart disease. *Industrial Medicine,* 1970, *39,* 383–397.

FRENCH, J. R. P., JR., RODGERS, W. L., & COBB, S. Adjustment as person-environment fit. In G. Coelho, D. Hamburg & J. Adams (eds.), *Coping and adaptation.* New York: Basic Books, 1974.

FRENCH, J. R. P., JR., TUPPER, C. J., & MUELLER, E. F. *Work load of university professors.* Ann Arbor: Institute for Social Research, 1965.

FROBERG, J., KARLSSON, C.-G., LEVI, L., LIDBERG, L., & SEEMAN, K. Conditions of work: Psychological and endocrine stress reactions. *Archives of Environmental Health,* 1970, *21,* 789–797.

GARDELL, B. Reactions at work and their influence on nonwork activities: An analysis of a sociopolitical problem in affluent societies. *Human Relations,* 1976, *29,* 885–904.

GAVIN, J. F. Employee perceptions of the work environment and mental health: A suggestive study. *Journal of Vocational Behavior,* 1975, *6,* 217–234.

GECHMAN, A. S., & WIENER, Y. Job involvement and satisfaction as related to mental health and personal time devoted to work. *Journal of Applied Psychology,* 1975, *60,* 521–523.

GEMMILL, R., & HEISLER, W. J. Machiavellianism as a factor in managerial job strain, job satisfaction, and upward mobility. *Academy of Management Journal,* 1972, *15,* 51–62.

GLASS, D. C. Stress, behavior patterns, and coronary disease. *American Scientist,* 1977, *65,* 177–187.

GLASS, D. C., & SINGER, J. E. *Urban stress: Experiments on noise and social stressors.* New York: Academic, 1972.

GULIAN, E. Fatigue and neuroticism: A differential approach. *Revista de Psihologie* (Bucharest), 1974, *20,* 15–30.

HALBERG, F., & NELSON, W. Some aspects of chronobiology relating to the optimization of shift work. In P. G. Rentos & R. D. Shepard (eds.), *Shift work and health.* Washington, D.C.: U.S. Government Printing Office, 1976.

HAMNER, W. C., & TOSI, H. Relationship of role conflict and role ambiguity to job involvement measures. *Journal of Applied Psychology,* 1974, *59,* 497–499.

HARRIS, W., & MACKIE, R. R. *A study of the relationship among fatigue, hours of service, and safety of operations of truck and bus drivers.* Washington, D.C.: U.S. Department of Transportation, 1972.

Harrison, R. V. Job stress as person-environment misfit. Paper presented to the annual meeting of the American Psychological Association, Washington, D.C. 1976.

Haynes, S. G., Feinleib, M., & Kannel, W. B. The relationship of psychosocial factors to coronary heart disease in the Framingham Study. Parts I and II. *American Journal of Epidemiology,* 1978, *107,* 362–402.

————. The relationship of psychosocial factors to coronary heart disease in the Framingham Study. Part III: Eight-year incidence of coronary heart disease. *American Journal of Epidemiology,* 1980, *111,* 37–58.

Hinkle, L. E., Jr. The effect of exposure to culture change, social change, and changes in the interpersonal relationships on health. In B. S. Dohrenwend & B. P. Dohrenwend (eds.), *Stressful life events: Their nature and effects.* New York: Wiley, 1974.

Hite, A. L. Some characteristics of work roles and their relationships to self-esteem and depression. *Dissertation Abstracts International,* 1976, *36*(7B), 3609B.

Holzer, C. E., III, Warheit, G. J., & Kuldau, J. M. *Life stress and continuity of depressive symptoms.* New York: American Psychiatric Association, 1978.

House, J. S. The relationship of intrinsic and extrinsic work motivations to occupational stress and coronary heart disease risk. *Dissertation Abstracts International,* 1972, *33*(5A). 2514A.

————. Occupational stress and coronary heart disease: A review and theoretical integration. *Journal of Health and Social Behavior,* 1974, *15,* 12–27.

House, J. S., McMichael, A. J., Wells, J. A., Kaplan, B. H., & Landerman, L. R. Occupational stress and health among factory workers. *Journal of Health and Social Behavior,* 1979, *20,* 139–160.

Ilfeld, F. W., Jr. Current social stressors and symptoms of depression. *American Journal of Psychiatry,* 1977, *134,* 161–166.

Iris, B., & Barrett, G. V. Some relations between job and life satisfactions and job importance. *Journal of Applied Psychology,* 1972, *56,* 301–304.

Ivancevich, J. M., & Donnelly, J. H. Relation of organizational structure to job satisfaction, anxiety-stress, and performance. *Administrative Science Quarterly,* 1975, *20,* 272–280.

Jacobson, D. Fatigue-producing factors in industrial work and preretirement attitudes. *Occupational Psychology,* 1972, *46,* 193–200.

Jahoda, M. The impact of unemployment in the 1930s and the 1970s. *Bulletin of the British Psychological Society,* 1979, *32,* 309–314.

James, L. R., & Jones, A. P. Organizational climate: A review of theory and research. *Psychological Bulletin,* 1974, *81,* 1096–1112.

————. Organizational structure: A review of structural dimensions and their conceptual relationships with individual attitudes and behavior. *Organizational Behavior and Human Performance,* 1976, *16,* 74–113.

Jenkins, C. D. Recent evidence supporting psychologic and social risk factors for coronary disease. *New England Journal of Medicine,* 1976, *294,* (Part I), 987–994; (Part 2), 1033–1038.

Jenkins, C. D., Rosenman, R. H., & Friedman, M. Replicability of rating the coronary-prone behavior pattern. *British Journal of Preventive and Social Medicine,* 1968, *22,* 16–22.

Johansson, G., & Lindstrom, B. *Paced and unpaced work under salary and piece-rate conditions.* University of Stockholm, Department of Psychology report no. 359. 1975.

Jolly, J. A. Job change: Its relationship to role stresses and stress symptoms according to personality and environment. *Dissertation Abstracts International,* 1979, *40*(5), 2418B.

Kahn, R. L. Conflict, ambiguity, and overload: Three elements in job stress. *Occupational Mental Health,* 1973, *3,* 2–9.

Kahn, R. L., & French, J. R. P., Jr. Stress and conflict: Two themes in the study of stress. In J. E. McGrath (ed.), *Social and psychological factors in stress.* New York: Holt, 1970.

KAHN, R. L., WOLFE, D. M., QUINN, R. P., SNOEK, J. D., & ROSENTHAL, R. A. *Organizational stress: Studies in role conflict and ambiguity.* New York: Wiley, 1964.

KARCHER, C. J. Normative integration of the industrial setting. *Dissertation Abstracts International,* 1978, *38*(7A), 4384A.

KASL, S. V., & COBB, S. Blood pressure changes in men undergoing job loss: A preliminary report. *Psychosomatic Medicine,* 1970, *32,* 19–38.

KASL, S. V., & FRENCH, J. R. P., JR. The effects of occupational status on physical and mental health. *Journal of Social Issues,* 1962, *18,* 67–89.

KASL, S. V., GORE, S., & COBB, S. The experience of losing a job: Reported change in health, symptoms, and illness behavior. *Psychosomatic Medicine,* 1975, *37,* 106–122.

KATZELL, R. A., YANKELOVICH, D., FEIN, M., OORNATI, O. A., & NASH, A. *Work, productivity, and job satisfaction.* New York: Psychological Corporation, 1975.

KELLAM, S. G. Stressful life events and illness: A research area in need of conceptual development. In B. S. Dohrenwend & B. P. Dohrenwend (eds.) *Stressful life events: Their nature and effects.* New York: Wiley, 1974.

KIMBALL, W. H. Psychological correlates of tension headaches. *Dissertation Abstracts International,* 1979, *39*(10B), 5073B.

KORMAN, A. *Industrial and organizational psychology.* Englewood Cliffs: Prentice-Hall, 1971.

KORNHAUSER, A. *Mental health of the industrial worker.* New York: Wiley, 1965.

KROES, W. H. *Society's victim, the policemen: An analysis of job stress in policing.* Springfield: Thomas, 1976.

KROES, W., HURRELL, J., & MARGOLIS, B. Job stress in police administrators. *Journal of Police Science and Administration,* 1974, *2,* 381–387.

LEDERER, L. G. Psychologic and psychopathologic aspects of behavior during airline pilot transition training. *Revue de Médicine Aeronautique et Spatiale* (Paris), 1973, *12,* 299–300.

LEVINE, H. Health and work shifts. In P. G. Rentos & R. D. Shepard (eds.), *Shift work and health.* Washington, D.C.: U. S. Government Printing Office, 1976.

LIKERT, R. *New patterns of management.* New York: McGraw-Hill, 1961.

LOCKE, E. A. The nature and causes of job satisfaction. In M. D. Dunnette (ed.), *Handbook of industrial and organizational psychology.* Chicago: Rand-McNally, 1976.

LONDON, M. & KLIMOSKI, R. J. Self-esteem and job complexity as moderators of performance and satisfaction. *Journal of Vocational Behavior,* 1975, *6,* 293–304.

MacKINNON, N. J. Role strain: An assessment of a measure and its invariance of factor structure across studies. *Journal of Applied Psychology,* 1978, *63,* 321–328.

MANGIONE, T. W., & QUINN, R. P. Job satisfaction, counterproductive behavior, and drug use at work. *Journal of Applied Psychology,* 1975, *60,* 114–116.

MARGOLIS, B. L., KROES, W. H., & QUINN, R. P. Job stress: An unlisted occupational hazard. *Journal of Occupational Medicine,* 1974, *16,* 659–661.

MARSHALL, J. Stress amongst nurses. In C. L. Cooper & J. Marshall (eds.), *White collar and professional stress.* New York: Wiley, 1980.

McFARLAND, R. A. Influence of changing time zones on air crews and passengers. *Aerospace Medicine,* 1974, *45,* 648–658.

McGRATH, J. E. Stress and behavior in organizations. In M. D. Dunnette (ed.), *Handbook of industrail and organizational psychology.* Chicago: Rand McNally, 1976.

MECHANIC, D. Discussion of research programs on relations between stressful life events and episodes of physical illness. In B. S. Dohrenwend & B. P. Dohrenwend (eds.), *Stressful life events: Their nature and effects.* New York: Wiley, 1974.

MEERS, A., MAASEN, A., & VERHAEGEN, P. Subjective health after six months and four years of shift work. *Ergonomics,* 1978, *21,* 857–859.

MENDELOFF, A., & DUNN, J. P. *Digestive diseases.* Cambridge: Harvard University Press, 1971.

MILES, R. H., & PETTY, M. M. Relationships between role clarity, need for clarity, and job tension and satisfaction for supervisory and nonsupervisory roles. *Academy of Management Journal,* 1975, *18,* 877–883.

MOCH, M. K., BARTUNEK, J., & BRASS, D. J. Structure, task characteristics, and experienced role stress in organizations employing complex technology. *Organizational Behavior and Human Performance,* 1979, *24,* 258–268.

MORRIS, J. N., HEADY, J. A., & BARLEY, R. G. Coronary heart disease in medical practitioners. *British Medical Journal,* 1952, (4757), 503–520.

MOTT, P. E. Social and psychological adjustment to shift work. In P. G. Rentos & R. D. Shepard (eds.), *Shift work and health.* Washington, D.C.: U.S. Government Printing Office, 1976.

MOTT, P. E., MANN, F. C., McLOUGHLIN, Q., & WARWICK, D. P. *Shift work: The social psychological consequences.* Ann Arbor: University of Michigan Press, 1965.

MULLEN, S. A., DAVIDSON, J. J., & JONES, H. B., JR. *Potential threat to licensed nuclear activities from insiders.* Washington, D.C.: U.S. Nuclear Regulatory Commission, 1980.

MUMFORD, L. *The myth of the machine.* Vol. 1: *Technics and human development.* New York: Harcourt, 1967.

————. *The myth of the machine.* Vol. 2: *The pentagon of power.* New York: Harcourt, 1970.

MURPHY, L. R., & HURRELL, J. J., JR. Machine pacing and occupational stress. In R. M. Schwartz (ed.), *New developments in occupational stress.* Cincinnati: National Institute for Occupational Safety and Health, 1980.

MURRAY, R. M. Psychiatric illness in doctors. *Lancet* (London), 1974, *151,* 1211–1213.

NEVES, I. F. Social adaptation and accidents on the job. *Revista Interamericaa de Psicología,* 1969, *3,* 139–162.

ORTH-GOMER, K. Ischemic heart disease and psychological stress in Stockholm and New York. *Journal of Psychosomatic Research,* 1979, *23,* 165–173.

OSTBERG, O. Interindividual differences in circadian fatigue patterns of shift workers. *British Journal of Industrial Medicine,* 1973, *30,* 341–351.

OWEN, J. D. The economics of shift work and absenteeism. In P. G. Rentos & R. D. Shepard (eds.), *Shift work and health.* Washington, D.C.: U.S. Government Printing Office, 1976.

PALMORE, E. B. Predicting longevity: A follow-up controlling for age. *Gerontologist,* 1969, *9,* 247–250.

PEARSE, R. *What managers think about their managerial careers.* New York: American Management Association, 1977.

PINNEAU, S. R. Effects of social support on occupational stresses and strains. Paper presented to the annual meeting of the American Psychological Association, Washington, D.C., 1976.

PORTER, L. W., & DUBIN, R. *The organization and the person: Final report of the Individual Occupational Linkages Project.* Washington, D.C.: U.S. Office of Naval Research, 1975.

POWELL, M. Age and occupational change among coal-miners. *Occupational Psychology,* 1973, *47,* 37–49.

QUINN, R. P. *Locking-in as a moderator of the relationship between job satisfaction and worker health.* Ann Arbor: University of Michigan, Survey Research Center, 1972.

————. What makes jobs monotonous and boring? Paper presented to the annual meeting of the American Psychological Association, Chicago, 1975.

QUINN, R. P., SEASHORE, S. KAHN, R., MANGIONE, T., CAMPBELL, D., STAINES, G., & McCULLOUGH, M. *Survey of working conditions: Final report on univariate and bivariate tables.* Washington, D.C.: U.S. Government Printing Office, 1971.

QUINN, R., & SHEPARD, L. *The 1972-73 quality of employment survey.* Ann Arbor: University of Michigan, Survey Research Center, 1974.

RAHE, R. H., GUNDERSON, E. K. E., PUGH, W., RUBIN, R. T., & ARTHUR, R. J. Illness prediction studies: Use of psychosocial and occupational characteristics as predictors. *Archives of Environmental Health,* 1972, *25,* 192-197.

RAMOS, A. A. The relationship of sex and ethnic background to job-related stress of research and development professionals. *Dissertation Abstracts International,* 1975, *36*(3)A, 1862A.

REINHART, G. R., IV. Social structure and self-destructive behavior. *Dissertation Abstracts International,* 1978, *38*(7A), 4390A.

RENSHAW, R. An exploration of the dynamics of the overlapping worlds of work and family. *Family Process,* 1976, *15,* 143-165.

RENTOS, P. G., & SHEPARD, R. D. (eds.). *Shift work and health: A symposium.* DHEW (NIOSH) Publication no. 76-203. Washington, D.C.: U.S. Government Printing Office, 1976.

RONAN, W. W., COBB, J. M., GARRETT, T. L., LAZARRI, J. D., MOSSER, D. R., & RACINE, A. E. Occupational level and mental health: A note. *Journal of Vocational Behavior,* 1974, *5,* 157-160.

ROSE, R. M., JENKINS, C. D., & HURST, N. W. Health change in air traffic controllers: A prospective study. *Psychosomatic Medicine,* 1978, *40,* 142-165.

RUSSEK, H. I. Emotional stress and coronary heart disease in American physicians. *American Journal of Medical Sciences,* 1960, *240,* 711-721.

————. Emotional stress as a cause of coronary heart disease. *Journal of the American College Health Association,* 1973, *22,* 120-123.

RYZHKOVA, M. N., LANSKIY, V. P., NEVSKAYA, Y. M., & SIMONOVA, T. A. Metodicheskiye voprosi psikholigiyenicheskikh issledovaniy v professiyakh nervonapryazhen-nogo truda. [Methodical questions of psychohygienic research on professions entailing stressful work.] *Gigyena Truda i Professional'nyye Zabolevaniya* (Moscow), 1978, *8,* 24-27.

SALES, S. M., & HOUSE, J. Job dissatisfaction as a possible risk factor in coronary heart disease. *Journal of Chronic Diseases,* 1971, *23,* 861-873.

SCHMIDT, W. H. Basic causes of organizational stress: Causes and problems. In R. M. Schwartz (ed.), *Occupational stress: Proceedings of the conference on occupational stress.* Washington, D.C.: U.S. Government Printing Office, 1978.

SCHRIESHEIM, C. A., & MURPHY, C. J. Relationships between leader behavior and subordinate satisfaction and performance: A test of some situational moderators. *Journal of Applied Psychology,* 1976, *61,* 634-641.

SELYE, H. *The stress of life.* New York: McGraw-Hill, 1956.

————. *Stress in health and disease.* London: Butterworths, 1976.

SHEPPARD, H. L., & HERRICK, N. Q. *Where have all the robots gone? Worker dissatisfaction in the '70s.* New York: Free Press, 1972.

SHIROM, A., EDEN, D., SILBERWASSER, S., & KELLERMAN, J. J. Job stress and risk factors in coronary heart disease among five occupational categories in kibbutzim. *Social Science and Medicine,* 1973, *7,* 875-892.

SINGER, J. N. Job strain as a function of job and life stresses. *Dissertation Abstracts International,* 1975, *36*(6B), 3109B.

SMITH, M., COLLIGAN, M., & HURRELL, J. Three incidents of industrial mass psychogenic illness. *Journal of Occupational Medicine,* 1978, *20,* 399-400.

SMITH, M. J., COLLIGAN, M. J., & HURRELL, J. J., JR. A review of psychological stress research carried out by NIOSH, 1971 to 1976. In R. M. Schwartz (ed.), *New developments in occupational stress.* Cincinnati: National Insititue for Occupational Safety and Health, 1980.

SPECTOR, P. E. Relationships of organizational frustration with reported behavioral reactions of employees. *Journal of Applied Psychology,* 1975, *60,* 635-637.

Susser, M. Causes of peptic ulcer: A selective epidemiological review. *Journal of Chronic Diseases,* 1967, *20,* 435–456.

Swain, A. D., & Guttmann, H. E. *Handbook of human reliability analysis with emphasis on nuclear power plant applications.* Washington, D.C.: U.S. Nuclear Regulatory Commission, 1980.

Tasto, D., & Colligan, M. *Health consequences of shiftwork.* DHEW (NIOSH) publication no. 78–154. Washington, D.C.: U.S. Government Printing Office, 1978.

Taylor, P. J. The effects of shift work on worker health. *Industrial Medicine and Surgery,* 1973, *42,* 13–19.

Theorell, T. Life events before and after the onset of a premature myocardial infarction. In B. S. Dohrenwend & B. P. Dohrenwend (eds.), *Stressful life events: Their nature and effects.* New York: Wiley, 1974.

Theorell, T., Lind, E., & Floderus, B. The relationship of disturbing life-changes and emotions to the early development of myocardial infarctions and other serious illnesses. *International Journal of Epidemiology,* 1975, *4,* 281–293.

Tung, R. L., & Koch, J. L. School administrators: Sources of stress and ways of coping with it. In C. L. Cooper & J. Marshall (eds.), *White collar and professional stress.* New York: Wiley, 1980.

Vertin, P. G. *Bedrijfsgeneeskundige Aspecten van het Ulcus Pepticum.* Eindhoven: Hermes, 1954.

Waldron, J. The coronary-prone behavior pattern, blood pressure, employment, and socio-economic status in women. *Journal of Psychosomatic Research,* 1978, *22,* 79–87.

Weiner, H. *Psychobiology and human disease.* New York: Elsevier, 1977.

Wilkes, B., Stammerjohn, L., & Lalich, N. *Job demands and worker health in machine-paced poultry inspection.* NIOSH final project report can. no. 0–9277766. Washington, D.C.: U.S. Government Printing Office, n.d.

Work in America: Report of a special task force to the Secretary of Health, Education, and Welfare. Cambridge: MIT Press, 1973.

Zung, W. W. A self-rating depression scale. *Archives of Genral Psychiatry,* 1965, *12,* 63–70.

26

Variability of Stress Effects among Men Experiencing Job Loss

Stanislav V. Kasl   Sidney Cobb

THE DAY IS YET TO COME WHEN A REVIEWER of stress research is challenged because he overestimated the extent of conceptual and methodological disagreement in the stress field. The term "stress" continues to be used in fundamentally different ways: (1) as an environmental condition, (2) as the appraisal of an environmental situation, (3) as the response to that condition, and (4) as some relationship between environmental demands and the person's ability to meet these demands. Passionate pleas for uniformity of usage or for the adaption of one particular definition go unheeded. Most likely, this is because no one has been able to develop a compelling argument for a concept or approach that would be suitable for all the areas and levels of human functioning in which stress research is conducted.

However, a good deal of convergence of opinion does exist regarding the overall strategy of human stress research. This consensus deals with the need to incorporate an idiographic, subjective approach to stress formulations into the study of the health impact of stressful conditions or experiences. For example, McGrath's (1970) widely used definition of stress as "a (perceived) substantial imbalance between demand and response capability, under conditions where failure to meet demand has important (perceived) consequences" (p. 20) incorporates both individual differences ("response capability") and subjective perceptions.

Though this idiographic, subjectivistic approach to stress may be necessary in order to capture the complexity of the problem, it does cause many conceptual and methodological headaches. First, it maintains the confusing overlap between various concepts and formulations, and we cannot make clear distinctions, such as between stress as an environmental condition and stress as some form of response or among stress, appraisal of stress, and coping. Moreover, it drives us away from the study of actual ("objective") environmental conditions and weakens our ability to reconstruct the causal chain from health outcomes back to some pathogenic aspect of the environment. Next, it seduces us into studying the easy but

Research for this chapter was supported, in part, by grants from the National Institute of Mental Health (K3–MH–16709 and K5–MH–16709), from the U.S. Public Health Service (5–R01–CD00120 and 5–R01–HS–00010), and from the U.S. Department of Labor (91–26–72–23), and by a NIOSH purchase order (76–1261).

methodologically suspect associations between perceived and self-reported stimulus conditions and perceived and self-reported responses or outcomes. And finally, in general, it adds an open-ended indeterminacy to our research designs, since we are less certain that, in a particular setting in which we are studying the stress-disease connection, we have assessed all the relevant and important mediating and modifying variables.

These dilemmas in stress research lead to difficult decisions regarding study design strategies to be used with a particular problem under investigation. No one design can, of course, realistically hope to capture all the etiological complexities of the stress-disease linkage and thus all designs will have some limitations. However, certain limitations have been particularly common in the stress-disease area and their potential for generating misleading etiological interpretations particularly strong: (1) the use of a simplistic assessment instrument (such as the many variations on deriving weighted total scores for reported stressful life events), which can create innumerable measurement problems; (2) the use of a retrospective, cross-sectional design when only prospective, longitudinal observations can possibly illuminate the underlying dynamics, and (3) the use of acute manipulations under experimental control when we wish to observe chronic, long-term effects in the field.

This chapter presents selected findings from a longitudinal study of plant closing and job loss in order to illustrate the complexity of results one may encounter in the study of stress effects in the field setting. In this way we hope to advance our substantive understanding of the effects of unemployment and job change; to increase our general sensitivity to the need for research designs that are responsive to the complexity of the phenomenon under study; and to identify specific dimensions of complexity that are likely to be troublesome in diverse stress-disease investigations.

BACKGROUND

Several major types of transition involving the work role could be assessed for their health impact: initial entry into the labor force; change in one's place of work, job, or career; loss of a job and being unemployed; withdrawal from the labor force in order to perform other roles (such as parent or homemaker); reentry into the labor force; and retirement. Among these, retirement is the transition that has received by far the most attention (Kasl, 1980). Job loss has been less adequately investigated, the emphasis has been primarily on indicators of mental health and well-being, and many of the studies date from the 1930s, which decade, of course, enjoyed less sophistication in social research (Kasl, 1979a).

Much of the recent research on unemployment has utilized a macroeconomic approach, linking aggregated data on economic change (particularly percentage of workers unemployed) to fluctuations in other indicators, also aggregated for a whole state or country (Brenner, 1971, 1973, 1975, 1979; Bunn, 1979). This proliferation of the business cycle study is taking place in splendid isolation from methodological criticism of the whole approach. Some have questioned the interpretation of the associations, but not the basic methodology (Eyer, 1977, 1980); others have questioned it as an approach to detecting the physical and mental health costs of unemployment (Kasl, 1979b; Marshall & Funch, 1979; Ratcliff, 1980); and still others have raised broad methodological criticisms of the whole approach of utilizing ecological data (Firebaugh, 1978; Stavraky, 1976). The concern with "ecological fallacy" is, of course, not very new (Robinson, 1950).

Clearly, there is a need for exploring the strengths and weaknesses of different methodologies and of different levels of analysis. The recent work of Catalano and Dooley

(Catalano & Dooley, 1979a, b; Dooley & Catalano, 1979, 1980) and of Sklar (1980) shows much promise both of clarifying the troublesome issue of generalization across levels of analysis and of establishing research strategies for studying the health impact of business cycle changes and of the individual experience of unemployment.

In this situation, any attempt to review briefly the evidence on health impact of unemployment would quickly become a methodological analysis of research strategies. The evidence itself is rather inconclusive and difficult to package, particularly if we were also to try to incorporate the complex evidence that came out of our earlier analyses and reports of plant closing and job loss (Cobb & Kasl, 1977; Kasl, 1979a; Kasl & Cobb, 1979, 1980; Kasl, Gore, & Cobb, 1975). In this chapter we do not propose to seek closure regarding the evidence on health impact of job loss. Rather, we wish selectively to examine some of the findings in order to gain insight into the methodological and substantive complexity of studying stressful experiences in the field.

METHODS

Our study was a longitudinal investigation of the health and behavioral effects of job loss and of the ensuing unemployment and/or job change experience. It reflected a research strategy of trying to identify significant social events of stressful nature that are predictable and thus can be studied in their natural setting with sufficient scientific rigor. The design may also be seen as an approach to the study of life events that emphasized the need to examine a single event in depth, rather than diverse events distributed over a span of time, such as might obtain when one uses the Schedule of Recent Experience (Holmes and Rahe, 1967) to monitor periodically events reported by study subjects.

We were able to identify two plants that were going to shut down permanently; all employees would lose their jobs. In this way, we were able to accumulate a cohort of men whom we could then follow at regular intervals up to 2 years as these men went through the stages of anticipation of job loss, plant closing and employment termination, unemployment (for most), probationary reemployment, and stable reemployment. Our target population was limited to male blue-collar workers at these two plants. All subjects were married, were in the age range of 35–60, and had worked at the company at least 3 years. Of the men eligible for study, 79% agreed to participate. The men were seen in their homes by public health nurses, on the following schedule of visits. Each phase included a pair of visits two weeks apart.

> *Phase 1:* The first visit took place some four to seven weeks before the scheduled plant closing; the men were still on their old jobs but they were well aware of the impending shutdown.
> *Phase 2:* The second visit took place some five to seven weeks after the plant closing. At this point, the men either were unemployed or had found a new job but were still in the probationary period of employment.
> *Phase 3:* The visits during this phase took place some four to eight months after the plant closing. Some men were seen only once, but roughly 60% of the men received two visits during this phase. For these men, we used the average of the two values for each study variable in the data analysis. During phase 3, more and more men found new jobs; some were still unemployed; and a few had made another job change.
> *Phase 4:* Here the visits took place one year after the plant closing. Most men had

achieved a stable reemployment situation, but some were experiencing further job changes and a few remained unemployed.

Phase 5: The last visit took place some two years after the original plant closing. A sizable minority of men had experienced additional job changes and unemployment during the year preceding this visit.

In our presentation of results, we refer to the first 2 phases as *anticipation,* and *termination.*

During the course of each visit the nurse collected blood and urine specimens; measured blood pressure, pulse rate, height, and weight; and used a structured interview and questionnaire to collect diverse social-psychological and health data. The interview schedule investigated the subject's current employment situation, his economic circumstances, his subjective evaluation of his job and financial situation, his mental health and affective reactions, and his physical health. Because there was a great deal of identical data being collected at each phase, two nurse visits were necessary; these visits came two weeks apart and during this period the men kept a daily health diary.

Most of our data were derived from standardized, explicit (precoded) interview schedule and questionnaire measures developed over a four-month period of pretesting. The public health nurses, all of them experienced interviewers, recieved an additional two to three weeks' training in the use of the study's interview schedule and questionnaires. This training was designed primarily to insure uniformity of interview behavior and strict adherence to the interview schedule, its questions, and its built-in probes.

The men who lost their jobs came from two companies. One was a paint manufacturing plant located in a large metropolitan area. The men were largely machine operators, laboratory assistants, or shipping department clerks; the work was relatively light for most. The other plant was located in a rural community of some 3000 people. It manufactured display fixtures used by wholesale and retail concerns; the men were machine operators, assembly line workers, and a few tool and die workers.

The study design also called for the use of controls, who were continuously employed men in comparable jobs. They were followed for almost the same length of time and exactly the same assessment procedures were used.

The controls came from four different companies and were quite comparable to the subjects on major demographic characteristics, type of work, and rural-urban location of the plant. One employer was a large university; the men were largely machinists and carpenters in the main tenance department. The second company manufactured parts for heavy trucks; it was located in a large metropolitan area and the men were machine operators and assembly line workers. The other two companies were rural manufacturing concerns, where the men, again, were primarily machine operators and assembly line workers.

Table 26-1 presents the major sociodemographic characteristics of the terminees—the men who lost their jobs—and the controls. The two groups were generally comparable and none of the differences reported in Table 26-1 proved to be significant. It is worth noting that the terminees had worked at the company almost 20 years on the average. Considered along with their age, this would suggest that the plant closing meant for most of them a separation from the primary place of employment of their adult work career. The bottom of Table 26-1 shows that terminees and controls were also comparable on diverse additional variables, such as Crowne and Marlowe's (1964) measure of the need for social approval, useful as an indicator of defensiveness in self-report; Block's (1965) Ego Resilience Scale, a

TABLE 26-1
A Comparison of Terminees and Controls

	Terminees	Controls
Companies involved	1 urban	2 urban
	1 rural	2 rural
Number of men in study	100	74
Initial participation rate (% of target population)	82	75
Mean age	48.1	50.1
Mean years of schooling	9.5	10.0
Mean number of children	2.9	3.3
Nonwhite (%)	8	11
Mean years at (original) company	19.4	21.1
Mean hourly wage (initial)	$2.96	$3.58
Mean Duncan code of occupational status (Reiss, 1961)	28.2	32.2
Mean employability (combines age, education, nurse's rating of health, and Duncan code of highest previous job held)	2.5($\pm$.5)	2.6($\pm$.5)
Terminees and controls also comparable on:		
Need for social approval (Crowne & Marlowe, 1964)		
Ego resilience (Block, 1965)		
Flexibility-rigidity (Gough, 1957)		
Self-rated health at initial visit		

measure of general adjustment; The California Psychological Inventory (CPI) flexibility-rigidity scale (Gough, 1957); and global self-rating of health on the initial visit.

Let us briefly characterize the unemployment experience of the men during the 24-month follow-up period. Overall, the men experienced an average of about 15 weeks of unemployment during the 24 months; for most of them, this was the period between the plant closing and their starting on a new full-time job. However, 20% of the men were unemployed two or more times. In the urban setting, the experience during the first year was less severe: 25% experienced no unemployment (i.e., they found a new job at once) and another 50% had less than 2 months of unemployment. In the rural setting, the men had a more difficult time finding a job; even some 3–4 months after the plant closing, one-third of the men were without a job. By the end of the first year, the men in the rural setting had experienced an average of 12 weeks of unemployment, in contrast to 7 weeks for the urban terminees. During the second year, the situation was reversed: more men in the urban than in the rural setting experienced additional periods of unemployment. Thus, by the end of the 24-month period, the cumulative experience of the men in the two companies was about the same.

A separate analysis of the social context of the two companies revealed that in the urban setting, where the men lived scattered throughout the city, the plant itself was an important focus of a sense of community and social support (Gore, 1973). When the plant closed down, this "community" died (Slote, 1969). But in the rural setting, the small town and the people in it were the major source of a sense of community and social support for the men, whereas the plant had never become fully integrated into community life. When the plant closed, the community and its social organization remained largely intact and social interaction with former co-workers who were friends was not significantly disrupted.

These differences in the course of the unemployment experience and in the social setting of the urban and rural companies have to be kept in mind as the results are presented and discussed. The reader is referred to Cobb and Kasl (1977) for full details of the study methodology.

RESULTS AND DISCUSSION

The remainder of this chapter describes some of the variability and complexity of the stress effects of the job loss experience and then draws some implications from these regarding the role of the social setting, personal characteristics, and stages of adaptation. Furthermore, we shall examine the problem of causal inferences posed by these results.

Before we embark on a presentation of results, we wish to give the reader a sense of the general findings, those that may be thought of as characterizing the average impact of the experience. The salient ones are summarized here:

The men who became unemployed did not blame themselves for this result; however, for those who continued being unemployed (6 months or more), self-blame did go up (Cobb & Kasl, 1977).

Job satisfaction data for reemployed men, collected 12 months after the plant closing, showed equal or higher job satisfaction for the new job, compared to the old. Strikingly higher satisfaction with co-workers and supervisors on the new job was particularly surprising, given the 20 years of seniority at the old plant (Cobb & Kasl, 1977).

Analysis of intraperson differences between occasions when a man was unemployed and when he was reemployed revealed a clear-cut impact of employment status on sense of economic deprivation and specific work role deprivation dimensions (e.g., "Chance to use skills you are best at;" "Feelings of security about the future"). However, on diverse indicators of mental health status (e.g., depression, anxiety-tension, psychophysiological symptoms), no significant differences attributable to employment status could be detected (Kasl, 1979a; Kasl & Cobb, 1979).

Measures based on a two-week health diary, such as *days complaint* (a count of the number of days out of 14 on which the respondent checked off on the health diary that he "did not feel as well as usual") and *days disability* (number of days checked off that he "did not carry on usual activities"), did show significant fluctuations over time, but they could not be linked to employment-unemployment status changes (Kasl, Gore, & Cobb, 1975).

Analyses of cardiovascular risk factors (blood pressure, serum cholesterol, cigarette smoking, body weight) did not at any point reveal a level of cardiovascular risk among men losing their jobs exceeding the risk among controls (Kasl & Cobb, 1980).

The vast majority of the dependent variables in this study (physiological and mental health and work role deprivation) showed a similar pattern of dynamic changes: between phase 1 and phase 2, they were reliably sensitive to the difference in employment status, that is, when going from anticipation to unemployment, as opposed to prompt reemployment; between phase 2 and phase 3, men continuing to remain unemployed tended to return to baseline levels, as did the men who were becoming reemployed at that time. This pattern suggests that the men did not maintain a state of arousal, distress, and sense of work role deprivation as long as the unemployment experience lasted; rather, they showed evidence of adaptation, so that following an initial period of unemployment those remaining unemployed could not be distinguished from those finding a new job.

Overall, this set of results may be seen against a background of research on low skill blue-collar jobs (Kasl, 1974, 1978). Many workers adapt to dull and monotonous jobs by disengaging and by giving up expectations that work will be a meaningful human activity. Thus, aside from the financial considerations, the adaptive demands of the loss of the work role may be only self-limiting, with a correspondingly minimal impact, among such disengaged blue-collar workers.

Effects of Urban versus Rural Setting

One of the powerful sources of variation in results that we encountered had to do with the location of the plant (Cobb & Kasl, 1977). In Table 26–2 we present some of the data on correlates of the job loss experience. The first half of the table deals with correlates of an objective index, number of weeks of unemployment experienced during the first year (for most men, this was the period between losing their original job and becoming reemployed for the first time). Three variables of labor-economic interest had highly similar correlations in both settings (and were highly significant for the combined sample): longer unemployment was related to lower employability; presence of additional wage earners in the family; and the respondent's greater readiness to seek medical attention for given symptoms, based on a brief scale from Mechanic and Volkart (1961). However, the subjective correlates of this objective indicator showed a strikingly different picture in the two settings; specifically, only the urban men showed the expected associations. The three scales included a four-item measure of job loss stress ("Rate job loss"; "How long before things back to normal") that compared job loss to other life events, along with a chart to evaluate distress around the time

TABLE 26–2
Correlates of the Job Loss Experience in the Urban and the Rural Setting

	Urban plant ($n = 46$)	Rural plant ($n = 54$)	Significance of difference in correlations (two-tail test)
	Correlates of number of weeks of unemployment experienced during first year of follow-up		
Variables of labor-economic interest			
Employability (see Table 25–1)	−.35	−.41	n.s.
Number of wage earners in the family	.29	.26	n.s.
Readiness for illness behavior	.29	.26	n.s.
The subjective experience (at phase 4)			
Job loss stress (4 items; see text)	.45	−.12	< .005
Relative economic deprivation	.38	−.06	< .05
Work role deprivation (12 items; see text)	.46	−.10	< .005
	Correlates of job loss stress		
Stable personality			
Ego resilience	−.25	−.29	n.s.
Flexibility-rigidity	.29	.28	n.s.
Depression (average over all phases)	.44	.40	n.s.
Contextual variables			
Nurse's rating of health	.43	−.10	< .01
Symptoms on health history	.38	.10	$p = .15$
Perceived social support	−.06	−.34	$p = .16$

of the plant closing; a two-item subjective index from Aiken, Ferman, and Sheppard (1968) on relative economic deprivation; and a measure of work role deprivation, a set of 12 pairs of ratings on work related dimensions for which the subject indicated "how things are now" and "how he would like them to be" (Cobb & Kasl, 1977). Clearly, only in the urban setting was length of unemployment correlated with amount of subjective impact.

The lower half of Table 26–2 shows correlates of the job loss stress index. The correlates that reflect stable personality characteristics showed similar associations in both settings (highly significant for the combined sample): greater stress ratings were obtained from men lower on ego resilience, higher on flexibility, and higher on average depression level. However, the bottom of Table 26–2 suggests that other influences on the job stress ratings perhaps were setting-specific: in the urban setting men in poorer health tended to report more stress, while in the rural setting this was true of those who reported lower social support (based on a 13-item index reflecting the man's perceptions of social support from his wife and, to a lesser extent, from friends and relatives).

Overall, the results in Table 26–2 strongly suggest that the dynamics of experiencing plant closing and job loss were quite different in the two settings. Let us examine some additional findings that strengthen this conclusion.

In Table 26–3 we consider the acute effects of the job loss experience; here we can compare the changes in selected indicators between anticipation and phase 2, controlling for whether the change was to unemployment or to reemployment. The first three columns of Table 26–3 address this issue for all 100 men losing their jobs. In all instances one can see a differential impact linked to employment status at phase 2. Men who were unemployed at that time showed either a large increase in a particular variable (when there had been no anticipation effect at phase 1) or a small increase that continued the elevated levels associated with an anticipation effect. Men who were already reemployed at phase 2 mostly showed a decline in the various indicators. All the differential changes were reliable. The remainder of the table further stratifies these findings by the setting of the plant. This finer breakdown suggests that the differential impact of reemployment and unemployment on economic deprivation was similar in both settings; on three intercorrelated mental health indicators (depression, anxiety, and low self-esteem), the differential impact of the employment status variable was greater in the urban setting; the impact on the index of suspicion was stronger in the rural setting, primarily because of the large decline among those finding prompt reemployment; and, according to the physiological data, the employment status variable had a stronger impact in the urban setting with respect to serum uric acid and in the rural setting with respect to diastolic blood pressure.

Overall, the results in Tables 26–2 and 26–3 support the argument that the urban-rural distinction is an important one in attempting to describe and document the impact of the job loss experience. However, we cannot pretend to understand the reasons for these urban-rural differences. We have already noted two differences reflected in this contrast: in the rural setting, the job market was quite limited and the prospect of reemployment was therefore limited; however, in the rural setting, the plant closing did not destroy the social community of co-workers, and there was a greater possibility for sharing the experience and enjoying mutual social support. It is also likely that there are rural-urban differences in the meaning of work: there is some evidence that small-town workers are less alienated from middle-class work norms than are urban workers (Hulin & Blood, 1968; Turner & Lawrence, 1968). The notion of a greater attachment to the work role in the rural setting is consistent with our finding that the work role deprivation scales were more sensitive to unemployment among the rural men, while the mental health scales tended to be more sensitive among the urban men (Kasl & Cobb, 1979).

TABLE 26-3

Changes between Phase 1 and Phase 2 in Selected Mental Health and Physiological Variables: The Role of Urban-Rural Location of Plant

	Mean changes from phase 1 (anticipation) to phase 2[a]							
	All men		*Significance of differential change due to employment status at phase 2*	*Urban plant*		*Rural plant*		*Significance of interaction: employment status by urban-rural setting*
	UNEMPLOYED AT PHASE 2	REEMPLOYED AT PHASE 2		UNEMPLOYED AT PHASE 2	REEMPLOYED AT PHASE 2	UNEMPLOYED AT PHASE 2	REEMPLOYED AT PHASE 2	
Relative economic deprivation[b]	1.74	.11	<.001	1.16	−.06	1.92	.49	n.s.
Depression[b]	.30	−.43	<.01	.88	−.46	.07	−.37	<.05
Anxiety-tension[b]	.19	−.45	<.01	.52	−.50	.06	−.36	<.10
Low self-esteem[b]	.22	−.42	<.05	.96	−.33	−.06	−.58	n.s.
Suspicion[b]	.17	−.55	<.05	−.09	−.08	.25	−1.43	<.01
Pulse rate (beats/minute)	2.43	−2.22	<.005	4.47	−2.29	1.63	−1.87	n.s.
Diastolic blood pressure (mmHg)	1.36	−3.07	<.01	−2.60	−2.83	2.53	−3.50	<.05
Serum cholesterol (mg/100ml)	9.24	−2.40	<.05	11.92	−4.96	8.30	1.94	n.s.
Serum uric acid (mg/100ml)	.09	−.55	<.001	.20	−.89	.05	−.01	<.001

[a] Positive score indicates an increase over time; negative score indicates a decrease.

[b] Scale values are in standard scores (M = 0, SD = 1), based on normative data from controls.

453

The Role of Perceived Social Support

Another major source of variation in our results reflected the modifier role of perceived social support (Kasl & Cobb, 1977). This 13-item index consisted of 6 items on perceived social support from wife, 2 items on support from friends and relatives, 3 items on frequency of social interaction with friends and relatives, and 2 items dealing with the perceptions of the social environment as one in which sociability can be expressed and problems can be discussed. When this scale was originally developed for this study (Cobb, Brooks, Kasl, & Connelly, 1966), we could comfortably view it as state of the art, if not somewhat novel. However, the recent rapid developments in conceptualization and measurement of social support and social networks have made our measure rather outdated.

The major findings involving this measure provided a fair amount of support for the general proposition that among men who went through a more severe plant closing–job loss experience, higher levels of perceived social support tended to ameliorate the negative impact of the experience, for both psychological and physiological indicators (Cobb & Kasl, 1977; Gore, 1978).

Social support influenced the relationship between length of unemployment and the job loss stress index (see Table 26-2). Among men with low levels of perceived social support, those below median on unemployment had a mean job stress level of $-.33$, compared to .44 for those above median (these values are standard scores); among men high on social support, men with shorter unemployment had mean job stress (.11) not much different from that among men with longer unemployment ($-.10$). The interaction effect between social support and length of unemployment was significant ($p < .025$).

Level of perceived social support was not associated with length of unemployment, i.e., a high level did not facilitate job seeking. However, social support did modify the influence of other variables on success in job seeking. For example, higher age, poorer self-rated health, and poorer nurse's rating of health (all at the initial interview) were more strongly related to length of subsequent unemployment among men high on social support (r's of .45, .60, and .73, respectively) than among men low on social support (r's of .05, .21, and .33, respectively). All three pairs of correlations were significantly different. This would seem to suggest that among older men in poorer health, higher level of social support may have acted as a deterrent to job seeking efforts.

Clearly, then, social support may act as a simple buffer, but it may also interact with other variables in complex ways. Additional findings to be presented now continue the theme of variability of stress effects of the job loss experience and illuminate the complex role social support may play in adjustments to unemployment.

One facet of complexity is that in some cases the modifying role of the social support variable was *specific to the setting;* that is, it interacted with the urban-rural plant location. Table 26-4 presents the results with respect to serum cholesterol changes between phase 1 and phase 2; these changes were adjusted for the effect of employment status (seen in Table 26-3) and number of job changes experienced during the first year (i.e., stability of employment), a separate influence on cholesterol described previously (Kasl & Cobb, 1980). It can be seen that lower levels of social support in the urban setting and higher levels of support in the rural setting tended to be associated with decreasing levels of serum cholesterol between phases 1 and 2.

The story of the complex effects of social support cannot be told without also paying attention to the *stages of adaptation* to the whole plant closing–job loss–reemployment experience. For example, we noted that changes in diastolic blood pressure between phases 1

TABLE 26–4
Serum Cholesterol Changes in Relation to Level of Social Support and Urban-Rural Location

Change in serum cholesterol from phase 1 to phase 2[a]	Urban plant		Rural plant	
	Level of social support		*Level of social support*	
	LOW	HIGH	LOW	HIGH
Increase/no change	6	13	14	13
Decrease	14	6	9	17
% showing decrease	70.0	31.6	39.1	56.7
	Significance of interaction $p < .005$			

[a] Adjusted for effect of employment status at phase 2 and employment stability (number of job changes in first year).

and 2 were significantly sensitive to employment status at phase 2 (as seen in Table 26–3), as well as to level of social support, which seemed to act as a buffer: among men going from anticipation to unemployment, those with low support showed an increase (4.1), while those high on support showed a small decline (− 1.6); among men going from anticipation to reemployment, the decline was smaller from those lower on social support (− 1.2) than for those who were higher (− 5.0). This was a main effect on social support ($p < .025$), acting within both levels of the employment status variable. Between phases 2 and 3, the men could be classified as remaining unemployed, becoming reemployed, continuing at the same job, and remaining employed but changing jobs. At this point, diastolic blood pressure changes were no longer reliably sensitive either to the level of social support or to the typology of work status transitions.

Changes in serum uric acid yielded a different pattern of results, shown in Table 26–5. During the early transition, between phase 1 and 2, there was a strong main effect associated with employment status (seen in Table 26–3), but no reliable effect of level of social support. However, the changes between phase 2 and 3 showed a strong effect of social support within each category of employment transition, even as employment status ceased to show a reliably impact: in each of the four groups, lower social support was associated with an increase in serum uric acid, while high social support was linked to a decline (or to a smaller increase).

The contingency of the effect of social support on the stage of the job loss experience is dramatically indicated in Table 26–6 with respect to anxiety-tension. In the early transition, from phase 1 to phase 2, there was a paradoxical main effect of social support: men low on support showed a smaller increase or a larger decline within the two groups stratified by employment status. The significant interaction suggests that the effect of level of support was concentrated primarily in the group of men low on support experiencing prompt reemployment. In the later transition, between phase 2 and 3, the main effect of social support was the familiar buffer effect: men high on social support were more likely to show a decline in anxiety-tension. Furthermore, the significant interaction suggests that the benefits of high social support redounded primarily to the group whose employment picture had not yet stabilized—men continuing to be unemployed or working in unstable job situations.

The results in Table 26–6 with respect to anxiety-tension closely parallel findings on

TABLE 26-5
Changes in Serum Uric Acid in Relation to Employment Status, Social Support, and Stage of Adaptation

Type of transition	Mean changes in serum uric acid			Significance of main effects
	Social support			
	LOW	HIGH	TOTAL	
Phase 1 to phase 2				
Anticipation to unemployment	.08	.07	.09	Employment status, $p < .001$
Anticipation to reemployment	−.73	−.30	−.55	Social support, n.s.
Phase 2 to phase 3				
Continued unemployment	.06	−.61	−.37	
Unemployment to reemployment	.09	−.40	−.23	Employment status, n.s.
Stable continued reemployment	.24	−.29	−.01	Social support, $p < .001$
Unstable reemployment	.57	.17	.27	

456

TABLE 26-6
Changes in Anxiety-Tension in Relation to Employment Status, Social Support, and Stage of Adaptation

Type of transition	Mean changes in anxiety-tension[a]			Significance of effects
	Social support			
	LOW	HIGH	TOTAL	
Phase 1 or phase 2				
Anticipation to unemployment	.15	.21	.19	Employment status, $p < .01$
Anticipation to reemployment	−.81	.06	−.45	Social support, $p < .05$
				Interaction, $p < .05$
Phase 2 to phase 3				
Failure to stabilize: continued unemployment or unstable reemployment	.48	−1.02	−.27	Employment status, n.s.
Stabilizing: becoming reemployed or continuing stable employment	−.07	−.11	−.09	Social support, $p < .05$
				Interaction, $p < .05$

[a]Scale values are in standard scores ($M = 0$, $SD = 1$), based on normative data from controls.

457

other mental health indicators we have examined, such as depression. These results cannot be definitively interpreted, but we believe that the following line of reasoning is plausible. During the early stages, the mental health benefits of prompt reemployment are felt primarily by men low in social support—perhaps in the spirit of "I did it in spite of little help from others!" At the same time, the benefits of high social support among those becoming unemployed at phase 2 may be attenuated by a sense of reciprocal obligation: perceiving high support may go hand in hand with a greater sense of responsibility for providing for those whose support one feels. However, in the later phases of the experience, inadequate support in the face of continuing employment uncertainty appears to enhance the mental health costs. Among men who are well supported, the continuing uncertainty may come to mobilize fully the support mechanism, so that now the benefits are clearly manifest.

The Role of Personal Characteristics

In this section we wish to consider briefly the role that personality characteristics may play in modifying the stress effects of the job loss experience. For this purpose, we have chosen a variable called *psychological defense* (Cobb & Kasl, 1977). This measure identifies a man as *well defended* if he scores in the extreme 12% of any of four measures: the rigid end of the CPI flexibility-rigidity scale (Gough, 1957); the high end of the Crowne-Marlowe (1964) scale of the need for approval; the high end of Block's (1965) Ego Resilience Scale; and the oral end of the orality scale of Lazare, Klerman, and Armor (1966). Otherwise, the respondent is scored as *poorly defended*. Admittedly, this measure of psychological defense is a mixed bag lacking conceptual purity; however, it is a pragmatic combination of several measures that in separate analyses tend to show similar modifier effects. Complete data were available on 86 of the 100 men, 47 of whom were classified as poorly defended.

The role of psychological defense may be seen in several ways. First, we found an association with length of unemployment experienced during the first year of follow-up: poorly defended men were less likely to be above median on length of unemployment (38.3%) than were well-defended men (66.7%; $p < .01$) for the difference in percentages). Thus, presence of one or another of the defenses appeared to delay reemployment. Second, poorly defended men were likely to report greater job loss stress (see Table 26-2), and this effect held within each level of length of unemployment ($p < .001$); the association between psychological defense and job loss stress can be represented by biserial correlations of $-.36$ among men below median on length of unemployment and $-.47$ for men above median. Thus, it appears that the presence of psychological defenses puts a man at greater risk for longer unemployment but at the same time buffers him against experiencing greater job stress, normally associated with longer unemployment.

In examining another objective indicator of the severity of the job loss experience, number of job changes during the first year, we found no association with psychological defense: among poorly defended men, 44.7% were above median on job changes, compared to 43.6% of well-defended men. Furthermore, number of job changes was not correlated with job loss stress ($r = .04$). However, we observed an interesting interaction: among poorly defended men, greater job stress was somewhat associated with fewer job changes (biserial $r = -.14$), while among well-defended men, the association was positive and moderately strong (biserial $r = .47$); the difference in the association was reliable ($p < .05$). This pattern of findings would seem to suggest that the role of psychological defense is not constant across indicators of severity of the job loss experience, i.e., duration of unemployment versus number of job changes.

Table 26–7 presents the results of an analysis that examined the impact of the job loss experience on serum glucose levels in conjunction with the possible modifying role of psychological defense. Because it was impossible to collect fasting bloods and because the amount of food eaten during the past three hours was measured imprecisely, we chose to ignore the continuous nature of this variable and selected an arbitrary cutoff to designate elevated levels of serum glucose. (We explored further refinements in this analysis, such as deleting the four known diabetics or selecting a variable cutoff depending upon whether or not a meal had preceded the home visit, but these variations had very little impact on the results.) Table 26–7 clearly shows that the chance of experiencing elevated glucose levels at some point in the study increased with length of unemployment and/or number of job changes. However, this association was seen primarily among poorly defended men; well-defended men showed a much weaker gradient, which was not significant. Overall, these results support the utility of the construct of psychological defense, while demonstrating that the same personality characteristic may both aggravate the exposure to an environmental stressor and buffer its impact.

Problems with Causal Inferences

The study of the health impact of stressful life experiences and situations is overwhelmingly quasi-experimental and the limitations of such designs have been well analyzed and described (e.g., Cook & Campbell, 1979). However, our understanding of the limitations from such textbook analyses must be supplemented by experience with a particular design and a particular problem, since not all ambiguities of causal interpretation can be detected a priori from the general features of a design.

In the present study, two features of the design may be viewed as strengths. First, self-selection factors assigning men to experimental (plant closing) versus control conditions were at a minimum since both plants closed down through no fault of any of the men studied; moreover, they had worked there some 20 years on the average, thus further limiting the possibility of self-selection, say, of marginal workers seeking out marginal employment opportunities. Second, the study was longitudinal and prospective, starting before the plants closed.

On the other hand, at least two major limitations of the design affect causal interpretations. First, the design was not prospective enough: we have no true baseline data from the time before the plant closing was announced (or feared, anticipated, rumored, etc.). Moreover, the severity of the experience (such as weeks unemployed or number of job changes) perhaps was heavily dependent on self-selection factors, including dependent variables being utilized to assess impact. We are not addressing other limitations of the design here. For example, with respect to generalizability of the findings, we are acutely aware that our results on the impact of unemployment cannot be extrapolated to white-collar professional and managerial groups.

In this section we wish to use selective findings to illustrate how ambiguity makes causal interpretation difficult in this type of stress research. For example, in our analysis of the days complaint index (Kasl, Gore, & Cobb, 1975) we noted that eight men were experiencing some unemployment at either phase 4 or phase 5. For these two phases, their average days complaint (seasonally adjusted) was 3.34, which was highly significant and was about 1.1 standard deviations above the mean for the total group. However, these men had high levels all along: an average of 3.56 for all phases, or about 1.2 standard deviations above the mean for the total group. Clearly, then, the index of days complaint, though it appeared to pick up

TABLE 26-7
The Role of Psychological Defenses in Modifying the Impact of the Job Loss Experience of Serum Glucose Levels

	Severity of the experience (based on number of weeks unemployed and number of job changes)		
	Below median on both	Above median on either weeks unemployed or job changes	Above median on both
All men %of men with serum glucose level ≥ 130mg/dl at any time during study	7.7 (*n* = 26)	32.5 (*n* = 40) gamma = .63 *p* < .001	52.6 (*n* = 19)
Men low on defenses % of men with elevated serum glucose	5.0 (*n* = 20)	38.9 (*n* = 18) gamma = .90 *p* < .001	87.5 (*n* = 8)
Men high on defenses % of men with elevated serum glucose	16.7 (*n* = 6)	27.3 (*n* = 22) gamma = .13 n.s.	27.3 (*n* = 11)

minor acute conditions, was actually a rather stable indicator of health status, and poor health was predictive (self-selective) of longer unemployment. Unfortunately, the issue of impact versus self-selection was seldom this simple. In our analysis of mental health variables involving stratification on length of unemployment and level of social support (Kasl & Cobb, 1979), we noted that most of the indicators revealed poorest mental health in the group high on unemployment and low on social support—exactly as predicted by the buffer notion of social support. But this pattern was seen even at anticipation! This forces us to consider an alternate interpretation: high levels of distress at anticipation, in conjunction with low levels of social support, were predictive of longer unemployment. However, this still does not clarify the issue of whether these high levels at anticipation were an acute reaction to the impending plant shutdown or represented characteristic levels of distress for these men. Examining the data through the two years of follow-up further clarified this picture: on the various work role deprivation measures, this appeared to be an acute reaction and by phase 5 these men had average values; on the mental health indicators, such as depression or anxiety-tension, this group remained distinct even through phase 5, suggesting that characteristically high levels of distress (in conjunction with low support) were involved in predicting length of unemployment.

These results indicate that cross-sectional analyses comparing employed and unemployed men must be viewed with great suspicion. The observations that unemployed men are more unhappy (Bradburn, 1969; Campbell, Converse, & Rodgers, 1976), have higher rates of psychiatric disorder (Fried, 1969), and believe their lives to be controlled by environmental forces instead of by themselves (Tiffany, Cowan, & Tiffany, 1970)—these are inherently ambiguous observations in need of clarification with respect to causality.

The self-selection influence of the dependent variables was not restricted to the psychological measures. In our NIOSH report (Cobb & Kasl, 1977), for example, we noted that norephinephrine excretion rates at anticipation were related to length of subsequent unemployment: men with elevated rates were more likely to have a shorter unemployment. (Because of the effect of coffee consumption on norepinephrine rates, these results applied only to men who had had no caffeine containing beverage in the three hours preceding the urine sample.) This would suggest that the high level of physiological arousal at anticipation reflected an increased motivation (whether positive or negative) to find reemployment promptly. Thus, the norepinephrine rates were not as much an indicator of impact as a predictor of the length of the subsequent unemployment.

Even more interesting results were obtained with respect to serum uric acid levels, which suggested a *delayed* self-selection effect. We observed that among the 51 men who were unemployed at phase 2, the mean of those still unemployed at phase 3 was 6.73, compared to 5.73 for those reemployed by phase 3 ($p < .001$ for this difference). However, working backward we observed little change over time: men still unemployed at phase 3 had a mean of 6.86 at anticipation and 7.04 at phase 2, while those reemployed at phase 3 had means of 5.86 and 5.94 for anticipation and phase 2, respectively (the differences in each case were highly significant, $p < .001$). Thus, the initial levels at anticipation were predictive not of the proximal transition to phase 2 but of the more distal transition between phases 2 and 3.

The final set of results we wish to present concerns number of job changes during the first year. The results in Table 26–8 show that this variable had an impact on phase 1 to phase 2 changes, independent of the already described effect of employment status. With respect to serum cholesterol, the biggest increase was seen for men who experienced both unemployment and many job changes, and the biggest decrease was seen for those who experienced prompt reemployment and few job changes. Highly similar results were obtained

TABLE 26-8
The Influence of Number of Job Changes before They Occurred

Type of transition	Mean changes from phase 1 to phase 2			Significance of effects
	Number of job changes the first year			
	FEW	MANY	TOTAL	
Serum cholesterol				
Anticipation to unemployment	3.0	15.0	9.2	Employment status, $p < .05$
Anticipation to reemployment	−5.6	8.5	−2.4	Number of job changes, $p < .025$
Suspicion[a]				
Anticipation to unemployment	−.17	.82	.17	Employment status, $p < .05$
Anticipation to reemployment	−.92	−.21	−.55	Number of job changes, $p < .01$

[a]Scale values are instandard scores (M = 0, SD = 1), based on normative data from controls.

for a selected mental health variable, suspicion. The problem with these results is, fundamentally, that the variable of job changes described the period between phase 2 and phase 4, i.e., an experience that had not yet taken place! We are not sure how best to interpret these results and are sharing our puzzlement with the reader. It is possible that for the reemployed men, by phase 2 they knew whether or not the job they held was likely to represent stable employment; stable reemployment would bring a greater reduction in stress than would unstable reemployment. However, this explanation does not apply to the effect of number of job changes among men unemployed at phase 2. They presumably would have had a much more difficult time assessing the stability of the new job, which they had not yet found. Certainly, these results suggest that in longitudinal studies of stressful experiences we may not always be able to pin down precisely the temporal location of a particular variable used to assess an experience; the time at which the variable is assessed may be a poor indication of the actual time at which the variable exerts its influence.

CONCLUDING REMARKS

If a novelist sought to convey the overall plot and the subplots relating to each of his characters by offering the reader a series of numbers, each representing the weighted cumulative score for stressful life events experienced by the dramatis personae in the novel, we might well question his sanity and doubt his ability to support himself in his chosen career. In this chapter we suggested, in effect, that the criteria for merit of research examining the impact of stress on human health are similar to the criteria for a meritorious novel: attention to detail, to complexity, and to richness. Without them, the novelist can survive only if he has such a captivating and forceful and innovative story line that the details of execution are unimportant. Without them, the stress researcher can survive only if he is dealing with a disaster of such proportions that an impact is easily detectable in nearly everyone. However, such plots and such disasters are not daily occurrences.

Nevertheless, the novelist and the stress researcher must soon part company, since the latter cannot depend solely on his characters to tell the complete story. The detail, the complexity, and the richness provided directly by the subject are suspect. Such subjective accounts of what he is experiencing, how he is appraising it (personal control, predictability, familiarity, etc.), how he is coping, how events are affecting him—all these may be but different invitations to the subject to describe the nature and the amount of his distress. The link to actual (presumably objective) environmental conditions is weakened, if not severed, as is the link to the so-called objective characteristics of the person. The challenge here is two-fold: to develop relatively objective measurement procedures for subjective constructs and to develop complex data analysis strategies so that objective and relatively superficial indicators can reveal some of the subjective and idiosyncratic import that they may have for particular individuals.

REFERENCES

AIKEN, M., FERMAN, L. A., & SHEPPARD, H. L. *Economic failure, alienation, and extremism.* Ann Arbor: University of Michigan Press, 1968.

BLOCK, J. *The challenge of response sets.* New York: Appleton, 1965.

BRADBURN, N. *The structure of psychological well-being.* Chicago: Aldine, 1969.

Brenner, M. H. Economic changes and heart disease mortality. *American Journal of Public Health,* 1971, *61,* 606–611.

————. Fetal, infant, and maternal mortality during periods of economic instability. *International Journal of Health Services,* 1973, *3,* 145–159.

————. Trends in alcohol consumption and associated illnesses: Some effects of economic changes. *American Journal of Public Health,* 1975, *65,* 1279–1292.

————. Mortality and the national economy: A review and the experience of England and Wales, 1936–1976. *Lancet,* 1979, *2,* 568–573.

Bunn, A. R. Ischaemic heart disease mortality and the business cycle in Australia. *American Journal of Public Health,* 1979, *69,* 772–781.

Campbell, A., Converse, P. E., & Rodgers, W. L. *The quality of american life.* New York: Russell Sage, 1976.

Catalano, R., & Dooley, D. Does economic change provoke or uncover behavioral disorder? In L. A. Ferman & J. P. Gordus (eds.), *Mental health and the economy.* Kalamazoo: Upjohn Institute for Employment Research, 1979. (a)

————. The economy as stressor: A sectoral analysis, *Review of Social Economy,* 1979, *37,* 175–188. (b)

Cobb, S., Brooks, G. W., Kasl, S. V., & Connelly, W. E. The health of people changing jobs: a discription of a longitudinal study. *American Journal of Public Health,* 1966, *56,* 1476–1481.

Cobb, S., & Kasl, S. V. *Termination: The consequences of job loss.* DHEW (NIOSH) publication no. 77-224. Cincinnati: National Institute for Occupational Safety and Health, 1977.

Cook, T. D., & Campbell, D. T. *Quasi-experimentation.* Chicago: Rand McNally, 1979.

Crowne, D. P., & Marlowe, D. *The approval motive.* New York: Wiley, 1964.

Dooley, D., & Catalano, R. Economic, life, and disorder changes: Time-series analyses. *American Journal of Community Psychology,* 1979, *7,* 381–396.

————. Economic change as a cause of behavioral disorder. *Psychological Bulletin,* 1980, *87,* 450–468.

Eyer, J. Prosperity as a cause of death. *International Journal of Health Services,* 1977, *7,* 125–150.

————. Social causes of coronary heart disease. *Psychotherapy and Psychosomatics,* 1980, *34,* 75–87.

Firebauge, G. A rule for inferring individual level relationships from aggregated data. *American Sociological Review,* 1978, *43,* 557–572.

Fried, M. Social differences in mental health. In J. Kosa, A. Antonovsky, & I. K. Zola (eds.), *Poverty and health: A sociological analysis.* Cambridge: Harvard University Press, 1969.

Gore, S. The influence of social support in ameliorating the consequences of job loss. Doctoral dissertation, University of Pennsylvania, 1973.

————. The effect of social support in moderating the health consequences of unemployment. *Journal of Health and Social Behavior,* 1978, *19,* 157–165.

Gough, G. *The California Psychological Inventory manual.* Palo Alto: Consulting Psychologists, 1957.

Holmes, T. H., & Rahe, R. H. The social readjustment rating scale. *Journal of Psychosomatic Research,* 1967, *11,* 213–218.

Hulin, C. L., & Blood, M. R. Job enlargement, individual differences, and worker responses. *Psychological Bulletin,* 1968, *69,* 41–55.

Kasl, S. V. Work and mental health. In J. O'Toole (ed.), *Work and quality of life.* Cambridge: MIT Press, 1974.

————. Epidemiological contributions to the study of work stress. In C. L. Cooper & R. Payne (eds.), *Stress at work.* New York: Wiley, 1978.

—————. Changes in mental health status associated with job loss and retirement. In J. E. Barrett (ed.), *Stress and mental disorder*. New York: Raven, 1979. (a)

—————. Mortality and the business cycle: Some questions about research strategies when utilizing macro-social and ecological data. *American Journal of Public Health*, 1979, *69*, 784–788. (b)

—————. The impact of retirement. In C. L. Cooper & R. Payne (eds.), *Current concerns in occupational stress*. New York: Wiley, 1980.

KASL, S. V., & COBB, S. Some mental health consequences of plant closing and job loss. In L. A. Ferman & J. P. Gordus (eds.), *Mental health and the economy*. Kalamazoo: Upjohn Institute for Employment Research, 1979.

—————. The experience of losing a job: Some effects on cardiovascular functioning. *Psychotherapy and Psychosomatics*, 1980, *34*, 88–109.

KASL, S. V., GORE, S., & COBB, S. The experience of losing a job: Reported changes in health, symptoms, and illness behavior. *Psychosomatic Medicine*, 1975, *37*, 106–122.

LAZARE, A., KLERMAN, G. L., & ARMOR, D. J. Oral, obsessive, and hysterical personality patterns: An analysis of psychoanalytic concepts by means of factor analysis. *Archives of General Psychiatry*, 1966, *14*, 624–630.

MARSHALL, J. R. & FUNCH, D. P. "Mental illness and the economy": A critique and partial replication. *Journal of Health and Social Behavior*, 1979, *20*, 282–289.

McGRATH, J. E. A conceptual formulation for research on stress. In J. E. McGrath (ed.), *Social and psychological factors in stress*. New York: Holt, 1970.

MECHANIC, D., & VOLKART, E. H. Stress, illness behavior, and the sick role. *American Sociological Review*, 1961, *26*, 51–58.

RATCLIFF, K. S. On Marshall and Funch's critique of "mental illness and the economy." *Journal of Health and Social Behavior*, 1980, *21*, 389–391.

REISS, A. J., JR. (ed.) *Occupations and social status*. Appendix B. Glencoe: Free Press, 1961.

ROBINSON, W. S. Ecological correlations and the behavior of individuals. *American Sociological Review*, 1950, *15*, 351–357.

SKLAR, E. D. Community economic structure and individual well-being: A look behind the statistics. *International Journal of Health Services*, 1980, *10*, 563–579.

SLOTE, A. *Termination: The closing at Baker plant*. Indianapolis: Bobbs-Merrill, 1969.

STAVRAKY, K. The role of ecological analysis in studies of the etiology of disease: A discussion with reference to large bowel cancer. *Journal of Chronic Diseases*, 1976, *29*, 435–444.

TIFFANY, D. W., COWAN, J. R., & TIFFANY, P. M. *The unemployed: A social-psychological portrait*. Englewood Cliffs: Prentice-Hall, 1970.

TURNER, A. N., & LAWRENCE, P. R. *Industrial jobs and the worker*. Cambridge: Harvard University, Graduate School of Business Administration, 1968.

B. Psychosocial and Developmental Sources

27

Shyness and the Stresses of the Human Connection

Philip G. Zimbardo

SHYNESS IS A UNIVERSAL EXPERIENCE that often exerts a profoundly negative influence on the life of the shy person. It can function as a central self-schema that biases how socially and personally relevant information is gathered, interpreted, and acted upon. As a cognitive style, shyness influences expressive behaviors, as well as attributional processes that relate the individual to other people. Although experienced privately, chronic shyness appears to reflect cultural programming and individual responsiveness to social norms. Moreover, shyness may be maintained by a variety of social control agents whose task of behavior management is facilitated when children, students, workers, voters, or clients are passive or unassertive.

After nearly a decade of research into this fascinating phenomenon, my perspective on shyness has become broader rather than narrower. *Shyness* serves as my code word for all the forces within each of us, as well as those pressures from society, that combine to isolate us from one another. In this sense, shyness includes fear of (and prejudice toward) people who are different and social situations that are novel. Shyness may then become a factor in sustaining class, caste, and power differences. In the dialectic of freedom and security, as used by Fromm (1942) in his classic analysis of the rise of fascism, extreme shyness leads people so to abhor freedom that they are willing to trade it for the illusion of security.

In this chapter, I should like to mention the historical evolution of my interest in shyness; suggest alternative conceptions of shyness; describe Stanford University's multimeasure, multiresponse shyness research project; outline some basic findings on and perhaps nonobvious consequences of shyness; and finally, point to new directions in thinking and research regarding shyness.

The research described in this chapter was supported in part by the Office of Naval Research, NIMH, the Boys Town Center for Youth Development at Stanford University.

THE SILENT PRISON OF SHYNESS:
A CONCEPTUAL MODEL

My academic interest in shyness emerged from a series of interrelated concerns that had directed my earlier research in the areas of affiliation, social evaluation, deindividuation, imprisonment, and freedom.

Anxiety about the *social appropriateness* of one's reactions to a novel setting has been shown to suppress *affiliative needs* in favor of *social isolation* (Bromberg, 1967; Rapaport, 1963; Sarnoff, 1971; Sarnoff & Zimbardo, 1961). When we are uncertain whether others in a given situation are responding similarly to ourselves, the affiliative response exposes us to the possibility of direct negative evaluation. Thus, the basic quest to understand our reactions to situational demands may be countered by the powerful anxiety associated with possible rejection. Although we often rely upon social comparison information to get a subjective fix on our opinions, abilities, and emotions (Festinger, 1954), nevertheless at other times we suspend that concern for social feedback. We desire to stand out from others and to present a unique persona in anticipation of rewards, praise, status, support, empathy, and love (Snyder & Fromkin, 1980). We do otherwise when we associate danger or aversive consequences with being marked as an individual performer. When people wish to forego responsibility for their actions, to engage in socially unacceptable behaviors, or to act from motives of self-interest and self-indulgence, the preferred modus operandi is *deindividuation,* an altered state of consciousness and behavior that reduces the individual's uniqueness and public identifiability (Maslach, 1971). Under conditions that give rise to this subjective state, wherein uniqueness of self is surrendered, two mediating cognitive processes are altered. There is a reduced concern for *social evaluation,* along with a lessened preoccupation with *self-monitoring* (Prentice-Dunn & Rogers, 1980; Zimbardo, 1970). Under these circumstances, individuals have been observed to behave in ways that violate both traditional norms and their own personality histories.

Prisonlike settings in everyday life are characterized by the anonymity of the participants playing the roles of guard and prisoner (Zimbardo, Haney, Banks, & Jaffe, 1973). This anonymity, combined with a power differential, may result in a so-called guard mentality, which arbitrarily limits the essential freedoms of the prisoner. The powerless prisoner may rebel (and be punished) or comply (and not be noticed). The *imprisonment* metaphor—guard exerting coercive control to facilitate the goal of ready behavioral management, on the one hand, and prisoner acquiescing to losses in freedom of speech, actions, and associations, on the other—brings to mind the mentality of the shy person (Zimbardo, 1975; Zimbardo, Pilkonis, & Norwood, 1975). The shy individual acts in the dual role of guard who imposes restraints on the prisoner's freedom and of prisoner who, in accepting these limits, denigrates himself or herself. The prisoner suffers a loss of self-esteem by virtue of observing his or her sheepish compliance with rule based authority, which, in turn, undermines any sense of *autonomy* and *competence.*

Based on this line of reasoning (which provided the staging ground for my venture into the alien land of the shy), the following model of shyness is proposed. Shyness represents a heightened state of individuation characterized by excessive egocentric preoccupation and overconcern with social evaluation. The excessive self-monitoring results in a diversion of attentional processes away from external stimulus inputs and toward the so-called contents of the mind. The excessive concern for social feedback regarding one's performance is biased toward the negative pole of the evaluative continuum. At the core of shyness is basic anxiety over rejection by others, ontological insecurity, and loss of identity. Such anxiety is both a cause and a consequence of the individual's inability to accept himself or herself as a worthy, lovable, competent, self-regulating, and autonomous person. Three fundamental fears flow from this core anxiety: fear of being socially inappropriate (one's unacceptable differences from others will be publicly exposed); fear of failure (one's incompetence will be publicly exposed); and fear of intimacy (one's real, private self will prove vulnerable to criticism or indifference when publicly exposed).

The defensive posture of shyness is designed to minimize the daily stresses engendered by having to cope regularly with these fears. The chronically shy person inhibits, withdraws, avoids, and escapes. The possibility for social evaluation is minimized by not affiliating with others. When it is not possible to avoid social contact, the shy person may still present such a low profile as not to be noticed (deindividuating) or not to initiate action. The anticipated pain of social rejection can also be attenuated by prior self-rejection—by throwing the "first stone" before anyone else is even aware that criticism is appropriate. This self-debasement is the behavioral input to the development of low self-esteem. Paradoxically, however, the more chronic source of a sense of the self as inadequate comes from the excessively high standards (often perfectionist) held by shy persons. The *discrepancy* between unrealistic ideals of what they should be and how they ought to perform and their perceived actual self may generate intolerant, self-critical attitudes. A related consequence of adopting exaggerated criteria for self-performance is behavioral inhibition: the shy person refrains from performances that might not be "just right." All of this self-referential cognitive activity leads the shy person to adopt a dispositional, rather than a situational, view of the causes of behavior. Thus, there is a stronger tendency toward attributing observed behavior (of self and others) to inner traits and states than to external stimulus events. This judgmental bias feeds back further to sensitize the shy to dispositionally based evaluations of them by other critics.

I believe it not too fanciful to imagine that Shakespeare's "To be or not to be" and "All the world's a stage" speeches refer most directly to the shy. Their central preoccupation is with the conflict over whether to take action; often they desire to do so but are held back by internalized voices of critics prepared to issue bad reviews of their performance. As the reservoir of lost opportunities builds, so does resentment and anger at their own passivity and the insensitivity of others. Depression is one way this anger gets deflected away from an acting our modality. However, at times the suppressed anger may be manifest in uncontrollable rage that is out of proportion to the immediate situational provocation.

Because of their focus on the self as performer, surrounded by an audience of overly eager critics, the shy lose their spontaneity and ability to act without plans and public masks (*persona*). Social situations are always first nights, fraught with anxiety until proven otherwise. The modern literary notion of the *performing self* is used to identify the artist whose work is concerned with his or her own creation. Poirier (1971), in *The Performing Self,* could have been analyzing the shy performer when he noted that certain writers "treat any occasion as a 'scene' or a stage for dramatizing the self as performer"; for them, "performance is an exercise of Power," which "presumes to compete with reality itself for control of the minds exposed to it" (pp. 86–87). Parenthetically, Stevens (1978), a literary scholar, presented a strong case that "the rise of the artist as a subject of his own work" was a signal development of twelfth-century culture, not a modern artistic innovation emerging from our ego centered culture.

ALTERNATIVE CONCEPTIONS OF SHYNESS

Before turning to alternative psychological perspectives on shyness, I should mention the insightful definition proposed by the poet Neruda (1977):

> Shyness is a kink in the soul, a special category, a dimension that opens out into solitude. Moreover, it is an inherent suffering, as if we had two skins (epidermises) and the one underneath rebelled and shrank back from life. Of the things that make up a man, this quality, this damaging thing, is a part of the alloy that lays the foundation, in the long run, for the perpetuity of the self. (P. 34)

A more formal approach to the concept that has guided our research defines shyness as a learned tendency to avoid social situations, to fail to participate appropriately in social encounters, to feel anxious and uncomfortable during interactions with others, and to lack confidence in one's self-worth. Shyness thus may involve four components: thoughts ("I'll make a fool of myself"), feelings (anxiety, nervousness, etc.), physical reactions (blushing, heart pounding, constricted breathing, etc.), and overt behaviors (not smiling, avoiding eye contact, etc.).

In the view of Darwin (1890), shyness was "an odd state of mind" that is

> chiefly recognized by the face reddening, by the eyes being averted or cast down, and by awkward, nervous movements of the body. . . . Shyness seems to depend on sensitiveness to the opinion, whether good or bad, of others, more especially with respect to external appearance. Strangers neither know nor care anything about our conduct or character, but they may, and often do, criticise our appearance. . . . The consciousness of anything peculiar, or even new, in the dress, or any slight blemish on the person, and more especially on the face—points which are likely to attract the attention of strangers—makes the shy intolerably shy. On the other hand, in those cases in which conduct, and not personal appearance, is concerned, we are much more apt to be shy in the presence of acquaintances whose judgments we in some degree value than in that of strangers. . . . Some persons, however, are so sensitive that the mere act of speaking to almost any one is sufficient to rouse their self-consciousness, and a slight blush is the result. Disapprobation . . . causes shyness and blushing much more readily than does approbation. . . . Persons who are exceedingly shy are rarely shy in the presence of those with whom they are quite familiar, and of whose good opinion and sympathy they are quite assured; for instance, a girl in presence of her mother. . . . Shyness . . . is closely related to fear; yet it is distinct from fear in the ordinary sense. A shy man dreads the notice of strangers, but can hardly be said to be afraid of them; he may be as bold as a hero in battle, and yet have no self-confidence about trifles in the presence of strangers. Almost every one is extremely nervous when first addressing a public assembly, and most men remain so through their lives. (Pp. 330–332)

Empirical support for Darwin's last assertion of the fear of addressing a public assembly came from a survey of 3000 U.S. inhabitants regarding their worst fears (Wallace, Wallechinsky & Wallace, 1977). "What are you most afraid of?" was most likely to be answered: "Speaking before a group." This worst human fear was acknowledged by 41% of respondents. Fear of heights took second place, acknowledged by 32% of those surveyed, while fear of sickness, death, loneliness, and the dark came further down the list.

James (1890), in reflecting upon Darwin's analysis of shyness, questioned the survival value of this mode. Shyness and the related impulses of stagefright and "servile terror" (fear of the danger in failing to please significant others) cannot have been selected for their usefulness: "Apparently, they are pure hindrances, like fainting at the sight of blood or disease, sea-sickness, a dizzy head on high places. . . . They are *incidental* emotions, in spite of which we get along" (p. 432).

The early empirical foundation of shyness as a personality construct came from the psychometric studies of Flanagan (1935), Guilford and Guilford (1936), Cattell (1943, 1965, 1973; Cattell, Eber, & Tatsuoka, 1970), and Comrey (1961, 1966, 1970). Flanagan's (1935) analysis of the data from high school males yielded three personality factors: self-confidence, sociability, and dominance. The self-confidence factor was described as distinguishing the socially aggressive, thick-skinned individual from the self-conscious, shy, emotionally unstable person. Five personality factors emerged from the analysis by Guilford and Guilford (1936) of students' responses to 36 typical items from various introversion-extroversion questionnaires: dependence, dominance, carefulness, intellectual leadership, and social introversion. The last was renamed shyness, a trait characteristic of individuals who are shy, deliberate, and overconscientious.

Cattell (1965) called shyness one of the "characteristic expressions," or surface traits, that define the negative pole of a personality factor he labeled H, the *threctic temperament*. Threctic people (like Emily Dickinson) are presumed to be at the mercy of a sympathetic nervous system that is overly susceptible to threat and conflict. They are contrasted to the stouthearted, bold, brash *parmia type* (with Teddy Roosevelt as prototype), The threctic person is "intensely shy, tormented by an unreasonable sense of inferiority, slow and impeded in expressing himself, disliking occupations with personal contacts, preferring one or two close friends to large groups, and not able to keep in contact with all that is going on around him" (Cattell, Eber, & Tatsuoka, 1970: 91). Looking at the pattern of correlations obtained from his questionnaire analysis of shyness, Cattell (1965) concluded that shyness as a personality factor is largely inheritable (as much as intelligence is); associated with strict parental discipline; likely to increase strongly during the middle years for males (but only slightly for females); not modifiable by environmental events or interventions; and likely to decline with age—"shyness of an excessive kind tends naturally to cure itself" (p. 97).

Comrey (1970) based his identification of shyness as a core factor in his taxonomy of personality largely on respondents' self-evaluations on only four test items (e.g., "I find it difficult to talk with a person I have just met"). In his model, shyness scores are associated with different combinations of the following: seclusiveness, lack of social poise, avoidance of social contact and social activities, loss of words, self-consciousness, submissiveness, reserve, stage fright, inferiority, and fear of speaking.

Saraf (1980) offered the most recent psychometric analysis of the global construct of shyness. Twenty shyness related scale items were factor-analyzed along with a series of other scales assessing aspects of personality and self-consciousness. Five components of shyness were revealed: social avoidance, social self-consciousness, uncomfortableness, egocentricity, and embarrassment. Positive correlations were obtained between shyness and scale scores of neuroticism, social anxiety, and public self-consciousness. Negative correlations were found with extroversion and the factor of body cathexis and self-cathexis.

Speculations about the nature of shyness have, over time, come under a variety of conceptual labels. McDougall's (1924) notion of "sensitization of the sentiment of self-regard" describes the excessive preoccupation with self characteristic of the shy person. This general concept was extended by Sears (1937) to include unconscious "projection of the subject," by which one develops ideas of reference. Self-criticism is thereby transformed from "I criticize myself" into the negative social evaluation anticipated and feared by the shy: *"They* are criticizing me." In a psychoanalytic orientation, shyness originates in the preoccupation of the ego with itself, i.e., as narcissism (Kaplan, 1972). Beneath their self-effacing, unresponsive masks, shy psychoanalytic patients are seething with grandiose fantasies and unexpressed hostilities. Fenichel (1945) linked shyness with repressed needs to gain sexual pleasure through the sensations of looking ("scoptophilia"); "extreme cases occasionally occur in shy, inhibited persons who actually do not dare to look at their environment. . . . Generally, shyness may be called the specific fear corresponding to the scoptophilic impulse" (p. 72). In the play *Lady in the Dark* (Hart, 1941), we are shown how such repressed exhibitionism leads to social inhibitions that may influence a person's lifestyle.

The psychoanalytic interpretation of shyness is the foundation upon which the *DSM-III* (1980) built the construct of *social phobia*—the closest contact psychiatry publicly makes with the lay term "shyness."

> The essential feature [of this anxiety disorder] is a persistent, irrational fear of, and compelling desire to avoid, situations in which the individual may be exposed to scrutiny by others. There is also fear that the individual may behave in a manner that will be humiliating or embarrassing. Marked anticipatory anxiety occurs if the individual is confronted with the necessity of entering such a situation, and he or she therefore attempts to avoid it. The disturbance is a significant source of distress and is recognized by the individual as excessive or unreasonable. (P. 227)

The stressful nature of social phobia is outlined in the description of its usual course: "The disorder is usually chronic, and may undergo exacerabation when the anxiety impairs performance of the feared activity. This then leads to increased anxiety, which strengthens the phobic avoidance" (pp. 227–228). In the next section of this chapter, I will take exception to the misinformation *DSM-III* presents regarding the "apparently relatively rare" condition of social phobia.

Among the variety of measures used to assess social anxiety, none distinguishes shyness from other forms of social distress (Buss, 1980). A recent attempt to do so by Cheek and Buss (1981) separated the social fear and emotionality component of shyness from that of sociability. Shyness was negatively and significantly correlated with being sociable ($r = -.30$, $n = 912$). However, shyness is not just being unsociable. The two constructs revealed different patterns of relationship to other personality measures. Shyness was more closely related to "psychological insecurity" (Ainsworth & Ainsworth, 1958) than to sociability. Sociable people are publicly self-conscious, but not fearful, and are high in self-esteem. Shy people are publicly self-conscious as well, but fearful and low in self-esteem.

THE STANFORD SHYNESS PROJECT

This cursory overview of conceptions may create the erroneous impression that shyness has been a well-studied area of research. To the contrary, given the important role that shyness plays in shaping the daily lives of the shy and its interesting theoretical associations, shyness is one of the least studied aspects of psychological functioning. In a recent report, Read (1980) noted: "Despite the growth of developmental research over the past 20 years, the study of social and emotional development in children has continued to lag behind research on other aspects of development" Part of this lag may be traced to the overemphasis on motor, cognitive, and intellectual development. Children in industrialized, modern societies are socialized to be effective problem-solvers; the focus is on action and performance.

Should we not also promote the development of the "soft side" of humanity along with task enhancing abilities? However, getting the task done well (and the product out on time) has seemed more central to progress than has concern for process, for feelings and personal relationships.

Other possible reasons for neglecting shyness as an area of either systematic research or serious speculation in personality, social psychology, or developmental textbooks are the myths that surround it. Shyness has been thought to be an inherited disposition, a natural stage of childhood that we outgrow, a characteristic with positive virtues, a woman's problem more than a man's, and a condition not amenable to therapeutic tactics. Indeed, psychologists have been loathe to study any problem with such defining features: inherited, universal, transient, positive, female, intractable.

Since 1972, my students and I at Stanford University have been studying the origins, correlates, and consequences of shyness using a multimethod, multiresponse approach. We surveyed about 10,000 people of many ages and diverse backgrounds in the United States and in eight other cultures. Hundreds of people were interviewed at length, shy and non-shy, along with their parents, teachers, associates, and employers. We utilized field and laboratory observations, structured laboratory experiments, psychological test correlations, and some novel exploratory paradigms to get beneath the surface structure of shyness. Finally, as part of our investigation of extreme and dynamic aspects of shyness, we created one of the first facilities exclusively devoted to the treatment of shyness related problem behaviors. In 1976 Marnell, Kramer, and I started the Stanford Shyness Clinic to learn more about the profound effects of shyness, as well as to study alternative strategies for reducing the aversive impact of shyness.

The most general conclusions that have emerged from our research (some of which will be described more fully) challenge all the features of the mythology of shyness previously noted.

1. About 40% of all adults surveyed described themselves as shy in an important dispositional sense. The prevalence of shyness was greatest, about 60%, in Japan and Taiwan and lowest in Israel, where 30% of those surveyed nevertheless reported being shy.

2. Shyness is as common among men as it is among women, although for men it is a less desirable characteristic and thus is more often concealed.

3. Shyness is not a natural stage that most children pass through and leave behind as they grow out of adolescence. Our studies of children (from preschool through high school) indicated that 30–40% of preadolescents are shy (by self-, parent, or teacher descriptions) and about 50–60% of young teenagers are shy; the figure decreases to 40% thereafter (Zimbardo & Radl, 1981). About 40% of our respondents reported ceasing to be shy at some point in their adult lives, while 16% of those currently shy reported first becoming shy sometime after adolescence. Of course, many shy children remain steadfastly shy throughout their lives. Letters from shy people in their eighties who long to enjoy one non-shy day before they die are sad testimony against the notion that shyness tends "to cure itself."

4. Shyness is negative to those who are shy. It may have some positive connotations (for example, modesty, coyness, nonaggressiveness), but these are aspects mentioned more often by the non-shy than by the shy. The vast majority of those who describe themselves as shy report that they dislike being shy and consider shyness to create real problems for them. In our study of four year olds, we found that preschoolers had a coherent conception of shyness that corresponded in its negative features to that held by adults. (Zimbardo, Linsenmeier, Dahlgren, & Buckner, 1981).

The Stanford Shyness Survey

We designed a survey instrument to allow the respondent to report about his or her shyness along many dimensions: history, variability, frequency, and severity of shyness; comparison with peers; as well as elicitors, accompanying reactions, and personal consequences of shyness. In this way, respondents could provide an individualized portrait of their shyness without being constrained by our preconceived categories (Zimbardo, 1977; Zimbardo, Pilkonis, & Norwood, 1975). This feature also made it possible to translate the survey into foreign languages for meaningful cross-cultural comparisons. After we analyzed and coded the initial open-ended survey, we developed fixed response categories to facilitate instrument administration and response scoring.

In addition to increasing our understanding of the self-conceptions surrounding shyness, this survey instrument has been used as a device to identify subgroups of shy and non-shy individuals for more systematic study. After briefly describing some of the findings uncovered by this survey instrument, I will outline its validity in terms of objectively recorded behaviors that differentiate the shy from the non-shy.

The 40% current prevalence of shyness statistic escalated to over 80% when respondents were asked whether they had described themselves as shy at any time in their life (past, present, or always). Only 17% reported never labeling themselves shy, but instead saw themselves as *situationally shy,* that is, responding with feelings of shyness in specific social situations. A mere 1% of Americans reported never having experienced shyness reactions personally. Across all cultures we studied, these "tough-skinned" non-shys made up no more than 10% of any national group.

When forced to evaluate their decision to call themselves shy persons in light of the frequency of their shyness reactions, most respondents (51%) reported being shy only occasionally but considered those circumstances sufficiently important to justify the shy label (i.e., *dispositional shyness*). Of our sample, 44% had a sense of being shy half the time or more, while 5% said they were shy all the time, in all situations, and with virtually everybody!

The evidence used by the shy so to label themselves comes from four sources:

behavioral (silence, failure to make eye contact, gaze aversion, avoidance of others, avoidance of initiating social actions, low speaking voice)
cognitive (self-consciousness, concern for impression management, concern for social evaluation, negative self-evaluation, thoughts about the unpleasantness of the situation and about shyness in general)
affective (awareness of feelings of anxiety, distress, nervousness, embarrassment, and awkwardness)
physiological (increased pulse, blushing, perspiration, pounding heart, shallow or constricted breathing, "butterflies in the stomach")

The differences between self-labeled shy and not-shy individuals on these dimensions have been shown to be highly significant in an independent test by Fatis (1981). The more shy the individual, the more each type of reaction is used as evidence of being shy.

Types of Shyness

When he performed a cluster analysis on the rankings by chronically shy people of the most important aspects of their shyness, Pilkonis (1974a) discovered four distinctive clusters. The major concerns of shy people with *public performance deficits* were awkward behavior and failure to respond. Those emphasizing *subjective discomfort* were most focused upon their internal discomfort and fear of negative evaluation. A third group, characterized as *fearful, with behavioral deficits,* centered their fears on negative evaluation and failure to respond. People in the last of the four categories, the *avoiders,* most emphasized avoidance of social situations and failure to respond.

Pilkonis's (1974b) study explored some complexities of the global construct of shyness, which includes not only dispositionally and situationally shy persons but also the *publicly shy* (whose behavior fits the prototypic conception of the awkward, passive, unresponsive person) and the *privately shy* (who have learned to act as though they were not shy despite their internal arousal and discomfort). When survey respondents further characterize themselves along the introversion-extroversion continuum (Eysenck & Eysenck, 1968), most shys are introverted; however, there are also shy extroverts. The latter often occupy public positions, in which they must talk and interact with other people, but they do not especially enjoy these demands and avoid them whenever possible. These shy extroverts perform best when playing clearly defined roles in structured situations, especially when they are in a position to control the nature and extent of the conversation (e.g., a television or newspaper interviewer).

When college women were selected according to their shyness and sociability scores and paired with another person who was also shy-sociable, shy-unsociable, un-shy-sociable, or un-shy-unsociable, Cheek and Buss (1981) uncovered some interesting patterns of response. The shy-sociable subjects were *most* tense and inhibited (in observers' judgments) while their shy-unsociable counterparts were least tense and inhibited. The shy-sociable women stood out from the other three types on various measures: they talked least, spent least time looking at their partner, and spent most time in anxious self-manipulation. The conflict between their need for affiliation and their inability to make adequate social responses was invoked as the explanation for their tense and disorganized behavior pattern.

Shyness and Situational Elicitors

Shyness is triggered by people and situations that are seen as threatening to the esteem and optimal performance of the individual. Those most likely to provoke shyness reactions are strangers, people of the opposite sex, and authorities by virtue of their knowledge or status. The situations that induce shyness are those characterized as social, novel, or evaluative; situations that require assertiveness, that make the person the focus of attention, or that place the person in a lower status vis-à-vis others who are present also elicit shyness.

Thus, it would appear that shyness is aroused by cues that unfamiliar others with needed resources are evaluating the individual in a setting that provides few learned guidelines for appropriate and acceptable performance. When shy and not-shy subjects were observed during an experimental session in which situational influences were manipulated, Pilkonis (1977b) found powerful context effects. Shyness was, in general, more readily evoked by ambiguous, unstructured encounters than by structured episodes. Observers were able most reliably to identify shy and not-shy subjects when they were in the unstructured setting, rather than in the formal, structured setup, where they performed specific role behaviors. Shy males suffered most in the opposite-sex encounter presumably because of the normative expectation that males initiate responding; they showed decreased rates of talking, gazing, and eye contact. The anxiety of shy women was manifested by their greater frequency of head nodding and nervous smiling.

This public-private distinction between shy subgroups was also apparent in the phase of our experimental research in which subjects had to prepare and deliver a formal speech. Asking the publicly shy, who generally focus on the inadequacy of their behavior, to concentrate on this public performance only served to aggravate their behavioral difficulties. They showed more speech anxiety and less satisfaction with their speeches, which were rated by judges as having less stylistic appeal than those of the privately shy. The demand to focus outward on a structured, clearly defined task seemed to distract the privately shy from their self-consciousness and their excessive monitoring of internal events.

Pilkonis's (1977a) research provided early behavioral confirmation of self-reported differences between shy and not-shy survey respondents. Let us now examine other effects of shyness.

STRESS RELATED CONSEQUENCES OF SHYNESS

In his essay on shyness, Bulwer-Lytton (1863) presented the most extreme consequence that shyness may have for an individual—the figurative loss of one's tongue leading to the literal loss of one's head. Indeed, Bulwer-Lytton traced the murder of Hercules to his shyness.

> Plutarch has an essay upon that defect which he calls *Dusopia*—a word signifying an unhappy facility of being put out of countenance—viz., shamefacedness—shyness. Plutarch seems to consider that Dusopia consisted chiefly in the difficulty of saying No, and has a stock of anecdotes illustrating the tragic consequences which may result from the pusillanimous characteristic of Shyness. It not only subjects us to the loss of our money when a slippery acquaintance asks us for a loan which we are perfectly aware he never intends to repay, but sometimes life is the penalty of that cowardly shyness which can not say No to a disagreeable invitation. Antipater was invited to an entertainment by Demetrius, and, feeling ashamed to evince distrust of a man whom he himself had entertained the day before, went forebodingly to the shambles. Polysperchon had been bribed by Cassander to make away with Hercules, the young son whom Barsina bore to Alexander. Accordingly he invited Hercules to supper. So long as Hercules could get off the invitation by note or message, he valiantly excused himself; but when Polysperchon called in person, and said burlily, "Why do you refuse my invitation? Gods! can you suspect me of any design against your life?" poor Hercules was too shy to imply, by continued refusal, that such design was exactly what he suspected. Accordingly, he suffered himself to be carried away, and in the midst of the supper was murdered. (P. 49)

Among other disasters that shyness visits upon persons so afflicted, the following received mention by Bulwer-Lytton (1863):

> His servants disregard him . . . his very friendships wound him . . . he loses the object of his affection because he is too bashful to woo. . . . As soon as he is married, he is at his wife's mercy—a woman is seldom merciful to the man who is timid. (P. 51)

While these adverse consequences were stated in rather extreme terms, our survey respondents indicated that shyness

1. creates social problems, making it difficult to meet people, make friends, or enjoy potentially good experiences;
2. has negative emotional correlates, such as feelings of depression, isolation, and loneliness;
3. makes it difficult to be appropriately assertive or to express opinions and values;
4. limits positive evaluations by others of one's personal assets;

5. allows incorrect social evaluations to be made and to persist unchallenged; for example, one may unjustly be seen as snobbish, unfriendly, bored, or weak;
6. creates difficulties in thinking clearly and communicating effectively in the presence of others; and
7. encourages self-consciousness and an excessive preoccupation with one's reactions.

The interpersonal distancing of shy people is not merely psychological but can be measured physically. In a study by Carducci and Webber (1981), volunteers were asked to stand on a spot 18 feet away from either a male or a female experimenter. The subject then walked toward the other person up to the point that felt comfortable. In a second trial, the experimenter walked toward the subject until he or she indicated that the most comfortable distance had been reached. After measuring the preferred interpersonal distances, the experimenters administered our shyness survey and dichotomized the subjects by a median split into high and low shyness groups. The results indicted that shy people kept others at a greater distance than did those who were less shy. This difference was greater (by 12 inches) when a stranger of the opposite sex, rather than of the same sex, shared the physical space.

This tendency of shys to minimize interpersonal contact by erecting broader spatial buffer zones than do non-shys was demonstrated in a content-free interaction situation. Earlier physiological research on determinants of cardiovascular response (as a stress indicator) had revealed that the importance of the transactional involvement with other people was greater than the sheer content of what people talk about during interviews. (Singer, 1967). When other researchers varied a number of aspects of the interview situations, diastolic blood pressure of the interviewees was most affected by the more personal interactive situation (Williams, Kimball, & Williard, 1972). These findings support the hypothesis of Williams and associates that "the transactional process of interpersonal interaction acts as an intervening variable in mediating cardiovascular responses to stressful emotional stimuli" (p. 198) in the subject's current life situation. A recent study examined and confirmed the hypothesis that increasing levels of psychological disturbance are associated with greater anxiety concerning interpersonal contact (Meles, DiTomasso, & Turner, 1981). Patients with social phobias showed measurably higher levels of social anxiety than did simple phobics or normal controls. Obviously, the line of reasoning developed in this chapter would suggest that the degree of anxiety experienced by shy people in such transactions would be greater than that experienced by the non-shy. If so, this social anxiety and the individual's awareness of and attention paid to it should influence a variety of cognitive and behavioral processes. Anecdotal support for this proposition is seen in a personal account by a shy businessman who wrote me:

> One of the key things about shyness, as I have found, is that the worst effects of shyness cause a person to be so self-preoccupied that, truly, he simply misses what is going on, doesn't hear or see. For instance, I often find myself unable to follow what's going on in a conversation because I've been so nervously conscious of myself.

The interference of social anxiety with memory was demonstrated experimentally in a series of experiments in our laboratory (Hatvany, Souza e Silva, & Zimbardo, 1981). When a shy person is put into a social setting in which there is a possibility of being evaluated, he or she expriences a state of heightened "objective self-awareness' (Duval & Wicklund, 1972). Recall tasks that require focused attention on continuous informational input should then be performed more poorly by socially anxious shys whose attention is directed, in part, to their inner state. Our research revealed that recall is significantly impaired when dispositionally shy subjects believe they are under evaluative scrutiny, the task is unstructured, and the information to be processed is complex. It is the internal versus external focus of attention that mediates recall of external events. The shy person's attention is diverted away from task-relevant analyses by the anxiety arising from self-monitoring in anticipation of an unstructured social encounter of an evaluative nature.

Three approaches to reducing the deleterious effects upon performance created by the anxiety of being shy have worked well in research under my direction. They involve deflecting attentional focus, modifying the causal attributions for perceived shyness arousal, and creating norms for more equitable participation between shy and not-shy individuals who must interact on problem-solving tasks.

Recall was improved when shy male subjects were induced to externalized their attentional focus, away from self toward mastery of a well-structured task—even when evaluation was present (Hatvany, Souza e Silva, & Zimbardo, 1981).

Extremely shy women behaved as though they were not shy when specific arousal symptoms previously associated with their social anxiety were misattributed to a non-psychological source: high-frequency noise (Brodt & Zimbardo, 1981). Their verbal fluency and interactional assertiveness was comparable to that of not-shy women given the same treatment (isolated with a unfamilar male partner). Moreover, they enjoyed what was a distressing situation for their shy peers, who were *not* able to misattribute their shyness to a nonsocial source. In addition, over the course of interacting with a stranger, the level of physiological arousal (measured by heart rate) was significantly lower for those shy women given the misattribution treatment.

Finally, in ongoing research, we are studying participation and effectiveness of shy and not-shy individuals in problem-solving teams. In many social settings, some of the most powerful, yet subtle, mediators of the extent, type, and style of interaction are implicit group norms. Who talks when, for how long, and how often is established sometimes a priori by implicitly acknowledged rules giving priority and access to persons of with greater authority, status, or social power. Shy people tend to defer to those who are more ready to initiate conversation, state desired actions, or pose solutions. When problem-solving groups are composed of shy and not-shy participants, we can expect unbalanced rates of participation. The potential contribution of the shys will be underrepresented, while team solutions will be more heavily biased by the greater input from not-shy group members.

We developed a computerized system for mediating group discussions among problem-solving teams. When a person wishes to talk, he or she presses a request button. The subject's monitor indicates when that request is acceptable; by pressing a talk button, the person gains full access to the floor (or to the microphone). Whenever more than one person wishes to speak, the computer determines which individual's request to speak should be granted. The computer mediates the discussion by granting requests according to specified access rules. For example, the system can be made to give priority to the first individual to enter a request (first in–first out) or to those who have spoken least (equal time-sharing). This flexibility allows us to investigate the consequences of group norms governing turn taking during problem-solving discussions. In addition, it is possible to display various prompts to suppress excessive participators and to encourage infrequent participators (Zimbardo, Linsenmeier, Kabat, & Smith, 1981).

We found that initial level of requesting a talking turn was linearly related to shyness level. The very shy rarely did so, next came the moderately shy, followed by the moderately assertive, who trailed those subjects most often requesting the opportunity to talk, the highly assertive (Stodolsky, Zimbardo, & Bascom, 1978). Imposing the equal time-sharing group norm dramatically altered this pattern of participation. Given the more favorable conditions for gaining access to the floor, the moderately shy made many more requests to talk; in fact, they became the most active participators of any of the four groups. However, the extremely shy did not benefit from the assistance provided by our computerized handicapping system.

Participation rates also changed markedly when subjects were exposed to periodic prompts regarding the amount of time each of the four team members (two shy, two non-shy) had participated: the shy, low participators talked more and the vocal non-shys inhibited their overresponsiveness. (Zimbardo, Linsenmeier, Kabat, & Smith, 1981) We found that by combining this information on relative rates of participation with equal time-sharing algorithms, not only was group participation altered but so, too, were group performance and attitudes. Shy subjects became more involved and committed to the group's task, as indicated by substantial increases in their requests to talk. They changed their self-perception away from that of passive listener to active participator, and they were even seen as assuming a position of leadership.[1] These shifts in motivation, perception, and behavior (which occurred within a brief experimental session) should generalize to other group settings because of the positive reinforcement attending this new set of reactions. Such an approach could also modify the deeply rooted biases against equal participation that exist between the sexes, as well as between members of ethnic or racial majority and minority groups who must work together in teams.

THE FUTURE OF SHYNESS

Shyness is an important psychological process that can have profound effects upon many aspects of the shy person's life. This mode has been implicated in low job morale, sexual dysfunction, alcoholism, conformity, depression, and even the irrational rage that can lead to sudden murders (Lee, Zimbardo, & Bertholf, 1978; Zimbardo, 1977). The negative consequences of shyness thus spread beyond the individual to affect those with whom he or she interacts.

Shyness is unconsciously but insidiously programmed into each generation of children by most of our social institutions and their agents of social control. Parents, teachers, employers, politicians, and others, in the effort to make individuals more "manageable," encourage passivity, reticence, submission and obedience to authority, compliance to rules, and acceptance of the existing power structure. Shy people report that one of the major elicitors of their shyness is authority; they fear, not necessarily respect, authority. The shy child is the "good child," seen but not heard; the shy adult is the "model citizen," who never publicly complains, opposes the system, or stands up for his or her rights. In this way, the shy form the silent majority who become the conservative defenders of the status quo. Shyness abhors freedom; shy people prefer to function in clearly defined, familiar, structured situations in which roles are well regulated. Such people may be willing to trade their freedom for an illusion of security—a trade that dictators and power managers have always urged. Recall Hitler's injunction (in Mein Kampf, 1933) for all people to accept the National State's imposed status of individual shyness so that fascist power of "the undisputed authority" might better flourish: "The individual should accept his personal insignificance, dissolve himself in a higher power and then feel proud in participating in the strength and glory of this higher power."

There are many forces at work in societies throughout the world that will make us feel increasingly insignificant, impotent, and passive. We are being ever more isolated from the social supports of community, neighborhood, family, and friends. In acknowledging that shyness is an alien force that opposes the fullest realization of the human potential to care for, share with, and love one another, we reaffirm the very foundation of our humanity.

NOTES

1. The negative relationship between shyness and leadership is apparently formed in early childhood. Preschool teachers rate their four-year-old shy students lower in leadership ability than they rate their non-shy peers. In a unpublished study I conducted in 1977 at the U.S. Military Academy (with the cooperation of Captain H. S. Hammond), West Point cadets who rated themselves shy received lower leadership effectiveness scores than did non-shy cadets. These scores were composite ratings of leadership behavior made by as many as 60 different evaluators. The mean rank of the shys was 151 units lower than that of the non-shys (in a sample of 1192 cadets whose leadership ability was assessed independently of their shyness). Finally, shy college students at Stanford University working in our problem-solving teams perceived themselves as not taking the leadership role—and the non-shy members of their teams also saw them in the same way.

REFERENCES

AINSWORTH, M. D., & AINSWORTH, L. H. *Measuring security in personal adjustment.* Toronto: University of Toronto Press, 1958.

BRODT, S. E., & ZIMBARDO, P. G. Modifying shyness-related social behavior through symptom misattribution. *Journal of Personality and Social Psychology,* 1981, *41,* 437–449.

BROMBERG, P. M. The effects of fear and two modes of anxiety reduction on social affiliation and phobic ideation. *Dissertation Abstracts International,* 1968, *28*(11B), 4753–4754.

BULWER-LYTTON, E. *Caxtoniana: A series of essays on life, literature, and manners.* New York: Harper, 1863.

BUSS, A. H. *Self consciousness and social anxiety.* San Francisco: Freeman, 1980.

CARDUCCI, B. J., & WEBBER, A. W. Shyness as a determinant of interpersonal distance. *Psychological Reports,* 1979, *44,* 1075–1078.

CATTELL, R. B. The description of personality: The foundations of trait measurement. *Psychological Review,* 1943, *50,* 559–594.

————. *The scientific analysis of personality.* Baltimore: Penguin, 1965.

————. *Personality and mood by questionnaire.* San Francisco: Jossey-Bass, 1973.

CATTELL, R. B., EBER, H. W., & TATSUCKA, M. M. *Handbook for the Sixteen Personality Factor Questionnaire.* Champaign: IPAT, 1970.

CHEEK, J., & BUSS, A. H. Shyness and sociability. *Journal of Personality and Social Psychology,* 1981, *41,* 330–339.

COMREY, A. L. Factored homogenous item dimensions in personality. *Educational and Psychological Measurement,* 1961, *2,* 417–431.

————. *Manual for the Comrey Personality Scales.* San Diego: Educational and Industrial Testing Service, 1970.

COMREY, A. L., & JAMISON, K. Verification of six personality factors. *Educational and Psychological Measurement,* 1966, *26,* 945–953.

DARWIN, C. *The expression of the emotions in man and animals.* New York: Appleton, 1890.

Diagnostic and Statistical Manual of Mental Disorders (3d ed.). Washington, D.C.: American Psychiatric Association, 1980.

DUVAL, S., & WICKLUND, R. A. *A theory of objective self awareness.* New York: Academic, 1972.

EYSENCK, H. J., & EYSENCK, S. B. G. *Personality structue and measurement.* San Diego: Educational and Industrial Testing Service, 1968.

FATIS, M. Degree of shyness and self reported physiological, behavioral, and cognitive reaction. Manuscript, Mankato State University, 1981.

FENICHEL, O. *The psychoanalytic theory of neurosis.* New York: Norton, 1945.

FESTINGER, L. A theory of social comparison processes. *Human Relations,* 1954, *7,* 117–140.

FLANAGAN, J. C. *Factor analysis in the study of personality.* Stanford: Stanford University Press, 1935.

FROMM, E. *Escape from freedom.* New York: Holt, 1942.

GUILFORD, J. P., & GUILFORD, R. B. Personality factors S, E, and M, and their measurement. *Journal of Psychology,* 1936, *2,* 109–128.

HART, M. *Lady in the dark.* New York: Random House, 1941.

HATVANY, N., SOUZA E SILVA, M. C., & ZIMBARDO, R. P. Shyness and recall deficits: The relationship between attention and arousal. Manuscript, Stanford University, 1981.

HITLER, A. *My Battle,* Trans. of *Mein Kampf* by E. T. S. Dugdale, Boston: Houghton Mifflin, 1933.

JAMES, W. *The principles of psychology,* vol. 2. New York: Holt, 1890.

KAPLAN, D. M. On shyness. *International Journal of Psychoanalysis,* 1972, *53,* 439–453.

LEE, M., ZIMBARDO, P. G., & BERTHOLF, M. Shy murderers. *Psychology Today,* 1977, *11,* 69–148.

MASLACH, C. Social and personal bases of individuation. *Journal of Personality and Social Psychology,* 1971, *29,* 411–425.

McDOUGALL, W. *An outline of psychology* (2d ed.). London: Methuen, 1924.

MELES, D., DiTOMASSO, R., & TURNER, R. M. Assessment of social anxiety: A controlled comparison among social phobics, obsessive-compulsives, agoraphobics, sexual disorders, and simple phobics. Paper presented to the annual meeting of the Western Psychological Association, Los Angeles, 1981.

NERUDA, P. *Memoirs,* trans. H. St. Martins. New York: Farrar, Straus & Giroux, 1977.

PILKONIS, P. A. The behavioral consequences of shyness. *Journal of Personality,* 1977, *45,* 596–611. (a)

————. Shyness, public and private, and its relationship to other measures of social behavior. *Journal of Personality,* 1977, *45,* 585–595. (b)

POIRIER, R. *The performing self.* New York: Oxford University Press, 1971.

PRENTICE-DUNN, S., & ROGERS, R. W. Effects of deindividuating situational cues and aggressive models on subjective deindividuation and aggression. *Journal of Personality and Social Psychology,* 1980, *39,* 104–113.

RAPAPORT, C. Character, anxiety, and social affiliation. Doctoral dissertation, New York University, 1963.

READ, P. Socialization Research Revisited. *The Sage Foundation Report,* New York, June, 1980.

SARAF, K. Shyness: Body and self-cathexis. Doctoral dissertation, California School of Professional Psychology, Fresno, 1980.

SARNOFF, 1. *Testing Freudian concepts: An experimental social approach.* New York: Springer 1971.

SARNOFF, I., & ZIMBARDO, P. G. Anxiety, fear, and social affiliation. *Journal of Abnormal and Social Psychology,* 1961, *62,* 356–363.

SEARS, R. R. Experimental studies of projection. Part II: Ideas of references. *Journal of Social Psychology,* 1937, *8,* 389–400.

SINGER, M. T. Enduring personality styles and responses to stress. *Transactions of the Association of Life Insurance Medical Directors of America,* 1967, *51,* 150–173.

SNYDER, C. R., & FROMKIN, L. *Uniqueness.* New York: Plenum, 1980.

STEVENS, M. The performing self in twelfth century culture. *Viator, 9,* 1978, 193–212.

STODOLSKY, D., ZIMBARDO, P., & BASCOM, L. Automatic facilitation of dialogue in shy and not shy problem-solving teams. Paper presented to the annual meeting of the Western Psychological Association, San Diego, 1978.

WALLACE, L., WALLECHINSKY, D., & WALLACE, A. *The people's almanac presents the book of lists.* New York: Morrow, 1977.

WILLIAMS, R. B., KIMBALL, C. P., & WILLIARD, H. N. The influence of interpersonal interaction on diastolic blood pressure. *Psychosomatic Medicine,* 1972, *34,* 194–198.

ZIMBARDO, P. G. The human choice: Individuation, reason, and order versus deindividuation, impulse, and chaos. In W. J. Arnold & D. Levine (eds.), *Nebraska Symposium on Motivation.* Lincoln: University of Nebraska Press, 1970.

————. On transforming experimental research into advocacy for social change. In M. Deutsch & Hornstein (eds.), *Applying social psychology: Implications for research, practice, and training.* Hillsdale: Erlbaum, 1975.

————. *Shyness: What it is, what to do about it.* Reading: Addison-Wesley, 1977.

ZIMBARDO, P. G., HANEY, C., BANKS, W. C., & JAFFE, D. The mind is a formidable jailer: A Pirandellian prison. *New York Times Magazine,* 8 April 1973, pp. 38–60.

ZIMBARDO, P. G., LINSENMEIER, J., DAHLGREN, D., & BUCKNER, J. Conceptions of shyness among preschool children and their teachers. Manuscript, Stanford University, 1981.

ZIMBARDO, P. G., LINSENMEIER, J., KABAT, L., & SMITH, P. Improving team performance and participation via computer-mediated turn taking and informational prompts. ONR technical report no. Z-81-01. Stanford, 1981.

ZIMBARDO, P., PILKONIS, P., & NORWOOD, R. The social disease called shyness. *Psychology Today,* 1975, *8,* 68–72.

ZIMBARDO, P. G., & RADL, S. *The shy child.* New York: McGraw-Hill, 1981.

28

Marital Stressors, Coping Styles, and Symptoms of Depression

Frederic W. Ilfeld, Jr.

ONE'S MARITAL STATUS AND THE NATURE OF one's marital relationship can be significant sources of distress and have a profound connection with depressive symptomatology. Moreover, the coping style used in combating marital stressors may be a major determinant of stressor level. These are some of the main findings from a cross-sectional survey of 2299 Chicago adults on social stressors and coping. This chapter reviews the pertinent findings of this survey that speak to marital status and the marital relationship as a source of stress and those coping styles by which marital stressors may be best combated.

I begin with a definition of concepts and an overview of the survey design. Then I consider marital status and the extent to which this variable relates to level of depression. Next, I operationally define indicators of marital stressors and explore the close relationship of marital and parental stressors (in contrast to job, financial, and neighborhood stressors) to depression. Since of all these interpersonal stressors, those of marriage are the most closely connected to depression, I shall look more carefully into what factors are predictive of marital stressors. Factors reviewed in this regard include the respondent's style of coping with marital problems, behavior patterns within the marriage, personality factors of the respondent, other current social stressors, demographic variables, and a variety of marital circumstances.

DEFINITION OF CONCEPTS

The variables of main concern are symptoms of depression, an index of marital stressors, and a variety of coping styles. Precisely what is meant by each of these? As for *depression,* I am focusing on 10 symptoms derived from a factor analysis of a 29-item index of psychiatric symptoms (Ilfeld, 1976a). The parent scale of the 29-item index was the Hopkins Symptom Distress Checklist (Lipman, Rickles, Covi, Derogatis, Uhlenhuth 1969).

All respondents were asked about the frequency of each symptom over the previous week (response categories: never, once in a while, fairly often, or very often). The 10 symptoms of depression follow: have a poor appetite, feel lonely, feel bored or have little interest in things, lose sexual interest or pleasure, have trouble getting to sleep or staying asleep, cry easily or feel like crying, feel downhearted or blue, feel low in energy or slowed down, feel hopeless about the future, have thoughts about possibly ending my life. The particular advantages, the assessed validity, and the statistical properties of this depression subscale of the Psychiatric Symptom Index (PSI) are described elsewhere (Ilfeld, 1976a). As a test of internal consistency, the alpha coefficient for the depression subscale has been calculated to be .84, a quite acceptable level. Validity has been affirmed by three criteria: having sought professional help for emotional problems, having recently used psychoactive drugs, and the interviewer's rating of the respondent's degree of tension. Keep in mind that when I refer to depression, I am speaking of the level of depressive symptoms as measured by the 10-item subscale rather than a clinical diagnosis of depression.

Conceptually, I define *marital stressors* as circumstances or conditions of daily marital life that are generally considered problematic or undesirable (Ilfeld, 1976a), including nonfulfillment of role obligations, lack of reciprocity between the marital partners, and a feeling of nonacceptance by one's spouse. Note that this conception focuses more on stressful stimuli existing outside the individual rather than on a personal distress response occurring inside the respondent. I have chosen to look at the stimulus side of the stress equation more than the response side in defining the term "stressor" because of my particular interest in the dependent variables of depression and psychiatric symptomatology. The view taken in this chapter is also very different from that of most life events investigators (Dohrenwend & Dohrenwend, 1974; Rahe & Arthur, 1978).

In my definition, stressors are tied to a social role or situation usually consisting of an ongoing circumstance instead of discrete events, and the stressors are commonly regarded as problematic or undesirable. Note that social stressors are only *possible* stressors, since they are problematic for most, but not necessarily all, individuals. I believe this perspective has greater therapeutic potential than the standard approach because ongoing social stressors are more amenable to intervention and change than are many of the life crisis events. Research findings from other analyses of these same Chicago data (Pearlin & Lieberman, 1979), as well as my own clinical experience, show that the more common stressors in everyday life take a significant toll of suffering above and beyond the impact of fortuitous and dramatic life crises. Because they are current and not past events, these stressors may be more relevant for possible prevention and treatment programs.

Coping is a catchword for a diverse number of activities and processes, and the reader is referred elsewhere in this book, as well as to Coelho, Hamburg and Adams (1974) and to Moos (1976), for reviews. In another context, I (Ilfeld, 1980a) discussed different definitions of, and conceptual pitfalls related to, the process of coping and settled on a definition of *coping* as attempts by an individual to resolve life stressors and emotional pain. The boundaries of coping under this definition focus upon individual effort, including actions and cognitive processes. One may respond to the requirements of an external situation, as well as to one's own feelings about that situation. The question of whether coping precedes or follows stressors or emotional pain is not addressed in my definition. Coping may either anticipate or follow a stressful experience. While the function of a given coping effort must be resolution of either the stressful experience or the attendant emotional pain, this process is not necessarily in the awareness of the respondent. Accordingly, I have not specified whether coping is a conscious or an unconscious activity.

SURVEY DESIGN

Chicago was chosen not because it is typical of urban America; no one city is. However, Chicago does contain a mix of social, occupational, ethnic, racial, and religious groups in proportions that are comparable with the averages of the larger American cities.

In the summer of 1972, a probability sample of 2299 households was drawn from the Chicago–northwestern Indiana standard metropolitan statistical area, and a respondent from each household was interviewed. The interviewers were professionals who were trained in the particulars of our questionnaire. Only respondents between the ages of 18 and 64 years were chosen because we wanted to study adults who were most likely to be in the job market. The cluster size and the sample selection was 4 houses per block, with 11 additional houses listed in each block to substitute for households that did not qualify, could not be reached, or refused to be interviewed. Of those respondents initially approached, 31% either refused an interview or were unreachable despite three attempts at contact.

The 90-minute structured questionnaire investigated (1) background and demographic variables; (2) potential sources of social stress in neighborhood, job, economic activity, parenthood, singlehood, and marital relations; (3) the various means by which respondents coped with different stresses in their lives; and (4) psychological status (psychiatric symptoms, psychosomatic disorders, psychoactive drug use, and levels of self-esteem and self-efficacy). Prevalence data for these five measures of psychological status were reported elsewhere (Ilfeld, 1978).

We developed the indicators of current social stressors from detailed, largely open-ended, tape-recorded interviews with approximately 175 people. A range of life problems was compiled and questions on them were refined over a period of several years. The language in the questionnaire used to describe these social stressors was adopted from that used by the interviewees. Interviewers also asked about specific, concrete circumstances that had an immediacy from the respondent.

Nine social stressor indexes and their statistical characteristics were delineated (Ilfeld, 1976a); only a brief overview will be given here. For married respondents there were 17 questions regarding degree of fulfillment of basic role expectations (e.g., companionship, affection, finances, wage earning), issues of control and fairness of exchange between marital partners, and the respondent's feelings of self-actualization in marital relationship (see Table 28-1). The internal consistency of this marital stressor scale was quite high (alpha coefficient = .87), indicating that our respondents were experiencing marital discord in a global fashion; therefore, in my analyses I shall use the marital stressors scale as a totality rather than break it down into its three theoretical components. Employed respondents answered a 19-item job stressors scale that assessed the degree of adversity of work conditions, issues of income and job benefits and security, and problematic interpersonal relationships in the job setting. The scale on parental stressors covered diverse topics; the exact questions asked depended on the ages of the respondent's children (e.g., health difficulties, divergent moral or religious beliefs, unacceptable behavior, disobedience, poor school work, and improper treatment of parents). Financial and neighborhood stressor scales were administered to all respondents. The financial stressor scale included 9 questions about difficulties in paying monthly bills and about having enough money to afford adequate living quarters, household equipment, transportation, medical care, clothing, food, and leisure activities. In the neighborhood stressor index, respondents were asked to rate their neighborhood along a four-point scale of goodness as to personal safety, friendliness, cleanliness, schools, type of people, quietness, protection of property, and race relations.

TABLE 28-1
Current Marital Stressors

	Rank as most problematic[a]
1. My (husband/wife) insists on having (his/her) own way.	1
2. My (husband/wife) usually expects more from me than (he/she) is willing to give back.[b]	
3. I can rely on my (husband/wife) to help me with most of the problems that need to be taken care of in the family.[b]	
4. My (husband/wife) usually acts as if (he/she) were the only important person in the family.[b]	
5. Generally, I give in more to my (husband's/wife's) wishes than (he/she) gives in to mine.	3
6. My (husband/wife) is someone I can really talk with about things that are important to me.	4
7. My (husband/wife) is someone who is affectionate towards me.[b]	
8. My (husband/wife) is someone who spends money wisely.	2
9. My (husband/wife) is someone who is a good (wage earner/ housekeeper).[b]	
10. My (husband/wife) is someone who is a good sexual partner.[b]	
11. My (husband/wife) is someone who appreciates the job I do as a (wage earner/housekeeper).[b]	
12. My (husband/wife) seems to bring out the best qualities in me.	
13. My (husband/wife) appreciates me just as I am.	
14. My marriage doesn't give me enough opportunity to become the sort of person I would like to be.	
15. I cannot completely be myself around my (husband/wife).	
16. Do you have a disagreement over (his/her) drinking? (response categories: yes or no)	
17. What about your (husband/wife)—at present does (he/she) have any problem with health, any sickness, injury, or handicap? (If yes) How much does this bother you or upset you? (Response categories: very much, somewhat, only a little, or not at all)	

[a] Response categories: strongly agree, somewhat agree, somewhat disagree, strongly disagree.
Scoring formula: 1(responses to items 1 + 2 + 3 + 4 + 5 + 12 + 13 + 14 + 14 + 15) + 2 (6 + 7 + 8 + 9 + 10 + 11 + 16 + 17) / 75 × 100.
Statistical characteristics: mean, 15.2; standard deviation, 13.4; alpha coefficient, .87; deciles, 1, 4, 7, 9, 12, 15, 20, 25, 32.
[b] For rating which stressor was the most problemtatic, the respondents (n = 1523) were asked to choose only from among items 1–11. Items marked with an asterisk (*) were rarely selected as being most problematic.

Coping responses were probed in the 175 open-ended exploratory interviews: respondents were asked to describe how they were dealing with problems faced in the common roles of everyday life. In the large-scale survey, interviewers inquired about coping in a structured way, asking about the different things people did to "help them get along on their jobs," about techniques that married couples used to avoid difficulties or to settle differences between themselves, and about the "different things parents do when they find something in their children's behavior that is troublesome." Interviewers also asked, "When you are short of money, how do you think or do these things?" Gradually a variety of coping patterns and questions for each interpersonal role area were developed and refined; the coping scales were published recently (Ilfeld, 1980a). Factor analyses of coping responses uncovered three major patterns: taking direct action, rationalization-avoidance of the stressor, and acceptance of the stressful situation without attempting alteration. Respondents did not consistently use one coping style across all areas but employed a varied repertoire of responses. Demographic characteristics explained only a small amount of variation in the coping styles.

MARITAL STATUS AND SYMPTOMS OF DEPRESSION

Over the past 40 years a number of epidemiological studies viewing the prevalence of psychologic disorder were undertaken in normal populations. In most of these, psychiatric morbidity was expressed as a single global measure, based either on self-report, on previous treatment status, or on direct interview and observation. Several monographs have reviewed this data in depth. Dohrenwend and Dohrenwend (1969) examined research reports on "untreated as well as treated cases" in 44 community populations up through 1968. Reviewing the sociodemographic literature for the period 1969–1974, Warheit, Robbins, and McGinnis (1975) offered the following generalization regarding marital status: "Married persons have lower rates of disorder than unmarried ones. The widowed, separated, and divorced have higher rates than single persons" (p. 167). While most investigators would agree with this generalization, Dohrenwend and Dohrenwend (1969) argued that existing evidence does not conclusively show that sociocultural and sociopsychological factors such as marital status are important in the *etiology* of functional psychiatric disorders. They recommended quasi-experimental stategies to provide tests of the role of the socioenvironmental factors.

The Chicago survey was distinct from and improved on earlier work in that the dependent variables consisted of five measures of psychological status (Ilfeld, 1978). In this way we attempted to gain a more comprehensive understanding of the relationship between mental status and demographic factors. Warheit's (Warheit et al., 1975) conclusion was supported by our data for the dependent variables of psychiatric symptomatology, use of psychoactive medication, and levels of self-esteem and self-efficacy.

Here I shall present data illustrating the relationship between depressive symptomatology and marital status. As noted previously, when I refer to depression, I am referring to the level of symptoms measured by the 10-item index. For purposes of comparison, I have arbitrarily defined high symptoms of depression as the top 14% of the entire community sample. I am interested primarily in comparing groups of persons exhibiting more or fewer depressive symptoms to identify groups at high risk. Symptoms were least frequent in married persons (11% with high symptoms); single or widowed respondents had double this prevalence (20% and 21%, respectively); by far the highest rate of morbidity was found in individuals who were separated (30% high symptoms) or divorced (27% high symptoms) from their spouses. These findings remained stable when sex, age, and race were controlled. Grouping together all those respondents who were not married, one can see what issues were most troublesome for the single person, namely, "staying at home because you are afraid to go out at night," "being without anyone you can share experiences and feelings with," and "being without anyone to talk to about yourself." Other, but less troublesome, areas of concern were "not having the kind of sex life you would like," "feeling out of place in a social situation because you are single," and being away from one's children.

CURRENT SOCIAL STRESSORS
AND SYMPTOMS OF DEPRESSION

Relationships between life stress and psychiatric disorder have been found in a number of populations. Langner and Michael (1963) reported that the total number of life stressors influenced psychiatric disorder more than did any one particular life stress. Berkman (1971) replicated this finding; using an 8-item index of psychological well-being, he found that the greater the stress, the greater the psychiatric risk, regardless of socioeconomic status. In a longitudinal study, Dohrenwend (1967) noted that scores on the Langner (Langner & Michael, 1963) 22-item symptom inventory increased or decreased according to negative or positive life experience over the preceding two years. In another longitudinal study, Myers, (Lindenthal and Pepper 1972) reinterviewed 720 of an original sample of 938 adults in New Haven after a two-year interval. The respondents were questioned specifically as to 62 life events, as well as the presence of psychiatric symptomatology. This study found that a net increase of life events was associated with a worsening of symptoms; a net decrease of life events was associated with improvement of symptoms; and the greater the net change in the number of life events, the greater the movement on the symptom inventory. Results consistent with these findings were subsequently obtained by Uhlenhuth and associates (1974) and by Markush and Favero (1974).

In summary, stressful life events consistently have been found to be related to psychological problems in community residents. However, researchers have concentrated on past stressful changes or events, many of which are fortuitous and most of which are time limited. I suggest that the social stressors patterned into our everyday roles are marital partners, breadwinners, and parents are equally important in affecting mental status. Other researchers have emphasized past rather than present events primarily to solve methodological issues of whether stressors come before symptoms or vice versa. If one could show that the stressful events precede symptoms, then the direction of a cause and effect relationship would be more certain (Brown, 1974). However, my research (Ilfeld, 1976c) has indicated that current social stressors are usually present before symptom onset, which supports the contention that such stressors influence symptoms more than they are influenced by them. Survey respondents independently estimated duration of current social stressors and duration of their depressive symptoms. Each respondent was asked not to compare which came first but rather to give the duration and time that he/she had been experiencing a particular stress and/or depressive symptom. Stressors showed a significantly longer duration than did depressive symptoms.

Besides considering stressors as ongoing problematic circumstances rather than life events, another departure of the Chicago survey from previous research was a comparison of the potency of the different life stressors. Studies in the past have grouped various stressors into one global measure and then compared this measure to symptoms or some other psychiatric variable. The fact that life stress produces symptoms is no great revelation; it is more valuable to find out which kinds of stress under what conditions have the most impact.

I find current social stressors to have a rather strong association with depressive symptoms. Table 28–2 displays Pearson product-moment correlation coefficients between the several social stressors and depression. Not that the table breaks down the respondent sample into five subgroups, which makes it possible to compare the relative potency of different social stressors and also to view differential effects of any one social stressor across these populations.

TABLE 28-2
Correlations between Current Social Stressors and Symptoms of Depression

Current social stressor	Employed married fathers (365–472)[a]	Employed married mothers (146–180)	Unemployed married mothers (346–471)	Employed single men (103–110)	Employed single women (75–82)
Neighborhood	.10[b]	.28[d]	.08[b]	.29[c]	.14
Job	.25[d]	.21[c]	—	.27[c]	.11
Homemaking	—	.02	.37[d]	—	—
Finances	.24[d]	.28[d]	.20[d]	.36[d]	.40[d]
Parenting	.17[d]	.37[d]	.25[d]	—	—
Being Married/ single	.46[d]	.37[d]	.42[d]	.43[d]	.28[c]

[a] The number of subjects varies with each correlation. The number drops to the low point for the scale on parental stressors because only parents who had a child aged six or older were included; however, a sizable proportion of parents had no children over six.
[b] One-tailed test of significance: $p < .05$.
[c] One-tailed test of significance: $p < .01$.
[d] One-tailed test of significance: $p < .001$.

Several patterns stand out in Table 28-2, most particularly the close relationship between marital stressors and depression. Generally speaking, current social stressors were significantly related to depressive symptoms for each of the five respondent groups. Note, however, the differences in magnitude among the correlations. Current marital stressors had the highest correlations with depression (.37–.46). Parenting, job, and financial stresses had lower correlations with depression. Other findings of note are the differences among the five population groups. Employed married fathers were greatly affected by their marital situation but significantly less so by their parental or job situation. Employed married mothers, on the other hand, were equally affected by parental stresses and marital stresses. Depression was more highly correlated with current social stressors for employed single men than for employed single women.

These correlations held up even when a number of variables were introduced as controls, including age, education and income level, score on a denial scale, interviewer's rating of the respondent's frankness, number of memberships in social settings, and duration of social stressors. An even more precise view of symptoms and stressors could be gained by using partial correlation techniques, by which I assessed the relationship between depression and any one stressor area while controlling for the other stressor areas. With third- and fourth-order partial correlations, marital stressors continued to have the highest and most significant relationship with depression. Parental stressors (for mothers) and job stressors (for married men) were among other correlations with depression that retained statistical significance.

Current social stressors were not only closely related to symptoms but also differentially related. For four of the five population groups, stress in the primary adult relationship (i.e., stress of marriage or of being single) was the life area most closely related to depression, suggesting this as a focal point for preventive and therapeutic intervention. Viewed against the finding that marital and parental stressors bear the closest relationship to depressive symptoms, psychiatry's increasing emphasis on marital and family therapy seems very much on target (Berman & Leif, 1975; Grunebaum & Christ, 1976; Gurman & Kniskern, 1981). Mental health professionals can intervene in the social arenas that have the most powerful relationship to depression. In fact, there are now wide-scale efforts outside the mental health establishment to shore up the besieged structures of marriage and the family (e.g., marriage encounters sponsored by religious groups). On the other hand, the low association between neighborhood stressors and depressive symptoms calls into question some fundamental assumptions psychiatry has made about the importance of effecting change in the community setting. The Chicago study found that neighborhood problems were not directly related to depression; therefore, relieving neighborhood stressors, while possibly providing other benefits, should not be expected strikingly to lower the level of psychological distress in the community. In short, our findings support the major commitment of mental health efforts to the microsocial level of the family, not to the macrosocial level of community affairs.

PREDICTORS OF MARITAL STRESSORS

Given the close connection between marital stressors and depression, one wonders which variable would be most predictive of marital stressors. Discovering what factors are associated with marital stressors and accounting for their variance should have considerable clinical relevance. A wide range of conditions will be examined, including background factors and circumstances of marriage, demographics, other current social stressors, several personality variables, behavior patterns between the partners, and styles of coping with stressors in marriage. As we shall see, the data challenge some common myths about which of these variables best predict marital stressors.

The literature fails to elucidate the factors underlying marital stressors. Earlier I (Ilfeld, 1976a) determined that very little of the variance of marital stressors is explained by demographic dimensions such as age, sex, or socioeconomic status. In contrast, I found parental stressors to lessen with age, financial stressors to be closely related to low income, and neighborhood stressors to be predictable by race (black) and income (low). Gebhard (1978), using a sample of 3000 married persons seeking help for sexual problems, inquired into marital troubles. Neither age at marriage nor duration of marriage had any marked effect upon the presence of marital problems. Pearlin (1975), using the same Chicago data base in forming this chapter, found that personal distress in marriage in part could be traced to differences in spouses' status origins. People to whom status advancement is important and who have married mates of lower status are more apt to have sense of loss that leads, in turn, to high marital stress. However, this finding has limited practical value since it explains just a small amount of the variance of marital problems; only 5% of married persons regard status advancement as important and live with a spouse of lower status. Pearlin and Lieberman (1979), in a comprehensive paper, viewed stressors as normative transitions, nonnormative crises events, and persistent strains (this last category is equivalent to my concept of current social stressors). They noted that persistent social stressors accounted for the link between life events and personal distress. More pertinent for our purpose, however, is their finding that women are more vulnerable to the durable problems of marriage. However, Pearlin and Lieberman did not investigate the many other possible predictors of marital stressors.

By seeking out predictors of marital stressors I am not trying to ascertain direction of effect; a major limitation of cross-sectional surveys is that cause and effect relationships cannot be established. However, multiple regression analysis allows one to assess the predictive value of a wide variety of variables on the level of marital stressors (Ilfeld, 1980c). In this manner one can determine the power of prediction of individual independent variables upon the level of marital stressors. Moreover, through multiple regression analysis one can determine the amount of variance of marital stressors that is collectively explained by a group of independent variables (this variance is designated R^2 in Table 28-3 and 28-5).

A common belief holds that those background factors that both the respondent and the spouse bring to marriage, as well as some of the circumstances of their marriage, contribute strongly to marital stressors. The Chicago data showed this *not* to be the case (Ilfeld, 1980c). Eleven circumstances frequently thought to be associated with marital failure accounted for only 1% of the variance in marital stressors. Surprisingly, the following variables, which one might assume would have a major impact upon marriages, bore little relationship to stressors: differences between respondent and spouse in regard to age, education, and religion; length of marriage; first marriage versus remarriage for either party; and issues surrounding children and other persons living in the home.

Another multiple regression analysis ascertained the extent to which the demographic variables of sex, race, income, education, and age of the respondent predicted the level of marital stressors. All together these five major demographic variables accounted for only 3% of the variation in marital stressors.

Were the stresses of other interpersonal roles (such as parental, financial, neighborhood, and job) related to the level of marital stressors? The association was only modest, since problems in these four other role areas accounted for just 9% of the variance of marital stressors (Ilfeld, 1980c). Parental stressors most closely predicted marital problems, followed by financial and then by neighborhood stressors.

The personality attributes of self-efficacy, self-esteem, frankness, and denial were measured in this study, and their relationship to marital stressors was ascertained via multiple regression analysis. These four variables accounted for 19% of the variance of marital stressors, with levels of self-efficacy and self-esteem strongly and significantly inversely related to marital stressors.

Again, trying to ascertain the components of marital stressors, I looked at a variety of behavior patterns on the part of spouses. Answers were submitted to a multiple regression analysis (see Table 28-3). Thirty percent of the variance in marital stressors was accounted for by these nine behavior patterns ($R^2 = .30$), with the frequency of marital arguments by far the strongest predictor. Note that involvement and membership in a variety of social settings with the spouse had minimal predictive power.

The interviewers assessed styles of coping with problems of marriage by asking the respondent the series of questions listed in Table 28-4. These questions were subjected to a factor analysis, and four different factors, or styles of coping, emerged: *rationalization-resignation* (questions 1-6), *seeking outside help* (questions 7-9), *optimistic-action* (questions 10-13), and *withdrawal-conflict* (questions 14-16). The influence of these several coping styles upon stressors is revealed in Table 28-5. Their relationship was the strongest of all the groupings of variables, with 38% of the variance of marital stressors explained by these four styles of coping (see the R^2).

One coping mode was most predictive of low stressors. This I labeled optimistic-action because it has two dimensions: a hopeful and positive view about marriage (Table 28-4, questions 10 and 12) and behavior that is active and directly problem-solving (questions 11 and 13). One might wonder whether this optimistic-action style of coping was simply reflective of the degree of depression experienced by the respondent, in that high optimistic-action

TABLE 28–3
Predictors of Marital Stressors: Behavior Patterns

Behavior pattern	Standardized regression coefficient	R	R^2	F	df
Frequency of marital arguments	.25[a]				
Consensus of marital partners	−.18[a]				
When you have a personal problem, whom do you speak to first (spouse → others)	.14[a]				
How often you and your spouse go out together	−.14[a]				
How often your spouse goes out alone	.12[a]				
When you are feeling depressed whom do you choose to be with (spouse → other)	.10[a]				
Number of spouse's friends known by respondent	.10[a]				
Membership in social groups	−.07[a]				
How often you go out alone without spouse	−.02				
		.55	.30	68.80[a]	9/1449

[a]$p < .01$.

related more to a low level of depression than to low marital stressors. However, such was not the case. In the data analysis I noted the level of optimistic-action while controlling simultaneously for amounts of marital stressors and depressive symptomatology. The coping style of taking optimistic-action with one's spouse varied more with the stressor level than with the amount of symptomatology. Respondents with low marital stressors showed significantly greater use of optimistic-action than did respondents with high stressors, regardless of whether symptomatology was high or low (Ilfeld, 1980c).

Knowing those factors predictive of marital stressors should aid us to pinpoint our therapeutic interventions. The Chicago findings revealed a descending order of explanatory power for the following variables: respondent's style of coping with marital problems, behavior patterns within marriage, personality factors of the respondent, other current social stressors, demographic variables, and marital circumstances. The single most powerful variable was the coping style of optimistic-action, which predicted low marital stressors. These findings are somewhat surprising, since they contradict several common beliefs about marital stressors, such as the importance of background differences and the contribution of other social stressors (job, parenting, finances) to marital discord.

Style of coping most likely interacts in a reciprocal fashion with marital stressors. Although cross-sectional data do not allow a determination of cause and effect (i.e., whether coping style changes level of stressors more than level of stressors changes coping

TABLE 28-4
Factor Analysis of Marital Coping Styles

Here are some techniques that married couples use to avoid difficulties or to settle differences between themselves. How often do you:	Factor I rationalization-resignation	Factor II seeking outside help	Factor III optimistic-action	Factor IV withdrawal-conflict
1. Try to ignore difficulties by looking only at good things	.52	.04	.05	.12
2. Keep so busy you don't have time to think	.45	−.09	−.13	.13
3. Tell yourself the difficulties are not important	.60	.00	.00	.01
4. Try to overlook your (husband's/wife's) faults and pay attention only to the good points	.58	−.05	.30	.09
5. Wait for time to remedy the difficulty	.50	−.04	.01	.25
6. Just keep hurt feeling to yourself	.39	−.02	−.18	.20
7. Have you gone to a doctor, counselor, or other professional person in the past year for marriage advice	−.04	.46	.11	−.07
8. Have you asked for the advice of a friend or neighbor in the past year or so about getting along in marriage	−.04	.64	.08	−.06
9. Have you asked for advice about marriage from relatives in the past year or so	.02	.60	.07	−.06
10. Appreciate your own marriage more after seeing what other marriages are like	.10	.07	.44	−.04
11. Sit down and talk things out	−.20	.00	.61	−.14
12. Just get completely discouraged about changing anything	.36	−.24	−.36	.29
13. Try to find a fair compromise	.04	.03	.52	.04
14. Yell or shout to let off steam	.11	−.15	−.02	.33
15. Keep out of your (husband's/wife's) way for a while	.19	−.08	−.09	.67
16. Give in more than halfway	.31	−.08	.00	.35

TABLE 28-5
Predictors of Marital Stressors: Coping Styles

Coping style	Standardized regression coefficient	R	R[a]	F	*df*
Optimistic-action	$-.44$[a]				
Withdrawal-conflict	$.20$[a]				
Rationalization-resignation	$.15$[a]				
Seeking outside help	$.10$[a]	.62	.38	185.35[a]	5/1500

[a] $p < .01$.

style), these findings still carry clinical implications. Social background, circumstances of the marriage, and stressors in other social arenas simply do not provide much information about the condition of the marriage. On the other hand, the viewpoint a spouse has toward his/her marriage and the way in which he/she deals with marital problems appear to be the most promising area of intervention. As suggested by these preliminary correlational self-report data, major tasks of marital counseling appear to be (1) aiding the partners better to discriminate specific problem areas; (2) developing an optimistic viewpoint toward resolving marital conflict; (3) teaching and facilitating active, mutual problem-solving.

Several pathways for future research are indicated. Scales for measuring coping styles along such dimensions as the four reviewed in this chapter can be developed with more detail and precision (e.g., Ilfeld, 1980a, 1980b; Pearlin & Schooler, 1978). Information from the spouse and behavioral observations could supplement the respondent's reports. Responses obtained from both marital partners would provide a completely new order of data for understanding marital interaction and stressors. Longitudinal investigation would shed light on the natural courses of stressors, coping styles, and symptoms. Especially important here is whether marital stressors precede or follow from a particular coping style. Strategic intervention experiments could aid in unraveling the cause and effect relationships. Also, the use of scales of marital stressors and coping styles could clarify the process of different marital therapies (Berman & Lief, 1975; Grunebaum & Christ, 1976; Sage, 1976; Segraves, 1978).

Elsewhere I (Ilfeld, 1980b) compared the efficacy of different coping styles in several interpersonal roles. Marriage and parenting were found to be more controllable by individual coping efforts than were job and finances and, therefore, should be more strongly influenced by such processes as counseling and psychotherapy. However, the reader is cautioned that while the coping style of optimistic-action is most closely related to lower marital stress, this approach does not lead to low stress in all situations, as witnessed in the job area (Ilfeld, 1980b). In fact, other evidence indicates that some stressors are managed best by non-problem-solving and nonaction methods. A recently reported example is the effective use of denial in situations in which nothing can be done by the participant (Lazarus, 1981).

Further questions arise from these data. For instance, how do the duration of stress and its intensity influence the type of coping style utilized, as well as its effectiveness? How changeable are coping styles over time? Finally, might one teach those coping styles that are most effective and does the use of these newly introduced coping styles serve to lower the stressor level? These questions await in-depth longitudinal investigations dealing with both the natural course of coping and the results of therapeutic intervention.

REFERENCES

Berkman, P. Life stress and psychological well-being: A replication of Langner's analysis in the Midtown Manhattan Study. *Journal of Health and Social Behavior,* 1971, *12,* 35–45.

Berman, E., & Lief, H. Marital therapy from a psychiatric perspective: An overview. *American Journal of Psychiatry.,* 1975, *132,* 583–592.

Brown, G. Meaning, measurement, and stress of life events. In B. S. Dohrenwend & B. P. Dohrenwend (eds.), *Stressful life events: Their nature and effects.* New York: Wiley, 1974.

Coelho, G., Hamburg, D., & Adams, J. (eds.). *Coping and adaptation.* New York: Basic Books, 1974.

Dohrenwend, B. P. Social status, stress, and psychological symptoms. *American Journal of Public Health,* 1967, *57,* 625–632.

Dohrenwend, B. P. & Dohrenwend, B. S. *Social status and psychological disorder.* New York: Wiley, 1969.

Dohrenwend, B. S. & Dohrenwend, B. P. (eds.) *Stressful life events: Their nature and effects.* New York: Wiley, 1974.

Gebhard, P. Marital stress. In L. Levi (ed.). *Society, stress, and disease,* vol. 3. New York: Oxford University Press, 1978.

Grunebaum, H. & Christ, J. (eds.). *Contemporary marriage: Structure, dynamics, and therapy.* Boston: Little, Brown, 1976.

Gurman, A., & Kniskern, D. (eds.). *Handbook of family therapy.* New York: Brunner/Mazel, 1981.

Ilfeld, F. Characteristics of current social stressors. *Psychological Reports,* 1976, *36,* 1231–1247. (a)

————. Further validation of a psychiatric symptom index in a normal population. *Psychological Reports,* 1976, *39,* 1215–1228. (b)

————. Methodological issues in relating symptoms to social stressors. *Psychological Reports,* 1976, *39,* 1251–1258. (c)

————. Current social stressors and symptoms of depression. *American Journal of Psychiatry,* 1977, *134,* 161–166.

————. Psychological status of community residents along major demographic dimensions. *Archives of General Psychiatry,* 1978, *35,* 716–724.

————. Coping styles of Chicago adults: Description. *Journal of Human Stress,* 1980, *6,* 2–10 (a)

————. Coping styles of Chicago adults: Effectiveness. *Archives of General Psychology,* 1980, *37,* 1239–1243. (b)

————. Understanding marital stressors: the importance of coping style. *Journal of Nervous Mental Disorders,* 1980, *168,* 375–381. (c)

Lazarus, R. The costs and benefits of denial. In S. Breznitz (ed.). *Denial of stress.* New York: International Universities, 1982.

Langner, T. & Michael, S. *Life stress and mental health.* New York: Free Press, 1963.

Lipman, R., Rickles, K., Covi, L, Derogatis, L., & Uhlenhuth, E. Factors of symptom distress. *Archives of General Psychology,* 1969, *21,* 328–338.

Markush, R. & Favero, R. Epidemiologic assessment of stressful life events, depressed mood, and psychophysiological symptoms: A preliminary report. In B. S. Dohrenwend & B. P. Dohrenwend (eds.). *Stressful life events: Their nature and effects.* New York: Wiley, 1974.

Moos, R. (ed.). *Human adaptation: Coping with life crises.* Lexington: Heath, 1976.

Myers, J., Lindenthal, J. & Pepper, M. Life events and mental status: A longitudinal study. *Journal of Health and Social Behavior* 1972, *13,* 398–406.

Pearlin, L. Status inequality and stress in marriage. *American Sociological Review,* 1975, *40,* 344–357.

PEARLIN, L. & LIEBERMAN, M. A. Social sources of emotional distress. In R. Simmons, (ed.). *Research in Community Mental Health*. Greenwich: JAI, 1979.

PEARLIN, L. & SCHOOLER, C. The structure of coping. *Journal of Health and Social Behavior*, 1978, *19*, 2–21.

RAHE, R. & ARTHUR, R. Life change and illness studies: Past history and future directions. *Journal of Human Stress*, 1978, *4*, 3–15.

SAGER, C. *Marriage contracts and couple therapy*. New York: Brunner/Mazel, 1976.

SEGRAVES, R. Conjoint marital therapy. *Archives of General Psychiatry*, 1978, *35*, 450–454.

UHLENHUTH, E., LIPMAN, R. BALTER, M. & STERN, M. Symptom intensity and life stress in the city. *Archives of General Psychiatry*, 1974, *31*, 759–764.

WARHEIT, G., ROBBINS, L., McGINNIS, N. *A review of selected research on the relationship of socio-demographic factors to mental disorders and treatment outcomes, 1968–1974*. Rockville: National Institute of Mental Health, 1975.

29

The Stress of Caring:
Women as Providers of Social Support

Deborah Belle

THE WOMEN'S MOVEMENT OF RECENT YEARS has helped to intensify interest in women's experience of stress. Particular attention has been paid to women's experiences in their family roles and in their occupational roles (see the reviews in Dunlop, 1981; Lemkau, 1980; Maracek, 1978; Maracek & Ballou, 1981).

Within the major tradition of stress research, which focuses on the stress of life change, relatively little attention has been paid either to sex differences or to women's experiences of stress. As Makosky (1980) noted, most life events stress studies have focused on exclusively or predominantly male research populations: "Prisoners of war, football players, industrial employees, medical interns, physicians, and Navy personnel at sea, for example" (p. 114). Sex comparisons are rarely reported, and the standard inventories of stressful life events include a disproportionate number that apply more often to men than to women, while excluding crucial events that women are likely both to experience and to find stressful. Thus, being drafted or being promoted at work often appears on inventories of life events, while experiencing an abortion, a rape, or a change in child care arrangements generally does not.

Among researchers who have used an inventory of recent life events to compare the experiences of men and women, Dohrenwend (1973) reported that women had significantly higher life change scores, (life change scores were computed by rating life events for the amount of readjustment each required and then summing these ratings) while Markush and Favero (1974) and Uhlenhuth, Lipman, Balter & Stern (1974) reported no sex difference in the amount of life change experienced. These conflicting reports cannot easily be reconciled, as any study relying on a predetermined inventory of life events may well favor events that generally happen to one sex or the other. A good discussion of the limitations of life events research in relation to women's experience of stress appears in Makosky (1980).

Wilkins (1974) pointed to another limitation of much research on life change: researchers typically ask about events that have occurred in one's own life but do not inquire about the stresses in one's own life caused by events in the life of one's spouse. As Wilkins noted, "This *contagion of stress* from husband to wife, is widely appreciated, but hardly tested in a scientific sense" (p. 250). Women may be particularly subject to this "contagion of stress."

This chapter was written with the support of a grant (MH28830) from the National Institute of Mental Health.

Dohrenwend (1976) reported that when men and women were asked to list recent events that had occurred to themselves, members of their families, and other people important to them, there was a large sex difference in the proportion of events in which the interviewee was not the central figure. A higher proportion of the events reported by women had happened to family menbers or friends rather than to the respondents themselves. Such a finding hints at the different relation in which women may stand to other people in their social worlds.

Contemporary theories of women's psychology (e.g., Chodorow, 1974; Gilligan, 1977; Miller, 1976) emphasize women's embeddedness in social relationships, their "flexible ego boundaries," and their lack of rigid "self-other distinction" (Chodorow, 1974). From childhood on, women's moral sense emphasizes caring for others (Gilligan, 1977). Women become attuned to the needs of others, "better geared then men to first recognize others' needs and then to believe strongly that others' needs can be served" (Miller, 1976:61). Women's orientation to the experiences, needs, and wishes of others can, in extreme form, entail a "loss of self in overwhelming responsibility for and connection to others" (Chodorow, 1974:59). Their sense of connection to and responsibility for others also leads women to attend to and nurture other human beings and to provide them with what has been called "social support" or "information leading the subject to believe that he is cared for and loved, esteemed, and a member of a network of mutual obligations" (Cobb, 1976:300). Social support can include moral support and instrumental assistance.

Many studies have demonstrated that the recipients of such social support are strongly protected against the ill effects of stress (e.g., Cobb, 1976). For instance, such support appears to protect stressed individuals against depression (Brown, Bhrolchain & Harris, 1975), complications of pregnancy (Nuckolls, Cassel & Kaplan, 1972), and ill health following job loss (Gore, 1978).

For Cobb (1976), the prototype of all social support is given by mother to infant, yet after infancy the individual increasingly receives support from others.

> Social support begins *in utero,* is best recognized at the maternal breast, and is communicated in a variety of ways, but especially in the way the baby is held (supported). As life progresses, support is derived increasingly from other members of the family, then from peers at work and in the community, and perhaps, in case of special need, from a member of the helping professions. (Pp. 301–302)

Caplan (1976) painted a picture of reciprocal support in families, provided by undifferentiated "family members."

> We can see the significance of what occurs in most families where, shortly after members come home, they give detailed reports on their behavior at school, work, or in social situations, together with how others reacted to them, especially if these reactions were upsetting, surprising, or incomprehensible. In some families, such discussions take place regularly at mealtimes and have almost a ceremonial aspect. During these discussions, the other members of the group help the person evaluate not only his own reported behavior in the light of the family value system but also the meaning of the reactions of the people with whom he was involved. (p. 23)

While appealing and plausible, this genderless picture of social support does not square with what we know about sex roles either in families or in the larger society. While such support can be provided by anyone, in our society most support is provided by women. In fact, much of what we have understood as women's "expressive function" (Parsons & Bales, 1955) can also be labeled the *provision of social support to others* (Vanfossen, 1981).

Similarly, while many theorists of social support presume that social ties entail reciprocal obligations to provide support, one party to a relationship may well provide far more support than he or she receives. The image of the nurturant mother supporting her dependent babe in arms is useful in suggesting the asymmetric nature of many supportive human relationships. Women, in their family roles as providers of social support to children, husbands, and other kinfolk and in their work roles as providers of support to bosses, clients, and customers, often give more support than they receive. While the health preserving value of receiving social support is well established, less attention has been paid to the consequences of providing social support to others. Yet a review of research on the impact of women's family and work roles on their own mental and physical health suggests that women's support of others may not be without cost to the women themselves, particularly when those who provide support receive little support in turn. Therefore, this chapter considers the giving of social support to others without receiving support oneself (the *support gap*) a source of stress to women today.

FAMILY AND COMMUNITY LIFE

Maracek and Ballou (1981) noted that the costs and benefits of family life are linked to gender. Compared to single men, married men are at reduced risk for suicide (Durkheim, 1951), mental health problems requiring treatment (Belle, 1980), and substance abuse and delinquent behavior (Maracek & Ballou, 1981; Radloff, 1975). Yet marriage does not confer a strong protective advantage on women, and in some studies marriage appears to expose women to enhanced risk (Bernard, 1971; Radloff, 1975).

While many explanations have been offered on the differential advantage of marriage for men and women, it may be that men derive more protection from marriage than women because more of the support in marriage flows from women to men than vice versa. A study of help seeking among blue-collar husbands and wives found that husbands were more inclined to seek support from their wives than were wives to seek support from their husbands (Warren, 1975). To provide support effectively, one needs a good understanding of the intended recipient of this support. It is relevant, therefore, that Campbell, Converse, and Rodgers (1976) found husbands more likely than wives to report that their spouses understood them well and wives more likely than husbands to report that they understood their spouses well. Bernard (1981) argued that men lack training in the "supportive function" and reviewed many studies that found women in stress turning to other women, rather than to husbands, for emotional support and understanding (see also Bernard, 1976).

Most marriages involve children, and the asymmetrical nature of family roles is most apparent when households include young children, whose needs for social support are immense. The importance of providing social support for children can be inferred by comparing the experiences of children in institutional settings and prolonged foster care with those of children in adoptive or biological families.

While there is no reason that social support for children cannot come from fathers as well as mothers, a majority of men and women believe that women should have primary responsibility for child care (Nye, 1976). The primacy of maternal care is recognized in child custody arrangements following divorce: mothers become the custodial parent 9 times out of 10 (Bane, 1979). Despite the increased participation of women in the paid labor force, men's involvement in child care and housekeeping has changed little in recent years (Pleck, 1977, 1979). Rubin (1976) found a consensus among the couples she interviewed that it is a woman's job to take care of the household and the children, perhaps with help from the husband.

While responsibility for young children can bring great joy, the stress of caring for young children was amply demonstrated in several recent studies that examined women's emotional well-being over the life cycle (Brown, Bhrolchain, and Harris, 1975; Pearlin & Johnson, 1977; Radloff, 1975). The risk of depression and demoralization in mothers was found to increase as the number of children living at home increased and as the age of the youngest child declined. Patterson (1980) used the language of reinforcement and conditioning to discuss the experience of mothers. He noted that a mother's caretaking role exposes her to "high rates of aversive events" (p. 2). Mothers must monitor and respond to their young children almost continually, while even a reasonably well-behaved child is far from continually cooperative or "positively reinforcing." The frequent result of providing support to a child while receiving only erratic support in return is frustration and dysphoria.

Since providing support to young children is so demanding, mothers often seek the help and sympathy of other adults. As Henderson (1977) noted, "Caring for young children frequently increases a mother's own attachment requirements" (p. 190). Yet marital relationships often suffer just at the time when a wife needs her husband's support most. Campbell and co-workers (1976) find that women evaluate the marital relationship least positively when there is a young child at home, and Brown and associates (1975) reported that during this stage of the life cycle women are less likely than at other times to find that their husbands are supportive confidants. A mother is at greatest risk for demoralization and depression when she bears the entire responsibility of child care and when she does not receive adequate nurturance herself. When mothers of young children are able to confide in their husbands, their risk of depression diminishes sharply (Brown, Bhrolchain, & Harris, 1975); similarly, when mothers receive assistance with child care or housekeeping tasks from husbands or other adults, their risk of experiencing depressive symptoms is dramatically lower (Belle, 1982; Zur-Szpiro & Longfellow, 1982). In these days of high divorce rates, it is important to note that relatives, friends, and ex-husbands, as well as husbands, can provide the support that protects mothers from depression and demoralization (Hetherington, Cox, & Cox, 1978; Pearlin & Johnson, 1977). For women who do live with their husbands, the support of others may still make a crucial difference (Abernethy, 1973).

While caring for children can be stressful when children experience only the normal problems of growing up, it can become extremely stressful when children have behavioral or emotional problems. Interactions with children can become more aversive (Patterson, 1980), and given our culture's tendency to blame mothers when anything goes wrong with children, mothers may experience severe guilt (Weisskopf, 1978). Furthermore, although we expect that the dependence of children and their need for support will diminish with age, not all children eventually become independent. Those who do not, because of ill health, mental retardation, or emotional problems, are likely to remain with their mothers. Riddell (1980) described the continuing dependence of her retarded adult son and her continuing care for her child.

> I am still trying to find a way to let us both live independently, though I must keep a very close watch. My fear for him, like that of other mothers of mentally handicapped adults, is that he will outlive me or that I won't find a place for him where he has some choice in his lifestyle. My fear for me is that I will never have any choice in my lifestyle! (P. 89)

The continuing care of adult dependent children may require the sacrifice of many other activities and pleasures and may be particularly stressful when the child's problem precipitates the exit of the father from the family.

Even mothers whose adult children make no continuing demands for support may still be active "kin keepers." Patients who return to the community when mental hospitals "deinstitutionalize" them are often cared for by female relatives. When aged parents remain in the community and yet need assistance with the tasks of daily living, the responsibility generally falls to daughters or daughters-in-law. Not surprisingly, Lieberman (1978) found adult women more likely than men, especially among older groups of men and women, to report being troubled by age related changes in their parents.

Woman also may be called on to provide support to neighbors and friends. A recent study of social ties and psychological well-being among middle-aged adults found that for women in certain ethnic groups, having extensive social ties was associated with an overload of responsibility and with heightened psychological distress (Cohler & Lieberman, 1980). Similarly, a study of mothers raising young children on low incomes found that the more involved a woman was with her relatives and close friends, the more stress she experienced in regard to her social relationships (Belle, 1982).

WORK ROLES

In recent years more and more women have added occupational roles to their family and community responsibilities. The number of women in the paid labor force more than doubled since 1940, and the percentage of employed mothers quadrupled between 1940 and 1974 (U.S. Department of Labor, 1975). Most women workers are found in clerical, service, sales, and factory work or in professions that emphasize service to others, such as teaching, nursing, and social work. Such jobs often require the same kind of attention to the needs of others and the same outpouring of support that women provide within the family. It is precisely the opportunity to provide support to others that attracts so many women to these often poorly paid and unprestigious jobs and that leads others to encourage women to enter these occupations.

Recent research suggests that much of women's traditional work may be stressful and destructive of health. A study of the occupations of those who sought treatment for mental health problems found that those in the health care professions were overrepresented (Colligan, Smith, & Hurrell, 1977). Colligan and associates commented that "the responsibility of caring for and interacting with people who are ill or infirm can be emotionally demanding, subjecting the health professional to considerable stress" (p. 38). Not coincidentally, most of the health care professionals found to be at risk were women. Similarly, Haynes and Feinleib (1980) found that women clerical workers, particularly those whose bosses were "nonsupportive," had a higher rate of coronary heart disease than did other women workers or housewives.

The combination of work and family responsibilities results in stressful work overload for many women (Maracek & Ballou, 1981). Not only do working mothers spend many hours working and few hours in leisure pursuits, but their paid work and their work at home generally require attention to the needs of others. Women's sensitivity to such needs may make it extremely difficult to ignore or refuse requests for attention and nurturance from employers, work mates, and subordinates. One working mother described her dilemma: "If I could only have an hour in the middle of the day to just SIT in a room in my home entirely alone with no demands from my child, my husband, my dog or cat, my employer . . . just time to sit all alone" (quoted in National Commission on Working Women, 1979:4).

Given the lack of institutional assistance available to employed mothers and their families (Kamerman, 1979), the working mother may have little respite. It is not surprising, therefore, that the risk of heart disease is highest among working women who have several children and accordingly must provide high levels of support both at work and at home (Haynes & Feinleib, 1980).

MONEY AS A BUFFER AGAINST STRESS

If money cannot buy love, it can buy health sustaining relief from otherwise overwhelming demands. Women with higher incomes can afford to hire babysitters or to pay for center based day care. They can reserve more of their energy for child care and paid work through the use of appliances that make housekeeping easier. Women with access to income from sources other than their own employment also find it easier to stop working when family responsibilities become too heavy.

Whether employed or not, women who rear young children with low incomes are at high risk for depression (Brown, Bhrolchain, & Harris, 1975; Pearlin & Johnson, 1977; Radloff, 1975). Research findings also suggest that when the low-income mother suffers from depression, her ability to provide emotional support to her children is likely to deteriorate. Weissman and Paykel (1974) found that compared to women not suffering from depression, depressed mothers were less involved with and less affectionate toward their children and less likely to meet their children's demands for attention and communication. Longfellow, Zelkowitz & Saunders (1982) found that women experiencing more depressive symptoms were less responsive, less nurturant, and more punitive to their young children than were less depressed women. Mothers under socioeconomic stress are those most likely to abuse their children (Garbarino, 1976).

Since low-income mothers and their children are particularly high-risk groups, it is frightening to realize that over the past 15 years, women and their dependent children have come to account for an increasingly large proportion of America's poor and near poor, a phenomenon that has been called the "feminization of poverty" (Pearce, 1978). The escalating divorce rate, particularly when there are young children at home, has pushed many women and children into poverty (Ross & Sawhill, 1975). Few families receive regular child support payments from the absent father over the years following a divorce, and there is a widespread expectation that single parent women should be financially self-sufficient.

Yet women's earning power is vastly inferior to that of men. In the mid-1950s, a woman who worked full-time, year-round earned, on average, 63 cents for every dollar earned by a man who worked full-time, year-round. By the mid-1960s and 1970s this figure had declined to below 60 cents (Barrett, 1979). Sawhill (1976) calculated the number of predominantly female occupations in which a female high school graduate, age 25–34, would earn less than $3000 per year working full-time and the comparable percentage of predominantly male jobs with a similarly dismal earning potential. She found that while 20% of predominantly male occupations had such poverty level wages, over half the predominantly female occupations had such a low wage level.

In 1978 one in five families in the United States was headed by a single parent, versus one in nine in 1970. Almost one female-headed family in three is poor, six times the rate for families headed by a man (National Advisory Council on Economic Opportunity, 1980). If present trends should continue, the feminization of poverty would be complete in the year 2000—100% of the poverty population would then be comprised of female family heads and their dependent children (National Advisory Council on Economic Opportunity, 1980). Thus, to the extent that money can protect women against stress, this buffer is unavailable to vast and increasing numbers of family women.

DISCUSSION AND CONCLUSION

> It appears that social support can protect people in crisis from a wide variety of pathological states: from low birth weight to death, from arthritis through tuberculosis to depression, alcoholism, and the social breakdown syndrome. (Cobb, 1976:300)

> In our culture "serving others" is for losers, it is low-level stuff. Yet serving others is a basic principle around which women's lives are organized; it is far from such for men. (Miller, 1976:60)

In recent years much attention has been directed to people experiencing stress and to the factors that can protect individuals from the ill effects of stress. In this context, social support has been recognized as a potent health and life sustaining buffer against stress. This chapter has directed attention to the women who provide much of this crucial support and to the health consequences for them of doing so. Clearly, there can be considerable stress in providing support to others, particularly if support is not reciprocated.

To add insult to injury, much of women's supportive work is not recognized for the powerful social support that it is. Instead, to quote Miller (1976), such work is seen as "low-level stuff," which actually reduces the status of the women engaged in it. We have come a long way in recognizing the power of social support provided by one human being to another. The discovery of social support should now be followed by the recognition that, all along, this is work that women have performed.

Much social support research begins with the stated or unstated assumption that individuals are involved in reciprocal, symmetrical, mutually obligating ties. However, it is probably a rare human relationship in which each participant provides exactly as much support as he or she receives. Future research might address the consequences of relative equity or inequity in support exchanges within relationships. Certain relationships necessitate an unequal provision of support, particularly relationships with young children and with adults who are physically or emotionally ill. Research might investigate the types of social support that are most valuable in protecting adults in such relationships. The research on support to mothers of young children and on burnout in the human service professions has already begun this work.

Recognition of the stressfulness of a support gap for many women has several clinical and public policy implications. Just as women have sought to emulate men's skills by going to assertiveness training classes, men might emulate women's skills at social support by seeking "supportiveness training." The husband, son, father, or friend who can provide social support to the women (and men) in his life is capable of combating the health destroying stress that those close to him may experience. Women who feel intensely guilty when they refuse the requests of others for social support can be helped to protect their own health by setting reasonable limits on the demands to which they will respond (Hare-Mustin, 1978). Or, if they receive overwhelming demands to which they believe they must respond, they can be helped in seeking out alternative support systems for themselves and for those who depend on them for support. The ability to provide social support is a precious human resource, and it can be destroyed by overload. Public acknowledgment of men's rightful role in providing support is also important. When men's employers allow them time away from work to care for their ill children, and when men consider such care a parental, not a maternal, responsibility, there is less danger of a support gap.

The impoverishment of so many women, especially those who are responsible for young children, is a grave cause for public concern. Extrapolating from the research on women in poverty, we can predict that the growing numbers of impoverished mothers and children will mean more maternal depression, deteriorating family relationships, more child abuse, and perhaps higher levels of heart disease as women with several young children seek employment to boost their meager incomes. The combination of poverty and responsibility for young children is a deadly one for women and for their young children.

Policies have been formulated for female-headed families as though women's earning power equaled that of men. Yet without child support payments from the noncustodial spouse and without an adequate level of government assistance, many women who head families cannot support their families above the poverty line. Divorce settlements must acknowledge these economic realities, and government policies must not abandon families under severe economic stress. Those who undertake the important task of nurturing and supporting the future generation require sufficient economic and emotional support to make their job a manageable one.

REFERENCES

ABERNETHY, V. Social network and response to the maternal role. *International Journal of Sociology of the Family,* 1973, *3,* 86–92.

BANE, M. Marital disruption and the lives of children. In G. Levinger & O. Moles (eds.), *Divorce and separation.* New York: Basic Books, 1979.

BARRETT, N. Women in the job market: Occupations, earnings, and career opportunities. In R. Smith (ed.), *The subtle revolution: Women at work.* Washington, D.C.: Urban Institute, 1979.

BELLE, D. Who uses mental health facilities? In M. Guttentag, S. Salasin, & D. Belle (eds.), *The mental health of women.* New York: Academic, 1980.

————. Social ties and social support. In D. Belle (ed.), *Lives in stress: Women and depression.* Beverly Hills: Sage, 1982.

BARNARD, J. The paradox of the happy marriage. In V. Gornick & B. Moran (eds.), *Woman in sexist society: Studies in power and powerlessness.* New York: Basic Books, 1971.

————. Homosociality and female depression. *Journal of Social Issues,* 1976, *32,* 4, 213–238.

————. *The female world.* New York: Free Press, 1981.

BROWN, G., BHROLCHAIN, M. & HARRIS, T. Social class and psychiatric disturbance among women in an urban population. *Sociology,* 1975, *9,* 225–254.

CAMPBELL, A., CONVERSE, P., & RODGERS, W. *The quality of American life: Perceptions, evaluations, and satisfactions.* New York: Russell Sage, 1976.

CAPLAN, G. The family as a support system. In G. Caplan & M. Killilea (eds.), *Support systems and mutual help: Multidisciplinary explorations.* New York: Grune & Stratton, 1976.

CHODOROW, N. Family structure and feminine personality. In M. Rosaldo & L. Lamphere (eds.), *Women, culture, and society.* Stanford: Stanford University Press, 1974.

COBB, S. Social support as a moderator of life stress. *Psychosomatic Medicine,* 1976, *38,* 300–314.

COHLER, B., & LIEBERMAN, M. Social relations and mental health among three European ethnic groups. *Research on Aging,* 1980, *2,* 4, 445–469.

COLLIGAN, M., SMITH, M., & HURRELL, J. Occupational incidence rates of mental health disorders. *Journal of Human Stress,* 1977, *3,* 34–39.

DOHRENWEND, B. S. Social status and stressful life events. *Journal of Personality and Social Psychology,* 1973, *28,* 225–235.

————. Anticipation and control of stressful life events: An exploratory analysis. Paper presented to the annual meeting of the Eastern Psychological Association, New York City, 1976.

Dunlop, K. Maternal employment and child care. *Professional Psychology,* 1981, *12,* 67–75.

Durkheim, E. *Suicide,* trans. J. Spaulding & G. Simpson. New York: Free Press, 1951.

Garbarino, J. A preliminary study of some ecological correlates of child abuse: The impact of socio-economic stress on mothers. *Child Development,* 1976, *47,* 178–185.

Gilligan, C. In a different voice: Women's conceptions of the self and of morality. *Harvard Educational Review,* 1977, *47,* 481–517.

Gore, S. The effect of social support in moderating the health consequences of unemployment. *Journal of Health and Social Behavior,* 1978, *19,* 157–165.

Hare-Mustin, R. A feminist approach to family therapy. *Family Process,* 1978, *17,* 181–194.

Haynes, S., & Feinleib, M. Women, work, and coronary heart disease: Prospective findings from the Framingham Heart Study. *American Journal of Public Health,* 1980, *70,* 133–141.

Henderson, S. The social network, support, and neurosis: The function of attachment in adult life. *British Journal of Psychiatry,* 1977, *131,* 185–191.

Hetherington, E., Cox, M., & Cox, R. The aftermath of divorce. In J. H. Stevens, Jr., & M. Mathews (eds.), *Mother-child father-child relationships.* Washington, D.C.: National Association for the Education of Young Children, 1978.

Kamerman, S. Work and family in industrialized societies. *Signs,* 1979, *4,* 632–650.

Lemkau, J. Women and employment: Some emotional hazards. In C. Heckerman (ed.), *The evolving female: Women in psychosocial context.* New York: Human Sciences, 1980.

Lieberman, G. Children of the elderly as natural helpers: Some demographic differences. *American Journal of Community Psychology,* 1978, *6,* 489–498.

Longfellow, C., Zelkowitz, P., & Saunders, E. The quality of mother-child relationships. In D. Belle (ed.), *Lives in stress: Women and depression.* Beverly Hills: Sage, 1982.

Makosky, V. Stress and the mental health of women: A discussion of research and issues. In M. Guttentag, S. Salasin, & D. Belle (eds.), *The mental health of women.* New York: Academic, 1980.

Maracek, J. Psychological disorders in women: Indices of role strain. In I. Frieze, J. Parsons, P. Johnson, D. Ruble, & G. Zellman (eds.), *Women and sex roles: A social psychological perspective.* New York: Norton, 1978.

Maracek, J., & Ballou, D. Family roles and women's mental health. *Professional Psychology,* 1981, *12,* 39–46.

Markush, R., & Favero, R. Epidemiologic assessment of stressful life events, depressed mood, and psychophysiological symptoms: A preliminary report. In B. S. Dohrenwend & B. P. Dohrenwend (eds.), *Stressful life events: Their nature and effects.* New York: Wiley, 1974.

Miller, J. B. *Toward a new psychology of women.* Boston: Beacon, 1976.

National Advisory Council on Economic Opportunity. *Critical choices for the 80's.* Washington, D.C.: U.S. Government Printing Office, 1980.

National Commission on Working Women. *National survey of working women: Perceptions, problems, and prospects.* Washington, D.C.: National Commission on Working Women, 1979.

Nuckolls, K., Cassel, J., & Kaplan, B. Psychosocial assets, life crisis, and the prognosis of pregnancy. *American Journal of Epidemiology,* 1972, *95,* 431–441.

Nye, F. *Role structure and analysis of the family.* Beverly Hills: Sage, 1976.

Parsons, T., & Bales, R. *Family, socialization, and interaction process.* New York: Free Press, 1955.

Patterson, G. Mothers: The unacknowledged victims. *Monographs of the Society for Research in Child Development* (whole no. 186), 1980, *45.*

Pearce, D. Women, work, and welfare: the feminization of poverty. In K. W. Feinstein (ed.), *Working women and families.* Beverly Hills: Sage, 1979.

Pearlin, L., & Johnson, J. Marital status, life-strains, and depression. *American Sociological Review,* 1977, *42,* 704–715.

PLECK, J. The work-family role system. *Social Problems,* 1977, *24,* 417–427.

————. Men's "family work" role: Three perspectives and some new data. *Family Coordinator,* 1979, *28,* 481–488.

RADLOFF, L. Sex differences in depression: The effects of occupation and marital status. *Sex Roles,* 1975, *1,* 249–266.

RIDDELL, R. Life with my retarded son. *Ms.,* July 1980, pp. 84–89.

ROSS, H., & SAWHILL, I. *Time of transition: The growth of families headed by women.* Washington, D.C.: Urban Institute, 1975.

RUBIN, L. *Worlds of pain: Life in the working class family.* New York: Basic Books, 1976.

SAWHILL, I. Women with low-incomes. In M. Blaxall & B. Reagan (eds.), *Women and the workplace: The implications of occupational segregation.* Chicago: University of Chicago Press, 1976.

UHLENHUTH, E., LIPMAN, R., BALTER, M., & STERN, M. Symptom intensity and life stress in the city. *Archives of General Psychiatry,* 1974, *31,* 759–764.

U.S. Department of Labor, Women's Bureau. *1975 handbook of women workers.* Washington, D.C.: U.S. Government Printing Office, 1975.

VANFOSSEN, B. Sex differences in the mental health effects of spouse support and equity. *Journal of Health and Social Behavior,* 1981, *22,* 130–143.

WARREN, R. The work role and problem coping: sex differentials in the use of helping systems in urban communities. Paper presented to the annual meeting of the American Sociological Association, San Francisco, 1975.

WEISSKOPF, S. *Maternal guilt and mental health professionals: A reconfirming interaction.* University of Michigan occasional paper no. 5. 1978.

WEISSMAN, M., & PAYKEL, E. *The depressed woman.* Chicago: University of Chicago Press, 1974.

WILKINS, W. Social stress and illness in industrial society. In E. Gunderson & R. Rahe (eds.), *Life stress and illness.* Springfield: Thomas, 1974.

ZUR-SZPIRO, S., & LONGFELLOW, C. Fathers' support to mothers and children. In D. Belle (ed.), *Lives in stress: Women and depression.* Beverly Hills: 1982.

30

Social Disability and Stress

Elizabeth Taylor Vance

ONE OF THE MOST RELIABLE OBSERVATIONS regarding human refractoriness to, and recovery from, stress is that these capabilities correlate with broad social conditions of rearing. Thus, humans achieve higher levels of adaptability and resourcefulness when they have been reared with socioeconomic, ethnic, and sex group advantage than when they have not. The relationships between stress dispositions and social structural factors also suggest that *social competence* (the collection of capabilities that enables us to regroup and appropriately organize our forces across many types of situations and changes) is as essential to understanding human stress as are the factors in the stress response to psychological conflict and life threat.

Social competence is the antithesis of *stress proneness.* Ordinarily we identify competence with culturally specific and valued behavior contents such as acceptable levels of performance on standard intelligence tests, socially appropriate habits, and freedom from deviant behavior. But these criteria are inadequate to comprise all the facets of social variation in stress dispositions. Actually, social competence broadly reflects the presence and maintenance of the formal aspects of adaptive behavior, those aspects that facilitate effective cross-situational and cross-cultural performance and, with it, the maintenance of positive self-esteem. Because change and tasks are woven into the fabric of life and living (some are even socially age graded), the deficit in adaptive *forms* of behavior can be described as generalized *social disability;* that is, a lowered level and quality of performance in the face of change, an inability to moderate environmental effects, and a general proneness to fixate on states of perceived stress and frustration. One finds these effects in individuals who otherwise seem well adjusted to their cultural niches and familiar roles. Social competence and disability refer to the *how,* not the *what,* of behavior.

This formulation of competence and disability is based on a view of the developing organism that assumes that its activity is intrinsically adaptive or competence motivated in form and that it is in the organism's nature to initiate, organize, reorganize, integrate, and reintegrate again and again in the face of the novel. The view of the process itself is that so-called normal, expectable environments for human infants are those that are sufficiently responsive to enable the growing person to acquire a sense that environments are more or less affected by his initiatives. Coping and initiative remain remarkably indefatigable attributes of many repeatedly challenged and "stressed" persons possessed of this formative background. Therefore, theories about the factors involved in adaptive failure and disability have sought explanations in the characteristics of the early interface between person and environments that lie outside the normal, expectable range of interactions (Phillips, 1968; Vance, 1973; White, 1970).

EPIDEMIOLOGY AND STRESS PRONENESS

The explanatory variables chosen in this view of adaptive stress and social disability are suggested by epidemiological findings of pathology, as well as by theories regarding the requirements of healthy human development. A detailed review of the epidemiology of social disability and other relevant variables has been made elsewhere (Dohrenwend & Dohrenwend, 1974; Ehrenmyer-Kimling, 1970; Fontana, 1967; Vance, 1977). However, I shall provide some illustrations of one type of finding that led to the choice of variables described in this chapter.

Interpretation of incidence rates is prone to controversy and findings on some variables are more conflicting than are findings on others. Nevertheless, my reading of the patterns and consistencies in the literature leads me to believe that they represent strong support for the summary of relationships displayed in Tables 30–1 and 30–2. The tables relate two grossly defined levels of *impairment,* on the one hand (distinguished by duration of illness or single versus repeated episode), and four kinds of *biosocial status* (either socioeconomic status and family order and stability (i.e. family conflict) or sex gender and birth order), on the other.

Low socioeconomic status has long been correlated with severity of emotional disorder and interpreted by some as causal and by others as effect. The distribution of severity in Tables 30–1 and 30–2 suggests that socioeconomic status comprises complex causal factors that are not to be found exclusively in conditions of socioeconomic poverty. The distribution in these tables suggests either multiple etiologies for impairment or a pathogenic process common to a number of diverse social contexts or statuses. Thus the distribution in Table 30–1 suggests that while SES is a factor in impairment, the more proximal the severity and disorganization, as when family conflict is added to socioeconomic disadvantage, the more chronically impaired the person. It must also be noted that among the severely impaired are individuals who often appear to have had sound social environments. Impairment in this group is usually interpreted to reflect a heavier contribution from genetic factors, which unquestionably play a role in a very complex etiology.

TABLE 30–1
Level of Impairment for Social Class and Level of Family Conflict

Level of impairment	Low SES		High SES	
	High family conflict	*Low family conflict*	*High family conflict*	*Low family conflict*
Brief reactive impairment		x	x	
Chronic impairment	x			x

TABLE 30-2
Level of Impairment for Social Class, Sex, and Birth Order

Level of impairment	Low SES				High SES			
	Low birth order		High/middle birth order		Low birth order		High/middle birth order	
	M	F	M	F	M	F	M	F
Brief reactive impairment			x					x
Chronic impairment		x			x	x		

In Table 30-2 the distribution of impairment among the social factors indicates an adaptive advantage for high to middle birth order, although this trend holds only in large families (five or more siblings). A biological explanation of this trend seems unlikely when we look at two other trends in Table 30-2. Early experience associated with low birth order can be compensated for either by *high socioeconomic status* or by *masculine sex role*. On the other hand, high birth rank and high socioeconomic status add to help women in some way. The fact that high birth rank for low socioeconomic status men does not protect them from some risk for impairment might be interpreted as cultural variation in the meaning of, and formative experience in, high sibling rank for males, male gender being of less value in low socioeconomic status groups. On the other hand, the finding that some impaired women have high socioeconomic status and high sibling rank can suggest the contribution of women's sex role to impairment. In neither case, however, do we find such combinations heavily represented in chronically impaired populations.

These tables make use of findings on chronic states of decompensation and on vulnerability to repeated episodes of disorder in a relatively extreme form. Since they reflect only the extreme degree of adaptive failure, they can best be viewed against a continuum of behaviors all of which can be interpreted as varying levels of adaptation and competence.

The developmental factor underlying these distribution patterns is an ecologically unbalanced formative biosocial status. For all four affected groups (low socioeconomic status, feminine gender and identity, low birth order, and conflict-ridden family life), the environment is overly salient such that initiative and coping efforts are experienced *not* to work and effective integrations are rarely achieved by the young. Some ecologies seem to aid in the development of personality mediated activity, which increases the person's autonomy and flexibility in making transitions. Unbalanced ecologies of the kind characterizing these group experiences simply increase dependence upon the particular arrangements and expectations of the ecosystem.

The causes of social disability are buried in very complex early formal person-environment relationships (Vance, 1977). Out of these early relationships develop fairly stable personal organizations that affect the modes by which we experience as well as the way we are organized to respond. The experiencing as well action modes are stable (i.e., slow changing mediators of stress). Because one effect of social organization is to pattern our experiences, variations in social organization (e.g., community and family structure, and stability, rank ordering of status, privilege, rights, and reciprocities) influence the development of traits or stable modes for mediating stress.

I find useful Escalona's (1963, 1968) concept of *stable patterns of experience* (SPE), which summarizes the effective formative experience of a developing person interacting with a particular environment. The essence of this concept is that the state available to the individual when he confronts change determines his behavioral repertoire and the quality of it and that the entire range of states available to the person stabilizes at a very early age.

If individualized patterns of experience reflect stability in, or greater frequency of, one state over time, the development of behavioral and psychological resources, which include mediating integrative mechanisms, is irreversibly affected. Social disability is proposed to have its origins in the *internal* and *external* events relevant to early states in which personal integration does not frequently allow for coping with change or difficulty. Such a view is consistent with evidence that early social experience alters brain chemistry and organization and that social group rearing can have very capricious effects on the development of cortical integrative mechanisms (McV. Hunt, 1975).

ANTECEDENTS OF SOCIAL DISABILITY PATTERNS

Five variables are most likely to influence early SPEs in the direction of an orientation to inflexible environmental and stimulus controls of behavior. Consistent with the concept of SPE, this list includes both organismic and environmental inputs.

Level of Social Density, Orderliness, Rhythmicity, and Predictability

A number of very broad parameters of the environment such as density (crowding), order, predictability, and the rhythm of events appear to affect cortical organization, psychological states and behavior (see Vance, 1973). For example, we know that *rhythmicity* and *orderliness* in an infant's immediate environment affect the stabilization of his states in the first few days of life. These parameters of the environment continue to be important to states throughout the early years of development, even though patterns of experience may already be relatively stable by the end of the first year of life. Furthermore, distal environments are graded in salience along all parameters and remain important in affecting state as the child grows. As one example, observers described ghetto life to include all these parameters as follows: "The experience of an ever-shifting population that yields the expectation that acquaintances are temporary; the various sources of unpredictability that lead to unending searches for signs that will identify the reliable; the sense of instability, chaos, confusion and fragmentation of the world" (Schlesinger & Schatz, 1977). Whether conditions like these prevail within or outside the family, the SPE for a developing infant and child will be one in which the environment is more salient than inner plans and memories for integrating perceptions and responses with change or task demands.

Level of Stimulation and Complexity

Complexity does not appear to play a role either in the perception of stress or in the stress reaction in socially disabled individuals. On the other hand, studies of infant development clearly indicate that complexity and richness of *stimulation* are critical to early healthy development of the brain. (Hunt, 1961; Levine, 1961; Rosenzweig 1966; Thompson & Grusec, 1970). These environmental attributes increase the frequency of states in which cortical excitability is optimum for the organization of coping plans and in which arousal levels are most finely tuned to critical features of the environment. When these conditions prevail, there can be much early practice in the generating of hypotheses about transitions, novel events, and problems and much opportunity to store plans and learning sets. The child will have experienced a high frequency of states, which early comprise a positive affective component and confidence, such that subsequent exposure to transitions should be accompanied by a reduction in indecisiveness regarding approaches.

Activity

The picture we get of temperament effects on patterns of experience is fairly consistent with respect to *activity* level. The features of the environment are much more salient in the development of low active than of high active infants. Low activity seems to enhance focusing on, prolonged gazing on, and scanning of the immediate environment, and mobilization of behavior seems to depend on this external stimulation rather than on internal stimuli. Active infants seem to have more autonomous mechanisms for mobilizing. They exhibit a great deal of spontaneous behavior and highly diverse motor exploration. Very little in the way of external stimulation seems to be required to mobilize the entire response repertoire. In studies of patterns like these, Escalona (1968) found that very different levels of performance and motor organization were evident in children who differed in this way by the end of the first year of life.

In the ordinary home, routine caretaking would move babies of all types through a sufficient range of activity such that differences in patterns of experiences from this source would be minimized. When such input from consistent and tuned caretaking is not present, as in more chaotic or in conflict-ridden homes, differences in activity level would contribute to SPE significantly.

Derived Status

In the first years of life, the child's attachment to and dependence on powerful caretaking adults is a necessary part of development. The effect of that dependence is to make him highly sensitive to control by salient features and wishes of caretakers. As he acquires a growing sense of self in the first three years, his dependence becomes more differentiated and he begins to identify and model himself after powerful figures for the pupose of deriving a sense of status and competence from being like the other rather than from being dependent on the other. I suggest that the behavioral modes and features of others serve as the child's plans for coping. *Derived status* of this kind is useful to the child's development of initiative only so long as it is temporary and facilitates the graded development of a growing sense of reciprocity and initiative. Early relationships that encourage overly prolonged derived status or render achievement of *acquired status* difficult contribute to highly stabilized, low-status patterns of experience and external orientation. Such may very well be the case for many women, for the youngest children in large families (for whom strong identification with elder siblings is common), and for many disadvantaged black males.

Biochemical States

We do not as yet fully understand the role that hormones play in stable patterns of experience. However, we do know that sex hormones play an important role in the organization of the fetal cortex and again at puberty they contribute significantly to the different ways in which men and women organize experience. The distribution of hormonal influence in SPEs is probably continuous since the ratio of estrogen to testosterone is continuously graded in a population of men and women, with men and women showing considerable overlap and fluctuation over the life cycle. From what we know at this point, the sex differences in hormonal influence on states is greatest and most pervasive at adolescence. The increased levels of testosterone relative to estrogen are associated with behaviorally focused, instrumental impulse expression. Increased levels of estrogen relative to testosterone have widespread, diffuse psychic and mood effects that are experienced as cyclic, unpredictable changes in state. During an important formative period when SPE is affected by maturing estrogen levels, environmental salience is likely to be exaggerated.

There are two final issues regarding social disability and stress that I will touch on briefly here. One has to do with the nature of adaptive stress itself in contrast to stress that involves psychological or life threat. The second related issue has to do with the parameters of the personality most likely to be involved in social disability.

ADAPTIVE STRESS

Cogent distinctions have been made between the responses to *threat,* to *complexity,* and to *difficulty* (Murphy, 1964; White, 1974). While *coping* is the best way to describe the adaptive response to difficult and also novel stimulus patterns, *defense* is typically elicited by conditions of threat and *mastery* by complex configurations of events or experiences. It is difficulty and novelty with which we are confronted in transitions. The adaptive response forms to change are *initiating, coping,* and *experimenting.*

Now, we know that novel and dissonant events have arousing and activating effects that we call *stress* in the organimic sense and that an important factor in mobilizing or maintaining a behavioral sequence that is refractory to stress is the maintenance of an optimal arousal level. Furthermore, if a plan or set for a sequence of behavior is initiated by the appraisal of novelty or dissonance, the inbuilt behavior sequence triggered is ordinarily a coping, experimenting, exploring one that continues until the dissonance is reduced and new behavioral competencies are organized—*unless the behavior sequence is interrupted in some way.* Any parameter of psychobiological functioning that involves the rapid habituation of arousal would disrupt the execution of a flexible and organized experimenting sequence. Such are the elements and relationships in adaptive stress. Another source of adaptive stress has to do with the extent to which the organism values and gives priority to unselected or salient elements of the stimulus field so that all aspects of the field have unselected pull on responses. The effect of simultaneous and unordered demand of unselected elements of the stimulus field is to disrupt the organization of behavior.

Several of these adaptive stress relationships are evident in extreme form in chronic psychotic impairment (e.g., chronic schizophrenia). Chronic outcome in schizophrenia is expressed in *psychological deficit;* that is, deviant and inadequate *performance* on a wide range of psychological tests, tasks, and laboratory problems. By many, this performance deficit is now thought to be the result of a cognitive set or psychobiological pattern that is elicited under conditions of arousal to all magnitudes of general stimulation but particularly to transition events requiring a performance, a set to perform, and mobilization to maintain the set (Cromwell, 1975).

Normally, a set to respond provided by the predictability of an event has a positive integrating effect on performance. Such adaptive behavior does not appear to differ between chronic schizophrenics and normals unless the preparation interval is of sufficient length to require autonomous mediating mechanisms that maintain arousal over a period of time while the subject is waiting for the event to occur. Under these latter conditions, the performance of the chronic schizophrenic, in contrast to that of reactive psychotics and normals, always deteriorates. Findings such as these aid in the identification of the dispositions involved in social disability.

MEDIATORS OF STRESS IN SOCIAL DISABILITY

The literature on human development, psychopathology, and personality contains findings that point to a number of traits or influences that exaggerate the salience of environmental information relative to person organized information in response to stress experience. In the final portion of this chapter I shall mention four of these traits (see also Vance, 1977).

Openness to Experience

Zuckerman (1980) recently reviewed an extensive literature on individual differences in perceived anxiety as associated with changing levels of activation. There are very stable individual differences in patterns of relationships between rate of increase in perceived stress and change in level of activation in response to an event. A reasonable conclusion to be drawn from this literature is that the *tendency to enter into risky situations or to seek novel experiences* is a function of the interaction of subjective distress and arousal states. Generally, findings on the intolerance and avoidance of arousal in disorders marked by chronicity and behavioral inactivity are consistent with expectations that socially disabled individuals are intolerant of the high levels of arousal elicited by novel or dissonant stimulus patterns. On the other hand, they may actually augment the salience of the event.

Augmenting

Characteristically, socially disabled persons appear not to use memory as a context or perspective for weighing the significance of ongoing events (Vance, 1977). In Piagetian terms, they *center* on single dimensions or information sources (Flavell, 1963). In the laboratory, too, individual differences in electrocortical response that reflect the *augmenting* of a stimulus evoked cortical response suggest highly stable cortical styles of mediating novel events (Zuckerman, 1980). The stimulus enhancement seems to have psychological significance in that it is associated with chronicity of impaired initiative and competence as in chronic schizophrenia, while persons suffering from acute reactive disorders are more likely to be reducers (Zuckerman, 1980). It is very likely that some of the *perceived stress* in chronic impairment can be attributed to this cortical characteristic of augmenting.

Field Orientation

Field independence refers to the use of body stimuli for integrating experience, while *field dependence* refers to reliance on field cues for doing so (Witkin, Dyk, Patterson, Goodenough, & Karp, 1962). The field-body parameter of personal integration or states may serve in a way similar to that of a set that determines what and how behavior is organized. In a field-dependent orientation, the temporal ordering of responses is dependent upon moment by moment saliencies in the stimulus field, as well as upon the temporal characteristics of arousal following the appraisal of an event. If arousal is for any reason maintained in a field oriented person, behavior is highly stimulus dependent. On the other hand, should stress arousal characteristics of a field oriented person be such that there is rapid habituation of arousal to an event, as occurs in chronic schizophrenia, there is little of an internal state to support behavior. Field orientation therefore may be describing a relationship between a particular kind of cortical integrative mechanism and its effect on the general activation necessary to maintain a planned behavioral sequence. Using the field-body findings in this way fits quite well with my explanation of social disability stress.

Externality-Internality

One's belief about whether one can respond effectively to an event seems to have some generality, at least across a particular class of events such as the successful establishment of new relationships. This more or less generalized belief regarding social effectiveness has evaluative consequences for one's social behavior. *External salience* in perception dissociates appraisal from behavior (in contrast to *internality,* the perception that one's behavior modifies effects). If a perception is one of externality, an appraisal is not likely to be followed by initiating and experimenting. In this way, the belief serves as a threshold for an integrative sequence in coping with change.

CONCLUSION

This chapter presented evidence for the view that the status of the developing person in relation to his social environment may have effects on him that are relatively irreversible by most practical standards. If, indeed, stress impairment is built into the structure of behavior in sensitive periods early in life, it would be important to give a great deal more attention to the salience of the social environments of the young. What is required is a salience taxonomy of social environments *relative to individual differences* in mediating states. Furthermore, we need to know a great deal more about the relationship between these states and integrative mechanisms. Perhaps most of all, we need to know more about the subtle and diverse effects of power on the developing capability of the person to tolerate change and to make competent adaptations.

REFERENCES

CROMWELL, R. Assessment of schizophrenia. In M. R. Rosenzweig & L. W. Porter (eds.), *Annual Review of Psychology,* 1975, *26,* 593–620.

DOHRENWEND, B. P., & DOHRENWEND, B. S. Social and cultural influences on psychopathology. In M. R. Rosenzweig & L. W. Porter (eds.), *Annual Review of Psychology,* 1974, *25,* 417–452.

ERLENMEYER-KIMLING, L., VAN DEN BOSCH, E., & DENHAM, B. The problem of birth order and schizophrenia: A negative conclusion. *British Journal of Psychiatry,* 1969, *115,* 659–678.

ESCALONA, S. K. Patterns of infantile experience and the developmental process. *Psychoanalytic Study of the Child,* 1963, *18,* 197–244.

ESCALONA, S. *Roots of individuality.* Chicago: Aldine, 1968.

FLAVELL, J. H. *The developmental psychology of Jean Piaget.* Princeton: Van Nostrand, 1963.

FONTANA, A. F. Familial etiology of schizophrenia: Is a scientific methodology possible? *Psychological Bulletin,* 1966, *66,* 214–227.

HUNT, J. McV., *Intelligence and experience.* New York: Ronald, 1961.

————. Psychological development: Early experience. In M. R. Rosenzweig & L. W. Porter (eds.), *Annual Review of Psychology,* 1979, *30,* 103–144.

LEVINE, S. Psychophysiological effects of early stimulation. In E. L. Bliss (ed.) *Roots of behavior,* New York: Hoeber, 1961.

MURPHY, L. Factors in continuity and change in the development of adaptational styles in children. *Vita Humana,* 1964, *7,* 96–114.

PHILLIPS, L. *Human adaptation and the failures.* New York: Academic, 1968.

ROSENZWEIG, M. R. Environmental complexity, cerebral change and behavior. *American Psychologist,* 1966, *21,* 321–332.

SCHLESINGER, E. G., & SCHATZ, J. L. Competence and social disability: A conceptual framework for HBSE content. *Journal of Education for Social Work,* 1977, *13,* 84–90.

THOMPSON, W. R., & GRUSEC, J. Studies of early experience, In Paul Mussen (ed.), *Carmichael's manual of child psychology,* vol. 1. New York: Wiley, 1970.

VANCE, E. T. Social disability. *American Psychologist,* 1973, *28,* 498–511.

————. A typology of risk and the disabilities of low status. In G. Albee & J. Joffe (eds.), *The primary prevention of psychopathology,* vol. 1.

WHITE, R. W. Motivation reconsidered: The concept of competence. *Psychological Review,* 1959, *66,* 297–333.

————. Strategies of adaptation: An attempt at systematic description. In B. V. Coelho, D. A. Hamburg, & J. E. Adams (eds.), *Coping and adaptation.* New York: Basic Books, 1974.

WITKIN, H., DYK, R. W., PATERSON, H. F., GOODENOUGH, D. N., & KARP, S. A. *Psychological differentiation: Studies of development.* New York: Wiley, 1962.

ZUCKERMAN, M. Sensation seeking and its biological correlates. *Psychological Bulletin,* 1980, *88,* 187–214.

31

Adolescence and Stress

Anne C. Petersen   Ralph Spiga

ADOLESCENCE IS A FRUITFUL STAGE OF LIFE during which to examine stress. There are clear stresses impinging on individuals at this age, and patterns of responses to stress have developed to the point that they can be readily examined; moreover, such patterns are somewhat predictive of later stress responsiveness.

In this chapter we view stress from a developmental perspective. Development is a complex process involving interactions within the individual and between the individual and the environment. The systems view of development, sometimes called *biopsychosocial development* (Petersen, 1980), takes into account the complex interactions or transactions that occur among biological, cognitive, affective, and behavioral aspects within the individual, as well as between any of these aspects and features of the external social and physical environment. Furthermore, this process involves reciprocal influences between aspects. Individuals are stressed by the environment, but they also can create stress.

During adolescence there are clear changes in biological, cognitive, social, and affective functioning. At the same time, the immediate and the larger social environment of developing young people changes. Thus, many features essential for complete understanding of stress at adolescence are undergoing change. Indeed, the nature and timing of changes at adolescence are stressful to many young people.

In this chapter we propose to present a model for understanding stress at adolescence, review the evidence on the applicability of this model, and indicate some questions for future research.

THEORIES OF STRESS AT ADOLESCENCE

Although no theories have specifically addressed stress during adolescence, some theories have implications for understanding stress at this time. Prevalent in views of adolescent development is the notion that biological change causes severe disruption in psychological status. This theory, first proposed by Hall (1904) and later elaborated by Blos (1962), Freud (1958), and others, suggests that adolescents must pass through a near-psychotic state

The preparation of this paper was supported by grant MH30252 to A. Petersen. We are grateful for the comments and suggestions of R. Lerner.

because of the disruption experienced in biological status. There is little empirical evidence to support this perspective. First, several studies have shown that not all adolescents pass through the tumultuous phase so often described in clinical and popular literature (e.g., Douvan & Adelson, 1966; Grinker, Orinker, & Timberlake, 1962; Offer, 1969; Offer & Offer, 1975). Second, there is no evidence that biological changes directly effect psychological changes at this time (see Petersen & Taylor, 1980, for a complete discussion of this view). Further research may, of course, demonstrate direct effects of hormones on moods or other psychological manifestations in puberty, but currently we have no evidence to support such a view.

A second approach to understanding stress at adolescence is similar to the stressful life events approach that has focused primarily on the events of adulthood such as divorce, changing of jobs, or death (e.g., Dohrenwend & Dohrenwend, 1974). This approach might be extended to adolescents and generalized to include normative developmental changes as well as unpredictable events. Coleman's (1978) *focal theory* posits that adolescents become distressed when the usual developmental changes of adolescence take place concurrently rather than sequentially. In support of this view of stress at adolescence, Simmons, Blyth, Van Cleave, and Bush (1979) found that changing schools at seventh grade, beginning dating, becoming pubertal, and being a girl all contributed to increased difficulties. Girls who had begun menstruating, begun dating, and moved into a junior high school had lower self-esteem, more behavior problems, and lower grades than girls and boys (mutatis mutandis) who had not experienced such changes. Other research has shown that at this age unpredictable life experiences may have an impact on psychological status (Andreasen & Wasek, 1980; Coddington, 1979; Gersten, Langer, Eisenberg, & Orzik, 1974). For example, adolescents whose parents are divorced or alcoholic, who have lost a boyfriend or girlfriend, or who have lost a parent through death are more likely to report feeling down and blue, be truant, engage in sex, or be chronic runaways.

In our view, a model for explaining stress at adolescence must consider not only stressors at this time but also individual characteristics. The development that precedes the adolescent years surely may either strengthen or weaken the maturing individual. Previous development includes individual characteristics, as well as important features of the individual's environment, such as family influences, socioeconomic status, and nutrition. Since environments, as well as individual response styles, are likely to remain consistent into the adolescent years, there is substantial overlap between previous development and development at adolescence. Furthermore, an individual's responses to predictable stresses at adolescence are likely to be mediated by the degree of preparation for such changes, along with the timing of the changes.

THE STRESSES OF ADOLESCENT DEVELOPMENT

Biological Development

Pubertal development, with its physiological and psychosocial correlates, is presumed to have a vast impact on developing young people. Everything from juvenile delinquency to adolescent trumoil to moodiness in young adolescents has, at some time, been attributed to pubertal changes. Such attributions suggest a view of puberty as a stressful experience. As with many stresses, however, pubertal change involves the opportunity for psychosocial growth. Puberty signals growth to adult appearance, as well as the development of mature reproductive capacity. These changes can be viewed as opportunities for adaptation and are not necessarily negative. An important feature of puberty, particularly in studies of stress, is its inevitability and universality in healthy young people.

Petersen and Taylor (1980) described the internal and external changes that characterize puberty. Many hormones show fivefold increases over their prepubertal levels. While prepubertal boys and girls are similar in their levels of circulating gonadal hormones, mature boys have much higher levels of testosterone, the most potent male hormone, and mature girls have markedly elevated levels of estradiol, the most potent female hormone. In addition, hormones in girls begin the cyclic fluctuations that underlie the menstrual cycle. Because they are more visible, the changes in physical appearance during puberty may be even more important than the endocrine changes. Growth in height and weight accelerates and then terminates. Accompanying the increase in size are related increases in heart rate and blood pressure. In addition to obtaining adult size during this period, adolescents also achieve mature reproductive capacity.

Thus, puberty involves dramatic internal endocrine changes, as well as equally dramatic external physical changes. Except for infancy, no other life stage involves such extensive biological changes. What distinguishes puberty from infancy is that young people experience both these changes in themselves and the responses of others to the changes.

While pubertal change is quite dramatic, there is no evidence that these biological changes alone produce any behavioral effects in developing young people. Given the complex nature of human development, we are not surprised by the lack of evidence for direct hormonal effects. The visible physical changes of puberty, however, are likely to show influence by virtue of their social and psychological stimulus value and meaning. The way in which pubertal changes are understood and responded to by others probably mediates the individual's response to the biological events.

While we question the assumption that the internal biological changes associated with puberty directly affect other aspects of the developing adolescent, we nevertheless believe that the external, visible aspects of pubertal development in a cohort of young people set off the various other changes that occur at early adolescence. Some of the linkages between pubertal changes and other aspects of change occur at an individual level. For example, an adultlike appearance will initiate expectations from peers and adults for more adult behavior. But changes also take place on a societal level resulting from pubertal change. For example, schools in our society are organized, in part, to group adolescents according to average pubertal status. Junior high schools, and more recently middle schools, serve the function of removing pubertal youth from prepubertal children. High schools similarly isolate youth who are generally adult in appearance from pubertal youth.

Therefore, our society has two mechanisms for attaining adult status: biological maturation and social conventions such as rites of passage, as well as grade related social structural changes in schools and other youth serving institutions. Table 31–1 lists the changes in the biological and social spheres. Disjunctions between these two routes can themselves be stressful. A girl who is biologically mature in the fifth grade may appear to be older than her psychosocial self, which may be more consistent with socially detined adolescence. Similarly, a biologically immature boy may feel quite uncomfortable in the social setting of ninth grade because of the lack of synchrong between the biological and social timetables.

This view of pubertal change as primary to other changes at adolescence does not imply that other changes occur only after puberty. Secondary social changes such as the effect of the entire cohort experiencing puberty, have an impact beyond that associated with an in-

TABLE 31-1
Biological and Social Changes at Adolescence

Biological	Social
Endocrine	Rites of passage (religious confirma-
Reproductive capacity	tion, bar mitzvah; sweet sixteen
Secondary sex characteristics	parties, debutante balls)
Adult size	School structure
	Legal status (military conscription;
	drinking; driving; voting)

dividual's pubertal change. This means that an early maturer may experience a lag in expectations of adult behavior relative to an adolescent who reaches puberty "on time." Similarly, a late maturer may experience expectations for adult behavior despite a yet childish appearance.

Cognitive Change

Discussions of adolescence always mention the change believed to occur during these years in the quality of thinking. According to Piaget's (Inhelder & Piaget, 1968) paradigm, young people develop the capacity to think about thinking during the adolescent years. While we believe that these changes do occur in many youths, studies have shown that not all young people develop this capacity during adolescence. (e.g., Elkind, 1975). Indeed, only about half the adults in this country show this Piagetian-type capacity for abstract thinking (Elkind, 1975). The reasons for the failure of some adults in our society to show abstract thought remain unclear. Possibilities, however, include bias in the instruments used to assess abstract thought and lack of proper stimulation for the development of abstract thought. In any case, the capacity to reflect on one's thoughts does have implications for responsiveness to stress. Indeed, the emergence of the capacity for abstract thinking in relation to pubertal change may be a key factor in the nature of responses to that change. We would expect the nature of this interaction to be complex. On the one hand, it may be easier to cope with pubertal change viewed simply as a change in appearance, as a concrete thinker might do. On the other hand, the nature of the responses of others, particularly adults, to pubertal change *is* complex and this stage may be less confusing to a young adolescent who has the cognitive capacity to take the perspective of another person, to understand the broader meaning of pubertal change biologically and socially, and to recognize that the adolescent is not responsible for the responses of others. Given that there has been almost no research on this topic, we cannot be sure about what role cognitive change plays here. Does cognitive change amplify the stress associated with puberty or does it facilitate coping?

Social Change

Peers. During adolescence, particularly early adolescence, conformity to the peer group peaks (Berndt, 1979; Costanzo & Shaw, 1966). Young people show a shift in the persons having influence upon them, from parents to peers. Parents do not necessarily decline in importance to young people; rather, peers increase in importance.

The conformity seen in young adolescents may result from the changes in pubertal status. Among boys, greater size and increased strength are highly valued and important to group status, as well as to self-esteem (Kavrell & Jarcho, 1980). Among girls, the most important status criterion is being on time (Wilen, 1980). This need to be normative with respect to the timing of puberty explains the mixed results obtained in various studies, with some finding increased (e.g., Jones & Mussen, 1958) and others finding decreased (e.g., Stolz & Stolz, 1944) social status related to pubertal status. The key factor is the age, and hence the normative pubertal status, of girls studied. Studies of older girls find earlier maturation to be better, while studies of younger girls find the reverse (Faust, 1960).

But how does pubertal status affect peer conformity? We believe that the answer is suggested by Festinger's (1954) *theory of social comparison*. Festinger argued that uncertainty about what standards are being used leads individuals to turn to others who are similar to themselves in order to determine appropriate behavior. This notion was supported by a study that demonstrated that subjects made fearful by anticipation preferred the company of subjects who faced the possibility of electric shock; those not so aroused preferred no company (Schachter, 1959). Presumably, waiting for shock—a novel situation to undergraduates—increased the desire for social comparison, which was manifested by a need for affiliation.

Adolescents are in a situation similar to that faced by the subjects waiting for shock. The adolescent is confronted by changed and conflicting expectations, as well as by increased social demands. Uncertainty about the capacity to adapt causes the adolescent to look to peers not only for ways to adapt but also for comparisons against which to measure his or her actions. Most important, during this period of dramatic physical change, the standard for appropriate body shape and size is in flux and therefore body image creates confusion. The adolescent may use the visible progress of others as a yardstick against which to assess his or her own progress. The ambiguity of the adolescent's relation to his or her body and the social milieu together exert a powerful drive toward behavioral uniformity in the group.

Although the group of peers may help the individual adolescent to measure and validate progress, as well as to define his or her relationship to changed social and institutional demands, there may be some cost to the individual. Uniformity may be achieved at the expense of a reduced tolerance for even the slightest deviations from normative values. Thus, adolescents who deviate from the norm in terms of pubertal appearance, social skill, or values may be subject ot social ridicule, pressure, and censure. Unless alternative sources of social validation and support can be found, the loss of status and esteem implied by the social censure may lead to reduced self-regard and resentment (Pepitone & Wolpizeski, 1960). Furthermore, adolescents find themselves in peer situations with which they have no experience. For example, they must now behave wisely about drug use and sexuality, even though they often have had no instructions on or previous experiences with such matters.

School.　Another social change occurring during adolescence involves school structure. There are a variety of arrangements for grouping adolescents in schools and the rationales for these arrangements seem to relate to assumptions about the impact of pubertal change, as well as about sexual and other behaviors. Not only is the size of young people considered, but the likelihood of engaging in or being influenced to engage in various deviant behaviors is also of concern. Today both middle schools (grades six to eight or sometimes five to eight) and junior high schools (grades seven to eight or sometimes seven to nine) serve to separate pubertal youth from their older and younger peers. The ultimate reason for particular school arrangements probably depends more on finances and available buildings, although developmental or stress related arguments are often made.

These school structure issues are important for understanding stress at adolescence for two reasons. First, the social arrangements for adolescents are based implicitly or explicitly on assumptions about the best ways to meet the social and educational needs of youth and hence to facilitate coping and to relieve stress. Second, there is research evidence that school structures do have differentially stressful influence on adolescents.

Indeed, the school may provide major stress during the adolescent years. In early adolescence, young people in our society move from a single classroom, with one teacher and the same group of classmates, into a middle school or junior high school, where they pass from class to class, most often with different teachers and different students. For many young people, this transition may be smooth, but for others it appears to be untimely and stressful. The research of Simmons and colleagues (Simmons et al., 1979) referred to earlier, suggested that for adolescents experiencing other changes, the change in school environment at this age is particularly stressful.

Little research has focused on the transition from eighth or ninth grade into senior high school. Research with early adolescents, however, would suggest that this change also involves stress. The major difference between a junior high school and a senior high is size. For some young people, increased size means increased opportunities—for friends, for activities, for excelling. However, for other young people, particularly those for whom the demands of junior high school are difficult, senior high school may bring only larger and more frequent disappointments. Smaller school size has, in general, been found to contribute to higher achievement (Barker & Gump, 1964).

Parents. Relationships with parents also change during this time. Probably as much because of adult size as because of other factors (e.g., threats to sexuality, reminders of parental aging), the adolescent's relationships with his or her parents must undergo alterations. This transition in the nature of the adolescent-parent relationship may proceed smoothly, but it also may be very difficult. The capacity of the parents themselves to change appears pivotal in this adolescent transition.

Steinberg and Hill (1978) studied a sample of pubertal boys and found that family interaction pattern changed as a function of pubertal status, with the boys becoming more power assertive. The gain of the boys was made at the expense of the mothers. This result suggests to us that physical size, as well as sex role relations, may be important factors influencing conflict and interpersonal relationships at this age.

Interactions between parents and adolescents may be stressful because of sexual overtones. If a parent feels stimulated by the newly mature appearance of the adolescent, she or he may define certain behaviors such as expressions of affection or touching as sexual and therefore as incestuous and forbidden. While sexual encounters between child and parent may take place prior to puberty, the appearance in the adolescent of secondary sex characteristics may generate new and perhaps frightening feelings in the parent. If the parent is frightened and anxious, he or she may become less demonstrative, causing distress to the adolescent. Alternatively, the parent may express feelings of attraction for the adolescent, either explicitly or implicitly. Or a parent might transmit mixed messages. In any case, most adolescents are ill equipped to deal with such sexual messages; any of them is likely to cause anxiety and perhaps rebellious behavior on the part of the adolescent.

Particularly if the adolescent is a firstborn child, entry into adolescence may remind the parent of his or her own advancing age. For some parents this may be an unwelcome reminder. Such parents might respond to the adolescent's new status with denial or resent-

TABLE 31–2
Developmental Stresses of Adolescence

Puberty	Adult appearance and size
	Reproductive capacity
	Timing (especially if deviant)
	Internal endocrinological changes
	Asynchrony (among body parts, among adolescents)
Cognition	Capacity for abstract thought
Peer group	Conformity
	Pressure to try new experiences
School	Changing school structure and format
Parents	Parental responses to adult size of adolescent
	Sexual stimulation
	Implications for parents' aging
	Impending separation
Society	Hopes and expectations for youth
	Occupational choices and opportunities

ment. Another reaction might be to overestimate the adolescent's potency and threat, as was seen in the glorification of youthfulness particularly prevalent in the 1960s and seventies.

Finally, the adolescent status of the child reminds the parent that separation is pending, at least among most groups in our society. This prospect may be either welcomed or feared.

Society. Society itself stresses adolescents. Once young people begin to look like adults, they are expected to behave like adults. While this is a reasonable expectation, it often occurs abruptly. The change in expectations is probably a consequence of the definition by parents and teachers of the young person as adolescent. For example, adolescent interest in heterosexual behavior is expected. However, feelings of attraction for an opposite-sex peer may be anxiety producing because of the associated expectations about dating behavior. Expressing interest in a peer becomes linked to a variety of other feelings about proceeding in the right way and, most important, to the fear of rejection. Lack of experience with such behaviors, together with intense pressure, both internal and external, to perform them understandably causes great anxiety among young adolescents. Also stressful may be the actual options available to adolescents in terms of future educational and occupational opportunities.

The various developmental stresses of adolescence are summarized in Table 31–2. Many of these stresses are interrelated, as we discussed. In addition, individuals will be affected by stress to differing degrees. Some factors mediating developmental stress responses are discussed next.

MEDIATORS OF STRESS

The *timing* of the developmental stresses of adolescence can be an important factor in how the individual copes. Onset of puberty, for example, is important to the responses of both boys and girls. For boys, earlier timing is better, while for girls being on time is best (Tobin-Richards, Boxer, & Petersen, in press; Wilen & Petersen, in press). In Coleman's (1978) model, the concurrent timing of developmental changes is more difficult than sequential timing.

In general, it is believed that *preparation* for experiences leads to better coping and adaptation. There is some support for this belief in general (Bandura, 1977), as well as with adolescents (Petersen, in press). Indeed, many health interventions or education programs are based on these assumptions (Perry, in press).

Of course, *individual vulnerability* may amplify the effect of any stressor. The risk research of Garmezy, Devine, and Tellegen (1980) demonstrated that some children and adolescents are relatively invulnerable to stress while others succumb readily. The availability of *social supports,* particularly parents, can moderate the effects of stress and enhance coping. Petersen (1981) found that adolescents who reported having better relationships with parents and more frequent communication with them also had higher self-esteem and more positive emotional tone. Better relations and frequent communication with parents may effectively prepare the adolescent for stress. Parents may provide information about what to ignore, what to attend to, and how to cope with challenges or threats. Parents may reduce the adolescent's anger and rage by allowing expression of the difficulties and providing empathy. Peers may play the same role. Social support assists the adolescent's efforts at mastering stress.

Thus, the timing of developmental changes, the extent of preparation for the changes, individual vulnerability, and social supports all serve to mediate the effects of developmental stress in adolescence. These same mediators also operate with unpredictable stresses. Timing, (lack of) preparation, individual vulnerability, and social support have all been found to modify the experience of such stressful life events as the death of a loved one.

RESPONSES TO STRESS AT ADOLESCENCE

As we noted earlier, pubertal changes in bodily configuration stimulate a response from the adolescent's social milieu. This response entails the definition of many new roles, each with differing rights and responsibilities. Although the rights and responsibilities of some of these roles, like the teenage role, are similar for all members of the culture, the demands of many of these new roles are mediated by the unique developmental history of the individual, as well as by the specific social situation of the adolescent. Thus, the normative role stresses of adolescence are experienced differently by each individual.

The adolescent response to stressors is the outcome of a complex interplay between behavioral and physiological factors. The challenge of negotiating and adopting these roles requires from the adolescent an ability to observe situational cues; to comprehend the meaning of situational demands in relation to individual, famalial, peer, and societal values; to define and select from among alternative plans of action; and, finally, to consummate plans. The capacity of the adolescent to engage in this problem-solving process might be hampered by any of the adolescence-specific factors, as well as by general factors. An example of an adolescent-specific factor is limitation in cognitive development. A more likely developmental limitation, however, is the adolescent's inexperience with many of the situations confronted during these years (see Petersen, in press). Novelty and uncertainty may bring increased anxiety, as well as awkwardness in performing new tasks.

Behavioral Responses

Much of the adolescent's behavioral effort is directed at mastering the stresses accompanying puberty. The individual masters stress by reducing to tolerable limits the intrapsychic and affective arousal induced by stressors, by altering the relation of a stressor to, or by removing the threat (Caplan, 1981). Affective arousal, as well as conscious feelings of shame, anger, anxiety, and depression, is reduced by such defense mechanisms as isloation, denial, and intellectualization (Freud, 1966). Research has shown that these defenses reduce both the affective consequences of threat and the associated physiological arousal (Knight, Atkins, Eagle, Evans, Finkelstein, Fukushima, Katz, & Weiner, 1979).

The adolescent's ability to remove a threat is influenced by his or her feelings of efficacy (Bandura, 1977). Such feelings arise from past experiences of efficacy, as well as from self-confidence and self-esteem. This self-understanding allows the adolescent to sustain the effort demanded by the challenges of puberty.

Coping with stress is a reciprocal process, part of an ongoing transaction between the individual's behaviors and the external and internal environments (Roskies & Lazarus, 1980). Such a model presumes that the individual's actions change the environment, which in turn becomes the context for subsequent action (cf. Lerner & Busch-Rossnagel, 1981).

Physiological Responses

Some aspects of physiological response at adolescence may impair the decisionmaking process, though little research has addressed this possibility. Increased physiological arousal is the common response to experiences such as the stress of adolescence (Frankenhaeuser, 1975; Hennesscy & Levine, 1979; Warburton, 1980). Although low levels of physiological arousal facilitate cognitive functioning, higher levels impair cognitive functioning.

The neuroendocrine arousal response may also affect the emotional behavior of the individual (Anisman, 1979; Hamburg, Hamburg, & Barchas, 1975). Changes in endogenous amine levels as measured by amine metabolites in urine have been associated with depression and anger. However, this relationship is a complicated one and may involve interaction with such hormones as cortisol and adrenocorticotrophic hormone. Although young adolescents do not differ from adults in baseline levels of biogenic amines (Ordy, Kaack, & Brizce, 1975), research suggests that for younger animals the rate of depletion and resynthesis of these amines is more rapid in response to stress (Ritter & Pelzer, 1978). If these results are applicable to human adolescents, then pubertal youths may have more physiological elasticity in the face of stress.

The physiological responses to the stresses of adolescence may have implications for adult well-being. A pattern of behavior characterized by extreme competitiveness, hostility, and impatience has been identified as the type A personality (Friedman & Rosenman, 1974). A body of research on the *type A personality* has established that these persons are twice as likely to suffer a myocardial infarction and to show evidence of atherosclerosis earlier than persons not exhibiting the type A pattern (Blumenthal & Williams, 1979; Jenkins, 1976). Our own research (Spiga & Petersen, 1981) suggests that type A behavior intensifies as children move from grammar to junior high school. Butensky, Farralli, Heebner, and Waldron (1976) showed that the expression of components of this pattern, such as impatience and irritability, increased over the high school years and was greater for suburban school children (the latter finding was attributed to the greater number of role opportunities and related demands faced by this group). The Bogolusa Heart Study (Hunter, 1981) found that irritability and urgency, both components of the coronary-prone pattern, were related to baseline serum cholesterol and blood pressure levels in children 10–17 years of age. Although in type A adults, an association between components of the pattern and baseline cholesterol and blood pressure levels is not generally found, Hunter's finding might be explained by the fact that children at this age are likely to be facing increased academic demands, uncertainty about role requirements, and conflicts between their own values and the expectations of others. In adults, such indexes have been related to heart disease and elevated levels of serum cholesterol (House, 1975).

An understanding of the physiological responses to stress and their relation to stressors in the environment might enhance our understanding of the development of psychopathology in adolescence. For example, some clinicians argue that adolescent impulsiveness may reflect the biological changes accompanying or characterizing depression (Toolan, 1968). Alternatively, as suggested earlier, such behavior might result from anxiety caused by stressful new experiences, together with limited skills to respond appropriately; rapid changes in physiological responsiveness would also add to feelings of anxiety.

Affective Responses

The longitudinal changes in adolescent emotional tone and self-image observed by Petersen (1981) and by Simmons and associates (1979) may be a manifestation of the complex intrapsychic work required to master the stresses of puberty. Research with individuals who had experienced a trauma showed that their response was phasic (Horowitz, 1979). The phases, in order of occurrence, following the trauma are *denial, intrusion,* and *working through.* Each of these phases is characterized by changes in the functioning of the individual's attention cognition and ideation, emotions, physiology, and capacity for self-control. Immediately following trauma the individual may deny or avoid the ideational and emotional consequences of the event. During the next period, ideas and feelings about, as well as symbolic reenactments of, the distressing event intrude into conciousness. In the final phase of working through, the individual integrates information about his or her response to the trauma with prior understandings of self, of the way life is, and the relation between the two.

For some adolescents, the dramatic physical changes of puberty may initiate a similar sequence. The working through stage then becomes a process whereby the adolescent integrates his or her understandings of the implications of these physical changes with their social and vicariously acquired meanings. The constant transaction among physical changes, social events, and cognitive processing results in what is often referred to as "character" (Blos, 1968). The cognitive contents of this process have been best described by psychodynamically oriented writers (Blos, 1979; Kestenberg, 1967a, 1967b; 1968).

Clearly, not all adolescents experience puberty as a trauma. Indeed, for many young people these changes are accommodated and assimilated smoothly (Tobin-Richards, Boxer, & Petersen, in press). It will be important for future research to identify the adolescents for whom puberty is traumatic. One such group consists of early maturing girls (Petersen, 1981a); another may be anorexics.

CONCLUSION

This chapter argued that puberty is likely to influence psychological status because of the meaning that it has both socially and psychologically. We believe that pubertal change achieves its influence by affecting the adolescent's interaction with his or her social milieu. The social responses initiated by normative developmental changes include changes in institutional structures and social expectations.

In our model (Figure 31–1) the physiological, behavioral, and affective responses of the

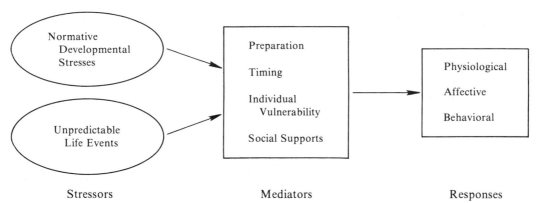

FIGURE 31-1. A model for stress and stress responsiveness at adolescence.

individual are the outcome of the interplay of these forces. Furthermore, the individual's responses to the stresses of puberty are mediated by the timing of puberty, by preparation, by individual vulnerability, and by social supports. While little is known from longitudinal studies about the specific relations among normative developmental changes, unpredictable life events, timing, and preparation, as well as behavioral, physiological, and affective responses, there is some evidence to support the model we have presented (e.g., Simmons et al., 1979). Both person and context measures need to be assessed in this model.

In the opening paragraph of this chapter we suggested that the adolescent's responses to stress might be predictive of later stress responsiveness. We think that the relation between adolescent and adult responsiveness can be understood only through a clear understanding of what stresses pubertal youths experience and how they master these stresses.

This chapter focused on stresses at adolescence related to puberty. These stresses are particularly important during early adolescence and may affect coping both during subsequent stages of adolescence and in adulthood. We do not mean to imply, however, that all stresses during adolescence are linked to puberty. The process of looking like an adult is the first step toward becoming an adult, but there are many other developmental tasks for the adolescent to master en route to adulthood. Lack of experience leads to deficits in skill and judgment, which in turn decrease feelings of efficacy and increase feelings of stress and anxiety. This sequence can be observed in a range of behaviors—from driving to interpersonal relationships to substance use.

A comprehensive model of stress in adolescence would consider all the new expectations on the adolescent, together with the individual's skills, self-esteem, and social supports. Such a model would permit assessment of developmental stress, situational stress, and individual stress, together with evaluation of coping resources in the individual and the environment. In this way, we might be able to identify who most needs intervention and how that intervention should be provided. The ultimate solution to stress at adolescence is adulthood, but many adult, as well as adolescent, years would be improved with effective intervention during adolescence.

REFERENCES

ANDREASEN, N. C. & WASEK, P. Adjustment disorders in adolescents and adults. *Archives of General Psychiatry,* 1980, *37,* 1166–1170.

ANISMAN, H. Neurochemical changes elicited by stress. In H. Anisman & G. Bignami (eds.), *Psychopharmacology of adversively motivated behavior.* New York: Plenum, 1978.

BANDURA, A. Self-efficacy: Toward a unifying theory of behavioral change. *Psychological Review,* 1977, *84,* 191–215.

BARKER, R. G., & GUMP, P. V. *Big school, small school.* Stanford: Stanford University Press, 1964.

BERNDT, T. J. Developmental changes in conformity to peers and parents. *Developmental Psychology,* 1979, *15,* 608–616.

BLOS, P. *On adolescence: A psychoanalytic interpretation.* New York: Free Press, 1962.

————. Character formation in adolescence. *The Psychoananlytic Study of the Child,* 1968, *23,* 245–263.

————. *The adolescent passage: Developmental issues.* New York: International Universities, 1979.

BLUMENTHAL, J. A., & WILLIAMS, R. B. Association of coronary heart disease and the type A pattern: An overview. Paper presented to the annual meeting of the American Psychological Association, New York City, 1979.

BLYTH, D. A., SIMMONS, R. G., & BUSH, D. The transition into early adolescence: A longitudinal comparison of youth in two educational contexts. *Sociology of Education,* 1978, *51,* 149–162.

BUTENSKY, A., FARRALLI, V., HEEBNER, D., & WALDRON, I. Elements of the coronary prone behavior pattern in children and teenagers. *Journal of Psychosomatic Research,* 1975, *20,* 439–444.

CAPLAN, G. Mastery of stress: Psychosocial aspects. *American Journal of Psychiatry,* 1981, *138,* 413–420.

CODDINGTON, R. D. Life events associated with adolescent pregnancies. *Journal of Youth and Adolescence,* 1978, *7,* 1–12.

COLEMAN, J. C. Current contradictions in adolescent theory. *Journal of Youth and Adolescence,* 1978, *7,* 1–11.

COSTANZO, P. R., & SHAW, M. E. Conformity as a function of age level. *Child Development,* 1966, *37,* 967–975.

DOHRENWEND, B. S. & DOHRENWEND, B. P. *Stressful life events: Their nature and effects.* New York: Wiley, 1974.

DOUVAN, E., & ADELSON, J. *The adolescent experience.* New York: Wiley, 1966.

ELKIND, D. Recent research on cognitive development in adolescence. In S. E. Dragastin & G. H. Elder Jr. (eds.), *Adolescence in the life cycle.* New York: Halstead, 1975.

FAUST, M. S. Developmental maturity as a determinant of prestige in adolescent girls. *Child Development,* 1960, *31,* 173–184.

FESTINGER, L. A. A theory of social comparison processes. *Human Relations,* 1954, *7,* 117–140.

FRANKENHAEUSER, M. Experimental approaches to the study of catecholamines and emotion. In L. Levi (ed.), *Emotions: Their parameters and measurement.* New York: Raven, 1975.

FRIEDMAN, M. & ROSENMAN, R. H. *Type A behavior and your heart.* New York: Knopf, 1974.

FREUD, A. Adolescence. In R. Eissler (ed.), *The psychoanalytic study of the child,* vol. 13. New York: International Universities, 1958.

————. *The ego and the mechanisms of defense.* New York: International Universities, 1966.

GARMEZY, N., DEVINE, V., & TELLEGEN, A. Research approaches to the study of stress-resistant children. Paper presented to the annual meeting of the American Psychological Association, Montreal, 1980.

GERSTEN, J. C., LANGER, T. S., EISENBERG, J. G., & ORZEK, L. Child behavior and life events. In B. S. Dohrenwend & B. P. Dohrenwend (eds.), *Stressful life events: Their nature and effects.* New York: Wiley, 1974.

GRINKER, R. R., GRINKER, R. R., JR., & TIMBERLAKE, I. Mentally healthy young males (homoclites). *Archives of General Psychiatry,* 1962, *6,* 311–318.

HALL, G. S. *Adolescence: Its psychology and its relations to physiology, anthropology, sociology, sex, crime, and education.* New York: Appleton, 1904.

HAMBURG, D., HAMBURG, B. A., & BARCHAS, J. D. Anger and depression in perspective of behavioral biology. In L. Levi (ed.), *Emotions—Their parameters and measurement*. New York: Raven, 1975.

HAMILTON, V., & WARBURTON, D. M. (eds.), *Human stress and cognition: An information processing approach*. New York: Wiley, 1980.

HENNESSY, J. W., & LEVINE, S. Stress, arousal, and the pituitary-adrenal system: A psychoendocrine hypothesis. In J. M. Sprague & A. N. Epstein (eds.), *Progress in psychobiology and physiological psychology*. New York: Academic, 1979.

HOROWITZ, M. J. *Stress response syndromes*. New York: Aronson, 1976.

————. *States of mind*. New York: Plenum, 1979.

HOUSE, J. S. Occupational stress as a precursor to coronary disease. In W. D. Gentry & R. B. WIlliams (eds.), *Psychological aspects of myocardial infarction and coronary care*. St. Louis: Mosby, 1975.

HUNTER, S. Physiology of stress in children. Paper presented to the Maryland State School Health Council, Ocean City, Maryland, 1981.

INHELDER, B., & PIAGET, J. *The growth of logical thinking from childhood to adolescence: An essay on the construction of formal operational structure*. New York: Basic Books, 1968.

JENKINS, C. D. Recent evidence supporting psychologic and social risk factors for coronary disease. *New England Journal of Medicine*, 1976, *294*, 987–1038.

JONES, M. C., & MUSSEN, P. H. Self-conceptions, motivations, and interpersonal attitudes of early- and late-maturing girls. *Child Development*, 1958, *29*, 491–501.

KAVRELL, S. H., & JARCHO, H. Self-esteem and body-image in early adolescence. Paper presented to the annual meeting of the American Psychological Association, Montreal, 1980.

KESTENBERG, J. Phases of adolescence with suggestions for a correlation of psychic and hormonal organization. Part I: Antecedents of adolescent organizations in childhood. *Journal of the American Academy of Child Psychiatry*, 1967, *6*, 426–463. (a)

————. Phases of adolescence with suggestions for a correlation of psychic and hormonal organization. Part II: Prepuberty, diffusion, and reintegration. *Journal of the American Academy of Child Psychiatry*, 1967, *6*, 577–614. (b)

————. Phases of adolescence with suggestions for a correlation of psychic and hormonal organization. Part III: Puberty growth, differentiation, and consolidation. *Journal of the American Academy of Child Psychiatry*, 1968, *7*, 108–151.

KNIGHT, R. B., ATKINS, A., EAGLE, C. J., EVANS, N., FINKELSTEIN, J. W., FUKOSHIMA, D., KATZ, J., & WEINER, H. Psychological stress, ego defenses, and cortisol production in children hospitalized for elective surgery. *Psychosomatic Medicine*, 1979, *41*, 40–50.

LERNER, R. M., & BUSCH-ROSSNAGEL, N. A. *Individuals as producers of their development: A life span perspective*. New York: Academic, 1981.

OFFER, D. *The psychological world of the teenager*. New York: Basic Books, 1969.

OFFER, D., & OFFER, J. *From teenage to young manhood*. New York: Basic Books, 1975.

ORDY, J. M., KAACK, B., & BRIZEE, K. B. Life span neurochemical changes in the human and non-human primate brain. In J. M. Ordy, B. Kaack, & K. B. Brizee (eds.), *Aging: Clinical, morphological, and neurochemical aspects in the aging nervous system*. New York: Raven, 1975.

PEPITONE, A., & WOLPIZESKI, C. Some consequences of experimental rejection. *Journal of Abnormal and Social Psychology*, 1960, *60*, 359–364.

PERRY, C. Adolescent health: An educational-ecological perspective. In T. J. Coates, A. C. Petersen, & C. Perry (eds.), *Adolescent health: Crossing the barriers*. New York: Academic, in press.

PETERSEN, A. C. Biopsychosocial development of sex-related differences. In J. Parsons (ed.), *Psychobiological bases of sex-role related behaviors*. Washington, D.C.: Hemisphere, 1980.

————. A developmental model for studying early adolescence. Manuscript, Laboratory for the Study of Adolescence, Chicago, 1981. (a)

————. Adolescent health: Developmental issues. In T. J. Coates, A. C. Petersen, & C. Perry (eds.), *Adolescent health: Crossing the barriers.* New York: Academic, in press b.

————. Menarche: Meaning of measures and measuring meaning. In S. Gotuo (ed.), *Menarche: An interdisciplinary view.* New York: Springer, in press.

PETERSEN, A. C., & TAYLOR, B. The biological approach to adolescence. In J. Adelson (ed.), *Handbook of adolescent psychology.* New York: Wiley, 1980.

RITTER, S., & PELZER, N. L. Magnitude of stress-induced brain norepinephrine depletion varies with age. *Brain Research,* 1978, *152,* 170–175.

ROSKIES, E., & LAZARUS, R. S. Coping theory and the teaching of coping skills. In P. O. Davidson & S. M. Davidson (eds.), *Behavioral medicine: Changing health life styles.* New York: Brunner/Mazel, 1980.

SAMORAGESKI, T. Age related changes in brain biogenic amines. In J. M. Ordy, B. Kaack, & K. B. Brizee (eds.), *Aging: Clinical, morphological, and neurochemical aspects in the aging nervous system.* New York: Raven, 1975.

SCHACHTER, S. *The psychology of affiliation.* Stanford: Stanford University Press, 1959.

SIMMONS, R. G., BLYTH, D. A., VAN CLEAVE, E. F., & BUSH, D. M. Entry into early adolescence: The impact of school structure, puberty, and early dating on self-esteem. *American Sociological Review,* 1979, *44,* 948–967.

SPIGA, R., & PETERSEN, A. C. The coronary prone behavior pattern in adolescence. Paper presented to the annual meeting of the American Educational Research Association, Los Angeles City, 1981.

STEINBERG, L. D., & HILL, J. P. Patterns of family interaction as a function of age, onset of puberty, and formal thinking. *Developmental Psychology,* 1978, *14,* 683–684.

STOLZ, H. R., & STOLZ, L. M. (eds.). Adolescent problems related to somatic variation. *Yearbook of the National Society for the Study of Education,* 1944, *43,* 81–99. In *Adolescence.* Chicago: University of Chicago Press, 1944.

TOBIN-RICHARDS, M., BOXER, A., & PETERSEN, A. C. The psychological impact of pubertal changes: Sex differences in perceptions of self during early adolescence. In J. Brooks-Gunn & A. C. Petersen (eds.), *Girls at puberty: Biological, psychological, and social perspectives.* New York: Plenum, in press.

TOOLAN, J. M. Depression in children and adolescents. *American Journal of Orthopsychiatry,* 1962, *32,* 404–414.

VAN HOUTEN, T., & GOLEMBIEWSKI, G. *Adolescent life stress as a predictor of alcohol abuse and/or runaway behavior.* Washington, D.C.: National Youth Alternatives Project, 1978.

WARBURTON, D. M. Physiological aspects of information processing and stress. In V. Hamilton & D. M. Warburton (eds.), *Human stress and cognition: An information processing approach.* New York: Wiley, 1980.

WILEN, J. The timing of pubertal changes and their psychological correlates. Paper presented to the annual meeting of the American Psychological Association, Montreal, 1980.

YAMAMOTO, K. Children's ratings of the stressfulness of experiences. *Developmental Psychology,* 1979, *15,* 580–581.

32

Challenge and Defeat: Stability and Change in Adulthood

Marjorie Fiske

CONSENSUS ON THEORIES AND METHODOLOGIES appropriate to the study of stress, coping, and adaptation is rare. Even more controversial is the complex and relatively new field of psychosocial change in adulthood, an area rich in literature of uneven merit. The objectives of this chapter on stress from a life course perspective must therefore be selective. My goal is to summarize evidence for continuity versus change both in the emotional and cognitive experience of what is stressful and in the buffers that help people deal with stress as they grow from young adulthood toward old age. In keeping with the flood of technological and social innovations, which affect all social strata, a recurrent theme will be social change as stress.

For centuries, theories of adult change were embedded in the humanities. Later, the biological sciences took up this subject. Empirical social and behavioral research on life course change appeared in Europe quite early in the nineteenth century and, as Reinert (1979) noted, Hall's works on adolescence (1904) and senescence (1922) were among the first reflections of interest in this country. Hall's contributions were followed by an early textbook of Hollingworth's (1927), a volume set firmly in a life span framework (Baltes, 1979). From then until the 1960s, interest in adult change was slight; the current multidisciplinary flourish spans little more than a decade. Some of this upsurge can be attributed to intriguing results from studies of children that were continued as the subjects grew to middle age and beyond. Such studies, especially those that include in-depth life histories, as well as structured tests, are at present the method of choice.

One-time surveys covering a broad age range and repeated with different samples frequently suggest life course change in attitudes, beliefs, and behavior, and many life course researchers have found results stimulating enough to pursue longitudinally. For example, some quite consistent differences among age cohorts and between the sexes in regard to stressful conditions in adult life have been reported. National surveys conducted by the University of Michigan's Institute for Social Research found that, among young adults, single women had much higher scores than did single men on indicators of psychological stress, but among young marrieds with no children, women ranked much lower on the stress index than did men. Widowed women in comparison with widowers (Campbell, Converse, & Rogers, 1976) also reported fewer stress symptoms. Among the divorced, on the other hand, in a 1957 survey by the institute, women were far more likely than men to report stress symptoms, and there was little change in this respect when the same questions were repeated with another sample about 20 years later (Institute for Social Research, 1979). A recent cross-sectional study of divorce (which has since become a longitudinal research program) also reported more distress among women than among men but only in the turbulent predecision period; once divorce proceedings had been initiated, men ranked higher on stress indicators (Chiriboga & Cutler, 1977). This sample ranged in age from 20 to 70, and among both men and women the youngest (in their twenties) were the least distressed, while those 50 and older were the most so.

The Michigan surveys cited earlier also reflect stresses linked to intervening social change. It appears that, in general, the lot of the young has deteriorated, while that of the old has improved. In 1957, about a third of the respondents reported that they worried always or a lot, with those 65 and older worrying the most. In a 1976 study, this life course trend was reversed: the oldest reported the least worry, while among people 21–39 nearly half ranked high on the worry scale, up from 30% in 1957 (Institute for Social Research, 1979). This pattern may not necessarily be susceptible to a straightforward interpretation, a possibility I consider later in discussing a longitudinal mental health study that identified the sociohistorical periods in which cohorts grew up and aged as at least as important in affecting life course change as was age per se.

The most comprehensive recent work on successive cross-sectional national surveys was done by Yankelovich (1981). This study, too, suggested differences across the stages of life in stressors and in stress responses. While in the 1960s mainly the young reported that they were searching for new meanings and for self-fulfillment, Yankelovich found such searching at present to be "an out-pouring of popular sentiment . . . an authentic grass roots phenomenon, involving as many as four-fifths of *all* adult Americans" (p. 39; italics supplied). Along with this search for change, and perhaps accounting for its feverish nature, come nostalgia and "a hungering for community" now lost. The one-fifth who maintained traditional values through to the 1980s (mainly rural dwellers—less privileged and somewhat older than the other respondents), whom Yankelovich called "weak formers," derived a sense of comfort from continuity. The four-fifths majority, though reporting symptoms of stress such as worry and anxiety, were not sufficiently distressed to return to old rules.

STRESS, COPING, AND MENTAL HEALTH

The extent to which cross-sectional studies, even if they repeat the same questions over time, may promote fallacies about life course change becomes apparent in both prestructured, quantitative and in-depth, longitudinal research. Let us consider the 20-year follow-up of the Midtown Manhattan Study, originally undertaken in 1955 (Srole, 1978; Srole, Langer, Michael, Opler, & Rennie, 1962). At the outset, the age range of the sample was 20–59; results pointed to a significant decline in mental health and adaptive modes with advancing age. If there is a general age linked deterioration, one would expect, with the youngest subjects now middle-aged and the oldest near 80, an even greater age linked impairment to prevail 20 years later. This was not the case.

Considered as simply another cross-sectional survey, the follow-up might seem to confirm the findings of the original study (Srole, et al., 1962). When, for example, the follow-up respondents were divided by age, the proportion severely impaired increased in successive age groups. The fallacy of such a conclusion can be demonstrated by comparing birthdate cohorts with themselves 20 years earlier. In such a comparison, age linked deterioration *decreases* (albeit not significantly) among all cohorts except the very youngest (20–29 at the baseline). The concept of the cohort, in fact, is the key to unraveling the paradox posed by these findings. Compared with people the same age in 1954, those aged 40–59 in 1974 had significantly fewer symptoms of mental impairment. Moreover, in each age cohort divided by sex, among men there was no significant difference in mental impairment rate between those who were 40–59 in 1954 and those who were the same age in 1974. On the other hand, among women, who in 1954 had nearly twice as many maladaptive symptoms as did their male cohort peers, there was a dramatic improvement, putting them by 1974 on a par with men of the same age. The link between psychological symptoms and self-appraisals of poor physical health being well established, it is not surprising that women improved in this sphere. In other words, subgroup analysis within a longitudinal framework shows that an age linked decline in coping and adaptation that appeared to hold true for women up to age 60 in 1954 was not found 20 years later. Here we see, across birthdate cohorts, evidence for consistency (among men) and change (among women) over a period that encompassed the latest version of a women's movement.

Subgroup qualitative analysis characterized Vaillant's (1977) follow-up study, at ages 47–52, of nearly 100 of the 268 elite-college men who initially participated in the Grant Study. The rich biographical material from baseline and intervening contacts enabled the author to trace unanticipated adaptive modes and levels of mental health at middle age. The Grant men were selected, by standards of the late 1930s and early 1940s, as outstanding in qualities and attributes considered predictive of high achievement and good adaptation in later life, yet several proved to be "perpetual boys" in the intervening quarter century. Others, from less privileged backgrounds and with fewer inner and outer resources while in college, became successful, mature, and loving adults. Throughout, Vaillant's work provides many clues as to why and how some of the Grant men developed strong and flexible adaptive modes, while others remained sophomoric; his in-depth case studies offer tentative answers to perplexing questions about change in the adult life course that cannot be illustrated in this short chapter.

While most people in all periods of life manage to sustain a bearable balance between change and stability, the extremes are worth noting. At one end are static people, who use socially or biographically inappropriate adaptive modes, such as Vaillant's (1977) perpetual boys or Yankelovich's (1981) weak formers, patterns recently evidenced by the so-called moral majority. At the other extreme are the top segment of Yankelovich's "strong formers", highly reminiscent of Lifton's (1976) "protean man."

In summing up the meaning of his own studies on the impact of several forms of change, or lack thereof, among people in a variety of life stages and cultures, Marris (1975) concluded that the human need for a degree of predictability (stability, continuity) is fundamental and universal. This need coexists with the equally fundamental need for innovation (change). His and other studies, in a variety of disciplines, have suggested that although there may be stressful exacerbation of the need for continuity as the individual grows older, the often positive changes of young adulthood and of the prime of life that bring with them a sense of discontinuity and loss of a real or imagined past may also produce stress.

FINDINGS FROM THE HUMAN DEVELOPMENT AND AGING PROGRAM

Longitudinal research conducted by the Human Development and Aging Program at the University of California, San Francisco, over nearly a quarter of a century has from the outset adopted a flexible paradigm of stress and adaptation. One of the principal objectives of this model has been to assess change and continuity in several domains. The current transitions study[1] grew directly out of 10 years of large-scale panel studies of normal and abnormal aging. This earlier research, begun in 1958, soon led to two conclusions: a stress adaptation paradigm is a very suitable model for reducing masses of data about older people who range in age from 60 to the late nineties (Lowenthal, Berkman, & Associates, 1967); moreover, to understand both stability and changeability in stress proneness, adaptive processes, and supportive resources, one needs to know much more about people in earlier periods of adulthood and about their childhood and adolescence as well. In the transitions study, the data on the latter are retrospective, based on in-depth life histories.

Having been the senior investigator in boths sets of studies, I cannot resist a rather sweeping generalization about changes in coping with aging; namely, there has been, among the middle and lower echelons of our society, a marked deterioration in the adaptive processes of late middle-aged and older people. The nature of this change might be summed up as retreatism, escapism, or a search for numbing, in pill form or otherwise. This trend has created a condition serious for both individual and society, for in their effort to protect themselves from the tensions and pressures of postindustrial technological culture, older people create a new form of stress for themselves, one unfortunately overlooked by most researchers: the passive stress of ennui. In reading the life histories of older people in the current studies, I felt nostalgic for the gusty personalities of the early 1960s. While these two longitudinal investigations are, of course, not strictly comparable, the reader may find support for this generalization in the remainder of the chapter.

Relative Deprivation and Stress Preoccupation in Adulthood

As Elder (1974, 1979) reported, severe deprivation in childhood or adolescence—his study looked at the Great Depression and its impact on family life and family structure—is about as likely to have good consequences in adulthood as poor. The often devastating effects of the depression on the child's family may provide a benchmark against which future familial and economic problems pale, in much the same way that experiencing the death of a close other when young may provide the individual with the reassuring knowledge that he or she can cope with the inevitable personal losses of middle and old age. Many people in Elder's (1979) middle-aged cohorts, like those in our study of transitions (Lowenthal, Thurnher, Chiriboga, & Associates, 1975), seemed to apply to their personal life course the sociological construct of *relative deprivation,* originally applied by scholars to self-assessments in relation to current reference groups. The individual, in other words, uses the former self as a referent other. But before exploring this relativity further, I should briefly note the difference between *exposure* to and preoccupation with, presumed stress in the life course.

Earlier work by the Human Development and Aging Program indicated that stress exposure, as well as stress preoccupation, varies enormously and changes over relatively short intervals (Lowenthal, Berkman and Associates, 1967). Furthermore, people who have been exposed to many stresses seem to differ from those who have experienced few. They are, for example, more complex, in both their inner and outer lives. While they have many inner and outer resources, at the same time they have more personal and social handicaps and deficiencies. Such people have broader perspectives, on both themselves and society, than do the lightly stressed and they are more growth oriented, insightful, and competent. In other words, they represent the kind of people who seek out a challenging lifestyle, which is bound to be stressful on occasion.

Persons who have experienced little stress, on the other hand, have more limited perspectives on themselves and the rest of the world; they also have fewer psychological and social handicaps and fewer inner and outer resources. Unlike people who have had a great many stressful experiences, they have long since adopted lifestyles that protect them from stress. When we divide these two groups into those who are and who are not very preoccupied with whatever stresses they are or were exposed to, we have a typology of four kinds of people, as Table 32–1 illustrates.

The *overwhelmed,* beset by many ostensibly stressful situations, dwell on them at length in discussing the ups and downs of their present and past; many, in fact, seem still to be living them through, even though their difficult experiences may have occurred in the remote past. The *challenged,* similarly besieged by many presumptive stresses or a few severe ones, are, in contrast, not excessively preoccupied with them. In recounting their life histories, they simply report, and perhaps briefly describe, such events and circumstances and then quickly move on to other topics that interest them more. The *self-defeating,* although they recount few stressful experiences, weight their life reviews heavily with themes of loss and deprivation, which they, like the overwhelmed, seem to be reliving with much of the original turmoil. On the other hand, the *lucky,* who also have had few or mild stresses, rarely discuss them, and loss is not a theme in their life stories. A few may report that they feel mysteriously protected or that luck has been on their side. While the more prosaic simply say, "I've been lucky, I guess," others speak of fate, the stars, or God, feeling that some mystical or magical force is protecting them. (In this context, it is perhaps important to recall that, according to recent surveys, a third of the people in the United States consider themselves to be born-again Christians [Vidal, 1978]; the proportions who report ESP experiences, consult astrologers, regularly read their horoscopes, or visit palm readers and other fortune-tellers regularly are equally impressive.)

In baseline assessments, about three-fifths of the subjects participating in the transitions study had expectable reactions to the situations judged stressful by the researchers who had developed the life events schedule used in the investigation. Slightly more than half the people who had experienced little stress were of the *lucky* type; Holmes and Rahe (1967) a slight majority of those who had experienced a great deal of stress were overwhelmed, that is, they have been highly stressed by normative standards, and dwell upon it at length. But this leaves a great many "deviants": about two-fifths of those who had experienced a great many of the presumed stresses fell into the challenged category; finally, among those exposed to very little stress, some 40% spoke as though their lives were an unending series of problems, i.e., they were self-defeating in orientation. Middle-aged men were far more likely to be challenged by considerable stress than were younger men, while both young and older lightly stressed men tended to consider themselves lucky. Severely stressed young women

TABLE 32–1
Stress Typology

	Preoccupation with stress	
Presumed stress	*Considerable*	*Little*
Frequent and/or severe	Overwhelmed	Challenged
Infrequent and/or mild	Self-defeating	Lucky

were more challenged than were middle-aged women (the ratio was three to one). Lightly stressed young women, unlike young men, reacted more negatively to little stress, whereas lightly stressed middle-aged women, like the middle-aged and the young men, tended to be in the lucky group. In situations of considerable stress, then, while many men rise to the occasion and are challenged, women seem to lose their stress tolerance: the great majority of the more severely stressed middle and late middle-aged women were overwhelmed. Details on operationalizing the preoccupation dimension of the typology appear in Lowenthal and Chiriboga (1973) (baseline) and Chiriboga (1977) (follow-up).

Subsequently, using data from several follow-up assessments of the sample, which represented four age groups ranging from high school seniors to people very close to retirement (see Lowenthal et al., 1975, on the sample's makeup), we were able to trace many changes. We found, for example, that middle-aged parents, now for the most part post–empty nest, reported the greatest increase in both positive and negative life events, while the now mainly retired oldest people reported more negative and fewer positive ones. The two younger groups reported fewer negative stressful events than did the two older, but, to our surprise, the young did not report as great an increase in positive changes as did the middle-aged. There were notable differences between these sexes at each life stage, too, and there also was evidence of change in stress preoccupation over a 10-year period (Chiriboga & Cutler, 1980). For example, newlyweds, who at the baseline had been highly preoccupied with positive life events, were now much less euphoric. By contrast, negatively preoccupied high school seniors had, by their late twenties, come to resemble those who had been newlywed at the baseline.

Aware of the pervasive assumption that the stresses of deprivation in childhood continue to have an impact on adaptive modes and stress levels in adulthood, we selected, as a simple indicator of life stress up to age 15, the loss or absence of one or both parents. What we found at the baseline was that in the two younger groups both men and women who had suffered such loss were less well adapted than were those who had not (Lowenthal & Chiriboga, 1975). Among the middle and late middle-aged, however, only women showed the effects of such deprivation. Subsequent follow-ups that used preoccupation with negative life events or circumstances as a criterion supported the original findings: middle-aged and older men (now averaging 66) who had lost one or both parents in childhood had further declined in stress preoccupation, while older women similarly deprived showed no change. At the 10-year follow-up in 1980, these sex differences were also maintained. Interestingly, there was also a trend toward less stress preoccupation among the younger men (now averaging 32), suggesting that for them the impact of childhood deprivation was wearing off.

Longitudinal findings also provide support for the thesis developed in our original stress typology (Lowenthal & Chiriboga, 1973) that people who are challenged by stress tend to adopt lifestyles that keep them challenged (Chiriboga & Cutler, 1980). The converse hypothesis that self-protectiveness (stress avoidance) increases with age in the lower-middle-income groups is indirectly supported, for we found an upswing in stress preoccupation as our two older groups reached their sixties and early seventies.

Change in Stress Mediators

Theory and empirical evidence from a number of disciplines suggest that there is more consistency in intrapersonal mediating resources than there is in outer supports, perceptions of what is stressful, preoccupation with stress, and adaptive processes. Thus far, two such resources have been identified that are especially significant throughout much of adulthood. Their nature is no cause for surprise—except, perhaps, among people who are skeptical about Freud's (possibly apocryphal) love and work thesis. Freud presumably referred to these capacities as criteria for adaptation and maturity. Their possible role as buffers of stress is reported by several contributing authors to the recently published book *Themes of Work and Love in Adulthood* (Smelser & Erikson, 1980). For purposes of this chapter, *love* is empirically examined in terms of the individual's beliefs about his or her own closest relationships, using the respondent's definitions of closeness, intimacy, mutuality, or having a confidant. *Work* is more broadly defined and includes commitments such as competence, mastery, and creativity.

While much research has been reported on social supports and networks at various life stages, particularly later life (for a review see Lowenthal & Robinson, 1976), most respondents attach more importance to their closest relationships, thus posing a far more difficult task for the researcher. The Human Development and Aging Program became interested in this sphere, as in many others, through its work on aging, conducted in the late 1950s and 1960s. The significance of a confidant surfaced serendipitously (Lowenthal & Haven, 1968), and in-depth exploration of self-defined intimate relationships became part of the design for the ensuing transitions study. The importance of intimacy was subsequently verified in conjunction with the stress typology. The contrast between challenged and overwhelmed men makes the point well. Of the four stress types, the challenged, who tend to be complex in several spheres of their lives, had the highest ratings of mutuality and emotional involvement among middle and late middle-aged men, while the overwhelmed men ranked lowest. Among middle-aged and older women, on the other hand, few were in the challenged category to being with, and many were self-defeating. Like women in most studies, female subjects in the transitions study reported higher levels of mutuality and close relationships, both intrafamilial and extrafamilial, but for them these capacities did not serve as buffers against stress.

Pauline and Robert Sears follow-up of Terman's sample of gifted children at age 62 provokes speculation about the notable differences between them and our considerably less privileged groups, in this instance the women. One hunch that proved to be well founded was that for many of this elite sample, both work and love were stress mediators (Sears, 1977). The sizable proportion of Terman's female subjects who had combined career with family were more satisfied with their family relationships and with life in general than were women who had devoted themselves to family and volunteer activities. Indeed, at the most recent follow-up, many of the latter expressed regret that they had not embarked on careers as younger women (Sears & Barbee, 1977). This suggests that a "balance model" (Lowenthal & Chiriboga, 1975) is helpful in understanding not only stressors (both positive and negative) and adaptation but also mediators. For example, we know that the stress-satisfaction axis can tilt from one side to the other at very short intervals. Having deep commitments in, say, two domains of life provides opportunity for sequential distancing and perspective. A mother's problems with her rebellious adolescent daughter may temporarily recede in the demands and engrossment of the work setting, and she may return home with a different mental and emotional set toward this particular stress from the set she manifested in the morning. By contrast, the woman who stays home or who does very routine paid work, as do about half the women in the transitions study, is likely to remain embroiled.

It is tempting to formulate a firm hypothesis that two or more strong commitments strengthen stress resistance in adulthood. Such hypothesis would find support in an important longitudinal project (Maas & Kuypers, 1974). Maas (1981), in response to my conjecture (Fiske, 1980b), reported that the working-class, family committed women in that study were aging more unhappily than were upper-middle-class women who, in addition to strong family concerns, were deeply involved in organizations outside the home. While the hypothesis was confirmed for younger subjects in the transitions study as they approached early middle age, among older men and women, strength and balance of commitments was no longer associated with stress resistance. Quite the contrary, among them the more complex people were aging most unhappily. This finding was somewhat more true of women than men; the explanation probably lies in the fact that their lower-class status added to the strong sex bias that continues to be found in blue-collar groups especially, poses barriers to fulfilling commitments that are not encountered by the more privileged.

Findings and hypotheses such as these convinced us that a commitment paradigm would be more helpful than the prevailing self-actualizing, growth oriented models and theories in elucidating patterns of behavior in adulthood. To this end, we constructed a model centered on the patterning, or configuration, sometimes hierarchical, of the fundamental concerns the individual harbors at a given time. This inner gestalt is drawn upon, consciously or not, to allot priority to one kind of choice or activity in preference to another. Thus far, the commitment framework embraces four domains (Fiske, 1980b, c): (1) curiosity, mastery, and creativity; (2) commitment to other people, including intimate relationships; (3) concerns that transcend self-in-present networks, including support and nurture of values such as integrity of the self, close others, and society at large; and (4) self-orientation or self-protectiveness, which may be either an age linked concern or a lifelong narcissism, pathological or otherwise (both forms would be expected to be associated with stress preoccupation).

A Commitment Paradigm

Among the more clear-cut patterns that have been traced is one of diversity, manifest among people who are about equally committed to a few of the first three domains. At the other extreme are people who put all their commitment eggs into one basket. Thus far, in tracing change in commitment structure through two follow-up assessments of our middle-aged and older groups, we have found at least as much change as continuity. Though most people in each stage had lived through the same type of normative life course transition in the intervening years, there was a great deal of variation in the ways in which their configurations were rearranged, as Figures 32–1 and 32–2 illustrate.

When we first talked with Mrs. M. R., she had been divorced for a few years. She held a responsible secretarial job, was studying for a professional degree, and was highly committed both to meeting the needs of her son, a high school senior who lived with her, and to attaining her work goals. Disillusioned by a difficult marriage and a later unhappy love affair, she was very protective of herself, in the hope of achieving a more satisfying life. At the 5-year follow-up she was 47, had nearly completed her education, and had been offered an interesting and prestigious new job. She no longer felt responsible for her son, who, happily married, was pursuing his own goals. As Figure 32–1 shows, both her interpersonal and mastery commitments had become strengthened, and she was no longer wrapped in a self-protective cocoon. We have not yet plotted her chart for the 10-year follow-up, but we do know that she is now thoroughly enjoying grandparenthood.

Mr. F. C., a former navy career man, presented a very different configuration (see

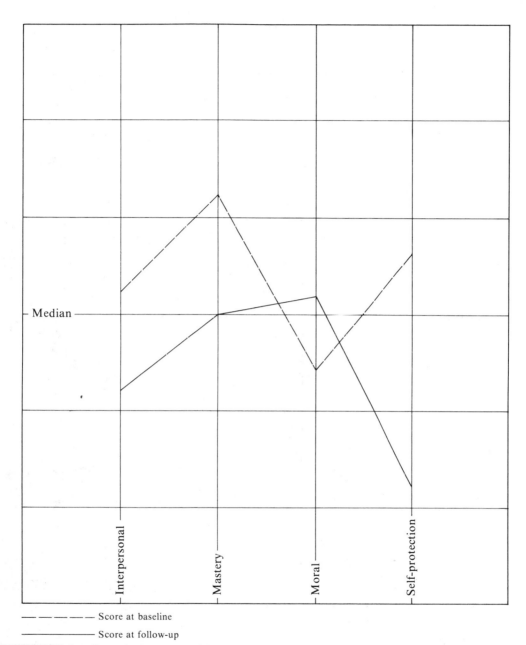

- — — — — Score at baseline
- ——————— Score at follow-up

FIGURE 32–1. Commitment scores: Mrs. M. R.

Figure 32–2). He had a modest business of his own when he was first contacted. A true child of the Great Depression, Mr. F. C. was concerned most with financial security, and at that time he was achieving this goal to his own satisfaction. Five years later, he had bought a new business and had become even more affluent. Despite this success and the resolution of difficulties in his relationship with one of his daughters, he had become much more cynical and was very bored. Mr. F. C. had all along found his marriage to be "not the greatest." During the interval, he had been hard hit by the realization that his life was quite empty despite con-

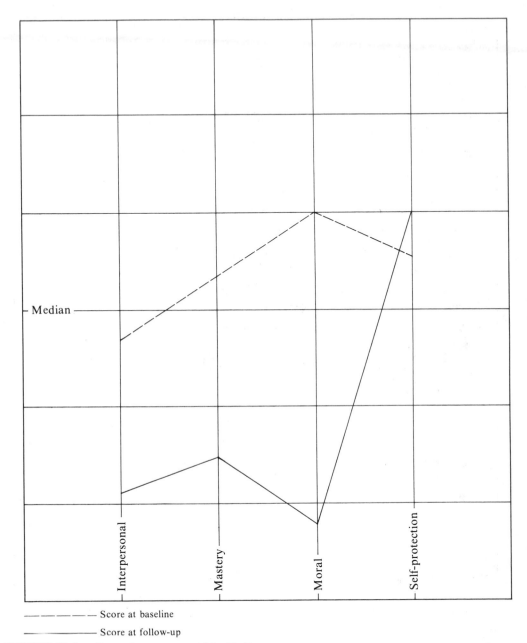

———————— Score at baseline

———————— Score at follow-up

FIGURE 32–2. Commitment scores: Mr. F. C.

siderable security and material comfort. At 50, he regretted not having had a professional career, found his work "not worthwhile," and admitted that "the money doesn't mean a goddam thing. . . . I'm just not a happy person." His decline in all commitments except to himself was the most drastic in his cohort of middle-aged men. The recent follow-up (not yet charted) found Mr. F. C. to be by his own account more affluent, still very bored, but quite happy. Since he also now considers his marriage somewhat better than most and describes his relationship with one of his daughters as "a dream," we suspect that his chart will show an increase in interpersonal commitment.

Another way to examine commitment change is to place each individual within the context of his or her life stage group and to examine change in each domain separately. Figures 32–3 and 32–4 show, respectively, change in commitment to mastery among the initially late middle-aged women (then in their late fifties) and among somewhat younger men, first confronting an empty nest (then in their late forties). As we can see in Figure 32–3, the late middle-aged women were more likely to have increased their self-expressive (mastery) commitments than to have reduced or relinquished them, several subjects to a very significant extent.

By contrast, only two empty nest men had increased their mastery commitments to any significant extent, and the graph for the entire male cohort is heavily weighted on the decline side. (Mr. F. C., number 27, had the steepest drop over the five-year period.)

Among most employed middle-aged men, commitments to competence and the accompanying satisfaction of effectance (White, 1965) can no longer be fulfilled in the work arena. When occupational peaking occurs, usually in the late thirties or early forties, men find themselves facing two decades or more of lack of challenge, if not sheer boredom in and hatred of their jobs. To these negative stresses, they themselves often add anxiety about retirement, even though this stage is far in the future. At the time of the five-year follow-up, inflation was already beginning to lean heavily upon our male respondents although the majority had selected their jobs in the first place with a keen eye for the security that pension

FIGURE 32–3. Change in commitment to mastery: preretired females. SD = standard deviation.

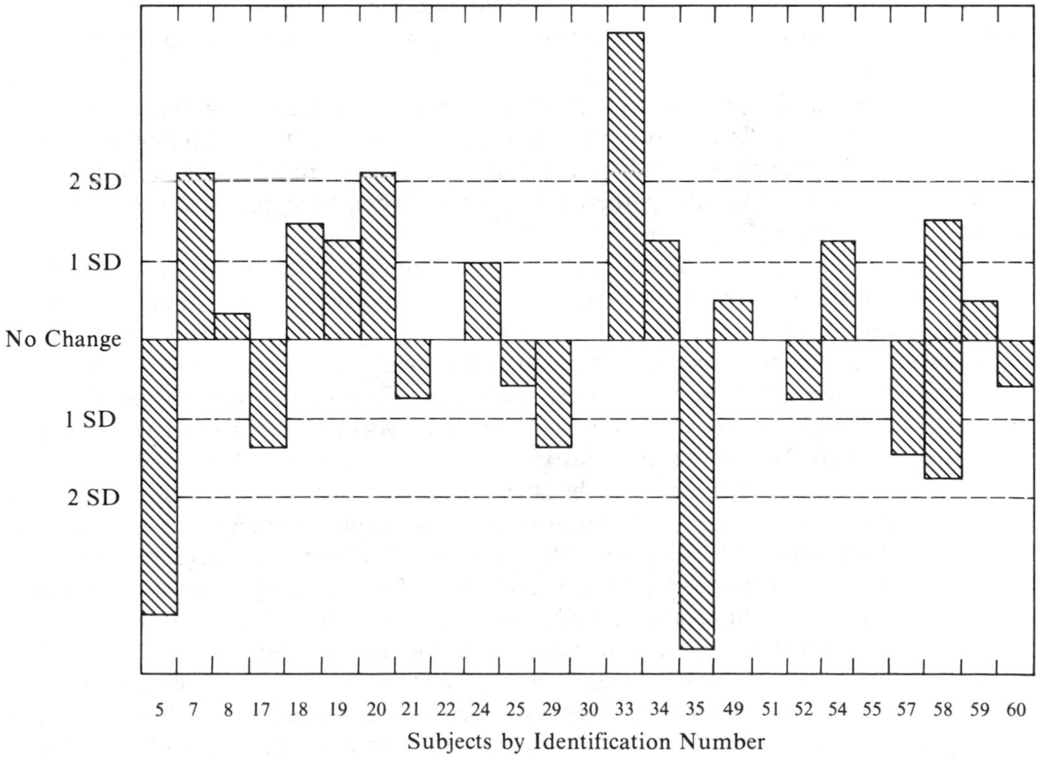

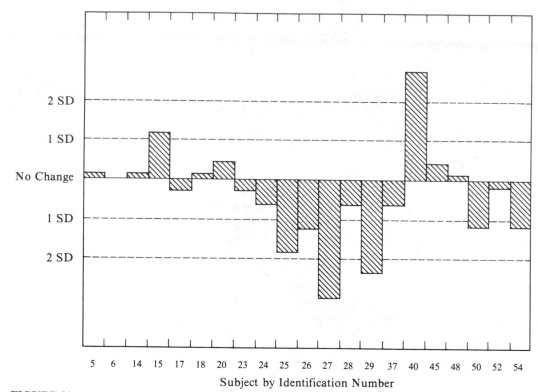

FIGURE 32–4. Change in commitment to mastery: empty nest males. SD = standard deviation.

plans and other benefits provide. Some were becoming anxious about another problem as well: how, in the immediate future, as well as during retirement could they retain, if not bolster, their self-esteem? That this worry may not be fully conscious is suggested in the change in projective materials, gathered at the time when their increasing interpersonal needs began to emerge (Thurnher, 1975).

This apparently age linked change is in the Jungian (Jung, 1933) tradition (as is the increase in mastery needs among women) and has been reported in other studies (Gutmann, 1969; Neugarten & Gutmann, 1968). The same trend appeared among the highly educated, self-assessing, often very successful men studied by Vaillant (1977) and by Sears (1977). These more privileged men, at both middle and late middle age, had come to value interpersonal relationships as much as, if not more than, their work, to which most had long been strongly committed. This change may be explained by reference to Erikson's (1950) concept of *generativity* as the main function of the later stages of life. In contrast, among men in the transitions study, the primary need appeared to be nurturance from and ego bolstering by others, especially their wives, at a time when women of the same age were seeking opportunities for autonomy and self-expression and lowering their commitments to the interpersonal sphere. Many of these women suffered bitter and painful inner conflict, for they realistically feared that if they became engrossed in any tasks or interests other than those that contributed to the husband's needs, their marriages might fail. Our five-year follow-up of the empty nest women demonstrated that some of them had compromised and in the process become more assertive and bossy at home—no way to nurture the already fragile egos of their husbands. Other women, however, did find opportunities for self-expression outside the home; about a third of this group got divorced (a few of these subsequently remarried). We have found no evidence of such sharply conflicting needs and trajectories between the sexes in more highly educated segments of American society, but among the people we have been studying in the transitions project such conflicts not only create new stress but undermine any buffering effect that personal commitments might have.

CONCLUSION

Since the Middle Ages, at least in Western societies, the self-conscious task of many young people, especially but not only university students, has been to acquire and to question the heritage bequeathed by their elders. Their teachers and leaders rarely felt threatened in their own beliefs and values because change in societal values and norms proceeded slowly. In this century, after World War I, elders seem to have become less secure. Since World War II, and especially in the past two decades, there has been both a resurgence of youthful questioning and an accelerated change in its content and consequences. After the short-lived retreatism of those who were young in the 1950s, the renewed opposition and activism among the youth of the 1960s was challenging to themselves and to some of their parents and teachers. Now, while there are no hippies or flower children in the Haight, and there are once again ambitious young people in the universities, most middle- and lower-middle-class parents find their offspring's style of living incomprehensible and distressing.

The choices and behaviors suitable for fulfilling any of the three substantive commitments (mastery, interpersonal, or moral-societal) require appropriate arenas, usually within social contexts. While access is fairly open through early middle age, by late middle age, except for the privileged and/or very talented, the avenues become severely restricted. Among average Americans, the pace of social and technological change exacerbates the stress of such roadblocks and their commitments come to seem obsolete. While they might agree with Erikson's conviction that generativity should be a major commitment after middle age, they cannot readily conceive of anything important that they might have to offer succeeding generations.

Some say that the best one can do is teach the young to be flexible and to bow with whatever winds of change may blow. Others suspect that the pace of technological change is now so rapid that the gap in values and knowledge between youngest and oldest adults may soon be unbridgeable, with each looking to the other like a creature from another world, a stressful circumstance for both. Late middle-aged parents, many of whom have living parents and parents-in-law, may soon become the most highly stressed of all, as they lose the sense of generational continuity with the young and become caretakers of the very old.

NOTES

1. This longitudinal study began in 1968. At the baseline the sample consisted of 216 men and women facing one of four normative adult transitions: departure from parental home, newly married, youngest child about to leave home, and people within a year or two of retirement. They lived in a homogeneous section of a metropolitan area and were (by design) primarily caucasian, blue- and white-collar workers. They have now been interviewed *in depth* and assessed by a variety of structured instruments five times. The most recent contact was in 1980.

REFERENCES

BALTES, P. B. Life-span developmental psychology: Some converging observations on history and theory. In P. B. Baltes & O. G. Brim, Jr. (eds.), *Life-span development and behavior,* vol. 2. New York: Academic, 1979.

CAMPBELL, A., CONVERSE, P. E., & RODGERS, W. L. *The quality of American life: Perceptions, evaluations, and satisfactions.* New York: Russell Sage, 1976.

CHIRIBOGA, D. A. Life event weighting systems: A comparative analysis. *Journal of Psychosomatic Research,* 1977, *21,* 415–422.

CHIRIBOGA, D. A., & CUTLER, L. Stress responses among divorcing men and women. *Journal of Divorce,* 1977, *1,* 95–106.

————. Stress and adaptation: A life span study. In L. Poon (ed.), *Aging in the 1980s: Selected contemporary issues in the psychology of aging.* Washington, D.C.: American Psychological Association, 1980.

ELDER, G. H., JR. *Children of the Great Depression.* Chicago: University of Chicago Press, 1974.

————. Historical change in life patterns and personality. In P. B. Baltes & O. G. Brim, Jr. (eds.), *Life-span development and behavior,* vol. 2. New York: Academic, 1979.

ERIKSON, E. H. Childhood and society. New York: Norton, 1950.

FISKE, M. Changing hierarchies of commitment in adulthood. In N. J. Smelser & E. H. Erikson (eds.), *Themes of work and love in adulthood.* Cambridge: Harvard University Press, 1980. (a)

————. The interplay of social and personal change in adulthood. Paper presented to the annual meeting of the Gerontological Society of America, San Diego, 1980. (b)

————. Tasks and crises of the second half of life: The interrelationship of commitment, coping, and adaptation. In J. E. Birren & R. B. Sloane (eds.), *Handbook of mental health and aging.* Englewood Cliffs: Prentice-Hall, 1980. (c)

GUTMANN, D. *The country of old men: Cross-cultural studies in the psychology of later life.* University of Michigan–Wayne State University, occasional paper no. 5. 1969. Institute of Gerontology.

HOLLINGWORTH, H. L. *Mental growth and decline: A survey of developmental psychology.* New York: Appleton, 1927.

HOLMES, T. H. & RAHE, R. H. The social readjustment rating scale. *Journal of Psychosomatic Research,* 1967, *11,* 213–218.

Institute for Social Research. Americans seek self-development, suffer anxiety from changing roles. *IRS Newsletter* (Ann Arbor), 1979, *7,* 4–5.

JUNG, C. G. The stages of life. In C. G. Jung, Modern man in search of a soul. New York: Harcourt, Brace, 1933.

LIFTON, R. J. *The life of self.* New York: Simon & Schuster, 1976.

LOWENTHAL, M. F., BERKMAN, P. L., & ASSOCIATES. *Aging and mental disorder.* San Francisco: Jossey-Bass, 1967.

LOWENTHAL, M. F., & CHIRIBOGA, D. Social stress and adaptation: Toward a life course perspective. In C. Eisdorfer & M. P. Lawton (eds.), *The psychology of adult development and aging.* Washington, D.C.: American Psychological Association, 1973.

————. Responses to stress. In M. F. Lowenthal, M. Thurnher, D. Chiriboga, & Associates, *Four stages of life: A comparative study of women and men facing transitions.* San Francisco: Jossey-Bass, 1975.

LOWENTHAL, M. F., & HAVEN, C. Interaction and adaptation: Intimacy as a critical variable. *American Sociological Review,* 1968, *33,* 20–30.

LOWENTHAL, M. F., & ROBINSON, B. Social networks and isolation. In R. Binstock & E. Shanas (eds.), *Handbook of aging and the social sciences.* New York: Van Nostrand, 1976.

LOWENTHAL, M. F., THURNHER, M., CHIRIBOGA, D., & ASSOCIATES. *Four stages of life: A comparative study of women and men facing transitions.* San Francisco: Jossey-Bass, 1975.

MAAS, H. S. Personal communication, 2 February 1981.

MAAS, H. S., & KUYPERS, J. A. *From thirty to seventy.* San Francisco: Jossey-Bass, 1974.

MARRIS, P. *Loss and change.* New York: Doubleday Anchor, 1975.

NEUGARTEN, B. L., & GUTMANN, D. L. Age-sex roles and personality in middle age: A thematic apperception study. In B. L. Neugarten (ed.), *Middle age and aging.* Chicago: University of Chicago Press, 1968.

REINERT, G. Prolegomenon to a history of life-span developmental psychology. In P. B. Baltes & O. G. Brim, Jr. (eds.), *Life-span development and behavior,* vol. 2. New York: Academic, 1979.

SEARS, P. S., & BARBEE, A. H. Career and life satisfaction among Terman's gifted women. In J. Stanley, W. George, & C. Solano (eds.), *The gifted and the creative: A fifty year perspective.* Baltimore: Johns Hopkins Press, 1977.

SEARS, R. Sources of life satisfactions of the Terman gifted men. *American Psychologist,* 1977, *32,* 119–128.

SMELSER, N. J., & ERIKSON, E. H. (eds.). *Themes of work and love in adulthood.* Cambridge: Harvard University Press, 1980.

SROLE, L. The Midtown Manhattan Study: Longitudinal focus on aging, genders, and life transitions. Paper presented to the annual meeting of the Gerontological Society, Dallas, 1978.

SCROLE, S., LANGNER, T. S., MICHAEL, S. T., OPLER, M. K., & RENNIE, T. A. C. *Mental health in the metropolis: The Midtown Manhattan Study.* New York: McGraw-Hill, 1962.

THURNHER, M. Continuities and discontinuities in value orientation. In M. F. Lowenthal, M. Thurnher, D. Chiriboga, & Associates, *Four stages of life: A comparative study of women and men facing transitions.* San Francisco: Jossey-Bass, 1975.

VAILLANT, G. *Adaptation to life.* Boston: Little, Brown, 1977.

VIDAL, G. Burt and Labelle and Jimmy and God. *New York Review of Books,* 29 June 1978, p. 21.

WHITE, R. W. *Lives in progress* (3d ed.). New York: Holt, 1975.

YANKELOVICH, D. *New rules in American life.* New York: Random House, 1981.

PART VI

COMMON PSYCHIATRIC AND SOMATIC CONDITIONS

33

Stress, Type A Behavior, and Coronary Disease

Ray H. Rosenman   **Margaret A. Chesney**

INDUSTRIALIZED SOCIETIES HAVE SUFFERED a marked increase of coronary heart disease (CHD) in the twentieth century, but with major population differences in these increased CHD rates that cannot be ascribed simply to greater longevity or improved diagnosis, to altered genetic predisposition, or even to the accepted risk factors for CHD. This chapter reviews the literature on a behavioral CHD risk factor that is associated with the industrialization of the twentieth century—the *Type A behavior pattern* (TABP). The inability of known risk factors to explain CHD prevalence, which precipitated the search for additional CHD risk factors, is discussed. The TABP, the psychosocial factor found by this search to be causally related to CHD, is described, along with the methods for its assessment. Research establishing the causal relationship of the Type A behavior pattern and its components to CHD is also reviewed. The relationship to TABP to sociodemographic and psychological variables is outlined. Following this review, the relationship of TABP both to other CHD risk factors and to biochemical and neurohormonal factors is discussed. The chapter concludes with a description of past research efforts to modify the Type A pattern and a recommendation for future interventions.

CORONARY HEART DISEASE RISK AND PSYCHOSOCIAL FACTORS

Environmental factors clearly play a dominant causal role in the increased rates of CHD. Coronary atherosclerosis and clinical CHD doubtless have a multifactorial etiology whose pathogenetic linkage is still imperfectly understood. It is generally believed that among causal and contributing factors are the habits of diet and physical activity, as well as the more established risk factors such as blood pressure, serum lipid-lipoproteins, and cigarette smoking. However, even taken together these factors fail to explain a substantial part of the numerical incidence of CHD, its differing societal rates, or individual specificity (Gordon & Verter, 1969). Indeed, many CHD patients do not exhibit high levels of risk factors, and most show no differences of diet or physical activity from patterns that prevail in the healthy population (Mann, 1977).

Research for this chapter was supported by grants from the National Institute of Mental Health (MH–31269) and from the National Heart, Lung, and Blood Institute (HL26042).

Cross-cultural studies have yielded conflicting evidence regarding the causal role of risk factors in CHD incidence. Various risk factors are at high levels in many populations with low rates of CHD (Bruhn & Wolf, 1970). When investigators adjust for differences in risk factors, U.S. males exhibit significantly higher CHD rates than do European men (Keys, Aravanis, Blackburn, Vanbuchem, Buzina, Djordjenic, Fidanza, Karvonen, Menotti, Puddu, & Taylor, 1972), and CHD rates in Framingham men are two to four times higher than those among men in Honolulu or Puerto Rico (Gordon, Garcia-Palmieri, Kagan, Kannel, & Schiffman, 1974), Yugoslavia (Kozarevic, Pire, Ravic, Dawber, Gordon, & Zukel, 1976), or Paris (Ducimetière, Cambien, Richard, Rakotovao, & Claude, 1980) at similar levels of the classical risk factors. Given these inconsistencies, it is not surprising that CHD risk factors, even taken together, account for less than half the numerical incidence of CHD in prospective studies (Keys et al., 1972). Nor can either the twentieth-century increased rates of CHD or the more recent decline of CHD mortality rates in some countries be ascribed simply to changes of diet, physical activity, or risk factors (Froelicher, Longo, & McIver, 1976). Finally, neither altered diet, nor physical conditioning, nor decrease of standard risk factors has been shown significantly to diminish the morbidity rates of CHD or reinfarction, despite the "remarkable aura of faith" in such treatment (Can I Avoid a Heart Attack?, 1974).

Critical reviews have suggested that classical risk factors are far from providing a total explanation of the twentieth-century increase of CHD, the different incidence in various Western countries, the occurrence of CHD in specific individuals, or the recent decline of CHD mortality in come countries (e.g., Corday & Corday, 1975). This has stimulated the search for other causes, as well as for improved prediction and prevention.

Many studies (see Jenkins, 1976, for review) have reviewed possible roles of many psychosocial factors, including such demographic, socioeconomic, psychological, and emotional factors as social class and status, educational level, religion, ethnic background, marital status, occupation, work overload, social and geographic mobility, status incongruity, anxiety, neuroticism, life events and change, life satisfactions and dissatisfactions, and emotional loss and deprivation. It can be concluded that certain factors do put subjects at higher risk for CHD, but few have been established as being causally related either to coronary atherogenesis or to risk of CHD

The most consistent evidence relates CHD with certain personality and behavioral traits. Van Dusch observed in 1868 that persons with loud vocal stylistics and excessive work involvement were predisposed to CHD. Osler (1892) strongly implicated stress and hard-driving behavior in CHD. Many years later, Menninger and Menninger (1936) observed CHD patients to be characterized by strongly aggressive behavior. Dunbar (1943) found them hard-driving and goal directed, and Kemple (1945) perceived them to be ambitious and compulsively striving to achieve goals that incorporated power and prestige. Arlow (1945) and Gildea (1949) observed similar behavior, and in 1950 Stewart correlated new conditions of stress in England with increased CHD rates. These observers noted remarkably similar behavior in CHD patients but failed to consider their milieu. It now appears that such behavior is typical of CHD patients and that this specific pattern of overt behavior, termed the Type A behavior pattern, clearly antedates CHD.

TYPE A BEHAVIOR PATTERN

Individuals who are engaged in a relatively chronic struggle to do and achieve more and more in less and less time, often in competition with other people or opposing forces in the environment (Rosenman, 1978), exhibit the set of behaviors that constitutes the Type A behavior pattern. The TABP includes such behavioral dispositions as ambitiousness, aggressiveness, competitiveness and impatience; specific behaviors such as alertness, muscle tenseness, rapid and emphatic speech stylistics; and emotional reactions such as enhanced irritation and expressed signs of anger. Type A persons differ from subjects with classic anxiety states, who, on finding challenges to be overwhelming, experience anxiety and often withdraw or seek support or counsel from others. Type A's confidently grapple with challenges, while anxious subjects retreat from similar situations.

Persons without such attributes are called *Type B*. Unlike Type A individuals, Type B's are rather relaxed, deferent, and satisfied; moreover, they exhibit unhurried behavior. Type B's rarely struggle, as do Type A's, to accomplish an endlessly growing number of things in ever decreasing amounts of time, and they respond less often to the same levels of challenge presented by the environment that elicit the TABP in Type A's.

The contemporary Western environment may have increased the prevalence of TABP by rewarding those who communicate and perform more rapidly and aggressively. Technological progress, accompanied by urbanization and the necessity for precise synchronization of interdependent human services, presents new challenges not experienced by earlier generations. Although TABP stems in part from certain personal or behavioral predispositions, it emerges when the environment's challenges elicit a particular set of behaviors. This requisite inclusion of the milieu implies that, if the challenges are severe enough, almost any person might so react that TABP emerges. Thus, the TABP is not a personality type but a set of behavioral responses typically including both an environmental and an intrinsic component.

It is important to distinguish TABP from the ill-defined concept of stress: this pattern is neither a stressor situation nor a distressed response but a style of overt behavior used to confront life situations. The TABP may be elicited by either pleasant or troubling situations, but it is particularly triggered by situations that are perceived as relevant challenges. The TABP is manifested by characteristic values, thoughts, and approaches to interpersonal relationships, as well as by characteristic gestures, facial expressions, motor activity and pace, stylistics of speech, and other mannerisms. It is prevalent in industrialized societies and is readily recognized by the behavioral facade that has been described in considerable detail (Rosenman, 1978; Rosenman & Friedman, 1974).

Other investigators have confirmed these observations about the behavior and emotional reactions of Type A individuals, also finding them to be orderly and well organized, self-controlled, self-confident, preferring to work alone when challenged, not easily distracted from task performance, outgoing, hyperalert, fast paced, competitive, tense and unrelaxed, impatient, aggressive, time conscious, deeply involved in vocation and unable to relax away from work, excessively striving with enhanced desire to control their environment, and hostile (Rosenmen & Chesney, 1980). The hostility that is characteristic of the TABP can be suppressed and elude the untrained observer. However, when the Type A individual is frustrated, the hostility may become overt.

ASSESSMENT OF TYPE A BEHAVIOR PATTERN BY THE STRUCTURED INTERVIEW

An interview was designed to provide a suitable challenge setting in which to assess an individual's response style (Rosenman, 1978; Rosenman, Friedman, Straus, Wurm, Kositchek, Hahn, & Werthessen, 1964). The intensity of TABP represents the reaction when such persons are challenged or aroused by relevant environmental stressors. These responses may not be felt or exhibited by Type A's when confronted by an environment that presents no salient challenge. For example, a usually rushed and hard-driving person might not exhibit TABP when relaxing on vacation. The Structured Interview (SI) was thus designed to provide a suitable challenge to elicit the TABP in predisposed individuals. The SI requires 15 minutes to administer and is audiotaped or videotaped for subsequent rating. Both interviewers and raters must be trained to provide a standardized, valid assessment.

Rating by the SI takes into account stylistics of speech (i.e., the way something is said by the subject), the content of answers (i.e., what is said), and overt psychomotor, nonverbal behaviors exhibited during the interview. While all three factors are taken into account, the content of responses and nonverbal behaviors are weighted less heavily, since Type A's often have little insight into their own behavior. Instead, emphasis is placed on the speech stylistics shown in the course of responding to the SI situation. The value of these speech stylistics for assessment of TABP has been confirmed (Schucker & Jacobs, 1977). Methodological studies of the SI have shown high levels of interrater agreement (Caffrey, 1968; National Institutes of Health, 1979) and stability of the Type A and B behavior patterns over time (Jenkins, Rosenman, & Friedman, 1968).

There has been an ongoing search for other methods of assessment since the SI is relatively subjective and requires training for its proper administration and rating. To assist in developing new assessment procedures and defining correlates of the TABP, researchers have given Type A and B subjects an array of psychometric questionnaires such as the Adjective Checklist of Gough and Heilbrun (1980), Thurstone Temperament Schedule (Thurstone, 1949), Eysenck Personality Inventory (Eysenck & Eysenck, 1968) SCL–90–R (Derogatis, 1977), State-Trait Anxiety Inventory (STAI) (Spielberger, Gorsuch & Lushene, 1970), Work Environment Scale (Insel & Moos, 1970), California Psychological Inventory (Gough, 1956), Minnesota Multiphasic Personality Inventory (Dahlstrom & Welsh, 1960), Cattell 16-Personality Factors Test (Cattell, Eber & Tatsuoka, 1970), and Barratt Impulsiveness Scale (Barratt, 1965). However, while strong construct validity for the TABP is supported by findings with these scales, results are influenced by the subject's insight and response bias. The hurry, poor insight, and inadequate self-appraisal of many Type A's are thought to lead to inaccuracy that limits the ability of questionnaires to serve as measures of TABP (Rosenman, Rahe, Borhani, & Feinleib, 1976).

Another assessment approach consists of questionnaires that attempt to duplicate the SI. Bortner (1969) designed a short scale that classified 70% of subjects into the same categories as did the SI. In a study conducted in Belgium, this scale correctly classified 75% of subjects (Kittel, Dornitzer, Zyzanski, Jenkins, Rustin, & Degré, 1978). Although promising, this and subsequent scales have been inadequately validated.

The best-studied questionnaire is the Jenkins Activity Survey (JAS), now available for clinical use (Jenkins, Rosenman, & Zyzanski, 1979). The JAS provides a composite Type A scale and three subscales: speed and impatience, job involvement, and hard-driving. The TABP assessed by the JAS is significantly related to CHD prevalence in many populations. JAS scores for TABP were predictive of new cases of CHD (Jenkins, Rosenman, & Zyzanski, 1974), risk of reinfarction in the Western Collaborative Group Study (Jenkins, Zyzanski, & Rosenman, 1976), and degree of basic coronary atherosclerosis (Zyzanski, Jenkins, Ryan, Flessas, & Everist, 1976) in some, if not all, studies (Blumenthal, Williams, Kong, Schangerb, & Thompson, 1978). However, compared to the SI, the JAS is a much weaker predictor of CHD incidence (Brand, Rosenman, Jenkins, Sholtz, & Zyzanski, 1978), of severity of coronary atherosclerosis (Blumenthal et al., 1976), and of challenge induced physiological arousal, which characterizes TABP (MacDougall, Dembroski, & Musante, 1979). The relative strength of the SI compared to that of questionnaires may be that the interview is based more upon direct observation of the behavior pattern than upon content of answers to questions.

RELATIONSHIP OF TYPE A BEHAVIOR PATTERN TO CORONARY HEART DISEASE

A significant association of TABP with CHD prevalence was found in both sexes that could not be ascribed to differences of diet or other risk factors (Friedman & Rosenman, 1959; Rosenman & Friedman, 1961). Many other investigators have confirmed this association (for reviews see Feinleib, Brand, Remington, & Zyzanski, 1978; Rosenman & Chesney, 1980). As was recently pointed out:

> Since response bias and sample selection can in many ways influence the results and interpretations in case-control studies these replications take on added meaning. They assume greater significance in that they speak to the following issues: (1) random phenomena rarely replicate; (2) a variety of population groups were studied, and not simply narrowly defined and selected cases vs. controls; and (3) epidemiological studies have often found that replicated associations based on prevalence data are prospectively related as well. (Feinleib et al., 1978:6)

Moreover, these confirmations proved significant when TABP was measured by the SI, the JAS (Jenkins et al., 1979), Bortner's scale (Bortner, 1979), the Type A scale used in the Framingham Study (Kannel & Gordon, 1974), or the activity scale of the Thurstone Temperament Schedule (Thurstone, 1949)—a scale that correlates significantly with the SI (Rosenman & Chesney, 1980).

Differences of TABP may in part explain considerably higher CHD rates in the densely populated, industrialized regions of the United States and England (Sigler, 1959) compared to farm belts, where consumption of animal and dairy fats is probably high, as well as apparently low rates in close-knit religious groups (Groen, Tjiong, Kamminger, & Willebrands, 1962). Such differences probably also help to explain higher rates in the United States compared to Europe (Keys et al., 1972) and in Framingham men compared to those in Yugoslavia (Kozarevic et al., 1976), Puerto Rico and Hawaii (Gordon et al., 1974), and Paris (Ducimetière et al., 1980).

The association between TABP and CHD has received major confirmation in prospective research. The Western Collaborative Group Study (WCGS) was a prospective epidemiological study of 3154 initially well men, aged 39–59 years at intake in 1960–1961, who were employed by 10 participating California companies (Rosenman et al., 1964). Subjects were comprehensively studied for all risk factors. The population and methodology are described elsewhere (Rosenman et al., 1964), as were findings at follow-up (Rosenman, Brand, Jenkins, Friedman, Strauss, & Wurm, 1975; Rosenman, Brand, Sholtz, & Friedman, 1976).

The 8.5-year follow-up found CHD in 257 men. Final results showed that men classified as Type A at intake were 2.37 times as likely to develop CHD over the follow-up period as were Type B subjects (Rosenman et al., 1975). When statistical multivariate adjustment for other risk factors was made, the relative Type A-B risk of CHD decreased to 1.97, the small difference (.40) between adjusted and nonadjusted relative risk being the amount of risk conferred by other standard risk factors, which showed small correlations with the TABP (Rosenman et al., 1976). The significant adjusted remainder (1.97) represented the relative risk for TABP that was independent of other risk factors. These findings indicate a synergistic pattern for CHD risk in which TABP operates with nearly a constant multiplicative effect applied to whatever background level results from other risk factors. Thus, TABP appears to double the risk of CHD at all levels of other risk factors. The observed associations could not be attributed to chance fluctuation since both adjusted and nonadjusted relative risk ratios achieved high statistical significance ($p < .001$) and were close to those later found at Framingham (Haynes, Feinleib, & Kannel, 1980).

The Framingham Study (Kannel & Gordon, 1974) yielded a multivariate risk equation for CHD prediction based on standard risk factors. The predicted risk levels in the WCGS highly correlated with those obtained with the Framingham data (Rosenman et al., 1976). Multiple logistic analysis of the direct association between CHD incidence and behavior pattern gave an approximate relative risk of 1.9 ($p < .0006$) and 2.1 ($p < .0015$) for Type A to Type B men, aged 39–40 and 50–59 years, respectively. Thus, substantial risk is associated directly with TABP and does not diminish in older, as compared with younger, men.

In the WCGS the association of TABP with CHD incidence prevailed for initial myocardial infarction, whether symptomatic or silent, as well as for angina pectoris (Rosenman et al., 1975). Although significant CHD incidence occurred in Type A men even at low risk factor levels, Type B subjects at similar levels exhibited relative CHD immunity (Rosenman, Friedman, Jenkins, Straus, Wurm, & Kositchek, 1966). The TABP also was strongly associated with recurring and fatal CHD events in the WCGS (Jenkins et al., 1976; Rosenman, Friedman, Jenkins, Straus, Wurm, & Kositchek, 1967).

Other investigators have confirmed the relationship between TABP and CHD incidence. As part of the study of CHD among Japanese men in Japan, Hawaii, and California, 2437 men in Hawaii completed the JAS in 1967–1968 (Cohen, Syme, Jenkins, Dagan, & Zyzanski, 1975). Despite the number classified as Type A, CHD rates were found to be associated with hard-driving and competitive behavior. Japanese men in Hawaii who had undergone cultural change were more prone to CHD, and those who were both culturally mobile and Type A had two to three times the CHD risk during follow-up (Brand, 1978). These results support the initial TABP construct as being an interplay between specific behaviors and an environment that challenges the susceptible individual.

The Thurstone Temperament Schedule (Thurstone, 1949) was used in the Minnesota study of businessmen. The activity scale of this instrument is concerned with the pace of daily activities such as eating, talking, walking, or driving. Subjects who score high on this scale enjoy rapid psychomotor pace even when they do *not* have to function at this accelerated pace, an excellent description of this TABP facet. This scale shows the highest correlations with TABP of any psychometric questionnaire (Rosenmen et al., 1976). A significant positive association was found between CHD incidence and activity scale scores in the Minnesota study (Brozek, Keys, & Blackburn, 1966), in which adrenergic response to the cold pressor test was the strongest predictor of CHD incidence (Keys, Taylor, Blackburn, Brozek, & Anderson, 1971).

Major confirmation also was obtained in the Framingham Study (Haynes, Feinleib, Levine, Scotch, & Kannel, 1978). A cohort of 1822 subjects was administered an extensive questionnaire in 1965–1967 that provided measures of behavior, situational stress, sociocultural mobility, and somatic strain. Among these items, the Framingham Type A Scale (FTAS) was significantly correlated with daily stress, emotional lability, tension, anger symptoms, and ambitiousness. The FTAS was significantly correlated with CHD prevalence in both sexes, after controlling for other risk factors. Subjects aged 40–74 and free of CHD ($n = 1674$) were then followed for 8 years in a prospective manner.

During follow-up, Type A men were found to be over twice as likely as Type B's to develop angina and myocardial infarction, with stronger associations in white- than in blue-collar workers (Haynes et al., 1980). The respective incidence of angina and infarction was 3.32 and 2.14 times higher in Type A than in Type B women. All such associations prevailed after controlling statistically for other risk factors.

In the WCGS CHD incidence was found to be particularly associated with competitive drive, impatience, and the potential for hostility (Matthews, Glass, Rosenman, & Bortner, 1977). Findings from this study support the hypothesis that it is not just hurried, hard-working, achievement oriented behavior that is causally related to CHD (Cohen et al., 1975). Indeed, it is possible to be a hard worker without manifesting individual competitiveness, as demonstrated by the Japanese, who exhibit a successful adaptation to the American standard of hard-working success without individual competitiveness or hostility (Cohen et al., 1975). The finding of a particular relationship between the competitive-hostile aspects of TABP and CHD incidence in the WCGS is supported by the association of these attributes in both sexes with the severity of basic coronary atherosclerosis (Williams, Thomas, Lee, Kong, Blumenthal, & Whalen, 1980) and the enhanced adrenergic response to challenge tasks in Type A subjects (Dembroski, MacDougall, Shields, Petitto, & Lushene, 1978).

The major clinical manifestations of CHD are complications of underlying coronary atherosclerosis. The TABP may be causally related to CHD incidence in several ways. First, it may help precipitate fatal coronary events. The role of psychological stress is well known in precipitating sudden coronary death by sympathetic nervous system triggering of ventricular fibrillation (Lown & Verrier, 1976). Subjects with CHD exhibit increased adrenergic output (Nestel, Verghese, & Lovell, 1967). It is relevant that exaggerated response to the cold pressor test was a strong predictor of CHD incidence in the Minnesota prospective study (Keys & Taylor, 1971), in which increased CHD incidence was linked to behaviors characteristic of TABP, as suggested by the association of CHD risk with high scores on the activity scale of the Thurstone Temperament Schedule (Brozek et al., 1966). The TABP is associated with enhanced catecholamine secretion in response to daily work challenges (Friedman, St. George, & Byers, 1960), as well as during specific psychological (Dembroski et al., 1978; Friedman, Byers, Diamant, & Rosenman, 1975) and physical (Simpson, Olewine, Jenkins, Ramsey, Zyzanski, Thomas, & James, 1974) challenges. In turn, TABP is associated with fatal CHD events (Rosenman et al., 1967) and with sudden coronary death from ventricular fibrillation (Friedman, Manwaring, Rosenman, Donlon, Ortega, & Grube, 1973). The potential for enhanced adrenergic output in Type A subjects is shown by their increased physiologic arousal during challenge tests (Dembroski et al., 1978; Friedman et al., 1975; Glass, 1977). As already noted, the anger and hostility facets of TABP are associated with augmented discharge of norepinephrine, increased incidence of CHD, and increased severity of coronary atherosclerosis. Some sequential mechanisms that might relate to triggering of coronary events, including sudden death, are well conceptualized by Nixon (1976).

A second mechanism by which TABP may be related to CHD incidence is through increased risk of coronary thrombosis. The role of psychological stress in precipitating myocardial infarction has been widely noted (Rosenman & Chesney, 1980), as has been its association with increased blood clotting and platelet aggregation (Haft & Fani, 1973). In this regard, TABP is associated with accelerated blood clotting (Friedman, Rosenman, & Carroll, 1958) and with increased platelet aggregation (Jenkins, Thomas, Olewine, Zyzanski, Simpson, & Hames, 1975).

The TABP is strongly associated not only with the incidence of CHD but also with the severity of basic coronary atherosclerosis. Thus, it is significantly correlated with the severity of coronary atherosclerosis observed by angiographic study (Blumenthal et al., 1978; Frank, Heller, Kornfield, Sporn, & Weiss, 1978; Zyzanski et al., 1976), as well as with the progression of coronary atherosclerosis (Krantz, Sanmarco, Selvester, & Matthews, 1975) in associations that prevail after multivariate statistical control for effects of other risk factors. These data confirm our observation of a significantly greater degree of coronary atherosclerosis in Type A men who died during the WCGS follow-up (Friedman, Rosenman, Straus, Wurm, & Kositchek, 1968).

RELATIONSHIP OF TYPE A BEHAVIOR PATTERN TO SOCIODEMOGRAPHIC AND PSYCHOLOGICAL VARIABLES

There is inadequate knowledge about the prevalence of TABP. The WCGS population in 1960 was comprised mainly of white-collar workers in two California urban centers, about half exhibiting TABP (Rosenman et al., 1964). More recent experience in one of the participating companies found higher prevalence (Chesney, Black, Chadwick, & Rosenman, 1981). Most persons can be classified as exhibiting mainly either TABP or the converse, Type B pattern, with 10-20% exhibiting midpoint patterns (Rosenman et al., 1964). As noted previously, TABP appears to be more prevalent in industrialized, densely populated urban areas than in smaller, rural communities. In an area devoted to relaxation, such as Hawaii, the prevalence of TABP is low (Cohen et al., 1975), which may help account for that state's much lower CHD rate than was found in Framingham in men at similar levels of other risk factors (Gordon et al., 1974).

Little correlation of TABP has been found with age except for lower prevalence at younger ages (Rosenman et al., 1964; Shekelle, Schoenberger, & Stamler, 1976). The TABP shows modest correlations with social class and level of education, accounting in part for small observed correlations with occupational status (Rosenman & Chesney, 1980; Waldron Zyzanski, Shekelle, Jenkins, & Tannebaum, 1978) and career advancement and achievement in both sexes (Waldron et al., 1978). Higher prevalence is generally observed in white- than in blue-collar workers (Howard et al., 1977; Rosenman, Bawol, & Oscherwitz, 1977; Shekelle, Schoenberger, & Stamler, 1976). Moreover, TABP was less prevalent in black than in white populations studied in Chicago (Shekelle, Schoenberger, & Stamler, 1976) and less prevalent among Japanese-American than among Caucasian men in Hawaii (Cohen et al., 1975).

The TABP must be differentiated from psychopathology. This pattern is not correlated on psychometric tests with anxiety, somatic complaints, or behavioral correlates of stress (Bortner, 1969; Caplan & Jones, 1975; Chesney et al., 1981). Thus, the TABP shows only small correlations with items on standard psychological stress tests (Bortner, 1969; Rosenman et al., 1976a) and none with psychopathology, despite TABP correlations with stressful life events and current tension (Caplan & Jones, 1975).

ANTECEDENTS OF TYPE A BEHAVIOR PATTERN

There is little evidence of a genetic component for the global TABP. A modest genetic component has been found for certain TABP behaviors, including drive, competitiveness, compulsiveness, dominance, sociability, and impulsiveness (Horn, Plomin, & Rosenman, 1976; Matthews & Krantz, 1976; Rosenman et al., 1976a).

Parental attitudes, behaviors, and performance standards influence offspring and probably play a role in the development of many TABP facets, including competitiveness and achievement striving (Matthews & Saal, 1978). Since adult modeling and conditioning processes significantly affect competitive and aggressive behavior in offspring, it is not surprising that there is familial similarity of TABP in children (Bortner, Rosenman, & Friedman, 1970) or more TABP in children of parents with higher educational levels and occupational status (Matthews & Saal, 1978), in children living in urban compared to rural areas (Butensky, Forelli, Heebner & Waldron, 1976), and in male compared to female children (Matthews, 1978). The TABP in children resembles that in adults, with exhibition of enhanced competitiveness, aggressiveness, restlessness, impatience, and achievement orientation (Butensky et al., 1976; Matthews, 1978). Thus, there are valid reasons to believe that environment plays a greater role than genetic factors in the dev8lopment of TABP (Rosenman et al., 1976), that this pattern often has origins in childhood (Matthews, 1978), and that cultural factors play an important antecedent role in the development of TABP (Cohen et al., 1975).

However, the antecedents vary across individuals, indicating that the behavioral classification derived from the SI or from scores on questionnaires such as the JAS does not necessarily represent a logical continuum. The TABP is often engendered by socioeconomic factors that do not play a role until occupational careers begin, a finding in keeping with lower prevalence at younger ages (Shekelle, Schoenberger & Stamler, 1976; Waldron et al., 1977). Doubtless, the TABP is bred in many people by occupational competitiveness, heavy work loads, conflicting demands, supervisory responsibilities, and associated factors (Howard, Cunningham, & Rechnitzer, 1977). The role of such factors is exemplified by the higher prevalence of TABP in women working full-time outside the home compared to women employed part-time or to housewives (Rosenman & Friedman, 1961; Waldron et al., 1978). Some relationships of TABP to the work setting were recently reviewed (Chesney & Rosenman, 1980).

RELATIONSHIP OF TYPE A BEHAVIOR PATTERN TO OTHER CORONARY HEART DISEASE RISK FACTORS, BIOCHEMICAL FINDINGS, AND NEUROHORMONAL FACTORS

The twofold relative Type A to B risk for CHD does not operate through other risk factors but is a strong independent predictive factor (Rosenman et al., 1976). In the WCGS and other studies, standard risk factors other than smoking (Jenkins, Rosenman, & Zyzanski, 1968) showed only small correlations with the behavior patterns (Rosenman, 1978; Rosenman et al., 1976).

Early in Type A research, a link was observed between TABP and serum cholesterol; significant rises in cholesterol were noted in accountants with deadlines to meet (Friedman et al., 1958). This confirmed effect of environmental deadlines (Rosenman & Friedman, 1974), which could not be attributed to diet, occurs in many persons in association with time pressure, occupational obligations, or annoyance over recent life events (cf. Rosenman & Friedman, 1963). Average serum cholesterols tend to be higher in Type A than Type B subjects in both sexes (Friedman & Rosenman, 1959; Rosenman & Friedman, 1961, 1963). Type

A's also exhibit higher fasting and postprandial serum triglyceride levels than do their Type B counterparts (Rosenman & Friedman, 1963), along with sludging of red blood cells in the bulbar conjunctival blood vessels for many hours after ingestion of a meal rich in either saturated or unsaturated triglycerides (Rosenman & Friedman, 1974). The association of psychological states with serum lipid-lipoprotein levels has been reviewed elsewhere (Jenkins, Hames, Zyzanski, Rosenman, & Friedman, 1969).

There are no Type A-B differences in plasma uric acid levels or in glucose metabolism, although Type A's may exhibit a hyperinsulinemic response to glucose, which nevertheless does not appear responsible for their higher serum triglyceride levels (Rosenman & Friedman, 1974). Psychological factors are related to the hypothalamic-pituitary-adrenal axis. Average plasma cortisol and thyroxine levels of Type A's and B's are similar. However, when Type A's were challenged with large doses of corticotropin, most excreted significantly less 17-hydroxycorticoid than did Type B's, suggesting that the Type A's might have been subject to long-standing, as well as current, excess discharge of adrenocorticotropic hormone (ACTH). Indeed, Type A's, compared to Type B subjects, exhibit higher plasma ACTH during waking hours (Rosenman & Friedman, 1974). Administration of ACTH temporarily abolished the elevation of serum triglycerides in many Type A subjects, but this response was not induced by hydrocortisone administration.

Plasma growth hormone levels are significantly lower in Type A than in Type B men, and plasma growth hormone response of Type A's to infusion of arginine is significantly less than in Type B's (Rosenman & Friedman, 1974). Growth hormone is necessary for maintenance of plasma cholesterol and administration of growth hormone to Type A men induced a prompt, although temporary, fall of serum cholesterol.

Catecholamines probably play an important role in mediating relationships between TABP and both coronary atherosclerosis and CHD incidence. As we have seen, increased CHD incidence is a twentieth-century phenomenon associated with the accelerated pace and pressure of life in industrialized societies. Raab (1953) early emphasized the role of catecholamines in twentieth-century Western life, and he recognized that adrenergic responses were enhanced in individuals with TABP, compared to more relaxed persons (Raab, 1966). Levi and Anderson (1975) pointed to dramatic changes in our environment that have not been accompanied by suitable modification of man's genetically determined psychobiological reaction pattern, which has become obsolete, and noted that the stress reactions that promoted survival for stone age man when confronting a wolf pack are inappropriate for modern man when confronting a traffic jam or other new stress. Nixon (1976) emphasized the tendency of Type A's, in particular, to show these reactions and exceed their homeostatic mechanisms, a pattern so well intuited by Osler (1892) and by Raab (1953).

In fact, it has been found that subjects with CHD exhibit enhanced catecholamine discharge in response to emotional and other stress and during physical exertion (Nestel, Verghese, & Lovell, 1967; Voudoukis, 1971). Such enhanced discharge is associated with aggressiveness, competitive drive, anger, and time urgency (Elmadjian, Hope, & Lamson, 1958), which are major TABP facets. The TABP is a response style that leads to chronic performance at maximum capacity, with hyperreactiveness to actual or perceived threats (Glass, 1977). Increased norephinephrine excretion by Type A subjects has been found in work settings (Friedman et al., 1960) and in competitive situations (Dembroski et al., 1978; Friedman et al., 1975; Simpson et al., 1974). Enhanced norepinephrine discharge is a phasic phenomenon during exposure to the environment that induces TABP in predisposed individuals, who have the desire or need to perform at maximum capacity in response to external challenges and threats. The Minnesota prospective study pointed to the importance of catecholamines, finding that the cold pressor test, which reflects adrenergic responsiveness, and hence catecholamine secretion, is strongly predictive of CHD incidence (Keys et al., 1971). This same study also found the major facets of TABP to be similarly associated with CHD incidence (Brozek et al., 1966). Increased response to the cold pressor test has been found in atherosclerotic disease (Voudoukis, 1971) and in Type A's (Dembroski et al., 1978).

The TABP is an interplay between certain behaviors and the environment, and the overt manifestations of this pattern represent characterological response of Type A's to a milieu perceived as a challenge. Enhanced discharge of norephinephrine occurs when relevant challenge requires rapid and competitive responses by such persons (Friedman et al., 1975; Simpson et al., 1974). Therefore, autonomic arousal is best studied in dynamic response than by static measurements. Static measurements have shown no Type A-B differences in heart rate or blood pressure (Rosenman et al., 1964; Shekelle, Schoenberger & Stamler, 1976). However, differences are often—but not invariably—observed in exposure to laboratory stressors. Specifically, Type A's compared to Type B's have been found to exhibit a greater rise of heart rate, systolic and/or diastolic blood pressure, and catecholamine secretion, along with increased peripheral vasoconstriction and EKG changes, during the Structured Interview, reaction-time tasks, cognitive puzzle-solving, exposure to noise and to uncontrollable aversive factors, psychomotor performance tests, and the cold pressor test (Dembroski et al., 1978; Friedman et al., 1975; Lovallo & Pishkin, 1980). In general, the enhanced response of Type A's is greater in males than in females (Sime & Parker, 1978) and when the challenge is of high rather than low order. Response elevation tends to be greatest in Type A's who exhibit the most competitiveness, impatience, and hostility, the attributes that particularly characterize relationships between TABP and CHP incidence (Haynes et al., 1980; Jenkins, Rosenman, & Friedman, 1966; Matthews et al., 1977) and between TABP and severity of coronary atherosclerosis (Williams et al., 1980). However, such increased responses have not been found by all investigators, in part because of methodological differences. The results suggest that Type A's do not have any intrinsic hyperreactivity but only hyperresponsiveness that may be caused by heightened perception of stressors as challenges.

At this juncture, little is known about relationships between TABP and other physiological factors that might relate to CHD. Type A's compared to Type B's exhibit an enhanced blood clotting time in connection with situational stress (Friedman et al., 1958), as well as enhanced platelet aggregation in such circumstances (Jenkins et al., 1975).

MODIFICATION OF TYPE A BEHAVIOR

Only recently have formal studies been undertaken to assess the effects of TABP modification for purposes of prevention. The need appears important since there is still inadequate evidence of significant reductions of CHD morbidity from programs that have altered diet (Mann, 1977) or habits of physical activity (Froelicher et al., 1976), reduced serum cholesterol or blood pressure (Rosenman, 1979), or eliminated smoking (Seltzer, 1977; Sparrow, Dawber, & Colton, 1978). The importance of these measures cannot be denied, although improved benefits may require their initiation in childhood. In adults, decrease of CHD incidence and reinfarction may require concurrent modification of TABP (Rosenman, 1978a, b).

The reduction of CHD projected by modification of TABP has been shown to be statistically significant (Rosenman et al., 1976), but effective modification is not simplistic.

Many Type A behaviors are considered to be strengths and rewarded as such in the Western world. Moreover, TABP is not associated with perceived psychological distress (Chesney & Rosenman, 1980a), and many consider aspects of TABP to be integral factors in modern occupational careers. Many Type A's derive security and pride from their behavior pattern and find it difficult to understand how the TABP may contribute to CHD, diminished productivity, or life dissatisfaction. Type A behaviors are often deeply ingrained, sometimes dating to childhood or to entry into a career, making it difficult for an impatient Type A to follow a program that can be related only to reduced risk in the future. For these reasons, clinical experience indicates that modification of TABP can be accomplished more readily in postinfarction than in healthy individuals (Rosenman & Friedman, 1977).

There are a number of relevant considerations to address regarding Type A modification (Roskies, 1980). The first concerns the identification of candidates for change. Modification of TABP is particularly important for patients with angina pectoris or prior myocardial infarction and for Type A subjects who are at higher risk by reason of either subclinical severe coronary atherosclerosis or high levels of other risk factors. In healthy individuals, modification may be appropriate for some Type A's with the characteristics that enhance coronary-prone TABP; for example, excessively competitive subjects who are chronically rushed and habitually hostile in response to environmental stressors. It should be understood that *modification does not mean an attempt to change a Type A into a Type B* but only to reduce excessive and adverse Type A responses for that person. Clinical experience has shown that such changes are associated with increased life satisfaction and often with improved productivity (Chesney & Rosenman, 1980a; Roskies, Kearney, Spevack, Surkis, Cohen, & Gilman, 1979).

The second consideration concerns which Type A behaviors should be modified since there is a need to select specific targets for intervention. It now seems fruitful to attempt modification of Type A behaviors that relate particularly to CHD, including *excessive* competitive drive, habitual severe impatience and time urgency, hostility, and hyperresponsiveness to environmental stressors (Chesney & Rosenman, 1980a).

The third consideration concerns methodology. As this chapter has emphasized, TABP is an interplay between certain behaviors and the environment. Successful adaptation to Western industrialization has been accomplished in Japan without the excessively rushed pace and individual competitiveness that probably explain neurohormonal links between TABP and CHD (Cohen et al., 1975; Matsumoto, 1970). In the West it is infrequently appropriate to advise occupational or other major lifestyle changes. It is possible, nevertheless, to alter methods of coping with stress (Chesney & Rosenman, 1980; Roskies, 1980) and to reduce autonomic hyperresponsiveness by such methodologies as muscular relaxation, meditation, biofeedback, autogenic training, anxiety management training, stress management training, and instruction in altered perception of stressors (Roskies & Lazarus, 1980).

Suinn (1979) developed an approach to TABP modification that teaches the subject a relaxation based strategy for coping with stress. Subjects are first relaxed and then trained to visualize an interaction that usually prompts Type A reactions. Once subjects begin to experience the arousal associated with Type A behavior, they are instructed to switch from the arousal state to a relaxed state. This visualization-arousal-relaxation sequence is practiced repeatedly until subjects can respond to arousal by substituting relaxation, a behavior thought to be protective of the cardiovascular system.

Roskies, Spevack, Surkis, Cohen, and Gilman (1978) used two different methods for modification of TABP. One was a psychoanalytically oriented and the other a behaviorally oriented training program for reduction of anxiety and tension. The follow-up revealed significantly less self-reported anxiety in subjects in the behavior therapy group. Others have not found that either Transcendental Meditation or progressive relaxation training is effective in altering TABP (Sime & Parker, 1978; Thompson, 1976).

Rahe and associates (Rahe, Ward, & Hayes, 1979) attempted TABP modification by group education and therapy in patients recovering from acute myocardial infarction, with impressive results at the four-year follow-up. Significantly fewer deaths and recurring CHD events were observed in the cognitive group therapy than in the control group in this pilot study, showing that modification of TABP may be effective for secondary CHD prevention.

Modification of TABP is most likely with a strategy that integrates cognitive, physiological, and behavioral methods (Chesney & Rosenman, 1980; Rosenman & Friedman, 1977). The cognitive aspects of the TABP (e.g., thoughts, perceptions, self-statements) can be addressed using cognitive restructuring procedures. Indeed, in one investigation such cognitive therapy was found to be superior to relaxation based stress management training (Jenni & Wollersheim, 1979). Other aspects of TABP can be best treated by direct modification of such overt behavior patterns as overscheduling appointments and taking excessive amounts of work home. Despite extensive cognitive and behavior changes, patients are inevitably confronted with situations that elicit TABP responses, including irritation and autonomic arousal. These responses can be controlled by relaxation based techniques for reducing autonomic arousal. Thus, successful modification of TABP must address all three factors to equip each patient with a set of coping strategies from which to select those that are most effective at the time of treatment, as well as those that may be more effective in the future.

The National Heart, Lung, and Blood Institute recently assembled a review panel critically to examine the evidence for the association between TABP and CHD.

> The Review Panel accepts the available body of scientific evidence as demonstrating that Type A behavior (as defined by the Structured Interview, JAS, and Framingham scale) is associated with an increased risk of clinically apparent CHD in employed, middle-aged U.S. citizens. This increased risk is over and above that imposed by age, systolic blood pressure, serum cholesterol, and smoking appears to be of the same order of magnitude as the relative risk associated with any of these factors. (Cooper, Detre, Weiss, Bristow, Carleton, Dustan, Elliot, Feinlieb, Jesse, Klocke, Schwartz, Shields & Stallones, 1981:1200–1215).

CONCLUSION

This chapter reviewed findings relevant to the Type A behavior pattern. This pattern of behavior was identified by the search for additional risk factors essential to understanding CHD etiology and developing treatment and prevention measures. The TABP does not equate with personality and emotional factors assessed by standard psychometric inventories but is instead an interplay of certain behaviors and emotional responses with the environment. The procedures for assessing TABP and the sociodemographic correlates of the behavior pattern were described. We also discussed research demonstrating the causal role of TABP in both clinical coronary heart disease and the severity of coronary atherosclerosis in both sexes. The TABP has a predictive strength that is independent of and equivalent to the standard risk factors for CHD. Moreover, the relationship of TABP to CHD has cross-cultural validity, specificity, and a biological gradient of pathogenicity. Finally, we surveyed research on and recommendations for modifying TABP in order to reduce the CHD risk it carries.

REFERENCES

Arlow, J. A. Indentification of mechanisms in coronary occlusion. *Psychosomatic Medicine,* 1945, *7,* 195–209.

Barratt, E. S. Factor analysis of impulsiveness and anxiety. *Psychological Reports,* 1965, *16,* 547–554.

Blumenthal, J. A., Williams, R., Kong, Y., Schanberg, S. M., & Thompson, L. W. Type A behavior and angiographically documented coronary disease. *Circulation,* 1978, *58,* 634–639.

Bortner, R. W. A short rating scale as a potential measure of Pattern A behavior. *Journal of Chronic Diseases,* 1969, *22,* 87–91.

Bortner, R. W., & Rosenman, R. H. The measurement of Pattern A behavior. *Journal of Chronic Diseases,* 1967, *20,* 525–533.

Bortner, R. W., Rosenman, R. H., & Friedman, M. Familial similarity in Pattern A behavior: Father and sons. *Journal of Chronic Diseases,* 1970, *23,* 39–43.

Brand, R. J. Coronary-prone behavior as an independent risk factor for coronary heart disease. In T. M. Dembroski, S. M. Weiss, J. L. Shields, S. G. Haynes, & M. Feinleib (eds.), *Coronary-prone behavior.* New York: Springer, 1978.

Brand, R. J., Rosenman, R. H., Jenkins, C. D., Sholtz, R. I., & Zyzanski, S. J. Comparison of coronary heart disease prediction in the Western Collaborative Group Study using the structured interview and the Jenkins Activity Survey assessments of the coronary-prone Type A behavior pattern. Unpublished manuscript, University of California, Berkeley, 1978.

Brozek, J., Keys, A., & Blackburn, H. Personality differences between potential coronary and non-coronary subjects. *Annals of the New York Academy of Sciences,* 1966, *134,* 1057–1064.

Bruhn, J. G., & Wolf, S. Studies reporting "low rates" of ischemic heart disease: A critical review. *American Journal of Public Health,* 1970, *60,* 1477–1495.

Butensky, A., Forelli, V., Heebner, D., & Waldron, I. Elements of the coronary-prone behavior pattern in children and teenagers. *Journal of Psychosomatic Research,* 1976, *20,* 439–444.

Caffrey, B. Reliability and validity of personality and behavioral measures in a study of coronary heart disease. *Journal of Chronic Diseases,* 1968, *21,* 191–204.

Can I avoid a heart attack? *Lancet,* 1974, *1,* 605–607.

Caplan, R. D., & Jones, K. W. Effects of work load, role ambiguity, and Type A personality on anxiety, depression, and heart rate. *Journal of Applied Psychology,* 1975, *60,* 713–719.

Cattell, R. B., Eber, H. W., & Tatsuoka, M. *Handbook for the sixteen personality factor questionnaire.* Champaign: Institute for Personality and Ability Testing, 1970.

Chesney, M. A., Black, G. W., Chadwick, J. H., & Rosenman, R. H. Psychological correlates of the coronary-prone behavior pattern. *Journal of Behavioral Medicine,* 1981, *4,* 217–230.

Chesney, M. A., & Rosenman, R. H. Strategies for modifying Type A behavior. *Consultant,* 1980, *20,* 216–222. (a)

————. Type A behavior in the work setting. In C. Cooper & R. Payne (eds.), *Current issues in occupational stress.* New York: Wiley, 1980. (b)

Cohen, J. B., Syme, S. L., Jenkins, C. D., Dagan, A., & Zyzanski, S. J. The cultural context of Type A behavior and the risk of CHD. *American Journal of Epidemiology,* 1975, *102,* 434.

Cooper, T., Detre, T., Weiss, S. M., Bristow, J. D., Carleton, R., Dustan, H. P., Elliot, R. S., Feinleib, M., Jesse, M. J., Klocke, F. J., Schwartz, G. E., Shields, J. M., & Stallones, R. A. Coronary-prone behavior and coronary heart disease: A critical review. *Circulation,* 1981, *63,* 1200–1215.

Corday, E. and Corday, S. R. Prevention of heart disease by control of risk factors: The time has come to face the facts. Editorial. *American Journal of Cardiology,* 1975, *35,* 330–335.

Dahlstrom, W. G., & Welsh, G. S. *An MMPI handbook: A guide to use in clinical practice and research.* Minneapolis: University of Minnesota Press, 1960.

DEMBROSKI, T. M., MACDOUGALL, J. M., SHIELDS, J. L., PETITTO, J., & LUSHENE, R. Components of Type A coronary-prone behavior pattern and cardiovascular responses to psychomotor challenge. *Journal of Behavioral Medicine,* 1978, *1,* 159–176.

DEROGATIS, L. R. *Symptom distress check list (rev. ed.).* Baltimore: Johns Hopkins University Press, 1977.

DUCIMETIÈRE, P., CAMBIEN, F., RICHARD, J. L., RAKOTOVAO, R., & CLAUDE, J. R. Coronary heart disease in middle-aged Frenchmen. *Lancet,* 1980, *1,* 1346–1349.

DUNBAR, H. F. *Psychosomatic diagnosis.* New York: Hoeber, 1943.

ELMADJIAN, F., HOPE, J. M., & LAMSON, E. T. Excretion of epinephrine and norepinephrine under stress. *Recent Progress in Hormone Research,* 1958, *14,* 513.

EYSENCK, H. J., & EYSENCK, S. B. G. *Eysenck personality inventory.* San Diego: Educational and Industrial Testing Service, 1968.

FEINLEIB, M., BRAND, R. J., REMINGTON, R., & ZYZANSKI, S. J. Association of the coronary-prone behavior pattern and coronary heart disease. In T. M. Dembroski, S. M. Weiss, J. L. Shields, S. G. Haynes, & M. Feinleib (eds.), *Coronary-prone behavior.* New York: Springer, 1978.

FRANK, K. A., HELLER, S. S., KORNFIELD, D. S., SPORN, A. A., & WEISS, M. B. Type A behavior and coronary heart disease: Angiographic confirmation. *Journal of the American Medical Association,* 1978, *240,* 761–763.

FRIEDMAN, M., BYERS, S. O., DIAMANT, J., & ROSENMAN, R. H. Plasma catecholamine response of coronary-prone subjects (Type A) to a specific challenge. *Metabolism,* 1975, *4,* 205–210.

FRIEDMAN, M., MANWARING, J. H., ROSENMAN, R. H., DONLON, G., ORTEGA, P., & GRUBE, S. M. Instantaneous and sudden death: Clinical and pathological differentiation in coronary artery disease. *Journal of the American Medical Association,* 1973, *225,* 1319–1328.

FRIEDMAN, M., & ROSENMAN, R. H. Association of specific overt behavior pattern with blood and cardiovascular findings. *Journal of the American Medical Association,* 1959, *169,* 1286–1296.

FRIEDMAN, M., ROSENMAN, R. H., & CARROLL, V. Changes in the serum cholesterol and blood-clotting time in men subjected to cyclic variation of occupational stress. *Circulation,* 1958, *17,* 852–861.

FRIEDMAN, M., ROSENMAN, R. H., STRAUS, R., WURM, M., & KOSITCHEK, R. The relationship of behavior Pattern A to the state of the coronary vasculature: A study of fifty-one autopsy subjects. *American Journal of Medicine,* 1968, *44,* 525–537.

FRIEDMAN, M., ST. GEORGE, S., & BYERS, S. O. Excretion of catecholamines, 17-ketosteroids, 17-hydroxycorticoids, and 5-hydroxyindole in men exhibiting a particular behavior pattern (A) associated with high incidence of clinical coronary artery disease. *Journal of Clinical Investigation,* 1960, *39,* 758–764.

FROELICHER, V. F., LONGO, M. R., & MCIVER, R. G. *The effects of chronic exercise on the heart and on coronary atherosclerotic heart disease: A literature survey.* Brooks Air Force Base: U.S. Air Force, Aerospace Medical Division, 1976.

GILDEA, E. Special features of personality which are common to certain psychosomatic disorders. *Psychosomatic Medicine,* 1949, *11,* 273–277.

GLASS, D. C. *Behavior patterns, stress, and coronary disease.* Hillsdale: Erlbaum, 1977.

GORDON, T., GARCIA-PALMIERI, M. R., KAGAN, A., KANNEL, W. B., & SCHIFFMAN, J. Differences in coronary heart disease in Framingham, Honolulu, and Puerto Rico. *Journal of Chronic Diseases,* 1974, *27,* 329–337.

GORDON, T., & VERTER, J. Serum cholesterol, systolic blood pressure, and Framingham relative weight as discriminators of cardiovascular disease. In W. B. Kannel & T. Gordon (eds.), *The Framingham Study: An epidemiological investigation of cardiovascular disease.* Washington, D.C.: U.S. Government Printing Office, 1969.

GOUGH, H. G. *California Psychological Inventory.* Palo Alto: Consulting Psychologists Press, 1956.

GOUGH, H. G., & HEILBRUN, A. B. *The adjective check list.* Palo Alto: Consulting Psychologists Press, 1980.

GROEN, J. J., TJIONG, B., KAMMINGER, C. E., & WILLBRANDS, A. F. The influence of nutrition, individuality, and some other factors, including various forms of stress, on serum cholesterol: An experiment of nine months' duration in 60 normal human volunteers. *Voeding,* 1962, *13,* 556.

HAFT, J. I., & FANI, K. Intravascular platelet aggregation in the heart induced by stress. *Circulation,* 1973, *47,* 353.

HAYNES, S. G., FEINLEIB, M., & KANNEL, W. B. The relationship of psychosocial factors to coronary heart disease in the Framingham Study. Part III: Eight-year incidence of CHD. *American Journal of Epidemiology,* 1980, *3,* 37–58.

HAYNES, S. G., FEINLEIB, M., LEVINE, S., SCOTCH, N., & KANNEL, W. B. The relationship of psychosocial factors to coronary heart disease in the Framingham Study: Prevalence of coronary heart disease. *American Journal of Epidemiology,* 1978, *107,* 384–402.

HORN, J. M., PLOMIN, R., & ROSENMAN, R. Heritability of personality traits in adult male twins. *Behavior Genetics,* 1976, *6,* 17–30.

HOWARD, J. H., CUNNINGHAM, D. A., & RECHNITZER, P. A. Work patterns associated with Type A behavior: A managerial population. *Human Relations,* 1977, *30,* 825–836.

INSEL, P. M., & MOOS, R. H. *Work environment scale.* Palo Alto: Consulting Psychologists Press, 1974.

JENKINS, C. D. Recent evidence supporting psychologic and social risk factors for coronary disease. *New England Journal of Medicine,* 1976, *294,* 987–1038.

JENKINS, C. D., HAMES, C. G., ZYZANSKI, S. J., ROSENMAN, R. H., & FRIEDMAN, M. Psychological traits and serum lipids. Part I: Findings from the California Psychological Inventory. *Psychosomatic Medicine,* 1969, *31,* 115–128.

JENKINS, C. D., ROSENMAN, R. H., & FRIEDMAN, M. Replicability of rating the coronary-prone behavior pattern. *British Journal of Preventive and Social Medicine,* 1968, *22,* 16–22.

JENKINS, C. D., ROSENMAN, R. H., & ZYZANSKI, S. J. Cigarette smoking: Its relationship to coronary heart disease and related risk factors in the Western Collaborative Group Study. *Circulation,* 1968, *38,* 1140–1155.

————. Prediction of clinical coronary heart disease by a test for the coronary-prone behavioral pattern. *New England Journal of Medicine,* 1974, *290,* 1271–1275.

————. *Jenkins Activity Survey.* New York: Psychological Corporation, 1979.

JENKINS, C. D., THOMAS, G., OLEWINE, D., ZYZANSKI, S. J., SIMPSON, M. T., & HAMES, S. G. Blood platelet aggregation and personality traits. *Journal of Human Stress,* 1975, *1,* 34–46.

JENKINS, C. D., ZYZANSKI, S. J., & ROSENMAN, R. H. Risk of new myocardial infarction in middle-aged men with manifest coronary heart disease. *Circulation,* 1976, *53,* 342–347.

————. *Jenkins activity survey.* New York: Psychological Corporation, 1979.

JENNI, M. A., & WOLLERSHEIM, J. P. Cognitive therapy, stress management training, and the Type A behavior pattern. *Cognitive Therapy and Research,* 1979, *3,* 61–73.

KANNEL, W. B., & GORDON, T. (eds.). *The Framingham study.* DHEW Publication (NIH) 74–599. Washington, D.C.: U.S. Government Printing Office, 1974.

KEMPLE, C. Rorschach method and psychosomatic diagnosis: Personality traits of patients with rheumatic disease, hypertension, cardiovascular disease, coronary occlusion, and fracture. *Psychosomatic Medicine,* 1945, *7,* 85–89.

KEYS, A., ARAVANIS, C., BLACKBURN, H., VANBUCHEM, F. S. P., BUZINA, R., DJORDJENIC, B. S., FIDANZA, F., KARVONEN, M. J., MENOTTI, A., PUDDU, V., & TAYLOR, H. L. Probability of middle-aged men developing coronary heart disease in 5 years. *Circulation,* 1972, *45,* 815–828.

KEYS, A., TAYLOR, H. L., BLACKBURN, H., BROZEK, J., & ANDERSON, J. T. Mortality and coronary heart disease among men studied for 23 years. *Annals of Internal Medicine,* 1971, *128,* 201–205.

KITTEL, F., DORNITZER, M., ZYZANSKI, S. J., JENKINS, C. D., RUSTIN, R. M., & DÉGRE, C. Two methods of assessing the Type A coronary-prone behavior pattern in Belgium. *Journal of Chronic Diseases,* 1978, *31,* 147–155.

KOZAREVIC, D., PIRC, B., RAVIC, Z., DAWBER, T. R., GORDON, T., & ZUKEL, W. J. The Yugoslavia cardiovascular disease study. Part II: Factors in the incidence of coronary heart disease. *American Journal of Epidemiology,* 1976, *104,* 133–140.

KRANTZ, D. S., SANMARCO, M. I., SELVESTER, R. H., & MATHEWS, K. Psychological correlates of progression of atherosclerosis in man. *Psychosomatic Medicine,* 1975, *41,* 467–475.

LEVI, L., & ANDERSSON, L. *Psychosocial stress: Population, environment, and quality of life.* New York: Spectrum, 1975.

LOVALLO, W. R., & PISHKIN, V. A psychophysiological comparison of Type A and B men exposed to failure and uncontrollable noise. *Psychophysiology,* 1980, *17,* 29–36.

LOWN, B., & VERRIER, R. L. Neural activity and ventricular fibrillation. *New England Journal of Medicine,* 1976, *294,* 1165–1170.

MACDOUGALL, J. M., DEMBROSKI, T. M., & MUSANTE, L. The structured interview and questionnaire methods of assessing coronary-prone behavior in male and female college students. *Journal of Behavioral Medicine,* 1979, *2,* 71–83.

MANN, G. V. Diet-heart: End of an era. *New England Journal of Medicine,* 1977, *297,* 644–650.

MATSUMOTO, Y. S. Social stress and coronary heart disease in Japan: A hypothesis. *Milbank Memorial Fund Quarterly,* 1970, *48,* 9–36.

MATTHEWS, K. A. Assessment and developmental antecedents of the coronary-prone behavior pattern in children. In T. M. Dembroski, S. M. Weiss, J. L. Shields, S. G. Haynes, & M. Feinleib (eds.), *Coronary-prone behavior.* New York: Springer, 1978.

MATTHEWS, K. A., GLASS, D. C., ROSENMAN, R. H., & BORTNER, R. W. Competitive drive, Pattern A, and coronary heart disease: A further analysis of some data from the Western Collaborative Group Study. *Journal of Chronic Diseases,* 1977, *30,* 489–498.

MATTHEWS, K. A., KRANTZ, D. S. Resemblances of twins and their parents in Pattern A behavior. *Psychosomatic Medicine,* 1976, *28,* 140–144.

MATTHEWS, K. A., & SAAL, F. E. The relationship of the Type A coronary prone behavior pattern to achievement, power, and affiliation motives. *Psychosomatic Medicine,* 1978, *40,* 631–636.

MENNINGER, K. A., & MENNINGER, W. C. Psychoanalytic observations in cardiac disorders. *American Heart Journal,* 1936, *11,* 10–26.

National Institutes of Health. The MRFIT behavior pattern study. Part I: Study design, procedures, and reproducibility of behavior pattern judgments. *Journal of Chronic Diseases,* 1979, *32,* 293–305.

NESTEL, P. J., VERGHESE, A., & LOVELL, R. R. H. Catecholamine secretion and sympathetic nervous responses to emotion in men with and without angina pectoris. *American Heart Journal,* 1967, *73,* 227–234.

NIXON, P. G. F. The human function curve, with special reference to cardiovascular disorders. *Practitioner,* 1976, *275,* 765–935.

OSLER, W. The Lumleian lectures on angina pectoris. *Lancet,* 1892, *1,* 839–844.

RAAB, W. *Hormonal and neurogenic cardiovascular disorders.* Baltimore: Williams & Wilkins, 1953.

————. (ed.), *Prevention of ischemic heart disease.* Springfield: Thomas, 1966.

RAHE, R. H., WARD, H. W., & HAYES, V. Brief group therapy in myocardial infarction rehabilitation: Three to four-year follow up of a controlled trial. *Psychosomatic Medicine,* 1979, *41,* 229–242.

ROSENMAN, R. H. The interview method of assessment of the coronary prone behavior pattern. In T. M. Dembroski, S. M. Weiss, J. L. Shields, S. G. Haynes, & M. Feinleib (eds.), *Coronary-prone behavior.* New York: Springer, 1978. (a)

————. The role of the Type A behavior pattern in ischemic heart disease: Modification of its effects by beta-blocking agents. *British Journal of Clinical Practice* (supp. 1), 1978, *32,* 58–65. (b)

————. Role of Type A behavior pattern in the pathogenesis of ischemic heart disease and modification for prevention. *Advances in Cardiology,* 1978, *25,* 1-12. (c)

————. The heart you save may be your own. In J. Chacko (ed.), *Health handbook.* Amsterdam: North-Holland, 1979.

ROSENMAN, R. H., BAWOL, R. D., & OSCHERWITZ, M. A 4-year prospective study of the relationship of different habitual vocational physical activity to risk and incidence of ischemic heart disease in volunteer male federal employees. In P. Milvy (ed.), *The marathon.* New York: New York Academy of Sciences, 1977.

ROSENMAN, R. H., BRAND, R. J., JENKINS, C. D., FRIEDMAN, M., STRAUS, R., & WURM, M. Coronary heart disease in the Western Collaborative Group Study: Final follow-up of 8½ years. *Journal of the American Medical Association,* 1975, *233,* 872-877.

ROSENMAN, R. H., BRAND, R. J., SHOLTZ, R. I., & FRIEDMAN, M. Multivariate prediction of coronary heart disease during 8.5 year follow-up in the Western Collaborative Group Study. *American Journal of Cardiology,* 1976, *37,* 903-910.

ROSENMAN, R. H., & CHESNEY, M. A. The relationship of Type A behavior pattern to coronary heart disease. *Activitas Nervosa Superior,* 1980, *22,* 1-45.

ROSENMAN, R. H., & FRIEDMAN, M. Association of specific behavior pattern in women with blood and cardiovascular findings. *Journal of the American Medical Association,* 1961, *24,* 1173-1184.

————. Behavior patterns, blood lipids, and coronary heart disease. *Journal of the American Medical Association,* 1963, *184,* 934-938.

————. Neurogenic factors in the pathogenesis of coronary heart disease. *Medical Clinics of North America,* 1974, *58,* 269-279.

————. Modifying Type A behavior pattern. *Journal of Psychosomatic Research,* 1977, *21,* 323-331.

ROSENMAN, R. H., FRIEDMAN, M., JENKINS, C. D., STRAUS, R., WURM, M., & KOSITCHEK, R. The prediction of immunity to coronary heart disease. *Journal of the American Medical Association,* 1966, *198,* 1159-1162.

————. Recurring and fatal myocardial infarction in the Western Collaborative Group Study. *American Journal of Cardiology,* 1967, *19,* 771-775.

ROSENMAN, R. H., FRIEDMAN, M., STRAUS, R., WURM, M., KOSITCHEK, R., HAHN, W., & WERTHESSEN, N. T. A predictive study of coronary heart disease: The Western Collaborative Group Study. *Journal of the American Medical Association,* 1964, *189,* 15-22.

ROSENMAN, R. H., RAHE, R. H., BORHANI, N. O., & FEINLEIB, M. Heritability of personality and behavior. *Acta Geneticae Medicae et Gemellologiae,* 1976, *25,* 221-224.

ROSKIES, E. Considerations in developing a treatment program for the coronary-prone (Type A) behavior pattern. In P. O. Davidson & S. M. Davidson (eds.), *Behavioral medicine: Changing health life styles.* New York: Brunner/Mazel, 1980.

ROSKIES, E., KEARNEY, H., SPEVACK, M., SURKIS, A., COHEN, C., & GILMAN, S. Generalizability and durability of treatment effects in an intervention program for coronary-prone (Type A) managers. *Journal of Behavioral Medicine,* 1979, *2,* 195-207.

ROSKIES, E., & LAZARUS, R. S. Coping theory and the teaching of coping skills. In P. O. Davidson & S. M. Davidson (eds.), *Behavioral medicine: Changing health life styles.* New York: Brunner/Mazel, 1980.

ROSKIES, E., SPEVACK, M., SURKIS, A., COHEN, C., and GILMAN, S. Changing the coronary-prone (Type A) behavior pattern in a non-clinical population. *Journal of Behavioral Medicine,* 1978, *1,* 201-216.

SCHUCKER, B., & JACOBS, D. R. Assessment of behavioral risks for coronary disease by voice characteristics. *Psychosomatic Medicine,* 1977, *39,* 219-228.

SELTZER, C. Smoking and coronary heart disease. *New England Journal of Medicine,* 1977, *228,* 1186.

SHEKELLE, R. B., SCHOENBERGER, J. A., & STAMLER, J. Correlates of the JAS Type A behavior score. *Journal of Chronic Diseases,* 1976, *29,* 381–394.

SIGLER, L. H. The mortality from arteriosclerotic and hypertensive heart diseases in the United States. Part I: Possible relation to distribution of population and economic status. *American Journal of Cardiology,* 1959, *1,* 605.

SIME, W. E., & PARKER, C. Physiological arousal in male and female students with either Type A or B behavior patterns. *Medicine and Science in Sports,* 1978, *10,* 51.

SIMPSON, M. T., OLEWINE, D. A., JENKINS, C. D., RAMSEY, F. H., ZYZANSKI, S. J., THOMAS, G., & JAMES, C. G. Exercise-induced catecholamines and platelet aggregation in the coronary-prone behavior pattern. *Psychosomatic Medicine,* 1974, *36,* 476–487.

SPARROW, D., DAWBER, T. R., & COLTON, T. The influence of cigarette smoking on prognosis after a first myocardial infarction: A report from the Framingham Study. *Journal of Chronic Diseases,* 1978, *31,* 425–433.

SPIELBERGER, C. D., GORSUCH, R. L., & LUSHENE, R. E. *State-trait anxiety inventory.* Palo Alto: Consulting Psychologists Press, 1970.

STEWART, I. M. G. Coronary disease and modern stress. *Lancet,* 1950, *2,* 867–878.

SUINN, R. M. Type A behavior pattern. In R. B. Williams & W. D. Gentry (eds.), *Behavioral approaches to medical treatment.* Cambridge: Ballinger, 1979.

THOMPSON, P. B. Effectiveness of relaxation techniques in reducing anxiety and stress factors in Type A, post-myocardial infarction patients. Doctoral dissertation, University of Massachusetts, 1976.

THURSTONE, L. L. *Thurstone temperament schedule.* Chicago: Science Research Associates, 1949.

VAN DUSCH, T. *Lehrbuch der Herzkrankheiten.* Liepzig: Engelman, 1868.

VOUDOUKIS, I. J. Exaggerated cold-pressor response in patients with atherosclerotic vascular disease. *Angiography,* 1971, *22,* 57–62.

WALDRON, I., ZYZANSKI, S., SHEKELLE, R. B., JENKINS, C. D., & TANNEBAUM, S. The coronary-prone behavior pattern in employed men and women. *Journal of Human Stress,* 1977, *3,* 2–18.

WILLIAMS, R. B., THOMAS, T. L., LEE, K. L., KONG, Y., BLUMENTHAL, J. A., & WHALEN, R. E. Type A behavior, hostility, and coronary atherosclerosis. *Psychosomatic Medicine,* 1980, *42,* 539–549.

ZYZANSKI, S. J., JENKINS, C. D., RYAN, T. J., FLESSAS, A., & EVERIST, M. Psychological correlates of coronary angiographic findings. *Archives of Internal Medicine,* 1976, *136,* 1234–1237.

34

Stress and Psychiatric Disorders

Judith Godwin Rabkin

ALTHOUGH THE ETIOLOGY OF THE PSYCHIATRIC DISORDERS has constituted a hotly controversial issue throughout the history of psychiatry, and questions about the relative influence of genetic and socioenvironmental factors have never been consensually resolved, few today would entirely exclude from consideration either one realm or the other. It is generally assumed that to varying degrees, depending on the particular syndrome, both biology and experience contribute to the risk of becoming ill, and genetic factors are being increasingly acknowledged as well. Under the label "experience" is usually included not only lifelong exposure and patterns but also the idea of a particular experience or event that is either etiologically or temporally associated with illness onset. In view of this nearly universal conceptualization of stress as a relevant consideration in illness onset, it is all the more surprising that the large majority of studies of stress and psychiatric disorder have failed to demonstrate a clinically significant association, although small, statistically significant relationships repeatedly have been found.

Many who have studied and worked in this field for any length of time believe that a substantial proportion of the research is sufficiently flawed in conceptualization and design so as to preclude identification of clear-cut relationships even if they do exist. Certainly, most of these problems are not specific to the study of stress and psychiatric disorders, and note is taken of them elsewhere in this volume. Both in order fairly to appraise the quality and validity of previous research and to improve the design of future work, I review in some detail those issues of concept and design particularly germane to the study of psychiatric disorders. After brief consideration of the officially recognized stress syndromes, I summarize the cumulative findings for the three major classes of functional disorder: anxiety disorders, schizophrenia, and depressive disorders. The extent and quality of study of these disorders vary considerably. Least has been done with anxiety disorders, and fewer than 20 controlled studies have explored the association between stress and schizophrenia, although some solid work has been published. In contrast, dozens of investigators have considered aspects of the relationship between stress and depressive disorder. Volume is related to level of sophistication of the issues addressed; thus, studies range from simple explorations of proportions of patients who report precipitating events to comparatively refined analyses of the role of concurrent personal and social variables in mediating the effects of exposure to stressors.

In the following discussion, the terms "life events" and "stressors" are used interchangeably. Both refer to discrete changes in life conditions that are consensually recognized as entailing some degree of distress, challenge, and/or hazard by the individual and members of his/her social group.

METHODOLOGICAL CONSIDERATIONS

As in the field of psychotherapy research, the study of stress and illness seems to have generated as much commentary as original research. Numerous reviewers have identified and described potential and actual sources of error in instruments and methods (e.g., Brown, 1974; Dohrenwend & Dohrenwend, 1978; Rabkin & Struening, 1976a). Perhaps partly as a result of such critical assessment, the quality of life events research is improving, although numerous issues remain unresolved. In this chapter, I will briefly note those particularly relevent to the study of psychiatric disorders.

Choice of Stress Model

A remarkable number of studies are minimally informative because of naive or inappropriate conceptions of stress and illness, indifference to the issue of psychiatric diagnosis, or some combination of these defects. With rare exceptions, investigators develop a model of stress and illness that is applied to all forms of psychiatric disorder, ignoring the possibility that different conceptualizations might be appropriate for psychiatric disorders with different historical antecedents and prodromal stages.

At least three major models of stress and illness have evolved in relation to the study of psychiatric disorders. Dohrenwend and Dohrenwend [1981] delineated seven models, but several of these are related to each other. In the simplest and historically earliest approach, the *innocent victim model,* the prospective patient by chance is exposed to stressful environmental events or circumstances that cause illness. This conception of illness and stress scarcely applies to most medical or psychiatric conditions as they are understood today, although it is valid with respect to rare and catastrophic situations such as prisoner of war or concentration camp internment. In such extreme conditions, the probability of both immediate and delayed illness is significantly increased for perfectly healthy people (Ursano, Boydstun & Wheatley, 1981). In sufficiently adverse circumstances, then, it is not a matter of *whether* but of *when* disorders will be manifested. In the current psychiatric nomenclature of *DSM-III* (1980), such reactions to unusual traumatic events are classified separately as post–traumatic stress disorder. In most other circumstances, however, this model is inadequate.

A model more generally relevant to the study of psychiatric disorder is called the *vulnerability hypothesis* (Dohrenwend & Dohrenwend, 1981). According to this model, chance exposure to stressors triggers illness onset in already vulnerable people. The source of vulnerability may vary according to the disorder or the investigator's point of view and may include childhood experiences, family relationships, or genetic predisposition. In addition, the resources available to the person, such as social supports, fiscal backing, or personal coping skills, are considered mediating factors that determine the impact of the stressor on the person and therefore affect the probability of his/her becoming ill. This is perhaps the most popular current model.

A third construction is structural, interactive, and probably most appropriate for at least some types of psychiatric illness. The *interactive model* is similar to the proneness, or vulnerability, hypothesis of Dohrenwend and Dohrenwend (1981). It suggests that because of preexisting deficiencies in coping and interpersonal skills, people who later become clinically ill either are unable to forestall the occurrence of undesirable life events or by their behavior actively provoke them while at the same time they lack the ability to make good events happen. Their long-standing limitations not only influence the number and quality of the life events they encounter but also determine the availability and extent of mediating factors such as access to social and family supports. This interactive conception seems more relevant to some illness types (e.g., schizophrenia) than others (e.g., panic disorder).

In short, it seems advisable to select the stress model most nearly related to the clinical condition under study in order to maximize the likelihood of finding meaningful associations between stress and illness.

Illness Definition: Clinical Diagnosis

Comparatively little attention has been devoted to the systematic diagnosis of psychiatric disorders in most stress research, a regrettable state of affairs that has detracted from the value of many studies. Many investigators have been content either to identify the presence or absence of disorder (or *casedness*) based on global ratings or interviews that are either structured or not, or else to classify research subjects in terms of number of symptoms reported. In the latter case they use various checklists, which may or may not be factor-analysed to identify symptom clusters and which cumulatively often measure demoralization rather than the presence of any particular psychiatric disorder (Dohrenwend, 1979). In such studies, the type of symptom is often not specified, or else respondents with different symptom clusters are combined to facilitate data analysis. This approach used to characterize studies of stress and medical conditions in which, for example, patients with skin problems and coronary heart disease were together classified as suffering from chronic disorders (Rabkin & Struening, 1976). While this failure to disaggregate groups is seldom seen now in studies of medical disorders, it remains all too common in studies of psychiatric disorders.

In addition to the application of systematic diagnostic criteria for psychiatric disorders, such as the Research Diagnostic Criteria of Spitzer, Endicott, and Robins (1978) or the *DSM-III* (1980) categories, the medical condition and current medication regimens of study participants warrant assessment, since both may contribute to cognitive and behavioral deviations that may be mistaken for signs of psychiatric disorder. Concurrent medical conditions may or may not be related to the stressors being studied, but in any case they should not be confused with manifestations of psychiatric disorder. Finally, it would be useful to distinguish between the presence of psychiatric disorder as such and the seeking of treatment for psychiatric problems. Since we know that at least as many people with psychiatric disorders remain untreated as receive treatment, and since there is no reason to assume that treated cases are a representative sample of all cases, this distinction may contribute to an understanding of the relation between stressors and illness as such.

Event Definitions

Originally, life events researchers used scales consisting of 40 or more items, such as marriage, birth of child, fired at work (Holmes & Rahe, 1967). The respondent's total score consisted of the sum (sometimes weighted) of items reported to have occurred during the preceding six months or year. However, many questions have been raised about the meaning of such a score, combining as it does so many disparate events. Although not routinely done, it would be useful for events to be differentiated in terms of whether they are anticipated or unanticipated, familiar or novel, desirable or undesirable, sudden or gradual, discrete or temporally prolonged, subjectively perceived as stressful by the patient or not so perceived, and fateful (outside one's control) or nonfateful. Is it possible for a respondent to experience a given event? Does the absence of an anticipated or desired event such as marriage represent a stressful experience? Does it matter whether the event constitutes a "role entrance" rather than a "role exit"? How close in timing must an event be to illness onset to be considered contributory? What is the difference between a life event and a condition or problem in living? When does an event, such as the chronic illness of a relative, stop being counted as an event? Should rare events be excluded because of reliability problems? Such unresolved questions generally concern the nature of the domain of life events to be sampled and represent problems in content validity and methods of measurement.

In addition to the formal characteristics of the items to be included, their content warrants consideration. Certain kinds of stressors would seem more likely to be linked with a particular disorder—e.g., losses and depressive disorders, frightening experiences and simple phobias. Some evidence, to be reviewed later, suggests that such relationships are more difficult to establish than may have been anticipated. Nevertheless, focused questions of this nature would seem more fruitful, either to demonstrate or to disprove theories of etiology, than a purely quantitative approach to the study of stress and psychiatric disorder.

Timing Definitions

Most chronic diseases (e.g., coronary heart disease, cancer) have a preliminary, subclinical phase that entails gradual organic and/or behavioral alterations, but few medical illnesses are defined in terms of the presence of a distinctive prodromal phase, as are some psychiatric disorders such as schizophrenia. Other psychiatric conditions cannot be diagnosed unless they have lasted a specified period of time (e.g., manic disorder). Historically, identification of a prodromal phase as a criterion for diagnosis has been more popular among European than among American psychiatrists, but in the past decade the concept has become more widely emphasized in this country as well. In *DSM-III* (1980), identification of a continuous phase of illness of at least six months' duration has become an essential prerequisite for the diagnosis of schizophrenia. This six-month phase may consist of prior acute illness or manifestation of a prodromal phase, which is defined in terms of behavioral changes such as impaired routine daily functioning, social withdrawal, diminished effectiveness at school or work, irritability, lack of drive, and personality changes (p. 189). In contrast to these relatively insidious alterations, onset of the active phase of schizophrenia is defined in terms of flagrant psychotic symptomatology: hallucinations, delusions, and disturbed thought processes.

In documenting the occurrence of life events preceding schizophrenic onset, the investigator cannot ignore changes in the prodromal phase even when onset is defined in terms of the acute phase, as is the usual research procedure. There is also the probability that a substantial proportion of patients do not suddenly become acutely ill but drift into illness without a clear-cut onset. How, then, is one to identify the occurrence and the impact of life events or the temporal sequence of event and behavioral change? In this context, it seems essential to differentiate between *fateful events*—those that are clearly unrelated to the patient's behavior—and *nonfateful events*—those that he/she may have instigated by personal action or inaction, such as divorce, loss of a job, or changes in social relationships or in financial status. While this strategy increases the plausibility of causal inferences, it does reduce considerably the number of life events apt to befall a person in a restricted time period, thus making it difficult to demonstrate differences between groups.

Another unresolved issue of timing concerns the optimal interval between event and illness selected for study, which can also be thought of as the distinction between measuring *incidence* (new cases) and *prevalence* (cases counted at a given point in time) of morbidity. Most investigators have studied the six months or year preceding illness in retrospective studies. Brown and Harris (1978) found the three-week interval immediately preceding illness onset to be the critical period differentiating patients from normal controls in terms of number of life events experienced. On the other hand, in a prospective study of former Vietnam prisoners of war, Ursano and colleagues (1981) found a relationship between severity of stress and proportion of men with psychiatric diagnoses five years later, although this distinction was not apparent at the time of repatriation. Among those who had experienced maximal stress, the proportion with psychiatric morbidity increased during this five-year interval, while there was a decline among those whose experience had been comparatively less harsh. While the documented effects of POW internment may not be generalizable to other classes of stressor, it seems likely that the distinction between transient and long-term disorders is useful.

Problems of Retrospective Design

The difficulties incurred by use of retrospective designs in the study of life events and illness have been observed in many contexts, but they seem particularly intrusive in the investigation of psychiatric disorders. These difficulties fall into three general areas: errors of recall that can attributed either to ordinary forgetting or to the condition of being ill; retrospective falsification to justify illness; and differences between the evidence generated by the study of cases and findings from prospective research or cohorts.

Several groups of investigators have demonstrated that people forget events, with greater forgetting associated with longer periods of recall (e.g., Jenkins, Hurst, & Rose, 1979). Even events as presumably memorable as hospitalization for medical conditions are increasingly underreported with the passage of time, so that in one survey 40% of respondents failed to report such an event one year later (Lilienfeld, 1976). Yager, Grant, Sweetwood, and Gerst (1981) compared reports by male psychiatric patients, male nonpatients, and their partners, for three separate two-month periods, of events experienced by the index person. For all groups, perfect agreement was obtained for only one-third of events reported by at least one member of the pair. All patients had chronic, rather than acute, illnesses so that illness status evidently did not play a role in recall.

When patients are interviewed during or at the end of acute illness episodes, the illness itself is likely to modify recall. In acute onset schizophrenia, for example, the patient's thinking, judgment, perception, language, and communication are profoundly affected, so that recall, identification, and interpretation of prior life events must operate through a "screen of pathology." More generally, patients who recently have become ill often seek to justify their illness, to make sense of it in terms of recent experiences or events that might have contributed to the condition. A dramatic example of "retrospective contamination" was offered by Brown (1974), who cited a study published before the genetic etiology of

Down's syndrome was established: mothers of Down's syndrome children reported more "shocks" early in pregnancy than did mothers of normal controls.

One of the problems with retrospective studies is not inherent in the method, namely, misinterpretation of results. Retrospective studies can show what proportion of those in a given illness or control group experience stress:

$$\text{rate} = \frac{\%\ \text{experiencing stressor(s)}}{\text{number ill}}$$

This equation provides a measure of association but no direct insight into etiology. In contrast, prospective studies indicate what proportion of those who experience stressors become ill:

$$\text{rate} = \frac{\%\ \text{ill}}{\text{number experiencing stressors}}$$

When results from retrospective studies are used to address etiological questions, problems then arise.

Despite the drawbacks associated with retrospective design, studies of stress and illness lend themselves to this approach. Events, after all, can be reported only after they have occurred, so that at least some data must be gathered retrospectively. The choices are three: to study those who have a particular characteristic (e.g., illness) in order to assess frequency of events; to study those who have experienced an event (e.g., bereavement, flood) and to follow them to see how many and who among them become ill; or to follow a randomly selected community cohort over a period of time to see who experiences stressors and who becomes ill. In the order presented, the three strategies become progressively more costly and sophisticated in their contributions to etiological insights. Most studies of stress and psychiatric disorder have used the first strategy, that of studying life events experienced and reported by different patient groups.

Sample Selection

In retrospective studies of life events, the selection of patients can strongly influence findings. The issue can be illustrated by considering the options possible in choosing a sample of schizophrenic patients. Because the investigator is concerned about pinpointing the timing of both events and illness onset, patients with good premorbid adjustment tend to be selectively included; reports by patients who have never done well at work, in school, or with other people are more difficult to interpret. Consequently, patients with acute onset and noticeable change in level of functioning are typically selected for study in order to facilitate dating of events. However, in the clinical tradition, acute onset is associated with a constellation of other variables, including presence of a precipitating event. If one then selects patients with acute onset and good premorbid functioning, is one increasing the probability of identifying recent precipitating events? Is the interviewer more persistent in efforts to define such an event? Is the patient more willing or able to report events? Such artifacts of data collection may account for an apparent association between the occurrence of a stressful life event and schizophrenic onset even if no association actually exists. Equivalent issues apply to the study of other syndromes.

Precipitant versus Hazard (Subjective versus Objective Stress)

A distinction infrequently drawn but undoubtedly meaningful in the study of life events and illness concerns the difference between *precipitant* and *hazard* (Beck & Worthen, 1972). In addition to seeking a stimulus, or precipitant, leading to an illness episode reported by either patient or relative, Beck and Worthen (1972) emphasized the utility of determining the degree of hazard signified by such an event according to other members of the same social group, as well as the correspondence between the hazard and the behavioral response.

It is commonly believed that people who become schizophrenic are exceptionally sensitive to perceived or actual threats to self-esteem and that psychotic episodes may follow situations not ordinarily regarded as objectively stressful or hazardous. As noted in a psychiatric textbook, "Those who have worked extensively with schizophrenics know that these patients . . . are very easily hurt by . . . behavior that, in most cases, would hardly be noticed by a person of normal sensitivity or, if noticed, certainly would not lead to traumatic experiences" (Lehmann, 1975: 891).

In life event studies, the distinction between precipitant and hazard is seldom observed, an omission that may lead to either conceptual or practical difficulties. When patients are asked about, or records searched for, life events immediately preceding a given illness episode, failure to make this distinction can generate misleading information.

Comment

No study of life events, stress, or psychopathology is entirely free of the foregoing problems of research method. However, more recent studies have taken many of these pitfalls into account. By seeking to identify consistent findings across studies, the methodological weaknesses of each individual study are minimized.

STRESS SYNDROMES

Included in the current psychiatric nosology of *DSM-III* (1980) are two syndromes specifically identified as a sequelae of "a recognizable stressor that would be expected to evoke significant symptoms of distress in most people" (pp. 200, 236). They are brief reactive psychosis and the post–traumatic stress disorder. The two are distinguished from each other by criteria regarding interval between precipitant and illness onset, by illness duration, and by type of symptoms. *Brief reactive psychosis* has a sudden onset immediately following exposure to stress, lasts at least a few hours but no more than two weeks, and has a clinical picture including emotional turmoil and at least one gross psychotic symptom. *Post–traumatic stress disorder* is classified as an anxiety disorder. In contrast to brief reactive psychosis, this condition may occur months or years after the precipitating event, and the disorder may last indefinitely. In addition, there is a distinctive clinical picture, including recurrent dreams or daytime flashbacks in which the trauma is reexperienced; emotional numbing; and one or more of several other symptoms, such as survival guilt, insomnia, or impaired concentration, not present before exposure to stress.

In both disorders, the precipitant is conceptualized as "outside the range of usual human experience," thus excluding the life events customarily studied in the stress literature. There is, however, a separate body of research on extreme situations, including man-made and natural disasters such as concentration camp internment, military combat, and floods and fires. This literature illustrates the reciprocal relationship between stressors, on the one hand, and social and individual characteristics, on the other. The more severe the stressor, the less significant are such characteristics in determining the likelihood and nature of response. When conditions are sufficiently harsh, breakdown is virtually universal (Horowitz, 1976), and individual variations are reflected only in the length of time before the reaction occurs and perhaps in recovery time. In contrast, when the stress is milder, social supports and individual characteristics can contribute to an understanding of why some people become ill and others do not.

Although it is suggested in *DSM-III* that "unstable" individuals are more likely to develop psychiatric disorders in response to stress than are others, and psychiatrists generally believe that stressful events within the realm of ordinary living cannot "cause madness in a person previously of sound mind" (Hudgens, 1974: 120), the empirical evidence is extremely limited. One is seldom in a position to have antecedent psychiatric assessments for survivors of major traumatic events, so that measures of change are not usually available. However, one recent study of six repatriated Vietnam prisoners of war who for various reasons had received extensive psychiatric assessments before their capture did address this issue (Ursano, 1981). Three men were found to be in superb psychological condition; three others had some sort of psychophysiological problem not severe enough to interfere with their military careers. No relationship was found between health status before and after internment, disproving the notion, as Singer (1981) pointed out in discussing this paper, that severe traumas "drive people out of their minds" or that those who develop psychiatric disorders after stress exposure "were covert or masked neurotics all the while" (p. 345).

The diagnostic criteria provided by *DSM-III* should facilitate the study of stress response syndromes, so that we learn more about the interaction among predisposing personal characteristics, social conditions, and response to stress.

STRESS AND ANXIETY DISORDERS

Defining Anxiety Disorders

Far-reaching changes in the diagnosis and classification of anxiety disorders have been introduced in the past decade by the Feighner Criteria (Feighner, 1972), the Research Diagnostic Criteria (Spitzer et al. 1978), and, most decisively, by *DSM-III* (1980). In the first two editions of the American Psychiatric Association's *Diagnostic and Statistical Manual* (1952, 1968), anxiety was presented as the chief characteristic of all neurotic disorders, and two subtypes, anxiety neurosis and phobic neurosis, were identified. In addition, transient situational disturbances, classified separately, referred to "acute reaction(s) to overwhelming environmental stress" in "individuals without any apparent underlying mental disorders" (1968: 48).

The authors of *DSM-III* reorganized, redefined, and provided operational criteria for anxiety disorders, which are now grouped into two major and nine minor classes. Phobic disorders include agoraphobia with or without panic attacks, as well as social and simple phobias. Anxiety states include panic disorder, generalized anxiety disorder, obsessive-compulsive disorder, post–traumatic stress disorder, and a residual category of atypical anxiety disorder. This new nosology permits more precision and specificity in sample composition, which should facilitate research on the role of stress in each of these syndromes.

Research findings in this area are very limited, perhaps to some extent because of the shifting diagnostic conceptualizations. Few controlled studies have been conducted, and much of the available evidence, such as it is, has come from clinical reports. Investigators have not progressed beyond the basic question of whether a relationship exists between life events and illness onset. Since more work has been done regarding stress and phobic disorders than other anxiety syndromes, these data will be reviewed to exemplify what is known to date about stress and anxiety disorders. For a comprehensive review of this literature, see Rabkin & Klein (1980).

Problems of Method

A major problem specific to the study of phobic disorders is the relative unavailability of new cases. Patients characteristically have been ill for years when they are identified for study or treatment, and, in fact, the most severely functionally disabled often seek medical help for varying periods of time before eventual referral to a psychiatrist (Klein, 1980). Treatment studies often report that the average illness duration of these patients is 8–10 years (Zitrin, Woerner, & Klein, 1981). Thus, it is difficult accurately to assess circumstances associated with illness onset no matter how carefully thought out are other design aspects.

Research Evidence

Despite long-standing recognition of the syndrome of phobic disorders and widespread assumptions by clinicians of the etiological role of stress in phobias, only in recent years have investigators begun to compile evidence concerning the presence and nature of such precipitants. Studies can be grouped into two categories: those in which the investigator assumes that each illness has a precipitant and the task is simply to identify it and those in which the investigator first asks whether or not illness onset is preceded by an identifiable stressor.

Studies in the first category usually consist of tabular presentations of events preceding illness onset for patients seen in various psychiatric treatment settings. Characteristically, neither definitions of stress nor diagnostic procedures are presented. Weekes's (1978) report is typical:

> For the majority of 528 agoraphobic men and women in my survey, the precipitating cause of their agoraphobia was stress . . . either sudden stress . . . or prolonged . . . stress created by some difficult life situation. . . . only 5% could offer no cause. (P. 358)

A more specific listing of 10 types of stressful factors was reported by Sim and Houghton (1966). They found that the most common precipitants of phobic disorder in their sample of 191 patients with agoraphobia and other phobias were bereavement and "sudden shock."

In studies such as these, absence of control groups, together with lack of precision in definition of terms concerning both stress and diagnosis, renders findings virtually uninterpretable. Furthermore, the question itself is of dubious validity since we know that nearly any illness or behavior change will be identified with a precipitant if the patient is asked to produce one. In general, then, this category of research is not a promising source of insight into the etiology of phobic disorders.

The second group of studies addresses the question of whether or not stressful events precede onset of phobic disorders. While these research designs represent an advance over the approach taken in the preceding category, systematic measurement of stressors continues to be weak or absent.

One of the better studies in this area—and one of the few to use a control group—was conducted by Buglass, Clarke, and Kreetman (1977). They studied 30 agoraphobic housewives and 30 controls enrolled in a general medical clinic. Their patients all experienced at least moderate functional impairment, which was found to vary markedly during illness course. In only 7 patients (23% of the sample) could discrete precipitating events be identified, and only 2 of these (7%) reported a particular fearful experience occurring away from home. The authors concluded that their data showed "no evidence that a specific stimulus commonly initiates the phobia" (p. 84). Turning to a consideration of personality style, in order to verify the widespread assumption of dependence in the pre-illness history of phobic patients, they found no differences between patients and controls in indexes of developmental signs of dependence (e.g., history of separation anxiety, problems of school adjustment, or unusual conformity).

In several other studies, about two-thirds of phobic patients reported a precipitating stressor, although the researchers themselves did not always agree with the patients' assessments (Roberts, 1964; Shafar, 1976; Woerner, 1980). Among patients with phobic disorders, those with agoraphobia appear to be least likely to report a specific illness precipitant, although far more work remains to be done before firm conclusions can be drawn.

Comment

Despite both clinical and lay expectations that phobic disorders are triggered, if not caused, by a particular stressor, investigators have not found a strong association. The available evidence is limited in terms of both design and definitional clarity. Base rates and control groups are scarcely evident, and even in studies that do differentiate phobic disorder from other anxiety disorders, the samples are often heterogeneous and time elapsed since illness onset is characteristically measured in years. Although initial results are not as encouraging as one might have anticipated, well-designed studies remain to be conducted so that it is premature to conclude that stress plays no significant role in the genesis of phobic disorders.

STRESS AND SCHIZOPHRENIA

Investigators working in this area have so far focused on determining whether patients with schizophrenia experience more or less stress before illness onset or subsequent exacerbations than do either patients with other psychiatric disorders or community controls. Studies are included in this review if their samples consisted of schizophrenic patients diagnosed according to specified criteria and considered as a distinct diagnostic group, if a comparison group was employed, and if data sources and time periods surveyed were reported by the investigators. For a detailed review, see Rabkin (1980).

As a general rule, investigators of stressful environmental conditions have been cautious in attributing an etiological role to such conditions and tend instead to emphasize their influence on the timing of the illness episode. This is most certainly the case in studies of stress and schizophrenia, in which life events are regarded as precipitating the onset of acute schizophrenic illness. Accordingly, the hypotheses presented in the studies reviewed here focus on the precipitating role of stressful events in already vulnerable people. Specifically, investigators have looked at whether schizophrenics, compared either to normal comparison groups or to other psychiatric subgroups, report events that are more severe, more frequent, of a singular nature, or in a specific category.

In order to facilitate comparison of findings, I have classified studies into three groups: comparison of life events reported by schizophrenics and other psychiatric patients; comparison of reports by schizophrenics and normals; and comparison of events reported by schizophrenic patients with and without subsequent relapses and comparison of events reported by chronic schizophrenic patients in the community and by controls.

Schizophrenics and Other Psychiatric Patients

The cumulative findings of studies in this area provide the following answers about the relationship between stressful life events and psychiatric syndromes. First, there is no evidence that events reported by schizophrenics are more frequent than those reported by other diagnostic groups preceding illness onset. Moreover, the one study that evaluated magnitude of stress associated with events found that events reported by schizophrenic patients were less objectively hazardous or "troublesome" than those reported by depressives (Beck & Worthen, 1972). Finally no investigator has gathered evidence to indicate that the events reported by schizophrenic patients either are of a singular nature or fall into categories different from those associated with other psychiatric patients.

Given the discrepancies in design and the unevenness of methodological rigor of these studies, one cannot justifiably conclude that they have disproved the possibility of an association between stressful life events and schizophrenia onset; rather, they have failed to provide positive evidence for such a link. At least three variables need further attention in order to clarify and to permit comparison of findings: magnitude of objective hazard associated with reported events, their fatefulness (i.e., independence of the patient's behavior), and the unit of time in which they occurred.

Schizophrenics and Normals

Studies in this group have compared events reported by schizophrenic patients and by normal samples drawn from the general population. Considered together, results do not point to any decisive agreement regarding the size of effect of stressful life events in precipitating illness. Brown and colleagues (Brown & Birley, 1968; Brown & Harris, 1978; Brown, Harris, & Peto, 1973), suggested that life events are significant factors that influence the timing, if not the probability, of illness. Jacob and Myers (1976) were more conservative in their evaluation of the role of recent life events, and Serban (1975) was least convinced about their influence. The only evidence of a positive effect is Brown and Birley's (1968) finding that more life events are reported by schizophrenics in the three weeks immediately preceding illness both in comparison to normals during the same period of time and in comparison to their own reports for earlier time periods. This single finding requires replication and further analysis before its significance can be assessed. In addition, the question of cumulative factors requires clarification. Serban's (1975) point that the so-called precipitating factors related to illness onset would not in themselves have such an effect in the absence of an inflated stress level was also noted by Brown and Birley (1968) and warrants additional study.

Schizophrenics with and without Relapses

Longitudinal studies have compared events reported by schizophrenic patients with and without subsequent relapses, as well as events reported by chronic schizophrenic patients in the community and normal controls (Birley & Brown, 1970; Leff, Hirsch, Gaind, Rhode & Stevens, 1973; Michaux, Gansereit, McCabe & Kurland, 1967; Schwartz (1975) & Myers, 1977). Overall, these investigators found reports of more events to be associated with relapse, although in each study some patients who did not report events also relapsed. Among chronic schizophrenics in the community, report of more events was related to greater psychiatric impairment. From these imperfect and preliminary studies, one may conclude that in schizophrenia, life events contribute an incremental component to the stress level of discharged patients, which is, in many cases, associated with subsequent rehospitalization.

Comment

Notwithstanding pervasive methodological problems and lack of equivalence in study designs, the weight of the evidence currently available suggests that schizophrenics do not report significantly more life events preceding illness onset than do other psychiatric patients or normal respondents, nor are the events they report of a singular nature or qualitatively unlike those reported by others. However, the few studies of life events and the probability of relapse suggests that relapsing schizophrenics report more events than do those who continue in remission. Cumulatively, these results tentatively indicate that life events contribute incrementally to an already inflated stress level and so influence the timing, if not the probability, of illness episodes. Whether or not the size of their effect is clinically meaningful remains to be demonstrated.

STRESS AND DEPRESSIVE DISORDERS

In the field of stress research, more investigators have studied depression than all other psychiatric disorders combined. As a result, the research is considerably more advanced, having progressed beyond efforts to demonstrate an association between stress and illness, which characterizes work with other syndromes. The number of studies and the range of issues addressed preclude a systematic review here. Instead, I will consider some of the major questions that have been raised, together with the available evidence.

Does the Occurrence of Stress Differentiate Depressed Patients from Others?

Depressed and Other Patients. In the studies cited in the section on stress and schizophrenia, several investigators reported that depressed patients report more life events than do schizophrenic patients, although a minority failed to find such a difference. In addition, Barrett (1979) found that depressed symptomatic volunteers reported more events in particular categories than did people with anxiety disorders. The cumulative evidence suggests that depressed patients do report more events in the period preceding the start of an illness episode.

Depressed Patients and the General Population. Depressed patients also report more life events than do normal controls, especially immediately before illness onset (Brown, Harris, & Peto, 1973; Lloyd, 1980; Paykel, 1979). As noted earlier, Brown and his colleagues (1973) found that the three-week period directly preceding illness was the critical juncture, distinguishing depressed patients from controls.

While these differences are neither large nor consistently reported, the available evidence suggests an association between increased frequency of life events and onset of depressive illness, in comparison both to other patient groups and to the general population. Overall, it seems justifiable to conclude that life events do play a role in the genesis of depressive disorders.

How Important Are Stressors in the Onset of Depression?

While an association has been established, its effect is small. The correlations between stressful life events and illness onset found in most studies are usually below .30, at best accounting for less than 10% of the variance in illness (Dohrenwend & Dohrenwend, 1981; Rabkin & Struening, 1976). While life events alter the risk for depression (Paykel, 1979), the difference in practical terms is unimpressive. Hudgens (1974) noted that most people do not become mentally ill even when terrible things happen to them, as evidenced by a recent report that less than one-quarter of repatriated Vietnam prisoners of war had diagnosable psychiatric disorders upon release (Ursano et al., 1981). Milder stressors experienced in ordinary living are even less likely to induce illness. Paykel (1974) estimated, for example, that less than 10% of role exits are followed by clinical depression, and Clayton (1979) found that one year after bereavement, only 16% of her sample were clinically depressed.

In addition to the fact that most people who experience losses, role exits, and other events presumably associated with depression do not in fact become ill, many who become depressed have not experienced a precipitating event of this or any other kind. In other words, as Holmes (1979), put it, some of the high-risk people remain well and one-third of the low-risk people get sick. Evidently, while often present, precipitating stress is neither necessary nor sufficient to account for depressive onset, and simply noting the presence or absence of stressful events contributes little to our ability to predict and control their pathological effects.

Is the Presence of Precipitating Stress Useful in Identifying Depressive Subtypes?

Clinicians have long recognized that there are different kinds of depressive disorders, although there is notably less agreement about how best to classify subtypes. One of the earliest and most widely accepted schemes distinguished between *reactive* and *endogenous* depressions, defined, respectively, by the presence or the absence of a stressor. Several other classification systems currently under study also include a distinction between categories that seem parallel; for example, Winokur's (1978) classification of familial pure depressive disorder versus depressive spectrum disorder, which is based entirely on family history of psychiatric disorder, and Klein's (1980) four-part conceptualization, which includes endogenomorphic depression, chronic dysphoria, atypical depression, and disappointment reaction, based on clinical symptoms and clinical history.

Investigators have not found life events to differentiate between subtypes in any of these classifications. Paykel (1979) reviewed his own data and found a correlation of .15 between symptom type and frequency of stress; patients with endogenous depression reported less life stress than did patients with nonendogenous depression. The size of this relationship was, however, far too small to have any practical meaning, accounting for less than 3% of the variance in illness subtype. Paykel concluded, "The so-called endogenous symptom pattern certainly does occur as a group of symptoms which cluster together, but the label is unfortunate: absence of stress is not a prominent feature" (p. 78). Others have also made this observation (e.g., Leff, Roach, & Bunney, 1970; Schless & Mendels, 1977).

Winokur (1979) also failed to find systematic differences in frequency of life events and patients with *depressive spectrum disorder* (diagnosed by a family history of antisocial personality and/or alcoholism) compared to patients with *familial pure depressive disorder* (family history of depression only). He suggested that instead of simple counts of events, the patient's response to their occurrence should be assessed. Similarly, Klein's (1980) endogenomorphic subtype could not be distinguished by the absence of precipitants, which were found in all groups. Barrett (1979) did find that patients with chronic depression reported fewer fateful events than did those with major or intermittent depression (using categories from the Research Diagnostic Criteria [Spitzer et al., 1978], but he was not studying new cases and his small samples and multiple comparisons render such findings tentative at best. Overall, depressive subtypes are not differentiated by frequency of stressful precipitants in the classification systems so far studied.

Does the Type of Event Matter?

A number of investigators have demonstrated that losses and exits from social roles cluster before depressive onset, as do undesirable events in general, although role entrances and desirable events do not show this clustering. This specificity is, however, weak: such events also cluster before the onset of other disorders, both psychiatric and medical. Furthermore, they seem to account for only about 25% of precipitating events among depressed patients. Altogether, there is some reason to suggest that event specificity is not as great as we might wish on theoretical grounds. These null findings do not mean that content of stressors is irrelevant but, rather, that no consistent and strong associations yet have been identified.

Do Childhood Losses Serve as Predisposing Factors in Adult Depressive Disorders?

In the same month, Crook and Eliot (1980) and Lloyd (1980) reviewed this literature in prestigious journals and arrived at discordant conclusions. Crook and Eliot (1980) examined more than 20 controlled studies published in the past two decades concerning the relationship between parental death during childhood and adult depression. They concluded that "parental death during childhood has not been established as a factor of etiological significance in adult depression or any subtype of adult depression studied to date'' (p. 252). They noted further that studies reporting such an association were, without exception, methodologically flawed, while those showing no differences in parental loss among adult depressives and normal controls were reasonably well designed. Lloyd (1980), on the other hand, reviewed the same body of literature and concluded that death of a parent in childhood ''generally increases depressive risk by a factor of about 2 or 3. In addition, early loss events also seem to be related to the severity of the subsequent depression and to attempted suicide'' (p. 529). The argument, analyses, and evidence presented by Crook and Eliot are more persuasive to me and are supported by more recent data published by Tennant, Smith, Bebbington, and Hurry (1981), who studied community residents and patients from the same neighborhood. They found no relationship between parental death in childhood and adult psychiatric impairment of any kind, either among untreated community residents or among patients. At present, the issue remains unresolved, although the explanatory power of this variable seems less promising now that a substantial number of studies have failed to establish its utility.

Do Mediating Variables Influence Illness Risk after Exposure to Stressors?

The literature on the buffering effects of personal and social variables on the likelihood of becoming ill has been reviewed extensively elsewhere (Dohrenwend & Dohrenwend, 1977; Rabkin & Struening, 1976b). It seems clear that exposure to stressors alone is almost never a sufficient explanation for illness in ordinary human experience, just as genetic studies have shown that biological vulnerability alone does not produce psychiatric disorder. Other factors that require consideration include characteristics of the stressful situation, individual biological and psychological attributes, and social supports available to the individual at risk.

Characteristics of the stressor presumed to mediate its impact include such dimensions as its magnitude, duration, novelty, and predictability. Relevant personality variables include coping skills, personality style, age at exposure, biological vulnerabilities, and response thresholds. Social factors include availability of benevolent and supportive relatives and friends, access to helping resources, social influence and social class, community attitudes, and prevailing group morale.

Consideration of such mediating factors in relation to stress exposure leads to a multifactorial model of illness that includes a temporal sequence. It seems probable that such an approach ultimately will facilitate our understanding of who becomes ill in what circumstances.

Comment

Several factors undoubtedly contribute to the inconsistencies in reported findings and the weakness of observed associations. First is the problem of diagnostic heterogeneity within depressed samples, both in terms of symptom cluster and in terms of length of illness. In many studies it is not clear whether subjects have depressive symptoms or a diagnosable mood disorder. When the latter is established, the distinction between unipolar and bipolar illness is seldom noted. In addition, few investigators have distinguished between onset of illness (first episode) and illness recurrence (other than first episode). There is some reason to believe that life events may influence illness course (later episodes) even if their etiological role in initial onset is unclear, as suggested in the literature on schizophrenia.

In this and other contexts, it is becoming increasingly apparent that a simple count of reported stressful precipitants is not fruitful. Improved strategies include adoption of a multifactorial model taking into account the effects of historical and concurrent burdens and buffers. Another interesting approach is to test hypotheses regarding the role of particular combinations of events within specified periods of time. This strategy is exemplified by Dohrenwend and Dohrenwend's (1979) *pathogenic triad*. They postulated that depression is more likely to occur following the advent within a short period of time of fateful loss events (e.g., death of spouse), events that exhaust the individual physically (e.g., major medical illness), and disruption of social supports (e.g., geographical move). The combined impact of such events would be associated with a greater incidence of psychopathology in previously healthy people than would be observed either in the absence of such events or in their separate occurrence or in their association with other categories. While the utility of this approach remains to be tested, it is innovative and promising.

A dimension of vulnerability that has been insufficiently studied in this area concerns biological vulnerability. As van Praag (1979) pointed out, it is quite possible that certain biogenic amine deficiencies may be a predisposing rather than a causal factor in depressive illness. Buchsbaum, Coursey, and Murphy (1976) suggested that low platelet monoamine oxidase activity in apparently normal people may serve as a biological marker for increased vulnerability to psychiatric disorder in the presence of stressful conditions. A family history of psychiatric disorder (schizophrenia, affective disorder) may be another useful index of heightened vulnerability. Integration of biological risk factors with social and personal mediating variables may increase the prospects of predicting who is more likely to become ill in response to exposure to stress.

In summary, it has been demonstrated sufficiently often that some relationship exists between life events and depressive disorders, accounting for a small portion of the variance associated with illness onset. The next steps in this field should entail examination of the circumstances in which and for whom such events are enhanced or minimized.

REFERENCES

AMERICAN PSYCHIATRIC ASSOCIATION. *Diagnostic and statistical manual of mental disorders.* Washington, D.C.: American Psychiatric Association, 1952.

————. *Diagnostic and statistical manual of mental disorders* (2d ed.). Washington, D.C.: American Psychiatric Association, 1968

————. *Diagnostic and statistical manual of mental disorders* (3d ed.). Washington, D.C.: American Psychiatric Association, 1980.

Barrett, J. E. The relationship of life events to the onset of neurotic disorders. In J. E. Barrett (ed.), *Stress and mental disorder.* New York: Raven, 1979.

BECK, J., & WORTHEN, K. Precipitating stress, crisis theory, and hospitalization in schizophrenia and depression. *Archives of General Psychiatry,* 1972, *26,* 123–129.

BIRLEY, J. L., & BROWN, G. Crises and life changes preceding the onset or relapse of acute schizophrenia. *British Journal of Psychiatry,* 1970, *116,* 327–333.

BROWN, G. Meaning, measurement, and stress of life events. In B. S. Dohrenwend & B. P. Dohrenwend (eds.), *Stressful life events.* New York: Wiley, 1974.

Brown, G., & Birley, J. Crises and life changes and the onset of schizophrenia. *Journal of Health and Social Behavior,* 1968, *9,* 203–214.

Brown, G. W., & Harris, T. *Social origins of depression: A study of psychiatric disorder in women.* London: Tavistock, 1978.

Brown, G., Harris, T., & Peto, J. Life events and psychiatric disorders. Part II: Nature of causal link. *Psychological Medicine,* 1973, *3,* 159–176.

Buchsbaum, M. S., Coursey, R., & Murphy, D. L. The biochemical high-risk paradigm: Behavior and familial correlates of low platelet monoamine oxidase activity. *Science,* 1976, *194,* 339–341.

Buglass, D., Clarke, J., & Kreitman, N. A study of agoraphobic housewives. *Psychological Medicine,* 1977, *7,* 73–86.

Clayton, P., & Darvish, H. Course of depressive symptoms following the stress of bereavement. In J. E. Barrett (ed.), *Stress and mental disorder.* New York: Raven, 1979.

Crook, T., & Eliot, J. Parental death during childhood and adult depression: A critical review of the literature. *Psychological Bulletin,* 1980, *87,* 252–259.

Dohrenwend, B. P. Problems in defining and sampling the relevant population of stressful life events. In B. S. Dohrenwend & B. P. Dohrenwend (eds.), *Stressful life events.* New York: Wiley, 1974.

————. Stressful life events and psychopathology: Some issues of theory and method. In J. E. Barrett (ed.), *Stress and mental disorder.* New York: Raven, 1979.

Dohrenwend, B. P., & Dohrenwend, B. S. The conceptualization and measurement of stressful life events: An overview of the issues. In J. Strauss, H. Babigian, & M. Roff (eds.), *The origins and course of psychopathology.* New York: Plenum, 1977.

Dohrenwend, B. S., & Dohrenwend, B. P. Some issues in research on stressful life events. *Journal of Nervous and Mental Disease,* 1978, *166,* 7–15.

————. Life stress and illness: Formulation of the issues. In B. S. Dohrenwend & B. P. Dohrenwend (eds.), *Stressful life events and their contexts.* New York: Watson, 1981.

Feighner, J., Robins, E., Guze, S., Woodruff, R., Winokur, G., & Munoz, R. Diagnostic criteria for use in psychiatric research. *Archives of General Psychiatry,* 1972, *26,* 57–63.

Holmes, T. General discussion. In J. E. Barrett (ed.), *Stress and mental illness.* New York: Raven, 1979.

Holmes, T. & Rahe, R. The Social readjustment rating scale. *Journal of Psychosomatic Research,* 1967, *11,* 213–218.

Horowitz, M. *Stress response syndromes.* New York: Aronson, 1976.

Hudgens, R. Personal catastrophe and depression. In B. S. Dohrenwend & B. P. Dohrenwend (eds.), *Stressful life events.* New York: Wiley, 1974.

Jacobs, S., & Myers, J. Recent life events and acute schizophrenic psychosis: A controlled study. *Journal of Nervous and Mental Disease,* 1976, *162,* 75–87.

Jenkins, C. D., Hurst, M. W., & Rose, R. M. Life changes: Do people really remember? *Archives of General Psychiatry,* 1979, *36,* 379–384.

Klein, D. F. Anxiety reconceptualized. *Comprehensive Psychiatry,* 1980, *21,* 411–427.

Klein, D. F., Gittelman R., Quitkin, F., & Rifkin A. *Diagnosis and drug treatment of psychiatric disorders.* Baltimore: Williams and Wilkins, 1980.

Leff, J., Hirsch, S., Gaind, R., Rhode, P., & Stevens, B. Life events and maintenance therapy in schizophrenic relapse. *British Journal of Psychiatry,* 1973, *123,* 659–660.

Leff, M., Roatch, J., & Bunney, W. Environmental factors preceding onset of severe depressions. *Psychiatry,* 1970, *33,* 293–311.

Lehmann, H. Schizophrenia: Clinical features. In A. Freedman, H. Kaplan, & B. Sadock (eds.), *Comprehensive textbook of psychiatry* (2d ed.), vol. 1. Baltimore: Williams & Wilkins, 1975.

Lilienfeld, A. *Foundations of epidemiology.* New York: Oxford University Press, 1976.

LLOYD, C. Life events and depressive disorder reviewed (in two parts). *Achives of General Psychiatry,* 1980, *37,* 529–548.

MICHAUX, W., GANSEREIT, K., McCABE, O., & KURLAND, A. The psychopathology and measurement of environmental stress. *Community Mental Health Journal,* 1967, *3,* 358–371.

PAYKEL, E. Life stress and psychiatric disorder: Applications of the clinical approach. In B. S. Dohrenwend & B. P. Dohrenwend (eds.), *Stressful life events.* New York: Wiley, 1974.

————. Causal relationships between clinical depression and life events. In J. E. Barrett (ed.), *Stress and mental disorder.* New York: Raven, 1979.

RABKIN, J. G. Stressful life events and schizophrenia: A review of the research literature. *Psychological Bulletin,* 1980, *87,* 408–425.

RABKIN, J. G., & KLEIN, D. F. Stress and phobic disorder: Review of empirical findings and research recommendations. Paper prepared for the Stress and Illness Panel of the Steering Committee for Research on Stress in Health and Disease, National Academy of Sciences, Washington, D.C.: 1980.

RABKIN, J. G., & STRUENING, E. L. Life events, stress, and illness. *Science,* 1976, *194,* 1013–1020. (a)

————. Social change, stress, and illness: A selective literature review. *Psychoanalysis and Contemporary Science,* 1976, *5,* 573–624. (b)

ROBERTS, A. Housebound housewives: A follow-up study of a phobic anxiety state. *British Journal of Psychiatry,* 1964, 110, 191–197.

SCHLESS, A., & MENDELS, J. Life stress and psychopathology. *Psychiatry Digest,* 1977, 25–35.

SCHWARTZ, C., & MYERS, J. K. Life events and schizophrenia: II. Impact of life events on symptom configuration. *Archives of General Psychiatry,* 1977, *34,* 1242–1245.

SERBAN, G. Stress in normals and schizophrenics. *British Journal of Psychiatry,* 1975, *126,* 397–407.

SHAFAR, S. Aspects of phobic illness: A study of 90 personal cases. *British Journal of Medical Psychology,* 1976, *49,* 221–236.

SIM, M., & HOUGHTON, H. Phobic anxiety and its treatment. *Journal of Nervous and Mental Disease,* 1966, *143,* 484–491.

SINGER, M. T. Viet Nam prisoners of war, stress, and personality resiliency. *American Journal of Psychiatry,* 1981, 138, 345–346.

SPITZER, R., ENDICOTT, J., & ROBINS, E. *Research Diagnostic Criteria.* New York City: New York State Psychiatric Institute, 1978.

TENNANT, C., SMITH, A., BEBBINGTON, P., & HURRY, J. Parental loss in childhood. *Archives of General Psychiatry,* 1981, *38,* 309–314.

URSANO, R. The Viet Nam era prisoner of war: Precaptivity personality and the development of psychiatric illness. *American Journal of Psychiatry,* 1981, *138,* 315–318.

URSANO, R., BOYDSTUN, J., & WHEATLEY, R. Psychiatric illness in U.S. Air Force Viet Nam prisoners of war: A five-year follow-up. *American Journal of Psychiatry,* 1981, *138,* 310–314.

VAN PRAAG, H. M. Psychopsychiatry: Can psychosocial factors cause psychiatric disorders? *Comprehensive Psychiatry,* 1979, *20,* 215–225.

WEEKES, C. Simple, effective treatment of agoraphobia. *American Journal of Psychotherapy,* 1978, *32,* 357–369.

WINOKUR, G. General discussion. In J. E. Barrett (ed.), *Stress and mental disorder.* New York: Raven, 1979.

WINOKUR, G., BEHAR, D., VANVALKENBURG, C., & LOWRY, M. Is a familial definition of depression both feasible and valid? *Journal of Nervous & Mental Disease,* 1978, *166,* 764–768.

WOERNER, M. Unpublished data, Long Island Jewish Hillside Medical Center, 1980.

YAGER, J., GRANT, I., SWEETWOOD, H., & GERST, M. Life event reports by psychiatric patients, nonpatients, and their partners. *Archives of General Psychiatry,* 1981, *38,* 343–347.

ZITRIN, C., WOERNER, M., & KLEIN, D. F. Differentiation of panic anxiety from anticipatory anxiety and avoidance behavior. In D. F. Klein & J. G. Rabkin (eds.), *Anxiety: New research and changing concepts.* New York, Raven, 1981.

35

Stress and Alcohol

Herbert Peyser

THE INGESTION OF ETHYL ALCOHOL is a means of coping with stress that is uniquely human. It is one aspect of an overall method that has been used by man everywhere throughout his history, namely, the consumption of intoxicating chemicals that alter the physiology of the body and, in particular, the physiology of the central nervous system. As technology advances, more and more powerful and effective chemical agents are produced, and as the zeitgeist moves ever further in the direction of the medicalization of various types of human misery, mankind is turning increasingly to these drugs.

The drugs involved can be grouped into three categories: (1) the stimulants and hallucinogens, including cocaine, the amphetamines, methylphenidate (Ritalin) in the first subgroup, marijuana (cannabis), LSD (lysergic acid diethylamide), PCP (phencyclidine), and mescaline in the second subgroup; (2) the narcotics, comprising all the injectable opiates such as heroin, morphine, and dilaudid, the synthetic equivalents such as meperidine (Demerol) and methadone, and the so-called lesser opiates and opiatelike drugs such as codeine, oxycodone (Percodan), hydrocodone, pentazocine (Talwin), and propoxyphene (Darvon); and (3) the sedative-hypnotics, which constitutes a large and varied group, including all the barbiturates (e.g., Seconal, Amytal, Nembutal), methalqualone (Quaalude), meprobamate (Miltown), glutethimide (Doriden), methyprylon (Noludar), ethchlorvynol (Placidyl), chloral hydrate, paraldehyde, bromides, certain anesthetics such as diethyl ether, all the benzodiazepines (known as minor tranquilizers)—including diazepam (Valium), chlordiazepoxide (Librium), flurazepam (Dalmane), and oxazepam (Serax)—and, finally, the most widespread drug of all, ethyl alcohol.

All these drugs can produce psychological dependence or habituation, but the drugs in categories 2 and 3 can also produce physical dependence—true addiction—with tolerance (i.e., larger and more frequent doses are required to produce the same effect) and a physical withdrawal or abstinence syndrome on acute cessation of the drug. The drugs of these latter two categories are all cross-addicting and cross-tolerant for the other drugs within the *same* category (despite chemical dissimilarities and different receptors and points of action in the nervous system); they are not cross-addicting or cross-tolerant for drugs of other categories and cannot *physically* substitute for them (although drugs in categories 2 and 3 may potentiate each other, and chronic alcohol intake can increase sensitization to morphine, for example). Within the same category, however, one drug can more or less physically substitute for another.

These drugs pose great dangers to the addicted individual beyond the threat of overdose and beyond their toxic effects. The withdrawal syndrome presents a problem, and that of category 3 drugs, which often includes convulsions and deleria, is far more dangerous than the withdrawal associated with category 2. This experience can be life threatening, unlike the withdrawal syndrome of category 2. Another danger is that of tolerance, where the effective dose must progressively approach lethal levels.

The sociology and psychology of the abusers of each of these three categories differ, although more and more polydrug abusers, crossing the categories, are being seen.

The most common and best-studied addictive drug is ethanol. There are injunctions against overuse of alcohol on the walls of the amphitheater at Delphi and ethanol is discussed in ancient Egyptian papyri. The Code of Hamurabi (*c.* 1700 B.C.) warns against abuse of alcohol. Yet alcohol is, and has been, part of man's great religions, from the Dionysian rituals to the Catholic mass and Holy Communion. Alcohol also is deeply involved in secular communal activities, as well as many elegant and esthetic experiences, and it has been an integral part of man's more joyous and more intimate moments. In short, alcohol pervades our lives.

This chapter discusses alcohol as the prototype of chemical means to cope with stress. Although in a more restricted and specific sense, it is the prototype of category 3 drugs only, alcohol does represent the best example of "better living through chemistry."

ALCOHOL AND ALCOHOLISM

It is important here to distinguish between the *effects of alcohol* and the disorder of *alcoholism* (or sedativism), which is the consequence of the use of alcohol (or sedatives) in certain people so predisposed by genetic, physiological, psychological, sociological, historical, or other such factors. The disease itself, regardless of how and what triggers it and whether its onset is acute or insidious, will sooner or later take over with a life of its own and will proceed along a given course (or a limited but specific variety of courses), with a unitary set of signs, symptoms, behavioral changes, and objective findings (Gitlow, 1980).

Probably no one factor can cause the disorder, which is a complex entity (Falk & Tang, 1977), and it should be noted that although two-thirds to three-fourths of all Americans have drunk alcohol on some occasion, only 5% or so will acquire the disease (Calahan, Cisin, & Crossley, 1969). That is, of course, a large enough number to cause much difficulty and distress, and alcohol has been, for example, the leading reason for hospitalization in New York County and the leading reason for in-hospital patient days there.[1] The suicide rate among alcoholics is 58 times that of the general population. Alcoholism's social and economic fallout is staggering: drinking is implicated in half of all fatal automobile accidents and the effects on industry, with days and talent lost, is incalculable, perhaps over $10 billion annually (U.S. Department of Health Education, and Welfare, 1980). The estimated annual cost to the United States of substance abuse problems in general is $50 billion in health and medical expenses, diminished job productivity, motor vehicle accidents, and violent crimes; these disorders account for nearly 30% of all mental health problems in the nation (U.S. Department of Health, Education, and Welfare, 1980).

I shall not consider the disease process per se here but the direct effects of alcohol itself, a phenomenon that is a part of the illness of alcoholism, probably the initiator and precipitant, and one of the factors that keeps the illness going. Ethyl alcohol is both a response to and a method of dealing with stress and, pari passu, a cause of further stress. This aspect is crucial to the development and course of the disorder of alcoholism. The pharmacological action of alcohol is both sedative and a central nervous system depressant, which is utilized by the individual under stress for the purpose of coping with that stress; and excitatory, which effect appears clinically as the depressant, sedative phase wears off. This latter effect of alcohol is a cause of further stress, requiring additional sedation and other methods of coping.

ALCOHOL AS A RESPONSE TO STRESS

The first consideration, then, is recourse to alcohol in response to stress. Everyday clinical observation and popular opinion agree that alcohol relieves tension and enables one to cope with stress. Physicians prescribe alcohol in small doses in cases of arteriosclerotic coronary artery disease, taking advantage of the drug's sedative (central nervous system depressant) qualities. Furthermore, there is some suggestive cross-cultural evidence that hunting societies with, presumably, subsistence insecurity, and agricultural societies with threats to the food supply evidence more prolonged drinking episodes and higher levels of intoxication than do secure agricultural societies (Horton, 1943). All in all, drinking to reduce stress seems to be a clearly established phenomenon.

The basic psychological effects of alcohol are usually grouped into three categories: euphoriant effects, disinhibiting effects, and anxiety and depression relieving effects (Kissin, 1974). These observations have been supported in the literature by alcoholics who report drinking for the personal effect on moods and emotions (Mulford & Miller, 1960). Alcoholics also report mood changes, increased aggression and sexuality, and decreased responsibility when intoxicated (Tamerin, Weiner, Poppen, Steinglass & Mendelson, 1971). These are only a few of the reports in the literature, but they are characteristic and reveal that the findings are quite general and consist of phenomenological observations and subjectively derived statements.

Although there are no established correlations of specific types of stress with the tendency to use alcohol as a response to stress, research has been done on predisposing personality characteristics in this regard; for example, field dependence (Witkin, Karp, & Goodenough, 1959) and dependence-independence conflicts (Blane, 1968). Finney, Smith, Skeeters, and Auvenshine (1971) found, for instance, that alcoholics tend to have a high need for emotional support, with craving for affection; they exhibit passive dependence, make aggressive demands, show impulsivity with easy decisionmaking, yield quickly to temptation, and engage in efforts at control by repression, suppression, faith, and inspiration. These results, though interesting, are too general to help us understand who will use alcohol in response to stress, how and why drinking will help, and what this pattern will do to the individual involved. It is also not clear what factors are causative in the use of the drug and what factors result from the use of alcohol and the consequences of its use.

It should be noted that the mood changes associated with the relief of discomfort often appear with the first drinking episode and remain something the alcoholic will later remember and report, on his recovery, at Alcoholics Anonymous meetings and elsewhere. The relief seems almost magical: for the first time, the person finds that he or she can talk to the opposite sex or to the boss, speak up in school or at parties, dance well in public, or have freer sexual intercourse with a lover.

On a deeper psychological level these effects can be related to ethanol's sedative, central nervous system depressant effects, with disinhibition and obtunding of awareness. In all probability, decreased alertness is the fundamental effect. In a psychoanalytic framework, one would say that in that face of the ego that is turned toward the external world, we see a truly anesthetic effect, with diminished intensity of perception of external (noxious, in particular) stimuli flowing in (indeed, alcohol has been used as an anesthetic). On the other hand, in that face of the ego that is turned inward, we see diminished intensity of stimuli flowing, so to speak, from memory and the other internal representatives of reality (resulting in denial) and, more important, diminished intensity of stimuli flowing from the internal representatives of authority (the superego.). Thus, we see, secondary to this last effect, disinhibition and release of sexual, aggressive, and assertive tendencies. The lessening, so to speak, of the superego's self-critical influences helps account for the diminution in anxiety and depression and the development of euphoria, apparent self-esteem, courage, and confidence.

PHYSIOLOGICAL CORRELATES

There are certain correlates of this hypothesis on the cellular, subcellular, and intercellular levels. Alcohol acts in the brain on the neuronal and synaptic membranes, stimulating in *very* low concentrations and depressing in higher concentrations. It has effects on neurohumoral release, affecting synaptic transduction (Grenell, 1978), a property shared by all drugs of categories 2 and 3. This effect correlates quite directly with electroencephalographic findings of a transitory excitatory stage with very small doses of alcohol, and depression with higher, more usual doses (Horsey & Akert, 1953; Nakai, 1964). The EEG changes involve increase in percent time of and slowing in alpha frequency. These effects are well correlated with the degree of intoxication and changes in the level of consciousness (Begleiter & Platz, 1974) but not with the quality of mood changes, which, being more personal and idosyncratic and the disinhibition and release being secondary to the depressant and obtunding effects, would obviously vary from person to person, from time to time, and from situation to situation. The slowing of the alpha rhythm parallels the blood alcohol level curve, especially in the initial, or ascending, part of the curve. A correlated effect is the decreased efficiency of the intellectual and cognitive processes (attention, memory, awareness, and comprehension).

The basis for these physiological changes must lie, at least in great part, in alcohol's effects on the transmission of nerve impulses across the various synapses, affecting in one way or another the different aggregations of neurons with their differing functions. Alcohol has varying effects on the different transmitters, a phenomenon that has yet to be fully elucidated. It is known, for example, that ethanol causes inhibition of the neuronal reuptake of norepinephrine discharged into the synapse on nerve stimulation; the drug also influences the reuptake of circulating norepinephrine. Moreover, alcohol seems to cause activation of noradrenergic neurons and therefore increased plasma and urine norepinephrine levels. There appears to be a similar block in the adrenal medulla's reuptake of epinephrine (Feldstein, 1971). On the other hand, ethanol potentiates the inhibition of cortical neurons by gamma-aminobutyric acid (GABA) in the cat. Benzodiazepines and barbiturates also potentiate GABA mediated neurotransmission and have an anxiolytic effect, although the former drug group has specified receptor binding sites to which neither barbiturates nor ethanol binds. Interestingly enough, long-term alcohol administration decreases GABA concentrations in the brain and alters the density of GABA receptors. This finding is consistent with the phenomenon of tolerance (i.e., long-term users of ethanol must use larger amounts of alcohol to obtain the GABA potentiation necessary to achieve an antianxiety effect or to avoid withdrawal symptoms (Nestoros, 1980). The norepinephrine effects may, at least in part, contribute to the excitatory action and the GABA effects to the sedative-depressant action.

Of course, one must be cautious in drawing conclusions relating activities at the synapse to clinical manifestations. Multiple neurotransmission systems are involved in a very complex network of activity. For example, both pentobarbital, a sedative-hypnotic, and GABA increase the binding of diazepam (Valium, a benzodiazepine) to benzodiazepine receptors in the central nervous system. At the same time, pentobarbital potentiates the GABA enhanced binding of diazepam to these receptors by increasing the affinity of the drug for the receptor. Finally, there is evidence of an endogenous inhibitor (or inhibitors) of GABA enhanced benzodiazepine binding (Skolnick, Moncada, Barken, & Paul, 1981).

Alcohol seems initially to depress the midbrain and its reticular activating system (a highly polysynaptic structure), and then the system's ascending and descending portions. The former portion, when so affected, causes disinhibition of the cortex, with increase in the amplitude of its electrical activity; thus, the cortex is progressively released from integrating controls and cognitive organization (Kalant, 1962). Inasmuch as the reticular activating system is an alerting and arousal system, this physiological effect correlates well with clinical observations, and one sees these depressant effects extending in a progressively downward manner from the cortex, through the thalamic and hypothalamic systems (affecting the autonomic functions), further down the brainstem and lower areas, and finally to the medulla and its vital centers (producing the symptoms of shock) (Himwich, 1956).

There is some evidence of primary cortical depression with alcohol (Diperri, Dravid, Schweigerdt, & Himwich, 1968), the drug nevertheless has an excitatory effect on the central cortex of the cat (Sauerland & Harper, 1970). This effect is possibly secondary to the depression of the ascending reticular activating system, which releases the cortex, but is also possibly due to direct excitatory action by ethanol, or both. Some workers have reported greater sensitivity (to alcohol) of the association cortical areas, the accessory somatosensory area, for example (Diperri, Dravid, Schweigerdt, & Himwich, 1968). All this evidence tends to correlate well with clinical findings. The sedative effects can be accounted for, as noted here, and the excitatory aspects will be considered later.

EXPERIMENTAL WORK AT THE ORGANISMIC LEVEL

The next step, demonstration of these sedative-depressant effects in experimental work at the organismic level, presents problems whether research involves animals in laboratories or humans in experimental situations. Indeed, one might find it difficult, if not impossible, to apply formulations concerning disinhibition of superego functions, for example, to laboratory animals. It would also be difficult to work out such an experiment in humans in a game type of situation: there are too many variables.

Thus, the literature involving work on this level is not clear. Experiments with laboratory animals showed that alcohol relieves fear and inhibitions, for example, in approach-avoidance situations (Wallgren & Barry, 1970). Alcohol consumption also increases in conflict rats given electric shocks (Wright, Pekanmaki & Malin, 1971). Shock alone has increased alcohol intake in rats (Myers & Cicero, 1968), as has audiogenic stress (Geber & Anderson, 1967) and spinning stress (Brown, 1968). Alcohol and meprobamate can relieve stress associated with frustration of extinction in rats (Myers, 1961). Other experiments have supported these results (Anisman & Waller, 1974; Mills & Bean, 1978; Mills, Bean & Hutcheson, 1977; Hill & Goldstein, 1974; Hatton & Vieth, 1974), and alcohol's effects have been noted to be additive to those of a barbiturate and vice versa (Chung & Brown, 1976). Social stress such as crowding of rats also increases alcohol consumption (Hannon & Donlong-Bantz, 1976). In primates, experimental uncertainty can result in increased alcohol intake (Orloff & Masserman, 1978).

Other work has indicated that stress counteracts the depressant effect of alcohol (Wallach & Barry, 1966) and thus it can be shown that the arousal phenomenon is involved in the effects of alcohol on the central nervous system. Activity and stress can reverse the effects of depression of the brainstem reticular activating system caused by alcohol up to a threshold dose, after which this effect is no longer capable of being reversed (Wallgren & Tirri, 1963; Myrsten, 1977).

On the other hand, Myers and Holman (1967) found that electrical shock did not increase alcohol intake in rats, nor did the stress of insoluble tasks (Persensky, Senter, & Jones, 1969). Cicero (1969) showed that alcohol selection increased when animals were exposed to the psychological stress of an unpredictable environment but not when they were exposed to unavoidable shock, a purely physical stress; uncertainty seemed to be the critical factor. Approach-avoidance conflict in rats produced gastric and duodenal ulceration, but alcohol administered experimentally did not protect against these effects (Schmidt, Kangas & Solomon, 1971). Other experiments also seem to disagree with the hypothesis that alcohol is consumed to alleviate stress and implicate other, non–stress related factors (Bond, 1978).

Cappell and Herman (1972) reviewed the literature involving stress in animals and concluded that only in the areas of conflict and experimental neurosis was good support found for alcohol's being used as a tension reducer. In other areas the evidence was negative, equivocal, or contradictory. In a review of animal studies, Myers and Veale (1972) also found that electric shock to the foot pads of an animal does not necessarily act as a stressor that prompts alcohol consumption, nor does crowding, cold, injections of formaldehyde, adrenalectomy, or other physical stress alone. Nevertheless, they reported that psychological or behavioral stress may increase an animal's intake of alcohol; for example, this pattern appeared in monkeys that had to press a lever continuously to avoid shock. Other experimenters disagreed. They concluded that a clear behavioral technique to produce addictive type drinking in primates and other animals has yet to be devised (Myers & Veale, 1972).

PROBLEMS WITH THE ANIMAL AND HUMAN MODELS OF ALCOHOLISM

A critique of the animal model and related experimental work by Falk and Tang (1977) focused on oversimplification in research and preconceived ideas on the part of experimenters about the absoluteness of the priority of alcohol. Falk and Tang suggested that alcohol ingestion involves a balance between desire and the opposing positive and negative motivations. The problems of alcohol abuse, dependence, and alcoholism are very complex entities. Furthermore, there is confusion over what stress is in this regard: psychological (e.g., anxiety) or physiological (e.g., withdrawal agitation). Alcohol dependent animals sometimes prefer concentrated sweet solutions to alcohol, just as human alcoholics in a laboratory situation often will prefer money to alcohol in the short run and will decrease their alcohol intake if punished by isolation or if required to do great amounts of work to obtain alcohol. In both humans and animals, withdrawal symptoms may fail to cause drinking. Here, too, sweet solutions may be preferred by animals. Alcohol intake in humans continues despite an increase in anxiety, agitation, sleep disturbance, and dysphoria. As noted earlier and discussed later in more detail, alcohol, taken to relieve stress, creates further tension, as well as dysphoria. In addition, constitutional and genetic factors must be taken into consideration, for some people are more sensitive to the physiological and pathological effects of alcohol (accounting, perhaps, for some national and racial differences in alcoholism rates). However, there is no proof that such people are at greater risk of developing alcoholism. In the disease, true physical dependence is often a later development, not part of the prolonged antecedent phase of occasional or periodic overindulgence. Indeed, a complex of environmental variables initiate and maintain drinking behavior (social, monetary, and work factors, for example); when these are removed, the laboratory animal or human subject stops drinking. There is a long and unpromising history of attempts to induce animals to ingest alcohol voluntarily in significant and stable amounts over a period of time. The complexity of this behavior pattern is evident when one considers that neither the agent (alcohol) nor the individuals' propensities nor the environment alone is critical: the agent produces powerful effects and can be a strong reinforcing factor; the individual can develop a bias to alcohol because the history of exposure causes social facilitation and conditioned pharmacological effects; finally, the environment may come into play, encouraging or discouraging addiction.

In one study, human alcoholics reported susceptibility for relapse when feeling depressed (93%), nervous (90%), worried (88%), bad (78%), under stress (77%), and after failure (72%), but not so frequently when feeling successful (35%), happy (30%), good (23%), or relaxed (18%) (Ludwig, Cain, Wikler, Taylor, & Bendfeldt, 1977). It should be noted that on occasion positive mood states and actual accomplishments may constitute a stress when the individual does not feel entitled to them or worthy of them; he must then pay the price for them and becomes "a character wrecked by success" (Freud, 1958). Paradoxically, then, seemingly positive mental states, conditions and situations can, in reality, constitute negative ones. That which seems non-stressful may actually be stressful, and vice versa. With this in mind, one can readily appreciate how difficult it is to reproduce such situations with animals and even with humans in laboratory conditions, and how difficult it is to extrapolate from the laboratory to real life. At any rate the above reports are all subjective ones, possibly containing rationalizations, and were not tested under laboratory conditions where, as noted, the results are limited; the situation there is not one of real life, merely a game.

Results from behavioral studies, then, though suggestive, are not conclusive and the literature is indeed ambiguous. Mendelson, Mello, & Solomon (1968) reported *reduction* of drinking following exposure to external stress, and Nathan and associates (Nathan, Lowenstein, Solomon & Rossi, 1970; Nathan, Zare, Ferneau & Lowenstein, 1970) showed drinking patterns of alcoholic subjects to be relatively unaffected by a condition of isolation that increased anxiety and depression (these effects having been subjectively assessed by the subjects).

BEHAVIORAL EVIDENCE FOR ALCOHOL'S USEFULNESS IN STRESS

There is, nevertheless, behavioral evidence of alcohol's usefulness in coping with stress, often despite the consequences of the drinking. Allman (1971) found alcoholics to drink most during stress associated with socialization and least with isolation stress, but the drinking reportedly increased depression, anxiety, and symptoms of psychopathology and decreased group structure and subjects' capacity to mobilize themselves. Nicol and associates (Nicol, Gunn, Gristwood, Foggitt, & Watson, 1973) reported that among violent men drinking was a common response to stress but often resulted in subsequent disinhibition of violence. Korman, Knopf, and Austin (1960) tested male students with alcohol or placebo at learning tasks (nonsense syllables) and shock; they concluded that small amounts of alcohol had analgesic and sedative effects, facilitating psychological performance under stress conditions. Goddard (1958) found that alcohol abolished the normal increase in urine noradrenaline during glider flights. Other drugs of this class have similar effects. Meprobamate (400mg.) enabled normal male subjects to deceive experimenters utilizing a polygraph apparatus (recording electrodermal, respiratory, and cardiovascular activity); other subjects receiving nothing or placebo in this double-blind study were unable to do so. The conclusion was that such drugs reduce the phasic physiological response to disturbing stimuli rather than simply lower tonic levels of arousal (Waid, Orne, Cook, & Orne, 1981).

Miller and associates (Miller, Hersen, Eisler & Hilsman, 1974) studied the effects of social stress on alcohol consumption in alcoholics and nonalcoholics and concluded that it seems doubtful that any simple interaction between stress and alcoholism or arousal and alcoholism will be demonstrated. The phenomenon of tolerance on the physiological level and on the psychological level, the total, *real* meaning of the situation to the subject, must be considered. Additionally, stress in one circumstance may push an individual to drink, but the presence of even potential negative reinforcement, implicit if not explicit, may—at least in the short run—push both the alcoholic and the nonalcoholic subject away from alcohol. Sedation can result in disinhibition, producing behavior that may appear, paradoxically, to be the effects of stimulation. Furthermore, alcohol not only serves as a means of dealing with stress but also constitutes a cause of further stress. It not merely functions to relieve tension, anxiety, depression, and other dysphoric states, but it produces them as well and both effects can occur concurrently, confusing the presenting picture.

ALCOHOL AS A CAUSE OF STRESS

That alcohol causes tension can be clearly seen on the neurophysiological and behavioral levels both in animals and in humans. McQuarrie and Fingle (1958) demonstrated cerebral cortical hyperexcitability and seizure susceptibility in rats following the sedative effects of alcohol; the degree of hyperexcitability was directly related to dose and to duration of exposure to alcohol. Microelectrode implantations indicated that increased amplitude of electrocortical activity was associated with the depressant effect on the reticular formation; this effect remained masked during the earlier, clinical depressant phase, appearing only as that pattern wore off (Kalant, 1962). Similar results characterize withdrawal in humans. Abrupt withdrawal of alcohol following a stable, prolonged period of significant alcohol ingestion causes the appearance in 12–48 hours of marked anxiety and tremulousness clinically and, in the EEG, moderate to high-voltage, rhythmic slow waves and a marked drop in alpha percentage. Later, random spikes and paroxysmal bursts of slow-wave, high-voltage activity appear, along with transient, mild dysrhythmia. Clinically, there may be progression to autonomic irregularities, convulsive seizures, hallucinosis, and even a full-blown delirium tremens (Wikler, Pescor, Fraser & Isbell, 1956). During at least the first 48 hours of withdrawal, there is a significant global reduction in mean cerebral blood flow. There is a relationship between the decrease and the length of the preceding period of heavy drinking and also between the decrease and the intensity of certain symptoms, such as clouded sensorium (in particular, high temporal and low parietal blood flows are related to increased symptoms). Finally, increased regional cerebral blood flow values were found in the temporal, sylvian, and occipital regions in two men reporting auditory and visual hallucinations (Berglund & Risberg, 1981).

Clearing of the clinical picture is fairly rapid over several days. Abnormal EEG responses to photic stimulation reach their peak about two days after withdrawal; these are infrequent after the fifth day. This parallels the time course of the clinical syndrome. There is no prolonged EEG impairment. It should be noted that the provocative event is the sharp drop in blood alcohol from a high level maintained over at least several days, so that the withdrawal picture can occur even in the presence of active drinking, but in lesser amounts (Wikler, Pescor, Fraser & Isbell, 1956). This has important implications for the detoxification process, in which the level of sedative-hypnotic in the blood is slowly lowered.

The clinical picture can be reproduced in rats. Liljequist and Engel (1977) reported that rats fed alcohol for nine months and then abruptly withdrawn from alcohol acutely developed hyperexcitability, along with rigidity, tremors, and convulsions. There was, in addition, a delayed withdrawal effect, with increased coordinated locomotor activity and hyperexcitability for about a week. The authors noted the similarity of this pattern to amphetamine activity and suggested that it was perhaps related to increased dopamine sensitivity linked to prolonged alcohol administration.

Sleep research in humans has produced similar data (Rundell, Williams, & Lester, 1977). Alcohol initially effects a brisk sleep onset, with decreased REM (rapid eye movement) stages and increased SWS (slow-wave stages). As the blood alcohol drops (after a moderate dose of alcohol) during the second half of the night, the REM periods increase, as does sleep disturbance. In recently withdrawn alcoholics, sleep continues to be disturbed, with brief arousals and with changes in the stages of sleep: decreased SWS (especially stage IV), increased stage I and REM, shortened inter-REM intervals, and frequent REM interruptions. These changes are reported to last in chronic alcoholics as long, in some instances, as one to two years, the length and severity of the sleep disturbance being related to age and to the duration of the excessive drinking. We can see, therefore, why there might exist a push within the individual, on a neurophysiological level, toward more alcohol or other sedative-hypnotics for additional sedation; such sedation will, in turn, subsequently produce additional agitation and hyperexcitability, requiring further sedation, and so on.

More recent work on withdrawal of ethanol in rats has shown similar brain hyperexcitability, measured by electrodes recording visually evoked potentials in the visual cortex, reticular formation, and thalamus, greatest in the former (Begleiter & Porjesz, 1977). Challenge doses of alcohol caused an immediate recurrence of hyperexcitability up to five weeks after withdrawal. The same phenomenon can be shown in other animals. Similarly in humans, although there is a return to obvious baseline brain hyperexcitability four days subsequent to withdrawal, alcoholics, as opposed to nonalcoholics, have a predisposition to withdrawal symptoms, particularly noticeable following challenge doses of alcohol (Begleiter & Porjesz, 1977).

There is, then, evidence of latent, long-term effects of prolonged alcohol intake; long-term aberration in the central and autonomic nervous systems, psychomotor performance, the emotions, etc., can best be shown after challenge doses of alcohol, which quickly cause impairment of central inhibitory mechanisms. Thus, a latent physical dependence can be said to persist in an attenuated form long beyond the immediate clinical withdrawal phase, and this dependence can be seen as constituting a long-term stress or, at least, a predisposition to abnormal response to stress. This phenomenon has its clinical implications in accounting, at least in part, for the prolonged period of emotional difficulties experienced during the recovery of the alcoholic and the tendency to relapse at any point in that recovery. Even small amounts of alcohol, with minimal stress, can contribute to a relapse.

CLINICAL SIGNIFICANCE OF ALCOHOL AND STRESS

As noted, the hyperexcitability will tend to push the individual in the direction of requiring more sedation by alcohol or other members of the sedative-hypnotic class of drugs. Yet, although this process can produce the symptoms of alcohol abuse, it is not enough in itself to cause the addiction (alcohol dependence) and the fullblown picture of the disorder. Other factors must play roles as well: genetic, sociological, psychological, environmental, etc. No one factor has been isolated as sufficient in itself.

Once the disorder is established and regardless of its course (inexorably progressive, periodic with remissions, stable, or recovering—at least temporarily), two other sets of stresses enter the picture, in addition to central nervous system hyperexcitability. One involves the direct effects of alcohol (and associated vitamin and nutritional deficiencies) on the organs and organ systems of the body, producing physical illnesses; Laennec's cirrhosis, Wernicke-Korsakoff's syndrome, alcoholic dementia, esophageal varices, gastrointestinal bleeding, and pancreatitis are among the best known (Seixas, 1980). Also involved here are organic functional disorders such as blackouts (brief amnesic periods; during such episodes the alcoholic may exhibit antisocial or inappropriate behavior); ataxia and poor coordination (causing automobile and industrial accidents); and behavioral release phenomena (the emergence of socially inappropriate sexual and aggressive impulses associated with disinhibition). Such behavior may be dangerous or embarrassing, diminishing the alcoholic's self-esteem, and may drive away friends, employers, co-workers, family, lovers, etc. Although alcohol may be taken initially to increase socialization (through disinhibition), isolation is the usual, later result of the disorder, with disruptions in and loss of job, personal, and social relationships.

The urgent quality of the need to drink results in the second set of stresses. The person becomes progressively removed from ordinary emotional interests and increasingly involved with drinking itself. Social withdrawal and isolation ensue as the individual concentrates all his energies on obtaining and drinking alcohol. As long as the compulsion outweighs the negative factors—the physical consequences of alcohol, the disapprobation and even rejection by the social environment, the loss of job, career, finances, lovers, friends, family, health, appearance, privileges, licenses, self-respect, even curtailment of liberty—the drinking will continue. Denial, minimization, and self-deception will be used to deal with many of these factors, especially where the self is concerned, and lying, deception, evasion, stealing, and other aspects of the deterioration of the character will emerge to deal with problems involving other people. All these behavioral activities will be found in the overt picture of severe alcoholism.

These are important phenomena for doctors, counselors, therapists, and concerned others to be aware of: threatened loss of one or more of the social, personal, or material desiderata at stake constitutes the leverage that can be used to bring about the proper motivation for the alcoholic to seek treatment, to enter into and to remain in an appropriate recovery program.

In summary, then, the use of alcohol develops in response to stress and serves to alleviate it, but as the pattern progresses into alcoholism drinking becomes a source of stress as well. This latter factor can be used to motivate the alcoholic into sobriety. The recovering alcoholic must learn to face life's difficulties without the use of intoxicants and thus to change. To change means to effect changes in the personality and in the modes of adaptation—and only this constitutes true and full sobriety.

NOTE

1. In 1978 in New York County there were 7612 hospital discharge diagnoses of alcoholism, 4.66% of total hospital discharge diagnoses, ranking first on the list; there were 60,037 alcoholism patient days, 2.99% of total hospital patient days, also ranking first. The significance of these numbers grows when one realizes that they included only alcoholism detoxification and not alcohol related medical diseases, alcoholic psychoses or convulsive disorders, undiagnosed alcoholism, or other alcohol related illnesses, nor to any other substance dependencies, which themselves ranked third in total diagnoses. Unpublished data, New York County Health Services Review Organization, 1978.

REFERENCES

ALLMAN, L. R. Group Drinking Under Stress: Effects of Alcohol Intake, Psychopathology, Mood and Group Process. Doctoral dissertation, Rutgers University, 1971.

ANISMAN, H. AND WALLER, T. G. Effects of inescapable shock and shock-produced conflict on self selection of alcohol in rats. *Pharmacology and Biochemistry of Behavior,* 1974, *2,* 27–33.

BEGLEITER, H. AND PLATZ, A. The effects of alcohol on the central nervous system in humans. In B. Kissin & H. Begleiter (eds.), *The biology of alcoholism. Vol. 2: Physiology and behavior.* New York: Plenum, 1974.

BEGLEITER, H. AND PORJESZ, B. Persistence of brain hyperexcitability following chronic alcohol exposure in rats. In M. Gross (ed.), *Alcohol intoxication and withdrawal. Vol 3b: Studies in alcohol dependence.* New York: Plenum, 1977.

BERGLUND, M. AND RISBERG, J. Regional cerebral blood flow during alcohol withdrawal. *Archives of General Psychiatry,* 1981, *38,* 351–355.

BLANE, H. T. *The personality of the alcoholic: Guises of dependency.* New York: Harper & Row, 1968.

BOND, N. W. Shock induced alcohol consumption in rats: Role of initial preference. *Pharmacology and Biochemistry of Behavior,* 1978, *9,* 39–42.

BROWN, R. V. Effects of stress on voluntary alcohol consumption in mice. *Quarterly Journal of Studies on Alcohol,* 1968, *29,* 49–53.

CALAHAN, D., CISIN, I. H., AND CROSSLEY, H. M. *American drinking practices: A national study of drinking behavior and attitudes.* Rutgers Center of Alcohol Studies monograph no. 6. 1969.

CAPPELL, H. AND HERMAN, C. P. Alcohol and tension reduction; a review. *Quarterly Journal of Studies on Alcohol,* 1972, *33,* 33–64.

CHUNG, H. AND BROWN, D. R. Alcohol-Hexobarbital interaction in rats under acute stress. *Life Sciences,* 1976, 18, 123–128.

CICERO, T. J. Self-selection of ethanol in rats: Behavioral, physiological, and neurochemical mechanisms. Doctoral dissertation, Purdue University, 1969.

DIPERRI, R., DRAVID, A., SCHWEIGERDT, A. AND HIMWICH, H. E. Effects of alcohol on evoked potentials of various parts of the central nervous system of the cat. *Quarterly Journal of Studies on Alcohol,* 1968, *29,* 20.

FALK, J. L. AND TANG, M. Animal model of alcoholism: Critique and progress. In M. Gross (ed.), *Alcohol intoxication and withdrawal, Vol. 3b; Studies in alcohol dependence.* New York: Plenum, 1977.

FELDSTEIN, A. Effect of ethanol on neurohumoral urine metabolism. Chap. 4. In B. Kissin & H. Begleiter (eds.), *The Biology of Alcoholism, Vol. 1: Biochemistry.* New York: Plenum, 1971.

FINNEY, J. C., SMITH, D. F., SKEETERS, D. E., AND AUVENSHINE, C. D. MMPI and alcoholic scales.*Quarterly Journal of Studies on Alcohol,* 1971, *32,* 1055–1060.

FREUD, S. Some character types met with in psychoanalytic work. Part II: Those wrecked by success. In J. Strachey (ed.), *The standard edition of the works of Sigmund Freud,* vol. 14. London: Hogarth, 1958.

GEBER, W. F. AND ANDERSON, T. A. Ethanol inhibition of audiogenic stress induced cardiac hypertrophy. *Experientia* (Basel), 1967, *23,* 734–736.

GITLOW, S. E., Chap. 1: An Overview. In S. Gitlow & H. Peyser (eds.) *Alcoholism: A practical treatment guide.* New York: Grune & Stratton, 1980.

GODDARD, P. J. Effect of alcohol on excretion of catechol amines in conditions giving rise to anxiety. *Journal of Applied Physiology,* 1958, *13,* 118–120.

GRENELL, R. G. Effects of alcohol on the neuron. In B. Kissin & H. Begleiter (eds.), *The Biology of Alcoholism. Vol. 2: Physiology and behavior.* New York: Plenum, 1978.

HANNON, R. AND DONLONG-BANTZ, K. Effect of housing density on alcohol consumption by rats. *Journal of Studies on Alcohol,* 1976, *37,* 1556–1563.

HATTON, G. I. AND VIETH, A. Stress-Related and diurnal alcohol drinking in rats. *Bulletin of Psychosomatic Society,* 1974, *4,* 195–196.

HILL, S. Y. AND GOLDSTEIN, R. Effects of p-chlorphenylalanine and stress on alcohol consumption by rats. *Quarterly Journal of Studies on Alcohol,* 1974, *35,* 34–41.

HIMWICH, H. E. Alcohol and brain physiology. In G. Thompson (ed.), *Alcoholism.* Springfield: Thomas, 1956.

HORSEY, W. J. AND AKERT, K. The influence of ethyl alcohol on the spontaneous electrical activity of the cerebral cortex and subcortical structures of the cat. *Quarterly Journal of Studies on Alcohol,* 1953, *14,* 363.

HORTON, D. J. The functions of alcohol in primitive society: A cross-cultural study. *Quarterly Journal of Studies on Alcohol,* 1943, *4,* 199–320.

KALANT, H. Some recent physiological and biochemical investigations on alcohol and alcoholism. *Quarterly Journal of Studies on Alcohol,* 1962, *23,* 52.

KISSIN, B. The pharmocodynamics and natural history of alcoholism. In B. Kissin & H. Begleiter (eds.), *The biology of alcoholism. Vol. 3: Clinical pathology.* New York: Plenum, 1974.

KORMAN, M., KNOPF, I. J. AND AUSTIN, R. B. Effects of alcohol on serial learning under stress conditions. *Psychological Reports,* 1960, *7,* 217–220.

LILJEQUIST, S. AND ENGEL, J. Behavioral changes after chronic ethanol treatment. In M. Gross (ed.), *Alcohol intoxication and withdrawal. Vol. 3b: Studies in alcohol dependence.* New York: Plenum, 1977.

LUDWIG, A. M., CAIN, R. G., WIKLER, A., TAYLOR, R. M., AND BENDFELDT, R. Physiologic and situational determinants of drinking behavior. In M. Gross (ed.), *Alcohol intoxication and withdrawal. Vol. 3b: Studies in alcohol dependence.* New York: Plenum, 1977.

McQUARRIE, D. G. AND FINGLE, E. Effects of single doses and chronic administration of ethanol on experimental seizures in mice. *Journal of Pharmacology,* 1958, *124,* 264.

MENDELSON, J. H., MELLO, N. K. AND SOLOMON P. Small group drinking behavior: An experimental study of chronic alcoholics. In A. Wikler (ed.), *The Addictive States.* Baltimore: Williams & Wilkins, 1968.

MILLER, P. M., HERSEN, M., EISLER, R. M. AND HILSMAN, G. Effects of social stress on operant drinking of alcoholics and social drinkers. *Behavioral Research and Therapy,* 1974, *12,* 67–72.

MILLS, K. C. AND BEAN, J. W. The caloric and intoxicating properties of fluid intake as components of stress-induced ethanol consumption in rats. *Psychopharmacology,* 1978, *57,* 27–31.

MILLS, K. C., BEAN, J. W. AND HUTCHESON, J. S. Shock induced ethanol consumption in rats. *Pharmacology and Biochemistry of Behavior,* 1977, *6,* 107–115.

MULFORD, H. A., AND MILLER, D. E. Drinking in Iowa. Part III: Definitions of alcoholism related to drinking behavior. *Quarterly Journal of Studies on Alcohol,* 1960, *21,* 267–281.

MULFORD, H. A., AND MILLER, D. E. Drinking in Iowa. Part IV: Preoccupation with alcohol and definitions of alcohol, heavy drinking, and trouble due to drinking. *Quarterly Journal of Studies on Alcohol.* 1960, *21,* 279–291.

MULFORD, H. A. AND MILLER, D. E. Drinking in Iowa. Part V: Drinking and Alcoholic Drinking. *Quarterly Journal of Studies on Alcohol,* 1960, *21,* 483–499.

MYERS, R. D. Effects of meprobamate on alcohol preference and on the stress of response extinction in rats. *Psychological Reports,* 1961, *8,* 385–392.

MYERS, R. D., AND CICERO, T. J. Effects of tybamate on ethanol intake in rats during psychological stress in an avoidance task. *Archives of Internal Pharmacodynamics,* 1968, *1175,* 440–446.

MYERS, R. D. AND HOLMAN, R. B. Failure of stress of electric shock to increase ethanol intake in rats. *Quarterly Journal of Studies on Alcohol,* 1967, *28,* 132–137.

MYERS, R. D. AND VEALE, W. L. The determinants of alcohol preference in animals. In B. Kissin & H. Begleiter (eds.), *The Biology of Alcoholism. Vol. 2: Physiology and Behavior.* New York: Plenum, 1972

MYRSTEN, A. L. Interaction of alcohol with psychological stress. In M. Gross (ed.), *Alcohol intoxication and withdrawal. Vol. 3b: Studies in alcohol dependence.* New York: Plenum, 1977.

NATHAN, P. E., LOWENSTEIN, L. M., SOLOMON, P. AND ROSSI, A. M. Behavioral analysis of chronic alcoholism. *Archives of General Psychiatry,* 1970, *22,* 219.

NATHAN, P. E., ZARE, N. C., FERNEAU, E. W., JR., AND LOWENSTEIN, L. M. Effects of congener differences in alcoholic beverages on the behavior of alcoholics. *Quarterly Journal of Studies on Alcohol,* 1970, Suppl. no. 5, 87–100.

NAKAI, Y. Effects of intravenous infusion of central depressants on the evoked potentials of the auditory cortex in cats. *Japanese Journal of Pharmacology* (Kyoto), 1964, *14,* 235.

NESTOROS, J. N. Ethanol specifically potentiates GABA-mediated neurotransmission in feline cerebral cortex. *Science,* 1980, *209,* 708–710.

NICOL, A. R., GUNN, J. C., GRISTWOOD, J., FOGGITT, R. H. AND WATSON, J. P. The relationship of alcoholism to violent behavior resulting in long term imprisonment. *British Journal of Psychiatry,* 1973, *123,* 47–51.

ORLOFF, E. R. AND MASSERMAN, J. H. Effects of abstinence on self-selection of ethanol induced by uncertainty in monkeys. *Journal of Studies on Alcohol,* 1978, *39,* 499–504.

PERSENSKY, J. J., SENTER, R. J. AND JONES, B. B. Alcohol consumption in rats after experimentally induced neurosis. *Psychosomatic Science,* 1969, *15,* 159–160.

RUNDELL, O. H., WILLIAMS, L. AND LESTER, B. K. Sleep in alcoholic patients: Longitudinal findings. In M. Gross (ed.), *Alcohol intoxication and withdrawal. Vol. 3b: Studies in alcohol dependence.* New York: Plenum, 1977.

SEIXAS, F. The Medical complications of alcoholism. In S. Gitlow & H. Peyser (eds.), *Alcoholism: A practical treatment guide.* New York: Grune & Stratton, 1980.

SAUERLAND, E. K. AND HARPER, R. M. Effects of ethanol on EEG spectra of the intact brain and isolated forebrain. *Experimental Neurology,* 1970, *27,* 490.

SCHMIDT, K.M., KANGAS, J. A. AND SOLOMON, G. F. The effects of ethanol on the development of gastric ulceration in the rat. *Journal of Psychosomatic Research,* 1971, *15,* 55–61.

Skolnick, P., Moncada, V., Barker, J. L. and Paul, S. M. Pentobarbital: Dual actions to increase brain benzodiazepine receptor affinity. *Science,* 1981, *211,* 1448–1450.

Tamerin, J. S., Weiner, S., Poppen, R., Steinglass, P., and Mendelson, J. H., Alcohol and memory: Amnesia and short-term memory function during experimentally induced intoxication, *American Journal of Psychiatry,* 1971, *127,* 1659–1664.

U.S. Department of Health, Education, and Welfare. *The alcohol, drug abuse, and mental health national data book.* DHEW publication no. 86–938. Washington, D.C.: U.S. Govenment Printing Office, 1980.

Waid, W. M., Orne, E. C., Cook, M. R. and Orne, M. T. Meprobamate reduces accuracy of physiological detection of deception. *Science,* 1981, *212,* 71–73.

Wallach, C. G. and Barry, H. III. Fear modifies drug effects on avoidance and escape during gradual shock increments. *Proceedings of the American Psychological Association,* 1966, 121–122.

Wallgren, H., and Barry, H., III. *Actions of alcohol* (2 vols.). New York: Elsevier, 1970.

Wallgren, H. and Tirri, R. Studies on the mechanism of stress-induced reduction of alcohol intoxication in rats. *Acta Pharmacologica Toxicologica* (Copenhagen), 1963, *20,* 27–38.

Wikler, A., Pescor, F. T., Fraser, H. F. and Isbell, H. Electroencephalographic changes associated with chronic alcoholic intoxication and the alcohol abstinence syndrome. *American Journal of Psychiatry,* 1956, *113,* 106.

Witkin, H. A., Karp, S. A., and Goodenough, D. R. Dependence in alcoholics, *Quarterly Journal of Studies on Alcohol,* 1959, *20,* 493–504.

Wright, J. M. von, Pekanmaki, L. and Malin, S. Effects of conflict and stress on alcohol intake in rats. *Quarterly Journal Studies on Alcohol,* 1971, *32,* 420–433.

36

Stress and Headaches

Joseph D. Sargent

THE CLASSIFICATION OF HEADACHE is a complex exercise with many nuances. A reductionistic approach to the etiology of functional headache would use severity as the common denominator for classification (Bakal & Kaganov, 1979). Generally, my own clinical experience has confirmed the clinical wisdom of those who served on the Ad Hoc Committee on the Classification of Headache (1962). Not all headaches listed in the committee's classification are related to psychological stress and so it is important to review this scheme to point out specific headache types thought to be related to this mode of stress. These conditions represent the focus of this chapter.

The headache classification constructed by the committee is given in Table 36–1. Groups 1–5 are those on which attention will be focused since groups 6–15 are clearly related to physical disorders that produce physiological stress. In group 1, *classic migraine* and *common migraine* will be considered separately from the other vascular headaches. Psychologi-

TABLE 36–1
Classification of Headache

1. Vascular headache of migraine type:
   - A. "Classic" migraine
   - B. "Common" migraine
   - C. "Cluster" headache
   - D. "Hemiplegic" and "opthalmoplegic" migraine
   - E. "Lower-half" headache
2. Muscle contraction headache
3. Combined headache: vascular and muscle contraction
4. Headache of nasal vasomotor reaction
5. Headache of delusional, conversion, or hypochondriacal states
6. Nonmigrainous vascular headaches
7. Traction headache
8. Headache due to overt cranial inflammation
9–13. Headache due to disease of ocular, aural, nasal and sinusal, dental, or other cranial or neck structures
14. Cranial neuritides
15. Cranial neuralgias

Source: Ad Hoc Committee on the Classification of Headache (1962:717); reprinted with permission.

TABLE 36–2
Classification of Headache

Vascular Headache	Muscle contraction (psychogenic) headache	Traction and inflammatory headache

A. Migraine
  1. Classic
  2. Common
  3. Hemiplegic
  4. Opthalmoplegic (complicated migraine)
	A. Cervical osteoarthritis	A. Mass lesions (tumors, edema, hematomas, cerebral hemorrhage)

B. Cluster (histamine)	B. Chronic myostitis	B. Diseases of the eye, ear, nose, throat, teeth
C. Toxic vascular	C. Depressive equivalents and conversion reactions	C. Infection
D. Hypertensive		D. Arthritis, phlebitis E. Cranial neuralgias F. Occlusive vascular disease

Source: Dalessio (1979:144); reprinted with permission of the author and of Oxford University Press.

cal stress is thought to be closely linked with these disorders, while *cluster headache,* a malady affecting mostly males, probably has little relationship to this type of stress. *Hemiplegic migraine* and *opthalmoplegic migraine* are exceedingly rare conditions; *lower-half headache* is a poorly understood disorder. *Muscle contraction headache,* probably a misnomer, is most certainly associated with psychological stress, although the patient may deny emotional factors; *combined headache,* featuring elements of migraine and muscle contraction headaches, is also closely related to the same type of stress. *Headaches caused by upper respiratory disease* are separated into two etiological groups: those linked to the spread of effects of noxious stimuli in nasal and sinus structures and those secondary to nasal vasomotor reaction, a condition thought to be related to psychological stress. Finally, *headaches associated with delusional, conversional,* or *hypochrondriacal states* are rare in most medical practices since such psychiatric disorders are not searched for in patients with headaches unless they are under the care of psychiatrists or psychologists. A troublesome aspect in analyzing this category is to determine how these headaches differ clinically from those in groups 1 and 2. Are they merely muscle contraction or vascular headaches occurring in association with underlying psychiatric disorders? From my perspective, stress generated by these psychological disorders should be seen simply as another triggering factor causing these headaches.

Dalessio (1979) developed another headache classification based on different pathophysiologic mechanisms. Table 36–2 illustrates his scheme.

EVOLUTION OF HEADACHE RESEARCH

Graham and Wolff (1938) were the first to show that the pulsations of the temporal artery are increased during the headache phase. Their work was based on observations of the effect of ergotamine tartrate on extracranial vessels in relief of migraine. Ergotamine tartrate diminished the increased amplitude of the arterial pulsation, with corresponding relief of the headache. These results seemed reasonable in view of previous work with histamine, which had clearly shown that stretched extracranial arteries are capable of producing pain (Clark, Hough, & Wolff, 1936; Pickering & Hess, 1933). Schumacher and Wolff (1941), using methods to increase intracranial pressure through the administration of amyl nitrite, reached the following conclusions:

> The essential migraine phenomena result from dysfunction of cranial arteries and represent contrasts in vascular mechanisms and vascular beds. Pre-headache disturbances follow occlusive vasoconstriction of cerebral arteries, where the headache results from dilation and distension chiefly of branches of external carotid arteries. (P. 214)

Hence the birth of the vascular theory of migraine.

A chance cerebral angiogram done on a patient while in a classical migraine attack showed a diminution in the size of the internal carotid system, with reflux into the vertebral vessels during the prodromal phase; at the beginning of the headache phase, blood flow returned to normal (Dukes & Vieth, 1964). O'Brien (1971) showed a profound reduction in blood flow in the cerebral cortex, in the prodromal phase; this change lasted much longer than the aura, may occur without symptoms, and is generalized and bilaterally distributed. This evidence indicates that each attack of migraine is biphasic; the occurrence of the aura is an accidental expression of a more generalized process.

Wolff (1963) proposed in his neurogenic theory of migraine headache that vasodilation of the cerebral circulation occurs whenever adequate blood supply to the brain is endangered. If cerebrovascular dilation is great enough, the extracranial arteries will dilate and release a number of chemical factors. Edema and a lowering of pain threshold will occur. What initiates vasoconstriction is not clear.

In recent years, investigators have postulated that an agent, or agents, causing vasoconstriction may initiate the headache sequence. Sicuteri (1967) proposed that such substances are amines, including norepinephrine, epinephrine, and serotonin—all powerful vasoconstrictors. Other substances implicated in the headache sequence are acetyl choline, adenosine triphosphate, bradykinin, and histamine (Ostfield, 1960). Serotonin may be the most important agent since, under some circumstances, it can also act as a vasodilator (Page, 1954). In the migraine attack, some subjects excrete increased amounts of catecholamine end products, particularly 5–HIAA (5–hydroxyimdoleacetic acid) from serotonin and VMA (vahillymahdelic acid) from norepinephrine and epinephrine (Sicuteri, 1967). Lance, Anthony, and Hintenberger (1967) showed a corresponding reduction in blood serotonin levels at the onset of a migraine attack.

According to Friedman and Elkind (1963), methysergide maleate (Sansert) has proven to be the most useful prophylactic agent in migraine. Interestingly, this medicine is an antiserotonin agent that has two actions: inhibition of central vasomotor reflex effects and accentuation of peripheral vasoconstriction produced by catecholamines. Ergotamine tartrate, in addition to its well-known peripheral vasoconstrictor effect, has significant central action, as demonstrated in man and animals (Graham & Wolff, 1938; Rothlin, 1923; Rothlin & Cerletti, 1949; Wolff, 1963). Friedman (1972) concluded that the "traditional view that migraine consists of phases of vasoconstriction and vasodilation is far too simplified, and it is apparent that migraine is a complex vasomotor disturbance" (p. 399). Because the migraine syndrome is a multifaceted clinical disorder, some investigators have postulated a dysfunction in the hypothalamus as the provocative element in the attack. Pearce (1969) suggested that the hypothalamus can profoundly influence the autonomic control of the peripheral vasculature and postulated "a periodic central disturbance of hypothalamic activity or a labile threshold accounting for the periodicity of the migraine attack and providing a mechanism whereby emotional disturbances could be mediated by pathways from the limbic system to the hypothalamus" (p. 9).

Herburg (1967) proposed an etiological role for the variation of hypothalamic activity in migraine. He relied on three groups of clinical observations: (1) the peripheral vasomotor involvement seen in the temporal arteries, conjunctivae, and skin; (2) metabolic and vegetative disturbances such as variations in water balance, food intake, mood, and sleep; and (3) the "accentuated secondary drives" of the migraine personality, which have been related to hypothalamic activity. Rao and Pearce (1971), using metyrapone and insulin hypoglycemia tests, failed to demonstrate in migraine subjects a disturbance in the hypothalamic-pituitary-adrenal axis; however, a consistently observed pattern of "hypoglycemia unresponsiveness" suggested a possible hypothalamic dysfunction.

Tunis and Wolff (1954) concluded from their studies that "concurrent vasoconstriction of nutrient arteries and increased muscle contraction result in headache" (p. 423). They found it "likely that the large group of normotensive and hypertensive persons with headaches associated with emotional conflict, tension and contraction of cranial and cervical muscles are those most likely to exhibit the combination of muscle contraction and vasoconstriction" (p. 433). The inference can be drawn that their subjects had muscle contraction headaches although this is not stated specifically.

The actual role of sustained muscle contraction as a cause for muscle contraction headaches has been called into question. Electromyographic (EMG) readings, which should be an accurate reflection of muscle contraction, do not differ substantially between people who do not and those who do suffer from muscle contraction headaches. Bakal (1975) emphasized this point in an in-depth review of headache. Some migraineurs show high EMG readings (Bakal & Kaganov, 1979; Cohen, 1978), and are diagnosed as combined headaches. These same authors have made a logical argument for the treatment of migraine and muscle contraction headaches using only EMG biofeedback.

Our understanding of the pathophysiology of muscle contraction headache has advanced little since the studies of Tunis and Wolff (1954). However, the knowledge that has been gained suggests that the principal etiological mechanism may be related to the vasoconstriction of the nutrient arteries. Looking exclusively at the symptoms presented by headache sufferers, Bakal and Kaganov (1979) and Ziegler (1978) raised serious questions regarding the clinician's ability to distinguish between migraine and muscle contraction headaches. As long as the medical history is the only reliable way to distinguish types of functional headache, this question will persist.

CURRENT THEMES IN HEADACHE RESEARCH AND TREATMENT

Currently there are four approaches in the research and treatment of headache:

1. psychoanalytic
2. pharmacophysiological
3. behavioral
4. psychophysiologic

Behavioral medicine has incorporated the psychophysiological approach, but the latter differs sufficiently from the behavioral method to warrant a separate discussion.

Psychoanalytic Approach

The prevailing concept that the migraineur has a specific personality type has been challenged. In the traditional view, the migraineur is a tense, ambitious, hard-working, obsessive-compulsive perfectionist who has stored up much hostility with few outlets for its expression. Unfortunately, the issue of repressed anger is common to many psychosomatic disorders, such as essential hypertension, coronary artery disease, and asthma, and therefore cannot be used as a distinguishing clinical feature for those complaining of migraine headache. Vincent (1960) and Sperling (1964) pointed out the importance of psychosexual formulations in understanding migraine headaches from this viewpoint. These formulations are derived from a theory of personality development espoused by Freud and contributed to later by other psychoanalytic theoreticians.

Henryk-Gutt and Rees (1973), after examining 50 males and 50 females suffering with migraine, concluded that psychological stresses appear to act as important precipitants of migraine attacks but do not necessarily predispose to migraine. These authors were unable to confirm earlier suggestions that migraine sufferers are neither overly obsessional nor overly ambitious. Furthermore, they stated that previous descriptions of migraine personality may have relied on self-selected groups not fully representative of the population suffering with migraine. Drawing on his clinical experience, Pearce (1977) reported that emotional disturbance was the single most common triggering mechanism in migraine and the most important cause of frequent and severe attacks. Again, he found nothing specific about the emotional stimulus nor a consistent personality type in migraine subjects.

Psychoanalytic formulations in the literature are usually based on one or, at most, several intensively studied case histories. Therefore, the findings may not be applicable to the broad spectrum of migraineurs. However, in my experience, this approach has something to offer clinically to chronic, severely disabled migraine sufferers who have responded poorly to other treatment modalities. Rees (1973) suggested that the migraine sufferer can benefit from interviews with a physician and from the doctor-patient relationship. The decision to provide individual psychotherapy requires a thorough assessment of many factors. This point was previously emphasized by Brenner, Friedman, and Carter (1949).

Interestingly, tension, or muscle contraction, headache has not received as much attention in the psychoanalytic literature as has migraine. Ziegler (1978) noted this lack and pointed out the ambiguity in the term "tension." Does it refer to the involved musculature or to psychological events? Friedman (1979) argued that there is no specific personality type prone to this type of headache but explained that certain individuals tend to express conflict through the muscular system, with headache as one manifestation of this process. He advised caution in correlating possible sources of tension with the onset of a specific headache: "The conflicting emotional factors that contribute to muscle contraction headaches are complex and may often be unrelated to obvious and immediate sources of tension or anxiety in the patient's life" (p. 110). Thus, it may be appropriate for a patient significantly disabled by this type of headache to seek insight through psychotherapy.

The psychoanalytic approach would have its greatest impact in understanding psychogenic headache, particularly conversion headache. Packard (1980) stated, "The coincidence of an acute emotional state and the appearance of headache is suggestive of a conversion headache, especially if the connection between the psychological event and the symptom is unrecognized by the patient'' (p. 267). The literature with respect to this headache is sparse.

Pharmacophysiological Approach

The earlier observations of Duke and Dieth (1964) and O'Brien (1971) have been carried forward by Skinhøj (1973), and Edmeads (1977), using the intracarotid xenon-133 technique, and by Sakai and Meyer (1979), utilizing the xenon-133 inhalation technique pioneered by O'Brien. These latter studies support the two-phase concept of migraine: *vasoconstriction* of the intracranial vasculature in the preheadache phase and *vasodilation* of the extracranial and intracranial vasculature during the headache phase.

Mathew, Hrastnik, and Meyers (1976) showed that regional cerebral blood flow with the xenon-133 inhalation technique was normal in the headache phase in patients with muscle contraction and psychogenic headaches. Regional cerebral blood flow was reduced, but not significantly, in patients with both cerebrovascular insufficiency and headache, as compared to those with cerebrovascular insufficiency without headache.

The most intriguing question in migraine is what initiates vasoconstriction. This problem, most likely, led Wolff (1963) to adopt his neurogenic theory of migraine. The literature is full of descriptions of various conditions that serve to trigger the sequence of events that constitute the migraine headache. Sicuteri (1967) proposed a serotonin theory for migraine, but other substances within the brain may be equally important (e.g., norepinephrine and epinephrine). Bruyn (1980) presented a good overview of this problem and marshaled considerable anatomical, clinical, and biochemical data to support the neurogenic theory of migraine, particularly at the hypothalamic level. Yamamoto and Meyer (1980), in their investigations, developed the likely possibility of an adrenoceptor site disorder in migraine.

Herburg (1978) pointed out that the sympathetic nerve supply originating in the spinal cord comes to an abrupt end soon after the small arteries have penetrated the brain substance. Therefore, it has been assumed that the sympathetic nervous system plays only a minor role in normal and abnormal cerebral circulation. However, I (Sargent, 1981) pointed out elsewhere that the brain has its own intrinsic sympathetic nerve supply, which could greatly influence the intracerebral vasculature.

Another intriguing aspect of the pathophysiology of migraine is the exact nature of the mechanism for vasodilation of the extracranial arterial system during the headache phase. Wolff (1963) originally spoke about his "headache stuff," fluid obtained from around the area of the dilated arteries, which produced migraine headaches when injected into the extracranial arteries of nonmigrainous subjects. To date, the exact ingredients of "headache stuff" has not been elucidated.

The characterization of migraine as a generalized vasomotor disturbance is another, equally fascinating aspect of the problem. Appenzeller (1969) has been one of the principal proponents of this view. "Migraine equivalents," episodic attacks of symptoms other than headache occurring in migraineurs, constitute another murky area.

Lately much has been written challenging the concept of tension headache as being solely or even primarily a disorder of spastic muscle. This debate highlights our lack of understanding of the pathophysiology of headache. The recent discovery of endorphins undoubtedly will lead to the development of new medications for headache (Reed, 1980) and illuminate this complex area (for a review of pharmacological issues in headache see Dalessio, 1980).

Behavioral Therapy

Benson, Klemchuk, and Graham (1974) stated that the regular elicitation of the *relaxation response* through the practice of Transcendental Meditation has limited usefulness for severe migraine and cluster headaches. The role of relaxation response in less severe headache remains to be investigated. More recently, Benson, Kotch, Crassweller, and Greenwood (1977) suggested that the relaxation response may be useful in counteracting overactivity of the sympathetic nervous system. The relaxation response is the antithesis to the flight-or-fight response and protects against "overstress." Tasto and Hinkle (1973) showed improvement in tension headaches with muscle relaxation. Warner and Lance (1975), using muscle relaxation, obtained similar results with migraine and chronic headache. Fowler (1975) provided both a rationale for the use of operant conditioning in headache and evidence for its efficacy. Paulley and Haskell (1975) showed significant improvement in migraineurs taught relaxation exercises and aspects of the migraine personality (previously discussed under the psychoanalytic approach) under the guidance of a physiotherapist in group sessions. Mitchell and Mitchell (1971) found that *combined desensitization* (applied relaxation, assertiveness training, and systematic desensitization) was more effective in headache control than either applied relaxation alone or a no-treatment control condition. Mitchell and White (1977) demonstrated that instruction in various self-management skills was helpful in reducing headaches. Andreychuk and Skriver (1975) showed that hypnotic training was effective in decreasing migraine. Using a cognitive skills approach to headache, Holroyd and Andrasik (1978) found that a group taught cognitive coping skills, a second group using cognitive and relaxation coping skills, and a third participating in a "headache discussion condition" showed greater improvement in headache control than did a symptom monitoring control group. Finally, the conceptualization of Greenspoon and Olson (1980), utilizing biofeedback in a behavior modification framework, is of some interest.

Psychophysiologic Approach

It has been fascinating to observe the growth in the use of biofeedback and self-regulation techniques for headache over the decade since the publication of articles by Budzynski, Stoyva and Adler (1970) and by Sargent, Green, and Walters (1972). Biofeedback is the technique of using instruments to display physiological information in a meaningful way so that an individual can manage his body at will, which is self-regulation. Clinically, self-regulation has not proven to be a panacea for functional headache, but it has nevertheless developed a definite role in this area. Scientific verification of the clinical efficacy of self-regulation has been hard to come by, perhaps because our research methodologies do not capture the complexity of the clinical situation. For example, there is no doubt that EMG self-regulation is the treatment of choice for the tension headache sufferer with elevated EMG readings (Budzynski, Stoyva, Adler, & Mulhanney, 1973), but clinically the number of individuals with tension headaches and elevated EMG readings are few. This method has not been particularly successful in patients with tension headaches and normal EMG readings.

Blanchard and Young (1974) produced the earliest comprehensive review of the efficacy of biofeedback training in various clinical problems. In their evaluation of EMG feedback training, they indicated that the combination of EMG feedback training and home practice in relaxation was effective in controlling tension headaches. Budzynski (1978) argued that although Blanchard and Young's (1974) conclusion had merit, the durability of clinical gains remained in question.

Blanchard and Young (1974) found that it was difficult to assess the role of *thermal training* (a technique combining autogenic training and feedback of skin temperature from the hands) in controlling migraine headaches, as described by Sargent, Green, and Walters (1972). After examining a broader collection of data, Fahrion (1978) offered a much more optimistic assessment of this technique. However, Kewman and Roberts (1980) and Cohen, McArthur, and Rickles (1980) found data in their controlled-outcome studies that suggested that thermal training had nonspecific effects on migraine headache activity. Blanchard, Theobald, Williamson, Silver, and Brown (1978) reported that relaxation training and thermal training at one-, two-, and three-month follow-ups seemed to have no differential effect on any of the headache dependent measures. Blanchard and associates postulated that in teaching patients to assume a more relaxed attitude, both methods use a common pathway. I think that the authors were unable to demonstrate a specific change for thermal training because their subjects had not yet achieved voluntary control over hand vasculature *(voluntary control* is defined as the ability to bring reliably about a change of feeling in the hands in a matter of seconds under all usual life circumstances).

Dalessio, Kunzel, Sternbach, and Sovak (1979) showed that thermal training was not associated with the conditioning of a single autonomic response but was related to a general decrease of sympathetic outflow, with improvement of migraine symptoms. Kentsmith, Strider, Copenhaver, and Jacques (1976), using a combination of meditation, biofeedback, and relaxation training, showed a reduction in the level of plasma dopamine-B-hydroxylase activity and migraine headache. Plasma dopamine-B-hydroxylase activity varies directly with the activity of the sympathetic nervous system. Mathew, Ho, Kralik, Taylor, and Claghorn (1980) demonstrated a decrease in plasma catecholamine levels and platelet monoamine oxidase activity by EMG biofeedback training in 15 anxious but otherwise normal subjects. Dalessio (1978) implicated the release of vasoactive substances from their reservoirs in the circulation (mainly platelets) in the painful vasodilation associated with migraine. And so, the work of Mathew and colleagues (1980) has implications beyond the possible role of relaxation in the control of headache.

Another control technique involves the teaching of migraineurs to vasoconstrict the temporal artery on the side of the headache. This approach has had success in controlling migraine headache (Bild & Adams, 1980; Koppman, McDonald, & Kunzel, 1974).

Olton and Noonberg (1980) presented a thorough discussion of the issues and literature related to the application of biofeedback and self-regulation to tension and migraine headaches and should be consulted for a detailed review of current methods.

STATE OF THE ART AND ISSUES FOR FUTURE RESEARCH

A curious paradox emerged in preparing this review: the literature is filled with multiple success stories, but the day-to-day clinical evaluation and treatment of headache is a demanding and often frustrating endeavor that requires ingenuity and flexibility in approach. The first step in the evaluation and treatment process is to make the diagnosis. As long as there are no physical, biochemical, or radiological markers for diagnosis of each headache type, the clinician must depend on obtaining a careful history from the patient. Skill in diagnostic interviewing is acquired only by experience with patients under many different circumstances. As one who has had to make difficult diagnostic decisions, I slowly have come to appreciate the clinical wisdom demonstrated in the classification of headaches devised by the Ad Hoc Committee on the Classification of Headache (1962) and think that this scheme should not be altered without solid evidence challenging its premises. For me, that evidence has not surfaced.

To date, the most useful tool, beyond the physical examination, and the medical history, in distinguishing causation of headaches is computerized tomography of the head. This tool should not be taken out of the hands of the clinician because of spurious arguments concerning cost-effectiveness. A missed diagnosis of a treatable intracranial space occupying lesion is more devastating and costly to both patient and physician than the performance of a CAT-scan of the head. Of course, I do not advocate that CAT-scans be used indiscriminately with headache sufferers. More investigation is required to assess the curious finding of increased incidence of cerebral atrophy found in CAT-scan of migraine and tension headache sufferers (Sargent, Lawson, Solbach, & Coyne, 1979).

Future research should also include epidemiologic studies to define more clearly the characteristics of various headache populations. Such studies could test the assumption of genetic predisposition to migraine, assess genetic versus environmental etiology of functional headache, and, perhaps, lay to rest the specter of a specific migraine personality. The assessment of placebo effects is also essential. Benson and Epstein (1975) pointed out that placebo has both positive and negative effects on treatment outcome. Meyers's use of the xenon-133 inhalation technique to study intracranial and extracranial blood flow in different clinical conditions and blood flow response to various medications and physiologic conditions is an exciting and promising avenue of research. Finally, researchers will continue to produce data on the biochemical composition of the human brain, and ideas for the development of new classes of drugs for headache (for example, endorphins) undoubtedly will come from these studies.

As society looks for ways to change its dependence on drugs to solve individual and collective ills, more emphasis in research and treatment will be placed on behavioral and psychophysiological modalities. To realize the full potential of these fields, our thoughts concerning research design and strategy will need to change so as to capture the complex interaction between the patient and the person treating the patient. The time for the single-case design, as outlined by Barlow and Herson (1973) and by Barlow, Blanchard, Hayes, and Epstein (1977), has come. Sheridan (1980) argued for another research strategy that should prove very productive. He stated that "designs should be representative with respect to subjects, contingencies, durations, instrumentation and, in effect, the entire treatment protocol" (p. 112). Such meaningful, relevant research will come only from researchers with experience in the clinical issues. The multiple baseline, within-subject, controlled design, outlined by Drury, DeRisi, and Liberman (1979), is of interest in the formulation of new research strategies.

Today's research in headache should use more sophisticated measurements and longer periods of follow-up to determine efficacy of treatment. Follow-up should last 6–12 months or longer because of the variability in headache activity. Follow-up limited to telephone calls and questionnaires is not as desirable as face-to-face assessments.

In surveying the literature, I have tried to be as complete as possible. Of course, some worthwhile papers and studies have been omitted; the reader is referred to the comprehensive reviews in Dalessio (1980) and in Olton and Noonberg (1980).

REFERENCES

Ad Hoc Committee on the Classification of Headache. Classification of headache. *Journal of the American Medical Association,* 1962, *179,* 717–718.

Andreychuk, P., & Skriver, C. Hypnosis and biofeedback in the treatment of migraine headache. *International Journal of Clinical and Experimental Hypnosis,* 1975, *23,* 172.

Appenzeller, O. Vasomotor function in migraine. *Headache,* 1969, *9,* 147–155.

Bakal, D. A. Headache: A biopsychological perspective. *Psychological Bulletin,* 1975, *82,* 369–392.

Bakal, D. A., & Kaganov, J. A. Symptom characteristics of chronic and non-chronic headache sufferers. *Headache,* 1979, *19,* 285–289.

Barlow, D. H., Blanchard, E. B., Hayes, S. C., & Epstein, L. H. Single case designs and clinical biofeedback experimentation. *Biofeedback and Self-regulation,* 1977, *2,* 221.

Barlow, D. H., & Herson, M. Single-case experimental designs. *Archives of General Psychiatry,* 1973, *29,* 319.

Benson, H., & Epstein, M. D. The placebo effect. *Journal of the American Medical Association,* 1975, *239,* 1225.

Benson, H., Klemchuk, H. P., & Graham, J. R. The usefulness of the relaxation response in the therapy of headache. *Headache,* 1974, *14,* 49.

Benson, H., Kotch, J. B., Crassweller, K. D., & Greenwood, M. M. Historical and clinical considerations of the relaxation response. *American Scientist,* 1977, *65,* 441.

Bild, R., & Adams, H. E. Modification of migraine headaches by cephalic blood volume pulse and EMG biofeedback. *Journal of Counseling and Clinical Psychology,* 1980, *48,* 51.

Blanchard, E. B., Theobald, D. E., Williamson, D. A., Silver, B. V., & Brown, D. A. Temperature biofeedback in the treatment of migraine headaches. *Archives of General Psychiatry,* 1978, *35,* 581–588.

Blanchard, E. B., & Young, L. D. Clinical applications of biofeedback training. *Archives of General Psychiatry,* 1974, *30,* 573–589.

Brenner, C., Friedman, A. P., & Carter, S. Psychologic factors in the etiology and treatment of chronic headache. *Psychosomatic Medicine,* 1949, *11,* 53.

Bruyn, G. W. The biochemistry of migraine. *Headache,* 1980, *20,* 235–246.

Budzynski, T. Biofeedback in the treatment of muscle-contraction (tension) headache. *Biofeedback and Self-regulation,* 1978, *3,* 409–434.

Budzynski, T., Stoyva, J., & Adler, C. Feedback-induced muscle relaxation: Application to tension headache. *Journal of Behavior Therapy and Experimental Psychiatry,* 1970, *1,* 205–211.

Budzynski, T. H., Stoyva, J. M., Adler, C. S., & Mullhaney, D. J. EMG biofeedback and tension headache: A controlled outcome study. *Psychosomatic Medicine,* 1973, *35,* 484–496.

Clark, D. H., Hough, B., & Wolff, H. J. Experimental studies on headache: Observations on histamine headaches. *Archives of Neurology and Psychiatry,* 1936, *35,* 1054–1069.

Cohen, M. J. Psychophysiological studies of headache: Is there similarity between migraine and muscle contraction headaches? *Headache,* 1978, *18,* 189–196.

Cohen, M. J., McArthur, D. L., & Rickles, W. H. Comparison of four biofeedback treatments for migraine headache: Physiological and headache variables. *Psychosomatic Medicine,* 1980, *42,* 463–480.

Dalessio, D. J. Migraine, platelets, and headache prophylaxis. *Journal of the American Medical Association,* 1978, *239,* 52.

————. Classification and mechanism of migraine. *Headache,* 1979, 114–121.

————. *Wolff's headache and other head pain.* New York: Oxford University Press, 1980.

Dalessio, D. J., Kunzel, M., Sternbach, R., & Sovak, M. Conditioned adaptation-relaxation reflex in migraine therapy. *Journal of the American Medical Association,* 1979, *242,* 2102.

DRURY, R. L., DeRISI, W. J., & LIBERMAN, R. P. Temperature biofeedback treatment for migraine headache: A controlled multiple baseline study. *Headache,* 1979, *19,* 278–284.

DUKES, H. T., & VIETH, R. G. Cerebral arteriography during migraine prodrome and headache. *Neurology,* 1964, *14,* 636.

EDMEADS, J. Cerebral blood flow in migraine. *Headache,* 1977, *17,* 148–152.

FAHRION, S. L. Autogenic biofeedback treatment for migraine research and clinical studies. *Research and Clinical Studies in Headaches,* 1978, *5,* 47–71.

FOWLER, R. S. Operant therapy for headaches. *Headache,* 1975, *15,* 63.

FRIEDMAN, A. P. Migraine headaches. *Journal of the American Medical Association,* 1972, *223,* 1399.

————. Muscle contraction headache. *American Family Practice,* 1979, *20,* 709.

FRIEDMAN, A. P., & ELKIND, A. H. Appraisal of methysergide in the treatment of vascular headaches of the migraine type. *Journal of the American Medical Association,* 1963, *184,* 125.

GRAHAM, J. R., & WOLFF, H. G. The mechanism of migraine headache and the action of ergotamine tartrate. *Archives of Neurology and Psychiatry,* 1938, *39,* 737–763.

GREENSPOON, J., & OLSON, J. N. Some further considerations of a conceptual framework for biofeedback. *American Journal of Clinical Biofeedback,* 1980, *2,* 123.

HENRYK-GUTT, R., & REES, W. L. Psychological aspects of migraine. *Journal of Psychosomatic Research,* 1973, *17,* 141–153.

HERBURG, L. J. The hypothalamus and the etiology of migraine. In R. Smith (ed.), *Background to migraine.* London: Heineman, 1967.

————. Migraine and the locus coeruleus. *Migraine News,* 1978, *36,* 1.

HOLROYD, K. A., & ANDRASIK, F. Coping and the self-control of chronic tension headache. *Journal of Consulting and Clinical Psychology,* 1978, *46,* 1036–1045.

KENTSMITH, D., STRIDER, F., COPENHAVER, J., & JACQUES, D. Effects of biofeedback upon suppression of migraine symptoms and plasma dopamine-B-hydroxylase activity. *Headache,* 1976, *16,* 173–177.

KEWMAN, D., & ROBERTS, A. M. Skin temperature, biofeedback, and migraine headaches. *Biofeedback and Self-regulation,* 1980, *5,* 327.

KOPPMAN, J. W., McDONALD, R. D., & KUNZEL, M. G. Voluntary regulation of temporal artery diameter by migraine headaches. *Headache,* 1974, *14,* 133–138.

LANCE, J. W., ANTHONY, M., & HINTERBERGER, H. The control of cranial arteries by Homoral Mechanism and its relation to migraine syndrome. *Headache,* 1967, *7,* 93.

MATHEW, M. T., HRASTNIK, F., & MEYER, J. S. Regional cerebral blood flow in the diagnosis of vascular headache. *Headache,* 1976, *16,* 252–260.

MATHEW, R. J., HO, B. T., KRALIK, D. T., TAYLOR & CLAGHORN, J. L. Catecholamines and migraine: Evidence based on biofeedback induced changes. *Headache,* 1980, *20,* 247.

MITCHELL, K. R., & MITCHELL, D. M. Migraine, an exploratory treatment: Application of programmed behavior therapy techniques. *Journal of Psychosomatic Research,* 1971, *15,* 137.

MITCHELL, K. R., & WHITE, R. E. Behavioral self-management: An application to the problem of migraine headaches. *Behavior Therapy,* 1977, *8,* 213.

O'BRIEN, M. D. The relationship between aura symptoms and cerebral blood flow changes in the problem of migraine. In D. J. Dalessio, T. Dalsgaard-Nielsen, & S. Diamond (eds.), *Proceedings of the 1971 International Headache Symposium.* Basel: Sandoz, 1971.

OLTON, D. S., & NOONBERG, A. R. *Biofeedback: Clinical Applications in Behavioral Medicine.* Englewood Cliffs: Prentice-Hall, 1980.

OSTFIELD, A. M. Migraine headache: Its physiology and biochemistry. *Journal of the American Medical Association,* 1960, *174,* 110.

PACKARD, R. C. Conversion headache. *Headache,* 1980, *20,* 266.

PAGE, I. H. Serotonin (5-hydroxy-tryptamine). *Physiological Review,* 1954, *34,* 563.

PAULLEY, J. W., & HASKELL, D. A. L. The treatment of migraine without drugs. *Journal of Psychosomatic Research,* 1975, *19,* 367.

PEARCE, J. *Migraine: Clinical features, mechanisms, and management.* Springfield: Thomas, 1969.

————. Migraine: A psychosomatic disorder. *Headache,* 1977, *17,* 125–128.

PICKERING, G. W., & HESS, W. Observations on the mechanisms of headache produced by histamine. *Clinical Science,* 1933, *51,* 77.

RAO, L. S., & PEARCE, J. Hypothalamic-pituitary-adrenal axis studies in migraine with special reference to insulin sensitivity. *Brain,* 1971, *94,* 289–298.

REED, M. Endorphin update. *Headache,* 1980, *20,* 146.

REES, W. L. Personality and psychodynamic mechanisms in migraine. *Psychotherapy and Psychosomatics,* 1974, *23,* 111.

ROTHLIN, E. Recherches experimentales sur l'ergotamine, alcaloi de specifique de l'ergot de seigle. *Archives of International Pharmacodynamics,* 1923, *27,* 459.

ROTHLIN, E., & CERLETTI, A. Untersucmumgere Die Krieslauf Wirkumg Des Ergotamine. *Helvetica Physiologica et Pharmacologica Acta,* 1959, *7,* 333.

SAKAI, F., & MEYER, J. S. Abnormal cerebrovascular reactivity in patients with migraine and cluster headache. *Headache,* 1979, *19,* 257–266.

SARGENT, J. D. The integration of psychosomatic self-regulation for headache into medically recognized therapies. In R. J. Mathew (ed.), *Biological basis for treatment of migraine: Pharmacological and biofeedback considerations.* New York: Spectrum, 1981.

SARGENT, J. D., GREEN, E. E., & WALTERS, E. D. The use of autogenic feedback training in a pilot study of migraine and tension headaches. *Headache,* 1972, *12,* 120–125.

SARGENT, J. D., LAWSON, R. C., SOLBACH, P., & COYNE, L. Use of CT scans in an out-patient headache population: An evaluation. *Headache,* 1979, *19,* 388.

SCHUMACHER, G. A., & WOLFF, H. G. Experimental studies of headache. *Archives of Neurology and Psychiatry,* 1941, *45,* 199–214.

SHERIDAN, C. L. Outline of a research strategy for biofeedback-based therapy. *American Journal of Clinical Biofeedback,* 1980, *3,* 107.

SICUTERI, F. Vasoneuroreactive substances and their implications in vascular pain. In A. P. Friedman (ed.), *Research and clinical studies of headache.* Baltimore: Williams & Wilkins, 1967.

SKINHØJ, E., Hemodynamic studies within the brain during migraine. *Archives of Neurology,* 1973, *29,* 95–98.

SKINØJ, E., & PAULSON, O. B. Regional blood flow in internal carotid distribution during migraine attack. *British Medical Journal,* 1969, *3,* 569.

SPERLING, M. A Further contribution to the psychoanalytic study of migraine and psychogenic headaches. *International Journal of Psychoanalysis,* 1964, *45,* 549–557.

TASTO, D. L., & HINKLE, J. E. Muscle relaxation treatment for tension headaches. *Behavioral Research and Therapy,* 1973, *1,* 347–349.

TUNIS, M. M., & WOLFF, H. G. Studies on headache. *Archives of Neurology and Psychiatry,* 1954, *71,* 425–434.

VINCENT, N. F. Psychodynamics of a patient with migraine. *American Journal of Psychotherapy,* 1960, *14,* 589.

WARNER, G., & LANCE, J. W. Relaxation therapy in migraine and chronic headache. *Medical Journal of Australia,* 1975, *1,* 298–301.

WOLFF, H. G. *Headache and other head pain* (2d ed.). New York: Oxford University Press, 1963.

YAMAMOTO, M., & MEYER, J. S. Hemicranial disorder of vasomotor adrenoceptors in migraine and cluster headache. *Headache,* 1980, *20,* 321–335.

ZIEGLER, D. K. Tension headache. *Medical Clinics of North America,* 1978, *62,* 495–505.

PART **VII**

EXTREME STRESSORS

37

Stress and Disaster

Mary Evans Melick   **James N. Logue**

Calvin J. Frederick

THE EFFECTS OF STRESS associated with major life events and other social factors on the health and well-being of individuals have been extensively investigated by researchers in the sociomedical fields. Particular attention has been paid to the specific effects of life events on health (Andrews, Tennant, Hewson, & Schonell, 1978; Blazer, 1980; Goldberg & Comstock, 1976; Theorell, Lind, & Flodreus, 1975), and major reviews on the stress of life events (Dohrenwend & Dohrenwend, 1974; Gunderson & Rahe, 1974; Levi, 1971; Rabkin & Struening, 1976) and on stress in general have recently appeared. Although many studies have shown that the experience of certain life events or clusters of these events can have deleterious effects on subsequent health status, there is still some question about the causal connection between such events and subsequent illness because of conflicting results and the inability to generalize across studies (Goldberg & Comstock, 1976), in addition to major methodologic difficulties (Rabkin & Struening, 1976).

As pointed out by Rabkin and Struening (1976), most individuals working in the field of life events research have adopted either the original 43-item life events checklist known as the Schedule of Recent Experience (Hawkins, Davies & Holmes, 1957; Rahe, Meyer, Smith, Kjaer & Holmes, 1964) or the later version, the Social Readjustment Rating Scale (SRSS) (Holmes & Masuda, 1974; Holmes & Rahe, 1967), or some modification of these instruments to quantify the stress associated with recent life events. In reviewing life events research, Rabkin and Struening (1976) limited their discussion to changes that are primarily personal in nature and excluded changes resulting from widespread social processes. This personal orientation is characteristic of most life events research, which uses life events scales to quantify individual stress levels. Disaster research may be considered a unique category of stress and life events research since the experience of disaster will impact not only on many factors usually considered in the more general research area but also on factors that are common only to the disaster experience. In addition, many of the life events experienced by the postdisaster population are shared by others, thereby creating a community of survivors.

We wish to thank Theresa LaBarge for her patience and diligence in typing this manuscript and Dr. Frank Lundin for his critique of the text.

Kinston and Rosser (1974) defined disaster as a "situation of massive collective stress" (p. 438). As indicated in this definition, the stress associated with disaster transcends the personal level. For this reason, empirical studies of disaster have focused on victims from disaster affected communities. Because of the nature of the disaster experience, the event has been studied as a single unique stressor; as an independent variable, disaster has characteristically been dichotomous in nature, with disaster victims, the exposed group, composed of individuals somehow directly affected by the initial impact and controls including those not so affected. However, the recovery period following disaster impact gives rise to numerous additional stressors. Some of these stressors are part of the SRSS set of items, although many others are unique to the disaster situation. Examples of unique stressors include evacuation, loss of personal items, residence in temporary living quarters, performance of cleanup and other physical labor associated with restoring the original condition of the affected area, and exposure to dangerous environmental conditions such as lack of food and clean water, raw sewage, and dust. It should be noted at this point that because of geographic proximity, friendship and kinship ties, and involvement in community organizations, including businesses, both victims and controls in some studies will experience, to some extent, the changed conditions brought about by community disasters.

In the past, disasters have usually been considered rare events that affect individuals and communities on a random basis. As the population increases, however, and as the number of man-made or technological disasters increases, the likelihood of being a disaster victim, at least once, also increases. Futhermore, specific geographic locations can be characterized as high-risk disaster areas, and, for individuals living in such areas, being a disaster victim one or more times can be considered a certainty.

KEY CONCEPTS

Since disasters represent situations of massive collective stress (Kinston & Rosser, 1974), they involve social groupings such as communities. Under the Disaster Relief Act of 1974, a major disaster is defined as "any hurricane, tornado, storm, flood, high-water, wind-driven water, tidal wave, tsunami, earthquake, volcanic eruption, landslide, snow storm, drought, fire, explosion, or other catastrophe in any part of the continental United States, or its territories, which causes damage of sufficient severity and magnitude to warrant major disaster assistance..." (Federal Register, 1976: p.52053). Making use of this definition, the president of the United States declared 326 events as federal *major* disasters between January 1, 1971, and June 3, 1980. Between July 22, 1974, and June 3, 1980, an additional 80 events were declared federal *emergency* disasters, reflecting an event of noteworthy severity and scope.

The majority of events noted in the federal government's definition of disasters are often referred to as acts of God (i.e., natural disasters); these events are often weather related, unscheduled, and nonpreventable. However, not all events considered disasters are of this nature. The other major category, man-made disasters, includes both technological accidents or events, such as the Three Mile Island nuclear plant accident, and situations such as war and concentration camp internment. Some would expand the category of man-made disasters to include conditions such as famine or chronic economic deprivation and its correlates.

Continuing technological developments and population concentrations are likely to increase the frequency and scope of man-made disasters. A recent example of a technological incident is the discovery of the threat to the health of the residents of the Love Canal area of

Niagara Falls, New York, where a housing development had been built in the vicinity of a chemical dump. Love Canal was declared a federal emergency disaster in 1978 and again in 1980, and the dump has been recognized as a public health threat by the New York State Department of Health (Nailor, Tarlton & Cassidy, 1978). The recognition of this problem resulted in the acknowledgment that many similar sites, which may now or in the future result in detrimental health effects, currently exist in the United States. The federal Environmental Protection Agency considers hazardous wastes "probably the most serious environmental problem in the United States today" ("Hazardous Waste Regulated," 1980:1); while the U.S. House Commerce Subcommittee on Oversight and Investigations reported identification of 3383 chemical disposal sites, containing over 750 million tons of waste dumped since 1950 (Richards, 1979). The existence of such hazardous waste sites, in addition to the settlement of areas considered flood plains, lends support to the contention that disasters, particularly technological disasters, can confidently be assumed to be of increasing importance in the future.

For purposes of intervention and analysis, disasters have been divided into several time periods. Powell and Rayner (1952) suggested the following categories: (1) warning, (2) threat, (3) impact, (4) inventory, (5) rescue, (6) remedy and (7) recovery. Until recently, most studies of disaster have focused on the first six periods, extending from immediately before the disaster to two to four weeks postdisaster. A body of literature describes the ways in which individuals and groups respond to the threat of disaster and how they organize for rescue and relief of the disaster population. Research on the periods immediately surrounding impact has been beneficial in disproving myths that have been fostered concerning human behavior in mass disasters. Quarantelli and Dynes (1970), for example, have demonstrated that panic is uncommon in disaster situations. Recently, considerable research has been conducted during the recovery period, that extended interval during which individuals and the community either recover previous stability or adapt to the conditions brought about by the disaster (Powell & Rayner, 1952). One major focus of this work has been the long-range health effects of stress associated with disaster. This research has investigated the relationship among disaster related variables, such as the nature of the disaster and the length of impact, personal variables, including demographic and life experience variables, social support variables, and physical and mental health status.

INTEREST IN DISASTERS

Catastrophic situations of both natural and man-made origin have plagued entire communities since the beginning of recorded history. Flooding, in particular, has been noted in religion and mythology as a problem from earliest times. Indeed, the oldest version of the Great Flood was written down by the Sumerians. Ancient documents indicate that earthquakes and tidal waves were particularly devastating occurrences. In A.D. 526, 250,000 persons were killed by an earthquake in Antioch, Syria; a millennium later, 830,000 died in Shaanxi, China, following such an event.

Looking at the modern era, we note that temblors occurred in the 1970s in Peru, Nicaragua, Guatemala, Pakistan, the Philippines, Algeria, China, and Italy; most of these quakes took the lives of more than 5000 persons. The largest loss of life ever recorded in any disaster resulted from flooding of the Huang River in China in 1931. As a result of this flood, 3.7 million people died. In 1976, an earthquake in Tangshan, China, was responsible for the death of more than 655,000 persons. Earthquakes have caused considerable damage in the United States also. Probably the greatest earthquake ever experienced in the continental United States occurred in New Madrid, Missouri in 1811, when shock waves knocked down chimneys in Cincinnati, Ohio, 400 miles away. A major earthquake with a magnitude of 8.3 on the Richter scale has been predicted in the area of the San Andreas fault in California sometime within the next 20 years (plans are being made to provide needed services and to conduct research in the event of its occurrence).

Formal research relating to human stress in disasters has been carried out largely by sociologists. This has influenced the aspects of disaster which have been studied. Today, although cognizance has been taken of the geographic and physical damage associated with disasters, prevention and preparedness planning shows little consideration for psychological factors, except for broadly focused medical concerns. In the main, physical and financial consequences of disasters have been obvious, while sociological and community sequelae have appeared somewhat less visible. Psychological factors, however, have been the least apparent of all. And government support of these aspects of disaster has been provided in corresponding fashion. Thus, physical damage and monetary loss have received most support. The process of physical reconstruction and rehabilitation have followed disasters with varying amounts of success. Since large populations continue to congregate near hazardous areas such as river basins, coastlines, and seismic-prone land shelves, major disasters are likely to continue to constitute important national hazards.

A series of studies conducted in the early 1950s by the National Academy of Sciences–National Research Council pointed clearly to the medical and psychological needs of disaster victims, but two decades passed before any definitive action was taken to address such problems. Raker, Wallace, and Rayner (1956) commented that the behavior of persons under extreme stress is likely to be less efficient than usual, including the performance of simple or routine tasks. This behavior can be so inefficient that it becomes pathological or quasipathological. The common denominator in this behavioral deterioration seems to be its regressive quality. At least two other studies under the auspices of the National Academy of Sciences series discussed overt emotional problems of children involved in major disasters (Perry & Perry, 1959; Perry, Silber & Block, 1956).

It was not until a number of particularly striking events occurred in the early 1970s that the psychological aspects of major catastrophes received any significant attention from health researchers and service providers. These events included an earthquake in California's San Fernando valley in 1971, flooding from Hurricane Agnes in Pennsylvania, and heavy rains in both Rapid City, South Dakota, and Buffalo Creek, West Virginia, in 1972. The Three Mile Island (TMI) accident, in Middletown, Pennsylvania, in 1979, further dramatized the need for state and federal intervention. A relatively small amount of discretionary money was made available for human services by the National Institute of Mental Health (NIMH). Since the chief governmental agency in charge of disaster relief was the Federal Disaster Assistance Administration (now part of the Federal Emergency Management Agency, or FEMA), an interagency agreement was mandated into law, through P.L. 93–288, section 413, to supply crisis counseling and counselor training for victims in affected communities. Authority was thereby delegated to the NIMH to implement this vital program of meeting long neglected human needs. However, line item research money is still not available for these presidentially declared disaster areas.

Academic interest in this field has grown considerably over the past few decades. The natural hazards research done at the University of Colorado by sociologists White and Haas (1975) is a good example. And since 1963 a Disaster Research Center has operated at Ohio

State University. In Belgium, the School of Public Health of Louvain University supports a Center of Disaster Epidemiology. Social and community responses to disaster have been studied by Chapman (1954), Form and Nosow (1958), Fritz (1961), Bates, Fosterman, Parenthen, and Tracy (1963), Dynes (1968), Drabek (1969), and Quarantelli (1979). Most of these investigators drew conclusions from observations of community response and social behavior. (Unfortunately, in many cases mental health experts were not brought into the field soon enough, with the result that emotional disorders were missed or inaccurately assessed as problems of living.) Tyhurst (1951, 1957) was among the first to categorize disaster reactions into phases. He delineated three stages: *impact, recoil,* and the *post-traumatic period*. This work has been expanded subsequently by Titchener and Kapp (1976), Lifton and Olson (1976), Zusman (1976), and Frederick (1977a, 1977b, 1980). Although one of the first accounts of the crisis management of psychic trauma in a disaster was published by Lindemann (1944) after the Coconut Grove fire in Boston, the American Psychiatric Association listed *post-traumatic stress disorder* as an official entity only in the third edition of its *Diagnostic and Statistical Manual* (1980). This disorder specifically includes psychic impairment from disasters as one of its elements.

Disaster research has been supported by the NIMH on an ad hoc basis. For example, Howard (1972) and Ahearn (1973) assessed intervention procedures in two earthquakes; Quarantelli (1979) investigated the characteristics and consequences of the delivery of mental health services in some 15 communities throughout the United States. Tierney and Baisden (1979) surveyed crisis intervention programs for disaster victims in 17 small communities. Quarantelli and Tierney and Baisden found administrative weaknesses and inadequate mental health care systems. Peck (1980) investigated social behavior during the 1977 New York City blackout and found that persons of lower socioeconomic status suffered from ongoing fears of personal loss and being victimized by violent crime. The Three Mile Island accident provided impetus for a research contract to (Bromet, Parkinson, Schulberg, Dunn, & Gondek, 1980), who compared plant workers, mothers of young children, and mental health clients at TMI with matched controls in another nuclear plant location that had had no accident. More recently, the state of Washington was awarded a postdisaster mental health grant by NIMH to assist victims of the 1980 Mount Saint Helens volcanic eruptions. Other than these studies, very little research into the mental health or behavioral consequences of disasters has been supported.

Since the passage of the Disaster Relief Act of 1974, the NIMH has provided crisis counseling services, supported by FEMA, in some 20 presidentially declared disaster areas in the United States and its territories. There has been an average of 36 such disasters annually, with nearly 200,000 families applying for assistance each year. At least 15% of all families affected suffer from such mental distress as to require treatment. Glass (1959), Popovic and Petrovic (1964) and Zusman (1976), among others, have pointed out that roughly 25% of the affected population may be expected to behave efficiently and another 25% to show inappropriate and disturbed responses. The remaining 50% will exhibit varying degrees of disturbance and efficiency in dealing with the rigors of disaster conditions. Both short- and long-term disorders may result.

Although FEMA, through the Disaster Relief Act of 1974, made $250,000 available to each state to develop a disaster preparedness program, many states have neglected mental health in their plans. The findings just reported indicate that every state should update its disaster preparedness plan to include an effective, comprehensive mental health component. In so doing, the state will be in a better position both to obtain supplemental federal funds when needed and to serve the needs of its citizens.

AN APPROPRIATE DISASTER–STRESS–ILLNESS MODEL

Theoretical models that depict the relationship between stressful life events and illness have recently appeared in the literature (Cobb, 1974; Rahe, 1974). The extension of these efforts to the relationship between disaster and illness appears appropriate. A disaster-stress-illness model was recently proposed to explain the effects of the Hurricane Agnes flood on the physical and mental health of disaster victims; with very slight modification, this model could be applied to certain technological disasters that affect communities (Logue, Melick, & Streuning, 1981).

The model begins with the disaster impact, or initial stressor. Following impact, the series of events that occurs during the recovery period may produce an even greater stressor or a perceived "second disaster" (Erikson, 1976). This second disaster may then give rise to a somatic stress situation for a given individual, which finally may or may not result in some manifest mental or physical disorder. In addition to the disaster related stressors (independent variables) and subsequent health outcomes (dependent variables), a series of mediating variables may modify in positive or negative ways the effects of the stressors on overall health. The model thus postulates how the stress associated with disaster experiences may ultimately give rise to mental or physical disorders or disease.

As pointed out by Cassel (1976), "It is most unlikely that any given psychosocial process or stressor will be etiologically specific for any given disease, at least as currently classified" (p. 109). The important point is that a range of health outcomes, both mental and physical, need to be assessed in studies of stress or disaster since individuals may be more susceptible to health sequelae in one domain than in another.

The discussion of an appropriate disaster-stress-illness model has demonstrated that separately studying the mental and physical health effects resulting from disaster is very artificial. As we have noted, some victims in a given disaster situation may be especially vulnerable in the physical health area, while others may experience mental health difficulties. It is possible that the distinction between mental and physical health effects by various researchers has clouded the issue of what mental health effects, if any, may be associated with disaster (Logue, 1980).

Other disaster researchers have done some very interesting work on conceptual models (Berren, Beigel, & Ghertner, 1980; Perry & Lindell, 1978). A theoretical model such as that proposed by Logue, Melick and Struening (1981) or by Perry and Lindell (1978) is most important to the design of an empirical study since it delineates variables in addition to the disaster (the independent variable) and its mental health effects or health effects in general (the dependent variables). These other variables may mediate the effect of the disaster on subsequent health status in either negative or positive ways. Social support is such a mediating variable. Lin, Simeone, Ensel, and Kuo (1979) defined social support as that "support accessible to an individual through social ties to other individuals, groups, and the larger community" (p. 109).

Three categories of variables are necessary to construct a general model of an individual's reaction to disaster: characteristics of the disaster, range of health outcomes, and variables that modify the effect of the disaster on health. The need for a comprehensive investigation of health outcomes in any well-executed empirical study on the effects of disaster should be fairly obvious. Mediating variables such as social support have been described well in both stress and disaster models in the literature (Logue, Melick & Struening, 1981; Perry & Lindell, 1978). Thus only the characteristics of the disaster itself and the interaction of disaster and mediating variables require further discussion here.

First, whether a disaster is natural or man-made, some events seem to be generally accepted by the victims as acts of God. In many other cases, however, victims tend to attach blame for the event to someone or something. The Buffalo Creek flood, Love Canal, and Three Mile Island may all be characterized as preventable events. On a priori grounds, one may expect preventable disasters to be more stressful than nonpreventable events for victims. Few attempts have been made until recently (Frederick, 1981b) to compare the effects of human induced violence or terrorism and the effects of natural disasters upon victims. The phases of these different types of disasters and the resulting psychological symptoms and social processes seem to differ significantly. For a discussion of these differences see Frederick (1981b).

Second, the time factor associated with disaster impact and subsequent stages is most important with respect to potential health sequelae. For example, in research on the effects of the Agnes flood, Logue (1978) demonstrated that the average perceived duration of the recovery period for victims was about 18 months. With man-made events such as the Love Canal incident, however, it may be very difficult to attach a time estimate to disaster impact or recovery. As we noted previously, federal emergency declarations were made in 1978 and again in 1980, but as early as 1977, or even earlier, people in the affected neighborhood suspected that their health was in danger.

These two issues—nature of the disaster and time factor—may be incorporated into two categories of disaster related variables: objective losses and perception or evaluation of the experience. For example, the 1974 tornado in Xenia, Ohio, resulted in extensive objective loss but minimal perceived stress (Tierney & Baisden, 1979). Other natural disasters, such as the Buffalo Creek and Agnes floods, may generate extensive stress in both categories. Recent technological events such as Love Canal and Three Mile Island, on the other hand, result in little objective loss but in high perceived loss or stress.

Other issues that need to be examined include whether the community is prepared for the event, possibly because of earlier encounters with disaster, whether evacuation has taken place on a large scale, and whether the event appears to have an irrevocable effect on the victim's life, as in the case of Love Canal and possibly Buffalo Creek. Recent comparisons of the outcomes of various types of disasters have increased our knowledge of the variables that may be associated with long-term modifications in the health and well-being of postdisaster populations. For example, seeing corpses and immersion in a "culture of death" (Lifton, 1967) and/or integration into a community of survivors may influence postdisaster mental health. Frederick's (1980) comparative work on various types of events emphasized the importance of some of these modifying factors, for example, aircraft disasters create special stresses, while other man-made or human induced disasters, such as terrorism, generate other kinds of stress. A unique aspect of airplane crashes is the lack of community among the victims. They do not usually know each other and leave the scene permanently after the event. The immediate and short-term crises are of particular importance in such catastrophes, but long-term effects may be experienced by airline personnel. Stresses from terrorism, on the other hand, may affect small or large groups ordinarily characterized by communal interaction. The psychological effects are invariably deleterious, despite some support from other victims in the group. Social support is important, however, in every catastrophic event.

While researchers may find it difficult to measure all potential disaster-related independent variables, a theoretical model helps to delineate the various components of the disaster experience that should be examined. In order for a theoretical model to be useful, however, it must be applied. This requirement has been neglected in many empirical studies and may be partly responsible for some of the apparent inconsistencies among studies of disaster effects on mental health. Plans to apply a conceptual model should be incorporated into the study design. Analytic strategies that adopt a multivariate (designed to determine the relationship among multiple independent and dependent variables) rather than an univariate (examination of the relationship between a single independent and dependent variable) approach are especially important in order to control for confounding factors, determine the joint effect of many independent variables, including the disaster experience, on health outcome, and identify high-risk groups. This approach has been illustrated in recent works on the joint effects of a natural disaster, major life events, and low psychosocial assets on mental health (e.g., Logue, Melick, & Streuning, 1981).

METHODS OF ASSESSING PHYSICAL HEALTH

To date, various aspects of physical health, ranging from minor symptoms to death, have been assessed in postdisaster populations. Measures of illness behavior have also been studied: office visits to a physician (Abrahams, Price, Whitlock, & Williams, 1976) or nurse (Wert, 1979), emergency room visits and emergency hospital admissions (Faich & Rose, 1979), and hospital referral and admission rates and surgical rates (Bennet, 1970) before and after disasters.

Immediately following a disaster, much emphasis is placed on the physical condition of the population, with reports published on the number of dead and injured. In the remedy period, the focus shifts to the outbreak or control of infectious diseases, while studies of the recovery period tend to address secondary illnesses. *Secondary illnesses* occur after disaster impact and are in some way causally related to the disaster but do not result from injury occurring during impact or infection resulting from disruption of food and water supplies. These illnesses are often considered to be stress related.

Objective measures of physical health—such as death (Bennet, 1970; Craven, Glass, Gregg, Winkler, and Heath, 1979; Glass, O'Hare, and Conrad, 1979; Lorraine, 1954), diagnosed physical ailments like myocardial infarction (Faich & Rose, 1979), or presence of disease, as determined by physical examination (Eitinger, 1971)—have occasionally been used in the long-term follow-up of disaster victims. Several recent studies looked at the number of spontaneous abortions (Nailor, Tarlton, & Cassidy, 1978; Janerich, Stark, Greenwald, Burnett, Jacobson, & McCusker, 1981), the incidence of liver dysfunction or blood mercury levels (Nailor, Tarlton, & Cassidy, 1978), and rates of leukemia or lymphoma reported in health records (Janerich, Stark, Greenwald, Burnett, Jacobson, & McCusker, 1981) to assess the health effects of natural or technological disasters. Many more studies, however, have used self-reports in determining the health effects of disasters. These studies either have administered health questionnaires (Parker, 1977) or symptom and condition checklists (Logue, 1978) or have asked the respondent about symptoms of disease and episodes of illness (Abrahams, Price, Whitlock, & Williams, 1976; Ciocco & Thompson, 1961; Lifton, 1967; Melick, 1976; Penick, Powell, & Sieck, 1976; Takuma, 1978). In some cases, victims have been asked to compare their health before the disaster with their postdisaster health (Logue, 1978; Melick, 1976). Self-report is preferable to objective measures for several reasons. First, self-report more accurately reflects the respondent's health-illness experience, a subjective phenomenon than do medical records. In addition, several problems exist in using medical records: it is often difficult to gain access to these records; they often have been shown to be incomplete or to contain conflicting information; and they often are destroyed in the disaster.

To our knowledge, no study to date has succeeded in presenting a comprehensive picture of physical illness in the recovery period. Such a study would need to employ a control group, make use of a longitudinal design, and most likely employ both subjective and objective means of assessing a broad range of health outcomes. Such a study would specifically need to assess severity of illness, length of illness, and treatment measures.

PHYSICAL HEALTH STATUS
OF POSTDISASTER POPULATIONS

It is difficult and perhaps inappropriate to consider the physical and mental health status of individuals separately. Our own research has considered individuals from a more holistic perspective, but some investigators have (e.g., Faich & Rose, 1979; Parker, 1977; Penick, Powell, & Sieck, 1976; Raphael, 1977) focused primarily on either the physical or the mental symptoms experienced by postdisaster populations. For that reason, this chapter examines physical and mental health status as discrete.

In the space allotted, it is not possible to review in detail the outcomes of all postdisaster studies focused on health. Logue, Melick, and Hansen (1981) presented a comprehensive review of this literature. An overview of the field indicates that in some cases the nature of physical symptoms or illnesses is related to the interval between the disaster and the assessment of its effects. For example, 25% of Parker's (1977) postcyclone respondents indicated deterioration in physical health 10 weeks following the disaster, while only 11% indicated this situation 14 months after the cyclone. The majority of Takuma's (1978) sample of earthquake victims similarly complained of ill health shortly after the quake, but their symptoms decreased over a 7-week period. The second factor that has been related to symptoms or illnesses is the nature of the disaster. This is especially true of technological disasters. For example, high rates of leukemia, birth defects, and cataracts might be expected following a nuclear disaster (e.g., Lifton, 1967). Paigen (1980) reported high rates of miscarriage, stillbirth, and birth defects in women living in the area of the Love Canal chemical dump. Paigen's report has recently been challenged by a study completed by the New York State Health Department (Janerich, Burnett, Feck, Hoff, Nasca, Polednak, Greenwald, & Vianna, 1981) which concluded that there was no evidence for higher cancer rates associated with living near the Love Canal in comparison with the rest of the state outside New York City. The higher rate of respiratory cancer noted in this investigation appeared to be related to a high rate for the city of Niagara Falls, in which the Love Canal area is located.

In addition to the findings previously cited, short-term health effects were found by Faich and Rose (1979) in their study of a Rhode Island blizzard. They noted that hospital admissions for myocardial infarction increased and that mortality from all causes and, in particular ischemic heart disease, increased in the five days following the storm. Glass, O'Hare, and Conrad's (1979) study of the effects of the storm in neighboring Massachusetts, however, failed to find any outbreaks of infectious disease or increase in mortality in the week following the storm.

Studies of the long-term effects of disaster have followed up affected populations for periods ranging to 30 years. Many of these studies have reported significant health problems that, through comparison with similar but nonexposed populations, seem to be related to the disaster experience. Ciocco and Thompson (1961), for example, studied a community nearly 9 years following an acute air pollution episode. They found that individuals who had become ill at the time of the initial survey, shortly following the incident, showed higher rates of mortality and morbidity than did other persons living in the same area. Bennet (1970) found a host of health differences between flood respondents (n = 316) and nonflood controls (n = 454) in the year following the Bristol floods of 1968. Some of the differences he noted in the flood group were an increased likelihood of dying within 12 months, increased surgical rates for flood group males, and overall poorer health among flood respondents. Other studies of postflood populations (compared to controls) have found longer duration of illnesses (Melick, 1976), increase in number of visits to general practitioners and hospitals for the year following the flood (Abrahams, Price, Whitlock, & Williams, 1976), and significantly greater history of a variety of symptoms or conditions of illness for the respondent and her immediate family and greater likelihood of hypertension in the respondent's husband in the 4 years following the flood (Logue, 1978). Logue (1978) and Melick (1976) also found that flood respondents perceived that the flood had had a more deleterious effect on their health than did nonflood respondents in the same communities. Long-term physical health effects were noted 30 years following concentration camp imprisonment (Eitinger, 1971).

METHODS OF ASSESSING MENTAL HEALTH

Assessments of mental health fall largely into two categories: interview schedules and standardized psychological scales or instruments, on the one hand, and clinical interviewing, on the other. Thus, the Three Mile Island accident was studied by several investigators who used standardized and accepted instruments of psychological measurement. Bromet and associates (1980), used the Schedule for Affective Disorders and Schizophrenia Lifetime Scale (SADS–L) (Endicott & Spitzer, 1978) to assess the presence or absence of severe mental disorder. The 90-item Self-report Symptom Inventory (Derogatis, 1973) was given to assess such psychological symptoms as anxiety, phobias, anger, and psychophysiological disturbances. Kasl, Chisholm, and Eskenazi (1981) used a one-hour telephone interview, followed by mailed questionnaires and face-to-face interviews. These investigators also used the Demoralization Scale (Link & Dohrenwend, 1980) to evaluate self-esteem and a modification of the Langner 22-item Screening Score of psychiatric impairment to assess psychophysiological symptoms. Following the Buffalo Creek Dam disaster, Titchener and Kapp (1976) used intensive clinical interviewing, Rorschach ink blots, and other projective clinical instruments. Statistical information from the records kept by various agencies and organizations (e.g., psychiatric hospitals, community mental health centers and state officers of mental health) would be useful principally in epidemiological studies, rather than clinical research studies, to assess mental health.

Since the passage of P.L. 93-288, section 413, the Disaster Relief Act of 1974, many state and local agencies have submitted proposals for crisis intervention projects in disaster affected communities. In developing these proposals, it was necessary to document various needs assessment procedures with respect to postdisaster mental health sequelae and the results of such procedures. As Tierney and Baisden (1979) pointed out, such assessments can be based on either formal surveys or clinical evaluations. However, since these approaches may not be the most appropriate methods of needs assessment given the circumstances surrounding the affected community, indirect indicators such as official statistics or records from organizations and agencies involved with disaster relief or even contacts with community informants may be more valuable.

MENTAL HEALTH EFFECTS OF DISASTER

A growing body of case studies, controlled surveys, and reviews that include details on the mental health sequelae of disasters (Fritz, 1961; Kinston & Rosser, 1974; Logue, 1978; Melick, 1976; NIMH, 1976; Wilson, 1962) indicates that disasters may give rise to a variety of psychological symptoms, including acute grief, anxiety, anger, hostility, resentment, depression, and loss of ambition among adults. The "disaster syndrome" originally described by Wallace (1956) has frequently been observed shortly after impact and has been characterized as an "absence of emotion, inhibition of activity, docility, indecisiveness, lack of responsiveness and automatic behavior, together with the physiological manifestations of autonomic arousal" (Kinston & Rosser, 1974:442). As pointed out by Chapman (1962), various disaster studies have noted this phenomenon among survivors of disasters to vary from none up to one-third of victims. (Data on the demographic characteristics of the victims experiencing this syndrome and the length of time that symptoms persist are generally lacking).

Other indicators of psychological disturbance include marital and family discord, increase in the use of tranquilizers and psychoactive medications, and excessive consumption of alcohol (Farberow, 1978, 1981; NIMH, 1976). In children, mental health effects may include phobias, prolonged sleep disturbances and nightmares, loss of interest in school, and lack of responsibility.

Although short-term mental health problems have been fairly well documented in the literature, long-term health effects are only beginning to be studied and the area is somewhat controversial. Western (1972) and Kinston and Rosser (1974) pointed out the limited number of systematic quantitative studies on this subject. They also noted that very few epidemiologic studies, such as Bennet's (1970) study of the long-term effects of the 1968 Bristol floods, have been reported.

A recently completed review of disaster epidemiology by Logue, Melick, and Hansen (1981) summarized the literature on long-term effects of disaster on health. Although a variety of long-term mental health effects were reported in these studies, probably the only investigation that revealed severe psychological effects was the two-year follow-up of victims of the 1972 Buffalo Creek flood in West Virginia (Lifton & Olson, 1976; Newman, 1976; Rangell, 1976; Titchener & Kapp, 1976). In a study of the effects of the 1968 Bristol floods, Bennet (1970) reported that women in the flood group experienced significantly more psychiatric symptoms, such as anxiety, depression, irritability, and insomnia, than did women in the control group over the year following the flood. Following the Agnes flood in northeastern Pennsylvania, Melick (1976) noted a longer duration of emotional disturbances in flood group respondents and their families compared to controls; Logue (1978) studied the same disaster area and reported retrospectively that both emotional and physical distress lasted about a year longer among the flood group than among the controls. He further noted that at the time of the his survey, five years after the event, the flood group, compared to controls, exhibited higher levels of anxiety and were higher on an obsessive-compulsive scale. More recently, Dohrenwend, Dohrenwend, Kasl and Warheit (1979) demonstrated that workers at the Three Mile Island nuclear plant manifested greater levels of demoralization six months after the accident than did workers in an occupational control group. Bromet and associates' (Bromet, Parkinson, Schulberg, Dunn, & Gondek, 1980) follow-up study of TMI also indicated an increase in mental health problems over the one-year study period. Kasl, and associates (Kasl, Chisholm, & Eskenazi, 1981) recently published two articles concerning the impact of the TMI accident on the behavior and well-being of nuclear plant workers. Six months after the accident, anger, extreme worry, and some psychophysiological symptoms were evident. Demoralization was greater primarily among nonsupervisory workers, while the presence of a preschool child at home enhanced the impact of the accident primarily among supervisors.

CROSS–SECTIONAL VERSUS LONGITUDINAL STUDY

Much of the early work on human response to disaster consisted of crosssectional studies of disaster victims conducted within several weeks of the event. This led to a picture of disaster populations as experiencing anxiety, depression, and psychosomatic symptoms such as gastrointestinal upset and diarrhea. Chapman(1962), for example, reporting on illness in the remedy period noted that a sizable proportion of survivors manifested insomnia, digestive upsets, nervousness, and other signs of nervous tension. These symptoms tended to subside several days after the disaster impact. Knaus's (1975) report of responses to tropical storm Agnes focused on the period shortly after the flood, at which time victims were housed in temporary living quarters. During this period, depression was the most common mental health symptom, especially among the elderly. Despondence and confusion were other common reactions; disorientation, loss of self-confidence, and loss of self-esteem also occurred.

Not all studies conducted in the remedy period, however, have found mental or physical health problems. Spiegal (1957), studying the English flood of 1953, found that little physical or emotional illness occurred despite exposure, tension, and an influenza epidemic that was in progress when the flood came.

From data gathered during the remedy period by investigators using a cross-sectional design, it is difficult to make inferences about behavior in the recovery period. Accordingly, recent research efforts have made use of more stringent study designs and have collected data further in time from the event. Efforts have been made, for example, to introduce control groups (Logue, 1978; Melick, 1976; Parker, 1977) to employ longitudinal designs (Bromet, 1980; Taylor, 1977), and to use predisaster information about the victim population or a similar population (Parker, 1977) when assessing health in the recovery period. These techniques have increased our understanding of the long-term health consequences of disasters.

CONCLUDING REMARKS

A disaster is not a single event occurring in the life of an individual; rather, it is a series of events preceding and following impact whose sequelae are likely to be experienced over time by exposed individuals and by the community in which the disaster occurred. Because of the political, economic, psychological, and social interdependence of individuals in society, many people not defined as victims by rescuers or relief agencies may nevertheless be affected by the disaster. For example, the destruction of a community's economic base of support affects both disaster victims and nonvictims. In assessing the consequences of a disaster use should be made of a conceptual model to examine the relationships among major independent variables (nature of the disaster, length of impact), mediating variables (prior experience with disaster, kin and friendship ties, economic resources), and dependent, or outcome, variables (health outcomes, destruction or strengthening of the community). This type of model can be useful in planning the study, guiding data collection, and doing analysis. In the analysis phase, appropriate statistical procedures such as multiple contingency table analysis, analysis of variance or covariance, and regression analysis or discriminant function analysis should be implemented.

Research to date is not unanimous on the consequences of the disaster experience for survivors. The evidence, however, does seem to suggest some long-term sequelae. Disaster victims are able to identify the length of the recovery period, as well as significant negative and occasional positive outcomes of the disaster experience. Studies that have used mental health clinicians and clinical assessments have been especially clear in their presentation of adverse effects on mental health (Lifton & Olson, 1976; Newman, 1976; Titchener & Kapp, 1976) and on the sense of community (Erikson, 1976).

Additional research is needed in order to state with greater assurance the most likely physical and mental health outcomes of the disaster experience. Immediate, cross-sectional studies, as well as longitudinal investigations, are needed. One of the major problems in studying disasters is the need to be on site at the time of the disaster and to have an appropriate design in place; however, few federal agencies are willing to appropriate money to allow investigators to sit and wait until a disaster occurs so that it can be studied on site both during impact and during recovery. Understanding the effects of disasters upon the health of communities also requires an accurate assessment of change. Carefully selected controls are needed to determine whether any observed changes would have occurred in the absence of disaster. Baseline data collected over time can help establish whether changes have occurred in the variables being studied.

Both cross-sectional and longitudinal studies must use a wide range of techniques to assess physical and mental health. They should include valid and reliable assessment instruments that permit comparison across studies, mental health assessments by professionals, and specially created instruments to address stressors or mediating factors that may exist because of the nature of either the disaster or the affected population.

Further investigation also needs to be done on the temporal relationship and sequence of stressful experiences. This would include an analysis of the stressors characteristic of each identified disaster time period, as well as an examination of disasters with multiple impacts over time and those whose impact may be difficult to identify (e.g., technological incidents such as Love Canal).

Comparisons should also be made of the nature and outcomes of technological and natural disasters to determine similarities and differences in the short- and long-term health sequelae associated with these types of events. In particular, research is needed to show how the individual's perception of the disaster experience, whatever its nature, is correlated with subsequent overall health status. Research is also needed to compare the health of victims of disaster of lesser severity (e.g., federally declared emergency disasters) with victims of federally declared major disasters. This type of comparison will aid in answering the question of the effectiveness of disaster declaration as a criterion for selecting those most in need of emergency mental health services.

Finally, further research is needed to identify high-risk groups for physical and mental health problems. Epidemiological approaches, for example, pilot case-control studies, can be useful in delineating and ranking risk factors. Once high-risk groups have been identified, appropriate intervention strategies can be implemented to prevent the development of long-term sequelae. Of course, all such intervention programs should be evaluated to determine their effectiveness.

The study of human response to disaster is a fascinating area because of its potential for providing information on the effects of multiple stressors. Investigation of catastrophic events can benefit stress theory by assisting in the development and validation of stress adaptation models.

REFERENCES

Abrahams, M. J., Price, J., Whitlock, F. A., & Williams, G. The Brisbane floods, January 1974: Their impact on health. *Medical Journal of Australia*, 1976, *2*, 936–939.

Ahearn, F. L. Socio-psychological consequences of an earthquake. NIMH grant MH25379, final report, 1973.

American Psychiatric Association. *Diagnostic and statistical manual of mental disorders* (3rd ed). Washington, D.C.: 1980.

Andrews, G., Tennant, C., Hewson, C., & Schonell, M. The relation of social factors to physical and psychiatric illness. *American Journal of Epidemiology*, 1978, *108*, 27–35.

Bates, F. L., Fosterman, C. W., Parenthen, V. J., & Tracy, G. S. *The social and psychological consequences of a natural disaster: A longitudinal study of Hurricane Audrey.* Washington, D.C.: National Academy of Sciences, 1963.

Bennet, G. Bristol floods, 1968: Controlled survey of effects on health of local community disaster. *British Medical Journal*, 1970. *3*, 454–458.

Berren, M. R., Beigel, A., & Ghertner, S. A typology for the classification of disasters. *Community Mental Health Journal*, 1970, *16*, 103–111.

Blazer, D. Life events, mental health functioning, and the use of health care services by the elderly. *American Journal of Public Health*, 1980, *70*, 1174–1179.

Bromet, E., Parkinson, D., Schulberg, H. C., Dunn, L., & Gondek, P. C. *Three Mile Island: Mental health findings.* Washington, D.C.: National Institute of Mental Health, 1980.

Cassel, J. The contribution of the social environment to host resistance. *American Journal of Epidemiology*, 1976, *104*, 107–123.

Chapman, D. C. A brief introduction to contemporary disaster research, In G. W. Baker & D. W. Chapman (eds.), *Man and society in disaster.* New York: Basic Books, 1962.

———— (ed.). Human behavior in disaster: A new field of social research. *Journal of Social Issues*, 1954, *10*.

Ciocco, A., & Thompson, D. J. A follow-up of Donora ten years after: Methodology and findings. *American Journal of Public Health*, 1961, *51*, 155–164.

Cobb, S. A model for life events and their consequences. In B. S. Dohrenwend & B. P. Dohrenwend (eds.), *Stressful life events: Their nature and effects,* New York: Wiley, 1974.

Craven R. B., Glass, R. I., Gregg, M. B., Winkler, W. G., & Heath, C. W. *Assessment of tornado-related deaths and injuries, Texas and Oklahoma.* Atlanta: Center for Disease Control, 1979.

Derogatis, L. R., Lipman, R. S., & Covi, L. SCL-90: An outpatient psychiatric rating scale—preliminary report. *Psychopharmacology Bulletin*, 1973, *9*, 13–28.

Dohrenwend, B. P., Dohrenwend, B. S., Kasl, S. V., & Warheit, G. T. Technical staff analysis report on behavioral effects to the President's Commission on the Accident at Three Mile Island. Advance copy, October 31, 1979.

Dohrenwend, B. S., & Dohrenwend, B. P. (eds.). *Stressful life events: Their nature and effects.* New York: Wiley, 1974.

DRABEK, T. E. Social processes in disaster: Family evacuation. *Social Problems,* 1969, *16,* 336–349.

DYNES, R. R. *The functioning of expanding organization in community disaster.* DRC report no. 2. Columbus: Ohio State University, Disaster Research Center, 1968.

EITINGER, L. Organic and psychosomatic aftereffects of concentration camp imprisonment. *International Psychiatry Clinics,* 1971, *8,* 205–215.

ENDICOTT, J., & SPITZER, R. A diagnostic interview: The schedule for affective disorders and schizophrenia. *Archives of General Psychiatry,* 1978, *35,* 837–844.

ERIKSON, K. T. *Everything in its path: Destruction of community in the Buffalo Creek flood.* New York: Simon & Schuster, 1976.

FAICH, G., & ROSE, R. Blizzard morbidity and mortality: Rhode Island, 1978. *American Journal of Public Health,* 1979, *69,* 1050–1052.

FARBEROW, N. L. *Training manual for human service workers in major disasters.* Department of Health, Education and Welfare publication no. (ADM) 79–538. Washington, D.C.: U.S. Government Printing Office, 1978.

————. *Manual for child health workers in major disasters.* Department of Health and Human Services publication no. (ADM) 81–1070. Washington, D.C.: U.S. Government Printing Office, 1981.

Federal Register. Rules and regulations for implementation of Section 413 of the Disaster Relief Act of 1974. November 26, 1976, *41,* No. 229, 52053.

FORM, W. H., & NOSOW, S. *Community in disaster.* New York: Harper, 1958.

FREDERICK, C. J. Crisis intervention and emergency mental health, In W. E. Johnson (ed.), *Health in action.* New York: Holt, 1977. (a)

————. Current thinking about crisis or psychological intervention in United States disasters. *Mass Emergencies,* 1977, *2,* 43–50. (b)

————. Effects of natural vs. human-induced violence upon vicitms. *Evaluation and Change,* 1980, 71–75.

————. (ed). *Aircraft accidents: Emergency mental health problems.* DHHS publication no. (ADM) 81–956. Washington, D.C.: U.S. Government Printing Office, 1981. (a)

————. Violence and disasters: Immediate and long-term consequences. Paper presented to a work ing group conference on the psychosocial consequences of violence, The Hague, 1981. (b)

FRITZ, C. E. Disasters compared in six American communities. *Human Organization,* 1951, *16,* 6–9.

————. Disaster. In R. Merton & R. Nisbet (eds.), *Contemporary social problems.* New York: Harcourt, 1961.

GLASS, A. J. Psychological aspects of disaster. *Journal of the American Medical Association,* 1959, *171,* 222–227.

GLASS, R. I., O'HARE, P., & CONRAD J. L. Health consequences of the snow disaster in Massachusetts, February 6, 1978. *American Journal of Public Health,* 1979, *69,* 1047–1049.

GOLDBERG, E. L., & COMSTOCK, G. W. Life events and subsequent illness. *American Journal of Epidemiology,* 1976, *104,* 146–158.

GUNDERSON, E. K. E., & RAHE, R. H. (eds.) *Life stress and illness.* Springfield: Thomas, 1974.

HAWKINS, N. G., DAVIES, R., & HOLMES, T. H. Evidence of psychosocial factors in the development of pulmonary tuberculosis. *American Review of Tuberculosis and Pulmonary Diseases,* 1957, *75,* 768–780.

Hazardous waste regulated: Preventing more Love Canals. *Nation's Health,* June 1980, pp. 1–8.

HOLMES, T. H., & RAHE, R. H. The Social Readjustment Rating Scale. *Journal of Psychosomatic Research,* 1967, *11,* 213–218.

HOLMES, T. H., & MASUDA, M. Life change and illness susceptibility. In B. S. Dohrenwend & B. P. Dohrenwend (eds.), *Stressful life events: Their nature and effects.* New York: Wiley, 1974, pp. 45–72.

Howard, S. J. Mental health intervention in a major disaster. NIMH grant MH21649, final progress report, 1972.

Janerich, D. T., Burnett, W. S., Feck, G., Hoff, M., Nasca, P, Polednak, A. P., Greenwald, P., & Vianna, N. Cancer incidence in the Love Canal area. *Science,* 1981, *212,* 1404–1407.

Janerich, D. T., Stark, A. D., Greenwald, P., Burnett, W. S., Jacobson, H. I., & McCusker, J. Increased leukemia, lymphoma, and spontaneous abortion in western New York following a flood disaster. *Public Health Reports,* 1981, *96,* 350–356.

Kasl, S. V., Chisholm, R. F. & Eskenazi, B. The impact of the accident at Three Mile Island on the behavior and well-being of nuclear workers (in two parts). *American Journal of Public Health,* 1981, *71,* 472–495.

Kinston, W., & Rosser, R. Disaster: Effects on mental and physical state. *Journal of Psychosomatic Research,* 1974, *18,* 437–456.

Knaus, R. L. Crisis intervention in a disaster area: The Pennsylvania flood in Wilkes-Barre. *Journal of the American Osteopathic Association,* 1975, *75,* 297–301.

Langner, T. S. A 22-item screening score of psychiatric symptoms indicating impairment. *Journal of Health and Human Behavior,* 1962, *3,* 269–276.

Levi, L. (ED.) *Psychosocial environment and psychosomatic diseases,* Vol. 1. New York: Oxford University Press, 1971.

Lifton, R. J. *Death in life: Survivors of Hiroshima.* New York: Random House, 1967.

Lifton, R. J., & Olson, E. The human meaning of total disaster: The Buffalo Creek experience. *Psychiatry,* 1976, *39,* 1–18.

Lin, N., Simeone, R. S., Ensel, W. M., & Kuo, W. Social support, stressful events, and illness: A model and an empirical test. *Journal of Health and Social Behavior,* 1979, *20,* 108–119.

Lindemann, E. Symptomatology and management of acute grief. *American Journal of Psychiatry,* 1944, *101,* 141–148.

Link, B., & Dohrenwend, B. P. Formulation of hypotheses about the true prevalence of demoralization in the United States. In B. P. Dohrenwend, B. S. Dohrenwend, M. S. Gould, et al. (eds.), *Mental illness in the United States: Epidemiological estimates.* New York: Praeger, 1980.

Logue, J. N. Long-term effects of a major natural disaster: The Hurricane Agnes flood in the Wyoming valley of Pennsylvania, June 1972. Doctoral dissertation, Columbia University, 1978.

————. Mental health aspects of disaster. Paper presented to the fifth Annual National Hazards Research Workshop, Boulder, 1980.

Logue, J. N., Melick, M. E., & Hansen, H. Disaster epidemiology: Research issues and directions. *Epidemiological Reviews,* 1981, *3,* 140–162.

Logue, J. N., Melick, M. E. & Struening, E. A study of health and mental health status following a major natural disaster. In R. Simmons (ed.), *Research in community and mental health: An annual compilation of research,* Vol. 2. Greenwich:, JAI, 1981

Lorraine, N. S. R. Canvey Island flood disaster, February, 1953. *Medical Officer,* 1954, *91,* 59–62.

Melick, M. E. Social, psychological and medical aspects of stress-related illness in the recovery period of a natural disaster. Doctoral dissertation, State University of New York at Albany, 1976.

————. Life change and illness: Illness behavior of males in the recovery period of a natural disaster. *Journal of Health and Social Behavior,* 1978, *19,* 335–342.

Nailor, M. G., Tarlton, F., & Cassidy, J. J. Love Canal: *Public health time bomb - A special report to the Governor and Legislature.* Albany: New York State Department of Health, 1978.

National Institute of Mental Health. *Disaster assistance and emergency mental health.* DHEW publication no. (ADM) 76-327. Washington, D.C.: U.S. Government Printing Office, 1976.

Newman, C. J. Children of disaster: Clinical observations at Buffalo Creek. *American Journal of Psychiatry,* 1976, *133,* 306–312.

PAIGEN, B. Love Canal residents under stress: Psychological effects may be greater than physical harm. *Science,* 1980, *208,* 1242–1244.

PARKER, G. Cyclone Tracy and Darwin evacuees: On the restoration of the species. *British Journal of Psychiatry,* 1977, *130,* 548–555.

PECK, H. Personal communication, 1980.

PENICK, E. C., POWELL, B. J., & SIECK, W. A. Mental health problems and natural disaster: Tornado victims. *Journal of Community Psychology,* 1976, *4,* 64–67.

PERRY, H. S., & PERRY, S. E. *The school house disasters: Family and community as determinants of the child's response to disaster.* National Research Council, disaster study no. 11. National Academy of Sciences. National Research Council. Washington, D.C.: National Academy of Sciences, 1959.

PERRY, H. S., SILBER, E., & BLOCK, D. A. *The child and his family in disaster: A study of the 1953 Vicksburg tornado.* National Research Council, publication no. 394, Washington, D.C: National Academy of Sciences, 1956.

PERRY, R. W., & LINDELL, M. K. The psychological consequences of natural disaster: A review of research on American communities. *Mass Emergencies,* 1978, *3,* 105–115.

POPOVIC, M., & PETROVIC, D. After the earthquake. *Lancet,* 1964, *2,* no. 7370, 1169–1171.

POWELL, J. W., & RAYNER, J. *Progress notes: Disaster investigation, July 1, 1951 - June 30, 1952.* Edgewood: Army Chemical Center Corps, Medical Laboratories, 1952.

QUARANTELLI, E. L. Delivery of mental health services in disasters. NIMH grant MH26619, final report, 1979.

QUARANTELLI, E. L., & DYNES, R. R. Organizational and group behavior in disasters. *American Behavioral Scientist,* 1970, *13,* 325–426.

RABKIN, J. G., & STRUENING, E. L. Life events, stress, and illness. *Science,* 1976, *194,* 1013–1020.

RAHE, R. H. The pathway between subjects' recent life changes and their near-future illness reports: Representative results and methodological issues. In B. S. Dohrewend & B. P. Dohrenwend (eds.), *Stressful life events: Their nature and effects.* New York: Wiley, 1974.

RAHE, R. H., MEYER, M., SMITH, M., KJAER, G., & HOLMES, T. H. Social stress and illness onset. *Journal of Psychosomatic Research,* 1964, *8,* 35–44.

RAKER, J. W., WALLACE, A. C. & RAYNER, J. F. *Emergency medical care in disasters.* National Research Council. Publication No. 457. Washington, D.C.: National Academy of Sciences, 1956.

RANGELL, L. Discussion of the Buffalo Creek disaster: The course of psychic trauma. *American Journal of Psychiatry,* 1976, *133,* 313–316.

RAPHAEL, B. The Granville train disaster: Psychological needs and their management. *Medical Journal of Australia,* 1977, *1,* 303–305.

RICHARDS, B. House investigation pinpoints 3383 chemical dumps. *Washington Post,* 2 November 1979, p. 49.

SPIEGAL, J. P. The English flood of 1953. *Human Organization,* 1957, *16,* 3–5.

SPITZER, R. L., & ENDICOTT, J. *NIMH clinical research branch collaborative program on the psychobiology of depression: Schedule for Affective Disorders and Schizophrenia - Lifetime version,* (3d ed.). New York: New York State Psychiatric Institute, Biometrics Research Division, 1978.

TAKUMA, T. Human behavior in the event of earthquakes. In E. L. Quarantelli (ed.), *Disasters: Theory and research.* Beverly Hills: Sage, 1978.

TAYLOR, V. Good news about disaster. *Psychology Today,* 1977, *11,* 93, 94, 124, & 126.

THEORELL, T., LIND, E., & FLODREUS, B. The relationship of disturbing life-changes and emotions to the early development of myocardial infarctions and other serious illnesses. *International Journal of Epidemiology,* 1975, *4,* 281–293.

Tierney, K. J. & Baisden, B. *Crisis intervention programs for disaster victims in smaller communities.* DHEW publication no. (ADM) 79–675. Washington, D.C.: U.S. Government Printing Office, 1979.

Titchener, J. L. & Kapp, F. T. Family and character change at Buffalo Creek. *American Journal of Psychiatry,* 1976, *133,* 295–299.

Tyhurst, J. S. Individual reactions to community disaster: The natural history of psychiatric phenomena. *American Journal of Psychiatry,* 1951, *107,* 23–27.

————. Psychological and social aspects of civilian disasters. *Canadian Medical Association Journal,* 1957, *76,* 385–393.

Wallace, A. F. C. *Tornado in Worcester: An explanatory study of individual and community behavior in an extreme situation.* National Research Council publication no. 392. Washington, D.C.: National Academy of Sciences, 1956.

Wert, B. J. Stress due to nuclear accident: A survey of an employee population. *Occupational Health Nursing,* 1979, *27,* 16–24.

Western, K. A. The epidemiology of natural and man-made disasters: The present state of the art. Dissertation, University of London, 1972.

Wilson, R. N. Disaster and mental health. In G. W. Baker & D. W. Chapman (eds.), *Man and society in disaster.* New York: Basic Books, 1962.

White, G., & Haas, E. *Assessment of research on natural hazards.* Cambridge: MIT Press, 1975.

Zusman, J. Meeting mental health needs in a disaster. In H. J. Parad, H. P. Resnik, & L. G. Parad (eds.). *Emergency and disaster management.* Bowie: Charles, 1976.

38

Stresses of War:
The Example of Viet Nam

Arthur S. Blank, Jr.

WAR IS UNIQUE among sources of extreme psychic stress first because it is massive in scope and frequency, affecting much of humanity throughout the ages, and second because it is altogether man-made and therefore in principle preventable. A third characteristic of war as a source of stress, however, is manifested in the modern era of psychological research: this human activity tends greatly to be ignored. For example, in Europe and the United States during the past century, the psychological literature on the impact of war has been relatively scanty. Researchers avoid precise accounts of the nature of war stress, in favor of a focus on unwillingness to fight and individual vulnerabilities to stress (1).

In this chapter I shall directly confront war experiences as they affected some of the 4 million American men and women who served in Indochina between 1964 and 1975. This example is chosen for three reasons: first, I was a participant; second, the psychological difficulties of Viet Nam veterans are currently undergoing intensive examination throughout the nation via a federally sponsored system of readjustment counseling centers, established following recognition of hundreds of thousands of cases of lingering stress disorder in veterans since the end of the war in 1975; and, third, as a holocaust experience for both Indochinese and Americans, the impact of the Viet Nam War constitutes a rich source for research into and understanding of stress reactions and disorder generally.

Having clinically evaluated over 1000 veterans of this war, and closely monitored research, I shall catalogue some portion of the great variety of war stress encountered in Viet Nam. This presentation attempts to penetrate a space between two kinds of literature on the war. On the one hand are first-person accounts—passionate and incisive renderings by soldiers of what happened to them and their comrades (2,3,4,5). On the other hand is the clinical and research literature, which usefully treats stress reactions and disorders but usually only fleetingly mentions the details of the actual stress (6,7).

STRESSES TYPICAL OF ALL WARS

Miserable Living Conditions

Persons in combat are deprived of the ordinary elements of food, clothing, shelter, and cleanliness of civilized peacetime life. Good food is often absent; water, scarce. There is also intense exposure to the land and weather.

Fatigue

Loss of sleep, impossibility of routines, arduous work, and long hiking with heavy equipment produce extreme fatigue in combat soldiers.

Sensory Assault

The senses are assaulted in various ways, for example, from artillery, bombs, helicopters, and planes. Temporary or permanent hearing loss incurred by artillerymen is an example of an effect of this category of stress.

The Fighting Itself

Combat involves a continuous threat of annihilation by either enemy or friendly fire. Personnel are under fire from ambushes, night patrols, in firebases under seige, on river boat patrol, in planes and helicopters, attacked by rifles, machine guns, mortars, artillery, bombs, booby traps, mines. One may be shot at by a sniper, hit by friendly artillery falling short, strafed by gunships, hit by napalm, or blown away while disarming a mine or booby trap.

Wounds

Soldiers may lose body parts, suffer head wounds that leave skull deformities or cause brain dysfunction, or sustain spinal cord injury from bullets or shrapnel that results in permanent paralysis. Witnessing the wounding of others is a major source of war stress. This sometimes reaches macabre realms, as when buddies nearby are blown up by direct hits from grenades or persons are set afire by napalm. War involves a regular exposure to mutilation and death, agony, and gruesomeness; wounding or blowing up of children or other noncombatants, whether accidentally caused or not, can be a lasting source of stress. The exposure to wounds can be especially intensive in medical personnel, both in the field and in hospitals removed from the field. Many persons deal with dead bodies in war: medevac pilots and medics, hospital corpsmen, doctors, nurses, and graves registration (morgue) personnel, who clean up and prepare bodies for shipment home (sometimes for months on end). An immersion in death is also experienced by those who dig the graves and bury the bodies in stateside cemeteries, as well as by those with the responsibility of going to the homes telling families about the death of a relative.

Special Stresses of the Combat Situation

A number of peculiar situations can develop in combat, partly distinguishable from the fighting itself, that can have stressful effects.

Capture and Torture. Being captured by the enemy is a distinct situation for the soldier. The POW may be tortured or threatened with torture. Just the threat of capture and torture, especially if one has a near miss, forms a major source of stress. This was especially the case in the Viet Nam War because of the widespread supposition, founded on actual incidents, of hideous mutilation in instances of capture, including genital mutilation and beheading.

Isolation. As in any war, in Viet Nam some troops were isolated for long periods, by design or by accident, as in cutoff special forces outposts accessible only by air. In the guerilla war situation, even outposts accessible by land were often subject to cutoff by attack.

Acute Survivorship. The experience of very narrowly escaping death when others are killed has special stress qualities, as when one's replacement in a combat unit is killed a day or so after one has departed or when all one's comrades in a patrol are killed by an ambush. For some individuals, these events may mobilize peculiarly intense survivor guilt.

Authoritarian Organization. Although comfortable and relieving for some persons, immersion in the authoritarian social organization of the military in wartime, with its qualities of required automatic obedience, etc., is traumatic. For some involuntary troops—draftees—the authoritarian military fabric is particularly stressful.

Command Incompetence. In any war, commanders are often competent and provide leadership that maintains psychological, as well as physical, health. However, in an extraordinarily stressful context, a commander may prove incompetent, even dangerously so, leading to unnecessary risks, casualties, deaths, and chaotic conditions in the unit.

Observers. Certain categories of participants in combat commonly share the role of a relatively passive observer, exposed to the events of the war in great detail and repetitively, but not authorized to act, react, or operate aggressively against the enemy in ways that could discharge anxiety and anger. The intense continuous inhibition, combined with exposure to the war, may serve as a critical stress. Persons in such a stance include photographers, journalists, casualty clerks, writers of award certificates, psychiatrists, chaplains, communications operators, and intelligence officers.

UNUSUAL STRESSES FOUND IN THE VIET NAM WAR

Guerilla Warfare

To a considerable extent, the enemy in Viet Nam was indistinguishable from the people of the country (9). The forces of the National Liberation Front were elusive, uncatchable, either because they were here tonight and gone in the daytime or because they were mixed in various ways with the general population. American troops regularly had the experience of finding traces of enemy troops in villages where only women and children and elderly people were present upon arrival, and of discovering that longtime Vietnamese associates, supposedly friendly and working for the Saigon government, were after all working for the other side. This elusiveness of the enemy on all levels produced extreme frustration.

Lack of Clear Objectives

A feature of ordinary warfare that helps sometimes to make it bearable is the chance for soldiers to accomplish something, especially the actual conquest of territory. In Viet Nam, it was never clear for long what was to be accomplished. Ground was taken, then given up, then retaken, only to be given up again. Territory was conquered, then turned over to the Saigon forces, who let it slip away again. Rice or other foodstuffs were ordered destroyed and thus denied to the other side, but such efforts never produced demonstrable results, an especially stressful fact for troops who may have spent weeks or months in such activity. At other times, the goal presented to the soldier was that of winning the hearts and minds of the people of the country, especially through health, sanitation, or related work, combined with military operations. These efforts proved fruitless in the experience of many troops.

Limitations on Offensive Actions

For career military persons and for those committed to the war effort, the extraordinary limitations on offensive actions in Viet Nam were a source of frustrating stress; for example, the off-again, on-again bombing which went on throughout the war. A common complaint was that on the one hand the U.S. government persistently claimed that the war resulted from an invasion of the south by the north, yet somehow the north could never be invaded in return. Medical personnel dealt with this stress insofar as increased numbers of casualties occurred following the end of each cease-fire, a result of enemy regrouping that had occurred during the cease-fire.

Terrorism

All of Viet Nam was the combat zone; what varied was only the degree. Trucks drove up to buildings and blew off the front with plastique, as happened with the Victoria officers' quarters in Saigon on April 1, 1966, with 3 Americans and 3 Vietnamese killed, and 112 Americans injured by glass and 37 injured by other parts of the building falling on them (10). Grenades with only a rubber band holding on the handle were quietly dropped into a parked jeep's gas tank—to explode and burn up the vehicle and its human contents as soon as the gas ate through the rubber band. One could be mortared anywhere, drive over and be exploded by a French convoy mine buried for 18 years, or be fatally shot away either out in the bush or down an alley in a town. One could be shot at by a sniper on the veranda of a villa, riding along a supposedly safe road in a car, or flying low in a helicopter on the way to land at a big American airbase.

Masking tape criss-crossed every window of every U.S. building in every major town and city of Viet Nam. The reason was to minimize flying glass in case of terrorist explosion. All major and most minor installations had elaborate security setups, with checkpoints, fences, sandbags, guards, floodlights, guard dogs, and mirrors on long handles with which MPs could check the underside of entering vehicles for bombs that might have been placed underneath. As Herr (1978) wrote: "They blew up the My Canh floating restaurant [on the riverfront in Saigon], waited for it to be rebuilt and moved to another spot on the river, and then blew it up again.... they bombed the first U.S. Embassy.... There were four known VC sapper battalions in the Saigon-Cholon area, dread sappers, guerilla superstars, they didn't even have to do anything to put the fear out" (p. 41).

There was heavy-gauge wire grille over the windows of U.S. buses and trucks to keep out grenades. Poisons of various kinds were put into drinks in Vietnamese bars. I saw a soldier in a Saigon hospital who had been riding a cycle downtown near a building that was blown up. He was knocked off the cycle, rendered unconscious, had amnesia for the next half hour, then developed anxiety, nightmares, hand tremor, headaches, loss of appetite, and insomnia. All symptoms remained stable for two months, until, upon his arrival in Danang, a Buddhist uprising broke out and he was shot at by a machine gunner while riding in a truck.

No road was reliable; if it was not paved, it could be mined. Any morning could start out with a mine there that hadn't been there the evening before. If it was a paved highway with no holes, there were the snipers. Grenades were thrown by children and old people, live babies were found booby-trapped; and identity cards were forged so that enemy agents could enter American compounds as employees. As a result of all these and other circumstances, Viet Nam was poisoned with terror for many Americans.

Climate and Topography

Added to the miserable living conditions characteristic for all life in the field in any war, Viet Nam's climate and land provided additional stress, especially for the soldier reared in a temperate zone. The intense heat was an assault, with temperatures often well over 100. Alternating with the tropical sun were monsoon rains and floods, which brought insects, mud, and immersion foot and other problems. Jungle warfare brought other stresses too numerous to mention here.

Miscellaneous Bizarre Physical Dangers

Viet Nam provided the soldier with other exotic physical stresses, with concomitant psychic stress. Poisonous snakes, including cobras and krait snakes, posed special difficulties. Although antivenom was sometimes available, in the combat situation, particularly at night, it was not often possible to capture and identify the snake by which one had been bitten and thus it was impossible to get specific treatment. Tigers were a problem in certain areas, with attacks on GIs and local people not uncommon. Unfortunately rabies was also common in Viet Nam; rats, dogs, monkeys, and other animals had rabies and had to be dealt with cautiously. One group of Navy people were hospitalized because of multiple jellyfish stings sustained when their boat was sunk in a Mekong River branch.

Tropical Diseases

Contracting or being exposed to tropical diseases was sometimes a source of psychological stress. Malaria, heat stroke, dysentery, and dengue fever were not uncommon among American troops. Although diagnosis became refined as the war went on, one army medic contracted tropical sprue, which could not be diagnosed through three months of hospitalizations in Saigon, the Pacific, and Washington, D.C.

Immersion in an Extraordinarily Poor Third World Society

For some troops, especially those who readily empathized with the Vietnamese, exposure to the conditions of life in the country was in itself highly stressful. This is highlighted by such phenomena as garbage—piles of garbage of enormous proportions, generated by the American military, and constantly being picked over by Vietnamese for any objects of value, but also for food; raw sewage; blindness, and various deformities, from both disease and war wounds, present amongst people of all ages throughout cities, towns, and the countryside.

Chaos

Disorder is a feature of any combat zone; however, in Viet Nam the contradictions of military strategy apparently created peculiar chaos in the soldier's life. The guerilla character of the war contributed to the confusion. Airfields, for example, were often the scene of unprecedented confusion and disorder. Tan Son Nhut at times was the world's busiest airport—with American and Vietnamese military aircraft in operation, Phantom jets returning from bombing runs to share a landing strip with an Air France 707, and communications equipment faltering because of climate and overuse, all complicated by Vietcong sniper fire from off the end of a runway from time to time.

PSYCHOLOGICAL STRESSES SECONDARY TO THE GENERAL POLITICAL CHARACTER OF THE WAR

The reader is probably well-aware of the peculiar features, from a political standpoint, of the American war in Viet Nam. What requires considerable further clarification, however, are the specific sociopolitical qualities of the war which functioned directly as psychic stressors. These factors, when delineated and understood, can generally be viewed as facets of an absence—an absence of the usual massive sense of honor, purpose, and glory that, present and necessary for most military personnel in other wars, serves to buffer the traumatic stress of the war experience.

The Experience of Absurd Waste

Regardless of their political attitudes about the validity of the overall American purpose in Viet Nam, many troops daily confronted waste, corruption, and absurdity in the conduct of the war. Drug use, black market activities by officers and senior noncoms, fraggings (killing of commanders by enlisted men), implicit arrangements between troops and their leaders to avoid combat because of its purposelessness, and other situations gave a quality of absurdity to the entire war experience and led to a profound sense of meaningless waste from which some have not recovered.

Government Deceit and Misjudgment

As chronicled, for example, in *The Pentagon Papers* (13), deception and miscalculation were standard on the part of U.S. government leaders during the Viet Nam War and were experienced in various direct ways by troops. Thus, soldiers stationed in Cambodia read newsclips sent from home that no U.S. troops were in Cambodia. Others were forced to lie to their commanders about bombing activities, as happened with air force personnel at Bien Hoa during the secret U.S. bombing of Cambodia (14). Still others were responsible for false body counts. Career military persons experienced an assault on their professional identity because of such events. Others experienced an assault on inner images involving trust and confidence in national leadership and the moral rectitude of American institutions.

Massive National Conflict

The well-known, intense national conflict about the Viet Nam War directly affected troops; it was an integral stress for them, as well as for many civilians. Some families had one son serving in Viet Nam and another militantly opposing the war stateside. Whether the individual soldier was himself or herself, pro-war or antiwar, a substantial portion of the American people were on the other side. And in Viet Nam itself sharp divisions about the war characterized the troops.

Defeat

The Viet Nam War was lost by the United States, a significant stress for the participants. It was the first instance in our national history of a defeat at war (the Korean War ended in a draw). Like other major historical events, this defeat profoundly affected the individuals involved. For some, the fact of defeat has constituted a major fault in the psychological defensive structure surrounding the war experience.

ATROCITY

The term "atrocity" refers to destruction that goes beyond the usual boundaries of war, lying outside the requirements of military strategy. Meaningless and cruel destruction, atrocity is present to a degree in all wars. It is unique in its impact on veterans who have witnessed it, heard of it up close, or participated in it. In Viet Nam there was atrocity directed against the land. Defoliation of forests and fields with herbicides (like Agent Orange), plausible at the time for military reasons, has turned out in retrospect not only to have been useless for military purposes but also to have produced lasting damage to the land in Indochina, the people of the country (possibly via continuing birth defects and cancer), and possibly to Americans who were exposed.

Meaningless destruction of human life was also experienced by troops in Viet Nam: captives pushed out of helicopters, shooting and napalming of noncombatants, massacres, etc. Aptly described as an "atrocity-producing situation" by Lifton, the war left some participants with brutalized sectors of personality (15), a subtle and lasting stress.

ADDITIONAL EMOTIONAL TRAUMA

This account of the stresses of the war experience itself concludes with five additional sources of stress, four of which are common to all wars, one of which was more or less peculiar to Viet Nam. These stresses often remain hidden until the subjective experience of the veteran is examined carefully, for they involve inner conflicts and events which often pass by unnoticed.

Failure to Live Up to One's Expectations

Many soldiers have clear and high expectations of themselves as they enter a war situation, striving for courage, if not heroism, in their actions. In battle, however, they may run, hide, fail to shoot, or otherwise fail to perform as anticipated. Such events may insert massive guilt and regret into an individual's life, which can take years to work out (16).

Overwhelming Fear Reactions

Occasionally in the combat situation, soldiers have overwhelming fear reactions, leading to trembling, diarrhea, vomiting, and other responses. In addition to the traumatic experience of powerlessness, a sense of humiliation may itself constitute lasting trauma.

Self-inflicted Wounds

Sometimes in war, troops are driven to inflict wounds upon themselves as a way of getting out of the combat situation. This may have various psychological ramifications, including shame over "cowardice," and the undoing of previously adequate defenses against masochism. Thus, such wounds can be a source of ongoing stress.

Accidental Killing of Comrades or Civilians

Experiencing loss of judgment, the heat and confusion of battle, etc., soldiers sometimes accidentally kill their buddies or noncombatants from the other side. I know of one case in Viet Nam in which a soldier machine-gunned well over 100 school children, altogether by accident, who had entered a wooded area and could not be distinguished from an attack force of soldiers.

Vietnamese Left Behind

Because of the peculiarities of the Viet Nam War, some Americans sustained personal losses such as Vietnamese friends left behind and never seen again. A special example of this type of stress affects men who fathered and left behind children in Viet Nam. This source of stress has been exacerbated by the impossibility of contact with persons in Viet Nam since the end of the war.

STRESSES OF THE IMMEDIATE HOMECOMING PERIOD

Veterans were subjected to additional stresses upon coming home. These can be categorized under two headings, as follows.

Absence of Sanction, Presence of Hostility

Sanction, approval, praise, appreciation, and festive welcoming are important elements in beginning a returned warrior's healing of the emotional trauma of war. These responses were absent from the reception accorded most Viet Nam returnees. Much of society was diverted from attention to the veteran by vigorous controversy over the war, which had torn at the structure of our nation for over a decade. Pro-war and antiwar civilians alike had developed anger and disgust over the war itself, which sometimes was displaced onto the veteran. It was not rare for returnees from Viet Nam to be shouted at, ridiculed, and spat upon in airports and other public places. This led, among other results, to the remarkable phenomenon of soldiers' hastily changing into civilian clothes and throwing away uniforms en masse at disembarkation points.

Absence of Normal Debriefing

Upon return from a war, soldiers commonly engage in prolonged and profound discussion of the events of the war with each other, with family, and with friends. Talking out traumatic experiences contributes to their working through. This process was severely disrupted, and most studies demonstrate that the large majority of Viet Nam veterans were unable to have such conversations with anyone. Apparently only in small towns, where community and social network ties are perhaps more intimate and retrievable, did this process sometimes go on (17). Many factors contributed to the absence of normal debriefing, including the veteran's shame or disgust about the war and wish to precipitiously forget it.

LONG-TERM FACTORS EXACERBATING THE EFFECTS OF WAR STRESS

Since the end of the war in 1975, four major factors have intensified the stresses impinging on Viet Nam veterans.

Further Fading of a Sense of Purpose

Apparently with time there has been a further fading on the part of veterans of any sense of redeeming purpose in the war. A major survey conducted by Lou Harris Associates for the Veterans Administration revealed in 1980 that 47% of Viet Nam veterans in the sample felt in general that the United States should have stayed out of Viet Nam. Thirteen percent did not express an opinion, leaving a minority of 40% who thought that the United States had done the right thing in getting into the fighting in Viet Nam (18). A study completed by the Center for Policy Research in 1981 revealed roughly the same percentages (17). However, even beyond the large segment of veterans who explicitly think that the war was wrong, the prevailing impression of clinicians currently working with veterans is that among those who consider the American intervention to have been proper and just, many reveal underlying feelings of waste and purposelessness when given a neutral and accepting forum in which to express any and all thoughts about the experience. Although refined studies remain to be done on the matter, it can be reasonably hypothesized that both explicit and hidden feelings that the war lacked purpose are continuing to undermine the healing process in many veterans constituting a source of ongoing stress.

Impossibility of Further Contact with Viet Nam

Viet Nam was the first war in which Americans have not been able to go back to the scene of fighting. The whole experience, therefore, is insanely frozen in time. Many veterans need contact with the reality of Viet Nam today in order to work out the inner imprints of the experience there. They need to see the people, the land, the buildings, the paddies, the trees, and the changes effected by peace and reconstruction. They need to see in *that* way that the war is over by viewing the land and the people now when they are free to look steadily and clearly, without the intervening murky screen of war. After World War II and the Korean War, the combat zone was overrun by American journalists and photographers, so that even those who could not visit the zone had the benefit of a great flow of words and pictures about the postwar evolution of the place and the people. Viet Nam veterans have been cut off from the further history of Viet Nam, which is an additional source of stress.

Unavailability of Psychotherapeutic Treatment

For many reasons, there has been a severe and pervasive inability of the mental health professions to provide effective psychotherapeutic treatment for all degrees of stress reaction in Viet Nam veterans. With very few exceptions, until the advent of special outreach programs launched by Disabled American Veterans and the Veterans Administration in 1978 and 1979, respectively, it was not possible for veterans to obtain psychotherapy or counseling that took account of the war experience. The reasons for this lack have been recounted elsewhere (6,7,17,19). Briefly, they include countertransference problems deriving from therapists' unresolved conflicts about the war, aversion to hearing about gruesome and tragic events, a long interval since the last major incidence of war stress disorder, and sociopolitical failure to respond to the issue as a public health problem.

Continuing Blackout of the War as History

The longest war in America's history (11 years) continues to be largely ignored in our academic and public life. Although in early 1981, the press manifested a new attention to Viet Nam veterans and three books were published providing first-person accounts (all receiving prominent reviews), there continues to be an almost total absence of published, searching, scholarly investigation of the Viet Nam War. The Viet Nam veteran appears to be a kind of keeper of the nation's history of the war. As Rosen (1981) noted: ''Vietnam veterans have become the chief mnemonic device in our efforts to remember a war already eight years behind us. It is through their painful adjustments to civilian life that we recall one cruel irony of that unholiest of foreign entanglements: many of its veterans are still fighting it'' (20,21,22,23). Thus, the present historical and political status of the war is a continuing source of stress for some veterans.

MAJOR DELAYED AND CHRONIC STRESS SYNDROMES SEEN IN VIET NAM VETERANS

From my clinic experience with over 1000 veterans, I developed a classification of the most common manifestations of stress disorder in this population.

Type I. Manifesting Primarily by Psychological Symptoms

Classical traumatic neurosis symptoms. Flashbacks, nightmares, irritability, rage spells, anxiety, insomnia, depression.

Depression. Without other symptoms, masking impacted grief about war experiences and related conflicts (Shatan, 1981).

Psychosomatic syndromes. Headache, low back syndrome, ulcer, migraine, irritable colon, hypertension.

Violent paranoid states. Without psychotic symptoms, or indicators of pre-war border-line personality disorder, these veterans manifest diffuse hostility, suspiciousness, paranoia, irritability, and crowd phobia. This state represents a persistence of the paranoid, hyper-vigilant state that was lifesaving for many participants in the terrorized guerilla atmosphere of Viet Nam.

Addictive disorders. Addiction to alcohol (25), marijuana, heroin, cocaine, thrills, risks, gambling—including gambling with fate as in chronic high-speed driving.

Exacerbated character disorders. Dramatic exacerbation of character problems, such as impulsive behavior or sociopathy, present in minor degree before the war.

Suicides and homicides. These are categorized separately for two purposes: to highlight them as problems, and also to indicate our lack of knowledge of the diagnostic background of Viet Nam veterans who kill themselves or others. Fortunately, the number of homicides is quite small. That may not be the case for suicides; there is not a single study of the incidence of suicide in Viet Nam veterans; but there is a persistent, almost universal impression among clinicians who work with this group, that the incidence of suicide is high and continuing.

Psychotic syndromes. Previously reported in 1973, in the past two years at Viet Nam Vet Centers and V.A. medical facilities, we have begun to see cases of psychotic-level symptomatology, usually misdiagnosed as schizophrenia, based on war trauma (26). This outcome, long-recognized in the literature (27) from previous wars, has remained largely hidden in Viet Nam veterans until recently.

Type II. Manifesting Primarily by General Alteration in Life Course

Underachievement. Lacking significant symptoms, these veterans' lives are characterized by chronic underachieving or instability in education or work. They consistently settle for less, settle for dullness. The underachievement may go undetected until it begins to dissipate in the context of effective treatment that deals with the war.

Wandering lifestyle. Though not necessarily underachieving in any obvious way, the veteran goes from job to job, school to school, town to town without progression toward any goal.

Crime. Some veterans commit antisocial acts not as a result of preexisting criminality but as a part of stress disorder. Sudden outbursts in veterans with no criminal record, based on repetitions of war events, with or without conscious imagery related to the war, may occur.

Type III. Problems Manifested Primarily in Relatedness to Significant Others

Difficulties in intimacy with wife or lover.

Special interferences in relating to children. One's own or others' are an especially painful, subtle, and confusing manifestation in Viet Nam veterans. The problems are usually traceable to episodes of wounding, killing, or harming of children in Viet Nam, done by the veteran, or observed, or simply heard about repeatedly.

Marked changes in relatedness to the country and its institutions. Many veterans have lost their patriotism and sustained marked changes in their citizen identity. This may lead to extreme detachment from the political process in all its aspects. Loss of political attachment may have occurred because the soldier in Viet Nam felt himself sacrificed by military and civilian leaders who, out of ignorance or cynicism, did not allow him to win a just war or, from the opposing perspective, sent him to fight an unjust war.

General alienation. Affected veterans display a pervasive and generalized detachment from most processes of life—marriage, career, social and political institutions, community, and friends. Some seem frozen at age 20, have not learned more adult skills for living, and are unsophisticated in subtle and diffuse ways.

Type IV

Veterans in this group have experienced a profound shattering of images of self and humanity. They are victims of the "broken connection" (28). Radical suffering or intense exposure to mutilation, death, and absurd, meaningless misery has caused a basic fault to appear in the individual's link to civilization. Manifestations of this phenomenon vary widely. These Viet Nam veterans have much in common with the survivors of Nazi death and concentration camps. They have lost some of their basic faith in the capacity of humanity for goodness, as described in Holocaust survivors by Des Pres (29).

CONCLUSION

In the summer of 1981, the U.S. Congress, by unanimous votes in both houses, renewed the mandate of the nationwide system of Viet Nam veteran counseling centers to provide outreach and assistance to hundreds of thousands of veterans suffering from war stress disorder and related problems (30). This effort will provide a continuing focus for the study and treatment of stress reactions in the years ahead.

REFERENCES

1. Smith, J. R. "A Survey of 125 Years of the Psychological Literature on Reactions to Combat," (mimeo), Durham, Duke University, Department of Psychology, 1981.

2. CAPUTO, P. *A Rumor of War,* New York, Ballantine, 1977.

3. HASFORD, G. *The Short-Timers,* New York, Bantam, 1979.

4. HEINEMANN, L. *Close Quarters,* New York, Popular Library, 1977.

5. KARLIN, W., PAQUET, B. T., & ROTTMANN, L. *Free Fire Zone,* Coventry, 1st Casualty Press, 1973.

6. FIGLEY, C. (ed.). *Stress Disorders Among Vietnam Veterans.* New York, Brunner/Mazel, 1978.

7. FIGLEY, C. & LEVENTMAN, S. *Strangers At Home,* New York, Praeger, 1980.

8. GLASS, A. J. "Principles of Combat Psychiatry," 117:27, *Military Medicine,* 1955.

9. FITZGERALD, F. *Fire In the Lake,* New York, Random House, Vintage, 1972.

10. WITHERS, J. H. "Personal Protection During the Bombing of the Victoria Bachelor Officers' Quarters," *Military Medicine,* 131:1285–1290, 1966.

11. HERR, M. *Dispatches,* New York, Avon, 1978.

12. MAHEDY, W. "We've Got To Get Out Of This Place," *Christian Century,* 26 September 1979, p. 922.

13. SHEEHAN, N., ET AL. *The Pentagon Papers,* New York, Bantam Books, 1971.

14. SHAWCROSS, W. *Sideshow,* New York, Pocket Books, 1979.

15. LIFTON, R. J. *Home From the War,* New York, Simon & Schuster, 1973.

16. SMITH, J. R. "Vietnam Veterans: Rap Groups and the Stress Recovery Process," (mimeo), Department of Psychology, Duke University, 1980.

17. LAUFER, R. S., ET AL. *Legacies of Viet Nam: Comparative Adjustment of Veterans and Their Peers,* (House Committee Print No. 14, 97th Congress, 1st Session, U.S. Government Printing Office, Washington, D.C., 1981.

18. UNITED STATES CONGRESS COMMITTEE ON VETERANS AFFAIRS. *Myths and Realities: A Study of Attitudes Toward Vietnam Era Veterans,* Washington, D.C., Veterans Administration, 1980.

19. BLANK, A. S. JR. *1st Training Conference Papers, Operation Outreach,* Washington, D.C., Veterans Administration (mimeo), 1979.

20. COLEMAN, C. *Sergeant Back Again,* New York, Harper & Row, 1980.

21. SANTOLI, A. *Everything We Had,* New York, Random House, 1981.

22. BAKER, M. *Nam,* New York, Morrow, 1981.

23. ROSEN, R. D. "Open Wounds: A Vietnam Legacy," *Boston Phoenix,* 26 May, 1981, p. 2.

24. BLANK, A. S. JR. "THE PRICE OF CONSTANT VIGILANCE: THE VIET NAM ERA VETERAN," *Frontiers of Psychiatry,* 11:12, no. 2, February 1, 1981.

25. LACOURSIERE, R. B., GODFREY, E., and RUBY, LORNE M. "Traumatic Neurosis in the Etiology of Alcoholism: Viet Nam Combat and Other Trauma," 137:8, *American Journal of Psychiatry,* 1980.

26. VAN PUTTEN, T., & EMORY, W. H. "Traumatic Neuroses in Vietnam Returnees." *Archives of General Psychiatry,* 1973, *29,* 699.

27. KARDINER, A. *The Traumatic Neuroses of War,* Washington, D.C., National Research Council, 1941.

28. LIFTON, R. J. *The Broken Connection,* New York: Simon & Schuster, 1979.

29. DES PRES, *The Survivor,* New York, Pocket Books, 1976.

30. UNITED STATES Committee on Veterans' Affairs, "Veterans' programs extension and improvements act of 1981," Senate report no. 97-89. 15 May, 1981.

31. SHATAN, CHAIM. Militarized Mourning and Ceremonial Vengeance. Paper delivered at the American Psychoanalytic Association Meetings, New York City, 1981.

39

Consequences of Modern Terrorism

J. Bastiaans

THE HUMAN BEING BY NATURE has a need for freedom to think, feel, and act. The sensation of freedom rests on the conviction that one controls one's own actions and has options. Freedom is pursued in particular by those who have experienced the lack thereof. Between total freedom and total constraint lie numerous levels of restraint associated with greater or lesser acceptance. Knowledge of freedom characterizes the mentally and physically healthy individual, and when deprivation of freedom is experienced at a relatively advanced stage of life, the consequences are significant. The effects are more severe the greater the duration and the intensity of this deprivation.

Many of those who have experienced a loss of freedom live in fear that this situation might occur again. In such cases, the person may seek protection against such fears by placing restraints on someone else's freedom. This pattern is evident daily, in both smaller and larger groups, at various levels—local, national, or international.

Experiencing violations of one's freedom also causes mental isolation. Here the individual consciously or unconsciously locks himself into mental invulnerability structures of a psychotic, psychoneurotic, or psychosomatic nature. This type of isolation is found in autism, narcissism, character neuroses, depersonalization, or psychosomatic character formation. The patient so affected becomes isolated from the world of his inner emotions by an excessive use of self-restraint. Along these lines, one could view many psychiatric patients as not being free. Their mental isolation may have its roots in traumatizing events or in unresolved conflicts.

In modern life, terrorism is a widespread threat. Victims of terrorism usually are exposed to so many stressors that they may suffer aftereffects for months and even years. Threats of annihilation may cause even the most healthy individual to become a psychiatric or psychosomatic patient.

As a result of the many sieges and hostage taking acts witnessed all over the world in recent years, much attention has been paid to victimization in the context of terrorism. One of the most striking examples was the holding of 53 American hostages in Iran for more than a year. In the past decade, Holland had to deal with many terroristic acts, and much research has been conducted thereon. In light of their experience, Dutch scientists have been repeatedly invited to function as advisors on the aftercare of victims in many countries.

THE DUTCH EXPERIENCE WITH TERRORISM IN THE 1970s

Hostage situations are extremely threatening and arduous for the victims and their relatives and friends. In such situations the hostages pledge their lives for the fulfillment of certain conditions imposed by the terrorists. The act of being held hostage isolates the individual or the group from a trusted and familiar environment. Such isolation is difficult in itself and devastating when linked to the threat of death.

In the 1970s, the Netherlands was shocked by hostage taking on a large scale. The main episodes are listed here:

The occupation of the French embassy in The Hague
In 1974, 11 hostages were held for four days by 3 members of the Japanese Red Army.
The siege at Scheveningen prison
In October 1974, 22 persons, members of a choir, were taken hostage by 4 prisoners. This experience lasted five days.
The hijacking of the train at Wijster
In December 1975, a Dutch train, consisting of two coaches, was brought to a halt by 4 South Moluccans. Some passengers escaped. Three were killed by the South Moluccans. Twelve days later the hijackers surrendered and the remaining 32 hostages were released.
The occupation of the Indonesian consulate in Amsterdam
In December 1975, a group of South Moluccans took 36 persons hostage in the Indonesian consulate in Amsterdam. Among the hostages were 14 children. One victim died. Fifteen days later the terrorists surrendered and the remaining hostages were freed.
The hijacking of a KLM DC9 airplane
In September 1976, the *City of Madrid,* on flight from Nice to Amsterdam, was hijacked by 3 Palestinians. Following touchdowns in Tunisia and Cyprus, the hostages, after hours of negotiation, were released.
The hijacking of the train near De Punt
In May 1977, a Dutch train was seized by 9 South Moluccans; 96 passengers were taken hostage. In the first hours, 42 were released. Twenty days later, marines took the train by storm. In this action, 2 hostages and 6 hijackers lost their lives.
The seige at Bovensmilde
Simultaneously with the hijacking of the train near De Punt, 4 South Moluccans took 5 teachers and 125 school children hostage at the junior school in Bovensmilde. Twenty Moluccan school children were soon released. Twenty days later, marines took the school by storm. The teachers and the remaining children were freed.

In December 1975 the Netherlands witnessed both the hijacking near Wijster and the occupation of the Indonesian consulate in Amsterdam. Concern was expressed for the need to investigate the effects on victims and to improve facilities for their support and treatment. On the advice of experts, the Centrale Beleids-en Ondersteuningsgroep (CBOG) was set up in January 1976 to provide aftercare to ex-hostages. The project also embraced the following research objectives:

1. to record the psychic and somatic changes experienced by people exposed to acts of terrorism

2. to distinguish changes caused by exposure to terrorism from conditions aggravated by this experience
3. to distinguish positive and negative changes associated with the hostage experience
4. to determine psychic and somatic changes in relatives, friends, and co-workers of hostages
5. to evaluate the assistance provided to hostages, including their assessments of services, as well as to compile a manual for use in future hostage situations
6. to predict psychic and somatic problems that ex-hostages and their closest contacts might experience (e.g., difficulty in handling stress, long-term health effects)

Crelinsten (1977a) reported the results of an international conference on terrorism held in Evian at the time of the train hijacking near De Punt and the seizure of the school in Bovensmilde. This report helped structure the scientific investigation undertaken by the CBOG. Likewise, the CBOG enlisted the cooperation of the International Center for Comparative Criminology in Montreal. Another important resource of the CBOG study was the model of the *KZ syndrome,* developed by myself after having treated hundreds of World War II survivors with psychiatric and psychosomatic manifestations of war stress (Bastiaans, 1957). Before reviewing the results of the CBOG investigation on terrorism, I shall outline this model. Bear in mind that at the start of their study, the CBOG scientists expected that the effects on ex-hostages would be similar to those experienced by prisoners of war and by people who have survived man-made and natural disasters.

THE KZ SYNDROME

The KZ (concentration camp) syndrome is a sequence of four distinct phases; Table 39–1 and Figure 39–1 illustrate these phases.

Phase 1: The Shock Phase

The *shock phase* usually is initiated by arrest, harsh interrogation, ill treatment, or imprisonment. Extreme shock implies loss of consciousness; less extreme shock may imply extreme depersonalization and ego paralysis. In this phase, the self-defense mechanisms cannot be used. When consciousness has not been significantly lowered, extreme feelings of powerlessness tend to dominate. These feelings may be so overwhelming that at later stages they give rise to fixations in conscious or unconscious states of powerlessness.

Phase 2: The Alarm Phase

The *alarm phase,* or contrashock phase, is a condition of intrapsychic lability marked by all the signs and symptoms of psychophysiological arousal. Typical manifestations are neurasthenia and extreme nervousness, in combination with fear, sleeplessness, and restlessness. The main feelings in the alarm phase are pain, guilt, and shame. These emotions have a feedback, as well as a warning, function, insofar as they prepare the individual for his task of coping.

TABLE 39-1.
Symptom Formation in Response to Traumatizing Stress

Phases of adaptation syndrome	Emotional	Intellectual
Shock	Fainting, no emotions	Paralysis of intellectual functioning in dream or coma
Alarm	Alarm emotions and feelings; affects, anxiety, pain, terror, panic, extreme insecurity and nervousness, hyperesthesia, agitation, hesitation, doubt	Hyperactivity in perception and thinking
Adaptation with accent on fight	Overactivity, destruction vs. construction, ranging from from hostile action to protest; sadism and overproduction	Intellectual overactivity
Adaptation with accent on fight and flight	Depression, masochism, disappointment; manifest or masked mourning	Insufficient investment of intellectual capacities in action, production, communication; everything lacks sense
Adaptation with accent on flight	Indifference, dislike or disgust of action, work, contact; feeling lonely; emotional autism and apathy	Failing functioning in orientation, perception, memory, conceptualization, thinking
Exhaustion	Feelings of weakness, asthenia, sleep paralysis, feeling of impotence	Chronic asthenia of intellectual functions; narrowing of mental horizon

Increased need for security, protection, contact, oral satisfaction, compensation

Phase 3: The Adaptation Phase

The *adaptation phase* can go in either of two directions: it may lead to a healthy adaptation, but it may also end in pathological mechanisms that prevent adaptation to reality. The primary biological mechanisms are fight or flight. Excessive flight may lead to depression, while excessive fight may lead to overt hostility or psychopathic aggressiveness. Controlled fight can result in overcontrolled coping, which leads in turn to psychosomatic syndrome formation. Psychiatric and psychosomatic syndromes are usually the consequences of forced adaptation.

Phase 4: The Exhaustion Phase

The *exhaustion phase* is usually reached when adaptation or coping procedures have succeeded. In this phase, the victim experiences symptoms of asthenia, tiredness, and

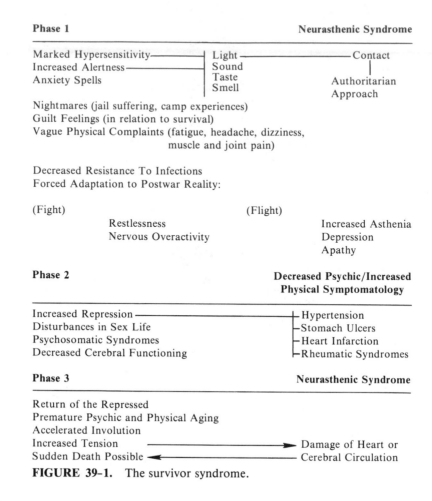

Phase 1   **Neurasthenic Syndrome**

Marked Hypersensitivity——————| Light ——————————Contact
Increased Alertness——————| Sound |
Anxiety Spells | Taste   Authoritarian
                                  | Smell   Approach
Nightmares (jail suffering, camp experiences)
Guilt Feelings (in relation to survival)
Vague Physical Complaints (fatigue, headache, dizziness,
                    muscle and joint pain)

Decreased Resistance To Infections
Forced Adaptation to Postwar Reality:

(Fight)   (Flight)
            Restlessness   Increased Asthenia
            Nervous Overactivity   Depression
                                              Apathy

Phase 2   **Decreased Psychic/Increased**
                                               Physical Symptomatology

Increased Repression ——————————| Hypertension
Disturbances in Sex Life |—Stomach Ulcers
Psychosomatic Syndromes |—Heart Infarction
Decreased Cerebral Functioning |—Rheumatic Syndromes

Phase 3   **Neurasthenic Syndrome**

Return of the Repressed
Premature Psychic and Physical Aging
Accelerated Involution
Increased Tension   ————————————————▶ Damage of Heart or
Sudden Death Possible ◀———————————— Cerebral Circulation

FIGURE 39-1. The survivor syndrome.

general weakness, in combination with a diversity of signs common to psychological and psychosomatic regression.

Discussion of the Syndrome

Having been exposed to war stress, often for years, soldiers and former inmates of prisons and concentration camps were in a state of complete exhaustion at the end of World War II. Those who tried to resume normal activities as soon as possible after an initial period of physical recovery frequently suffered psychic and psychosomatic decompensation in later years. Clinical observation of such people suggested the importance of a prolonged recovery period. In view of what is known about KZ pathology, it could be predicted that victims of such terroristic acts as hijackings would suffer, in the poststress period, from similar symptoms and face similar difficulties in returning to a normal way of life.

THE MAIN RESULTS OF THE DUTCH INVESTIGATION

The CBOG began its investigation of terrorism by sending letters of introduction to ex-hostages (283) and their relatives (Bastiaans, Jaspers, van der Ploeg, van den Berg-Schaap,

& van den Berg, 1979). Fifty-nine percent (168 ex-hostages) agreed to be interviewed about their experiences; 13 ex-hostages (5%) refused; and 50 (17%) could be evaluated only by questionnaire (15 people in this group completed and returned the questionnaire). The remainder ($n = 52$) were excluded from the study because they were unable to speak Dutch or could not be reached. The investigators also obtained completed questionnaires from two-thirds of the physicians attending the ex-hostages, half the social workers on their cases, and nearly three-fourths of the CBOG staff.

The interviews were conducted by psychologists in the homes of the ex-hostages. A semistructured format, permitting some free conservation, focused on how the subjects had experienced their captivity, how they had coped, what consequences they were aware of, what care they had received upon their release, and what help they presently desired.

The questionnaires covered roughly the same areas; however, the attending physicians were asked, with the ex-hostages' permission, to evaluate the victims according to the Dutch Personality Questionnaire.

Negative Consequences for Ex-hostages

Tenseness, insomnia, fears, and phobias were the prominent negative effects in the four weeks following the event. The intensity of negative effects in the short run was greater for women than for men. Long-term negative effects, that is to say, those appearing after the first month, were experienced by two-thirds of the ex-hostages. Symptoms included irritability, increased lability, fears, phobias, and, in most cases, vague physical complaints, as well as insomnia, feelings of unsafety, feelings of being misunderstood, and preoccupation with having been taken hostage. The long-term effects were more pronounced for women than for men, and the intensity of effects was greater the longer the captivity had lasted, the younger the hostage, and the less education he or she had had. There was a clear connection in terms of intensity between short-term and long-term negative effects. Finally, among half the ex-hostages, new acts of terrorism reactivated the fears, thoughts, etc., they had experienced in confinement.

Positive Consequences for Ex-hostages

Short-term positive effects were mentioned by two-thirds of the ex-hostages. For the long term, positive effects were mentioned by half the group. The main positive effect concerned the ability to see things as relative.

Effects on Family Members

The intensity of short-term negative effects was rather low for members of the ex-hostages' families, but two-thirds of family members suffered long-term negative effects. Though similar to those reported by the ex-hostages, these effects were less intense, as were the positive consequences noted by family members. Family members, like hostages, showed a strong connection in terms of intensity between short- and long-term negative effects. Finally, new acts of terrorism had a negative effect on family members.

Effects on Social and Family Relationships

One-fifth of respondents reported a worsening of relations with intimates (e.g., misunderstanding of each other's experiences and an increase of quarrels and conflicts). One-third reported positive consequences (e.g., honest exchanges of experiences, greater emotional involvement); the experience of being offered help in getting through the whole event was also viewed as positive.

Help Seeking by Family Members in the Hostage Period

On-site aid centers were available in five of the seven hostage situations listed earlier. One-third of the family members spent more than half their time in such centers. However, 41% either did not visit the aid center at all or came only once. In such centers, contact with fellow sufferers and assistants was appreciated most. Two-thirds of the relatives expressed a positive opinion of the assistance that had been offered to them; only 6% were not satisfied. The relatives of the long held De Punt hostages greatly appreciated the comprehensive information that had been available at the center.

About half the family members consulted their own family doctors during the hostage period. For the De Punt hostages this figure was 80%. Seventy-one percent were satisfied with the doctor's assistance; 9% were not.

Finally, 8% of the relatives asked for assistance from government authorities or social workers not affiliated with the aid centers. Fifty-three percent got no response from these sources.

Short- and Long-term Care of Ex-hostages

Immediately after release, one-third of the ex-hostages received no professional assistance. Support services were better organized in the more recent episodes of terrorism. Of the ex-hostages 59% expressed a positive opinion of immediate aid; 14%, negative. Appreciation was highest in the groups that had received the comprehensive help (Wijster, De Punt, Bovensmilde).

With regard to aftercare, about half the ex-hostages were offered help from several sources (e.g., social workers, government authorities). One-fifth were offered no help at all. In most cases, the number of contacts with social workers was limited: 56% had fewer than 5 consultations; 21% had more than 10. Most consultations (largely conversations) took place over a period of some months. Only 9% of ex-hostages who received treatment needed aftercare longer than a year. In the case of the French embassy and the Scheveningen prison, aftercare was offered too late; for this reason, many of the ex-hostages made little or no use of the available services. Almost half the ex-hostages reported satisfaction with the help that had been offered; about one-fifth had a negative opinion of aftercare; the rest were neither explicitly positive nor explicitly negative about the services. The hostages of the short Wijster siege and the ex-hostages from Scheveningen prison expressed the least satisfaction with services. Lack of continuity in aftercare proved to be disadvantageous for these groups, as well as for the Bovensmilde ex-hostages.

The Family Doctor's Role in Hostage Situations

The CBOG investigation paid special attention to the family doctor's role in short- and long-term care. Although most of the doctors did not consider their task more difficult in the hostage situation than in other crisis situations, almost half of them thought themselves not adequately trained for this specific function. Those who did think themselves adequately prepared attributed their skill to personal interest and involvement, as well as to previous experience with situations of stress. With regard to the nature and the gravity of the effects associated with the hostage experience, the doctors' opinions agreed almost entirely with those of the ex-hostages. Finally, 20% of the ex-hostages increased the frequency of visits to doctors, while there was a decrease in 8% of cases. The frequency of consultations did not depend on any confidential relationship between doctor and patient.

Coping Behavior in the Context of the Family

Another focus of attention was how family members experienced the act of terrorism. Information seeking and adhering to normal routines were considered by respondents the best coping mechanisms. Seeking diversion and affiliating were considered important as well.

In the first few weeks after the events, 15% of family members and ex-hostages tried hard to ignore the experience. Avoidance behavior was most pronounced among the ex-hostages of the Indonesian consulate; least, among the long held De Punt hostages. As a rule, preoccupation with the event decreased in intensity after the first few weeks. In the short run, however, 40% of ex-hostages and their relatives focused on the ordeal. Finally, the experiences of the ex-hostages usually were discussed more than those of the family.

Predicting the Consequences of the Hostage Experience

To a certain extent it appears possible to predict whether negative effects will occur after termination of the terrorist act.[1]

Effects on Ex-hostages. The more negative experiences the hostages had gone through and the more frightened they had felt, the more negative effects they manifested after release regardless of the degree of support from and contact with fellow hostages. Negative effects were less pronounced among better educated people. Age, too, was a good predictor, though not as reliable as education. The older they were, the less ex-hostages suffered from negative effects. Moreover, the better their physical condition before the event, the less ex-hostages suffered from negative effects afterward. Certain correlations emerged with personality traits: the higher the score on rigidity or neuroticism, the stronger the negative effects. The interviewers also reported that more active and conscious use of various coping mechanisms during the event correlated with fewer negative effects after release.

Effects on Family Members. Family members who were more frightened and who discussed the hostage situation more intensively visited the reception centers more frequently. Relatives taking more medicine before the event also visited the centers more often.

Use of aftercare by ex-hostages could be predicted on the basis of experiences during and following the crisis. Hostages who had not used avoidance and those who suffered from more pronounced negative effects tended to make use of available services, as did those who had had more negative experiences during captivity and who had been less active at that time. The longer the captivity, too, the greater the reliance on aftercare. Finally, the higher the score on neuroticism and aggrievance and the lower the score on social inadequacy, the more use was made of aftercare.

Among family members, more negative expectations about outcome and more fear correlated with stronger postcrisis negative effects. As was the case with the ex-hostages, demographic characteristics—especially schooling—appeared to be important: more education usually meant fewer negative effects. The longer the captivity, the stronger the negative effects manifested by family members. Likewise, when psychosocial problems had existed before the captivity, negative effects were more clear among relatives. The interviewers had the impression that postcrisis negative effects were stronger both when the physical condition of family members had been problematic before the event and when daily routine and sleeping habits had been disrupted during the hostage period.

The Role of Authorities in Hostage Situations

The CBOG investigation solicited the opinion of the ex-hostages and the members of their families on the role of the authorities vis-à-vis the crisis. Twenty-four percent of the ex-hostages and 31% of the relatives held a negative opinion of the authorities; 40% of the ex-hostages and 33% of the relatives expressed a positive opinion. The remainder had no opinion. Of the ex-hostages, 55% reported having had no expectations about the government's role in the crisis. A small group (7%) had expected preventive measures. This attitude was especially prevalent among the parents whose children had been taken hostage at Bovensmilde; this group greatly feared a recurrence of the event. Half the ex-hostages and two-thirds of the relatives reported that the government had not met their expectations; only 25% of the ex-hostages and 10% of the relatives were for the most part satisfied. Clearly, the less that expectations had been met, the more negative were the opinions of the authorities. Thus, those who reported no expectations of the government had a more positive opinion, whereas about half the people who had had such expectations expressed a negative opinion. The stronger the negative opinion, the greater the expectations had been.

The Role of the Media in Hostage Situations

Two-thirds of the relatives were approached by journalists during the terrorist episode, but only 21% agreed to talk with the press. The greater part of those contacted had a negative opinion of the approach method used. Those who did speak to the press expressed more negative than positive opinions. Their dissatisfaction related primarily to the published accounts. At the same time, relatives expressing favorable opinions believed that the information given to the journalists had been reported accurately. In general, 67% of the relatives expressed a negative opinion of the way in which events had been reported during the hostage period. Only 3% had a positive opinion.

After the hostage period, 83% of the ex-hostages and 69% of their families were approached by the press. Fifty-two percent of the ex-hostages and 29% of their families agreed to speak to reporters, although in most cases not immediately after release. The overall opinion of the functioning of the press after the terrorist act was negative.

RECOMMENDATIONS

The report prepared for the Dutch government by the CBOG included a number of recommendations on immediate aid, aftercare, the training of crisis care providers, and future research directions (Bastiaans et al., 1979).

Immediate Aid

In a hostage crisis, the government must act to end the situation as quickly as possible and to organize appropriate aid for the hostages' relatives and for the hostages themselves, both in the short run and over the longer term. In addition, assistance should be offered to former hostages whose problems may be reactivated at this time.

Reception Centers for Family Members

Supportive care for family members is a necessity. Crisis centers can help relatives deal with the immediate situation and provide aftercare as required. Nonclassified information on negotiations and other aspects of the terrorist situation is useful to relatives.

The report also recommended that relatives actively participate in the organization of services, etc., at the reception centers. Relatives who cannot come to the center, for whatever reason, ought to be contacted, possibly by the emergency aid center, and to be provided the same assistance outlined earlier.

Care for Victims upon Release

As soon as the hostages are released, they should be given access to appropriate services. Some may need hospital rest for a short period; others, medical treatment. Psychiatric or psychological help should be available. In some cases, ex-hostages or their relatives may ask for such consultations, but in other cases, social workers, physicians, etc., may have to recommend therapy.

At this time, ex-hostages and their relatives must be protected from the press. Moreover, ex-hostages who live alone should be advised not to spend the first few days following release on their own. Reception centers should give the ex-hostages and the members of their families ample opportunity to talk and to relax. Center personnel can facilitate interactions, preventing the types of conflict that tend to arise when people are severely stressed.

Short- and Long-term Assistance to Ex-hostages

The CBOG investigation found that active assistance is highly appreciated by its beneficiaries. The family doctor may fulfill an important function, for example, by visiting ex-hostages and their families on his own initiative.

Immediate aid should be followed up by effective aftercare. Health workers and other personnel involved in postrelease treatment should be able to identify individuals at high risk for long-term negative effects; their case reports constitute an important resource for aftercare providers.

Many people find it difficult to ask for help and, therefore, both in the short run and over the longer term ex-hostages should be made aware that services are available. Help should not be forced on ex-hostages, but they should be well informed about their options and care providers must be alert to symptoms of distress. Crisis intervention is a subtle art. Ex-hostages and their relatives may resent the label "patient" and avoid seeking help. They should be told that accepting some guidance after a period of severe stress by no means implies that they are considered mentally ill.

Training Care Providers

Care providers in crisis situations require both practical experience and formal training. Access to experts in various fields can help on-site and aftercare personnel tailor the services they deliver to victims and their relatives.

To improve the quality of care, it is imperative that research on hostage situations and their aftermath proceed. A central research institute, possibly acting in conjunction with regional institutes or departments, could conduct the relevant scientific investigations. The results could be used to prepare practical manuals for care providers. Such an institute also might develop methods to desensitize the victims of terrorism, refine crisis intervention and aftercare strategies, and provide training to professionals in the field. In light of the worldwide incidence of hijackings, bombings, sieges, and other acts of terrorism, the study of victims has assumed special urgency in recent years.

NOTES

1. Behavior during the hostage experience, though less predictable than 'aftereffects, correlated with certain indicators (especially for the victims of the earlier sieges). For example, the more stress the hostages had experienced at the beginning and the end of the crisis, the more vigorously they internalized the event after their release. The same pattern characterized people who during captivity had put less confidence in the world outside and had been more active and more involved with fellow hostages. The less educated hostages and those who scored higher on self-sufficiency tended to engage in avoidance behavior.

REFERENCES

BANDLER, R. J., MADARAS, G. R., & BEM, D. J. Self-observation as a source of pain perception. *Journal of Personality and Social Psychology,* 1968, *9,* 205–209.

BASTIAANS, J. Psychosomatische Gevolgen van Onderdrukking en Verzet. Master's thesis, Noord-Hollandse Uitgevers Mij., 1957.

————. General comments on the role of aggression in human psychopathology. In J. Ruesch, A. H. Schmale, & T. Spoerri (eds.), *Psychotherapy and psychosomatics.* Basel: Karger, 1972.

————. Het KZ-syndroom en de menselijke Vrijheid. Ned. T. v. Geneeskunde, 1974, *118.*

————. The Optimal use of anxiety in the struggle for adaptation. In C. D. Spielberger & I. G. Sarason (eds.), *Stress and anxiety,* vol. 5. New York: Wiley, 1977.

————. Life against life: The psychosomatic consequences of man-made disasters. In C. D. Spielberger, I. G. Sarason, & P. B. Defares, *Stress and anxiety,* vol. 9. New York: Wiley, 1981.

BASTIAANS, J., JASPERS, J. P. C., VAN DER PLOEG, H. M., VAN DEN BERG-SCHAAP, T. E., & VAN DEN BERG, J. F. *Rapport Psychologisch Onderzoek naar de Gevolgen van Gijzelingen in Nederland, 1974–1977.* The Hague: Staatsuitgeverij, 's-Gravenhage, 1979.

BASTIAANS, J., MULDER, D., VAN DIJK, W. K., & VAN DER PLOEG, H. M. *Mensen bij Gijzelingen.* 1981.

BASTIAANS, J., & VAN DER PLOEG, H. M. Control and regulation of aggression. *Psychotherapy and Psychosomatics,* 1978, *29,* 40–48.

COELHO, G., HAMBURG, D. A., & ADAMS, J. E. *Coping and adaptation.* New York: Basic Books, 1974.

CRELINSTEN, R. D. *Dimensions of victimization in the context of terroristic acts.* Montreal: International Center for Comparative Criminology, 1977. (a)

————. *Research strategies for the study of international political terrorism.* Montreal: International Center for Comparative Criminology, 1977. (b)

CRELINSTEN, R. D., & LABERGE-ALTMEJD, D. *The impact of terrorism and skyjacking on the operations of the criminal justice system.* Montreal: International Center for Comparative Criminology, 1977.

DIMSDALE, J. E. The coping behavior of Nazi concentration camp survivors. *American Journal of Psychiatry,* 1974, *131,* 792–797.

————. Coping: Every man's war. *American Journal of Psychotherapy,* 1978, *32,* 402–413.

FIGLEY, C. R. Mobilization. Part I: The Iranian crisis. *Final Report of the Task Force on Families of Catastrophe.* West Lafayette: Purdue University, Family Research Institute, 1980.

GLASS, D., & SINGER, J. *Urban stress: Experiments in noise and social stressors.* New York: Academic, 1972.

HAMBURG, D., & ADAMS, J. A perspective on coping behavior. *Archives of General Psychiatry,* 1967, *17,* 277.

HOKANSON, J. E., DE GOOD, D. E., FORREST, M. S., & BRITTAIN, T. M. Availability of avoidance behaviors for modulating vascular-stress responses. *Journal of Personality and Social Psychology,* 1971, *19,* 60–68.

HOPPE, K. D. The Master-slave seesaw relationship in psychotherapy. *Reiss Davis Clinical Bulletin,* 1971, *8,* 117–125.

JASPERS, J. P. C. Gijzelingen in Nederland: Een Onderzoek naar de psychiatrische, psychologische en andragologische Aspecten. Thesis, Swets & Zeitlinger B.V., Lisse, 1980.

LAZARUS, R. L. *Psychological stress and the coping process.* New York: McGraw-Hill, 1966.

MEICHENBAUM, D., & CAMERON, R. Stress inoculation: A skills training approach to anxiety management. Manuscript, University of Waterloo, 1973.

SCHACHTER, S. *The psychology of affiliation.* Stanford: Stanford University Press, 1959.

SELIGMAN, M. E. P. *Helplessness: On depression, development, and death.* San Francisco: Freeman, 1975.

SELYE, H. *Stress.* Philadelphia: Lippincott, 1974.

40

War Related Stress in Israeli Children and Youth

Norman A. Milgram

HUMANKIND HAS HAD TO COPE with the threat of war, war itself, and the aftermath of war from earliest times; investigation of the psychological effects of war related stress on military and civilian populations is a much more recent phenomenon. There has been some research on specific topics in adults, such as posttraumatic war neurosis in soldiers and psychiatric syndromes in former prisoners of war and in survivors of concentration and death camps. However, there has been little programmatic research on other topics in adults and even less research on children and youth. The few exceptions are Freud and Burlingham's (1943) work on children evacuated from London in World War II and Fraser's (1973) book on children in Northern Ireland. These important sources contain astute observations and clinical intuitions but lack quantitative data and objective conclusions. Moreover, these works examine only a few aspects of war related stress.

Comprehensive research and treatment programs for children and adolescents should focus on their behavior in a wide variety of war related stress situations. Appropriate conditions would be characterized by war related threat or by actual damage to or destruction of one's person or property; (2) those of family and friends; (3) one's perception of the familiar, the predictable, and the controllable; and (4) one's feelings of physical and psychological invulnerability.

It is very difficult to do research on, and to provide mental health services to, children in situations of extreme deprivation and destruction, which entail famine, disease, wholesale loss of life, destruction of property, and the breakdown of family, social, and political institutions. The basic needs of human survival at these times have priority over psychological needs. Conditions of life in war torn countries make mental health concerns appear misplaced and even trivial. Moreover, many societies suffering the ravages of war lack the mental health scientists and practitioners to engage in research and treatment. It is far easier to deal with the more mild war related stress reactions of children in largely intact Western societies.

Israel (and before it Palestine) is a Western oriented society that has lived in a state of

I wish to thank Dr. Charles Noblin, head of the Department of Psychology at the Virginia Polytechnic Institute and State University, for gracious cooperation in the preparation of this chapter.

war for over 100 years ago. This country may be regarded as a natural laboratory for the study of war related stress reactions in children and youth. Many investigators have capitalized on this fact. The present chapter summarizes research on children and adolescents with reference to the following topics:

1. growing up in exposed border communities, including those settlements that are unique to Israel: the *kibbutz,* the *moshav,* and the development town
2. loss of the soldier in war as it affects family members
3. the role of social institutions, including schools, social agencies, and private organizations, vis-à-vis children and adolescents in crisis situations
4. personality and attitude change in urban children and adolescents

EFFECTS OF WAR RELATED STRESS ON CHILDREN AND ADOLESCENTS IN BORDER COMMUNITIES

The stress of intermittent shelling and of terrorist attacks on Israeli children and youth has been the subject of numerous investigations. Given the established relationship among uncertainty, uncontrollability, and anxiety level (Stokols, 1979) and given the constant threat of these stressors in Israeli life, one might well expect children and adolescents growing up in exposed border communities to be more anxious and disturbed than their peers growing up in nonexposed communities in the interior.

Before I summarize the studies that bear on this question, a word of explanation is necessary about the different communities to which these studies refer. At one extreme we find comparisons of young people growing up in exposed and nonexposed *kibbutzim. Kibbutzim* are socialist collectives characterized by a high degree of community organization and self-sufficiency, by communal rearing of children, and by a strong ideological commitment. *Kibbutz* members are primarily of Western background—speaking English or other European languages and generally are well educated. At the other extreme one finds the *development towns,* which are often located close to *kibbutzim* but are characterized by a lower level of community organization and a weaker ideological commitment. Development town people are of North African or Asian background and Arabic speaking and are not highly educated. These Israelis experience considerable cultural turmoil and change because of differences between their Eastern cultural background and that of the dominant European culture.

A type of community midway between the *kibbutz* and the development town is the *moshav,* an agricultural settlement based on cooperative private enterprise. Each family owns a home and land and rears its children at home but cooperates in many community enterprises associated with agriculture and marketing. Many *moshav* members are of Eastern background, but they are less susceptible to cultural conflict because they live in extended, farm based families in their own communities.

Kibbutz and Moshav

In a study of exposed and nonexposed *kibbutzim,* Ziv and Israeli (1973) compared manifest anxiety scores of 10-year-old children ($n = 103$) from seven *kibbutzim,* located along the Jordanian border, that were under almost constant shelling at the time of testing

(May 1969) and of children (n = 90) from seven *kibbutzim* that were never under fire. Anxiety scores of both boys and girls were uniformly low in the entire sample.

The investigators offered several explanations for the absence of higher anxiety levels in the exposed group. First, according to Helson's (1964) theory of adaptation level, the shelling situation becomes, over time, part of the children's way of life. They learn to deal with this stress situation in a matter-of-fact, constructive way. The *kibbutzim,* for example, regularly conduct air raid drills; the children sleep in attractively decorated shelters even during periods of calm. Second, the *kibbutzim* routinely provide strong social support in all stressful situations through the presence of adults well known to the children. These include the *metaplot* (women who care for preschool children), the teachers and counselors of school children, and all other adult members of the *kibbutz.* All are known to the children in their formal and informal roles in this close-knit and ideologically committed group. These adults have themselves adapted successfully; they serve as good role models and also reinforce with praise and affection the responsible, mature, and independent behavior of the children. Finally, children typically develop a stronger need for affiliation with peers and adults in stressful situations (Schachter, 1959). This need is recognized by the *kibbutz* community and is amply met by the physical plant and the psychosocial rituals of *kibbutz* living: common dining and recreation halls, tightly clustured living quarters, and a familiarity based on years of living together.

To some extent, these conditions prevail in the *moshav,* and Milgram and Miller (1973) found no difference in manifest anxiety between 11-year-old children living in exposed *moshavim* along the Jordanian border and those living in *moshavim* in the middle of the country (50 children were studied in each setting). In fact, they reported a higher degree of personal autonomy in the exposed group: the children were more confident in their ability to overcome obstacles, to function independently of their parents, and to handle potentially frightening situations on their own. These findings suggest that in the life threatening war environment of the *moshav,* children are expected to exercise independence and to assume responsibility for themselves and are rewarded for doing so, just as on the *kibbutz.*

When comparisons are made, however, of an exposed *moshav* and an exposed *kibbutz,* the more cohesive structure of the *kibbutz* is an asset. Zuckerman-Bareli (1982) interviewed 100 *kibbutz* and 100 *moshav* members randomly selected from the 740 adult members of six settlements: three *kibbutzim* and three *moshavim* near the Lebanese border in the north of Israel. These settlements differed in the intensity and frequency of border incidents and their consequences. Interviews dealt with the persistence of adult fears and insomnia, with the curtailment of adult recreational activities outside the home in the evening, and with the restriction of children's play outside the home during the day in the period following a terrorist attack. These emotional and social variables may be regarded as indexes of residual anxiety and apprehension in the parents and, by inference, in their children.

Zuckerman-Bareli (1982) found that *moshav* members reported a higher frequency of these symptoms than did *kibbutz* members. Moreover, their emotional stress reactions were high, regardless of the severity of the incident that had affected their settlement. By contrast, the stress reactions of *kibbutz* members were commensurate with the severity of the incident. A detailed path analysis confirmed that certain stress resistant factors reduced the frequency of the anxiety indicators: Western background and education, *kibbutz* communal life, and associated socialist ideology. These factors contributed to higher overall satisfaction and stronger identification with the community and thereby to less personal anxiety and less behavior disturbance.

Development Town

Ayalon (1978) extended this generalization to the development town. Her descriptive study of 10 settlements that were infiltrated by terrorists during the period 1974–1975 included *kibbutzim, moshavim,* and development towns. These episodes were far more stressful than those described in the studies cited earlier. Obviously, the threat to one's person and to one's subsequent sense of security is greater when armed terrorists fire at close range on men, women, and children than when an occasional rocket or shell is fired from a distance in the direction of a settlement (Zuckerman-Bareli, 1979).

Ayalon (1978) reported that the community's reaction during and after these attacks reflected the degree of community cohesiveness. This variable was defined by the investigator in terms of the nature of communal life, quality of leadership, communication among community members, and extent of shared values. By this definition, the *kibbutz* was the most cohesive, the *moshav* second, and the development town least of all. Degree of cohesiveness was directly associated with other stress resistant factors such as the degree of foresight in regard to, and the preparation for coping with, stressful war events. The highly cohesive *kibbutz* quickly and quietly resumed daily routines shortly after an incursion in which some of its members had been injured and others killed; by contrast, community life in a development town remained extremely disorganized long after a terrorist incursion in which visiting teenagers *from another town* had been injured or killed.

The implication of these studies is that children's reactions to war stress are strongly influenced by the social cohesiveness of the community in which they live. Cohesive communities provide ground rules for acceptable behavior during crisis situations, support individuals and families in dire circumstances, and provide activities to adults and children during periods of relative calm and crisis that are constructive in their own right but also reduce anxiety and apprehension in the community.

When one compares exposed and nonexposed development towns with reference to intermittent shelling—the more mild form of terrorist activity—a similar picture emerges. Ziv, Kruglanski, and Shulman (1974) administered a series of tests to 521 children (grades four to eight) from two exposed development towns (Kiryat Shmona in the north and Bet Shaan on the Jordanian border) and to 297 children from two nonexposed development towns in the lower Galilee (Upper Nazareth and Migdal Ha'Emek). Since the exposed communities had enjoyed relative calm for 18 months at the time of testing, it was decided to measure reactions and attitudes that might reflect the earlier stress period. Accordingly, children were questioned about their identification with their town and community, their attitude toward the war and the Arabs, the kinds of dreams they liked to dream, and the Rosenzweig Picture Frustration Test.

Overall, prior exposure to war stress either did not have an adverse effect or actually had a salutary effect. For example, there was a stronger identification with community: exposed children wanted to remain in their own towns rather than move away and regarded town residents as more helpful and nicer than people elsewhere; even their dreams referred to improving the living conditions of their town. Admittedly, more exposed children preferred to dream about victory in war and the cessation of bombing, but less than 6% of all respondents cited these kinds of dream content. The desire for peace was cited by the highest percentage of children overall (44.1), with no significant difference between exposed and unexposed children. Interestingly, the degree of overt aggressiveness expressed toward the Arabs as enemies was as low in the exposed as in the nonexposed children probably because of the strong social sanction in Israeli society against hatred of the Arabs as a group. Finally, there were no differences on a Thurstone type scale of attitudes toward the war and the Arabs, with the overall mean in the direction of seeking peace and accommodation.

Children in this study were also asked to indicate whether they chose a classmate as a close friend because he was a good student, a helpful person, a good athlete, or a courageous person (Ziv, Kruglanski, & Shulman, 1974). The majority of children responded to the four characteristics in descending order: 40.9, 35.9, 15.8, and 7.4%, respectively. Those citing courage tended to be from the exposed rather than from the nonexposed towns. This finding suggests a constructive mechanism for coping with war related stress—having a friend whose courageous behavior would be reassuring and protective in crises—but one that characterized only a small minority of children.

The final result was a greater frequency of extrapunitive responses to pictures of frustrating situations and a correspondingly lower frequency of nonpunitive responses in exposed than in nonexposed children. In the context of strictures against openly expressing hostile feelings about Arabs, such feelings may have found expression in politically neutral projective cartoons. Possibly, the extrapunitive responses represented socially sanctioned aggression against the civilian and military authorities for failing to end the conflict. Whatever the explanation, the absolute magnitude of the difference was not great and the findings did not indicate a pathological trend (Ziv, Kruglanski, & Shulman, 1974).

Although self-report anxiety scales and attitude surveys do not reflect greater disturbance in exposed development town children, one might still argue that there is psychological disturbance beneath the surface that can be revealed by more subtle techniques. Rofé and Lewin examined the effects of intermittent shelling and occasional terrorist incursions on dreams and sleep (1982) and on daydreaming (1980) in 486 adolescents (aged 14–17) living in two development towns, Kiryat Smona in the north and Bet Shemesh in the center of the country. Nearly all were of North African or Asian background and were of working-class families with little education.

A long history of intermittent war threats in the former town might lead one to expect a greater frequency of nightmares, other unpleasant dream topics, and sleep disturbances and a greater desire to take revenge on the enemy. This hypothesis is consistent with the Freudian theory of catharsis, whereby the individual strives to reduce anxiety by symbolic representation of fears and wishes. Rofé and Lewin (1982) argued, however, that children and adolescents living in stressful environments from which they cannot escape attempt to reduce anxiety by shutting out war related material from conscious awareness; i.e., by adopting a repressive rather than a sensitive cognitive defense style (Byrne, 1964). Given some degree of communal support and adult reassurance, they will succeed in this defensive maneuver so that life becomes more tolerable and anxiety-free.

Impressive evidence was found for the latter hypothesis: shelled adolescents reported fewer horror filled and aggressive dreams than did nonexposed adolescents during periods of calm. All reported a higher frequency of such dreams during wartime, but here again the exposed adolescents reported relatively fewer aggressive dreams than did the controls. With respect to sleep disturbances, the exposed subjects went to bed earlier, fell asleep sooner, and slept longer. They were also more compromising in their political and military attitudes toward the Arabs, so that the possibility of an end to the state of war appeared greater.

Similar findings were obtained in a second study of these adolescents with reference to daydreaming (Rofé & Lewin, 1980). Exposed adolescents had fewer daydreams about the tragic consequences of war, fewer aggressive daydreams about the enemy, and in general fewer unpleasant daydreams of any sort. Only in daydreams about the destruction of the state of Israel were there no differences between groups, since daydreams about this eventuality were unacceptable to all Israelis regardless of locale or personality style.

Overall, more adolescents were at the repressor end of Byrne's (1964) scale in the exposed as compared to the nonexposed town, but the earlier conclusions still obtained when findings were statistically adjusted for personality style. One may conclude that even for sensitizers growing up in a war environment leads to the development of repression as a personality style and as a mechanism for dealing with stress. This consequence need not be viewed with dismay, since Rofé and Lewin (1982) also showed that adolescent repressors were regarded as better adjusted socially by both peers and teachers and better adjusted academically by their teachers than were sensitizers.

A Discordant Note

The possibility exists, however, of the return of the repressed in exposed children and adolescents. That is, repression may not be complete. Some symptomatic expression of underlying anxiety may occur on the physiological level and a greater magnitude of affective arousal may occur in response to cues reminiscent of life threatening experiences. One study bears on this question.

Kristal (1978) investigated the hypothesis of a latent traumatic neurotic response (Janis, 1971) in 66 exposed *moshav* children aged 10-12 living in the Jordan valley and in 71 peers living in nonexposed settlements. The former group had been shelled continuously during 1968-1971 but had enjoyed calm for the 2 years preceding Kristal's research. He found that the shelled children had a higher frequency of *bruxism* (teeth grinding), a psychosomatic condition associated with psychological tension. Second, shelled children reported higher anxiety than did their nonshelled peers after watching a stressful film simulating a terrorist attack on a settlement; the two groups did not differ, however, in manifest anxiety levels reported in a neutral situation.

Taking these findings at face value, one may conclude that previously exposed children may be paying a price physiologically for the earlier stressful period that they weathered without obvious symptom formation. Given the problematic nature of bruxism as a diagnosable condition, the numerous extraneous factors that may account for bruxism differences in children living in geographically separated intact communities, and the absence of a significant correlation between bruxism and anxiety arousal level in the Kristal (1978) study, it is imperative that this finding be replicated. Moreover, one cannot conclude from the emotional reaction to the film that the exposed children suffered incapacitating anxiety in that situation or would suffer incapacitating anxiety in a real-life terrorist attack on their community. The finding does suggest, however, sensitization—rather than desensitization—in the exposed group to more stressful experiences (e.g., a terrorist attack on their homes) than the shelling experience that had been their lot earlier.

Coping in the Kibbutz

One should not assume from the foregoing summary that the *kibbutz* maintains a relatively low level of anxiety and of emotional disturbance in its youngsters during and after a war crisis by complacent reliance on the properties of the social milieu. On the contrary, *kibbutz* members continually assess the reactions of their children to war related stress and the success or failure of their efforts in working with their children. When difficult situations arise, they frequently turn to consultants outside the *kibbutz* but usually associated with the *kibbutz* movement.

Thus, for example, a staff member of the Oranim Child Guidance Center was called in during a period of heavy shelling of a particular *kibbutz* on the Lebanese border in 1970 (Pergamenter, 1981). The preschool children had become visibly distressed and their *metaplot* were uncertain as to how to handle the situation. The consultant held group discussions with these women and quickly identified the problem: the underlying anxiety of some *metaplot* and their reluctance to acknowledge it to themselves, much less to their preschool charges. Once they were able to acknowledge their concerns for their husbands and their own children, they could begin to draw upon the resources of the *kibbutz* to bolster their flagging confidence. Thereafter, they could develop teaching and training strategies to enhance the sense of security of the children under their care. They set up telephone communication between their charges and their mothers and also communicated with their own children elsewhere on the *kibbutz*. They encouraged the children to decorate the shelters in which they had to sleep. They permitted expression of apprehension through class discussions and through drawings. In sum, group work with the outside consultant enabled the child care workers to cope more effectively with their own fears and to help their preschool charges cope more effectively with theirs.

Because of activities of this sort, the psychiatric director of the Kibbutz Child and Family Clinic in Tel Aviv—the agency responsible for providing mental health consultation and treatment to the members of some 150 *kibbutzim* nationwide—was able to assert that the incidence of psychological disturbance was no higher in the two years that followed the Yom Kippur War (1973) than it had been in the two years of relative calm that had preceded it (Kaffman, 1977). During the war itself the incidence of psychological disturbance decreased for many adolescent patients in treatment, who were now given greater responsibility on the *kibbutz* than in peacetime and who behaved in an exemplary fashion. After the war, however, according to Kaffman (1977), there was a recurrence of symptoms as life returned to normal.

THE EFFECT OF THE LOSS OF THE SOLDIER IN WARTIME ON FAMILY MEMBERS

The death of a loved one is invariably a painful experience for the survivors. How painful and for how long depends on the age of the deceased person, the circumstances of the death, the relationship of the deceased to the bereaved parties, and their particular vulnerabilities.

In Israel the tragedy of men, generally young or middle-aged, dying in war is somewhat mitigated by a national consensus that their deaths have not been in vain because they died in defense of their families, their people, and their state. Nevertheless, loss of loved ones in combat is a major cause of adult concern for children, possibly the most disturbing consequence of war for Israeli children.

Even the cohesive *kibbutz* provides no protection against the deleterious effects of losing one's father in war. According to Kaffman (1977), approximately one-half of *kibbutz* children between the ages of 2 and 10 who had lost their fathers displayed excessive and persistent mourning reactions and the majority of these children were referred for counseling or psychotherapy in the year that followed the Yom Kippur War. One may presume that children from the *moshavim,* the development towns, and the larger cities were no less disturbed by the loss of their fathers in war and required equally extensive mental health services. In fact, data from Lifschitz's (1975, 1978) studies, discussed subsequently, indicate that fatherless children from these settings were more adversely affected than fatherless *kibbutz* children.

Widows and Orphaned Children

The first line of treatment for war orphaned children has been to provide individual and group services to their mothers, the war widows. It is widely assumed that if the bereaved widow is helped to rebuild her life, she can help her children in rebuilding theirs. This assumption is all the more important because the vast majority of 1967 war widows have not remarried and the same situation is likely to prevail for the 1973 widows. In these one-parent homes, the personal-social development of the children is heavily dependent on the adjustment and functioning of the mother.

Self-help groups for war widows were established immediately following the Six-Day War (1967). On the basis of experience with these groups, it was possible rapidly to form many more such groups after the Yom Kippur War (1973). This work has been described by members of the Alfred Adler Institute of Tel Aviv (Bawly, 1982; Eloul, 1982; Katz, 1982; Kirschner, 1982), a private mental health training and service agency that assumed much of the responsibility for initiating and directing these groups in the metropolitan center of the country after 1973. Recent widows were contacted by widows of the 1967 war who had themselves participated in groups. The new groups met in the homes of the widows themselves. The primary emphasis was to share feelings, concerns, and plans related not only to the past and the present but also to the future. Members kept in constant contact with one another during the week and gave practical advice and help to one another in meeting their homemaking and childrearing commitments, as well as in preparing for their future roles as independent heads of their families.

Eloul (1982) reported that for some newly orphaned children the loss of parental presence and support was total, at least for a time. Not only was the father gone, but some mothers were so overwhelmed by grief that they ceased to function as parents. In other cases, paternal grandparents reacted to their son's death by rejecting his widow and contact with them was broken off.

A recurring problem in early group meetings was how and when to tell the children, especially preschoolers. It became clear that mothers who were evasive or who lied altogether only confused and upset their children. One four-year-old child was told that his father was in heaven. He subsequently became anxious whenever he heard an airplane overhead because he feared (it was learned subsequently) that the airplane might run his father over. He also got upset whenever it rained because the rain would make his father cold and wet. Another child of three years was told that his father had fallen. The word "fall" in Hebrew clearly implies death, but this child became disturbed whenever he went up or down stairs, fearing, as he later explained, that if he were to fall on the stairs something terrible would happen to him as it had to his father, who had fallen.

Numerous clinical case studies indicate that the grief reaction of the child or the adolescent is strongly influenced by that of the significant adults in his or her life (Aleksandrowicz, 1982; Wieder, 1975). In one case, a 12-year-old girl attempted to commit suicide out of desperation and anger because her mother was in interminable grief over the death of the oldest son in the family (Aleksandrowicz, 1982). The mother stopped living when the son died and resented any efforts by other family members to find enjoyment in life. She lavished affection on the memory of the son and neglected her living children and husband. The daughter's suicidal attempt altered this neurotic equilibrium and after a series of sessions with family members separately and together, the therapist reported that the family was beginning to work through the loss of the son.

A behaviorist orientation to the effect of adult behavior on the mourning behavior of fatherless children was formulated by Ashkenazi (1982). A practicing psychiatrist at the Children's Development Center at Beer Sheva, she found that children were being reinforced for immature and undesirable behaviors following the death of their fathers in the Yom Kippur War. She prepared a memorandum of behavioral do's and dont's for the use by family members and teachers. Constructive and positive child behaviors were to be reinforced, while regressive and other undesirable behaviors were to be extinguished by studied indifference and other techniques. Adults were to be made aware that their own behavior provided a model for that of their children. A follow-up of 18 mothers who had approached the center for advice showed that they were managing well and did not require further help in this regard. In fact, some of the children now had fewer behavior problems than they had manifested before the father's death.

In some cases mourning may be insufficient. If a soldier is reported as missing in action (MIA), the family cannot declare him dead and begin mourning; the uncertainty of this situation may be overpowering (Teichman, Spiegel, & Teichman, 1978). Some wives collapse under this burden and cease functioning, while their children assume responsibility for the household. Drawing on her clinical experience with relatives of MIA soldiers and other grieving families in the Yom Kippur War, Wieder (1975) recommended active intervention with families considered at high risk for maladaptive adjustment on the basis of initial screening contacts.

Amir and Sharon (1982) conducted a major research study of 1967 and 1973 war widows and identified a constellation of characteristics associated with high-risk widows and by inference with high-risk fatherless children. These included a lower-class, traditional family background, migration to Israel from North Africa or Asia, and poor education. Women who met this description often received a great deal of family support during the early stages of widowhood—perhaps too much support—but were prevented afterward from building a new life for themselves and their children because of strong normative traditions requiring them to remain at home and to conduct themselves in circumscribed ways. Western women, by contrast, had a more difficult time initially (Palgi, 1973) but subsequently acquired new skills, assumed responsibilities formerly handled by their husbands, and achieved a greater degree of self-actualization and greater satisfaction in their lives. In moving from wife to widow to woman, the low-risk widows were able to provide a better model for and a happier home to their children (N. Golan, 1975).

Bereaved Parents and Siblings

Not all cases of interminable mourning can be resolved. In the final analysis, according to Aleksandrowicz (1982), the outcome depends more on the nature and strength of the pre-existing love relationships between the mourner and other surviving family members than on the skill of the therapist. In some cases one can only help the family resign itself to the loss of two members, one physically lost and the other emotionally lost to the family. This tends to be the case more often with the family of origin than with the family of procreation.

The death of a son is trauma from which many parents never recover emotionally.

Some have argued that older people lack the emotional flexibility and resources that are available to the young (the siblings, widow, and children of the deceased). A more compelling reason is that the death of a child before that of his or her parents is a violation of the natural order, the way the world is supposed to run. Some people cannot tolerate this blow to their belief in a just world (Lerner & Miller, 1978).

Gay (1982) reported a high percentage of physical and psychological disturbances in 74 parents (mostly couples) three years after the loss of a son. The superficial functioning of these people at work or at home was adequate, but the psychic pain was palpable when tapped. For example, many had drastically curtailed their social activities. For every bereaved parent asserting that the loss had made him or her stronger or brought the parents closer together, many more asserted the opposite. Moreover, despite the obvious need of many parents for help, efforts at setting up self-help groups of bereaved parents have not been highly successful (Gay, 1982; Granot, 1975). Gay (1982) recommended that in the future such groups include parents who have suffered the loss of a son in a previous military conflict and have coped with this tragedy.

The adjustment problems of bereaved parents are relevant to this discussion because their behavior strongly affects the grief reactions and subsequent adjustment of the surviving siblings. Granot (1975) and Aleksandrowicz (1982) cited the neglect experienced by siblings, the unfavorable way they may be compared to the idealized deceased son, and the ambivalent feelings toward the deceased with which they must cope (usually by themselves). Helping the bereaved parents to rebuild their own lives contributes greatly to the healthy development of the surviving sibling(s) within the family.

The coping of parents with the loss of a son becomes especially important in the context of treatment approaches directed toward adolescent siblings. There is on record one study of group work with bereaved adolescents following the Yom Kippur War (Morawetz, 1982). Five sessions were conducted with 11 adolescents (aged 13–17) whose brothers had died several months earlier. These sessions had two major themes. The first was the search for existential meaning in the brother's death and for delineating the consequences of this meaning in the survivor's future life. Religious beliefs, Zionist ideology, pacifism, humanism, hedonism—all these issues were raised, reformulated, reaffirmed, and attacked in the course of the group sessions. The second theme was the change in the family structure brought about by the brother's death. Many group members felt that they were now closer to their parents; they also felt a sense of responsibility to help their parents with the suffering that they were undergoing. While group members considered the sessions worthwhile, they were not eager to prolong them. When the five-session contract was completed, only a few reappeared for a follow-up session a few months later. They were not interested in understanding their motivations or the consequences of their behavior. They were too close in time to the traumatic event to acknowledge their personal problems in coping with it. They wished to focus on the present and plan for the future and to forget about the pains of the past. If the reactions of this group are at all representative of the larger population of adolescent siblings of deceased soldiers, then group psychotherapy is at best a short-term instrument for ventilation. In these circumstances, the family assumes special importance.

Research on Fatherless Children

The consequences of losing a father in war on young children were examined in a series of research studies. Smilansky (1982) identified 203 fatherless elementary school children in

32 schools (not all fathers had died in war) and compared them with same-sex classmates on a number of measures of academic, intellectual, and social-emotional adjustment. She found a six-point decrement on a group intelligence test; a decrement in verbal achievement in the classroom, primarily for fatherless girls; a greater decrement in verbal achievement in the younger children (grades one to three) even when years of bereavement were held constant; poorer emotional adjustment as judged by teachers' ratings of the children (fatherless children had lower self-esteem, were more shy and quiet, gave up more easily, and tended toward depression and mood swings); and more frequent rejection in sociometric choices made by their classmates.

A number of explanations may be offered for these findings. With the death of the father there may be a decline in attention and concentration, inefficient encoding and retrieval of information, etc., because of either preoccupation with the father's death or depressed mood. These reactions may be more impressive in the lower academic grades, when formal skills are first being acquired, than later on. Second, girls may grieve more than boys either because social conventions permit or even require them to do so or because they identify more with their grieving mothers. Girls are also more likely to be called upon by the grieving mother to help with household chores or the care of younger children. In families of Middle Eastern origin—60% of Smilansky's (1982) sample—the commitment of the girl to the home is considered stronger than her commitment to school. Third, although one might imagine that fatherless children would be regarded with special sympathy and friendship by their peers and receive high acceptance and low rejection scores in sociometric choice situations, the reverse was found. Possibly these children did behave differently—as the teachers' behavior ratings would appear to indicate—and their less attractive behavior may have adversely affected their sociometric status in the eyes of their classmates. Another possibility not to be casually dismissed is that children from intact families are reluctant to identify with fatherless classmates for fear of becoming like them.

While Smilansky's (1982) study included children whose fathers had died in peacetime as well as in wartime, Lifschitz (1974, 1975, 1976, 1978; Lifschitz, Berman, Galili & Gilad, 1977) did a number of studies restricted to the loss of the father in war. Lifschitz, Berman, Galili & Gilad (1977) assessed the short-term effect of the loss of father in the Yom Kippur War on 48 middle-class children aged 5–15. Three to six months after the loss, boys were found to be more problematic than girls in the judgment of their mother, teacher, and an independent classroom observer—especially boys from the *moshav* or the city. *Kibbutz* boys and girls were least affected. Lifschitz found that the more affectionate the mother's approach to the child and the more similar he was considered to be to one of the two parents (but especially the idealized father) as judged by the mother, the more adjusted he appeared to be.

Lifschitz (1975) also reported on a treatment program. She personally recommended a series of interventions to mothers and teachers that were designed to provide the child with an affectionate and supporting environment, with opportunities for new, diverse activities, and with opportunities for meeting new people, especially older children or adults who might serve as a "big brother." Mothers were advised to find new interests for themselves both in and outside the home. Teachers were counseled to reinforce the child's strengths and to direct his or her negative or destructive tendencies into constructive channels. A six-month follow-up showed an improvement in behavior for those children who had been free of behavior disturbance prior to the father's death.

In a second study with preadolescent orphans, Lifschitz (1974) found that the boys who functioned the best following the death of their fathers were those who continued to see themselves as similar to their fathers and who also were perceived as similar to their fathers by their mothers. The fathers were regarded as desirable figures by the mothers either because they tended to idealize the dead or because they had married these men for their desirable characteristics. In any event, the perceived similarity of son to father by the son and his mother augurs well for the external support of the boy by his mother and for stability of positive identification in the boy himself.

Lifschitz (1975) also studied fatherless children 3–6 years after the father's death. She compared each of 34 middle-class, urban children aged 9–14 with 3 two-parented controls from the same classroom matched on relevant variables—102 control children in all. No differences were found in perceptual organization of unstructured visual stimuli, assessed by the Rorschach or in perceptual differentiation of meaningful social milieus, evaluated with the Bieri Cognitive Complexity Test. However, there was a difference between fatherless and control children in the direction of the relationship between perceptual organization and perceptual differentiation on the measures used. For the fatherless children, those who perceived themselves as similar to their mothers organized Rorschach stimuli better than did children who perceived themselves as different from their mothers. For the children from intact families, the reverse was true: the children who best organized the Rorschach stimuli were those who differentiated themselves most from their mothers.

The findings from Lifschitz's (1974, 1975) studies suggest that children growing up in intact families achieve greater perceptual organization by asserting independence from their parents. By contrast, children who have lost their fathers emphasize whatever identifications are available—the mother as physically present and the father as present in memory—to develop their capacities (Lifschitz, 1976).

In her most recent study of fatherless children, Lifschitz (1978) reported on the adjustment of children whose fathers had died in the Six-Day War and in the Yom Kippur War. Preschool orphans were found to lack self-direction and were less creative and more destructive than only-child controls from intact families. For older children (aged 5–8), few differences were noted except that girls assumed greater personal responsibility for successful events in their lives (internal locus of control) and gave other evidence of positive compensatory mechanisms. In the 8–14 age range, the recently bereaved were more cognitively constricted than the children bereaved 8 years earlier. Finally, being associated with a supportive social framework (e.g., *kibbutz,* religious group, extended family) was related to better adjustment.

Halpern (1982) found that fatherless children brought together for recreational activities by the former comrades-in-arms of their fathers enjoyed the opportunity to be with other orphaned children. As indicated by their responses to an open-ended interview, these 42 children, aged 6–12, perceived themselves to be in a self-help group. However, they, unlike adults in similar settings, did not discuss the basis for the group's composition with one another but dealt in indirect ways with the issue of having lost their fathers.

The observation that children are reluctant to cope directly (especially verbally) with the loss of a father has been made by a number of investigators (Eloul, 1982; S. Golan, 1975; Teichman, Spiegel, & Teichman, 1978). Often, such behavior is misinterpreted by adults as evidence of emotional shallowness or selfishness. It is reassuring to parents to be told during the early stages of mourning that there are enormous individual differences in children's behavior in response to the death of a loved one and to be admonished to release children from the burden of adult expectations, perceptions, and interpretations.

THE ROLE OF PUBLIC AND PRIVATE INSTITUTIONS
IN PROVIDING INTERVENTION
FOR CHILDREN IN ISRAEL

In a protracted crisis such as war, it is considered imperative by Israelis that the education of the young continue and that children occupy themselves with familiar educational and recreational routines. This rule rests on the assumption that children—like adults—tolerate crisis situations best when there is minimal dislocation from familiar surroundings, peers, authority figures, and the customary routines of daily living. Moreover, when children are occupied constructively and are cared for efficiently, their mothers and older siblings are free to assist the war effort as civilian volunteers and to maintain the home and the community while the majority of adult males are at the front.

The school system is regarded not only as a peacetime institution that should continue to function during war but also as a wartime provider of mental health services to the children themselves and through them to their families. A number of psychologists have developed guidelines for the effective and comprehensive functioning of the schools during wars or local crises. Benyamini (1976) prepared detailed guidelines for the graduated deployment of mental health personnel in the school system. He described three levels of intervention—the individual, the group, and the institution. Mild problems—disorientation, confusion, low morale, difficulties in concentration—are best handled at the institutional level by consulting with the principal and the teaching staff. Problems of moderate severity—fear, panic, hyperactivity, difficulty in following through with familiar routines—are best hand-led at the group level by conducting orientation and discussion sessions with teachers and with children. Severe problems—incapacitation, intense fear, depression, and apathy—are best handled at the level of the individual teacher or child, with a spectrum of psychiatric or psychological treatments for acute psychopathological reactions.

Benyamini (1976) cautioned mental health workers against investing their energies in the individual at the expense of the group and the institution. Individual professional treatment may be the preferred mode of intervention for mental health workers whose anxiety is reduced by their doing in wartime what they do best during peacetime. Benyamini and especially Caplan (1974) asserted, however, that the conventional mental health practices of peacetime are generally wasteful, ineffective, and even damaging in wartime. In some crisis situations, the very presence of mental health workers in their professional roles is disconcerting, if not demoralizing, to school children, their teachers, and their families. Benyamini urged workers carefully to diagnose the needs of the system, the level of intervention, and the severity of emerging problems and judiciously and cautiously to work with the appropriate target population.

In the context of crisis situations, one concern about conducting business as usual inevitably arises. If it is important to maintain peacetime routines, is it also wise to introduce crisis related material either into the formal curriculum or into informal classroom discussions and activities? Many parents and educators prefer to ignore war events for fear of upsetting children. Others argue, however, that avoidance of stressful issues is probably more upsetting to children because they are exposed to adults—their mothers, older siblings, teachers, commentators on radio and television—who are themselves disturbed and probably are conveying their anxieties without conscious intention. In these situations, adults have an advantage over children: they have been exposed to clarifications and reassurances and have been able to engage in cognitive appraisals of the war related stressors that serve to reduce anxiety. By remaining silent about war related stressors, adults do not protect children; they merely deny them the means to cope, namely, informed cognitive appraisal, shared ventilation of concern, and cognitive and emotional reassurances about eventual outcomes (Baider & Rosenfeld, 1974; S. Golan, 1975; Koubovi, 1982; Pergamenter, 1982).

Koubovi (1982) recommended that *therapeutic teaching,* a technique developed for teaching mental hygiene in peacetime, be applied to wartime situations. Her method involves selecting literary texts that contain war related topics and conducting classroom discussions around these topics. Such an approach steers a middle course between uncontrolled, unstructured ventilation of feelings (which can be disturbing to children) and defensive avoidance of unpleasant current events (which can be disturbing in a different manner). The proposed method provides a formal context and pretext for directing children's cognitive and affective reactions to real-life material and for controlled ventilation of feelings. Koubovi argued that her method promotes intellectualization and the achieving of distance from upsetting issues in a supportive group setting.

Another medium that lends itself to therapeutic instruction is art. Schwarcz (1982) described the art productions of kindergarten and elementary school children in a *kibbutz* struck by Syrian rockets during the Yom Kippur War. He asserted that drawings permit both controlled expression of inner concerns and a sharing of these concerns with other children, who can view and comment on all the drawings. Schwarcz concluded that an art program that explicitly encourages children to draw specific war related themes is beneficial for several reasons. First, the fact that their teachers openly request artistic and verbal expressions of the children's apprehensions and comprehensions about war is reassuring to children. Since it is commonly held that people tend to deny or suppress topics that they fear they cannot handle, the raising of these topics in the classroom by teachers is a clear statement to the children that responsible adults are not afraid to approach these topics and are confident that the children can also cope with them. Second, an art program not only permits expression of inner turmoil but also encourages children to mobilize inner resources to gain self-control over the inner turmoil. Third, the public display of art productions and the discussions that accompany these exhibits serve to identify the children who need help in coping, as well as the children who can provide such help to peers.

Art was also one component of the approach used by the outside consultant with the distraught *metaplot* in a report cited earlier (Pergamenter, 1982). Children's drawings were obtained both prior to and during group work sessions with the *kibbutz* child care personnel. There was a striking similarity between what went on in the group discussions and what appeared in the children's drawings. As the sessions began, the *metaplot* were reluctant to deal with their own fears and anxieties about terrorist attack, so that the children had to deal with their own feelings unaided. The result—drawings of vulnerable shelters under attack. As group work proceeded, the shelters were seen as protective and impregnable, as permitting children to visit parents through passageways. By the end of the sessions, the shelters had become a safe haven for as long as necessary. Apparently, children's perception of a stressful reality mirrors that of the significant adults in their environment; both children and adults cope better with stressful situations if they identify the source of the stressful threat, if they engage in or witness activities undertaken to answer the threat to their security, and if they engage in palliative activities that enhance emotional control (Lazarus, 1966).

Klingman (1978) recently developed an anticipatory guidance system for implementation in schools in advance of natural or man-made disasters. He based this approach on work by Caplan (1964) and Glass (1959). Klingman's method uses specially designed classroom study units by teachers, along with simulation and simulation games for the teaching staff, conducted by mental health professionals. The classroom units include descriptions of common behavioral reactions of children under stress, some elementary psychological first-aid instructions, stories and poems to stimulate discussion of the children's personal experiences, ideas for dramatic play and for small-group discussion, etc. A parental guidance program was also instituted on an experimental basis in several schools. The program was designed to help parents better understand their children's stress reactions in a variety of situations, including but not restricted to war or terrorist attack.

Several years later, this approach was applied in the schools of Naharia immediately following a terrorist incursion from the sea in which four townspeople died (Klingman, 1980). The local school psychological service organized consultation and treatment teams to work with teachers, children, and parents. The psychological service identified 60 elementary school children with continuing pathological symptoms and provided them with a graduated program of small-group counseling (6–8 children per group). In the course of these sessions the children were encouraged to ventilate freely, to relive suppressed events, to express angry feelings through art and written forms against the terrorists for attacking them and against the authorities for not protecting them, to learn relaxation techniques, actively to reconstruct their own role during the attack, to revisit the scene of the attack, and to return to normal living (their own room and bed, etc.)—in this order. Guidance was also provided to their parents.

PRIVATE ORGANIZATIONS WITH NEW ROLES IN CRISIS SITUATIONS

Some crises affect people as workers. In such situations, the factory or the company may be the best institution to provide a variety of mental health and other services to the injured parties. One striking example was the mobilization of the Egged Bus Cooperative (a worker owned public transportation company) following the terrorist seizure of an Egged bus carrying members of the cooperative and their families on a Saturday outing. Zafrir (1982), chief psychologist of the cooperative, helped organize and then documented the numerous volunteer services provided by cooperative members and their families to the stricken families. For example, a bus cooperative official visited a hospitalized child who was hoarding food on the ward. With her father dead, the child feared that the family would not have enough to eat. The official explained that the cooperative would assume responsibility for the financial security of the family. Children returning home without parents were greeted by the extended company family and provided with the services necessary to begin the long process of rehabilitation and adjustment to a new reality. Such volunteer emergency services were possible because of the loyalty and affection shared by the cooperative members.

Volunteering in war related crises was not unique to special groups caring for their own. Volunteering was a widespread phenomenon during the Yom Kippur War. The duration of this war and the number of casualties made the mobilization of volunteers necessary. For example, most male adolescents in Israel were involved in volunteer activities. Chen, Shapira, Regev, and Fresko (1982) administered questionnaires to 1230 male high school students and reported that over 90% had contributed actively to the war effort in hospitals, factories, public services, and other forums. The majority sought volunteering opportunities together with their friends and in most cases were able to provide service in their company. The volunteer activities were beneficial both to the recipients of the help and to the helpers themselves, who reported a sense of satisfaction from their contribution. (Volunteering encompassed professionals as well as nonprofessionals. Mental health workers were mobilized on a volunteer basis to provide a variety of consultation and treatment services.)

WAR RELATED STRESS AND PERSONALITY AND ATTITUDE CHANGE IN URBAN CHILDREN AND ADOLESCENTS

The final section of this chapter summarizes studies that looked at changes in personality and attitudes in urban children and adolescents exposed to war stress. Zak (1982) administered the Cattell 16PF to 474 male high school seniors prior to the Yom Kippur War and to 133 of these young men and to 49 new high school seniors one year after the war. He found an increase in anxiety related personality traits and in uncertainty about the best course of action to satisfy one's needs—both in the test-retest comparison and in the comparison of the two age cohorts. He concluded that war is a stressful event exercising a consistent effect on the personality characteristics of young men even if they have not been in military service. (Other studies have documented the effect of combat and wartime military service on young men who did not suffer posttraumatic war neurosis [Kedem, Menat, & Feldman, 1975; Lieblich, 1982] and on young men who did [Dasberg, 1982; Falk, 1982; Halmosh, 1982].) Kedem, Gelman, and Blum (1975) found an increased interest in social and political issues in junior high school students six months after the war. Whether the postwar levels of these children and late adolescents will remain constant or decline to prewar levels can be answered only by longitudinal follow-up of these and other groups of young people in Israel.

Some personal-social characteristics are clearly labile and situation-specific. Invariably, manifest anxiety as reported by Israeli children has risen in times of crisis and dropped off afterward (Ziv, 1975). In a study comparing peacetime and wartime levels of anxiety, Milgram and Milgram (1976) found a substantial elevation of anxiety in 85 fifth- and sixth-grade urban children: the mean score nearly doubled. The greatest increment was noted in those children who had been lowest in peacetime anxiety—boys as compared with girls and middle-class children as compared with lower-class. In fact, some of the children with the highest peacetime levels of anxiety either showed no rise or actually showed a decline in wartime. The inverse relationship of peacetime and wartime anxiety levels was substantial ($-.57$) and could not be attributed to artifacts such as restricted ceiling of the anxiety scale.

This unanticipated finding contradicts the assumption that stressors are additive. According to proponents of the latter view (e.g., Zuckerman-Bareli, 1982), people who are high in peacetime trait anxiety because of the life stressors to which they are routinely exposed should become still higher during wartime, when additional stressors are imposed. An alternate view is that children who are initially highly anxious find in war a legitimate, socially shared focus for their anxiety and rise minimally, if at all; they might even decline, with objective, war related stressors binding the initially free-floating anxiety. Another possibility is that children originally low in anxiety may not have acquired coping mechanisms for handling high anxiety levels; in wartime they are hard pressed to cope with severe external stressors and, therefore, experience disproportionate affective arousal.

A second unanticipated finding in the Milgram and Milgram (1976) study was the absence of a relationship between wartime anxiety levels and the extent of active involvement of family members in the Yom Kippur War. One might well expect a higher anxiety level in a child whose father, older brother, or other close relative is in a combat area, has not communicated with the family for some time, or has been injured than in a child whose relatives are not in combat. This was not the case with either the elementary school children of the Milgram and Milgram (1976) study or the junior high school students of the Kedem, Gelman, and Blum (1976) study. Moreover, extent of family involvement seemed to be unrelated to the fear and anxiety levels reported by adults: wives of men at war (Cohen & Dotan, 1975) and university students whose relatives were involved in the Yom Kippur War (Goldberg, Yinon, Saffir, & Merbaum, 1977).

Breznitz (1980) suggested that in a small country like Israel everyone knows everyone else, more or less, so that all share in the apprehensions and grief reactions of those whose family members are in grave danger, are injured, or are killed. I would add, by way of explaining the anti-intuitive finding just reported, that there is no necessary relationship between the objective intensity of the war related stressors impinging on the individual and the subjective anxiety level that he or she reports. Furthermore, existing anxiety scales may fail to reflect differences in mild to moderate involvement; if the range of involvement scores also included extreme involvement such as the death of one family member or the irreversible injury of others, then one would expect a wider range of anxiety scores and a positive relationship between involvement and anxiety. It is reasonable to assume from the nature of Israeli society and the war stress to which it is exposed that there is considerable empathy by all for the suffering of some. Nevertheless, the anxiety and anguish of directly afflicted people must be greater than that of people only indirectly affected.

War related events also may affect personality development in another way. Kurtz and Davidson (1974) reported a case study of an 11-year-old boy with severe episodes of somnabulism after his father's return home from a war related hospitalization. Before the injury, the father, a professional soldier, had been away from home for long periods of time. The mother had turned to the patient, the youngest son, to fill a vacuum in her own life and had thereby intensified his Oedipal longings. In the course of short-term therapy, the child gained insight into his ambivalent attitude toward both parents and his desire to shift allegiances to the father. Therapy was successful and the boy was found to be more independent and self-assertive at a follow-up 18 months after termination of therapy than he had been before the appearance of the somnabulism. In sum, the frequent absences of the father had intensified a maladaptive Oedipal attachment to the mother; subsequently, the father's injury precipitated an emotional crisis, which afforded the boy an opportunity for confronting personal problems and for achieving considerable change in personality and in behavior.

Two conclusions may be drawn from this case. The first is that a particular war related episode will be interpreted dynamically by a child in terms of the constellation of forces operating in his or her life space at the time. Like the missing piece of a jigsaw puzzle, the event may confirm or disprove a psychopathological hypothesis and bring about a new, anxiety provoking disequilibrium. Second, the new intrapersonal situation can become the occasion for seeking help and for self-exploration. Golan (1982) argued that many stress reactions in war or other disasters can generate positive developmental and transitional crises, providing the opportunity for and the promise of personal growth.

Lieblich (1982) reached substantially the same conclusions in her Gestalt therapy groups with young adults. She found that war themes frequently occured in the dreams of group members—beginning in some cases a year or more after the war. Members verbalized their conflicts about heroism-cowardice or aggression–guilt feelings and their guilt about surviving while their comrades-in-arms had been killed. These conflicts reflected not only the individual's particular wartime experiences but also his or her prewar experiences and ongoing personality problems.

CONCLUSION

The topic of survival and of coping with war related stress is at the core of Israeli consciousness. It is not, however, an alien topic to citizens of other countries that have suffered the ravages of war in this century. Nor should it be an alien topic to citizens of countries that have hitherto been spared. In the broadest sense, the very threat of war impinges on society as a whole. Concerns of children and adolescents about a nuclear holocaust or the dire consequences of so-called conventional warfare, as well as the effect of military service on those who serve and their families, are only a few of the war related stress topics with which scientists and practitioners should become involved.

> It is man's fate to live in an imperfect world and while striving for its perfection, to cope with its imperfections. In coping man calls upon the emotional resources of the human spirit and the tools and knowledge of the scientific spirit . . . in the effort . . . to make the best of the human predicament in war and in the peace that follows. (Milgram, 1975:41)

REFERENCES

ALEKSANDROWICZ, D. R. Interminable mourning as a family process. In C. D. Spielberger, I. G. Sarason, & N. A. Milgram (eds.), *Stress and anxiety,* vol. 8. Washington, D.C.: Hemisphere, 1982.

AMIR, Y., & SHARON, I. Factors in the adjustment of war widows in Israel. In C. D. Spielberger, I. G. Sarason, & N. A. Milgram (eds.), *Stress and anxiety,* vol. 8. Washington, D.C.: Hemisphere, 1982.

ASHKENAZI, Z. The application of principles of operant conditioning to war widows and their children. In C. D. Spielberger, I. G. Sarason, & N. A. Milgram (eds.), *Stress and anxiety,* vol. 8. Washington, D.C.: Hemisphere, 1982.

AYALON, O. Potential victims of violence. Paper presented to the Second International Conference on Psychological Stress and Adjustment in Time of War and Peace, Jerusalem, 1978.

BAIDER, L., & ROSENFELD, E. Effect of parental fears on children in wartime. *Social Casework,* 1974, *55,* 497–503.

BAWLY, I. Widow to widow: A personal account. In C. D. Spielberger, I. G. Sarason, & N. A. Milgram (eds.), *Stress and anxiety,* vol. 8. Washington, D.C.: Hemisphere, 1982.

BENYAMINI, K. School psychological emergency intervention: Proposals for guidelines based on recent Israeli experience. *Mental Health and Society,* 1976, *3,* 22–32.

BREZNITZ, S. Stress in Israel. In H. Selye (ed.), *Selye's guide to stress research,* vol. 1. New York: Van Nostrand, 1980.

BYRNE, D. Repression-sensitization as a dimension of personality. In B. A. Maher (ed.), *Progress in experimental personality research,* vol. 1. New York: Academic, 1964.

CAPLAN, G. *Principles of preventive psychiatry.* New York: Basic Books, 1964.

————. *Support systems and community mental health behavior.* New York: Behavioral Publications, 1974.

CHEN, M., SHAPIRA, R., REGEV, H., & FRESKO, B. Volunteering behavior and its correlates in adolescent males during the Yom Kippur War. In C. D. Spielberger, I. G. Sarason, & N. A. Milgram (eds.), *Stress and anxiety,* vol. 8. Washington, D.C.: Hemisphere, 1982.

COHEN, A. A., & DOTAN, J. Interpersonal behavior and mass communication consumption in the family as a means of coping with stress in war and peace: The effects of socioeconomic status and the absence of the adult male. Paper presented to the First International Conference on Psychological Stress and Adjustment in Time of War and Peace, Tel Aviv, 1975.

DASBERG, H. Belonging and loneliness in relation to mental breakdown in battle. In C. D. Spielberger,

I. G. Sarason, & N. A. Milgram (eds.), *Stress and anxiety,* vol. 8. Washington, D.C.: Hemisphere, 1982.

ELOUL, J. A description of group work with war widows. In C. D. Spielberger, I. G. Sarason, & N. A. Milgram (eds.)., *Stress and anxiety,* vol. 8. Washington, D.C.: Hemisphere, 1982.

FALK, A. The role of guilt feelings in war neurosis. In C. D. Spielberger, I. G. Sarason, & N. A. Milgram (eds.), *Stress and anxiety,* vol. 8. Washington, D.C.: Hemisphere, 1982.

FRASER, M. *Children in conflict.* London: Secker & Warburg, 1973.

FREUD, A., & BURLINGHAM, D. T. *War and children.* New York: Medical War Books, 1943.

GAY, M. The adjustment of parents to wartime bereavement. In C. D. Spielberger, I. G. Sarason, & N. A. Milgram (eds.), *Stress and anxiety,* vol. 8. Washington, D.C.: Hemisphere, 1982.

GLASS, A. J. Psychiatric aspects of disaster. *Journal of the American Medical Association,* 1959, *171,* 188–191.

GOLAN, N. Wife to widow to woman. *Social Work,* 1975, *20,* 369–375.

————. The influence of developmental and transitional crises on victims of disasters. In C. D. Spielberger, I. G. Sarason, & N. A. Milgram (eds.), *Stress and anxiety,* vol. 8. Washington, D.C.: Hemisphere, 1982

GOLAN, S. Children whose fathers died. *Kibbutz* memorandum received by N. A. Milgram, Tel Aviv University, 1975.

GOLDBERG, J., YINON, Y., SAFFIR, M., & MERBAUM, M. Fear in periods of stress and calm among Israeli students. *Behavioral Therapy and Experimental Psychiatry,* 1977, *8,* 5–9.

GRANOT, T. *Group work with bereaved parents.* Tel Aviv: Israeli Ministry of Defense, Rehabilitation Branch, 1975.

HALMOSH, A. F. Some dynamic aspects of treatment in resistant emotional war casualties. In C. D. Spielberger, I. G. Sarason, & N. A. Milgram (eds.), *Stress and anxiety,* vol. 8. Washington, D.C.: Hemisphere, 1982.

HALPERN, E. Children's support systems in coping with orphanhood: Child helps child in a natural setting. In C. D. Spielberger, I. G. Sarason, & N. A. Milgram (eds.), *Stress and anxiety,* vol. 8. Washington, D.C.: Hemisphere, 1982.

HELSON, H. *Adaptation level theory: The experimental and systematic approach to behavior.* New York: Harper, 1964.

JANIS, I. L. *Stress and frustration.* New York: Harcourt, 1971.

KAFFMAN, M. *Kibbutz* civilian population under war stress. *British Journal of Psychiatry,* 1977, *30,* 489–494.

KATZ, M. Background and development of the project (war widows in Israel). In C. D. Spielberger, I. G. Sarason, & N. A. Milgram (eds.), *Stress and anxiety,* vol. 8. Washington, D.C.: Hemisphere, 1982.

KEDEM, P., GELMAN, R., & BLUM, L. The effect of the Yom Kippur War on the attitudes, values, and locus of control of young adolescents. Paper presented to the First International Conference on Psychological Stress and Adjustment in Time of War and Peace, Tel Aviv, 1975.

KEDEM, P., MENAT, Y., & FELDMAN, B. Changes in attitudes, values, and power of concentration of male university students as a function of personality variables and military service during the Yom Kippur War. Paper presented to the First International Conference on Psychological Stress and Adjustment in Time of War and Peace, Tel Aviv, 1975.

KIRSCHNER, E. Data on bereavement and rehabilitation of war widows. In C. D. Spielberger, I. G. Sarason, & N. A. Milgram (eds.), *Stress and anxiety,* vol. 8. Washington, D.C.: Hemisphere, 1982.

KLINGMAN, A. Children in stress: Anticipatory guidance in the framework of the educational system. *Personnel and Guidance Journal,* 1978, *55,* 22–26.

————. Intervention via school psychological services following terrorist attack. Manuscript, Haifa University, 1980.

KOUBOVI, D. Therapeutic teaching of literature during the war and its aftermath. In C. D. Spielberger, I. G. Sarason, & N. A. Milgram (eds.), *Stress and anxiety*, vol. 8. Washington, D.C.: Hemisphere, 1982.

KRISTAL, L. Bruxism: An anxiety response to environmental stress. In C. D. Spielbeger & I. G. Sarason (eds.), *Stress and anxiety*, vol. 5. Washington, D.C.: Hemisphere, 1978.

KURTZ, H., & DAVIDSON, S. Psychic trauma in an Israeli child: Relationship to environmental security. *American Journal of Psychotherapy*, 1974, *28*, 438–444.

LAZARUS, R. S. *Psychological stress and the coping process*. New York: McGraw-Hill, 1966.

LERNER, M. J., & MILLER, D. T. Just world research and the attribution process: Looking back and ahead, *Psychological Bulletin*, 1978, *85*, 1030–1051.

LIEBLICH, A. Living with war in Israel: A summary of Gestalt therapy work. In C. D. Spielberger, I. G. Sarason, & N. A. Milgram (eds.), *Stress and anxiety*, vol. 8. Washington, D.C.: Hemisphere, 1982.

LIFSCHITZ, M. Social differentiation and integration of fatherless adolescents. *Megamot: Israeli Journal for the Behavioral and Social Sciences*, 1974, *20*, 347–372.

————. Social differentiation and organization of the Rorschach in fatherless and two-parented children. *Journal of Clinical Psychology*, 1975, *35*, 126–130.

————. Long-range effects of father's loss: The cognitive complexity of bereaved children and their school adjustment. *British Journal of Medical Psychology*, 1976, *49*, 189–197.

————. Growing up without a father. Paper prepared for presentation to the Second International Conference on Psychological Stress and Adjustment in Time of War and Peace, Jerusalem, 1978.

LIFSCHITZ, M., BERMAN, D., GALILI, A., & GILAD, D. Bereaved children: The effects of mother's perception and social system organization on their short range adjustment. *Journal of Child Psychiatry*, 1977, *16*, 272–284.

MILGRAM, N. Psychological stress and adjustment in time of war and peace. *Tel-Aviv University Review*, 1975, 38–41.

MILGRAM, N. A., & MILLER, M. S. The influence of extended shelling on the levels of manifest anxiety and autonomy of children. Manuscript, Bar-Ilan University, 1973.

MILGRAM, R. M., & MILGRAM, N. A. The effect of the Yom Kippur War on anxiety level in Israeli children. *Journal of Psychology*, 1976, *94*, 107–113.

MORAWETZ, A. The impact on adolescents of the death in war of an older sibling. In C. D. Spielberger, I. G. Sarason, & N. A. Milgram (eds.), *Stress and anxiety*, vol. 8. Washington, D.C.: Hemisphere, 1982.

PALGI, P. Socio-cultural expressions and implications of death, mourning, and bereavement in Israel arising out of the war situation. *Israel Annals of Psychiatry and Related Disciplines*, 1973, *11*, Whole No. 3.

PERGAMENTER, R. Crisis intervention with child-care personnel (*metaplot*) in an Israeli border kibbutz. In C. D. Spielberger, I. G. Sarason, & N. A. Milgram (eds.), *Stress and anxiety*, vol. 8. Washington, D.C.: Hemisphere, 1982.

ROFÉ, Y., & LEWIN, I. Daydreams in a war environment. *Journal of Mental Imagery*, 1980, *4*, 59–75.

————. The effect of war environment on dreams and sleep habits. In C. D. Spielberger, I. G. Sarason, & N. A. Milgram (eds.), *Stress and anxiety*, vol. 8. Washington, D.C.: Hemisphere, 1982.

SCHACHTER, S. *The psychology of affiliation*. Stanford: Stanford University Press, 1959.

SCHWARCZ, J. H. Guiding children's creative expression in the stress of war. In C. D. Spielberger, I. G. Sarason, & N. A. Milgram (eds.), *Stress and anxiety*, vol. 8. Washington, D.C.: Hemisphere, 1982.

SMILANSKY, S. The adjustment in elementary school of children orphaned from their fathers. In C. D. Spielberger, I. G. Sarason, & N. A. Milgram (eds.), *Stress and anxiety,* vol. 8. Washington, D.C.: Hemisphere, 1982.

STOKOLS, D. A congruence analysis of human stress. In I. G. Sarason & C. D. Spielberger (eds.), *Stress and anxiety,* vol. 6. Washington, D.C.: Hemisphere, 1979.

TEICHMAN, Y. The stress of coping with the unknown regarding a significant family member. In C. D. Spielberger & I. G. Sarason (eds.), *Stress and anxiety,* vol. 5. Washington, D. C.: Hemisphere, 1978.

TEICHMAN, Y., SPIEGEL, Y., & TEICHMAN, M. Volunteers' reports about crisis intervention work with families of servicemen missing in action. *American Journal of Community Psychology,* 1978, *6,* 315-325.

WIEDER, S. Parallel reactions of widows and their young children following the death of their fathers in the Yom Kippur War. Paper presented to the First International Conference on Psychological Stress and Adjustment in Time of War and Peace, Tel Aviv, 1975.

ZAFRIR, A. Community therapeutic intervention in treatment of civilian victims after a major terrorist attack. In C. D. Spielberger, I. G. Sarason, & N. A. Milgram (eds.), *Stress and anxiety,* vol. 8. Washington, D.C.: Hemisphere, 1982.

ZAK, I. Stability and change of personality traits: Possible effects of the Yom Kippur War on Israeli youth. In C. D. Spielberger, I. G. Sarason, & N. A. Milgram (eds.), *Stress and anxiety,* vol. 8. Washington, D.C.: Hemisphere, 1982.

ZIV, A. Empirical findings on children's reactions to war stress. Paper presented to the First International Conference on Psychological Stress and Adjustment in Time of War and Peace, Tel Aviv, 1975.

ZIV, A., & ISRAELI, R. Effects of bombardment on the manifest anxiety levels of children living in the kibbutz. *Journal of Consulting and Clinical Psychology,* 1973, *40,* 287-291.

ZIV, A., KRUGLANSKI, A., & SHULMAN, S. Children's psychological reactions to wartime stress. *Journal of Personality and Social Psychology,* 1974, *30,* 24-30.

ZIV, A., & NEBENHAUS, S. Frequency of wishes for peace of children during different periods of war intensity. *Megamot: Israeli Journal of Behavioral Sciences,* 1973, *19,* 423-427.

ZUCKERMAN-BARELI, C. Effects of border tension on residents of an Israeli town. *Journal of Human Stress,* 1979, *5,* 29-40.

————. The effect of border tension on the adjustment of *kibbutzim* and *moshavim* on the northern border of Israel: A path analysis. In C. D. Spielberger, I. G. Sarason, & N. A. Milgram (eds.), *Stress and anxiety,* vol. 8. Washington, D.C.: Hemisphere, 1982.

41

Migration and Stress

Judith T. Shuval

THE RELATIONSHIP BETWEEN STRESS AND MIGRATION may be considered on two levels that differ analytically in terms of the assumed direction of cause and effect. On the one hand, stress of various sorts may be said *to cause* migration; on the other, stress may be viewed as *caused by* migration. As noted, this distinction is essentially analytical since both processes may in fact occur with regard to any specific stream of migration. This chapter focuses primarily on stress as a potential outcome of migration, although some attention is also given to the causative role of stress in stimulating that process.

MIGRATION: SOME THEORETICAL CONSIDERATIONS

Before considering the relationship between migration and stress, it will be useful to present a theoretical view of migration as a general social process. Since the large number of descriptive studies that have been carried out in the past 20–30 years have not yielded a single, coherent model concerning migration (Brody, 1970; Davis, 1974; Jackson, 1969; Jansen, 1970; Lee, 1969; Price, 1969), I will draw together several theoretical themes and attempt to integrate them in a comprehensive model of the migration process (Shuval, 1982).

Migration may be viewed as a dynamic process that involves a decision to leave one place of residence for another. In the most general sense, migration refers to moves of any distance, from one block to the next or one continent to the next. The intention of the move is long-term, if not permanent, residence in the new social setting, so that nomadic wanderings are generally not considered a category of migration. At the same time, Richmond (1969) noted the motility of contemporary migration: relatively inexpensive means of transportation and the wide applicability of many occupational skills have made recent migration less of a permanent commitment than resettlement was in the past. Thus, a new location may be viewed as tentative for a period of time and, under certain conditions, migration may continue to another, more attractive destination or even back to the migrant's original location.

On the macrolevel migration may be said to have implications and repercussions not only for the individuals involved but for two social systems as well: that at the locus of origin and that at the destination. Departure or entry of groups requires readjustment in each of the two social systems. (Mangalam & Schwarzweller, 1970). The extent of these implications depends on the size of the migrating population relative to the populations at the origin and the destination. The greater their proportion of each of these groups, the more far-reaching the social adaptation required of the total social system at the relevant point.

The number of persons involved is as relevant as the position they occupied or will occupy at either end of the migration process. Brain drain is a type of migration that tends to deplete the society of origin of highly trained persons and that may require redeployment in the occupational structure. Migration of dissidents from the Soviet Union eases the potential tension they generate in that society and improves social control (Gitelman, 1972, 1977). At the destination, a process of readjustment takes place when specific racial, ethnic, or occupational groups, which shift the balance of relationships, enter the social system. Thus, viewed on the macrolevel, migration may be said to be a process generating social change in at least two social systems.

The decision to migrate is made in the final analysis on an individual level but, like other decisions, within a context of salient reference groups and social norms. On the whole, social networks in which individuals are embedded tend to tie them to a given locus of residence (Hull, 1979). But when such groups see migration as desirable or even as normative, pressure is generated to encourage individuals to move. Thus, migration may become a norm in certain social situations and sweep along individuals whose inclination to migrate is initially low. On the other hand, the decision to migrate may run counter to prevailing norms and therefore require tenacity and nonconformity in the individual.

The decision to leave a given location has been described as a product of complementary push and pull factors (Lee, 1969). These vary in their relative intensity, but when a decision to migrate is reached, the overall balance is such as to make the destination appear more attractive than the place of origin to the potential migrant. Given the inertia of most people, there need to be situational or value factors that are perceived as undesirable in the place of origin and these must be of sufficient salience to motivate people to disengage from the social context in which they are embedded. In the classic case these factors have included religious or political persecution, economic deprivation, ideological rejection of the dominant norms, or other forms of alienation. These negative factors are subjectively defined by the potential migrant and include situations of relative deprivation in which the objective status of the individual may appear quite satisfactory to others.

The mutual dependence of the push and pull factors is seen in the fact that even the strongest push will fail to disengage an individual from his place of origin unless he can identify an alternative accessible location in which the relevant negative factor is absent, markedly weaker, or avoidable. Therefore, there is a certain symmetrical relationship between factors that motivate people to leave a permanent residence and those that attract them to another specific locus (e.g., unemployment versus job opportunities, religious persecution versus religious freedom, marginal status versus full social acceptance). From this viewpoint, push and pull factors are frequently opposite sides of the same coin.

A lack of symmetry occurs when the destination appears to the potential migrant to be characterized by special, highly salient attractive qualities, so that even if certain of the negative qualities of his place of origin persist at the destination, these attractive qualities may play a powerful role in dicisionmaking.

A decision to migrate is mediated by the individual's resources. However negative the perceived conditions in the place of origin and however attractive the destination, a decision to move also requires certain material means, as well as skills that include initiative, organizational abilities, and knowledge.

Needless to say, all migrants are not equal participants in the decisionmaking process. When an unaccompanied adult migrates, most of the decisionmaking is indeed his own. But some migrants may be passive participants in a decision reached by others. The most evident of these are dependents such as children and elderly persons. But when a marriage is characterized by asymmetrical power relations, wives tend to be less actively involved in the decisionmaking process. Such participation is undoubtedly related to the subsequent process of adjustment in the new social setting because of the motivational and cognitive-perceptual patterns it implies.

All migration is selective. The population moving from one setting or country to another is rarely representative of the population from which it is drawn; however, the criteria of selection vary (Lee, 1969). In some cases, the selection will be "positive," resulting in highly educated, ambitious, adventurous, and adaptable migrants. In other cases, migrants may be characterized by failure in their place of origin, low education, present or potential social or psychological pathology, lack of occupational skills, or susceptibility to illness. A mixture of these traits often occurs, although it is usually possible to descern a dominant pattern of positive or negative selection. Processes of selection determine the kinds of personal resources migrants being with them in the form of education, skills, and personality traits. Their level of sensitivity and susceptibility to different stresses is also a function of selection processes.

The selection process is mediated by freedom of exit from the place of origin and policies concerning admission to the destination. On a formal level there are often barriers to leaving and requirements—educational or occupational—for entry.

In the Soviet Union, for example, Jewish emigrants must pass through two separate and unrelated stages of selection in gaining permission to leave. The first is self-determined: individuals or families make a decision, which is expressed by their formal application for a permit to emigrate. For this application to be considered, a *vyzov* is required, that is, an affidavit attesting to an invitation from a familily member in Israel. Between 1968 and 1978, 318,914 such affidavits were sent from Israel but only a third utilized for de facto emigration (*Insight,* 1977). Lack of use of the affidavits can be explained by a variety of other restrictions imposed by the Soviet authorities, by a change of mind on the part of potential emigrants, or by the decision among some of the latter to keep the *vyzov* in case of later need (Gitelman, 1972, 1977). The application to emigrate from the Soviet Union requires no small amount of risk taking, often involving job loss, expulsion of children from school or university, ostracism by colleagues and friends, threats and open hostility, condemnation in the media, and the need to move to other housing. The Soviet authorities demand that applicants for permits provide a character reference from their place of employment, permission from parents, permission from a former spouse (in case of divorce), and certification from their house committee. All of these requirements are open to delay and may expose the applicant to harassment. Self-selection at this stage therefore involves courage, determination, alienation from Soviet society, self-confidence, Jewish identity, or some combination of these factors (Shuval, 1982).

The Soviet authorities at this point institute a second selection process by granting exit permits to a subgroup of would-be emigrants. Permission appears to vary by region and republic in the Soviet Union, as well as over time (*Insight,* 1977). Those most likely to obtain exit permits include people viewed as less skilled, older people, people whose work is considered nonessential or not secret, people who do not have relatives in the security establishment or in high party positions, dissidents, and troublemakers. It has been suggested that some local officials may be eager to grant exit permits to Jews, who generally assimilate into

Russian culture rather than into that of local ethnic groups: emigration thus removes "agents" of Russification. Such emigration also frees jobs for local people and broadens the opportunities for occupational mobility. There is an impression that the Soviet authorities are responsive to some extent to protests or political pressure from the West and grant exit visas in response. In the 1970s, the Soviet Union's need for expanded trade relations with the West made the U.S.S.R. particularly sensitive to the Jackson Amendment, which linked free emigration of Soviet citizens with "most favored nation" recognition by the United States. In any case, potential emigrants are a fairly varied population and it is probably impossible to establish precisely what criteria are actually used by the Soviet authorities in granting exit permits (Shuval, 1982).

An immigrant's entry into a new society is a gradual process. The length of the time span that is relevant depends on the substantive issues being considered. At what point in time does an immigrant turn into a veteran? The relevant time span may be defined in terms of months, years, or even generations. What seems to be important is the dynamic quality of the process.

Different stages in the process have different characteristics, so that issues that are important at one stage may disappear at another. For example, knowledge of a new language has differential meaning in terms of behavior and interaction with others when an immigrant is in a new country 6 months, 5 years, or 20 years. The same is true for primary relations between immigrants and veteran members of the host society: these generally develop relatively late in the integration process (Gordon, 1964). Although the orderly progression described by Park and Burgess (1921) from contact to competition and conflict and finally to accommodation does not seem to characterize all situations, the migrant's experience undoubtedly varies by stage.

There are a variety of approaches with regard to the conceptual definition of integration in a new social system. Terms such as socialization, resocialization, acculturation, accommodation, and normative behavior have been widely used but, in most cases, inadequately spelled out either conceptually or empirically (Price, 1969). Does the term "integration" refer to the dispersal of immigrants in the institutional structure? To their conformity to the prevalent norms of the society? To an absence of pathological behavior among them? To their feelings of identification, well-being, familiarity, acceptance, hopefulness? To their interaction on a primary level with other members of the society? To lack of conflict between them and other groups? These issues refer to a variety of *contents* of the integration concept. All can be studied, but they refer to different aspects of integration.

It is also essential to determine which point of view is being considered with regard to the integration of immigrants. Several are undoubtedly relevant. One salient point of view is, or course, that of the immigrants themselves: How do they feel about the new society? Do they see it as their permanent home or is it more of a way station in a series of moves? Another point of view is that of veteran residents: Do they accept newcomers or do they view them with hostility—as potential competitors or disrupters of the staus quo? Are they apathetic? Finally, one may consider the viewpoint of the society as a whole in terms of its dominant values and their relationship to the issue of immigration. These values have both manifest and latent components expressed by more and less formal means.

It would seem essential to view integration into a new society as a multidimensional process. Migration can be considered in terms of a variety of subprocesses, each focusing on a different aspect of life in the new society. Thus, there are many pathways and mechanisms by means of which immigrants enter a new social system. At any point in time integration in one life area is not necessarily correlated with integration in others: some areas more highly correlated with each other than are others, but there seems to be no consistency across populations or situations to permit one to establish necessary correlations. Furthermore, change in one life area may not be correlated with change in other areas (Shuval, Markus, & Dotan, 1973; Shuval, Markus, Dotan, 1975).

The implications of such a multidimensional conceptual approach are that there is little to be gained from seeking one overall measure of integration. The problem is to establish which points of view are to be considered and which life areas are deemed relevant for understanding the process and to seek the empirical relationships among them at various points in time. Composite indexes of integration, such as the one used by Rose (1969), involve arbitrary weighting of the measures from which the composite is derived. They are, therefore, of limited use. It would seem preferable to focus on different meanings and factors depending on the temrporal stage in a group's process of entry into the social system. Focusing on one specific area, for example, the occupational sphere, is of course legitimate provided one bears in mind that it is only one of several life areas that could be considered. While behavior in this area is not positively correlated with behavior in all other areas, it *is* generally highly correlated with morale, identification, and feelings about the new society, which gives special salience to employment in the overall process of migration (Shuval, Markus, & Dotan, 1973).

The integration process in all its dimensions may involve conflict no less than solidarity. The process does not necessarily reestablish an earlier equilibrium but may result in a redefinition of the social situation in terms quite different from those initially characterizing the society (Mangalam & Schwarzweller, 1970). Indeed, the numerous differing interests and values that inhere in the meeting of groups and subgroups suggest that the process is unlikely to be smooth. Thus, one can assume that the various groups of actors in the situation are characterized by different interests and goals as a result of their differential position in the social system and these may not always be complementary. No less important are value conflicts inherent in the orientation of any one group.

Immigrants are just as likely to come into contact with the problems and pathologies of the institutional structure as they are to encounter its more stable elements. Chronic problems to which veterans have accommodated often plague newcomers during their initial stages in the society. It has even been suggested that acceptance of certain chronic pathologies of a society be used as one index of integration! Furthermore, weak or imperfectly functioning institutional structures may be strained by the arrival of an immigrant population, so that the group itself may serve as an additional cause of the society's dysfunction. An example of this would be a social service that was overutilized before the arrival of an immigrant group (Shuval, 1982).

In a rapidly changing society, newcomers are generally not presented with a coherent set of norms to which conformity is expected. Differentiation of the host society in terms of ethnic, social class, regional, occupational, or political subgroups results in a variety of norms to which immigrants are differentially exposed depending on the groups with which they come into contact.

By channeling newcomers into specific subgroups or locations, a pluralistically structured society allows immigrants to learn the norms of one group but remain ignorant of the norms of others or of those held in common by all members of the society. If that subgroup happens to consist of other immigrants from the same place of origin, the resulting separation may serve to intensify feelings of isolation or conflict.

In the case of migrant professionals, such as physicians, who are familiar with the norms that are generally shared by members of that profession in the host society, acculturation is ostensibly comparatively simple. If both the country of origin and the host society belong to the same overall cultural and professional tradition, professional practice in the country of origin is controlled by similar norms to those prevalent in the new society. Thus, if Western style medicine is practiced in both societies, ideally little acculturation should be required since the same norms were presumably learned and followed in the country of origin. However, since the general cultural context, history, and structure of professional practice affect role performance, one can expect professionals to behave somewhat differently in two similar societies. To the extent that general values of the social system impinge on professional performance and to the extent that these values differ across countries, a process of acculturation will be necessary. The cultural distance between the groups determines the pace and quality of this process (Shuval, 1982; Stevens, Goddman, & Mick, 1979).

Whichever dimension of integration is considered, the process is an interaction between immigrants and the host society. There is a mutual process of adaptation in which immigrants and veterans respond to each other in a variety of patterns. Each side is dependent on the other and each changes in response to the other's behavior. From this point of view, it is just as important to understand attitudes and orientations to immigrants on the part of members of the host society and its various subgroups as it is to understand the orientations of the immigrants themselves. Focusing on the host society, Rose (1969) referred to the degree of societal openness as expressed, on the one hand, by formal rules and regulations concerning admission or granting of privileges and, on the other, by informal attitudes expressed by members of the host society toward immigrants; the latter include fear of competition, xenophobia, stereotyping, and the extent to which the host culture is able to tolerate deviance.

STRESS: A DEFINITION

The stress model that appears to be most useful in the present context is the one proposed by Levine and Scotch (1970). House (1974) noted that "stress occurs when an individual confronts a situation where his usual modes of behavior are insufficient and the consequences of not adapting are serious." Stated most generally, this theory proposes a multilinked chain among potential stressor situations, subjectively determined perception variables, and the availability and usability of personal and social coping mechanisms (French, Rodgers, & Cobb, 1974; Scott & Howard, 1970). Thus, homeostasis on the individual level will be disrupted when a person perceives a given situation to be disturbing, alarming, or threatening. If he is unable to mobilize personal or social resources to cope with the situation in such a manner as to restore homeostasis, his energy will be bound up dealing with this perceived disturbance; this preoccupation defines a stressful condition (Scott & Howard, 1970).

Levine and Scotch's (1970) approach emphasizes the subjective definition of stress by making it clear that situations are not objectively stressful but are socially or psychologically defined as such by individuals in terms of social and cultural norms. Thus, bereavement or divorce may be subjectively defined as extremely disturbing but also by some, under certain circumstances, as a relief or even as a positive challenge (House, 1974). The conditional quality of the stress model also emphasizes the importance of coping mechanisms. These may be individual (personal skills, personality traits, intelligence, knowledge) or social (formal institutions, informal groups, social norms and values). The availability and usability of coping mechanisms constitute the link that determines whether a situation that is perceived as disturbing will in fact result in stress for the individual (Pearlin & Schooler, 1978).

Mechanic (1978) distinguished between two types of coping: *defense processes,* which are psychological mechanisms to redefine, deny, repress, or possibly distort a disturbing reality, and *instrumental coping behavior,* which utilizes skills and knowledge for problem-solving in an effort to change or ameliorate the stressful situation. Defense processes may enable the individual to live with a difficult situation, e.g., chronic illness, but neurotic or more serious consequences may accompany this adaptation. In contrast, instrumental coping seeks to alter a disturbing situation. Clearly, coping depends on early socialization and on prior experiences with the given situation or with settings perceived as similar.

In sum, *stress* is said to exist to the extent that an individual defines a salient situation as disturbing for himself and is unable to recruit effective coping mechanisms to remove or reduce the disturbance. Two simultaneous conditions are necessary for stress to be present or to increase: a subjective definition of a situation as disturbing and an inability—for whatever reason—to cope with the condition. The centrality of social and psychological factors in determining stress is seen in the fact that both these conditions (i.e., what one defines as disturbing and what resources one can utilize for coping) are largely socially determined. It is therefore clear that migration as a social process does not necessarily induce stress. While social change is structurally built into the process, a variety of subjective responses and definitions of the situation may take place. In accordance with the model, stress occurs only when migrants define some aspect of their situation as disturbing and when they are unable to recruit significant personal or social resources to cope with that disturbance. Such a combination of circumstances may indeed occur in certain migration situations but not in all.

CHANGE AS A STRUCTURAL CHARACTERISTIC OF MIGRATION

Change is inherent in all migration and may be considered a structural characteristic of the process. Such change may, under the circumstances proposed in the model just outlined, be viewed as a potential stressor. Three forms of change characterize the migration process: physical, social, and cultural.

Physical Change

Migration often involves movement from one geographical location to another. The migrant may experience changes in climate, sanitation level, and dietary habits, as well as exposure to pollution, new pathogens, and exotic diseases. Changes in climate, in conjunction with the new culture, may induce changes in lifestyle that express themselves in patterns of sleep (e.g., siesta), nutrition, timing of meals (e.g., when the main meal of the day is taken), clothing, housing, or general pace of activity. All these physical changes may, under certain circumstances, serve as stressors (Hull, 1979; Wessen, 1971).

Social Change

All migrants disengage from a network of social relations in the society they are leaving. In the case of migration of whole kin groups, disengagement may be minimal, but in other cases there are numerous breaks in social relationships. Disruption of long-standing ties may or may not be perceived as disturbing by the migrant; accordingly, disengagement will cause the migrant to feel isolated and unsupported or relieved and unencumbered. Separation may be viewed as permanent, as when leaving aged parents in the Soviet Union, or as temporary, as when the person left behind can come to visit the migrant in his new residence or the migrant himself can revisit his original home. In some cases, the disengagement may be perceived as disturbing only after a lapse of time: a young migrant, initially exhilarated by the freedom from ties to parents and other kin, may begin to feel disturbed by the absence of relatives after a period of separation. Experiences in the host society—difficulties in establishing new social networks, employment problems, or other frustrations—may sharpen the sense of loneliness at a later stage.

The relevant coping mechanism for this feeling is a new social network that serves as a functional alternative to the earlier one. Immigrants experience different levels of difficulty in developing such alternative relations in their new location; meaningful primary relations with veterans in a new social context frequently form only slowly (Gordon, 1964). In many cases, social relations develop among migrants of the same origin, either because of residential proximity or because of deliberate choice. When entire kin groups or whole communities migrate, membership within such groups provides consideable support. But when migrants seek to move into the larger social context of the host society, their success will be determined by its receptiveness to newcomers.

Cultural Change

All migrants need to learn new norms and values and to abandon or adapt their old ones. The culture gap between the places of origin and destination determines the amount of learning that must be undergone. But even when the gap is minimal, as in the case of migration from one part of a city to another, the sensitive migrant will nevertheless feel subtle culture changes. Learning skills, youth, flexibility, and readiness for change serve as individual coping mechanisms for this need. Individual coping by immigrants is mediated by attitudes and behavior of the host population, which may range from acceptance, tolerance, and encouragement to disdain, ridicule, or hostility toward immigrants' efforts to learn the new language, norms, and values. Some host societies in which the culture gap is considered large may provide formal institutions for instruction in the local language and culture, but most acculturation takes place informally.

Styles of interpersonal relations are culturally defined and often require a process of readjustment. For example, expected levels of intimacy among friends, relations with officials in bureaucratic settings, and sytles of politeness vary widely from society to society and may require migrants to change many patterns of behavior. An immigrant from the Soviet Union stated the issue poignantly with regard to the expected level of intimacy in his new home.

> [In the Soviet Union] life is hopeless and dark. So the relationship among people, relations of the "soul," is very developed and this adorns (ykrashchaet) the life of the individual. In America a man is free but alone in his little corner. In Russia there is no freedom, so in order to escape the influence of the environment, people hide in groups of two or twenty or thirty people. . . . When life became unbearable we banded together in groups and such strong friendships developed in these groups and there was so much self-sacrifice, that spiritual contact was stronger than in family relations. This was the natural defence of the soul against tyranny. . . . This cannot be repeated in a free country. . . . Here life is too multi-faceted (mnogogranna), but that's the price you pay for freedom of the West. (Quoted in Gitelman, 1979).

MIGRATION AND COPING

The model notes the critical role on the individual level of perception in defining any situation, as well as the existence of effective and appropriate coping mechanisms to deal with stressors. Each of these elements may be affected by the migration process.

Expectations are crucial in determining perception. Realistic expectations based on accurate information of the new situation tend to buffer negative definitions of conditions at the destination. Highly educated migrants tend to have more knowledge of the destination than do less educated migrants.

Migrants' coping mechanisms are affected by the migration process itself in a number of ways. First, as noted, selection patterns determine the type and effectiveness of resources emigrants bring with them; these resources not only are material but also take the form of skills, status, knowledge, and personality traits (flexibility, adaptive capacity, readiness for change, etc.). When selection is negative, migrants may have low levels of such resources and, consequently, poor coping capacity (and vice versa). But regardless of the type or effectiveness of resources that migrants import into the host society, the structural processes of change described earlier may affect coping mechanisms in diverse ways. For example, the migrant may find his existing coping mechanisms inadequate to deal with new stressors. Unless he can strengthen them or develop alternative, more suitable coping mechanisms, stress will result. The change process—physical, social, and cultural—may of itself weaken coping mechanisms that functioned effectively in the past, so that they no longer function effectively in the new situation. Finally, the social change process may subject the migrant to new stresses for which he has no prior set of coping mechanisms. New strategies must then be developed if stress is to be avoided.

Stress is not easy to measure directly and proxy variables viewed as outcomes of stress are frequently used instead. If a phenomenon such as illness (physical or mental) or social deviance is linked to migration, it is often assumed that stress is the mediating variable that is eluding identification or measurement. There is considerable evidence linking migration with both infectious and chronic diseases and especially with mental illness (Abramson, 1966; Antonovsky, 1971; Aviram & Levav, 1975; Halevi, 1963; Hull, 1979; Kuo, 1976; Odegaarde, 1932; Scotch, 1943; Shuval, 1981; Stromberg, Peyman, & Dowd, 1974; Syme, Hyman, & Enterline 1964; Wessen, 1971).

VULNERABILITY OF MIGRANTS

Because migrants are differentially exposed to stressors and because their coping abilities are often directly affected by the process of migration itself, the entry into a new social setting and the newcomer's location in it are directly related to the level of stress he will experience. The very status of migrant may result in exposure to special stressors by virtue of the position accorded that status in the host society. I shall consider this issue on both a structural and a normative level.

Structural Issues

In general migrants are not dispersed at random in a social system but tend to be located in specific occupational and geographical niches that determine their socioeconomic status in the society. On the occupational level, migrants' distribution often reflects the host society's need for particular types of manpower; indeed, much migration takes place in response to demand for specific skills or types of workers. Accordingly, migrants tend to be located in particular occupational spheres, frequently in high concentrations and sometimes to the exclusion of nonmigrant workers. The types of jobs available vary widely, from unskilled laborers to skilled technicians or professionals. This process is often accompanied by local geographic concentration. The nonrandom residence patterns of migrants reflect both their location in specific occupational niches in a social system that requires residence in certain areas and the availability of suitable housing at an appropriate price level. Housing shortages may force migrants into undesirable neighborhoods or into substandard housing. In some situations housing is provided by employers. Although its quality varies widely, such housing frequently tends to be inferior. Thus, the structural location of the migrant in the social system exposes him to different stressors depending on the characteristics of the location.

Occupational and geographic concentration contributes to the visibility of migrants, and this affects both the migrant group itself and other populations in the society. Insofar as the migrants are concerned, a common structural location carries implications for self-identification, solidarity, and feelings of commonality. Such feelings sometimes exacerbate stress by encouraging or reinforcing perceptions of exploitation and deprivation. But a sense of cohesion may also result, promoting positive group identification and social support, which are mechanisms that alleviate stress.

Attitudes of groups in the host society toward migrants may range from acceptance and tolerance to hostility or overt aggression. In any case, visibility of the migrants makes possible a clearer focus on them by the host population or by subgroups in it. Expressions of prejudice, intolerance, aggression, or xenophobia may serve as stressors, especially when the migrant group is perceived as competing with, or advantaged relative to, longtime members of the society. Conversely, positive and accepting attitudes by host groups serve to alleviate stress (Rose, 1969).

Another structural dimension on which migrants are not randomly distributed is the power and influence hierarchy in the host society. At the time of entry, migrants tend to be low on these factors. Even professional immigrants, whose socioeconomic status is relatively high, are likely to be characterized by low power and influence as a result of being new to the society. The accumulation of power is generally a function of time, so that veterans or natives are by definition able to mobilize more of it. For migrants who enjoyed and utilized power before their move, its absence may serve as a stressor in the new society.

Absence of power may express itself on the simplest level by lack of citizenship. For period of time the migrant may be unable to vote, hold office, acquire property, or qualify for certain jobs. Once formal citizenship has been acquired, migrants may still encounter barriers in the economic and political spheres, where positions of power are occupied by veterans, who have little interest in relinquishing such influence to newcomers. A political organization of migrant groups may provide channels for migrants to acquire power and influence within such groups and through them eventually in the broader political context.

On the informal level, migration often results in a shift in the balance of power within families and other informal social contexts. Thus, persons who traditionally have wielded power in the family, e.g., grandparents or fathers, may find themselves stripped of their accustomed roles as a result of different patterns of family life in the new society. Unless alternative rewards are found for the demoted traditional leaders, they are likely to experience stress.

There is a dynamic quality to structurally determined stressors. As noted earlier, migrants may be located in vulnerable positions in the new social system, which in itself exposes them to stress. However, the length of time they are so located varies. Migrants often accept low status or deprivation as inevitable or even as justifiable during their initial period in the new location. But when migration has been voluntary, there is generally a strong expectation of change for the better. If improvement is perceived as slow or absent, such lack of change may serve as a stressor, especially in host societies with value systems emphasizing egalitarianism or achievement. Any subgroup in such a value context that feels it is not really succeeding tends to be under stress, and migrants are especially vulnerable to such feelings.

Normative Issues

On the simplest normative level it may be assumed that the potential for stress varies directly with differences between norms and values in the place of origin and those in the new setting. In an effort to minimize such differences, migrants often seek locations that are relatively similar culturally to their place of origin (Murphy, 1955) or settle near compatriots who migrated earlier. Thus, culture shock, or the confrontation between very different norms and values, may be viewed as a stressor; response to this stress depends, as in other cases, on the coping mechanisms available to the migrant.

Expectations also function as a mediating variable controlling the immigrant's response to new norms and values. Realistic expectations and accurate knowledge—however different the new culture may be from the old—tend to moderate the effect of such differences.

Different norms may serve as stressors not only because they are new to the immigrant and put pressure on him to change but also because they run counter to familiar guidelines; for example, norms of greater aggressiveness for people socialized to nonaggressive behavior, norms of restraint and control for people socialized to expressiveness, and norms of a future time orientation for people socialized to an orientation to the past.

Furthermore, the content of certain norms or values may be especially problematic for persons of migrant status by virtue of that very status. Thus, norms of achievement may serve as stressors for migrants who are blocked from conforming to that norm by language barriers or ignorance of social niceties. Merton (1949) described the forms of anomie that occur when there is a gap between values and means to attain them. This model is undoubtedly appropriate for migrants confronting norms for which there are structural barriers to conformity.

Norms concerning migration also play a role with regard to stress. When migration is itself a norm, as, for example, in Israel, the migrant is not in a deviant role. In societies that see migration as unusual, however, the entering migrant is a stranger who has deviated from prevailing norms merely by relocating. Stevens, Goddman, and Mick (1978) dramatized this issue by noting that migrant physicians in the United States are referred to as aliens. In Israel, on the other hand, large segments of the population immigrated in the recent past, so that language idiosyncracies, foreign accents, and lack of familiarity with certain elements of the culture are widespread and quite readily accepted. Other things being equal, there is likely to be less stress when the host population is composed largely of recent migrants than when the resident population is composed predominantly of natives.

Some Research Issues

Most research on migration has focused on migrants at their destination and has addressed itself to the issue of stress or its outcomes at that geographical location. For example, many investigators have asked whether migrants exhibit relatively high rates of illness, hospitalization, crime, or other social pathology. This question of course relates to social policies on admission of immigrants. If it can be demonstrated that migrants are indeed characterized by high levels of social or physical pathology, the host society can make a strong case for limiting entry. In Israel, however, the criteria for admission rest on ideological grounds rather than on instrumental considerations of migrants' contribution to the host society and the costs they impose on it (Shuval, 1982).

The constraint of studying migrants at their destination naturally stems from the fact that conclusive identification of migrants can take place only after they have in fact left their place of origin and arrived at their destination. The alternative strategy is to study self-identified potential migrants—people who have registered for exit visas or otherwise demonstrated an intention to leave. For logistic reasons this procedure—despite the useful findings it could yield—has rarely been followed.

Focusing on migrants in the host setting and attempting to link migration with stress require consideration of the selection mechanisms at the place of origin to determine the differential susceptibility of migrants to stress. Testing this hypothesis requires data on populations in the place of origin, as well as at the destination. Odegaarde's (1931) early work comparing Norwegian migrants to Minnesota with residents of both Norway and Minnesota was a classic test of this hypothesis (see also Malzberg & Lee, 1956).

In order to demonstrate that migrants are relatively susceptible to stress as a result of selection, it is necessary to determine criteria of selection that are relevant to susceptibility and to show that migrants differ significantly on these measures from the population at the point of origin. For example, compared to controls at the place or origin, are migrants more prone to mental or physical illness, more deviant in behavior, or less able to cope? Such negative selection could explain relatively high stress at the destination. The difficulty in testing this hypothesis is considerable. At best, demographic data on the population at the original location may be available, but psychological or social indicators of comparative susceptibility generally are neither collected nor reliably recorded. Thus, even if one could determine that certain demographically defined subgroups were overrepresented among migrants from a given country or region—women, unskilled workers, elderly persons—the link between such characteristics and susceptibility to stress would be largely conjectural.

Using migrant populations at the destination as the data base makes it difficult to identify the motivational and decisionmaking patterns that preceded migration. After migration has taken place, such information is by definition retrospective and suffers from all the weaknesses of this type of data.

Ideally, several of these research issues could be addressed by a longitudinal, multistage design that started at the place of origin and included various population groups at different times: samples of the base population from which migrants were self-selected at the place of origin; the subset of persons who formally identified themselves as potential migrants at the place of origin; actual migrants at the place of origin prior to leaving; migrants in the host society shortly after arrival and at subsequent points in time; and samples of nonmigrants in the host society. All these groups would need to be evaluated with regard to motivations, decisionmaking, expectations, available resources, norms, values, perceptions, feelings about host and migrant population, and evidence of stress or its outcomes. Such a design poses formidable practical problems. However, Israel's Ministry of Absorption has shed considerable light on the migration experience by systematically monitoring the process of absorption in a longitudinal investigation (Israel Ministry of Immigrant Absorption, 1975, 1976, 1977, 1978, 1979, 1980).

CONCLUSION

Migration is a process of transition from the place of origin to the destination. The decision to migrate entails balancing attractive and undesirable features at both these points. The selection of individuals and groups from the host population is influenced by their resources, which in turn affect their vulnerability to stress at the destination. The integration of migrants into a new social system is a multidimensional process that is not necessarily smooth and may be characterized by conflict as a result of competing interests and values between newcomers and longtime residents.

In considering stress, I emphasized the effectiveness of coping mechanisms, both personal and social. Stress is subjectively defined on an individual level, so that any objective condition may or may not result in stress, depending on the individual's definition of the situation and his style of coping.

I discussed the specific link between migration and stress on several levels. Change, which is viewed as inherent in migration, may under certain circumstances be defined as a stressor. Change may take place on a physical, a social, or a cultural level. Furthermore, migrants, by virtue of their special status, may be vulnerable to stress as a result of structural and normative aspects of the migration process that cause them to be located in certain niches of the host society. On a structural level, migrants may be located geographically and socially in positions that expose them differentially to stressors of a physical and/or social nature (poor physical conditions, stereotypes, hostility, low power, etc.). The norms to which conformity is required may also serve as stressors when these conflict with norms learned earlier.

Finally, I pointed out that coping mechanisms that may have served the migrant in his place of origin may not be effective or appropriate in the new social context. Certain roles required by the host society may place the newcomer in situations for which he has no prior coping mechanisms available and, therefore, these must be developed.

The methodological problems of research in this field center heavily on a situational constraint: virtually all research concerning migrants has been based on populations already settled in a new society. This constraint poses difficulties in addressing the issue of selection processes among migrants since data concerning the relevant comparative groups in the place of origin may not be available or accessible. Furthermore, the post facto status of the migrant raises serious questions about the reliability of retrospective information he may provide concerning motivations, perceptions, and expectations prior to his removal. Since entry into a new social system is a prolonged process, during which levels of stress may vary considerably, longitudinal research would seem necessary if this area is to be addressed appropriately.

REFERENCES

ABRAMSON, J. H. Emotional disorder, status inconsistency, and migration. *Milbank Memorial Fund Quarterly,* 1966, *44,* 23–48.

ANTONOVSKY, A. Social and cultural factors in coronary heart disease: An Israel–North American sibling study. *Israel Journal of Medical Sciences,* 1971, *7,* 1578–1583.

AVIRAM, U. & LEVAV, I. Psychiatric epidemiology in Israel: Analysis of community studies. *Acta Psychiatrica Scandinavica,* 1975, *52,* 295–311.

BRODY, E. B. (ed.). *Behavior in new environments.* Beverly Hills: Sage, 1970.

Cassel, J. T. Social science theory as a source of hypotheses in epidemiological research. *American Journal of Public Health,* 1964, *54,* 1482–1488.

Davis, K. The migration of human populations. *Scientific American,* 1974, *231,* 93–107.

French, J. P. R., Jr., Rodgers, W., & Cobb, S. Adjustment as person-environment fit. In G. V. Coelho, D. A. Hamburg, & J. E. Adams (eds.), *Coping and adaptation: Interdisciplinary perspectives.* New York: Basic Books, 1974.

Freid, M. Deprivation and migration. In E. B. Brody (ed.), *Behavior in new environments.* Beverly Hills: Sage, 1970.

Gitelman,, Z. *Jewish nationality and Soviet politics.* Princeton: Princeton University Press, 1972.

————. Soviet Jewish emigrants: Why are they choosing America? *Soviet Jewish Affairs,* 1977, *7,* 31–46.

————. Political resocialization of Soviet and American Immigrants in Israel. Manuscript, University of Michigan, Ann Arbor, 1979.

Gordon, M. Assimilation in American life. New York: Oxford University Press, 1964.

Halevi, H. S. Frequency of mental illness among Jews in Israel. *International Journal of Social Psychiatry,* 1963, *9,* 268–282.

House, J. S. Occupational stress and coronary heart disease: A review. *Journal of Health and Social Behavior,* 1974, *15,* 12–27.

Hull, D. Migration, adaptation, and illness: A review. *Social Science and Medicine,* 1979, *13A,* 25–36.

Insight, 1977, *5*(3).

Israel Ministry of Absorption. *Immigrant absorption.* Jerusalem, 1975, 1976, 1977, 1978, 1979, 1980.

Jackson, J. A. (ed.). *Migration.* New York: Cambridge University Press, 1969.

Jansen, C. J. *Readings in the sociology of migration.* New York: Pergamon, 1970.

Kantor, M. B. *Mobility and mental health.* Springfield: Thomas, 1965.

Kuo, W. Theories of migration and mental health: An empirical testing on Chinese Americans. *Social Science and Medicine,* 1976, *10,* 297–306.

Lee, E. A theory of migration. In J. A. Jackson (ed.), *Migration.* New York: Cambridge University Press, 1969.

Levine, S., & Scotch, N. A. (eds.). *Social stress.* Chicago: Aldine, 1970.

Malzberg, B., & Lee, E. *Migration and mental disease.* New York: Social Science Research Council, 1956.

Mangalam, J., & Schwarzweller, H. Some theoretical guidelines toward a sociology of migration. *International Migration Review,* 1970, *4,* 5–21.

Mechanic, D. *Medical sociology.* New York: Free Press, 1978.

Merton, R. K. *Social theory and social structure.* New York: Free Press, 1949.

Murphy, H. B. M. *Flight and resettlement.* Paris: UNESCO, 1955.

Odegaarde, Emigration and insanity. *Acta Psychiatrica et Neurologica* (suppl. 4), 1932, 1–206.

Park, R., & Burgess, E. Introduction to the science of sociology. Chicago: University of Chicago Press, 1921.

Pearlin, L. I., & Schooler, C. The structure of coping. *Journal of Health and Social Behavior,* 1978, *19,* 2–21.

Price, C. The study of assimilation. In J. A. Jackson (ed.), *Migration,* New York: Cambridge University Press, 1969.

Richmond, A. Migration in industrial societies. In J. A. Jackson (ed.), *Migration.* New York: Cambridge University Press, 1969.

Rose, A. Migrants in Europe. Minneapolis: University of Minnesota Press, 1969.

SCOTCH, N. A. Socio-cultural factors in the epidemiology of Zulu hypertension. *American Journal of Public Health,* 1943, *53,* 1205–1213.

SCOTT, R., & HOWARD, A. Models of stress. In S. Levine & N. A. Scotch (eds.), *Social stress.* Chicago: Aldine, 1970.

SHUVAL, J. T. The contribution of social and psychological phenomena to an understanding of the aetiology of disease and illness. *Social Science and Medicine,* 1981, *15,* 337–342.

————. *Newcomers and colleagues: Soviet immigrant physicians in Israel.* New York: Academic, 1982.

SHUVAL, J. T., MARKUS, E. J., and DOTAN, J. *Patterns of adjustment of Soviet immigrants to Israel.* Jerusalem: Israel Institute of Applied Social Research, 1973.

————. *Patterns of integration over time: Soviet immigrants in Israel.* Jerusalem: Israel Institute of Applied Social Research, 1975.

STEVENS, R., GODDMAN, L. W., & MICK, S. S. *The alien doctors.* New York: Wiley, 1978.

STROMBERG, J., PEYMAN, H., & DOWD, J. E. Migration and health: Adaptation experiences of Iranian immigrants to the city of Teheran. *Social Science and Medicine,* 1974, *8,* 309–323.

SYME, L. S., HYMAN, M. M., & ENTERLINE, P. E. Some social and cultural factors associated with the occurrence of coronary heart disease. *Journal of Chronic Diseases,* 1964, *17,* 277–289.

WESSEN, A. E. The role of migrant studies in epidemiological research. *Israel Journal of Medical Sciences,* 1971, *7,* 1584–1591.

PART **VIII**

TREATMENT AND SUPPORTS

42

The Nature of Effective Coping and the Treatment of Stress Related Problems: A Cognitive-Behavioral Perspective

Roy Cameron   Don Meichenbaum

STRESS IS A CONCEPT that, though ill defined, has nonetheless attracted a great deal of scientific interest. The rapidly proliferating literature on stress is not only vast but also diverse. The diversity exists because stress and adaptation have been conceptualized from many points of view. Anthropological (e.g., Cannon, 1942), biological (e.g., Selye, 1956), cultural (e.g., Zborowski, 1969), ethological (e.g., Tinbergen, 1974), and psychological (e.g., Lazarus, 1966) perspectives are all represented in the literature. Moreover, individuals within disciplines have thought about stress in different ways, studied different phenomena, used different methodologies, and made different assumptions.

This conceptual diversity has made it difficult to define the term "stress." Thirty years ago Beach (1950) observed that "if the word is going to refer to everything from homeostatic mechanisms . . . to cerebral activity . . . , we are apt to arrive at a very inclusive but equally indefinite concept" (p. 119). His statement was prophetic: we do not seem to have made notable progress in clarifying the definition. Mason (1975b) more recently echoed Beach's concern when he noted that "the general picture in the field can still only be described as one of confusion" since the "term 'stress' has been used variously to refer to 'stimulus' . . . , 'response' . . . , 'interaction' . . . and more comprehensive combinations of these factors" (p. 29).

A *transactional model of stress* appears to be emerging as a broad integrative framework in this complex area. This model has been developed largely by Lazarus and his colleagues (Lazarus, 1966; Lazarus & Cohen, 1977; Lazarus, Cohen, Folkman, Kanner, & Schaeffer, 1980; Lazarus & Launier, 1978; Roskies & Lazarus, 1980). According to this view, stress is said to occur in the face of *"demands that tax or exceed the resources of the system* or, to put it in a slightly different way, demands to which there are no readily available or automatic adaptive responses" (Lazarus & Cohen, 1977:109). The transactional perspective emphasizes *cognitive appraisals* and *coping responses*. A stressful transaction begins with a primary cognitive appraisal that a situation requires an effective response to

We are grateful to John Conway, Myles Genest, and Dennis Turk for their comments on an earlier draft of this chapter.

avoid or reduce physical or psychological harm and a secondary appraisal that no completely effective response is immediately available. The person makes the best response possible. The response (or its absence) has environmental repercussions, and the external situation tends to be altered. This prompts reappraisal of the situation and potential coping responses, with this reappraisal in turn affecting the ongoing response to the situation. The model thus suggests that persons actively define and shape stressful transactions by means of their cognitive appraisals and their coping responses.

This model of stress is noteworthy because it appears to have general and fundamental significance within the stress field. For instance, Mason (1975a) and Lazarus (1975) presented data indicting that the *general adaptation syndrome* described by Selye (1956) may be precipitated not by noxious physical stimuli per se but rather by the psychological reaction to physical stimuli. Deleterious physiological changes resulting in damage, ranging from stomach ulceration (Weiss, 1977) to death (Richter, 1957), appear to be mediated by psychological mechanisms that seem to involve cognitive appraisal and coping. There is evidence that human neuroendocrine responses in stressful situations are influenced by the nature of the person-environment transaction (Frankenhaeuser, 1975, 1980). Developmental psychobiologists have discovered that there may be critical developmental periods during which different types of interactions between organisms and their environments result in "permanent and profound" individual differences in adrenocortical response to environmental stress that persist into adulthood (Levine, 1975). Findings such as these suggest that even basic biological stress research may be enriched by the transactional perspective.

The model is appealing also because it provides a conceptual link between stress research and contemporary cognitive-behavioral treatment strategies, which are designed to promote realistic or adaptive appraisals of problems and effective coping responses. Roskies and Lazarus (1980) discussed in some detail the affinity between the transactional model of stress and cognitive behavior therapy. The objectives of the present chapter are to outline a model of effective coping and an approach to treating stress related problems by training effective coping skills. The models of coping and treatment we describe are consistent with the transactional model of stress and reflect our cognitive-behavioral approach to clinical problems.

TOWARD A COGNITIVE-BEHAVIORAL MODEL OF EFFECTIVE COPING PROCESSES

Our understanding of coping processes is far from complete. The lack of solid data arises in part from the inherent difficulties in the empirical study of coping. It is unethical to induce high levels of stress in humans in a laboratory situation. Even if this were not so, laboratory based experimental research tends to constrain response alternatives (Bowers, 1973) so that any view of coping processes that emerged from such research undoubtedly would be incomplete and distorted. The alternative is to conduct naturalistic studies. Cohen and Lazarus (1979) published a thoughtful and detailed discussion of difficulties in studying coping that must be surmounted if meaningful empirical work is to flourish. During the course of their discussion, they noted that the study of coping would be facilitated by a classification system that enabled researchers to categorize coping acts for purposes of description and analysis.

A number of taxonomies of coping behavior have been developed. Some of these are explicitly based on or consistent with a transactional model of stress. For instance, Moos and Tsu (1977) classified coping responses employed by people adjusting to physical illness.

They identified and described seven classes of coping skills: (1) denying or minimizing the seriousness of a crisis, (2) seeking relevant information, (3) requesting reassurance and emotional support, (4) learning specific illness related procedures, (5) setting concrete, limited goals, (6) rehearsing alternative outcomes, and (7) finding a general purpose or pattern of meaning in the course of events.

A second taxonomy for classifing coping strategies has been developed by Lazarus and his colleagues (Lazarus et al., 1980). Whereas the taxonomy presented by Moos and Tsu (1977) refers specifically to coping with stresses related to physical illness, Lazarus's classification system is more general. Lazarus and Launier (1978) classified coping efforts according to *mode* (direct action, action inhibition, information search, or intrapsychic) and *function* (instrumental alteration of the problem or palliative regulation of the emotional response). They noted that each of the major coping modes subsumes a wide range of discrete coping strategies.

Lazarus and Launier's (1978) scheme takes into account *coping resources,* as well as *coping strategies.* The former refer to relatively stable factors that affect both the range of coping options available to an individual and the predisposition to utilize available responses. The Lazarus group (Folkman, Schaeffer, & Lazarus, 1980) identified six categories of coping resources, some inherent in the person (health and energy, morale, problem-solving skills, system of beliefs) and some environmentally based (social support, material resources). Pearlin and Schooler (1978) also discussed stable coping resources and liabilities. They presented data that led them to identify three dimensions (self-denigration, lack of a sense of mastery, and lack of a sense of positive self-esteem) associated with subjective stress levels in a variety of personal and vocational contexts.

We would like to introduce a somewhat different perspective on coping. Although our approach is compatible with the classification schemes described earlier, we are interested in the *process of effective coping* rather than the classification of all possible responses or resources. This perspective reflects our interest in stress and coping as clinical problems. Effective treatment presupposes some (at least tentative) understanding of the nature of adaptive functioning, the goal toward which therapy is to progress. Our aim is to outline a process model of coping that bridges the gap between transactional models of stress and recent conceptual developments in cognitive-behavioral modification.

Our model is derived from a cognitive-functional analysis of the coping process. In brief, *cognitive-functional analysis* starts with the assumption that most human functioning involves a complex integration of cognitive, affective, and behavioral processes. We further assume that it is possible to delineate both the component processes of effective sequences of behavior and the ways in which effective functioning can be disrupted. This type of analysis has been described in more detail elsewhere (Cameron, 1976; Kinsbourne, 1971; Meichenbaum, 1977; Schwartz & Gottman, 1976). A cognitive-functional analysis appears to have considerable value for both theoretical and clinical purposes. From a theoretical point of view, it takes into account the possibility that people who have what appears to be the same overt problem may in fact have different underlying deficits. For instance, Kinsbourne (1971) indicated that a logical analysis of reading suggests that there are at least nine specific cognitive deficits that could underlie an inability to read. This sort of analysis of underlying deficits makes it possible to avoid mistakenly grouping together people with different underlying problems. Even though there may be similarity in overt presenting problems across individuals, it is important *not* to assume that the group is homogeneous. Not only is cognitive-functional analysis useful for research purposes, but also greatly facilitates clinical assessment since it pinpoints specific deficits, thus providing a sound basis for planning interventions tailored to the needs of the individual client.

It is important to emphasize at the outset that a cognitive-functional assessment is conducted with reference to a particular individual engaged in a specific task. This approach is necessary because both the resources and deficiencies specific to the individual and the demands peculiar to the task combine to define the optimal coping chain for any given person in any given situation. This implies that there is a virtually limitless number of ways in which effective coping may manifest itself across situations and across persons. Our intention is not to delineate all the possibilities. Our goal is rather to introduce a *way of thinking* about stress and coping and a *framework* for conceptualizing general factors that contribute to (or interfere with) the process of effective functioning.

At a gross level of analysis there appear to be at least four fundamental prerequisites for effective coping. First, coping is (most often) likely to be facilitated by a veridical, or at least an adaptive, appraisal of the world, oneself, and the commerce between the two. Efforts to cope may well be misguided to the extent that the "true" nature of things is misconstrued. Second, given a reasonable appraisal, effective coping presupposes an adequate repertoire of responses (or skills) for dealing with the ongoing demands of life. Third, given that the first two prerequisites are met, the person must actually deploy appropriate coping responses as required. Fourth, upon completion of a stress coping sequence, effective coping implies an efficient return to a baseline level of functioning rather than unnecessary protraction of the episode. Ineffective coping could arise because of failure at any of the four stages just described. We shall discuss each of these four components of effective coping in turn.

Accurate Appraisal

Life is fraught with ambiguity. The events we observe and the processes of which we are a part may be interpreted in more than one way. In the words of Kelly (1969), "Whatever exists can be reconstrued" (p. 227). Similarly, Frank (1974) noted that everyone interprets experience on the basis of "a set of more or less implicit assumptions about himself and the nature of the world in which he lives" (p. 27). Frank used the term "assumptive world" to refer to this set of assumptions. He suggested that assumptive worlds differ across people, with the result that different people may construe the same objective phenomenon in diverse ways. Raimy (1975) indicated that this view of people as interpreters of their world has played a central role in the thinking of many other eminent students of human behavior, ranging from Immanuel Kant to H. S. Sullivan.

Although experience may be interpreted in many ways, some interpretations are presumably more adaptive than others. As an interpreter of experience, a person is in a position analogous to that of a scientist. The objectives of interpreting experience (like the objectives of science) are to understand, to predict, and, where possible and desirable, to control. This way of looking at things implies that interpretations are valid to the extent that they are supported (and not contradicted) by convincing data. Moreover, it implies that interpretations are valuable insofar as they make sense of experience in terms that allow predictions to be made about what is likely to transpire and point the way to potentially effective means of intervening in the flow of events.

This view of the person as scientist is central to our model of coping. Our general thesis is that maximally effective coping depends upon a person's functioning like a scientist in interpretating and experimenting with the world of experience. This view is certainly not original or new. It is implicitly or explicitly embodied in the work of many other psychologists, including those mentioned previously. The similarity between lay thinking and scientific thinking was the subject of a delightful essay published by Huxley in 1938. Huxley (1938) wrote, "The method of scientific investigation is nothing but the expression of the necessary mode of working of the human mind" (p. 1311). He went on to elaborate the thesis that common sense is the same, in principle, as scientific thinking.

Our process model of effective coping, then, suggests that the quality of human transactions with the environment will depend in the first instance upon the adequacy of the person's interpretations of experience. Successful coping efforts presuppose interpretations that minimize distortion and blind spots. We should not gloss over the fact that this tenet may require qualification. There is evidence that distortions can sometimes be adaptive. Allport (1968) related an amusing anecdote, reportedly true, that illustrates the adaptive potential of distortion. According to Allport's account, a man lay near death in a provincial Austrian hospital. He was told that his physicians could not diagnose his problem, but that he could probably be cured if a diagnosis could be made. He was further told that a great diagnostician would soon visit the hospital and that this gifted physician might be able to identify the problem. When the diagnostician came, he stopped briefly at the patient's bedside, muttered "moribundus," and moved on. Several years later the patient contacted the diagnostician to thank him for his diagnosis, adding, "They told me that if you could diagnose me I'd get well, and so the minute you said 'Moribundus' I knew I'd recover" (p. 124).

The argument that distortion sometimes may be adaptive has received more formal support from a variety of sources. For instance, in a classic investigation, Wolff, Friedman, Hofer, and Mason (1964) studied the parents of children who had leukemia. They found that the amount of 17-hydroxycorticosteroid excreted was higher among parents who acknowledged the reality of the situation than among those judged to be denying the seriousness of the problem. Also, there is evidence that placebos may sometimes trigger bona fide physical repsonses that have a salutary effect (Levine, Gordon, & Fields, 1978; Wolf, 1950), an effect derived from a misperception. A final provocative report was published recently by Lewinsohn, Mischel, Chaplin, and Barton (1980). These investigators found evidence that depressed people see themselves more objectively (or at least more like others see them) than do nondepressed people, who tend to have a more positive view of themselves than others have of them. These findings prompted the authors to speculate that perhaps "to feel good about ourselves we may have to judge ourselves more kindly than we are judged" (p. 212).

Although there may be some situations in which distortion is adaptive, it seems probable that interpretations consistent with available evidence generally will be more adaptive in the long run than those that are skewed. Indeed, it seems likely that distorted interpretations will often actually induce or exacerbate stress. This may occur in a number of ways.

First, misinterpreting a benign situation as threatening may trigger what amounts to unnecessary, self-inflicted stress. If such situations are appraised more carefully

> the dreaded possiblities turn out to be highly improbable or imaginary, or it is discovered that the fears were generalized from another situation that was quite different from the present one. Often, discriminating the realistic from the unrealistic fears can make one feel much better. (Miller, 1980:146)

Raimy (1975) and Valins and Nisbett (1976) published interesting accounts of how misinterpretations of benign information can lead to psychological distress.

Second, since we respond behaviorally, as well as affectively, to our interpretations, we are likely to behave inappropriately in situations that we have misread. This pattern may set in motion an objectively stressful chain of events. Wagar's (1963) statement that "the ultimate function of prophecy is not to tell the future, but to make it" (p. 66) comes to mind here. The person who anticipates stress in a situation in which such an anticipation is unfounded may precipitate a self-fulfilling prophecy by behaving inappropriately, thereby triggering stress engendering reactions in others. Jones (1977) reviewed in some detail the research pertaining to such phenomena.

Third, failure accurately to appraise a situation by underestimating threat potential may be maladaptive if the misperception forestalls self-protective action. For instance, a person who underestimates the significance of physical symptoms may delay seeking medical assistance, thereby aggravating the problem. Or the student who underestimates the importance of negative feedback may fail to work diligently in order to reestablish good standing.

An Adequate Response Repertoire

Effective coping requires that a person not only perceive the world clearly but also respond in ways that defuse threat. Appropriate response depends in the first instance upon the person's having the capability to make an effective response. Some behaviors are so universally required in our society that absence of adequate response skills is likely to be debilitating and to constitute a source of considerable stress, as defined in transactional terms. By definition, anyone deficient in skills regularly required to meet recurrent, common, unavoidable demands cannot be an effective coper. Conversely, for the person who has developed the skills required to respond effectively to the normal demands of life, stress will be less pervasive. A number of generally useful skills come to mind immediately. These include skills related to assertive behavior, communication skills, and palliative skills (e.g., self-relaxation), which have wide application in situations in which the best option is to moderate our reaction to a stressful transaction over which we have no control.

The assessment of a coping response repertoire is a complex task. The most obvious and crucial problem concerns the interpretation of negative results. If the target response is not produced in the assessment situation, does this mean that the response is not in the person's repertoire? Or did the person merely fail to deliver an available response? There may be no way to decide between these two alternatives with complete confidence. It is clear, however, that the repertoire deficit interpretation is credible only to the extent that the assessment has occurred under conditions "most favorable for demonstration of the ability in question" (Wallace, 1966:134). The important issue of how to assess competencies cannot be considered in detail here. However, more extended discussions of strategies for assessing response capabilities have been offered by Wallace (1966), Goldfried and D'Zurilla (1969), and Schwartz and Gottman (1976).

Appropriate Deployment of Coping Responses

Let us assume that an adequate response for meeting a demand is available in a person's repertoire. Adequate coping will not occur unless the response is actually deployed. Failure to produce an available response may be due to "production deficiency" or to "mediational deficiency" (Flavell, 1970; Reese, 1962). In the first instance, the response failure occurs because there is no appropriate cognitive cue to activate the response. In the second instance, the activating cue is present but the response nonetheless fails to occur.

In a stressful situation it simply may not occur to a person to employ a potentially effective response *(production deficiency)*. This experience appears to be so commonplace as to be self-evident. A few years ago a personal experience brought home this type of coping failure in a very vivid way. One of us (R. C.) had been asked to review a paper. I had planned to get up early Saturday morning and to complete the task by the time the rest of the family wakened. The paper was interesting but involved an unorthodox and complex statistical analysis; it was difficult to determine whether the analysis was appropriate. The children woke, and I snarled at them when the interrupted me with their cheery greeting. This was clearly inappropriate, so there was an apology and an explanation of the problem. Four-year-old Melanie had an idea along these lines: "Why not tell [the editor] what you think, but tell him there's part of it you don't understand for sure?" It was a good solution, fair to all concerned, and easy to implement. The response was obvious enough for a four year old to see but it simply did not register as a possibility until Melanie suggested it.

Sometimes available coping responses are not activated even though an appropriate mediating cue is present *(mediational deficiency)*. Facilitative cognitive mediators are most likely to fail to activate available responses when the facilitative cue is overbalanced by inhibitory mediators. Schwartz and Gottman (1976) found evidence that although nonassertive people had assertive responses in their repertoires and seemed to have cognitive cues to facilitate such responses, they nonetheless failed to take appropriate action. Apparently, their self-statements emphasizing the appropriateness of acting assertively were offset by inhibitory concerns about possible negative effects of assertive behavior.

Recovery from a Stress Coping Episode

Stressful situations typically terminate either because an effective response has met the environmental demand or because a demand that surpassed response capability has passed. At that point, there is no objective basis for stress. Rate of return to a normal pattern of psychological and physiological functioning might be construed as an index of coping effectiveness (as the return of heart rate to a normal level after exertion provides an index of fitness).

Frankenhaeuser (1980) recently emphasized the importance of this aspect of coping.

> It seems reasonable to regard the *duration* of the response evoked by temporary disturbances in life as a key determinant of their potential harmfulness. In other words, the speed with which a person "unwinds" after stressful transactions with his environment will influence the total wear and tear of the organism. (P. 58)

Levine (1975) reviewed work showing striking individual differences in the rate at which mice returned to normal physiological patterns after objectively stressful experiences (differences in recovery seemed to reflect early experiences). Frankenhaeuser (1980) reviewed a number of studies suggesting that individual differences in "unwinding" rate appeared to be associated with personality characteristics; for example, *type A people*—individuals whose behavior puts them at high risk for coronary heart disease (CHD)—were found to maintain high arousal levels during periods of inactivity interspersed between periods of mental work, whereas type B's (low risk for CHD) raised and lowered arousal level depending upon demand. Other findings reported by Frankenhaeuser suggest that improvements in psychological and physical condition (after vacation) may result in more rapid arousal decrease after stressful episodes.

To the best of our knowledge, not much is known about specific psychological factors that might influence the unwinding process. It is obvious that unwinding will be impaired if a particular coping response or a failure to cope precipitates further stressful transactions. For instance, in commenting on the plight of soldiers who withdraw from battle with shellshock, Menninger (1967) noted that

> an individual's adjustment always means his reaction to a reaction, to a reaction, etc. And when an individual has fallen or wavered, his struggle back to the line of march is often handicapped by the attitudes which have been created in the environment by the development of his illness. (P. 291)

There may well be factors under voluntary control that affect the rate of unwinding. For instance, Frankenhaeuser's (1980) data suggested that maintaining good physical condition could result in more rapid arousal reduction. It is conceivable that the habit of mentally rehearsing failures and concurrently engaging in self-denigrating thoughts might interfere with at least some dimensions of the unwinding process, whereas distraction or detached retrospective analysis might promote rapid unwinding. Goleman and Schwartz (1976) found that subjects trained to meditate demonstrated more rapid recovery from stress related arousal than did subjects not trained to meditate. Further investigation of factors that contribute to efficient unwinding appears to be warranted.

The view of effective coping we have sketched has been presented as a linear model; that is, the processes seem to follow a temporal sequence. However, it should be noted that there is an interplay among the various processes such that activities associated with later stages affect the ongoing activities described in relation to earlier stages. For instance, production of an adequate coping response results in reappraisal of the threat implicit in the unfolding transaction.

THE TRAINING OF COGNITIVE AND BEHAVIORAL COPING SKILLS

A number of years ago, we developed a treatment approach we called *stress inoculation training* (Meichenbaum & Cameron, 1972). The goal was to train general coping skills that could be used under conditions of high stress and anxiety. Treatment consisted of three phases. First, there was an *educational phase* designed to lead the client to construe the problem as one that could be managed by acquiring appropriate coping skills. Next, there was a *rehearsal phase,* during which the client was introduced to and practiced cognitive and behavioral coping responses. Finally, there was an *application phase* that involved practicing the coping skills in a series of graded stressful situations. This approach proved to be more effective than systematic desensitization in the treatment of phobic avoidance and anxiety.

The basic three-phase stress inoculation paradigm has been adapted for use with a variety of clinical problems in both individual and group treatment formats. Problems addressed have included speech anxiety (Meichenbaum, Gilmore, & Fedoravicius, 1971), anger reactions (Novaco, 1975), and pain (Holroyd, 1980; Turk & Genest, 1979; Turk, Meichenbaum, & Genest, in press). A number of comprehensive overviews of this work are available (e.g. Meichenbaum, 1977; Meichenbaum & Jaremko, in press; Turk, Meichenbaum & Genest, in press).

A general model of the process of cognitive-behavioral coping skill training has been evolving from the original stress inoculation paradigm (Meichenbaum, 1976, 1977;

Meichenbaum & Cameron, in press). For heuristic purposes, the process of change is conceptualized as consisting of three phases reminiscent of the three phases of stress inoculation training. Although the names used for the various phases have changed as the model has evolved, we shall refer to the phases as the *conceptualization phase,* the *skill acquisition and activation phase,* and the *rehearsal and application phase.* We should acknowledge at the outset that in practice the three phases tend to blend together, so that the model is a heuristic device rather than a precise outline of the course of therapy. The general goal of therapy is to promote effective coping, as described earlier in the chapter.

Phase 1: Conceptualization

A major task of the first phase of treatment is for the therapist and client to evolve a shared understanding of the presenting problem in terms that set the stage for coping skill training (phase 2). Data collection and interpretation are the primary activities associated with this initial diagnostic phase. Cognitions and behaviors that contribute to the difficulty are identified. The data of the client's experience typically fit nicely with the transactional model of stress as his or her appraisal processes and coping efforts are examined. Once the client's experience has been organized into a transactional framework, there is a natural progression to the training of coping respones, which occurs in the next phase of therapy. We have discussed this process of developing a shared conceptualization elsewhere (Turk, Meichenbaum, and Genest, in press). This material will not be reiterated here.

When the original stress inoculation treatment paradigm was developed (Meichenbaum & Cameron, 1972), the conceptualization (or educational) phase of therapy was seen primarily as a prelude to intervention. Subsequently, it has become evident that important therapeutic changes may begin during this first phase. Specifically, there are rich opportunities for developing and refining the client's appraisal skills as diagnostic data are gathered and interpreted. The present discussion of the initial phase of treatment will be restricted to this theme.

We suggested earlier that effective coping is likely to be facilitated by accurate appraisal, which enables a person to understand, predict, and be in a position to influence ongoing transactions. If it is granted that accurate appraisal is of such fundamental significance, it becomes important to identify cognitive habits and skills that lead to reasonable interpretations. The following factors seem likely to promote realistic appraisal: a conscious recognition that any given appraisal is not necessarily accurate or complete; the habit of generating alternative hypotheses and interpretations; an inclination to collect data pertinent to the evaluation of hypotheses under consideration; and, if ambiguity cannot be resolved, the ability to evaluate the relative heuristic value of competing alternative hypotheses. To the extent that such attitudes and skills are developed, the person will tend to revise appraisals in an ongoing way in order to bring them into line with available data and to look for heuristically useful conceptualizations.

Even as therapist and client gather and interpret diagnostic data, the therapist may begin teaching the client to think more scientifically. The therapist can proceed with this task by providing an explicit description of the process of clarifying appraisals; modeling a tentative, hypothetical, self-correcting approach as diagnostic data are reviewed; brainstorming with the client to generate alternative hypotheses about available data; discussing how further diagnostic data could be collected deliberately to decide among plausible interpretations; and prompting the client to consider the heuristic value of plausible alternative interpretations (e.g., "If we think about it that way, where are we led?"). Note that this process is not conducted as if one were lecturing an introductory psychology class about the scientific method; instead, patient and therapist engage in a therapeutic dialogue, with the therapist using Socratic questions, reflection, amplification, juxtaposition of the client's data, and so forth. See Turk, Meichenbaum, and Genest (in press) for a detailed account of these clinical techniques. The client's appraisal processes may also be refined by identifying biases that regularly result in distortion. Although idiosyncratic biases may emerge during the diagnostic formulation phase, two biases appear to be so pervasive and important as to be particularly noteworthy.

The first is a bias toward *dispositional* as opposed to *situational* attributions. In a classic paper, Jones and Davis (1965) presented empirical evidence that we tend to underestimate the extent to which situational factors influence behavior. If one is concerned with altering transactional patterns, and clients inevitably are, situational analyses are almost always of more practical value than are dispositional attributions. For instance, the husband who attributes his marital dissatisfaction to his own reserved nature, in combination with his wife's bitchiness, sees little potential for change. If he considers the possibility that the behaviors he labels bitchiness in his wife are influenced significantly by his own behavior and other situational variables, he may be able to see some concrete steps he can take to improve the relationship. Cognitive-behavioral assessments emphasize an analysis of situational determinants of behavior. Training clients to conduct such analyses for themselves and helping them to appreciate both the heuristic value of such analyses and the bias against situational attributions may equip them to be more effective interpreters of their experience.

Bias toward *confirmatory data* also is commonplace. Some empirical evidence points to a tendency to bias attention toward data that confirm hypotheses and to avoid seeking out or noticing disconfirmatory information (Mahoney & DeMonbreun, 1977; Synder & Swann, 1978). In the latter study, for instance, subjects were provided with hypotheses about the personalities of other individuals ("targets"). Some subjects were led to hypothesize that the target was extroverted; others, that the target was introverted. When subjects were asked to test their hypotheses, they preferentially searched for evidence that would confirm the initial hypothesis. Moreover, the biased search strategy of the subject influenced the behavior of the target such that the target responded by producing behaviors consistent with the original hypothesis of the subject. In a similar vein, a person who sees the world as competitive may behave competitively, thus eliciting similar behavior from others, with this pattern confirming the original assumption that people are competitive (Kelley & Stahelski, 1970). Frank (1974) used the term "pseudoconfirmation" to refer to this process in which an initial biased assumption prompts us to behave in a way that is almost certain to evoke a reaction that will confirm the assumption. Training clients to cultivate the habit of searching for and attempting to generate disconfirmatory data is likely to enhance the client's capacity to be self-correcting and to see things more accurately.

Phase 2: Skill Acquisition and Activation

During the first phase of therapy the client has learned to become a better observer and interpreter of experience as diagnostic data are collected and discussed. To the extent that interpretative skills have been developed, the client is equipped to make reasonable and useful appraisals of situations. Moreover, client and therapist have used the diagnostic data to arrive at a shared understanding of the client's problem in transactional terms.

The next step is for the client to learn to respond more effectively in situations in which coping responses have proved to be inadequate. Our analysis of effective coping sequences suggested that response inadequacy may stem either from a deficit in the response repertoire or from a failure to deploy available responses. Insofar as the performance inadequacy results from lack of skill, therapy focuses on skill acquisition during this second phase. If the relevant skill is in the repertoire, the focus is on increasing facilitative mediators and reducing inhibition in order to activate the response.

A great deal has been written about the training of cognitive-behavioral coping skills. A number of comprehensive reviews are available (e.g., Goldfried, 1980; Mahoney & Arnkoff, 1978; Meichenbaum, 1977; Meichenbaum & Jaremko, in press; Rosenthal & Bandura, 1978; Turk, Meichenbaum, & Genest, in press). It is clearly beyond the scope of this chapter to summarize this extensive literature. However, we would like to single out for discussion, two classes of behavior that may be regarded as coping skills although they have received little attention. We have in mind behaviors that prevent the occurrence of stressful transactions and behaviors related to unwinding after stressful episodes.

The transactional model of stress emphasizes that people not only respond to, but also create, their environments. This "reciprocal determinism" (Bandura, 1977b) introduces the possibility of preventative actions. It is easiest to envision this possibility with reference to interpersonal stresses. Much of the stress experienced by clients arises when they find themselves unable to "straighten out" significant relationships that have gone awry. Rosenthal and Bandura (1978) suggested that "teaching clients . . . to amplify social cues that bring out the best in other people's repertoires seems a plausible goal" (p. 625). If clients are able to acquire such skills, they increase the probability of eliciting friendly, cooperative behavior in their transactions and decrease the likelihood of evoking the sorts of hostile responses that generally characterize stressful, conflictual interactions. To the extent that clients develop such skills, they may not only decrease stress but actually increase life satisfaction. Developing "switching responses" that prevent incipient conflictual transactions from escalating and shift the focus in a positive direction may also be useful. For example, a client may be able to diffuse a brewing marital conflict by saying, "I realize I've been focusing on who's to blame. I don't think that's going to get anywhere. I'd like to think about how we can come up with a mutually agreeable solution." Our original stress inoculation paradigm was designed to help people react adaptively in stressful situations. The transactional model underscores the possibility of training people to behave in ways that prevent stressful transactions from arising and increase the rate of positive transactions.

As noted previously, we have much to learn about the process of unwinding after stressful experiences. Therefore, it is difficult to know either how important the unwinding process is or how to facilitate it. Although we lack basic knowledge in this area, it seems reasonable to be attentive to the client's recovery from distressing episodes. If there is evidence of cognitive or behavioral habits that appear to interfere with the unwinding process, it may be useful to nurture more adaptive patterns. For instance, the client who repeatedly reviews a stressful incident while making self-denigrating comments may be able to shift to a more dispassionate retrospective analysis with a view to learning from the experience.

Once it is established that the client has the requisite coping skills, any coping response failures that arise presumably result either from a deficiency of facilitative mediating cues, or from inhibitory cognitions, or from disruptive affective experiences. At this point, the objective is to help the client activate coping responses as they are called for. One strategy for developing facilitative mediators of coping responses is to have the client carefully monitor the stressful transactional sequence with a view to identifying specific experiences or events that may serve as cues to cope. Such cues are most likely to be effective mediators if they are regularly a part of the transactional sequence. They are also perhaps more likely to be effective if they are *early* components in a maladaptive sequence, so that the person can alter the transaction before affect has intensified and before other persons in the environment have begun high-intensity complementary reactions to the maladaptive behavior chain. A second general strategy for developing mediators is to encourage a general habit of cueing oneself to stop, interpret the situation, and consider response alternatives when stress is experienced. This set, coupled with a recognition that *something* (at least palliative coping) constructive can be done in response to *any* situation, may serve as a general mediator that orients the person to consider specific coping alternatives.

There are also a variety of potentially valuable strategies for reducing inhibitory cognitions that block production of coping responses. Many inhibitions result from the anticipation that the response would result in negative consequences that outweighed possible benefits. Such anticipations are often unfounded. If so, information clarifying this may be helpful. For instance, in a recent clinical situation a nonorgasmic wife said she stopped herself from being physically active during sex because she believed her husband would disapprove of her moving. When she asked him about this, she found that quite the opposite was true. She gradually took more initiative during sex, receiving an encouraging response from her husband each time. The verbal checking out seemed to result in enough disinhibition to initiate some cautious behavioral checking out, with this process building progressively until she was able to express herself freely without self-consciousness or restraint. Here the husband's response was crucial to the process of disinhibition. Discussions with significant others, and cueing them about the importance of positive responses to the inhibited behavior, may be critical to the success of the endeavor.

A second strategy is to use the inhibitory cognition as a cue to muster the arguments in favor of making the desirable response (i.e., to generate facilitative cues). It is interesting to recall that Schwartz and Gottman (1976) found that even assertive people made inhibitory self-statements about behaving assertively. What distinguished them from nonassertive people was that these negative thoughts were more than offset by facilitative self-statements.

A third strategy is to learn to use a coping response that is likely to elicit the desired consequence without eliciting the anticipated negative reaction. For instance, the person who inhibits assertive behavior for fear of offending may learn to make responses that are at once assertive and pleasant (polite, humorous, nonattacking).

Phase 3: Rehearsal and Application

Ideally, the client who has progressed through phases 1 and 2 has acquired interpretative and coping skills and has learned to activate these skills appropriately. At this point, treatment has covered all the basic elements of effective coping as we have described them. However, the task of therapy is not seen as complete until the client has had enough practice with the skills to consolidate treatment gains. Consolidation occurs as the client rehearses skills and applies them in ongoing stressful situations. Problems of maintenance and generalization of treatment gains continue to be a source of concern to clinicians (Meichenbaum & Cameron, in press). It is clear that we still have much to learn about how to promote the consolidation of therapeutic changes. Nonetheless, there are some promising leads.

Bandura's (1977) work on self-efficacy is notable here. Bandura postulated that the probability of engaging and persisting in coping behavior is determined in large measure by the degree to which a sense of self-efficacy has been established. A sense of self-efficacy involves confidence that the required behaviors can be produced *(efficacy expectation)* and that when produced they will result in the desired outcome *(outcome expectation)*. Bandura's analysis suggests that a sense of self-efficacy is likely to be strengthened if the therapist arranges for the client to engage in newly acquired coping responses in real-life circumstances in which there is a high probability both that the response will evoke the desired outcome and that the client can attribute success to personal capability rather than to external factors. The therapist may promote a sense of self-efficacy by reviewing success experiences with clients and prompting the client to analyze the specific coping behaviors that contributed to the success.

The problem of relapse was addressed recently by Marlatt and Gordon (1980) and by Wilson (1980). These authors emphasized the importance of a person's cognitive appraisal of a failure experience (or "slip") after successful treatment. If the person catastrophically interprets the slip as evidence that the treatment has come undone, this demoralizing appraisal may undermine coping efforts. In an attempt to reduce the risk of such occurrences, therapists may encourage clients mentally to rehearse coping reactions in response to such lapses. Marlatt and Gordon (1980) even suggested that treatment incorporate "programmed relapse" to develop coping responses and a sense of self-efficacy in the face of setbacks. It is important for clients to anticipate that they will continue to experience stress even if they are successfully treated (since stress is a normal part of life). The probability of maintaining treatment gains may be enhanced if the client anticipates discouragement, recognizes "relapse cues" (e.g., previously familiar maladaptive patterns that now can be viewed as warning signals), and develops strategies for handling them. Although we have not experimented with programmed relapse, clinical experience suggests that clients who overcome setbacks during treatment may develop a sense of self-efficacy in relation to their ability to get back on track after lapses.

Lazarus and Launier (1978) suggested that patterns of transactions gradually form basic personality characteristics in a manner analogous to the slow shaping of topographical structures by rain and the flow of rivers. One way of thinking about the final phase of therapy is to envision it as a period during which the therapist attempts to insure that the new channels of behavior are well enough established that the flow of future transactions will continue to carve the patterns more deeply. The kindling of a sense of self-efficacy related to coping responses, including responses for recovering from lapses, would appear to be an important prerequisite for such consolidation.

Another related objective of the rehearsal and application phase is to steer the patient away from a preoccupation with avoiding threats and toward a more positive search for opportunities for satisfying experiences. Bruner (1966) described the tendency of people who are not coping effectively to bias attention toward sources of threat and to react to neutral or even positive situations as threatening. He noted the incapacitating effect of this orientation: "So long as organization is dominated by so exigent an internal requirement—not missing anything dangerous lest one be overwhelmed by it—it is difficult to gain the detachment necessary to treat new materials and tasks in their own terms" (p. 138). As coping skills are rehearsed and feelings of self-efficacy built, such vigilance is relaxed, and there may be a reorientation toward life. Rather than scanning the world for lurking threats, the person may be encouraged to seek out opportunities. There is a movement away from preoccupation with avoidance of negative emotions and toward the active cultivation of what Frank (1974) called the "welfare emotions." Consolidation of treatment gains is likely to be enhanced if such a general shift in orientation can be accomplished.

CONCLUSION

In summary, we have attempted to present a general outline of coping and treatment processes as viewed from a cognitive-behavioral perspective. We recognized at the outset that this attempt would both tax and exceed our capacity to develop completely satisfactory, detailed models given the current state of knowledge. Coping and therapeutic processes are exquisitely subtle and complex. We regard the models presented as heuristic frameworks that may have some value for oganizing our thinking about these complicated processes. Undoubtedly the models will require revision and elaboration as our empirical knowledge base expands.

REFERENCES

ALLPORT, G. W. *The person in psychology*. Boston: Beacon, 1968.

BANDURA, A. *Principles of behavior modification*. New York: Holt, 1969.

————. Self-efficacy: Toward a unifying theory of behavior change. *Psychological Review,* 1977, *84,* 191–215. (a)

————. *Social learning theory*. Englewood Cliffs: Prentice-Hall, 1977. (b)

BEACH, F. A. Discussion. In H. G. Wolff (ed.), *Life stress and bodily disease*. Baltimore: Williams & Wilkins, 1950.

BOWERS, K. S. Situationism in psychology: An analysis and a critique. *Psychological Review,* 1973, *80,* 307–336.

BRUNER, J. S. *Toward a theory of instruction*. Cambridge: Harvard University Press, 1966.

CAMERON, R. Conceptual tempo and children's problem solving behavior: A developmental task analysis. Doctoral dissertation, University of Waterloo, 1976.

CANNON, W. B. Voodoo death. *American Anthropologist,* 1942, *44,* 169–181.

COHEN, F., & LAZARUS, R. S. Coping with the stresses of illness. In G. C. Stone, F. Cohen, & N. E. Adler (eds.), *Health psychology*. San Francisco: Jossey-Bass, 1979.

FLAVELL, J. H. Developmental studies of mediated memory. In H. W. Reese & L. P. Lipsitt (eds.), *Advances in child development and behavior,* vol. 5. New York: Academic, 1970.

FOLKMAN, S., SCHAEFFER, C., & LAZARUS, R. S. In V. Hamilton & D. M. Warburton (eds.), *Human stress and cognition*. New York: Wiley, 1980

FRANK, J. D. *Persuasion and healing* (rev. ed.). New York: Schocken, 1974.

FRANKENHAEUSER, M. Exprimental approaches to the study of catecholamines and emotion. In L. Levi (ed.), *Emotions: Their parameters and measurement*. New York: Raven, 1975.

————. Psychoneuroendocrine approaches to the study of stressful person-environment transactions In H. Selye (ed.), *Selye's guide to stress research,* vol. 1. New York: Van Nostrand, 1980.

GOLDFRIED, M. R. Psychotherapy as coping skills training. In M. J. Mahoney (ed.), *Psychotherapy process*. New York: Plenum, 1980.

GOLDFRIED, M. R., & D'ZURILLA, T. J. A behavioral-analytic model for assessing competence. In C. D. Spielberger (ed.), *Current topics in clinical and community psychology*. New York: Academic, 1969.

GOLEMAN, D. J., & SCHWARTZ, G. E. Meditation as an intervention in stress reactivity. *Journal of Consulting and Clinical Psychology,* 1976, *44,* 456–466.

HOLROYD, K. Stress, coping, and the treatment of stress-related illness. In J. R. McNamara (ed.), *Behavioral approaches in medicine: Application and analysis*. New York: Plenum, 1980.

HUXLEY, T. H. Darwinia. In C. F. Harrold & W. D. Templeman (eds.), *English prose of the Victorian era.* New York: Oxford University Press, 1938.

JONES, E. E., & DAVIS, K. E. From acts to dispositions: The attribution process in person perception. In L. Berkowitz (ed.), *Advances in experimental social psychology,* vol. 2. New York: Academic, 1965.

JONES, R. A. *Self-fulfilling prophecies.* Hillsdale: Erlbaum, 1977.

KELLEY, H. H., & STAHELSKI, A. J. Social interaction basis of cooperators' and competitors' beliefs about others. *Journal of Personality and Social Psychology,* 1970, *16,* 66–91.

KELLY, G. A. Personal construct theory and the psychotherapeutic interview. In B. Maher (ed.), *Clinical psychology and personality: The selected papers of George Kelly.* New York: Wiley, 1969.

KINSBOURNE, M. Cognitive deficit: Experimental analysis. In J. McGaugh (ed.), *Psychobiology.* New York: Academic, 1971.

Lazarus, R. S. *Psychological stress and the coping process.* New York: McGraw-Hill, 1966.

————. A cognitively oriented psychologist looks at biofeedback. *American Psychologist,* 1975, *30,* 553–561.

LAZARUS, R. S., & COHEN, J. B. Environmental stress. In I. Altman & J. F. Wohlwill (eds.), *Human behavior and environment,* vol. 2. New York: Plenum, 1977.

LAZARUS, R. S., COHEN, J. B., FOLKMAN, S., KANNER, A., & SCHAEFFER, C. Psychological stress and adaptation: Some unresolved issues. In H. Selye (ed.), *Selye's guide to stress research,* vol. 1. New York: Van Nostrand, 1980.

LAZARUS, R. S., & LAUNIER, R. Stress-related transactions between person and environment. In L. A. Pervin & M. Lewis (eds.), *Perspectives in interactional psychology.* New York: Plenum, 1978.

LEVINE, J. D., GORDON, N. C., & FIELDS, H. L. The mechanism of placebo analgesia. *Lancet,* 1978, *2,* 654–657.

LEVINE, S. Developmental psychobiology. In D. A. Hamburg & H. K. H. Brodie (eds.), *American handbook of psychiatry* (2d ed.), vol. 6. New York: Basic Books, 1975.

LEWINSOHN, P. M., MISCHEL, W., CHAPLIN, W., & BARTON, R. Social competence and depression: The role of illusory self-perceptions. *Journal of Abnormal Psychlogy,* 1980, *89,* 203–212.

MAHONEY, M. J., & ARNKOFF, D. Cognitive and self-control therapies. In S. L. Garfield & A. E. Bergin (eds.), *Handbook of psychotherapy and behavior change* (2d ed.). New York: Wiley, 1978.

MAHONEY, M. J., & DeMONBREUN, B. G. Psychology of the scientist: An analysis of problem solving bias. *Cognitive Therapy and Research,* 1977, *1,* 229–238.

MARLATT, G. A., & GORDON, J. R. Determinants of relapse: Implications for the maintenance of behavior change. In P. O. Davidson & S. M. Davidson (eds.), *Behavioral medicine.* New York: Brunner/Mazel, 1980.

MASON, J. W. Emotion as reflected in patterns of endocrine integration. In L. Levi (ed.), *Emotions: Their parameters and measurement.* New York: Raven, 1975. (a)

————. A historical view of the stress field (part II). *Journal of Human Stress,* 1975, *1,* 22–36. (b)

MEICHENBAUM, D. Toward a cognitive theory of self-control. In G. E. Schwartz & D. Shapiro (eds.), *Consciousness and self-regulation,* vol. 1. New York: Plenum, 1976.

————. *Cognitive-behavior modification: An integrative approach.* New York: Plenum, 1977.

MEICHENBAUM, D., & CAMERON, R. Stress inoculation: A skills training approach to anxiety management. Manuscript, University of Waterloo, 1972.

————. Cognitive behavior modification: Current issues. In C. M. Franks & G. T. Wilson (eds.), *Handbook of behavior therapy.* New York: Guilford, in press.

MEICHENBAUM, D., GILMORE, B., & FEDORAVICIUS, A. Group insight vs. group desensitization in treating speech anxiety. *Journal of Consulting and Clinical Psychology,* 1971, *36,* 410–421.

MEICHENBAUM, D., & JAREMKO, M. *Stress prevention and management.* New York: Plenum, in press.

Menninger, K. *The vital balance.* New York: Viking, 1967.

Miller, N. E. Effects of learning on physical symptoms produced by pychological stress. In H. Selye (ed.), *Selye's guide to stress research,* vol. 1. New York: Van Nostrand, 1980.

Moos, R. H., & Tsu, V. D. The crisis of physical illness: An overview. In R. H. Moos (ed.), *Coping with physical illness.* New York: Plenum, 1977.

Novaco, R. *Anger control: The development of an experimental treatment.* Lexington: Heath, 1975.

Pearlin, L. I., & Schooler, C. The structure of coping. *Journal of Health and Social Behavior,* 1978, *19,* 2–21.

Raimy, V. *Misunderstandings of the self.* San Francisco: Jossey-Bass, 1975.

Reese, H. W. Verbal mediation as a function of age level. *Psychological Bulletin,* 1962, *59,* 502–509.

Richter, C. On the phenomenon of sudden death in animals and man. *Psychosomatic Medicine,* 1957, *19,* 191–198.

Rosenthal, T., & Bandura, A. Psychological modeling: Theory and practice. In S. L. Garfield & A. E. Bergin (eds.), *Handbook of psychotherapy and behavior change* (2d ed.). New York: Wiley, 1978.

Roskies, E., & Lazarus, R. S. Coping theory and the teaching of coping skills. In P. O. Davidson & S. M. Davidson (eds.), *Behavioral medicine.* New York: Brunner/Mazel, 1980.

Schwartz, R. M., & Gottman, J. M. Toward a task analysis of assertive behavior. *Journal of Consulting and Clinical Psychology,* 1976, *44,* 910–920.

Selye, H. *The stress of life.* New York: McGraw-Hill, 1956.

Snyder, M., & Swann, W. B. Hypothesis-testing processes in social interaction. *Journal of Personality and Social Psychology,* 1978, *36,* 1207–1212.

Tinbergen, N. Ethology and stress diseases. *Science,* 1974, *185,* 20–23.

Turk, D. C., & Genest, M. Regulation of pain: The application of cognitive and behavioral techniques for prevention and remediation. In P. C. Kendall & S. D. Hollon (eds.), *Cognitive-behavioral interventions.* New York: Academic, 1979.

Turk, D. C., Meichenbaum, D., & Genest, M. *Pain and behavioral medicine: Theory, research, and a clinical guide.* New York: Guilford, in press.

Valins, S., & Nisbett, R. E. Attributional processes in the development and treatment of emotional disorders. In J. T. Spence, R. C. Carson, & J. W. Thibaut (eds.), *Behavioral approaches to therapy.* Morristown: General Learning Press, 1976.

Wallace, J. An abilities conception of personality: Some implications for personality measurement. *American Psychologist,* 1966, *24,* 132–138.

Wagar, W. W. *The city of man.* Boston: Houghton Mifflin, 1963.

Weiss, J. Psychological and behavioral influences on gastrointestinal lesions in animal models. In J. D. Maser & M. E. P. Seligman (eds.), *Psychopathology: Experimental models.* San Francisco: Freeman, 1977.

Wilson, G. T. Cognitive factors in lifestyle changes: A social learning perspective. In P. O. Davidson & S. M. Davidson (eds.), *Behavioral medicine.* New York: Brunner/Mazel, 1980.

Wolf, S. Effects of suggestion and conditioning on the action of chemical agents in human subjects: The pharmacology of placebos. *Journal of Clinical Investigation,* 1950, *29,* 100–109.

Wolff, G. T., Friedman, S. B., Hofer, M. A., & Mason, J. W. Relationship between psychological defenses and mean urinary 17-hydroxycorticosteriod excretion rates. Part I: A predictive study of parents of fatally ill children. *Psychosomatic Medicine,* 1964, *26,* 576–591.

Zborowski, M. *People in pain.* San Francisco: Jossey-Bass 1969.

43

Stress Response Syndromes and Their Treatment

Mardi J. Horowitz

THE COMPULSIVE REPETITION OF TRAUMATIC PERCEPTIONS is an observed phenomenon with a long history. Breuer and Freud (1895) greatly advanced the modern conceptualization of this pattern. Freud (1953) reemphasized and generalized their observation that "hysterics suffer from reminiscences," a form of compulsive repetition, and Schur (1976) gave a more contemporary summary. With an awareness of this literature, I began a clinical investigation of the phenomenon of unbidden images. But, as I made my own observations, I was surprised by the intensity of the phenomenon. It seemed possible that the intrusive quality of ideas related to a previous life event constituted a specific index of distress.

UNBIDDEN IMAGES: CLINICAL OBSERVATIONS

Before undertaking a systematic series of investigations of stress response syndromes, I had been interested in certain abnormalities of thought as they were made manifest by visual images. The central phenomenon in this mode of representation seemed to be the loss of voluntary control over the flow of information. Intrusiveness was of special interest because it was a quality that ranged across phenomenology and diagnosis, hallucinations, illusions, nightmares, obsessive thought images, flashbacks, and altered body images. Careful explanation of such unbidden images would shed some light on visual thinking, regulation of thinking, and failures of defensive processes.

A series of clinical investigations were begun that ranged from psychoanalysis of persons who complained of unbidden images to study of psychiatric patients and to people who had bizarre experiences associated with temporal lobe epilepsy. The contents, genesis, changes, and derivatives of recurrent unbidden imagery experiences were examined, with

This line of work on stress, especially on the phenomenon of intrusion, has been supported by a research scientist development award from NIMH (K3-22-573), a stress research grant from NIMH (MH 17373, 01-07), a stress and coronary heart disease grant from NHLBI (HL17580, 01-06), a program project grant from NICHD (AGOOOO2), and funds granted to the Center for the Study of Neuroses as a Clinical Research Center of NIMH (MH 30899). I would also like to thank the following colleagues for their assistance: Robert Wallerstein, Nancy Wilner, Nancy Kaltreider, Charles Marmar, Janice Krupnick, Phyllis Cameron, William Alvarez, Tony Leong, Matthew Holden, Kathryn DeWitt, and Daniel Weiss.

special interest in change: cessation of a recurrent image, alteration of its contents, and appearance of greater volitional control.

The details are published elsewhere (Horowitz, 1978). What is important here is the conviction, based on observations, that the contents of unbidden images are quite frequently based upon previous perceptual realities. This conviction was startling because I expected, given the patient populations selected and my training in theory, that these contents would emerge mainly as fantasy elaborations based on current intrapsychic conflicts. The contents did, of course, contain fantasy elaborations and served various impulsive and defensive purposes, but the frequency of contents repeating a traumatic perception of a serious life event that had actually occurred was impressive.

EXPERIMENTAL WORK ON INTRUSIVE THINKING AFTER PERCEPTION OF STRESS INDUCING STIMULI

It seemed that the connection between perception of stress inducing stimuli and subsequent experiences of intrusive thinking, especially in the same modality as the perception, might be strong enough to be called a general human response tendency. If this were so, the association between these phenomena could serve as an index of how stressful a set of people found a set of life experiences. Change in degree of distress could be monitored by following this index and noting the factors that mediated the process of working through a reaction to a serious life event. However, review of the voluminous experimental work on laboratory induced stress revealed an emphasis on biological response variables. While there were many data on ratings of emotional responses, such as degree of fear or anger after a stress inducing stimulus, there were few reports on subjective experiences. These were considered by some investigators as too fragile for scientific measurement and by others as too epiphenomenal to be important; yet, Antrobus and Singer (1969) had done very relevant work with such variables, and Lazarus (1966) and Janis (1969) had placed strong theoretical emphasis on cognitive variables.

In order to test the hypothesis that intrusive and repetitive thought is a general stress response tendency, I designed an experimental investigation that used films, a well-studied and replicable laboratory device for observing visual stress events. Intrusive and repetitive thoughts were defined in operational terms and then quantified by two methods: subjective self-report and content analysis of reported episodes of consciousness (Horowitz, 1975). A series of investigations was conducted. In a prototypical experiment, groups of subjects saw a stress film and a neutral contrast film in counterbalanced order. Measurements were taken at baseline, poststress, and postneutral periods. Over 300 subjects were selected by systematic sampling of various populations. The mental set given to subjects varied in terms of specific and general instructions on how to report episodes of consciousness, normal and abnormal slants as to the meaning of having intrusive images, and the context of attention deployment. The results confirmed the hypothesis.

For example, a cross-experimental data analysis was performed using the Finn (1970) Multivariate Analysis of Variance program for nonorthogonal designs. The change in conditions (neutral or stress) had a significant effect on the levels of reported quality of intrusiveness and repetitiveness of original stimuli. These two factors, one of form and one of content, correlated significantly and positively ($r = .51, p < .001, n = 133$).

Table 43–1 reports adjusted means for the effects of all factors and conditions on intrusions and film references. The population consisted of 133 subjects in various experiments who each had data on the variable in all conditions (baseline, neutral, and stress). Positive

TABLE 43-1
Combined Means as Adjusted according to Report Length

Factor	n	Intrusions			Film References		
		Base	*Neu-tral*	*Stress*	*Base*	*Neu-tral*	*Stress*
Population							
Military inpatients	23	−.44	−.16	.41	−1.69	−.88	−.08
Civilian students	82	−.83	−.40	1.38	−2.14	−.23	1.51
Health students	28	−.50	−.11	.39	−1.53	.08	1.61
Sex							
Men	99	−.66	−.33	.55	−1.81	−.13	−.98
Women	34	−.80	−.20	2.33	−2.29	−.69	2.05
Instructional demand							
Normal	24	−.72	−.30	1.73	−2.26	−.53	2.44
Abnormal	25	−.63	.02	1.79	−1.96	−.25	1.65
Specific	16	−.49	.01	.93	−1.70	.07	0.86
General	68	−.76	−.49	.48	−1.86	−.28	.78
Order							
Stress 1st	51	−.67	−.20	.57	−1.82	.16	.86
Neutral 1st	82	−.71	−.36	1.27	−2.00	−.55	1.50
Film							
"Subincision"	110	−.75	−.33	1.13	−1.98	−.15	1.53
Woodshop	23	−.44	−.16	.41	−1.69	−.88	−.08
Overall	133	−.69	−.30	1.00	−1.23	−.29	1.23

Source: Horowitz (1975).

scores for the adjusted means in Table 42-1 indicate the number of intrusions per subject above expectation, while negative scores indicate lower than expected levels. At the $p < .05$ cutoff level, only the change in conditions, from neutral to stressful, exerted a significant effect on both intrusions (MS = 57.5; df = 2; F = 20.7; $p < .001$) and film references (MS = 146.5; df = 2; F = 49.1; $p < .001$). Population differences (health sciences students, college students, and military health personnel), film order (stress or neutral first), sex of subjects, and instructional demands (general and specific; abnormal or normal slants) did not exert a significant effect.

The significant condition effect for intrusions can be accounted for by the stress film. Baseline film references were, of course, especially low because no film had yet been seen, and only occasional anticipatory remarks were scored. The neutral and stress condition film reference levels were significantly different.

While the large-scale analysis of variance found condition to be the only variable to exert a significant effect on levels of intrusion and film reference, the variance associated with instructional demand and sex approached significance ($p < .09$).

Analyses of variance and covariance were performed on film references and intrusions only as scored in the stress condition to observe more closely the effect of all other factors except condition on these two variables. The entire group of 302 subjects had yielded data in the stress condition and was, therefore, used for these analyses.

TABLE 43-2
Intrusions for All Factors in the Stress Condition (N = 302)

Source[a]	df	Using Unadjusted Means			Using Adjusted Means		
		MS	F	p	MS	F	p
ANOVA[b]							
Population	3	7.22	2.55	.06	4.96	1.85	< .14
Sex	1	37.34	13.18	< .001	35.10	13.09	< .001
Error	277	2.83			2.68		
ANOC (reduced model)							
Population	3				13.97	5.14	< .002
Sex	1				48.03	17.69	< .001
Error	294				2.72		

Source: Horowitz (1975).
[a] Analysis of variance is indicated by ANOVA; analysis of covariance, by ANOC.
[b] Instructions, order, film, and residual were not significant.

Table 43-2 presents the results of the two analyses for intrusions. The analysis of variance used intrusion means both adjusted and unadjusted for report length, while the analysis of covariance used number of words in a subject's report as the covariate of intrusions. This analysis and an additionally reduced analysis of covariance found sex and population to have a significant effect on intrusions.

Female subjects scored the highest levels of intrusions in the stress condition; civilian men scored higher than military nonpatients (health personnel) (see Table 43-3). Film reference data did not show a significant difference between the sexes or across population groups, although military psychiatric patients reported more film repetitions after the stress film than did military nonpatients. These data can be interpreted as either a disinclination of military nonpatients and, to a lesser extent, civilian men to disclose mental contents they might construe as weak or a greater tendency on the part of women and psychiatric patients to develop such response to stress.

TABLE 43-3
Average Level of Intrusions per Subject in Stress Condition[A]

	Military inpatients	Military nonpatients	Civilian students	Health students	Estimated
Population means					
Men	.41	− .11	.64	.44	.27
Women		.31	2.06	.78	1.64
Estimated	.41	− .09	1.24	.57	
n					
Men	51	92	64	27	234
Women	0	4	47	17	68
Total	51	96	111	44	302

Source: Horowitz (1975).
[a] Adjusted combined means.

INTRUSIONS TEND TO CORRELATE WITH DEGREE OF REPORTED STRESS

In the stress condition, persons who rated themselves high on negative emotions tended also to report high levels of intrusions. The adjusted intrusion scores in 133 subjects who did the same affect report measure during the stress condition correlated significantly and positively with a composite of negative affects ($r = .27$, $p < .001$) and significantly and negatively with a composite of positive affects ($r = -.16$, $p < .05$). The highest correlation with specific individual affects was with pain ($r = .38$, $p < .001$) and surprise ($r = .35$, $p < .001$). These correlations and others are found in Table 43-4. Of course, with large numbers of subjects, some low levels of correlation (e.g., $r = -.16$) may reach statistical significance but indicate only a small effect.

A group of 77 subjects also rated themselves after the stress film on 1–100 "thermometer" type scales for emotional and physical stress, following the method of Stevens (1966). Both scales correlated significantly and positively with intrusion levels. For emotional stress the correlation was $r = .39$, $p < .01$; for physical stress, $r = .34$, $p < .01$.

A subsequent experiment contrasted the effects of different types of stressful films (Horowitz & Wilner, 1976). The earlier series had involved two films, both depicting events of bodily injury, which tended to induce feelings of fear. In this later experiment, a film was included that showed no bodily injury, but rather the abandonment of a young boy by his father. This tended to induce feelings of anger and sadness. Both stress films, and an arousing erotic film, led to significantly higher levels of intrusive and repetitive thinking than did a neutral control film. Of interest here, this experiment included an inventory of life events for each subject (Horowitz, Schaefer, & Cooney, 1974). Thus, preexperiment experiences could be compared with reactions to witnessing the stressful stimuli in the study.

There was no correlation between response to the films and on overall presumptive stress score obtained by summing weights assigned to each experienced item on our life

TABLE 43-4
Correlation of Intrusions with Affective Variables in Stress Condition (N = 133)

Affect	Correlations with adjusted intrusions
Interest	$-.12$
Pleasantness	$-.20^a$
Happiness	$-.02$
Positive composite	$-.16^b$
Sadness	$.20^a$
Anger	$.05$
Disgust	$.14^b$
Contempt	$.07$
Surprise	$.35^c$
Fear	$.13$
Pain	$.38^c$
Nervousness	$.12$
Negative compositive	$.27^c$

Source: Horowitz (1975).
[a] $p < .01$.
[b] $p < .05$.
[c] $p < .001$.

events questionnaire. People who had had the highest frequency of deaths and separations in the past experienced the most sadness and fear after the separation film ($r = .44, p < .05$ for sadness; $r = .41, p < .05$ for fear).

FIELD STUDIES

Since the laboratory investigations supported the importance of intrusive thinking as one index of the degree of stress after a recent life event, it seemed valuable to design a self-rating instrument that would allow for repeated measurement of such variables (Horowitz, Wilner, & Alvarez, 1979). Open-ended interviews were conducted with people who had experienced diverse stress inducing life events. We hoped to add to the clinical experiences already assembled in the study of unbidden images and in everyday clinical practice. The sample included patients who had sought help after a recent loss or injury or who had sustained such events during the course of extended psychoanalysis or psychoanalytic psychotherapy (allowing for some prospective understanding of the mix between character and circumstances). Items for a self-report instrument were assembled from written reports and the clearest wording of redundant experiences was selected. The list that evolved in this way contained experiences of a particular quality, such as intrusiveness, worded so that they might apply to any event. To anchor the qualities of experience to a particular context, the life event specific to each person was entered at the top of the form and served as a referent for each of the statements on the list.

Clinical experience suggested that the various items be divided into two subgroups, intrusion and avoidance. The goal was a scale that would provide subscores for these response sets, as well as a total subjective stress score. Over a period of several years various forms of this item list were given both to psychotherapy patients with stress response syndromes and to nonpatient volunteers exposed to serious life events. The wording and the format were revised.

Through examination of the data it became evident that although we had asked for separate ratings of how often during the past week a particular experience had occurred, and what the peak intensity of that episode had been, the scores for frequency and intensity of episodes were relatively similar. In other words, the experience of a single, very intense intrusive image was similar in effect to multiple experiences of less intense and only mildly intrusive images. Therefore, although subjects were asked to respond to both variables in a study of the refined impact of event scale, only the higher score of either frequency or intensity was used as the indicator of the magnitude of the item (Horowitz, Wilner, & Alvarez, 1979).

In its form after pilot studies, the scale consisted of 20 items: 9 items described episodes of intrusion; 11 described episodes of avoidance. This scale was given to 66 adults who had sought psychotherapy at the University of California, outpatient department in response to a serious life event. These patients were referred to a clinic for specialized treatment of stress response syndromes. This clinic accepted patients with neurotic levels of psychopathology; those persons referred elsewhere either had overt psychoses, drug dependence, or alcoholism or were unwilling to give written consent to research review of their records.

The serious life event that had preceded the development of a stress response syndrome varied in this group. About half the patients ($n = 34$) had experienced bereavement, the remainder had suffered personal injuries resulting from accidents, violence, illness, or surgery. When scales completed by bereaved subjects were compared with those of subjects who had incurred personal injury, endorsements of items were found to be relatively similar. The subjects were 16 men and 50 women between 20 and 75 years of age, with a mean age of 34.

All items were endorsed frequently. Those most often endorsed, "Things I saw or heard suddenly reminded me of it" and "I got waves or pangs of intense or deep feelings about it," were acknowledged by 85% of the subject sample (see Table 43–5). Even the item with the lowest endorsement, "It seemed to me that I was reacting less than would be expected," was acknowledged by 38% of the 66 subjects. All six of the most frequently reported items had a mean weighted score of 3 or more, indicating that *as a group* these subjects experienced such episodes at a high level of frequency or intensity. This occurred even though the particular stressful event usually had been experienced several months earlier (mean of 5.5 months), while the time frame for endorsement of any scale item was limited to the past week.

The mean scores for each item were calculated separately for men and women, as well as for the total group. The sexes differed significantly in frequency or intensity on only 3 of 20 items. In each instance, women indicated a higher level of endorsement.

As shown in Table 43–5, the primary and secondary clusters included 15 of the 20 items, with two smaller residual clusters containing 5 items. The primary cluster contained items from the clinically derived intrusion subset, while the second cluster was composed of clinically derived avoidance items. This finding, added to the logic with which items were usually selected, supported the use of the intrusion and avoidance classifications.

Subsequently, the number of items was reduced by selecting only those that empirically clustered and had significant item to subscale correlations beyond the .01 level of significance. Next, comparison of scores derived by frequency and by intensity indicated a degree of similarity that made dual response for each item unnecessary. We retained only the frequency variable since subjects seemed able to score it more accurately than the intensity variable. Finally, wording of a few items was slightly modified further to reduce ambiguity.

After reduction of the scale to the 15 most powerful items, the split half reliability of the total scale was high ($r = 0.86$). Internal consistency of the subscales, calculated using Cronbach's alpha, was also high (intrusion = .78, avoidance = .82). A correlation of .42 ($p < 0.0002$) between intrusion and avoidance subscale scores indicated that the two subsets were associated but did not measure identical dimensions. In a later sample, test-retest reliability and sensitivity were found to be good (Horowitz, Wilner, & Alvarez, 1979).

In a subsequent series of studies, people with diverse life events were asked to fill out the revised impact of event scale.[1] Some were prospective patients at a special clinic for the treatment of individuals with posttraumatic stress disorders or adjustment reactions to serious life events. For these patients, the specific event was used as the referent for their impact of event scale. Other field populations were selected because of their participation in a preselected event such as death of a parent; we also studied medical and physical therapy students shortly after they had participated for the first time in cadaver dissection. Other respondents were women who had received news of the possibility of cancer and were about to undergo a breast biopsy. Each event for each group was the referent for their impact of event scales. Still other groups consisted of patients with head or neck cancer who, when they came for treatment, related the scale to the diagnosis of their disease some months earlier, and the people closest to these cancer patients, who filled out the scale as related to their recent experiences concerning the news that their relative had cancer (see Table 43–6).

The comparative impact of diverse events could be assessed on this kind of scale

TABLE 43–5
Impact of Event Scale: Frequency and Mean of Positive Report and Cluster Analysis of Items (n = 66)

Item	% endorsement	mean	(SD)	Item to subscale r	Logical cluster[a]
Cluster 1					
I had waves of strong feelings about it.	88	3.8	(1.9)	.57[b]	I
Things I saw or heard suddenly reminded me of it.	85	3.7	(1.9)	.57[b]	I
I thought about it when I didn't mean to.	76	3.3	(2.2)	.45[b]	I
Images related to it popped into my mind.	76	3.2	(2.2)	.39[b]	I
Any reminder brought back emotions related to it.	76	3.0	(2.1)	.62[b]	I
I have difficulty falling asleep because of images or thoughts related to the event.	64	2.6	(2.4)	.35[b]	I
I had bad dreams related to the event.	44	1.7	(2.2)	.41[b]	I
Cluster 2					
I knew that a lot of unresolved feelings were still there, but I kept them under wraps.	71	3.0	(2.2)	.46[b]	A
I avoided letting myself get emotional when I thought about it or was reminded of it.	70	2.8	(2.1)	.62[b]	A
I wished to banish it from my store of memories.	65	2.8	(2.3)	.49[b]	A
I made an effort to avoid talking about it.	61	2.2	(2.0)	.59[b]	A

718

Item	n	Mean	(SD)	r	Type
My emotions related to it were kind of numb.	59	2.1	(2.1)	$.42^b$	A
I felt unreleased about it, as if it hadn't happened or as if it wasn't real.	58	2.2	(2.3)	$.48^b$	A
I stayed away from things or situations that might remind me of it.	53	2.2	(2.3)	$.57^b$	A
I didn't let myself have thoughts related to it.	50	1.8	(2.2)	$.65^b$	A
Cluster 3					
I kept wondering why it had to happen to me or to persons near me and not someone else.	59	2.6	(2.3)	.18	I
I used alcohol, drugs, or a lot of activity to help me forget.	54	2.0	(2.2)	.29	A
It seemed to me that I was reacting less than would be expected.	38	1.3	(2.0)	.20	A
Cluster 4					
I found myself almost waiting for something like that to happen again.	44	1.6	(2.1)	.29	I
I found myself making plans and decisions which were inappropriate in light of the event.	41	1.5	(2.0)	.08	A

Source: Horowitz, Wilner, & Alvarez (1979). Copyright 1979 by The American Psychosomatic Society, Inc. Reprinted with permission.

[a] I = intrusion item; A = avoidance item.
[b] $p < .01$.

TABLE 43-6
Populations

Groups	Life event	Total	Women	Men	Age mean	Time since event (weeks) Mean	(SD)
			n				
Stress clinic patients	Loss to self or of others	77	67	10	35.3	24.2	(33.6)
Bereavement field subjects	Death of a parent	36	18	18	37.9	7.6	(2.4)
Surgical patients	Breast biopsy for possible cancer	68	68	0	41.8	1.0	(0)
Medical patients	Diagnosis of cancer of head or neck beyond simple surgical cure	54	17	37	56.5	4.8	(3.1)
Collaterals of medical patients	Above in related person	36	22	14	53.9	4.9	(3.6)
Medical students	First exposure to and dissection of cadaver	69	23	46	23.6	2.0	(0)
Physical therapy students	First exposure to and dissection of cadaver	25	20	5	25.3	2.0	(0)

because the instrument focuses on qualities of experience that allow it to be anchored for reference to any specific event. As might be expected, the least stressful of the events was cadaver dissection. The experience of possibly having cancer was much more distressing, even though the first news of the disease in these people was more remote in time than the experience of the cadaver dissection for the health students. Respondents with the highest levels of distress as evidenced by intrusive and avoidant experiences were people seeking help for psychological stress associated with a serious life event.

The levels of intrusion and avoidance were significantly different across the groups by ANOVA and Scheffe contrast statistical examinations. The means ranged from a high of 23 for intrusion levels among the stress clinic help seeking patients, the majority of whom had posttraumatic stress disorders, to a low of 2.4 for the physical therapy students after cadaver dissection. Equivalent avoidance levels ranged from 19.4 in the stress clinic patients to 2.1 for the physical therapy students. But these are mean levels, and a clinically more relevant consideration has to do with how many people have high, medium, or low distress. In order to derive such approximations, we establish clinical criteria for symptom levels on the impact of event scale.

A low level was established below the indifference point on the ascending scores accord-

TABLE 43–7
Percentage of Persons at Three Levels of Distress on the Intrusion Subscale of the Impact of Event Scale

	Level of Distress		
	Low	*Medium*	*High*
Stress clinic patients (on entry to therapy) ($n = 77$)	10	16	74
Bereavement field subjects (two months after death of a parent) ($n = 36$)	28	39	33
Surgical patients (within one week of breast biopsy) ($n = 68$)	66	22	12
Medical patients (one month after cancer diagnosis) $n = 54$)	59	22	19
Collaterals of medical patients (one month after diagnosis) ($n = 36$)	42	31	28
Medical students (two weeks after beginning cadaver dissection) ($n = 69$)	86	13	1
Physical therapy students (two weeks after beginning cadaver dissection) ($n = 25$)	92	8	0

ing to these criteria for low and medium levels of symptoms reported on the impact of event scale:

Low level: As a clinician you would not be concerned about persons who fall within this range because, while they might have some complaints or signs from time to time, the outlook is for ready improvement. There is no indication for further diagnostic, evaluative, or treatment procedures.

Medium level: As a clinician you would be concerned with this level of complaints and/or signs because they may give a global indication of conditions that warrant further evaluation.

In a similar manner, the indifference level between medium and high ratings was established. High levels of symptoms on the scale were based on the following criteria:

High level: As a clinician, you feel that this level of signs and symptoms merits concern; that diagnostic, evaluative, or treatment procedures are clearly warranted; and that the person is more likely to be in a problem or pathological category.

Four clinicians arrived at these indifference points, and their independent judgments (within one gradation of each other) were averaged to serve as a threshold (Horowitz, Krupnick, Kaltreider, Wilner, Leong, & Marmar, 1981). For the Impact of Event Scale (IES), low scores were those below 8.5, high scores were those over 19, and medium scores ranged from

TABLE 43-8

Percentage of Persons at Three Levels of Distress on the Avoidance Subscale of the Impact of Event Scale

	Level of Distress		
	Low	Medium	High
Stress clinic patients (on entry to therapy) (n = 77)	21	27	52
Bereavement field subjects (two months after death of a parent) (n = 36)	61	17	22
Surgical patients (within one week of breast biopsy) (n = 68)	65	24	12
Medical patients (one month after cancer diagnosis) (n = 54)	56	32	13
Collaterals of medical patients (one month after diagnosis) (n = 36)	53	25	22
Medical students (two weeks after beginning cadaver dissection) (n = 69)	75	20	4
Physical therapy students (two weeks after beginning cadaver dissection) (n = 25)	96	4	0

TABLE 43-9
Intrusion Levels of Impact of Study Stress Scale

	Year 1		Year 2		Year 3	
	Mean	*(SD)*	*Mean*	*(SD)*	*Mean*	*(SD)*
Special intervention group (*n* = 226)	4.5	(5.6)	4.1	(6.3)	3.0	(5.1)
Usual care group (*n* = 260)	3.6	(5.1)	2.6	(5.1)	1.9	(4.9)

Source: Horowitz, Hulley, Alvarez, Billings, Benfari, Blair, Borhani, & Simon (1980).

9 to 19. Tables 43-7 and 43-8 indicate the percentage of subjects from each group at these levels of distress. These percentages allowed comparison of the degree of distress within diverse groups, experiencing diverse life events, for their given situations and contexts. The majority of stress clinic patients, on seeking help, were at high distress (74%). About one-fifth of the cancer patients and their relatives were at high distress by these criteria. Only one of the students was at an equivalent level of distress on the first confrontation with death through cadaver dissection. These variations indicated the sensitivity of even this self-report measure for intrusion.

Another investigation involved a large group of men who were given the usually unexpected news that they were at high risk for coronary heart disease. Half of this group was then randomly assigned to a special intervention program designed to reduce their risk factors, while the other half continued with their usual community sources of health care, knowing that they were at risk because of any combination of elevated serum cholesterol, excessive smoking, or high blood pressure. At yearly intervals after receiving this news, the men filled out a special derivative of the impact of event scale. The group that received the special intervention attended special meetings for risk reduction, which served to remind them of their risk and tended to reduce denial. Probably as a consequence, this group had significant elevations in the levels of intrusive ideas and feelings related to the news of their high risk. Of interest, this significantly higher level of intrusive experience persisted over each of the three years of follow-up. As reported by Horowitz and associates (1980), the levels for intrusion on the impact of study stress scale are as shown in Table 43-9. On ANOVA, the group effects were significantly different (MS = 480.0; df = 1; F = 8.4; P < .004). The decline over time was also significant (MS = 307.0; df = Z; F = 2.8; $p < .00001$). The group by year interaction was not significant. These data confirmed the importance of intrusive thinking as an indicator of the degree of current stress imposed by a past life event.

CLINICAL INVESTIGATIONS

A group at the University of California, Center for the Study of Neuroses, studied patients who presented with problems precipitated by a recent serious life event. Intrusive experiences were common chief complaints in these patients, and such symptoms represent an important defining characteristic of the new category of posttraumatic stress disorder in the American Psychiatric Association's *DSM-III* (1980) (see Table 43-10).

In 66 cases of stress response syndromes, intrusive symptoms were virtually universal according to both self-report and clinician's rating (Horowitz, Wilner, Kaltreider, and Alvarez, 1980). Differences were not noted between patients who had experienced the loss of someone close to them and those who had sustained a bodily injury or had had a near-fatal

TABLE 43–10
Diagnostic Criteria for Posttraumatic Stress Disorder

A. A recognizable stressor that would be expected to evoke significant symptoms of distress in almost all individuals

B. Re-experiencing the traumatic event either by
   (1) Recurrent and intrusive recollections of the event; or
   (2) Recurrent dreams of the event; or
   (3) Suddenly acting or feeling as if the traumatic event were occuring because of an association with an environmental or ideational stimulus

C. Numbing of responsiveness to, or involvement with, the external world, beginning some time after the traumatic event(s) as shown by either
   (1) Markedly diminished interest in one or more significant activities; or
   (2) Feelings of detachment or estrangement from others; or
   (3) Marked constriction of affective responses

D. At least two of the following (not present prior to the traumatic event)
   (1) Hyperalertness or exaggerated startle response;
   (2) Initial, middle, or terminal sleep disturbance;
   (3) Guilt about surviving when others have not, or about behavior required to achieve survival;
   (4) Memory impairment or trouble concentrating;
   (5) Avoidance of activities that arouse recollection of the traumatic event;
   (6) Intensification of symptoms by exposure to events that symbolize or resemble the traumatic event

Source: American Psychiatric Association (1980). Reprinted with permission.

experience. This study produced very little data on the differences among persons according to dispositional factors such as personality. Clinical judgment of personality style was included in the study, although the reliability of such assessments was not fully examined.

It will be necessary to accumulate a larger consecutive sample and to evolve a reliable method before any conclusions can be drawn on the interaction of information-processing styles and the experiential qualities of stress response states. Only the most tentative results can be reported herein, but they are worthy of mention in order to underscore the importance of the eventual inclusion of such variables.

Among the 66 patients in the sample, 14 had a good to excellent fit to the obsessional type and 13 had a good to excellent fit to the hysterical type. As would be expected from clinical theory, the hysterical group (12 women and one man) reported more symptoms than the obsessional group (11 women and three men). On the intrusion subset of the Impact of Event Scale, the hysterical group produced a mean score of 23 ± 8.0, as compared with a mean score of 17 ± 11.0 for the obsessional group. On the avoidance subset, the mean score for the hysterical group was 20 ± 10.0, as compared with 15 ± 13.0 for the obsessional group. Three of the 15 items of the Impact of Event Scale significantly differentiated the groups with levels of at least $p < .05$, with the hysterical group always higher. On responses to the Symptom Checklist and other variables, the groups were similar.

Two of the items on the Impact of Event Scale were in the intrusion subset. They were: (1) "Things I saw or heard suddenly reminded me of it," with a mean score for the hysterical group of 4.4 ± 1.0, as compared with the obsessional group, who had mean scores of 2.9 ± 2.1 ($t = 2.5$, $p < .05$); and (2) "Images related to it popped into my mind," with a mean score for the hysterical group of 4.2 ± 1.5, as compared with the obsessional group who had mean scores of 2.0 ± 2.2 ($t = 2.9$, $p < .05$). These data can be accounted for, perhaps, on the increased readiness of the hysterical personality to admit to emotional qualities of experience." (Horowitz, Wilner, Kaltreider, & Alvarez, 1980:91)

The clinical nature of intrusive experiences can be conveyed with a case vignette.

A young man was called by an acquaintance, who asked him for help, and described himself as feeling desperate. He said no, because he didn't want to get too entangled with this person, who was not a very close friend, and was seen as "too demanding." Later, the body of this acquaintance was found with a gun beside it. He had shot himself later that night.

The young man, who became a patient in our clinic, didn't go to the funeral because he did not want to get upset. A few weeks later, after keeping the event out of mind (which we, in retrospect, would call a denial and numbing period), he had an intrusive image while lying down to go to sleep. He lay in his bed, closed his eyes, and had a pseudo-hallucination of a felt presence of the dead acquaintance standing at the bedside looking calmly down at him. He felt very guilty and anxious. From then on he developed a syndrome in which he was unable to sleep except with the lights on and when he was exhausted. He was afraid to lie in bed and close his eyes. He did not wash his face because he was afraid that if he closed his eyes he would once again see the intrusive image of the face of the person who committed suicide.

People often go through a period of latency after a traumatic experience. Five or six months later, they may unexpectedly, with very minor triggers, begin to have intrusive thoughts or images with intense pangs of feeling. The word "pang" is particularly effective because it expresses the sharp, overwhelming intensity of these feelings. For example, people do not think they can tolerate the experience of bereavement if it were to continue. The feelings experienced at this time usually come in a wavelike form; the unbearable emotional quality passes, sometimes in seconds. The person is able to bear the feeling because it seems to occur in doses. One can also gain an idea of the intensity of intrusive experiences by comparing different groups who have shared the same life event but who respond to it differently. In another cohort studied at the center, the particular life event common to all adult subjects was the recent death of a parent. One group consisted of people who had sought treatment for a neurotic level of reaction to this life event. A nonequivalent field study contrast group was selected by a review of hospital death records. In a tactful way, the controls were asked to participate in the same evaluation procedures used with the patient sample. This allowed us systematically to contrast persons who had sought psychotherapy with people who had experienced the same event but did not seek therapy (Horowitz, Krupnick, Kaltreider, Wilner, Leong, & Marmar, 1981).

As might be expected, the group seeking psychotherapy had significantly higher levels of intrusive thinking on the Impact of Event Scale at the first evaluation. Their mean was 21.52, compared with a mean of 13.83 for the field subjects (SD = 7.99 and 9.05, respectively; $t = 3.66$, $p < .001$). Clinician rating of intrusion on a separate instrument was also significantly higher for the group seeking therapy (mean = 18.53 for patients versus 8.36 for field subjects; SD = 11.05 and 10.72, respectively; $t = 3.79$, $p < .0001$). These two ratings for the total sample also correlated significantly ($r = .69$). In terms of the thresholds mentioned earlier, only 3% of the patients were at a low or nonsymptomatic level for intrusive experiences; only 10% were at this level for the avoidance report portion of the impact of event scale. This compared with 28% and 61%, respectively, for the field subjects (chi square = 8.98, $p < .01$). Meanwhile, on clinician's ratings for intrusion, 17% of the patients were at a low or nonsymptomatic level compared with 67% of the field subjects. The remainder of both groups were at medium or high symptomatic levels.

As in prior studies, female subjects tended to have higher ratings on both intrusion and avoidance than did males ($r = .39$ for the correlation between level and sex for intrusion, .35 for avoidance, both significant at $p < .01$). Age did not correlate, nor did marital status or number of children.

THEMATIC CONTENTS OF INTRUSIVE THOUGHTS AND FEELINGS

Prior perceptions of stress inducing events are often combined with reactive thoughts, forming a constellation of external and internal bits of information that are the elements of intrusive experiences. These constellations of ideas and feelings have a thematic valence, often reflected in the quality of the felt emotions. The main emotional ingredients are familiar from clinical experience: anger, sadness, fear, and guilt about the occurrence of serious life events and the possibility of their repetition. A large clinical sample of persons intensely interviewed after similar life events allows one to determine the generality of these common tendencies. Among the latter is one that is sometimes neglected because it is hard to deal with: rage that the event has taken place at all.

Most clinicians are quite ready to help a person work through his or her fear that a painful event in the past may repeat itself. They are also quite ready to help patients work on their fear of merger with others who are victims, their guilt over survival, and the shame and rage they feel that they, or a loved one, were vulnerable to harm. Rage at the source of an event is especially difficult, however, because it often involves an unjust or irrational component that is avoided in communication and recognition but is a common human response.

Krupnick and I worked on developing operational definitions for the themes most commonly noted in our case material on post–traumatic stress disorder (1981). We examined 15 cases in which the stress event was the death of a loved one and 15 in which it was a personal injury such as an amputation, an assault, or a near-fatal experience. The frequency of conflicts involving eight common themes in stress response syndromes, as averaged for two judges following a manual of operational definitions for each theme in reviewing written case material, is reported in Table 43–11. As expected, all themes, especially discomfort over vulnerability and rage at the source, were quite common. The main differences between the groups involved sadness over loss (more common in bereavement cases) and fear of repetition (more common after personal injury).

TABLE 43-11
Frequency of Eight Major Themes

Theme	Bereavement cases ($n = 15$)	Personal Injury Cases ($n = 15$)	Combined ($n = 30$)
Discomfort over vulnerability	13 (87%)	11 (73%)	24 (80%)
Rage at the source	12 (80%)	11 (73%)	23 (77%)
Feelings of responsibility	9 (60%)	12 (80%)	21 (70%)
Fear of repetition	7 (47%)	13 (87%)	20 (67%)
Sadness over loss	14 (93%)	4 (27%)	18 (60%)
Discomfort over aggressive impulses	7 (47%)	9 (60%)	16 (53%)
Fear of loss of control over aggressive impulses	6 (40%)	7 (47%)	13 (43%)
Rage at those exempted	6 (40%)	4 (27%)	10 (33%)

Source: Krupnick & Horowitz (1981). Copyright 1981, American Medical Association. Reprinted with permission.

EXPLANATION OF INTRUSIVE IDEAS AND FEELINGS

The data presented so far have suggested that a quality of thinking—intrusive entry into consciousness—is an important psychological index of stress. Intrusive thoughts are a general tendency in wide populations, as noted in experimental, field, and clinical studies. Some of the themes that provide the content are not only perceptual residues of the experience but also major affectively colored attitudes. As Table 43–12 shows, these intrusive episodes (as measured by self-report) decline with time and working through (Horowitz & Wilner, 1980).

TABLE 43–12
Impact of Event Scale Data on Intrusion over Time and Treatment

Impact of event scale	Entry (*n* = 45)	Therapy hour 4 (*n* = 25)	Therapy hour 8 (*n* = 23)	Therapy hour 12 (end of therapy) (*n* = 45)	Follow-up (*n* = 45)
Intrusion items mean score	20	16	12	11	10

Source: Horowitz & Wilner (1980).

What is it that eventually alters mental states from those characterized by either intrusion or denial to those in which a serious life event can be contemplated or put out of mind in a volitional manner? Apparently, there is a gradual integration of both memories and associations activated by the incident. Until that time, the event and activated and reactive attitudes are maintained in an active memory system that seems to have an intrinsic property of repetition. Because each repetition evokes painful experiences, defensive processes are instituted. The result is an unstable dynamic conflict, so that after repeated representation of the active memories, the experience is regarded as intrusive.

The detailed exposition of this theory has been presented elsewhere (Horowitz, 1976) and has led to some revision of the classical theory of the differentiation between normal and pathological grief (Horowitz, Wilner, Marmar, & Krupnick, 1980). A synopsis of one aspect of this theory appeared in *Human Stress and Cognition* (Horowitz, 1980).

> Serious life events such as a loss or injury present news that will eventually change inner models. But change is slow; time is essential for review of the implications of the news and available options for response. The mind continues to process important new information until the situation or the models change, and reality and models of reality reach accord. This important tendency to integrate reality and schemata can be called a *completion tendency.*
>
> Until completion occurs, the new information and reactions to it are stored in active memory. According to this theory, active memory contents will be transformed into representations wherever that process is not actively inhibited (Horowitz and Becker, 1972). This tendency for repeated representations will end only when these are no longer stored in active memory. In the instance of very important contents, termination in active memory will not occur with decay but only when information processing is complete. At that point, the news will be a part of long-term models and revised inner schemata.
>
> As ideas related to the stress event are represented, there will be a very natural comparison of the news with relevant schemata. Because a stress event is, by definition, a significant change, there will be a discrepancy between the implications of the news, and these schemata. This discrepancy evokes emotion. Serious life events, and the repetition of information related to them, are so different from inner models of attachment that very painful emotional responses occur; emotional states of such power that controls are activated to prevent the threat of unendurable anguish or flooding. . . .

News and immediate responses to serious life events remain stored in active memory because, on first encounter, the meanings seem to have great personal importance. Because the contents are strongly coded in active memory they tend to be represented intensely and frequently. With each recurrence of the information, comparisons are made again, and emotional activation increases. Emotional responses are also represented, and so become part of the constellation stored in active memory. When other tasks are more immediately relevant, or when emotional responses such as fear, guilt, rage, or sorrow are a threat, controls are initiated. This feedback modulates the flow of information and reduces emotional response.

Excessive controls interrupt the process, change the state of the person to some form of denial and may prevent complete processing of the event. Failures of control lead to excessive levels of emotion, flooding and retraumatization, causing entry into intrusive states. Optimal controls slow down recognition processes and so provide tolerable doses of new information and emotional responses. They lead to working states or less intense oscillations between denial and intrusive states. In this optimal condition some intrusiveness will occur with repeated representation. Some denial will occur when controls operate more pervasively, but the overall result will be adaptive, in that completion will eventually occur. Inner models will eventually conform to the new reality, as in the process of completion of mourning. When this happens, information storage in active memory will terminate.

At any given time, different sets of meanings of a stress event will exist in different stages. For example, fear of repetition, or fear of merger with a victim might be a recurrent intrusive experience, while survivor-guilt themes might be completely inhibited and for the moment avoided in experience. Later, in situations of greater safety, this theme might be allowed to enter awareness, and be represented as an intrusive experience.

This model accounts for compulsive repetition, phasic states of intrusion and denial or numbing, variation in the level of experience between different constellations of response, and eventual resolution of stress response syndromes. While general stress response tendencies can be abstracted in this way, persons also respond uniquely. This is due in part to how their developmental history colours personal meanings of an event and to how their current life tasks and environment are effected by the event. Individual variation in response to the same type of life event is also partly due to variations in the habitual style and capacity for control. (Pp. 248–251. Reprinted by permission of John Wiley & Sons, Ltd.)

TREATMENT OF STRESS RESPONSE SYNDROMES

Treatment can be conceptualized as an effort to assist patients in their own natural completion process. This will usually involve efforts to work through conflicts that have stymied the patient's own attempts toward this goal. It will also involve examination of latent conflicts that have been activated by association to this recent event and its present implications. This process has been reported in detail elsewhere (Horowitz, 1976) but can be summarized by a citation from Horowitz and Kaltreider (1979). The therapist who sees a patient can organize treatment around three goals:

1. The patient needs to retain a sense of his competence and self-worth. This necessitates his accepting whatever unalterable limitations are placed on his life plans by the loss or injury. This should be done without loss of hope or a sense of meaning in life.

2. The person should continue realistic and adaptive actions, including maintenance of available relationships and development of new, adaptively useful ones.

3. In working through the reactions to such a serious life event, the situation should be used for additional growth and maturation.

The Pattern of Treatment

After a serious life event, persons usually reconsider the meanings and plans for response to that event in a manner that is systematic, step by step, and dosed. When emotional responses become excessive, or threaten flooding, the person initiates control operations. The recollection of the unfinished processing of sets of meanings will tend to counteract these controls. When the person cannot handle both the repetition compulsion and the defensive counters, he seeks help. The therapist establishes a working alliance through which he assists the patient in working through his natural responses to the event and to the overall situation. In addition, efforts may be directed at modification of pre-existing conflicts, developmental difficulties, and defensive styles that made the person unusually vulnerable to traumatization by this particular experience.

Therapy depends, in part, on establishing a safe relationship. Once this is done, work within the therapy alters the status of the patient's controls. With a safe relationship and gradual modification of controls, the patient can then proceed to reappraise the serious life event, and the meanings associated with it, and make the necessary revisions of his inner models of himself and the world. As this reappraisal and revision takes place, the person is in a position to make new decisions and to engage in adaptive actions. He can practice the altered models until they gradually become automatic. Overlapping with these processes is the necessity for working through reactions to the approaching loss of the therapist and the therapy.

As the person is able to accommodate to new levels of awareness, this process repeats itself. When he can relate in a still more mutual and intimate manner, he can examine himself more deeply, and controls can be modified further. Additional work of this sort may modify aspects of character structure.

Within the time limits of a brief psychotherapy, the therapist works to establish conditions which will be helpful to the processing of the painful event. There is an early testing by the patient of both the safety of the relationship and the therapist's ability to help him cope with symptoms. These symptoms can seem less overwhelming when the therapist provides support, suggests some immediate structuring of time and events, prescribes medication if anxiety or insomnia is too disruptive, and gives "permission" for the patient to dose his feelings rather than to doggedly attempt to work them through as quickly as possible. Such interventions are often called for even during the period of acute medical hospitalization after trauma.

Patients who are more handicapped by their symptoms of avoidance can be helped by encouragement from the therapist to recollect the stress event with associations and abreactions, while working toward changing attitudes that made the controls necessary.

Frequently, symptoms subside rapidly with the establishment of a good working alliance. Then, the relationship of the stress event to the patient's various self concepts can become a focus. Introduction of the plans for termination of therapy several sessions before the final one leads to a re-experience of loss, often with a return of symptoms. But this time, loss can be faced gradually, actively rather than passively, and in a communicative helping relationship. Specific interpretations of the link of the termination experience to the stress event are made and the final hours center on this theme. At termination, the patient will usually still have symptoms, in part because of the time needed to process a major loss and because of anxiety about the loss of the relationship with the therapist. Follow up evaluations suggest to us that the therapy serves as a catalyst for both symptomatic and structural change over the ensuing year or more. This very global and generalized overview for a model 12 hour therapy as it has been applied in our center [see Table 43-13].

Patients sometimes become aware, in the course of these brief therapies, of a particular style they have for not thinking about events, and they are able to deliberately alter that situation. It may be possible for them, by continued work on their own after therapy, to live out changes that may gradually be incremental in altering habitual controls.

When a person experiences the impact of a serious life event, such as a loss or injury, his most advanced, adaptive role relationships can be threatened. He may regress to earlier role relationships, or the meaning of the event itself may tend to create some new role relationship, perhaps with unattractive, dangerous, or undesirable characteristics. The person may then enter a series of painful, strongly affective states based on altered self images and the changed role relationship. As a consequence of therapeutic facilitation of normal processes, the disturbing role relationships or self images can once again be subordinated to more adaptive, mature self images and role relationships. Intensive work using a brief therapy model may both alter the symptomatic response to a stressful life event and facilitate further progress along developmental lines. (Pp. 374–376. Reprinted with permission of W. B. Saunders Company, Publishers.)

TABLE 43-13
An Example of Timing in Brief Psychotherapy

Session	Relationship issues	Patient activity	Therapist activity
1	Initial positive feeling for helper	Patient tells story of event	Preliminary focus discussed
2	Lull as sense of pressure is reduced	Event related to life of patient	Takes psychiatric history
3	Patient tests therapist	Patient adds associations	Realignment of focus; interpretation of resistances with empathic recognition of reasons why they are currently reasonable based on past relationships
4	Therapeutic alliance deepened		Further interpretation of defenses and warded off contents linking of latter to stress event and responses
5		Work on what has been avoided	
6			Time of termination discussed
7–11	Transference reactions interpreted when seen and indicated, and linked to other configurations	Continued working through of central conflicts and issues of termination as related to the life event and reactions to it	Clarification and interpretation related to central conflicts and termination; clarification of unfinished issues and recommendations
12'	Saying goodbye	Realization of work to continue on own	Acknowledgment of real gains and real *future* work in continued mourning and formation of new schemata

Source: Horowitz & Kaltreider (1979). Reprinted with permission of W. B. Saunders Company, Publishers.

CONCLUSION

Intrusive thinking can be used as an index of the degree of distress resulting from a serious life event when the thought is linked by content to themes and emotions related to that event. Such an approach may give false positive results when distress related to some other area of stress and conflict is displaced onto a traumatic constellation of memories. Such an approach may also give false negatives when unconscious maneuvers of denial and disavowal work sufficiently well to prevent intrusive ideas and feelings. But accepting and understanding these limitations, researchers can include intrusive thinking in experimental, field, and clinical investigations of stress as a useful variable, amenable to time series sampling. The manner of inquiry can range from self-reports, such as the impact of event scale, through in-depth clinical interviews. In treatment, the contents of mental life that have an intrusive quality may provide a guide for fruitful areas of investigation.

NOTES

1. These studies were carried out in collaboration with Frances Cohen, Barbara Kent, Nancy Wilner, Anthony Leong, Nancy Horowitz, and Michael Paglarouli and will be presented in forthcoming publications.

REFERENCES

American Psychiatric Association. Diagnostic and statistical manual of mental disorders (DSM III) (Third Edition). Washington, D.C.: American Psychiatric Association, 1980.

ANTROBUS, J. S., SINGER, J. L. Mind wandering and cognitive structure. Paper presented to the New York Academy of Science, October, 20, 1969.

ANTROBUS, J. S., SINGER, J. L., & GREENBERG, S. Studies in the stream of consciousness: Experimental enhancement and suppression of spontaneous cognitive processes. *Percept Motor Skills* 1966, *23*, 399–417.

BREUER, J., & FREUD, S. Studies on hysteria. In J. Strachey (ed.), *The standard edition of the complete psychological works*, vol. 2. London: Hogarth, 1957.

FINN, R. H. A note on estimating the reliability of categorical data. *Educational and Psychological Measurement*, 1970, *3*, 71–76.

FREUD, S. Beyond the pleasure principle. In J. Strachey (ed.), *The standard edition of the complete psychological works*, vol. 18. London: Hogarth, 1953.

HOROWITZ, M. J. Intrusive and repetitive thoughts after experimental stress: A summary. *Archives of General Psychiatry*, 1975, *32*, 1457–1463.

―――. *Stress response syndromes*. New York: Aronson, 1976.

―――. *Image formation and cognition* (2d ed.). New York: Appleton, 1978.

―――. Psychological response to serious life events. V. Hamilton & D. Warburton (eds.), In *Human stress and cognition:* New York: Wiley, 1980.

HOROWITZ, M. J., & BECKER, S. Cognitive response to stress: Experimental studies of a "compulsion to repeat trauma." In R. Holt & E. Peterfreund (eds.), *Psychoanalysis and contemporary science*. New York: Macmillan, 1972.

HOROWITZ, M. J., HULLEY, S., ALVAREZ, W., BILLINGS, J., BENFARI, R., BLAIR, S., BORHANI, N., & SIMON, N. News of risk for early heart disease as a stressful event. *Psychosomatic Medicine*, 1980, *42*, 37–46.

HOROWITZ, M. J., KRUPNICK, J., KALTREIDER, K., WILNER, N., LEONG, A., & MARMAR, C. Initial psychological response to death of a parent. *Archives of General Psychiatry*, 1981, *38*, 316–323.

HOROWITZ, M. J., & KALTREIDER, N. Brief therapy of stress response syndromes. *Psychiatric Clinics of North America*, 1979, *2*, 365–378.

HOROWITZ, M. J., SCHAEFER, C., & COONEY, P. Life event scaling for recency of experience. In E. Gundersen & R. Rahe (eds.), *Life stress and illness*. Springfield: Thomas, 1974.

HOROWITZ, M. J., & WILNER, N. Stress films, emotion, and cognitive response. *Archives of General Psychiatry*, 1976, *30*, 1339–1344.

―――. Life events, stress, and coping. In L. Poon (ed.), *Aging in the 80's*. Washington, D.C.: American Psychiatric Association, 1980.

HOROWITZ, M. J., WILNER, N., & ALVAREZ W. Impact of event scale: A measure of subjective stress. *Psychosomatic Medicine,* 1979, *41,* 209–218.

HOROWITZ, M. J., WILNER, N., KALTREIDER, K., & ALVAREZ, W. Signs and symptoms of post-traumatic stress disorder. *Archives of General Psychiatry,* 1980, *37,* 85–92.

HOROWITZ, M. J., WILNER N., MARMAR, C., & KRUPNICK, J. Pathological grief and the activation of latent self-images. *American Journal of Psychiatry,* 1980, *137,* 1157–1162.

JANIS, I. *Stress and frustration.* New York: Harcourt, 1969.

KRUPNICK, J., & HOROWITZ, M. J. Stress response syndromes: Recurrent themes. *Archives of General Psychiatry,* 1981, *38,* 428–435.

LAZARUS, R. *Psychological stress and the coping process.* New York: McGraw-Hill, 1966.

MALAN, D. *Frontier of brief therapy.* New York: Plenum, 1976.

SCHUR, M. *The id and the regulatory process of the ego.* New York: International Universities, 1966.

SIFNEOS, P. E. *Short-term psychotherapy and emotional crises.* Cambridge: Harvard University Press, 1972.

STEVENS, S. S. A metric for the social consensus. *Science,* 1966, *151,* 530–541.

44

Evaluation and Management of Stress in General Medicine: The Psychosomatic Approach

Hoyle Leigh

THE EVOLUTION OF PSYCHOSOMATIC MEDICINE

The concept of psychosomatic medicine has undergone major evolutionary changes in the past several decades. In the 1930s and 1940s, Alexander (1950) proposed a conflict-specific theory of psychosomatic disorders based on psychoanalytic investigation of patients with illnesses frequently observed to be related to psychologic stress and conflict (see also Alexander [1950], Reiser [1975], Lipowski [1968], Kimball [1970], Leigh & Reiser [1977]). He theorized that specific unresolved psychologic conflicts were accompanied by prolonged specific autonomic arousal, representing the somatic concomitant of repressed affects. When life situations (stress) activated or intensified the unresolved conflict, a *psychosomatic disorder,* such as peptic ulcer, would ensue, caused by tissue damage arising from the prolonged and intense autonomic arousal. For example, Alexander postulated that in the case of duodenal ulcer a life situation that activated conflicted longings for love would be accompanied by gastric hyperactivity and so contribute to peptic ulceration in the presence of specific constitutional vulnerability.

Alexander's formulations gave rise to the notion that certain medical diseases were particularly psychosomatic—i.e., psychologic factors were especially important in their etiology. For example, ulcerative colitis, bronchial asthma, essential hypertension, migraine headache, neurodermatitis, thyrotoxicosis, and rheumatoid arthritis were considered to be psychosomatic disorders par excellence. Although Alexander's approach was helpful in elucidating the psychodynamic meanings of many medical conditions, there were inherent problems: the retrospective nature of the investigative method, confusion between correlation and causation, and, most important, a tendency for premature closure of investigation when the psychodynamic meaning was understood (without studying further the genetic, immunologic, or infectious factors).

Wolff and Wolf (1947), who were Alexander's contemporaries made important contributions by using the research laboratory and experimental methods to investigate psychosomatic relationships. They argued that adaptive, defensive psychophysiologic patterns might result in tissue damage and illness if the stressful situation were prolonged. For example, the physiologic correlate of the psychologic defensive wish to get rid of an unpleasant idea, which, in turn, is precipitated by exposure to a certain person (stress), might be associated with hyperfunction of the organ of ejection-riddance, the colon, and resultant diarrhea.

The past three decades ushered in a new blossoming of investigations using experimental methods, aided by newly gained knowledge in biochemistry and computer technology. For example, in the classic psychosomatic disorders, such as peptic ulcer, it became possible to define and investigate the relation between constitutional, or genetic, vulnerability and psychosocial stress factors. Weiner, Thaler, Reiser, and Mirsky (1957) showed in the late 1950s that a genetically determined trait, serum pepsinogen level, could be used as an indicator of vulnerability to peptic ulcer conditions under nonspecific stress like basic training in the army. In their study, those who developed peptic ulcer were found to have the personality configuration that followed Alexander's formulations. In addition, and without exception, they also had constitutionally high serum pepsinogen levels, and the stress of basic training for them was such that activation of the specific conflict described by Alexander ensued. It is now clear that predisposing constitutional factors are present in other disorders such as hypertension and coronary disease.

While these and other investigations in the 1950s through the 1970s showed the importance of constitutional factors in somatic diseases, it also became clear that stress arising from the environment plays a major role in the development of a number of somatic diseases, including those that had not been considered particularly psychosomatic. For example, Henry, Stephens, Axelrod, and Mueller (1971) and Henry, Stephens, and Watson (1975) were able to construct a psychosocial environment in which mice almost invariably developed hypertension and another environment in which susceptible mice strains inevitably developed breast carcinoma. The hypertension environment was a cage system in which the animals were under constant threat of dominance challenge and had to compete for food in a territorial manner. The cancer environment involved a situation of forced breeding, in which the mice were kept in a constant state of readiness to reproduce, while offspring were always removed after delivery. This resulted in a disorganization of the social structure and 100% incidence of mammary cancer in the susceptible female subjects.

Epidemiologic studies repeatedly showed that environmental stresses, especially bereavement, have an important role in the development of disease, as well as in illness behavior. A 1967 study in Wales (Rees & Lutkins, 1967) showed that mortality after loss of a first-degree relative was seven times that in an age matched control group. Other studies (Jacobs & Ostfeld, 1979) confirm increased mortality after bereavement, although the risk may not be quite as high as sevenfold.

Engel and Schmale (1967; Schmale, 1972) postulated that a specific psychologic state, which they called the "giving up–given up complex," characterized by feelings of helplessness and hopelessness, may be a particularly favorable setting for pathogenesis of general medical disease. This state, of course, is most likely to occur at a time of personal loss or severe stress.

Holmes and Rahe (1968) showed, in a number of populations, that those individuals who experienced a large number of life changes (such as bereavement, marriage, divorce, change in residence) had a higher risk of developing almost any kind of physical illness (see also Rahe, 1972). They attempted to quantify the stress value of some commonly encountered life changes, developing the concept of *life change units*.

Behavioral patterns of individuals significantly contribute to the pathogenesis of a number of diseases. Smoking and drinking are the most salient examples. There is a clear relationship between changes in smoking and drinking behavior and environmental stress.

The *type A behavior pattern,* characterized by a hard-driving, unable to relax, hurried, and deadline oriented lifestyle, is associated with an increased risk to develop coronary disease (Friedman & Rosenman, 1959).

These several lines of investigation contributed to the evolution of psychosomatic medicine from a conflict-specific, disease-specific, or stress-specific model to a general systems model (Table 44-1) applicable to all diseases. As more recent investigations have showed, all medical diseases must be understood in terms of the person's constitution and developmental history and the current interaction between the behavioral and physiologic aspects of the person and between the person and the environment. Psychosomatic medicine has ceased to be the study of specific psychosomatic disorders but is, rather, a comprehensive approach to all patients with disease or disorder that pays special emphasis to the interaction between biological and psychosocial dimensions.

THE PSYCHOSOMATIC APPROACH AND CONSULTATION–LIAISON PSYCHIATRY

Consultation-liaison psychiatry applies the psychosomatic approach in the evaluation and management of patients in the general medical setting. The consultation-liaison psychiatrist works collaboratively with the internist or surgeon in the comprehensive evaluation process, including the assessment of stressors in the patient's environment, any changes in behavior (e.g., sleep, drinking habits) or mood (e.g., depression, anxiety) that might have contributed to the disease, and aspects of the patient's personality that may prove to be important in planning a management strategy. Another important role of the consultation-liaison psychiatrist is to help educate the nonpsychiatric physician and other health care workers in the comprehensive psychosomatic approach to patients.

THE PATIENT EVALUATION GRID

Evaluation and management of stress is, of course, an important aspect of the psychosomatic approach. Leigh, Feinstein and Reiser (1980) and Leigh and Reiser (1980) proposed a Patient Evaluation Grid (PEG) as an operational method of evaluating patients comprehensively. The PEG consists of three dimensions (biological, personal, environmental) intersected by three time contexts (current, recent, background), as shown in Table 44-1.

The *biological dimension* contains information on such components of the patient as tissues, organs, and disease. The *personal dimension* refers to the psychological and behavioral aspects of the patient as a person. The *environmental dimension* contains information related to the physical and social environment of the patient, including family, work, and environmental toxins.

The *current context* refers to the current state of the patient in each of the dimensions—physical state, mental status, and family relationships. The *recent context* pertains to recent changes and events—recent surgery, development of symptoms and signs, changes in sleep pattern, recent onset of depression, and life changes such as bereavement or change in residence. The *background context* refers to relatively long-standing factors such as genetic givens, personality type and habitual coping mechanisms, and cultural factors like sick role expectations and religious influences.

TABLE 44-1
Patient Evaluation Grid (PEG).

Dimensions	Current *(current states)*	Contexts Recent *(recent events and changes)*	Background *(culture, traits, constitution)*
Biological	Symptoms Physical examination Vital signs Status of related organs Medications Disease	Age Recent bodily changes Injuries, operations Disease Drugs	Heredity Early nutrition Constitution Predisposition Early disease
Personal	Chief complaint Mental status Expectations about illness and treatment	Recent illness, occurrence of symptoms Personality change Mood, thinking, behavior Adaptation-defenses	Developmental factors Early experience Personality type Attitude to illness
Environmental	Immediate physical and interpersonal environment Supportive figure, next of kin Effect of help seeking	Recent physical and interpersonal environment Life changes Family, work, others Contact with ill persons Contact with doctor or hospital	Early physical environment Cultural and family environment Early relations Cultural sick role expectation

Source: Leigh, Feinstein, and Reiser, 1980.

Whereas the current context represents the most pressing needs and immediate constraints in evaluating and managing the patient, the recent context embraces the contributing and precipitating factors in the illness. The background context information represents relatively stable factors that must be taken into account in attempting to approach the patient. Stress is an important consideration, then, in the recent context.

EVALUATION OF STRESS

An environmental event *(stressor)* is stressful if it has an impact on the individual. Stress may be likened to a load that causes strain on a recipient structure (for example, the bending of a steel bridge as a heavy truck passes over it). The degree of distortion or strain is indicative of the load *(stress)* caused by the stressor.

Stress as a noxious stimulus causing strain may exist in any of the three dimensions—biological, personal, or environmental. In fact, one may conceptualize any disease or disorder as a *stress-responsive phenomenon*. In this discussion, however, I use the term "stress" to indicate an *external, environmental stimulus*.

Intervening variables in the stress response sequence include psychological defense mechanisms (e.g., denial operating at the perceptual level, repression blocking activation of certain memories), the state of the autonomic and neuroendocrine apparatus (e.g., hyperactive hypothalamus, limbic system disorder), learned patterns of behavior at both the action and the speech level, and the status of target organs (e.g., congenital organ vulnerability, acquired weakness of organs such as atherosclerotic coronary arteries).

In the presence of severe stress, common outcomes are the emotions of anxiety and depression, with associated physical symptoms and individual-specific target organ dysfunction.

Anxiety is recognized by subjective symptoms and objective signs. Feelings of dread and fear, accompanied by evidence of sympathetic arousal (sweating, rapid heart rate, and tension in the skeletal muscles), are common features of anxiety. The function of anxiety is protective: this response signals a danger situation (Leigh & Reiser, 1980) either in the environment or within the personality system. Psychodynamic conflict is the main cause for anxiety arising from within the personality system; this pattern represents the classic diffuse and vague sense of dread without identifiable external stimulus. (Freud, 1926) Anxiety may also be experienced *after* a danger situation has passed or *after* exposure to a major traumatic situation (e.g., post-traumatic stress disorder following an earthquake or a severe burn). Anxiety experienced after trauma may respresent danger signals arising from the severe strain that the person has developed, including autonomic and endocrine arousal and tissue damage. Reliving of the trauma, with concomitant anxiety, may also represent an unconscious attempt at mastery of the traumatic experience.

Given the signs and symptoms of anxiety in a patient, the clinician must determine whether the source of anxiety is in the environment, in the personality system, or in the biological dimension. Careful history taking, especially concerning recent and anticipated changes and events, will usually shed light on possible environmental stressors. In the absence of environmental stressors, factors in the biological dimension causing anxiety symptoms must be ruled out before a diagnosis of anxiety arising from psychological conflicts can be made. Any disease of the central nervous system (e.g., epilepsy), the neuroendocrine system (e.g., hyperthyroidism), the autonomic nervous system (e.g, pheochromocytoma), or metabolism (e.g., hypoglycemia), as well as exogenous drugs (e.g., phencyclidine) and their withdrawal (e.g., delirium tremens), can cause symptoms and signs of anxiety. Thus, any patient presenting with anxiety must have a thorough medical evaluation, including laboratory tests, before specific antianxiety or stress management plans are instituted.

In some patients, history may show the presence of a major stressor in the environment without any evidence of strain. For example, some patients who are admitted to the coronary care unit with myocardial infarction deny feeling apprehensive at all (Hackett, Cassem, & Wishnie, 1968). At least in the coronary care unit, such major deniers, who can successfully block out stressful stimuli, have been shown to have better prognosis than those who feel anxiety. On the other hand, patients who are to undergo elective surgery do better if they experience anticipatory anxiety (Janis, 1958). In other instances, there may be a dissociation between the subjective experience of anxiety and its physiological aspects. For example, a patient may experience minimal feelings of apprehension while anticipating a major personal change, although his blood pressure may show a marked increase. Such dissociation may be caused either by massive repression or other defense mechanisms that do not successfully block perception or because of a hypersensitive (vulnerable) autonomic nervous system or the target organ (in this case, arterioles).

As discussed earlier, certain target organ diseases once were considered either psychosomatic or stress related. While hyperfunction of certain organs is clearly seen in individuals undergoing stress (e.g., increased heart rate, increased or decreased gastrointestinal motility, increase in blood pressure) actual disease of these organs involves other factors that may be more important in pathogenesis than stress. These factors include heredity and infection. This implies that a patient with a target organ disease must be evaluated in a comprehensive way, including evaluation of the biological, personal, and environmental dimensions.

Although some general stress-responsive reactions, like anxiety, appear in most individuals, other reactions to stress may be unique to the individual. For example, some individuals may show gastric hyperacidity, others may have diarrhea or constipation, and still others may have tachycardia. These individual-specific responses to stress (Lacey & Lacey, 1965) are probably determined in early life by constitution and learning (Reiser, 1975). It is important for the clinician to know the individual-specific stress response patterns in his patients because the presence of a typical pattern for the patient at a given time may indicate the presence of environmental stressors or intrapsychic conflicts, while symptoms atypical of the individual's pattern should alert the clinician to the possibility of a newly developed disease.

Depressive mood often ensues when an individual undergoes a loss or when an individual is exposed to a stressor that is difficult or impossible to overcome. Depression, in this sense, may be seen as a signal or recent or impending loss or defeat (grief). The sense of helplessness and hopelessness, described by Engel and others (Engel, Schmale, 1967; Schmale, 1972), is often assoicated with a particularly favorable setting for the onset of nonspecific disease. Depression with helpless and hopeless feelings often follows severe anxiety; in such cases, the individual assumes that he is helpless about the stressor. Depressive mood has been shown not only to increase morbidity but also to worsen prognosis and to prolong recovery from any disease (Leigh & Reiser, 1980).

Depressed mood, however, does not always indicate the presence of an environmental stressor. Like anxiety, depression may be caused by factors within either the personality or the biological dimension. In fact, severe depression (the depressive syndrome) usually involves a constitutional factor, as well as possible environmental or intrapsychic factors. Severe depression is characterized by neurovegetative signs, along with subjective symptoms such as feeling sad, down, and blue. Apathy may also be a main feature, as well as an inability to enjoy things that used to give pleasure to the individual. Likewise, loss of self-esteem and guilt feelings are common. The neurovegetative signs of depression include sleep disturbance (especially early morning awakening), loss of appetite and weight loss, loss of sexual interest, fatigue, and vague aches and pains.

Patients who evidence the symptoms and signs of serious depression must be evaluated comprehensively. First, biological dimension factors must be considered because many diseases of the central nervous system and endocrine system can cause signs and symptoms of depression. For example, hyperparathyroidism, Cushing's syndrome, multiple sclerosis, and viral infections are often associated with depression. Occult neoplasms, especially cancer of the tail of the pancreas, must also be ruled out since they often present with depressive symptomatology; the high index of suspicion in such conditions may be lifesaving for many patients. A number of drugs may also cause depression—most antihypertensive agents, reserpine, in particular, and hormone preparations (e.g., cortisol, birth control pills). Careful drug history is thus indicated in a patient showing symptoms of depression.

In the personal dimension, an important consideration is past history of depressive episodes. Patients with the common psychiatric disorder of major depression usually have recurrent episodes of depression. Since self-destructive thoughts are often entertained, but not verbalized, by depressed individuals, the clinician should ask specifically about suicidal thoughts and plans. Presence of serious suicidal ideation warrants psychiatric hospitalization. Severe guilt feelings and serious loss of self-esteem are usually associated with major depression.

Psychosocial events such as personal loss, threatened loss, and insurmountable future problems are common stressors in the environmental dimension. Except in cases of clear bereavement, the presence of an environmental stressor should not be taken as sufficient evidence that the depressive syndrome is purely a reactive one not requiring medical attention. Serious depression usually warrants psychiatric evaluation and combined drug treatment and psychotherapy after possible medical causes have been ruled out.

STRESS MANAGEMENT

Stress management in the general medical patient includes treatment of the strain (anxiety, depression, somatic symptoms, target organ disease) and prevention of excessive strain (through improved coping strategies, relaxation training, etc.). When a thorough evaluation shows the presence of severe anxiety associated with an environmental stressor, treatment plans should be devised in the biological, personal, and environmental dimensions (Leigh & Reiser, 1980).

Biological dimension treatment modalities include antianxiety drugs and biofeedback for specific muscle relaxation. Benzodiazepines such as diazepam (Valium) and chlordiazepoxide (Librium) are commonly used antianxiety drugs. In cases of anxiety associated with an external stressor, antianxiety drugs should be used only to reduce paralyzing anxiety—and only as an emergency measure on a temporary basis. Continued use of antianxiety agents may result in tolerance and addiction, with iatrogenic anxiety syndrome if abrupt withdrawal is attempted. Electromyelographic (EMG) biofeedback may be useful if skeletal muscle tension associated with anxiety is a prominent feature.

Antianxiety therapy in the personal dimension includes psychotherapy, counseling, hypnosis, and instruction in relaxation. The psychotherapeutic technique may be exploratory, geared to identification and resolution of intrapsychic conflicts that may be the source of anxiety. For many patients, supportive psychotherapy or counseling can reduce the experience of anxiety by enhancing coping abilities and providing interpersonal support. Behavioral therapies like desensitization and reciprocal inhibition may be used to reduce anxiety associated with environmental stimuli. These approaches are especially effective in phobias and with exaggerated anxiety response in the face of mild stimuli. (Spiegel & Spiegel, 1978; Benson, 1975) Both hypnosis and relaxation training tend to reduce the experience of anxiety by attaining a state of relaxation. These techniques, then, may be used as treatment for the strain and as preventive measures.

In the environmental dimension, anxiety may be treated by removing the individual from the stressful situation (e.g., hospitalization, vacation). More frequently, mobilization of environmental support systems such as family and friends is more feasible and effective.

Any of the preceding treatment modalities may be used alone or in combination, according to the needs of the individual patient. The consultation-liaison psychiatrist is usually called in to evaluate anxiety syndromes in medical patients and to recommend treatment. Then, the psychiatrist and the primary physician enter into a collaborative management relationship regarding the patient.

The treatment of depression follows similar lines. Antidepressant therapy is usually indicated and effective in serious depression. Tricyclic antidepressants such as imipramine (Tofranil) and amitriptyline (Elavil) are commonly used drugs. Unlike antianxiety agents, antidepressants do not have a tolerance effect and are not addicting. However, sudden termination may cause mild to moderate withdrawal symptoms. Antidepressants usually require two to four weeks for full effect and must be continued for approximately six months when used to treat major depression. Supportive psychotherapy is essential in a depressed patient, and an additive benefit occurs in combination with drug therapy (Weissman, Prusoff, DiMascio et al., 1979). Environmental therapy for depression includes hospitalization, supportive groups, and mobilization of family support. Hospitalization may be critical in suicidal patients.

Patients with somatic symptoms such as tachycardia, diarrhea, or tension headache may respond to treatment modalities geared to anxiety—psychotherapy, relaxation training, biofeedback (of heart rate for tachycardia, EMG for tension headache)—and to antianxiety agents when symptoms are especially severe. Specific drugs for symptom relief may also be necessary (e.g., propranolol for tachycardia).

Target organ diseases, formerly considered psychosomatic disorders, should also be treated comprehensively. The primary treatment may need to be directed toward the target organ itself; for instance, colectomy in ulcerative colitis, antihypertensive drugs in essential hypertension, or diet and drugs in peptic ulcer. If stress seems to be playing a major role in the exacerbation of the target organ disease, then specific treatments for the aspects of stress (e.g., anxiety, depression), outlined earlier, may be instituted in addition to the medical regimen.

Preventive measures for stress-responsive disorders (strain) are designed to improve the individual's coping ability. Since stress tends to reduce normal problem-solving ability, it is especially helpful to strengthen the patient's coping ability in a preventive fashion (Hansell, 1976; Caplan, 1974; Caplan, 1981).

General measures to improve coping ability in the biological dimension include any health promoting strategy, including healthy diet, moderate exercise, weight control, etc. Physical fitness provides the healthy internal environment in which the brain functions.

In the personal dimension, general stress reducing techniques such as relaxation training and self-hypnosis may be useful. When these self-relaxation exercises are practiced on a regular basis, they tend to neutralize the accumulating strain caused by stressors. In addition, these measures may foster a sense of mastery, which seems to play a very important role in preventing the noxious effects of stress.

In the well-known executive monkey experiments, monkeys were trained to press bars constantly to avoid electric shock in a complex and highly demanding operant conditioning program with many contingencies (Brady, 1958). In this very stressful situation of high demand, the monkeys developed bleeding gastric ulcers and died, while yoked controls who were shocked the same amount but did not have to press bars to avoid shock did not develop bleeding ulcers. In another experiment, rats who were trained to avoid shock by bar-pressing did not develop bleeding ulcers, while yoked control rats who were exposed to inescapable shock developed bleeding ulcers (Weiss, 1968). In the latter experiment, the rats trained to press bars to avoid shock had *feedback* in the form of light; that is, the light indicating impending shock was turned off as the bar was pressed (in the executive monkey situation, there was no direct feedback concerning adequate performance). One might speculate that the executive rats had a sense of mastery or control.

Measures to increase the sense of mastery, then, include experiencing successful solution to problems (feedback). Recreational activities generally increase one's sense of mastery through a combination of relaxation, problem-solving (especially in games), and sense of control (as in exercise) and reward (pleasure derived from the activity). Specific strategies can be developed to increase the sense of mastery and to decrease anxiety for specific stressors, such as impending surgery. Such strategies may utilize anticipatory information and guidance (Egbert, Battit, Welch et al., 1964) or cognitive training to divert attention from present discomfort and focus attention on pleasant thoughts and memories (Langer, Janis, Wolfer, 1975). Again, recreational activity can increase the sense of control by diverting attention away from the stressor. General education may itself be important in increasing coping ability. In men with complex ventricular premature contractions, those with eight years of formal education or less had three times the risk of sudden coronary death associated with men who had more education (Weinblatt, Ruberman, Goldberg et al., 1978).

In the environmental dimension, social support plays a critical role in preventing stress-responsive disorder. A study of stress and complications of pregnancy found that the groups with *much stress and much social support* had a 33.3% incidence of complications, compared to 90.9% in the *much stress and little support* group (Nuckolls, Cassel, & Kaplan, 1972). Many other studies have indicated that social and family support and/or a confiding relationship help ameliorate the noxious effects of environmental stress, including anxiety and depression, and increase the coping ability of the stressed individual. Controlled environmental change (e.g., vacation) also increases the sense of mastery and may divert the individual's attention from environmental stressors while producing relaxation.

FUTURE RESEARCH DIRECTIONS

Just as psychosomatic research has evolved from the study of the specific psychologic factors (conflicts) in specific medical diseases to the elucidation of psychosocial factors in all medical (and psychiatric) diseases, future studies will focus on the general role of stress in providing a favorable internal environment for the development of disease. Research is particularly needed to elucidate the mediating emotional states (i.e., anxiety and depression). Much work has already been done to determine the neurochemical changes in anxiety states and in depression (for a review see Leigh & Reiser, 1980). Target organ symptoms associated with anxiety, such as syncope, may be explained on the basis of relatively simple hemodynamic factors (Engel, 1962). Tension headache and hyperventilation syndrome likewise have relatively simple underlying mechanisms.

How stress contributes to general susceptibility to illness and how depression contributes to general morbidity and mortality are questions that still challenge us. Studies in psychoneuroendocrinology (Mason, 1975) and psychoimmunology (Bartrop, Lazarus, Luckhurst et al., 1977) are beginning to shed some light on the mechanism by which host resistance might be reduced at times of stress. Bartrop and associates (1977) found that bereaved individuals had depressed T-cell function at five weeks but not at 2 weeks after bereavement. The T-cells, lymphocytes originally derived from the thymus gland, mediate cellular and delayed hypersensitivity reactions. The difference between bereaved spouses and controls was tenfold. This difference was not mediated by hormones such as cortisol. Other reports have indicated that the natural killer activity (through which cancerous cells, for example, are killed by our immune cells) mediated by T-cells is decreased in college students undergoing stress and having difficulty coping (for a review see Rogers, Dubey, & Reich, 1979).

Since lymphocytes are known to have receptors for neurotransmitters such as catecholamines, prostaglandins, somatostatin, histamine, and insulin, the autonomic changes accompanying anxiety and depression could play a role in the changes in immune mechanisms under stress. Epinephrine and norepinephrine, important hormones in the stress response syndrome, decrease the immune response and inhibit delayed cutaneous hypersensitivity.

This is a very cursory overview of psychoimmunology. We are becoming aware, with each discovery, that there is a complex and exquisite homeostatic mechanism in the universe of the immune cells (T-cells, B-cells, killer cells, suppressor cells, etc.), which is, in turn, in a state of balance with the endocrine system. Since Selye's (1950) studies on the role of corticosteroids in stress, there has been an ever increasing knowledge of hormonal changes in stress. Many hormones, besides corticosteroids, respond to stress in individual-specific patterns. An important intervening mechanism in the endocrine response is the degree of success of psychological defense mechanisms. For example, some individuals respond to a stressor with a *decrease* in the level of cortisol rather than with an increase, which is the common pattern. Testosterone, pituitary grow hormone, and thyroxine are other hormones that respond to stress. Mason (1982) found that individuals who showed extreme values in several hormones (either high or low) were at a higher risk of developing disease than were those who had moderate values. This suggests that susceptibility to disease may not be a simple function of increased or decreased levels of one hormone, but rather the net result of a complex interaction among hormones and target organs. On the other hand, an unstable central nervous system (e.g., hypothalamus) may be the constitutional vulnerability.

In depth studies on the cellular and hormonal changes in stress must be supplemented by research on the overall relationship among the variables and their association with disease. Why a killer cell fails to do its job with a cancerous cell in a given individual is a function not only of the killer cell but also of the toxic and endocrine factors that may have caused the cancer in the first place and may be preventing the killer cell from functioning optimally through endocrine (cortisol) and/or autonomic (sympathetic arousal—catecholamines) mechanisms.

Exactly what combinations of changes in hormones, autonomic nervous system, and immune mechanisms result in disease? What determines the nature of disease? Do specific patterns of changes tend to contribute to specific diseases? For example, would greater changes in immune (compared to endocrine) mechanisms be likely to contribute to infectious and neoplastic diseases, while greater changes in endocrine function might result in hypertension and coronary disease? These are some of the questions that await further research.

The attempt to understand pathogenesis should parallel a clinical approach that evaluates the interrelated biological, personal, and environmental factors that affect patients. Through this comprehensive approach, as exemplified by the PEG, new patterns of associations between psychosocial factors and disease may be discovered, which, in turn, may lead to further studies of underlying biochemical and cellular mechanisms.

REFERENCES

ALEXANDER, F. *Psychosomatic medicine.* New York: Noron, 1950.

BARTROP, R. W., LAZARUS, L., LUCKHURST, E. ET AL. Depressed lymphocyte function after bereavement. Lancet *I:* 834–836, 1977.

BENSON, H. The relaxation response. New York, Morrow, 1975.

BRADY, J. V. Ulcers in "executive" monkeys, *Sci Am 199:* 95–100, 1958.

CAPLAN, G. Support systems and community mental health. New York, Behavioral Publications, 1974.

————. Mastery of stress: Psychosocial aspects. *Am. J. Psychiatry 138:* 413–420, 1981.

EGBERT, L. D., BATTIT, G. E., WELCH, C. E., ET AL. Reduction of postoperative pain by encouragement and instruction of patients. *New Eng J Med 270:* 825–827, 1964.

ENGEL, G. L. *Fainting* (2d ed). Springfield Thomas, 1962.

ENGEL, G. L. & SCHMALE, A. R. Psychoanalytic theory of somatic disorder: Conversion specificity and the disease onset situation. *J. Am Psychoanal Assoc 15:* 344–365, 1967.

FREUD, S. (1926) Inhibitions, symptoms, and anxiety. In Strachey, J. (ed.), *The Standard Edition of the Complete Psychological Works of Sigmund Freud.* London, Hogarth, 1953, vol. 20.

FRIEDMAN, M. & ROSENMAN, R. H. Association of specific overt behavior pattern with blood and cardiovascular findings. *J of the Am Med Assoc 96:* 1286–1296, 1959.

HACKETT, T. P., CASSEM, N. Y., & WISHNIE, H. A. The coronary care unit: An appraisal of its psychologic hazards. *N. Engl J Med 279:* 1365–1370, 1968.

HANSELL, N. The Person-In-Distress: On the biological dynamics of adaptation. New York, Behavioral Publications, 1976.

HENRY, J. P., STEPHENS, P. M., AXELROD, J., & MUELLER, R. A. Effects of psychosocial stimulation on the enzymes involved in the biosynthesis and metabolism of noradrenaline and adrenaline. *Psychosom Med 33:* 227–237, 1971.

HENRY, J. P., STEPHENS, P. M., & WATSON, F. M. Force breeding, social disorder, and mammary tumor formation in CBA/USC mouse colonies: A pilot study. *Psychosom Med 37:* 227–283, 1975.

HOLMES, R. H. & RAHE, R. H. The social readjustment rating scale. *J. Psychosom Res 11:* 213, 1968.

JACOBS, S. & OSTFELD, A. An epidemiological review of the mortality of bereavement *Psychosom Med 39:* 344–357, 1979.

JANIS, I. L. *Psychological stress.* Wiley, New York, 1958.

KIMBALL, C. P. Conceptual developments in psychosomatic medicine, 1939–1969. *Ann Intern Med 73:* 307–316, 1970

LACEY, J. I., LACEY, B. C. Verification and extension of the principle of autonomic response-stereotype. *Am J Psychol 71:* 50–73, 1965.

LANGER, E. J., JANIS, I. L., & WOLFER, J. A. Reduction of psychological stress in surgical patients. *J Exp Soc Psychol 11:* 155–165, 1975.

Leigh, H., Feinstein, A. R., & Reiser, M. F. The Patient Evaluation Grid: A systematic approach to comprehensive care. *Gen Hosp. Psychiat 2:* 3–9, 1980.

Leigh, H. & Reiser, M. F. Major trends in psychosomatic medicine: The psychiatrist's evolving role in medicine: *Ann Intern Med 87:* 233–239, 1977.

Leigh, H. & Reiser, M. F. *The patient: Biological, psychological, and social dimensions of medical practice.* Plenum. New York, 1980.

Lipowski, Z. J. Review of consultation psychiatry and psychosomatic medicine. III: Theoretical issues. *Psychosom Med 30:* 395–422, 1968.

Mason, J. W. Clinical psychophysiology: Psychoendocrine mechanism, in Reiser, M. F. (ed). *American Handbook of Psychiatry* 2nd ed. Vol. 4. *Organic disorder and psychosomatic medicine,* New York, Basic Books, 1975.

Mason, J. W. Personal communication, 1982.

Nuckolls, K. B., Cassel, J., & Kaplan, B. H. Psychosocial assets, life crisis, and the prognosis of pregnancy. *Am J Epidemiol 95:* 431–441, 1972.

Paclidis, N., & Chirigos, M. Stress-induced impariment of macrophage turmoricidal function. *Psychosom Med 42:* 47–54, 1980.

Rahe, R. H. Subjects' recent life changes and their near future illness susceptibility. *Adv Psychosom Med 8:* 2–19, 1972.

Rees, W. D., & Lutkins, S. G. Mortality of bereavement. *Br. Med J 4:*13–16, 1967.

Reiser, M. F. Changing theoretical concepts in psychosomatic medicine, in *American Handbook of Psychiatry,* 2nd ed., vol. 4, edited by Reiser, M. F. New York, Basic Books, 1975, pp. 477–500.

Rogers, M. P., Dubey, D., & Reich, P. The influence of the psyche and the brain on immunity and disease susceptibility: A critical reveiw. *Psychosom Med 41:* 147–164, 1979.

Schmale, A. H. Giving up as a final common pathway to changes in health. *Adv. Psychosom Med 8:*20–40, 1972.

Selye, H. The Physiology and Pathology of Exposure to Stress, Montreal, Acta, 1950.

Spiegel, H. & Spiegel, D. *Trance and treatment: Clinical uses of hypnosis.* New York, Basic Books, 1978.

Weiner, H., Thaler, M., Reiser, M. F., & Mirsky, I. A. Etiology of duodenal ulcer: Relation of specific psychological characteristics to rate of gastric secretion (serum pepsinogen) *Psychosom Med 19:*10, 1957.

Weinblatt, E., Ruberman, W., Goldberg, J. D., et al. Relation of education to sudden death after myocardial infarction, *New Engl J Med 299:* 60–65, 1978.

Weiss, J. M. Effects of coping responses on stress. *J Comp Physiol Psychol 65:* 251–260, 1968.

Weissman, M. M., Prusoff, B. A., DiMascio, A., et al. The efficacy of the treatment of acute depression episodes, *Am. J. Psychiatry 136:* 555–558, 1979.

Wolf, S., Wolff, H. G. *Human gastric function,* 2nd ed. New York: Oxford University Press, 1947.

45

A Coping-Rest Model of Relaxation and Stress Management

Johann Stoyva   **Cathy Anderson**

ONE'S FIRST REACTION TO THE TERM "STRESS MANAGEMENT" is likely to be skepticism: perhaps this is simply another of those shimmering illusions conjured up by the ebullient and indefatigable purveyors of pop psychology. Indeed, there are some genuine problems with the term. To begin with, quite a mix of techniques seem to be involved. Do these various techniques have anything in common? Do they possess any theoretical coherence? Moreover, the term "stress" itself is amorphous. It has been applied to practically everything of an aversive nature, indeed, to virtually anything we dislike. One wonders, too, with something this amorphous, exactly how to go about managing it!

Despite these difficulties, we believe that stress management is a legitimate field of endeavor. This area is taking shape in response to widely perceived needs and problems in our society and is, in fact, evolving quickly. Consequently, an assessment of stress management could be a useful enterprise. First, we would like to discuss and present a point of view regarding the term "stress," with particular reference to the distinction between coping and rest. Second, we would like to describe and briefly to evaluate a number of procedures currently used in stress management. Like the term "psychotherapy," stress management is a global conception and therefore difficult to evaluate as a whole (see Bergin & Strupp, 1972, on psychotherapy evaluation). Accordingly, the second part of this chapter focuses upon the task of breaking down the global term "stress management" into particular procedures, or components. We believe this components approach should be useful both in the teaching and in the evaluation of these procedures.

A COPING–REST MODEL OF ADAPTIVE EFFORTS

Our own thinking about the term "stress" goes back to earlier experiments concerning the use of elecromyographic (EMG) feedback in the induction of muscular relaxation. In this work, we were pleased to note that a well-mastered relaxation response was often useful in

We wish to thank various colleagues for their comments on this chapter, in particular John Carlson of the University of Hawaii, Richard Seaton of the University of British Columbia, and Sven Svebak of the University of Bergen, Norway.

reducing various symptoms related to psychological stress. Profound relaxation seemed to be a condition with effects opposite in nature to those of psychological stress (Stoyva & Budzynski, 1974). Yet, we also thought that the management of stress related disorders must entail more than simply engaging in relaxation training. For example, a critic could ask: "Here you are dealing with people facing severe real-life challenges at work or at home, in military situations or in athletic contests, and what you do is train them to go limp! How can this be considered adaptive behavior?" Criticisms of this nature, as well as extensive work with patients suffering from various psychosomatic and stress related symptoms, led us to view stress management more broadly. In working with patients, we realized that any one mode of intervention has only limited impact.

Because of difficulties such as the foregoing, we developed a conceptual framework for thinking about the individual's response to stress and about what goes on in stress management as it is customarily practiced. In essence, we proposed that the individual's reaction to stress can be regarded as consisting of two major phases. There is an *active coping phase* and a *rest phase*. Both are necessary, as is a fairly frequent alternation between the two. In fact, our daily existence can be thought of as a series of shifts from one mode to the other (see Figure 45-1). Sometimes the shifts are difficult to accomplish, i.e., the transition becomes sticky. Note that in the proposed model, the term "coping" refers to active coping attempts. It can be further noted that this alternation between coping endeavors and rest is reflected at many different levels of behavioral and physiological organization. At the gross behavioral level, the fundamental and dramatic contrast between wakefulness and sleep may be noted, a shift that is especially clear in the higher forms of life such as birds and mammals. Waking is the time of active coping efforts; sleep is the time of behavioral quiescence.[1] A coping-rest cycle is also seen in the three major bodily effector systems. In the skeletal-muscular system, there is an alternation between muscular contraction (involved in active coping efforts) and muscular relaxation, an alternation that is at the core of how this system operates. In the autonomic nervous system, there is a division into two great branches, the sympathetic nervous system and the parasympathetic nervous system. The former acts to support vigorous physical action, with high energy utilization; the latter system functions to promote digestion, relaxation, sleep, and the rebuilding of energy sources. In the neuroendocrine system there is considerable evidence for the occurrence of periods of activation and nonactivation; for example, in the case of hormone responses to various psychological stressors (Mason, 1972). According to Mason (1972), pituitary-adrenocortical activity is increased under conditions in which there appears to be an undifferentiated state of arousal, alerting, or involvement, "perhaps in anticipation of activity or coping" (p. 23). Particularly effective in trig-

FIGURE 45-1

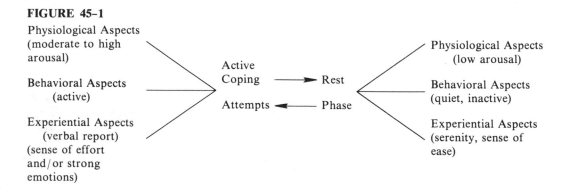

Physiological Aspects
(moderate to high
arousal)

Behavioral Aspects
(active)

Experiential Aspects
(verbal report)
(sense of effort
and/or strong
emotions)

Active
Coping ⟶ Rest
Attempts ⟵ Phase

Physiological Aspects
(low arousal)

Behavioral Aspects
(quiet, inactive)

Experiential Aspects
(serenity, sense of
ease)

gering pituitary-adrenocortical activity are situations involving novelty, uncertainty, suspenseful anticipation, or "trying". A related series of experiments of Frankenhaeuser (1978) indicated that the neuroendocrine system in humans is highly responsive to perceived stress. In particular, situations requiring a marked degree of active coping behavior generate large increases in catecholamine levels. Finally, when we consider the experimental level, it may be noted that during active coping attempts the individual is likely to sense excitement, exhibit focused attention, or be aware of mental effort. During relaxation, one is likely to experience tranquility, an absence of striving, or even drowsiness as a shift toward sleep occurs.[2]

Central to our position is the idea that a high proportion of psychosomatic and stress-susceptible patients are strongly or excessively involved with the active coping mode. More conservatively put, this pattern is very common among the sample of patients ordinarily seen in the practice of stress management. A related and very important point is that these patients often appear to be defective in the ability to shift readily from the coping to the resting mode. Illustrations of these characteristics can be observed in many disorders.

Pervasive Anxiety

Patients suffering from chronic, pervasive anxiety show many signs of high physiological arousal, such as elevated heart rate and blood pressure, respiratory irregularities, excessive sweating, cold hands and feet, as well as increased skeletal muscle tension (Lader & Marks, 1971; Malmo, 1975). Malmo and his colleagues (Malmo, Shagass, & Davis, 1950) adduced evidence suggesting that such patients show a defect in turning to resting physiological levels after exposure to brief aversive stimulation; i.e., they exhibit a slowness of return to prestimulation baseline values in various physiological indicators (see also Lader & Marks, 1971). It has also been noted that anxious patients, compared to normals, are defective in habituating to aversive stimulation. Lader (1969) summarized these various observations.

Response Specificity

When stressed, patients with psychosomatic disorders react more strongly than do normals in their symptomatic system. This phenomenon, a principal finding in psychophysiological research over the past several decades, has been noted in many psychosomatic disorders: essential hypertension, Raynaud's syndrome, migraine headache, peptic ulcers, asthma, and rheumatoid arthritis (Sternbach, 1966).

Poor Sleepers and Insomniacs

In a study comparing poor sleepers and good sleepers, Monroe (1967) noted that the former showed various signs of elevated physiological arousal during sleep. Compared to the good sleepers, they showed heightened levels of heart rate, respiration, and electrodermal activity.

Type A Personality

It is by now well documented that the *type A behavior pattern* constitutes a significant risk factor in coronary artery disease (see Chapter 33). The type A individual, as depicted by Friedman and Rosenman (1974), shows many signs of strongly favoring the coping mode. Glass (1977) documented that such individuals not only react very strongly to various stressors but also place great emphasis upon achieving control over their environment.

Summary of Argument

Patients with psychosomatic or stress linked disorders are likely to show signs of high physiological arousal, and they are likely, under stress, to react strongly in the symptomatic system and to show evidence of being deficient in the ability to shift from the coping to the rest mode (e.g., slowness of habituation to, and recovery from, stressful stimulation). A corollary inference is that such patients, if studied on a round-the-clock basis, show activity in the symptomatic system for a higher percentage of the time that do normal subjects. We suggest that this defect in the capacity to shift to a rest condition is the principal reason that various relaxation procedures have so often proved successful in the alleviation of stress related symptoms.

THREE–SYSTEM EXTENSION OF THE COPING–REST MODEL

As has already been hypothesized, the individual's reaction to stress may be viewed as a *process occuring over time;* there is an oscillation between episodes of rest and episodes of active coping attempts. We further propose that each wing of the coping-rest dichotomy can itself be partitioned in a way that reflects the complex and multidimensional nature of the stress response. In other words, the coping-rest alternation is not only a physiological phenomenon but is manifest in behavior and cognition as well (see Figure 45-1).

Such a tripartite conceptualization of the individual's reaction to threat was proposed by Rachman (1978) with regard to anxiety. He developed some ideas that were advanced earlier by Lang (1968). In arguing for a three-level or a three-system approach to anxiety, Rachman maintained that anxiety is not a "unified lump" but a phenomenon with behavioral, physiological, and experimental aspects. The same thesis, we think, can be developed for stress management. It one considers the various procedures commonly employed in stress management (see Table 45-1), it is apparent that they reflect the multidimensional nature of the stress response. Some techniques, such as relaxation training and biofeedback, emphasize modification of physiological responses. Others, such as the self-statements approach and imagery techniques, focus on cognitive changes. In assertiveness training and social skills learning, behavior change is emphasized. In other words, the clinical work presently going on in stress management already reflects the three-system conceptualization of the individual's reaction to stress. This conceptualization should have utility both in the diagnostic and in the treatment phases of stress management. It enables us to ask in which system or systems the patient's stress reaction has gone awry. Similarly, during treatment, we would want to focus on changing the maladaptive response. Thus, if misperceptions and distorted beliefs seem mainly to be the problem, we would consider

TABLE 45-1
Stress Management Procedures and the Coping-Rest Model

Primary focus on rest phase	Primary focus on coping phase
Relaxation training	Assertiveness training
Progressive relaxation	Social skills retraining and
Autogenic training	motor skills retraining
EMG feedback	Self-statements
Meditation (Zen, TM)	Imagery
Specific biofeedback	Guided waking imagery
Hand temperature	Autogenic abreaction
Electrodermal response (EDR)	Covert reinforcement and
EMG from particular muscle group	covert sensitization
Systematic desensitization	Behavior rehearsal

cognitive interventions. If physiological arousal looked excessive, relaxation training or biofeedback would be initiated. Finally, we would want to ask whether any change in the maladaptive response had in fact occurred, and whether it persisted. In other words, the conception proposed here would be relevant not only to diagnosis and treatment but to the assessment phase of stress management as well.

The foregoing theoretical framework—a coping-rest model of the stress response in combination with a three-system analysis—reflects an attempt to grapple with a complex phenomenon (of which there are many in psychology). It is intriguing to note that a number of clear antecedents for such a model exist. Rachman (1978), as already mentioned, found it useful to divide the phenomenon of fear into physiological, cognitive, and behavioral components. Similarly, Davidson and Schwartz (1976) conceptualized relaxation as consisting of somatic, cognitive, and attentional components. Phillips (1977) argued that pain, such as headache pain, can be viewed as consisting of cognitive, behavioral, and physiological aspects (and that, consequently, we should not expect high correlations between headache pain and a particular physiological measure such as forehead EMG level).

A logically similar conception to that of Rachman (1978) and of Davidson and Schwartz (1976), but arising from a different area of psychology, was advanced by Stoyva and Kamiya (1968). In discussing contemporary studies of dreaming, they proposed that there is no single, totally valid indicator of dreaming as a mental experience. Instead, there are several imperfect indicators of the dream experience—verbal report, rapid eye movements, and certain electroencephalographic (EEG) stages. These indicators can be used in combined fashion to make inferences about dreaming. Moreover, discrepancies among the indicators can serve to generate hypotheses.

A three-system conception of stress management should provide a more sophisticated approach to the area since it encourages one not to overlook signficant aspects of the stress response in favor of some monolithic strategy, whether this be relaxation training, self-statements, or something else. Also, as Rachman (1978) emphasized, a three-system conception serves to raise questions and stimulate research. He pointed out that the various indicators of fear are often discrepant. But this need not be an occasion for hand wringing. Instead, anomalies can help us deal more resourcefully with the patient's disorder. For example, a patient may state that he does not feel afraid but yet show behavioral and physiological signs of fear, thereby suggesting either that strong denial mechanisms are at work or that he is deficient in perceiving (or labeling) his own emotional reactions. Another individual may show the physiological and cognitive signs of fear, yet gamely proceed to cope with the source of the threat (the courage model).[3]

Rachman (1978) also suggested that the degree of synchrony among indicators may change over the course of treatment. In systematic desensitization, for example, the physiological indicators are normally the first to change in the direction of lowered arousal; then the fear behavior changes; lastly the verbal report of fear is diminished. Consequently, one would expect greater synchrony among the three systems after successful completion of the (desensitization) treatment than during the treatment process itself.

Similarly, we believe that it will prove valuable to view stress management as addressed to a process occuring over time. Such an emphasis is encouraged by the coping-rest conception of the stress response. Has coping behavior been improved? And, especially, has the ability to shift from the coping mode to the rest mode been enhanced? Is there evidence that the three systems have moved in the direction of diminished reactivity to stress?

In the remaining portion of this chapter we would like to consider individual stress management techniques within the framework of the coping-rest model.

STRESS MANAGEMENT: RETRAINING THE CAPACITY TO REST

As already discussed, the various interventions in stress management may, for the most part, be broken down into those that address primarily the active coping phase of the stress response and those that focus upon the rest phase (see Table 45-1). An important advantage of this approach is that it encourages us to begin the task of breaking down the global term "stress management" into a number of specific and operational procedures. Each type of intervention can then be considered upon its own merits with respect to evaluating its efficacy. We can then evaluate the evidence that a particular intervention procedure is useful for a particular symptom or disorder. Over time, we should acquire increasingly refined estimates as to which procedure is likely to be useful with which type of patient. Although the task is onerous, we think it is of undeniable long-run importance that we confront the challenge of demonstrating efficacy. We cannot afford the attitude recently expressed by the breathless advocate of another new therapy emanating from southern California, who told us that, "Things are moving too fast for us to do much research!"

The various procedures described in this section reflect the reality that the individual's response to stress is a many-sided phenomenon, a point strongly emphasized throughout this volume. And what has become known as stress management actually represents a still evolving mix of procedures. Major sources of influence include biofeedback technology and the older relaxation therapies, as well as behavior therapy and its cognitive variants.

Relaxation Training

Several of the best-known stress management procedures involve systematic training in relaxation. Probably it is because relaxation is in key ways directly antithetical to the active coping (striving) mode that procedures utilizing relaxation are so frequently successful in the alleviation of stress related symptoms. Various types of relaxation procedures have been developed. Some of the major ones are progressive relaxation (Jacobson, 1929, 1938); autogenic training (Luthe, 1969; Schultz, 1932); electromyographic feedback (Budzynski &

Stoyva, 1969; Budzynski, Stoyva, & Peffer, 1980); and meditation, as, for example, in Zen (Hirai, 1974) or in the modified Transcendental Meditation developed by Benson (1975).

The main points of emphasis vary somewhat from one technique to the other, suggesting that the various techniques address slightly different components of the relaxation response (Davidson & Schwartz, 1976). At any rate, considerable evidence has accumulated that relaxation procedures (especially those involving whole body relaxation) can be useful in diminishing stress related symptoms such as chronic anxiety, sleep-onset insomnia, tension headache, migraine headache, localized muscular tensions, the cramping involved in dysphagia, and (sometimes) temporomandibular joint (TMJ) syndrome (see Rugh, Perlis, & Disraeli, 1977).

Examination of the various methods of relaxation reveals that they have many features in common: there is usually some emphasis on muscular relaxation; regular and frequent practice of the response is emphasized; the individual is encouraged to use relaxation in everyday stressful situations; and the trainee is given some cognitive procedure for producing mental quieting. In autogenic training, for instance, the trainee repeats a phrase such as "My arms and legs are heavy and warm." The phrase varies with the particular exercise being practiced.

Probably the strongest point of similarity in these various procedures is their emphasis upon *passive attention,* a volitional phenomenon that is the opposite of a striving or effort response (Stoyva, 1973). For example, in autogenic training, the patient is taught passive concentration. In EMG feedback training, the client soon realizes that he must learn to do the opposite of trying hard. In Zen, there is much emphasis upon reaching a nonstriving condition. The disciple must "learn to try not to try." This "trying not to try," which indeed sounds paradoxical on a verbal level, can readily be sensed when EMG feedback (and many other types of biofeedback training) is undertaken. The fact that this passive attention, or passive volition, dimension has emerged so strongly in various kinds of relaxation training is an intriguing observation. It may well be that for patients suffering from an excess of the active coping response, cultivation of a condition opposite in nature to active coping (nonstriving) would generate a number of beneficial effects.

Recent evidence suggests that *absence of effort signals* emanating from the central nervous system (CNS) may be the critical feature of muscular relaxation. A study at the University of Colorado Medical Center by Stilson, Matus, and Ball (1980) led to the conclusion that relaxation is not brought about mainly by a reduction of proprioceptive input from the peripheral skeletal-muscular muscle system to the CNS; rather, the critical feature seems to be the absence of effort signals from the CNS. More precisely, these investigators suggested that the condition of muscular relaxation is characterized by *conscious monitoring of an absence of effort signals* from the brain. Such a condition can certainly be thought of as opposite in character to the coping mode.

Evidence of Efficacy. Admittedly, there will be some argument as to which of the various relaxation techniques is the most powerful. This, however, is essentially a technical matter (see Stoyva, 1979). In the short history of biofeedback and stress management, the crucial initial question has generally been whether there would be any significant effect at all with a behavioral and nonpharmacological intervention. Once positive evidence has been generated on this question, we can then begin the task of evaluating the various methods of inducing relaxation. It is conceivable, for example, that some types of patients may need only a fairly simple, verbally induced form of relaxation training. Others—for example, patients suffering from pervasive anxiety—may require a skillfully managed biofeedback training in combination with other types of relaxation in order to achieve a good relaxation response (Budzynski & Stoyva, 1975).

A large body of evidence collected mostly over the past decade indicates that mastery of relaxation is a robust and clinically useful response. Since space does not permit detailed discussion of these studies, this information will be presented only in summary form, with special emphasis on controlled-outcome studies.

Biofeedback. We believe that a major practical consequence of developments in biofeedback has been the demonstration of the clinical usefulness of relaxation training, a fact of central significance for stress management. Since in stress management, the two techniques are generally used in tandem, studies with a bearing on their efficacy are described together in the following sections. Also, because extensive recent reviews of clinical biofeedback applications are available, only a summary of the material most pertinent to stress management is presented in this chapter (Basmajian, 1979; Olton & Noonberg, 1980; Stoyva, 1979; Yates, 1980).

Tension Headache. In recent years, relaxation procedures have been widely used in the treatment of tension headache (also known as muscle contraction headache). Studies are virtually unanimous that relaxation procedures act to decrease the amount of headache pain. Nuechterlein and Holroyd (1980) summarized 20 investigations carried out in the decade subsequent to the original report from this laboratory (Budzynski, Stoyva, & Adler, 1970); nearly half these reports were controlled studies. All but a few of these twenty investigations found that relaxation training brought about significant reductions in headache activity. There is controversy, however, about whether EMG feedback is necessary for the requisite degree of relaxation. Nuechterlein and Holroyd (1980) concluded that verbally induced relaxation works about as well and costs less.

Insomnia. The literature of both progressive relaxation and autogenic training report successful application to cases of sleep-onset insomnia. In recent years, several controlled studies also employed all-night EEG monitoring. Of four reports, one was negative; the other three, positive. Hauri (1978) observed negative results with EMG assisted relaxation training. Positive results, however, were reported by Borkovec (1977), Freedman and Papsdorf (1976), and Coursey, Frankel, and Gaarder (1980). Borkovec used a modified form of progressive relaxation; the other two studies employed primarily frontal EMG feedback.

Chronc Anxiety. Two controlled studies indicated that EMG feedback training can be helpful for patients suffering from chronic anxiety. Given the refractory character of this affliction, the results are quite encouraging. Townsend, House, and Addario (1975) compared chronically anxious patients given EMG feedback training to a matched group receiving group psychotherapy. The feedback group showed significant decreases in EMG levels, mood disturbance, and anxiety, a pattern that did not occur in the group psychotherapy subjects. In another study of chronic anxiety, LaVallée, Lamontagne, Pinard, Annable, and Tétreault (1977) compared EMG feedback assisted relaxation with Valium; EMG feedback treatment without Valium led to a more prolonged therapeutic effect than did the tranquilizing medication.

Essential Hypertension. Reports concerning beneficial effects of relaxation training upon blood pressure date at least as far back as the 1930s (Jacobson, 1938; Schultz & Luthe, 1959). In the past few years, several controlled studies appeared. Patel and North (1975) employed a crossover design; Taylor, Farquhar, and Nelson (1977) utilized two control groups. Jacob, Kramer, and Agras (1977), in a review article, concluded that relaxation procedures indeed exert a genuine treatment effect upon blood pressure beyond that attributable to placebo responding.

There are discrepant reports, however. Surwit and Shapiro (1977) failed to show significant decreases in blood pressure over a five-week training period—nearly all the change occurred during the baseline habituation phase. Similar results were noted by Stoyva, Anderson, Vaughn, Budzynski, and MacDonald (1980).

Is Biofeedback Necessary in Relaxation Training? Some debate exists as to whether biofeedback is necessary for the induction of relaxation (Silver & Blanchard, 1978; Yates, 1980). In our laboratory, viewing the matter from a practical standpoint, we have long stressed that EMG feedback be employed in an integrated fashion, especially in combination with elements from autogenic training and progressive relaxation—a procedure we have referred to as the "shaping of low arousal" (Stoyva & Budzynski, 1974).

Biofeedback techniques, as contrasted to verbal induction of relaxation, do offer certain practical advantages in the operation of a stress management clinic.

1. How does one know whether relaxation has been achieved? This is hard to determine in the absence of measurement—something that most biofeedback devices routinely incorporate.

2. With biofeedback instrumentation, patients are more likely to be aware that they are beginning to master an antistress response, or at least making some progress toward this goal, a realization that can act as a potent source of motivation.

3. If there are difficulties in learning to relax, perhaps not so common with college student experimental subjects but a routine occurrence with clinic patients, then biofeedback techniques offer a variety of flexible strategies for coping with the problem. Instead of just offering continued exhortations "to stay with it," we can describe an alternative strategy to the patient or a variant on an old one (Budzynski, Stoyva, & Peffer, 1980).

4. Finally, if older, nonbiofeedback approaches to relaxation are so useful, why was their impact on psychology and psychiatry quite modest until the 1970s? There is much more to teaching mastery of a relaxation response than simply admonishing a patient to relax, a point Jacobson (1938) himself emphasized repeatedly. Biofeedback lends itself to the development of specific operations; the training can be borken down into a sequence of small steps and criteria for each step can be described, a feature that acts to standardize biofeedback relaxation training and makes it less dependent on the virtuosity of a particular therapist.

Systematic Desensitization

Since anxiety is often present in psychosomatic and stress related disorders (Alexander, 1950), methods of systematically dealing with anxiety can be an important part of the treatment program. One well-known anxiety reduction procedure was developed by Wolpe (1973). In it, strong emphasis is placed on the ability to reach or maintain a calm condition despite the presence of perceived threat or anxiety. Apropos the coping-rest model, it is worth noting that Wolpe (1973) argued that an excessive autonomic response lies at the core of neurotic anxiety. After desensitization is successful, the patient is able calmly to think about things that formerly produced great anxiety. Along with a feeling of reduced anxiety, there is a waning or even a disappearance of the excessive autonomic reaction (Wolpe, 1980).

Evidence of Efficacy. Systematic desensitization is quite a robust procedure and has successfully weathered a large number of controlled-outcome studies (Rachman, 1978; Wolpe, 1973), even though, as Yates (1975) pointed out, the necessity of any single one of its constituents is uncertain. This procedure has been extensively described in the literature; detailed discussions can be found in Wolpe (1973) and in Goldstein and Foa (1980).

A number of reports have noted the successful use of desensitization in certain psychosomatic disorders—at least as one component of the treatment approach. Wolpe (1980) summarized many instances in which systematic desensitization has been helpful in psychosomatic disturbances, including bronchial asthma, migraine headache, and various gastrointestinal disorders. Fundamentally, his position is that if the behavioral analysis indicates anxiety to be a culprit in precipitating the psychosomatic symptom, then systematic desensitization is an eminently reasonable and often useful intervention.

STRESS MANAGEMENT: RESHAPING THE COPING RESPONSE

Assertiveness Training

A common clinical observation is that many types of psychosomatic patients show an inability to express emotions. This inability may consist either of an inability to express emotions or an inability even to sense the presence of emotions. The psychoanalyst Sifneos (1973) coined the term "alexithymia" for this putative defect. It seems reasonable to think that if the inability to express affect is a contributing factor in the development of a psychosomatic or stress related disorder, than procedures aimed at correcting this difficulty could be useful therapeutically.

A good candidate for a corrective procedure is assertiveness training, a technique that focuses on both behavioral and cognitive aspects of the stress response. Initially developed by the behavior therapists Salter (1949) and Wolpe (1958), this procedure essentially involves learning the expression of appropriate affect, as well as the assertion of one's reasonable rights. It should be emphasized that assertiveness training is not training in aggression, either verbal or physical. Rather, it may be viewed as learning the skills of emotional expression. An extensive discussion of this procedure can be found in Fodor (1980).

A particular variant of assertiveness training with great promise involves teaching the patient new ways of handling anger reactions. Since anger, hate, and suppressed rage are prominent features of many psychosomatic disturbances (Alexander, 1950), it seems plausible that assertiveness training employed in the adaptive reshaping of anger impulses may prove an important tool. Navaco (1975) developed procedures especially for the modification of anger and rage responses.

Evidence of Efficacy. An important question is whether there is any systematic evidence, apart from many clinical accounts, that assertiveness training may be useful in particular psychosomatic disorders? Although much work needs to be done, some intriguing reports exist. Brooks and Richardson (1980) used "emotional skills training" in the alleviation of duodenal ulcer. Having concluded that the two emotional factors of prime importance in duodenal ulcer are the presence of strong anxiety and stress reactions and inhibited expression of emotions, including nonassertive behavior and unexpressed feelings of resentment, the investigators adopted interventions addressed to these contributing factors.

Experimental patients first received four sessions of anxiety management training, which included restructuring of irrational beliefs, replacement of worry type self-statements with more positive self-statements, as well as progressive relaxation. During the assertiveness training phase, patients focused upon learning prudent self-expression to replace feelings of chronic resentment. Patients were also instructed in the daily rehearsal of the new behavior in both home and work situations.

Compared to controls, treatment subjects showed reduced levels of anxiety, fewer days of ulcer pain, and reduced antacid consumption. Most dramatic was the much lower rate of ulcer recurrence in the experimental group. At a 42-month follow-up, only one of the nine available treatment patients had had a recurrence, but five of the eight controls had suffered recurrence. Admittedly, since a mix of procedures was used, one cannot precisely determine the part played by assertiveness training, but the study is most encouraging nonetheless.

A psychodynamically oriented investigation inadvertently provided evidence that assertiveness training may be helpful in certain psychocutaneous afflictions, that is, emotionally triggered skin disorders (Seitz, 1953). Twenty-five patients with pruritic syndrome were encouraged to express their hostile feelings during an interview with Seitz; they were also told, however, not to act out their aggressions in daily life. Eleven patients disobeyed the injunction, and in this group the skin disorder cleared up! Wolpe (1980) suggested that the assertiveness training produced some deconditioning of the anxiety reactions precipitating the skin condition (although one wonders whether deconditioning of anger reactions might not have been an equally potent influence).

Overall, the literature cited supports Wolpe's (1980) view that if behavior analysis indicates that strong but unexpressed emotions are contributing to psychosomatic disorder, then assertiveness training is a plausible intervention strategy.

Social Skills and Motor Skills Retraining

Since these procedures have been described extensively in the behavior therapy literature (e.g., Goldstein & Foa, 1980), they will not be discussed in this chapter.

Self-statements

Another stress management strategy that focuses upon the reshaping of maladaptive coping responses derives from the cognitive behavior therapies and involves changing the statements that people make to themselves, especially what they say to themselves in stress situations. According to Meichenbaum (1976), the originator of this technique, the things we say to ourselves are important as guides to behavior, will modify our emotional reactions, and influence our conduct in stress situations. It is also assumed that learning principles can be used to modify both one's self-statements (the cognitive component) and their behavioral and emotional concomitants.

Meichenbaum (1976) reported that his technique of *stress inoculation* has proven useful in a generalized way as a means of combating anxiety. Clients find the procedure helpful in more than one type of stressful situation. The self-statements approach was also utilized in the Brooks and Richardson (1980) study, in which duodenal ulcer patients learned a combination of stress management procedures. For a detailed description of this cognitive behavior therapy approach, as well as supporting evidence, the reader is referred to Meichenbaum (Chapter 42).

Imagery Techniques

Another body of techniques addressed mainly to altering the cognitive aspects of stress responses involves imagery. Although of great interest, these techniques will be discussed only briefly. More extensive descriptions can be found in Singer's (1975) useful book, in which he summarized both European and American sources. Emphasis is given to procedures arising from psychodynamic and behavioral therapies.

Although imagery techniques are often employed by stress management therapists, one approaches this area with ambivalence. In part, this uneasiness springs from the unsettling awareness that imagery techniques have been embraced by a freewheeling assortment of lay psychologists such as Emil Coué, Dale Carnegie, and Norman Vincent Peale, not to mention a diverse throng of contemporary "mind controllers" and self-styled healers. A more serious source of uneasiness is ignorance of the specific processes at work. What are the mechanisms by which imagery affects the stress response? Are there specific, identifiable causal sequences at work? We have much to learn about these matters.

A sampling of the better researched imagery techniques that have been utilized in psychotherapy, and sometimes in stress management, follows.

Guided Waking Imagery. In this technique, devised by the psychoanalyst Leuner (1969), the patient it taught to visualize a standard series of scenes such as a meadow, a mountain, a house, and a swamp. Later, the patient's imaginings are examined for sources of conflict, irrational beliefs, and interpersonal problems.

Autogenic Abreactions. Here the patient is asked to assume an attitude of passive acceptance toward his mental experiences (Luthe & BLUMBERGER, 1977). In this condition, the patient is to verbalize, without restriction, all the thoughts, feelings, and sensations that occur to him. Strong affect, often with marked involvement of both facial and somatic musculature, is likely to emerge. The session continues until the effective discharge has run its course. It seems likely that autogenic abreaction may be useful with alexithymic patients: the expression of thought and affect in the clinic situation might constitute an important bridge on the path to improved emotional expression.

Covert Sensitization. This is one of several procedures devised by Cautela (1980). These techniques are based on the reinforcement paradigm and involve what has become known as the *continuity assumption,* or the postulate that imagery processes can be modified according to the same principles that govern the modification of overt, visible behavior. In covert sensitization, the patient first imagines engaging in some behavior he wishes to change, say, an addiction. This is quickly followed by the imagining of a highly unpleasant event. Thus, the addictive behavior becomes paired with a highly aversive event and therefore is less likely to occur in the future.

Covert Behavior Rehearsal. In this method, the individual systematically visualizes the desired correct coping behavior (Mahoney, 1974). This technique has seen much use in sports.

Summary. It is difficult to make any overall statement about the use of imagery in stress management, but there are some fascinating observations buried in the literature. A little-known experiment by Chappel and Stevenson (1936) involved a positive imagery technique with peptic ulcer patients. Unusual for clinical studies of that era, a control group was employed. The experimental patients were told that whenever they became anxious they were to think about pleasant experiences. There were dramatic differences between the two groups. At a three-year follow-up, over 90% of the experimental subjects had maintained their treatment gains. In contrast, all 20 control patients reported a significant return of symptoms within two months. Strangely enough, this remarkable report seems not to have been followed up by either the authors or anyone else.[4]

Controllability

A hitherto neglected aspect of stress management, but one that may be central to the whole endeavor, is the concept of controllability, the feeling that the individual has some influence either over the situation in which he finds himself or over his reaction to it. Indeed, the very phrase "stress management" implies some degree of controllability. In many stress management procedures, the idea of increasing control—or even the *sense* of control—can be seen quite clearly as, for instance, in relaxation training, in biofeedback, and in assertiveness training.

The sense of control—perhaps self-control would be a better term—is emerging as a powerful component not only of stress management but of many behavioral interventions and psychodynamic therapies as well (Strupp, 1970). Its role in affective disorders, especially, is now supported by experimental evidence. For example, in the Seligman (1975) model of reactive depression, the sense of controllability is accorded a central position. Feelings of depression are generated when the individual is faced by aversive outcomes that still threaten to engulf him.

Similarly, in an extensive review and analysis of behavioral approaches to anxiety, Rachman (1978) stressed the importance of a sense of controllability as a major determinant of both fear and courage. In his conception, anxiety is likely to be present when we face situations in which the outcome is both uncertain and important to us. Anxiety and reactive depression may well be linked phenomena, at least conceptually. The initial stage, characterized by uncertainty of outcome, is one of anxiety. But if, despite much effort by the individual, there is no change in his circumstances—the unpleasant or even tragic events still inevitably bear down upon him—then depression may result.

In World War II studies of courage and fear in military fliers (summarized by Rachman, 1978), the controllability factor emerged as a major dimension along with a sense of competence and group membership ("not letting your buddies down"). Studies later conducted on the original Project Mercury astronauts produced similar findings (Rachman, 1978). For the Mercury astronauts, all former test pilots, the element of controllability was very important in their attitude to the whole enterprise. As a matter of fact, several leading test pilots declined to participate in the Mercury program because the pilot's role in it was very small—more that of an experimental animal. The original vehicle was simply a windowless capsule. According to the novelist Tom Wolfe (1980), virtuoso test pilots were reluctant to assume the status of "spam in a can." At the astronauts' insistence, mission scientists added manual controls and a window to the capsule, as well as renaming it a spacecraft.

Our own hypothesis is that the sense of controllability is an important part of stress management procedures and has considerable therapeutic potential. It is clearly present in a number of the procedures we have described. Biofeedback techniques lend themselves especially well to providing the individual with a sense of controllability. In psychosomatic and stress linked disorders, the patient works at acquiring control over some variable or response thought to be contributing to his affliction. As Budzynski and Stoyva (1973) noted, EMG feedback procedures can be arranged so as to provide a feeling of accomplishment and modest success even early in training. When relaxation training is thoroughly conducted the individual begins to realize that he has a way of moderating his reactions to the experience of psychological stress. Rachman (1978) suggested that knowledge of such a capacity will act to reduce anticipatory fear reactions. Much of what takes place in assertiveness training involves self-control. Novaco (1975: App. III) listed a number of self-statements for dealing with excessive anger reactions: "This is going to upset me but I know how to deal with it." "I can manage the situation. I know how to regulate my anger." "You don't need to prove yourself." "Take it easy. Don't get pushy." Both self-statements and stress inoculation place heavy emphasis on the substitution of coping type statements for negative and self-deprecating ones. Finally, Singer (1975) suggested that the very idea that one can acquire some control over one's own thoughts and imagery is important in the therapeutic use of imagery. And Cautela (1980) explicitly identified his imagery techniques, such as covert sensitization, as means of improving control over one's own behavior, usually over self-destructive behavior like addiction.

There is intriguing recent evidence that simply the illusion of control may exert beneficial effects. Stern, Miller, Ewy, and Grant (1980) noted that subjects who were led to believe by means of bogus information feedback that they were successfully lowering their heart rates showed a reduction in stress type symptoms, especially those of a cardiovascular nature. It seems possible that the feeling of control may be an important part of what we have called "placebo responding." Stoyva (1979b) suggested that this phenomenon is probably not a unitary entity but, rather, a cluster of processes, of which the feeling of developing control over factors affecting one's disorder is an important and potentially manipulable component of therapeutic interventions. At any rate, it seems that since stress management promotes a sense of control over oneself and one's reaction to aversive stimuli, this dimension should have considerable potential for further development. The controllability factor would also be specifically relevant to the coping-rest conception. The knowledge that one can moderate one's reaction to a stressor, and also that one knows better than before how to cope with the stressor, should augment one's sense of competence and diminish fear (see Bandura, 1977, on the concept of self-efficacy).

CONCLUSION

The Efficacy Issue

There is a growing body of evidence from controlled studies that a number of the procedures described in this chapter show at least a degree of clinical efficacy. Relaxation training can reduce anxiety, often relieve sleep-onset insomnia, and decrease tension headache pain and sometimes that of migraine—common stress symptoms. Systematic desensitization is effective in eliminating phobias and circumscribed anxieties. Although not much evidence is yet available, assertiveness training may be useful when psychosomatic symptoms are generated by strong but poorly expressed emotions. Evidence is accumulating that the self-statements technique can sometimes be useful, although work needs to be done concerning the conditions under which it is reliable. A similar conclusion holds for the various imagery techniques that have been described.

By evaluating the components of stress management, it should be possible to eliminate, or at least to deemphasize, those that show no specific therapeutic effect. It will also be possible—and this is frequently being done already—to combine procedures in the interest of strengthening overall therapeutic affects, although systematic work on the evaluation of combined procedures is scant.

Evidence for the Coping-Rest Model

Are there any data in support of the coping-rest conception? One might object that the model is simply a taxonomic device. There is some truth to this claim. The model does provide a conceptual framework and thus, to some extent, a rationale for many of the currently used stress management techniques. A particular stress management intervention can be considered in terms of which aspect of the stress reaction it purports to modify and whether there is any reason to think that this goal is being accomplished.

Are there any experimental observations that lend support to the coping-rest model? Although the picture is far from complete, a number of observations in the literature are compatible with this conceptualization.

First, there is some evidence that relaxation training acts to reduce arousal level and that the effects persist beyond the training session itself. Using patients as their own controls in an A-B-A design, Agras, Taylor, Kraemer, Allen, and Schneider (1980) noted that blood pressures were reduced during nights following relaxation sessions. Blood pressures of the three patients who showed the longest initial effects of training averaged 12.5/7.3mmHg less during nights following relaxation sessions than during nights following no treatment. In other words, the effects of relaxation in the direction of lowered arousal persisted beyond the training period itself. Two Norwegian investigators, Alnaes and Skaug (see Luthe, 1969, vol. IV, pp. 76-78), observed that cortisol concentrations decreased in long-term autogenic trainees after they engaged in twenty minutes of passive concentration on heaviness and warmth exercises. Control subjects in a hypnosis group and in a normal rest group failed to show this regular pattern of decrease. Wolpe (1980), the originator of systematic desensitization, has argued that a learned maladaptive autonomic response is at the core of anxiety. By implication, successful reduction of anxiety would also imply a reduction of autonomic arousal. A number of studies are consistent with such an interpretation, for example, the early and well-known study of Paul (1966). In a controlled study of public speaking phobia, Paul reported that compared to control patients, those who had undergone densensitization showed reduced heart rate and galvanic skin response.

The model postulates that patients seen in stress management are often defective in the ability to shift from the coping mode to the rest mode. We hypothesize that this ability should improve with stress management training. As far as we are aware, there has been no systematic test of this hypothesis.

Finally, another inference from the coping-rest model is that if the ability to shift from the coping to the resting phase has improved, then over the course of the day—and perhaps during sleep as well—the individual will operate at a lower arousal level than prior to treatment. The hypertension experiment of Agras and associates (1980), is consistent with such an interpretation. The patients who displayed the largest reductions in blood pressure during their training were the ones who also showed significant pressure reductions during sleep. For a systematic test of this aspect of the coping-rest model, the use of portable monitoring devices would be extremely valuable. An example of such a device would be the EMG unit developed by Rugh (see Rugh, Perlis, & Disraeli, 1977) for round-the-clock monitoring of masseter EMG levels in TMJ patients.

NOTES

1. Dreams are a possible exception. There have been several suggestions in both the old and the new sleep literature that dreaming may be a type of coping effort (Kety, Evarts, & Williams, 1967). It

may be noted, too, that in infants, rapid eye movement sleep is sometimes called active sleep because of the child's vigorous activity, both physiological and behavioral.

2. The issue of whether or not these various systems act in concert has been the focus of spirited controversy. Hess (1954) and Gellhorn (1967) emphasized the synchrony between autonomic and skeletal-muscular systems. The terms "ergotropic" and "trophotropic" were coined by Hess (1954) to indicate the coordinated action of these systems. Many psychophysiologists, on the other hand, have stressed that the correlation between responses in different systems is disconcertingly low and that correlations even between different measures in the same system—the autonomic nervous system, for example—are very low (Lacey, 1967; Sternbach, 1966). Neuroendocrine measures, moreoever, are likely to exhibit diurnal cyclicity and long-term "tidal" changes rather than acute changes. Mason (1972) emphasized that there is coordinated action among systems but the organization of it is highly complex. The pattern among responses is more than a synchronous ebb and flow that would generate high one-to-one correlations. For further discussion of these problems see Roessler and Engel (1977).

3. Another example of important information yielded by the discrepancy between verbal report and physiological indicators is provided by the case of lie detection. Here, the combined use of two different types of indicator can provide information not readily available through either measure taken singly.

4. A growing body of research indicates that jogging and other forms of aerobic exercise (cycling, hiking, swimming) can frequently be a useful part of a stress program. Personal observations suggest that these activities influence the resting as well as the active coping phase of the stress response. Studies in recent years have pointed to the value of regular exercise as a means of decreasing anxiety and reducing depression (Folkins & Sime, 1981).

REFERENCES

AGRAS, W. S., TAYLOR, C. B., KRAEMER, H. C., ALLEN, R. A., & SCHNEIDER, J. A. Relaxation training: Twenty-four-hour blood pressure reductions. *Archives of General Psychiatry,* 1980, *37,* 859–863.

ALEXANDER, F. *Psychosomatic medicine.* New York: Norton, 1950.

BANDURA, A. Self-efficacy: Toward a unifying theory of behavioral change. *Psychological Review,* 1977, *84,* 191–215.

BARBER, T. X. Suggested ("hypnotic") behavior: The trance paradigm versus an alternative paradigm. In T. X. Barber (ed.) *Advances in altered states of consciousness and human potentialities,* vol. 1. New York: Psychological Dimensions, 1976.

BASMAJIAN, J. V. *Biofeedback: Principles and practice for clinicians.* Baltimore: Williams & Wilkins, 1979.

BENSON, H. *The relaxation response.* New York: Morrow, 1975.

BERGIN, A. E., & STRUPP, H. H. *Changing frontiers in the science of psychotherapy.* Chicago: Aldine-Atherton, 1972.

BORKOVEC, T. D. Insomnia. In R. B. Williams & W. D. Gentry (eds.), *Behavioral approaches to medical treatment.* Cambridge: Ballinger, 1977.

BROOKS, G. R., & RICHARDSON, F. C. Emotional skills training: A treatment program for duodenal ulcer. *Behavior Therapy,* 1980, *11,* 198–207.

BUDZYNSKI, T. H., & STOYVA, J. M. An instrument for producing deep muscle relaxation by means of analog information feedback. *Journal of Applied Behavior Analysis,* 1969, *2,* 231–237.

―――――. Biofeedback techniques in behavior therapy. In N. Birbaumer (ed.), *Fortschritte der Klinischen Psychologie.* Vol. 3: *Neuropsychologie der Angst.* Berlin: Urban & Schwarzenberg, 1973.

―――――. EMG-Biofeedback bei unspezifischen und spezifischen Angstzustanden. In H. Legewie & L. Nusselt (eds.), *Fortschritte der Klinischen Psychologie.* Vol 6: *Biofeedback-Therapie: Lern-*

methoden in der Psychosomatik, Neurologie, und Rehabilitation. Berlin: Urban & Schwarzenberg, 1975.

BUDZYNSKI, T. H., STOYVA, J. M., & ADLER, C. S. Feedback-induced muscle relaxation: Application to tension headache. *Behavior Therapy and Experimental Psychiatry,* 1970, *1,* 205–211.

BUDZYNSKI, T. H., STOYVA, J. M., ADLER, C. S., & MULLANEY, D. J. EMG-biofeedback and tension headache: A controlled outcome study. *Psychosomatic Medicine,* 1973, *35,* 484–496.

BUDZYNSKI, T. H., STOYVA, J. M., & PEFFER, K. E. Biofeedback techniques in psychosomatic disorders. In A. Goldstein & E. Foa (eds.), *Handbook of behavioral interventions.* New York: Wiley, 1980.

CAUTELA, J. R. Covert conditioning in clinical practice. In A. Goldstein & E. Foa (eds.), *Handbook of behavioral interventions.* New York: Wiley, 1980.

CHAPPELL, P. M., & STEVENSON, T. Group psychological training in some organic conditions. *Mental Hygiene,* 1936, *20,* 588–597.

COURSEY, R. D., FRANKEL, B. L., GAARDER, K. R., & MOTT, D. D. A comparison of relaxation techniques with electrosleep therapy for chronic sleep-onset insomnia: A sleep-EEG study. *Biofeedback and Self-regulation,* 1980, *5,* 57–73.

DALESSIO, D. J. (ed.) *Wolff's headache and other head pain.* New York: Oxford University Press, 1972.

DAVIDSON, R. J., & SCHWARTZ, G. E. The psychobiology of relaxation and related states: A multiprocess theory. In D. I. Mostofsky (ed.), *Behavior control and modification of physiological activity.* Englewood Cliffs: Prentice-Hall, 1976.

DUBOS, R. *Man adapting.* New Haven: Yale University Press, 1965.

FODOR, I. G. The treatment of communication problems with assertiveness training. In A. Goldstein & E. Foa (eds.), *Handbook of behavioral interventions.* New York: Wiley, 1980.

FOLKINS, C. H., & SIME, W. E. Physical fitness training and mental health. *American Psychologist,* 1981, *36,* 373–389.

FRANKENHAEUSER, M. Psychoneuroendocrine approaches to the study of emotion as related to stress and coping. In H. E. Howe & R. A. Dienstbier (eds.), *1978 Nebraska Symposium on Motivation,* Lincoln, Nebraska: University of Nebraska Press, 1978.

FREEDMAN, R., & PAPSDORF, J. D. Biofeedback and progressive relaxation treatment of sleep-onset insomnia: A controlled, all-night investigation. *Biofeedback and Self-regulation,* 1976, *2,* 253–271.

FRIEDMAN, M., & ROSENMAN, R. *Type A behavior and your heart.* New York: Knopf, 1974.

GELLHORN, E. *Principles of autonomic-somatic integrations.* Minneapolis: University of Minnesota Press, 1967.

GELLHORN, E., & KIELY, W. F. Mystical states of consciousness: Neurophysiological and clinical aspects. *Journal of Nervous and Mental Disease,* 1972, *154,* 399–405.

GLASS, D. C. Stress, behavior patterns, and coronary disease. *American Scientist,* 1977, *65,* 177–187.

GOLDSTEIN, A., & FOA, E. (eds.). *Handbook of behavioral interventions.* New York: Wiley, 1980.

HAURI, P. Biofeedback techniques in the treatment of serious, chronic insomniacs. In *Proceedings of the Biofeedback Society of America.* Denver: Biofeedback Society of America, 1978.

HESS, W. R. *Diencephalon.* New York: Grune & Stratton, 1954.

HIRAI, T. *Psychophysiology of Zen.* Tokyo: Igaku, 1974.

JACOB, R. G., KRAEMER, H. C., & AGRAS, W. S. Relaxation therapy in the treatment of hypertension: A review. *Archives of General Psychiatry,* 1977, *34,* 1417–1427.

JACOBSON, E. *Progressive relaxation* (2d ed.). Chicago: University of Chicago Press, 1938.

KETY, S. S., EVARTS, E. V., & WILLIAMS, H. L. (eds.). *Sleep and altered states of consciousness.* Baltimore: Williams & Wilkins, 1967.

LACEY, J. I. Somatic response patterning and stress: Some revisions of activation theory. In M. H. Appley & R. Trumbull (eds.), *Psychological stress.* New York: Appleton, 1967.

LADER, M. H. Psychophysiological aspects of anxiety. In M. H. Lader (ed.), *Studies of anxiety*. Ashford: Headley, 1969.

LADER, M., & MARKS, I. *Clinical anxiety*. London: Heinemann, 1971.

LANG, P. J. Fear reduction and fear behavior: Problems in treating a construct. *Research in Psychotherapy*, 1968, *3*, 90-102.

LAVALLÉE, Y. J., LAMONTAGNE, Y., PINARD, G., ANNABLE, L., & TÉTREAULT, L. Effects of EMG feedback, diazepam, and their combination on chronic anxiety. *Journal of Psychosomatic Research*, 1977, *21*, 65-71.

LEUNER, H. Guided affective imagery (GAI): A method of intensive psychotherapy. *American Journal of Psychotherapy*, 1969, *23*, 4-22.

LUTHE, W. (ed.). *Autogenic therapy* (6 vols.). New York: Grune & Stratton, 1969.

LUTHE, W., & BLUMBERGER, S. Autogenic therapy. In E. D. Wittkower & H. Warnes (eds.), *Psychosomatic medicine: Its clinical applications*. New York: Harper & Row, 1977.

MAHONEY, M. J. *Cognition and behavior modification*. Cambridge, Mass.: Balinger, 1974.

MALMO, R. B. *On emotions, needs, and our archaic brain*. New York: Holt, 1975.

MALMO, R. B., SHAGASS, C., & DAVIS, J. F. A method for the investigation of somatic response mechanisms in psychoneurosis. *Science*, 1950, *112*, 325-328.

MASON, J. W. Organization of psychoendocrine mechanisms. In N. S. Greenfield & R. A. Sternbach (eds.), *Handbook of psychophysiology*. New York: Holt, 1972.

MEICHENBAUM, D. Cognitive factors in biofeedback therapy. *Biofeedback and Self-regulation*, 1976, *1*, 201-216.

MITCHELL, K. R. The treatment of migraine: An exploratory application of time limited behavior therapy. *Technology*, 1969, *14*, 50.

MONROE, L. J. Psychological and physiological differences between good and poor sleepers. *Journal of Abnormal Psychology*, 1967, *72*, 255-264.

NOVACO, R. W. *Anger control: The development and evaluation of an experimental treatment*. Lexington: Heath, Lexington Books, 1975.

NUECHTERLEIN, K. H., & HOLROYD, J. C. Biofeedback in the treatment of tension headache. *Archives of General Psychiatry*, 1980, *37*, 866-873.

OLTON, D. S., & NOONBERG, A. R. *Biofeedback: Clinical applications in behavioral medicine*. Englewood Cliffs: Prentice-Hall, 1980.

PATEL, C. H., & NORTH, W. R. Randomized control trial of yoga and biofeedback in management of hypertension. *Lancet*, 1975, *2*, 93-95.

PAUL, G. L. *Insight versus desensitization in psychotherapy*. Stanford: Stanford University Press, 1966.

PHILIPS, C. A psychological analysis of tension headache. In S. J. Rachman (ed.), *Contributions to medical psychology*. New York: Pergamon, 1977.

RACHMAN, S. J. *Fear and courage*. San Francisco: Freeman, 1978.

ROESSLER, R., & ENGEL, B. The current status of the concepts of physiological response specificity and activation. In Z. J. Lipowski, D. R. Lipsitt, & P. C. Whybrow (eds.). *Psychosomatic medicine: Current trends*. New York: Oxford University Press, 1977.

RUGH, J., PERLIS, D., & DISRAELI, R. (eds.). *Biofeedback in dentistry*. Phoenix: Semantodontics, 1977.

SALTER, A. *Conditioned reflex therapy*. New York: Capricorn, 1949.

SCHULTZ, J. H. *Das Autogene Training: Konzentrative Selbstentspannung*. Stuttgart: Thieme, 1932.

SCHULTZ. J. H., & LUTHE, W. *Autogenic training: A psychophysiological approach in psychotherapy*. New York: Grune & Stratton, 1959.

SEITZ, P. F. Dynamically-oriented brief psychotherapy: Psychocutaneous excoriation syndrome. *Psychosomatic Medicine*, 1953, *15*, 200-242.

SELIGMAN, M. E. *Helplessness: On depression development and death.* San Francisco: Freeman, 1975.

SIFNEOS, P. E. The prevalence of "alexithymic" characteristics in psychosomatic patients. *Psychotherapy and Psychosomatics,* 1973, *22,* 255–262.

SILVER, B. V., & BLANCHARD, E. B. Biofeedback and relaxation training in the treatment of psychophysiological disorders: Or are the machines really necessary? *Journal of Behavioral Medicine,* 1978, *1,* 217–239.

SINGER, J. L. *Imagery and daydream methods in psychotherapy and behavior modification.* New York: Academic, 1975.

STERN, G. S., MILLER, C. R., EWY, H. W., & GRANT, P. S. Perceived control: Bogus pulse rate feedback and reported symptom reduction for individuals with accumulated stressful life events. *Biofeedback and Self-regulation,* 1980, *5,* 37–49.

STERNBACH, R. A. *Principles of psychophysiology: An introductory text and readings.* New York: Academic, 1966.

STILSON, D. W., MATUS, I., & BALL, G. Relaxation and subjective estimates of muscle tension: Implications for a central efferent theory of muscle control. *Biofeedback and Self-regulation,* 1980, *5,* 19–36.

STOYVA, J. M. Biofeedback techniques and the conditions for hallucinatory activity. In F. J. McGuigan & R. Schoonover (eds.), *The psychophysiology of thinking.* New York: Academic, 1973.

————. Musculoskeletal and stress-related disorders. In O. F. Pomerleau & J. P. Brady (eds.), *Behavioral medicine: Theory and practice.* Baltimore: Williams & Wilkins, 1979. (a)

————. Issues in clinical biofeedback. In J. Stoyva, T. Barber, J. Kamiya, N. Miller, & D. Shapiro (eds.), *Biofeedback and Self-control, 1977–78: An Aldine annual.* Chicago: Aldine, 1979. (b)

STOYVA, J. M., ANDERSON, C. D., VAUGHN, L. J., BUDZYNSKI, T. H., & MACDONALD, K. Relaxation training in mild to moderate essential hypertension. In *Proceedings of the Biofeedback Society of America.* Denver: Biofeedback Society of America, 1980.

STOYVA, J. M., & BUDZYNSKI, T. H. Cultivated low arousal: An anti-stress response? In L. V. DiCara (ed.), *Recent advances in limbic and autonomic nervous systems research.* New York: Plenum, 1974.

STOYVA, J. M., & KAMIYA, J. Electrophysiological studies of dreaming as the prototype of a new strategy in the study of consciousness. *Psychological Review,* 1968, *75,* 192–205.

STRUPP, H. Specific versus nonspecific factors in psychology and the problem of control. *Archives of General Psychiatry,* 1970, *23,* 393–401.

SURWIT, R. S. Biofeedback: A possible treatment of Raynaud's disease. In L. Birk (ed.), *Biofeedback: Behavioral medicine.* New York: Grune & Stratton, 1973.

TAYLOR, C. B., FARQUHAR, J. W., & NELSON, E. The effects of relaxation therapy upon high blood pressure. *Archives of General Psychiatry,* 1977, *34,* 339–342.

TOWNSEND, R. E., HOUSE, J. F., & ADDARIO, D. A comparison of biofeedback-mediated relaxation and group therapy in the treatment of chronic anxiety. *American Journal of Psychiatry,* 1975, *132,* 598–601.

WALLACE, R. K., & BENSON, H. The physiology of meditation. *Scientific American,* 1972, *226,* 84–90.

WOLFE, T. *The right stuff.* New York: Bantam, 1980.

WOLPE, J. *Psychotherapy by reciprocal inhibition.* Stanford: Stanford University Press, 1958.

————. *The practice of behavior therapy.* New York: Pergamon, 1973.

————. Behavior therapy for psychosomatic disorders. *Psychosomatics,* 1980, *21,* 379–385.

YATES, A. J. *Theory and practice in behavior therapy.* New York: Wiley, 1975.

————. *Biofeedback and the modification of behavior.* New York: Plenum, 1980.

YEMM, R. Temporomandibular dysfunction and masseter muscle response to experimental stress. *British Dental Journal,* 1969, *127,* 508–510.

46

The Effects of Social Supports on Responses to Stress

Morton A. Lieberman

THIS CHAPTER EXAMINES SOCIAL SUPPORTS using findings from a series of my studies. In this regard it is not an ordinary review of the literature; that task has been performed well by many others (Cobb, 1976; Gore, 1978; Heller, 1978; Kaplan, Cassel, & Gore, 1977; Lin, Simeone, Ensel, & Kuo, 1979; Pinneau, 1976). Nor is it a statement of large theoretical propositions. Rather, it is an attempt to articulate the boundaries among sets of ideas, problems of method, and information generated by two ongoing projects. These projects have yielded considerable information about the role of social resources in stress mitigation. Each of these substudies, conducted by myself, my colleagues, and, most often, my students, has addressed the role of social support in mitigating the effects of social stress or in facilitating positive change.

THE RESEARCH BASE

The Transitions Study has been under way since 1974. In that year, under the direction of Leonard I. Pearlin, interviews were conducted with 2300 people representative of the adult population of the census defined urbanized area of Chicago. These interviews had three main foci: the assessment of a wide range of problems and hardships people experience as workers and breadwinners, as husbands and wives, and as parents; the identification of resources and responses they bring to bear in coping with these life strains; and the enumeration of symptoms indicative of emotional stress and psychological disturbance.

In 1976–1977 Pearlin and I identified a subsample from the transitions sample of over 1100 people whose social characteristics differed only slightly from those of the original population. The follow-up survey, like the first, was broadly concerned with life problems and challenges, along with their psychological effects. The project was enlarged, however, to include a variety of events that had occurred between the points of interview, such as life

Studies reported in this chapter were supported by grants from the Administration on Aging (90–A644), the National Institute on Aging (5–P01–HG00123 and 5–R01–MH 30742), and the University of Chicago Cancer Control Center (3–R18–CA1640–0151) and by a research scientist award (1–Morton A. Lieberman K05–MH20342).

cycle transitions, major crises, and role strains. Information was gathered on respondents social networks and social resources, as well as on the specific way in which individuals utilized their social network for help.

The second project, the Self-help Study (with Leonard Borman), addressed the origins, formation, development, processes, and impact of self-help organizations. We studied groups experiencing particular afflictions or crises—first-time mothers, mothers of twins, open-heart-surgery patients, widows and widowers, parents who had lost children—in short, life circumstances likely represent a range of life stresses. The samples also included afflicted individuals who had access to self-help groups but chose not to join. A distinction exists between informal social resources and the kind of resources offered by self-help. The latter are highly bounded systems, requiring more formal and specified exchange than is ordinary in kith or kin relationships. We chose to examine social networks in depth in the self-help project because we believed that one of the major change mechanisms in self-help groups is their ability to provide social linkages to relevant networks of people who can become friends and confidants. Information from the self-help project relevant to stress inducing events, the availability and use of social resources, and the consequence or impact of such utilization was examined.

BACKGROUND—THEORY AND ISSUES

Although academic interest in social support goes back to the very beginnings of sociology, recent empirical investigation has highlighted the conditions under which the person's social world will be functionally related to physical and mental health issues. Addressed are such issues as the role of social supports in reducing the number of complications of pregnancy for women under high life stress; the prevention of posthospital psychological reactions in children who have had a tonsillectomy; recovery from surgery; recovery from illness such as congestive heart failure, tuberculosis, or myocardial infarction; reducing the need for steroid therapy in adult asthmatics; protecting against clinical depression in the face of adverse events; reducing psychological distress and physiological symptomatology following job loss; mitigating the effects of bereavement; protecting against the development of emotional problems associated with aging; reducing physiological symptomatology in highly stressful job environments; and promoting adherence to medical regimes (Hamburg & Killilea, 1979).

Such a vigorous outpouring of empirical research would ordinarily suggest a line of inquiry that is beginning to take on coherence. Unfortunately, that is not the case. The problems of comparability of results across studies appear to have escalated with the increased frequency with which such studies have been conducted. The list of caveats would be indeed long, including the classical problems of assessing stress consequences (outcome measures), sampling, and the derivation of causal relationships from cross-sectional data. These problems of research design are well known and have been articulated by many others. More specific, however, to the assessment of social supports or social resources are the problems inherent in defining the particular characteristics of social settings important in elucidating the stress mediation hypothesis.

The classical work of sociology's founding fathers (with, of course, some important exceptions like George Simmel) produced macrotheories using surrogate indicators of social integration. The concept of *social network,* a specific social envelope, has brought increased precision, moving us away from macrosocial indicators to measures of targeted individuals.

Social network is the context in which social resources are contained. The characteristics of social network, such as size, density, composition, rate and content of exchange, and interconnectedness of members, have been examined for their impact on adjustment. Each of these social network characteristics can be assessed through an external frame of reference; they can be determined without recourse to the respondent's reflections. Although in fact the overwhelming majority of social network studies have used the respondent as informant, the perspective is external, not phenomenological.

Social support, or *social resource,* represents a much narrower concept than network. Most of the current stress mediation research emphasizes social resources. The assessment of social support depends upon an assessment of people's perception of their social network as containing individuals in whom they can confide, on whom to rely, and so forth. Investigators have significantly shifted the definition of the social context by ascertaining the respondent's views about specific kinds of interactions or transactions. One of the major confusions in social support research is the failure to make the distinction between data measurable by an external frame of reference and data that can be generated only through a phenomenological set. As we shall see in the studies to be presented, different conclusions are possible depending on the approach taken. Both, however, are situationally nonspecific; they are general indexes of the person's social context. Other investigations construe social resources as situationally specific. They strive to identify the people who are asked for help in a specific situation or crisis faced by the respondent. Measures of social network, social resources, or situationally specific help are not independent; certain characteristics of the person's social network largely determine the degree to which such a social network is perceived as containing relevant social resources. Without such a generalized perception, it is unlikely in a specific set of circumstances that the person will turn to, or will be turned to by, relevant others with functionally useful or emotionally relevant provisions that address the dilemma or the consequences of the dilemma facing the person.

The field is increasingly moving not only toward specification of the social resources relevant to particular circumstances but also toward definition of the kinds of aid received (i.e., the nature of the exchange) and the people in the person's social network likely to figure in functional or emotional exchanges. Although somewhat different frameworks have been offered on the nature of exchange (Cobb, 1976; Pinneau, 1976), all such schemes tend to include emotional concern, instrumental aid, as well as information exchanges.

By examining findings from two ongoing projects, I hope in this chapter to highlight the central questions that are associated with the use of other people in stress reduction. *Stress* is viewed as the product of certain life events or conditions that can lead to a variety of consequences—coping efforts and defense strategies, feelings of distress, altered quality of functioning in the major life roles, and psychological and physiological symptoms. The findings reported in this chapter are concerned with neither the nature of these events nor the conditions that elicit stress responses but, rather, with the role that other people play in helping the stressed person to cope with, mitigate, avoid, or contain the sequelae of stressful events or conditions. The traditional response to studying how others provide aid has been to compartmentalize help in terms of formal and informal resources. The role of professionals whose task it is to aid the distressed person represents a well-articulated set of inquiry; psychotherapy research and social service evaluations are but two examples. A different group of investigators has looked at the role that informal networks—kith and kin—can play in stress reduction. The sociological and epidemiological tradition reflective of this line of inquiry creates a distinct set of issues. One theme of the chapter is to question the value of this distinction and the attendant split in research traditions.

HELP SEEKING: THE USE OF SOCIAL RESOURCES

Basic to both traditions is an interest in specifying the conditions under which people turn to others. One answer to this question is contained in investigations of stress inducing circumstances. Explanations vary: some focus on the intensity of the stress; others are concerned with the nature of the stress inducing circumstances, for example, whether the event is a normative transition or an unexpected event. Another response is to consider whether certain problems or conditions may be more likely to be sanctioned by society or legitimized for seeking help. Are the events creating stress public or private? Are they communal or individual? Is this event a problem labeled by society as one that is beyond the control of the person? Yet another approach involves the examination of individual characteristics, ranging from place of the person in the social structure to personality variables.

In a review of the empirical literature, Gourash (1978) found that epidemiological studies have established that the majority of people who report experiencing troublesome life events do seek help for their problems (Gurin, Veroff, & Feld, 1960; Lowenthal, Thurnher, & Chiriboga, 1975). The key factors that differentiate those who do and those do not seek help are age and race. Helpseeking has been shown to decline consistently with age (Gurin, Veroff, & Feld, 1960) and to be more prevalent among whites than blacks (Baker, 1977; Gurin, Veroff, & Feld, 1960; Rosenblatt & Mayer, 1972).

People who solicit help are usually looking for comfort, reassurance, and advice (Gurin, Veroff, & Feld, 1960; Weiss, 1973; Zimbardo & Formica, 1963). Initially they tend to turn to family and friends; relief agencies or professional service organizations are contacted only as a last resort (Booth & Babchuk, 1972; Croog, Lipson, & Levine, 1972; Litman, 1974; Quarentelli, 1960). The sole use of professional services occurs much less frequently then either exclusive reliance on family and friends or help seeking from both the social network and professional sources (Rosenblatt & Mayer, 1972).

Although people who seek help within the social network appear to represent a cross-section of the general population, those who eventually go to human service agencies are readily identified by a common core of characteristics. Investigators of discretionary medical and dental care; mental health, social service, and legal facilities; and self-help groups have found repeatedly that users tend to be young, white, educated, middle-class, and female (Beck, 1961; Hollingshead & Redlich, 1958; Kadushin, 1969; Kammeyer & Bolton, 1968; Katz & Bender, 1976; Kravits, 1972; Sue, McKinney, Allen, & Hall, 1974; Srole, Langner, Michael, Oppler, & Rennie, 1962). More recent investigations, however, have suggested that social class may no longer differentiate between those who do and those who do not use professional services. In studies of people experiencing emotional distress, education and income were not found to correlate with the use of mental health facilities (Baker, 1977; Tischler, Henesz, Myers, & Boswell, 1975). Both studies suggested that the success of efforts to link public services and lower-class consumers accounts for the lack of association between socioeconomic variables and help seeking behavior.

No one type of problem invariably precipitates the search for assistance, but there appear to be some common linkages between certain types of problems and sources of help. The social network is the primary resource for general worries and unhappiness, with spouses the focal helpers for worries and friends the major resource for unhappy emotions (Gurin, Veroff, & Feld, 1960). Family, friends, and neighbors are the predominant source of aid in national (Quarentelli, 1960) and family crises (Boswell, 1969; Croog, Lipson, & Levine, 1972). Within the middle and working classes, the social network is a major provider of economic assistance (Burchinal, 1959; Sussman, 1960). Professional help is sought for problems ranging from severe emotional distress (Gurin, Veroff, & Feld, 1960; Kadushin, 1969) to discrete strains suffered under the press of work or family roles (Beck, 1961; Kammeyer & Bolton, 1968; Levine & Preston, 1970; Lurie, 1974).

Most people perceive their social network as a major source of help (Litwak & Szelenyi, 1969; Wellman, 1976a,b). Empirical evidence suggests that these perceptions are generally accurate (Croog, Lipson, & Levine, 1972; Quarentelli, 1960). In many instances, people turn to professional agencies only when assistance is not available within the network (Kasal, Gore, & Cobb, 1975; Quarentelli, 1960).

A parallel body of research has demonstrated the central role of the social network in decisionmaking and referral to formal services. Several investigations found that family members, friends, or co-workers comprised at least 75% of the people named as influential in an individual's decision to seek health services (Booth & Babchuk, 1972; Lee, 1969). In addition, these same individuals were reported to be instrumental referral agents once the decision to seek professional assistance had been made.

Another function of networks is the transmission of values and norms that facilitate or discourage the use of professional services. Freidson (1969) suggested that many people (e.g., accountants, lawyers, teachers) participate in a network characterized by values and norms congruent with those of people who deliver services. Such people may consequently use professional services regardless of the availability of a supportive social network. This mechanism of network influence, however, has received scant empirical attention. Kadushin (1969) found that urban adults entered psychoanalysis by meeting people actively involved with psychotherapy or by making contact with local sophisticated cultural circles. In an epidemiological study of psychological well-being, Gurin, Veroff, and Feld (1960) found that the elderly comprised the one subgroup of the general population most likely to follow norms of self-reliance; thus, they tended not to seek assistance for their problems.

In the sample from the Transitions Study, analyses were conducted to determine the social and psychological correlates of those who turned to others when faced with crises or stress (Brown, 1978). Major normative transitions, unexpected crises, and role related strain were considered in Brown's (1978) sample of stress inducing events. A variety of hypotheses were tested to determine factors leading people to seek social resources in response to these stresses, strains, and events—the magnitude of strain, personal resources, characteristics of the social network, and attitudes toward seeking assistance, as well as some general attitudes regarding people (trust). Although some of the usual demographic characteristics were found (age and race related to assistance seeking), the study did not confirm those hypotheses that relate help seekers to fewer personal resources, more extensive social resources, and milder psychological constraints compared to those who do not seek assistance. Rather, the most dramatic finding was that those not seeking assistance fell into bipolar groups. One group, termed self-reliance on the basis of their reports regarding why they did not seek assistance, had the lowest strains and the best personal resources of any group in the sample. They possessed strong informal networks and showed few reservations about discussing problems with others. Opposite to this group were those who were termed reluctant nonseekers on the basis of their reason for not seeking assistance. They had the least effective coping repetoires, perceived their informal networks as unsupportive and unreliable, and had strong reservations about discussing their problems with others.

These findings should alert us to a likely confound in social resource utilization studies. Although by and large the smallest portion of our population (11% compared to 22% reluctant nonseekers), self-reliant group constituted a substantial minority who possessed quality social networks and appropriate attitudes toward reaching out to others but did not choose to avail themselves of their social resources. Studies that compare people who actively use their social resources with those who do not under similar conditions with similar perceptions of the stressfulness of that event may be biased from the outset. Much still needs to be learned about the so-called self-reliant type. Are these individuals who rarely, if ever, avail themselves of help from others, or are our results simply a reflection of the particular circumstances into which we inquired? Such answers await the third round of our longitudinal study.

Who utilizes social supports when faced with stress has only indirect interest. Findings in this area set the stage for what has become the central issue for most current investigators: the role of social resources in mitigating or avoiding stress.

A GENERAL TEST OF SOCIAL RESOURCES AS STRESS BUFFERS

The second wave of the Transitions Study ($N = 1106$) indicated that the majority of respondents (85%) experienced at least one of the following events between 1972 and 1977: an expectable transition such as birth (15%), the departure of children from the home (16%), the changing demands of aging parents (38%), or an unexpected crisis such as the death of someone close other than a spouse (48%), illness of spouse (27%), illness of a child (28%), or unemployment (9%). Those who indicated that they were highly troubled by the event were questioned about the source and type of help received. Individuals who sought help from their social network were likely to turn to their mates for advice and assistance. Friends and relatives were the next most frequently chosen helpers, with co-workers, parents, and children a distinct third. If respondents sought professional help, physicians were by far the most frequently chosen helpers for health related events; otherwise, clergy were as likely to be chosen as helpers as were physicians.

Our investigation focused on the differences in adaptation between those who did and those who did not use social resources when confronted with a stressful event; nine measures of adaptation were used—anxiety and depression symptoms, strain in marital, occupational, and economic roles, and perceived stress in these roles (Lieberman & Mullan, 1978). Change was measured on the nine indexes of adaptation by using a residualized change score, with the baseline (time 1) as a co-variant. A series of analyses systematically examined characteristics that could influence the effectiveness of social resources by creating nonrandomness in this design. The sources of bias examined were demographic characteristics, level of perceived stress of the event, psychological resources characteristic of the person, actual access to help, and time elapsed since the event. The problem of comparison of control groups was addressed by making use of a longitudinal design and equating the treated and untreated groups on a variety of relevant help seeking characteristics. While our study was not a true experiment in that differences probably exist between those who use social resources and those who do not, the study did statistically control for a number of characteristics that might have biased the sample.

The findings clearly pointed to the expected differences in the sample between those who utilized social resources and those who did not. People's perceptions of how troubled or bothered they were by the same event was highly associated with turning to kith, kin, or professionals for aid. However, when factors such as event perception; population characteristics like age, sex, race, and social class; access to help; internal resources or general coping effectiveness; perception of the self in terms of control over the environment; as well as the time since the event were statistically controlled so that the groups were equivalent, we could find no evidence that obtaining help from kith, kin, or professionals reduced distress for any of the stress events. In other words, we could find no support for social resources as stress buffers.

We believe our results were unlikely to be biased by sampling; our sample was as close to a random sample as is reasonably possible in a longitudinal study. Nor, as is so often the case, do we believe that the lack of findings resulted from inadequate outcome measures. Given our homeostatic model, we utilized indexes covering a fairly wide range of important human functioning, representing both transitional mental health measures and more specific behavioral indexes of role functioning. The availability of baseline measures prior to the distressing crisis or transition, as well as the breadth of these measures, led us to conclude that the findings were probably not unduly biased because of the outcome measure. Nor do we believe that our design was overly biased by the characteristics of the control group. Specification of a control group based on statistical equivalence is, of course, only as good as the assumption that all the important adjustments were made to equate those who turned to others at a time of crisis from those who did not. Available information from the literature on help seekers was reflected in our choice of sources of bias regarding those who utilized social resources and those who did not. The major source of unexamined information that could critically affect our findings is the lack of specification about the kind of help given, its duration and quality, and the relationship between the respondent and the help giver.

The study's findings, generated from a random sample of adults, a design not biased by post hoc measures (i.e., a baseline prior to the stress inducing event and the use of social resources), as well as psychometrical robust outcome measures, point to the central problem in the field. Generalized findings about the effectiveness of social resources may not be within our grasp. Simple generalizations—people who have social resources use them and thereby experience less distress—may not be possible to make in this complex, multidetermined area of human inquiry. At this point we need a high degree of specification about the who, what, when, and how much of social resources, as well as about the particular life circumstances eliciting the use of support.

THE EFFECTIVENESS OF SOCIAL SUPPORTS

Each of the studies discussed subsequently examined the effects of source and kind of support under a particular stress condition (child loss, widowhood, and parenting). Collectively, they pursued the role of social resources in stress mitigation and identified some conceptual and methodological dilemmas central to this research area.

Sources of Support

Sherman and Lieberman examined the source of functional help and the effective helping mechanisms in a sample of 663 parents who had lost a child. The sample was generated by obtaining mailing lists from 18 chapters of Compassionate Friends, a self-help group for bereaved parents. Members, as well as nonmembers, were studied.

Social resources data were generated by asking the respondent to list all the people they had turned to for help with problems following the death of their child and to indicate who had been the most helpful (the primary helper), as well as who had failed to provide help.

The activities of the primary helper were ascertained by asking how the person had helped—by listening or asking questions (talk); pointing out new ways to look at things or giving information (cognitive), or taking or suggesting action (action). The relationship among source of help, type of help, and effect was assessed by measures of mental health and social role function. We used indexes of depression and anxiety, such as the Hopkins Symptom Checklist (Derogatis, Lipman, & Rickles, 1971), as well as the Life Satisfaction Index (Neugarten, Havinghurst, & Tobin, 1961). For social roles we used a measure of marital satisfaction and a measure of marital strain developed in the Transitions Study (Pearlin & Lieberman, 1979).

The sample was comprised mostly of women (72%) married at the time of the survey; they ranged in age from 21 to 75, with a mean of 44 years. They represented a middle-class and upper-middle-class population. All but 4% of the sample had turned to others for help. The rule was multiple sources of help—people had sought out friends and relatives, as well as professionals and self-help groups. Eighteen percent had used only their informal networks; 42%, both formal and informal sources of help; 12%, self-help in addition to informal sources; and 25%, professional help as well as self-help.

The initial analysis related all sources and types of help to mental health and marital relationship measures. By and large, these analyses proved uninformative; such an overall analysis may have masked the relationships between support and outcome since most individuals had turned to a variety of sources of help, which made it difficult to disentangle the specific source or even specific type. A reanalysis based on primary helpers produced indeterminate results (21% perceived the spouse as the primary helper; 13%, other relatives, 20%, friends, 18%, professionals; 10%, self-help; and 10%, no one). Trends, however, between source of help and mental health indexes led to a reanalysis using precise specification of outcome by linking an idiographic perspective with nomothetic indexes (see Lieberman & Borman, 1979, for a discussion of this method). Respondents were classified according to the primary problem experienced following the child's death (mental health or psychological issues, marital problems, and parental concerns). Thus, for example, we examined outcomes measured by anxiety, depression, and life satisfaction only among those who reported their primary problem as psychological.

We found significant effects ($p < .001$) between outcomes and source of help in two problem areas: mental health and marriage. Specifically, the spouse was the most effective source of help for psychological problems. Friends were the second most effective helpers for psychological problems, followed by professionals and self-help groups. Relatives who helped seemed to be the least effective in mediating psychological stress. For marital role, not surprisingly, the spouse's help was essential for a positive outcome. Self-help groups appeared to be more successful than professional sources in reducing strain in a marriage. Friends were much more helpful in the psychological realm than in the marital area, while relatives, unhelpful for psychological problems, proved more helpful than friends in the marital area. It is not the total amount of help that is salient, but rather the fit between a particular kind of problem and the help provider.

Helping processes—talk, insight, or action—were not associated with outcome. Even when interaction effects between the primary helper and the type of help were examined, only 4 out of 15 interactions reached significance levels of .10 or better.

What can we learn from this study? Under extreme stress such as child loss it is rare to find individuals without usable social resources. Overall amount of help provided does not have an impact on the person's marital relationship or well-being; the crucial factor is who provides the help. The spouse is central. Mean scores on marital and mental health measures dramatically illustrate this point. When the spouse was the primary helper, mean life satisfaction was 11.2 (the figures for other help sources follow: relatives, 7.8; friends, 9.5; professionals, 8.9; self-help, 8.0). Unfortunately, sample limitations precluded a clear-cut determination of whether the effect of not having a spouse available can be overridden by other sources of help. The issue of substitution will be examined in a later section of this chapter.

The study also illustrates some important methodological and conceptual dilemmas in examining social resources. In highly stressful situations most people utilize their social resources. Unless we are willing to accept a field that is based upon a small minority—the truly isolated—our measures need to be highly specific and detailed. There is no apparent link between amount of social resources and stress reduction. In fact, because individuals tend to draw on a number of people for help, we began to have some purchase on our data only when we examined social resources through a phenomenological set. Only under those conditions could we find a relationship to outcome. And finally, we were appreciably helped in producing significant findings by outcome specifications. To assume that under any given life crisis all individuals will be preoccupied with the same dilemmas seems to fly in the face of reality. Investigators can maximize the possibility of discovering linkages between social resources and stress mitigation if they acknowledge that help is specific and relative to a particular psychological dilemma.

The Special Role of the Spouse: Sources of Support Reconsidered

A different strategy for studying the role of social supports was used by Reibstein (1981)). A subsample of 236 first-time mothers over the age of 25 was selected from a sample of 600 respondents drawn from women who had participated in Lamaze instruction. Approximately half the participants joined mothers' self-help groups subsequent to the birth. The participants were highly educated, upper-middle-class women who had considerable investment in their work roles. Reibstein hypothesized, based on a model of role learning interactions that the relevant social resource would be peer support. Indexes of social resource interactions were developed to indicate opportunities for modeling and social comparison as mothers with women like themselves; discussions and ventilation of feelings about role problems; and approval for performance in the new role. The extent to which peers, the respondent's own mother, and her mother-in-law offered such opportunities was assessed. Husband's instrumental support and affirmation of the mothering role were also determined.

Outcomes were assessed by measures of maternal role strain and role dissatisfaction. Individual variations in parenting were ascertained by measures of level of support needs as well as level of infant strain.

No appreciable relationship between peer group interaction and maternal dissatisfaction or maternal role strain was found. In fact, the few low correlations that were statistically significant went in the opposite direction; the more women discussed and ventilated their feelings about the maternal role, the more likely they were to be distressed and to show strain.

In contrast to the lack of a positive association between peer support and maternal distress and satisfaction, husbands appeared to play a critical role; the more they involved themselves in discussions of important personal problems with their wives and approved of the new mother in her role of mother and housewife, the more satisfied the women were with their roles and the less maternal strain they experienced.

The finding on the role of peer groups was quite surprising. It counteracts the common view that social resources, particularly those individuals in the social network similar to the person, can aid in lowering distress. What is most impressive in these data was the strong and consistent effect of the marital relationship on women's well-being. For those women whose husbands did not provide the needed resources, we could develop no evidence that suggested that other resources could substitute. To be sure, our homogeneous population did not represent a situation in which husbands were absent physically. It may very well be that when the salient support person is available but does not provide needed resources, substitution becomes almost impossible; this may not be the case when the critical relationship no longer exists.

Spouse as Confidant

A detailed examination of the role of spouse was provided by Brown (1981) using Transitions Study data. His central question was to determine the role of confiding relationships in coping with a variety of life events and role strains. Confidant relations were defined by asking: "Among your friends and relatives, excluding your spouse, is there someone you feel you can tell just about anything to, someone you can count on for understanding and advice?" Married respondents were considered to have a confiding marital relationship if they strongly agreed that "my spouse is someone I can really talk with about things that are important to me." A variety of other social resource measures were also examined, including the proximity of primary relationships (close friends and relatives), the network's diversity (different types of informal associates) and activity (frequency of contact), cohesiveness of the neighborhood, the strength of predispositions to confide and seek help, and the network's intimacy (general degree of confiding and perceived dependability for emergency help). To assess impact, three measures were used: the Rosenberg (1965) Self-Esteem Scale, the anxiety and depression subscales of the Hopkins Symptom Checklist (Derogatis, Lipman, & Rickles, 1971), and a Psychological Distress Scale on the degree of emotional upset triggered by life events and the frustrations enumerated by the respondent.

Eighty-five percent of the respondents had a confidant other than the spouse and slightly over one-half claimed to have more than one such relationship. Friends were most commonly selected for intimate relationships (75%). Over one-fourth claimed a sibling as a confidant, 18% chose a parent, 10% named a child, and 16% selected a more distant relative. Those possessing a confidant interacted with informal associates more frequently, sought the counsel of a variety of network members with greater regularity, felt more at ease revealing problems and personal information to others, and expressed greater confidence that informal associates would respond. They were more likely to be younger than older, more likely to be female, and somewhat more likely to be well educated.

Using the three outcome dimensions—distress, self-esteem, and symptoms—an analysis controlling for time 1 (baseline levels) and for the effects of age, gender, and race indicated significant differences among those who had confidants and those who did not; the lack of confidant was related to higher levels of psychological distress, lower levels of self-esteem, and a trend toward higher symptoms. In other words, the 15% of the respondents who had no confidants outside the marital relationship were less able to adapt to the various life stresses they faced.

When, however, individuals who had no confidant but were able to confide in their spouses were examined, a different picture emerged. Of the 15% who did not have confidants outside the marital relationship, only a small minority , 4%, had no confiding relationship. Comparisons among respondents who had both types of confidant, relied only on friends and relatives, relied only on spouse, or had no confiding relationship indicated that the small (4%) subgroup who reported no confidants showed high levels of distress, low levels of self-esteem, and high levels of symptoms. In fact, the group that was best off consisted of those who had a confiding marital relationship, regardless of whether they had confiding relationships outside the marriage.

This study indicates that the spouse is the key confidant; when he or she is not perceived as available, other confiding relationships cannot effectively substitute. The finding that the number of individuals who did not have confiding relationships was quite small suggests that investigation of social resources' contribution to stress mitigation is unlikely to be productive if investigators simply focus on the availability of confidants. Previous studies that showed the importance of confiding relationships probably were based on the population extremes; such studies may have high levels of practical consequences, but low levels of theoretical interest.

The Relationship between Psychological Needs and the Effectiveness of Social Supports

A study of recent widows by Bankoff (1981) demonstrated how the specific psychological issues associated with a crisis are related to the functional utility of social resources. The sample was drawn from a self-help study of two organizations aiding widows: NAIM and Theos. Survey respondents included active and former members, as well as invited widows who had chosen not to join. A subsample of 483 women widowed 35 months or less who had not remarried was used to study social resources. Their average age was 50; 60% were employed; half were Catholic, half were Protestant; typically they were high school graduates; finally, the women had lived close to 30 years in the community (urban, suburban, or rural) in which they were currently residing and had an average of 3 children.

Two distinct phases in reaction to widowhood were hypothesized and operationally defined according to length of widowhood and self-reports of grieving. The two phases, bereavement and transition, found confirmation using measures of psychological distress; the widows in the bereavement phase had lower overall psychological well-being (Bradburn, 1969); higher symptoms of anxiety and depression (Derogatis, Rickles & Lipman, 1971); and lower life satisfaction (Neugarten, Havighurst, & Tobin, 1961). The distinct psychological characteristics (there were no demographic differences between these two subsamples) were further supported by analyses of widows' response to the following question: "What is the main problem your are experiencing as a widow?" Widows in the bereavement phase differed in their focal concerns from those in the transition phase: grief related, 49% for the bereavement phase, 22% for the transition phase; role change, 22% and 3%, respectively; interpersonal, 10% and 21%, respectively; projected future concerns, 3% and 6% respectively; and concrete, 2% and 3% respectively.

Social support was indexed by the source of support (parents, in-laws, children, other relatives, married friends, single or widowed friends, and neighbors) and the type of support offered (intimacy, companionship for social interaction and activities, approval of a new lifestyle, emotional support, assurance of emergency assistance, and guidance).

The most frequent providers of support during the bereavement, as well as the transition, phase were the widow's children, followed by widowed or single friends. Parents were slightly more frequent sources during the bereavement phase, while widowed friends were slightly more frequent during the transition phase. The least frequent were in-laws and neighbors.

The major analysis related overall amount, type, and source of support to a general measure of psychological well-being. During the bereavement phase the amount of support widows received did not affect their well-being; however, there was a significant (univariate regression $p < .05$) association for widows in the transition phase between amount of support and well-being. The magnitude of this relationship was relatively small ($r^2 = .06$). In a comparable analysis, when Bankoff examined source of support (parents, in-laws, children, married friends, widowed friends, neighbors, and close relatives), the r^2 increased substantially (bereavement phase $r^2 = .16$; transition, $r^2 = .17$). An analysis based upon type of support suggested a modest increase relative to the finding for overall support. Thus, the source of support is more important than the overall amount of support provided.

Source of Support. Correlations between sources of support and well-being indicated that during the early stage of bereavement, support from the widow's parents and widowed or single friends was critical, followed by support from married friends and neighbors (Bankoff, 1981). Although the most frequently cited source of support was children, they, as well as in-laws and other relatives, did not contribute to well-being during the bereavement phase. The transition phase revealed a markedly different set of associations between source of support and well-being. Kin—inlaws, children, and other relatives—become an effective source of support. It should be noted that the overall amount of support provided by the various relevant others was not distinctive in the two phases; rather, it was the relationship between the source of support and well-being that was different. For example, married friends, who contributed to the well-being of the widows in the bereavement phase, were totally absent in the relationship to well-being for transition widows.

Bankoff next turned to type of support. She asked about the frequency with which the widow interacted with her social network, the frequency of intimate exchanges, and the frequency of approval of behavior provided by others for new social roles; as well as about the perceived availability of others for support, emergency help, and advice and/or guidance. The most significant factor seemed to be whether the widow believed that specific people in her world could be counted upon to provide needed psychological resources, not such transactions themselves. Indeed, more widows expressed confidence that their social network would provide the needed resource than attested to having engaged in frequent social interaction for emotional support. For example, more than twice as many widows believed that they could count on their social network for significant emotional support than reported frequent intimate interactions. The dependability of the network does not necessarily indicate that the person is actually turning to others for help.

Type of Support. What is the relationship between type of support and well-being? For widows in the bereavement phase, only one (availability of others for emotional support) of the six forms of support correlated significantly with well-being; the less emotional support the widow saw herself as having available, the more dysphoric affect she experienced. In contrast, among transition widows there was a significant association between well-being and frequency of intimate contact, frequency of approval for new social behavior, and amount of contact. The more interactions involving intimacy, approval, and contact, the happier the widow.

Thus, during the early phase of widowhood, having others one can count on provides a modicum of relief. The realities of interaction seem less critical than its perception. In contrast, as the widow moves through grieving to reengagement with the world and begins addressing different psychological tasks, contact with others, particularly contact in which important personal problems can be shared and approval for new lifestyle provided, becomes a required social resource. It should be noted that the overwhelming majority of the widows studied had at least one or more significant individuals to whom they could turn for emotional and instrumental resources.

Support Substitution. Did those widows in Bankoff's 1981 sample who did not have access to a specific type of relationship found in general to be the most beneficial have other relationships that were especially effective in mitigating the psychological trauma of widowhood? The single most important people in the bereavement phase widow's network were her own parents. To determine whether other social resources could substitute, Bankoff compared the level of well-being among widows who had no living parents, widows who had living, nonsupporting parents, and widows whose parents were seen as dependable resources. She found the poorest adjustment among widows who had living parents who were not seen as providing emotional support. Using multiple classification analysis, she found a significant effect in a positive direction: single or widowed friends could provide support in lieu of parents, but only for those widows who did not have living parents. In other words, the low level of well-being found among the widows who had little or no parental support was to some extent offset by the availability of single or widowed friends for those widows with no living parents; support from such friends did not benefit widows with living parents who were as preceived as not providing emotional support. Thus, substitution appears possible when the person's network lacks the requisite others when, however, these people exist but do not provide the needed resources, no other individuals apparently can provide substitution sufficient to improve the level of adjustment.

The study of widows again points to the specificity of social resources. In Bankoff's relatively homogeneous sample, significant differences in the specific source of support and, to some extent, the type of support offered were the psychological tasks facing the widow. The study also underscores the importance of how an investigator assesses social support. Perceptions of significant others who are available are not the same as data generated by asking participants to act as an observer of their own interactions, that is, to assess frequency of particular kinds of exchange. As was demonstrated in this study, different psychological qualities are being assessed. The study also raises the issue of substitution. Perhaps there are implicit norms about the appropriate source of support in specific situations. If those designated people do not come forward, then no matter who else does, psychological rejection is experienced. When such designated individuals are not physically available, the implications may not be rejection, and other sources can become functionally relevant.

MECHANISMS OF SOCIAL SUPPORT

Until now this chapter has addressed the effectiveness of social supports and particular circumstances that may require support—who, what, and when issues. I have not as yet considered process: how do effective social resources alter the stress inducing conditions of life? In order to address this issue, I first need to portray a framework explicating the linkage between potentially stressful life circumstances and their effect on adaptation.

A Stress Framework

Figure 46–1 summarizes the overall process framework (Pearlin & Lieberman, 1979; Pearlin, Lieberman, Mennaghan, & Mullan, 1981). The Transitions Study findings have so

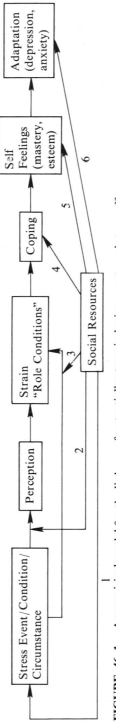

FIGURE 46-1. An empirical model for the linkage of potentially stress inducing events and stress effects

far led to such a model for best understanding the effects of stressful life events. At this point, investigation must go beyond the relationship of the event to the stress response, or even the event and its perception (meaning), to the consequences of the event. In part, life events have a deleterious impact on individuals through their impact on the more enduring, ongoing relationships characterized in our study by role (Pearlin & Lieberman, 1979). In a recent paper (Pearlin, Lieberman, Mennaghan and Mullan, 1981), we examined the processes by which job disruption leads to depression. We found that job loss intensifies economic strain, which in turn is influenced by coping. These factors, in turn, have implications for self-esteem and mastery, which play an important role in depression. This complex chain represents a more realistic account of how life circumstances bear upon a person's level of adjustment.

Theoretically, social resources can influence both the occurrence and the effects of stress in a variety of ways:

1. Social resources can decrease the likelihood of the occurrence of stressful events.
2. If the event occurs, interaction with significant others can modify or alter the individual's perception of the particular event and hence mitigate the stress potential.
3. Stress levels are partially contingent on the degree to which a potentially stressful event alters role functioning. Social resources can alter the relationship between role strain and the stress inducing event.
4. Social resources can influence coping strategies and in this way modify the linkage between stress event and effect.
5. To the degree that stressful events erode self-esteem and feelings of personal mastery, social resources can modify such effects.
6. There may be a direct influence of social resources on adaptation level.

Thus, an explanation of the processes through which social resources can buffer the consequences of stress must be complex. Findings from the Transitions Study will now be presented that address some of the ways in which social supports influence the occurrence or impact of stress.

The Role of Social Support in Reducing the Occurrence of Life Stress

Information from the Transitions Study points to a significant association between both the extensiveness ($r = .24$) and the intimacy ($r = .10$) of a person's social network, on the one hand, and the number of crises and transitions encountered, on the other. This is an obvious relationship, since the vast majority of life events involve both positive and negative changes with regard to others; people who have a constricted social network are less likely to experience a large number of life events. The occurrence, however, of such life events is only part of the picture of stress. Respondents were asked to indicate the degree to which the life events they reported were troublesome or bothersome. I found no relationship between the extensiveness of the social network and the number of troublesome or stress inducing life events. No evidence was found that either social network characteristics or the degree to which such networks functioned in the person's life as social supports (the measure of confiding or intimacy and our measure of being able to count on people under emergency situations) lessened the negative perceptions and hence the stress inducing level of such life events.

Since a significant portion of the effect of life events in producing maladaptive responses depends upon the degree to which such events alter the fabric of everyday life (operationally defined as the degree of strain in the major adult roles), the relationship between role strain and social resources was examined. In general, I found that the social resource measures of activity and dependability were significantly related to overall role strain (.24 and .30).

A detailed look at specific role strains and social network–social resource indicated a number of significant relation between all the indicators of social network–social resource and level of role strain. The more active the social network, the more intimate the social network, and the more dependable the social network, the lower the role strain. The most effective social resource appeared to be reliability or dependability; the least, intimacy. These correlations were modest but statistically significant (.15–.30 range). A key to understanding the relationship between stress inducing events and their effects on depression is an understanding of the degree to which such events alter the ongoing envelope of life, the day-to-day context. Individuals who perceive their social world as containing significant others who can be counted on or who are dependable in crises or emergency situations are less likely to be affected by the stress inducing events of life.

I have so far suggested that there is a moderate but significant association between certain characteristics of a person's social network and his or her perceptions of the functional social resources that might serve to mitigate exposure to the strains of everyday life; measured by the presses individuals encounter in occupational, economic, parental, and marital roles. Highly interactive social networks were associated with lower strain in all four role areas, and the perception of one's social network as providing a dependable source of help appeared to diminish the experience of strain within the aforementioned role areas.

Another way of examining social networks and social resources is to determine their effect on individuals with high levels of role strain. To what degree is the person's perception (the meaning) of role strain influenced by social resources? It was found that individuals who perceived their social network as reliable in providing emergency help were less likely to be troubled or bothered by economic strain ($\chi^2 = .001$, gamma $= .47$); similarly, individuals in the sample who had high levels of occupational strain but who saw their social network as more reliable were less troubled by such strain ($\chi^2 = .02$, gamma $= .30$). A similar result was found for economic strain ($\overline{X} = .05$, gamma $= .40$). No such relationship was found in the two more personal areas of life, parental and marital roles, nor did a relationship obtain between perception of stress and the social network's breadth and activity.

Thus, there is some evidence that good levels of social resources and highly interactive social networks will buffer individuals from day-to-day occupational and economic stresses and will diminish the person's perception of stress in the event of high levels of role strain. Large and active social networks and perceived adequate social resources, however, have no apparent influence on the occurrence of such events.

CONCLUSIONS

Stress mitigation is an empirical reality to the extent that the investigator can specify the psychological issues elicited by the stress inducing event or condition, specify the source of social support, specify the nature of the exchange in the support relationship, and, to some extent, pick the right outcome measures. Large generalizations about the role of social supports are not possible at this time.

Early research showed that highly isolated people tend to adjust poorly to stress. However, the number of isolated individuals in a normal population is extremely small, so this level of analysis is limited in scope and import. The realities of normative samples have forced investigators to develop increasingly subtle measures of actual or perceived social support transactions; such changes have not always altered the investigators' underlying sociological theory, these theories have provided the beacon that has lit the way, but perhaps represent models that have outlived their usefulness. The emphasis by some current researchers on social-psychological constructs, particularly exchange theory, represents just such a movement. Many of the findings reported from the two projects were illuminated by such a theoretical tradition. As our findings accrued, however, it appeared that what is required are models that address the psychology of relationships if we are to move increasingly toward explication of the process by which the availability and utilization of social networks can mitigate the occurrence or the effects of stress inducing circumstances.

To some extent this is not a new suggestion; other investigators have attempted to characterize support relationships. Cobb (1976) for example, conceptualized support within a social-psychological framework into emotional, esteem, and network support. Kahn and Antenucci (1980), as well as Pinneau (1976), addressed the same issue using broadly similar relationship categories. Unfortunately, these ideas have not as yet been fully explored empirically. The findings reported in this chapter do not corroborate the notion that nature of support is central to stress reduction. The robust findings were not type of exchange, but source of any kind of support. These findings, as well as our inability generally to demonstrate the effectiveness of substitute helpers, suggest that social supports may best be understood by invoking symbol theories of relationship rather than interactional ones. Encouragement for moving in this direction comes from our observation that more often than not the most cogent relationship between social support and stress mitigation can be found in the perception by individuals that they have a reliable and accessible social network—regardless of whether this network is used.

The call for development of a purely psychological theory of social support is also not new. For example, attachment theory has intrigued investigators as a possible source for explaining how social supports provide psychological help. Such a reconceptualization has its problems since attachment theory assumes a relatively enduring person trait. As an investigatory model for adults, attachment theory is not contextual but would sort populations into groups of individuals who have fundamental lacks, laid down rather early in life. Thus, the study of social supports could become static and non-contextual, relying totally on person explanations. Despite this dilemma, attachment theory, or more general statements of object relationships theory, may provide a useful perspective for process explanations about the role that significant others can play in warding off stressful situations or altering the responses thereto.

It may, on the other hand, be premature to foresake a social-psychological or interaction theory of social support. The findings reported on the nature of support transactions may represent early and rather primitive frameworks for understanding the subtlety of such interactions. Our findings are reminiscent of results reported for psychotherapy processes, aptly named nonspecific therapeutic factors (Frank, 1961). Even in such well-studied helping relationships as psychotherapy, specification of what constitutes help is difficult and intricate. Perhaps taking a page from that notebook of inquiry, examinations of the subtleties of relationships that characterize a person's social network may yet prove to be robust.

In general, this is a field that has overemphasized a rather simple and yet profound question: does a person's social network play a role in adaptation? Early efforts sought empirically to demonstrate such a role. Two general issues underlie current research. First, how does social network utilization mediate between stressful circumstances and the consequences of stress? Do social supports exert their influence as main effects or as buffers? As suggested earlier in this chapter, the role of social supports in this process is complex and does in large part depend upon the complexity of intervening variables used to explain the linkage between circumstances or events and stress responses. Second, others have emphasized the specification of support processes, inquiring into the nature of the transaction between the person and his or her social resources. These issues are obviously intertwined, although heretofore they have tended to be examined separately.

If the field is to move in the directions outlined here, research strategies must be found that combine the best of epidemiological sampling with provisions for the subtlety that comes from the study of lives. Survey strategies are limited in explicating processes of which we theoretically have only a glimmer; just as clearly, the highly skewed samples characteristic of clinical research often fail to illuminate processes found in nonaberrant populations.

REFERENCES

BANKOFF, E. The informal social network and the adaptation to widowhood. Doctoral dissertation, University of Chicago, 1981.

BAKER, O. V. Effects of social integration on the utilization of mental health services. Paper presented to the annual meeting of the American Psychological Association, San Francisco, 1977.

BECK, D. F. Patterns of use of family agency service. Paper presented to the biennial meeting of the Family Service Association of America, 1961.

BOOTH, A., & BABCHUK, N. Seeking health care from new resources. *Journal of Health and Social Behavior,* 1972, *13,* 90–99.

BOSWELL, D. M. Personal crises and the mobilization of the social network. In J. C. Mitchell (ed.), *Social networks in urban situations.* Manchester: Manchester University Press, 1969.

BRADBURN, N. *The structure of psychological well-being.* Chicago: Aldine, 1969.

BROWN, B. B. Social and psychological correlates of help-seeking behavior among urban adults. *American Journal of Community Psychology,* 1978, *6,* 425–439.

————. A friend in need: The impact of having a confidant. Unpublished paper, Department of Educational Psychology, Univ. of Wisconsin, Madison, 1981.

BURCHINAL, L. G. Comparisons of factors related to pregnancy-provoked and non-pregnancy-provoked youthful marriages. *Midwest Sociologist,* 1959, *21,* 92–96.

COBB, S. Social support as a moderator of life stress. *Psychosomatic Medicine,* 1976, *38,* 300–314.

CROOG, S., LIPSON, A., & LEVINE, S. Help patterns in severe illnesses: The roles of kin network, nonfamily resources, and institutions. *Journal of Marriage and the Family,* 1972, *34,* 32–41.

DEROGATIS, L. S., LIPMAN, L. C., & RICKLES, K. Neurotic symptom dimensions. *Archives of General Psychiatry,* 1971, *24,* 454–464.

FRANK, J. *Persuasion and healing.* Baltimore: John Hopkins Press, 1961.

FREIDSON, E. Client control and medical practice. *American Journal of Sociology,* 1969, *65,* 374–382.

GORE, S. The effect of social support in moderating the health consequences of unemployment. *Journal of Health and Social Behavior,* 1978, *19,* 157–165.

GOURASH, N. Helpseeking: A review of the literature. *American Journal of Community Psychology,* 1978, *6,* 432–440.

GURIN, G., VEROFF, J., & FELD, S. *Americans view their mental health.* New York: Basic Books, 1960.

HAMBURG, B. A., & KILLILEA, M. Relation of social support, stress, illness, and use of health services. Background paper for *Healthy people: The surgeon general's report on health promotion and disease prevention,* 1979.

HELLER, A. The effects of social support: Prevention and treatment implications. In A. P. Goldstein & F. H. Kanfer (eds.), *Maximizing treatment gains: Transference enhancement and psychotherapy.* New York: Academic, 1978.

HOLLINGSHEAD, A., & REDLICH, F. *Social class and mental illness.* New York: Wiley, 1958.

KADUSHIN, C. *Why people go to psychiatrists.* Chicago: Atherton, 1969.

KAHN, R. L., & ANTENUCCI, T. Convoys over the life course: Attachment, roles, and social support. In P. B. Baltes and O. Brim (eds.), *Life-span development and behavior,* vol. 3. Boston: Lexington, 1980.

KAMMEYER, K., & BOLTON, C. Community and family factors related to the use of a family service agency. *Journal of Marriage and the Family,* 1968, *30,* 488–498.

KAPLAN, B. H., CASSEL, J. C., & GORE, S. Social support and health. *Medical Care,* 1977, *15,* 47–58.

KASAL, S. V., GORE, S., & COBB, S. The experience of losing a job: Reported changes in health symptoms and illness behaviors. *Psychosomatic Medicine,* 1975, *37,* 106–121.

KATZ A. H., & BENDER, E. I. Self-help groups in Western society: History and prospects. *Journal of Applied Behavioral Science,* 1976, *12,* 265–282.

KRAVITS, J. Attitudes toward the use of discretionary physician and dental services by race, controlling for income and age. Doctoral dissertation, University of Chicago, 1972.

LEE, N. *The search for an abortionist.* Chicago: University of Chicago Press, 1969.

LEVINE, F., & PRESTON, E. Community resource orientation among low income groups. *Wisconsin Law Review,* 1970, *1,* 80–113.

LIEBERMAN, M. A., & BORMAN, L. *Self-help groups for coping with crises.* San Francisco: Jossey-Bass, 1979.

LIEBERMAN, M. A., & MULLAN, J. T. Does help help? *American Journal of Community Psychology,* 1978, *6,* 449–517.

LIN, N. R., SIMEONE, S., ENSEL, W. M., & KUO, W. Social support, stressful life events, and illness: A model and an empirical test. *Journal of Health and Social Behavior,* 1979, *20,* 108–119.

LITMAN, T. J. The family as a basic unit in health and medical care: A social-behavioral overview. *Social Science and Medicine,* 1974, *8,* 494–519.

LITWAK, E., & SZELENYI, I. Primary group structures and their functions. Kin, neighbors, and friends. *American Sociological Review,* 1969, *34,* 465–581.

LOWENTHAL, M. F., THURNHER, M., & CHIRIBOGA, D. *Four stages of life.* San Francisco: Jossey-Bass, 1975.

LURIE, O. Parents' attitudes toward children's problems and toward use of mental health services: Socioeconomic differences. *American Journal of Orthopsychiatry,* 1974, *44,* 109–120.

NEUGARTEN, B., HAVIGHURST, R., & TOBIN, S. The measurement of life satisfaction. *Journal of Gerontology,* 1961, *16,* 134–143.

PEARLIN, L. I., & LIEBERMAN, M. A. Social sources of emotional distress. In R. Simmons (ed.), *Research in community and mental health.* Greenwich: JAI, 1979.

PEARLIN, L. I., LIEBERMAN, M. A., MENNAGHAN, E., & MULLAN, J. T. The stress process. *Journal of Health and Social Behavior,* 1981, *22,* 337–356.

PINNEAU, R. S. Effects of social support on occupational stress and strain. Paper presented to the annual meeting of the American Psychological Association, Washington, D.C., 1976.

QUARENTELLI, E. L. A note on the protective function of the family in disasters. *Journal of Marriage and Family Living,* 1960, *22,* 263–264.

REIBSTEIN, J. Adjustment to the maternal role in mothers leaving careers: The impact of their interaction with role colleagues. Doctoral dissertation, University of Chicago, 1981.

ROSENBERG, M. *Society and the adolescent self-image,* Princeton: Princeton University Press, 1965.

ROSENBLATT, A., & MAYER, J. E. Helpseeking for family problems: A survey of utilization and satisfaction. *American Journal of Psychiatry,* 1972, *28,* 126–130.

SHERMAN, B. R., & LIEBERMAN, M. A. Effective social supports for bereaved parents. Manuscript, Committee on Human Development, University of Chicago, Chicago, Ill., 1981.

SROLE, L., LANGNER, T. S., MICHAEL, S. T., OPLER, M. K., & RENNIE, T. A. C. *Mental health in the metropolis.* New York: McGraw-Hill, 1962.

SUE, S., McKINNEY, H., ALLEN, D., & HALL, J. Delivery of community mental health services to black and white clients. *Journal of Consulting and Clinical Psychology,* 1974, *42,* 974–801.

SUSSMAN, M. B. Intergenerational family relationship and social role changes in middle age. *Journal of Gerontology,* 1960, *15,* 71–75.

TISCHLER, G. L., HENESZ, J. C., MYERS, J. K., & BOSWELL, P. C. Utilization of mental health services: Patienthood and the prevalence of symptomatology in the community. *Archives of General Psychiatry,* 1975, *32,* 441–445.

WEISS, R. S. Helping relationships: Relationships of clients with physicians, social workers, priests, and others. *Social Problems,* 1973, *20,* 319–328.

WELLMAN, B. Community ties and support systems: From intimacy to support. In L. Bourne, R. McKinnon, & J. Simmons (eds.), *The form of cities in central Canada.* Toronto: University of Toronto Press, 1976.(a)

————. *Urban connections.* Toronto: University of Toronto, Center for Urban and Community Studies, 1976(b).

ZIMBARDO, P., & FORMICA, R. Emotional comparison and self-esteem as determinants of affiliation. *Journal of Personality,* 1963, *31,* 151–162.

Index